# PROTEIN-BASED NANOPARTICLES IN DRUG DELIVERY

# PROTEIN-BASED NANOPARTICLES IN DRUG DELIVERY

*Edited by*

PRASHANT KESHARWANI

*Department of Pharmaceutical Sciences, Dr. Harisingh Gour Vishwavidyalaya University, Sagar, Madhya Pradesh, India*

ELSEVIER

ACADEMIC PRESS

An imprint of Elsevier

Academic Press is an imprint of Elsevier
125 London Wall, London EC2Y 5AS, United Kingdom
50 Hampshire Street, 5th Floor, Cambridge, MA 02139, United States



ISBN: 978-0-443-33639-3

For information on all Academic Press publications visit our website at
https://www.elsevier.com/books-and-journals

*Publisher:* Andre Wolff
*Acquisitions Editor:* Andre Wolff
*Editorial Project Manager:* Soumya Yadav
*Production Project Manager:* Vijayaraj Purushothaman
*Cover Designer:* Bakyalakshmi S.

Typeset by TNQ Tech

# Contents

**Contributors xi**

# I

## Foundations of protein-based drug delivery

### 1. Fundamentals of protein-based nanocarrier development: drug encapsulation, targetability, stimuli-response and *in vivo* behavior

Genada Sinani, İmren Esentürk-Güzel, Meltem Ezgi Durgun, Yıldız Özsoy, and Sevgi Güngör

1. Introduction 3
2. Protein-based nanocarrier systems 4
3. Characterization parameters of protein-based nanocarriers 12
4. Applications of protein-based nanocarriers as drug delivery system 16
5. Targeting strategies for protein-based nanocarriers 26
6. Superiorities and limitations for protein-based nanocarriers 28
7. *In vivo* behavior of protein-based nanocarriers 29
8. Treatment potentials for protein-based nanoparticles 31
9. Future perspectives 38

References 39

### 2. Unlocking the potential of protein-based drug delivery: Discovery, characteristics, and real-world applications

Ali Nematollahzadeh and Navid Ahadi-Jomairan

1. Tracing the evolution of protein-based drug delivery 51
2. Characteristics of protein-based therapeutics 62
3. Challenges in protein drug delivery 68
4. Technological advances in protein drug delivery 73
5. Future directions and emerging trends 77

References 80

### 3. History, introduction, properties, and applications of protein-based drug delivery

Uyen N.P. Nguyen and Tien T. Dang

1. Introduction 83
2. The history of the discovery and development of protein-based drug delivery 85
3. Types of materials of protein nanoparticles 87
4. Design considerations 92
5. The role of protein-based drug delivery in therapeutic applications 96
6. Conclusion 100

References 100

Further reading 112

### 4. Methods of preparation, characterization parameters, and pharmaceutical application for protein based nanoparticles

Sara Yazdani, Gholamreza Pazuki, Mehrdad Mozaffarian, and Naghmeh Hadidi

1. Introduction 113
2. Methods of preparation 115
3. Characterization parameters 119
4. Pharmaceutical applications 125
5. Conclusion 128

References 129

## 5. Design, development, and drug delivery applications of self-assembling nanocarriers from engineered proteins

Tanvir Ahmed and Kazi Tasnuva Alam

1. Introduction 139
2. Protein engineering for nanocarrier development 141
3. Design and fabrication of self-assembling protein nanocarriers 149
4. Drug loading and encapsulation strategies 155
5. Applications of self-assembling protein nanocarriers 160
6. Clinical translation potential of protein-based drug delivery systems 167
7. Challenges and limitations of using protein-based nanoparticles 168
8. Conclusion 169
References 170

## 6. Mechanism of protein-based nanoparticle interactions

Özlem Kaplan, Kevser Bal, Numan Eczacioglu, and Mehmet Koray Gök

1. Introduction 179
2. Environmental, physical, and biological interaction mechanisms of protein-based nanoparticles 181
3. Modifications and targeting strategies for protein-based nanoparticles 192
4. Drug loading and release mechanisms for protein-based nanoparticles 193
5. Conclusion 200
References 200

# II

# Applications of protein-based nanoparticles in drug delivery

## 7. Protein nanoparticles in cancer therapy

Soodabeh Shafiee, Mitra Samadi, Marzieh Peyman, and Zahra Mohammadpour

1. Introduction 211
2. Utilization of PNPs in cancer therapeutic modalities 212
3. Tumor-targeting strategies for PNP delivery 217
4. TME-responsive PNPs for cancer therapy 218
5. Protein nanoparticle platforms 224
6. Protein nanoparticles marketed and under clinical trial 254
7. Concluding remarks 257
References 258

## 8. Protein nanoparticles in cancer imaging

Swagat Ranjan Maharana, Kiran Mahapatra, Aiswarya Pati, Sheary Somam Tete, Archana Padhiary, Binata Nayak, Safdar Ali, Showkat Ahmad Mir, and Mehboob Hoque

1. Introduction 273
2. Protein nanoparticles used in cancer optical imaging 275
3. Mechanism of optical imaging for the detection of cancer 280
4. Example protein nanoparticles in cancer optical imaging 280
5. Advantages of protein nanoparticles in cancer optical imaging 284
6. Disadvantages of PNPs in cancer optical imaging 285
7. Future prospects of protein nanoparticles in cancer optical imaging 285
8. Protein nanoparticles in positron emission tomography 286
9. Future perspectives 291
References 291

## 9. Protein-based nanotechnologies as cancer theranostics

Anamika Verma, Abhishesh Kumar Mehata, Kavipriya Murugaiyan, and Aravind Kumar Rengan

1. Introduction 297
2. Protein-based nanomaterials in cancer theranostics 299
3. Therapeutic applications of protein-based nanoparticles 302
4. Diagnostic applications of protein-based nanoparticles 308
5. Protein-based nanoparticles aided multifunctional platforms 310
6. Case studies and recent advances 315

7. Challenges and limitations 319
8. Summary and future directives 322
Acknowledgments 322
References 322

## 10. Protein-based nanoparticles for the delivery of genetic materials

Ahmad Vaez, Majid Salehi, Ali Mohammad Amani, and Hadi Samadian

1. Introduction 327
2. Protein NPs potentials in gene therapy 333
3. Challenges and future prospects 341
Conflicts of interest 341
AI disclosure 341
References 341

## 11. Human serum albumin—based nanocarriers for drug delivery

Ali Nematollahzadeh and Navid Ahadi-Jomairan

1. Properties and significance of human serum albumin 349
2. Fabrication methods of HSA-based nanocarriers 350
3. Drug loading mechanisms 357
4. Mechanisms of drug release 361
5. Challenges and limitations of HSA nanocarriers 368
6. Future perspectives of HSA-based nanoemulsions 370
7. Conclusion 371
References 372

## 12. Bovine serum albumin-based nanocarriers for drug delivery

Davi Siqueira da Silva de Souza, Giovana Cristina Zambuzi, Gabriela Bevilaqua, Rafael César Russo Chagas, Lucimara Lopes Da Silva, and Kelly Roberta Francisco

1. Introduction 377
2. Relevant BSA properties for use as nanocarriers 384
3. BSA-based nanocarrier synthesis methods 388
4. Applications of BSA nanocarriers in drug delivery 390
5. Unresolved questions and emerging challenges 393
6. Recent advances and future perspectives 397
7. Conclusions 399
Acknowledgments 400
Conflicts of interest 400
References 400

## 13. Milk protein/casein-based nanocarriers for drug delivery

Mona M. Agwa, Hesham S.M. Soliman, Heba Elmotasem, Hossam M. El-Masry, and Sally Sabra

1. Introduction 409
2. Structural manifestation 410
3. Methods of preparation 411
4. Drug delivery applications of casein nanocarriers 413
5. Application of casein-based nanofibers 426
6. Conclusion 428
References 428

## 14. Silk-based nanocarriers for drug delivery

Panoraia I. Siafaka, Androulla N. Miliotou, Ioannis D. Karantas, Emre Şefik Çağlar, Mehmet Evren Okur, and Neslihan Üstündağ Okur

1. Introduction 435
2. Silk: Structure, types, properties, and preparation methods 436
3. Silk-based nanocarriers 439
4. Silk NCs for gene therapy and protein delivery 449
5. Conclusions 455
References 456

## 15. Zein-based nanocarriers for drug delivery

Mohammad Hossein Karami and Omid Moini Jazani

1. Introduction 465
2. Preparation of zein-based nanoparticles 466
3. Characterization of zein-based nanoparticles 471
4. Treatment of zein nanoparticles 472
5. The difficulties and solutions of using zein-based nanocarriers for targeted cancer treatment 475
6. Responsive zein-based DDSs 478
7. Hybrid zein-based DDSs 480

8. Applications of zein nanoparticles 481
9. Zein-based nanotechnology applications in cancer therapy 483
10. Zein-based delivery system for active substances targeting type II diabetes 485
11. Perspectives and conclusions 486
CRediT authorship contribution statement 487
Declaration of competing interest 487
References 487

## 16. Gliadin-based nanocarriers for drug delivery

Joseph D. Tanfani, Harsh Anchan, Mahima Singh, and Kamal Jonnalagadda

1. Brief overview of nanocarriers in drug delivery 499
2. Chemical structure and composition 500
3. Role in celiac disease 502
4. Manufacture of gliadin nanocarriers 502
5. Gliadin extraction 503
6. Preparation of gliadin nanocarriers 504
7. Nanocarrier stabilization 506
8. Characterization of gliadin nanocarriers 508
9. Clinical applications 509
10. Challenges and future perspectives 511
11. Outlook for future research and development 512
12. Conclusion 513
References 513
Further reading 517

## 17. Lectin based nanocarriers for drug delivery

Engin Kaptan

1. Overview of lectins 519
2. Targeted delivery of drugs using lectins 521
3. Lectin-based nanocarrier systems 524
4. Advantages of lectin-based nanocarriers 527
5. Challenges and considerations 533
6. Overview of current research 534
7. Conclusion 539
AI disclosure 540
References 540

## 18. Elastin like polypeptides (ELPs) based nanocarriers for drug delivery

Ridhima Goel and Vijaya Sarangthem

1. Introduction 547
2. Design and synthesis of ELP-based nanocarriers 549
3. ELP-based architectures in drug delivery 554
4. Applications of ELP-based nanocarriers 559
5. Future directions and conclusion 566
References 566

## 19. Virus-like particle (VLP)-based nanocarriers for drug delivery

Aiswarya Pati, Sheary Somam Tete, Archana Padhiary, Swagat Ranjan Maharana, Kiran Mahapatra, Binata Nayak, Safdar Ali, Showkat Ahmed Mir, and Mehboob Hoque

1. Introduction 571
2. Development of nanocarrier 572
3. Biological nanocarriers 573
4. Virus-based nanocarriers 574
5. Packaging drug molecules into VLPs 578
6. Applications of VLPs 588
7. VLPs—pros and cons 597
8. Future perspective 597
References 598

## 20. The role of sol-gel routes in the nanoparticle—protein interactions in drug delivery systems

Cícero Coelho de Escobar and João Henrique Z. dos Santos

1. Introduction 611
2. Silica-based nanomaterials for drug delivery via the sol-gel process 612
3. Nanoparticles for protein delivery systems via sol-gel routes 616
4. Challenges in toxicity, biocompatibility, and potential side effects in nanoparticle protein delivery via sol-gel routes 629
5. Concluding remarks 631
Acknowledgments 632
References 632

# III

# Recent advances and regulatory aspects of protein-based nanoparticles in drug delivery


## 21. Recent advancement in the codelivery of proteins and small-molecule drugs for targeted therapy

Sahar Salehi and Seyed Morteza Naghib

1. Introduction 639
2. Different drug delivery formulations 640
3. Molecular targeted drugs in the treatment of cancer 644
4. Protein drug delivery 647
5. Combination therapy of small-molecule drugs and protein 649
6. Other advances in codelivery of proteins and small-molecule drugs 657
7. Conclusion 660

References 661

## 22. Antibody—drug conjugated (ADC) nanoparticles for target-specific drug delivery nanocarriers in drug delivery

Mahsa Nikbakht, Morteza Hosseini, Hodjattallah Rabbani, and Masoud Montazer

1. An overview of drug delivery 667
2. Antibody—drug conjugates 674
3. Nanoparticle functionalization with antibody 683
4. Conclusion and future perspectives 688

References 688
Further reading 690

## 23. Recent updates in protein nanoparticle vaccine platforms

Samira Sabzi, Shahla Shahbazi, Roghayeh Mohammadzadeh, Fatemeh Mottaghitalab, and Mehdi Farokhi

1. Introduction 691
2. The advantages of PNP vaccines 693
3. Immune response activation 693
4. The immunological impact of adjuvants 695
5. Application of PNPs-based vaccines in infectious diseases and cancer 696
6. Important PNP-based vaccines 697
7. Safety and efficacy of PNP vaccines 710
8. Conclusion, challenges, and future directions 712

Declaration of competing interest 712
Acknowledgments 713
References 713

## 24. Recent advances in protein based nano delivery systems in overcoming the challenges associated with metastatic cancers

Mohammad Doroudian, Sana Rahimian, Elham Abbasgholinejad, and Hossein Najafi

1. Introduction 723
2. Challenges in metastatic cancer treatment 727
3. Structural properties and mechanisms of drug delivery in protein-based nanoparticles 730
4. Mechanisms of drug delivery 731
5. Functional groups and their roles 742
6. Hydrophilicity and hydrophobicity applications in medicine 744
7. Future trends in drug delivery 753
8. Conclusion 756

References 756

## 25. Conclusion and future prospective of protein-based nanoparticles

Alookika Agarwal, Payel Shil, K.G. Abishek, Garima Gupta, Prakash Kumar Sarangi, Muskan Leharwani, Prashant Kesharwani, Ulduza Gurbanova, Aziz Eftekhari, and Rambabu Dandela

1. Introduction 773
2. Current state of protein-based nanoparticles 779
3. Future prospects of protein-based nanoparticles in drug delivery 784
4. Potential areas of expansion 791
5. Conclusion 798

Acknowledgment 799
References 800
Further reading 806

**Index 807**

# Contributors

**Elham Abbasgholinejad** Department of Cell and Molecular Sciences, Faculty of Biological Sciences, Kharazmi University, Tehran, Iran

**K.G. Abishek** Department of Industrial and Engineering Chemistry, Institute of Chemical Technology, Indian Oil Campus, Bhubaneswar, Odisha, India

**Alookika Agarwal** Department of Industrial and Engineering Chemistry, Institute of Chemical Technology, Indian Oil Campus, Bhubaneswar, Odisha, India

**Mona M. Agwa** Department of Chemistry of Natural and Microbial Products, Pharmaceutical and Drug Industries Research Institute, National Research Centre, Giza, Cairo, Egypt

**Navid Ahadi-Jomairan** Chemical Engineering Department, University of Mohaghegh Ardabili, Ardabil, Iran

**Tanvir Ahmed** Department of Pharmaceutical Sciences, North South University, Dhaka, Bangladesh

**Safdar Ali** Applied Biochemistry Lab, Department of Biological Sciences, Aliah University, Kolkata, West Bengal, India

**Ali Mohammad Amani** Department of Medical Nanotechnology, School of Advanced Medical Sciences and Technologies, Shiraz University of Medical Sciences, Shiraz, Iran

**Harsh Anchan** Department of Pharmaceutical Sciences, Philadelphia College of Pharmacy, Saint Joseph's University, Philadelphia, PA, United States

**Kevser Bal** Istanbul University-Cerrahpasa, Faculty of Engineering, Department of Chemical Engineering, Istanbul, Türkiye

**Gabriela Bevilaqua** Department of Physical Chemistry, Institute of Chemistry, State University of Campinas (UNICAMP), Campinas, SP, Brazil

**Emre Şefik Çağlar** Department of Pharmaceutical Biotechnology, Faculty of Pharmacy, University of Health Sciences, Istanbul, Turkey

**Rafael César Russo Chagas** Laboratory of Biosorption and Chemical Synthesis - Labiosin, Federal University of São João del Rei (UFSJ), Divinópolis, MG, Brazil

**Cícero Coelho de Escobar** Centro de Engenharias – Universidade Federal de Pelotas, Rua Benjamin Constant, Pelotas, RS, Brazil

**Rambabu Dandela** Department of Industrial and Engineering Chemistry, Institute of Chemical Technology, Indian Oil Campus, Bhubaneswar, Odisha, India

**Tien T. Dang** Institute of Advanced Technology, Vietnam Academy of Science and Technology, Ho Chi Minh City, Vietnam

**Mohammad Doroudian** Department of Cell and Molecular Sciences, Faculty of Biological Sciences, Kharazmi University, Tehran, Iran

**João Henrique Z. dos Santos** Instituto de Química – Universidade Federal do Rio Grande do Sul, Porto Alegre, RS, Brazil

**Meltem Ezgi Durgun** Department of Pharmaceutical Technology, Faculty of Pharmacy, Istanbul Health and Technology University, Istanbul, Türkiye

**Numan Eczacioglu** Karamanoglu Mehmetbey University, Faculty of Engineering, Department of Bioengineering, Karaman, Türkiye

**Aziz Eftekhari** Department of Biochemistry, Faculty of Science, Ege University, Izmir, Turkiye; Nanobiomedicine Research Center, Azerbaijan Medical University, Baku, Azerbaijan

**Hossam M. El-Masry** Department of Chemistry of Natural and Microbial Products, Pharmaceutical and Drug Industries Research Institute, National Research Centre, Giza, Cairo, Egypt

**Heba Elmotasem** Pharmaceutical Technology Department, Pharmaceutical and Drug Industries Research Institute, National Research Centre, Giza, Cairo, Egypt

**İmren Esentürk-Güzel** Department of Pharmaceutical Technology, Hamidiye Faculty of Pharmacy, University of Health Sciences, Istanbul, Türkiye

**Mehdi Farokhi** National Cell Bank of Iran, Pasteur Institute of Iran, Tehran, Iran

**Kelly Roberta Francisco** Center for Science and Technologies for Sustainability, Federal University of São Carlos, Sorocaba, SP, Brazil; Center for Natural and Human Sciences, Federal University of ABC, Santo André, SP, Brazil

**Ridhima Goel** Department of Medical Oncology Laboratory, All India Institute of Medical Sciences, New Delhi, India

**Mehmet Koray Gök** Istanbul University-Cerrahpasa, Faculty of Engineering, Department of Chemical Engineering, Istanbul, Türkiye

**Sevgi Güngör** Department of Pharmaceutical Technology, Faculty of Pharmacy, Istanbul University, Istanbul, Türkiye

**Garima Gupta** School of Allied Medical Sciences, Lovely Professional University, Phagwara, Punjab, India

**Ulduza Gurbanova** Institute of Molecular Biology, Ministry of Science and Education of the Republic of Azerbaijan, Baku, Azerbaijan

**Naghmeh Hadidi** Department of Clinical Research and EM Microscope, Pasteur Institute of Iran (PII), Tehran, Iran

**Mehboob Hoque** Clinical and Applied Genomics Lab, Department of Biological Sciences, Aliah University, Kolkata, West Bengal, India

**Morteza Hosseini** Nanobiosensors Lab, Department of Life Science Engineering, Faculty of New Sciences & Technologies, University of Tehran, Tehran, Iran

**Omid Moini Jazani** Department of Chemical Engineering, Faculty of Engineering, University of Isfahan, Isfahan, Iran

**Kamal Jonnalagadda** Department of Pharmaceutical Sciences, Philadelphia College of Pharmacy, Saint Joseph's University, Philadelphia, PA, United States

**Özlem Kaplan** Alanya Alaaddin Keykubat University, Rafet Kayıs Faculty of Engineering, Department of Genetics and Bioengineering, Antalya, Türkiye

**Engin Kaptan** Istanbul University Faculty of Science, Department of Biology, Section of Molecular Biology, Istanbul, Turkey

**Mohammad Hossein Karami** Department of Chemical Engineering, Faculty of Engineering, University of Isfahan, Isfahan, Iran

**Ioannis D. Karantas** Apostolos Loukas Medical Centre, Nicosia, Cyprus

**Prashant Kesharwani** Next-Generation Translational Nanomedicine Laboratory, Department of Pharmaceutical Sciences, Dr. Harisingh Gour Vishwavidyalaya (A Central University), Sagar, Madhya Pradesh, India; University Institute of Pharma Sciences, Chandigarh University, Mohali, Punjab, India

**Muskan Leharwani** Next-Generation Translational Nanomedicine Laboratory, Department of Pharmaceutical Sciences, Dr. Harisingh Gour Vishwavidyalaya (A Central University), Sagar, Madhya Pradesh, India

**Kiran Mahapatra** School of Life Sciences, Sambalpur University, Jyotivihar, Odisha, India

**Swagat Ranjan Maharana** School of Life Sciences, Sambalpur University, Jyotivihar, Odisha, India

**Abhishesh Kumar Mehata** Department of Biomedical Engineering, Indian Institute of Technology, Hyderabad, Telangana, India

**Androulla N. Miliotou** Department of Health Sciences, School of Life & Health Sciences, University of Nicosia, Nicosia, Cyprus

**Showkat Ahmad Mir** School of Life Sciences, Sambalpur University, Jyotivihar, Odisha, India

**Zahra Mohammadpour** Medical Nanotechnology Department, Breast Cancer Research Center, National Cancer Institute, ACECR, Tehran, Iran

**Roghayeh Mohammadzadeh** Department of Microbiology and Virology, School of Medicine, Mashhad University of Medical Sciences, Mashhad, Iran

**Masoud Montazer** Nanobiosensors Lab, Department of Life Science Engineering, Faculty of New Sciences & Technologies, University of Tehran, Tehran, Iran

**Fatemeh Mottaghitalab** Nanotechnology Research Centre, Faculty of Pharmacy, Tehran University of Medical Sciences, Tehran, Iran

**Mehrdad Mozaffarian** Department of Chemical Engineering, Amirkabir University of Technology, Tehran, Iran

**Kavipriya Murugaiyan** Department of Biomedical Engineering, Indian Institute of Technology, Hyderabad, Telangana, India

**Seyed Morteza Naghib** Nanotechnology Department, School of Advanced Technologies, Iran University of Science and Technology (IUST), Tehran, Iran

**Hossein Najafi** Department of Industrial and Environmental Biotechnology, National Institute of Genetic Engineering and Biotechnology (NIGEB), Tehran, Iran

**Binata Nayak** School of Life Sciences, Sambalpur University, Jyotivihar, Odisha, India

**Ali Nematollahzadeh** Chemical Engineering Department, University of Mohaghegh Ardabili, Ardabil, Iran

**Uyen N.P. Nguyen** Institute of Advanced Technology, Vietnam Academy of Science and Technology, Ho Chi Minh City, Vietnam

**Mahsa Nikbakht** Nanobiosensors Lab, Department of Life Science Engineering, Faculty of New Sciences & Technologies, University of Tehran, Tehran, Iran

**Mehmet Evren Okur** Department of Pharmacology, Faculty of Pharmacy, University of Health Sciences, Istanbul, Turkey

**Yıldız Özsoy** Department of Pharmaceutical Technology, Faculty of Pharmacy, Istanbul University, Istanbul, Türkiye

**Archana Padhiary** School of Life Sciences, Sambalpur University, Jyotivihar, Odisha, India

**Aiswarya Pati** School of Life Sciences, Sambalpur University, Jyotivihar, Odisha, India

**Gholamreza Pazuki** Department of Chemical Engineering, Amirkabir University of Technology, Tehran, Iran

**Marzieh Peyman** Medical Nanotechnology Department, Breast Cancer Research Center, National Cancer Institute, ACECR, Tehran, Iran; Department of Nanotechnology, Faculty of Advanced Sciences and Technology, Tehran Medical Sciences Islamic Azad University, Tehran, Iran

**Hodjattallah Rabbani** Monoclonal Antibody Research Center, Avicenna Research Institute, ACECR, Tehran, Iran

**Sana Rahimian** Department of Cell and Molecular Sciences, Faculty of Biological Sciences, Kharazmi University, Tehran, Iran

**Aravind Kumar Rengan** Department of Biomedical Engineering, Indian Institute of Technology, Hyderabad, Telangana, India

**Sally Sabra** Department of Biotechnology, Institute of Graduate Studies and Research, Alexandria University, Alexandria, Egypt

**Samira Sabzi** Medical Microbiology Research Center, Qazvin University of Medical Sciences, Qazvin, Iran

**Majid Salehi** Tissue Engineering and Stem Cells Research Center, Shahroud University of Medical Sciences, Shahroud, Iran; Department of Tissue Engineering, School of Medicine, Shahroud University of Medical Sciences, Shahroud, Iran

**Sahar Salehi** Department of Biomedical Engineering, Shahab Danesh University, Qom, Iran

**Mitra Samadi** Department of Molecular Genetics, Faculty of Biological Sciences, Tarbiat Modares University, Tehran, Iran; Genetics Department, Breast Cancer Research Center, National Cancer Institute, ACECR, Tehran, Iran

**Hadi Samadian** Research Center for Molecular Medicine, Hamadan University of Medical Sciences, Hamadan, Iran

**Prakash Kumar Sarangi** College of Agriculture, Central Agricultural University, Imphal, Manipur, India

**Vijaya Sarangthem** Department of Biochemistry and Cell Biology, Cell and Matrix Research Institute, Kyungpook National University, School of Medicine, Daegu, Republic of Korea

**Soodabeh Shafiee** Recombinant Proteins in Cancer Department, Breast Cancer Research Center, National Cancer Institute, ACECR, Tehran, Iran

**Shahla Shahbazi** Department of Molecular Biology, Pasteur Institute of Iran, Tehran, Iran

**Payel Shil** Department of Industrial and Engineering Chemistry, Institute of Chemical Technology, Indian Oil Campus, Bhubaneswar, Odisha, India

**Panoraia I. Siafaka** Department of Life Sciences, School of Sciences, Program of Pharmacy, European University Cyprus, Nicosia, Cyprus

**Lucimara Lopes Da Silva** Department of Chemical Engineering, Federal University of Technology - Paraná, Londrina, PR, Brazil

**Genada Sinani** Department of Pharmaceutical Technology, Faculty of Pharmacy, Altinbas University, Istanbul, Türkiye

**Mahima Singh** Department of Pharmaceutical Sciences, Philadelphia College of Pharmacy, Saint Joseph's University, Philadelphia, PA, United States

**Hesham S.M. Soliman** Pharmacognosy Department, Faculty of Pharmacy, Capital University (Previously Helwan University), Cairo, Egypt; Faculty of Pharmacy, Egypt-Japan University of Science and Technology, New Borg El Arab, Alexandria, Egypt

**Davi Siqueira da Silva de Souza** Center for Science and Technologies for Sustainability, Federal University of São Carlos, Sorocaba, SP, Brazil

**Joseph D. Tanfani** Department of Pharmaceutical Sciences, Philadelphia College of Pharmacy, Saint Joseph's University, Philadelphia, PA, United States

**Kazi Tasnuva Alam** Department of Pharmaceutical Sciences, North South University, Dhaka, Bangladesh

**Sheary Somam Tete** School of Life Sciences, Sambalpur University, Jyotivihar, Odisha, India

**Neslihan Üstündağ Okur** Department of Pharmaceutical Technology, Faculty of Pharmacy, University of Health Sciences, Istanbul, Turkey

**Ahmad Vaez** Biotechnology Research Center, Shiraz University of Medical Sciences, Shiraz, Iran; Department of Tissue Engineering, School of Advanced Medical Sciences and Technologies, Shiraz University of Medical Sciences, Shiraz, Iran; Histomorphometry and Stereology Research Center, Shiraz University of Medical Sciences, Shiraz, Iran

**Anamika Verma** Department of Biomedical Engineering, Indian Institute of Technology, Hyderabad, Telangana, India

**Sara Yazdani** Department of Chemical Engineering, Amirkabir University of Technology, Tehran, Iran

**Giovana Cristina Zambuzi** Center for Natural and Human Sciences, Federal University of ABC, Santo André, SP, Brazil

# PART I

# Foundations of protein-based drug delivery

CHAPTER

# 1

# Fundamentals of protein-based nanocarrier development: drug encapsulation, targetability, stimuli-response and *in vivo* behavior

*Genada Sinani*[1], *İmren Esentürk-Güzel*[2], *Meltem Ezgi Durgun*[3], *Yıldız Özsoy*[4] *and Sevgi Güngör*[4]

**[1]Department of Pharmaceutical Technology, Faculty of Pharmacy, Altinbas University, Istanbul, Türkiye; [2]Department of Pharmaceutical Technology, Hamidiye Faculty of Pharmacy, University of Health Sciences, Istanbul, Türkiye; [3]Department of Pharmaceutical Technology, Faculty of Pharmacy, Istanbul Health and Technology University, Istanbul, Türkiye; [4]Department of Pharmaceutical Technology, Faculty of Pharmacy, Istanbul University, Istanbul, Türkiye**

## 1. Introduction

The development of nanocarrier drug systems has enabled the overcoming of limitations associated with conventional dosage forms. Amphiphilic copolymers or surfactants have been utilized in the production of these systems from their initial formulations to the present. Research conducted with the nanocarriers produced has elucidated the biological responses that occur or have the potential to occur in the body. This has prompted researchers to explore the use of more natural-based substances, proteins among other polymers in the production of nanocarriers (Lin et al., 2023; Elzoghby et al., 2012). The advent of novel developments, including investigative advances in physiological and biochemical research, the identification of new pathways, and the elucidation of receptor structures, has given rise to the concept of employing proteins in the fabrication of nanocarriers.

Protein-based nanocarriers offer distinct advantages, particularly high biocompatibility and minimal immunological responses, attributable to their biodegradability. In addition

*Protein-Based Nanoparticles in Drug Delivery*
**https://doi.org/10.1016/B978-0-443-33639-3.00002-7**

to these benefits, protein-based nanocarriers possess several advantages, including their capacity for high drug binding, their versatility in accommodating both hydrophilic and lipophilic drugs, and their ability to regulate particle size and drug release (Elzoghby et al., 2012; Malekzad et al., 2018). The potential of protein-based nanocarriers to enhance the pharmacokinetic properties of a wide range of drugs, encompassing drugs with diverse pharmacological effects, is a significant area of interest. This versatility extends to various fields, including tissue engineering and biomedical applications. This chapter will address the following topics: proteins utilized in nanocarrier production, the types, production methods and characterization parameters of protein-based nanocarriers and, and, *in vivo* behavior of these systems.

# 2. Protein-based nanocarrier systems

## 2.1 Proteins used in nanocarriers

Proteins can be classified according to multiple criteria. These classification systems may be based on criteria such as their animal or plant origin (Elzoghby et al., 2012; Malekzad et al., 2018), their composition (Elzoghby et al., 2012; Maviah et al., 2020), or their solubility (the most widely accepted classification) (Martínez-López et al., 2020). Alternatively, they may be categorized based on their biological function. In this chapter, the focus is on the classification of proteins utilized in the production of nanocarriers, with the classification criteria being based on their composition and solubility. This classification system categorizes proteins into three primary classifications: simple proteins or holoproteins, conjugated or complex proteins or heteroproteins, and derived proteins. Table 1.1 provides a comprehensive classification of proteins and the groups of proteins that are most frequently utilized in nanocarrier production. A more detailed description of some proteins is given later in this chapter.

### *2.1.1 Albumin*

Albumin is a water-soluble globular protein. It is utilized in the development of drug delivery systems due to its prolonged residence time in the body, high stability, and capacity to overcome biological barriers (Martínez-López et al., 2020; Ji et al., 2024a). It is especially preferred for targeting hydrophobic drugs. Their capacity to serve as both active (*via* ligand-functionalization) and passive (*via* the enhanced permeability and retention (EPR) effect) drug targeting confers a substantial advantage (Garg et al., 2023). Albumin is classified into two distinct categories: serum albumin and lactalbumin (Martínez-López et al., 2020).

### *2.1.2 Serum albumin*

Human serum albumin (HSA) and bovine serum albumin (BSA) are the most widely used and well-known varieties of albumin (Elzoghby et al., 2012). Due to their high drug binding capacity and ability to overcome biological barriers, highly soluble HSA and BSA have been used for years in drug delivery systems for tumoral and genetic diseases (Salatin et al., 2015). Notably, the most significant and successful work in this field is the formulation of paclitaxel-albumin, which is licensed under the trade name Abraxane (Martínez-López et al., 2020).

**TABLE 1.1** Proteins frequently used in nanocarrier production, their classification, sources and properties.

| Protein type | Subtype | | Protein name | Origin | Advantage | References |
|---|---|---|---|---|---|---|
| Haloproteins | Globular | Albumin | Serum albumin | Animal | • High drug binding capacity<br>• Ability to overcome biological barriers<br>• Used for years in drug delivery systems | Elzoghby et al. (2012) |
| | | | Lactalbumin | Animal | • Applicable in the encapsulation of both hydrophilic and hydrophobic drugs, as well as in the development of nutraceuticals | Pisoschi et al. (2018); Layman et al. (2018) |
| | | Globulins | Legumin & Vicilin | Plant | • Derived from legumes<br>• Suitable for use in the development of cutaneous and transdermal drug delivery systems because of the ability to form gel structures | Elzoghby et al. (2012); Chen et al. (2022) |
| | | | Lactoglobulin | Animal | • Functions as a pivotal carrier agent, particularly for hydrophobic drugs<br>• Enables the formation of nanocarriers without the necessity of synthetic surfactants | Purwanti et al. (2016) |
| | | | Soy protein | Plant | • Applicable in the encapsulation of both hydrophilic and hydrophobic drugs, as well as in the development of nutraceuticals<br>• Substitute for animal-sourced products | Huang et al. (2025) |
| | | Prolamin | Zein | Plant | • Derived from corn<br>• Well-suited for the delivery of hydrophobic drugs | Elzoghby et al. (2012) |
| | | | Gliadin | Plant | • Derived from maize<br>• High mucoadhesion, and capacity for the formation of biofilms | Arangoa et al. (2001); Umamaheshwari et al. (2004) |
| | | | Hordein | Plant | • Derived from barley<br>• Primary application is in the domain of nutraceutical development and the design of drug delivery systems | Sha et al. (2024) |

*(Continued)*

**TABLE 1.1** Proteins frequently used in nanocarrier production, their classification, sources and properties.—cont'd

| Protein type | Subtype | | Protein name | Origin | Advantage | References |
|---|---|---|---|---|---|---|
| | | | Kafirin | Plant | • Derived from sorghum<br>• Possesses film-forming ability<br>• Due to its elevated degree of hydrophobicity, it finds particular application in the targeting of hydrophobic drugs and the development of nutraceuticals | Maviah et al. (2020); Emmambux et al. (2004) |
| | | Glutenin | | Plant | • Utilized in the development of drug delivery systems, particularly in conjunction with gliadin to regulate drug release | Elzoghby et al. (2012) |
| | | Histone | Protamine & Salmine | Animal | • Has a natural affinity for negatively charged nucleic acids | Sim et al. (2017) |
| | Scleroprotein | Elastin | | Animal | • Primarily employed in tissue engineering; however, it is also utilized in the fabrication of carrier systems for hydrophobic drugs | Elzoghby et al. (2012); Daamen et al. (2007) |
| | | Collagen | | Animal | • Used in transdermal drug delivery systems because of the mucoadhesive properties.<br>• Promoting tissue regeneration renders it a valuable component in the development of wound healing systems | Ahmad et al. (2024); Mathew-Steiner et al. (2021) |
| | | Fibroin | | Plant | • High mechanical resistance, long-term stability, and biocompatibility<br>• Selected to develop long-term release carrier systems and tissue engineering | Salatin et al. (2015) |
| Heteroproteins | Phosphoprotein | Casein | | Animal | • Excipient of nanocarrier systems for hydrophobic drugs due to its self-emulsifying properties | Fathi et al. (2018) |
| | Metalloprotein | Gelatin | | Animal | • Has a high degree of encapsulation ability<br>• Significant advantages in the development of nanocarriers and in modifying the developed nanocarriers with desired properties<br>• Applicable in the encapsulation of both hydrophilic and hydrophobic drugs | Maviah et al. (2020); Narayanaswamy et al. (2016); Tarhini et al. (2017a) |

| | | | | | |
|---|---|---|---|---|---|
| | Glycoprotein | Lactoferrin | Animal | • Can be used as an active substance is primarily driven by its antimicrobial and anticancer properties<br>• Potential to reduce the necessity for emulsion agents in the formulation of nanocarrier systems | García-Montoya et al. (2012); Baghdadi et al. (2024) |
| | Lectin (Agglutinin) | | Plant | • A protein that demonstrates a high degree of affinity for sugar complexes that are bound to proteins and lipids<br>• Well-suited for the development of nanocarriers for anticancer drugs due to its capacity to recognize glycans on the surface of cancer cells and to bind with them in a specific manner | Lavín de Juan et al. (2017); Silva (2024) |
| Derivatized proteins | Polypeptides | Lysozyme | Animal | • Can be used as an active substance is primarily driven by its antimicrobial properties<br>• A good excipient, particularly in the context of renal and pulmonary drug targeting | Massa et al. (2015); Franssen et al. (1991); Haas et al. (1997); Zhou et al. (2014); Devrim Gökberk and Erdinç (2023) |

Two receptors for serum albumin have been identified in the human body. These receptors are glycoprotein 60 (GP60) and secreted acidic-cysteine-rich protein (SPARC) (Ji et al., 2024b). Of particular significance is GP60, also known as albondin, which facilitates the transvascular permeability of albumin across the endothelial cell layer. SPARC, an osteonectin, is a receptor that is more abundant in many tumor cells than in normal tissue cells and plays a significant role in cancer progression (Tai and Tang, 2008). Consequently, SPARC is regarded as a pivotal pathway in the development of albumin-based antitumor drugs.

### 2.1.3 *Lactalbumin*

It is a globular protein derived from milk and has high nutritional value. It is classified into two subtypes: α and β (de Oliveira Bianchi et al., 2024; Shafaei et al., 2017). It has the ability to bind calcium and other metal ions at a high rate. This property renders it a preferred candidate not only in the realm of drug targeting but also in the development of nutraceuticals (Layman et al., 2018). The formation of gels and emulsions, along with their high biocompatibility, renders them suitable for use in the development of carrier systems for both hydrophilic and hydrophobic drugs (Pisoschi et al., 2018).

### 2.1.4 *Zein*

Zein is obtained from corn. Due to its hydrophobic nature, it is particularly well-suited for the delivery of hydrophobic drugs (Elzoghby et al., 2012). Its resistance to digestive enzymes contributes to its effectiveness as a mean to enhance the oral administration of drugs. It functions as a protective barrier against enzymatic biodegradation, thereby enhancing the potency of the encapsulated drug within the gastrointestinal tract and prolonging its stability (Zhong et al., 2009).

### 2.1.5 *Histones*

Due to their positive charge, these particles exhibit a natural affinity for negatively charged nucleic acids (Sim et al., 2017). Consequently, they are particularly employed in gene therapy studies. One notable example is protamine, which is derived from Histone H1 (Lewis et al., 2004). Salmine, a protamine subtype that is characterized by its arginine richness and abundance in fish sperm, is particularly utilized in ribonucleic acid (RNA)-related studies (Roque, 2004).

### 2.1.6 *Fibroin*

It is obtained from silk. These materials possess a number of advantageous properties, including high mechanical resistance, long-term stability, and biocompatibility (Salatin et al., 2015). Consequently, they are frequently selected for enhancing the stability of sensitive medications and for developing long-term release carrier systems. Its prevalence in nanofiber production is attributable to its amenability to electrospinning, a method that facilitates its large-scale manufacturing. Additionally, it is frequently utilized in implant production (Uzel et al., 2023).

## 2.2 Nanocarrier types developed as protein-based drug delivery systems

### 2.2.1 *Nanoparticles*

These colloidal systems are formed by the adsorption or conjugation of natural or recombinant proteins. These systems have the capacity to target both hydrophilic and lipophilic drugs, with the utilization of appropriate proteins (Shin et al., 2024). Nanoparticles are characterized by their biocompatibility and biodegradability. They exhibit high drug loading efficiency (Lin et al., 2023). A notable example of this class of products is Abraxane, a commercial formulation of paclitaxel-loaded albumin nanoparticles (Martínez-López et al., 2020).

### 2.2.2 *Nanocapsules*

The subject of this study is a type of nanocarrier with a core-shell structure. The core of the nanocarrier contains the drug in either liquid or solid form (Lin et al., 2023). These delivery systems function as reservoirs, enabling the regulated release of the drug substance. The capsule's protective barrier significantly enhances the stability and bioavailability of the drug. This attribute contributes to enhanced pharmacokinetic properties, thereby ensuring the effective and targeted delivery of the drug substance. These properties endow them with a notable advantage in the targeted delivery of antimicrobial (Cruz et al., 2021) and anticancer drugs (Ghalandari et al., 2014).

### 2.2.3 *Micelles*

These are systems in which proteins self-assemble above a critical micelle concentration. These systems are composed of a hydrophobic core and a hydrophilic shell that surrounds it (Durgun et al., 2020). This structural characteristic renders them well-suited to serve as carriers for lipophilic drugs. The ability to regulate the release of drugs and the high degree of biocompatibility are significant advantages. Casein micelles have been extensively studied for oral and intravenous drug administration (Lin et al., 2023), while elastin-like protein micelles have been explored for temperature-sensitive drugs (van Strien et al., 2023).

### 2.2.4 *Nanogels*

Nanogels are systems that exhibit the capacity for swelling in aqueous media due to their three-dimensional cross-links (Lin et al., 2023). They offer several advantages, including high drug loading efficiency, biocompatibility and biodegradability, as well as the ability to control and sustain the release of the encapsulated drug. Additionally, they can protect the drug from degradation by pH, temperature, or enzymes (Chander et al., 2021). The broad range of potential applications for these nanogels encompasses wound healing, targeted delivery of anticancer drugs, and other fields of research.

### 2.2.5 *Nanofibers*

Nanofibers are thin, thread-like structures formed by proteins using electrospinning techniques. These fibers facilitate the sustained and localized delivery of drugs, enabling the precise application of therapeutic agents over extensive surfaces. In particular, tissue engineering studies employing silk fibroin protein are prevalent (Uzel et al., 2023). Additionally, casein nanofibers have demonstrated potential for utilization in oral drug targeting applications (Selvaraj et al., 2018).

### 2.2.6 *Protein cages and virus-like particles (VLPs)*

Protein cages are hollow, self-assembling nanostructures composed of viral capsid proteins or ferritin-like proteins (Stupka and Heddle, 2020; Molino and Wang, 2014; Nooraei et al., 2021). These structures have found application in the encapsulation of drugs, genes, or imaging agents. They are notable for their stability, high drug loading efficiency properties and biodegradability.

## 2.3 Production methods of protein based nanocarriers

Despite the existence of various types of nanocarriers, the underlying production methodologies are largely analogous. However, there are also specific methods employed to produce certain tyepes of nanocarriers. One such example is the application of electrospinning in the synthesis of nanofibers (Uzel et al., 2023). Consequently, the techniques employed in the production of protein-based nanocarriers are examined as a discrete topic, rather than within the broader context of nanocarriers (Martínez-López et al., 2020; Elzoghby et al., 2015).

The production technique exerts a direct influence on the nanocarrier's particle size, drug loading efficiency, stability, and drug release kinetics. Consequently, a judicious selection of the production method can yield a nanocarrier with the desired properties (Martínez-López et al., 2020). Furthermore, the nature of the protein or proteins utilized, whether they are naturally occurring or genetically engineered, is a crucial factor in determining the most suitable production method. The applicability of the selected production method to the proteins to be used is an important criterion. The following are the primary methods for producing protein-based nanocarriers.

### *2.3.1 Desolvation (precipitation)*

The process is predicated on the principle of protein precipitation and nanoparticle formation, which occurs as a result of the gradual addition of a desolvation agent, such as ethanol or acetone, to an aqueous protein solution. The addition of a crosslinking agent, such as glutaraldehyde or genipin, to the medium serves to stabilize the precipitated nanoparticles (Martínez-López et al., 2020; Elzoghby et al., 2015). This method finds application in the preparation of a variety of nanoparticle types, including albumin, gelatin, and β-lactoglobulin nanoparticles, and is suitable for both hydrophilic and hydrophobic drugs (Elzoghby et al., 2012). Noteworthy advantages include its simplicity and scalability, high drug loading efficiency, and particle size tunability depending on solvent type and concentration. Noteworthy disadvantages include potential toxic effects stemming from the organic solvent residue utilized during its production and the necessity for cross-linking, which underscores the need for caution in its application (Elzoghby et al., 2015).

### *2.3.2 Coacervation-phase separation*

The basis of this process is the dissolution of proteins in water, followed by the formation of nanoparticles through pH modification or the addition of substances such as sodium sulfate (Elzoghby et al., 2015; Lohcharoenkal et al., 2014; Ramos et al., 2022). The method is particularly well-suited for the production of nanocarriers intended for oral or intravenous administration and compatible with carrier systems comprising gelatin, casein, and albumin proteins (Elzoghby et al., 2012). It has been demonstrated to be effective for sensitive biomolecules, exhibiting a high degree of drug loading efficiency. A notable advantage of this method is that it does not involve the use of organic solvents. However, as with the desolvation method, cross-linker addition is necessary to stabilize the nanoparticles formed (Martínez-López et al., 2020).

### 2.3.3 *Emulsification-solvent evaporation*

The mixture of the aqueous protein solution and the drug solution in the organic phase results in the formation of an oil-in-water (O/W) or water-in-oil (W/O) emulsion (Elzoghby et al., 2015). The organic phase is then subjected to evaporation, resulting in the formation of an aqueous dispersed system comprising nanocarriers. A notable drawback of this method is the instability of the nanocarriers formed. To address this challenge, the application of high-speed homogenization or ultrasonication prior to the evaporation of the organic phase has been proposed (Li et al., 2021). This approach aims to stabilize emulsion by disrupting the nanocarriers. The utilization of organic solvents poses an additional challenge. However, its employment in the synthesis of lipophilic drugs confers substantial benefits. It is employed in the synthesis of nanocarriers derived from albumin (Kudarha and Sawant, 2017), silk fibroin (Zhu et al., 2024), and casein (Du et al., 2022).

### 2.3.4 *Nanoprecipitation*

The fundamental principle underlying this process is the observation that, upon the gradual addition of an organic phase comprising proteins and drugs to an aqueous phase, a process of solvent diffusion occurs, resulting in the precipitation of nanocarriers (Martínez Rivas et al., 2017). This method is particularly well-suited for nanocarrier systems that utilize zein (Elzoghby et al., 2015), gliadin (Alqahtani et al., 2020). Notable advantages include its fast, simple, and adjustable production scale, as well as its controllability of particle size. However, the necessity of organic solvents and the incompatibility with hydrophilic drugs impose limitations on its application.

### 2.3.5 *Electrospinning deposition*

The fundamental principle underlying this process entails the application of a high-voltage electric field, which results in the evaporation of the solvent, thereby leaving the nanocarrier behind (Uzel et al., 2023). This method finds application in the domain of drug delivery, with silk fibroin (Uzel et al., 2023), gliadin (Bahrami et al., 2023), and gelatin (El-Seedi et al., 2023) serving as the primary materials. A notable advantage of this method is the ability to adjust the particle size with great precision, obviating the necessity for the addition of a cross-linking agent. However, the equipment necessary for its implementation is costly and challenging to scale up (Uzel et al., 2023).

### 2.3.6 *Self-assembly*

The protein and the pharmaceutical agent are dissolved in a solvent. Subsequently, nanocarrier systems are spontaneously formed under the influence of hydrophobic interactions, hydrogen bonding, and electrostatic forces depending on pH and temperature changes (Elzoghby et al., 2015). These nanocarrier systems find application in the production of elastin-like polypeptides (Martínez-López et al., 2020), casein micelles (Martínez-López et al., 2020), and virus-like particles (VLPs) (Nooraei et al., 2021). The development of biocompatible and biodegradable nanocarriers that do not necessitate the use of organic solvents is possible; however, it should be noted that the release of the drug is not adjustable according to specific needs.

#### 2.3.7 *Nano spray drying*

The process of interest is a high-speed drying process. In this process, protein and drug solutions are atomized into fine droplets and rapidly dried to form nanocarriers (Elzoghby et al., 2015). The production of nanocarriers with a stable structure is possible. The process is rapid, and its execution at the desired scale is feasible. However, the escape of rapidly drying powders into cyclones can reduce efficiency (Sosnik and Seremeta, 2015). The production of nanocarriers utilizes protein sources such as albumin (Kudarha and Sawant, 2017), silk fibroin (Gu et al., 2024), and lactoferrin (Marques et al., 2023).

#### 2.3.8 *Crosslinking (chemical and enzymatic)*

This is a prevalent technique employed in the synthesis and stabilization of protein-based nanocarriers. The method is based on the formation of covalent or non-covalent bonds between protein molecules, which endows nanocarriers with resistance to enzymatic degradation and increased mechanical strength (Elzoghby et al., 2015; Sun et al., 2023). The cross-linking method, which can be achieved through chemical or enzymatic treatment, has the capacity to yield a broad spectrum of products, ranging from the fabrication of drug delivery systems (Elzoghby et al., 2015) to the production of biomedical equipment utilized in tissue engineering (Domeradzka et al., 2016).

#### 2.3.9 *Microfluidic technology*

This advanced method enables precise and scalable production of protein-based nanocarriers through the manipulation of liquids at the microscale. This technique has been shown to enhance several key characteristics of nanoparticle production, including the degree of homogeneity, the efficiency of encapsulation, and the precision of controlled drug release (Meng et al., 2018). The method's hallmark is its high degree of reproducibility, enabling precise control over the size and uniformity of the nanocarriers. The versatility of this method extends to both hydrophilic and hydrophobic drugs. However, the cost of the equipment used is quite high and the efficiency is quite low. Additionally, there is a risk of clogging the microchannels utilized for nanocarrier production, which can compromise the efficacy of the process (H. Zhang et al., 2023a).

#### 2.3.10 *Nab technology (nanoparticle albumen dependent technology)*

The manufacturing method employed in the production of the commercial product Abraxane involves the use of high-pressure homogenization to bind drugs to albumin nanoparticles, thereby enhancing their tumor targeting ability (Martínez-López et al., 2020; Lluch et al., 2014).

## 3. Characterization parameters of protein-based nanocarriers

The primary objectives of designing protein-based nanocarriers as a drug delivery system are to control drug release, surface properties, and particle size in order to achieve the desired results. Hence, it is important to characterize the nanocarriers in order to regulate their expected behavior in both *in vitro* and *in vivo* conditions (Jain and Thareja, 2019). The particle size, polydispersity index (PDI), particle morphology, surface charge, particle structure, drug loading capacity, encapsulation efficiency, *in vitro* drug release, and stability are the main factors used to determine the characteristics of protein nanocarriers (Li et al., 2024; Alshawwa et al., 2022; Verma et al., 2018).

## 3.1 Particle size and polydispersity

Particle size is one of the most critical characteristics of nanocarriers and the other is PDI value, which indicates the homogeneity of particles based on their size. These influence the nanocarriers' properties of dispersibility, stability, retention/release, attachment, bioadhesion and processes of phagocytosis, circulation half-life, cellular distribution, cellular uptake and endocytosis (Alshawwa et al., 2022). Larger surface areas and better stability against aggregation and phase separation are typically associated with smaller particle sizes. On the contrary, the retention and chemical stability of encapsulated drugs frequently decreases with a reduction in particle sizes. Regarding the PDI value, it is preferable to be as low as possible for providing uniform-sized particles and a more stable nanocarrier system with more expected properties (Li et al., 2024). Dynamic light scattering (DLS), laser diffraction spectroscopy, photon-correlation spectroscopy, differential centrifugal sedimentation and microscopic techniques are used in the mean size determination (Verma et al., 2018; Jain et al., 2018) and the PDI value is determined using a particle sizer integrated software (Alshawwa et al., 2022). Esim et al. (2022) developed pH-responsive lipid-coated albumin nanoparticles encapsulated with drugs of carboplatin and decitabine for overcoming platinum resistance in ovarian cancer. The mean diameter of the albumin nanoparticles was analysed by DLS and found to be $350 \pm 12$ nm, which is good for EPR effect.

## 3.2 Particle morphology

The shape of protein-based nanocarriers is defined using a variety of microscopic analysis including optical microscopy (OM), scanning electron microscopy (SEM), transmission electron microscopy (TEM), atomic force microscopy (AFM) and confocal laser scanning microscopy (CLSM). Using OM, the determination of the characteristics of smaller particles than the wavelength of light becomes difficult while using OM. Advanced techniques such as SEM are employed to visualize the surface morphology of the particles and TEM is employed to examine the internal structure of the nanocarriers by directing an electron beam through the sample. Also, CLSM is used for examining the shapes of nanocarriers for encapsulation by loading with fluorescence substances. AFM is the only technique utilized to monitor surface topography such as roughness (Maviah et al., 2020; Layman et al., 2018). In a study, whey protein isolate (WPI) and zein proteins were prepared as core-shell complex nanoparticles for potential use in drug delivery applications. The WPI-zein complex nanoparticles displayed a distinct core-shell structure, indicating that WPI was successfully adsorbed onto the surface of zein nanoparticles using the pH-shifting method. At higher WPI concentrations, the complex nanoparticles maintained a regular spherical shape with smaller sizes. As the mass ratio of WPI to zein decreased, larger, irregular particle aggregates were formed, followed by bridging flocculation. TEM imaging highlighted the crucial influence of the WPI to zein mass ratio on the preparation of stable, small-sized complex nanoparticles (Agwa et al., 2022).

## 3.3 Surface charge and hydrophilicity

Effectiveness, stability, cellular absorption, and *in vivo* distribution are all impacted by the surface properties of nanocarriers, such as surface charge and hydrophilicity, which vary greatly in their degree of adsorption of certain proteins, such as opsonins. One important parameter that represents the electrical characteristics of particles is the zeta-potential, which is frequently measured in relation to pH. The most popular method for determining the zeta-potential value is electrophoretic light scattering. The value of the zeta-potential defines their interactions with each other and with other compounds (Li et al., 2024; Alshawwa et al., 2022). In general, nanocarriers with a $\zeta$-potential more than $\pm 30$ mV have been reported to exhibit stability within the carrier, as the surface charge inhibits particle aggregation (Hong et al., 2020). However, the presence of oppositely charged particles within a system may facilitate flocculation. For effective drug delivery, nanocarriers should ideally possess a neutral and hydrophilic surface to minimize plasma protein adsorption and escape from the components of the reticuloendothelial system PEGylation could be employed to reduce the adsorption of opsonins on protein-based nanocarriers (Li et al., 2024; Alshawwa et al., 2022; Jain et al., 2018). In a study, Gharbavi et al. developed a microemulsion and nanoparticle hybrid nanocarrier system for paclitaxel delivery in breast cancer treatment. Folic-acid conjugated BSA nanoparticles were used as the fraction of the microemulsions' aqueous part, which stimulates the surface and steady the nanocarriers through the negative charge. The average zeta-potential of the BSA nanocarrier systems ranged from $-4.15$ to $-18.20$ mV. Also, BSA was modified *via* PEGylation to enhance surface hydrophilicity (Gharbavi et al., 2020).

## 3.4 Particle structure

The structural analysis of protein-based nanocarriers is conducted to assess the nature of the proteins as well as any modifications in their conformation, folding, and chemical bonding. Fourier transform infrared spectroscopy (FTIR) is based on the principle that molecules absorb infrared radiation at specific frequencies, which are characteristic of their molecular structure. This technique facilitates the precise characterization of protein structures in solution, offering enhanced spatial and temporal resolution. X-ray diffraction (XRD) is another used technique for examining crystalline materials in terms of their phase composition, crystallite size, morphology, lattice structure, and other relevant properties (Verma et al., 2018).

## 3.5 Drug loading capacity and encapsulation efficiency

When evaluating the effectiveness of nanocarriers as delivery systems, two important factors are their loading capacity and encapsulation efficiency. Encapsulation efficiency indicates the percentage of drug loaded into the nanoparticles relative to the total amount initially given, while loading capacity indicates the maximum amount of drug (g/g) that can be incorporated into the nanocarriers. An efficient nanocarrier system must have a high drug loading capacity since it reduces the quantity of matrix material required for administration. Drugs can be loaded into the nanocarriers by either integrating the drug during the nanocarrier developing process (incorporation method) or soaking into the drug dispersion after preparation (adsorption/absorption approach) (Li et al., 2024; Işıklan et al., 2021). The kind of protein, particle structure, pH, and temperature are some of the variables that influence the encapsulation and loading characteristics of protein nanoparticles. Physical, chemical, or enzymatic changes can frequently improve these qualities. Physical modification methods designed for this purpose include thermal, high-pressure, freezing, and microwave treatments. Chemical or enzymatic modifications involve controlled hydrolysis, crosslinking, and conjugation techniques (Li et al., 2024). Işıklan et al. developed gelatin-including magnetic graphene oxide (GO) nanosheets in order to use in photothermal therapy and paclitaxel delivery. The developed formulations enhanced biocompatibility, increased cell attachment and entry and had a drug loading capacity of $19.54 \pm 1.54\%$ and high drug entrapment efficiency of $81.21 \pm 2.75\%$ due to gelatin polymer *via* its functional groups making the character of the materials amphiphilic (Işıklan et al., 2021).

## 3.6 *In vitro* drug release

The most important properties of polymer-based nanocarrier systems which affect the therapeutic efficiency are *in vitro* drug release and protein degradation. To develop formulation and assess batch-to-batch variability, *in vitro* drug release studies are performed. In addition, compliance with the regulations and alignments with the specific label claims are ensured. Although there is not any regulatory standard for this purpose, various methods are used to assess *in vitro* drug release from nanocarriers. *In vitro* drug release tests generally involve placing nanocarriers in a release medium and taking samples at specific times. The drug concentration is determined after delivery using appropriate analytical procedures such as ultraviolet-visible (UV) spectrophotometry or high-performance liquid chromatography (HPLC). The most popular *in vitro* drug release method is dialysis, which comes in three forms: reverse, side-by-side, and regular. The other methods include sample and separation (the types of which are membrane filters, centrifugation, ultracentrifugation, and ultrafiltration), continuous flow and dynamic dissolution micro-dialysis (Alshawwa et al., 2022). Drug release from protein-based nanocarriers is influenced by factors like protein degradation, drug diffusion through nanoparticle pores, desorption from the polymer surface, and external field-triggered pulsed delivery (Tarhini et al., 2017; Hong et al., 2020; Tarhini et al., 2017). In a study, silk fibroin nanoparticles loaded with rifampin were produced to treat pulmonary tuberculosis. Only $36 \pm 1.8\%$ of the drug was released in Phosphate Buffered Saline (PBS) after 24 hours, according to *in vitro* release testing due to the stability of the nanoparticles. On the other hand, when macrophage lysate was provided as a supplement, drug release increased to $55.0 \pm 1.2\%$, and sustained release was obtained when fresh lysate was added regularly. Enzyme activity of macrophage lysate was thought to be the cause of this enhanced release. Silk fibroin is slowly degraded *in vitro*, but certain enzymes can accelerate its biodegradation *in vivo* (Mitra et al., 2022).

### 3.7 Stability

A crucial factor in applying protein nanocarriers as delivery systems is their stability under many environmental conditions including pH, heat, light and enzyme activity. Environmental stability is typically assessed by determining the differences in particle size and zeta potential under these conditions. The stability of nanoparticles is mostly determined by their surface properties, especially their charge and hydrophobicity (Li et al., 2024). Cross-linking techniques can be used to increase stability and ensure long-term drug delivery in protein-based nanocarrier systems. Protein-based nanoparticles are usually prepared using a series of cross-linkers such as chemical, ionic, thermal and enzymatic cross-linkers (Işıklan et al., 2021). One of the most popular cross-linkers to improve stability, mechanical strength and drug release kinetics is glutaraldehyde. Chen et al. prepared dual-response gelatin nanoparticles loaded with doxorubicin (DOX) and indocyanine green (ICG) to treat breast cancer. Glutaraldehyde (GA) was added to these nanoparticles to increase their mechanical strength and stability and they were aimed to be sensitive to temperature and matrix metalloproteinase-2 stimuli. Drug release studies showed that non- and low-crosslinked nanoparticles had higher cumulative DOX release (57.3% and 44.8%, respectively), while high-crosslinked nanoparticles exhibited minimal increase in release. As a result, low-crosslinked nanoparticles were selected for further *in vivo* and *in vitro* antitumor evaluations (Chen et al., 2021).

## 4. Applications of protein-based nanocarriers as drug delivery system

Proteins are biodegradable by nature and have high compatibility with biological systems. Because of their properties of improving bioavailability and penetrating mucosal barriers, nanocarriers are widely used in drug delivery. Protein-based nanocarriers have attracted special attention among other types for their easy modifiable and metabolizable characteristics, and biodegradability. Moreover, due to their amphiphilicity and large number of binding sites, protein-based nanocarriers have a great capacity to encapsulate drugs. Through various interactions such as covalent bonding, electrostatic attraction, hydrogen bonding and hydrophobic forces, these nanocarriers contribute to drug binding. Consequently, Protein-based nanocarriers are essential in the development and progression of drug delivery systems (Tarhini et al., 2017; Sripriyalakshmi et al., 2014; Wen et al., 2022).

The different types of protein-based nanocarriers for drug delivery applications are given in Table 1.2.

Among nanocarriers, nanoparticles synthesized easily from a range of naturally derived or engineered proteins have become a promising platform for drug delivery applications (Jain et al., 2018). Patel et al. studied the application of HSA as a drug delivery system and solvent for four novel benzothiazinone (BTZ) compounds when administered to the lungs. When BTZ compounds were treated with albumin, their solubility increased up to

**TABLE 1.2** Drug delivery applications of different types of protein-based nanocarriers.

| Protein | Nanocarrier type | Drug loaded | Target disease/ Purpose | Description/Results | References |
|---|---|---|---|---|---|
| Bovine serum albumin (BSA) | Nanoparticle | Berberine (BBR) | Cancer | • To improve water solubility and bioavailability, BBR was loaded into BSA nanoparticles by desolvation method.<br>• The drug loading capacity of nanoparticles with an average size of 166 nm was 7.78% and the entrapment efficiency was 85.65%.<br>• These nanoparticles may be a useful way to deliver BBR intracellularly, which may increase its anticancer efficacy. | Solanki et al. (2021) |
| Human serum albumin (HSA) | Nanoparticle | Benzothiazinone (BTZ) | Tuberculosis | • The purpose of the study was to assess the effectiveness of HSA as a drug delivery system and solubilizing agent for the pulmonary administration of antimycobacterial BTZ drugs.<br>• HSA-based nanoparticles with a zeta potential of −31 mV and a particle size of 169 nm showed an encapsulation efficiency ranging from 37% to 60%.<br>• More than half of the drugs was released in 4 hours due to protease-triggered drug release.<br>• In a macrophage model infected with *M. tuberculosis in vitro*, the nanoparticles demonstrated potent antimycobacterial activity. | Patel et al. (2020) |
| Lactalbumin | Nanosphere | siPlk1 and curcumin (CUR) | Cancer | • Curcumin (CUR) and siPlk1 were co-loaded into α-lactalbumin (α-Lac) nanocarriers, which self-assembled into nanospheres (NS) after partially hydrolyzing into amphiphilic peptides.<br>• To target integrins that are overexpressed in HeLa cells, the CRGDK peptide was attached to the nanospheres. High intracellular glutathione levels in cancer cells caused the drug to be released from the nanospheres.<br>• The co-delivered nanosphere platform revealed synergistic antitumor action and excellent tumor targeting, according to both *in vitro* cell viability tests and *in vivo* antitumor evaluations. | Li et al. (2019) |

(*Continued*)

TABLE 1.2 Drug delivery applications of different types of protein-based nanocarriers.—cont'd

| Protein | Nanocarrier type | Drug loaded | Target disease/ Purpose | Description/Results | References |
|---|---|---|---|---|---|
| Zein | Nanoparticle | Enrofloxacin/ ciprofloxacin/ metronidazole/ nitrofurantoin/ norfloxacin | Gastrointestinal infections | • By adding succinyl groups or changing –COOH groups, zinc nanoparticles with modified hydrophobicity were produced *via* nanoprecipitation.<br>• More hydrophilic drugs, such as norfloxacin and nitrofurantoin, showed higher release (~75% and ~65%, respectively) under intestinal conditions, where gastrointestinal infections occur.<br>• The antibiotic-loaded Zein nanoparticles enhanced bacterial inactivation against Escherichia coli and Salmonella typhimurium infections. | Peña-Bahamonde et al. (2023) |
| Gliadin (Gli) | Nanogel | Methotrexate | Cancer | • Gli nanoparticles and sodium caseinate (CAS) were used to produce nanogels *via* a pH-cycle method, which served as a carrier for methotrexate (MTX).<br>• The nanogels were spherical, with 146 nm in diameter, 0.19 polydispersity index, and 23 mV a zeta-potential.<br>• MTX had a 27.35% loading capacity and a pH-dependent release rate, with a faster release at 5.0 than at 7.2.<br>• The excellent cytotoxicity of the nanogels against cancer cells was shown by *in vitro* MTT studies. | Xu et al. (2022) |
| Hordein | Core-shell nanoparticles | Quercetin (Que) | Colon cancer | • Hordein/pectin nanoparticles developed with an emphasis on colon-specific release for the oral administration of quercetin (Que).<br>• These nanoparticles enhanced encapsulation efficiency of Que and offered superior defense against salt and UV rays.<br>• After 6 hours, $80.60 \pm 1.78\%$ of Que was released from the nanoparticles in intestinal fluid. | (Xiaomin Zhang et al., 2023b) |
| Kafirin | Nanoparticles | Curcumin (CUR) | Drug delivery applications | • Curcumin (CUR) was encapsulated using kafirin and zein nanoparticles.<br>• Compared to zein nanoparticles, cur was released from kafirin nanoparticles more slowly, resulting in a sustained-release mechanism.<br>• The stability of CUR in gastric fluid was preserved by its binding with kafirin, and the release in intestinal fluid was further reduced by covering the nanoparticles with gum Arabic. | Ye et al. (2024) |

| | | | | | |
|---|---|---|---|---|---|
| Legumin/vicilin (LV) | Nanoparticles | Folic acid (FA) | Drug delivery applications | • Glutaraldehyde crosslinked LV protein-based nanoparticles were self-assembled using poloxamer 188 *via* pH-coacervation method.<br>• Loading capacity of the nanoparticles was 26.3 mg/g, encapsulation efficiency of 13.5%, and the mean size was about 50 nm.<br>• The release of folic acid was modified by the presence of enzymes and pH.<br>• These nanoparticles were promising for applications involving controlled drug delivery and were non-toxic to Caco-2 cells. | Fang et al. (2024) |
| β-lactoglobulin | Nanoparticle, nanofiber, and nanotube | Vancomycin | Drug delivery applications | • Vancomycin loaded β-lactoglobulin nanocarriers including nanoparticles, nanofibers, and nanotubes were prepared.<br>• The nanocarriers were high pH responsive, with maximum vancomycin loading at pH 7.4.<br>• The nanotubes had the highest drug-loading efficiency, followed by nanofibers and nanoparticles.<br>• Nanofibers showed the lowest drug release rate at pH 7.4, indicating greater stability. | Ahadi-Amandi et al. (2025) |
| Soy protein isolate | Nanoparticles | Curcumin (CUR) | Drug delivery applications | • Soy protein isolate/cellulose nanocrystal nanoparticles, which have a low PdI (0.14) and a small size (197.7 nm), were developed for the delivery of curcumin (CUR).<br>• Across a pH (3–9), temperature (30–90°C), and salt content (0–40 mmol/L) range, the nanoparticles showed stability. During simulated gastrointestinal digestion, they demonstrated a sustained release and a high encapsulation efficiency (88.3%).<br>• According to the results, cellulose nanocrystal nanoparticles together with soy protein isolate appear to be an appropriate delivery approach for hydrophobic bioactive substances. | Wang et al. (2020) |

*(Continued)*

TABLE 1.2 Drug delivery applications of different types of protein-based nanocarriers.—cont'd

| Protein | Nanocarrier type | Drug loaded | Target disease/ Purpose | Description/Results | References |
|---|---|---|---|---|---|
| Glutenin | Nanoparticles | Retinoic acid (RA) | Breast cancer | • To improve retinoic acid (RA) delivery to MCF-7 breast cancer cells, folic acid-conjugated RA-loaded glutenin nanoparticles were developed.<br>• The spherical and 185 nm-sized nanoparticles had a loading capacity of 9.9% and an encapsulation efficiency of 83.5%.<br>• By promoting endocytosis, they allowed RA to enter the cells. The released RA dVemonstrated therapeutic potential for the treatment of breast cancer by dramatically raising reactive oxygen species levels and damaging the integrity of the mitochondrial membrane. | Rajeshkumar et al. (2024) |
| Human histones | Nanococktail | Doxorubicin (DOX) | Multidrug resistant tumors | • Using DOX, the NIR dye IR825, and human histones, a therapeutic nanococktail known as DIR825@histone was developed for nucleus-targeted chemophotothermal treatment of multidrug-resistant malignancies.<br>• Through transcytosis, the nanoparticles effectively entered cells, penetrated malignant tissues, and targeted cell nuclei. The therapeutic method was improved by the efficient photothermal performance DIR825@histone and thermally induced drug release. | Guo et al. (2022) |
| Protamine | Nanoemulsion and nanocapsules | Cyclosporine-A (CsA) | Transdermal drug delivery applications | • For the delivery of CsA to the skin, protein-based nanosystems such as nanoemulsion (NE) and three different kinds of nanocapsules (NC–1P, NC-2P, and NC-i) were prepared.<br>• These nanosystems contained CsA (60%–80%) in their oily core and released the drug in a controlled manner. They had low polydispersity index, 200–300 nm particle diameters, and zeta potentials between −16 and + 35 mV.<br>• Using Franz diffusion cells, the protamine setting in the shell affected the retention of CsA skin. | Alvarez-Figueroa et al. (2019) |

| | | | | | |
|---|---|---|---|---|---|
| Elastin | Nanogel | Decursin (DEC) | Prostate cancer | • To treat castration-resistant prostate cancer, injectable elastin nanogels were prepared to deliver DEC, a small molecule inhibitor that targets the Wnt/β-catenin system.<br>• The nanogels demonstrated low toxicity, flexibility, and good biocompatibility. According to vitro studies, the DU145 cell line exhibited considerable cytotoxicity and a sustained, pH-dependent DEC release over a period of 120 hours.<br>• An advantage over free DEC was provided by the improved permeability and retention (EPR) effect, which made targeted drug delivery to prostate cancers easier. | Rather et al. (2024) |
| Collagen | Nanofiber | Artemisinin (ART) | Malaria | • Polycaprolactone (PCL)/collagen nanofibers loaded with ART were prepared to treat malaria.<br>• These electrospun nanofibers prevented drug recrystallization and showed prolonged drug release.<br>• A Fickian release mechanism was obtained, and the release persisted for up to 48 hours. | Huo et al. (2021) |
| Silk fibroin | Nanoparticles | Rifampicin | Pulmonary tuberculosis | • Using a pH-induced self-assembly method, silk fibroin nanoparticles coated with rifampicin were produced for pulmonary drug delivery against Mycobacterium.<br>• High drug loading (21.0 ± 2.1%), high cellular absorption (66.2 ± 2.1%), and an ideal size of 165 ± 38 nm at pH 3.8 were all demonstrated by these nanoparticles.<br>• Additionally, they showed good aerosol characteristics, with a mass median aerodynamic diameter of 3.82 ± 0.71 μm.<br>• The nanoparticles demonstrated prolonged drug release in macrophage lysates after being effectively absorbed by macrophages through clathrin- and caveolae-mediated endocytosis. | Mitra et al. (2022) |

*(Continued)*

**TABLE 1.2** Drug delivery applications of different types of protein-based nanocarriers.—cont'd

| Protein | Nanocarrier type | Drug loaded | Target disease/ Purpose | Description/Results | References |
|---|---|---|---|---|---|
| Gelatin | Nanoparticles | Galunisertib | Colorectal cancer | • To detect and treat colorectal cancer, a hybrid system comprising diatomite and gold nanoparticles was prepared. The platform, which was capped with gelatin shells, increased Galunisertib's drug loading capacity, which varied between 2.4 and 5.6 μg·mg−1. Because gelatin-degrading enzymes are overexpressed in the tumor microenvironment, this system made it possible to monitor both drug release and gelatin degradation using spectroscopic techniques.<br>• The gelatin capping material made drug release responsive to external stimuli, allowing for targeted drug delivery. | Tramontano et al. (2021) |
| Casein | Micelles | Benzydamine | Drug delivery applications | • Benzydamine-loaded casein nanoparticles were created using a spray-drying method. The micelles had particle sizes ranging from 135.9 to 994.2 nm, with drug loading varying between 16.02% and 57.41%, and encapsulation efficiency ranging from 34.61% to 78.82%.<br>• Spray drying transformed benzydamine from crystalline to amorphous form, which enhanced its dissolution rate. The nanocarriers facilitated the sustained release of benzydamine. | Zahariev et al. (2021) |
| Whey protein | Nanoparticles in film | Frankincense essential oil (FRK) | Wound healing | • Using a spray-drying method, FRK, which was isolated from Bosolica papyrifera oliogum resin, was encapsulated into whey protein nanoparticles.<br>• The FRK-loaded nanoparticles were then embedded into FRK resin *via* solvent casting to have a bionanocomposite film.<br>• The nanoparticles had a spherical diameter of about 151 nm and an encapsulation efficiency of 75.9%. The film outperformed the nanoparticles alone in terms of tensile strength and sustained release of FRK essential oil.<br>• Additionally, it demonstrated strong antimicrobial properties, little hemolytic activity, and superior wound-healing capacity *in vivo*. | Agwa et al. (2022) |

| | | | | | |
|---|---|---|---|---|---|
| Lactoferrin | Nanoparticles | Curcumin (CUR) | Neurodegenerative diseases | • To provide neuroprotection, lactoferrin nanoparticles loaded with curcumin (CUR) were used for developing a nose-to-brain delivery system. The hydrophobic region of lactoferrin was bound to CUR without the use of cross-linking agents or toxic reagents.<br>• The nanoparticles had a size of $84.8 \pm 6.5$ nm and a zeta potential of $+22.8 \pm 4.3$ mV. Their permeability coefficient ($4.36 \pm 0.79 \times 10^{-6}$ cm/second) was 50 times higher than that of CUR suspension.<br>• *In vivo*, intranasal administration led to an increase in CUR delivery, with 59.7% of the drug directly reaching the brain. | Li et al. (2023) |
| Wheat germ agglutinin (WGA) | Nanostructured lipid carriers (NLC) | Quercetin (QU) | Intracellular infective diseases | • A nanostructured lipid carrier (NLC) containing WGA protein surface-functionalized (~200 nm, PDI >0.3) was developed and characterized.<br>• It provided controlled drug release by successfully encapsulating quercetin (QU), a lipophilic model molecule.<br>• The functionalization of the WGA protein improved macrophage phagocytosis. | Hädrich et al. (2022) |
| Lysozyme | Nanoparticles | Metformin (MET) | Cancer | • Metformin-loaded nanoparticles with shellac cores and lysozyme coating were prepared. A 3D tumor cell culture extracellular matrix (ECM) was partially broken down by the lysozyme, increasing porosity and nanoparticle penetration.<br>• The antitumor efficacy of the MET-loaded nanoparticles was assessed *in vitro* using a three-dimensional human hepatic tumor model. | Wang, Madden and Paunov (2024) |

140-fold. The HSA nanoparticles, which were prepared using a modified desolvation method, had an average particle size of 169 nm and a zeta potential of −31 mV. They showed drug encapsulation efficiencies ranging from 37% to 60%. More than 50% of the drug was released within 4 hours due to protease-triggered BTZ release. The nanoparticles improved antimycobacterial activity in an *in vitro M. tuberculosis*-infected macrophage model and demonstrated efficacy *in vivo* through intranasal administration in *M. tuberculosis*-infected mice (Patel et al., 2020).

Advanced nanocarriers are used to increase the effectiveness of regulating treatment and to reduce side effects by responding to changing physiological conditions and external stimuli in cancer treatment. α-Lactalbumin nanospheres were developed by Li et al. to co-load curcumin and small interfering RNA (siPlk1) to enhance their anticancer activity.Since these nanospheres were designed to respond to the acidic pH and redox conditions present in tumor cells, curcumin and siPlk1 were released into the cytoplasm immediately. The effect of EPR and the acquisition of overexpressed integrins in tumors was improved. In addition, downregulation of Plk1 pathway led to significant tumor suppression through a synergistic mechanism. Cellular uptake was enhanced due to the amount of overexpressed integrins in tumors and EPR effect. In addition, downregulation of Plk1 pathway led to significant tumor suppression through a synergistic mechanism (Alvarez-Figueroa et al., 2019).

Nanogels, which provide high encapsulation efficiency and drug loading capacity due to their swelling tendency, hold promise for precise drug delivery. The inverse mini emulsion method was used to create elastin-based nanogels cross-linked with bis(sulfosuccinimidyl) suberate (BS3). These nanogels showed a high drug loading capacity of 49% and an encapsulation efficiency of 91% when loaded with decursin targeting the Wnt/β-catenin pathways in prostate cancer. The nanogels showed exceptional stability with an average size of 152.9 nm and a zeta potential of $-52.67 \pm 1.6$ mV. Targeted release in the tumor microenvironment was achieved by *in vitro* studies showing pH-dependent drug release, which was extended to a period of 120 hours with increased swelling in acidic conditions (Rather et al., 2024).

By assembling *via* temperature and pH dependent aggregation without using crosslinking agents, β-lactoglobulin was included to form pH sensitive nanocarriers such as nanoparticles, nanofibers, and nanotubes. Due to the amphiphilic nature of β-lactoglobulin, these nanocarriers loaded with vancomycin showed significant affinity for both hydrophobic and amphiphilic ligands. The most effective drug loading was demonstrated by nanotubes, followed by nanofibers and nanoparticles. Nanofibers showed the lowest drug release rate indicating superior stability, whereas all nanocarriers showed pH sensitive controlled drug release at pH 7.4. These β-lactoglobulin based nanocarriers provide a promising method for the delivery of antibiotics (Murphy et al., 2025).

Micelle type casein nanocarriers were prepared for benzydamine delivery using coacervation method and spray drying. The αs1, αs2 and β-caseins formed the micelle core and glycosylated κ-casein stabilized the outer layer. The micelle particle diameters ranged from 135.9 to 994.2 nm, while encapsulation and drug loading efficiencies ranged from 34.61% to 78.82% and 16.02%–57.41%, respectively. Both hydrophobic and hydrophilic interactions were possible due to micelle pH-dependent activity and surface charge-induced structural changes. The study demonstrated the potential of these nanocarriers for long-term benzydamine delivery (Zahariev et al., 2021).

Nanocarriers are useful in skin drug delivery applications to take advantage of the benefits of the proteins. Alvarez-Figueroa et al. developed four protamine-based nanocarrier formulations to enhance cyclosporine-A (CsA) skin delivery. The formulations included nanoemulsion and nanocapsules prepared *via* one-step, two-step, and injection methods, with particle sizes between 200 and 300 nm, low polydispersity, and zeta potentials ranging from −16 to +35 mV. The nanocarriers efficiently encapsulated CsA (60%–80%) and provided controlled drug release. Injection-prepared nanocapsules were the smallest. All formulations improved CsA's transdermal delivery, with protamine in the shell influencing skin retention. These protamine-based nanocarriers hold promise for transdermal CsA administration, particularly for treating dermal inflammation (Alvarez-Figueroa et al., 2019).

Nanostructured lipid carriers (NLC) system provides the advantages of protection drugs from degradation, enhanced bioavailability, and targeted drug release. In a study, novel glycosylated amphiphilic nanostructured lipid carriers (NLCs) (~200 nm, PDI >0.3) were utilized to conjugate wheat germ agglutinin (WGA) on their surface. WGA promotes phagocytosis by binding to receptors in the alveolar epithelium. The aim was to enhance intracellular drug delivery to treat intracellular infections. NLCs contained curcumin and WGA protein surface functionality greatly improved macrophage phagocytosis (Hädrich et al., 2022).

## 4.1 Commercialized albumin-based nanocarriers in clinical application

To date, two products based on nanoparticle albumin bound (nab) technology have been commercialized, Abraxane and Fyarro.

Abraxane (nab paclitaxel) is an injectable ~130-nm nanoparticle formulation of paclitaxel, a taxane antimicrotubule hydrophobic agent, bounded to human serum albumin that was approved by Food and Drug Administration (FDA) in 2005 for the treatment for metastatic breast cancer. It is the first approved formulation utilizing the nab technology for clinical use (FDA, 2005, Abraxane Approval Package). It has been demonstrated that Abraxane enhanced tumor accumulation and safety profile of paclitaxel compared to solvent-based formulation already in clinical application. Noteworthy, the utilization of the polyethoxylated castor oil (Cremophor EL) as a solubilizer in the conventional formulation was related to several side effects such as liver metabolism changes and altered pharmacokinetics (Murphy et al., 2025). Currently, Abraxane is used for multiple indications in oncology including advanced (metastatic) breast and pancreatic cancer and advanced non–small cell lung cancer.

Fyarro (nab rapamycin), which obtained marketing authorization with orphan designation by FDA in 2021, is the second product approved utilizing the nab delivery platform for drug delivery. Fyarro is a human albumin-bound formulation of the poorly water-soluble drug rapamycin, also known as sirolimus. It is the first and only FDA-approved treatment for adults with advanced malignant perivascular epithelioid cell tumors (PEComa) (FDA, 2021, Fyarro Approval). It inhibits the tumor growth by blocking the mechanistic target of rapamycin (mTOR) pathway of cellular signaling. According to the results of phase II clinical studies in patients with malignant PEComa, intravenous treatment with nab rapamycin demonstrated rapid and durable responses, and manageable adverse events. The study results supported the treatment with *nab*-sirolimus as a new treatment option for the disease (Wagner et al., 2021). Clinical trials aiming to evaluate nab-sirolimus for other types of cancers including advanced or recurrent endometrioid-type endometrial cancer and neuroendocrine tumors (NETs) are ongoing (ClinicalTrials.gov).

## 5. Targeting strategies for protein-based nanocarriers

Targeted protein-based nanocarriers have drawn a lot of interest because of their capacity to transport medications or therapeutic substances to the specific cells or tissues as well as their biocompatibility and biodegradability. Various studies have been carried out to enhance their targeting efficiency through the rapid liver and renal clearance and thus therapeutic outcomes (Sandra et al., 2019). The targeting ability of drug loaded protein-based nanocarriers can be increased based on two main strategies: passive targeting and active targeting (MaHam et al., 2009).

### 5.1 Passive targeting

Due to the EPR effect, which is caused by leaky vasculature and reduced lymphatic drainage, nanocarriers can accumulate in tumor tissues. Particle size, surface charge, and surface properties are some examples of factors that can affect biodistribution and *in vivo* circulation time. Through the EPR effect, the long-term circulation of nanoparticles in the bloodstream is essential to promote their accumulation in diseased tissues (Zahariev et al., 2021). The size of nanoparticles has a significant impact on the effectiveness of passive targeting, especially when it comes to the EPR effect in tumor tissues. Abnormal blood arteries with larger fenestrations are a feature of the tumor vasculature that allows nanoparticles to preferentially accumulate in an ideal size range in tumor tissue. Rigid, and spherical nanoparticles between 50 and 200 nm generally show the strongest propensity for long-term circulation, as they are large enough to avoid rapid absorption by the liver and spleen while avoiding renal clearance. In addition, after intravenous injection, proteins with molecular weights greater than the renal threshold (40 kDa) tend to preferentially accumulate in neoplastic tissues (Li et al., 2023; Hädrich et al., 2022). Moreover, changing the surface charge of nanocarriers can improve cellular uptake by enhancing their contact with negatively charged cell membranes. More efficient cellular uptake has been demonstrated by nanoparticles with higher surface charge and greater surface-to-volume ratio (Wang et al., 2024a, 2024b). By delaying clearance *via* reticuloendothelial system (RES) and providing essential stealth properties, protein-based nanocarriers with steric hindrance and biocompatibility enable prolonged circulation. The hydrodynamic size of the nanoparticles rises when polyethylene glycol (PEG) is added to protein-based nanocarriers, which decreases opsonization and the particles' subsequent clearance by RES. Because this alteration produces a thick hydrophilic covering of long PEG chains that shields the core from nonspecific hydrophobic interactions with serum proteins (such opsonins), it ultimately contributes to decreased uptake by RES (Sandra et al., 2019).

## 5.2 Active targeting

One of the most popular active targeting approaches is ligand-conjugated targeting. The increased uptake into diseased tissues is facilitated by the binding of protein ligands to overexpressed receptors on tumor or endothelial cells. Ligand-conjugated nanocarriers are coupled to specific receptors overexpressed in specific tissues using antibodies (e.g., DI17E6, hKC4), peptides (e.g., arginylglycylaspartic acid (RGD), epidermal growth factor (EGF)), vitamins (e.g., folic acid and biotin), small molecules (e.g., retinoic acid), carbohydrates (e.g., heparin), hormones (e.g., luteinizing hormone-releasing hormone), enzymes (e.g., collagenase), and polymers (e.g., polyethylenimine (PEI) and the thermoresponsive polymer poly(N-isopropylacrylamide-co-acrylamide)-block-polyallylamine). Electrostatic interactions or covalent chemical conjugation procedures are frequently used to attach these ligands to functional groups on the surface of protein nanocarriers (Işıklan et al., 2021; Sandra et al., 2019). In a recent study, ibrutinib was delivered to cancer cell lines HeLa, BT-474 and SKBR3 using folic acid-conjugated silk nanoparticles, specifically by upregulating folate receptors. After 24 hours, cellular uptake studies revealed that folic acid-functionalized nanoparticles were completely internalized into cancer cells, in contrast to unfunctionalized nanoparticles. According to these results, the nanocarrier formed may be useful to specifically deliver drugs to cancer cells overexpressing the folate receptor (MaHam et al., 2009).

Protein-based nanoparticles are notably capable of being internalized by tumor cells through receptor-mediated endocytosis or transcytosis. For example, albumin selectively interacts with the membrane-associated Glycoprotein 60 (gp60), also referred to as albondin. Upon binding to albondin on endothelial cell surfaces, albumin triggers its internalization and active transport. Specifically, albondin can associate with the intracellular caveolin-1, initiating the inward folding of the cell membrane to form transcytosis vesicles called caveolae. These vesicles transport albumin and other plasma components into the extravascular site. Consequently, anticancer drugs encapsulated or conjugated within albumin nanoparticles are concurrently delivered to the encompassing region of the tumor cell (Iqbal et al., 2021). Functionalized aptamers are an additional alternative for active targeting that can improve drug efficacy and sensitivity. Aptamers are single-stranded oligonucleotides that are ideal ligands for targeting tumor cells or other disease-associated biomarkers due to their high affinity and specificity for their specific targets. An aptamer can be covalently attached to a protein-based nanoparticle to target specific receptors or antigens overexpressed on diseased cell membranes. Targeting overexpressed receptors on tumor cells was made achievable by incorporating the Anti-nucleoin aptamer (AS1411) onto the surface of DOX-loaded BSA nanoparticles. When compared to untreated nanoparticles, the aptamer-modified nanoparticles demonstrated increased cellular uptake and anticancer activity against MCF-7 cells (Iqbal et al., 2021).

Developing stimuli-responsive systems, such as employing pH-responsive proteins in nanocarriers, is one of the alternative targeting options (Rather et al., 2024). Alternatives include the development of hybrid nanocarrier systems, such as protein-polymer, protein-lipid, and protein-metal hybrid nanoparticles, or the use of magnetic nanoparticles, ultrasound, and light-triggered release to provide active targeting by external stimuli (Sandra et al., 2019; Georgilis et al., 2020; Elzoghby et al., 2013).

## 6. Superiorities and limitations for protein-based nanocarriers

Protein based nanoparticles show favorable characteristics for diagnostic, therapeutic and vaccination purposes compared to other types of nanoparticles due to their unique structural and biological properties. Firstly, they show inherent biocompatibility and biodegradability considering that their composition is based on natural proteins. They generally degrade into non-toxic degradation products and are less likely to trigger unwanted immune responses (Georgilis et al., 2020). Secondly, they are versatile, show great source availability and allow cost-effective large-scale manufacturing at mild conditions. Thirdly, the presence of hydrophilic and hydrophobic groups in the structure of proteins allow binding/encapsulation of several therapeutic agents with different physicochemical properties. In several studies, protein nanoparticles have shown high loading capacity particularly for hydrophobic drugs the delivery of which is challenging. Nevertheless, drug loading depends on protein type and method of nanoparticle preparation, thus a rationale system and preparation design should be done to achieve high drug loading (Tarhini et al., 2017; Elzoghby et al., 2013).

In addition, improved performance can be achieved by controlled and stimuli responsive (e.g., pH, enzyme, etc.) drug release. It is important to mention that proteinic structures are natural targets for various types of proteases present in the human body. In a study by Yu et al. (2018), protein nanoparticles showing proteases-sensitive drug release were developed. Following systemic administration in rats, the nanoparticles demonstrated efficient delivery of a neuroprotective peptide (NR2B9c) and a cytolytic peptide (melittin) for treatment of stroke and cancer, respectively and showed good safety profile. Lastly, it is possible to tailor the surface of nanoparticles to enhance distribution, to provide active targeting, reduce off-target cell interaction and minimize side effects. Moreover, proteins such as albumin and transferrin show inherent affinity for specific receptors in cells which can lead to enhanced interaction of nanoparticles with cells overexpressing the specific receptors. In this context, active targeting of nanoparticles is possible through intrinsic targeting ability of individual proteins. For example, transferrin-based nanoparticles are advantageous for targeted delivery to the brain (Obozina et al., 2023; Nogueira-Librelotto et al., 2017). Overall, due to their biodegradability, functional versatility and ability to provide sustained and targeted delivery protein nanoparticles serve as a highly suitable delivery platform for different drugs and show superiority especially in terms of safety compared to other nanocarriers composed of synthetic polymer or inorganic materials.

Beside their numerous advantages, translation of protein-based nanocarriers into clinical settings faces its own challenges. Particularly, processing of proteins, formulation, manufacturing, stability, biodistribution and regulatory-related issues should be carefully addressed for developing commercial protein-based nanocarriers for medical applications.

Proteins are structurally sensitive to extreme conditions such as pH, ionic strength, high temperature, mechanical stress which can lead to protein denaturation and aggregation. While adjusting the temperature and pH of the environment can be an alternative to prepare protein nanoparticles (Ghadami et al., 2021), if the aforementioned factors are not optimized chemical and physical degradation of proteins can occur, ultimately resulting in alternations in protein structure and particle size. Consecutively, stability related issues lead to loss of nanoscale properties due to aggregation and negatively affect therapeutic effect (Tanjung et al., 2024; Siri et al., 2019). Lyophilization is widely employed to increase the stability of protein nanoparticles during storage. The utilization of appropriate stabilizers (e.g., sucrose, mannitol or trehalose) is critical in preventing aggregation and ensure long-term storage stability of nanoparticles (Anhorn et al., 2008).

Other challenges that nanoparticles face in physiological environment, is destabilization of their structure and nanoparticle aggregation. Moreover, nonspecific adsorption of blood components (e.g., albumin, fibrinogen and immunoglobulins, etc.) resulting in the formation of a layer around the particle called "protein corona" is an additional barrier that alters the physicochemical characteristics of nanoparticles and their *in vivo* performance, such as biodistribution, clearance and targeting ability (Lim et al., 2024; Xiao et al., 2022) While it is well established that nanoparticle characteristics (e.g., composition, size, hydrophobicity, charge, etc.) govern the formation of protein corona, the studies investigating the formation of protein corona specifically around protein nanoparticles are limited (Ilinskaya and Dobrovolskaia, 2017). Generally, hydrophobic particles, including protein nanoparticles, show increased adsorption of plasma proteins onto their surface compared to hydrophilic ones (Pustulka et al., 2020).

To minimize protein corona formation, enhance bioavailability and reduce clearance of nanoparticles, PEGylation approach, i.e., modification of the particle surface with the hydrophilic polymer PEG is extensively utilized (Suk et al., 2016). PEGylated gelatin nanoparticles showed enhanced blood circulation time and distribution is solid tumor following i.v. admistration in mice compared to non-PEGylated nanoparticles (Kaul and Amiji, 2004). More recently, it was reported that PEGylated gelatine nanoparticle could be utilized for co-delivery of therapeutic agents of chemotherapy (Amjadi et al., 2019). Even though human serum albumin is characterized by long half-life and low immunogenicity, albumin-based nanoparticles can be further pegylated to enhance their performance. A more sustained release of the drug tamoxifen was observed from pegylated human serum albumin-based nanoparticles compared to non-pegylated ones (Kouchakzadeh et al., 2014). In a recent study, pegylated human serum albumin-based nanoparticles were evaluated for coadministration of brain-derived neurotrophic factor (BDNF) and neurotrophic Factor 3 (NT3) which has a short half-life for age-related macular degeneration. Following intravitreal injection in mice, BDNF and NT3 levels within the retina were significantly increased on the initial day post administration of nanoparticles compared to BDNF and NT3, alone and were still detectable 28 days following administration (Dąbkowska et al., 2024). Interestingly, albumin has been used as a coating material for other nanocarriers systems. Surface-bound albumin has shown to enhance delivery of nanoparticles in several studies (Hyun et al., 2018; Chubarov, 2022).

Finally, limitations related to regulatory procedures should be addressed. Although several nano-based medicines have been successfully employed into clinical practice so far, the quality standards and regulatory guidelines for nanomedicines are still limited (Patra et al., 2018).

## 7. *In vivo* behavior of protein-based nanocarriers

The protein-based nanoparticles are preferred nano-based delivery systems for *in vivo* delivery of several hydrophobic and hydrophilic therapeutic agents (i.e., small and high molecular weight drugs). They have shown to improve treatment outcomes in terms of safety and efficacy. Since the introduction into clinical settings of albumin-bound paclitaxel loaded 130 nm sized particles (Abraxane) that outperformed in terms of efficacy and intratumor delivery the Cremophor-based paclitaxel while avoiding its Cremophor/ethanol-associated toxicities (Desai et al., 2006), different protein nanoparticles such as human serum albumin (Spada et al., 2021), gelatine (Yasmin et al., 2017), silk protein fibroin (Jain et al., 2018), etc. have been evaluated *in vivo* in preclinical models or/and human studies. In addition to therapeutic and diagnostic applications which are discussed herein, protein nanoparticles can be successfully utilized as vaccine platforms for various diseases, as reviewed in (Pandey et al., 2024; Nguyen and Tolia, 2021).

## 7.1 The parameters affecting *in vivo* performance of protein-based nanocarriers

Route of administration, physicochemical properties of nanoparticles and protein corona formation are major factors that have critical impact on the *in vivo* performance of protein-based nanocarriers as described below.

### 7.1.1 *Route of administration*

The route of administration affects the biodistribution and efficacy of nanoparticles. Each administration route has its own specific physiological and structural characteristics that should be considered for optimum drug delivery (Fuchs and Coester, 2010). While the *in vivo* performance of protein nanoparticles following parenteral administration is widely evaluated, other routes including nasal, pulmonary and oral route have also been explored (Hoogenboezem and Duvall, 2018; Choi et al., 2015; Hashem et al., 2018).

Recently, fluorescent albumin nanoparticles were found to translocate throughout different mouse organs and tissues following nasal, oral and intravenous administration and main accumulation was observed in the brain and intestine for nasal or oral administration (Morozova et al., 2023). Compared to human serum albumin solution, human serum albumin nanoparticles (smaller than 150 nm) fabricated *via* a desolvation technique showed increased intestinal uptake and transport in Caco-2 monolayers at equivalent concentrations. The nanoparticulate formulation did not demonstrate any toxicity at concentrations as high as 140 μg/mL suggesting its suitability for oral drug delivery (Hashem et al., 2018). In another study, albumin nanoparticles showed high biocompatibility over a wide dose range as well as suitable biodistribution profile following pulmonary delivery. Albumin nanoparticles (~190 nm) remained in the lung for extended periods of time compared to albumin in solution (~7 nm). The accumulation in the secondary organs (i.e., liver and kidneys) was small. Moreover, the nanoparticulate formulation was cleared more slowly than solution formulation (e.g., $64.1 \pm 8.5\%$ vs. $40.6 \pm 3.3\%$ at $t = 48h$, respectively) (Woods et al., 2015). The aforementioned studies provide valuable insights on uptake, distribution and clearance of protein nanoparticles necessary for their realistic development as nanomedicines.

### 7.1.2 *Nanoparticle characteristics*

Beside of the route of administration, nanoparticle stability, circulation in blood, uptake by cells, targeting capacity, cytotoxicity and clearance can be influenced by several factors related to nanoparticle characteristics. Composition, size, hydrophobicity, surface charge, morphology are critical parameters that affect the *in vivo* fate of nanoparticles (Xiao et al., 2022; Wei et al., 2018). Brown et al. (2020) investigated the effect of composition, size, shape, and stiffness of different nanoparticles on their penetration across the blood–brain barrier. It is reported that composition of particulate nanocarrier had the greatest impact on uptake and transport across a blood-brain barrier model. Among the different nanocarriers studied, 456 nm-sized transferrin spherical nanoparticles performed better than human serum albumin nanoparticles, liposomes and nonspherical polystyrene nanoparticles of different sizes and shapes (Brown et al., 2020). However, results obtained from *in vitro* studies should be correlated with *in vivo* performance of nanoparticles.

#### *7.1.3 Protein corona formation*

Protein corona (i.e., adsorption of blood components to nanoparticle surface) is another important factor that can affect the behavior, clearance and targeting capabilities of nanoparticles, including protein nanoparticles, upon exposure to biological environment (Xiao et al., 2022; Salvati et al., 2013). To understand the effect of hydrophobicity and charge of protein nanoparticles on macrophage uptake, Pustulka et al. prepared albumin, cationic albumin, and ovalbumin cross-linked nanoparticles showing variable surface characteristics and investigated their adsorbed protein coronas. The authors concluded that the protein corona varied in corona mass and composition between nanoparticles. It also influenced the nanoparticle internalization *in vitro* in J774A.1 macrophages (Pustulka et al., 2020). In another study, the protein corona on respiratory syncytial virus (RSV) and herpes simplex virus type 1 (HSV–I), affected the immune cell activation and viral pathogenesis (Ezzat et al., 2019). The effect between physicochemical characteristics and protein corona formation on the *in vivo* bioactivity and fate of protein nanoparticles remains yet to be further explored in more detail and in a comparative basis.

Clinical trials investigating protein-based nanoparticles for treatment purposes are given in Table 1.3. Noteworthy, most of the clinical trials involve nanoparticle albumin-bound (nab) drug formulations. The number of clinical trials when "albumin-bound nanoparticle" is used as a search term by Feb 2025 is 201. It is important to mention that a significant number of studies evaluate the use of nanoparticle albumin-bound drug in combination with other therapeutic agents. For the sake of brevity, only selected examples from clinical trials involving nab particles are added to Table 1.3. Clinical trials investigating ferritin nanoparticles for human immunodeficiency virus (HIV) (NCT06267872 and NCT05903339), Epstein–Barr Virus (NCT05683834 and NCT04645147) and SARS-CoV-2 (NCT04784767) (ClinicalTrials.gov) vaccination have also been excluded.

As mentioned earlier, different types of protein nanocarriers have been investigated as potential nanocarriers for several diseases, mainly for neurodegenerative disorders, infections and extensively cancer therapy. The *in vivo* evaluation of protein nanocarriers for the aforementioned purposes has been discussed below. Additionally, highlights from selected studies evaluating protein-based nanoparticles *in vivo* have been summarized in Table 1.4.

## 8. Treatment potentials for protein-based nanoparticles

### 8.1 Treatment of tumors

Ideally, for an efficacious and safe treatment of tumors, following parenteral administration anticancer agents should reach the target tumor site, affect the tumor cells without

**TABLE 1.3** Clinical studies involving protein-based nanoparticles registered in ClinicalTrials.gov.

| Protein | Nanocarrier type | Drug loaded | Target disease/Condition | Clinical trial ID<br>Clinical trial title | Phase | Clinical status |
|---|---|---|---|---|---|---|
| Albumin | Nanoparticles | Rapamycin | Advanced cancers | NCT02646319<br>Nanoparticle albumin-bound rapamycin in treating patients with advanced cancer with mtor mutations | Early Phase 1 | Completed |
| Albumin | Nanoparticles | Rapamycin | Recurrent or refractory solid tumors | NCT02975882<br>Nanoparticle albumin-bound rapamycin, temozolomide, and irinotecan hydrochloride in treating pediatric patients with recurrent or refractory solid tumors | Phase 1 | Completed |
| Albumin | Nanoparticles | Paclitaxel | Breast cancer, renal cell carcinoma | NCT03961698<br>Evaluation of IPI-549 combined with front-line treatments in pts. with triple-negative breast cancer or renal cell carcinoma | Phase 2 | Active, not recruiting |
| Albumin | Nanoparticles | Rapamycin | Advanced soft tissue sarcoma, locally advanced soft tissue sarcoma, metastatic soft tissue sarcoma | NCT03660930<br>Nab-sirolimus and pazopanib hydrochloride in treating patients with advanced nonadipocytic soft tissue sarcomas | Phase 1<br>Phase 2 | Active, not recruiting |
| Albumin | Nanoparticles | Sirolimus | PEComa, Malignant<br>TSC1 TSC2 mTOR pathway abberation | NCT03817515<br>Expanded access for ABI-009 in patients with advanced PEComa and patients with a malignancy with relevant genetic mutations or mTor pathway activation | – | Approved for marketing |
| Albumin | Nanoparticles | Paclitaxel | Pancreatic cancer, advanced or metastatic<br>brca1/2 mutation<br>palb2 gene mutation | NCT06783140<br>Study of NABPLAGEM versus Nab-paclitaxel/gemcitabine in BRCA1/2 or PALB2 pancreatic cancer (PLATINUM-CAN) | Phase 2<br>Phase 3 | Not yet recruiting |
| Albumin | Nanoparticles | Paclitaxel | Advanced lung non-small cell carcinoma,<br>Stage IIIB/IIIC/IV lung cancer AJCC v8 | NCT06096844<br>Chemotherapy combined with immunotherapy versus immunotherapy alone for older adults with stage IIIB-IV lung cancer, The ACHIEVE Trial | Phase 3 | Recruiting |
| Albumin | Nanoparticles | Paclitaxel | Breast cancer | NCT04137653<br>Treatment of triple-negative breast cancer with albumin-bound paclitaxel as neoadjuvant therapy: a prospective RCT | Phase 3 | Recruiting |

| | | | | | | |
|---|---|---|---|---|---|---|
| Gelatin | Nanoparticles | Doxycycline | Immediate implant placement | NCT06809829 Evaluation of doxycycline nanoparticle with gelatin sponge on immediate implant in esthetic region | Not Applicable | Recruiting |
| Casein | Micelles | Vitamin D3 | Vitamin D deficiency | NCT01807845 Bioavailability of vitamin d encapsulated in casein micelles, compared to its bioavailability in a synthetic emulsifier currently used for supplementation and enrichment | Not Applicable | Unknown status |
| Casein | Micelles | Vitamin D | Healthy individuals | NCT01259570 Bioavailability of vitamin d encapsulated in casein micelles, compared to its bioavailability in the milk-fat, or in a synthetic emulsifier currently used for supplementation and enrichment | Not Applicable | Unknown status |
| Zein | Nanocapsules | – | PreDiabetes, overweight and obesity | NCT05560412 Zein Nanoparticles for Glycemic Control (GLUCOCAPS) | Not Applicable | Completed |
| Whey | Nanoparticles | – | Periodontitis chronic localized slight | NCT06401798/Locally delivered whey protein nanoparticles gel in stage II Grade B periodontitis | Not Applicable | Recruiting |

TABLE 1.4 *In vivo* studies evaluating protein-based nanoparticles for treatment purposes.

| Protein | Nanocarrier type | Drug loaded | Target disease/ Condition | Administration route | *In vivo* model | Main results | References |
|---|---|---|---|---|---|---|---|
| Bovine serum albumin (RGD-modified) | Nanoparticles | Celastrol | Rheumatoid arthritis | Intravenous | Collagen-induced arthritis mouse | Suppression of the inflammatory response and reduction of the toxic effects of drug | Liu et al. (2024) |
| Bovine serum albumin | Nanoparticles | hMDA-7 plasmid | Pancreatic cancer | Subcutaneous | Pancreatic cancer mouse (BALB/c) model | Decrease in tumor size, significant suppression of VEGF expression | Zhu et al. (2017) |
| Bovine serum albumin | Nanoparticles | Amphotericin B | Leishmaniasis | Intraperitonal | Mouse (male BALB/c mice) model of cutaneous leishmaniasis | Significant reduction in the lesion thickness at the infected footpad | Casa et al. (2018) |
| Chitosan-gelatin-EGCG | Nanoparticles | si-TMEM44-AS1 | Gastric cancer | Intraperitoneal | Xenograft mouse (BALB/c) model of gastric cancer | Enhancment of therapeutic effect with good biocompatibility | Zhou et al. (2022) |
| Gelatin | Nanoparticles | Antibacterial photothermal peptide AMP-Cypate | Chronic wounds | Local application by microneedle patches | Diabetic foot ulcer rat model | Eradiation of the bacterial infection and complete wound healing in a rat model | Lei et al. (2022) |
| Human serum albumin | Nanoparticles | Basic fibroblast growth factor (bFGF) | Wound healing | Topical (dropping of formulation at the wound area) | Specific Pathogen-Free Sprague–Dawley male rats | Acceleration of tissue regeneration characterized by highly organized extracellular matrix and enhancement of angiogenesis | Son et al. (2023) |

| | | | | | | | |
|---|---|---|---|---|---|---|---|
| Melanin-gelatin | Nanoparticles | – | Dual-modal photoacoustic (PA) imaging and nuclear magnetic resonance (MRI) imaging | Intravenous | 4T1 tumor-bearing mice | Good biocompatibility, preferable biodistribution and clearance | Li et al. (2022) |
| Silk Sericin/ Superparamagnetic iron oxide nanoparticles (SPION) | Nanoparticles | ROR1 siRNA | Triple-negative breast cancer | Intravenous | Triple-negative breast cancer model in female BALB/c mice | Effectient downregulation of ROR1 gene expression resulting in inhibition of disease progression | Shirangi et al. (2022) |
| Zein- poly(L-lysine) | Dendrons | Doxorubicin and siRNA | Osteosarcoma | Intravenous | Athymic BALB/c | Growth inhibition of AEG-1-positive osteosarcoma with minimal adverse effects | Pang et al. (2024) |

adversely affecting normal cells and release drugs in an optimized/controlled manner for best therapeutic effect. Protein nanoparticles seem to satisfy largely these requirements. They are well-suited for the delivery of different drugs because of the multiple drug binding sites present in their structure and can enhance the bioavailability of poorly soluble drugs, such as in Abraxane. Thus, protein-based nanoparticles have been evaluated extensively *in vivo* for therapeutic, diagnostic or theragnostic purposes for tumors, i.e., cancer (Lohcharoenkal et al., 2014; Sadeghi et al., 2020).

Among protein-based nanocarriers, albumin-based ones are explored the most due to several benefits (Spada et al., 2021). Albumin is the most abundant plasma protein and it is stable at a wide pH range (pH 4–9) and temperatures as high as 60°C. Moreover, it can inherently bind to cell-surface receptors (e.g., glycoprotein 60) and mediate endothelium transcytosis, as well as may engage with neonatal Fc receptor and improve delivery across mucosal barriers (Habibi et al., 2022). Notably, albumin-based nanocarriers show caveolae-mediated endocytosis through caveolin-1 which is overexpressed in cancer cells and increase transportation and accumulation of drugs to tumors. In this context, it is suggested that Cav-1 can be a predictive biomarker for response to albumin-delivered anticancer therapeutics (Chatterjee et al., 2017).

So far, albumin nanoparticles have been evaluated *in vivo* for treatment of different types of cancers, including breast cancer (Taheri et al., 2012), lung metastatic cancer (Han et al., 2014), pancreatic cancer (Giordano et al., 2017), ovarian cancer (Tillmanns et al., 2013). Particularly, the results from different groups indicate that albumin nanoparticles seem promising for the delivery of drugs to the brain for treating brain tumors due to their BBB-penetrating characteristics *via* albumin-binding protein pathways (Lin et al., 2016; Gregory et al., 2020; Dadparvar et al., 2011).

Protein nanoparticles can be also potential delivery systems for drug resistant cancers. The *in vivo* evaluation of antitumor effect of gemcitabine-loaded albumin on gemcitabine-resistant pancreatic cancer showed enhanced antitumor effect with nanoparticle formulation compared to gemcitabine alone possibly because albumin-based nanoparticles can be transported into tumor cells through endocytosis and thus, overcome resistance (Guo et al., 2018).

Favorably, transferrin-based nanoparticles also can show inherent active tumor-targeting capacity to different cancer cells. Transferrin binds to transferrin-receptors overexpressed on the surface of several cancer cells enhancing the uptake of the drug-loaded transferrin nanoparticles. Self-assembled IR780-loaded transferrin nanoparticles exhibited effective tumor-targeting for imaging and phototherapy both *in vitro* and *in vivo* in a mouse model of tumor. This study also indicated that transferrin targeting ability was not compromised due to nanoparticle formation (Wang et al., 2016).

The antitumoral effect of nanoparticles can be enhanced through further surface functionalization for specific targeting to cancer cells. When doxorubicin-loaded bovine serum albumin nanoparticle surface was modified with hyaluronic acid which can interact with CD44 receptors in metastatic breast cancer cells, maximum accumulation in tumor and better tumor reduction were observed compared to free doxorubicin (Pulakkat et al., 2016). Also, development of stimuli-sensitive formulations can enhance efficacy and safety of nanocarriers. Acid labile transferrin and albumin conjugates of doxorubicin showed improved antitumor activity compared to free doxorubicin and significantly reduced toxicity in a carcinoma mouse model (Kratz et al., 2000).

In addition, hybrid protein nanoparticles composed of zein as the core and whey as the shell of the nanoparticle with a particle size of 200–250 nm, showed encapsulation efficiency of >70% for the anticancer agent fenretinide. The particles sustained the release of drug up to 24 hours in simulated gastrointestinal fluids and improved the permeability across Caco-2 cell monolayers. A significant increase in the half-life of fenretinide was observed while its bioavailability was increased by 7-fold *in vivo* in mice. The results indicated that hybrid zein-whey nanoparticles could be suitable for pediatric oral drug delivery of the anticancer agent without any significant immunogenicity (Islam et al., 2019).

## 8.2 Treatment of neurodegenerative diseases

Treatment of neurodegenerative disorders is challenging due to the presence of blood brain barrier which limits the entry of drugs to the brain leading to poor bioavailability. While there is no definitive treatment for most neurodegenerative disorders yet, ongoing preclinical and clinical research suggests that nanoparticle-based systems provide an advantageous alternative for delivery of drugs to the brain (Lamptey et al., 2022).

Self-assembled lactoferrin-conjugated linoleic acid micelle-based nanocarriers, showed improved *in vivo* biodistribution in brain tissue following oral administration. Enhanced cognitive abilities were observed in $AlCl_3$-induced Alzheimer's-animal model with decreased $A\beta_{1-42}$ level, decreased brain oxidative stress, inflammation and apoptosis in brain tissue. The glycoprotein lactoferrin may attach to the lactoferrin receptors (LfR) that are overexpressed on the surface of the brain endothelial cells and consequently, aid the transport of the nanocarrier through the blood-brain barier (BBB) *via* LfR-mediated transcytosis (Agwa et al., 2020).

In particular, the nasal route provides an excellent site for administering drugs to the brain because it can maximize treatment efficacy while minimizing systemic side effects (Huang et al., 2024). Nose-to-brain delivery of albumin-based nanoparticles loaded with R-flurbiprofen, a drug showing neuroprotective effects in Alzheimer's disease, demonstrated higher brain-to-plasma ratio profile compared to intranasal and oral administration of R-flurbiprofen solution (Wong and Ho, 2018). In another study, clioquinol, a metal-ion chelating agent and donepezil, an acetylcholinesterase (AChE) inhibitor coencapsulated in HSA nanoparticles modified with transcriptional activator protein (TAT) and monosialotetrahexosylganglioside (GM1), reduced $A\beta$ deposition, ameliorated neuron morphological alternations, rescued memory deficits, and improved acetylcholine regulation ability *in vivo* following nasal administration in mice. This study provided insights for future opportunities to use combination therapy for neurodegenerative disorders (Yang et al., 2020). Also, intranasal delivery of drug loaded gelatin nanoparticles could protect against cell apoptosis providing a treatment option for Parkinson's disease (Lu et al., 2015). In conclusion, protein-based nanocarriers can be suitable carriers to treat neurodegenerative disorders.

## 8.3 Treatment of infections

Despite advancements in medicine, improved therapy options to treat infections are still required particularly for serious and challenging infections, such as tuberculosis. Different protein nanoparticles have emerged as promising delivery systems for antibiotics, antifungals and antivirals. For example, *in vivo* evaluation in tuberculosis-infected mice of mannosylated gelatin nanoparticles (Mn-GNPs) with size of 380 nm showed improvement in the bioavailability of isoniazid, the first line drug used in the treatment of tuberculosis, and reduced its hepatotoxicity (Saraogi et al., 2011). In another study, inhalation therapy with human serum albumin nanocarriers loaded with the antimycobacterial drug benzothiazinone demonstrated significant reduction in bacterial burden at much lower drug doses and a shorter therapeutic duration compared to oral therapy indicating that bioavailability of benzothiazinone can be enhanced through pulmonary delivery (Patel et al., 2020). Protein-based nanocarriers can present a solution to overcome drug resistance and improve the effectiveness of drug therapy against infections (Madkhali, 2023).

In addition, protein-based nanocarriers can be potential candidates to deliver antibiotics, growth factors, etc. for wound healing reducing infections and promoting faster tissue regeneration. Enhanced wound healing and regeneration has been observed in a study utilizing human serum albumin-based protein nanoparticles (164–182 nm) prepared *via* desolvation method for the delivery of basic fibroblast growth factor (Son et al., 2023). Particularly, silk fibroin- and silk serin-based nanoformulations have emerged as promising biomaterials with antimicrobial properties for applications in wound healing (Indrakumar et al., 2024; Wang et al., 2024a)

## 9. Future perspectives

Protein-based nanocarriers have emerged with multiple advantages for therapeutic, diagnostic and vaccination applications. Natural, engineered and synthetic proteins can be utilized in their preparation, thus offering not only versatility but also opportunity to develop multifunctional nanocarriers. The natural protein-based nanocarriers derived from animal-based or plant-based proteins such as albumin, ferritin, zein, etc. have shown significant potential to enhance the efficacy and safety of several small-molecule drugs and biopharmaceuticals which can be loaded efficiently into these nanocarriers. Therefore, improved *in vivo* performance and treatment outcomes can be achieved. They can overcome current challenges related to low *in vivo* bioavailability, stability and biodistribution of pharmaceuticals for different applications, particularly in oncology. The inherit targeting capability of proteins such as albumin and ferritin make protein-based nanocarriers superior to other drug delivery systems and minimizes the requirement for complex chemical modifications.

The approval of the first protein-bound formulation, Abraxane (nab paclitaxel) in 2005 by FDA, not only showed that bounding of hydrophobic drugs to nanoparticle albumin could significantly improve efficacy of treatment while reducing side effects but also accelerated preclinical and clinical research on transferring the nanoparticle albumin bond (nab) technology to other drugs. However, the second medicine based on nanoparticle albumin-bound technology was approved by FDA only years later. Fyarro (nab sirolimus) approved in 2021 by FDA, is the first mechanistic target of rapamycin (mTOR) inhibitor for locally advanced unresectable or metastatic malignant perivascular epithelioid cell tumor

(PEComa). Despite these achievements, the nab technology is still not fully understood, which can delay the development of other albumin-based formulations.

While proteins such as gelatin, albumin, etc. are already successfully used in pharmaceutical formulations and show good safety profile, challenges in terms of their source still exists. For example, there is risk of transmission of infectious agents with human albumin derived from human blood even though it is considered extremely rare. Also, concerns about the source of gelatin due to cultural and religious beliefs exists. Thus, alternative sources for production of pharmaceutical-grade proteins are being evaluated. Particularly, utilization of recombinant seems promising. Also, it is still needed to develop novel protein-based nanocarriers that show improved protein stability. Formulation strategies such as coating of the nanocarrier or crosslinking approaches might be applied.

In addition to formulation and process development challenges, insufficient testing strategies for preclinical and clinical assessment of nanocarriers (i.e., nanomedicines) and regulatory guidance can slow their introduction into medical practice. Efficient collaboration between academia, research laboratories, industry and regulatory agencies can anticipate the translation of protein nanocarriers from bench-to-bedside.

The unique characteristics of protein-based nanocarriers, the increasing knowledge on their properties, *in vitro* and *in vivo* behavior, and evolving regulatory aspects can hopefully result in other innovative clinically approved products that offer benefits for diagnosis, treatment and prevention of diseases in the future.

## References


Agwa, M.M., Abdelmonsif, D.A., Khattab, S.N., Sabra, S., 2020. Self- assembled lactoferrin-conjugated linoleic acid micelles as an orally active targeted nanoplatform for Alzheimer's disease. Int. J. Biol. Macromol. 162, 246–261. https://doi.org/10.1016/j.ijbiomac.2020.06.058.

Agwa, M.M., Sabra, S., Atwa, N.A., Dahdooh, H.A., Lithy, R.M., Elmotasem, H., 2022. Potential of frankincense essential oil-loaded whey protein nanoparticles embedded in frankincense resin as a wound healing film based on green technology. J. Drug Deliv. Scie. Technol. 71, 17732247. https://doi.org/10.1016/j.jddst.2022.103291.

Ahadi-Amandi, K., Ghadami, S.A., Bijari, N., 2025. Development and evaluation of nanocarriers of β-lactoglobulin for drug delivery: a comparative study of protein-based nanoparticle, nanofiber, and nanotube. Polym. Bullet. https://doi.org/10.1007/s00289-025-05654-1.

Ahmad, K., Meng, Y., Fan, C., Din, A.S.U., Jia, Q., Ashraf, A., Zhang, Y., Hou, H., 2024. Collagen/gelatin and polysaccharide complexes enhance gastric retention and mucoadhesive properties. Int. J. Biol. Macromol. 266. https://doi.org/10.1016/j.ijbiomac.2024.131034.

Alqahtani, M.S., Syed, R., Alshehri, M., 2020. Size-dependent phagocytic uptake and immunogenicity of gliadin nanoparticles. Polymers 12 (11), 2576. https://doi.org/10.3390/polym12112576.

Alshawwa, S.Z., Kassem, A.A., Farid, R.M., Mostafa, S.K., Labib, G.S., 2022. Nanocarrier drug delivery systems: characterization, limitations, future perspectives and implementation of artificial intelligence. Pharmaceutics 14 (4), 19994923. https://doi.org/10.3390/pharmaceutics14040883.

Alvarez-Figueroa, M.J., Abarca-Riquelme, J.M., González-Aramundiz, J.V., 2019. Influence of protamine shell on nanoemulsions as a carrier for cyclosporine-A skin delivery. Pharmaceut. Dev. Technol. 24 (5), 630–638. https://doi.org/10.1080/10837450.2018.1550789.

Amjadi, S., Hamishehkar, H., Ghorbani, M., 2019. A novel smart PEGylated gelatin nanoparticle for co-delivery of doxorubicin and betanin: a strategy for enhancing the therapeutic efficacy of chemotherapy. Mater. Sci. Eng. C 97, 833–841. https://doi.org/10.1016/j.msec.2018.12.104.

Anhorn, M.G., Mahler, H.-C., Langer, K., 2008. Freeze drying of human serum albumin (HSA) nanoparticles with different excipients. Int. J. Pharm. 363, 162–169. https://doi.org/10.1016/j.ijpharm.2008.07.004.

Arangoa, M.A., Campanero, M.A., Renedo, M.J., Ponchel, G., Irache, J.M., 2001. Gliadin nanoparticles as carriers for the oral administration of lipophilic drugs. Relationships between bioadhesion and pharmacokinetics. Pharmaceut. Res. 18 (11), 1521–1527. https://doi.org/10.1023/A:1013018111829.

Baghdadi, R.A., Abdalla, A.N., Abourehab, M.A.S., Tulbah, A.S., 2024. Evaluation of the effects of a dasatinib-containing, self-emulsifying, drug delivery system on HT29 and SW420 human colorectal carcinoma cells, and MCF7 human breast adenocarcinoma cells. J. Taibah Univ. Med. Sci. 19 (4), 806–815. https://doi.org/10.1016/j.jtumed.2024.07.002.

Bahrami, Z., Pedram-Nia, A., Saeidi-Asl, M., Armin, M., Heydari-Majd, M., 2023. Bioactive gliadin electrospinning loaded with Zataria multiflora Boiss essential oil: improves antimicrobial activity and release modeling behavior. Food Sci. Nutr. 11 (1), 307–319. https://doi.org/10.1002/fsn3.3062.

Brown, T.D., Habibi, N., Wu, D., Lahann, J., Mitragotri, S., 2020. Effect of nanoparticle composition, size, shape, and stiffness on penetration across the blood–brain barrier. ACS Biomater. Sci. Eng. 6, 4916–4928. https://doi.org/10.1021/acsbiomaterials.0c00743.

Casa, D.M., Scariot, D.B., Khalil, N.M., Nakamura, C.V., Mainardes, R.M., 2018. Bovine serum albumin nanoparticles containing amphotericin B were effective in treating murine cutaneous leishmaniasis and reduced the drug toxicity. Exp. Parasitol. 192, 12–18. https://doi.org/10.1016/j.exppara.2018.07.003.

Chander, S., Kulkarni, G.T., Dhiman, N., Kharkwal, H., 2021. Protein-based nanohydrogels for bioactive delivery. Front. Chem. 9. https://doi.org/10.3389/fchem.2021.573748.

Chatterjee, M., Ben-Josef, E., Robb, R., Vedaie, M., Seum, S., Thirumoorthy, K., Palanichamy, K., Harbrecht, M., Chakravarti, A., Williams, T.M., 2017. Caveolae-mediated endocytosis is critical for albumin cellular uptake and response to albumin-bound chemotherapy. Cancer Res. 77, 5925–5937. https://doi.org/10.1158/0008-5472.CAN-17-0604.

Chen, X., Zou, J., Zhang, K., Zhu, J., Zhang, Y., Zhu, Z., Zheng, H., Li, F., Piao, J.G., 2021. Photothermal/matrix metalloproteinase-2 dual-responsive gelatin nanoparticles for breast cancer treatment. Acta Pharmaceut. Sin. B 11 (1), 271–282. https://doi.org/10.1016/j.apsb.2020.08.009.

Chen, Y., Wang, T., Zhang, Y., Yang, X., Du, J., Yu, D., Xie, F., 2022. Effect of moderate electric fields on the structural and gelation properties of pea protein isolate. Innov. Food Sci. Emerg. Technol. 77, 102959. https://doi.org/10.1016/j.ifset.2022.102959.

Choi, S.H., Byeon, H.J., Choi, J.S., Thao, L., Kim, I., Lee, E.S., Shin, B.S., Lee, K.C., Youn, Y.S., 2015. Inhalable self-assembled albumin nanoparticles for treating drug-resistant lung cancer. J. Contr. Release 197, 199–207. https://doi.org/10.1016/j.jconrel.2014.11.008.

Chubarov, A.S., 2022. Serum albumin for magnetic nanoparticles coating. Magnetochemistry 8, 13. https://doi.org/10.3390/magnetochemistry8020013.

ClinicalTrials.gov. https://clinicaltrials.gov/.

Cruz, C.H.B., Marzuoli, I., Fraternali, F., 2021. Virus-inspired designs of antimicrobial nanocapsules. Faraday Discussions 232, 448–462. https://doi.org/10.1039/d1fd00041a.

Daamen, W., Veerkamp, J., Vanhest, J., Vankuppevelt, T., 2007. Elastin as a biomaterial for tissue engineering. Biomaterials 28 (30), 4378–4398. https://doi.org/10.1016/j.biomaterials.2007.06.025.

Dąbkowska, M., Stukan, I., Kosiorowska, A., Szatanik, A., Łuczkowska, K., Machalińska, A., Machaliński, B., 2024. In vitro and *in vivo* characterization of human serum albumin-based PEGylated nanoparticles for BDNF and NT3 codelivery. Int. J. Biol. Macromol. 265, 130726. https://doi.org/10.1016/j.ijbiomac.2024.130726.

Dadparvar, M., Wagner, S., Wien, S., Kufleitner, J., Worek, F., von Briesen, H., Kreuter, J., 2011. HI 6 human serum albumin nanoparticles—development and transport over an in vitro blood–brain barrier model. Toxicol. Lett. 206, 60–66. https://doi.org/10.1016/j.toxlet.2011.06.027.

de Oliveira Bianchi, J.R., Fabrino, D.L., Quintão, C.M.F., dos Reis Coimbra, J.S., Santos, I.J.B., 2024. Self-assembled α-lactalbumin nanostructures: encapsulation and controlled release of bioactive molecules in gastrointestinal in vitro model. J. Sci. Food Agri. 104 (15), 9592–9602. https://doi.org/10.1002/jsfa.13784.

Desai, N., Trieu, V., Yao, Z., Louie, L., Ci, S., Yang, A., Tao, C., De, T., Beals, B., Dykes, D., Noker, P., Yao, R., Labao, E., Hawkins, M., Soon-Shiong, P., 2006. Increased antitumor activity, intratumor paclitaxel concentrations, and endothelial cell transport of cremophor-free, albumin-bound paclitaxel, ABI-007, compared with cremophor-based paclitaxel. Clin. Cancer Res. 12, 1317–1324. https://doi.org/10.1158/1078-0432.CCR-05-1634.

Devrim Gökberk, B., Erdinç, N., 2023. Design, optimization, and characterization of lysozyme-loaded poly(ε-caprolactone) microparticles for pulmonary delivery. J. Pharmaceut. Innov. 18 (1), 325–338. https://doi.org/10.1007/s12247-022-09648-8.

Domeradzka, N.E., Werten, M.W.T., Wolf, F.A.d., de Vries, R., 2016. Protein cross-linking tools for the construction of nanomaterials. Curr. Opin. Biotechnol. 39, 61–67. https://doi.org/10.1016/j.copbio.2016.01.003.

Du, X., Jing, H., Wang, L., Huang, X., Mo, L., Bai, X., Wang, H., 2022. pH-shifting formation of goat milk casein nanoparticles from insoluble peptide aggregates and encapsulation of curcumin for enhanced dispersibility and bioactivity. LWT 154, 112753. https://doi.org/10.1016/j.lwt.2021.112753.

Durgun, M.E., Güngör, S., Özsoy, Y., 2020. Micelles: promising ocular drug carriers for anterior and posterior segment diseases. J. Ocul. Pharmacol. Therapeut. 36 (6), 323–341. https://doi.org/10.1089/jop.2019.0109.

El-Seedi, H.R., Said, N.S., Yosri, N., Hawash, H.B., El-Sherif, D.M., Abouzid, M., Abdel-Daim, M.M., Yaseen, M., Omar, H., Shou, Q., Attia, N.F., Zou, X., Guo, Z., Khalifa, S.A.M., 2023. Gelatin nanofibers: recent insights in synthesis, bio-medical applications and limitations. Heliyon 9 (5), 24058440. https://doi.org/10.1016/j.heliyon.2023.e16228.

Elzoghby, A.O., Samy, W.M., Elgindy, N.A., 2012. Protein-based nanocarriers as promising drug and gene delivery systems. J. Contr. Release 161 (1), 38–49. https://doi.org/10.1016/j.jconrel.2012.04.036.

Elzoghby, A., Helmy, Samy, Elgindy, 2013. Novel ionically crosslinked casein nanoparticles for flutamide delivery: formulation, characterization, and *in vivo* pharmacokinetics. Int. J. Nanomed. 1721. https://doi.org/10.2147/IJN.S40674.

Elzoghby, A.O., Elgohary, M.M., Kamel, N.M., 2015. Implications of protein- and peptide-based nanoparticles as potential vehicles for anticancer drugs. Adv. Protein Chem. Struct. Biol. 98, 169–221. https://doi.org/10.1016/bs.apcsb.2014.12.002.

Emmambux, M.N., Stading, M., Taylor, J.R.N., 2004. Sorghum kafirin film property modification with hydrolysable and condensed tannins. J. Cereal. Sci. 40 (2), 127–135. https://doi.org/10.1016/j.jcs.2004.08.005.

Esim, O., Hascicek, C., Gedik, M.E., Gunaydin, G., Dogan, A.L., 2022. Carboplatin and decitabine loaded lipid-coated albumin nanoparticles for an efficient treatment of platinum-resistant ovarian cancer. J. Drug Deliv. Sci. Technol. 76, 17732247. https://doi.org/10.1016/j.jddst.2022.103801.

Ezzat, K., Pernemalm, M., Pålsson, S., Roberts, T.C., Järver, P., Dondalska, A., Bestas, B., Sobkowiak, M.J., Levänen, B., Sköld, M., Thompson, E.A., Saher, O., Kari, O.K., Lajunen, T., Sverremark Ekström, E., Nilsson, C., Ishchenko, Y., Malm, T., Wood, M.J.A., Power, U.F., Masich, S., Lindén, A., Sandberg, J.K., Lehtiö, J., Spetz, A.-L., El Andaloussi, S., 2019. The viral protein corona directs viral pathogenesis and amyloid aggregation. Nat. Commun. 10, 2331. https://doi.org/10.1038/s41467-019-10192-2.

Fang, C., Kanemaru, K., Carvalho, W.S.P., Fruehauf, K.R., Zhang, S., Das, P.P., Xu, C., Lu, Y., Rajagopalan, N., Kulka, M., Makeiff, D.A., Serpe, M.J., 2024. Self-assembled poloxamer-legumin/vicilin nanoparticles for the nanoencapsulation and controlled release of folic acid. Int. J. Biol.Macromol. 268. https://doi.org/10.1016/j.ijbiomac.2024.131646.

Fathi, M., Donsi, F., McClements, D.J., 2018. Protein-based delivery systems for the nanoencapsulation of food ingredients. Comprehen. Rev. Food Sci. Food Saf. 17 (4), 920–936. https://doi.org/10.1111/1541-4337.12360.

Food and Drug Administration, 2005. Drug Approval Package, Abraxane (Paclitaxel Protein-Bound Particles), NDA #021660. https://www.accessdata.fda.gov/drugsatfda_docs/nda/2005/21660_abraxane_approv.pdf.

Food and Drug Administration, 2021. FDA Approves Sirolimus Protein-Bound Particles for Malignant Perivascular Epithelioid Cell Tumor. https://www.fda.gov/drugs/resources-information-approved-drugs/fda-approves-sirolimus-protein-bound-particles-malignant-perivascular-epithelioid-cell-tumor#:~:text=On%20November%2022%2C%202021%2C%20the,epithelioid%20cell%20tumor%20(PEComa).

Franssen, E.J.F., van Aterdam, R.G.M., Visser, J., Moolenaar, F., de Zeeuw, D., Meijer, D.K.F., 1991. Low molecular weight proteins as carriers for renal drug targeting: naproxen–lysozyme. Pharm. Res. 8 (10), 1223–1230. https://doi.org/10.1023/A:1015835325321.

Fuchs, S., Coester, C., 2010. Protein-based nanoparticles as a drug delivery system: chances, risks, perspectives. J. Drug Deliv. Sci. Technol. 20, 331–342. https://doi.org/10.1016/S1773-2247(10)50056-X.

García-Montoya, I.A., Cendón, T.S., Arévalo-Gallegos, S., Rascón-Cruz, Q., 2012. Lactoferrin a multiple bioactive protein: an overview. Biochim. Biophys. Acta Gen. Subj. 1820 (3), 226–236. https://doi.org/10.1016/j.bbagen.2011.06.018.

Garg, U., Jain, N., Kaul, S., Nagaich, U., 2023. Role of albumin as a targeted drug carrier in the management of rheumatoid arthritis: a comprehensive review. Mol. Pharmaceut. 20 (11), 5345–5358. https://doi.org/10.1021/acs.molpharmaceut.3c00581.

Georgilis, E., Abdelghani, M., Pille, J., Aydinlioglu, E., van Hest, J.C.M., Lecommandoux, S., Garanger, E., 2020. Nanoparticles based on natural, engineered or synthetic proteins and polypeptides for drug delivery applications. Int. J. Pharm. 586, 119537. https://doi.org/10.1016/j.ijpharm.2020.119537.

Ghadami, S.A., Ahmadi, Z., Moosavi-Nejad, Z., 2021. The albumin-based nanoparticle formation in relation to protein aggregation. Spectrochim. Acta Mol. Biomol. Spectrosc. 252. https://doi.org/10.1016/j.saa.2021.119489.

Ghalandari, B., Divsalar, A., Saboury, A.A., Parivar, K., 2014. The new insight into oral drug delivery system based on metal drugs in colon cancer therapy through β-lactoglobulin/oxali-palladium nanocapsules. J. Photochem. Photobiol. B Biol. 140, 255–265. https://doi.org/10.1016/j.jphotobiol.2014.08.003.

Gharbavi, M., Danafar, H., Sharafi, A., 2020. Microemulsion and bovine serum albumin nanoparticles as a novel hybrid nanocarrier system for efficient multifunctional drug delivery. J. Biomed. Mater. Res. A 108 (8), 1688–1702. https://doi.org/10.1002/jbm.a.36935.

Giordano, G., Pancione, M., Olivieri, N., Parcesepe, P., Velocci, M., Di Raimo, T., Coppola, L., Toffoli, G., D'Andrea, M.R., 2017. Nano albumin bound-paclitaxel in pancreatic cancer: current evidences and future directions. World J. Gastroenterol. 23, 5875. https://doi.org/10.3748/wjg.v23.i32.5875.

Gregory, J.V., Kadiyala, P., Doherty, R., Cadena, M., Habeel, S., Ruoslahti, E., Lowenstein, P.R., Castro, M.G., Lahann, J., 2020. Systemic brain tumor delivery of synthetic protein nanoparticles for glioblastoma therapy. Nat. Commun. 11, 5687. https://doi.org/10.1038/s41467-020-19225-7.

Gu, K., Tong, Y., Mi, R., Leng, S., Huang, H., Yao, J., Chen, X., Shao, Z., 2024. The production of soluble regenerated silk fibroin powder with high molecular weight and silk protein-based materials. Giant 19, 100313. https://doi.org/10.1016/j.giant.2024.100313.

Guo, Z., Wang, F., Di, Y., Yao, L., Yu, X., Fu, D., Li, J., Jin, C., 2018. Antitumor effect of gemcitabine-loaded albumin nanoparticle on gemcitabine-resistant pancreatic cancer induced by low hENT1 expression. Int. J. Nanomed. 13, 4869–4880. https://doi.org/10.2147/IJN.S166769.

Guo, J., Tan, D., Lou, C., Guo, S., Jin, X., Qu, H., Jing, L., Li, S., 2022. A tumor-penetrable drug nanococktail made from human histones for interventional nucleus-targeted chemophotothermal therapy of drug-resistant tumors. Bioact. Mater. 9, 554–565. https://doi.org/10.1016/j.bioactmat.2021.07.018.

Haas, M., Kluppel, A.C.A., Wartna, E.S., Moolenaar, F., Meijer, D.K.F., De Jong, P.E., De Zeeuw, D., 1997. Drug-targeting to the kidney: renal delivery and degradation of a naproxen-lysozyme conjugate in vivo. Kidney Int. 52 (6), 1693–1699. https://doi.org/10.1038/ki.1997.504.

Habibi, N., Mauser, A., Ko, Y., Lahann, J., 2022. Protein nanoparticles: uniting the power of proteins with engineering design approaches. Adv. Sci. 9. https://doi.org/10.1002/advs.202104012.

Hädrich, G., Vaz, G.R., Bidone, J., Yurgel, V.C., Teixeira, H.F., Gonçalves Dal Bó, A., da Silva Pinto, L., Hort, M.A., Ramos, D.F., Junior, A.S.V., Almeida da Silva, P.E., Dora, C.L., 2022. Development of a novel lipid-based nanosystem functionalized with WGA for enhanced intracellular drug delivery. Pharmaceutics 14 (10), 19994923. https://doi.org/10.3390/pharmaceutics14102022.

Han, J., Wang, Q., Zhang, Z., Gong, T., Sun, X., 2014. Cationic bovine serum albumin based self-assembled nanoparticles as siRNA delivery vector for treating lung metastatic cancer. Small 10, 524–535. https://doi.org/10.1002/smll.201301992.

Hashem, L., Swedrowska, M., Vllasaliu, D., 2018. Intestinal uptake and transport of albumin nanoparticles: potential for oral delivery. Nanomedicine 13, 1255–1265. https://doi.org/10.2217/nnm-2018-0029.

Hong, S., Choi, D.W., Kim, H.N., Park, C.G., Lee, W., Park, H.H., 2020. Protein-based nanoparticles as drug delivery systems. Pharmaceutics 12 (7), 1–28. https://doi.org/10.3390/pharmaceutics12070604.

Hoogenboezem, E.N., Duvall, C.L., 2018. Harnessing albumin as a carrier for cancer therapies. Adv. Drug Deliv. Rev. 130, 73–89. https://doi.org/10.1016/j.addr.2018.07.011.

Huang, Q., Chen, Y., Zhang, W., Xia, X., Li, H., Qin, M., Gao, H., 2024. Nanotechnology for enhanced nose-to-brain drug delivery in treating neurological diseases. J. Contr. Release 366, 519–534. https://doi.org/10.1016/j.jconrel.2023.12.054.

Huang, R., Song, H., Sen, L., Guan, X., 2025. Selection strategy for encapsulation of hydrophilic and hydrophobic ingredients with food-grade materials: a systematic review and analysis. Food Chem. 25, 102149. https://doi.org/10.1016/j.fochx.2024.102149.

Huo, P., Han, X., Zhang, W., Zhang, J., Kumar, P., Liu, B., 2021. Electrospun nanofibers of polycaprolactone/collagen as a sustained-release drug delivery system for artemisinin. Pharmaceutics 13 (8), 19994923. https://doi.org/10.3390/pharmaceutics13081228.

Hyun, H., Park, J., Willis, K., Park, J.E., Lyle, L.T., Lee, W., Yeo, Y., 2018. Surface modification of polymer nanoparticles with native albumin for enhancing drug delivery to solid tumors. Biomaterials 180, 206–224. https://doi.org/10.1016/j.biomaterials.2018.07.024.

Ilinskaya, A.N., Dobrovolskaia, M.A., 2017. Interaction between Nanoparticles and Plasma Proteins: Effects on Nanoparticle Biodistribution and Toxicity . Springer Science and Business Media LLC. Springer Science and Business Media LLC, pp. 505–520. https://doi.org/10.1007/978-3-319-41421-8_15.

Indrakumar, S., Dash, T.K., Mishra, V., Tandon, B., Chatterjee, K., 2024. Silk fibroin and its nanocomposites for wound care: a comprehensive review. ACS Polymers Au 4, 168–188. https://doi.org/10.1021/acspolymersau.3c00050.

Iqbal, H., Yang, T., Li, T., Zhang, M., Ke, H., Ding, D., Deng, Y., Chen, H., 2021. Serum protein-based nanoparticles for cancer diagnosis and treatment. J. Control. Release 329, 997–1022.

Işıklan, N., Hussien, N.A., Türk, M., 2021. Synthesis and drug delivery performance of gelatin-decorated magnetic graphene oxide nanoplatform. Coll. Surf. A Physicochem. Eng. Asp. 616, 18734359. https://doi.org/10.1016/j.colsurfa.2021.126256.

Islam, M.S., Reineke, J., Kaushik, R., Woyengo, T., Baride, A., Alqahtani, M.S., Perumal, O., 2019. Bioadhesive food protein nanoparticles as pediatric oral drug delivery system. ACS Appl. Mater. Interfaces 11, 18062–18073. https://doi.org/10.1021/acsami.9b00152.

Jain, A.K., Thareja, S., 2019. In vitro and in vivo characterization of pharmaceutical nanocarriers used for drug delivery. Artif. Cells Nanomed. Biotechnol. 47 (1), 524–539. https://doi.org/10.1080/21691401.2018.1561457.

Jain, A., Singh, S.K., Arya, S.K., Kundu, S.C., Kapoor, S., 2018. Protein nanoparticles: promising platforms for drug delivery applications. ACS Biomater. Sci. Eng. 4, 3939–3961. https://doi.org/10.1021/acsbiomaterials.8b01098.

Ji, H., Zheng, Z., Li, S., Xiao, X., Tang, W., Zhang, X., Guo, Q., He, Q., Cai, S., Jiang, P., Wang, H., Li, L., Xiao, X., Wang, L., 2024a. Research progress of serum albumin in the field of drug delivery. Interdiscipl. Med. 2 (3), 28326245. https://doi.org/10.1002/INMD.20240010.

Ji, Q., Zhu, H., Qin, Y., Zhang, R., Wang, L., Zhang, E., Zhou, X., Meng, R., 2024b. GP60 and SPARC as albumin receptors: key targeted sites for the delivery of antitumor drugs. Front. Pharmacol. 15. https://doi.org/10.3389/fphar.2024.1329636.

Kaul, G., Amiji, M., 2004. Biodistribution and targeting potential of poly(ethylene glycol)-modified gelatin nanoparticles in subcutaneous murine tumor model. J. Drug Target. 12, 585–591. https://doi.org/10.1080/10611860400013451.

Kouchakzadeh, H., Shojaosadati, S.A., Shokri, F., 2014. Efficient loading and entrapment of tamoxifen in human serum albumin based nanoparticulate delivery system by a modified desolvation technique. Chem. Eng. Res. Des. 92, 1681–1692. https://doi.org/10.1016/j.cherd.2013.11.024.

Kratz, F., Roth, T., Fichiner, I., Schumacher, P., Fiebig, H., Unger, C., 2000. In vitro and *in vivo* efficacy of acid-sensitive transferrin and albumin doxorubicin conjugates in a human xenograft panel and in the MDA-MB-435 mamma carcinoma model. J. Drug Target. 8, 305–318. https://doi.org/10.3109/10611860008997908.

Kudarha, R.R., Sawant, K.K., 2017. Albumin based versatile multifunctional nanocarriers for cancer therapy: fabrication, surface modification, multimodal therapeutics and imaging approaches. Mater. Sci. Eng. C 81, 607–626. https://doi.org/10.1016/j.msec.2017.08.004.

Lamptey, R.N.L., Chaulagain, B., Trivedi, R., Gothwal, A., Layek, B., Singh, J., 2022. A review of the common neurodegenerative disorders: current therapeutic approaches and the potential role of nanotherapeutics. Int. J. Mol. Sci. 23, 1851. https://doi.org/10.3390/ijms23031851.

Lavín de Juan, L., Recio, V.G., López, P.J., Juan, T.G., Cordoba-Diaz, M., Cordoba-Diaz, D., 2017. Pharmaceutical applications of lectins. J. Drug Deliv. Sci. Technol. 42 (17732247), 126–133. https://doi.org/10.1016/j.jddst.2017.05.018.

Layman, D.K., Lönnerdal, B., Fernstrom, J.D., 2018. Applications for a-lactalbumin in human nutrition. Nutr. Rev. 76 (6), 444–460. https://doi.org/10.1093/nutrit/nuy004.

Lei, X., Li, M., Wang, C., Cui, P., Qiu, L., Zhou, S., Jiang, P., Li, H., Zhao, D., Ni, X., Wang, J., Xia, J., 2022. Degradable microneedle patches loaded with antibacterial gelatin nanoparticles to treat staphylococcal infection-induced chronic wounds. Int. J. Biol. Macromol. 217, 55–65. https://doi.org/10.1016/j.ijbiomac.2022.07.021.

Lewis, J.D., Saperas, N., Song, Y., Zamora, M.J., Chiva, M., Ausió, J., 2004. Histone H1 and the origin of protamines. Proc. Natl. Acad. Sci. U. S. A. 101 (12), 4148–4152. https://doi.org/10.1073/pnas.0308721101.

Li, D., Shi, M., Bao, C., Bao, W., Zhang, L., Jiao, L., Li, T., Li, Y., 2019. Synergistically enhanced anticancer effect of codelivered curcumin and siPlk1 by stimuli-responsive α-lactalbumin nanospheres. Nanomedicine. 8 (1), 595–612. https://doi.org/10.2217/nnm-2018-0291.

Li, Y., Xu, G., Li, W., Lv, L., Zhang, Q., 2021. The role of ultrasound in the preparation of zein nanoparticles/flaxseed gum complexes for the stabilization of pickering emulsion. Foods 10 (9), 1990. https://doi.org/10.3390/foods10091990.

Li, T., Yang, Y., Jing, W., Yan, Z., Che, J., Xu, H., Hu, X., Zhang, R., 2022. Melanin-gelatin nanoparticles with both EPR effect and renal clearance for PA/MRI dual-modal imaging of tumors. Biomater. Adv. 134, 112718. https://doi.org/10.1016/j.msec.2022.112718.

Li, L., Tan, L., Zhang, Q., Cheng, Y., Liu, Y., Li, R., Hou, S., 2023. Nose-to-brain delivery of self-assembled curcumin-lactoferrin nanoparticles: characterization, neuroprotective effect and in vivo pharmacokinetic study. Front. Bioeng. Biotechnol. 11. https://doi.org/10.3389/fbioe.2023.1168408.

Li, C., Chen, L., McClements, D.J., Peng, X., Xu, Z., Meng, M., Ji, H., Qiu, C., Long, J., Jin, Z., 2024. Encapsulation of polyphenols in protein-based nanoparticles: preparation, properties, and applications. Crit. Rev. Food Sci. Nutr. 64 (31), 11341–11355. https://doi.org/10.1080/10408398.2023.2237126.

Lim, S.H., Wong, T.W., Tay, W.X., 2024. Overcoming colloidal nanoparticle aggregation in biological milieu for cancer therapeutic delivery: perspectives of materials and particle design. Adv. Colloid Interface Sci. 325, 103094. https://doi.org/10.1016/j.cis.2024.103094.

Lin, T., Zhao, P., Jiang, Y., Tang, Y., Jin, H., Pan, Z., He, H., Yang, V.C., Huang, Y., 2016. Blood–brain-barrier-penetrating albumin nanoparticles for biomimetic drug delivery *via* albumin-binding protein pathways for antiglioma therapy. ACS Nano 10, 9999–10012. https://doi.org/10.1021/acsnano.6b04268.

Lin, Q., Ge, S., McClements, D.J., Li, X., Jin, Z., Jiao, A., Wang, J., Long, J., Xu, X., Qiu, C., 2023. Advances in preparation, interaction and stimulus responsiveness of protein-based nanodelivery systems. Crit. Rev. Food Sci. Nutr. 63 (19), 4092–4105. https://doi.org/10.1080/10408398.2021.1997908.

Liu, S., Liu, M., Xiu, J., Zhang, T., Zhang, B., Cun, D., Yang, C., Li, K., Zhang, J., Zhao, X., 2024. Celastrol-loaded bovine serum albumin nanoparticles target inflamed neutrophils for improved rheumatoid arthritis therapy. Acta Biomater. 174, 345–357. https://doi.org/10.1016/j.actbio.2023.11.028.

Lluch, A., Álvarez, I., Muñoz, M., Seguí, M.A., Tusquets, I., García-Estévez, L., 2014. Treatment innovations for metastatic breast cancer: nanoparticle albumin-bound (NAB) technology targeted to tumors. Crit. Rev. Oncol. Hematol. 89 (1), 62–72. https://doi.org/10.1016/j.critrevonc.2013.08.001.

Lohcharoenkal, W., Wang, L., Chen, Y.C., Rojanasakul, Y., 2014 (2014. Protein nanoparticles as drug delivery carriers for cancer therapy. BioMed Res. Int. 1–12. https://doi.org/10.1155/2014/180549.

Lu, C.T., Jin, R.R., Jiang, Y.N., Lin, Q., Yu, W.Z., Mao, K.L., Tian, F.R., Zhao, Y.P., Zhao, Y.Z., 2015. Gelatin nanoparticle-mediated intranasal delivery of substance P protects against 6-hydroxydopamine-induced apoptosis: an in vitro and in vivo study. Drug Design Dev. Ther. 9, 1955–1962. https://doi.org/10.2147/DDDT.S77237.

Madkhali, O.A., 2023. Drug delivery of gelatin nanoparticles as a biodegradable polymer for the treatment of infectious diseases: perspectives and challenges. Polymers 15, 4327. https://doi.org/10.3390/polym15214327.

MaHam, A., Tang, Z., Wu, H., Wang, J., Lin, Y., 2009. Protein-based nanomedicine platforms for drug delivery. Small 5 (15), 1706–1721. https://doi.org/10.1002/smll.200801602.

Malekzad, H., Mirshekari, H., Sahandi Zangabad, P., Moosavi Basri, S.M., Baniasadi, F., Sharifi Aghdam, M., Karimi, M., Hamblin, M.R., 2018. Plant protein-based hydrophobic fine and ultrafine carrier particles in drug delivery systems. Crit. Rev. Biotechnol. 38 (1), 47–67. https://doi.org/10.1080/07388551.2017.1312267.

Marques, A.M., Bourbon, A.I., Rodrigues, R.M., Teixeira, J.A., Pastrana, L.M., Cerqueira, M.A., 2023. Lactoferrin as a carrier of iron: Development and physicochemical characterization. Food Hydrocoll. 142. https://doi.org/10.1016/j.foodhyd.2023.108772.

Martínez Rivas, C.J., Tarhini, M., Badri, W., Miladi, K., Greige-Gerges, H., Nazari, Q.A., Galindo Rodríguez, S.A., Román, R.Á., Fessi, H., Elaissari, A., 2017. Nanoprecipitation process: from encapsulation to drug delivery. Int. J. Pharmaceut. 532 (1), 66–81.

Martínez-López, A.L., Pangua, C., Reboredo, C., Campión, R., Morales-Gracia, J., Irache, J.M., 2020. Protein-based nanoparticles for drug delivery purposes. Int. J. Pharmaceut. 581.

Massa, H.M., Lim, D.J., Kurono, Y., Cripps, A.W., 2015. Middle ear and Eustachian tube mucosal immunology. In: Mucosal Immunolgy, fourth ed., pp. 1923–1942. https://doi.org/10.1016/B978-0-12-415847-4.00101-4.

Mathew-Steiner, S.S., Roy, S., Sen, C.K., 2021. Collagen in wound healing. Bioengineering 8 (5). https://doi.org/10.3390/bioengineering8050063.

Maviah, M.B.J., Farooq, M.A., Mavlyanova, R., Veroniaina, H., Filli, M.S., Aquib, M., Kesse, S., Boakye-Yiadom, K. O., Wang, B., 2020. Food protein-based nanodelivery systems for hydrophobic and poorly soluble compounds. AAPS PharmSciTech 21 (3), 15309932. https://doi.org/10.1208/s12249-020-01641-z.

Meng, H., Deng, S., You, Y., Chan, H.F., 2018. The role of microfluidics in protein formulations with pre-programmed functional characteristics. Biologics Targets Ther. 12, 191–197. https://doi.org/10.2147/btt.s126725.

Mitra, K., Chadha, A., Muthuvijayan, V., Doble, M., 2022. Self-assembled inhalable immunomodulatory silk fibroin nanocarriers for enhanced drug loading and intracellular antibacterial activity. ACS Biomater. Sci. Eng. 8 (2), 708–721.

Molino, N.M., Wang, S.W., 2014. Caged protein nanoparticles for drug delivery. Curr. Opin. Biotechnol. 28, 75–82. https://doi.org/10.1016/j.copbio.2013.12.007.

Morozova, O., Isaeva, E., Klinov, D., 2023. Biodistribution of fluorescent albumin nanoparticles among organs of laboratory animals after intranasal and peroral administration. Curr. Issues Mol. Biol. 45, 8227–8238. https://doi.org/10.3390/cimb45100519.

Murphy, G., Brayden, D.J., Cheung, D.L., Liew, A., Fitzgerald, M., Pandit, A., 2025. Albumin-based delivery systems: Recent advances, challenges, and opportunities. J. Control. Release 380, 375–395. https://doi.org/10.1016/j.jconrel.2025.01.035.

Narayanaswamy, R., Kanagesan, S., Pandurangan, A., Padmanabhan, P., 2016. Basics to Different Imaging Techniques, Different Nanobiomaterials for Image Enhancement. Elsevier BV, pp. 101–129. https://doi.org/10.1016/b978-0-323-41736-5.00004-2.

Nguyen, B., Tolia, N.H., 2021. Protein-based antigen presentation platforms for nanoparticle vaccines. npj Vaccines 6, 70. https://doi.org/10.1038/s41541-021-00330-7.

Nogueira-Librelotto, D.R., Codevilla, C.F., Farooqi, A., Rolim, C.M.B., 2017. Transferrin-conjugated nanocarriers as active-targeted drug delivery platforms for cancer therapy. Curr. Pharm. Des. 23, 454–466. https://doi.org/10.2174/1381612822666161026162347.

Nooraei, S., Bahrulolum, H., Hoseini, Z.S., Katalani, C., Hajizade, A., Easton, A.J., Ahmadian, G., 2021. Virus-like particles: preparation, immunogenicity and their roles as nanovaccines and drug nanocarriers. J. Nanobiotechnol. 19 (1), 14773155. https://doi.org/10.1186/s12951-021-00806-7.

Obozina, A.S., Komedchikova, E.N., Kolesnikova, O.A., Iureva, A.M., Kovalenko, V.L., Zavalko, F.A., Rozhnikova, T.V., Tereshina, E.D., Mochalova, E.N., Shipunova, V.O., 2023. Genetically encoded self-assembling protein nanoparticles for the targeted delivery in vitro and in vivo. Pharmaceutics 15, 231. https://doi.org/10.3390/pharmaceutics15010231.

Pandey, K.K., Sahoo, B.R., Pattnaik, A.K., 2024. Protein nanoparticles as vaccine platforms for human and zoonotic viruses. Viruses 16, 936. https://doi.org/10.3390/v16060936.

Pang, J., Huang, L., Lian, Y., Yuan, Z., Wang, F., Zhang, L.-M., 2024. Co-delivery of siAEG-1 and doxorubicin to treat osteosarcoma via nanomicelles for azide–alkyne "click" conjugation of poly( -lysine) dendrons onto Zein. Int. J. Biol. Macromol. 264, 130729. https://doi.org/10.1016/j.ijbiomac.2024.130729.

Patel, A., Redinger, N., Richter, A., Woods, A., Neumann, P.R., Keegan, G., Childerhouse, N., Imming, P., Schaible, U.E., Forbes, B., Dailey, L.A., 2020. In vitro and *in vivo* antitubercular activity of benzothiazinone-loaded human serum albumin nanocarriers designed for inhalation. J. Contr. Release 328, 339–349. https://doi.org/10.1016/j.jconrel.2020.08.022.

Patra, J.K., Das, G., Fraceto, L.F., Campos, E.V.R., Rodriguez-Torres, M. del P., Acosta-Torres, L.S., Diaz-Torres, L. A., Grillo, R., Swamy, M.K., Sharma, S., Habtemariam, S., Shin, H.-S., 2018. Nano based drug delivery systems: recent developments and future prospects. J. Nanobiotechnol. 16, 71. https://doi.org/10.1186/s12951-018-0392-8.

Peña-Bahamonde, J., Herrera, G., Lupini, S., Arabaghian, H., Rodrigues, D.F., 2023. Zein nanoparticles for controlled intestinal drug release for the treatment of gastrointestinal infections. ACS Appl. Nano Mater. 6 (23), 21707–21720. https://doi.org/10.1021/acsanm.3c03923.

Pisoschi, A.M., Pop, A., Cimpeanu, C., Turcuş, V., Predoi, G., Iordache, F., 2018. Nanoencapsulation techniques for compounds and products with antioxidant and antimicrobial activity - a critical view. Eur. J. Med. Chem. 157, 1326–1345. https://doi.org/10.1016/j.ejmech.2018.08.076.

Pulakkat, S., Balaji, S.A., Rangarajan, A., Raichur, A.M., 2016. Surface engineered protein nanoparticles with hyaluronic acid based multilayers for targeted delivery of anticancer agents. ACS Appl. Mater. Interfaces 8, 23437–23449. https://doi.org/10.1021/acsami.6b04179.

Purwanti, N., Ichikawa, S., Neves, M.A., Uemura, K., Nakajima, M., Kobayashi, I., 2016. β-lactoglobulin as food grade surfactant for clove oil-in-water and limonene-in-water emulsion droplets produced by microchannel emulsification. Food Hydrocoll. 60, 98–108. https://doi.org/10.1016/j.foodhyd.2016.03.024.

Pustulka, S.M., Ling, K., Pish, S.L., Champion, J.A., 2020. Protein nanoparticle charge and hydrophobicity govern protein corona and macrophage uptake. ACS Appl. Mater. Interfaces 12 (43). https://doi.org/10.1021/acsami.0c12341.

Rajeshkumar, R.R., Panneerselvam, T., Pavadai, P., Pandian, S.R.K., Kumar, A.S.K., Sankaranarayan, M., Kabilan, S. J., Kunjiappan, S., 2024. Folate receptor-targeted camptothecin-loaded PLGA-glutenin nanoparticles for effective breast cancer treatment. J. Polym. Environ. 32 (12), 6440–6460. https://doi.org/10.1007/s10924-024-03391-6.

Ramos, R., Bernard, J., Ganachaud, F., Miserez, A., 2022. Protein-based encapsulation strategies: toward micro- and nanoscale carriers with increased functionality. Small Sci. 2 (3). https://doi.org/10.1002/smsc.202100095.

Rather, G.A., Selvakumar, P., Srinivas, K.S., Natarajan, K., Kaushik, A., Rajan, P., Lee, S.R., Sing, W.L., Alkhamees, M., Lian, S., Holley, M., Do Jung, Y., Lakshmanan, V.K., 2024. Facile synthesis of elastin nanogels encapsulated decursin for castrated resistance prostate cancer therapy. Sci. Rep. 14 (1), 20452322. https://doi.org/10.1038/s41598-024-65999-x.

Roque, A., 2004. The preferential binding of histone H1 to DNA scaffold-associated regions is determined by its C-terminal domain. Nucleic Acids Res. 32 (20), 6111–6119. https://doi.org/10.1093/nar/gkh945.

Sadeghi, S., Lee, W.K., Kong, S.N., Shetty, A., Drum, C.L., 2020. Oral administration of protein nanoparticles: an emerging route to disease treatment. Pharmacol. Res. 158, 104685. https://doi.org/10.1016/j.phrs.2020.104685.

Salatin, S., Jelvehgari, M., Maleki-Dizaj, S., Adibkia, K., 2015. A sight on protein-based nanoparticles as drug/gene delivery systems. Therapeut. Deliv. 6 (8), 1017–1029. https://doi.org/10.4155/tde.15.28.

Salvati, A., Pitek, A.S., Monopoli, M.P., Prapainop, K., Bombelli, F.B., Hristov, D.R., Kelly, P.M., Åberg, C., Mahon, E., Dawson, K.A., 2013. Transferrin-functionalized nanoparticles lose their targeting capabilities when a biomolecule corona adsorbs on the surface. Nat. Nanotechnol. 8, 137–143. https://doi.org/10.1038/nnano.2012.237.

Sandra, F., Khaliq, N.U., Sunna, A., Care, A., 2019. Developing protein-based nanoparticles as versatile delivery systems for cancer therapy and imaging. Nanomaterials 9 (9). https://doi.org/10.3390/nano9091329.

Saraogi, G.K., Sharma, B., Joshi, B., Gupta, P., Gupta, U.D., Jain, N.K., Agrawal, G.P., 2011. Mannosylated gelatin nanoparticles bearing isoniazid for effective management of tuberculosis. J. Drug Target. 19, 219–227. https://doi.org/10.3109/1061186X.2010.492522.

Selvaraj, S., Thangam, R., Fathima, N.N., 2018. Electrospinning of casein nanofibers with silver nanoparticles for potential biomedical applications. Int. J. Biol. Macromol. 120, 1674–1681. https://doi.org/10.1016/j.ijbiomac.2018.09.177.

Sha, X., Sun, H., Li, Y., Wu, J., Zhang, H., Yang, R., 2024. The prolamins, from structure, property, to the function in encapsulation and delivery of bioactive compounds. Food Hydrocoll. 149, 109508. https://doi.org/10.1016/j.foodhyd.2023.109508.

Shafaei, Z., Ghalandari, B., Vaseghi, A., Divsalar, A., Haertlé, T., Saboury, A.A., Sawyer, L., 2017. β-Lactoglobulin: an efficient nanocarrier for advanced delivery systems. Nanomed. Nanotechnol. Biol. Med. 13 (5), 1685–1692. https://doi.org/10.1016/j.nano.2017.03.007.

Shin, J., Cole, B.D., Seyedmohammad, M., Lim, S.I., Jang, Y., 2024. Protein nanocarriers capable of encapsulating both hydrophobic and hydrophilic drugs. Methods Mol. Biol. 2720, 143–150. https://doi.org/10.1007/978-1-0716-3469-1_10.

Shirangi, A., Mottaghitalab, F., Dinarvand, S., Atyabi, F., 2022. Theranostic silk sericin/SPION nanoparticles for targeted delivery of ROR1 siRNA: synthesis, characterization, diagnosis and anticancer effect on triple-negative breast cancer. Int. J. Biol. Macromol. 221, 604–612. https://doi.org/10.1016/j.ijbiomac.2022.09.020.

Silva, M.L.S., 2024. Lectin-modified drug delivery systems – recent applications in the oncology field. Int. J. Pharm. 665, 124685. https://doi.org/10.1016/j.ijpharm.2024.124685.

Sim, S., Wang, P., Beyer, B.N., Cutrona, K.J., Radhakrishnan, M.L., Elmore, D.E., 2017. Investigating the nucleic acid interactions of histone-derived antimicrobial peptides. FEBS Lett. 591 (5), 706–717. https://doi.org/10.1002/1873-3468.12574.

Siri, M., Grasselli, M., Alonso, S. del V., 2019. Media interaction and stability of a gamma irradiated albumin nanoparticle. J. Biotechnol. 306, 169–176. https://doi.org/10.1016/j.jbiotec.2019.10.001.

Solanki, R., Patel, K., Patel, S., 2021. Bovine serum albumin nanoparticles for the efficient delivery of berberine: preparation, characterization and in vitro biological studies. Colloids Surf. A Physicochem. Eng. Asp. 608, 125501. https://doi.org/10.1016/j.colsurfa.2020.125501.

Son, B., Kim, M., Won, H., Jung, A., Kim, J., Koo, Y., Lee, N.K., Baek, S.-H., Han, U., Park, C.G., Shin, H., Gweon, B., Joo, J., Park, H.H., 2023. Secured delivery of basic fibroblast growth factor using human serum albumin-based protein nanoparticles for enhanced wound healing and regeneration. J. Nanobiotechnol. 21, 310. https://doi.org/10.1186/s12951-023-02053-4.

Sosnik, A., Seremeta, K.P., 2015. Advantages and challenges of the spray-drying technology for the production of pure drug particles and drug-loaded polymeric carriers. Adv. Coll. Interface Sci.. 223, 40–54. https://doi.org/10.1016/j.cis.2015.05.003.

Spada, A., Emami, J., Tuszynski, J.A., Lavasanifar, A., 2021. The uniqueness of albumin as a carrier in nanodrug delivery. Mol. Pharm. 18, 1862–1894.

Sripriyalakshmi, S., Jose, P., Ravindran, A., Anjali, C.H., 2014. Recent trends in drug delivery system using protein nanoparticles. Cell Biochem. Biophys. 70 (1), 17–26. https://doi.org/10.1007/s12013-014-9896-5.

Stupka, I., Heddle, J.G., 2020. Artificial protein cages – inspiration, construction, and observation. Curr. Opin. Struct. Biol. 64, 66–73. https://doi.org/10.1016/j.sbi.2020.05.014.

Suk, J.S., Xu, Q., Kim, N., Hanes, J., Ensign, L.M., 2016. PEGylation as a strategy for improving nanoparticle-based drug and gene delivery. Adv. Drug Deliv. Rev. 99, 28–51. https://doi.org/10.1016/j.addr.2015.09.012.

Sun, P., Sun, W., Wei, Z., Wu, S., Xiang, N., 2023. Soy protein nanoparticles prepared by enzymatic cross-linking with enhanced emulsion stability. Soft Matter 19 (11), 2099–2109. https://doi.org/10.1039/d2sm01461k.

Taheri, A., Dinarvand, R., Ahadi, F., Khorramizadeh, M.R., Atyabi, F., 2012. The *in vivo* antitumor activity of LHRH targeted methotrexate–human serum albumin nanoparticles in 4T1 tumor-bearing Balb/c mice. Int. J. Pharm. 431, 183–189. https://doi.org/10.1016/j.ijpharm.2012.04.033.

Tai, I.T., Tang, M.J., 2008. SPARC in cancer biology: its role in cancer progression and potential for therapy. Drug Resist. Updates 11 (6), 231–246. https://doi.org/10.1016/j.drup.2008.08.005.

Tanjung, Y., Dewi, M., Gatera, V., Barliana, M., Joni, I.M., Chaerunisaa, A., 2024. Factors affecting the synthesis of bovine serum albumin nanoparticles using the desolvation method. Nanotechnol. Sci. Appl. 17, 21–40. https://doi.org/10.2147/NSA.S441324.

Tarhini, M., Greige-Gerges, H., Elaissari, A., 2017. Protein-based nanoparticles: from preparation to encapsulation of active molecules. Int. J. Pharm. 522, 172–197. https://doi.org/10.1016/j.ijpharm.2017.01.067.

Tillmanns, T.D., Lowe, M.P., Walker, M.S., Stepanski, E.J., Schwartzberg, L.S., 2013. Phase II clinical trial of bevacizumab with albumin-bound paclitaxel in patients with recurrent, platinum-resistant primary epithelial ovarian or primary peritoneal carcinoma. Gynecol. Oncol. 128, 221–228. https://doi.org/10.1016/j.ygyno.2012.08.039.

Tramontano, C., Miranda, B., Chianese, G., De Stefano, L., Forestiere, C., Pirozzi, M., Rea, I., 2021. Design of gelatin-capped plasmonic-diatomite nanoparticles with enhanced galunisertib loading capacity for drug delivery applications. Int. J. Mol. Sci. 22 (19). https://doi.org/10.3390/ijms221910755.

Umamaheshwari, R.B., Ramteke, S., Jain, N.K., 2004. Anti-Helicobacter pylori effect of mucoadhesive nanoparticles bearing amoxicillin in experimental gerbils model. AAPS PharmSciTech 5 (2), 60–68. https://doi.org/10.1208/pt050232.

Uzel, E., Durgun, M.E., Esentürk-Güzel, İ., Güngör, S., Özsoy, Y., 2023. Nanofibers in ocular drug targeting and tissue engineering: their importance, advantages, advances, and future perspectives. Pharmaceutics 15 (4). https://doi.org/10.3390/pharmaceutics15041062.

van Strien, J., Escalona-Rayo, O., Jiskoot, W., Slütter, B., Kros, A., 2023. Elastin-like polypeptide-based micelles as a promising platform in nanomedicine. J. Control. Release 353, 713–726. https://doi.org/10.1016/j.jconrel.2022.12.033.

Verma, D., Gulati, N., Kaul, S., Mukherjee, S., Nagaich, U., 2018. Protein based nanostructures for drug delivery. J. Pharmaceut. 1–18. https://doi.org/10.1155/2018/9285854.

Wagner, A.J., Ravi, V., Riedel, R.F., Ganjoo, K., Van Tine, B.A., Chugh, R., Cranmer, L., Gordon, E.M., Hornick, J.L., Du, H., Grigorian, B., Schmid, A.N., Hou, S., Harris, K., Kwiatkowski, D.J., Desai, N.P., Dickson, M.A., 2021. Nab-sirolimus for patients with malignant perivascular epithelioid cell tumors. J. Clin. Oncol. 39 (33), 3660–3670. https://doi.org/10.1200/JCO.21.01728.

Wang, K., Zhang, Y., Wang, J., Yuan, A., Sun, M., Wu, J., Hu, Y., 2016. Self-assembled IR780-loaded transferrin nanoparticles as an imaging, targeting and PDT/PTT agent for cancer therapy. Sci. Rep. 6, 27421. https://doi.org/10.1038/srep27421.

Wang, S., Lu, Y., Ouyang, X.k., Ling, J., 2020. Fabrication of soy protein isolate/cellulose nanocrystal composite nanoparticles for curcumin delivery. Int. J. Biol. Macromol. 165, 1468–1474. https://doi.org/10.1016/j.ijbiomac.2020.10.046.

Wang, S.-L., Zhuo, J.-J., Fang, S.-M., Xu, W., Yu, Q.-Y., 2024a. Silk sericin and its composite materials with antibacterial properties to enhance wound healing: a review. Biomolecules 14, 723. https://doi.org/10.3390/biom14060723.

Wang, A., Madden, L.A., Paunov, V.N., 2024b. Enhanced anticancer effect of lysozyme-functionalized metformin-loaded shellac nanoparticles on a 3D cell model: role of the nanoparticle and payload concentrations. Biomater. Sci. 12 (18), 4735–4746. https://doi.org/10.1039/d4bm00692e.

Wei, Y., Quan, L., Zhou, C., Zhan, Q., 2018. Factors relating to the biodistribution and clearance of nanoparticles and their effects on in vivo application. Nanomedicine 13, 1495–1512. https://doi.org/10.2217/nnm-2018-0040.

Wen, C., Zhang, J., Zhang, H., Duan, Y., 2022. New perspective on natural plant protein-based nanocarriers for bioactive ingredients delivery. Foods 11 (12). https://doi.org/10.3390/foods11121701.

Wong, L.R., Ho, P.C., 2018. Role of serum albumin as a nanoparticulate carrier for nose-to-brain delivery of R-flurbiprofen: implications for the treatment of Alzheimer's disease. J. Pharm. Pharmacol. 70, 59–69. https://doi.org/10.1111/jphp.12836.

Woods, A., Patel, A., Spina, D., Riffo-Vasquez, Y., Babin-Morgan, A., de Rosales, R.T.M., Sunassee, K., Clark, S., Collins, H., Bruce, K., Dailey, L.A., Forbes, B., 2015. *In vivo* biocompatibility, clearance, and biodistribution of albumin vehicles for pulmonary drug delivery. J. Contr. Release 210, 1–9. https://doi.org/10.1016/j.jconrel.2015.05.269.

Xiao, Q., Zoulikha, M., Qiu, M., Teng, C., Lin, C., Li, X., Sallam, M.A., Xu, Q., He, W., 2022. The effects of protein corona on *in vivo* fate of nanocarriers. Adv. Drug Deliv. Rev. 186, 114356. https://doi.org/10.1016/j.addr.2022.114356.

Xu, W., Zheng, S., Sun, H., Li, Z., Xi, R., Luo, D., Li, Y., Shah, B.R., 2022. Green-step fabrication of gliadin/sodium caseinate nanogels for methotrexate release, cytotoxicity and cell phagocytosis. J. Drug Deliv. Sci. Technol. 67. https://doi.org/10.1016/j.jddst.2021.103028.

Yang, H., Mu, W., Wei, D., Zhang, Y., Duan, Y., Gao, J., Gong, X., Wang, H., Wu, X., Tao, H., Chang, J., 2020. A novel targeted and high-efficiency nanosystem for combinational therapy for alzheimer's disease. Adv. Sci. 7. https://doi.org/10.1002/advs.201902906.

Yasmin, R., Shah, M., Khan, S.A., Ali, R., 2017. Gelatin nanoparticles: a potential candidate for medical applications. Nanotechnol. Rev. 6, 191–207. https://doi.org/10.1515/ntrev-2016-0009.

Ye, Z., Wang, Y., Shen, P., Sagis, L.M.C., Landman, J., 2024. Effect of gum Arabic coating on release behavior of curcumin-loaded kafirin and zein composite nanoparticles. Food Hydrocoll. 156. https://doi.org/10.1016/j.foodhyd.2024.110254.

Yu, X., Gou, X., Wu, P., Han, L., Tian, D., Du, F., Chen, Z., Liu, F., Deng, G., Chen, A.T., Ma, C., Liu, J., Hashmi, S.M., Guo, X., Wang, X., Zhao, H., Liu, X., Zhu, X., Sheth, K., Chen, Q., Fan, L., Zhou, J., 2018. Activatable protein nanoparticles for targeted delivery of therapeutic peptides. Adv. Mater. 30. https://doi.org/10.1002/adma.201705383.

Zahariev, N., Marudova, M., Milenkova, S., Uzunova, Y., Pilicheva, B., 2021. Casein micelles as nanocarriers for benzydamine delivery. Polymers 13 (24), 20734360. https://doi.org/10.3390/polym13244357.

Zhang, H., Yang, J., Sun, R., Han, S., Yang, Z., Teng, L., 2023a. Microfluidics for nano-drug delivery systems: from fundamentals to industrialization. Acta Pharmaceut. Sin. B 13 (8), 3277–3299. https://doi.org/10.1016/j.apsb.2023.01.018.

Zhang, X., Wei, Z., Sun, Y., Luo, T., Xue, C., 2023b. Preparation of core–shell hordein/pectin nanoparticles as quercetin delivery matrices: physicochemical properties and colon-specific release analyses. Food Res. Int. 170, 112971. https://doi.org/10.1016/j.foodres.2023.112971.

Zhong, Q., Tian, H., Zivanovic, S., 2009. Encapsulation of fish oil in solid zein particles by liquid-liquid dispersion. J. Food Process. Preserv. 33 (2), 255–270. https://doi.org/10.1111/j.1745-4549.2009.00390.x.

Zhou, P., Sun, X., Zhang, Z., 2014. Kidney–targeted drug delivery systems. Acta Pharm. Sin. B 4 (1), 37–42. https://doi.org/10.1016/j.apsb.2013.12.005.

Zhou, M., Dong, J., Huang, J., Ye, W., Zheng, Z., Huang, K., Pan, Y., Cen, J., Liang, Y., Shu, G., Ye, S., Lu, X., Zhang, J., 2022. Chitosan-gelatin-EGCG nanoparticle-meditated LncRNA TMEM44-AS1 silencing to activate the P53 signaling pathway for the synergistic reversal of 5-FU resistance in gastric cancer. Adv. Sci. 9. https://doi.org/10.1002/advs.202105077.

Zhu, Q., Pan, X., Sun, Y., Wang, Z., Liu, F., Li, A., Zhao, Z., Wang, Y., Li, K., Mi, L., 2017. Biological nanoparticles carrying the Hmda-7 gene are effective in inhibiting pancreatic cancer in vitro and *in vivo*. PLoS One 12, e0185507. https://doi.org/10.1371/journal.pone.0185507.

Zhu, L., Dai, Y., Feng, Y., Zhang, Q., You, R., Li, X., 2024. Chemical-free fabrication of silk fibroin microspheres with silk I structure. Int. J. Biol. Macromol. 278 (Pt 4), 134927. https://doi.org/10.1016/j.ijbiomac.2024.134927.

CHAPTER

# 2

# Unlocking the potential of protein-based drug delivery: Discovery, characteristics, and real-world applications

*Ali Nematollahzadeh and Navid Ahadi-Jomairan*
**Chemical Engineering Department, University of Mohaghegh Ardabili, Ardabil, Iran**

## 1. Tracing the evolution of protein-based drug delivery

The development of protein-based drug delivery systems is rooted in the recognition of the unique properties and potential of proteins as therapeutic agents. Initial discoveries in protein science set the stage for their applications in medicine. Proteins were first recognized as critical biological molecules in the 18th century due to their ability to coagulate under heat or acid treatments. The term "protein" was coined in 1838 by Jöns Jakob Berzelius, derived from the Greek word "proteios," meaning "primary" or "foremost" (Dimitrov, 2012).

The first significant breakthrough in using proteins therapeutically came with the advent of serum therapy in the late 19th century. This pioneering treatment, developed by Emil von Behring (1989), neutralized bacterial toxins and saved countless lives from diphtheria. Von Behring's efforts culminated in receiving the first Nobel Prize in Medicine in 1901 (Dimitrov, 2012).

In the 20th century, the field advanced with the discovery and use of insulin, which marked a milestone for therapeutic proteins. Insulin was first extracted and used successfully to treat diabetes in 1922. However, its initial production faced challenges due to limited supply from animal sources and immune reactions in some patients (Leader et al., 2008). The development of recombinant DNA technology in the late 1970s revolutionized protein therapeutics, allowing for large-scale production of human insulin in bacteria. Approved by the US FDA in 1982, recombinant insulin was the first commercially available recombinant protein and significantly reduced immunogenicity issues (Dimitrov, 2012; Leader et al., 2008;

*Protein-Based Nanoparticles in Drug Delivery*
https://doi.org/10.1016/B978-0-443-33639-3.00011-8

Johnson, 1983). The recombinant DNA production of human insulin was a complex and groundbreaking process involving several key steps. Initially, the human insulin gene needed to be synthesized, a task undertaken by the City of Hope Medical Center, which successfully completed the synthesis. Following this, the genes encoding the A and B chains of insulin were inserted into a safe strain of *Escherichia coli* (*E. coli*) K-12. This genetically engineered bacterium was then capable of expressing the insulin chains. In the laboratory setting, specifically within the Lilly Research Laboratories, the expressed A and B chains were isolated and purified. Subsequent steps involved combining these chains through disulfide bonds to form the complete human insulin molecule. The purification process was meticulously carried out using advanced techniques such as high-performance liquid chromatography (HPLC), ensuring the removal of impurities and the verification of the insulin's structural integrity (Johnson, 1983).

The field of drug delivery has witnessed significant milestones that have propelled the development of modern therapeutic approaches, particularly in the realm of protein-based drug delivery. Here, we outline key breakthroughs that have shaped this area over recent decades:

## 1.1 Early discoveries and initial applications

### *1.1.1 The introduction of protein-based controlled-release systems*

The concept of controlled-release drug delivery systems gained momentum with the development of Spansule technology in the 1950s, which represented a significant advancement in extending and controlling drug release. Spansules, as encapsulated granules with varying coating thicknesses, are designed to release medication at predetermined intervals, ensuring a prolonged therapeutic effect. This innovation provided a foundation for subsequent developments in drug release mechanisms, such as diffusion-controlled and osmosis-controlled systems, which regulate drug administration to maintain consistent plasma drug concentrations. These approaches minimize fluctuations in drug levels, thereby improving patient compliance and therapeutic efficacy while reducing side effects and the frequency of dosing (Park et al., 2022; Kumar and Badola, 2021).

### *1.1.2 PEGylation and improved stability*

The development of PEGylation (polyethylene glycol conjugation) was a groundbreaking advancement in protein therapeutics. This technique improved the stability and half-life of protein drugs by reducing immunogenicity and proteolytic degradation. The first PEGylated protein, Adagen, set a precedent that led to further developments such as PEGylated liposomal formulations such as Doxil and PEGylated siRNA therapies (Park et al., 2022; Carter, 2011).

PEGylation, the attachment of polyethylene glycol (PEG) chains to proteins, peptides, or small molecules, is a widely used strategy in drug delivery to enhance the pharmacological properties of therapeutic agents. By linking nontoxic, FDA-approved PEG polymers to proteins, PEGylation increases the size of the molecule, reducing kidney filtration and thereby prolonging its circulation time in the bloodstream. This modification also enhances solubility due to the hydrophilic nature of PEG and decreases the accessibility of the protein to proteolytic enzymes and antibodies, reducing degradation and immunogenicity. As a result,

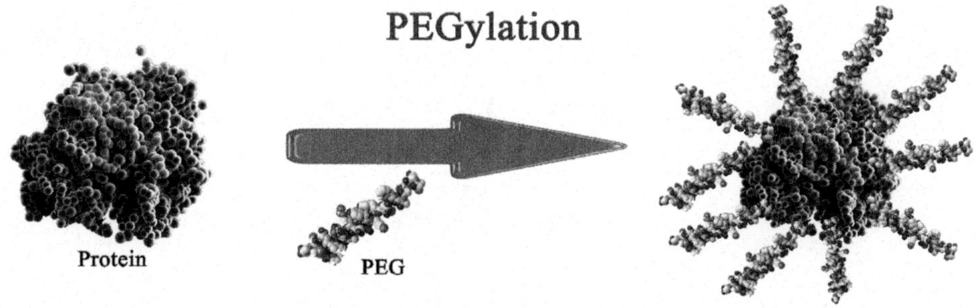


FIGURE 2.1 PEGylated protein.

PEGylation significantly improves the stability of therapeutic proteins and peptides, making them more effective and safer for clinical use (Veronese and Pasut, 2005).

Initially described in the 1970s, PEGylation has evolved with advances in chemistry to allow targeted modifications of specific functional groups on proteins, such as amino or thiol groups. This selective conjugation minimizes structural changes and retains the biological activity of the native protein. For example, PEGylated drugs such as Pegasys and Neulasta demonstrate improved therapeutic efficacy through increased stability and reduced dosing frequency. However, challenges such as reduced activity of PEGylated proteins and potential accumulation of high-molecular-weight PEGs in the liver highlight the need for further refinements. Despite these limitations, PEGylation remains a pivotal technique for improving the pharmacokinetics, solubility, and safety of therapeutic molecules, enabling their successful application in treating diseases such as cancer, hepatitis, and genetic disorders (Veronese and Pasut, 2005). Figure 2.1 represents a PEGylated protein, where polyethylene glycol (PEG) chains are attached to the surface of the protein. The protein core is illustrated with densely packed colored spheres, while the extended chains surrounding it depict the PEG molecules. These chains create a protective barrier around the protein, likely enhancing its stability, solubility, and reducing interactions with external agents such as enzymes or immune components. This structural representation highlights the molecular-level integration of PEG into therapeutic proteins, demonstrating the impact of PEGylation on their biophysical properties.

### *1.1.3 Recombinant protein technologies*

The use of recombinant DNA technology was a transformative step that enabled the mass production of human proteins such as insulin. This shift not only improved the scalability and affordability of protein-based drugs but also significantly reduced immunogenic reactions compared with animal-derived proteins (Leader et al., 2008; Carter, 2011). Recombinant technology facilitated the creation of more than 130 protein-based therapeutics, broadening the scope of treatments available for chronic conditions (Leader et al., 2008). Figure 2.2 illustrates the process of creating recombinant DNA, a key technique in genetic engineering. It starts with a plasmid, depicted in two colors with a specific cloning site marked in red. The plasmid is then cut open at this cloning site using restriction enzymes, a step shown as "Digestion." Following this, foreign DNA, colored green, is introduced and ligated into the opened plasmid, creating a new combined DNA sequence termed "Recombinant DNA." This recombinant plasmid can now be introduced into organisms such as bacteria, enabling them to

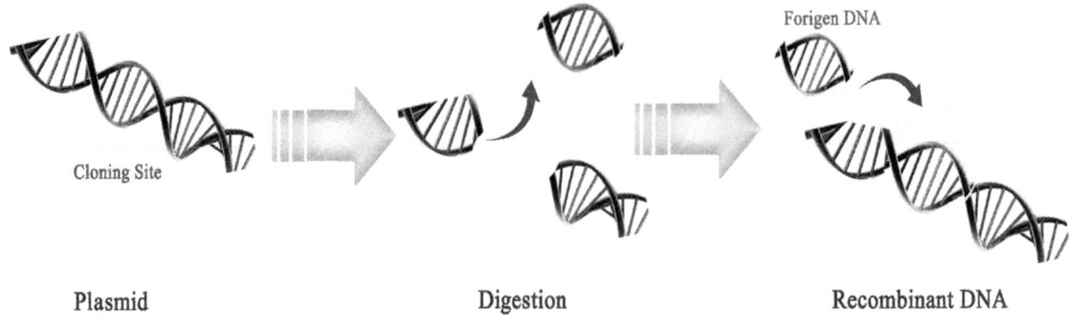


FIGURE 2.2 Recombinant DNA technology.

produce new proteins or perform new genetic functions, a cornerstone method used in developing medicines, agricultural products, and various biotechnological applications.

### 1.1.4 *Nanoparticle-based delivery systems*

Nanotechnology brought a new dimension to drug delivery by facilitating targeted and controlled drug transport. Nanoparticles, including lipid nanoparticles, enhanced the precision and stability of protein drugs. These innovations have been pivotal in enabling drugs to overcome biological barriers and increase therapeutic efficacy, exemplified by their role in COVID-19 vaccine delivery (Park et al., 2022; Vargason et al., 2021). Hassanzadeh et al. explored the physical and chemical properties of bovine serum albumin (BSA) nanoparticles, including size, morphology, and zeta potential measurements. These analyses suggest aspects of the nanoparticles' stability. Specifically, the zeta potential measurements, which reflect colloidal stability, were reported for the optimized samples to be between −41 and −51 mV. Such values indicate relatively high stability of the nanoparticles in solution, as zeta potentials above ±30 mV generally signify good colloidal stability. Although the primary focus of their research was the optimization of synthesis and drug delivery capabilities, particularly for the controlled release of the antibiotic cefazolin, the zeta potential data indirectly provide insights into the colloidal stability of the nanoparticles within their suspension (Hassanzadeh et al., 2021). Figure 2.3 provides a schematic representation of the particle size reduction process for BSA (bovine serum albumin) nanoparticles created by the conventional desolvating method. This illustration depicts the application of a high shear rate during synthesis, which is instrumental in breaking down larger aggregated protein particles into smaller, more uniform nanoparticles. The diagram likely shows the passage of these aggregates through the small gap between the rotor and stator of a homogenizer, where they are subjected to intense shear forces that facilitate the reduction in particle size. This schematic is essential for understanding how mechanical forces can be leveraged to optimize nanoparticle size for better drug delivery capabilities (Hassanzadeh et al., 2021).

## 1.2 The rise of recombinant protein therapeutics

Recombinant protein therapeutics have redefined the field of modern medicine, introducing substantial advancements in the treatment landscape for numerous diseases and

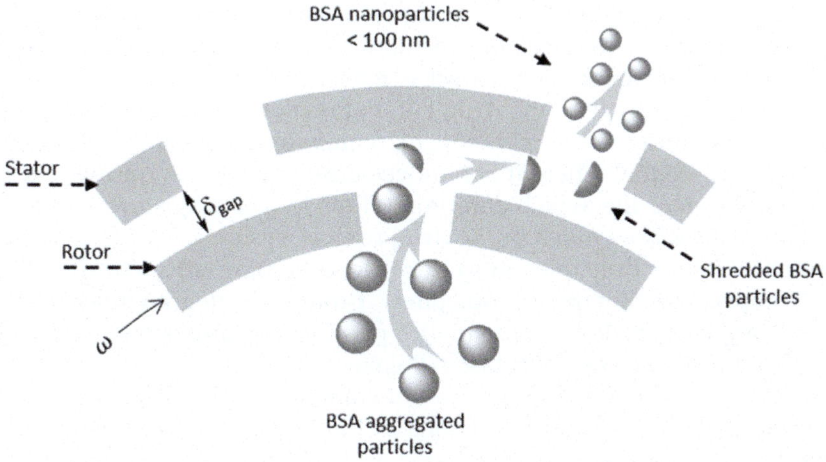


FIGURE 2.3 Schematic representation of BSA particle size reduction via the conventional desolvation method (S. Hassanzadeh, Ali N., B. Mirzayi, S. Fatemeh Kaboli, Protein-based nanoparticles synthesized at a high shear rate and optimized for drug delivery applications. J. Mol. Liq.. 335 (2021), 116133, https://doi.org/10.1016/j.molliq.2021.116133).

complex medical conditions. This transformative journey began in the early 1980s, catalyzed by significant breakthroughs in genetic engineering and recombinant DNA technology. This section delves into the historical development, profound impact, and key milestones associated with recombinant protein therapeutics, supplemented by insights from comprehensive literature and pivotal references.

### 1.2.1 *Early developments and initial breakthroughs*

The approval of human insulin in 1982 by the US Food and Drug Administration (FDA) marked a groundbreaking event in therapeutic biotechnology. This achievement underscored the potential of recombinant DNA technology to synthesize human proteins that mirrored their endogenous counterparts, ensuring enhanced efficacy and reduced immunogenic reactions compared with proteins sourced from animals (Leader et al., 2008; Carter, 2011).

As previously discussed, initial developments in recombinant protein production primarily leveraged *Escherichia coli* as the host organism. The rationale behind this choice lay in its well-documented genetic framework, ease of genetic manipulation, and rapid proliferation rates. The success of recombinant human insulin established a blueprint for subsequent proteins, including recombinant growth hormones and blood coagulation factors, which revolutionized treatment protocols for various endocrine and hematological disorders (Bruno et al., 2013; Jain, 2020).

### 1.2.2 *Expansion and diversification*

Building on the foundational success of insulin, the pipeline for recombinant proteins expanded rapidly. By the 1990s, the scope had broadened to include more structurally complex proteins, such as monoclonal antibodies and fusion proteins. These developments were facilitated by innovative protein engineering techniques, such as PEGylation—the covalent attachment of polyethylene glycol—which enhanced pharmacokinetics and reduced immunogenicity by shielding proteins from proteolytic degradation (Vargason et al., 2021; Chen and Zeng, 2016). Pharmacokinetics is the study of how a drug moves through the body, focusing on its absorption, distribution, metabolism, and excretion. It examines what the body does to the drug from the moment it is administered until it is eliminated. The key stages include absorption, where the drug enters the bloodstream; distribution, where it is transported to tissues and organs; metabolism, mainly in the liver, where the drug is chemically altered; and excretion, where it is removed from the body, typically via urine or bile. Key concepts such as half-life, which determines how long a drug stays active, and bioavailability, which measures how much of the drug reaches systemic circulation, are essential in pharmacokinetics. These principles are critical in designing effective drugs, determining dosages, and improving therapeutic outcomes. Proteolytic degradation is the process by which proteins are broken down into smaller peptides or amino acids through the action of enzymes called proteases or peptidases (Polaka et al., 2022).

The diversification of therapeutic proteins included various categories such as enzymes (molecules that accelerate chemical reactions in the body), cytokines (signaling molecules that regulate the immune system), and blood factors (key proteins involved in the blood clotting process). This expansion paved the way for more targeted treatments for conditions such as hemophilia (a genetic disorder that causes bleeding due to clotting factor deficiencies), chronic granulomatous disease (a rare immune disorder that impairs immune cells' ability to fight infections), and metabolic disorders (conditions in which the body cannot properly produce or break down specific molecules). A pivotal aspect of this progress was the ability to modify protein structures—such as by engineering additional glycosylation sites (the attachment of sugar molecules to proteins to enhance stability and half-life)—thereby optimizing therapeutic attributes for improved clinical outcomes (Vargason et al., 2021; Bruno et al., 2013; Jain, 2020).

### 1.2.3 Technological advancements

Technological strides in recombinant protein production extended beyond microbial systems to more intricate eukaryotic systems, such as yeast, insect, and mammalian cell cultures. These eukaryotic systems provided the critical capability for posttranslational modifications necessary for protein stability, folding, and bioactivity. For example, the development of darbepoetin-α, an engineered erythropoietin analog with increased glycosylation, significantly improved its half-life and therapeutic efficacy, showcasing the impact of strategic protein modifications (Vargason et al., 2021; Bruno et al., 2013).

Advanced methodologies, including phage display and hybridoma technology, were pivotal in the generation of fully human monoclonal antibodies, which overcame the limitations posed by murine-derived antibodies that elicited higher immunogenic responses in patients. These technological innovations marked a significant shift in the development of biologics, particularly in the realms of oncology and autoimmune disease management (Carter, 2011). Figure 2.4 illustrates the biopanning (affinity selection) process of phage display, a technique used to discover peptides or proteins that bind specifically to a target molecule. In this process, a phage library displaying a vast array of random peptides on its surface is exposed to a target, such as a protein or receptor. Phages that bind to the target are retained, while nonbinding phages are washed away. The bound phages are then eluted (removed from the target) and amplified in bacteria to produce more copies of the selected phages. These phages are then sequenced to identify the peptides that were displayed on

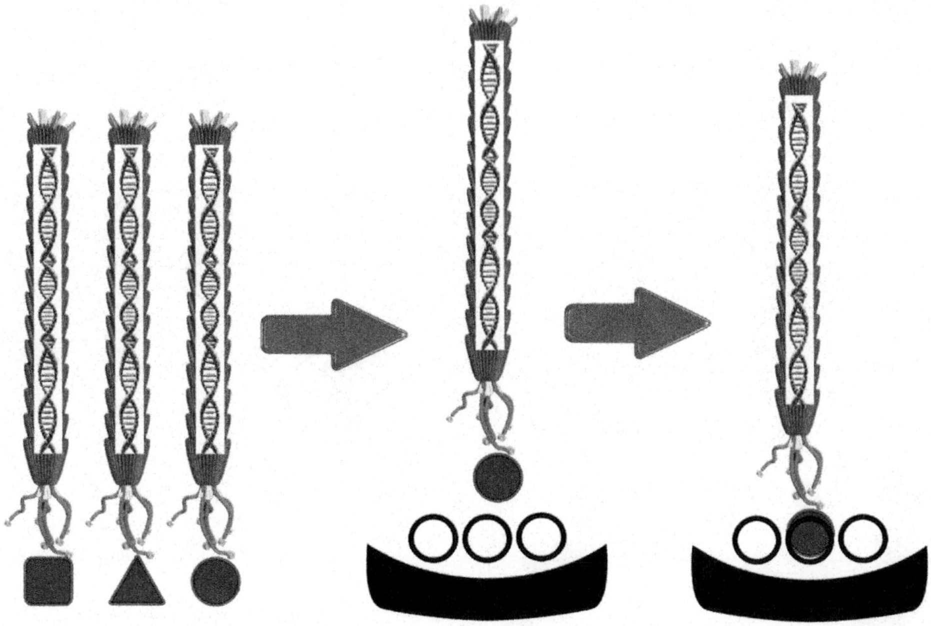


FIGURE 2.4 Biopanning (affinity selection) of phage-displayed random peptide library for protein targeting using phage display technology. Regeared from ref (D. Shiuan, D.-F. Tai, K.-J. Huang, Z. Yu, F. Ni, J. Li, Target-based discovery of therapeutic agents from food ingredients. Trends Food Sci. Technol.. 09242244. 105 (2020), 378–384, https://doi.org/10.1016/j.tifs.2020.09.013).

their surfaces, which are likely to have strong affinity for the target. This technique is powerful because the phenotype (the displayed peptide) is directly linked to the genotype (the DNA inside the phage), making it possible to easily identify the binding peptides and study their potential for therapeutic or diagnostic applications. Phage display is widely used for discovering therapeutic peptides, antibodies, and enzyme inhibitors (Shiuan et al., 2020).

The development of recombinant protein conjugation techniques, such as antibody–drug conjugates (ADCs), has significantly advanced cancer therapy by integrating the targeting specificity of monoclonal antibodies with the potent cytotoxic effects of chemotherapeutic agents (Leader et al., 2008; Chen and Zeng, 2016). This innovative strategy enables the precise delivery of cytotoxic drugs directly to tumor cells, reducing the impact on healthy tissues and minimizing side effects. Taxanes, a class of hydrophobic cytotoxic drugs, are integral in cancer treatment, functioning by disrupting microtubule dynamics, as illustrated in Fig. 2.5A, which outlines the structure of the cell, highlighting the crucial role of microtubules in various cellular processes. During mitosis, as depicted in Fig. 2.5B, microtubules form the spindle apparatus, which ensures proper chromosome segregation, a process facilitated by centrioles. Taxanes target beta-tubulin on the inner surface of microtubules (Fig. 2.5C), stabilizing them and blocking their normal dynamic function, resulting in the

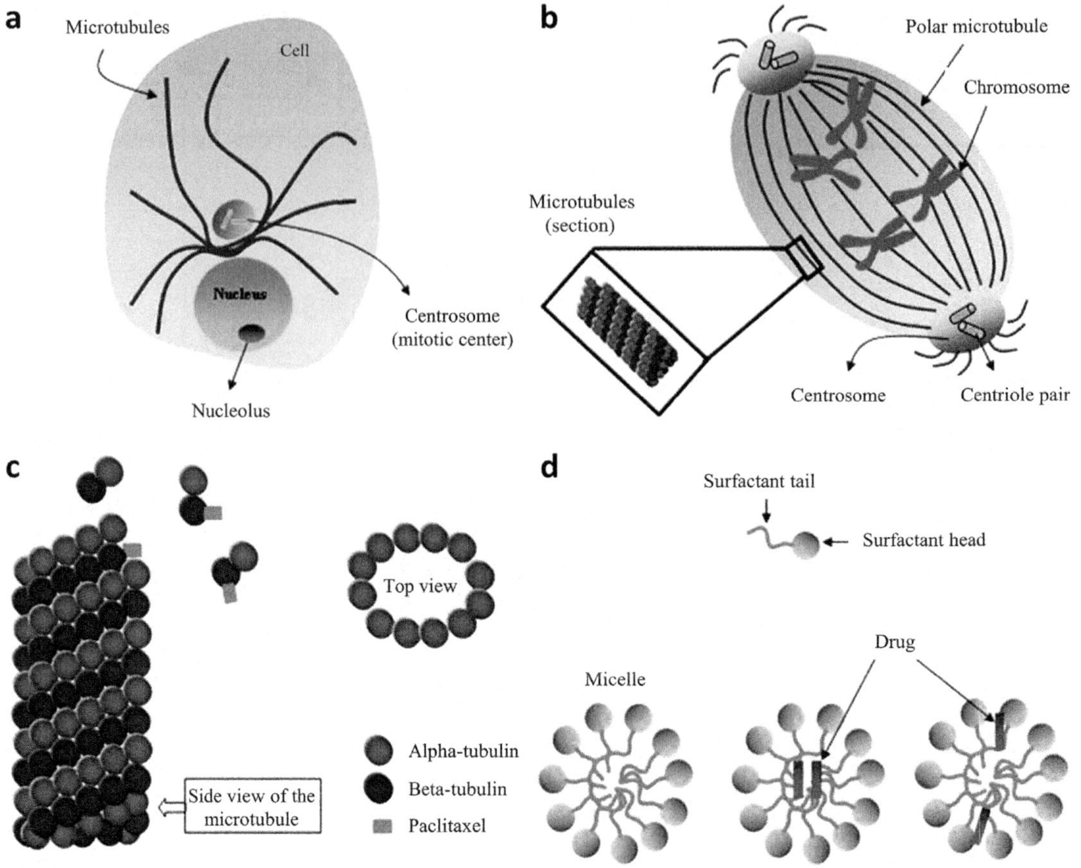


FIGURE 2.5 Microtubule dynamics and cytotoxic drug delivery systems (G.F.V. Ismael, D.D. Rosa, M.S. Mano, A. Awada, Novel cytotoxic drugs: Old challenges, new solutions. Cancer Treat. Rev.. 34 (1) (2008), 81–91, https://doi.org/10.1016/j.ctrv.2007.08.001).

formation of dysfunctional microtubules. However, due to their hydrophobic nature, taxanes require solubilizing agents such as Cremophor EL (CrEL), as shown in Fig. 2.5D. While CrEL improves drug solubility, it is associated with adverse effects, including hypersensitivity reactions and peripheral neuropathy (Ismael et al., 2008).

To overcome these challenges, alternative drug delivery systems, such as albumin nanoparticles, polyglutamates, and prodrugs, have been explored. When combined with the targeting precision of ADCs, these strategies improve the solubility and specificity of cytotoxic agents, thereby enhancing therapeutic efficacy and minimizing side effects, offering promising new approaches for cancer treatment (Ismael et al., 2008).

### *1.2.4 Impact on modern medicine*

Recombinant protein therapeutics have become indispensable in the management of diseases that were previously difficult to treat. Monoclonal antibodies, for instance, have emerged as vital tools in targeted cancer therapies, enabling highly specific interactions with tumor antigens and facilitating more personalized and effective treatment regimens (Leader et al., 2008; Chen and Zeng, 2016). These biologics have also extended their utility to chronic and rare genetic disorders by replacing deficient or dysfunctional proteins, thereby restoring essential biological functions (Carter, 2011; Vargason et al., 2021). One of the most compelling advantages of recombinant proteins over conventional small-molecule drugs is their remarkable specificity, which often results in fewer off-target effects and improved safety profiles. This specificity is also linked to accelerated clinical development timelines, allowing for swifter regulatory approvals compared with traditional drugs (Jain, 2020; Akash et al., 2015). The recombinant approach has thus bridged significant gaps in therapeutic innovation, making complex treatments more accessible and effective.

## 1.3 Fundamental concepts of protein therapeutics

Protein therapeutics have transformed modern medicine by introducing biologics that offer high specificity and efficacy in treating a wide range of diseases. These therapeutic proteins can replace or supplement endogenous proteins, modulate biological processes, or serve as targeting agents to deliver drugs to specific sites. The uniqueness of proteins lies in their complex structures, diverse functions, and specific interactions within the human body, allowing for targeted and sophisticated therapeutic applications (Park et al., 2022; Jain, 2020).

### *1.3.1 Key characteristics and benefits*

One of the primary advantages of protein therapeutics over traditional small-molecule drugs is their ability to perform complex biological functions that are difficult to replicate with chemical compounds. Proteins act in highly specific ways, interacting with targets through multiple points of contact, thus reducing the likelihood of off-target effects and adverse reactions (Bruno et al., 2013). This specificity minimizes interference with other biological processes, contributing to the often-favorable safety profile of protein-based treatments (Leader et al., 2008).

In diseases where there is a deficiency or abnormality in a particular protein, therapeutic proteins can restore the balance by replacing or augmenting the missing functions. Moreover, protein therapeutics are generally well-tolerated by the body, as they are derived from or mimic natural human proteins. This biocompatibility reduces immunogenicity and improves patient outcomes (Jain, 2020).

### *1.3.2 Therapeutic classes and mechanisms of action*

Protein therapeutics can be classified based on their pharmacological activity, including the following:

- Replacement therapies: For conditions involving deficient or defective proteins, therapeutic proteins can replace the missing functionality, as seen in insulin therapy for diabetes (Leader et al., 2008; Jain, 2020).
- Targeted delivery: Proteins such as monoclonal antibodies are used to target specific cells or molecules, enhancing treatment specificity, particularly in cancer therapy (Park et al., 2022; Bruno et al., 2013).

- Modulation of biological pathways: Proteins such as cytokines and growth factors act on cellular pathways to modulate immune responses or stimulate tissue repair (Akash et al., 2015).

Tissue repair involving proteins often centers on the role of extracellular vesicles (EVs), which are lipid bilayer–enclosed particles secreted by cells. These vesicles deliver proteins, nucleic acids, and lipids to recipient cells, modulating cellular functions and physiological processes critical to repair. EV-associated proteins enhance tissue repair by preventing apoptosis, reducing oxidative stress, modulating immune responses, and promoting angiogenesis. For example, proteins on EVs like VEGF (vascular endothelial growth factor) activate endothelial cells to foster new blood vessel growth, while antiinflammatory proteins encourage immune cell polarization to minimize damage. The therapeutic potential of EV-proteins lies in their ability to directly engage with cellular receptors or deliver functional cargo intracellularly, offering a targeted approach to regeneration and repair in diseases or injuries (Roefs et al., 2020).

### 1.3.3 *Advances in delivery and engineering*

Protein therapeutics face unique delivery challenges, particularly in terms of stability and bioavailability. Innovations such as PEGylation and Fc fusion technologies have been developed to enhance the half-life and reduce the immunogenicity of therapeutic proteins, allowing for improved efficacy and patient compliance (Carter, 2011). Additionally, nanoparticles and microparticles are being explored as carriers to protect proteins from degradation and facilitate targeted delivery (Park et al., 2022; Vargason et al., 2021). Fc-fusion proteins are a specialized class of biopharmaceuticals that combine the pharmacological properties of biological ligands with the functionality of the Fc (fragment crystallizable) domain of immunoglobulins. These proteins are engineered by linking biological moieties, such as peptides, receptors, or enzymes, to the Fc domain of IgG, enhancing their therapeutic efficacy by extending plasma half-life, improving stability, and modulating immune interactions (Duivelshof et al., 2021). Figure 2.6 highlights the key applications of bifunctional fusion proteins in drug delivery, emphasizing their ability to improve therapeutic outcomes through three primary mechanisms. (1) One of the main advantages is the extension of plasma half-life. By reducing access to proteases, decreasing renal filtration, or altering intracellular routing via receptor-mediated recycling, bifunctional fusion proteins can maintain their presence in circulation for longer periods, thereby minimizing the need for frequent dosing and enhancing drug efficacy. (2) Additionally, bifunctional fusion proteins facilitate the absorption of drugs across epithelial bilayers. This is achieved by binding to specific receptors that undergo transcytosis, enabling the drug to cross-barriers such as the blood–brain barrier or the gastrointestinal epithelium. (3) Lastly, these fusion proteins enable targeted drug delivery to in vivo sites that either overexpress or uniquely express specific receptors or antigens. This targeting capability allows for precision delivery of therapeutic agents to disease sites, such as tumors or inflamed tissues, while minimizing off-target effects on healthy tissues. These properties make bifunctional fusion proteins an invaluable tool in drug delivery systems (Chen et al., 2013).

The development of protein therapeutics represents a convergence of biotechnology, molecular biology, and pharmacology, enabling the creation of highly specific, effective

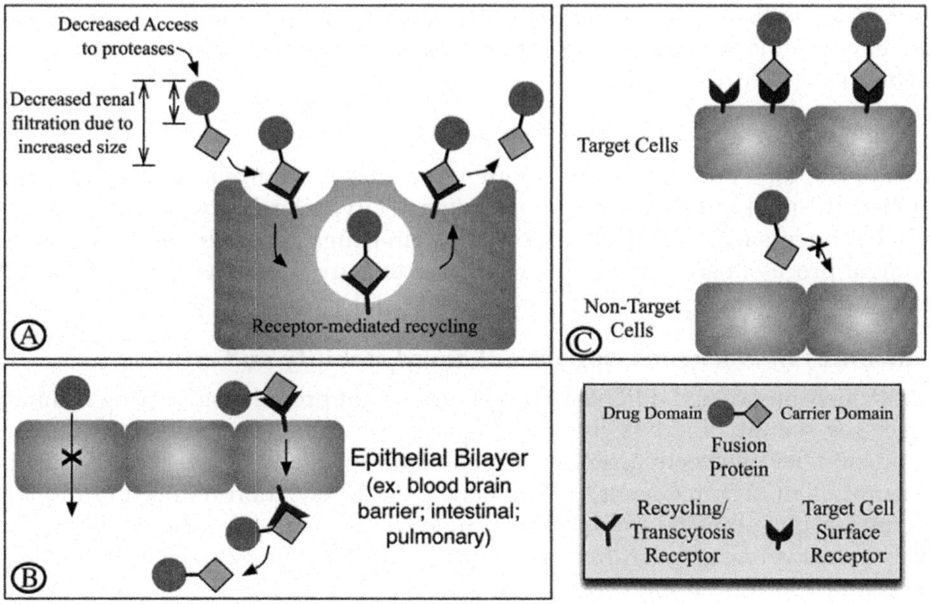


FIGURE 2.6 Applications of bifunctional fusion proteins in drug delivery: mechanisms for extended half-life, epithelial absorption, and targeted therapy (X. Chen, J.L. Zaro, W.C. Shen, Fusion protein linkers: Property, design and functionality. Adv. Drug Deliv. Rev.. 65 (10) (2013), 1357–1369, https://doi.org/10.1016/j.addr.2012.09.039).

treatments with broad clinical applications. As protein engineering advances, therapeutic proteins are expected to become more sophisticated, with applications in personalized medicine and regenerative therapies on the horizon (Bruno et al., 2013).

## 1.4 Key advantages over small-molecule drugs

Protein-based therapeutics offer several key advantages over traditional small-molecule drugs, primarily due to their unique structural and functional properties. Unlike small molecules, which often provide generalized treatment approaches, proteins can be tailored for highly specific functions, which translates to increased efficacy and reduced side effects. These distinctions make protein therapeutics especially valuable in treating complex diseases that involve intricate molecular pathways. Because proteins are naturally occurring in the human body, they are generally better tolerated by patients compared with foreign chemical compounds. Many protein drugs, such as recombinant proteins, closely resemble their natural counterparts, reducing the likelihood of immune responses. This characteristic is especially advantageous for chronic diseases, where long-term treatment is essential (Carter, 2011; Chen and Zeng, 2016).

### *1.4.1 Replacement therapy potential*

Proteins are well-suited for use in replacement therapy, particularly in cases where a gene mutation or deficiency causes a lack of essential proteins. For instance, insulin, growth hormones, and clotting factors can be directly replaced with recombinant protein versions, allowing effective management of conditions that were previously challenging to treat with small molecules (Akash et al., 2015).

#### 1.4.2 *Accelerated approval and market access*

Regulatory bodies, such as the FDA, often grant faster approval to protein therapeutics compared with small molecules due to their specificity, tolerability, and the pressing need for novel treatments in complex conditions. Protein drugs generally undergo a streamlined development process, partly due to their reduced toxicity profile, which enables faster clinical trials and regulatory review (Vargason et al., 2021).

#### 1.4.3 *Advances in bioengineering for enhanced stability and efficacy*

As previously mentioned, PEGylation is an important protein engineering technique used to enhance the stability and half-life of therapeutic proteins. However, if we look at PEGylation from another perspective, it offers several additional advantages beyond just prolonging the duration of action. One of the key benefits of PEGylation reduced immunogenicity. By attaching a polyethylene glycol (PEG) molecule to a protein, the PEGylation process effectively "shields" the protein from the immune system, preventing it from being recognized and attacked as a foreign substance. This is particularly valuable in the treatment of chronic conditions where long-term administration of protein therapeutics is required, as it reduces the likelihood of immune responses that could decrease the effectiveness of the treatment or cause adverse reactions. Additionally, PEGylation can also improve the solubility of proteins. Many therapeutic proteins have poor solubility in aqueous environments, which can complicate their formulation and delivery. By attaching PEG, the hydrophilic properties of the protein are enhanced, leading to improved solubility and easier administration. This is especially important for proteins that need to be administered intravenously or in high concentrations. Moreover, PEGylation helps reduce protein aggregation. Aggregation can occur when proteins clump together, which can affect their functionality and lead to undesirable side effects. PEGylation helps prevent this aggregation by providing a protective coating that stabilizes the protein structure (Dimitrov, 2012; Jain, 2020).

## 2. Characteristics of protein-based therapeutics

### 2.1 Structural and functional characteristics of proteins

Proteins' complex structures and multifunctional nature are fundamental to their role as therapeutics. The structure–function relationship in proteins enables diverse and highly specific biological functions, which are harnessed for therapeutic use. In the following, we delve into the structure, stability, functionality, and advances in engineering of protein therapeutics.

#### 2.1.1 *Protein structure and stability*

Proteins are composed of amino acid chains folded into specific three-dimensional structures, forming functional domains critical for therapeutic effectiveness. These structures range from simple α-helices and β-sheets to complex globular and fibrous forms that allow precise interactions with molecular targets. This structural diversity supports their therapeutic functions but also renders proteins sensitive to environmental factors such as pH, temperature, and enzymatic activity (Leader et al., 2008; Bruno et al., 2013). Protein stability is a key challenge in therapeutic applications. The complex tertiary and quaternary structures of proteins are vulnerable to denaturation and degradation, particularly when administered systemically. To enhance stability, PEGylation (attachment of polyethylene glycol chains) is frequently used. PEGylation increases solubility, reduces proteolytic degradation, and extends circulation half-life, making PEGylated proteins less immunogenic and improving therapeutic efficacy (Park et al., 2022). Other methods, such as glycosylation, help stabilize proteins by modifying surface characteristics and reducing the likelihood of aggregation (Akash et al., 2015).

Figure 2.7 shows the four levels of protein structure: primary, secondary, tertiary, and quaternary, each of which is crucial for determining a protein's function. (1) Primary structure refers to the linear sequence of amino acids in a protein, which is determined by the gene's DNA sequence. Any changes in this sequence can affect the protein's function, potentially leading to diseases or dysfunction. (2) Secondary structure describes the local folding of the polypeptide chain into shapes such as the α-helix and β-pleated sheet, held together by hydrogen bonds. These formations are essential for maintaining the protein's stability and functionality. (3) Tertiary structure refers to the three-dimensional shape of the protein, created by interactions between the side chains (R groups) of amino acids. These interactions include hydrogen bonds, ionic bonds, and hydrophobic forces, which are critical for the protein's biological activity. (4) Quaternary structure occurs when multiple polypeptide chains come together to form a functional protein complex. Not all proteins have this structure, as many function as a single polypeptide with only primary, secondary, and tertiary structures (Delfi et al., 2021; de Almeida Paiva et al., 2022). Understanding these structural levels is key to grasping how proteins execute their biological roles. Since proteins are involved in nearly all cellular processes, knowing how their structure relates to their function is essential for the development of targeted therapies, especially with the increasing availability of genomic

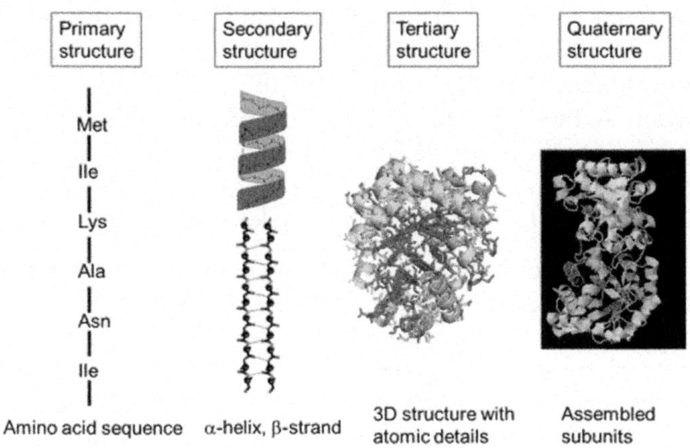


**FIGURE 2.7** Overview of protein structure: primary, secondary, tertiary, and quaternary levels and their role in function (V. de Almeida Paiva, I.de S. Gomes, C.R. Monteiro, M. Ventura Mendonça, P.M. Martins, C.A. Santana, V. Gonçalves-Almeida, S.C. Izidoro, R.C.de Melo-Minardi, S.de A. Silveira, Protein structural bioinformatics: An overview. Comput. Biol. Med.. 147 (2022), 105695, https://doi.org/10.1016/j.compbiomed.2022.105695).

data. The growing identification of new proteins highlights the need for computational tools to predict protein functions efficiently.

### 2.1.2 *Pharmacokinetics and pharmacodynamics of protein-based therapeutics*

Protein-based therapeutics hold significant promise in addressing complex diseases due to their unique PK/PD profiles. Here, we expand on the absorption, distribution, metabolism, and excretion (ADME) aspects that shape their pharmacokinetics and discuss how their biological specificity influences pharmacodynamics.

### 2.1.3 *Pharmacokinetics of protein therapeutics*

- **Absorption:** Protein-based drugs are generally administered via parenteral routes (intravenous, subcutaneous, or intramuscular) because their large molecular size and susceptibility to proteolytic enzymes hinder effective absorption through oral administration. Subcutaneous and intramuscular injections allow for slow, sustained release, but intravenous administration often provides the most controlled bioavailability. To counteract degradation in biological environments, encapsulation within protective carriers such as nanoparticles is utilized. For instance, high-shear synthesized BSA nanoparticles have been optimized to enhance stability and drug-loading efficiency, which is crucial for maintaining bioavailability (Hassanzadeh et al., 2021; Bruno et al., 2013).
- **Distribution:** Unlike small molecules, proteins primarily remain in extracellular spaces and are distributed across the vascular and interstitial compartments. Their distribution is often limited due to large molecular sizes and hydrophilic properties, which prevent cellular internalization. Targeted delivery platforms, such as PEGylation and the development of Fc-fusion proteins, have been employed to increase distribution efficiency and prolong circulation times. Studies using BSA hollow nanospheres and protein-based drug carriers show improved distribution and site-specific release, enhancing therapeutic outcomes without affecting nontarget tissues (Dimitrov, 2012; Park et al., 2022; Lotfalian et al., 2021).
- **Metabolism and excretion:** Protein-based drugs are metabolized primarily by proteolytic enzymes and are generally eliminated through lysosomal degradation rather than traditional hepatic and renal pathways. This unique pathway minimizes drug–drug interactions commonly seen in small molecules metabolized by cytochrome P450 enzymes. However, their molecular weight and propensity for aggregation can result in accumulation in organs such as the liver and spleen. Encapsulation and surface modifications, such as PEGylation, have been shown to reduce immunogenicity and prolong half-life by delaying proteolytic degradation, as observed in studies on protein nanoparticles and Fc-fusion modifications (Carter, 2011; Akash et al., 2015).

Figure 2.8 provides an overview of the various pharmacokinetic processes involved in protein-based therapeutics. These processes include absorption via different routes such as gastrointestinal, dermal, and pulmonary pathways. It also highlights the distribution of these therapeutics across extracellular spaces and emphasizes the use of targeted delivery platforms, such as nanoparticles, to improve distribution efficiency and facilitate tumor-specific delivery. Finally, metabolism and excretion of protein-based drugs primarily occur

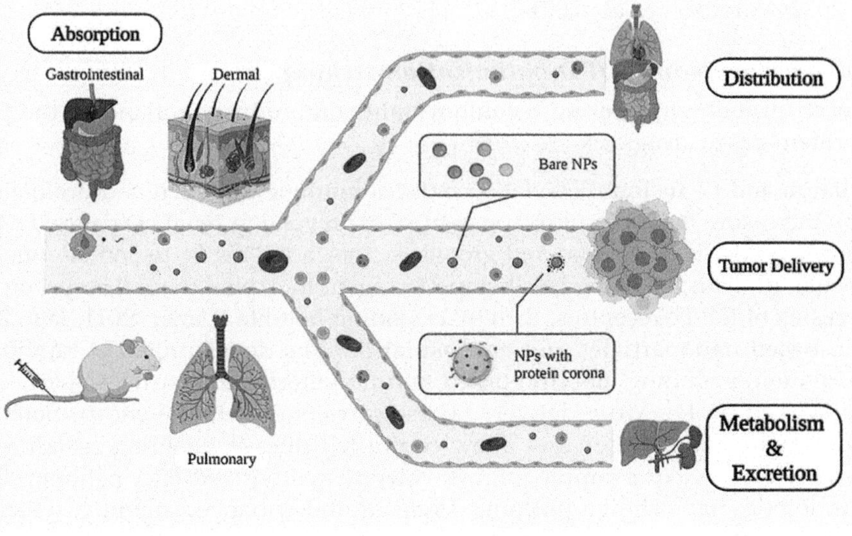


FIGURE 2.8 Pharmacokinetics of protein-based therapeutics, highlighting absorption, distribution, and metabolism/excretion (L. Yuan, Q. Chen, J.E. Riviere, Z. Lin, Pharmacokinetics and tumor delivery of nanoparticles. J. Drug Deliv. Sci. Technol.. 17732247. 83 (2023), 104404, https://doi.org/10.1016/j.jddst.2023.104404).

through proteolytic degradation, with elimination through lysosomal pathways and organs such as the liver and spleen. This figure clearly illustrates these stages and underscores the role of advanced technologies in enhancing the pharmacokinetics of protein therapeutics (Yuan et al., 2023).

### 2.1.4 *Pharmacodynamics of protein-based drugs*

Protein-based therapeutics often exhibit high target affinity and specificity, leading to distinct and predictable pharmacodynamic responses.

- **Target specificity and mechanism of action:** Proteins can interact with biological targets in a highly specific manner due to multiple binding sites, leading to effects that are often superior to small molecules in terms of precision. Monoclonal antibodies (mAbs), for example, are designed to bind to specific antigens, eliciting immune responses that can target pathogens or tumor cells without affecting surrounding healthy tissues. This mechanism reduces the risk of off-target effects, a significant advantage over conventional drugs (Leader et al., 2008; Bruno et al., 2013).
- **Dose–response relationship and therapeutic window:** The therapeutic effect of protein-based drugs is often nonlinear, with saturable binding at higher doses. This property creates a narrow therapeutic window where the effective dose is close to the maximum tolerated dose. Protein modifications such as glycoengineering have been introduced to optimize the therapeutic window by increasing bioavailability and reducing immunogenicity, ensuring efficacy without triggering adverse immune responses. For example, glycosylation and PEGylation of proteins can minimize

immune activation and extend half-life, optimizing the dose–response profile (Park et al., 2022; Vargason et al., 2021).

### 2.1.5 Advancements in PK/PD optimization techniques

Advanced protein engineering techniques are continuously enhancing the PK/PD profiles of protein-based drugs:

- **PEGylation and Fc fusion:** PEGylation reduces immune detection and prolongs circulation time by increasing the molecule's apparent size, preventing renal clearance. Fc fusion, commonly used with cytokines and growth factors, adds the Fc region of antibodies to therapeutic proteins, allowing the therapeutic agent to exploit natural recycling mechanisms of the Fc receptors, thereby extending half-life (Carter, 2011; Jain, 2020).
- **Protein-based nanoparticles and encapsulation:** The development of nanoparticle encapsulation, including albumin-based and polymeric nanoparticles, has revolutionized protein drug delivery. These carriers protect the encapsulated protein from enzymatic degradation and allow controlled release, enabling sustained therapeutic effects. For example, high-shear-rate synthesized BSA nanoparticles loaded with antibiotics have shown prolonged release and enhanced stability, which is beneficial for controlled drug delivery and minimizing toxicity (Hassanzadeh et al., 2021; Lotfalian et al., 2021).
- **Glycoengineering:** By altering glycosylation patterns, glycoengineering adjusts a protein's pharmacokinetic and immunogenic properties. This modification not only improves stability and bioavailability but also enhances the therapeutic agent's receptor binding affinity, optimizing efficacy (Akash et al., 2015).

### 2.1.6 Physical instability: denaturation and aggregation

Protein denaturation and aggregation pose major challenges, often exacerbated by processing or physiological conditions. Denaturation results from unfolding under thermal, pH, or mechanical stresses, exposing hydrophobic regions that promote aggregation. Aggregation not only reduces bioactivity but can also provoke immune responses, limiting therapeutic effectiveness (Leader et al., 2008; Bruno et al., 2013).

To address these issues, nanoparticle formulations have been used to stabilize proteins in delivery applications. For example, albumin-based nanoparticles synthesized under high-shear conditions maintain structural integrity by reducing particle size and promoting uniform distribution, which helps prevent aggregation (Hassanzadeh et al., 2021). Furthermore, by optimizing pH during nanoparticle synthesis—usually above the protein's isoelectric point—charge repulsion can be leveraged to maintain particle stability and prevent aggregation (Lotfalian et al., 2021). This is particularly valuable for proteins such as bovine serum albumin (BSA), commonly used in nanoparticle systems for controlled release (Akash et al., 2015).

### 2.1.7 Chemical instability: Oxidation, deamidation, and proteolysis

Chemical degradation can significantly impact therapeutic proteins by altering amino acid residues and modifying active sites. Oxidation, particularly of methionine and cysteine residues, is a common cause of degradation in protein therapeutics, often induced by reactive oxygen species (ROS) in the bloodstream. Oxidized proteins may lose binding affinity, become more immunogenic, or aggregate more readily (Dimitrov, 2012; Leader et al., 2008).

Deamidation, where asparagine and glutamine residues convert into aspartic or glutamic acid, respectively, changes the protein's charge and can affect stability and solubility. Proteolysis, meanwhile, is a form of enzymatic degradation that occurs predominantly in the bloodstream due to proteolytic enzymes. PEGylation, attaching polyethylene glycol (PEG) chains to protein molecules, is widely used to protect therapeutic proteins from proteolysis and oxidation by forming a hydrophilic barrier that also extends circulation time (Park et al., 2022; Carter, 2011). Glycosylation, which involves attaching carbohydrate chains, can similarly reduce immunogenicity and degradation by proteolytic enzymes (Akash et al., 2015).

### 2.1.8 *Strategies for enhancing stability*

Effective strategies to enhance protein stability in drug delivery systems include physical encapsulation, chemical modification, and environmental optimization:

- **PEGylation and cross-linking**: PEGylation and cross-linking are standard methods to improve stability. PEGylated proteins are more resistant to aggregation and enzymatic breakdown, while cross-linking proteins (e.g., with glutaraldehyde) enhance thermal and mechanical stability. In BSA-based nanoparticle systems, for instance, glutaraldehyde cross-linking prevents premature breakdown, maintaining therapeutic effectiveness (Dimitrov, 2012; Lotfalian et al., 2021).
- **Nanoparticle encapsulation:** Encapsulation within nanoparticles shields proteins from external stressors, protecting them from enzymatic degradation and improving bioavailability. Albumin nanoparticles provide an example where stability is enhanced through controlled release, which minimizes the "burst release" effect and enables a sustained release over extended periods, beneficial for drugs such as paclitaxel (Hassanzadeh et al., 2021; Lotfalian et al., 2021).
- **Optimization of environmental conditions:** Maintaining stability also involves careful control of pH, ionic strength, and temperature during formulation. For example, maintaining a pH above the isoelectric point of albumin nanoparticles reduces aggregation by promoting electrostatic repulsion between particles (Bruno et al., 2013; Akash et al., 2015). Additionally, high-shear preparation methods produce smaller, more stable nanoparticles, making them ideal for intravenous applications (Hassanzadeh et al., 2021).

### 2.1.9 *In vitro and in vivo degradation studies*

The stability of protein-based therapeutics is further evaluated through in vitro and in vivo degradation studies, which simulate physiological conditions and assess the release kinetics of the therapeutic protein. These studies are crucial to understand the degradation pathway and ensure the therapeutic protein reaches its target in an active form. For example, BSA-based nanoparticles have shown controlled, sustained release of drugs in vitro, indicating their potential to reduce initial burst release and extend drug availability over time. Studies with paclitaxel-loaded hollow albumin nanoparticles demonstrated higher cytotoxic effects on lung cancer cells over extended periods, suggesting their potential for use in cancer therapies with controlled release (Hassanzadeh et al., 2021; Lotfalian et al., 2021).

#### 2.1.10 *Advanced engineering and emerging techniques for stability*

Protein stability has benefited from recent advancements in protein engineering and nanoparticle technology. Techniques such as directed evolution and computational modeling enable the design of proteins with improved stability profiles tailored to specific delivery systems. Directed evolution accelerates the identification of protein variants with higher stability under physiological conditions, while computational modeling predicts beneficial modifications to prevent aggregation or degradation (Jain, 2020; Akash et al., 2015). Additionally, hierarchical structuring, as seen in the design of hollow protein-based nanospheres, enhances drug loading capacity and stability, addressing common limitations in drug delivery (Lotfalian et al., 2021).

## 3. Challenges in protein drug delivery

### 3.1 Bioavailability and absorption barriers

Protein-based therapeutics present unique challenges in terms of bioavailability and absorption, largely due to their structural complexity, size, susceptibility to enzymatic degradation, and the physiological barriers they encounter. The following is an expanded discussion of these challenges, supported by details from recent research advancements.

#### 3.1.1 *Structural complexity and large molecular size*

Protein drugs are generally large, complex molecules, making it difficult for them to cross cellular membranes and enter systemic circulation through passive absorption. Unlike small-molecule drugs, which can permeate cell membranes via simple diffusion, proteins require specialized carriers or transporters to traverse barriers such as the intestinal epithelium (Leader et al., 2008; Bruno et al., 2013). This large molecular size also limits absorption routes. Oral administration is generally ineffective for protein drugs because they cannot penetrate the epithelial cell layer in the gastrointestinal (GI) tract. Instead, protein drugs are typically administered parenterally (e.g., via injection), bypassing the absorption barriers but raising issues with patient compliance and potential injection-related complications (Carter, 2011).

#### 3.1.2 *Susceptibility to enzymatic degradation*

The GI tract contains proteolytic enzymes (e.g., pepsin, trypsin, and chymotrypsin) designed to break down proteins, which poses a major hurdle for oral protein drug delivery. These enzymes quickly degrade therapeutic proteins, limiting their effectiveness. For example, therapeutic insulin, when orally administered, is broken down before it reaches the bloodstream, thus losing its biological activity (Akash et al., 2015; Lotfalian et al., 2021). Some recent advancements involve encapsulation techniques and the use of enzyme inhibitors to protect protein drugs from enzymatic degradation. One promising approach is encapsulating proteins within nanoparticles, which provide a protective shield against enzymatic breakdown while enabling controlled release of the therapeutic agent (Park et al., 2022; Hassanzadeh et al., 2021).

#### 3.1.3 *Poor bioavailability and rapid clearance*

Due to rapid clearance by the liver and kidneys, protein drugs often have short half-lives, reducing their bioavailability. Once in the bloodstream, many proteins are recognized as foreign substances and are cleared by the reticuloendothelial system (RES) or filtered out by the kidneys if they are small enough. This rapid clearance necessitates frequent dosing, which can lead to reduced patient adherence and increased costs (Vargason et al., 2021; Bruno et al., 2013). One strategy to improve bioavailability involves modifying the molecular structure of proteins to resist clearance. PEGylation, for instance, adds polyethylene glycol (PEG) to the protein surface, making it more hydrophilic and thus less recognizable to the immune system. PEGylation has shown significant success in extending half-lives of protein drugs such as PEGylated interferons (Dimitrov, 2012; Akash et al., 2015).

### *3.1.4 Technological advances to enhance bioavailability*

- **Nanoparticles and liposomes:** Protein drugs are often encapsulated within nanoparticles or liposomes to shield them from enzymatic degradation and immune clearance. For example, bovine serum albumin (BSA)–based hollow nanospheres offer high drug-loading capacity and controlled release properties. These structures, with adjustable shell thickness and drug diffusion rates, allow for sustained release and reduced initial burst effects, maintaining therapeutic levels over time (Hassanzadeh et al., 2021; Lotfalian et al., 2021).
- **Microparticles and microspheres:** Larger protein-based drugs can be encapsulated in microspheres, which dissolve slowly, allowing the drug to be released over an extended period. Studies on albumin-based microparticles have demonstrated sustained release profiles that reduce dosing frequency while enhancing patient compliance (Jain, 2020).
- **PEGylation and Fc fusion:** These modifications extend the half-life of protein drugs in circulation. PEGylation forms a hydrophilic layer around the protein, reducing opsonization by immune cells, while Fc fusion links the protein to the Fc region of an antibody, exploiting Fc receptor recycling to extend half-life (Carter, 2011).

### *3.1.5 Overcoming the immune response*

Many protein drugs are recognized as foreign antigens by the immune system, triggering immune responses that can neutralize their therapeutic effect. Additionally, repeated administration of a protein drug can lead to antibody formation, causing hypersensitivity or reduced efficacy over time (Leader et al., 2008; Akash et al., 2015). To mitigate immune responses, researchers have developed protein engineering strategies such as glycoengineering to alter the glycosylation patterns on protein drugs, making them less immunogenic. Another approach involves the use of Fc fusions, which exploit immune system tolerance mechanisms associated with the Fc region of antibodies, reducing the likelihood of immune recognition (Vargason et al., 2021; Jain, 2020).

### *3.1.6 Absorption-enhancing carriers and alternative routes*

Alternative delivery methods are being explored to improve absorption and bioavailability. For instance:

- **Transdermal delivery:** Attempts have been made to deliver proteins through the skin using patches or microneedles. These methods bypass the GI tract and offer controlled release, though they are limited by the protein size that can penetrate the skin layers (Hassanzadeh et al., 2021).

- **Intranasal delivery:** This method exploits the vascularized nasal mucosa to deliver protein drugs directly to systemic circulation, reducing exposure to digestive enzymes and offering a noninvasive alternative to injections (Leader et al., 2008; Park et al., 2022).

## 3.2 Immune response and safety concerns

Protein-based therapeutics present unique benefits in targeting and specificity but are also associated with significant immune-related challenges. Immune responses to therapeutic proteins can severely impact treatment efficacy, safety, and patient tolerance. The following are detailed aspects of the immunogenicity and safety challenges in protein drug delivery and the strategies being developed to address them.

### *3.2.1 Immunogenicity of therapeutic proteins*

The immune system can identify therapeutic proteins as foreign agents, leading to immunogenic responses that compromise drug effectiveness and patient safety (Dimitrov, 2012; Park et al., 2022). Immunogenicity occurs when epitopes (antigenic determinants) on therapeutic proteins trigger antibody production. These antibodies can neutralize the therapeutic protein, clear it from circulation, or cause cross-reactions with similar endogenous proteins (Bruno et al., 2013). Immunogenicity is particularly prevalent in nonhuman proteins or proteins with structural differences from native human proteins. For example, foreign glycosylation patterns in proteins produced by nonhuman expression systems (such as bacterial or yeast cells) can significantly increase immunogenic potential (Leader et al., 2008; Jain, 2020). Even subtle structural changes due to recombinant production processes can lead to immune recognition and subsequent neutralization by the immune system.

### *3.2.2 Adverse immune reactions and safety concerns*

Immune responses to therapeutic proteins range from mild to life-threatening reactions, such as anaphylaxis. Mild reactions may include fever and rashes, while severe reactions involve cytokine release and systemic inflammation (Vargason et al., 2021; Chen and Zeng, 2016; Akash et al., 2015). One key mechanism by which these adverse reactions occur is through the formation of immune complexes. When therapeutic proteins bind to antibodies, they can form large complexes that activate the complement cascade, leading to inflammation, vascular leakage, and potential tissue damage (Chen and Zeng, 2016; Akash et al., 2015). Repeated exposure to therapeutic proteins can result in sensitization, where memory immune cells recognize the therapeutic protein upon readministration, leading to faster and stronger immune responses. This effect complicates long-term treatment regimens and may render the therapy ineffective over time (Dimitrov, 2012; Leader et al., 2008).

### *3.2.3 Strategies to minimize immunogenicity and enhance safety*

Various strategies have been employed to reduce the immunogenicity and improve the safety profile of protein therapeutics:

- **PEGylation and surface modifications:** PEGylation, or attaching polyethylene glycol (PEG) chains to a protein's surface, is one of the most effective methods to shield immunogenic epitopes. PEGylated proteins exhibit reduced recognition by immune cells and longer circulation times due to decreased enzymatic degradation. This modification has been successful in creating less immunogenic versions of drugs such as interferon and granulocyte colony-stimulating factor (Bruno et al., 2013; Chen and Zeng, 2016).

- **Humanization of therapeutic proteins:** Humanization involves modifying nonhuman proteins, particularly monoclonal antibodies, to closely resemble human proteins in their amino acid sequences and glycosylation patterns. By reducing the presence of foreign structures, humanized proteins are less likely to trigger an immune response. This technique is especially critical for monoclonal antibodies, which originally came from mouse models and had high immunogenicity in human patients (Carter, 2011; Jain, 2020).
- **Encapsulation in nanoparticles and liposomes:** Encapsulation technologies help deliver therapeutic proteins without direct exposure to immune cells. Nanoparticle and liposome encapsulation provides a protective barrier, allowing proteins to circulate longer and reducing immediate immune recognition. Controlled release systems within these carriers also enable sustained drug delivery, minimizing peak concentrations that could otherwise provoke a strong immune response (Park et al., 2022; Chen and Zeng, 2016).
- **Glycoengineering and protein engineering:** Glycoengineering allows for the manipulation of glycosylation sites to create human-like glycan patterns on therapeutic proteins. This reduces immune recognition and can also enhance protein stability. In addition, site-directed mutagenesis and protein engineering enable modifications at specific amino acids to reduce immunogenicity without affecting protein function (Carter, 2011; Vargason et al., 2021).
- **Tolerance-inducing therapies:** Researchers are exploring tolerance-inducing approaches, such as coadministration with immunosuppressive agents or using low-dose regimens that gradually increase to higher doses. These strategies aim to acclimate the immune system to therapeutic proteins, particularly in chronic therapies where long-term use is essential (Leader et al., 2008).

## 3.3 Formulation and delivery method constraints

Protein-based therapeutics offer precise targeting and high specificity, yet they face substantial challenges in formulation and delivery. The structural complexity, instability, and sensitivity of proteins demand specialized formulations and delivery systems to preserve their functionality, enhance bioavailability, and ensure therapeutic effectiveness.

### 3.3.1 *Instability and degradation in formulation*

Proteins are sensitive to environmental conditions such as temperature, pH, and mechanical stress, which can lead to denaturation, aggregation, and loss of biological activity (Carter, 2011; Bruno et al., 2013). Maintaining stability during formulation, storage, and administration is challenging due to proteins' complex folding patterns and the need to preserve their tertiary and quaternary structures.

Several formulation strategies aim to address these stability issues:

- **Lyophilization:** This freeze-drying technique reduces water content, which helps maintain protein structure and stability during storage. However, lyophilization requires careful control to prevent protein damage from freezing and drying stresses (Akash et al., 2015).

- **Buffer optimization:** Formulations often include specific buffers and stabilizers that maintain an optimal pH, minimizing protein degradation and aggregation during storage (Park et al., 2022).
- **Use of surfactants and cryoprotectants:** These agents can protect proteins from surface-induced denaturation and stress during formulation. Surfactants such as polysorbates are commonly added to protein formulations to prevent aggregation, while cryoprotectants such as trehalose shield proteins from freezing damage (Chen and Zeng, 2016).

### 3.3.2 *Delivery route limitations*

Proteins are typically administered via parenteral routes (e.g., intravenous, subcutaneous) because of their poor oral bioavailability. Oral delivery poses significant challenges due to the harsh conditions in the gastrointestinal (GI) tract and the large size and hydrophilicity of protein molecules, which hinder their absorption across the intestinal epithelium (Leader et al., 2008; Jain, 2020).

- **Oral delivery constraints:** In the GI tract, proteins are susceptible to degradation by proteolytic enzymes and the acidic environment of the stomach. Additionally, they struggle to cross the epithelial barrier in the intestines. Although various approaches, such as enteric coatings and enzyme inhibitors, are under investigation, efficient oral delivery remains an unmet need in protein drug development (Dimitrov, 2012).
- **Alternative delivery methods:** Beyond parenteral administration, methods such as inhalation, transdermal, and nasal delivery are being explored. However, these routes face their own limitations. For instance, inhaled proteins need to be formulated as fine particles, stable against respiratory tract enzymes, and capable of reaching the targeted site in the lungs, which complicates formulation and delivery (Bruno et al., 2013).

### 3.3.3 *Challenges with controlled and sustained release*

Controlled and sustained release is particularly challenging for proteins, which often have short half-lives and require frequent dosing. To reduce dosing frequency and enhance patient compliance, researchers have developed various delivery systems:

- **Polymer-based delivery systems:** Biodegradable polymers such as PLGA (poly(lactic-co-glycolic acid)) can encapsulate proteins, allowing for slow release over time. However, protein instability within polymer matrices remains a problem, as encapsulated proteins may denature or aggregate during the polymer's degradation (Vargason et al., 2021; Akash et al., 2015).
- **Hydrogel systems:** Hydrogels can create a moist environment that stabilizes proteins and allows for gradual release. These materials are useful in injectable formats, but achieving consistent release rates while maintaining protein stability is complex (Chen and Zeng, 2016).
- **Microparticles and nanoparticles:** Microparticle and nanoparticle systems can protect proteins from degradation and enable controlled release. These particles may be

modified to target specific tissues, yet their production can be challenging and costly, requiring precise control to maintain protein activity (Leader et al., 2008; Jain, 2020).

#### 3.3.4 *Aggregation and immunogenicity concerns in formulation*

Protein aggregation is a common challenge in protein formulations, particularly for high-concentration solutions needed for injectable routes. Aggregates can lead to immunogenic responses, where the immune system recognizes the aggregated protein as foreign and mounts an immune response.

- **Aggregation prevention:** Formulation approaches to prevent aggregation include adjusting protein concentration, using additives (e.g., stabilizers or surfactants), and controlling environmental factors during storage and delivery. The use of PEGylation (attachment of polyethylene glycol chains) can also reduce aggregation by increasing solubility and reducing protein–protein interactions (Carter, 2011; Chen and Zeng, 2016).
- **Avoiding immunogenicity:** Aggregates can trigger immune responses, making it essential to minimize aggregation during formulation. Techniques such as controlled freeze-drying and encapsulation within liposomes or nanoparticles help isolate the protein from aggregation-prone environments (Dimitrov, 2012; Akash et al., 2015).

#### 3.3.5 *Formulation scalability and cost*

Manufacturing protein formulations at scale while maintaining quality and stability is costly and complex. Protein-based therapeutics require high-quality production environments to prevent contamination, degradation, and loss of activity. Scaling up these processes often introduces additional challenges in maintaining consistency, especially in the context of encapsulation, freeze-drying, and sterile filling (Vargason et al., 2021).

- **Production challenges:** Producing proteins in large quantities often necessitates expensive bioreactors, rigorous purification processes, and specialized storage. Techniques such as recombinant DNA technology have streamlined production but still require precise control over factors such as pH and temperature throughout the production pipeline (Park et al., 2022; Akash et al., 2015).
- **Cost of delivery technologies:** Advanced delivery technologies, such as nanoparticles and sustained-release systems, add to the overall production costs, limiting accessibility and application. Optimizing these methods to balance efficacy with affordability is a key area of ongoing research (Leader et al., 2008; Vargason et al., 2021).

## 4. Technological advances in protein drug delivery

### 4.1 PEGylation and Fc fusion techniques

As the field of protein therapeutics advances, several innovative technologies have been developed to overcome the challenges of stability, immunogenicity, and pharmacokinetics. Among the most transformative are PEGylation and Fc fusion, which enhance the delivery and effectiveness of protein drugs. These techniques optimize therapeutic proteins to increase circulation time, reduce immune reactions, and improve targeted efficacy.

### *4.1.1 PEGylation: extending circulation and reducing immunogenicity*

PEGylation, the attachment of polyethylene glycol (PEG) polymers to therapeutic proteins, has revolutionized protein drug delivery by addressing multiple pharmacokinetic and pharmacodynamic challenges:

- **Extended half-life and improved pharmacokinetics:** The addition of PEG increases the molecular size and hydrodynamic volume of proteins, which minimizes renal filtration and extends the protein's half-life in circulation. By increasing molecular weight, PEGylated proteins are less rapidly cleared from the bloodstream, resulting in prolonged therapeutic action and reducing the frequency of dosing. PEGylation has thus improved patient compliance in treatments that would otherwise require frequent administration (Dimitrov, 2012; Akash et al., 2015).
- **Shielding from the immune system:** PEG chains create a protective, hydrophilic layer around proteins, making them less recognizable to immune cells and reducing immunogenicity. This "stealth" effect helps PEGylated proteins evade immune surveillance, preventing the rapid clearance typically mediated by phagocytic cells and allowing the therapeutic protein to act longer and more effectively. This property is particularly valuable for chronic treatment regimens, where repeated exposure to a therapeutic protein can otherwise lead to sensitization and antibody production (Chen and Zeng, 2016).
- **Increased solubility and stability:** Many proteins, especially those with hydrophobic regions, are prone to aggregation and denaturation, which can lead to loss of efficacy and immunogenicity. PEGylation increases the solubility of proteins in aqueous environments by masking hydrophobic surfaces, reducing the likelihood of aggregation. Additionally, the PEG layer can provide stability against proteolytic enzymes, further enhancing the drug's resilience in physiological conditions (Park et al., 2022; Carter, 2011).
- **Site-specific PEGylation for optimized efficacy:** Advances in PEGylation technology have led to site-specific PEGylation methods, where PEG chains are covalently attached to specific amino acid residues or termini of the protein. This targeted approach preserves the protein's active sites, maintaining efficacy while still reaping the benefits of PEGylation. Site-specific PEGylation is achieved through various techniques, such as selective chemical reactions or genetic engineering, ensuring that the functional parts of the protein remain accessible to target binding (Leader et al., 2008; Bruno et al., 2013).
- **Applications in therapeutics:** PEGylation has been successfully applied to multiple therapeutics, including PEGylated interferons used in hepatitis treatments and PEGylated G-CSF (granulocyte colony-stimulating factor) for neutropenia. PEGylated drugs such as Pegfilgrastim (a PEGylated form of G-CSF) and Peginterferon have shown improved patient outcomes, reduced dosing frequency, and lower immunogenicity compared with their non-PEGylated counterparts (Chen and Zeng, 2016; Akash et al., 2015).

### *4.1.2 Protein-based therapies in cancer treatment*

Cancer is one of the primary areas where protein-based therapeutics have made significant strides. Monoclonal antibodies and therapeutic proteins target specific cancer cell antigens with minimal effects on healthy cells, unlike traditional chemotherapy, which affects rapidly dividing cells indiscriminately (Park et al., 2022; Bruno et al., 2013).

- **Monoclonal antibodies (mAbs):** Engineered to recognize cancer-specific antigens, mAbs such as trastuzumab (herceptin) for HER2-positive breast cancer or rituximab for B cell lymphomas bind selectively to cancer cells, marking them for immune destruction. The specificity of mAbs reduces side effects and enhances treatment efficacy (Leader et al., 2008; Akash et al., 2015).
- **Immunooncology agents:** Proteins such as checkpoint inhibitors (e.g., pembrolizumab) block inhibitory signals in cancer cells, reactivating immune responses. These agents have shown promise in treating cancers that evade immune detection, providing a new approach to immunotherapy (Dimitrov, 2012; Chen and Zeng, 2016).

### 4.1.3 *Diabetes management with protein-based therapeutics*

Diabetes, particularly type 1 diabetes, is managed with protein-based drugs such as insulin, which was one of the first therapeutic proteins developed. Innovations in insulin formulations and delivery systems now allow for extended-release versions, reducing the frequency of injections required for blood glucose control.

- **Long-acting insulin analogs:** Insulin analogs, such as insulin glargine, provide a steady release over 24 h, offering more consistent glucose control and fewer injections. This reduces the burden on patients with diabetes and lowers the risk of blood glucose fluctuations (Carter, 2011; Akash et al., 2015).
- **Glucagon-like peptide 1 (GLP-1) agonists:** Drugs such as exenatide and liraglutide mimic the GLP-1 hormone, enhancing insulin secretion and delaying gastric emptying to regulate blood glucose levels. These drugs are especially beneficial in managing type 2 diabetes, improving glycemic control with minimal hypoglycemia risk (Leader et al., 2008; Vargason et al., 2021).

### 4.1.4 *Autoimmune disease treatment with targeted protein therapy*

Autoimmune diseases, where the immune system mistakenly attacks the body's own cells, benefit from protein-based therapies that suppress specific immune responses without compromising overall immunity. These drugs reduce inflammation and immune overactivity, providing relief from conditions such as rheumatoid arthritis and multiple sclerosis.

- **Tumor necrosis factor (TNF) inhibitors:** TNF inhibitors such as infliximab and adalimumab block TNF, a cytokine involved in inflammation, and are widely used in treating rheumatoid arthritis and Crohn's disease. By targeting a specific inflammatory pathway, TNF inhibitors reduce symptoms and slow disease progression (Jain, 2020; Chen and Zeng, 2016).
- **Interleukin (IL) inhibitors:** Therapies targeting specific interleukins (e.g., IL-6 or IL-1) are used in conditions such as juvenile arthritis and lupus. These inhibitors provide targeted suppression of immune activity, lowering the risk of general immunosuppression (Park et al., 2022; Bruno et al., 2013).

#### 4.1.5 *Protein therapy for genetic disorders*

Protein-based drug delivery also addresses the underlying causes of genetic disorders by replacing or supplementing deficient or malfunctioning proteins, as in enzyme replacement therapies (ERTs) for conditions such as Gaucher's disease and Fabry disease.

- **Enzyme replacement therapy (ERT):** ERT supplies patients with missing or defective enzymes, restoring normal metabolic function. For example, ERT for Gaucher's disease (using imiglucerase) helps reduce symptoms such as anemia and organ enlargement by breaking down lipid accumulations in cells (Carter, 2011; Vargason et al., 2021).
- **Hemophilia treatment:** Hemophilia patients lack specific clotting factors, leading to severe bleeding episodes. Recombinant clotting factors, such as factor VIII for hemophilia A, provide effective management, reducing bleeding risk and improving quality of life (Dimitrov, 2012; Akash et al., 2015).

#### 4.1.6 *Neurodegenerative diseases and emerging protein therapeutics*

Protein-based therapeutics are showing promise in neurodegenerative diseases, such as Alzheimer's and Parkinson's, where traditional small-molecule drugs have had limited success. Antibodies targeting amyloid plaques or other pathological proteins are being developed to slow disease progression.

- **Antiamyloid and Antitau therapies:** Monoclonal antibodies targeting amyloid-β (e.g., aducanumab) aim to reduce amyloid plaque buildup in Alzheimer's disease. These therapies represent a potential breakthrough in neurodegeneration, though further research is needed to confirm their efficacy (Leader et al., 2008; Chen and Zeng, 2016).
- **Neurotrophic factors:** Protein-based neurotrophic factors support neuron survival and regeneration, offering potential therapeutic effects in neurodegenerative diseases. Delivery challenges remain, but advancements in delivery methods are making these treatments more viable (Vargason et al., 2021).

#### 4.1.7 *Protein-based nanoparticles for enhanced delivery and tumor targeting*

Protein-based nanoparticles offer unique benefits in targeted cancer therapy due to their biocompatibility, high loading capacity, and versatility in functionalization. These nanoparticles encapsulate therapeutic proteins, shielding them from enzymatic degradation and extending circulation time, which is crucial for effective cancer targeting. Additionally, protein-based nanoparticles can be engineered with ligands that bind specifically to receptors on cancer cells, increasing targeting precision. In recent studies, nanoparticles synthesized at high shear rates have shown enhanced stability and controlled release properties, ideal for delivering proteins such as tumor necrosis factor-alpha (TNF-α), a potent antitumor cytokine. These nanoparticles protect TNF-α from systemic clearance and release it selectively in the acidic tumor microenvironment, enhancing its antitumor effects while minimizing systemic toxicity. Hierarchically structured protein nanoparticles are particularly promising, as they allow for sequential or multidrug loading, facilitating combination therapies that simultaneously deliver immune activators and cytotoxic agents (Chen and Zeng, 2016; Akash et al., 2015). Furthermore, recent developments in high-shear synthesized protein nanoparticles have shown that these particles can maintain structural integrity and payload stability under physiological conditions, making them suitable for systemic administration and enhancing the delivery of fragile protein therapeutics to tumors (Leader et al., 2008; Vargason et al., 2021).

#### *4.1.8 Protein-based vaccines for infectious diseases*

Protein-based vaccines utilize purified proteins or subunit fragments from pathogens, providing a nonreplicating approach that stimulates the immune system without the risk of infection. These vaccines activate both humoral and cellular immunity, as protein antigens presented on MHC class I and II molecules can effectively recruit T helper cells and cytotoxic T cells.

- **Subunit and recombinant protein vaccines:** Subunit vaccines focus on epitopes or immunodominant antigens, such as surface glycoproteins. For instance, the hepatitis B virus (HBV) vaccine contains the surface antigen HBsAg, inducing a robust humoral response that provides long-lasting immunity (Dimitrov, 2012; Leader et al., 2008). Recombinant technologies enable the expression of these proteins in bacterial or yeast systems, making production scalable and reducing contamination risks. Protein-based vaccines for SARS-CoV-2 similarly use the spike protein (S-protein) to produce neutralizing antibodies, offering targeted immunity against the virus (Bruno et al., 2013).
- **Adjuvant enhancements:** Since protein antigens are typically less immunogenic than live-attenuated or inactivated viruses, they require adjuvants to boost immune responses. Aluminum-based adjuvants create a depot effect, prolonging antigen presentation and enhancing the recruitment of antigen-presenting cells (APCs). More advanced adjuvants, such as MF59 and AS01, induce local cytokine release, enhancing APC activation and cytokine production, which improves T cell priming and B cell activation for robust immunity (Vargason et al., 2021; Akash et al., 2015).

## 5. Future directions and emerging trends

### 5.1 Next-generation protein therapeutic

Advancements in protein-based therapeutics aim to improve specificity, stability, and patient accessibility. Next-generation protein therapeutics are tackling limitations of traditional therapies with innovative approaches in nanostructuring, responsive delivery systems, and individualized medicine. These developments hold promise for more effective, safer, and personalized treatments across various disease areas.

#### *5.1.1 Engineered protein scaffolds and hierarchically structured nanoparticles*

Newer protein scaffolds, such as DARPins (designed ankyrin repeat proteins) and Affibodies, are smaller and more stable alternatives to traditional antibodies. These engineered scaffolds enhance tissue penetration and specificity, which is especially beneficial for solid tumors and dense tissues. Hierarchically structured protein-based nanospheres (HNS) further elevate therapeutic potential, enabling the encapsulation of hydrophobic drugs such as paclitaxel with controlled release properties. Composed of materials such as bovine serum albumin (BSA), these HNS particles offer high drug-loading capacity, enhanced stability, and sustained release, optimizing therapeutic impact at targeted sites (Dimitrov, 2012; Lotfalian et al., 2021).

#### 5.1.1.1 Responsive and Stimuli-Triggered Delivery Systems

Stimuli-responsive protein delivery systems activate in response to specific environmental triggers, such as pH or temperature shifts, for localized release. These systems use pH-sensitive polymers and biocompatible proteins that activate only in desired conditions, such as the acidic tumor microenvironment or inflamed tissues. For example, BSA-based nanoparticles have shown promising results in releasing their drug payloads only in the acidic regions associated with cancer, minimizing systemic exposure and enhancing targeted efficacy (Bruno et al., 2013; Jain, 2020; Lotfalian et al., 2021).

### 5.1.2 *Protein corona and improved nanoparticle stability*

The protein corona technique, where a nanoparticle is coated with a protein layer, such as albumin, enhances stability, reduces immunogenicity, and improves bioavailability. Protein corona formation allows nanoparticles to blend more effectively with biological systems, reducing immune clearance and increasing retention at disease sites. This approach is particularly valuable for improving the circulatory stability of nanoparticle-based drug delivery systems, leading to prolonged therapeutic effects (Lotfalian et al., 2021).

#### 5.1.2.1 Precision drug delivery through protein nanoparticles

Personalized medicine also involves delivering proteins in a way that maximizes their effectiveness while reducing systemic exposure. Protein-based nanoparticles and other delivery systems can be engineered to respond to specific conditions within the body, such as pH or enzymatic activity in tumor tissues. These nanoparticles protect the protein drug from premature degradation and ensure targeted delivery to diseased cells, improving the safety and efficacy of personalized protein therapies. Additionally, nanoparticle carriers can be functionalized with ligands or antibodies specific to the patient's tumor markers, enabling highly precise delivery (Jain, 2020; Lotfalian et al., 2021).

### 5.1.3 *Regulatory and commercial considerations*

As protein-based therapeutics continue to advance, navigating regulatory and commercial landscapes becomes increasingly crucial. The complexity of protein drugs—due to their biological origin, intricate structures, and specific storage requirements—presents unique regulatory and commercialization challenges compared with traditional small-molecule drugs. Ensuring safety, efficacy, and consistent quality while maintaining commercial viability requires careful attention to regulatory compliance, manufacturing processes, and market positioning.

### 5.1.4 *Manufacturing and quality control*

The production of protein-based drugs requires specialized facilities and stringent quality control measures. Manufacturing processes must maintain the structural integrity, purity, and biological activity of proteins, often requiring advanced technologies such as bioreactors, controlled environments, and specialized purification techniques.

- **Batch consistency and quality assurance:** Protein drugs are highly sensitive to variations in production conditions, and even minor changes can impact efficacy and safety. Regulatory bodies mandate strict guidelines for good manufacturing practices (GMP), ensuring consistency and quality across batches. Advanced analytics, such as mass spectrometry and chromatography, are employed to verify the structural fidelity of each batch (Park et al., 2022; Vargason et al., 2021).
- **Cold chain logistics and storage:** Protein therapeutics often require cold chain logistics to preserve their stability during transport and storage. Maintaining the cold chain from manufacturing facilities to the point of care is crucial, as exposure to inappropriate temperatures can lead to denaturation and loss of function. These logistical requirements add to the cost and complexity of commercialization, particularly for global distribution (Dimitrov, 2012; Akash et al., 2015).

### 5.1.5 Market access and pricing

The high cost of developing and manufacturing protein drugs influences market access and pricing strategies. Compared with small-molecule drugs, protein therapeutics require substantial investment in R&D, production infrastructure, and regulatory compliance, leading to higher market prices. As a result, pricing and reimbursement become central considerations in ensuring patient access and commercial success.

- **Pricing and reimbursement:** Protein drugs are often priced at a premium due to their therapeutic benefits and production costs. Securing reimbursement from healthcare systems and insurance providers is essential for broad market access. Health technology assessments (HTAs) conducted by payers evaluate the cost-effectiveness of protein therapies, influencing reimbursement decisions and pricing strategies (Bruno et al., 2013; Jain, 2020).
- **Intellectual property and exclusivity:** Patent protections and exclusivity rights are critical for recouping the high costs associated with developing protein-based drugs. Patents provide innovators with a limited period of market exclusivity, allowing them to recover R&D investments. However, once patents expire, biosimilar manufacturers can enter the market, increasing competition and reducing prices. Regulatory agencies provide exclusivity periods for biologics, creating a balance between innovation incentives and patient access to affordable therapies (Leader et al., 2008; Chen and Zeng, 2016).

### 5.1.6 Commercialization strategies for protein-based therapeutics

Successfully commercializing protein drugs requires strategic planning to address the unique demands of the biologics market. Companies must consider factors such as market differentiation, patient education, and stakeholder engagement to achieve a competitive edge.

- **Stakeholder engagement and education:** Educating healthcare providers, patients, and payers on the benefits, safety, and administration of protein therapeutics is crucial. Given the novelty and complexity of many protein drugs, stakeholders may require detailed information about dosing, side effects, and long-term benefits. Effective educational programs can foster acceptance and adoption, especially for therapies with complex administration methods (Park et al., 2022; Carter, 2011).

- **Collaborations and partnerships:** Given the high development costs, partnerships between biotechnology companies, academic institutions, and pharmaceutical firms are increasingly common. Collaborations can accelerate development, share resources, and expand market reach. These alliances are particularly valuable for smaller biotech firms, enabling them to leverage the commercialization experience and global reach of established pharmaceutical companies (Vargason et al., 2021; Akash et al., 2015).

### *5.1.7 Future directions in regulatory and commercial strategies*

As the protein therapeutics landscape continues to evolve, regulatory frameworks and commercial strategies are adapting to accommodate new innovations in gene-editing proteins, biosimilars, and personalized medicine.

- **Adaptive regulatory pathways:** Regulatory agencies are exploring adaptive pathways that allow for accelerated approval of breakthrough protein therapies, particularly those targeting rare or life-threatening conditions. Adaptive frameworks provide flexible, evidence-based regulatory routes, balancing safety with rapid access for patients in need (Dimitrov, 2012; Leader et al., 2008).
- **Value-based pricing models:** The rise of personalized and targeted therapies has led to an emphasis on value-based pricing, where the cost of treatment aligns with patient outcomes. This approach is increasingly relevant for protein drugs that offer significant benefits but come with high price tags. By focusing on outcomes, value-based models help ensure sustainable pricing while maximizing patient access (Vargason et al., 2021; Akash et al., 2015).

These regulatory and commercial considerations are crucial in ensuring the success and accessibility of protein-based therapeutics. Adapting to regulatory requirements, maintaining stringent quality control, and developing sustainable pricing models will continue to be essential as the field advances.

## References

Akash, M.S.H., Rehman, K., Tariq, M., Chen, S., 2015. Development of therapeutic proteins: Advances and challenges. Turk. J. Biol. 39 (3), 343–358. https://doi.org/10.3906/biy-1411-8.

Behring, Von, 1989. Serum therapy in the science and art of healing. Scand. J. Immunol. 30 (1).

Bruno, B.J., Miller, G.D., Lim, C.S., 2013. Basics and recent advances in peptide and protein drug delivery. Ther. Deliv. 4 (11), 1443–1467. https://doi.org/10.4155/tde.13.104.

Carter, P.J., 2011. Introduction to current and future protein therapeutics: A protein engineering perspective. Cell Res. 317 (9), 1261–1269. https://doi.org/10.1016/j.yexcr.2011.02.013.

Chen, Z., Zeng, A.P., 2016. Protein Engineering approaches to chemical biotechnology. In: Current Opinion in Biotechnology. Elsevier Ltd, China, pp. 198–205. https://doi.org/10.1016/j.copbio.2016.07.007. http://www.elsevier.com/locate/copbio.

Chen, X., Zaro, J.L., Shen, W.C., 2013. Fusion protein linkers: Property, design and functionality. Adv. Drug Deliv. Rev. 65 (10), 1357–1369. https://doi.org/10.1016/j.addr.2012.09.039.

de Almeida Paiva, V., Gomes, I.de S., Monteiro, C.R., Ventura Mendonça, M., Martins, P.M., Santana, C.A., Gonçalves-Almeida, V., Izidoro, S.C., Melo-Minardi, R.C.de, Silveira, S.de A., 2022. Protein structural bioinformatics: An overview. Comput. Biol. Med. 147, 105695. https://doi.org/10.1016/j.compbiomed.2022.105695.

Delfi, M., Sartorius, R., Ashrafizadeh, M., Sharifi, E., Zhang, Y., De Berardinis, P., Ali, Z., Varma, R.S., Tay, F.R., Smith, B.R., Makvandi, P., 2021. Self-assembled peptide and protein nanostructures for anti-cancer therapy:

Targeted delivery, stimuli-responsive devices and immunotherapy. Nano Today 38, 101119. https://doi.org/10.1016/j.nantod.2021.101119.

Dimitrov, D.S., 2012. Therapeutic proteins. Methods Mol. Biol. 899 (10643745), 1–26. https://doi.org/10.1007/978-1-61779-921-1_1.

Duivelshof, B.L., Murisier, A., Camperi, J., Fekete, S., Beck, A., Guillarme, D., D'Atri, V., 2021. Therapeutic Fc-fusion proteins: Current analytical strategies. J. Sep. Sci. 44 (1), 35–62. https://doi.org/10.1002/jssc.202000765. http://onlinelibrary.wiley.com/journal/10.1002/(ISSN)1615-9314.

Hassanzadeh, S., Ali, N., Mirzayi, B., Fatemeh Kaboli, S., 2021. Protein-based nanoparticles synthesized at a high shear rate and optimized for drug delivery applications. J. Mol. Liq. 335, 116133. https://doi.org/10.1016/j.molliq.2021.116133.

Ismael, G.F.V., Rosa, D.D., Mano, M.S., Awada, A., 2008. Novel cytotoxic drugs: Old challenges, new solutions. Cancer Treat. Rev. 34 (1), 81–91. https://doi.org/10.1016/j.ctrv.2007.08.001.

Jain, K.K., 2020. An overview of drug delivery systems. In: Methods in Molecular Biology. Humana Press Inc., Switzerland, pp. 1–54. https://doi.org/10.1007/978-1-4939-9798-5_1. http://www.springer.com/series/7651.

Johnson, I.S., 1983. Human insulin from recombinant DNA technology. Science. 00368075 219 (4585), 632–637. https://doi.org/10.1126/science.6337396.

Kumar, A., Badola, D., 2021. A review on controlled drug release formulation: Spansules. World J. Pharm. Pharmaceut. Sci.

Leader, B., Baca, Q.J., Golan, D.E., 2008. Protein therapeutics: A summary and pharmacological classification. Nat. Rev. Drug Discov. 7 (1), 21–39. https://doi.org/10.1038/nrd2399.

Lotfalian, S., Ali, N., Ghasemi, S., 2021. Hierarchically structured protein-based hollow-nanospheres for drug delivery. React. Funct. Polym. 160, 104821. https://doi.org/10.1016/j.reactfunctpolym.2021.104821.

Park, H., Otte, A., Park, K., 2022. Evolution of drug delivery systems: From 1950 to 2020 and beyond. J. Contr. Release 342, 53–65. https://doi.org/10.1016/j.jconrel.2021.12.030.

Polaka, S., Tella, J.D., Tekade, M., Sharma, M.C., Tekade, R.K., 2022. Impact of ageing on the pharmacokinetics and pharmacodynamics of the drugs pharmacokinetics and toxicokinetic considerations - Vol II. Elsevier, India. https://doi.org/10.1016/B978-0-323-98367-9.00008-1, 241–261. https://www.sciencedirect.com/book/9780323983679.

Roefs, M.T., Sluijter, J.P.G., Vader, P., 2020. Extracellular vesicle-associated proteins in tissue repair. Trends Cell Biol. 30 (12), 990–1013. https://doi.org/10.1016/j.tcb.2020.09.009.

Shiuan, D., Tai, D.-F., Huang, K.-J., Yu, Z., Ni, F., Li, J., 2020. Target-based discovery of therapeutic agents from food ingredients. Trends Food Sci. Technol. 105, 378–384. https://doi.org/10.1016/j.tifs.2020.09.013, 09242244.

Vargason, A.M., Anselmo, A.C., Mitragotri, S., 2021. The evolution of commercial drug delivery technologies. Nat. Biomed. Eng. 5 (9), 951–967. https://doi.org/10.1038/s41551-021-00698-w.

Veronese, F.M., Pasut, G., 2005. PEGylation, successful approach to drug delivery. Drug Discov. Today 10 (21), 1451–1458. https://doi.org/10.1016/S1359-6446(05)03575-0.

Yuan, L., Chen, Q., Riviere, J.E., Lin, Z., 2023. Pharmacokinetics and tumor delivery of nanoparticles. J. Drug Deliv. Sci. Technol. 83 (17732247), 104404. https://doi.org/10.1016/j.jddst.2023.104404.

CHAPTER

# 3

# History, introduction, properties, and applications of protein-based drug delivery

*Uyen N.P. Nguyen and Tien T. Dang*

**Institute of Advanced Technology, Vietnam Academy of Science and Technology, Ho Chi Minh City, Vietnam**

## 1. Introduction

Efficient medication delivery is complicated by the necessity for therapeutic agents to endure various transport hurdles and binding sites throughout the body. Biomolecular medications, including proteins and oligonucleotides, traditionally encounter constraints in therapeutic efficacy, chiefly due to their brief half-lives caused by proteolysis and renal clearance (Bae et al., 2015; Peng et al., 2016). In circulation, drugs can be rapidly filtered by the kidneys or cleared by the reticuloendothelial system (RES) before reaching their target site. For injectable administration, the vasculature offers a direct path to diseased areas, but also exposes them to potential detours and elimination. High doses and frequent administrations are often required to circulate drugs through the vasculature and achieve diffusion into the tissue interstitium (Hubbell and Chilkoti, 2012). Oral administration is the most convenient, safe, and commonly accepted method. However, bioactive compounds must be insoluble in the stomach to prevent significant losses from stomach acid, pepsin, and pancreatic enzymes in the small intestine (Garrait et al., 2014). These traditional methods are inadequate for chronic conditions that demand long-term, controlled drug delivery systems (DDS) that are nontoxic and provide precise dosing over time.

Innovations in medicine and evolving treatment strategies highlight the need for more advanced drug delivery methods. Three primary strategies have been widely developed to modify the pharmacokinetic (PK) and pharmacodynamic (PD) properties of a drug: (i) using a prodrug where a small moiety is covalently attached to mask bioactivity, only activating at the disease site in response to specific stimuli; (ii) encapsulating the drug in a delivery vehicle that modulates PK and PD; and (iii) employing implantable drug-eluting

*Protein-Based Nanoparticles in Drug Delivery*
**https://doi.org/10.1016/B978-0-443-33639-3.00017-9**

depots or devices (Li et al., 2019). Nanotechnology has gained increasing popularity in recent years because it not only involves miniaturizing materials but also creating nanomaterials (NMs) with unique physicochemical properties distinct from their bulk counterparts. In nanocarrier-based delivery, the drug is encapsulated within a nanocarrier, allowing it to interact with the carrier material. Upon ingestion, the drug is gradually released from the nanocarrier in a controlled manner, achieving a sustained release over time. This method initially allows for a rapid release to achieve a minimum therapeutic concentration, followed by a continuous release that maintains the required therapeutic level for effective treatment (Aliabadi et al., 2018).

Two major factors underpin the unique behavior of NMs compared to larger-scale forms: surface and quantum effects (Roduner, 2006). NMs exhibit distinct surface effects compared to micromaterials or bulk materials due to three primary characteristics: (a) dispersed NMs possess significantly larger surface areas and higher particles per unit mass, (b) a greater proportion of atoms are located on the surface, and (c) surface atoms in NMs have fewer direct neighbors. These differences lead to notable variations in chemical and physical properties between NMs and their larger counterparts (Roduner, 2006). Increased surface area and higher surface-to-volume ratios generally enhance reactivity by expanding the reaction surface (Buzea et al., 2007). The dispersity of NMs is a critical factor affecting surface properties, as strong particle interactions may lead to agglomeration and aggregation, declining surface area, and disrupting nanoscale characteristics (Ashraf et al., 2018). Adjustments can be made to the hydrophilicity or hydrophobicity of the NM or by optimizing the pH and ionic strength of the suspension medium (Fubini et al., 2010). By formulating drugs as nanoparticles or NM-based solutions, or "nanomedicines," it is now possible to enhance activity and reduce toxicity, effectively increasing the therapeutic index (Aliabadi et al., 2018; Chen and Mitra, 2019).

Researchers have investigated numerous synthetic and natural carrier molecules for DDS based on proteins and peptides (Tong et al., 2020). Protein nanoparticle delivery involves the utilization of various protein-based materials that bind to drugs, providing protection from degradation until they reach their target receptors, while also controlling the timing of their release. Proteins play a crucial role in nearly all biological processes, ranging from the transport of small molecules to cellular signaling and the structural organization within cells (Dietzen, 2018). Their well-defined architecture, remarkable biocompatibility, and ability to interact specifically with target receptors make them highly adaptable materials for biomedical purposes. Concurrently, natural protein assemblies, including virus-like particles (VLPs), have been the subject of research for several decades (Friedmann, 1992). Protein-based nanoparticles can be derived from both natural materials, such as keratin, collagen, elastin, and silk (Carvalho et al., 2018), and engineered or synthetic compounds (Fig. 3.1) (Jiang et al., 2012).

The first generation of protein-based drug delivery emerged in the early 1970s, using albumin-based microparticles as diagnostic tools in nuclear medicine for circulation studies (Scheffel et al., 1972). By the late 2000s, advancements in mild formulation techniques enabled the field to expand beyond albumin, incorporating more functional proteins and enzymes with diverse applications (Jiang et al., 2014; Xia et al., 2013; Lee et al., 2020; Kaltbeitzel and Wich, 2023). The artificial assembly of proteins into nanometer-sized particles has been extensively explored in the literature to address several limitations of individual proteins,

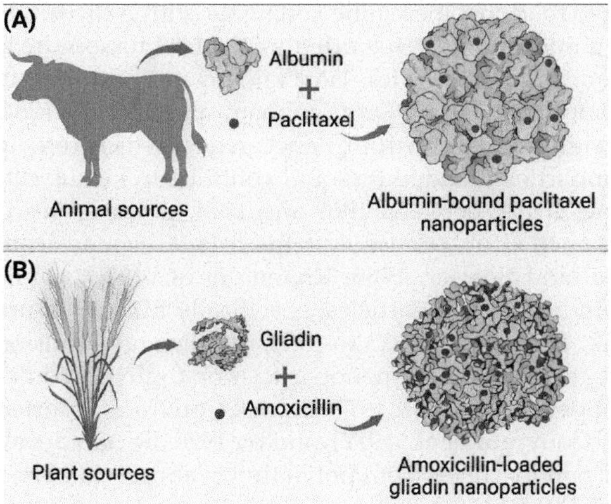


FIGURE 3.1 (A) Albumin, sourced from either bovine or human origins, has been used as a delivery platform for paclitaxel by incorporating the drug into albumin nanoparticles. (B) Similarly, gliadin, a wheat protein, has been used to form amoxicillin-loaded gliadin nanoparticles by combining amoxicillin with gliadin.

such as extending circulation time, enhancing cellular uptake, and facilitating spatial proximity for cascade reactions (Herrera Estrada and Champion, 2015; Tarhini et al., 2017; Hong et al., 2020). In protein-based nanoparticle design, targeting mechanisms often leverage the affinity of cells for the protein components. Furthermore, peptide bonds facilitate the linkage of small molecules and macromolecules to nanoparticles, enhancing the biocompatibility of nonbiocompatible moieties (Varanko et al., 2020). This biocompatibility results from properties like water dispersibility, pH stability, and low cytotoxicity, making proteins and peptides key elements in nanoparticle design due to their physiological relevance and clinical potential compared to synthetic polymers (Garrait et al., 2014). Depending on the intended diagnostic or therapeutic utilization, nanoparticles can be delivered through various routes, including transdermally (Sharma, 2019), subcutaneously (Tomasini et al., 2024), nasally (Chatzitaki et al., 2020), intramuscularly (Hassett et al., 2019), or via intravenous injection (Trac and Chung, 2021). Recently, significant efforts have been directed toward the development of dynamic protein nanoparticles that respond to their environment, for instance, disassembling into native protein building blocks upon cellular uptake, which shows promising potential for applications in protein therapy (Liu et al., 2019; Ma et al., 2019; Steiert et al., 2020).

# 2. The history of the discovery and development of protein-based drug delivery

## 2.1 In the early 1970s

In 1953, Hermann Staudinger was awarded the Nobel Prize in Chemistry for his work on "Makromoleküle" (macromolecules), which laid the foundation for the field of polymer chemistry (Fig. 3.2). This milestone was followed in 1955 by Jatzkewitz, who prepared the first polymer–drug conjugate, a polyvinylpyrrolidone–mescaline conjugate with a dipeptide (glycyrrhizin, GL) spacer between the drug and polymer, regarded as the first nanoparticle therapeutic (Jatzkewitz, 1955). The discovery of lipid vesicles, later known as liposomes, in the 1960s marked the advent of nanotechnology-based DDS (Bangham and Horne, 1964; Bangham et al., 1965). These innovations signified the birth of nanocarriers, which remain the most prominent class of marketed nanoparticle therapeutics and continue to be subjects of extensive research (Petros and Desimone, 2010). Between 1969 and 1971, polymer beads were studied for the development of sustained drug release systems using suspension or "bead" polymerization techniques (Khanna and Speiser, 1969; Khanna et al., 1970), while 1972 saw the preparation of the first protein-based nanoparticles, specifically human serum albumin (HSA) microspheres (Scheffel et al., 1972). From 1973 to 1976, micelle and emulsion polymerization techniques were used to create drug-loaded nanoparticles and microcapsules (Birrenbach and Speiser, 1976; Merkle and Speiser, 1973). In 1977, Patrick Couvreur reported the lysosomotropic effects of nanoparticles (Couvreur et al., 1977), and by 1979, he had developed the first rapidly biodegradable acrylic nanoparticles from poly(ethyl cyanoacrylate) and poly(methyl cyanoacrylate) (Couvreur et al., 1979, 1982). In conclusion, by the late 1970s, a fundamental understanding of controlled drug delivery had emerged, including various drug release mechanisms such as dissolution, diffusion, osmosis, and ion exchange. Technologies developed during this first generation of controlled drug delivery facilitated the creation of numerous oral delivery systems with twice- and once-daily dosing.

## 2.2 From the 1980s to the present

The second generation of controlled drug delivery technologies emerged in the 1980s. During the second generation, smart polymers and hydrogels were developed, enabling DDS to respond to environmental triggers such as pH, temperature, or glucose levels (Hussein et al., 2022; Samal et al., 2014; Yamato et al., 2003). Biodegradable microparticles, solid implants, and in situ gel-forming implants were also introduced for delivering peptides and proteins over extended periods. Despite these advancements, fewer than 10 clinical products for peptide and protein delivery were developed, highlighting the challenges of product development in this area. The final decade of the second generation saw the growing focus on nanotechnology-based DDS, with the *Journal of Controlled Release* playing a central role in shaping these advancements (Park, 2014) (Fig. 3.2).

In 1986, Robert Gurny published the first research article on the use of nanoparticulate systems for ocular drug delivery (Gurny et al., 1985). By 2000, when the nanotechnology revolution gained momentum, the term "nanoparticle" was already well established, particularly in the context of nanoparticle-based DDS. Although the fundamental properties of nanoparticles in drug delivery have remained largely unchanged, nanoparticles have been promoted for over a decade as a transformative tool for drug delivery. Numerous studies have shown that nanoparticle systems accumulate more at tumor sites than nonparticulate formulations, primarily due to the enhanced permeation and retention (EPR) effect (Maeda et al., 1985; Matsumura and Maeda, 1986). However, it must be understood that this increase in nanoparticle accumulation at tumor sites is marginal, and the total drug delivered to the tumor represents only a small fraction of the administered dose (Park, 2013; Kwon et al.,

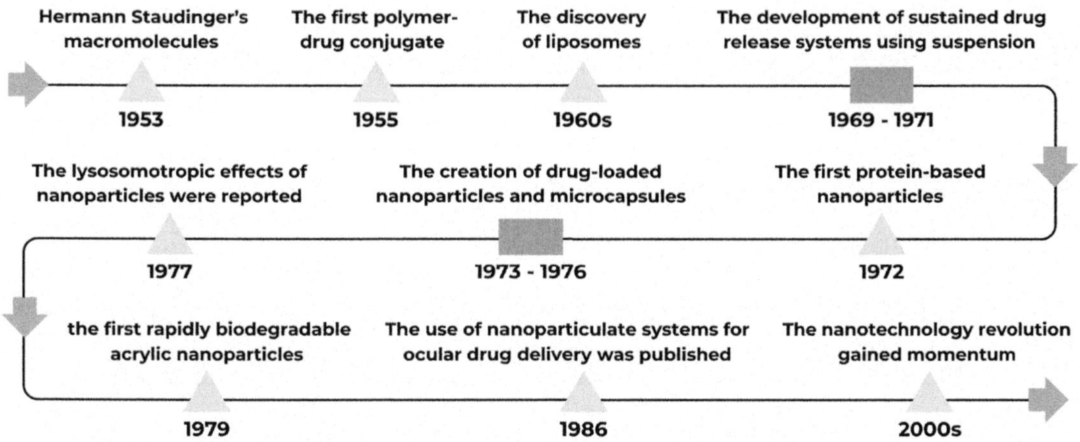


FIGURE 3.2 The progression of protein nanoparticle development over time.

2012; Stirland et al., 2013; Hollis et al., 2013). While more efficient targeted DDS are needed, research in drug delivery must also address other important areas.

## 3. Types of materials of protein nanoparticles

### 3.1 Animal protein

#### *3.1.1 Collagen*

Collagen, the most abundant structural protein in the vertebrate body, accounts for 20%–30% of total body protein (Fig. 3.3). Its fundamental structure consists of tropocollagen, a triple-helix molecule formed by three intertwined polypeptide chains, stabilized by various noncovalent bonds. Type I collagen, in particular, is a key component of the extracellular matrices found in skin, arteries, bones, and corneas (Dai et al., 2015; Dehouck et al., 1994; Gao, 2016; Dal Magro et al., 2018). While collagen performs a variety of physiological functions and is highly durable in vivo, it is prone to degradation in vitro, largely due to the dissociation of natural crosslinks during extraction and purification (Rafat et al., 2008). Its high biocompatibility and versatility make it an ideal material for drug delivery applications, as it can be processed into hydrogels, microparticles, and films (Friess, 1998). However, one challenge in handling collagen is its heat sensitivity. High temperatures are often required to render collagen water-soluble, but such heat is unsuitable for preserving drugs and other substances incorporated into microparticles and films. Thus, alternative solvents such as organic acids are used (Friess, 1998). To enhance its resistance to enzymatic and hydrothermal degradation, collagen can be chemically crosslinked, improving its mechanical stability. Chemical crosslinking methods fall into two main categories: bifunctional and amide type (Rafat et al., 2008; Ghezzi et al., 2017). A significant drawback of many crosslinking agents is the potential for cytotoxicity or chromogenic effects from residual molecules. Although amide-type crosslinkers do not pose cytotoxic risks, most crosslinking agents

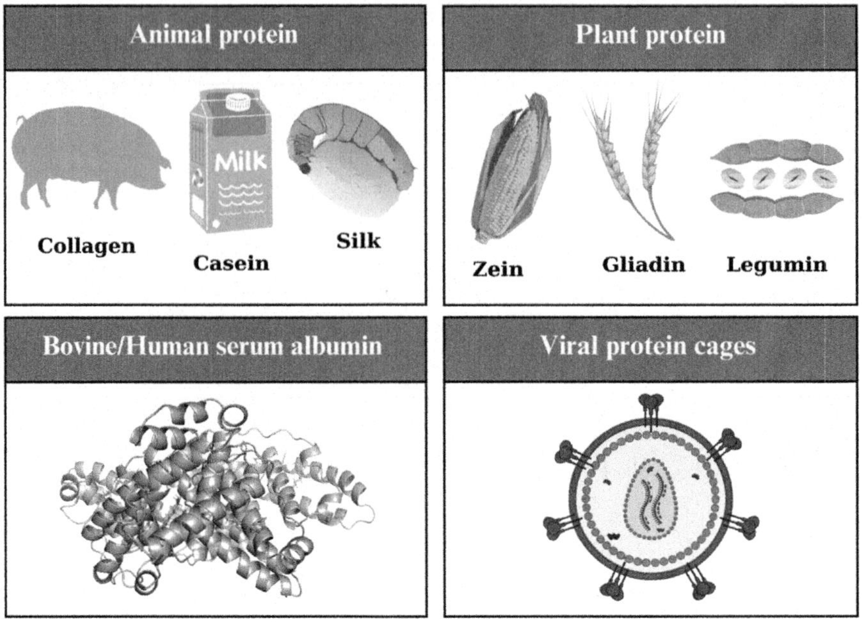


FIGURE 3.3 Types of materials of protein nanoparticles.

may be released into the environment during degradation (Osidak, 2022). By carefully selecting safe crosslinking methods, it is possible to improve collagen's drug stability and retention time, thereby enhancing its potential for drug delivery applications.

### *3.1.2 Casein*

Casein is the primary protein found in milk (Amenabar et al., 2013; Assfalg et al., 2016). Due to the presence of both hydrophilic and hydrophobic residues, caseins are amphiphilic proteins that can form block copolymers, with a strong propensity for self-assembling into micelles ranging in size from 50 to 500 nm, with an average hydrodynamic radius of 250 nm (Zong et al., 2018; Molino and Wang, 2014). The diverse structural and physicochemical properties of caseins make them suitable candidates for use as DDS. These properties include the ability to bind to various ions and molecules, excellent self-assembly and surface activity, emulsification capability, water-binding and gel-forming capacity, as well as remarkable stability (Lundqvist et al., 2004; Stayton et al., 2003; Carril et al., 2017). Casein nanomicelles have been employed as carriers for several anticancer drugs, such as curcumin, mitoxantrone, vinblastine, docetaxel, and paclitaxel. Additionally, caseins exhibit a protective effect, which is crucial for safeguarding sensitive drug compounds (Carrillo-Carrion et al., 2017; Guan et al., 2015). However, caseins do present some limitations, such as concerns regarding immunosuppression and allergic reactions. While casein in milk is broken down into amino acids during digestion and absorbed by the body, in cases where casein proteins are administered intravenously, potential immune responses must be considered (Dobrovolskaia et al., 2009; Schaefer et al., 2012; Chong et al., 2015).

### 3.1.3 *Silk fibroin*

Silk is a natural protein polymer produced by certain insect larvae, such as silkworms and spiders. Its primary components include fibroin, a linear protein that forms the core structure, and sericin, an adhesive protein that encapsulates the fibroin core (Ho et al., 2015). Fibroin induces a less inflammatory response at the degradation site relative to widely utilized biocompatible synthetic polymers such as polylactic acid. Fibroin nanoparticles can safeguard proteins and peptides, including conjugated insulin and vascular endothelial growth factor, in blood serum and enzyme-rich solutions such as trypsin, thereby extending the release of these substances (Pace et al., 1995; Kambhampati et al., 2019; Mahmoudi et al., 2011). Silk's controlled release properties are governed by two mechanisms: diffusion of the payload and the solubilization or degradation of the silk material (Din Wani and Veerabhadrappa, 2018). Genetically engineered silk proteins result in highly stable composite materials with enhanced elasticity and strength, similar to native dragline spider silk fibers. Various types of silks, including those from *Bombyx mori*, Tussah, and Eri, have been used in drug delivery applications (Dal Magro et al., 2018).

### 3.1.4 *Bovine serum albumin*

As the most prevalent plasma protein, albumin possesses unique qualities, including stability across a wide pH range (4–9), the maintenance of plasma colloidal osmotic pressure, nutrient transport within cells, pH stabilization, and solubilization of hydrophobic fatty acids (Michnik et al., 2005). Its properties support improved aqueous solubility for hydrophobic drugs when bound to albumin, thereby enhancing the PK property of such drugs within the physiological environment (Patel and Datta, 2007). Bovine serum albumin (BSA), with a molecular weight of 69,323 Da and an isoelectric point (pI) of 4.7 at 25 °C in water, is a versatile natural protein capable of forming complexes of various shapes (Tantra et al., 2010; Hu et al., 2006). BSA nanoparticles can be synthesized through desolvation followed by glutaraldehyde fixation or heat denaturation, yielding spherical nanoparticles with an average diameter of 492 nm. Heat-denatured nanoparticles exhibit favorable cytocompatibility and have been investigated for their drug-loading capacity and controlled release behaviors as drug carriers (Elsadek and Kratz, 2012; Rodrigues et al., 2013; Elzoghby et al., 2012). BSA nanoparticles are recognized for their clinical potential due to their low toxicity, low immunogenicity, ease of purification, natural abundance, and propensity for tumor accumulation. The aforementioned properties, along with notable biocompatibility and the convenience of injection distribution, render BSA a formidable choice for nanoparticle production (Cui et al., 2016).

## 3.2 Plant proteins

### 3.2.1 *Zein*

Zein, a primary storage protein rich in prolamine, is found in the endosperm of corn kernels (Sousa, 2012; Paliwal and Palakurthi, 2014). Zein contains both hydrophobic and hydrophilic domains but is generally regarded as a hydrophobic protein due to its insolubility in water and solubility in solvents such as ethanol, acetone, and acetylacetone. The nonpolar helical interior of zein, enriched with glutamine, allows it to self-assemble into particles and layers (Sousa, 2012). Consequently, zein demonstrates chemical and thermoplastic properties that are stable under heat and varying pH levels (Nonthanum et al., 2012). Their additional qualities, including biodegradability, mechanical strength, and water resistance, make them highly desirable for DDS, as well as for use in coatings for food and pharmaceuticals (Sousa, 2012). Moreover, zein can form aggregates and entrap substances like drugs or amino acids, making it an effective matrix for sustained drug release (Berardi et al., 2018).

### 3.2.2 *Gliadin*

In bread wheat, gliadin and glutenin are the two major storage proteins, comprising 70% of gluten (Biesiekierski, 2017). The alcohol-insoluble fraction was later identified as glutenin (Urade et al., 2018). Due to the presence of glutamine (Cedervall et al., 2007) and hydrophobic amino acids (Xu et al., 2021; Zou et al., 2019), gliadin forms numerous hydrogen bonds with the mucosal layer, while interacting with cell membranes through hydrophobic interactions. These characteristics grant gliadin excellent biocompatibility, biodegradability, nontoxicity, and stability, making it well-suited for drug delivery applications. The mucoadhesive properties of gliadin make it particularly advantageous for oral DDS, allowing it to adhere to mucosal surfaces (Wu et al., 2018).

As such, gliadin is an appropriate material for the preparation of nanoparticles for delivering hydrophobic and amphiphilic drugs (Gil et al., 2021; Wang et al., 2016). Its interaction with biological membranes, due to its abundance of neutral and hydrophobic amino acids, further enhances its potential as an oral delivery vehicle for lipophilic drugs (Mehanna and Mneimneh, 2020). Gliadin nanoparticles provide an efficient drug delivery strategy for targeting the upper gastrointestinal tract, with one of their potential applications being the treatment of *Helicobacter pylori*, as they exhibit strong affinity for this region (Wang et al., 2019; Mukherjee et al., 2014). In vivo studies have demonstrated that amoxicillin-loaded gliadin nanoparticles were more effective at eradicating *Helicobacter pylori* compared to free amoxicillin (Umamaheshwari et al., 2004). Gliadin nanoparticles have also shown potential for delivering anticancer drugs, such as inducing the death of breast cancer cells (Gulfam et al., 2012). Gliadin nanoparticles loaded with cyclophosphamide exhibited prolonged drug release over 48 h, compared to gliadin–gelatin-loaded nanoparticles.

### 3.2.3 *Legumin*

Legumin is a major storage protein found in soybean seeds, belonging to the 11S globulin protein family (Cho and Jones, 2019). Legumin-derived nanoparticles possess bioadhesive characteristics and an extensive surface area, facilitating significant contact with biological surfaces (Irache et al., 1995). During the coacervation process, the solubility of legumin decreases, inducing phase separation to form nanoparticles. Mirshahi et al. (2002) have attempted to develop micro- and nanoparticle-based legumin colloidal delivery systems (Mirshahi et al., 2002). Chemical crosslinking via pH coacervation and glutaraldehyde has been explored to improve yield, particle size, and surface charge, while avoiding the use of organic solvents. While these nanoparticles displayed good stability in Phosphate-Buffered Saline (PBS) (pH 7.4), the yield was as low as 27% of the original material. However, the particles demonstrated good stability when stored under neutral pH conditions. Legumin-based nanoparticles are characterized by small size, excellent stability, and low antigenicity;

however, further research is required to optimize their production yield and to explore their potential in biomedical applications.

## 3.3 Human serum albumin

HSA is a globular protein predominantly found in the circulatory system, consisting of approximately 585 amino acids (Langer et al., 2003; Jahanban-Esfahlan et al., 2016). HSA is commonly employed for delivering various substances to specific tissues within the body. It demonstrates remarkable stability across a broad pH range (pH 4–9), at elevated temperatures (60 °C for up to 10 h), and in the presence of organic solvents (Elsadek and Kratz, 2012; Elzoghby et al., 2012; Kratz, 2008). Being of biological origin, HSA offers advantages in terms of biodegradability, nontoxicity, nonimmunogenicity, and high solubility (Saleh et al., 2019). Due to these properties, HSA can noncovalently bind to a range of drugs and peptides, offering high stability and multiple high-affinity binding sites for loading therapeutic agents at significant concentrations (Fasano et al., 2005; Sudlow et al., 1975; Bertucci and Domenici, 2002). HSA nanoparticles have been applied extensively in various fields, including the treatment of cardiovascular calcifications in the media of large- and medium-sized arteries (Keuth et al., 2020). The characteristics of HSA nanoparticles, such as size and polydispersity, vary based on production conditions (Jahanban-Esfahlan et al., 2016; Ascoli et al., 2006), and it has been observed that reducing the ethanol addition rate during synthesis results in the formation of smaller nanoparticles (Langer et al., 2003). Following the approval of Abraxane (albumin-paclitaxel nanoparticles), clinical trials have demonstrated its significant efficacy in treating advanced pancreatic cancer (Jameson et al., 2020) and a manageable safety profile with antitumor responses in breast cancer patients (Adams et al., 2019; Gianni et al., 2018). Additionally, Redin et al. developed HSA nanoparticles loaded with bevacizumab, a chemotherapeutic agent used in the treatment of cancers and certain eye diseases (Luis de Redín et al., 2018).

## 3.4 Viral protein cages

Protein cages are structures derived from viruses or VLPs, typically ranging in size from a few nanometers to several tens of nanometers. These virus cages represent the structural shell, or capsid, of a virus, devoid of its nucleic acid content. The size, shape, and stability of these cages depend on the specific type of virus. Protein cages consist of a limited number of subunits that assemble into porous nanospherical structures, featuring three key regions: the inner surface, the outer surface, and the space between the subunits. All three regions can be chemically or genetically modified without altering the overall structure of the cage, enabling their use in medical diagnostics and treatments (Puzyn et al., 2011).

One unique advantage of protein cages compared to other protein structures is their uniform size, which facilitates precise drug loading, an important PK feature in drug formulations. Viral protein cages are highly stable across various chemical environments, allowing for multiple chemical modifications. As a result, they can be engineered to perform simultaneous functions in cancer chemotherapy (Walkey et al., 2014; Eigenheer et al., 2014). Their nanometer scale prevents them from passing through the endothelial layer of normal blood vessels, thereby prolonging their half-life in the bloodstream. However, they are small enough to penetrate the fenestrated vessels of tumor tissue, allowing for effective delivery of chemotherapy drugs directly to tumor cells. Moreover, their small size enables these particles to evade liver macrophages, further enhancing their potential as therapeutic carriers (Tavanti et al., 2019; Zanganeh et al., 2016).

## 4. Design considerations

Systemically delivered nanoparticles face multiple physiological barriers, including navigating the bloodstream, reaching disease sites, and interacting with target cells. In addition, natural processes, including those in the kidneys, liver, spleen, and immune cells, clear foreign substances from the bloodstream, reducing the circulation time of intravenously injected nanoparticles (Sun et al., 2014; Nie, 2010). However, the rapidly growing or dysfunctional endothelium in tumors and atherosclerosis creates large gaps, allowing nanoparticles to pass through and accumulate in affected areas. Additionally, when the nanoparticles are delivered around the tumor region, they are retained locally due to impaired lymphatic drainage. This process is known as the EPR effect, and it allows passive targeting and selective accumulation of nanoparticles (Byrne et al., 2008; Lobatto et al., 2011).

Tumor blood vessels are abnormally structured and highly permeable (50–70 times that of normal vessels (Din et al., 2017)), allowing plasma to leak into the tumor tissue. Due to the absence of lymphatic vessels in tumors (Pereira et al., 2018), interstitial fluid pressure (IFP) accumulates within tumors, creating a high-pressure environment within the tumor that impedes nanoparticle accumulation (Stylianopoulos et al., 2018; Jain et al., 2007; Soltani et al., 2011). This high IFP, along with clearance by the mononuclear phagocyte system (MPS), are key barriers to effective nanoparticle delivery (Jain and Stylianopoulos, 2010). One of the key challenges in developing nanoparticles as protein delivery carriers is to extend their circulation half-life in the bloodstream while retaining their intended functionality. Nanoparticles frequently combine to minimize surface energy, which might induce opsonization in the bloodstream, rendering them more identifiable to defense systems such as the MPS and leading to their clearance from circulation by immune cells, significantly diminishing their efficacy (Gref et al., 1994; Anderson et al., 2004; Yoo et al., 2010). Triggering endogenous defense systems may result in nanoparticle removal within hours or minutes (Lee et al., 2010; Litzinger et al., 1994; Singh et al., 2006). Extending circulation time increases nanoparticle accumulation in tumors, but this is influenced by factors like nanoparticle size and geometry, which affect how they interact with blood vessels (Mascheroni and Schrefler, 2018; Blanco et al., 2015).

### 4.1 Size

Studies showed that nanoparticles with submicron size have more advantages than microparticles for DDS (Singh et al., 2006; Popović et al., 2010; Choi et al., 2010). The optimal nanoparticle size for efficient drug delivery in tumors is typically between 12 and 60 nm, allowing for effective transvascular transport while extravasation and minimizing clearance in normal tissues (Stylianopoulos, 2013). In tumors with large interendothelial junctions, nanoparticles up to 100 nm may be considered to increase the payload (Jain and

Stylianopoulos, 2010; Chauhan et al., 2012; Stylianopoulos and Jain, 2015). Particles smaller than 500 nm tend to move parallel to the vessel wall and are minimally affected by the red blood cells (RBCs), while very small nanoparticles can intersperse within RBC clusters near the centerline (Lee et al., 2013). Larger nanoparticles encounter lateral stresses in the bloodstream, resulting in their proximity to the vessel wall. The lateral migration of nanoparticles toward endothelial walls facilitates interactions and adhesion between the nanoparticles and the vascular surface (Lee et al., 2013). Large nanoparticles exhibit less extravasation into tissues compared to smaller particles; yet, they are not eliminated as swiftly, resulting in prolonged circulation durations (Perrault et al., 2009; Choi et al., 2007).

Renal clearance is very rapid for particles smaller than 6 nm in diameter, while larger nanoparticles are generally cleared by the liver RES (Choi et al., 2007; Dai et al., 2018). Interstitial convection of particles is driven by IFP gradients in the tumor and is impeded by the electrostatic, hydrodynamic, and steric interactions in the interstitial space (Pluen et al., 2001; Stylianopoulos et al., 2010). Particle diffusion is inversely related to size and is also affected by interactions between the nanoparticles and extracellular fibers. Furthermore, because of steric hindrance, larger particles have very limited penetration into tumor tissue (Tang et al., 2015). The optimal size of nanoparticles for tissue penetration varies by system. Nevertheless, given the large amount of heterogeneity that exists within a given tumor, identifying a nanoparticle formulation optimal for all tumor applications has proved difficult (Stylianopoulos, 2013).

Computational modeling has been used to predict how nanoparticle size affects behavior in dynamic flows, such as motion, margination, and interaction with cells. For example, nanoparticles larger than 500 nm are influenced by gravity, while smaller ones are governed by Brownian motion (Gentile et al., 2008). Furthermore, van der Waals forces, buoyancy parameters, electrostatic interactions, and steric interactions can lead to a "critical radius" where the time for margination of particles toward a surface in shear flow will be the longest (Decuzzi et al., 2005). Examining the cellular uptake of particles with different sizes by Caco-2 cells, found that nanoparticles with a diameter of 100 nm had a 2.5- and 6-fold uptake rate, respectively, compared with 1 and 10 μm microparticles (Desai et al., 1997). Mathematical modeling and experimental results using gold and silver nanoparticles in the size range of 2–100 nm demonstrate that particles of 40–50 nm more efficiently bind and induce receptor-mediated endocytic processes (Jiang et al., 2008). Smaller particles (12–50 nm) being most appropriate for transvascular and extravascular transport, while nanoparticles larger than 50 nm, however, often fail to reach the cell nucleus (Rudolph et al., 2003). Thus, nanoparticles in the 12–50 nm range are generally most effective for crossing vessel walls and penetrating tumor tissue.

## 4.2 Shapes

The nanoparticle shape significantly influences their interactions with biological tissues, including circulation, tissue penetration, cellular uptake, and clearance (Peer et al., 2007; Geng et al., 2007). Nonspherical nanoparticles, such as rod-shaped particles, have been found to penetrate diseased tissues more efficiently than spherical ones, as their shape aids in faster movement through tissue and better accumulation at the site (Park et al., 2008). Anisotropic nanoparticles, such as rods and discs, exhibit better margination and wall adhesion in dynamic flow compared to spherical nanoparticles due to hydrodynamic and Brownian forces (Shah et al., 2011; Tao et al., 2011). In addition, rod-like nanoparticles stay in the bloodstream up to 10 times longer than spherical particles (Geng et al., 2007), whereas ellipsoid-shaped nanoparticles drift away from the vessel core more easily (Li et al., 2015). Elongated nanoparticles are more effective than spherical ones for transvascular flux due to better margination and reduced resistance to movement through endothelial junctions (Decuzzi et al., 2005; Zhou et al., 2013). They also distribute more efficiently in the tumor interstitial space (Chauhan et al., 2011) with deeper penetration and accumulation due to lower steric and hydrodynamic interactions with collagen fibers (Pluen et al., 1999). However, spherical gold nanoparticles have higher cellular uptake than rod-shaped and hollow particles, as demonstrated by studies comparing different nanoparticle forms (Bartczak et al., 2012; Chithrani et al., 2006). For nanoparticles smaller than 100 nm, spherical particles are internalized more effectively than rod-shaped ones (Huang et al., 2010). However, as particle size increases, those with higher aspect ratios (like rods) show better internalization, especially when aligned perpendicularly to the cell membrane (Stylianopoulos and Jain, 2015). Li et al. employed a dissipative particle dynamics (DPD) model to assess various geometries and discovered that spherical nanoparticles exhibited the greatest cellular uptake, followed by cubic and rod-shaped particles, but disk-like particles predominantly adhered to the cell surface (Li et al., 2015).

## 4.3 Charge

Nanoparticle surface charge plays a crucial role in drug delivery, influencing transport to and within tumors, solubility, stability, cellular uptake, and cytotoxicity (Wilhelm, 2016). Charged nanoparticles may activate plasma complement proteins (factor H and C3b), which can further accelerate their clearance from the bloodstream (Yu et al., 2012a; Salvador-Morales et al., 2009). Surface charge density can also affect nanoparticle clearance (Choi et al., 2007; Zamboni et al., 2012). The positive charge of cationic particles attracts negatively charged proteins in the bloodstream, causing them to adsorb to the particle surface. This facilitates their recognition by the immune system and their subsequent removal (Zein et al., 2020). Additionally, because endothelial basal lamina has a negative charge, positively charged nanoparticles are easily absorbed, limiting their circulation (Chauhan et al., 2012; Stylianopoulos et al., 2013). Conversely, negatively charged nanoparticles are repelled by certain regions like the endothelial basal lamina (Dellian et al., 2000; Campbell et al., 2002). For these reasons, nanoparticles with neutral charge are better for vascular transport (Peer et al., 2007).

Electrostatic interactions with the negatively charged glycocalyx of vascular endothelial cells can allow cationic nanoparticles to extravasate more readily than their anionic or neutral counterparts (Dellian et al., 2000; Campbell et al., 2002). Because many charged species exist in the tumor environment, including cationic collagen and anionic hyaluronic acid, electrostatic interactions also affect how nanoparticles distribute in the tumor interstitium (Lieleg et al., 2009). The coarse-grained molecular dynamics (CGMD) method showed that cationic nanoparticles exhibit stronger adhesion to cell membranes compared to neutral particles (Li and Gu, 2010). Positively charged nanoparticles also increase the tilt angle of lipid molecules, enlarging the lipid head group area, while negatively charged nanoparticles tend to create more ordered regions in the lipid bilayers. These findings highlight the significant influence of surface charge on nanoparticle adsorption mechanisms (Harush-Frenkel et al., 2008).

## 4.4 Chemistry

An effective method for increasing the delivery of low-solubility drugs to tumors is to encapsulate the drug within a nanocarrier that has a hydrophobic or amphiphilic surface (Li *et al.*, 2015; Senapati et al., 2018). To improve the delivery of nanoparticles to the tumor, nanoparticles can be engineered with surface chemistry that includes hydrophilic surface coatings to prevent the formation of a protein corona and subsequent phagocytosis (Yang and Ma, 2010). Additionally, modifying the surface with polysaccharides can improve cellular uptake (Guardia et al., 2012). These techniques are employed to create "stealth" nanoparticles (Owens and Peppas, 2006), helping them avoid nonspecific adsorption of opsonins. These methods include coating nanoparticles with biocompatible and hydrophilic polymers like polyethylene glycol (PEG), as well as small organic molecules such as zwitterionic molecules, or biomimetic surfaces (e.g., RBC membrane, human CD47) (Yu et al., 2012b; Rodriguez et al., 2013). Coating the surface with PEG leads to increased time of particle circulation (Papahadjopoulos et al., 1991; Klibanov et al., 1990). The functionalization with PEG depends on the length of the polymer chains and their density at the surface (Perrault et al., 2009). Clinical applications have shown that administration of PEGylated particles can induce production of anti-PEG antibodies, further enhancing clearance (Shimizu et al., 2012; Garay et al., 2012).

Other coatings, such as zwitterionic species and carbohydrates, appear to be promising (Garca et al., 2010; García et al., 2014), as are engineered intralipid formulations (Liu et al., 2013) or liposomes, which have been used to deliver lipids (Jang et al., 2016). Micelle nanoparticles and liposome-based carriers have been successful in suspending such drugs in aqueous media (Huh et al., 2005; Liu et al., 2006). Liposomes can overcome the effects of surface charge and block the uptake of gold nanorods by the MPS (Sun et al., 2017). Hydrophilic polysaccharides can be grafted onto hydrophobic polymers or to hydrophobic molecules to improve the performance of surfaces (Sun et al., 2014). In addition, computational modeling showed that increasing the hydrophilic surface enhances penetration (Zhang et al., 2015; Gupta and Rai, 2017). This underscores the need to develop alternative methods for reducing the clearance of nanoparticles in vivo.

Although the EPR effect allows for passive targeting, the abnormal tumor microenvironment limits nanoparticle distribution. To enhance nanoparticle retention at disease sites, targeting ligands such as antibodies, small molecules, and peptides can be attached to the nanoparticle surface, a strategy known as active targeting (Li and Huang, 2008). In the case of neurodegenerative diseases, delivering therapeutics to the central nervous system (CNS) is particularly challenging due to the blood–brain barrier (BBB), which tightly controls the passage of molecules into the brain. Targeting overexpressed receptors such as transferrin and insulin receptors on brain endothelial cells allows for receptor-mediated endocytosis, helping nanoparticles cross the BBB and deliver drugs to the brain (Jain et al., 2007). Once nanoparticles reach their target cells, they are taken up through endocytosis and then release their drug payloads within specific subcellular compartments like the cytosol, mitochondria, or nucleus. To achieve this result, the surface coatings and targeting ligands on nanoparticles must be optimized. Furthermore, nanoparticles can be designed to respond to specific stimuli within the cellular environment, such as changes in pH or redox conditions, to trigger on-demand drug release (Xiao et al., 2015; Kabanov and Vinogradov, 2009; Uhrich et al., 1999).

### 4.5 Elasticity

Nanoparticle rigidity (elasticity) significantly affects pharmacokinetics and pharmacodynamics. The studies showed that less rigid nanoparticles stay longer in circulation and resist phagocytosis better than rigid ones (Anselmo et al., 2015). Stiff nanoparticles tend to move toward the CFL, enhancing transvascular transport (Kumar and Graham, 2012). Meanwhile, softer nanoparticles penetrate tumors more efficiently by moving through the extracellular matrix (ECM) more easily (Deng et al., 2018). Furthermore, limited nanoparticle penetration into tumor tissue is an important obstacle to the efficacy of cancer chemotherapy agents, and nanoparticle mechanics can affect this step. The computational model of Yi and Gao showed that softer nanoparticles with specific binding receptors have higher cellular uptake due to increased surface contact and better receptor diffusion compared to stiffer particles (Yi and Gao, 2017). Anselmo et al. (2015) found that stiffer nanoparticles are bound/internalized more readily than their softer counterparts after 8–12 h. These varied results underscore the necessity for further investigation into the influence of mechanical characteristics on nanoparticle efficacy.

## 5. The role of protein-based drug delivery in therapeutic applications

### 5.1 Cancer therapy

Various protein-based nanoparticles are utilized in cancer immunotherapy, each with its unique therapeutic significance (Verma et al., 2020; Wang et al., 2021). Between 2002 and 2016, protein nanoparticles comprised a substantial portion of clinical trials (51% of trials); however, their representation significantly decreased to over 26% in the 2016–2021 period, with liposomal formulations correspondingly increasing to 44% of all trials (Fig. 3.4) (Namiot et al., 2023). Upon entering the tumor interstitium, nanoparticles undergo cellular internalization, where protein nanoparticles can release their cargo. Endocytosis is the primary mechanism for the translocation of nanoparticles across the cell membrane, influenced by their biophysical properties (Blanco et al., 2015). Comparative analyses of protein-bound medications and their unbound equivalents indicate favorable success rates, while protein-bound pharmaceuticals may elicit less severe adverse effects than their free counterparts (Bobo et al., 2016). However, a challenge arises from the nonspecific delivery of therapeutics to unintended cells expressing albumin receptors. Furthermore, preserving the activity of the therapeutic cargo can be difficult, as enzyme cargos may lose functionality during the nanoparticle preparation process, particularly through methods like desolvation (Hong et al., 2020).

Protein nanoparticles are predominantly employed in developing anticancer therapies. They also provide a promising pathway for oral peptide delivery, as seen with nanoparticles

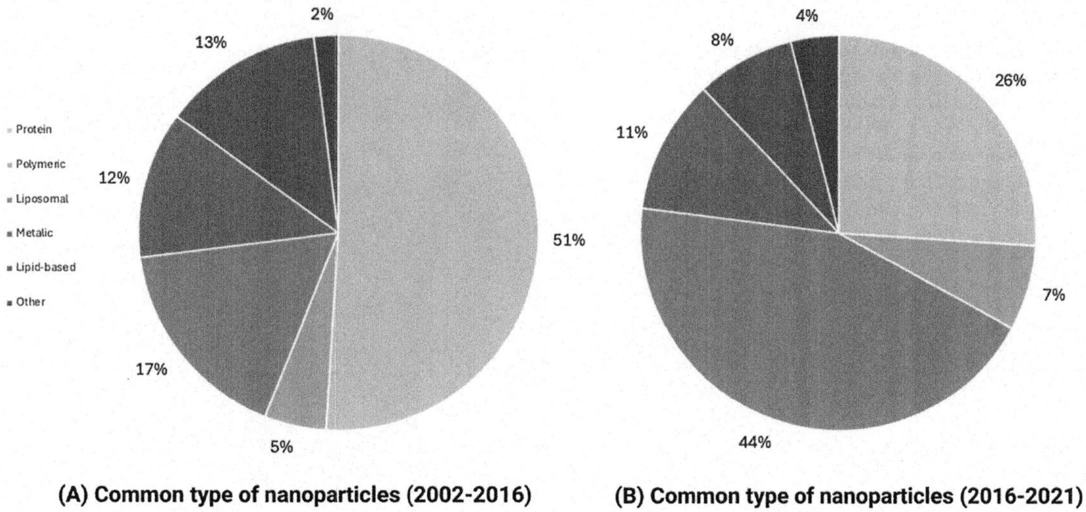


**FIGURE 3.4** (A) This pie chart shows the distribution of nanoparticle types in clinical trials from 2002 to 2016. During this period, protein nanoparticles were the most prevalent, comprising 51% of clinical trials. The "other" category includes carbon- and silica-based nanoparticles, as well as nanostructured hormone formulations. (B) This figure illustrates the types of nanoparticles in trials from 2016 to 2021. Compared to 2002–2016, the usage of protein nanoparticles declined from 51% to 26%, likely due to an increase in liposomal drug trials, which rose from 17% to 44%. The "other" category includes quantum dots, micellar nanoparticles, and exosomes (Namiot et al., 2023).

encapsulating insulin (Verma et al., 2018). Albumin nanoparticles have demonstrated cellular uptake in cancer cells via the caveolae pathway (Kudarha and Sawant, 2021; Asrorov et al., 2024). Furthermore, albumin has been shown to facilitate endothelial transcytosis of both protein-bound and unbound plasma components by binding to a 60-kDa glycoprotein receptor (Gp60, or albondin) on cell surfaces (Miele et al., 2009). Abraxane is a notable example of nanometer albumin-bound technology approved by the U.S. Food and Drug Administration (FDA) for treating advanced nonsmall cell lung cancer and metastatic breast cancer (Kudlowitz and Muggia, 2014). Abraxane (Fig. 3.5) offers a higher therapeutic index than paclitaxel alone (Iwamoto, 2013). It has been approved for first-line treatment in metastatic pancreatic adenocarcinoma in combination with gemcitabine, as well as metastatic nonsmall cell lung carcinoma alongside carboplatin (Kudlowitz and Muggia, 2014). This albumin-bound drug capitalizes on the potential tumor-targeting properties of albumin, and its use bypasses the need for premedication with antihistamines and corticosteroids (Shi, 2020). Today, various albumin-based drugs and imaging agents are available on the market, while numerous others are undergoing clinical trials for a range of applications (Zhang et al., 2006).

Cationic bovine serum albumin (CBSA) nanoparticles have been investigated for lung cancer treatment as an innovative siRNA delivery system, forming stable nanoscale particles with siRNA (Han et al., 2014). CBSA facilitates siRNA accumulation in the lungs, where Bcl-2 siRNA is delivered into the circulation via CBSA, hence inducing cancer cell apoptosis by gene-silencing mechanisms (Ghosh et al., 2021). Meanwhile, Ontak, an engineered protein nanoparticle combining interleukin-2 (IL-2) with the translocating and active domains

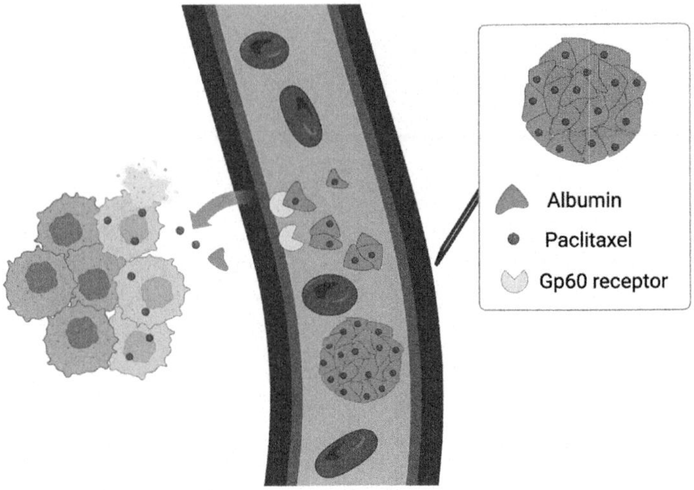


FIGURE 3.5 Abraxane (nanoparticle albumin-bound paclitaxel) exemplifies a protein nanoparticle system in which the hydrophobic drug is stabilized and encased by an albumin shell. Following administration into the bloodstream, the particles rapidly dissociate, allowing individual albumin proteins to transport the drug specifically to the tumor site through Gp60 receptors (Kaltbeitzel and Wich, 2023).

of diphtheria toxin, is beneficial for cutaneous T-cell lymphoma due to its T-cell-targeting specificity and lysosomal escape mechanism. Ontak is internalized via endocytosis through IL-2 receptor-bearing cells, making it the first FDA-approved genetically constructed fusion protein (Weissig et al., 2014; Foss, 2000).

## 5.2 Enzyme replacement therapy

Enzyme replacement therapy (ERT) has been applied to treat certain diseases caused by enzyme deficiency or low enzymatic activity (Desnick and Schuchman, 2012; Grabowski et al., 1998; Alegra et al., 2012). However, ERT faces three main challenges: (i) introducing foreign proteins into the body can trigger severe immune responses, (ii) degradation of the exogenous enzyme by the body's own proteases reduces treatment efficacy and necessitates higher doses, and (iii) systemic administration increases dosage requirements and risks side effects as enzymes distribute into healthy tissues (González-Davis et al., 2023). Enzymatic nanoreactors, which encapsulate enzymes within VLPs, present a promising alternative for ERT. VLPs can be produced using native hosts [bacteria (Sanchez-Sanchez, 2015), plants (Nuñez-Rivera et al., 2020), and animals (Thrane et al., 2015)] and recombinant systems, offering versatile production (Effio and Hubbuch, 2015).

VLPs provide three modifiable interfaces: outer surface, intersubunit, and inner surface (Douglas and Young, 2006). The inner surface, in particular, has been used to encapsulate various materials such as metals (Hooker et al., 2007; Duran-Meza, 2020), drugs (Ren et al., 2007), DNA (Verma and Weitzman, 2005), and proteins (Lipin et al., 2008), enabling applications in materials science, catalysis, and drug delivery. VLPs, which consist of empty viral capsids, can enter mammalian cells without replicating, making them ideal for therapeutic purposes. Encapsulated enzymes within VLPs act as nanoscale bioreactors, allowing substrates and products to pass through VLP pores and enabling isolated multistep reactions (Sánchez-Sánchez et al., 2014; Selivanovitch et al., 2021).

VLPs can also be modified for specific cell targeting (Koudelka et al., 2015). For instance, Gama et al. (2021) demonstrated the encapsulation of the Galactose-1-phosphate uridylyltransferase (GALT) enzyme in brome mosaic virus (BMV) using charge complementarity. These GALT nanoreactors were effectively internalized by various human cell lines, including hepatocytes, fibroblasts, and kidney cells (Gama et al., 2021). The inherent compatibility of VLPs with biological fluids makes them highly suitable for carrying and delivering enzymatic activity in ERT. Additionally, their stability, solubility, and surface functionalization potential allow for targeted delivery to specific organs or cell compartments, reducing protease degradation and immune recognition while extending enzyme lifespan in vivo. This positions VLP-based enzymatic nanoreactors as a valuable strategy for enhancing the effectiveness of ERT (González-Davis et al., 2023).

## 5.3 Vaccines

Nanoparticles are extensively utilized for vaccine delivery, which is advancing rapidly. The nanomedicine landscape has evolved significantly, propelled by the global introduction of Moderna and Pfizer-BioNTech's lipid nanoparticle mRNA COVID-19 vaccines (Creech et al., 2021; Haynes, 2021). Polymeric and liposomal particles are often employed as carriers and adjuvants. Notably, paclitaxel is frequently used in clinical trials, accounting for 23% of cases (Namiot et al., 2023). Polymeric nanoparticles show promise in vaccine and antibiotic delivery due to their structural versatility and relatively straightforward design and fabrication (El-Say and El-Sawy, 2017). Since 2019, over 35 novel nanoparticle technologies have entered clinical trials (Anselmo and Mitragotri, 2019). Of these, three protein-based nanoparticles are currently being investigated as non-mRNA vaccine candidates (Table 3.1).

**TABLE 3.1** Nanoparticle vaccines currently in active clinical trials, as listed in the ClinicalTrials.gov database.

| Name | Company | Particle type | Payload | Investigated application | ClinicalTrials.gov ID |
|---|---|---|---|---|---|
| GBP510 | SK Bioscience Co. | Self-assembling protein nanoparticle immunogens | Various immunogens | COVID-19 vaccine | NCT0474273 (Ph I/II)—Completed NCT04750343 (Ph I/II)—Completed |
| NanoFlu | Novavax | Recombinant hemagglutinin protein nanoparticle with saponin-based Matrix-M adjuvant | Recombinant hemagglutinin protein | Influenza vaccine | NCT04120194 (Ph III)—Completed |
| SARS-CoV-2 rS/Matrix-M1 adjuvant | Novavax | Recombinant spike protein nanoparticle with saponin-based Matrix-M1 adjuvant | Recombinant spike protein | COVID-19 vaccine | NCT04611802 (Ph III)—Completed NCT04368988 (Ph I/II)—Completed NCT04533399 (Ph IIA/B)—Completed NCT04583995 (Ph III)—Completed |

## 6. Conclusion

Protein nanoparticles serve as effective delivery carriers with numerous advantages and applications in material transport. Compared to other colloidal carriers, protein nanoparticles offer greater stability and are easier to produce. Moreover, their potential for in vivo application is substantial, as proteins from various sources may be easily transformed into nanoparticles via a straightforward, economical, and environmentally benign manufacturing process that utilizes fewer chemicals than those necessary for nanoparticles derived from alternative materials. The benefits and limitations of protein nanoparticles vary depending on the materials and synthesis processes involved, with albumin being the most widely used protein in drug delivery applications. In addition, protein nanoparticles enhance protein transfer efficiency by enabling control over characteristics such as size, shape, and surface charge. They also regulate protein drug loading and release efficiency according to nanoparticle properties and the concentration or type of drug used. Despite promising initial results and the significant future potential of protein nanoparticles, comparative data on their performance and therapeutic efficiency versus other delivery systems remain limited. Consequently, further research is needed, and selecting the most suitable materials and processes on a case-by-case basis is essential for the development of efficient protein nanoparticles.

## References

Adams, S., Diamond, J.R., Hamilton, E., Pohlmann, P.R., Tolaney, S.M., Chang, C.W., Zhang, W., Iizuka, K., Foster, P.G., Molinero, L., Funke, R., Powderly, J., 2019. Atezolizumab plus nab-paclitaxel in the treatment of metastatic triple-negative breast cancer with 2-year survival follow-up: A phase 1b clinical trial. JAMA Oncol. 5 (3), 334–342. https://doi.org/10.1001/jamaoncol.2018.5152.

Alegra, T., Vairo, F., de Souza, M.V., Krug, B.C., Schwartz, I.V.D., 2012. Enzyme replacement therapy for Fabry disease: A systematic review and meta-analysis. Genet. Mol. Biol. 35 (4 Suppl. 1), 947–954. https://doi.org/10.1590/S1415-47572012000600009.

Aliabadi, M., Yunessnia Lehi, A., Shagholani, H., Ali, G., 2018. Planar polymer-graphene oxide nanohybrid as a 5-fluorouacil carrier in pH-responsive controlled release. J. Drug Deliv. Sci. Technol. 43, 103–106. https://doi.org/10.1016/j.jddst.2017.09.020.

Amenabar, I., Poly, S., Nuansing, W., Hubrich, E.H., Govyadinov, A.A., Huth, F., Krutokhvostov, R., Zhang, L., Knez, M., Heberle, J., Bittner, A.M., Hillenbrand, R., 2013. Structural analysis and mapping of individual protein complexes by infrared nanospectroscopy. Nat. Commun. 4 (1). https://doi.org/10.1038/ncomms3890.

Anderson, N.L., Polanski, M., Pieper, R., Gatlin, T., Tirumalai, R.S., Conrads, T.P., Veenstra, T.D., Adkins, J.N., Pounds, J.G., Fagan, R., Lobley, A., 2004. The human plasma proteome. Mol. Cell. Proteomics 3 (4), 311–326. https://doi.org/10.1074/mcp.M300127-MCP200.

Anselmo, A.C., Mitragotri, S., 2019. Nanoparticles in the clinic: An update. Bioeng. Transl. Med. 4 (3). https://doi.org/10.1002/btm2.10143.

Anselmo, A.C., Zhang, M., Kumar, S., Vogus, D.R., Menegatti, S., Helgeson, M.E., Mitragotri, S., 2015. Elasticity of nanoparticles influences their blood circulation, phagocytosis, endocytosis, and targeting. ACS Nano 9 (3), 3169–3177. https://doi.org/10.1021/acsnano.5b00147.

Ascoli, G.A., Domenici, E., Bertucci, C., 2006. Drug binding to human serum albumin: Abridged review of results obtained with high-performance liquid chromatography and circular dichroism. Chirality 18 (9), 667–679. https://doi.org/10.1002/chir.20301.

Ashraf, M.A., Peng, W., Zare, Y., Rhee, K.Y., 2018. Effects of size and aggregation/agglomeration of nanoparticles on the interfacial/interphase properties and tensile strength of polymer nanocomposites. Nanoscale Res. Lett. 13 (1). https://doi.org/10.1186/s11671-018-2624-0.

Asrorov, A.M., Mukhamedov, N., Kayumov, M., Yashinov, A.S., Wali, A., Yili, A., Mirzaakhmedov, S.Y., Huang, Y., 2024. Albumin is a reliable drug-delivering molecule: highlighting points in cancer therapy. Med. Drug Discov. 22, 100186. https://doi.org/10.1016/j.medidd.2024.100186.

Assfalg, M., Ragona, L., Pagano, K., D'Onofrio, M., Zanzoni, S., Tomaselli, S., Molinari, H., 2016. The study of transient protein–nanoparticle interactions by solution NMR spectroscopy. Biochimica et Biophysica Acta (BBA) - Proteins and Proteomics 1864 (1), 102–114. https://doi.org/10.1016/j.bbapap.2015.04.024.

Bae, K.H., Lee, F., Xu, K., Keng, C.T., Tan, S.Y., Tan, Y.J., Chen, Q., Kurisawa, M., 2015. Microstructured dextran hydrogels for burst-free sustained release of PEGylated protein drugs. Biomaterials 63, 146–157. https://doi.org/10.1016/j.biomaterials.2015.06.008.

Bangham, A.D., Standish, M.M., Watkins, J.C., 1965. Diffusion of univalent ions across the lamellae of swollen phospholipids. J. Mol. Biol. 13 (1), 238–252. https://doi.org/10.1016/S0022-2836(65)80093-6.

Bangham, A.D., Horne, R.W., 1964. Negative staining of phospholipids and their structural modification by surface-active agents as observed in the electron microscope. J. Mol. Biol. 8 (5), 660–668. https://doi.org/10.1016/S0022-2836(64)80115-7.

Bartczak, D., Muskens, O.L., Nitti, S., Sanchez-Elsner, T., Millar, T.M., Kanaras, A.G., 2012. Interactions of human endothelial cells with gold nanoparticles of different morphologies. Small 8 (1), 122–130. https://doi.org/10.1002/smll.201101422.

Berardi, A., Bisharat, L., AlKhatib, H.S., Cespi, M., 2018. Zein as a pharmaceutical excipient in oral solid dosage forms: State of the art and future perspectives. AAPS PharmSciTech 19 (5), 2009–2022. https://doi.org/10.1208/s12249-018-1035-y.

Bertucci, C., Domenici, E., 2002. Reversible and covalent binding of drugs to human serum albumin: Methodological approaches and physiological relevance. Curr. Med. Chem. 9 (15), 1463–1481. https://doi.org/10.2174/0929867023369673.

Biesiekierski, J.R., 2017. What is gluten? J. Gastroenterol. Hepatol. 32, 78–81. https://doi.org/10.1111/jgh.13703.

Birrenbach, G., Speiser, P.P., 1976. Polymerized micelles and their use as adjuvants in immunology. J. Pharmaceut. Sci. 65 (12), 1763–1766. https://doi.org/10.1002/jps.2600651217.

Blanco, E., Shen, H., Ferrari, M., 2015. Principles of nanoparticle design for overcoming biological barriers to drug delivery. Nat. Biotechnol. 33 (9), 941–951. https://doi.org/10.1038/nbt.3330.

Bobo, D., Robinson, K.J., Islam, J., Thurecht, K.J., Corrie, S.R., 2016. Nanoparticle-based medicines: a review of FDA-approved materials and clinical trials to date. Pharm. Res. 33 (10), 2373–2387. https://doi.org/10.1007/s11095-016-1958-5.

Buzea, C., Pacheco, I.I., Robbie, K., 2007. Nanomaterials and nanoparticles: Sources and toxicity. Biointerphases 2 (4), MR17. https://doi.org/10.1116/1.2815690.

Byrne, J.D., Betancourt, T., Brannon-Peppas, L., 2008. Active targeting schemes for nanoparticle systems in cancer therapeutics. Adv. Drug Deliv. Rev. 60 (15), 1615–1626. https://doi.org/10.1016/j.addr.2008.08.005.

Campbell, R.B., Fukumura, D., Brown, E.B., Mazzola, L.M., Izumi, Y., Jain, R.K., Torchilin, V.P., Munn, L.L., 2002. Cationic charge determines the distribution of liposomes between the vascular and extravascular compartments of tumors. Cancer Res. 62 (23), 6831–6836.

Carril, M., Padro, D., Pino, P.del, Carrillo-Carrion, C., Gallego, M., Parak, W.J., 2017. In situ detection of the protein corona in complex environments. Nat. Commun. 8 (1). https://doi.org/10.1038/s41467-017-01826-4.

Carrillo-Carrion, C., Carril, M., Parak, W.J., 2017. Techniques for the experimental investigation of the protein corona. Curr. Opin. Biotechnol. 46, 106–113. https://doi.org/10.1016/j.copbio.2017.02.009.

Carvalho, J.A., Abreu, A.S., Ferreira, V.T.P., Gonçalves, E.P., Tedesco, A.C., Pinto, J.G., Ferreira-Strixino, J., Beltrame Junior, M., Simioni, A.R., 2018. Preparation of gelatin nanoparticles by two step desolvation method for application in photodynamic therapy. J. Biomater. Sci. Polym. Ed. 29 (11), 1287–1301. https://doi.org/10.1080/09205063.2018.1456027.

Cedervall, T., Lynch, I., Lindman, S., Berggård, T., Thulin, E., Hanna, N., Dawson, K.A., Linse, S., 2007. Understanding the nanoparticle–protein corona using methods to quantify exchange rates and affinities of proteins for nanoparticles. Proc. Natl. Acad. Sci. 104 (7), 2050–2055. https://doi.org/10.1073/pnas.0608582104.

Chatzitaki, A.-T., Jesus, S., Karavasili, C., Andreadis, D., Fatouros, D.G., Borges, O., 2020. Chitosan-coated PLGA nanoparticles for the nasal delivery of ropinirole hydrochloride: In vitro and ex vivo evaluation of efficacy and safety. Int. J. Pharm. 589, 119776. https://doi.org/10.1016/j.ijpharm.2020.119776.

Chauhan, V.P., Popović, Z., Chen, O., Cui, J., Fukumura, D., Bawendi, M.G., Jain, R.K., 2011. Fluorescent nanorods and nanospheres for real-time in vivo probing of nanoparticle shape-dependent tumor penetration. Angewandte Chemie - International Edition 50 (48), 11417–11420. https://doi.org/10.1002/anie.201104449.

Chauhan, V.P., Stylianopoulos, T., Martin, J.D., PopoviÄ, Z., Chen, O., Kamoun, W.S., Bawendi, M.G., Fukumura, D., Jain, R.K., 2012. Normalization of tumour blood vessels improves the delivery of nanomedicines in a size-dependent manner, 17483395 Nat. Nanotechnol. 7 (6), 383–388. https://doi.org/10.1038/nnano.2012.45.

Chen, K., Mitra, S., 2019. Incorporation of functionalized carbon nanotubes into hydrophobic drug crystals for enhancing aqueous dissolution. Colloids Surf. B Biointerfaces 173, 386–391. https://doi.org/10.1016/j.colsurfb.2018.09.080.

Chithrani, B.D., Ghazani, A.A., Chan, W.C.W., 2006. Determining the size and shape dependence of gold nanoparticle uptake into mammalian cells. Nano Lett. 6 (4), 662–668. https://doi.org/10.1021/nl052396o.

Cho, Y.H., Jones, O.G., 2019. Assembled protein nanoparticles in food or nutrition applications. Adv. Food Nutr. Res. 88, 47–84. https://doi.org/10.1016/bs.afnr.2019.01.002.

Choi, H.S., Liu, W., Liu, F., Nasr, K., Misra, P., Bawendi, M.G., Frangioni, J.V., 2010. Design considerations for tumour-targeted nanoparticles. Nat. Nanotechnol. 5 (1), 42–47. https://doi.org/10.1038/nnano.2009.314.

Choi, H.S., Liu, W., Misra, P., Tanaka, E., Zimmer, J.P., Ipe, B.I., Bawendi, M.G., Frangioni, J.V., 2007. Renal clearance of quantum dots. Nat. Biotechnol. 25 (10), 1165–1170. https://doi.org/10.1038/nbt1340.

Chong, Y., Ge, C., Yang, Z., Garate, J.A., Gu, Z., Weber, J.K., Liu, J., Zhou, R., 2015. Reduced cytotoxicity of graphene nanosheets mediated by blood-protein coating. ACS Nano 9 (6), 5713–5724. https://doi.org/10.1021/nn5066606.

Couvreur, P., Tulkenst, P., Roland, M., Trouet, A., Speiser, P., 1977. Nanocapsules: A new type of lysosomotropic carrier. FEBS (Fed. Eur. Biochem. Soc.) Lett. 84 (2), 323–326. https://doi.org/10.1016/0014-5793(77)80717-5.

Couvreur, P., Kante, B., Roland, M., Guiot, P., Bauduin, P., Speiser, P., 1979. Polycyanoacrylate nanocapsules as potential lysosomotropic carriers: preparation, morphological and sorptive properties. J. Pharm. Pharmacol. 31 (1), 331–332. https://doi.org/10.1111/j.2042-7158.1979.tb13510.x.

Couvreur, P., Kante, B., Grislain, L., Roland, M., Speiser, P., 1982. Toxicity of polyalkylcyanoacrylate nanoparticles II: Doxorubicin-loaded nanoparticles. J. Pharmaceut. Sci. 71 (7), 790–792. https://doi.org/10.1002/jps.2600710717.

Creech, C.B., Walker, S.C., Samuels, R.J., 2021. SARS-CoV-2 vaccines. JAMA, J. Am. Med. Assoc. 325 (13), 1318–1320. https://doi.org/10.1001/jama.2021.3199.

Cui, W., Wang, A., Zhao, J., Li, J., 2016. Biomacromolecules based core/shell architecture toward biomedical applications. Adv. Colloid Interface Sci. 237, 43–51. https://doi.org/10.1016/j.cis.2016.10.001.

Dai, Q., Yan, Y., Ang, C.-S., Kempe, K., Kamphuis, M.M.J., Dodds, S.J., Caruso, F., 2015. Monoclonal antibody-functionalized multilayered particles: Targeting cancer cells in the presence of protein coronas. ACS Nano 9 (3), 2876–2885. https://doi.org/10.1021/nn506929e.

Dai, Q., Wilhelm, S., Ding, D., Muhammad Syed, A., Sindhwani, S., Zhang, Y., Chen, Y.Y., MacMillan, P., Chan, W. C.W., 2018. Quantifying the ligand-coated nanoparticle delivery to cancer cells in solid tumors. ACS Nano 12 (8), 8423–8435. https://doi.org/10.1021/acsnano.8b03900.

Dal Magro, R., Albertini, B., Beretta, S., Rigolio, R., Donzelli, E., Chiorazzi, A., Ricci, M., Blasi, P., Sancini, G., 2018. Artificial apolipoprotein corona enables nanoparticle brain targeting. Nanomed. Nanotechnol. Biol. Med. 14 (2), 429–438. https://doi.org/10.1016/j.nano.2017.11.008.

Decuzzi, P., Lee, S., Bhushan, B., Ferrari, M., 2005. A theoretical model for the margination of particles within blood vessels. Ann. Biomed. Eng. 33 (2), 179–190. https://doi.org/10.1007/s10439-005-8976-5.

Dehouck, B., Dehouck, M.P., Fruchart, J.C., Cecchelli, R., 1994. Upregulation of the low density lipoprotein receptor at the blood-brain barrier: Intercommunications between brain capillary endothelial cells and astrocytes. J. Cell Biol. 126 (2), 465–473. https://doi.org/10.1083/jcb.126.2.465.

Dellian, M., Yuan, F., Trubetskoy, V.S., Torchilin, V.P., Jain, R.K., 2000. Vascular permeability in a human tumour xenograft: molecular charge dependence. Br. J. Cancer 82 (9), 1513–1518.

Deng, H., Song, K., Zhang, J., Deng, L., Dong, A., Qin, Z., 2018. Modulating the rigidity of nanoparticles for tumor penetration. Chem. Commun. 54 (24), 3014–3017. https://doi.org/10.1039/c8cc00398j.

Desai, M.P., Labhasetwar, V., Walter, E., Levy, R.J., Amidon, G.L., 1997. The mechanism of uptake of biodegradable microparticles in Caco-2 cells is size dependent. Pharm. Res. 14 (11), 1568–1573. https://doi.org/10.1023/A:1012126301290.

Desnick, R.J., Schuchman, E.H., 2012. Enzyme replacement therapy for lysosomal diseases: Lessons from 20 Years of experience and remaining challenges. Annu. Rev. Genom. Hum. Genet. 13 (1), 307–335. https://doi.org/10.1146/annurev-genom-090711-163739.

Dietzen, D.J., 2018. Amino Acids, Peptides, and Proteins Principles and Applications of Molecular Diagnostics. Elsevier, United States, pp. 345–380. https://doi.org/10.1016/B978-0-12-816061-9.00013-8.

Din, F.U., Aman, W., Ullah, I., Qureshi, O.S., Mustapha, O., Shafique, S., Zeb, A., 2017. Effective use of nanocarriers as drug delivery systems for the treatment of selected tumors. Int. J. Nanomed. 12, 7291–7309. https://doi.org/10.2147/IJN.S146315.

Din Wani, S.U., Veerabhadrappa, G.H., 2018. Silk fibroin based drug delivery applications: Promises and challenges. Curr. Drug Targets 19 (10), 1177–1190. https://doi.org/10.2174/1389450119666171227205525.

Dobrovolskaia, M.A., Patri, A.K., Zheng, J., Clogston, J.D., Ayub, N., Aggarwal, P., Neun, B.W., Hall, J.B., McNeil, S. E., 2009. Interaction of colloidal gold nanoparticles with human blood: effects on particle size and analysis of plasma protein binding profiles. Nanomed. Nanotechnol. Biol. Med. 5 (2), 106–117. https://doi.org/10.1016/j.nano.2008.08.001.

Douglas, T., Young, M., 2006. Viruses: Making friends with old foes. Science 312 (5775), 873–875. https://doi.org/10.1126/science.1123223.

Duran-Meza, A.L., 2020. Encapsidation of different plasmonic gold nanoparticles by the CCMV CP. Molecules 25 (11), 2628. https://doi.org/10.3390/molecules25112628.

Effio, C.L., Hubbuch, J., 2015. Next generation vaccines and vectors: Designing downstream processes for recombinant protein-based virus-like particles. Biotechnol. J. 10 (5), 715–727. https://doi.org/10.1002/biot.201400392.

Eigenheer, R., Castellanos, E.R., Nakamoto, M.Y., Gerner, K.T., Lampe, A.M., Wheeler, K.E., 2014. Silver nanoparticle protein corona composition compared across engineered particle properties and environmentally relevant reaction conditions. Environ. Sci. Nano 1 (3), 238–247. https://doi.org/10.1039/c4en00002a.

El-Say, K.M., El-Sawy, H.S., 2017. Polymeric nanoparticles: Promising platform for drug delivery. Int. J. Pharm. 528 (1–2), 675–691. https://doi.org/10.1016/j.ijpharm.2017.06.052.

Elsadek, B., Kratz, F., 2012. Impact of albumin on drug delivery - New applications on the horizon. J. Contr. Release 157 (1), 4–28. https://doi.org/10.1016/j.jconrel.2011.09.069.

Elzoghby, A.O., Samy, W.M., Elgindy, N.A., 2012. Albumin-based nanoparticles as potential controlled release drug delivery systems. J. Contr. Release 157 (2), 168–182. https://doi.org/10.1016/j.jconrel.2011.07.031.

Fasano, M., Curry, S., Terreno, E., Galliano, M., Fanali, G., Narciso, P., Notari, S., Ascenzi, P., 2005. The extraordinary ligand binding properties of human serum albumin. IUBMB Life 57 (12), 787–796. https://doi.org/10.1080/15216540500404093.

Foss, F.M., 2000. DAB389IL-2 (ONTAK): A novel fusion toxin therapy for lymphoma. Clin. Lymphoma 1 (2), 110–116. https://doi.org/10.3816/CLM.2000.n.009.

Friedmann, T., 1992. A brief history of gene therapy. Nat. Genet. 2 (2), 93–98. https://doi.org/10.1038/ng1092-93.

Friess, W., 1998. Collagen - biomaterial for drug delivery. Eur. J. Pharm. Biopharm. 45 (2), 113–136. https://doi.org/10.1016/S0939-6411(98)00017-4.

Fubini, B., Ghiazza, M., Fenoglio, I., 2010. Physico-chemical features of engineered nanoparticles relevant to their toxicity. Nanotoxicology 4 (4), 347–363. https://doi.org/10.3109/17435390.2010.509519.

Gama, P., Cadena-Nava, R.D., Moreno, K.J.-, Pérez-Robles, J., Vazquez-Duhalt, R., 2021. Virus-based nanoreactors with GALT activity for classic galactosemia therapy. ChemMedChem 16 (9), 1438–1445. https://doi.org/10.1002/cmdc.202000999.

Gao, H., 2016. Progress and perspectives on targeting nanoparticles for brain drug delivery. Acta Pharm. Sin. B 6 (4), 268–286. https://doi.org/10.1016/j.apsb.2016.05.013.

Garay, R.P., El-Gewely, R., Armstrong, J.K., Garratty, G., Richette, P., 2012. Antibodies against polyethylene glycol in healthy subjects and in patients treated with PEG-conjugated agents. Expet Opin. Drug Deliv. 9 (11), 1319–1323. https://doi.org/10.1517/17425247.2012.720969.

Garrait, G., Beyssac, E., Subirade, M., 2014. Development of a novel drug delivery system: Chitosan nanoparticles entrapped in alginate microparticles. J. Microencapsul. 31 (4), 363–372. https://doi.org/10.3109/02652048.2013.858792.

Garca, I., Marradi, M., Penadés, S., 2010. Glyconanoparticles: Multifunctional nanomaterials for biomedical applications. Nanomedicine 5 (5), 777–792. https://doi.org/10.2217/nnm.10.48.

García, K.P., Zarschler, K., Barbaro, L., Barreto, J.A., O'Malley, W., Spiccia, L., Stephan, H., Graham, B., 2014. Zwitterionic-coated "stealth" nanoparticles for biomedical applications: Recent advances in countering biomolecular corona formation and uptake by the mononuclear phagocyte system. Small 10 (13), 2516–2529. https://doi.org/10.1002/smll.201303540.

Geng, Y., Paul, D., Cai, S., Tsai, R., Tewari, M., Minko, T., Discher, D.E., 2007. Shape effects of filaments versus spherical particles in flow and drug delivery. Nat. Nanotechnol. 2 (4), 249–255. https://doi.org/10.1038/nnano.2007.70.

Gentile, F., Curcio, A., Indolfi, C., Ferrari, M., Decuzzi, P., 2008. The margination propensity of spherical particles for vascular targeting in the microcirculation. J. Nanobiotechnol. 6 (1). https://doi.org/10.1186/1477-3155-6-9.

Ghezzi, C.E., Marelli, B., Omenetto, F.G., Funderburgh, J.L., Kaplan, D.L., Karamichos, D., 2017. 3D functional corneal stromal tissue equivalent based on corneal stromal stem cells and multi-layered silk film architecture. PLoS One 12 (1), e0169504. https://doi.org/10.1371/journal.pone.0169504.

Ghosh, S., Javia, A., Shetty, S., Bardoliwala, D., Maiti, K., Banerjee, S., Khopade, A., Misra, A., Sawant, K., Bhowmick, S., 2021. Triple negative breast cancer and non-small cell lung cancer: Clinical challenges and nano-formulation approaches. J. Contr. Release 337, 27–58. https://doi.org/10.1016/j.jconrel.2021.07.014.

Gianni, L., Mansutti, M., Anton, A., Calvo, L., Bisagni, G., Bermejo, B., Semiglazov, V., Thill, M., Chacon, J.I., Chan, A., Morales, S., Alvarez, I., Plazaola, A., Zambetti, M., Redfern, A.D., Dittrich, C., Dent, R.A., Magazzu, D., De Fato, R., Valagussa, P., Tusquets, I., 2018. Comparing neoadjuvant nab-paclitaxel vs paclitaxel both followed by anthracycline regimens in women with ERBB2/HER2-negative breast cancer-the evaluating treatment with neoadjuvant abraxane (ETNA) trial a randomized phase 3 clinical trial. JAMA Oncol. 4 (3), 302–308. https://doi.org/10.1001/jamaoncol.2017.4612.

Gil, J.F., Mesa, V., Estrada-Ortiz, N., Lopez-Obando, M., Gómez, A., Plácido, J., 2021. Viruses in extreme environments, current overview, and biotechnological potential. Viruses 13 (1). https://doi.org/10.3390/v13010081.

González-Davis, O., Villagrana-Escareño, M.V., Trujillo, M.A., Gama, P., Chauhan, K., Vazquez-Duhalt, R., 2023. Virus-like nanoparticles as enzyme carriers for enzyme replacement therapy (ERT). Virology 580, 73–87. https://doi.org/10.1016/j.virol.2023.01.017.

Grabowski, G.A., Leslie, N., Wenstrup, R., 1998. Enzyme therapy for Gaucher disease: the first 5 years. Blood Rev. 12 (2), 115–133. https://doi.org/10.1016/s0268-960x(98)90023-6.

Gref, R., Minamitake, Y., Peracchia, M.T., Trubetskoy, V., Torchilin, V., Langer, R., 1994. Biodegradable long-circulating polymeric nanospheres. Science 263 (5153), 1600–1603. https://doi.org/10.1126/science.8128245.

Guan, G., Zhang, S., Liu, S., Cai, Y., Low, M., Teng, C.P., Phang, I.Y., Yuan, C., Koh, L.D., Srinivasan, B.M., Zheng, Y., Zhang, Y.-W., Han, M.-Y., 2015. Protein induces layer-by-layer exfoliation of transition metal dichalcogenides. J. Am. Chem. Soc. 137 (19), 6152–6155. https://doi.org/10.1021/jacs.5b02780.

Guardia, P., Di Corato, R., Lartigue, L., Wilhelm, C., Espinosa, A., Garcia-Hernandez, M., Gazeau, F., Manna, L., Pellegrino, T., 2012. Water-soluble iron oxide nanocubes with high values of specific absorption rate for cancer cell hyperthermia treatment. ACS Nano 6 (4), 3080–3091. https://doi.org/10.1021/nn2048137.

Gulfam, M., Kim, J.-eun, Lee, J.M., Ku, B., Chung, B.H., Chung, B.G., 2012. Anticancer drug-loaded gliadin nanoparticles induce apoptosis in breast cancer cells. Langmuir 28 (21), 8216–8223. https://doi.org/10.1021/la300691n.

Gurny, R., Boye, T., Ibrahim, H., 1985. Ocular therapy with nanoparticulate systems for controlled drug delivery. J. Contr. Release 2 (C), 353–361. https://doi.org/10.1016/0168-3659(85)90057-4.

Gupta, R., Rai, B., 2017. Effect of size and surface charge of gold nanoparticles on their skin permeability: A molecular dynamics study. Sci. Rep. 7. https://doi.org/10.1038/srep45292.

Han, J., Wang, Q., Zhang, Z., Gong, T., Sun, X., 2014. Cationic bovine serum albumin based self-assembled nanoparticles as siRNA delivery vector for treating lung metastatic cancer. Small 10 (3), 524–535. https://doi.org/10.1002/smll.201301992.

Harush-Frenkel, O., Rozentur, E., Benita, S., Altschuler, Y., 2008. Surface charge of nanoparticles determines their endocytic and transcytotic pathway in polarized MDCK cells. Biomacromolecules 9 (2), 435–443. https://doi.org/10.1021/bm700535p.

Hassett, K.J., Benenato, K.E., Jacquinet, E., Lee, A., Woods, A., Yuzhakov, O., Himansu, S., Deterling, J., Geilich, B. M., Ketova, T., Mihai, C., Lynn, A., McFadyen, I., Moore, M.J., Senn, J.J., Stanton, M.G., Almarsson, Ö., Ciaramella, G., Brito, L.A., 2019. Optimization of lipid nanoparticles for intramuscular administration of mRNA vaccines. Mol. Ther. Nucleic Acids 15, 1–11. https://doi.org/10.1016/j.omtn.2019.01.013.

Haynes, B.F., 2021. A new vaccine to battle COVID-19, 15334406 N. Engl. J. Med. 384 (5), 470–471. https://doi.org/10.1056/NEJMe2035557.

Herrera Estrada, L.P., Champion, J.A., 2015. Protein nanoparticles for therapeutic protein delivery. Biomater. Sci. 3 (6), 787–799. https://doi.org/10.1039/C5BM00052A.

Ho, Y.T., Poinard, B., Yeo, E.L.L., Kah, J.C.Y., 2015. An instantaneous colorimetric protein assay based on spontaneous formation of a protein corona on gold nanoparticles. Analyst 140 (4), 1026–1036. https://doi.org/10.1039/c4an01819b.

Hollis, C.P., Weiss, H.L., Leggas, M., Evers, B.M., Gemeinhart, R.A., Li, T., 2013. Biodistribution and bioimaging studies of hybrid paclitaxel nanocrystals: Lessons learned of the EPR effect and image-guided drug delivery. J. Contr. Release 172 (1), 12–21. https://doi.org/10.1016/j.jconrel.2013.06.039.

Hong, S., Choi, D.W., Kim, H.N., Park, C.G., Lee, W., Park, H.H., 2020. Protein-based nanoparticles as drug delivery systems. Pharmaceutics 12 (7), 604. https://doi.org/10.3390/pharmaceutics12070604.

Hooker, J.M., Datta, A., Botta, M., Raymond, K.N., Francis, M.B., 2007. Magnetic resonance contrast agents from viral capsid shells: A comparison of exterior and interior cargo strategies. Nano Lett. 7 (8), 2207–2210. https://doi.org/10.1021/nl070512c.

Hu, Y.J., Liu, Y., Sun, T.Q., Bai, A.M., Lu, J.Q., Pi, Z.B., 2006. Binding of anti-inflammatory drug cromolyn sodium to bovine serum albumin. Int. J. Biol. Macromol. 39 (4–5), 280–285. https://doi.org/10.1016/j.ijbiomac.2006.04.004.

Huang, X., Teng, X., Chen, D., Tang, F., He, J., 2010. The effect of the shape of mesoporous silica nanoparticles on cellular uptake and cell function. Biomaterials 31 (3), 438–448. https://doi.org/10.1016/j.biomaterials.2009.09.060.

Hubbell, J.A., Chilkoti, A., 2012. Nanomaterials for drug delivery. Science 337 (6092), 303–305. https://doi.org/10.1126/science.1219657.

Huh, K.M., Lee, S.C., Cho, Y.W., Lee, J., Jeong, J.H., Park, K., 2005. Hydrotropic polymer micelle system for delivery of paclitaxel. J. Contr. Release 101. https://doi.org/10.1016/j.jconrel.2004.07.003.

Hussein, M., El-Husseiny, Mady, E.A., Hamabe, L., Abugomaa, A., Shimada, K., Yoshida, T., Tanaka, T., Yokoi, A., Mohamed, E., Tanaka, R., 2022. Smart/stimuli-responsive hydrogels: Cutting-edge platforms for tissue engineering and other biomedical applications. Mater. Today Bio 13, 100186. https://doi.org/10.1016/j.mtbio.2021.100186.

Irache, J.M., Bergougnoux, L., Ezpeleta, I., Gueguen, J., Orecchioni, A.M., 1995. Optimization and in vitro stability of legumin nanoparticles obtained by a coacervation method. Int. J. Pharm. 126 (1–2), 103–109. https://doi.org/10.1016/0378-5173(95)04103-6.

Iwamoto, T., 2013. Clinical application of drug delivery systems in cancer chemotherapy: Review of the efficacy and side effects of approved drugs. Biol. Pharm. Bull. 36 (5), 715–718. https://doi.org/10.1248/bpb.b12-01102.

Jahanban-Esfahlan, A., Dastmalchi, S., Davaran, S., 2016. A simple improved desolvation method for the rapid preparation of albumin nanoparticles. Int. J. Biol. Macromol. 91, 703–709. https://doi.org/10.1016/j.ijbiomac.2016.05.032.

Jain, R.K., Stylianopoulos, T., 2010. Delivering nanomedicine to solid tumors. Nat. Rev. Clin. Oncol. 7 (11), 653–664. https://doi.org/10.1038/nrclinonc.2010.139.

Jain, R.K., Tong, R.T., Munn, L.L., 2007. Effect of vascular normalization by antiangiogenic therapy on interstitial hypertension, peritumor edema, and lymphatic metastasis: Insights from a mathematical model. Cancer Res. 67 (6), 2729–2735. https://doi.org/10.1158/0008-5472.CAN-06-4102.

Jameson, G.S., Borazanci, E., Babiker, H.M., Poplin, E., Niewiarowska, A.A., Gordon, M.S., Barrett, M.T., Rosenthal, A., Stoll-D'Astice, A., Crowley, J., Shemanski, L., Korn, R.L., Ansaldo, K., Lebron, L., Ramanathan, R.K., Von Hoff, D.D., 2020. Response rate following albumin-bound paclitaxel plus gemcitabine plus cisplatin treatment among patients with advanced pancreatic cancer: A phase 1b/2 pilot clinical trial. JAMA Oncol. 6 (1), 125–132. https://doi.org/10.1001/jamaoncol.2019.3394.

Jang, D.J., Moon, C., Oh, E., 2016. Improved tumor targeting and antitumor activity of camptothecin loaded solid lipid nanoparticles by preinjection of blank solid lipid nanoparticles. Biomed. Pharmacother. 80, 162–172. https://doi.org/10.1016/j.biopha.2016.03.018.

Jatzkewitz, H., 1955. Peptamin (glycyl-L-leucyl-mescaline) bound to blood plasma expander (polyvinylpyrrolidone) as a new depot form of a biologically active primary amine (mescaline). Z. Naturforsch. 10, 27–31.

Jiang, W., Kim, B.Y.S., Rutka, J.T., Chan, W.C.W., 2008. Nanoparticle-mediated cellular response is size-dependent. Nat. Nanotechnol. 3 (3), 145–150. https://doi.org/10.1038/nnano.2008.30.

Jiang, W., Xu, X.P., Gong, J.M., Tu, S.T., 2012. Influence of repair length on residual stress in the repair weld of a clad plate. Nucl. Eng. Des. 246, 211–219. https://doi.org/10.1016/j.nucengdes.2012.01.021.

Jiang, Y., Liang, M., Svejkar, D., Hart-Smith, G., Lu, H., Scarano, W., Stenzel, M.H., 2014. Albumin-micelles via a one-pot technology platform for the delivery of drugs. Chem. Commun. 50 (48), 6394. https://doi.org/10.1039/c4cc00616j.

Kabanov, A.V., Vinogradov, S.V., 2009. Nanogels as pharmaceutical carriers: Finite networks of infinite capabilities. Angewandte Chemie - International Edition 48 (30), 5418–5429. https://doi.org/10.1002/anie.200900441.

Kaltbeitzel, J., Wich, P.R., 2023. Protein-based nanoparticles: from drug delivery to imaging, nanocatalysis and protein therapy. Angewandte Chemie - International Edition 62 (44). https://doi.org/10.1002/anie.202216097.

Kambhampati, S., Jia, L., Evans, B.S., Allen, D.K., 2019. Accurate and efficient amino acid analysis for protein quantification using hydrophilic interaction chromatography coupled tandem mass spectrometry. Plant Methods 15 (1). https://doi.org/10.1186/s13007-019-0430-z.

Keuth, J., Nitschke, Y., Mulac, D., Riehemann, K., Rutsch, F., Langer, K., 2020. Reversion of arterial calcification by elastin-targeted DTPA-HSA nanoparticles. Eur. J. Pharm. Biopharm. 150, 108–119. https://doi.org/10.1016/j.ejpb.2020.03.007.

Khanna, S.C., Speiser, P., 1969. Epoxy resin beads as a pharmaceutical dosage form I: Method of preparation. J. Pharmaceut. Sci. 58 (9), 1114–1117. https://doi.org/10.1002/jps.2600580916.

Khanna, S.C., Jecklin, T., Speiser, P., 1970. Bead polymerization technique for sustained-release dosage form. J. Pharmaceut. Sci. 59 (5), 614–618. https://doi.org/10.1002/jps.2600590508.

Klibanov, A.L., Maruyama, K., Torchilin, V.P., Huang, L., 1990. Amphipathic polyethyleneglycols effectively prolong the circulation time of liposomes. FEBS (Fed. Eur. Biochem. Soc.) Lett. 268 (1), 235–237. https://doi.org/10.1016/0014-5793(90)81016-H.

Koudelka, K.J., Pitek, A.S., Manchester, M., Steinmetz, N.F., 2015. Virus-based nanoparticles as versatile nanomachines. Annu. Rev. Virol. 2 (1), 379–401. https://doi.org/10.1146/annurev-virology-100114-055141.

Kratz, F., 2008. Albumin as a drug carrier: design of prodrugs, drug conjugates and nanoparticles. J. Contr. Release 132 (3), 171–183. https://doi.org/10.1016/j.jconrel.2008.05.010.

Kudarha, R.R., Sawant, K.K., 2021. Chondroitin sulfate conjugation facilitates tumor cell internalization of albumin nanoparticles for brain-targeted delivery of temozolomide via CD44 receptor-mediated targeting. Drug Deliv. Transl. Res. 11 (5), 1994–2008. https://doi.org/10.1007/s13346-020-00861-x.

Kudlowitz, D., Muggia, F., 2014. Nanoparticle albumin-bound paclitaxel (nab-paclitaxel): Extending its indications. Expet Opin. Drug Saf. 13 (6), 681–685. https://doi.org/10.1517/14740338.2014.910193.

Kumar, A., Graham, M.D., 2012. Margination and segregation in confined flows of blood and other multicomponent suspensions. Soft Matter 8 (41), 10536–10548. https://doi.org/10.1039/c2sm25943e.

Kwon, I.K., Lee, S.C., Han, B., Park, K., 2012. Analysis on the current status of targeted drug delivery to tumors. J. Contr. Release 164 (2), 108–114. https://doi.org/10.1016/j.jconrel.2012.07.010.

Langer, K., Balthasar, S., Vogel, V., Dinauer, N., von Briesen, H., Schubert, D., 2003. Optimization of the preparation process for human serum albumin (HSA) nanoparticles. Int. J. Pharm. 257 (1–2), 169–180. https://doi.org/10.1016/s0378-5173(03)00134-0.

Lee, H., Hoang, B., Humphrey, F., Reilly, R.M., Allen, C., 2010. In vivo distribution of polymeric nanoparticles at the whole-body, tumor, and cellular levels. Pharm. Res. 27 (11), 2343–2355. https://doi.org/10.1007/s11095-010-0068-z.

Lee, T.R., Choi, M., Kopacz, A.M., Yun, S.H., Liu, W.K., Decuzzi, P., 2013. On the near-wall accumulation of injectable particles in the microcirculation: Smaller is not better. Sci. Rep. 3. https://doi.org/10.1038/srep02079.

Lee, Y.W., Luther, D.C., Goswami, R., Jeon, T., Clark, V., Elia, J., Gopalakrishnan, S., Rotello, V.M., 2020. Direct cytosolic delivery of proteins through coengineering of proteins and polymeric delivery vehicles. J. Am. Chem. Soc. 142 (9), 4349–4355. https://doi.org/10.1021/jacs.9b12759.

Li, Y., Gu, N., 2010. Thermodynamics of charged nanoparticle adsorption on charge-neutral membranes: A simulation study. J. Phys. Chem. B 114 (8), 2749–2754. https://doi.org/10.1021/jp904550b.

Li, S.D., Huang, L., 2008 7. Pharmacokinetics and biodistribution of nanoparticles. Mol. Pharm. 5. https://doi.org/10.1021/mp800049w.

Li, Y., Kröger, M., Liu, W.K., 2015. Shape effect in cellular uptake of PEGylated nanoparticles: Comparison between sphere, rod, cube and disk. Nanoscale 7 (40), 16631–16646. https://doi.org/10.1039/c5nr02970h.

Lieleg, O., Baumgärtel, R.M., Bausch, A.R., 2009. Selective filtering of particles by the extracellular matrix: An electrostatic bandpass. Biophys. J. 97 (6), 1569–1577. https://doi.org/10.1016/j.bpj.2009.07.009.

Li, C., Wang, J., Wang, Y., Gao, H., Wei, G., Huang, Y., Yu, H., Gan, Y., Wang, Y., Mei, L., Chen, H., Hu, H., Zhang, Z., Jin, Y., 2019. Recent progress in drug delivery. Acta Pharm. Sin. B 9 (6), 1145–1162. https://doi.org/10.1016/j.apsb.2019.08.003.

Lipin, D.I., Chuan, Y.P., Lua, L.H.L., Middelberg, A.P.J., 2008. Encapsulation of DNA and non-viral protein changes the structure of murine polyomavirus virus-like particles. Arch. Virol. 153 (11), 2027–2039. https://doi.org/10.1007/s00705-008-0220-9.

Litzinger, D.C., Buiting, A.M.J., van Rooijen, N., Huang, L., 1994. Effect of liposome size on the circulation time and intraorgan distribution of amphipathic poly(ethylene glycol)-containing liposomes. BBA - Biomembranes 1190 (1), 99–107. https://doi.org/10.1016/0005-2736(94)90038-8.

Liu, J., Lee, H., Huesca, M., Young, A., Allen, C., 2006. Liposome formulation of a novel hydrophobic aryl-imidazole compound for anti-cancer therapy. Cancer Chemother. Pharmacol. 58 (3), 306–318. https://doi.org/10.1007/s00280-005-0161-x.

Liu, B., Ianosi-Irimie, M., Thayumanavan, S., 2019. Reversible click chemistry for ultrafast and quantitative formation of protein-polymer nanoassembly and intracellular protein delivery. ACS Nano 13 (8), 9408–9420. https://doi.org/10.1021/acsnano.9b04198.

Liu, L., Kevin Hitchens, T., Ye, Q., Wu, Y., Barbe, B., Prior, D.E., Li, W.F., Yeh, F.-C., Foley, L.M., Bain, D.J., Ho, C., 2013. Decreased reticuloendothelial system clearance and increased blood half-life and immune cell labeling for nano- and micron-sized superparamagnetic iron-oxide particles upon pre-treatment with Intralipid. Biochim. Biophys. Acta Gen. Subj. 1830 (6), 3447–3453. https://doi.org/10.1016/j.bbagen.2013.01.021.

Lobatto, M.E., Fuster, V., Fayad, Z.A., Mulder, W.J.M., 2011. Perspectives and opportunities for nanomedicine in the management of atherosclerosis. Nat. Rev. Drug Discov. 10 (11), 835–852. https://doi.org/10.1038/nrd3578.

Luis de Redín, I., Boiero, C., Martínez-Ohárriz, M.C., Agüeros, M., Ramos, R., Peñuelas, I., Allemandi, D., Llabot, J.M., Irache, J.M., 2018. Human serum albumin nanoparticles for ocular delivery of bevacizumab. Int. J. Pharm. 541 (1–2), 214–223. https://doi.org/10.1016/j.ijpharm.2018.02.003.

Lundqvist, M., Sethson, I., Jonsson, B.H., 2004. Protein adsorption onto silica nanoparticles: Conformational changes depend on the particles' curvature and the protein stability. Langmuir 20 (24), 10639–10647. https://doi.org/10.1021/la0484725.

Ma, Y., Zhao, Y., Kumar Bejjanki, N., Tang, X., Jiang, W., Dou, J., Khan, M.I.nullah, Wang, Q., Xia, J., Liu, H., You, Y.-Z., Zhang, G., Wang, Y., Wang, J., 2019. Nanoclustered cascaded enzymes for targeted tumor starvation and deoxygenation-activated chemotherapy without systemic toxicity. ACS Nano 13 (8), 8890–8902. https://doi.org/10.1021/acsnano.9b02466.

Maeda, H., Ueda, M., Morinaga, T., Matsumoto, T., 1985. Conjugation of poly(styrene-co-maleic acid) derivatives to the antitumor protein neocarzinostatin: pronounced improvements in pharmacological properties. J. Med. Chem. 28 (4), 455–461. https://doi.org/10.1021/jm00382a012.

Mahmoudi, M., Shokrgozar, M.A., Sardari, S., Moghadam, M.K., Vali, H., Laurent, S., Stroeve, P., 2011. Irreversible changes in protein conformation due to interaction with superparamagnetic iron oxide nanoparticles. Nanoscale 3 (3), 1127–1138. https://doi.org/10.1039/c0nr00733a.

Mascheroni, P., Schrefler, B.A., 2018. In silico models for nanomedicine: Recent developments. Curr. Med. Chem. 25 (34), 4192–4207. https://doi.org/10.2174/0929867324666170417120725.

Matsumura, Y., Maeda, H., 1986. A new concept for macromolecular therapeutics in cancer chemotherapy: mechanism of tumoritropic accumulation of proteins and the antitumor agent smancs. Cancer Res. 46 (8), 6387–6392.

Mehanna, M.M., Mneimneh, A.T., 2020. Updated but not outdated "Gliadin": a plant protein in advanced pharmaceutical nanotechnologies. Int. J. Pharm. 587.

Merkle, H.P., Speiser, P., 1973. Preparation and in vitro evaluation of cellulose acetate phthalate coacervate microcapsules. J. Pharmaceut. Sci. 62 (9), 1444–1448. https://doi.org/10.1002/jps.2600620910.

Michnik, A., Michalik, K., Drzazga, Z., 2005. Stability of bovine serum albumin at different pH. J. Ther. Anal. Calorim. 80 (2), 399–406. https://doi.org/10.1007/s10973-005-0667-9.

Miele, E., Spinelli, G.P., Miele, E., Tomao, F., Tomao, S., 2009. Albumin-bound formulation of paclitaxel (Abraxane® ABI-007) in the treatment of breast cancer. Int. J. Nanomed. 4 (1), 99–105.

Mirshahi, T., Irache, J.M., Nicolas, C., Mirshahi, M., Faure, J.P., Gueguen, J., Hecquet, C., Orecchioni, A.M., 2002. Adaptive immune responses of legumin nanoparticles. J. Drug Target. 10 (8), 625–631. https://doi.org/10.1080/1061186021000066237.

Molino, N.M., Wang, S.W., 2014. Caged protein nanoparticles for drug delivery. Curr. Opin. Biotechnol. 28, 75–82. https://doi.org/10.1016/j.copbio.2013.12.007.

Mukherjee, S., Chowdhury, D., Kotcherlakota, R., Patra, S., Vinothkumar, B., Bhadra, M.P., Sreedhar, B., Patra, C.R., 2014. Potential theranostics application of bio-synthesized silver nanoparticles (4-in-1 system). Theranostics 4 (3), 316–335. https://doi.org/10.7150/thno.7819.

Namiot, E.D., Sokolov, A.V., Chubarev, V.N., Tarasov, V.V., Schiöth, H.B., 2023. Nanoparticles in clinical trials: analysis of clinical trials, FDA approvals and use for COVID-19 vaccines. Int. J. Mol. Sci. 24 (1). https://doi.org/10.3390/ijms24010787.

Nie, S., 2010. Understanding and overcoming major barriers in cancer nanomedicine. Nanomedicine 5 (4), 523–528. https://doi.org/10.2217/nnm.10.23.

Nonthanum, P., Lee, Y., Padua, G.W., 2012. Effect of γ-zein on the rheological behavior of concentrated zein solutions. J. Agric. Food Chem. 60 (7), 1742–1747. https://doi.org/10.1021/jf2035302.

Nuñez-Rivera, A., Fournier, P.G.J., Arellano, D.L., Rodriguez-Hernandez, A.G., Vazquez-Duhalt, R., Cadena-Nava, R.D., 2020. Brome mosaic virus-like particles as siRNA nanocarriers for biomedical purposes. Beilstein J. Nanotechnol. 11, 372–382. https://doi.org/10.3762/bjnano.11.28.

Osidak, E.O., 2022. Corneal stroma regeneration with collagen-based hydrogel as an artificial stroma equivalent: A comprehensive in vivo study. Polymers 14 (19).

Owens, D.E., Peppas, N.A., 2006. Opsonization, biodistribution, and pharmacokinetics of polymeric nanoparticles. Int. J. Pharm. 307 (1), 93–102. https://doi.org/10.1016/j.ijpharm.2005.10.010.

Pace, C.N., Vajdos, F., Fee, L., Grimsley, G., Gray, T., 1995. How to measure and predict the molar absorption coefficient of a protein. Protein Sci. 4 (11), 2411–2423. https://doi.org/10.1002/pro.5560041120.

Paliwal, R., Palakurthi, S., 2014. Zein in controlled drug delivery and tissue engineering. J. Contr. Release 189, 108–122. https://doi.org/10.1016/j.jconrel.2014.06.036.

Papahadjopoulos, D., Allen, T.M., Gabizon, A., Mayhew, E., Matthay, K., Huang, S.K., Lee, K.D., Woodle, M.C., Lasic, D.D., Redemann, C., 1991. Sterically stabilized liposomes: improvements in pharmacokinetics and antitumor therapeutic efficacy. Proc. Natl. Acad. Sci. 88 (24), 11460–11464. https://doi.org/10.1073/pnas.88.24.11460.

Park, K., 2013. Facing the truth about nanotechnology in drug delivery. ACS Nano 7 (9), 7442–7447. https://doi.org/10.1021/nn404501g.

Park, K., 2014. Controlled drug delivery systems: Past forward and future back. J. Contr. Release 190, 3–8. https://doi.org/10.1016/j.jconrel.2014.03.054.

Park, J.H., Von Maltzahn, G., Zhang, L., Schwartz, M.P., Ruoslahti, E., Bhatia, S.N., Sailor, M.J., 2008. Magnetic iron oxide nanoworms for tumor targeting and imaging. Adv. Mater. 20 (9), 1630–1635. https://doi.org/10.1002/adma.200800004.

Patel, S., Datta, A., 2007. Steady state and time-resolved fluorescence investigation of the specific binding of two chlorin derivatives with human serum albumin. J. Phys. Chem. B 111 (35), 10557–10562. https://doi.org/10.1021/jp072544u.

Peer, D., Karp, J.M., Hong, S., Farokhzad, O.C., Margalit, R., Langer, R., 2007. Nanocarriers as an emerging platform for cancer therapy. Nat. Nanotechnol. 2 (12), 751–760. https://doi.org/10.1038/nnano.2007.387.

Peng, Z., Li, S., Han, X., Al-Youbi, A.O., Bashammakh, A.S., El-Shahawi, M.S., Leblanc, R.M., 2016. Determination of the composition, encapsulation efficiency and loading capacity in protein drug delivery systems using circular dichroism spectroscopy. Anal. Chim. Acta 937, 113–118. https://doi.org/10.1016/j.aca.2016.08.014.

Pereira, E.R., Kedrin, D., Seano, G., Gautier, O., Meijer, E.F.J., Jones, D., Chin, S.M., Kitahara, S., Bouta, E.M., Chang, J., Beech, E., Jeong, H.S., Carroll, M.C., Taghian, A.G., Padera, T.P., 2018. Lymph node metastases can invade local blood vessels, exit the node, and colonize distant organs in mice. Science 359 (6382), 1403–1407. https://doi.org/10.1126/science.aal3622.

Perrault, S.D., Walkey, C., Jennings, T., Fischer, H.C., Chan, W.C.W., 2009. Mediating tumor targeting efficiency of nanoparticles through design. Nano Lett. 9 (5), 1909–1915. https://doi.org/10.1021/nl900031yCanada.

Petros, R.A., Desimone, J.M., 2010. Strategies in the design of nanoparticles for therapeutic applications. Nat. Rev. Drug Discov. 9 (8), 615–627. https://doi.org/10.1038/nrd2591.

Pluen, A., Netti, P.A., Jain, R.K., Berk, D.A., 1999. Diffusion of macromolecules in agarose gels: comparison of linear and globular configurations. Biophys. J. 77 (1), 542–552. https://doi.org/10.1016/s0006-3495(99)76911-0.

Pluen, A., Boucher, Y., Ramanujan, S., McKee, T.D., Gohongi, T., di Tomaso, E., Brown, E.B., Izumi, Y., Campbell, R. B., Berk, D.A., Jain, R.K., 2001. Role of tumor–host interactions in interstitial diffusion of macromolecules: Cranial vs. subcutaneous tumors. Proc. Natl. Acad. Sci. 98 (8), 4628–4633. https://doi.org/10.1073/pnas.081626898.

Popović, Z., Liu, W., Chauhan, V.P., Lee, J., Wong, C., Greytak, A.B., Insin, N., Nocera, D.G., Fukumura, D., Jain, R. K., Bawendi, M.G., 2010. A nanoparticle size series for in vivo fluorescence imaging. Angew. Chem. Int. Ed. 49 (46), 8649–8652. https://doi.org/10.1002/anie.201003142.

Puzyn, T., Rasulev, B., Gajewicz, A., Hu, X., Dasari, T.P., Michalkova, A., Hwang, H.-M., Toropov, A., Leszczynska, D., Leszczynski, J., 2011. Using nano-QSAR to predict the cytotoxicity of metal oxide nanoparticles. Nat. Nanotechnol. 6 (3), 175–178. https://doi.org/10.1038/nnano.2011.10.

Rafat, M., Li, F., Fagerholm, P., Lagali, N.S., Watsky, M.A., Munger, R., Matsuura, T., Griffith, M., 2008. PEG-stabilized carbodiimide crosslinked collagen–chitosan hydrogels for corneal tissue engineering. Biomaterials 29 (29), 3960–3972. https://doi.org/10.1016/j.biomaterials.2008.06.017.

Ren, J., Nichols, C.E., Chamberlain, P.P., Weaver, K.L., Short, S.A., Chan, J.H., Kleim, J.-P., Stammers, D.K., 2007. Relationship of potency and resilience to drug resistant mutations for GW420867X revealed by crystal structures of inhibitor complexes for wild-type, Leu100Ile, Lys101Glu, and Tyr188Cys mutant HIV-1 reverse transcriptases. J. Med. Chem. 50 (10), 2301–2309. https://doi.org/10.1021/jm061117m.

Rodrigues, N.F., Van Tilburg Bernardes, E., Rocha, R.P., Da Costa, L.C.F., Coutinho, A.C.A., Dos Santos Muniz, M., Pereira, A.A.O.C., Da Silva, P.H.B., Malaquias, L.C.C., Coelho, L.F.L., 2013. Bovine serum albumin nanoparticle vaccine reduces lung pathology induced by live Pseudomonas aeruginosa infection in mice. Vaccine 31 (44), 5062–5066. https://doi.org/10.1016/j.vaccine.2013.08.078.

Rodriguez, P.L., Harada, T., Christian, D.A., Pantano, D.A., Tsai, R.K., Discher, D.E., 2013. Minimal "self" peptides that inhibit phagocytic clearance and enhance delivery of nanoparticles. Science 339 (6122), 971–975. https://doi.org/10.1126/science.1229568.

Roduner, E., 2006. Size matters: Why nanomaterials are different. Chem. Soc. Rev. 35 (7), 583–592. https://doi.org/10.1039/b502142c.

Rudolph, C., Plank, C., Lausier, J., Schillinger, U., Müller, R.H., Rosenecker, J., 2003. Oligomers of the arginine-rich motif of the HIV-1 TAT protein are capable of transferring plasmid DNA into cells. J. Biol. Chem. 278 (13), 11411–11418. https://doi.org/10.1074/jbc.m211891200.

Salvador-Morales, C., Zhang, L., Langer, R., Farokhzad, O.C., 2009. Immunocompatibility properties of lipid–polymer hybrid nanoparticles with heterogeneous surface functional groups. Biomaterials 30 (12), 2231–2240. https://doi.org/10.1016/j.biomaterials.2009.01.005.

Saleh, T., Soudi, T., Shojaosadati, S.A., 2019. Aptamer functionalized curcumin-loaded human serum albumin (HSA) nanoparticles for targeted delivery to HER-2 positive breast cancer cells. Int. J. Biol. Macromol. 130, 109–116. https://doi.org/10.1016/j.ijbiomac.2019.02.129.

Samal, S.K., Dash, M., Dubruel, P., Van Vlierberghe, S., 2014. Smart polymer hydrogels: Properties, synthesis and applications smart polymers and their applications. Elsevier Ltd, Belgium, pp. 237–270. https://doi.org/10.1533/9780857097026.1.237.

Sanchez-Sanchez, l., 2015. Design of a VLP-nanovehicle for CYP450 enzymatic activity delivery. J. Nanobiotechnology 13.

Sánchez-Sánchez, L., Cadena-Nava, R.D., Palomares, L.A., Ruiz-Garcia, J., Koay, M.S.T., Cornelissen, J.J.M.T., Vazquez-Duhalt, R., 2014. Chemotherapy pro-drug activation by biocatalytic virus-like nanoparticles containing cytochrome P450. Enzym. Microb. Technol. 60, 24–31. https://doi.org/10.1016/j.enzmictec.2014.04.003.

Schaefer, J., Schulze, C., Marxer, E.E.J., Ulrich, F.S., Wohlleben, W., Bakowsky, U., Lehr, C.-M., 2012. Atomic force microscopy and analytical ultracentrifugation for probing nanomaterial protein interactions. ACS Nano 6 (6), 4603–4614. https://doi.org/10.1021/nn202657q.

Scheffel, U., Rhodes, B.A., Natarajan, T.K., Wagner, H.N., 1972. Albumin microspheres for study of the reticuloendothelial system. J. Nucl. Med. 13 (7), 498–503.

Selivanovitch, E., LaFrance, B., Douglas, T., 2021. Molecular exclusion limits for diffusion across a porous capsid. Nat. Commun. 12 (1). https://doi.org/10.1038/s41467-021-23200-1.

Senapati, S., Kumar Mahanta, A., Kumar, S., Maiti, P., 2018. Controlled drug delivery vehicles for cancer treatment and their performance. Signal Transduct. Targeted Ther. 3 (1). https://doi.org/10.1038/s41392-017-0004-3.

Shah, S., Liu, Y., Hu, W., Gao, J., 2011. Modeling particle shape-dependent dynamics in nanomedicine. J. Nanosci. Nanotechnol. 11 (2), 919–928. https://doi.org/10.1166/jnn.2011.3536.

Sharma, M., 2019. Transdermal and Intravenous nano drug delivery systems. Elsevier BV, pp. 499–550. https://doi.org/10.1016/b978-0-12-814029-1.00018-1.

Shi, Y., 2020. Clinical translation of nanomedicine and biomaterials for cancer immunotherapy: Progress and perspectives. Adv. Therapeut. 3 (9).

Shimizu, T., Ichihara, M., Yoshioka, Y., Ishida, T., Nakagawa, S., Kiwada, H., 2012. Intravenous administration of polyethylene glycol-coated (PEGylated) proteins and PEGylated adenovirus elicits an anti-PEG immunoglobulin M response. Biol. Pharm. Bull. 35 (8), 1336–1342. https://doi.org/10.1248/bpb.b12-00276.

Singh, R., Pantarotto, D., Lacerda, L., Pastorin, G., Klumpp, C., Prato, M., Bianco, A., Kostarelos, K., 2006. Tissue biodistribution and blood clearance rates of intravenously administered carbon nanotube radiotracers. Proc. Natl. Acad. Sci. 103 (9), 3357–3362. https://doi.org/10.1073/pnas.0509009103.

Soltani, M., Chen, P., Androulakis, I.P., 2011. Numerical modeling of fluid flow in solid tumors. PLoS One 6 (6), e20344. https://doi.org/10.1371/journal.pone.0020344.

Sousa, F.F.O., 2012. Asteria luzardo-álvarez, josé blanco-méndez, manuel martín-pastor, NMR techniques in drug delivery: Application to zein protein complexes. Int. J. Pharm. 439 (1–2), 41–48. https://doi.org/10.1016/j.ijpharm.2012.09.046.

Stayton, P.S., Drobny, G.P., Shaw, W.J., Long, J.R., Gilbert, M., 2003. Molecular recognition at the protein-hydroxyapatite interface. Crit. Rev. Oral Biol. Med. 14 (5), 370–376. https://doi.org/10.1177/154411130301400507.

Steiert, E., Ewald, J., Wagner, A., Hellmich, U.A., Frey, H., Wich, P.R., 2020. pH-Responsive protein nanoparticles via conjugation of degradable PEG to the surface of cytochrome c. Polym. Chem. 11 (2), 551–559. https://doi.org/10.1039/c9py01162e.

Stirland, D.L., Nichols, J.W., Miura, S., Bae, Y.H., 2013. Mind the gap: A survey of how cancer drug carriers are susceptible to the gap between research and practice. J. Contr. Release 172 (3), 1045–1064. https://doi.org/10.1016/j.jconrel.2013.09.026.

Stylianopoulos, T., 2013. EPR-Effect: Utilizing size-dependent nanoparticle delivery to solid tumors. Ther. Deliv. 4 (4), 421–423. https://doi.org/10.4155/tde.13.8.

Stylianopoulos, T., Munn, L.L., Jain, R.K., 2018. Reengineering the physical microenvironment of tumors to improve drug delivery and efficacy: from mathematical modeling to bench to bedside. Trends Cancer 4 (4), 292–319. https://doi.org/10.1016/j.trecan.2018.02.005.

Stylianopoulos, T., Jain, R.K., 2015. Design considerations for nanotherapeutics in oncology. Nanomed. Nanotechnol. Biol. Med. 11 (8), 1893–1907. https://doi.org/10.1016/j.nano.2015.07.015.

Stylianopoulos, T., Diop-Frimpong, B., Munn, L.L., Jain, R.K., 2010. Diffusion anisotropy in collagen gels and tumors: the effect of fiber network orientation. Biophys. J. 99 (10), 3119–3128. https://doi.org/10.1016/j.bpj.2010.08.065.

Stylianopoulos, T., Soteriou, K., Dai, F., Jain, R.K., 2013. Cationic nanoparticles have superior transvascular flux into solid tumors: Insights from a mathematical model. Ann. Biomed. Eng. 41 (1), 68–77. https://doi.org/10.1007/s10439-012-0630-4.

Sudlow, G., Birkett, D.J., Wade, D.N., 1975. The characterization of two specific drug binding sites on human serum albumin. Mol. Pharmacol. 11 (6), 824–832.

Sun, T., Zhang, Y.S., Pang, B., Hyun, D.C., Yang, M., Xia, Y., 2014. Engineered nanoparticles for drug delivery in cancer therapy. Angew. Chem. Int. Ed. 53 (46), 12320–12364. https://doi.org/10.1002/anie.201403036.

Sun, X., Yan, X., Jacobson, O., Sun, W., Wang, Z., Tong, X., Xia, Y., Ling, D., Chen, X., 2017. Improved tumor uptake by optimizing liposome based RES blockade strategy. Theranostics 7 (2), 319–328. https://doi.org/10.7150/thno.18078.

Tang, J., Li, L., Howard, C.B., Mahler, S.M., Huang, L., Xu, Z.P., 2015. Preparation of optimized lipid-coated calcium phosphate nanoparticles for enhanced in vitro gene delivery to breast cancer cells. J. Mater. Chem. B 3 (33), 6805–6812. https://doi.org/10.1039/C5TB00912J.

Tao, L., Hu, W., Liu, Y., Huang, G., Sumer, B.D., Gao, J., 2011. Shape-specific polymeric nanomedicine: emerging opportunities and challenges. Exp. Biol. Med. 236 (1), 20–29. https://doi.org/10.1258/ebm.2010.010243.

Tantra, R., Tompkins, J., Quincey, P., 2010. Characterisation of the de-agglomeration effects of bovine serum albumin on nanoparticles in aqueous suspension. Colloids Surf. B Biointerfaces 75 (1), 275–281. https://doi.org/10.1016/j.colsurfb.2009.08.049.

Tarhini, M., Greige-Gerges, H., Elaissari, A., 2017. Protein-based nanoparticles: from preparation to encapsulation of active molecules. Int. J. Pharm. 522 (1–2), 172–197. https://doi.org/10.1016/j.ijpharm.2017.01.067.

Tavanti, F., Pedone, A., Menziani, M.C., 2019. Multiscale molecular dynamics simulation of multiple protein adsorption on gold nanoparticles. Int. J. Mol. Sci. 20 (14). https://doi.org/10.3390/ijms20143539.

Thrane, S., Janitzek, C.M., Agerbæk, M.Ø., Ditlev, S.B., Resende, M., Nielsen, M.A., Theander, T.G., Ali, S., Sander, A.F., Tsuboi, T., 2015. A novel virus-like particle based vaccine platform displaying the placental malaria antigen VAR2CSA. PLoS One 10 (11), e0143071. https://doi.org/10.1371/journal.pone.0143071.

Tomasini, L., Ferrere, M., Nicolas, J., 2024. Subcutaneous drug delivery from nanoscale systems. Nat. Rev. Bioeng. 2 (6), 501–520. https://doi.org/10.1038/s44222-024-00161-w.

Tong, X., Pan, W., Su, T., Zhang, M., Dong, W., Qi, X., 2020. Recent advances in natural polymer-based drug delivery systems. React. Funct. Polym. 148, 104501. https://doi.org/10.1016/j.reactfunctpolym.2020.104501.

Trac, N., Chung, E.J., 2021. Overcoming physiological barriers by nanoparticles for intravenous drug delivery to the lymph nodes. Exp. Biol. Med. 246 (22), 2358–2371. https://doi.org/10.1177/15353702211010762.

Uhrich, K.E., Cannizzaro, S.M., Langer, R.S., Shakesheff, K.M., 1999. Polymeric systems for controlled drug release. Chem. Rev. 99 (11), 3181–3198. https://doi.org/10.1021/cr940351u.

Umamaheshwari, R.B., Ramteke, S., Jain, N.K., 2004. Anti-Helicobacter pylori effect of mucoadhesive nanoparticles bearing amoxicillin in experimental gerbils model. AAPS PharmSciTech 5 (2). http://www.aapspharmscitech.org/view.asp?art=pt.050232&pdf=yes.

Urade, R., Sato, N., Sugiyama, M., 2018. Gliadins from wheat grain: an overview, from primary structure to nanostructures of aggregates. Biophy. Rev. 10 (2), 435–443. https://doi.org/10.1007/s12551-017-0367-2.

Varanko, A., Saha, S., Chilkoti, A., 2020. Recent trends in protein and peptide-based biomaterials for advanced drug delivery. Adv. Drug Deliv. Rev. 156, 133–187. https://doi.org/10.1016/j.addr.2020.08.008.

Verma, I.M., Weitzman, M.D., 2005. Gene therapy: Twenty-first century medicine. Annu. Rev. Biochem. 74, 711–738. https://doi.org/10.1146/annurev.biochem.74.050304.091637.

Verma, D., Gulati, N., Kaul, S., Mukherjee, S., Nagaich, U., 2018. Protein based nanostructures for drug delivery. J. Pharm. 2018, 1–18. https://doi.org/10.1155/2018/9285854.

Verma, M.L., Dhanya, B.S., Sukriti, Rani, V., Thakur, M., Jeslin, J., Kushwaha, R., 2020. Carbohydrate and protein based biopolymeric nanoparticles: Current status and biotechnological applications. Int. J. Biol. Macromol. 154, 390–412. https://doi.org/10.1016/j.ijbiomac.2020.03.105.

Walkey, C.D., Olsen, J.B., Song, F., Liu, R., Guo, H., Olsen, D.W.H., Cohen, Y., Emili, A., Chan, W.C.W., 2014. Protein corona fingerprinting predicts the cellular interaction of gold and silver nanoparticles. ACS Nano 8 (3), 2439–2455. https://doi.org/10.1021/nn406018q.

Wang, H., Shang, L., Maffre, P., Hohmann, S., Kirschhöfer, F., Brenner-Weiß, G., Ulrich Nienhaus, G., 2016. The nature of a hard protein corona forming on quantum dots exposed to human blood serum. Small 12 (42), 5836–5844. https://doi.org/10.1002/smll.201602283.

Wang, Y., Li, M., Xu, X., Tang, W., Xiong, L., Sun, Q., 2019. Formation of protein corona on nanoparticles with digestive enzymes in simulated gastrointestinal fluids. J. Agric. Food Chem. 67 (8), 2296–2306. https://doi.org/10.1021/acs.jafc.8b05702.

Wang, Z., Zhi, K., Ding, Z., Sun, Y., Li, S., Li, M., Pu, K., Zou, J., 2021. Emergence in protein derived nanomedicine as anticancer therapeutics: More than a tour de force. Semin. Cancer Biol. 69, 77–90. https://doi.org/10.1016/j.semcancer.2019.11.012.

Weissig, V., Pettinger, T.K., Murdock, N., 2014. Nanopharmaceuticals (part 1): products on the market. Int. J. Nanomed. 9, 4357–4373. https://doi.org/10.2147/IJN.S46900.

Wilhelm, S., 2016. Analysis of nanoparticle delivery to tumours. Nat. Rev. Mater. 1 (5).

Wu, W., Kong, X., Zhang, C., Hua, Y., Chen, Y., 2018. Improving the stability of wheat gliadin nanoparticles – effect of gum Arabic addition. Food Hydrocoll. 80, 78–87. https://doi.org/10.1016/j.foodhyd.2018.01.042.

Xiao, C., Ding, J., Ma, L., Yang, C., Zhuang, X., Chen, X., 2015. Synthesis of thermal and oxidation dual responsive polymers for reactive oxygen species (ROS)-triggered drug release. Polym. Chem. 6 (5), 738–747. https://doi.org/10.1039/C4PY01156B.

Xia, Y., Tang, S., Olsen, B.D., 2013. Site-specific conjugation of RAFT polymers to proteins via expressed protein ligation. Chem. Commun. 49 (25), 2566–2568. https://doi.org/10.1039/c3cc38976f.

Xu, L., Jiang, S., Wu, J., Zou, Q., 2021. An in silico approach to identification, categorization and prediction of nucleic acid binding proteins. Briefings Bioinf. 22 (3). https://doi.org/10.1093/bib/bbaa171.

Yamato, M., Konno, C., Koike, S., Isoi, Y., Shimizu, T., Kikuchi, A., Makino, K., Okano, T., 2003. Nanofabrication for micropatterned cell arrays by combining electron beam-irradiated polymer grafting and localized laser ablation. J. Biomed. Mater. Res. - Part A 67. https://doi.org/10.1002/jbm.a.10078.

Yang, K., Ma, Y.Q., 2010. Computer simulation of the translocation of nanoparticles with different shapes across a lipid bilayer. Nat. Nanotechnol. 5 (8), 579–583. https://doi.org/10.1038/nnano.2010.141.

Yi, X., Gao, H., 2017. Kinetics of receptor-mediated endocytosis of elastic nanoparticles. Nanoscale 9 (1), 454–463. https://doi.org/10.1039/c6nr07179a.

Yoo, J.W., Chambers, E., Mitragotri, S., 2010. Factors that control the circulation time of nanoparticles in blood: Challenges, solutions and future prospects. Curr. Pharm. Des. 16 (21), 2298–2307. https://doi.org/10.2174/138161210791920496.

Yu, M.K., Park, J., Jon, S., 2012a. Magnetic nanoparticles and their applications in image-guided drug delivery. Drug Deliv. Transl. Res. 2 (1), 3–21. https://doi.org/10.1007/s13346-011-0049-8.

Yu, M.K., Park, J., Jon, S., 2012b. Targeting strategies for multifunctional nanoparticles in cancer imaging and therapy. Theranostics 2 (1), 3–44. https://doi.org/10.7150/thno.3463.

Zamboni, W.C., Torchilin, V., Patri, A.K., Hrkach, J., Stern, S., Lee, R., Nel, A., Panaro, N.J., Grodzinski, P., 2012. Best practices in cancer nanotechnology: perspective from NCI nanotechnology alliance. Clin. Cancer Res. 18 (12), 3229–3241. https://doi.org/10.1158/1078-0432.CCR-11-2938.

Zanganeh, S., Spitler, R., Erfanzadeh, M., Alkilany, A.M., Mahmoudi, M., 2016. Protein corona: Opportunities and challenges. Int. J. Biochem. Cell Biol. 75, 143–147. https://doi.org/10.1016/j.biocel.2016.01.005.

Zein, R., Sharrouf, W., Selting, K., 2020. Physical properties of nanoparticles that result in improved cancer targeting. J. Oncol. 2020. https://doi.org/10.1155/2020/5194780.

Zhang, X., He, Q., Cui, Y., Duan, L., Li, J., 2006. Human serum albumin supported lipid patterns for the targeted recognition of microspheres coated by membrane based on ss-DNA hybridization. Biochem. Biophys. Res. Commun. 349 (3), 920–924. https://doi.org/10.1016/j.bbrc.2006.08.157.

Zhang, H., Ji, Q., Huang, C., Zhang, S., Yuan, B., Yang, K., Ma, Y.Q., 2015. Cooperative transmembrane penetration of nanoparticles. Sci. Rep. 5. https://doi.org/10.1038/srep10525.

Zhou, Z., Ma, X., Jin, E., Tang, J., Sui, M., Shen, Y., Van Kirk, E.A., Murdoch, W.J., Radosz, M., 2013. Linear-dendritic drug conjugates forming long-circulating nanorods for cancer-drug delivery. Biomaterials 34 (22), 5722–5735. https://doi.org/10.1016/j.biomaterials.2013.04.012.

Zong, C., Xu, M., Xu, L.-J., Ting, W., Ma, X., Zheng, X.-S., Hu, R., Ren, B., 2018. Surface-enhanced Raman spectroscopy for bioanalysis: Reliability and challenges. Chem. Rev. 118 (10), 4946–4980. https://doi.org/10.1021/acs.chemrev.7b00668.

Zou, Q., Xing, P., Wei, L., Liu, B., 2019. Gene2vec: Gene subsequence embedding for prediction of mammalian N 6 -methyladenosine sites from mRNA. RNA 25 (2), 205–218. https://doi.org/10.1261/rna.069112.118.

# Further reading

Jacob, B., Belton, P., Venema, P., Linden, E.van der, de Vries, R., Qi, S., 2016. Controlled release from zein matrices: Interplay of drug hydrophobicity and pH. Pharm. Res. 33 (3), 673–685. https://doi.org/10.1007/s11095-015-1818-8.

Qiang, F., Sun, J., Zhang, W., Sui, X., Yan, Z., He, Z., 2009. Nanoparticle albumin - bound (NAB) technology is a promising method for anti-cancer drug delivery. Recent Pat. Anticancer Drug Discov. 4 (3), 262–272. https://doi.org/10.2174/157489209789206869.

Shang, L., Zou, R., Tu, Y., Wu, J., Landry, M.P., 2017. Cholesterol-directed nanoparticle assemblies based on single amino acid peptide mutations activate cellular uptake and decrease tumor volume. Chem. Sci. 8 (11), 7552–7559. https://doi.org/10.1039/C7SC02616A.

Ying, L., Lian, Y., Zhang, L.T., Aldousari, S.M., Hedia, H.S., Asiri, S.A., Liu, W.K., 2016. Cell and nanoparticle transport in tumour microvasculature: the role of size, shape and surface functionality of nanoparticles. Interface Focus 6 (1), 20150086. https://doi.org/10.1098/rsfs.2015.0086.

CHAPTER

# 4

# Methods of preparation, characterization parameters, and pharmaceutical application for protein based nanoparticles

*Sara Yazdani*[1], *Gholamreza Pazuki*[1], *Mehrdad Mozaffarian*[1] *and Naghmeh Hadidi*[2]

[1]Department of Chemical Engineering, Amirkabir University of Technology, Tehran, Iran;
[2]Department of Clinical Research and EM Microscope, Pasteur Institute of Iran (PII), Tehran, Iran

## 1. Introduction

Protein-based nanoparticles (PBNPs) are nanoscale particles composed of proteins or protein complexes, which have gained significant attention in the pharmaceutical field due to their unique properties and versatile applications. These nanoparticles are defined by their biocompatibility, biodegradability, and ability to interact specifically with biological systems, making them ideal carriers for drug delivery (DeFrates et al., 2018). Unlike synthetic polymers or inorganic nanoparticles, PBNPs offer the advantage of being derived from natural sources, which reduces the risk of toxicity and immunogenicity. Their size, typically ranging from 10 to 1000 nm, allows them to navigate biological barriers and deliver therapeutic agents directly to targeted sites with high precision (Ding et al., 2021). The significance of PBNPs in pharmaceuticals lies in their potential to improve the efficacy and safety of treatments by enabling controlled release, targeted delivery, and enhanced stability of encapsulated drugs. As a result, they are being increasingly explored for a wide range of applications, including cancer therapy, vaccine delivery, and treatment of chronic diseases, thereby positioning them as a promising platform for next-generation therapeutics (Elzoghby, Samy and Elgindy, 2012b; Nagarajan et al., 2019).

*Protein-Based Nanoparticles in Drug Delivery*
https://doi.org/10.1016/B978-0-443-33639-3.00006-4

The development of PBNPs has evolved over several decades, with roots tracing back to early explorations of biocompatible materials for drug delivery (Aljabali et al., 2022). Initially, the focus was on using natural proteins, such as albumin and gelatin, for encapsulating and delivering therapeutic agents, capitalizing on their inherent biocompatibility and availability (Kuna et al., 2024). In the 1970s and 1980s, the concept of using proteins as carriers gained momentum as researchers began to recognize the advantages of protein nanoparticles, such as their ability to be metabolized and their functional versatility (Pandey and Balekar, 2018; Gouveia et al., 2023). Advancements in biotechnology and nanotechnology in the 1990s further accelerated the development of PBNPs (Lee et al., 2000; Smith, 1998). Techniques such as desolvation, coacervation, and self-assembly were refined, allowing for more precise control over particle size, shape, and surface properties (Wang et al., 2022; Tong et al., 2012). The introduction of recombinant protein technology enabled the production of engineered proteins with tailored properties, expanding the potential applications of PBNPs (Diaz et al., 2018). In recent years, the field has witnessed significant progress with the advent of targeted drug delivery systems and personalized medicine, where protein nanoparticles are designed to deliver drugs with high specificity to disease sites, minimizing side effects. The historical development of PBNPs reflects a growing understanding of their potential to revolutionize drug delivery, leading to their current prominence in pharmaceutical research and clinical applications (Aljabali et al., 2022; Mitchell et al., 2021).

PBNPs have emerged as a critical innovation in drug delivery and therapeutic applications, offering several advantages over other nanoparticle systems. Some of the primary advantages lie in their biocompatibility and biodegradability characteristics, which significantly reduce the risk of adverse reactions compared to synthetic nanoparticles (Wang and Uludag, 2008). Proteins, being natural biological molecules, are less likely to provoke immune responses and can be metabolized by the body, minimizing long-term toxicity (Matteis, 2017). Additionally, the versatility of protein structures allows for the precise engineering of nanoparticles with specific functional groups that enhance targeting capabilities, drug loading efficiency, and controlled release profiles (Li and Champion, 2022). Unlike other systems, PBNPs can be designed to respond to various physiological triggers, such as pH or temperature changes, enabling site-specific drug delivery that improves therapeutic outcomes while reducing off-target effects. Their ability to carry both hydrophilic and hydrophobic drugs, as well as bio-macromolecules such as nucleic acids, distinguishes them further as a superior choice for a wide range of therapeutic applications (Lin et al., 2023; Jain et al., 2018).

Current trends in the development of PBNPs are increasingly focused on personalized medicine and precision therapeutics. Advances in protein engineering and nanotechnology are enabling the creation of nanoparticles tailored to individual patient's needs, with specific targeting moieties that can recognize and bind to disease markers at the molecular level (Petros and Desimone, 2010). This precision enhances the efficacy of treatments, particularly in challenging areas such as cancer therapy, where targeted delivery to tumor cells is crucial, while sparing healthy tissues. Additionally, the integration of PBNPs with other nanomaterials, such as lipids or polymers, is leading to the development of hybrid systems that combine the strengths of multiple approaches for enhanced therapeutic performances (Hong et al., 2020).

Looking ahead, the future prospects for PBNPs are promising, with ongoing research exploring their applications in gene therapy, immunotherapy, and regenerative medicine. The potential to deliver complex therapies, such as CRISPR-based gene editing tools, or to modulate immune responses in diseases such as cancer and autoimmune disorders, should position PBNPs at the forefront of next-generation therapeutics (Jacob et al., 2022).

## 2. Methods of preparation

See Fig. 4.1.

### 2.1 Desolvation method

The desolvation method is a widely used technique for the preparation of PBNPs and is valued particularly for its simplicity and effectiveness in producing stable particles (Hong et al., 2020). This method involves the gradual addition of a desolvating agent such as ethanol or acetone to a protein solution, leading to the reduction of the protein's solubility (Etorki et al., 2016). As the solubility decreases, the protein's molecules aggregate to form nanoparticles. Typically, the process begins with the dissolution of a given protein, such as albumin or gelatin, in an aqueous buffer medium at an appropriate pH. The desolvating agent is then added dropwise under constant stirring, which induces controlled aggregation of the protein's molecules. To stabilize the formed nanoparticles, cross-linking agents such as glutaraldehyde are often introduced, which covalently bond the protein molecules, enhancing the structural integrity of nanoparticles (Weber et al., 2000; Jahanban-Esfahlan et al., 2016). Optimization of the desolvation process is critical for achieving the desired nanoparticle characteristics, such as size, shape, and surface charge. Key parameters that influence the outcome include concentration of the protein solution, rate of desolvating agent addition, type and concentration of cross-linking agent, pH, and ionic strength of the solution. Fine-tuning these parameters allows for precise control over nanoparticle size, typically ranging from 50 to 300 nm, which is crucial for their functionality in drug delivery applications. For instance, a slower rate of desolvation agent addition tends to produce smaller and more uniform nanoparticles, while the choice of a cross-linker and its concentration can significantly affect surface properties and stability of PBNPs for various therapeutic applications. One of the primary applications of PBNPs is in drug delivery, where nanoparticles

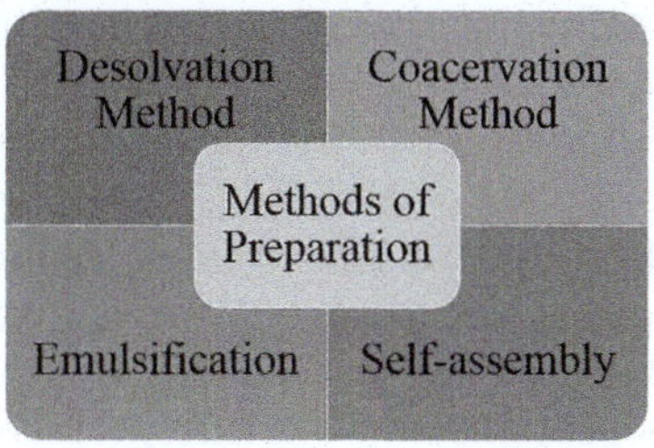


**FIGURE 4.1** Four different methods for preparing the PBNPs.

serve as carriers for a range of therapeutic agents, including small molecules, peptides, and nucleic acids. This method is particularly advantageous in the formulation of nanoparticles for anticancer drug delivery, where precision in targeting and drug release kinetics is essential. Additionally, desolvation-based nanoparticles have been explored for vaccine delivery, where their ability to present antigens in a controlled manner can enhance immune responses. Overall, the desolvation method remains a cornerstone in the production of PBNPs, offering versatility and efficiency in the preparation of nanoparticles for diverse pharmaceutical applications (Wang and Uludag, 2008).

## 2.2 Coacervation method

The coacervation method is another prominent technique used for the preparation of PBNPs and is particularly valued for its ability to encapsulate bioactive compounds with high efficiency (Dissanayake and Bandara, 2024). The process, typically induced by changes in pH, temperature, or the addition of a nonsolvent, involves the phase separation of a colloidal dispersion into two liquid phases: a coacervate-rich phase containing the protein and a coacervate-poor phase (Rane et al., 2013). The basic principle of coacervation relies on the self-assembly of protein molecules, driven by electrostatic interactions, hydrophobic forces, and van der Waals interactions (Pathak et al., 2017). In a typical process, a protein such as gelatin or albumin is dissolved in an aqueous solution, and the conditions are adjusted to promote coacervation, usually by adding a desolvating agent or changing the pH. The protein molecules then aggregate into dense, coacervate droplets, which can be stabilized by cross-linking agents such as glutaraldehyde or by adjusting the ionic strength of the solution. These droplets are then solidified into nanoparticles, which can encapsulate drugs or other bioactive molecules during the coacervation process (Tarhini et al., 2017; Davidov-Pardo et al., 2015).

Several variables affect particle formation in the coacervation method, including concentration and type of protein, pH and ionic strength of the solution, temperature, and the type and concentration of desolvating or cross-linking agents (Eghbal and Choudhary, 2018). For example, the pH of the solution plays a crucial role in determining the charge of protein molecules, which in turn influences the coacervation process. A pH close to the isoelectric point of the protein typically enhances coacervation by reducing the electrostatic repulsion between protein molecules, leading to more efficient aggregation (Comert et al., 2016). Similarly, the ionic strength of the solution can modulate the coacervation process by screening electrostatic interactions, thereby affecting the size and uniformity of nanoparticles (Liu et al., 2022). Temperature is another critical factor, as it can influence the phase separation kinetics and the stability of the formed nanoparticles. Additionally, the rate of addition and concentration of the cross-linking agent can determine the degree of cross-linking, which impacts the mechanical stability and drug release properties of nanoparticles (Alavarse et al., 2022; Martínez-López et al., 2020).

The coacervation method offers several advantages, including the ability to encapsulate a wide range of therapeutic agents, high encapsulation efficiency, and the potential for controlled release of encapsulated drug. It is particularly advantageous for encapsulating hydrophilic molecules, such as proteins and peptides, which can be challenging to encapsulate using other methods (Ban and Kim, 2022). Additionally, coacervation allows for the formation of nanoparticles with tunable size and surface characteristics, making it suitable for targeted drug delivery applications. However, the method also has limitations, such as the potential for protein denaturation during the process, which can affect the bioactivity of the encapsulated therapeutic agent. Furthermore, the application of cross-linking agents such as glutaraldehyde, while essential for stabilizing the nanoparticles, can introduce toxicity issues that require to be thoroughly resolved. Despite these challenges, the coacervation method remains a versatile and effective approach for the preparation of PBNPs, particularly in applications requiring high encapsulation efficiency and precise control over nanoparticle properties (Jiang et al., 2023; Forenzo and Larsen, 2023; Rosales and Fabi, 2023).

## 2.3 Emulsification

Emulsification is a widely utilized method for the preparation of PBNPs and is particularly recognized for its ability to produce nanoparticles with controlled size and morphology (Jiménez-Cruz et al., 2015; Saif et al., 2023). The emulsification process involves dispersing a protein solution in an immiscible organic phase, typically oil, to form an emulsion. This emulsion is then stabilized using surfactants or emulsifiers, which prevent the coalescence of droplets. Following emulsification, the organic solvent is evaporated or extracted, leading to the formation of solid protein nanoparticles as the dispersed phase solidifies (López-Montilla et al., 2002; Angardi et al., 2022). This method is particularly effective for encapsulating hydrophobic drugs within protein nanoparticles, offering a protective environment that enhances drug stability and bioavailability (Ye and Chi, 2018).

There are two primary types of emulsification techniques: single emulsion and double emulsion (Ding et al., 2019). The single emulsion technique involves the dispersion of an aqueous protein solution into an organic phase, resulting in water-in-oil (W/O) emulsion. This method is straightforward and is often used for the encapsulation of hydrophobic drugs. On the other hand, the double emulsion technique is a more complex process that involves the formation of a water-in-oil-in-water (W/O/W) emulsion. In this technique, an aqueous protein solution containing the drug is first emulsified in an organic solvent to create the primary W/O emulsion. This primary emulsion is then re-emulsified in a second aqueous phase, resulting in the W/O/W double emulsion (Windhab et al., 2005; Pradhan and Rousseau, 2012). The double emulsification technique is particularly advantageous for encapsulating hydrophilic drugs or biomolecules that are otherwise difficult to encapsulate in single emulsion systems (Ding et al., 2019).

Several factors influence the particle size and stability of the nanoparticles produced via emulsification (Guttoff et al., 2015). The concentration and type of surfactant or emulsifier are critical, as they stabilize the emulsion droplets and prevent them from coalescing, directly impacting the uniformity and size of nanoparticles (Ravera et al., 2021). The ratio of aqueous to organic phases also plays a significant role; a higher ratio typically results in smaller droplets, and consequently, smaller nanoparticles. Additionally, the method and energy input used for emulsification, such as ultrasonication or high-speed homogenization, can significantly affect the size distribution of the particles. Higher energy input generally leads to smaller and more uniform nanoparticles (Ravera et al., 2021). Furthermore, the rate of solvent evaporation or extraction can influence the final size and stability of nanoparticles, as rapid solvent removal may lead to the formation of smaller, more stable particles. Temperature, pH, and ionic strength of the aqueous phase are also important factors that can affect the stability and morphology of the resulting nanoparticles. By carefully optimizing these variables, the emulsification method can produce PBNPs with tailored properties for a wide range of pharmaceutical applications (Naik et al., 2012; Xingang Wang et al., 2020b).

## 2.4 Self-assembly

Self-assembly is a sophisticated and efficient method for the preparation of PBNPs, leveraging the natural tendency of proteins to organize into well-defined nanostructures under specific conditions (Zottig et al., 2020; Thiruvengadathan et al., 2013). The mechanism of self-assembly is driven by noncovalent interactions, including hydrogen bonding, hydrophobic interactions, electrostatic forces, and van der Waals interactions, which guide the spontaneous organization of protein molecules into nanoparticles (Yadav et al., 2020; Grzelczak et al., 2019). This process is highly dependent on the inherent properties of the protein, such as its amino acid sequence and tertiary structure, which determine the nature and strength of these interactions. During self-assembly, proteins can form into various nanostructures, including micelles, nanospheres, and fibrils, depending on the environmental conditions, such as pH, temperature, ionic strength, and solvent composition. The process can be triggered or enhanced by external stimuli, such as changes in pH or temperature, making it a versatile method for nanoparticle preparation (Yadav et al., 2020; Tomadoni et al., 2020).

Designing a self-assembly system is centered on selecting the appropriate protein and controlling the environmental conditions to achieve the desired nanoparticle characteristics. The choice of protein is crucial, as it must possess the ability to self-assemble under specific conditions while maintaining the functional integrity of the encapsulated drug (Hosseinkhani et al., 2013). Engineering the protein structure through genetic modification or chemical conjugation can enhance its self-assembly properties or introduce functionalities that improve loading, targeting, or release of drugs (Stevens et al., 2021). Additionally, protein concentration and rate of assembly can be controlled to fine-tune the size, shape, and stability of nanoparticles. For instance, lower protein concentrations may lead to the formation of smaller nanoparticles, while higher concentrations can result in larger aggregates. The incorporation of other materials, such as polymers or lipids, can also be considered to create hybrid nanoparticles with enhanced performance characteristics (Parveen et al., 2017).

Several case studies have demonstrated the successful application of self-assembly in the creation of PBNPs for drug delivery (Kaltbeitzel and Wich, 2023; Ferrer-Miralles et al., 2015). For example, self-assembled nanoparticles from elastin-like polypeptides have been designed to respond to temperature changes, allowing for targeted delivery of chemotherapeutic agents to tumors with minimal off-target effects (Macewan and Chilkoti, 2014). Another example is the self-assembly of silk fibroin proteins, which have been employed to create nanoparticles for controlled release of antibiotics, enhancing their therapeutic efficacy and reducing side effects (Yavuz et al., 2019). In another case, ferritin, a naturally occurring protein, has been utilized to self-assemble into nanocages that can encapsulate and deliver anticancer drugs directly to tumor cells, demonstrating significant improvements in drug targeting and efficacy (Tesarova et al., 2020). These examples highlight the versatility and potential of self-assembly in the design of PBNPs, making it a promising method for developing advanced drug delivery systems tailored to specific therapeutic needs.

## 3. Characterization parameters

### 3.1 Particle size and distribution

Particle size and distribution are fundamental characterization parameters that play a pivotal role in determining the performance, stability, and biological interactions of PBNPs, particularly in pharmaceutical applications (Davidov-Pardo et al., 2015). The size of these nanoparticles can range from a few to several hundred nanometers, depending on the method of preparation and desired therapeutic or diagnostic function. Nanoparticles on the smaller end of the spectrum often exhibit a higher surface area-to-volume ratio, which can enhance their interaction with biological systems, increase solubility, and improve bioavailability. This can lead to more effective drug delivery, as smaller particles are better able to navigate the complex biological environments and reach target cells or tissues (Kopp et al., 2017). However, the advantages of small size must be carefully balanced with stability. Larger particles may exhibit better physical and chemical stability but are more prone to rapid clearance by the reticuloendothelial system (RES), particularly in organs such as the liver and spleen, which reduces their circulation time in the bloodstream. The interplay between size and stability becomes especially important when considering the pharmacokinetics and pharmacodynamics of the nanoparticle-based drug delivery systems (Wang et al., 2013). The distribution of particle size, often referred to as polydispersity index (PDI), is another crucial factor to evaluate. A narrow size distribution, indicated by a low PDI, signifies uniformity in particle size, which is desirable for reproducible and predictable biological behavior. Homogeneous particle size contributes to consistent drug release profiles, predictable bio-distribution, and optimized targeting efficiency. By contrast, a broad size distribution could lead to variability in therapeutic outcomes, as different-sized particles may exhibit distinct biological fates. This heterogeneity may result in unequal cellular uptake, varied circulation times, and inconsistent drug release, potentially reducing the efficacy of the nanoparticle system (Danaei et al., 2018). Dynamic light scattering (DLS) and nanoparticle tracking analysis (NTA) are the commonly employed techniques to measure particle size and distribution. DLS is widely used for its ability to provide rapid, high-throughput analysis of particle size in solutions, although it tends to skew toward larger particles in polydisperse samples (Knysh et al., 2023). On the other hand, NTA allows for visualization and tracking of individual nanoparticles, providing detailed insights into both size and distribution (Wells et al., 2024). Both techniques are essential tools in ensuring the accurate characterization of nanoparticles and confirming that their size and distribution align with the desired specifications for a given pharmaceutical application (Chan et al., 2017).

Additionally, the particle size of PBNPs significantly influences their biological behavior, including cellular uptake, intracellular trafficking, and endocytosis mechanism (Madni et al., 2021). Smaller particles are typically internalized via clathrin-mediated endocytosis, while larger particles might engage caveolae-mediated pathways or macropinocytosis. The route of entry can affect the intracellular fate of nanoparticles, including their ability to escape endosomal entrapment and reach their target organelles, such as the cytosol or nucleus (Means et al., 2022). Moreover, size plays a crucial role in determining nanoparticles' ability to penetrate biological barriers, such as the blood–brain barrier (BBB) or the gastrointestinal tract. Nanoparticles in the range of 10–100 nm are often ideal for achieving passive targeting through the enhanced permeability and retention (EPR) effect, especially in tumor tissues, which exhibit leaky vasculature (Shinde et al., 2022). Conversely, larger particles may have difficulty penetrating these barriers and may instead accumulate in nontarget tissues, reducing the therapeutic effect and increasing the potential for off-target toxicity (Domínguez, Suárez-Merino and Goñi-De-Cerio, 2014).

## 3.2 Surface charge (zeta potential)

Surface charge, typically measured as zeta potential, is a crucial parameter in the characterization of PBNPs, as it influences their stability, interactions with biological systems, and overall performance in pharmaceutical applications. Zeta potential reflects the net electrical charge at the interface between the nanoparticle surface and its surrounding medium, and it provides insights into colloidal stability (Karmakar, 2019). Nanoparticles with high positive or negative zeta potential values tend to repel each other due to electrostatic forces, which helps prevent aggregation. In contrast, nanoparticles with low zeta potential values may experience reduced repulsive forces, increasing the likelihood of aggregation and destabilization while in suspension. Ensuring adequate colloidal stability is essential for maintaining the integrity of PBNPs, particularly during storage and transport (Shrestha et al., 2020). The surface charge of PBNPs is also pivotal in determining their interactions with cells, tissues, and biological fluids. Positively charged nanoparticles are typically more likely to interact with the negatively charged cell membranes, facilitating cellular uptake through electrostatic attraction. This characteristic makes cationic nanoparticles particularly effective for drug delivery, gene therapy, or vaccine applications, where enhanced uptake is critical. However, this increased interaction also carries the potential risk of toxicity, as excessive positive surface charge can lead to membrane destabilization and cell lysis, thereby triggering unwanted immune responses (Forest and Pourchez, 2017). In contrast, negatively charged or neutral nanoparticles tend to exhibit reduced cellular uptake but often show enhanced biocompatibility and prolonged circulation times in the bloodstream, as they are less likely to be cleared rapidly by the mononuclear phagocyte system (MPS) (Adjei et al., 2014). The zeta potential of PBNPs can be modulated by altering the composition of the nanoparticle's surface or by modifying the pH and ionic strength of the surrounding medium. For instance, the presence of functional groups such as amines, carboxylates, or sulfates on a nanoparticle's surface can significantly alter zeta potential, allowing for precise tuning of surface charge to meet the requirements of a specific application (Sanità et al., 2020). Additionally, the pH of the surrounding medium plays a key role in determining the ionization state of these functional groups, thereby affecting the surface charge. PBNPs, being highly sensitive to environmental conditions, may undergo charge alterations due to the inherent characteristics of protein components, as well as through postsynthesis modifications such as PEGylation or conjugation with targeting ligands (Shimanovich et al., 2014; Sahandi Zangabad et al., 2017). Zeta potential measurement, typically performed using electrophoretic light scattering (ELS), provides a quick and reliable vehicle to assess the charge properties of nanoparticles. The results of such measurements offer valuable insights into the expected behavior of nanoparticles in biological environments, including their interaction with serum proteins, cell membranes, and other biological components (Varenne et al., 2015). Protein corona formation, wherein proteins from biological fluids adsorb onto the nanoparticle surface, can further alter zeta potential, impacting the nanoparticles' biodistribution, circulation half-life, and immune recognition (Acet, 2024). This dynamic nature of surface charge highlights the importance of careful evaluation of zeta potential under biologically relevant conditions to ensure that PBNPs maintain their functionality throughout their lifecycle, from formulation to therapeutic delivery (Acet, 2024). The surface charge also plays a vital role in nanoparticles' ability to cross biological barriers. For instance, positively charged nanoparticles may have an enhanced ability to traverse the BBB compared to their negatively charged counterparts due to electrostatic interaction with the negatively charged endothelial cells lining the BBB. This characteristic makes surface charge optimization a key consideration in the design of PBNPs for targeted drug delivery to the central nervous system (CNS) (Zhou et al., 2018; Ceña and Játiva, 2018).

## 3.3 Morphology and surface properties

Morphology and surface properties are critical aspects of PBNPs that significantly influence their behavior, stability, and functionality in pharmaceutical applications. The morphology of PBNPs typically refers to their shape and structure, which can range from spherical to rod-like, tubular, or irregular forms. The shape of nanoparticles is largely determined by the preparation method, the nature of the used protein, and any surface modifications that may be applied. Morphological characteristics, such as aspect ratio and surface texture, play crucial roles in determining how these nanoparticles interact with biological systems, including their cellular uptake, bio-distribution, and clearance (Zhang et al., 2021). For instance, spherical nanoparticles are often more readily internalized by cells through endocytosis compared to rod-shaped or elongated particles, which may require enhanced circulation times but provide reduced cellular uptake (Hadji and Bouchemal, 2022). Surface properties, including roughness, hydrophilicity/hydrophobicity balance, and chemical functionality, are equally vital in dictating the biological fate of PBNPs. The surface roughness of nanoparticles can affect protein corona formation, which involves the adsorption of proteins from biological fluids onto the nanoparticle's surface. This protein corona can significantly alter the biological identity of nanoparticles, impacting their biodistribution, targeting efficiency, and immune recognition. A smooth surface might lead to a more uniform protein corona, while a rougher surface may attract different types of proteins, influencing how the nanoparticle behaves in vivo (Song et al., 2018; Khan et al., 2022).

Hydrophilicity and hydrophobicity are key surface properties that determine the interaction of nanoparticles with biological membranes and fluids. PBNPs with hydrophilic surfaces tend to exhibit better stability in aqueous environments and are less prone to aggregation, making them suitable for intravenous administration. Hydrophilic surfaces also reduce nonspecific protein adsorption, which can prolong circulation time in the bloodstream by evading the immune system. On the other hand, nanoparticles with hydrophobic surfaces may interact more readily with cell membranes, potentially enhancing cellular uptake but also increasing the risk of aggregation and rapid clearance by the immune system (Jain et al., 2018; Yu et al., 2016). Surface functionalization further extends the control over the nanoparticle's behavior. Modifications, such as PEGylation (the attachment of polyethylene glycol chains) (Yazdani, Mozaffarian, Pazuki, Hadidi, et al., 2022a) or conjugation of targeting ligands, can be employed to tailor surface properties for specific applications. PEGylation, for instance, imparts a "stealth" property to nanoparticles, reducing their recognition by the immune system, thereby extending their circulation time. Meanwhile, the attachment of targeting moieties, such as antibodies or peptides, allows for selective interaction with specific cell types, enhancing the precision of drug delivery (Yazdani, Mozaffarian, Pazuki and Hadidi, 2022b; Hussain et al., 2019).

Techniques such as transmission electron microscopy (TEM) and scanning electron microscopy (SEM) are commonly used to visualize the morphology of PBNPs at nanoscale levels (Verma et al., 2020). These imaging techniques provide detailed information on the size, shape, and surface texture of nanoparticles, allowing researchers to fine-tune their design for specific pharmaceutical applications (Verma et al., 2020; Gupta et al., 2024).

## 3.4 Encapsulation efficiency and drug loading

Encapsulation efficiency and drug loading are critical parameters in the development and evaluation of PBNPs, directly influencing their therapeutic efficacy and overall performance in drug delivery systems (Wang and Uludag, 2008; Tarhini et al., 2017). Encapsulation efficiency refers to the percentage of drug or bioactive compound that is successfully incorporated within the nanoparticle matrix during the formulation process. High encapsulation efficiency is desirable, as it maximizes the amount of active ingredient that can be delivered to the target site, thereby enhancing therapeutic outcomes (Martínez Rivas et al., 2017). Several factors influence encapsulation efficiency, including physicochemical properties of the drug, the employed preparation method, and characteristics of the protein used to create the nanoparticles (Tarhini et al., 2017). For instance, hydrophobic drugs are often more effectively encapsulated in protein matrices due to favorable interactions with hydrophobic domains of the protein's structure, whereas hydrophilic drugs may require different strategies, such as the application of surfactants or cosolvents, to achieve high encapsulation rates (Ristroph and Prud'homme, 2019). Drug loading, on the other hand, refers to the amount of drug incorporated into nanoparticles relative to the total weight of the nanoparticle formulation (Ahlin Grabnar and Kristl, 2011). This parameter is crucial for determining the dosage and therapeutic efficacy of nanoparticles. Optimal drug loading must strike a balance between achieving sufficient therapeutic concentrations while maintaining the stability and functionality of PBNPs. Excessive drug loading can lead to structural alterations or destabilization of nanoparticles, compromising their integrity and release profiles. Conversely, inadequate drug loading may result in suboptimal therapeutic results (Yin et al., 2022; Felice et al., 2014).

The preparation method significantly impacts both encapsulation efficiency and drug loading. Techniques such as solvent evaporation, coacervation, and nano-precipitation are commonly employed to encapsulate drugs within PBNPs. Each method offers distinct advantages and limitations (Jiménez-Cruz et al., 2015). For example, solvent evaporation is often used for hydrophobic drugs but may not be suitable for sensitive biomolecules due to potential exposure to organic solvents. In contrast, coacervation techniques can effectively encapsulate both hydrophobic and hydrophilic drugs by forming a phase-separated structure that retains the active compound within the protein's matrix (Blocher McTigue and Perry, 2020). Characterization of encapsulation efficiency and drug loading is typically performed through analytical techniques such as high-performance liquid chromatography (HPLC), UV-Vis spectroscopy, or mass spectrometry (Scheeren et al., 2018). These methods enable researchers to quantify the amount of drug loaded into the nanoparticles and assess the efficiency of the encapsulation process. The application of these analytical techniques is crucial for optimizing formulation parameters and ensuring that nanoparticles meet the desired specifications for clinical applications (Fan et al., 2021; Yaneva and Georgieva, 2017).

## 3.5 Release kinetics

Release kinetics of PBNPs is a critical aspect of drug delivery systems, as it dictates the temporal profile of therapeutic agent release and thereby influences the efficacy and safety of treatment regimens (Shuying Wang et al., 2020a). Understanding the mechanisms underlying drug release from nanoparticles is essential for optimizing therapeutic outcomes, ensuring the drug is delivered at the right dose and duration to achieve the desired pharmacological effect. The release kinetics can be influenced by several factors, including physicochemical properties of the encapsulated drug, characteristics of the protein's matrix, and environmental conditions governing deployment of nanoparticles (Lee and Yeo, 2015).

Typically, the release of drugs from PBNPs can be described by various kinetic models, such as zero-order, first-order, or Higuchi models, each providing insights into the release mechanism (Viswanadha et al., 2024). Zero-order kinetics suggests a constant release rate, while first-order kinetics indicates a release rate that decreases over time (Laracuente et al., 2020). Higuchi kinetics, on the other hand, is commonly observed in systems, where drug release is controlled by diffusion processes. The selection of an appropriate model is crucial for predicting the release behavior and for tailoring the formulation to meet specific therapeutic needs (Fard and Fard, 2022).

The structure and composition of the protein's matrix play significant roles in determining the release kinetics. For instance, hydrophilic proteins tend to facilitate faster drug release due to enhanced diffusion of the drug through aqueous channels formed within the nanoparticle's matrix. Conversely, hydrophobic proteins can create a more robust network that may slow down the release, allowing for sustained delivery over extended periods (Ding and Li, 2017). Additionally, cross-linking density within a protein's matrix can also impact release rates; higher cross-linking may result in slower drug release due to tighter networks hindering drug diffusion (Le Devedec et al., 2018). Environmental factors, such as pH, temperature, and ionic strength, can significantly influence release kinetics as well (Dragan and Cocarta, 2016). PBNPs designed for specific applications may be engineered to respond to changes in these parameters. For example, pH-sensitive nanoparticles can release their payload in response to the acidic environment of tumor tissues or inflamed areas, thereby enhancing targeted delivery and minimizing systemic side effects. Similarly, temperature-sensitive formulations can exploit the differences in physiological temperatures to trigger drug release in specific tissues or conditions (Dragan and Cocarta, 2016).

In vitro studies are commonly employed to evaluate release kinetics, providing preliminary data that can be correlated with in vivo behavior. Methods such as dialysis, Franz diffusion cells (Kumar et al., 2024), or release in simulated biological fluids allow researchers to monitor drug release profiles over time, helping to identify the optimal conditions for drug delivery (Jug et al., 2018; Nemutlu et al., 2019). However, it is essential to note that in vitro release profiles may not always predict in vivo behavior accurately due to complex interactions within biological systems, including protein corona formation, enzymatic degradation, and variations in tissue permeability (Shabbits et al., 2002).

Ultimately, the goal of optimizing release kinetics in PBNPs is to achieve a controlled, predictable, and sustained release of therapeutic agents. This can enhance the therapeutic index by maintaining drug concentrations within the therapeutic window while minimizing toxicity (Zhao et al., 2016). By leveraging advanced formulation strategies, including the incorporation of stimuli-responsive elements or developing hybrid systems that combine multiple release mechanisms, researchers can design PBNPs that provide tailored release profiles suited for specific clinical applications (Zhao et al., 2016).

## 3.6 Biocompatibility and toxicity

Biocompatibility and toxicity are paramount considerations in the development and application of PBNPs, particularly in the context of drug delivery systems. Biocompatibility refers to the ability of a material to interact with biological systems without eliciting an adverse immune response or causing toxicity (Kyriakides, 2021). This characteristic of PBNPs is intrinsically linked to the nature of the protein used, as proteins are naturally occurring biomolecules that typically exhibit lower immunogenicity compared to synthetic polymers or metals. However, even naturally derived proteins can induce immune responses, particularly if they are modified or if the body recognizes them as a foreign entity. Therefore, a comprehensive evaluation of biocompatibility is essential to ensure nanoparticles can safely circulate in the body, deliver their therapeutic payload, and degrade without causing harm (Hong et al., 2020; Chua et al., 2012).

The size, shape, surface charge, and functionalization of PBNPs significantly influence their biocompatibility and toxicity profiles (Sanità et al., 2020). Smaller nanoparticles often exhibit enhanced cellular uptake, but their small size may also facilitate interactions with unintended biological targets, leading to potential toxicity. Similarly, surface charge plays a crucial role in determining how nanoparticles interact with cell membranes and biological fluids. Positively charged nanoparticles may enhance cellular uptake but can also lead to cytotoxic effects due to membrane destabilization. Neutral or negatively charged nanoparticles tend to exhibit improved biocompatibility, as they are less likely to provoke an immune response or cause cell lysis (Carnovale et al., 2016; Deng and Gao, 2016).

Toxicity assessments for PBNPs typically involve a combination of in vitro and in vivo studies. In vitro cytotoxicity assays, such as The MTT (3-[4,5-dimethylthiazol-2-yl]-2,5 diphenyl tetrazolium bromide) or Lactate Dehydrogenase (LDH), are often conducted using various cell lines to evaluate cell viability, proliferation, and membrane integrity upon exposure to nanoparticles (Bahadar et al., 2016). These studies provide critical insights into the potential toxicity of formulations. However, in vivo studies are also necessary to evaluate the biocompatibility of nanoparticles in complex biological environments. Animal models can help assess systemic toxicity, bio-distribution, and immune responses, providing a more comprehensive understanding of how PBNPs behave within living organisms (Silva Lima and Videira, 2018; Zamboni et al., 2018).

Additionally, the potential for protein corona formation—where proteins from biological fluids adsorb onto the surface of nanoparticles—can influence both their biocompatibility and toxicity. Protein corona can alter the identity of nanoparticles, impacting their interactions with cells and immune systems (Liu et al., 2020). For instance, the adsorption of opsonins can enhance phagocytosis, leading to accelerated clearance by the MPS, while the binding of serum proteins may reduce toxicity and improve circulation time (OWENSIII and PEPPAS, 2006; Gustafson et al., 2015).

# 4. Pharmaceutical applications

## 4.1 Drug delivery systems

PBNPs have garnered significant attention as vehicles for drug delivery due to their intrinsic biocompatibility, biodegradability, and tunable properties. These nanoparticles can be derived from naturally occurring proteins such as albumin, gelatin, and silk fibroin, or engineered from synthetic proteins, providing a versatile platform for delivering a wide range of therapeutic agents. Their structure allows for efficient drug encapsulation, protecting drugs from premature degradation and enabling controlled release in specific physiological environments (Varanko et al., 2020). One of the most prominent examples of PBNPs in drug delivery is albumin-based nanoparticles, particularly those derived from human serum albumin (HSA) (Elzoghby, Samy and Elgindy, 2012a). Albumin's natural role in the body as a carrier of hydrophobic molecules makes it an ideal candidate for drug delivery (Elzoghby, Samy and Elgindy, 2012a). The widely known Abraxane formulation, which uses albumin-bound paclitaxel, has been used to treat metastatic breast cancer as well as other cancers. This formulation improves the solubility of paclitaxel, a hydrophobic drug, without the need for toxic solvents, reducing the side effects and enhancing the therapeutic index (Desai, 2016; Gradishar, 2006). The nanoparticle's small size enables it to accumulate in tumors via the EPR effect, allowing for a more effective targeting of cancer cells (Gradishar, 2006). Another example is gelatin nanoparticles, which have been explored for the delivery of both small molecules and large biological drugs such as proteins and nucleic acids. Gelatin nanoparticles are known for their excellent biodegradability and their ability to be chemically modified to optimize drug release kinetics (Sahoo et al., 2015; Yasmin et al., 2017). For instance, gelatin-based nanoparticles have been investigated for the delivery of doxorubicin, a common chemotherapy drug, enhancing its targeted delivery to tumor tissues and reducing systemic toxicity (Fatima et al., 2024). Silk fibroin nanoparticles represent another promising class of PBNPs. Silk fibroin, derived from the silk of *Bombyx mori* (silkworms), is a natural protein with remarkable mechanical properties, biodegradability, and biocompatibility. Silk-based nanoparticles can be designed for controlled drug release, and their surface can be functionalized for targeted delivery (Zhao et al., 2015; Yadav, 2024). Studies have demonstrated the potential of silk fibroin nanoparticles in delivering **curcumin**, a hydrophobic anticancer agent, improving its stability and bioavailability. These nanoparticles provide sustained release over time, making them ideal for chronic diseases that require long-term therapy (Crivelli et al., 2019). PBNPs can also be engineered to respond to specific stimuli such as pH, enzymes, or redox conditions, which is highly beneficial for site-specific drug delivery (Karimi, Ghasemi, et al., 2016b). For instance, casein-based nanoparticles, derived from milk protein, have been studied for the delivery of chemotherapeutic drugs. Casein nanoparticles exhibit pH-sensitive behavior, which can be utilized for drug release in the acidic microenvironment of tumors, thus improving drug efficacy and reducing damage to healthy tissues (Shapira et al., 2010; Zahariev et al., 2023).

Overall, PBNPs offer immense potential in drug delivery systems due to their versatility in drug encapsulation, ability to target specific tissues, and capacity for controlled and stimuli-responsive drug release. These advantages make them suitable candidates for delivering a wide range of therapeutic agents, especially in challenging areas such as cancer therapy (Hong et al., 2020).

## 4.2 Gene therapy

Gene therapy, which involves the delivery of genetic material to correct or modulate defective genes, has gained considerable momentum as a treatment for genetic disorders, cancers, and other diseases (Sayed et al., 2022). However, one of the critical challenges in gene therapy is the safe and efficient delivery of nucleic acids, such as DNA, mRNA, or small interfering RNA (siRNA), to target cells without causing significant off-target effects or degradation (Sayed et al., 2022; Cesur-Ergün and Demir-Dora, 2023). PBNPs have emerged as promising carriers for gene delivery due to their biocompatibility, biodegradability, and ability to encapsulate and protect nucleic acids, while enabling efficient cellular uptake and gene expression (Shukla et al., 2023). One of the most commonly used PBNPs in gene therapy is **albumin-based nanoparticles**. Albumin, a naturally occurring protein in the human body, is widely studied due to its nontoxic, nonimmunogenic properties, making it an ideal delivery system. Albumin nanoparticles can be functionalized with ligands to target specific cells and tissues, and their surface can be modified to improve nucleic acid binding (Prajapati and Somoza, 2021; Qu et al., 2024). Albumin nanoparticles have been used in gene therapy applications to deliver **plasmid DNA (pDNA)** and **siRNA** to target cancer cells, improving gene silencing and reducing tumor growth (Prajapati and Somoza, 2021; Son et al., 2013). Studies have demonstrated that albumin nanoparticles can significantly enhance cellular uptake of siRNA, protect it from nuclease degradation, and facilitate endosomal escape, which is crucial for effective gene silencing (Shajari et al., 2017; Subhan and Torchilin, 2020). Another example is the application of **protamine-based nanoparticles**. Protamine, a small, naturally occurring protein, has strong cationic properties, enabling it to bind efficiently to negatively charged nucleic acids (Jarzebska et al., 2021). Protamine-based nanoparticles have been investigated for delivering both DNA and RNA in gene therapy (Jarzebska et al., 2021). As an example, **protamine-DNA complexes** have been developed for delivering therapeutic genes to cancer cells, where they induce apoptosis and suppress tumor growth. Protamine's ability to form stable complexes with nucleic acids and facilitate cellular internalization has made it a valuable tool in gene delivery systems, particularly in enhancing transfection efficiency and reducing cytotoxicity (Ruseska, 2021; Li and Huang, 1997). **Gelatin nanoparticles** are another class of PBNPs that have been widely explored for gene delivery. Gelatin's natural biodegradability and ease of chemical modification make it an attractive carrier for gene therapy. Gelatin nanoparticles can encapsulate genetic materials and release them in a controlled manner, allowing for sustained gene expression (Elzoghby, 2013). Gelatin-based systems have been used to deliver **DNA vaccines** and **therapeutic genes** for cardiovascular diseases and cancer therapy (Milano, 2023). As an example, gelatin nanoparticles loaded with **vascular endothelial growth factor DNA** have been utilized to promote angiogenesis in ischemic tissues, demonstrating improved gene expression and tissue repair (Beheshtizadeh et al., 2023). In addition to these naturally occurring proteins, **engineered protein nanoparticles** are gaining attention in gene therapy. **Virus-like particles (VLPs)**, which are protein nanoparticles that mimic the structure of viruses but lack viral genetic material, have been developed for gene delivery applications. VLPs can encapsulate nucleic acids and deliver them to specific cells with high efficiency (Mejía-Méndez, no date). For instance, VLPs based on **hepatitis B core protein** have been engineered to deliver **siRNA** to cancer cells, where they efficiently silence target genes, resulting in tumor suppression (Chen et al., 2020).

In summary, PBNPs represent a versatile and promising platform for gene therapy. Their ability to encapsulate and protect genetic material, enhance cellular uptake, and offer targeted and controlled release makes them suitable candidates for a wide range of gene therapy applications, including cancer, genetic disorders, and cardiovascular diseases. Protein-based delivery systems are poised to play a crucial role in the future of gene therapy based on the ongoing advancements in protein engineering and nanoparticle designs (Diaz et al., 2018; Unzueta et al., 2015).

## 4.3 Tissue engineering

Tissue engineering is a multidisciplinary field aimed at developing substitute biological entities to restore, maintain, or improve tissue function (Gomes et al., 2017). PBNPs have emerged as promising components in this field due to their biocompatibility, biodegradability, and tunable physical and chemical properties. These nanoparticles can act as scaffolding materials, promoting cellular adhesion, proliferation, and differentiation, as well as delivering bioactive molecules such as growth factors, drugs, or genetic materials to the engineered tissues (Zielińska et al., 2023; George and Ravindran, 2010). One of the primary roles of PBNPs in tissue engineering is their incorporation into **scaffolds**, which serve as a framework to support cell attachment and tissue regeneration (Biru, 2022). PBNPs can be embedded within or conjugated to larger scaffold matrices, where they help regulate the release of signaling molecules that promote tissue growth and repair. As an example, **gelatin nanoparticles** have been widely explored in bone and cartilage tissue engineering due to their ability to support cell adhesion and their natural degradation profile, which mimics the body's extracellular matrix (ECM) (Echave et al., 2017). Gelatin nanoparticles can be loaded with growth factors such as **bone morphogenetic protein-2** to enhance osteogenic differentiation and promote bone regeneration (Agrawal and Sinha, 2017). Silk-based scaffolds integrated with silk nanoparticles have been shown to promote regeneration of bones and nerve tissues by providing structural support while allowing for controlled release of bioactive molecules

(Tandon et al., 2020). Studies have demonstrated that silk nanoparticles loaded with **nerve growth factors** can enhance neuronal differentiation and regeneration, making them suitable for applications in neural tissue engineering (Li et al., 2022). PBNPs also play a crucial role in **hydrogel-based systems** for tissue engineering. Hydrogels, which are hydrophilic polymeric networks that mimic the ECM's properties, are widely used for encapsulating cells and promoting tissue growth. The incorporation of PBNPs into hydrogels enhances their mechanical properties, degradation rates, and bioactivity (Davari, 2022; Gomez-Florit et al., 2020). As an example, **albumin nanoparticles** embedded within hydrogels can be used to deliver growth factors in a sustained manner, aiding in wound healing and skin regeneration (Son et al., 2023). Albumin's natural ability to bind hydrophobic molecules also allows for the incorporation of hydrophobic drugs, broadening further the potential applications of these nanoparticle-laden hydrogels in tissue repair (Karimi, Bahrami, et al., 2016a).

In conclusion, PBNPs offer immense potential in tissue engineering due to their ability to act as scaffolds, deliver bioactive molecules, and modulate cellular behavior. Their versatility and biocompatibility make them suitable for a wide range of tissue engineering applications, including bone, cartilage, nerve, and cardiovascular tissue regeneration. PBNPs are poised to play a pivotal role in the future of regenerative medicine and tissue engineering, based on the ongoing advancements in nanoparticle fabrication and surface functionalization.

## 5. Conclusion

PBNPs have gained significant attention as versatile nanocarriers in the biomedical field due to their inherent biocompatibility, biodegradability, and functional tunability. Throughout this chapter, we have explored various aspects of PBNPs, including their methods of preparation, characterization parameters, and their diverse pharmaceutical applications, particularly in drug delivery, vaccine development, gene therapy, and tissue engineering. The application of these nanoparticles in pharmaceutical sciences highlights their potential to overcome key challenges such as poor solubility, drug instability, and limited bioavailability, while enabling targeted and controlled delivery of therapeutic agents. The preparation of PBNPs relies on a variety of techniques, each offering distinct advantages based on the nature of the protein and the desired application. Methods such as desolvation, emulsification, and self-assembly allow for fine-tuning nanoparticle's size, shape, and surface properties, which are critical factors in determining their interaction with biological systems. Moreover, the functionalization of these nanoparticles through covalent or noncovalent modifications can enhance their stability and improve targeting capabilities, making them highly adaptable for therapeutic purposes. The characterization of PBNPs is equally crucial in ensuring their functionality and efficacy. Parameters such as particle size, zeta potential, surface morphology, and encapsulation efficiency are central to understanding their behavior in biological environments. Techniques such as DLS, SEM, and Fourier-transform infrared spectroscopy (FTIR) provide essential insights into physicochemical properties of nanoparticles, which in turn influence their bio-distribution, cellular uptake, and release kinetics.

The pharmaceutical applications of PBNPs are vast and diverse. In drug delivery, PBNPs offer the ability to encapsulate both hydrophobic and hydrophilic drugs, providing protection from degradation and enhancing controlled release at the target site. Their application in vaccine delivery has been shown to significantly improve antigen stability and immune responses, offering new opportunities for the development of the next-generation vaccines. In gene therapy, PBNPs serve as effective carriers for nucleic acids, facilitating the safe and efficient delivery of genetic material, while minimizing off-target effects. Furthermore, in tissue engineering, PBNPs can be integrated into scaffolds or hydrogels to promote cell proliferation, differentiation, and tissue regeneration, as well as offer solutions for various medical regenerative applications. Despite the promising potential of PBNPs, challenges still remain in optimizing their scalability, stability, and reproducibility for large-scale production and clinical use. Issues such as the stability of protein carriers in vivo, the potential for immunogenic responses, and the controlled release of therapeutic payloads need to be addressed through further research and development. Additionally, regulatory considerations regarding the safety, efficacy, and biocompatibility of PBNPs must be thoroughly examined to facilitate their translation from laboratory to clinical settings.

In conclusion, PBNPs represent a highly promising platform for the advancement of drug delivery systems and other biomedical applications. Their unique properties, combined with ongoing advances in nanoparticle engineering and surface functionalization, position them at the forefront of nanomedicine. As research continues to address the current challenges and explore novel applications, it presents PBNPs with the potential to revolutionize therapeutic approaches by offering more efficient, targeted, and personalized treatments for a wide range of diseases.

## References

Acet, Ö., 2024. A Review for uncovering the "protein-nanoparticle alliance": implications of the protein corona for biomedical applications. Nanomaterials 14 (10).

Adjei, I.M., Sharma, B., Labhasetwar, V., 2014. Nanoparticles: Cellular uptake and cytotoxicity. Adv. Exp. Med. Biol. 811, 74–91. https://doi.org/10.1007/978-94-017-8739-0_5.

Agrawal, V., Sinha, M., 2017. A review on carrier systems for bone morphogenetic protein-2. J. Biomed. Mater. Res. B Appl. Biomater. 105 (4), 904–925. https://doi.org/10.1002/jbm.b.33599.

Ahlin Grabnar, P., Kristl, J., 2011. The manufacturing techniques of drug-loaded polymeric nanoparticles from preformed polymers. J. Microencapsul. 28 (4), 323–335. https://doi.org/10.3109/02652048.2011.569763.

Alavarse, A.C., Frachini, E.C.G., da Silva, R.L.C.G., Lima, V.H., Shavandi, A., Petri, D.F.S., 2022. Crosslinkers for polysaccharides and proteins: Synthesis conditions, mechanisms, and crosslinking efficiency, a review. Int. J. Biol. Macromol. 202, 558–596. https://doi.org/10.1016/j.ijbiomac.2022.01.029.

Aljabali, A.A.A., Rezigue, M., Alsharedeh, R.H., Obeid, M.A., Mishra, V., Serrano-Aroca, Á., El-Tanani, M., Tambuwala, M.M., 2022. Protein-based nanomaterials: a new tool for targeted drug delivery. Ther. Deliv. 13 (6), 321–338. https://doi.org/10.4155/tde-2021-0091.

Angardi, V., Ali, E., Yücel, Ö., 2022. Critical review of emulsion stability and characterization techniques in oil processing. J. Energy Resour. Technol. 144 (4). https://doi.org/10.1115/1.4051571.

Bahadar, H., Maqbool, F., Niaz, K., Abdollahi, M., 2016. Toxicity of nanoparticles and an overview of current experimental models. Iran. Biomed. J. 20 (1), 1–11.

Ban, E., Kim, A., 2022. Coacervates: Recent developments as nanostructure delivery platforms for therapeutic biomolecules. Int. J. Pharm. 624, 122058. https://doi.org/10.1016/j.ijpharm.2022.122058.

Beheshtizadeh, N., Gharibshahian, M., Bayati, M., Maleki, R., Strachan, H., Doughty, S., Tayebi, L., 2023. Vascular endothelial growth factor (VEGF) delivery approaches in regenerative medicine. Biomed. Pharmacother. 166, 115301. https://doi.org/10.1016/j.biopha.2023.115301.

Biru, E.I., 2022. Graphene oxide–protein-based scaffolds for tissue engineering: recent advances and applications. Polymers 14 (5).

Blocher McTigue, W.C., Perry, S.L., 2020. Protein encapsulation using complex coacervates: what nature has to teach us. Small 16 (27). https://doi.org/10.1002/smll.201907671.

Carnovale, C., Bryant, G., Shukla, R., Bansal, V., 2016. Size, shape and surface chemistry of nano-gold dictate its cellular interactions, uptake and toxicity. Prog. Mater. Sci. 83, 152–190. https://doi.org/10.1016/j.pmatsci.2016.04.003.

Ceña, V., Játiva, P., 2018. Nanoparticle crossing of blood-brain barrier: a road to new therapeutic approaches to central nervous system diseases. Nanomedicine 13 (13), 1513–1516. https://doi.org/10.2217/nnm-2018-0139.

Cesur-Ergün, B., Demir-Dora, D., 2023. Gene therapy in cancer. J. Gene Med. 25 (11).

Chan, M.Y., Dowling, Q.M., Sivananthan, S.J., Kramer, R.M., 2017. Particle sizing of nanoparticle adjuvant formulations by dynamic light scattering (DLS) and nanoparticle tracking analysis (NTA). Methods Mol. Biol. 1494, 239–252. https://doi.org/10.1007/978-1-4939-6445-1_17.

Chen, W., Hartzell, E.J., Lieser, R.M., Sullivan, M.O., 2020. Modular hepatitis b virus-like particle platform for biosensing and drug delivery. ACS Nano 14 (10), 12642–12651. https://doi.org/10.1021/acsnano.9b08756.

Chua, B.Y., Al Kobaisi, M., Zeng, W., Mainwaring, D., Jackson, D.C., 2012. Chitosan microparticles and nanoparticles as biocompatible delivery vehicles for peptide and protein-based immunocontraceptive vaccines. Mol. Pharm. 9 (1), 81–90. https://doi.org/10.1021/mp200264m.

Comert, F., Malanowski, A.J., Azarikia, F., Dubin, P.L., 2016. Coacervation and precipitation in polysaccharide–protein systems. Soft Matter 12 (18), 4154–4161. https://doi.org/10.1039/C6SM00044D.

Crivelli, B., Bari, E., Perteghella, S., Catenacci, L., Sorrenti, M., Mocchi, M., Faragò, S., Tripodo, G., Prina-Mello, A., Torre, M.L., 2019. Silk fibroin nanoparticles for celecoxib and curcumin delivery: ROS-scavenging and anti-inflammatory activities in an in vitro model of osteoarthritis. Eur. J. Pharm. Biopharm. 137, 37–45. https://doi.org/10.1016/j.ejpb.2019.02.008.

Danaei, M., Dehghankhold, M., Ataei, S., Hasanzadeh Davarani, F., Javanmard, R., Dokhani, A., Khorasani, S., Mozafari, M.R., 2018. Impact of particle size and polydispersity index on the clinical applications of lipidic nanocarrier systems. Pharmaceutics 10 (2), 57. https://doi.org/10.3390/pharmaceutics10020057.

Davari, N., 2022. Protein-based hydrogels: promising materials for tissue engineering. Polymers 14 (5).

Davidov-Pardo, G., Joye, I.J., Mcclements, D.J., 2015. Food-grade protein-based nanoparticles and microparticles for bioactive delivery: Fabrication, characterization, and utilization. Adv. Protein Chem. Struct. Biol. 98, 293–325. https://doi.org/10.1016/bs.apcsb.2014.11.004.

DeFrates, K., Markiewicz, T., Gallo, P., Rack, A., Weyhmiller, A., Jarmusik, B., Hu, X., 2018. Protein polymer-based nanoparticles: fabrication and medical applications. Int. J. Mol. Sci. 19 (6), 1717. https://doi.org/10.3390/ijms19061717.

Deng, J., Gao, C., 2016. Recent advances in interactions of designed nanoparticles and cells with respect to cellular uptake, intracellular fate, degradation and cytotoxicity. Nanotechnology 27 (41), 412002. https://doi.org/10.1088/0957-4484/27/41/412002.

Desai, N., 2016. Nanoparticle Albumin-Bound Paclitaxel (Abraxane®) Albumin in Medicine: Pathological and Clinical Applications. Springer Singapore, United States, pp. 101–119. https://doi.org/10.1007/978-981-10-2116-9_6.

Diaz, D., Care, A., Sunna, A., 2018. Bioengineering strategies for protein-based nanoparticles. Genes 9 (7), 370. https://doi.org/10.3390/genes9070370.

Ding, C., Li, Z., 2017. A review of drug release mechanisms from nanocarrier systems. Mater. Sci. Eng. C 76, 1440–1453. https://doi.org/10.1016/j.msec.2017.03.130.

Ding, S., Zhang, N., Lyu, Z., Zhu, W., Chang, Y.-C., Hu, X., Du, D., Lin, Y., 2021. Protein-based nanomaterials and nanosystems for biomedical applications: A review. Mater. Today 43, 166–184. https://doi.org/10.1016/j.mattod.2020.11.015.

Ding, S., Serra, C.A., Vandamme, T.F., Yu, W., 2019. Nicolas Anton, double emulsions prepared by two–step emulsification: History, state-of-the-art and perspective. J. Contr. Release 295, 31–49. https://doi.org/10.1016/j.jconrel.2018.12.037.

Dissanayake, T., Bandara, N., 2024. Protein-based encapsulation systems for codelivery of bioactive compounds: Recent studies and potential applications. Curr. Opin. Food Sci. 57, 101181. https://doi.org/10.1016/j.cofs.2024.101181.

Domínguez, A., Suárez-Merino, B., Goñi-De-Cerio, F., 2014. Nanoparticles and blood-brain barrier: The key to central nervous system diseases. J. Nanosci. Nanotechnol. 14 (1), 766–779. https://doi.org/10.1166/jnn.2014.9119Spain.

Dragan, E.S., Cocarta, A.I., 2016. Smart macroporous IPN hydrogels responsive to ph, temperature, and ionic strength: Synthesis, characterization, and evaluation of controlled release of drugs. ACS Appl. Mater. Interfaces 8 (19), 12018–12030. https://doi.org/10.1021/acsami.6b02264.

Echave, M.C., Burgo, L.S., Pedraz, J.L., Orive, G., 2017. Gelatin as biomaterial for tissue engineering. Curr. Pharm. Des. 23 (24), 3567–3584. https://doi.org/10.2174/0929867324666170511123101.

Eghbal, N., Choudhary, R., 2018. Complex coacervation: Encapsulation and controlled release of active agents in food systems. LWT 90, 254–264. https://doi.org/10.1016/j.lwt.2017.12.036.

Elzoghby, A.O., 2013. Gelatin-based nanoparticles as drug and gene delivery systems: Reviewing three decades of research. J. Contr. Release 172 (3), 1075–1091. https://doi.org/10.1016/j.jconrel.2013.09.019.

Elzoghby, A.O., Samy, W.M., Elgindy, N.A., 2012a. Albumin-based nanoparticles as potential controlled release drug delivery systems. J. Contr. Release 157 (2), 168–182. https://doi.org/10.1016/j.jconrel.2011.07.031.

Elzoghby, A.O., Samy, W.M., Elgindy, N.A., 2012b. Protein-based nanocarriers as promising drug and gene delivery systems. J. Contr. Release 161 (1), 38–49. https://doi.org/10.1016/j.jconrel.2012.04.036.

Etorki, A.M., Gao, M., Sadeghi, R., Maldonado-Mejia, L.F., Kokini, J.L., 2016. Effects of desolvating agent types, ratios, and temperature on size and nanostructure of nanoparticles from α-lactalbumin and ovalbumin. J. Food Sci. 81 (10), E2511. https://doi.org/10.1111/1750-3841.13447.

Fan, Y., Marioli, M., Zhang, K., 2021. Analytical characterization of liposomes and other lipid nanoparticles for drug delivery. J. Pharmaceut. Biomed. Anal. 192, 113642. https://doi.org/10.1016/j.jpba.2020.113642.

Fard, A.M., Fard, M.M., 2022. Modeling drug release. Eurasian Journal of Science and Technology 1, 14–33.

Fatima, W., Batool, S.R., Mushtaq, F., Aslam, M., Ali Raza, Z., Nazeer, M.A., 2024. Controlled release of doxorubicin from gelatin-based nanoparticles: theoretical and experimental approach. Mater. Adv. 5 (6), 2347–2358. https://doi.org/10.1039/d3ma00825h.

Felice, B., Prabhakaran, M.P., Rodríguez, A.P., Ramakrishna, S., 2014. Drug delivery vehicles on a nano-engineering perspective. Mater. Sci. Eng. C 41, 178–195. https://doi.org/10.1016/j.msec.2014.04.049.

Ferrer-Miralles, N., Rodríguez-Carmona, E., Corchero, J.L., García-Fruitós, E., Vázquez, E., Villaverde, A., 2015. Engineering protein self-assembling in protein-based nanomedicines for drug delivery and gene therapy. Crit. Rev. Biotechnol. 35 (2), 209–221. https://doi.org/10.3109/07388551.2013.833163.

Forenzo, C., Larsen, J., 2023. Complex coacervates as a promising vehicle for mRNA delivery: a comprehensive review of recent advances and challenges. Mol. Pharm. 20 (9), 4387–4403. https://doi.org/10.1021/acs.molpharmaceut.3c00439.

Forest, V., Pourchez, J., 2017. Preferential binding of positive nanoparticles on cell membranes is due to electrostatic interactions: A too simplistic explanation that does not take into account the nanoparticle protein corona. Mater. Sci. Eng. C 70, 889–896. https://doi.org/10.1016/j.msec.2016.09.016.

George, A., Ravindran, S., 2010. Protein templates in hard tissue engineering. Nano Today 5 (4), 254–266. https://doi.org/10.1016/j.nantod.2010.05.005.

Gomes, M.E., Rodrigues, M.T., Domingues, R.M.A., Reis, R.L., 2017. Tissue engineering and regenerative medicine: new trends and directions - a year in review. Tissue Eng. B Rev. 23 (3), 211–224. https://doi.org/10.1089/ten.teb.2017.0081.

Gomez-Florit, M., Pardo, A., Domingues, R.M.A., Graça, A.L., Babo, P.S., Reis, R.L., Gomes, M.E., 2020. Natural-based hydrogels for tissue engineering applications. Molecules 25 (24), 5858. https://doi.org/10.3390/molecules25245858.

Gouveia, M.G., Wesseler, J.P., Ramaekers, J., Weder, C., Scholten, P.B.V., Bruns, N., 2023. Polymersome-based protein drug delivery – quo vadis? Chem. Soc. Rev. 52 (2), 728–778. https://doi.org/10.1039/d2cs00106c.

Gradishar, W.J., 2006. Albumin-bound paclitaxel: a next-generation taxane. Expet Opin. Pharmacother. 7 (8), 1041–1053. https://doi.org/10.1517/14656566.7.8.1041.

Grzelczak, M., Liz-Marzán, L.M., Klajn, R., 2019. Stimuli-responsive self-assembly of nanoparticles. Chem. Soc. Rev. 48 (5), 1342–1361. https://doi.org/10.1039/c8cs00787j.

Gupta, P., Rai, N., Verma, A., Gautam, V., 2024. Microscopy based methods for characterization, drug delivery, and understanding the dynamics of nanoparticles. Med. Res. Rev. 44 (1), 138–168. https://doi.org/10.1002/med.21981.

Gustafson, H.H., Holt-Casper, D., Grainger, D.W., Ghandehari, H., 2015. Nanoparticle uptake: the phagocyte problem. Nano Today 10 (4), 487–510. https://doi.org/10.1016/j.nantod.2015.06.006.

Guttoff, M., Saberi, A.H., Mcclements, D.J., 2015. Formation of vitamin D nanoemulsion-based delivery systems by spontaneous emulsification: Factors affecting particle size and stability. Food Chem. 171, 117–122. https://doi.org/10.1016/j.foodchem.2014.08.087.

Hadji, H., Bouchemal, K., 2022. Effect of micro- and nanoparticle shape on biological processes. J. Contr. Release 342, 93–110. https://doi.org/10.1016/j.jconrel.2021.12.032.

Hong, S., Choi, D.W., Kim, H.N., Park, C.G., Lee, W., Park, H.H., 2020. Protein-based nanoparticles as drug delivery systems. Pharmaceutics 12 (7), 604. https://doi.org/10.3390/pharmaceutics12070604.

Hosseinkhani, H., Hong, P.D., Yu, D.S., 2013. Self-assembled proteins and peptides for regenerative medicine. Chem. Rev. 113 (7), 4837–4861. https://doi.org/10.1021/cr300131h.

Hussain, Z., Khan, S., Imran, M., Sohail, M., Shah, S.W.A., 2019. Marcel de Matas, PEGylation: a promising strategy to overcome challenges to cancer-targeted nanomedicines: a review of challenges to clinical transition and promising resolution. Drug Deliv. Transl. Res. 9 (3), 721–734. https://doi.org/10.1007/s13346-019-00631-4.

Jacob, E.M., Borah, A., Sakthi Kumar, D., 2022. CRISPR/Cas9 Nano-Delivery Approaches for Targeted Gene Therapy Nanotechnology in the Life Sciences. Springer Science and Business Media B.V., Japan, pp. 27–64. https://doi.org/10.1007/978-3-031-12658-1_2.

Jahanban-Esfahlan, A., Dastmalchi, S., Davaran, S., 2016. A simple improved desolvation method for the rapid preparation of albumin nanoparticles. Int. J. Biol. Macromol. 91, 703–709. https://doi.org/10.1016/j.ijbiomac.2016.05.032.

Jain, A., Singh, S.K., Arya, S.K., Kundu, S.C., Kapoor, S., 2018. Protein nanoparticles: promising platforms for drug delivery applications. ACS Biomater. Sci. Eng. 4 (12), 3939–3961. https://doi.org/10.1021/acsbiomaterials.8b01098.

Jarzebska, N.T., Mellett, M., Frei, J., Kündig, T.M., Pascolo, S., 2021. Protamine-based strategies for RNA transfection. Pharmaceutics 13 (6), 877. https://doi.org/10.3390/pharmaceutics13060877.

Jiang, L., Zeng, Y., Li, H., Lin, Z., Liu, H., Richardson, J.J., Gao, Z., Wu, D., Liu, L., Caruso, F., Zhou, J., 2023. Peptide-based coacervate protocells with cytoprotective metal–phenolic network membranes. J. Am. Chem. Soc. 145 (44), 24108–24115. https://doi.org/10.1021/jacs.3c07748.

Jiménez-Cruz, E., Arroyo-Maya, I.J., Hernández-Arana, A., Cornejo-Mazón, M., Hernández-Sánchez, H., 2015. Protein-Based Nanoparticles. Springer Science and Business Media LLC, pp. 69–79. https://doi.org/10.1007/978-3-319-13596-0_5.

Jug, M., Hafner, A., Lovrić, J., Lusina Kregar, M., Pepić, I., Vanić, Ž., Cetina-Čižmek, B., Filipović-Grčić, J., 2018. An overview of in vitro dissolution/release methods for novel mucosal drug delivery systems. J. Pharmaceut. Biomed. Anal. 147, 350–366. https://doi.org/10.1016/j.jpba.2017.06.072.

Kaltbeitzel, J., Wich, P.R., 2023. Protein-based nanoparticles: from drug delivery to imaging, nanocatalysis and protein therapy. Angew. Chem., Int. Ed. 62 (44). https://doi.org/10.1002/anie.202216097.

Karimi, M., Bahrami, S., Ravari, S.B., Sahandi Zangabad, P., Mirshekari, H., Bozorgomid, M., Shahreza, S., Sori, M., Hamblin, M.R., 2016a. Albumin nanostructures as advanced drug delivery systems. Expet Opin. Drug Deliv. 13 (11), 1609–1623. https://doi.org/10.1080/17425247.2016.1193149.

Karimi, M., Ghasemi, A., Zangabad, P.S., Rahighi, R., Masoud Moosavi Basri, S., Mirshekari, H., Amiri, M., Shafaei Pishabad, Z., Aslani, A., Bozorgomid, M., Ghosh, D., Beyzavi, A., Vaseghi, A., Aref, A.R., Haghani, L., Bahrami, S., Hamblin, M.R., 2016b. Smart micro/nanoparticles in stimulus-responsive drug/gene delivery systems. Chem. Soc. Rev. 45 (5), 1457–1501. https://doi.org/10.1039/c5cs00798d.

Karmakar, S., 2019. Particle size distribution and zeta potential based on dynamic light scattering: Techniques to characterize stability and surface charge distribution of charged colloids. Recent Trends Mater. Phys. Chem. 28, 117–159.

Khan, S., Sharifi, M., Gleghorn, J.P., Babadaei, M.M.N., Bloukh, S.H., Edis, Z., Amin, M., Qian, B., ten Hagen, T.L.M., Falahati, M., Cho, W.C., 2022. Artificial engineering of the protein corona at bio-nano interfaces for improved cancer-targeted nanotherapy. J. Contr. Release 348, 127–147. https://doi.org/10.1016/j.jconrel.2022.05.055.

Knysh, A., Sokolov, P., Nabiev, I., 2023. Dynamic light scattering analysis in biomedical research and applications of nanoparticles and polymers. Federation Journal of Biomedical Photonics and Engineering 9 (2). https://doi.org/10.18287/JBPE23.09.020203.

Kopp, M., Kollenda, S., Epple, M., 2017. Nanoparticle-protein interactions: Therapeutic approaches and supramolecular chemistry. Accounts Chem. Res. 50 (6), 1383–1390. https://doi.org/10.1021/acs.accounts.7b00051.

Kumar, M., Sharma, A., Mahmood, S., Thakur, A., Mirza, M.A., Bhatia, A., 2024. Franz diffusion cell and its implication in skin permeation studies. J. Dispersion Sci. Technol. 45 (5), 943–956. https://doi.org/10.1080/01932691.2023.2188923.

Kuna, K., Reddy Baddam, S., Kalagara, S., Akkiraju, P.C., Tade, R.S., Enaganti, S., 2024. Emerging natural polymer-based architectured nanotherapeutics for the treatment of cancer. Int. J. Biol. Macromol. 262, 129434. https://doi.org/10.1016/j.ijbiomac.2024.129434.

Kyriakides, T.R., 2021. Biocompatibility of nanomaterials and their immunological properties. Biomed. Mater. 16 (4).

Laracuente, M.L., Yu, M.H., McHugh, K.J., 2020. Zero-order drug delivery: State of the art and future prospects. J. Contr. Release 327, 834–856. https://doi.org/10.1016/j.jconrel.2020.09.020.

Le Devedec, F., Boucher, H., Dubins, D., Allen, C., 2018. Factors controlling drug release in cross-linked poly(valerolactone) based matrices. Mol. Pharm. 15 (4), 1565–1577. https://doi.org/10.1021/acs.molpharmaceut.7b01102.

Lee, J.H., Yeo, Y., 2015. Controlled drug release from pharmaceutical nanocarriers. Chem. Eng. Sci. 125, 75–84. https://doi.org/10.1016/j.ces.2014.08.046.

Lee, R.J., Springer, M.L., Blanco-Bose, W.E., Shaw, R., Ursell, P.C., Blau, H.M., 2000. VEGF gene delivery to myocardium: Deleterious effects of unregulated expression. Circulation 102 (8), 898–901. https://doi.org/10.1161/01.CIR.102.8.898.

Li, S., Huang, L., 1997. In vivo gene transfer via intravenous administration of cationic lipid-protamine-DNA (LPD) complexes. Gene Ther. 4 (9), 891–900. https://doi.org/10.1038/sj.gt.3300482.

Li, Y., Champion, J.A., 2022. Self-assembling nanocarriers from engineered proteins: Design, functionalization, and application for drug delivery. Adv. Drug Deliv. Rev. 189, 114462. https://doi.org/10.1016/j.addr.2022.114462.

Li, Z., Meng, Z., Zhao, Z., 2022. Silk fibroin nanofibrous scaffolds incorporated with microRNA-222 loaded chitosan nanoparticles for enhanced neuronal differentiation of neural stem cells. Carbohydr. Polym. 277, 118791. https://doi.org/10.1016/j.carbpol.2021.118791.

Lin, Q., Ge, S., McClements, D.J., Li, X., Jin, Z., Jiao, A., Wang, J., Long, J., Xu, X., Qiu, C., 2023. Advances in preparation, interaction and stimulus responsiveness of protein-based nanodelivery systems. Crit. Rev. Food Sci. Nutr. 63 (19), 4092–4105. https://doi.org/10.1080/10408398.2021.1997908.

Liu, N., Tang, M., Ding, J., 2020. The interaction between nanoparticles-protein corona complex and cells and its toxic effect on cells. Chemosphere 245, 125624. https://doi.org/10.1016/j.chemosphere.2019.125624.

Liu, Y., Liang, Q., Liu, X., Raza, H., Ma, H., Ren, X., 2022. Treatment with ultrasound improves the encapsulation efficiency of resveratrol in zein-gum Arabic complex coacervates. LWT 153, 112331. https://doi.org/10.1016/j.lwt.2021.112331.

López-Montilla, J.C., Herrera-Morales, P.E., Pandey, S., Shah, D.O., 2002. Spontaneous emulsification: mechanisms, physicochemical aspects, modeling, and applications. J. Dispersion Sci. Technol. 23 (1–3), 219–268. https://doi.org/10.1080/01932690208984202.

Macewan, S.R., Chilkoti, A., 2014. Applications of elastin-like polypeptides in drug delivery. J. Contr. Release 190, 314–330. https://doi.org/10.1016/j.jconrel.2014.06.028.

Madni, A., Rehman, S., Sultan, H., Khan, M.M., Ahmad, F., Rafi Raza, M., Rai, N., Parveen, F., 2021. Mechanistic approaches of internalization, subcellular trafficking, and cytotoxicity of nanoparticles for targeting the small intestine. AAPS PharmSciTech 22 (1). https://doi.org/10.1208/s12249-020-01873-z.

Martínez Rivas, C.J., Tarhini, M., Badri, W., Karim, M., Greige-Gerges, H., Agha Nazari, Q., Rodríguez, S.A.G., Román, R.Á., Fessi, H., Elaissari, A., 2017. Nanoprecipitation process: From encapsulation to drug delivery. Int. J. Pharm. 532 (1), 66–81. https://doi.org/10.1016/j.ijpharm.2017.08.064.

Martínez-López, A.L., Pangua, C., Reboredo, C., Campión, R., Morales-Gracia, J., Irache, J.M., 2020. Protein-based nanoparticles for drug delivery purposes. Int. J. Pharm. 581, 119289. https://doi.org/10.1016/j.ijpharm.2020.119289.

Matteis, 2017. Exposure to inorganic nanoparticles: routes of entry, immune response, biodistribution and in vitro/in vivo toxicity evaluation. Toxics 5 (4).

Means, N., Kumar Elechalawar, C., Chen, W.R., Bhattacharya, R., Mukherjee, P., 2022. Revealing macropinocytosis using nanoparticles. Mol. Aspect. Med. 83, 100993. https://doi.org/10.1016/j.mam.2021.100993.

Mejía-Mendez, J.L., Virus-like particles: fundamentals and biomedical applications. Int. J. Mol. Sci., 23.

Milano, F., 2023. Current trends in gelatin-based drug delivery systems. Pharmaceutics 15 (5).

Mitchell, M.J., Billingsley, M.M., Haley, R.M., Wechsler, M.E., Peppas, N.A., Langer, R., 2021. Engineering precision nanoparticles for drug delivery. Nat. Rev. Drug Discov. 20 (2), 101–124. https://doi.org/10.1038/s41573-020-0090-8.

Nagarajan, S., Radhakrishnan, S., Kalkura, S.N., Balme, S., Miele, P., Bechelany, M., 2019. Overview of protein-based biopolymers for biomedical application. Macromol. Chem. Phys. 220 (14). https://doi.org/10.1002/macp.201900126.

Naik, J.B., Lokhande, A.B., Mishra, S., Kulkarni, R.D., 2012. Development of sustained release micro/nano particles using different solvent emulsification techniques: a review. Int. J. Pharma Bio Sci. 3 (4), 573–590.

Nemutlu, E., Eroğlu, İ., Eroğlu, H., Kır, S., 2019. In vitro release test of nano-drug delivery systems based on analytical and technological perspectives. Curr. Anal. Chem. 15 (4), 373–409. https://doi.org/10.2174/1573411014666180912125931.

Owensiii, D., Peppas, N., 2006. Opsonization, biodistribution, and pharmacokinetics of polymeric nanoparticles. Int. J. Pharm. 307 (1), 93–102. https://doi.org/10.1016/j.ijpharm.2005.10.010.

Pandey, P., Balekar, N., 2018. Target-specific Delivery: An Insight Drug Targeting and Stimuli Sensitive Drug Delivery Systems. Elsevier, India, pp. 117–154. https://doi.org/10.1016/B978-0-12-813689-8.00004-5.

Parveen, R., Shamsi, T.N., Fatima, S., 2017. Nanoparticles-protein interaction: Role in protein aggregation and clinical implications. Int. J. Biol. Macromol. 94, 386–395. https://doi.org/10.1016/j.ijbiomac.2016.10.024.

Pathak, J., Priyadarshini, E., Rawat, K., Bohidar, H.B., 2017. Complex coacervation in charge complementary biopolymers: Electrostatic versus surface patch binding. Adv. Colloid Interface Sci. 250, 40–53. https://doi.org/10.1016/j.cis.2017.10.006.

Petros, R.A., Desimone, J.M., 2010. Strategies in the design of nanoparticles for therapeutic applications. Nat. Rev. Drug Discov. 9 (8), 615–627. https://doi.org/10.1038/nrd2591.

Pradhan, M., Rousseau, D., 2012. A one-step process for oil-in-water-in-oil double emulsion formation using a single surfactant. J. Colloid Interface Sci. 386 (1), 398–404. https://doi.org/10.1016/j.jcis.2012.07.055.

Prajapati, R., Somoza, Á., 2021. Albumin nanostructures for nucleic acid delivery in cancer: current trend, emerging issues, and possible solutions. Cancers 13 (14), 3454. https://doi.org/10.3390/cancers13143454.

Qu, N., Song, K., Ji, Y., Liu, M., Chen, L., Lee, R., Teng, L., 2024. Albumin nanoparticle-based drug delivery systems. Int. J. Nanomed. 19, 6945–6980. https://doi.org/10.2147/ijn.s467876.

Rane, A.M., Schwing, J.A., Jonnalagadda, S., 2013. Coacervation and phase separation. In: Encyclopedia of Pharmaceutical Science and Technology, Six Volume Set (Print). CRC Press, pp. 497–511.

Ravera, F., Dziza, K., Santini, E., Cristofolini, L., Liggieri, L., 2021. Emulsification and emulsion stability: the role of the interfacial properties. Adv. Colloid Interface Sci. 288, 102344. https://doi.org/10.1016/j.cis.2020.102344.

Ristroph, K.D., Prud'homme, R.K., 2019. Hydrophobic ion pairing: Encapsulating small molecules, peptides, and proteins into nanocarriers. Nanoscale Adv. 1 (11), 4207–4237. https://doi.org/10.1039/c9na00308h.

Rosales, T.K.O., Fabi, J.P., 2023. Pectin-based nanoencapsulation strategy to improve the bioavailability of bioactive compounds. Int. J. Biol. Macromol. 229, 11–21. https://doi.org/10.1016/j.ijbiomac.2022.12.292.

Ruseska, I., 2021. Use of protamine in nanopharmaceuticals—a review. Nanomaterials 11 (6).

Sahandi Zangabad, P., Karimi, M., Mehdizadeh, F., Malekzad, H., Ghasemi, A., Bahrami, S., Zare, H., Moghoofei, M., Amin, H., Hamblin, M.R., 2017. Nanocaged platforms: modification, drug delivery and nanotoxicity. Opening synthetic cages to release the tiger. Nanoscale 9 (4), 1356–1392. https://doi.org/10.1039/c6nr07315h.

Sahoo, N., Sahoo, R.K., Biswas, N., Guha, A., Kuotsu, K., 2015. Recent advancement of gelatin nanoparticles in drug and vaccine delivery. Int. J. Biol. Macromol. 81, 317–331. https://doi.org/10.1016/j.ijbiomac.2015.08.006.

Saif, A., Anjum, L., Faisal, Z., Akram, N., Abbas Shah, Y., Irfan, R., Saeed, F., Afzaal, M., Shah, M.A., 2023. Recent advances in protein-based nanoparticles and their applications in the delivery of bioactive compounds. Int. J. Food Prop. 26 (2), 2866–2880. https://doi.org/10.1080/10942912.2023.2261662.

Sanità, G., Carrese, B., Lamberti, A., 2020. Nanoparticle surface functionalization: how to improve biocompatibility and cellular internalization. Front. Mol. Biosci. 7. https://doi.org/10.3389/fmolb.2020.587012.

Sayed, N., Allawadhi, P., Khurana, A., Singh, V., Navik, U., Kumar Pasumarthi, S., Khurana, I., Kumar Banothu, A., Weiskirchen, R., Kumar Bharani, K., therapy, G., 2022. Comprehensive overview and therapeutic applications. Life Sci. 294, 120375. https://doi.org/10.1016/j.lfs.2022.120375.

Scheeren, L.E., Nogueira-Librelotto, D.R., Fernandes, J.R., Macedo, L.B., Marcolino, A.I.P., Vinardell, M.P., Rolim, C. M.B., 2018. Comparative study of reversed-phase high-performance liquid chromatography and ultraviolet–visible spectrophotometry to determine doxorubicin in ph-sensitive nanoparticles. Anal. Lett. 51 (10), 1445–1463. https://doi.org/10.1080/00032719.2017.1380034.

Shabbits, J.A., Chiu, G.N.C., Mayer, L.D., 2002. Development of an in vitro drug release assay that accurately predicts in vivo drug retention for liposome-based delivery systems. J. Contr. Release 84 (3), 161–170. https://doi.org/10.1016/S0168-3659(02)00294-8.

Shajari, N., Mansoori, B., Davudian, S., Mohammadi, A., Baradaran, B., 2017. Overcoming the challenges of siRNA delivery: Nanoparticle strategies. Curr. Drug Deliv. 14 (1), 36–46. https://doi.org/10.2174/1567201813666160816105408.

Shapira, A., Markman, G., Assaraf, Y.G., Livney, Y.D., 2010. β-casein–based nanovehicles for oral delivery of chemotherapeutic drugs: drug-protein interactions and mitoxantrone loading capacity. Nanomed. Nanotechnol. Biol. Med. 6 (4), 547–555. https://doi.org/10.1016/j.nano.2010.01.003.

Shimanovich, U., Bernardes, G.J.L., Knowles, T.P.J., Cavaco-Paulo, A., 2014. Protein micro- and nano-capsules for biomedical applications. Chem. Soc. Rev. 43 (5), 1361–1371. https://doi.org/10.1039/c3cs60376h.

Shinde, V.R., Revi, N., Murugappan, S., Singh, S.P., Kumar Rengan, A., 2022. Enhanced permeability and retention effect: A key facilitator for solid tumor targeting by nanoparticles. Photodiagnosis Photodyn. Ther. 39, 102915. https://doi.org/10.1016/j.pdpdt.2022.102915.

Shrestha, S., Wang, B., Dutta, P., 2020. Nanoparticle processing: Understanding and controlling aggregation. Adv. Colloid Interface Sci. 279, 102162. https://doi.org/10.1016/j.cis.2020.102162.

Shukla, M., Verma, N.V., Mohanta, Z., Tripathi, S., Pandya, A., 2023. A review on tunable multi-functional Prussian blue nanoparticles; their promising biological applications & future directions. Coord. Chem. Rev. 496, 215414. https://doi.org/10.1016/j.ccr.2023.215414.

Silva Lima, B., Videira, M.A., 2018. Toxicology and biodistribution: the clinical value of animal biodistribution studies. Mol. Ther., Methods Clin. Dev. 8, 183–197. https://doi.org/10.1016/j.omtm.2018.01.003.

Smith, R.H., A policy framework for developing a national nanotechnology program. (1998),

Son, B., Kim, M., Won, H., Jung, A., Kim, J., Koo, Y., Lee, N.K., Baek, S.-H., Han, U., Park, C.G., Shin, H., Gweon, B., Joo, J., Ho Park, H., 2023. Secured delivery of basic fibroblast growth factor using human serum albumin-based protein nanoparticles for enhanced wound healing and regeneration. J. Nanobiotechnol. 21 (1). https://doi.org/10.1186/s12951-023-02053-4.

Son, S., Song, S., Lee, S.J., Min, S., Kim, S.A., Young Yhee, J., Huh, M.S., Chan Kwon, I., Jeong, S.Y., Byun, Y., Kim, S. H., Kim, K., 2013. Self-crosslinked human serum albumin nanocarriers for systemic delivery of polymerized siRNA to tumors. Biomaterials 34 (37), 9475–9485. https://doi.org/10.1016/j.biomaterials.2013.08.085.

Song, R., Murphy, M., Li, C., Ting, K., Soo, C., Zhong, Z., 2018. Current development of biodegradable polymeric materials for biomedical applications. Drug Des. Dev. Ther. 12, 3117–3145. https://doi.org/10.2147/dddt.s165440.

Stevens, C.A., Kaur, K., Klok, H.A., 2021. Self-assembly of protein-polymer conjugates for drug delivery. Adv. Drug Deliv. Rev. 174, 447–460. https://doi.org/10.1016/j.addr.2021.05.002.

Subhan, Md A., Torchilin, V.P., 2020. siRNA based drug design, quality, delivery and clinical translation. Nanomed. Nanotechnol. Biol. Med. 29, 102239. https://doi.org/10.1016/j.nano.2020.102239.

Tandon, S., Kandasubramanian, B., Ibrahim, S.M., 2020. Silk-based composite scaffolds for tissue engineering applications. Ind. Eng. Chem. Res. 59 (40), 17593–17611. https://doi.org/10.1021/acs.iecr.0c02195.

Tarhini, M., Greige-Gerges, H., Elaissari, A., 2017. Protein-based nanoparticles: from preparation to encapsulation of active molecules. Int. J. Pharm. 522 (1–2), 172–197. https://doi.org/10.1016/j.ijpharm.2017.01.067.

Tesarova, B., Musilek, K., Rex, S., Heger, Z., 2020. Taking advantage of cellular uptake of ferritin nanocages for targeted drug delivery. J. Contr. Release 325, 176–190. https://doi.org/10.1016/j.jconrel.2020.06.026.

Thiruvengadathan, R., Korampally, V., Ghosh, A., Chanda, N., Gangopadhyay, K., Gangopadhyay, S., 2013. Nanomaterial processing using self-assembly-bottom-up chemical and biological approaches. Rep. Prog. Phys. 76 (6), 066501. https://doi.org/10.1088/0034-4885/76/6/066501.

Tomadoni, B., Capello, C., Valencia, G.A., Gutiérrez, T.J., 2020. Self-assembled proteins for food applications: a review. Trends Food Sci. Technol. 101, 1–16. https://doi.org/10.1016/j.tifs.2020.04.015.

Tong, W., Song, X., Gao, C., 2012. Layer-by-layer assembly of microcapsules and their biomedical applications. Chem. Soc. Rev. 41 (18), 6103–6124. https://doi.org/10.1039/c2cs35088b.

Unzueta, U., Virtudes Céspedes, M., Vázquez, E., Ferrer-Miralles, N., Mangues, R., Villaverde, A., 2015. Towards protein-based viral mimetics for cancer therapies. Trends Biotechnol. 33 (5), 253–258. https://doi.org/10.1016/j.tibtech.2015.02.007.

Varanko, A., Saha, S., Chilkoti, A., 2020. Recent trends in protein and peptide-based biomaterials for advanced drug delivery. Adv. Drug Deliv. Rev. 156, 133–187. https://doi.org/10.1016/j.addr.2020.08.008.

Varenne, F., Botton, J., Merlet, C., Vachon, J.-J., Geiger, S., Infante, I.C., Chehimi, M.M., Vauthier, C., 2015. Standardization and validation of a protocol of zeta potential measurements by electrophoretic light scattering for nanomaterial characterization. Colloids Surf. A Physicochem. Eng. Asp. 486, 218–231. https://doi.org/10.1016/j.colsurfa.2015.08.044.

Verma, M.L., Dhanya, B.S., Sukriti, Rani, V., Thakur, M., Jeslin, J., Kushwaha, R., 2020. Carbohydrate and protein based biopolymeric nanoparticles: Current status and biotechnological applications. Int. J. Biol. Macromol. 154, 390–412. https://doi.org/10.1016/j.ijbiomac.2020.03.105.

Viswanadha, L.S., Arcot, Y., Lin, Y.-T., Akbulut, M.E.S., 2024. A comparative investigation of release kinetics of paclitaxel from natural protein and macromolecular nanocarriers in nanoscale drug delivery systems. JCIS Open 15, 100120. https://doi.org/10.1016/j.jciso.2024.100120.

Wang, B., He, X., Zhang, Z., Zhao, Y., Feng, W., 2013. Metabolism of nanomaterials in vivo : blood circulation and organ clearance. Accounts Chem. Res. 46 (3), 761–769. https://doi.org/10.1021/ar2003336.

Wang, C., Wu, J., Wang, C., Mu, C., Ngai, T., Lin, W., 2022. Advances in Pickering emulsions stabilized by protein particles: toward particle fabrication, interaction and arrangement. Food Res. Int. 157, 111380. https://doi.org/10.1016/j.foodres.2022.111380.

Wang, G., Uludag, H., 2008. Recent developments in nanoparticle-based drug delivery and targeting systems with emphasis on protein-based nanoparticles. Expet Opin. Drug Deliv. 5 (5), 499–515. https://doi.org/10.1517/17425247.5.5.499.

Wang, S., Liu, R., Fu, Y., John Kao, W., 2020a. Release mechanisms and applications of drug delivery systems for extended-release. Expet Opin. Drug Deliv. 17 (9), 1289–1304. https://doi.org/10.1080/17425247.2020.1788541.

Wang, X., Sun, T., Zhu, H., Han, T., Wang, J., Dai, H., 2020b. Roles of pH, cation valence, and ionic strength in the stability and aggregation behavior of zinc oxide nanoparticles. J. Environ. Manag. 267, 110656. https://doi.org/10.1016/j.jenvman.2020.110656.

Weber, C., Coester, C., Kreuter, J., Langer, K., 2000. Desolvation process and surface characterisation of protein nanoparticles. Int. J. Pharm. 194 (1), 91–102. https://doi.org/10.1016/s0378-5173(99)00370-1.

Wells, M.J.M., Chen, J.Y., Bodycomb, J., Wolgemuth, D., Stretz, H.A., Adam Zacheis, G., Bautista, M., Bell, K.Y., 2024. Multi-laser nanoparticle tracking analysis (NTA): a unique method to visualize dynamic (shear) and dynamic (Brownian motion) light scattering and quantify nonliving natural organic matter (NNOM) in environmental water. Sci. Total Environ. 949, 174985. https://doi.org/10.1016/j.scitotenv.2024.174985.

Windhab, E.J., Dressler, M., Feigl, K., Fischer, P., Megias-Alguacil, D., 2005. Emulsion processing—from single-drop deformation to design of complex processes and products. Chem. Eng. Sci. 60 (8–9), 2101–2113. https://doi.org/10.1016/j.ces.2004.12.003.

Yadav, R.H., 2024. A review of silk fibroin-based drug delivery systems and their applications. Eur. Polym. J. 216.

Yadav, S., Sharma, A.K., Kumar, P., 2020. Nanoscale self-assembly for therapeutic delivery. Front. Bioeng. Biotechnol. 8. https://doi.org/10.3389/fbioe.2020.00127.

Yaneva, Z., Georgieva, N., 2017. Physicochemical and Morphological Characterization of Pharmaceutical Nanocarriers and Mathematical Modeling of Drug Encapsulation/release Mass Transfer Processes Nanoscale Fabrication, Optimization, Scale-Up and Biological Aspects of Pharmaceutical Nanotechnology. Elsevier, Bulgaria, pp. 173–218. https://doi.org/10.1016/B978-0-12-813629-4.00005-X.

Yasmin, R., Shah, M., Ahmad Khan, S., Ali, R., 2017. Gelatin nanoparticles: a potential candidate for medical applications. Nanotechnol. Rev. 6 (2), 191–207. https://doi.org/10.1515/ntrev-2016-0009.

Yavuz, B., Chambre, L., Kaplan, D.L., 2019. Extended release formulations using silk proteins for controlled delivery of therapeutics. Expet Opin. Drug Deliv. 16 (7), 741–756. https://doi.org/10.1080/17425247.2019.1635116.

Yazdani, S., Mozaffarian, M., Pazuki, G., Hadidi, N., 2022a. Application of Flory-Huggins model in experimental and theoretical study of stability of amphotericin B on nanocarrier based on functionalized carbon nanotube. J. Mol. Liq. 360, 119519. https://doi.org/10.1016/j.molliq.2022.119519.

Yazdani, S., Mozaffarian, M., Pazuki, G., Hadidi, N., Gallego, I., Puras, G., Luis Pedraz, J., 2022b. Design of double functionalized carbon nanotube for amphotericin B and genetic material delivery. Sci. Rep. 12 (1). https://doi.org/10.1038/s41598-022-25222-1.

Ye, C., Chi, H., 2018. A review of recent progress in drug and protein encapsulation: Approaches, applications and challenges. Mater. Sci. Eng. C 83, 233–246. https://doi.org/10.1016/j.msec.2017.10.003.

Yin, S., Davey, K., Dai, S., Liu, Y., Bi, J., 2022. A critical review of ferritin as a drug nanocarrier: Structure, properties, comparative advantages and challenges. Particuology 64, 65–84. https://doi.org/10.1016/j.partic.2021.04.020.

Yu, M., Wu, J., Shi, J., Farokhzad, O.C., 2016. Nanotechnology for protein delivery: Overview and perspectives. J. Contr. Release 240, 24–37. https://doi.org/10.1016/j.jconrel.2015.10.012.

Zahariev, N., Draganova, M., Zagorchev, P., Pilicheva, B., 2023. Casein-based nanoparticles: a potential tool for the delivery of daunorubicin in acute lymphocytic leukemia. Pharmaceutics 15 (2), 471. https://doi.org/10.3390/pharmaceutics15020471.

Zamboni, W.C., Szebeni, J., Kozlov, S.V., Lucas, A.T., Piscitelli, J.A., Dobrovolskaia, M.A., 2018. Animal models for analysis of immunological responses to nanomaterials: Challenges and considerations. Adv. Drug Deliv. Rev. 136–137, 82–96. https://doi.org/10.1016/j.addr.2018.09.012.

Zhang, T., Xu, J., Chen, J., Wang, Z., Wang, X., Zhong, J., 2021. Protein nanoparticles for Pickering emulsions: A comprehensive review on their shapes, preparation methods, and modification methods. Trends Food Sci. Technol. 113, 26–41. https://doi.org/10.1016/j.tifs.2021.04.054.

Zhao, H., Lin, Z.Y., Yildirimer, L., Dhinakar, A., Zhao, X., Wu, J., 2016. Polymer-based nanoparticles for protein delivery: design, strategies and applications. J. Mater. Chem. B 4 (23), 4060–4071. https://doi.org/10.1039/C6TB00308G.

Zhao, Z., Li, Y., Xie, M.B., 2015. Silk fibroin-based nanoparticles for drug delivery. Int. J. Mol. Sci. 16 (3), 4880–4903. https://doi.org/10.3390/ijms16034880.

Zhou, Y., Peng, Z., Seven, E.S., Leblanc, R.M., 2018. Crossing the blood-brain barrier with nanoparticles. J. Contr. Release 270, 290–303. https://doi.org/10.1016/j.jconrel.2017.12.015.

Zielińska, A., Karczewski, J., Eder, P., Kolanowski, T., Szalata, M., Wielgus, K., Szalata, M., Kim, D., Shin, S.R., Słomski, R., Souto, E.B., 2023. Scaffolds for drug delivery and tissue engineering: The role of genetics. J. Contr. Release 359, 207–223. https://doi.org/10.1016/j.jconrel.2023.05.042.

Zottig, X., Côté-Cyr, M., Arpin, D., Archambault, D., Bourgault, S., 2020. Protein supramolecular structures: from self-assembly to nanovaccine design. Nanomaterials 10 (5), 1008. https://doi.org/10.3390/nano10051008.

CHAPTER

# 5

# Design, development, and drug delivery applications of self-assembling nanocarriers from engineered proteins

*Tanvir Ahmed and Kazi Tasnuva Alam*

**Department of Pharmaceutical Sciences, North South University, Dhaka, Bangladesh**

## 1. Introduction

The nanoparticle-based drug delivery system has emerged as a promising platform in pharmaceutical research, enhancing the delivery efficiency of encapsulated anticancer agents, therapeutic proteins, and various other drugs through nanoscale formulation and overcoming the barriers associated with biodistribution, stability, clearance, and unfavorable physicochemical properties (Varma et al., 2020). Among the diverse categories of substances used, such as carbon, metal, lipid, ceramic, polymers, micelles, and graphene, protein-nanocarrier systems have gained prominence due to their superior biocompatibility and biodegradability relative to synthesized molecules. Proteins, as fascinating biomacromolecules showing extensive variety and functionality, are recognized as important components of organisms, involved in all cellular processes, including metabolism, gene transcription and expression, response to stimuli, and molecular transport, which accounts for their substantial investigation in the domain of drug delivery. Due to their small dimensions, cells can readily take protein nanoparticles through endocytosis. They are highly biocompatible, biodegradable, and stable inside biological tissues, so they are less likely to be immunogenic and cause toxicity after administration. Moreover, protein nanoparticles offer ease of size control and surface modification, which corresponds with the main purpose of designing nanoparticle systems so that the nanocarriers can release drugs to perform specific activities in vivo. Furthermore, because of their nonantigenic property, protein-based nanosystems are used in targeted therapies for cancer and infectious diseases. Protein

*Protein-Based Nanoparticles in Drug Delivery*
**https://doi.org/10.1016/B978-0-443-33639-3.00023-4**

nanoparticles for the administration of drugs can be synthesized from several proteins, including silk fibroin, albumin, legumin, lipoprotein, gelatin, ferritin, and 30Kc19 (a cell-penetrating and protein-stabilizing protein derived from Bombyx mori (silkworm) hemolymph). Each of these types comes with its own set of pros and cons that are used for various purposes. Typically, four types of approaches are undertaken to generate protein nanocarriers, namely the chemical method (emulsion, complex coacervation), physical method (electrospray, nanospray), desolvation, and self-assembly techniques (Hong et al., 2020).

Self-assembly is common across several biological systems, resulting in the development of diverse complex biological structures found in nature. These intricate and sophisticated examples motivate scientists to develop analogous artificial systems using the fundamental components of life, including amino acids, lipids, carbon, polymers, and nucleic acids. This chapter aims to explore self-assembled nanocarriers derived from modified proteins used in modern drug delivery. The self-assembly approach is a bottom-up process where components spontaneously assemble and form ordered nanostructures by covalent or noncovalent interactions (Ariga et al., 2016). This enables the aggregation of structures into ordered arrays that are too small for individual manipulation. This innovative approach produces supramolecular structures, endowing distinctive features to its inorganic and organic components. Self-assembled nanomaterials have emerged as a valuable resource in biomedicine, particularly in medical diagnostics, biosensors, and drug delivery due to their simplicity, adaptability, spontaneity, scalability, reversibility, and cost-effectiveness. In comparison to alternative nanocarrier systems, self-assembled nanoparticles enhance drug bioavailability, extend drug delivery efficacy, facilitate targeted delivery, allow controlled release, and mitigate drug resistance, hence optimizing the therapeutic delivery process of agents to treat a wide range of diseases (Yadav et al., 2020). Among the many self-assembled nanoparticles, protein-based self-assembled ones are extensively studied and engineered due to their intrinsic biocompatibility, biodegradability, and stability. Moreover, peptides show considerable variety in chemical composition and the ability to transform into highly organized structures. This allows for the manipulation of final assemblies by controlling structural features at the nanometric scale, making them valuable building blocks for the formation of self-assembled nanostructures in drug delivery applications (Panda and Chauhan, 2014). Amino acids function as a versatile biochemical toolkit for the synthesis of peptide-based materials, displaying a wide array of physicochemical characteristics related to their size, charge, hydrophobicity, and polarity. Peptide self-assembly is primarily driven and regulated by noncovalent interactions. These interactions facilitate the self-assembly process and stabilize the secondary structure of proteins and peptides. Noncovalent interactions, including hydrophobic interactions, electrostatic forces, hydrogen bonding, van der Waals contacts, $\pi$–$\pi$ stacking, and coordination bonds, are the key contributors to the initiation of molecular self-assembly. There is an increasing interest in developing dynamic systems that can assemble and disassemble in response to external stimuli. Noncovalent interactions are fragile and highly responsive to changes in environmental variables, including pH, light, temperature, ionic strength, and solvent polarity. Hence, these factors work as triggers driving the self-assembling of peptides (Ariga et al., 2016; Lowik et al., 2010).

Scientists today adopt the cutting-edge technology of protein engineering to synthesize self-assembling peptide building blocks. Nanoparticles are engineered through chemical and genetic modifications to show specific properties, including drug encapsulation, targeting specificity, stimuli responsiveness, surface functionalization, and distinct physicochemical characteristics. Currently, strategies such as direct evolution, de novo design, solid-phase methods, ring-opening polymerization techniques, and genetic engineering are used to adjust the functionalities of proteins, resulting in modified protein structures that are more appropriate for their intended applications than the original forms. These engineered self-assembled proteins serve as effective drug carriers for a targeted and controlled release of therapeutic cargo, minimizing side effects, enhancing drug stability, and optimizing biodistribution (Ariga et al., 2016; Olshefsky et al., 2022).

This chapter seeks to disseminate the knowledge of the design, synthesis, and working of self-assembling nanocarriers from engineered proteins, along with an in-depth exploration of the protein engineering process, fabrication of self-assembling protein nanocarriers, their types, and diverse drug-loading techniques used. By the end of this chapter, readers will have a comprehensive understanding of the functionality, applications, and limitations of self-assembled protein nanocarriers in therapeutic drug delivery. They will also realize the vast scope of this innovative technique for optimizing drug delivery paradigms in biomedicine.

# 2. Protein engineering for nanocarrier development

## 2.1 Principles of protein engineering

Protein engineering is a powerful biotechnological process that involves modifying a protein's structure by substituting, inserting, or deleting nucleotides in the encoding gene, intending to develop proteins suitable for specific purposes (Engqvist and Rabe, 2019). Every protein possesses a distinct genetic code corresponding to a certain amino acid sequence. Researchers use genetic engineering techniques to alter codons and create various proteins with potentially enhanced functions. Moreover, technical innovations like X-ray crystallography and computer modeling assist researchers in formulating amino acid sequences that accurately fold into defined three-dimensional structures, thereby creating proteins with particular characteristics (Kuhlman and Bradley, 2019). For example, the modification of insulin structure exemplifies how protein engineering can transform peptide functionalities. It was observed that storage of a drug product containing individual native insulin molecules led to the formation of dimeric and hexameric structures, resulting in a delayed therapeutic effect. To address this issue, modifications to the amino acid sequence in the areas of protein linked to self-association reduced aggregation, thereby producing faster-acting insulins (Reynolds et al., 2013).

This fundamental principle of modifying the genetic code of proteins is used to alter different types of biomolecules in the biomedical industry to serve purposes relating to drug delivery, diagnostic imaging, tissue engineering, and biosensing. Protein engineering includes several methodologies such as rational design, guided evolution, semirational design, peptidomimetics, and de novo protein design. Researchers use these strategies to create innovative proteins or enhance the characteristics of existing proteins useful for different biomedical applications. Researchers subsequently evaluate newly engineered protein variations to ascertain those exhibiting favorable functions. To do this, they have devised effective screening techniques, including fluorescence-activated cell sorting

(FACS) and phage display technologies, to analyze extensive libraries of synthetic proteins and enzymes (Bansal and Kundu, 2022; Xiao et al., 2015).

## 2.2 Techniques for protein modification and functionalization

Protein structures are altered using several techniques, including rational design, directed evolution, semirational protein design, peptidomimetics, and de novo protein design.

Rational design is a conventional protein modification technique where researchers perform specific point mutations through insertions or deletions in the coding sequence, informed by structural and functional insights of the target protein. They generally alter coding areas associated with a protein's function.

This approach is less time-consuming compared to others, and protein-based vaccines can be effectively engineered using this technique. However, a significant limitation of this technique is the difficulty in precisely predicting the sequence–structure–function relationship, especially at the individual amino acid level (Sellés Vidal et al., 2023).

The directed evolution approach, a highly efficient and robust technique for protein engineering, earned Frances H. Arnold the Nobel Prize in Chemistry in 2018. It has become a cornerstone in protein engineering due to its capacity to imitate the natural evolutionary process to produce proteins with desirable features. This process involves random mutations in the gene of interest, followed by rigorous screening and optimization of protein functionality, such as selectivity and activity. Scientists commonly use error-prone PCR (polymerase chain reaction) to create a wide range of random mutations as a part of creating a library of protein variants. Moreover, methods like DNA shuffling and random insertions/deletions are also used. Following random mutagenesis, high-throughput screening (HTS) experiments are used to assess the extensive array of mutant proteins and select those showing preferred characteristics (stability, specificity, binding affinity, etc.). Afterward, the most effective gene variations are isolated and amplified for further mutagenesis. This method, although resource-intensive, does not require preexisting structural data of proteins and allows for the exploration of many mutations, making it applicable to a broad spectrum of proteins for research and therapeutic applications (Sellés Vidal et al., 2023; Wang et al., 2021).

Semirational protein design is a hybrid methodology in protein engineering that integrates elements of rational design with directed evolution techniques. This method involves targeting a specific area of the protein using existing structural and functional data, thus creating "smart" libraries. This focused strategy diminishes the unpredictability of conventional directed evolution while preserving the ability to explore a broader substrate spectrum, specificity, selectivity, and stability without compromising their catalytic efficacy (Chica et al., 2005).

Peptidomimetics is a biological technique for protein modification that includes several methods to replicate or inhibit the structural characteristics and biological functions of peptides or enzymes, resulting in the synthesis of metabolically stable peptide analogs. Peptidomimetics uses combinatorial methods that incorporate various synthetic biology techniques, leading to the fast creation of protein variants. This technique produces modified proteins showing improved stability, bioavailability, pharmacokinetic characteristics, and decreased immunogenicity. Therefore, peptides generated through this strategy have the potential to be used as carriers for therapeutic agents in biomedicine. Nonetheless, intricate design and high costs restrict the extensive adoption of this method (Vagner et al., 2008).

With the rapid progress in the integration of computational techniques with healthcare, de novo protein synthesis has emerged as one of the most revolutionary discoveries in the realm of protein engineering. In 2024, David Baker was awarded the Nobel Prize in Chemistry for computational protein design, which he shared with Demis Hassabis and John Jumper for their contributions to protein structure prediction. The de novo design methodology synthesizes proteins with precise structural and functional qualities from scratch, compared to other methods that modify native protein structures. New amino acid sequences are engineered to fold into predetermined three-dimensional structures with designated functions or to bind to certain targets. Furthermore, computational methods facilitate the prediction of protein sequences to yield highly effective results. For instance, machine learning techniques, specifically denoising diffusion probabilistic models (DDPM), facilitate photorealistic image production for visualizing protein folding and assist in de novo protein design. Moreover, advanced methods such as Rosetta and AlphaFold are used for predicting protein sequences. Furthermore, de novo design can generate small peptides capable of self-assembly and responsive to particular external stimuli such as pH, temperature, enzymes, light, etc. This innovative technology transcends the limitations of natural protein design and enables the creation of protein structures not commonly observed in nature. De novo design is gaining prominence in multiple domains of biomedicine, including drug delivery, therapeutic intervention, biosensors, and synthetic biology. However, researchers must still confront challenges related to intricate computational methods, operational complexity, and high costs (Watson et al., 2023).

## 2.3 Selection of proteins for nanocarrier design

Protein-based nanostructures for drug delivery systems are constructed from a variety of self-assembling proteins and can be further modified to acquire specific desirable characteristics. This section and Table 5.1 address the most common ones used in drug delivery applications.

Fibroin comprises 65%–85% of the total protein content in silk fibers. Fibroin is a semicrystalline configuration with heavy and light chains, generally obtained from the silk of the Bombyx mori silkworm. The heavy chain consists of 12 principal hydrophobic domains interconnected by 11 hydrophilic segments. Nano-carriers synthesized with this type of protein exhibit exceptional stability, flexibility, mechanical strength, and excellent biocompatibility and biodegradability. They are self-assembling proteins that can be customized to obtain desirable features. Furthermore, they can mitigate certain disadvantages of low molecular weight drugs by facilitating controlled drug release, inhibiting drug degradation, and producing little systemic toxicity in vivo. Nonetheless, the continual degeneration of silk II crystalline antiparallel β-sheet domains limits the overall effectiveness of this nanoparticle system (Bailey, no date).

Human serum albumin (HSA) is a globular protein mostly found in the bloodstream, consisting of roughly 585 amino acids. HSA is known for its function as a transport medium for various substances and for enhancing the solubility of hydrophobic drugs in the blood circulation (Langer et al., 2003). Moreover, HSA has remarkable stability in response to variations in pH, temperature, and organic solvents. Due to its biological origin, HSA is biocompatible, biodegradable, and nonimmunogenic. Furthermore, HSA shows a strong

**TABLE 5.1** Classification of self-assembling protein nanocarriers.

| SL No. | Protein type | Structural features | Assembly mechanism | Applications | References |
|---|---|---|---|---|---|
| 01 | Silk-based proteins (fibroin) | A semicrystalline fibrous structure consisting of heavy and light chains linked together via a single disulfide bond, rich in β-sheet regions | Self-assembly is induced by hydrophobic interactions and β-sheet folding | Drug delivery, vascular tissue regeneration, wound healing | Qi et al. (2017) |
| 02 | Human serum albumin (HSA) | Globular protein comprised of SA is comprised of 67% α-helices, 10% turns, 23% random coils, and no β-sheets, contains several binding sites with disulfide bonds stabilizing the HSA fold | Self-assembly is induced by hydrophobic interactions and the influence of external factors such as pH and temperature | Drug delivery, molecular diagnostics, and tissue engineering | Mishra and Heath (2021) |
| 03 | Ferritin | Hollow spherical structures consisting of an inner inorganic core and an outer polypeptide shell | Self-assembly is induced by variations in pH level and noncovalent bonds | Drug delivery, gene delivery | Liang et al. (2014) |
| 04 | Gelatin | Triple helix amorphous structure made up of three alpha chains and derived from collagen | Self-assembly is induced by temperature and electrostatic forces | Drug delivery, tissue engineering, wound healing | Kommareddy et al. (2003) |
| 05 | Casein micelles | Indistinct globular tertiary structure, micellar quaternary structure with a hydrophobic core and a peripheral hydrophilic layer | Self-assembly is driven by hydrophobic interactions and calcium and phosphate | Drug and nutrient delivery | Bhat et al. (2016) |
| 06 | Legumin | Globular storage protein | Self-assembly induced by factors like ionic strength, pH, and temperature | Drug delivery, gene delivery, and nutrient delivery | Cho and Jones (2019) |

affinity for multiple drugs and antibodies, thereby enabling the effective integration of these molecules through a matrix of HSA nanoparticles (Steinhauser et al., 2008). Saleh et al. produced HSA nanoparticles encapsulating curcumin using a desolvation process and gave them to HER-2-positive breast cancer cells, yielding nanoparticles with a size of $246.1 \pm 15.4$ nm and a zeta potential of $-25 \pm 2.7$ mV. The drug-loading efficiency of nanoparticles was 3.4%, while the encapsulation efficiency was 71.3%, indicating improvements in both the stability and solubility of curcumin. However, the increased production costs pose an obstacle to its widespread manufacturing and application in biomedicine (Saleh et al., 2019).

Ferritin is a self-assembling protein that is frequently used in nanotechnology. It has a hollow globular structure and a molecular weight of 474 kDa, made up of 24 subunits. The structure consists of a 6-nm inorganic core made of hydrated iron oxide ferrihydrite, which is surrounded by a spherical polypeptide shell referred to as apoferritin. Twenty-four identical ferritin subunits self-assemble to generate ferritin nanoparticles. The proteins show excellent pH stability, thermal stability, and high biodegradability, making them a preferred candidate for nanocarrier design. Liang et al. used H-ferritin (HFn)-nanocaged nanoparticles to administer doxorubicin (DOX), using a natural HFn nanocarrier that precisely targeted tumor cells, resulting in a substantial reduction in tumor growth following a single-dose treatment. Nonetheless, similar to HAS (Human Serum Albumin), the production cost of ferritin is high (Liang et al., 2014; Chasteen and Harrison, 1999).

Legumin is a type of plant-derived protein that may spontaneously aggregate into nanoparticles formed by the coacervation technique. The principal storage proteins of soybean seeds are abundant in sulfur-containing amino acids and comprise six subunits. Legumin-derived nanoparticles are capable of encapsulating folic acid, genetic material, and chemotherapeutic drugs. These particles have significant bioadhesive properties, therefore eliminating the possibility of tissue damage. Furthermore, they show low immunogenicity and great stability. However, the usefulness of these types of nanocarriers remains under investigation, providing scientists the opportunity to discover methods to optimize legumin-based nanocarriers for improved yield (Cho and Jones, 2019).

Gelatin is another type of protein for nanocarrier design that can self-assemble used cross-linkers such as phosphates and aldehydes. They are the first proteinaceous substances used in the synthesis of nanoparticles. Gelatin-based nanoparticles are extremely biodegradable, biocompatible, and safe when administered within the body. The advantageous characteristics of gelatin-based nanoparticles, combined with the considerable potential of nanosized delivery systems, make them a promising option for drug delivery. Gelatin, readily available, FDA-approved, and deemed a generally recognized safe protein, is used as a dietary supplement and plasma expander by intravenous infusion. Gelatin nanoparticles are extensively used for the encapsulation of DNA, RNA, and several biologically active compounds, including bovine serum albumin (BSA), basic fibroblast growth factor (bFGF), and bone morphogenetic protein 2 (BMP-2). Nonetheless, the low mechanical strength and rapid disintegration rate restrict their ability to achieve their full potential as the most effective nanocarriers for therapeutic applications (Hong et al., 2020; Kommareddy et al., 2003). Other types of self-assembling proteins currently under study for nanocarrier design include transferrin, lactoferrin, casein, collagen, and fibronectin.

Self-assembling protein nanocarriers have become preferred platforms for drug administration due to their inherent biocompatibility and biodegradability, structural consistency, and design versatility. Advancements in genetic engineering and synthetic biology enable the modification of these proteins through various genetic methods and computational techniques, allowing scientists to tailor the properties of nanocarriers for specific purposes.

## 2.4 Structural considerations in protein nanocarriers

In the development of efficient protein-based nanovehicles for therapeutic drug or gene delivery, it is essential to thoroughly assess the design and physical characteristics of the selected proteins. These factors are essential to guarantee the functioning, stability, and efficacy of the nanocarriers in facilitating targeted and controlled delivery. The following sections explore such significant characteristics of proteins.

### 2.4.1 Protein folding and stability

Protein folding represents a fundamental and captivating topic in structural biology, prompting substantial study into the identification of folding intermediates, real-time folding probes, computational modeling, and simulations. From these early studies, various models on the mechanism of protein folding were established. Despite significant advancements in knowledge during the past 4 decades since the study into the protein folding problem increased, this molecular enigma remains unresolved. It is now evident that the diverse hypothesized theories of protein folding are unlikely to function in a mutually exclusive manner, and that the folding mechanisms are expected to differ among proteins. However, the fundamental principle of protein folding has been understood by researchers at this point. Protein folding is a crucial prerequisite for protein functionality and, consequently, cellular function, wherein, following synthesis by a ribosome as a linear amino acid chain, it transitions from an unstable random coil to a more organized three-dimensional conformation. The core structure undergoes folding into the secondary structures of alpha helices and beta sheets. The secondary structure of the protein influences the tertiary structure, representing the protein's three-dimensional configuration. This fundamental characteristic of proteins indicates their biological activity and helps in sustaining the normal physiology of living organisms. On the contrary, misfolded proteins often generate toxic chemicals that lead to the development of various neurological disorders such as Parkinson's disease, Alzheimer's disease, and Huntington's disease (Kang and Kini, 2009).

The properties of different amino acids can affect the structural attributes and folding patterns of polypeptides. The positioning of residues, along with variations in the microenvironment and external factors such as temperature, pH, and organic solvents, can influence protein folding outcomes. Therefore, it is essential to oversee and regulate the stability of protein folding in order to prevent its misfolding (Kang and Kini, 2009). Protein folding stability is the equilibrium of free energy between the folded and unfolded forms of a protein, and it is a crucial determinant of the protein's structure and biological function. The underlying thermodynamics of folding can affect disease, govern protein evolution, and guide protein engineering; therefore, innovative methods are necessary to clarify these thermodynamics for each protein sequence and structure. Consequently, scientists developed cDNA display proteolysis, a technique for evaluating thermodynamic folding stability for up to 900,000 protein domains over the course of 1 week. This distinctive, scalable method can measure the environmental factors affecting protein stability, identify stability determinants in engineered proteins, and assess design methodologies and thermodynamic interactions across different protein sites (Tsuboyama et al., 2023). Furthermore, differential scanning calorimetry (DSC) characterizes protein stability in its native state by quantifying the heat necessary to denature a specific biomolecule, such as a protein. Molecules with elevated thermal transition midpoints ($T_m$) are regarded as more stable than those with diminished $T_m$. Additionally, circular dichroism (CD) spectroscopy and fluorescence-based assays are utilized for similar purposes (Johnson, 2013).

At present, numerous protein stability prediction tools (MAESTRO, DUET, FoldX, Rosetta, IMutant3, Hunter, etc.) are used to differentiate between stable and unstable, as well as active and inactive, protein variations. These computational technologies possess the capacity to facilitate the swift and cost-effective generation of proteins while addressing numerous constraints of traditional protein engineering methods (Broom et al., 2020).

### 2.4.2 *Self-assembly mechanisms*

The self-assembly of proteins is a prominent biological process wherein protein subunits spontaneously arrange into one or more highly ordered structures from a complex mixture, influenced by thermodynamic and kinetic factors, including noncovalent interactions such as van der Waals forces, electrostatic forces, hydrogen bonds, and stacking interactions. The ultimate configurations of protein assembly can manifest in several forms, including nanostructures, crystals, gels, filaments, or amorphous aggregates. The folding pathway of proteins depends on amino acids, the smallest building blocks. Protein structure has four levels: primary, secondary, tertiary, and quaternary. Their amino acid sequences dictate the folding and intramolecular bonding of the straight amino acid chain, resulting in proteins' distinctive three-dimensional structure. Hydrogen bonding between amino and carboxyl groups in nearby protein chains can generate particular folding patterns. The secondary structure of proteins includes stable folding motifs known as alpha helices and beta sheets. The tertiary structure of a protein refers to the three-dimensional folding and assembly of a polypeptide chain. Finally, proteins with numerous polypeptide chains or subunits constitute its higher-order quaternary structures. Most proteins, however, do not require quaternary structure because they are composed of a single polypeptide chain that only represents the tertiary level of structure. Peptides and proteins have gained significant interest in the development of self-assembled nanostructures owing to their intrinsic biocompatibility, biodegradability, simple design, and variability in shape and sequence. These biomolecules organize into distinct structures by chemical bonding at their surfaces, resulting in innovative shapes with various functionalities, including nanofibers, nanotubes, nanofibrils, cylindrical micelles, tubular nanostructures, nanospheres, and nanorods. The self-assembly of peptides is affected by the amino acid sequence and environmental factors such as pH, temperature, enzymes, light, redox potential, etc. Covalently triggered mechanisms yield nanostructures that lead to the formation of thermodynamically stable self-assembled compounds, which show an enhanced ability to encapsulate a diverse array of therapeutic agents and improve their targeted efficacy (Kang et al., 2018; Mandal et al., 2014). The key mechanisms for protein self-assembly are outlined in Table 5.2.

A subsequent classification based on energy dissipation during operation categorizes the self-assembly process as either static or dynamic. A static self-assembly process is defined as an ordered assembly that maintains equilibrium without energy dissipation, while a dynamic self-assembly process requires a self-organized structure that experiences energy loss. The folding of a globular protein signifies a static self-assembly process (Maheswari, no date).

### 2.4.3 *Functional domains for targeted delivery*

The presentation of functional domains on nanoparticle surfaces modulates specific biological interactions, including targeted delivery to tumor vasculature and immune-mediated

TABLE 5.2 Design strategies for self-assembling protein nanocarriers.

| SL No. | Design strategy | Key functional groups | Stability factors | Targeting approach | Advantages | Challenges | References |
|---|---|---|---|---|---|---|---|
| 01 | Hydrophobic interactions | Nonpolar residues, including leucine and phenylalanine | Hydrophobicity, protein folding stability | Passive targeting | Enhanced stability of the nanocarriers, improved encapsulation of hydrophobic drugs | Limited selectivity in precise targeting | Sánchez-Iglesias et al. (2012) |
| 02 | Hydrogen bond | Amide groups, carboxyl groups, hydroxyl groups | Environmental conditions | Interaction via hydrogen bonds | Improved specificity of the nanostructures | Complexity in controlled self-assembly, sensitive to varying environmental factors | Liu et al. (2021) |
| 03 | Electrostatic interactions | Charged amino acids such as lysine and arginine | pH, ionic strength, charge density | Electrostatic interaction with specific types of cells | Enhanced tuneability, versatility, and specificity of nanoparticles | Sensitivity to varying environmental factors | Zhou and Pang (2018) |
| 04 | Stimuli-responsive assembly | Stimuli-sensitive domains on the protein surface | pH, temperature, redox potential, light, enzyme, ultrasound | Interaction of stimuli-sensitive region with designated tissues | Dynamic control over self-assembly, multifunctionality, and targeted delivery | Complex biological environment | Mu et al. (2024) |
| 05 | Covalent crosslinking | Lysine, cystine, carboxyl groups | Crosslinking density | Targeting ligand attached to the nanocarrier surface | High biostability | Potential loss of biological activity | Jayachandran et al. (2022) |

responses to pathogen-derived antigens in nanoparticle-based delivery systems. Multiple regions or motifs in the protein nanostructure facilitate the targeted distribution of the encapsulated drugs. The ligand binding and surface modification domains facilitate the attachment of specific ligands, like peptides, polymers, antibodies, and aptamers, to the nanoparticle surface, thereby permitting tailored interaction with specific receptors in biological tissues. Polyethylene glycol (PEG) conjugated to albumin is a well-known nanocarrier system that provides significant targeted efficacy and regulated release of several chemotherapeutic drugs. Furthermore, certain stimuli-responsive linker molecules attached to the protein nanostructures enable the nanovehicle to selectively target specific tissues. For example, ionizable compounds are coupled with proteins that are activated by varying pH levels in physiological environments, facilitating targeted and regulated drug release. Additionally, hydrophobic and hydrophilic sequences are included to encapsulate certain drugs within the protein nanocarrier. These functionalities can be imparted to protein nanoparticles through various chemical and physical changes using covalent and noncovalent interactions. Furthermore, innovative protein engineering techniques offer structural and functional modifications of the nanocarrier, making it appropriate for the targeted administration of the encapsulated therapeutic agents (Olshefsky et al., 2022; Aljabali et al., 2022).

## 3. Design and fabrication of self-assembling protein nanocarriers

Self-assembled protein nanostructures show significant potential as biomaterials and for carrier-mediated drug delivery. Scientists have used the distinctive features of proteins to develop and engineer self-assembled nanocarriers by using several strategies. The design, mechanism, and functionalization of these types of carriers are discussed in the sections below.

### 3.1 Strategies for self-assembly in nanocarriers

The self-assembly of nanoparticles to develop nanocarriers relies mostly on covalent and noncovalent interactions, hydrogen bonds, and hydrophobic interactions between the protein molecules. These mechanisms are discussed in the sections below.

#### *3.1.1 Covalent versus noncovalent interactions*

Covalent and noncovalent interactions contribute to the self-assembly of nanocarriers, with each type serving a specific function in the formation, stability, and utility of the nanostructures. Generally, covalent bonds form when two atoms share electrons, forming the foundation for the majority of organic compounds. In the self-assembly of nanocarriers initiated by covalent bonding, multiple types of covalent reactions occur, corresponding to different active functional groups in the peptides. For instance, associated covalent interactions create disulfide bonds in thiol groups (-SH) and form and break amide bonds (–NH–CO). These types of bonds are robust and stable. Conversely, noncovalent interactions lack a common pair of electrons; rather, atoms attract due to opposite charges. These interactions encompass hydrophobic interactions, hydrogen bonding, electrostatic forces, van der Waals forces, and $\pi$–$\pi$ stacking. These strategies also drive the self-assembly of nanoparticles. These bonds are considerably weaker than covalent interactions (Liu et al., 2023).

The spontaneous covalent reaction after in situ self-assembly in water-based solutions can be considered as a self-synthesis of nanomaterials, improving colloidal resilience and stability in physiological systems while reducing toxicity. For example, the Schiff base bond is a dynamic covalent bond characterized by its reversibility and stability across different pH levels. This characteristic is particularly beneficial in delivering chemotherapeutic drugs for anticancer treatment and also in cancer theranostics. Furthermore, self-assembly by covalent bonding can generate nanostructures of adjustable dimensions. Covalent interactions, which facilitate self-assembly, play a crucial role in creating nanocarriers that show enhanced stability under diverse physiological settings, allowing for greater regulation of degradation rates, stimuli responsiveness, and surface functionalization of the nanocarriers (Liu et al., 2023; Ulrich, 2019).

Noncovalent interactions, while weaker than covalent interactions, possess the ability to easily break and reform, thereby providing flexibility to the nanostructure. Furthermore, these interactions can create well-defined nanostructures such as nanofibers and nanorods. These bonds are reversible and dynamic, demonstrating improved stimuli-responsive behavior, drug targeting, and mitigated toxicity. For example, enabling noncovalent self-assembly of proteins by hydrophobic interactions or modification of disulfide bonds can provide nontoxic, crosslinker-free, drug-encapsulated protein nanoparticles. Covalent and noncovalent interactions are essential in the design and development of various protein-based nanodrugs and drug delivery systems, tailored to the specific objectives of the carrier system. A combination of these interactions typically produces the most effective nanocarrier systems (Liu et al., 2023; Hassanin and Elzoghby, 2020).

### *3.1.2 Hydrophobic interactions and hydrogen bonding*

Hydrophobic interactions are a form of weak noncovalent bond that indicates the attractive forces between the nonpolar regions of molecules. In the design of protein-nanocarrier systems, hydrophobic interactions facilitate protein self-assembly through water-mediated interactions between the hydrophobic regions of the proteins. This strategy enables protein folding and confers stability to the proteins. These hydrophobic interactions are particularly significant in the self-assembly of protein-based nanoparticles for the encapsulation of hydrophobic drugs. Hydrophobic binding sites of proteins can interact with lipophilic drugs, facilitating the encapsulation of these hydrophobic bioactive agents within the core of a protein nanoparticle, while the hydrophilic surface stays in contact with the water-based medium. Protein nanoparticles can be stabilized through the formation of intermolecular disulfide bridges. This process occurs when free thiol groups are exposed, and unfolding is induced by reducing agents that act on intramolecular disulfide bonds. Hydrophobic interactions reportedly enhance the biostability, targeting capability, and stimulus responsiveness of protein nanocarriers. Anticancer agents such as DOX, celecoxib, and paclitaxel have been investigated during the creation of protein nanoassemblies. HSA is a frequently studied protein for the production of self-assembling nanocarriers through the incorporation of drugs inside the hydrophobic domains of HSA (Xia et al., 2014).

Hydrogen bonding is crucial in facilitating the self-assembly of protein nanoparticles. A hydrogen atom covalently bonded to an electronegative atom, such as nitrogen, oxygen, or fluorine, and another electronegative atom with a single pair of electrons form a hydrogen bond. In biomolecular self-assembly, hydrogen bonds promote the unidirectional growth of biomolecules, leading to the development of one-dimensional nanostructures. This sort of interaction is dynamic and provides integrity to the nanostructure, facilitates targeted self-assembly, and enhances stimulus reactivity. Protein-based micelles and hydrogels for nanocarriers are formed through self-assembly via hydrogen bonding between protein subunits. Intermolecular hydrogen bonding among several peptide subunits facilitates the formation of nanostructures. For example, peptides containing hydrogen-bonding motifs such as amide groups spontaneously organize into nanostructures such as nanofibers and nanospheres. Moreover, protein-polymer-based nanocarriers are engineered by self-assembly, facilitating the encapsulation of both hydrophobic and hydrophilic drugs (Kang et al., 2018; Wang et al., 2019).

## 3.2 Types of engineered protein nanocarriers

### 3.2.1 *Protein micelles*

Protein-derived polymeric micelles have garnered significant interest in the recent decade and transformed the biomedical therapeutic delivery field. Proteins are considered an advantageous option for micelle development due to their biocompatibility, safety, enhanced blood circulation, and ability to solubilize poorly soluble drugs. Soy, casein, gelatin, and albumin are commonly used proteins for micelle formation. Protein micelles are nanostructures developed by the self-assembly of amphiphilic proteins in aqueous conditions. The principal mechanism enabling the creation of micellar systems is hydrophobic attraction, whereas ionic repulsion or solvation forces function as opposing factors. The hydrophobic areas coalesce to reduce water exposure, creating the micelle core. The hydrophilic areas are exposed to the aqueous phase, constituting the micelle shell. This arrangement leads to a specific position where attractive and repulsive forces equilibrate, resulting in micelle production. Protein micelles undergo chemical modification to form protein–polymer conjugates using synthetic polymers like PEG, enhancing their stability, biocompatibility, and biodegradability as nanocarriers, thereby addressing the limitations of protein-based nanocarriers, which often experience a loss of inherent properties and biological activity. This functionalization enables precise targeting of tissues and minimizes in vivo toxicity. Moreover, protein micelles effectively traverse biological barriers and can be included in diverse formulation designs utilized in biomedical applications. Protein micelles are extensively researched and engineered to encapsulate hydrophobic drugs in their core and hydrophilic drugs in their shell. Furthermore, they are prospective candidates for nucleic acid (DNA, RNA, siRNA) encapsulation for gene delivery. Producing protein micelles at a commercial scale with uniform quality, however, poses significant challenges. In the future, numerous stimuli-responsive polymeric micelles and hybrid protein micelle nanocarriers are anticipated to be developed that will aim to address the limitations of current protein-based micelle nanocarriers (Yadav et al., 2020; Mustafai et al., 2023).

### 3.2.2 *Protein-based hydrogels*

Protein-based hydrogels are valuable materials for numerous medical applications due to their biocompatibility, biodegradability, and adaptability to chemical and biological modifications. Modern developments in protein engineering and synthetic biology have enabled the precise modification of protein sequences, hydrogel architectures, and the mechanical properties of hydrogels, thereby expanding the potential biomedical applications of protein hydrogels, particularly as efficient drug delivery systems. Hydrogels are three-dimensional structures capable of absorbing at least 10% water, either by weight or volume, within their polymer matrix. In the comparison of various biopolymers, proteins show the ability to adopt varied conformations and demonstrate a broader spectrum of chemical and biological functionalities, rendering them appealing as hydrogel materials for the construction of hydrogel-based nanocarriers. Silk, collagen, and elastin are extensively used proteins for the construction of protein-hydrogel nanostructures (Lee et al., 2023). Hydrogels derived from proteins are generally produced via diverse cross-linking methods, including physical cross-linking through polymer chain entanglements or noncovalent interactions, including hydrophobic interactions, hydrogen bonding, and electrostatic forces. These hydrogels are also synthesized using chemical cross-linking through covalent bonding or enzymatic cross-linking techniques (Li et al., 2016a).

To enhance various functionalities of the protein-hydrogel nanocarrier system, proteins are engineered with specific sequences or the incorporation of functional domains such as cysteine and lysine. This improves the mechanical properties of the nanocarriers and facilitates the self-assembly of proteins into hydrogels. Furthermore, these structures can be designed to improve the stimulus-responsiveness of the nanostructures. This can be accomplished by introducing acidic or basic residues to the protein conformation or altering the pH or ionic strength. Temperature influences protein interactions and triggers hydrogel formation. Hydrogels that form quickly at body temperature are particularly advantageous for application as injectable materials in drug delivery. Moreover, proteins with photosensitive modifications can undergo crosslinking through radical-based reactions to develop a three-dimensional network, facilitating faster self-assembly. Despite the remarkable potential of protein-based hydrogels as excellent vehicles for drug, protein, and gene delivery, the crosslinking agents and residues may induce toxicity and stability issues postadministration. These problems can be overcome by developing smart hydrogels and hybrid nanosystems (Lee et al., 2023).

### 3.2.3 *Protein nanocages*

Protein nanocarriers have been investigated as potential engineered vehicles for encapsulating and transporting drugs, nucleic acids, and proteins. The caged structure is constituted by the self-assembly of protein subunits and possesses three engineerable surfaces: the interior, the exterior, and the intersubunit. Therapeutic and diagnostic compounds can be encapsulated within nanocages, and their external surfaces have been optimized to improve biocompatibility and targeted efficacy. Alterations in intersubunit interactions have been demonstrated to influence the self-assembly characteristics, affecting the modulation of drug release. By effectively targeting the engineering sites within the protein nanocages, these structures can be optimized. A prevalent method involves the incorporation of cysteine residues to alter the interior of nanocages. This alteration facilitates the covalent attachment of drugs and other active compounds via disulfide bonds. The exterior can be altered via ligand attachment, such as peptides Arg–Gly–Asp (RGD) and aptamers, or by integrating with polymethylmethacrylate, PEG, poly(lactic-co-glycolic acid), and polyamidoamine, thereby enhancing the targeting affinity, biodegradability, and biocompatibility of the protein nanocage. Moreover, intersubunit modifications can be accomplished by altering protein–protein interactions and regulating the self-assembly mechanism through variations in salt, nucleic acid, metal ion, or pH levels. These engineered nanostructures can subsequently be used for many tailored applications for drug delivery (Bhaskar and Lim, 2017).

Ferritin, E2 protein, and virus-like particles (VLPs) are frequently used natural proteins in the design of nanocages. The iron in the central cavity of the globular, multisubunit-caged ferritin exists as small crystal-like particles in an organic ferric oxyhydroxide form. Ferritin shows stability under elevated temperatures and varying pH levels for brief durations, maintaining its caged quaternary structure composed of 24 subunits without substantial disruption. The ferritin nanocage shows controllable self-assembly and disassembly properties influenced by metal ions, facilitating the absorption and expulsion of active molecules from its protein framework (Uchida et al., 2007; Sana et al., 2015).

Protein nanocages serve as a multifaceted platform for biomedical applications. The main advantage of protein nanocages is their ability to precisely and spatially regulate functional groups that are positioned at particular places through chemical or genetic alterations. Despite several capabilities, the efficacy of cargo loading, stability in the bloodstream, and immunogenicity remain little known. Nonetheless, the advancement of protein-based nanocages can be further enhanced through the application of sophisticated technologies such as de novo design, hybrid nanocarrier systems, and stimuli-responsive nanocages for drug and gene delivery (Bhaskar and Lim, 2017).

### 3.2.4 *Protein–polymer hybrid nanocarriers*

Polymeric nanoparticles hold significant medical potential, with numerous therapeutic nanoparticles currently undergoing clinical studies. The use of these nanoparticles may improve the delivery of hydrophobic drugs, enable targeted drug administration to specific cells through ligand attachment, and support sustained release mechanisms. Protein–polymer hybrid nanocarriers are advanced delivery methods that combine the strengths of both proteins and natural or synthetic polymers. This combination enables the nanostructure to show improved biocompatibility, functional versatility, and encapsulation capacity. These hybrid nanostructures can be synthesized through covalent conjugation, self-assembly, or physical assembly techniques. PEG and its derivatives, biomimetic polymers, degradable polymers, and stimuli-responsive polymers represent a class of polymers studied concerning polymer–protein conjugation. Researchers have developed a versatile delivery platform that integrates self-assembled BSA with PEG for anticancer drug delivery, allowing targeted release, low immunogenicity, and favorable stability in vivo. Research on targeted polymer–protein drugs has gained prominence in recent years due to their highly effective tumor-targeting capabilities in cancer therapy. However, complex synthesis and scalability pose challenges to its widespread applicability. Therefore, researchers have to focus on creating viable manufacturing procedures alongside enhanced functionalization techniques to mitigate the existing constraints of these hybrid delivery systems (Sun et al., 2023; Ge et al., 2012).

## 3.3 Surface modification and functionalization for drug loading

### 3.3.1 *Ligand attachment*

The attachment of ligands to the surfaces of designed protein nanocarriers is a highly successful method for surface modification and functionalization in drug encapsulation. The functionalization of nanoparticles serves as an effective method for achieving targeted delivery to receptors present in specific cell types. Monoclonal antibodies, growth factors, and peptides like RGD and Trans-Activator of Transcription(TAT), along with synthetic polymers, are frequently used as ligands that bind to nanoparticle surfaces by various covalent and noncovalent interactions, including hydrophobic bonding and electrostatic interactions. Furthermore, proteins are engineered to incorporate ligand-binding domains or reactive sites. These conjugations not only increase the targeting affinity of the nanocarrier but also enhance the biocompatibility, solubility, and stability of drugs while mitigating the risk of nanotoxicity. Moreover, ligand attachment boosts cellular uptake of the therapeutic cargo and promotes drug accumulation at the targeted site. Ligands must be carefully attached to the surface of the nanoparticle in specific orientations and densities that preserve their bioactivity to provide the optimum ligand–receptor interactions (Thalhauser and Breunig, 2020; Singh et al., 2024). For example, self-assembling HSA exhibits superior ligand-binding characteristics; thus, reactive groups like amino, carboxyl, and thiol on the nanoparticle surface promote covalent ligand attachment and surface modification, enhancing targeting affinity and in vivo stability. Furthermore, gelatin can be cationized by incorporating amine residues into its carboxyl groups. This enhances their capacity to traverse the blood–brain barrier and be internalized by macrophages (Hong et al., 2020).

### 3.3.2 *PEGylation*

PEG is among the most frequently used polymers for the surface modification of nanoparticles. Due to its numerous physicochemical advantages, including nontoxicity, excellent solubility, and biocompatibility, PEG is a favored option for altering the surfaces of engineered protein-based nanocarriers. PEGylation on the surface of protein-derived nanocarriers can be accomplished by covalent interactions such as amide and disulfide bonds, as well as through noncovalent interactions such as hydrogen bonding, hydrophobic interactions, and electrostatic forces between one or more units of chemically activated PEG with specific sites of the protein nanostructure. PEGylation conceals antigenic epitopes through steric hindrance, thereby reducing the ability to induce immunity of the encapsulated drugs. Furthermore, this action inhibits the enzymatic degradation of proteins in vivo. PEG can improve the solubility and stability of proteins, which is beneficial for preserving the biocompatibility of nanocarriers within tissues. Crucially, the binding affinity of drugs to cell surface receptors can be significantly affected by PEG modification, which reduces nonspecific absorption by the phagocytic system and improves the targeting efficacy of protein-based delivery methods (Sun et al., 2023; Bailon and Won, 2009).

### 3.3.3 *Surface charge modulation*

The surface charge is a critical attribute of nanoparticles that influences their stability, interactions, and overall effectiveness in physiological environments. The surface charge of nanoparticles is quantified by zeta potential, which refers to the electric potential between the nanoparticle and the fluid in which it is suspended. The magnitude of surface charges has varying implications for the stability of a nanostructure in vivo. Nanoparticles possessing a high surface charge show repulsion from one another due to electrostatic forces, hence inhibiting aggregation. Various data indicate that a zeta potential over 30 mV ($\pm$) is associated with stability in the deposit, as the surface charge inhibits particle agglomeration.

Negatively charged or neutral nanoparticles typically signify low systemic toxicity. Therefore, the manipulation of surface charges can lead to the development of protein nanocarriers for specific applications. A protein nanoparticle's surface charge is determined by the sequence of its amino acids. Functionalization with charged molecules, ionization, or polymer coatings can modify the charge of engineered protein-based nanocarriers, facilitating various drug delivery objectives. For instance, in the targeted administration of chemotherapeutic drugs, the protein nanocarrier needs to possess a positive charge to effectively adhere to the negatively charged tumor cells (Newfang et al., 2015).

## 4. Drug loading and encapsulation strategies

Drug loading and encapsulation strategies are essential parameters in the design and fabrication of nanocarriers for drug delivery that directly influence the therapeutic efficacy, in vivo stability, targeting ability, and regulated release of the nanocarrier system. The following sections provide an overview of these characteristics.

### 4.1 Mechanisms of drug encapsulation in protein nanocarriers

Advancements in nanoscience have resulted in novel methods for encapsulating drugs into protein nanocarriers. Two techniques are frequently used to encapsulate drugs into nanocarrier systems. These includes covalent drug conjugation and noncovalent physical encapsulation. The following sections explore these two strategies.

#### 4.1.1 *Covalent drug conjugation*

Covalent drug conjugation defines the linkage or attachment of a drug to a drug carrier system via chemical bonds. The predominant bonds used to develop covalently linked drug conjugates are ester, amide, thiol, disulfide, and carbamate. Additionally, covalent links between therapeutics and nanodelivery systems have been developed using Schiff bases and polycyclic bonds. These bonds are biodegradable or dissociated within the body at disease locations. Furthermore, covalent linkers are used in the conjugation of drugs to a nanodelivery system. The selection of these linkers is dependent upon the specificity of drug release and the surrounding environment for the drug's release. This drug encapsulation method provides significant control over drug release and facilitates targeted administration of the therapeutic agent. Covalently conjugated drug nanocarriers can release drugs by cleaving covalent bonds in response to specific environmental stimuli, including pH, temperature, light, enzymes, and redox potential. In the design of protein-based nanocarriers, albumin-based drug conjugates are developed in which the anticancer agent paclitaxel is covalently linked through thiol groups present in HSA. Results have shown improved stability and targeting efficacy of this nanocarrier technology. Another example is the encapsulation of the chemotherapeutic agent, DOX. DOX is conjugated to silk fibroin nanoparticles via amide bonds by reacting its primary amine group with the carboxyl groups on silk fibroin, facilitating controlled release in cancer therapy. The biggest advantages of covalent bonding compared to physical encapsulation includes prolonged drug circulation in the body, greater biodistribution, sustained release, increased therapeutic efficacy, and less systemic toxicity (Lamidi et al., 2022; Kaminskas et al., 2012).

#### 4.1.2 *Physical encapsulation*

The physical encapsulation of drugs within a nanocarrier system involves hydrophobic interactions, electrostatic forces, and the physical trapping of therapeutics within the carrier matrix via processes such as emulsification, spray drying, freeze drying, electrospraying, desolvation, adsorption, and electrospinning. These procedures are very simple and maintain the bioactivity of both the therapeutic agent and the carrier. Furthermore, these techniques are suitable for the scalability of delivery systems for substantial production in industries. Physical encapsulation is a widely used method for loading drugs into nanocarriers; however, ionic complexation, precipitation, and dose dumping may arise if the effective interactions between the drug and the delivery system weaken due to charge shifts and short-range attractions among protein subunits. The challenges have led to physical encapsulation characterized by low loading efficiencies. Consequently, scientists are increasingly utilizing the covalent bonding of drugs to nanodrug delivery systems as a substitute for physical encapsulation in the loading of drugs into protein-based nanocarriers (Lamidi et al., 2022; Murtaja and Repka, 2023).

### 4.2 Control of drug release from protein nanocarriers

The release of drugs from protein nanocarriers is influenced and controlled by certain environmental signals, such as pH, temperature, light, enzymes, ultrasound, and redox potential, which induce conformational changes and other alterations in their structure. Scientists have labeled them as "stimuli-responsive smart nanomaterials." These strategies have emerged as a viable tool for directing the targeted release of encapsulated therapeutic compounds from protein-based nanosystems applicable to a wide range of diseases. The following sections discuss two of the most researched stimuli for controlling drug release from protein nanocarriers.

#### 4.2.1 *pH-responsive release mechanisms*

pH variations are evident in nearly every cellular compartment inside the human body. Moreover, bacteria, either directly or by enzyme secretion, might show either acidic or alkaline properties based on the physiological environment. Consequently, nanocarrier compounds leverage pH variations across distinct physiological settings to engineer pH-sensitive protein nanocarriers that release their encapsulated drugs for optimal therapeutic efficacy with minimal adverse effects and improved biostability and prolonged circulation inside the body. Drugs are released from nanocarriers by dissolution or swelling. The nanocarriers maintain stability in the bloodstream postadministration. Upon approaching the targeted cells with differing pH levels, they disintegrate, releasing the encapsulated drugs. For example, ferritin nanocages that encapsulate anticancer drugs show stability at neutral pH but deconstruct at acidic pH levels, thereby releasing the encapsulated drugs. In protein-based nanosystems, the surface of the nanostructure is changed with various pH-sensitive linkers, such as hydrazone, and polymers like poly (acrylic acid) and poly (L-lactic acid), to improve pH-sensitive responsiveness and targeted drug release. Protein micelles are frequently functionalized with these polymers, wherein the hydrophobic core of the micelle undergoes protonation at low or acidic pH, resulting in micelle breakdown and the liberation of the encapsulated therapeutic payload (Stringer et al., 2017).

Another form of drug release induced by pH is swelling, resulting from alterations in electrostatic interactions, cross-linking density, or hydrophilicity of certain nanocarriers. This enables the controlled and precise release of the encapsulated drugs. The predominant functional groups used in the manufacture of pH-sensitive nanoparticles are carboxyl and pyridine groups. In acidic conditions or at low pH values, nanocarriers conjugated with carboxyl groups exhibit a compact shape and reduced porosity. The carboxyl groups undergo protonation, leading to predominance of hydrophobic interactions, which results in the volume contraction of the nanocarrier and consequently facilitates drug release. Conversely, at elevated pH levels or in an alkaline environment, the nanostructure expands and attains maximum porosity, thereby diminishing diffusion resistance and facilitating drug release. For swelling caused by pyridine groups, a markedly opposite effect occurs. When pyridine groups are protonated at an acidic pH, the pyridinium groups experience internal charge repulsion. The overall size of the nanocarrier expands as a result of charge repulsion, leading to the release of the drug. At higher pH levels, the pyridine groups experience reduced ionization, leading to decreased charge repulsion among the pyridinium groups and a smaller overall diameter of the nanocarrier system, which aids in the release of the encapsulated drugs (Chen et al., 2010; Wang and Zhang, 2012).

pH-sensitive release mechanisms are particularly advantageous in cancer therapy, as the acidic environment of tumor cells can be exploited to release the anticancer drug from the protein-based nanocarrier precisely. Nonetheless, premature drug release, possible immunogenicity due to proteins, and scalability problems remain challenges that require solutions (Stringer et al., 2017).

### *4.2.2 Enzyme-mediated release*

In the human body, all biological and metabolic processes fundamentally depend on the release of drugs from a nanocarrier in an enzyme-responsive manner, which arises from specific enzyme-catalyzed chemical processes that lead to the decomposition, dissociation, or morphological changes of the parent nanoparticle. The core idea of enzyme-mediated drug release is that nanocarriers containing enzyme-sensitive components in their structure undergo transitions (degradation, cleavage, or conformational changes) upon exposure to specific enzymes, releasing encapsulated drugs. Among the enzymes examined, proteases exhibiting diverse responsiveness to various enzyme-sensitive components of nanoparticles have been extensively studied. The enzyme's action site can be positioned on any component of nanoparticle carriers, dependent upon the drug administration and release requirements, provided it possesses enzyme-sensitive capability. For example, nanocarrier systems are engineered with an enzyme-responsive core that, upon enzymatic action on the core's functionalities, can initiate drug release through structural alterations, including disintegration, charge shifting, macroscopic deformation, and the cleavage of covalent bonds. The matrix metalloproteinase (MMP) enzyme, predominantly overexpressed in tumor microenvironments, disintegrates gelatin-based nanocarriers. Drugs are covalently conjugated through enzyme-sensitive linkers. These linker molecules are cleaved at the targeted site of drug release. The delicate hydrophobic therapeutic short peptide T4 (NLLMAAS) is one example of this process. It was altered with PEG using an enzyme-responsive linker made of the amino acid sequence AAN. The linker is susceptible to cleavage in the tumor-associated microenvironment due to the overexpression of the cysteine protease legumain. Additionally, nanoparticles are engineered with enzyme-responsive ligands, including small molecules and polymers, to facilitate controlled drug release. The fabrication of nanoparticles with enzyme-responsive sites can yield various effects, including enhanced tissue penetration, decreased toxicity, extended circulation time, enhanced accumulation, and controlled release of drugs. These characteristics position them as potential candidates for future clinical applications in drug delivery (Li et al., 2020).

## 4.3 Optimization of drug-loading efficiency

Drug-loading efficiency quantifies the amount of drug successfully encapsulated or conjugated onto a protein nanocarrier relative to the initial preparation of the drug. Optimization of drug-loading efficiency is a critical step in developing an effective delivery system that achieves the intended therapeutic benefit. The following sections explore the factors influencing drug-loading efficacy and the methods for controlling and regulating drug loading in a protein-based nanocarrier system. In addition, Table 5.3 explores the drug loading and release kinetics of a few protein-based nanocarrier systems for better understanding.

### 4.3.1 *Protein–drug interaction kinetics*

Research on the kinetics of drug interactions with different proteins is important in comprehending the pharmacokinetic properties of these drugs and evaluating the drug-loading capacity of the carrier. Drugs are associated with protein nanocarriers by various covalent and noncovalent interactions, as discussed in the previous sections of this review. Key parameters, including the association rate constant of drug binding to a protein carrier, the dissociation rate constant of drug release from a protein carrier, and other equilibrium dynamics, are assessed using techniques such as surface plasmon resonance (SPR), filtration assays, stopped-flow techniques, and various chromatographic methods. The kinetic studies of these protein–drug interactions are vital in identifying the parameters controlling drug loading in the protein carriers. The amino acid sequence, surface charge, hydrophobicity, hydrophilicity, functional groups, and environmental stimuli are all factors that directly or indirectly influence drug loading in a protein-based nanocarrier system. Understanding these factors is essential for formulating strategies to enhance the binding affinity of therapeutics to proteins, attain high kinetic compatibility, and ultimately improve drug-loading efficacy. For example, scientists have developed a peak profiling technique to find the dissociation rate constants for the drugs carbamazepine and imipramine related to HSA. The results facilitated an improved understanding of the drug's pharmacokinetic features, enabling the engineering of protein structures for optimal binding efficacy (Of et al., 2012).

### 4.3.2 *Influence of nanocarrier size and shape*

Generally, nanoparticles are relevant to several biological targets due to their nanoscale dimensions, which enable them to penetrate diverse biological membranes and accumulate, indicating their potential to treat a broad spectrum of illnesses. The dimensions and

**TABLE 5.3** Drug loading and release kinetics of protein nanocarriers.

| SL No. | Nanocarrier type | Drug-loading strategies | Release profile | pH/enzyme sensitivity | Example of clinical application | References |
|---|---|---|---|---|---|---|
| 01 | Albumin-based nanocarrier | Covalent drug conjugation | Sustained release | Release of encapsulated drugs upon acidic pH levels and enzymatic triggers | Anticancer drug paclitaxel is covalently linked through thiol groups present in human serum albumin (HSA) for targeted therapy | Lamidi et al. (2022), Kaminskas et al. (2012) |
| 02 | Silk-based nanocarrier | Covalent drug conjugation | Controlled release | Release of encapsulated drugs upon varying pH levels and enzymatic triggers | Anticancer agent doxorubicin is conjugated to silk fibroin nanoparticles via amide bonds for regulated drug delivery | Lamidi et al. (2022), Kaminskas et al. (2012) |
| 03 | Ferritin nanocages | Physical encapsulation | Controlled release influenced by metal ions | Release of encapsulated drugs upon acidic/low pH levels | Several anticancer agents are loaded into the ferritin nanocages via physical trapping or hydrophobic and electrostatic interactions | Sana et al. (2015) |
| 04 | Gelatin-based nanocarrier | Covalent drug conjugation | Rapid release under acidic conditions | Release of encapsulated drugs upon acidic/low pH levels | Anticancer agent doxorubicin bound to amino, hydroxyl, and carboxyl functional groups to gelatin for tumor-targeted therapy | Jiang et al. (2023) |

morphology of nanocarriers serve as essential criteria in assessing the efficacy of medication loading onto a nanocarrier system. Several studies indicate that when proteins are added at or close to the isoelectric point (IEP), the size of the nanoparticles corresponds with the effectiveness of loading. Presently, the primary and swiftest technique for quantifying particle size is photon correlation spectroscopy (PCS) or dynamic light scattering (DLS). Small nanocarriers possess extensive surface areas that enhance the accessibility of active binding sites for pharmaceutical compounds. This promotes increased surface loading of drugs and accelerated diffusion into the nanocarriers, primarily used for the delivery of hydrophilic medications. Larger nanocarriers, despite possessing smaller surface areas, can encapsulate greater quantities of therapeutic payload and disseminate them at a slower rate. These are particularly helpful for loading hydrophobic drug molecules onto the nanoparticles. Additionally, the morphological characteristics of nanocarriers, including shape, affect the drug encapsulation capacity and loading mechanism that further guide the development of strategies for effective drug loading. For example, spherical protein nanocarriers are appropriate for the uniform biodistribution of drugs. Assessing and functionalizing the structure of nanocarrier systems is necessary for developing efficient drug-delivery vehicles. Quantification of the morphology of nanoparticles can be achieved through the utilization of techniques such as atomic force microscopy (AFM) and scanning electron microscopy (SEM). SEM possesses the nanoscale resolution essential for analyzing submicron dimensions, which is vital for assessing particle shape (Hong et al., 2020; Wang et al., 2016; Dunne et al., 2000).

#### 4.3.3 *Controlling drug-loading capacity*

A high drug-loading capacity is a prerequisite for a successful nanoparticle system, which necessitates a diminished amount of matrix material for administration. The solubility of solid-state drugs in the polymer matrix is affected by polymer structure, molecular mass, drug–polymer interactions, and terminal functional groups, all of which are vital to drug loading and entrapment efficiency. Furthermore, enhanced loading efficiency has been observed when the protein is loaded at or near its IEP, showing minimal solubility and maximal adsorption. Consequently, it is imperative to optimize protein–drug ratios and functionalize the nanocarrier structure through chemical modification, genetic engineering, or cross-linking to efficiently regulate the drug-loading capacity of a nanocarrier system (Tarhini et al., 2017).

## 5. Applications of self-assembling protein nanocarriers

The following sections and Table 5.4 discuss the biomedical applications of self-assembled protein nanocarriers.

### 5.1 Advanced drug delivery with self-assembled protein–polymer conjugates

Advanced drug delivery methods in nanomedicine seek to improve the efficacy and diminish the toxicity of systemically delivered therapeutic agents by precisely directing the drug to the designated site, therefore reducing off-target deposition and biodistribution of the drugs. The current toolkit for advanced drug delivery systems comprises nanogels,

**TABLE 5.4** Applications of self-assembling protein nanocarriers in drug delivery.

| SL No. | Area of application | Targeted disease | Protein carrier | Drug delivery route | Preclinical/ clinical status | References |
|---|---|---|---|---|---|---|
| 01 | Cancer therapy | Lung cancer, breast cancer, | Albumin, ferritin nanocages, gelatin | Intravenous | Clinical | Obozina et al. (2023) |
| 02 | Vaccination | Infectious diseases | Virus-like particles (VLPs), ferritin | Intravenous, intramuscular | Clinical | Obozina et al. (2023) |
| 03 | Gene therapy | Genetic disorders | VLPs, ferritin, legumin | Intravenous | Preclinical | Bhaskar and Lim (2017) |
| 04 | Tissue engineering | Tissue and organ repair, wound healing | Collagen, silk fibroin | Scaffold implantation | Preclinical | Manna et al. (2021) |
| 05 | Hormone replacement therapy | Diabetes | Albumin | Subcutaneous | Clinical | Karami et al. (2020) |

liposomes, and traditional block copolymers and is continually expanding. The development of self-assembled protein–polymer bioconjugates may facilitate the advancement of next-generation drug delivery systems and nanomedicines. Optimal drug delivery systems should be nonimmunogenic, nontoxic, capable of stabilizing the therapeutic agent, localizing delivery, crossing biological barriers, and facilitating triggered drug release. Considering these criteria, self-assembled protein–polymer conjugates serve as promising candidates for the engineering of delivery materials (Stevens et al., 2021).

### *5.1.1 Drug intracellular delivery*

Intracellular administration and release of functional protein therapies are difficult. Currently, approved protein–polymer therapeutics work extracellularly. A significant number of therapeutic drug targets are based on cellular mechanisms. Recent advancements have been made in the development of self-assembling protein–polymer conjugates to facilitate drug delivery across the cell membrane and enable the release of functional proteins into the cytosol. The Thayumanavan group devised a grafting method to produce self-assembled protein–polymer conjugates that release functional protein from the polymer into the cytoplasm without residue (Dutta et al., 2017, 2021). Spherical nanoassemblies are formed by conjugating a protein to a p-nitrophenylcarbonate (NPC)-ended polymer with a disulfide moiety. Using protein surface amines, the NPC forms a carbamate. The protein is released when the disulfide link clears, and the thiol hydrolyzes the carbamate under reducing conditions. As demonstrated by Dutta et al., this technique attaches polymers to cytochrome C, lysozyme, and ribonuclease A. After polymer encapsulation and release, all proteins maintained their secondary structure and enzymatic function. This method also delivered proteins to HeLa cell cytosols. The Thayumanavan group enhanced this method by creating protein–polymer nanoassemblies using reversible click chemistry (Liu et al., 2019). Salicylhydroxamic acid-modified polymers and protein moieties with boronic acid moieties can form protein–polymer conjugate nanoassemblies by clicking. Proteins of diverse shapes, sizes, and IEPs can be assembled using this nanoassembly method. Reversible and controllable, the conjugation can break down and release native proteins undetected. To improve pH and redox stimuli-responsiveness, assemblies can include self-immolating linkers. The authors showed that these nanoassemblies can deliver functional proteins to mammalian cell cytosols. The stimuli-responsive and traceless release of functional proteins across cell membranes making this an attractive method for intracellular drug delivery. Two recent investigations have successfully delivered therapeutic proteins to the cytosol present in tumor cells in mice using this delivery platform (Zhang et al., 2020; X. Li et al., 2020). Nanozymogen, a hypoxia-triggered nanoassembly, is an effective cancer treatment developed by Li et al. This nanoassembly used a hypoxia-dissociable polymer to codeliver a hypoxia-activatable RNase pro-protein and glucose oxidase (GOx) to treat cancer cells intracellularly (X. Li et al., 2020). In order to deliver DOX and RNase A concurrently for a synergistic cancer treatment, Zhang et al. developed a multistage nanoplatform. DOX and phenylboronic acid-modified RNase A were enclosed by a triblock copolymer consisting of mPEG, catechol, and tertiary amine. This was accomplished by hydrophobic interactions and pH-reversible dynamic covalent conjugation. The nanoassembly effectively transported DOX and RNase A to solid tumor sites, showing significant systemic stability, prolonged blood circulation, and enhanced tumor accumulation. Following internalization, pH-sensitive endosomal degradation liberated DOX and RNase A. Coadministered DOX and RNase A exhibited synergistic anticancer effects in both in vitro and in vivo mouse melanoma models. This study highlights the possibility of a multistage nanoplatform for simultaneous therapeutic delivery (Zhang et al., 2020). These results show that self-assembling protein–polymer conjugates are capable of overcoming the limitations of other drug delivery strategies. Reversible binding and protein function modification are possible with noncovalent or cleavable covalent polymer–protein interactions. Charged polymers and macromolecular scaffolds bind to protein surfaces and may be used in drug delivery (Stevens et al., 2021; Roy et al., 2010; Kale et al., 2009).

### *5.1.2 Triggered drug delivery*

Triggered drug release holds significant potential for temporal regulation in clinical applications. Locoregional stimulation optimizes medication release at the target region and reduces off-target release. Self-assembled protein–polymer conjugates are advantageous for controlled drug release owing to their responsiveness to environmental stimuli such as light, temperature, and ultrasound. The responsiveness to stimuli can regulate the release of therapeutic agents in self-assembled bioconjugates. Vanparijs et al. created a stimuli-responsive protein–polymer conjugate compound through 2-(Dimethylamino)ethyl methacrylate (DMDMA) growth from BSA (Vanparijs et al., 2015). The conjugate forms nanoparticles that respond to external triggers such as temperature and pH. When the temperature exceeds the lower critical solution temperature (LCST), DMDOMA transitions to an insoluble state, forming nanoparticles. Acidic or low pH solutions facilitate the hydrolysis of dioxolane units within polymer chains, resulting in the formation of diols, creating a hydrophilic conjugate that disassembles nanoparticles regardless of temperature. The hydrophobic immune stimulatory drug CL075 was delivered to dendritic cells in vitro by these conjugates. Encapsulation of CL075 with a protein–polymer hybrid and exposing it to dendritic cells obtained from mouse bone marrow for incubation. The presence of cell surface maturation markers MHCII and CD86 demonstrated that the assembly elicited a robust immune response in dendritic cells. This study shows the potential of partially soluble, acid-degradable protein–polymer conjugates for drug delivery. In addition, Wong et al. created stimuli-responsive protein–polymer conjugates that autonomously assemble into polymersomes (Wong et al., 2015). RAFT (reversible addition-fragmentation chain transfer polymerization) was used to conjugate PNIPAM with amilFP947, a green fluorescent protein. Elevating the solution temperature beyond PNIPAM's LCST resulted in the creation of polymersome structures, as detected by confocal and transmission electron microscopy. Phycoerythrin 545 (PE545) and DOX hydrochloride were added to polymersomes. The tiny molecules were located in distinct locations of the polymersome due to variances in hydrophilicity. Hydrophobic PE545 was found mostly inside the membrane, while DOX was present in both the membrane and the polymersome core. The polymersome's dual loading of hydrophilic and hydrophobic compounds indicates that the system can carry multiple therapies simultaneously. This triggered drug delivery device is notable due to this unique feature (Stevens et al., 2021) (Fig. 5.1).

## 5.2 Vaccines

### *5.2.1 Vaccine design using self-assembled peptides*

Self-assembled peptides exhibit diverse effects on the immune system. Some peptides do not induce measurable antibody responses, whereas others can provoke strong responses independently of additional adjuvants. The characterization and evaluation of strategies to avoid or induce an immune response using these materials is underdeveloped (Hubbell et al., 2009). The advancement of peptide-based vaccinations is impeded by the necessity to display antigens in their original conformation and the dependence on immuno-adjuvants that exhibit augmented capabilities alone under specific conditions (Rudra et al., 2010). In recent years, numerous patents have been submitted for the development of self-adjuvanting vaccines originating from self-assembled peptides (Stephenson et al., 2014; Temming et al., 2005). These materials provide scaffolds that enhance multivalency and molecular precision, enabling precise control over epitope location (Sun, 2018). Self-assembled nanostructures display increased antigen concentrations on their surfaces, leading to strong high-affinity and neutralizing IgG responses, as well as $CD8^+$ T-cell-mediated protection (Chen et al., 2013; Chesson et al., 2014). Because of their adjuvanticity—an effect that is affected by particle characteristics and which boosts the immune response—nanomaterials play a key role in vaccine administration (Zolnik et al., 2010; Hajizade et al., 2014). Numerous initiatives to create a vaccine using this class of biomaterials include peptides that form beta sheets and lipidated peptide amphiphiles. A different approach utilized repeats of the immunodominant peptide that self-assembled into nanoparticles. Kaba et al. created a self-assembled peptide nanovaccine composed of nanoparticles around 25 nm in size, noted for their high density of antigen presentation on the surface. In the absence of an extra adjuvant, a nanovaccine made of tandem repetitions of *Plasmodium berghei* circumsporozoite protein [(DPPPPNPN)2D], the B-cell immunodominant malaria parasite, produced a long-lasting protective immune response. Mice that received three doses of the vaccine candidates spaced 2 weeks apart showed protection for up to 15 months after the second challenge and 6 months after the last inoculation. When compared to antibodies

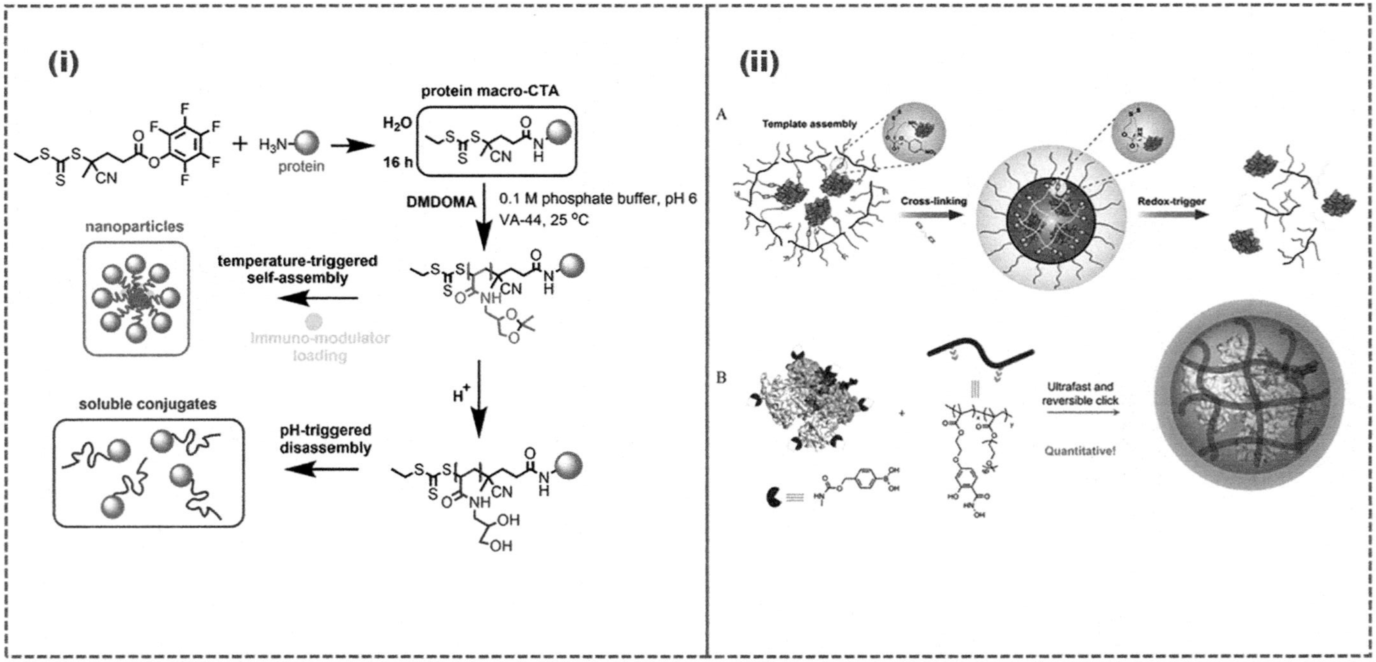


FIGURE 5.1 (i) Synthesis, self-assembly, and disassembly of transiently responsive protein-polymer conjugates by "grafting-from" RAFT polymerization molecular structure and schematic illustration. (ii) A diagram showing how the protein can be used as a template to construct a covalent polymer network, as well as its traceless and triggered release in a reducing environment. An illustration showing the synthesis and self-assembly of protein–polymer conjugates, as well as how the protein can be used as a template to construct a covalent polymer. *Adapted from C.A. Stevens, K. Kaur, H. A. Klok, Self-assembly of protein-polymer conjugates for drug delivery. Advanced Drug Delivery Reviews. 174 (2021), 447–460, https://doi.org/10.1016/j.addr.2021.05.002.*

produced using the adjuvant Montanide ISA-720, the $CD4^+$ T-cell-reliant antibodies showed higher avidity and an association with improved protection (Kaba et al., 2009; Eskandari et al., 2017).

### *5.2.2 Vaccine delivery using self-assembled peptides*

Traditional vaccines based on whole pathogens effectively prevent numerous diseases; however, they may be unsuitable or inadequate for certain diseases due to safety concerns, inadequate immune response, antigen instability, or limitations in engineering and manufacturing processes (Fries et al., 2021). Protein nanoparticle immunogens provide antigens in a repeating arrangement by genetic fusion or protein–peptide conjugation to nanoparticle scaffolds. They seek to surmount numerous constraints and have exhibited the capacity to elicit protective immunological responses (Rodrigues et al., 2021; Kanekiyo et al., 2015; Walls et al., 2020; Antanasijevic et al., 2020; Duan et al., 2018; Lagoutte et al., 2018; Choi et al., 2016). This approach employs multiple facets of the immune system that have evolved to recognize "particulate" pathogens distinguished by repetitive antigenic determinants. Initially, protein nanoparticles exhibit an optimal shape and size for uptake by peripheral or lymph node dendritic cells following intramuscular injection, specifically being spherical and approximately 20–150 nm in diameter (Reddy et al., 2006). Furthermore, the display of multivalent antigens enhances the detection of pathogen-associated molecular patterns; it has been shown that protein nanoparticle-mediated cross-linking of B cell receptors induces more robust immune responses compared to those triggered by soluble antigens (De Groot and Scott, 2007; Bachmann and Jennings, 2010; Kato et al., 2020). Live-attenuated and inactivated vaccines utilize these immunological phenomena; however, self-assembling protein nanoparticles are typically considered safer due to the lack of infectious agents. Protein nanoparticles facilitate the utilization of antigens that are engineered in manners potentially incompatible with viral or bacterial proliferation, exemplified by prefusion-stabilized RSV (respiratory syncytial virus) (McLellan et al., 2013; Mukhamedova et al., 2021). The immunogen of the modified protein nanoparticle may be more stable, increasing immunological exposure to the antigenic shape or epitope, which is targeted for an immune response (Pauthner et al., 2017; Cirelli et al., 2019; Sesterhenn et al., 2020; Marcandalli et al., 2019). The suitability of self-assembling protein nanoparticles for vaccine delivery needs, similar to VLP-based vaccinations, likely explains the progression of vaccines as the exclusive use of protein nanoparticles to achieve clinical stages. The delivery efficiency of vaccines is less limited by immunogenicity compared to other therapeutic applications (Walls et al., 2020; Marcandalli et al., 2019; Boyoglu-Barnum et al., 2021; Zhao et al., 2014; Joyce et al., 2016; Roldão et al., 2010; Jeong and Seong, 2017). Therefore, more information is needed about the emergence of antibody responses to nanoparticle scaffolds and their consequences (Olshefsky et al., 2022).

## 5.3 Anticancer drug delivery

Tumors represent a significant global health challenge, yet effective treatment options remain insufficient. There remains a necessity for innovative materials and methods in cancer treatment. Nanomaterials employed as drug delivery carriers exhibit high drug-loading efficiency, minimal drug loss, and enhanced stability to prevent rapid drug clearance from the body (Shi et al., 2011). Nanostructures can improve therapeutic efficacy and reduce side effects, making them promising anticancer drug delivery vehicles. Currently, anticancer drug delivery via peptide self-assembled nanostructures is a promising cancer treatment technique. Peptides self-assemble into nanoparticles, nanovesicles, nanotubes, nanomicelles, and nanofibers to produce hydrogels (Yu et al., 2015). These strategies can be used to treat cancer with various anticancer drugs. Amphiphilic peptides self-assemble into nanovesicles that transport hydrophobic anticancer drugs. The outer layer of these nanostructures can also be customized for drug delivery (Boekhoven et al., 2015). Direct tumor administration of injectable peptide self-assembled hydrogels may improve tumor therapy efficacy and safety (Yishay-Safranchik, Golan and David, 2014). By conjugating peptide self-assembled nanotubes with DOX, cancer treatment is highly effective (Silva et al., 2013). Preclinical and clinical experiments have introduced DOX, curcumin, fluorouracil, and paclitaxel to peptide self-assembled nanostructures for cancer treatment. The biodegradability and biocompatibility of peptide self-assembled nanostructures have improved cancer treatment. Peptide-based self-assembled nanofibers that create injectable hydrogels represent a promising approach for anticancer drug delivery systems. This technology permits chemotherapeutic medications to directly interact with cancer tissues at high concentrations, outperforming standard cancer treatments. The delayed release rates of these peptide hydrogels may improve safety and control. Stimuli-responsive hydrogels made from KLD motifs (Lys–Leu–Asp) can regulate DOX release (Yishay-Safranchik, Golan and David, 2014). Nanofibers self-assembled from EAK peptides (Glu–Ala–Lys) can encapsulate ellipticine, an anticancer medication. Self-assembly and drug delivery applications were analyzed using two methodologies. The UV-based technique is first. Electrostatic interactions helped conjugate the peptide with the anticancer medication ellipticine. This approach allows for the evaluation of drug-loading efficiency in peptide self-assembled nanostructures. The second technique analyzes conjugation efficiency using fluorescence. Ellipticine concentrations were monitored throughout self-assembly and administration using fluorescence. In vitro studies demonstrated that protonated self-assembled nanofibers encapsulating the anticancer drug ellipticine exhibit superior efficacy compared to crystalline forms. EAK peptide self-assembled nanoparticles and the two encapsulation methods can be employed to provide various anticancer agents (Lu et al., 2012). Upon conjugation with PEG and DOX, the dendrimer tetrapeptide GFLG (Gly–Phe–Leu–Gly) self-assembled into compact nanoparticles characterized by negatively charged surfaces. Drug loading and release assays demonstrated a drug-loading efficiency of 9.62 wt% and the possibility for enzyme-responsive drug delivery. In contrast to free DOX, fluorescent and cellular studies demonstrated a steady and successful cancer treatment. This study revealed no adverse effects and decreased DOX toxicity (Li et al., 2014). Peptide self-assembled multifunctional nanostructures with dual-functional liposomes have been created for the delivery of targeted cancer treatments. By combining active targeting agents and cell-penetrating peptides, this method may deliver anticancer medications. R6H4 was evaluated in this study as a pH-responsive anticancer drug delivery system. Hyaluronic acid was used to bind R6H4 peptides because of their rapid degradation. Tests conducted both in vitro and in vivo demonstrate that these nanocarriers enhance tumor-targeted drug delivery in the treatment of cancer (Jiang et al., 2012). A hybrid nanostructure was made from polylactide (PLA) and V6K2 peptides (von Maltzahn et al., 2003). These nanostructures can be coupled with paclitaxel and DOX to deliver cancer medications. Pure PLA nanoparticles measure 130 nm, while PLA-V6K2 self-assembled nanoparticles measure 100 nm. Compared to pure PLA, PLA-V6K2 nanoparticles exhibit significantly higher and more gradual encapsulation and anticancer drug release ratios. The findings reveal that PLA-V6K2 nanoparticles conjugated with anticancer drugs, as opposed to free DOX, paclitaxel, and pure PLA nanoparticle conjugates, are more harmful to cancer cells. According to this study, PLA-V6K2 nanoparticles are more effective at delivering chemotherapy drugs, which suggests that they could be used to treat cancer (Jabbari et al., 2013; Fan et al., 2017).

## 5.4 Gene drug delivery

Advances in biotechnology and genetic understanding of disease pathology have changed the diagnosis and treatment of many diseases. Researchers use recombinant plasmid DNA as a gene medication for targeted gene therapy. Patient healing may use gene-encoded functional proteins. Gene drug delivery for targeted gene-disease therapy must be cost-effective and noninvasive (Takakura et al., 2001). Despite the growing interest in gene therapy, nonviral gene medication delivery platforms need further development. Toxicity, immunogenicity, and inadequate cellular and nuclear absorption must be improved in gene drug nanocarriers (Thomas et al., 2003; Li et al., 2016b). Thus, gene drug delivery nanostructure design and production must prioritize cellular delivery, specificity, and loading efficacy. Cationic nanostructures are widely studied and used due to their effective cellular transport and nucleic acid loading (Ballarín-González and Howard, 2012). Due to their intrinsic features and precise production methods, peptide self-assembled nanostructures are promising gene drug delivery methods. Peptide-based self-assembled nanotubes may help distribute gene drugs by producing nanovesicles during endocytosis (Yan et al., 2007). Thus, many gene drug conjugations and peptide self-assembled nanostructures have been produced for gene delivery applications (McCarthy et al., 2014).

Surfactant peptide self-assembles into 50-nm nanotubes or nanovesicles. To improve gene medication delivery, this surfactant peptide was created from cationic lipid systems. Approximately 2 nm long peptide monomers. The peptide head contains one or two cationic and hydrophilic lysine and histidine amino acids. Following this, six amino acids, including Ala, Val, and Leu, form a hydrophobic peptide tail. When the pH reaches above the IEP, these nanostructures may self-assemble into nanosheets. These cationic peptides' self-assembly and charge properties allow nanostructures to couple negatively charged DNA and RNA for gene therapy delivery (von Maltzahn et al., 2003).

For gene therapy applications, a four-segment peptide conjugated to a lipopeptide has been developed to enhance gene transfection and delivery. Cysteine, histidine, lysine, and alkyl chains make up the peptide. These nanostructures self-assemble to deliver gene medicines to cells via histidine residues. Charged lysine residues at neutral pH helped gene drugs enter the nucleus. Following design, development, production, and assessment, these peptide self-assembled nanostructures displayed significant transfection efficiency for gene therapy through gene-drug delivery (Fan et al., 2017; Jazayeri, Prankerd and Pouton, 2009).

# 6. Clinical translation potential of protein-based drug delivery systems

Protein-based drug carriers represent a significant breakthrough in contemporary medicine, including benefits like specificity, biocompatibility, and the ability to create customized delivery systems. As a result, the clinical development of these systems is becoming increasingly important as the field develops, with a number of crucial areas of focus shaping this novel approach's future. A cisplatin-loaded gelatin microsphere formulation was created by Tomaya et al., and preliminary clinical data showed positive effects in 19 patients with advanced hepatocellular carcinoma, especially in the 1- and 3-month follow-up results. Every surgery was completed satisfactorily, and no negative side effects were noted (Toyama et al., 2012).

The beneficial role of casein micelles in the nanoencapsulation of vitamin D has been described in a study that also looked at the differences in vitamin D bioavailability when using casein micelles as opposed to synthetic emulsifiers like Tween 80, which are occasionally used by industries to incorporate vitamin D into milk. Ninety healthy adults between the ages of 18 and 65 who passed a medical screening were divided into three groups at random and given different fat-free dietary supplements: a placebo consisting of skim milk without vitamin D; skim milk with the same amount of vitamin D but emulsified with Tween 80; and skim milk fortified with 50,000 international units of vitamin D in a 150 g product using a conventional method. Blood samples were taken before the substance was consumed, as well as 1, 7, and 14 days after consumption. The initial findings demonstrate the advantageous characteristics of casein micelles and their crucial role in the targeted and efficient delivery of vitamin D.

According to a number of studies, albumin-based nanoparticles are used in clinical trials for anticancer treatments. One such example is the nanocomposite Abraxane, which is used as a treatment for breast, nonsmall cell lung, and pancreatic cancer. Additionally, a number of researchers have highlighted the use of albumin nanoparticles for the loading and targeted distribution of paclitaxel, a chemotherapeutic drug frequently used to treat different kinds of cancer: 503 patients with advanced, previously treated nonsmall cell lung cancer were randomized to one of two groups in a Phase III clinical trial (NCT01620190). On days 1, 8, and 15, 252 patients got 100 $mg/m^2$ of albumin NPs–paclitaxel, while on day 1 of a 21-day cycle, 251 patients received 60 $mg/m^2$ of Docetaxel, a conventional formulation. In contrast to 22% in the Docetaxel group, 2% of the NPs–paclitaxel group experienced severe adverse events, such as febrile neutropenia, after nearly 3 years of surveillance. Furthermore, 10% of the NPs–paclitaxel group and 1% of the Docetaxel group were found to have peripheral sensory neuropathy. Every result showed several benefits linked to the use of albumin NPs–paclitaxel composites (Yoneshima et al., 2021; Ferraro et al., 2024).

## 7. Challenges and limitations of using protein-based nanoparticles

Protein nanoparticles have many benefits in the field of drug delivery and regenerative medicine, but their use in pharmaceutical and medical research is limited (Lohcharoenkal et al., 2014; Huang et al., 2015; Elzoghby et al., 2011). Natural polymers like proteins are heterogeneous mixes of size and molecular weight. This feature reduces repeatability issues and product characteristic differences between production batches in mass manufacturing and pharmaceutical applications. Genetic engineering is being used to produce recombinant proteins to solve this issue (Wu et al., 2021; Pang et al., 2019). These approaches produce homogenous proteins with a predetermined molecular weight. Their structure lets targeting factors and other groups attach to their surface and modulate breakdown and drug release. Elastin proteins, including Elastin-Like Polypeptides (ELPs), Recombinant Human Serum Albumin (rHSA), and gelatin, have been produced for medication delivery. Genetic engineering raises protein manufacturing prices. Protein nanoparticles' immunogenicity is limited by the body's immunological reaction to foreign proteins. Albumin, gelatin, casein, and zein nanoparticles injected intravenously had little immune response. Achieving an optimal release pattern: Proteins' hydrophilic nature limits medication release over time. Water-absorbing nanoparticles cause swelling and fast medication dispersion outside the body. During protein nanoparticle synthesis, formaldehyde and glutaraldehyde are used as linkers (Kianfar et al., 2020; Kianfar, Researchers and Club, 2019; Kianfar et al., 2017; Kianfar et al., 2015). Protein nanoparticle research is focused on developing nontoxic linkers for interface molecules, which are harmful. Additionally, hydrophobic plant proteins can be used to create protein nanocarriers with sustained release. Nanoparticle synthesis using animal protein sources could spread animal diseases like bovine spongiform encephalopathy to humans (Kianfar, 2021).

## 8. Conclusion

Self-assembling nanocarriers derived from engineered proteins offer an exciting advancement in drug delivery, showcasing a distinctive combination of biocompatibility, functionality, and precision. These nanocarriers use the natural stability and structural flexibility of protein building blocks to create a variety of architectures capable of encapsulating, protecting, and delivering therapeutic agents with impressive specificity. Recent developments in protein engineering have enabled the tailoring of these nanocarriers to address significant challenges in drug delivery, including targeted delivery, controlled release, and the reduction of immunogenicity. The design, engineering, and production of self-assembling protein-based nanocarriers are reaching new heights, supported by innovations in bioconjugation, surface modification, and fusion protein technology. Each of these advancements improves the therapeutic potential of these carriers by enhancing their ability to navigate complex biological environments and respond to specific stimuli. By functionalizing targeting ligands into nanocarriers, precise delivery to cancer cells or particular tissues is made possible, reducing off-target effects and enhancing treatment efficiency. Although the promise of protein-based nanocarriers is considerable, challenges remain to be tackled, such as large-scale production, stability, and regulatory issues. Establishing standardized protocols and tackling these challenges through thorough in vivo studies will be crucial for clinical translation. Moreover, as we enhance our understanding of protein structures and molecular interactions, there exists significant potential to customize these nanocarriers for the delivery of not just small-molecule drugs, but also genetic materials like siRNA and mRNA, thereby expanding their use in personalized medicine. Self-assembling protein-based nanocarriers have the potential to revolutionize drug delivery, especially in fields that demand high specificity and controlled release. Ongoing collaboration across disciplines and cutting-edge research will be essential in realizing their complete potential, leading to the development of next-generation therapeutics that prioritize safety, effectiveness, and adaptability to intricate treatment requirements.

## References

Aljabali, A.A.A., Rezigue, M., Alsharedeh, R.H., Obeid, M.A., Mishra, V., Serrano-Aroca, Á., El-Tanani, M., Tambuwala, M.M., 2022. Protein-based nanomaterials: a new tool for targeted drug delivery. Ther. Deliv. 13 (6), 321–338. https://doi.org/10.4155/tde-2021-0091.

Antanasijevic, A., Ueda, G., Brouwer, P.J.M., Copps, J., Huang, D., Allen, J.D., Cottrell, C.A., Yasmeen, A., Sewall, L. M., Bontjer, I., Ketas, T.J., Turner, H.L., Berndsen, Z.T., Montefiori, D.C., Klasse, P.J., Crispin, M., Nemazee, D., Moore, J.P., Sanders, R.W., King, N.P., Baker, D., Ward, A.B., Evans, D.T., 2020. Structural and functional evaluation of de novo-designed, two-component nanoparticle carriers for HIV Env trimer immunogens. PLoS Pathog. 16 (8), e1008665. https://doi.org/10.1371/journal.ppat.1008665.

Ariga, K., Hill, J.P., Lee, M.V., Lee, Y., Chen, Y., 2016. NI. Tarasova, to study protein unfolding Self-assembled peptide nanostructures for functional materials. Nanotechnology 27, 1–37.

Bachmann, M.F., Jennings, G.T., 2010. Vaccine delivery: a matter of size, geometry, kinetics and molecular patterns. Nat. Rev. Immunol. 10 (11), 787–796. https://doi.org/10.1038/nri2868, 14741733.

e. Bailey, Eur. J. Pharmacol.. 1–7.

Bailon, P., Won, C.-Y., 2009. PEG-modified biopharmaceuticals. Expet Opin. Drug Deliv. 6 (1), 1–16. https://doi.org/10.1517/17425240802650568.

Ballarín-González, B., Howard, K.A., 2012. Polycation-based nanoparticle delivery of RNAi therapeutics: Adverse effects and solutions. Adv. Drug Deliv. Rev. 64 (15), 1717–1729. https://doi.org/10.1016/j.addr.2012.07.004.

Bansal, S., Kundu, B., 2022. Protein Engineering: Methods and Applications. Elsevier BV, pp. 641–668. https://doi.org/10.1016/b978-0-323-90264-9.00039-8.

Bhaskar, S., Lim, S., 2017. Engineering protein nanocages as carriers for biomedical applications. NPG Asia Mater. 9 (4). https://doi.org/10.1038/am.2016.128.

Bhat, M.Y., Ali Dar, T., Singh, L.R., 2016. Casein Proteins: Structural and Functional Aspects. InTech. https://doi.org/10.5772/64187.

Boekhoven, J., Zha, R.H., Tantakitti, F., Zhuang, E., Zandi, R., Newcomb, C.J., Stupp, S.I., 2015. Alginate-peptide amphiphile core-shell microparticles as a targeted drug delivery system. RSC Adv. 5 (12), 8753–8756. https://doi.org/10.1039/c4ra16593d.

Boyoglu-Barnum, S., Ellis, D., Gillespie, R.A., Hutchinson, G.B., Park, Y.J., Moin, S.M., Acton, O.J., Ravichandran, R., Murphy, M., Pettie, D., Matheson, N., Carter, L., Creanga, A., Watson, M.J., Kephart, S., Ataca, S., Vaile, J.R., Ueda, G., Crank, M.C., Stewart, L., Lee, K.K., Guttman, M., Baker, D., Mascola, J.R., Veesler, D., Graham, B.S., King, N.P., Kanekiyo, M., 2021. Quadrivalent influenza nanoparticle vaccines induce broad protection. Nature 592 (7855), 623–628. https://doi.org/10.1038/s41586-021-03365-x.

Broom, A., Trainor, K., Jacobi, Z., Meiering, E.M., 2020. Computational modeling of protein stability: Quantitative analysis reveals solutions to pervasive problems. Structure 28 (6), 717. https://doi.org/10.1016/j.str.2020.04.003.

Chasteen, N.D., Harrison, P.M., 1999. Mineralization in ferritin: an efficient means of iron storage. J. Struct. Biol. 126 (3), 182–194. https://doi.org/10.1006/jsbi.1999.4118.

Chen, W., Meng, F., Cheng, R., Zhong, Z., 2010. pH-Sensitive degradable polymersomes for triggered release of anticancer drugs: a comparative study with micelles. J. Contr. Release 142 (1), 40–46. https://doi.org/10.1016/j.jconrel.2009.09.023.

Chen, J., Pompano, R.R., Santiago, F.W., Maillat, L., Sciammas, R., Sun, T., Han, H., Topham, D.J., Chong, A.S., Collier, J. H., 2013. The use of self-adjuvanting nanofiber vaccines to elicit high-affinity B cell responses to peptide antigens without inflammation. Biomaterials 34 (34), 8776–8785. https://doi.org/10.1016/j.biomaterials.2013.07.063.

Chesson, C.B., Huelsmann, E.J., Lacek, A.T., Kohlhapp, F.J., Webb, M.F., Nabatiyan, A., Zloza, A., Rudra, J.S., 2014. Antigenic peptide nanofibers elicit adjuvant-free CD8+ T cell responses. Vaccine 32 (10), 1174–1180. https://doi.org/10.1016/j.vaccine.2013.11.047.

Chica, R.A., Doucet, N., Pelletier, J.N., 2005. Semi-rational approaches to engineering enzyme activity: Combining the benefits of directed evolution and rational design. Curr. Opin. Biotechnol. 16 (4), 378–384. https://doi.org/10.1016/j.copbio.2005.06.004.

Cho, Y.H., Jones, O.G., 2019. Assembled protein nanoparticles in food or nutrition applications. Adv. Food Nutr. Res. 88, 47–84. https://doi.org/10.1016/bs.afnr.2019.01.002.

Choi, B., Moon, H., Hong, S.J., Shin, C., Do, Y., Ryu, S., Kang, S., 2016. Effective delivery of antigen-encapsulin nanoparticle fusions to dendritic cells leads to antigen-specific cytotoxic T cell activation and tumor rejection. ACS Nano 10 (8), 7339–7350. https://doi.org/10.1021/acsnano.5b08084.

Cirelli, K.M., Carnathan, D.G., Nogal, B., Martin, J.T., Rodriguez, O.L., Upadhyay, A.A., Enemuo, C.A., Gebru, E.H., Choe, Y., Viviano, F., Nakao, C., Pauthner, M.G., Reiss, S., Cottrell, C.A., Smith, M.L., Bastidas, R., Gibson, W., Wolabaugh, A.N., Melo, M.B., Cossette, B., Kumar, V., Patel, N.B., Tokatlian, T., Menis, S., Kulp, D.W., Burton, D.R., Murrell, B., Schief, W.R., Bosinger, S.E., Ward, A.B., Watson, C.T., Silvestri, G., Irvine, D.J., Crotty, S., 2019. Slow delivery immunization enhances HIV neutralizing antibody and germinal center responses via modulation of immunodominance. Cell 177 (5), 1153. https://doi.org/10.1016/j.cell.2019.04.012.

De Groot, A.S., Scott, D.W., 2007. Immunogenicity of protein therapeutics. Trends Immunol. 28 (11), 482–490. https://doi.org/10.1016/j.it.2007.07.011.

Duan, H., Chen, X., Boyington, J.C., Cheng, C., Zhang, Y., Jafari, A.J., Stephens, T., Tsybovsky, Y., Kalyuzhniy, O., Zhao, P., Menis, S., Nason, M.C., Normandin, E., Mukhamedova, M., DeKosky, B.J., Wells, L., Schief, W.R., Tian, M., Alt, F.W., Kwong, P.D., Mascola, J.R., 2018. Glycan masking focuses immune responses to the HIV-1 CD4-binding site and enhances elicitation of VRC01-class precursor antibodies. Immunity 49 (2), 301. https://doi.org/10.1016/j.immuni.2018.07.005.

Dunne, M., Corrigan, O.I., Ramtoola, Z., 2000. Influence of particle size and dissolution conditions on the degradation properties of polylactide-co-glycolide particles. Biomaterials 21 (16), 1659–1668. https://doi.org/10.1016/s0142-9612(00)00040-5.

Dutta, K., Hu, D., Zhao, B., Ribbe, A.E., Zhuang, J., Thayumanavan, S., 2017. Templated self-assembly of a covalent polymer network for intracellular protein delivery and traceless release. J. Am. Chem. Soc. 139 (16), 5676–5679. https://doi.org/10.1021/jacs.7b01214.

Dutta, K., Kanjilal, P., Das, R., Thayumanavan, S., 2021. Synergistic interplay of covalent and non-covalent interactions in reactive polymer nanoassembly facilitates intracellular delivery of antibodies. Angew. Chem. 133 (4), 1849–1858. https://doi.org/10.1002/ange.202010412.

Elzoghby, A.O., Abo El-Fotoh, W.S., Elgindy, N.A., 2011. Casein-based formulations as promising controlled release drug delivery systems. J. Contr. Release 153 (3), 206–216. https://doi.org/10.1016/j.jconrel.2011.02.010.

Engqvist, M.K.M., Rabe, K.S., 2019. Applications of protein engineering and directed evolution in plant research. Plant Physiol. 179 (3), 907–917. https://doi.org/10.1104/pp.18.01534.

Eskandari, S., Guerin, T., Toth, I., Stephenson, R.J., 2017. Recent advances in self-assembled peptides: Implications for targeted drug delivery and vaccine engineering. Adv. Drug Deliv. Rev. 110–111, 169–187. https://doi.org/10.1016/j.addr.2016.06.013.

Fan, T., Yu, X., Shen, B., Sun, L., 2017. Peptide self-assembled nanostructures for drug delivery applications. J. Nanomater. 2017, 1–16. https://doi.org/10.1155/2017/4562474.

Ferraro, C., Dattilo, M., Patitucci, F., Prete, S., Scopelliti, G., Parisi, O., Puoci, F., 2024. Exploring protein-based carriers in drug delivery: a review. Pharmaceutics 16 (9), 1172. https://doi.org/10.3390/pharmaceutics16091172.

Fries, C.N., Curvino, E.J., Chen, J.L., Permar, S.R., Fouda, G.G., Collier, J.H., 2021. Advances in nanomaterial vaccine strategies to address infectious diseases impacting global health. Nat. Nanotechnol. 16 (4). https://doi.org/10.1038/s41565-020-0739-9.

Ge, J., Neofytou, E., Lei, J., Beygui, R.E., Zare, R.N., 2012. Protein-polymer hybrid nanoparticles for drug delivery. Small 8 (23), 3573–3578. https://doi.org/10.1002/smll.201200889.

Hajizade, A., Ebrahimi, F., Salmanian, A.H., Arpanaei, A., Amani, J., 2014. Nanoparticles in vaccine development. Journal of Applied Biotechnology Reports 1 (4), 125–134.

Hassanin, I.A., Elzoghby, A.O., 2020. Self-assembled non-covalent protein-drug nanoparticles: an emerging delivery platform for anti-cancer drugs. Expet Opin. Drug Deliv. 17 (10), 1437–1458. https://doi.org/10.1080/17425247.2020.1813713.

Hong, S., Choi, D.W., Kim, H.N., Park, C.G., Lee, W., Park, H.H., 2020. Protein-based nanoparticles as drug delivery systems. Pharmaceutics 12 (7), 1–28. https://doi.org/10.3390/pharmaceutics12070604.

Huang, W., Rollett, A., Kaplan, D.L., 2015. Silk-elastin-like protein biomaterials for the controlled delivery of therapeutics. Expet Opin. Drug Deliv. 12 (5), 779–791. https://doi.org/10.1517/17425247.2015.989830.

Hubbell, J.A., Thomas, S.N., Swartz, M.A., 2009. Materials engineering for immunomodulation. Nature 462 (7272), 449–460. https://doi.org/10.1038/nature08604.

Jabbari, E., Yang, X., Moeinzadeh, S., He, X., 2013. Drug release kinetics, cell uptake, and tumor toxicity of hybrid VVVVVVKK peptide-assembled polylactide nanoparticles. Eur. J. Pharm. Biopharm. 84 (1), 49–62. https://doi.org/10.1016/j.ejpb.2012.12.012.

Jayachandran, B., Parvin, T.N., Alam, M.M., Chanda, K., Mm, B., 2022. Insights on chemical crosslinking strategies for proteins. Molecules 27 (23). https://doi.org/10.3390/molecules27238124.

Jazayeri, J.A., Prankerd, R.J., Pouton, C.W., 2009. Preparation and in vitro evaluation of novel lipopeptide transfection agents for efficient gene delivery. Bioconjug Chem. American Chemical Society 19.

Jeong, H., Seong, B.L., 2017. Exploiting virus-like particles as innovative vaccines against emerging viral infections. J. Microbiol. 55 (3), 220–230. https://doi.org/10.1007/s12275-017-7058-3.

Jiang, T., Zhang, Z., Zhang, Y., Lv, H., Zhou, J., Li, C., Hou, L., Zhang, Q., 2012. Dual-functional liposomes based on pH-responsive cell-penetrating peptide and hyaluronic acid for tumor-targeted anticancer drug delivery. Biomaterials 33 (36), 9246–9258. https://doi.org/10.1016/j.biomaterials.2012.09.027.

Jiang, X., Du, Z., Zhang, X., Zaman, F., Song, Z., Guan, Y., Yu, T., Huang, Y., 2023. Gelatin-based anticancer drug delivery nanosystems: a mini review. Front. Bioeng. Biotechnol. 11. https://doi.org/10.3389/fbioe.2023.1158749.

Johnson, C.M., 2013. Differential scanning calorimetry as a tool for protein folding and stability. Arch. Biochem. Biophys. 531 (1–2), 100–109. https://doi.org/10.1016/j.abb.2012.09.008.

Joyce, M.G., Wheatley, A.K., Thomas, P.V., Chuang, G.Y., Soto, C., Bailer, R.T., Druz, A., Georgiev, I.S., Gillespie, R. A., Kanekiyo, M., Kong, W.P., Leung, K., Narpala, S.N., Prabhakaran, M.S., Yang, E.S., Zhang, B., Zhang, Y., Asokan, M., Boyington, J.C., Bylund, T., Darko, S., Lees, C.R., Ransier, A., Shen, C.H., Wang, L., Whittle, J.R., Wu, X., Yassine, H.M., Santos, C., Matsuoka, Y., Tsybovsky, Y., Baxa, U., Mullikin, J.C., Subbarao, K., Douek, D.C., Graham, B.S., Koup, R.A., Ledgerwood, J.E., Roederer, M., Shapiro, L., Kwong, P.D., Mascola, J. R., McDermott, A.B., 2016. Vaccine-induced antibodies that neutralize group 1 and group 2 influenza A viruses. Cell 166 (3), 609–623. https://doi.org/10.1016/j.cell.2016.06.043.

Kaba, S.A., Brando, C., Guo, Q., Mittelholzer, C., Raman, S., Tropel, D., Aebi, U., Burkhard, P., Lanar, D.E., 2009. A nonadjuvanted polypeptide nanoparticle vaccine confers long-lasting protection against rodent malaria. J. Immunol. 183 (11), 7268–7277. https://doi.org/10.4049/jimmunol.0901957.

Kale, T.S., Klaikherd, A., Popere, B., Thayumanavan, S., 2009. Supramolecular assemblies of amphiphilic homopolymers. Langmuir 25 (17), 9660–9670. https://doi.org/10.1021/la900734d.

Kaminskas, L.M., McLeod, V.M., Porter, C.J.H., Boyd, B.J., 2012. Association of chemotherapeutic drugs with dendrimer nanocarriers: an assessment of the merits of covalent conjugation compared to noncovalent encapsulation. Mol. Pharm. 9 (3), 355–373. https://doi.org/10.1021/mp2005966.

Kanekiyo, M., Bu, W., Joyce, M.G., Meng, G., Whittle, J.R.R., Baxa, U., Yamamoto, T., Narpala, S., Todd, J.P., Rao, S. S., McDermott, A.B., Koup, R.A., Rossmann, M.G., Mascola, J.R., Graham, B.S., Cohen, J.I., Nabel, G.J., 2015. Rational design of an Epstein-Barr virus vaccine targeting the receptor-binding site. Cell 162 (5), 1090–1100. https://doi.org/10.1016/j.cell.2015.07.043.

Kang, T.S., Kini, R.M., 2009. Structural determinants of protein folding. Cell. Mol. Life Sci. 66 (14), 2341–2361. https://doi.org/10.1007/s00018-009-0023-5.

Kang, G., Ewing-Nelson, S.R., Mackey, L., Schlitt, J.T., Marathe, A., Abbas, K.M.S.S., 2018. Physiol. Behav. 176.

Karami, E., Behdani, M., Kazemi-Lomedasht, F., 2020. Albumin nanoparticles as nanocarriers for drug delivery: Focusing on antibody and nanobody delivery and albumin-based drugs. J. Drug Deliv. Sci. Technol. 55, 101471. https://doi.org/10.1016/j.jddst.2019.101471.

Kato, Y., Abbott, R.K., Freeman, B.L., Haupt, S., Groschel, B., Silva, M., Menis, S., Irvine, D.J., Schief, W.R., Crotty, S., 2020. Multifaceted effects of antigen valency on B cell response composition and differentiation in vivo. Immunity 53 (3), 548. https://doi.org/10.1016/j.immuni.2020.08.001.

E. Kianfar, Y Researchers, S Club, Synthesizing of vanadium oxide nanotubes using hydrothermal and ultrasonic method. (2019),

Kianfar, E., 2021. Protein nanoparticles in drug delivery: animal protein, plant proteins and protein cages, albumin nanoparticles. J. Nanobiotechnol. 19 (1). https://doi.org/10.1186/s12951-021-00896-3.

Kianfar, E., Baghernejad, M., Rahimdashti, Y., 2015. Study synthesis of vanadium oxide nanotubes with two template hexadecylamin and hexylamine. Biol Forum 7.

Kianfar, E., Pirouzfar, V., Sakhaeinia, H., 2017. An experimental study on absorption/stripping $CO_2$ using monoethanol amine hollow fiber membrane contactor. J. Taiwan Inst. Chem. Eng. 80, 954–962. https://doi.org/10.1016/j.jtice.2017.08.017.

Kianfar, E., Hajimirzaee, S., mousavian, S., Soleimani Mehr, A., 2020. Zeolite-based catalysts for methanol to gasoline process: A review. Microchem. J. 156, 104822. https://doi.org/10.1016/j.microc.2020.104822.

Kommareddy, S., Shenoy, D.B., Amiji, M.M., 2003. Gelatin nanoparticles and their biofunctionalization. Nanotechnologies Life Sci 1.

Kuhlman, B., Bradley, P., 2019. Advances in protein structure prediction and design. Nat. Rev. Mol. Cell Biol. 20 (11), 681–697. https://doi.org/10.1038/s41580-019-0163-x.

Lagoutte, P., Mignon, C., Stadthagen, G., Potisopon, S., Donnat, S., Mast, J., Lugari, A., Werle, B., 2018. Simultaneous surface display and cargo loading of encapsulin nanocompartments and their use for rational vaccine design. Vaccine 36 (25), 3622–3628. https://doi.org/10.1016/j.vaccine.2018.05.034.

Lamidi, S., Olaleye, O.N., Polytechnic, L.S., Bankole, Y.O., Polytechnic, L.S., Obalola, A., 2022. We Are IntechOpen , the World ' S Leading Publisher of Open Access Books Built by Scientists , for Scientists. WwwIntechopenCom, pp. 0–12.

Langer, K., Balthasar, S., Vogel, V., Dinauer, N., von Briesen, H., Schubert, D., 2003. Optimization of the preparation process for human serum albumin (HSA) nanoparticles. Int. J. Pharm. 257 (1–2), 169–180. https://doi.org/10.1016/s0378-5173(03)00134-0.

Lee, K.Z., Jeon, J., Jiang, B., Subramani, S.V., Li, J., Zhang, F., 2023. Protein-based hydrogels and their biomedical applications. Molecules 28 (13). https://doi.org/10.3390/molecules28134988.

Li, N., Li, N., Yi, Q., Luo, K., Guo, C., Pan, D., Gu, Z., 2014. Amphiphilic peptide dendritic copolymer-doxorubicin nanoscale conjugate self-assembled to enzyme-responsive anti-cancer agent. Biomaterials 35 (35), 9529–9545. https://doi.org/10.1016/j.biomaterials.2014.07.059.

Li, H., Kong, N., Laver, B., Liu, J., 2016a. Hydrogels constructed from engineered proteins. Small 12 (8), 973–987. https://doi.org/10.1002/smll.201502429.

Li, Z., Liu, C., Zhang, D., Luo, S., Yamaguchi, Y., 2016b. Capillary electrophoresis of RNA in hydroxyethylcellulose polymer with various molecular weights. J. Chromatogr. B 1011, 114–120. https://doi.org/10.1016/j.jchromb.2015.12.057.

Li, X., Wei, Y., Wu, Y., Yin, L., 2020. Hypoxia-induced pro-protein therapy assisted by a self-catalyzed nanozymogen. Angew. Chem., Int. Ed. 59 (50), 22544–22553. https://doi.org/10.1002/anie.202004008.

Liang, M., Fan, K., Zhou, M., Duan, D., Zheng, J., Yang, D., Feng, J., Yan, X., 2014. H-ferritin–nanocaged doxorubicin nanoparticles specifically target and kill tumors with a single-dose injection. Proc. Natl. Acad. Sci. 111 (41), 14900–14905. https://doi.org/10.1073/pnas.1407808111.

Liu, B., Ianosi-Irimie, M., Thayumanavan, S., 2019. Reversible click chemistry for ultrafast and quantitative formation of protein–polymer nanoassembly and intracellular protein delivery. ACS Nano 13 (8), 9408–9420. https://doi.org/10.1021/acsnano.9b04198.

Liu, K., Zha, X.Q., Li, Q.M., Pan, L.H., Luo, J.P., 2021. Hydrophobic interaction and hydrogen bonding driving the self-assembling of quinoa protein and flavonoids. Food Hydrocoll. 118. https://doi.org/10.1016/j.foodhyd.2021.106807.

Liu, Y., Xing, R., Li, J., Yan, X., 2023. Covalently triggered self-assembly of peptide-based nanodrugs for cancer theranostics. iScience 26 (1), 105789. https://doi.org/10.1016/j.isci.2022.105789.

Lohcharoenkal, W., Wang, L., Chen, Y.C., Rojanasakul, Y., 2014. Protein nanoparticles as drug delivery carriers for cancer therapy. BioMed Res. Int. 2014, 1–12. https://doi.org/10.1155/2014/180549.

Lowik, D.W.P.M., Leunissen, E.H.P., Heuvel, M.V.D., Hansen, M.B., Hest, J.C.M.V., 2010. Stimulus responsive peptide based materials. Chem. Soc. Rev. 39 (9), 3394–3412. https://doi.org/10.1039/b914342b.

Lu, S., Wang, H., Sheng, Y., Liu, M., Chen, P., 2012. Molecular binding of self-assembling peptide EAK16-II with anticancer agent EPT and its implication in cancer cell inhibition. J. Contr. Release 160 (1), 33–40. https://doi.org/10.1016/j.jconrel.2012.03.009.

KU. Maheswari, Self-assembly of proteins .

Mandal, D., Nasrolahi Shirazi, A., Parang, K., 2014. Self-assembly of peptides to nanostructures. Org. Biomol. Chem. 12 (22), 3544–3561. https://doi.org/10.1039/C4OB00447G.

Manna, La, Natale, Di, Onesto, C., Marasco, V., 2021. Self-assembling peptides: from design to biomedical applications. Int. J. Mol. Sci. 22.

Marcandalli, J., Fiala, B., Ols, S., Perotti, M., Schueren, W.de van der, Snijder, J., Hodge, E., Benhaim, M., Ravichandran, R., Carter, L., Sheffler, W., Brunner, L., Lawrenz, M., Dubois, P., Lanzavecchia, A., Sallusto, F., Lee, K.K., Veesler, D., Correnti, C.E., Stewart, L.J., Baker, D., Loré, K., Perez, L., King, N.P., 2019. Induction of potent neutralizing antibody responses by a designed protein nanoparticle vaccine for respiratory syncytial virus. Cell 176 (6), 1420. https://doi.org/10.1016/j.cell.2019.01.046.

McCarthy, H.O., McCaffrey, J., Mccrudden, C.M., Zholobenko, A., Ali, A.A., McBride, J.W., Massey, A.S., Pentlavalli, S., Chen, K.H., Cole, G., Loughran, S.P., Dunne, N.J., Donnelly, R.F., Kett, V.L., Robson, T., 2014. Development and characterization of self-assembling nanoparticles using a bio-inspired amphipathic peptide for gene delivery. J. Contr. Release 189, 141–149. https://doi.org/10.1016/j.jconrel.2014.06.048.

McLellan, J.S., Chen, M., Joyce, M.G., Sastry, M., Stewart-Jones, G.B.E., Yang, Y., Zhang, B., Chen, L., Srivatsan, S., Zheng, A., Zhou, T., Graepel, K.W., Kumar, A., Moin, S., Boyington, J.C., Chuang, G.Y., Soto, C., Baxa, U., Bakker, A.Q., Spits, H., Beaumont, T., Zheng, Z., Xia, N., Ko, S.Y., Todd, J.P., Rao, S., Graham, B.S., Kwong, P.D., 2013. Structure-based design of a fusion glycoprotein vaccine for respiratory syncytial virus. Science 342 (6158), 592–598. https://doi.org/10.1126/science.1243283.

Mishra, V., Heath, R.J., 2021. Structural and biochemical features of human serum albumin essential for eukaryotic cell culture. Int. J. Mol. Sci. 22 (16). https://doi.org/10.3390/ijms22168411.

Mu, R., Zhu, D., Abdulmalik, S., Wijekoon, S., Wei, G., Kumbar, S.G., 2024. Stimuli-responsive peptide assemblies: Design, self-assembly, modulation, and biomedical applications. Bioact. Mater. 35, 181–207. https://doi.org/10.1016/j.bioactmat.2024.01.023.

Mukhamedova, M., Wrapp, D., Shen, C.H., Gilman, M.S.A., Ruckwardt, T.J., Schramm, C.A., Ault, L., Chang, L., Derrien-Colemyn, A., Lucas, S.A.M., Ransier, A., Darko, S., Phung, E., Wang, L., Zhang, Y., Rush, S.A., Madan, B., Stewart-Jones, G.B.E., Costner, P.J., Holman, L.S.A., Hickman, S.P., Berkowitz, N.M., Doria-Rose, N.A., Morabito, K.M., DeKosky, B.J., Gaudinski, M.R., Chen, G.L., Crank, M.C., Misasi, J., Sullivan, N. J., Douek, D.C., Kwong, P.D., Graham, B.S., McLellan, J.S., Mascola, J.R., 2021. Vaccination with prefusion-stabilized respiratory syncytial virus fusion protein induces genetically and antigenically diverse antibody responses. Immunity 54 (4), 769. https://doi.org/10.1016/j.immuni.2021.03.004.

Murtaja, Y., Repka, D., 2023. Application of Physical-Chemical Approaches for Encapsulation, pp. 1–17.

Mustafai, A., Zubair, M., Hussain, A., Ullah, A., 2023. Recent progress in proteins-based micelles as drug delivery carriers. Polymers 15 (4), 836. https://doi.org/10.3390/polym15040836.

Newfang, D.A., Johnson, G.T., Harbison, R.D., 2015. Nanoparticles. Hamilt Hardy's Ind Toxicol 5. Sixth Ed.

Obozina, A.S., Komedchikova, E.N., Kolesnikova, O.A., Iureva, A.M., Kovalenko, V.L., Zavalko, F.A., Rozhnikova, T.V., Tereshina, E.D., Mochalova, E.N., Shipunova, V.O., 2023. Genetically encoded self-assembling protein nanoparticles for the targeted delivery in vitro and in vivo. Federation Pharmaceutics 15 (1). https://doi.org/10.3390/pharmaceutics15010231.

I Of, D With, H. Serum, Using peak profiling and high-performance affinity interactions of drugs with human serum albumin. 1218 (2012),

Olshefsky, A., Richardson, C., Pun, S.H., King, N.P., 2022. Engineering self-assembling protein nanoparticles for therapeutic delivery. Bioconjug. Chem. 33 (11), 2018–2034. https://doi.org/10.1021/acs.bioconjchem.2c00030.

Panda, J.J., Chauhan, V.S., 2014. Short peptide based self-assembled nanostructures: Implications in drug delivery and tissue engineering. Polym. Chem. 5 (15), 4418–4436. https://doi.org/10.1039/c4py00173g.

Pang, X., Gong, K., Zhang, X., Wu, S., Cui, Y., Qian, B.Z., 2019. Osteopontin as a multifaceted driver of bone metastasis and drug resistance. Pharmacol. Res. 144, 235–244. https://doi.org/10.1016/j.phrs.2019.04.030.

Pauthner, M., Havenar-Daughton, C., Sok, D., Nkolola, J.P., Bastidas, R., Boopathy, A.V., Carnathan, D.G., Chandrashekar, A., Cirelli, K.M., Cottrell, C.A., Eroshkin, A.M., Guenaga, J., Kaushik, K., Kulp, D.W., Liu, J., McCoy, L.E., Oom, A.L., Ozorowski, G., Post, K.W., Sharma, S.K., Steichen, J.M., de Taeye, S.W., Tokatlian, T., Torrents de la Peña, A., Butera, S.T., LaBranche, C.C., Montefiori, D.C., Silvestri, G., Wilson, I. A., Irvine, D.J., Sanders, R.W., Schief, W.R., Ward, A.B., Wyatt, R.T., Barouch, D.H., Crotty, S., Burton, D.R., 2017. Elicitation of robust tier 2 neutralizing antibody responses in nonhuman primates by HIV envelope trimer immunization using optimized approaches. Immunity 46 (6), 1073. https://doi.org/10.1016/j.immuni.2017.05.007.

Qi, Y., Wang, H., Wei, K., Yang, Y., Zheng, R.-Y., Kim, I., Zhang, K.-Q., 2017. A review of structure construction of silk fibroin biomaterials from single structures to multi-level structures. Int. J. Mol. Sci. 18 (3), 237. https://doi.org/10.3390/ijms18030237.

Reddy, S.T., Swartz, M.A., Hubbell, J.A., 2006. Targeting dendritic cells with biomaterials: Developing the next generation of vaccines. Trends Immunol. 27 (12), 573–579. https://doi.org/10.1016/j.it.2006.10.005.

Reynolds, T., de Zafra, C., Kim, A., Gelzleichter, T.R., 2013. Overview of Biopharmaceuticals and Comparison with Small-Molecule Drug Development Nonclinical Development of Novel Biologics, Biosimilars, Vaccines and Specialty Biologics. Elsevier Inc., United States, pp. 3–33. https://doi.org/10.1016/B978-0-12-394810-6.00001-0.

Rodrigues, M.Q., Alves, P.M., Roldão, A., 2021. Functionalizing ferritin nanoparticles for vaccine development. Pharmaceutics 13 (10). https://doi.org/10.3390/pharmaceutics13101621.

Roldão, A., Mellado, M.C.M., Castilho, L.R., Carrondo, M.J.T., Alves, P.M., 2010. Virus-like particles in vaccine development. Expet Rev. Vaccine 9 (10), 1149–1176. https://doi.org/10.1586/erv.10.115.

Roy, D., Cambre, J.N., Sumerlin, B.S., 2010. Future perspectives and recent advances in stimuli-responsive materials. Prog. Polym. Sci. 35 (1–2), 278–301. https://doi.org/10.1016/j.progpolymsci.2009.10.008.

Rudra, J.S., Tian, Y.F., Jung, J.P., Collier, J.H., 2010. A self-assembling peptide acting as an immune adjuvant. Proc. Natl. Acad. Sci. U. S. A 107 (2), 622–627. https://doi.org/10.1073/pnas.0912124107.

Saleh, T., Soudi, T., Shojaosadati, S.A., 2019. Aptamer functionalized curcumin-loaded human serum albumin (HSA) nanoparticles for targeted delivery to HER-2 positive breast cancer cells. Int. J. Biol. Macromol. 130, 109–116. https://doi.org/10.1016/j.ijbiomac.2019.02.129.

Sana, B., Johnson, E., Lim, S., 2015. The unique self-assembly/disassembly property of Archaeoglobus fulgidus ferritin and its implications on molecular release from the protein cage. Biochim. Biophys. Acta Gen. Subj. 1850 (12), 2544–2551. https://doi.org/10.1016/j.bbagen.2015.08.019.

Sánchez-Iglesias, A., Grzelczak, M., Altantzis, T., Goris, B., Pérez-Juste, J., Bals, S., Van Tendeloo, G., Donaldson, S. H., Chmelka, B.F., Israelachvili, J.N., Luis, M., Liz-Marzán, 2012. Hydrophobic interactions modulate self-assembly of nanoparticles. ACS Nano 6 (12), 11059–11065. https://doi.org/10.1021/nn3047605.

Sellés Vidal, L., Isalan, M., Heap, J.T., Ledesma-Amaro, R., 2023. A primer to directed evolution: current methodologies and future directions. RSC Chem. Biol. 4 (4), 271–291. https://doi.org/10.1039/d2cb00231k.

Sesterhenn, F., Yang, C., Bonet, J., Cramer, J.T., Wen, X., Wang, Y., Chiang, C.I., Abriata, L.A., Kucharska, I., Castoro, G., Vollers, S.S., Galloux, M., Dheilly, E., Rosset, S., Corthésy, P., Georgeon, S., Villard, M., Richard, C.A., Descamps, D., Delgado, T., Oricchio, E., Rameix-Welti, M.A., Más, V., Ervin, S., Eléouët, J.F., Riffault, S., Bates, J.T., Julien, J.P., Li, Y., Jardetzky, T., Krey, T., Correia, B.E., 2020. De novo protein design enables the precise induction of RSV-neutralizing antibodies. Science 368 (6492). https://doi.org/10.1126/science.aay5051.

Shi, J., Xiao, Z., Kamaly, N., Farokhzad, O.C., 2011. Self-assembled targeted nanoparticles: Evolution of technologies and bench to bedside translation. Accounts Chem. Res. 44 (10), 1123–1134. https://doi.org/10.1021/ar200054n.

Silva, R.F., Silva, E.R., Ando, A., 2013. L-diphenylalanine microtubes as a potential drug-delivery system: characterization, release kinetics, and cytotoxicity. Langmuir : the ACS journal of Surfaces and Colloids 29, 10205–10212.

Singh, R., Srinivas, S.P., Kumawat, M., Daima, H.K., 2024. Ligand-based surface engineering of nanomaterials: Trends, challenges, and biomedical perspectives. Open 15. https://doi.org/10.1016/j.onano.2023.100194.

Steinhauser, I.M., Langer, K., Strebhardt, K.M., Spänkuch, B., 2008. Effect of trastuzumab-modified antisense oligonucleotide-loaded human serum albumin nanoparticles prepared by heat denaturation. Biomaterials 29 (29), 4022–4028. https://doi.org/10.1016/j.biomaterials.2008.07.001.

Stephenson, R., Varamini, P., Butcher, N., Minchin, R., Toth, I., 2014. Effect of lipidated gonadotropin-releasing hormone peptides on receptor mediated binding and uptake into prostate cancer cells in vitro. Nanomed. Nanotechnol. Biol. Med. 10 (8), 1799–1808. https://doi.org/10.1016/j.nano.2014.06.015.

Stevens, C.A., Kaur, K., Klok, H.A., 2021. Self-assembly of protein-polymer conjugates for drug delivery. Dvanced Drug Delivery Reviews 174, 447–460. https://doi.org/10.1016/j.addr.2021.05.002.

Stringer, K.L., Turan, B., McCormick, L., Durojaiye, M., Nyblade, L., Kempf, M.-C., Lichtenstein, B., 2017. JMT, Physiol Behav 176.

Sun, Q., Vaccine adjuvants from self-assembling peptides . Google Patents, Google Patents, (2018),

Sun, Q., Yang, Z., Qi, X., 2023. Design and application of hybrid polymer-protein systems in cancer therapy. Polymers 15 (9), 2219. https://doi.org/10.3390/polym15092219.

Takakura, Y., Nishikawa, M., Yamashita, F., Hashida, M., 2001. Development of gene drug delivery systems based on pharmacokinetic studies. Eur. J. Pharmaceut. Sci. 13 (1), 71–76. https://doi.org/10.1016/s0928-0987(00)00209-8.

Tarhini, M., Greige-Gerges, H., Elaissari, A., 2017. Protein-based nanoparticles: From preparation to encapsulation of active molecules. Int. J. Pharm. 522 (1–2), 172–197. https://doi.org/10.1016/j.ijpharm.2017.01.067.

Temming, K., Schiffelers, R.M., Molema, G., Kok, R.J., 2005. RGD-based strategies for selective delivery of therapeutics and imaging agents to the tumour vasculature. Drug Resist. Updates 8 (6), 381–402. https://doi.org/10.1016/j.drup.2005.10.002.

Thalhauser, S., Breunig, M., 2020. Considerations for efficient surface functionalization of nanoparticles with a high molecular weight protein as targeting ligand. Eur. J. Pharmaceut. Sci. 155, 105520. https://doi.org/10.1016/j.ejps.2020.105520.

Thomas, C.E., Ehrhardt, A., Kay, M.A., 2003. Progress and problems with the use of viral vectors for gene therapy. Nat. Rev. Genet. 4 (5), 346–358. https://doi.org/10.1038/nrg1066.

Toyama, T., Nitta, N., Ohta, S., Tanaka, T., Nagatani, Y., Takahashi, M., Murata, K., Shiomi, H., Naka, S., Kurumi, Y., Tani, T., Tabata, Y., 2012. Clinical trial of cisplatin-conjugated gelatin microspheres for patients with hepatocellular carcinoma. Jpn. J. Radiol. 30 (1), 62–68. https://doi.org/10.1007/s11604-011-0010-2.

Tsuboyama, K., Dauparas, J., Chen, J., Laine, E., Mohseni Behbahani, Y., Weinstein, J.J., Mangan, N.M., Ovchinnikov, S., Rocklin, G.J., 2023. Mega-scale experimental analysis of protein folding stability in biology and design. Nature 620 (7973), 434–444. https://doi.org/10.1038/s41586-023-06328-6.

Uchida, M., Klem, M.T., Allen, M., Suci, P., Flenniken, M., Gillitzer, E., Varpness, Z., Liepold, L.O., Young, M., Douglas, T., 2007. Biological containers: Protein cages as multifunctional nanoplatforms. Adv. Mater. 19 (8), 1025–1042. https://doi.org/10.1002/adma.200601168.

Ulrich, S., 2019. Growing prospects of dynamic covalent chemistry in delivery applications. Accounts Chem. Res. 52 (2), 510–519. https://doi.org/10.1021/acs.accounts.8b00591.

Vagner, J., Qu, H., Hruby, V.J., 2008. Peptidomimetics, a synthetic tool of drug discovery. Curr. Opin. Chem. Biol. 12 (3), 292–296. https://doi.org/10.1016/j.cbpa.2008.03.009.

Vanparijs, N., De Coen, R., Laplace, D., Louage, B., Maji, S., Lybaert, L., Hoogenboom, R., De Geest, B.G., 2015. Transiently responsive protein-polymer conjugates via a grafting-from RAFT approach for intracellular co-delivery of proteins and immune-modulators. Chem. Commun. 51 (73), 13972–13975. https://doi.org/10.1039/c5cc04809e.

Varma, L.T., Singh, N., Gorain, B., Choudhury, H., Tambuwala, M.M., Kesharwani, P., Shukla, R., 2020. Recent advances in self-assembled nanoparticles for drug delivery. Curr. Drug Deliv. 17 (4), 279–291. https://doi.org/10.2174/1567201817666200210122340.

von Maltzahn, G., Vauthey, S., Santoso, S., Zhang, S., 2003. Positively charged surfactant-like peptides self-assemble into nanostructures. Langmuir 19 (10), 4332–4337. https://doi.org/10.1021/la026526+.

Walls, A.C., Fiala, B., Schäfer, A., Wrenn, S., Pham, M.N., Murphy, M., Tse, L.V., Shehata, L., O'Connor, M.A., Chen, C., Navarro, M.J., Miranda, M.C., Pettie, D., Ravichandran, R., Kraft, J.C., Ogohara, C., Palser, A., Chalk, S., Lee, E.C., Guerriero, K., Kepl, E., Chow, C.M., Sydeman, C., Hodge, E.A., Brown, B., Fuller, J.T., Dinnon, K.H., Gralinski, L.E., Leist, S.R., Gully, K.L., Lewis, T.B., Guttman, M., Chu, H.Y., Lee, K.K., Fuller, D.H., Baric, R.S., Kellam, P., Carter, L., Pepper, M., Sheahan, T.P., Veesler, D., King, N.P., 2020. Elicitation of potent neutralizing antibody responses by designed protein nanoparticle vaccines for SARS-CoV-2. Cell 183 (5), 1367. https://doi.org/10.1016/j.cell.2020.10.043.

Wang, X.-Q., Zhang, Q., 2012. pH-sensitive polymeric nanoparticles to improve oral bioavailability of peptide/protein drugs and poorly water-soluble drugs. Eur. J. Pharm. Biopharm. 82 (2), 219–229. https://doi.org/10.1016/j.ejpb.2012.07.014.

Wang, B., Hu, L., Siahaan, T.J., 2016. Drug Delivery: Principles and Applications. Wiley. https://doi.org/10.1002/9781118833322.

Wang, L., Gong, C., Yuan, X., Wei, G., 2019. Controlling the self-assembly of biomolecules into functional nanomaterials through internal interactions and external stimulations: a review. Nanomaterials 9 (2), 285. https://doi.org/10.3390/nano9020285.

Wang, Y., Xue, P., Cao, M., Yu, T., Lane, S.T., Zhao, H., 2021. Directed evolution: Methodologies and applications. Chem. Rev. 121 (20), 12384–12444. https://doi.org/10.1021/acs.chemrev.1c00260.

Watson, J.L., Juergens, D., Bennett, N.R., Trippe, B.L., Yim, J., Eisenach, H.E., Ahern, W., Borst, A.J., Ragotte, R.J., Milles, L.F., Wicky, B.I.M., Hanikel, N., Pellock, S.J., Courbet, A., Sheffler, W., Wang, J., Venkatesh, P., Sappington, I., Torres, S.V., Lauko, A., De Bortoli, V., Mathieu, E., Ovchinnikov, S., Barzilay, R., Jaakkola, T. S., DiMaio, F., Baek, M., Baker, D., 2023. De novo design of protein structure and function with RFdiffusion. Nature 620 (7976), 1089–1100. https://doi.org/10.1038/s41586-023-06415-8.

Wong, C.K., Laos, A.J., Soeriyadi, A.H., Wiedenmann, J., Curmi, P.M.G., Justin Gooding, J., Marquis, C.P., Stenzel, M.H., Thordarson, P., 2015. Polymersomes prepared from thermoresponsive fluorescent protein–polymer bioconjugates: Capture of and report on drug and protein payloads. Angew. Chem. 127 (18), 5407–5412. https://doi.org/10.1002/ange.201412406.

Wu, P., Gao, W., Su, M., Nice, E.C., Zhang, W., Lin, J., Xie, N., 2021. Adaptive mechanisms of tumor therapy resistance driven by tumor microenvironment. Front. Cell Dev. Biol. 9. https://doi.org/10.3389/fcell.2021.641469.

Xia, X.X., Wang, M., Lin, Y., Xu, Q., Kaplan, D.L., 2014. Hydrophobic drug-triggered self-assembly of nanoparticles from silk-elastin-like protein polymers for drug delivery. Biomacromolecules 15 (3), 908–914. https://doi.org/10.1021/bm4017594.

Xiao, H., Bao, Z., Zhao, H., 2015. High throughput screening and selection methods for directed enzyme evolution. Ind. Eng. Chem. Res. 54 (16), 4011–4020. https://doi.org/10.1021/ie503060a.

Yadav, S., Sharma, A.K., Kumar, P., 2020. Nanoscale self-assembly for therapeutic delivery. Front. Bioeng. Biotechnol. 8. https://doi.org/10.3389/fbioe.2020.00127.

Yan, X., He, Q., Wang, K., Duan, L., Cui, Y., Li, J., 2007. Transition of cationic dipeptide nanotubes into vesicles and oligonucleotide delivery. Angew. Chem. 119 (14), 2483–2486. https://doi.org/10.1002/ange.200603387.

Yishay-Safranchik, E., Golan, M., David, A., 2014. Controlled release of doxorubicin and Smac-derived pro-apoptotic peptide from self-assembled KLD-based peptide hydrogels. Polym. Adv. Technol. 25 (5), 539–544. https://doi.org/10.1002/pat.3300.

Yoneshima, Y., Morita, S., Ando, M., Nakamura, A., Iwasawa, S., Yoshioka, H., Goto, Y., Takeshita, M., Harada, T., Hirano, K., Oguri, T., Kondo, M., Miura, S., Hosomi, Y., Kato, T., Kubo, T., Kishimoto, J., Yamamoto, N., Nakanishi, Y., Okamoto, I., 2021. Phase 3 trial comparing nanoparticle albumin-bound paclitaxel with docetaxel for previously treated advanced NSCLC. J. Thorac. Oncol. 16 (9), 1523–1532. https://doi.org/10.1016/j.jtho.2021.03.027.

Yu, Z., Xu, Q., Dong, C., Lee, S., Gao, L., Li, Y., D'Ortenzio, M., Wu, J., 2015. Self-assembling peptide nanofibrous hydrogel as a versatile drug delivery platform. Curr. Pharm. Des. 21 (29), 4342–4354. https://doi.org/10.2174/1381612821666150901104821.

Zhang, P., Zhang, Y., Ding, X., Shen, W., Li, M., Wagner, E., Xiao, C., Chen, X., 2020. A multistage cooperative nanoplatform enables intracellular co-delivery of proteins and chemotherapeutics for cancer therapy. Adv. Mater. 32 (46). https://doi.org/10.1002/adma.202000013.

Zhao, Q., Potter, C.S., Carragher, B., Lander, G., Sworen, J., Towne, V., Abraham, D., Duncan, P., Washabaugh, M. W., Sitrin, R.D., 2014. Characterization of virus-like particles in GARDASIL® by cryo transmission electron microscopy. Hum. Vaccines Immunother. 10 (3), 734–739. https://doi.org/10.4161/hv.27316.

Zhou, H.-X., Pang, X., 2018. Electrostatic interactions in protein structure, folding, binding, and condensation. Chem. Rev. 118 (4), 1691–1741. https://doi.org/10.1021/acs.chemrev.7b00305.

Zolnik, B.S., González-Fernández, A., Sadrieh, N., Dobrovolskaia, M.A., 2010. Minireview: Nanoparticles and the immune system. Endocrinology 151 (2), 458–465. https://doi.org/10.1210/en.2009-1082.

CHAPTER

# 6

# Mechanism of protein-based nanoparticle interactions

*Özlem Kaplan*[1], *Kevser Bal*[2], *Numan Eczacioglu*[3] *and Mehmet Koray Gök*[2]

[1]Alanya Alaaddin Keykubat University, Rafet Kayıs Faculty of Engineering, Department of Genetics and Bioengineering, Antalya, Türkiye; [2]Istanbul University-Cerrahpasa, Faculty of Engineering, Department of Chemical Engineering, Istanbul, Türkiye; [3]Karamanoglu Mehmetbey University, Faculty of Engineering, Department of Bioengineering, Karaman, Türkiye

## 1. Introduction

Proteins are key players in all existence on Earth; as Randy Schekman pointed out, they are responsible for the chemistry of life. They are naturally occurring, well-defined biopolymers and offer intriguing properties such as high biocompatibility, complete degradability, and specific interactions with receptors (Martínez-López et al., 2020; Lohcharoenkal et al., 2014; Verma et al., 2018). The interactions of proteins with nanoparticles (Kopac, 2021), biomaterials (Yang et al., 2013), polymers (Wei et al., 2014), ligands (Du et al., 2016), drugs (Huang et al., 2010), and even with themselves (Archakov et al., 2003) have therefore often been intensively investigated by researchers. Moreover, protein-based nanoparticles formed from proteins have recently gained prominence in their use as pharmaceutical devices. Protein-based nanoparticles are a versatile and rapidly growing area of research in many disciplines, such as biomedical applications of nanomaterials, drug delivery, biosensing applications, nanocatalysis, protein therapy, and so on (Baimanov et al., 2019; Kaltbeitzel and Wich, 2023; Jain et al., 2018). Considering the increase in the use of protein-based nanoparticles for therapeutic purposes and their sensitivity to physical–chemical changes in their environment (Herrera Estrada and Champion, 2015), it is crucial to investigate the effects of their interactions for biocompatibility and nanosafety evaluation, especially on drug delivery.

*Protein-Based Nanoparticles in Drug Delivery*
https://doi.org/10.1016/B978-0-443-33639-3.00010-6

These protein-based nanoparticles could make outstanding contributions to drug delivery systems as drug carriers and as the active therapeutic protein itself (Herrera Estrada and Champion, 2015). The range of available proteins provides versatile options (Huang et al., 2016). Thus, protein-based nanoparticles can also be used to deliver small drug molecules, nucleic acids, growth factors, and vaccines (Jain et al., 2018; Herrera Estrada and Champion, 2015). They are amphiphilic, allowing them to interact with hydrophilic and hydrophobic drugs and solvents. These approaches often aim to reduce toxicity by conjugating natural proteins with known drugs (Verma et al., 2018). For instance, human serum albumin protein-bound paclitaxel particles are one of the first FDA approved protein-based nanoparticles (in 2005, Abraxane) for the treatment of breast cancer. Furthermore, it has since been approved for other cancers, such as nonsmall cell lung cancer and pancreatic cancer. This is widely recognized as a significant milestone in the use of protein-based nanoparticle drugs. This formulation allows for better drug delivery to tumors, increasing its effectiveness and reducing some of the side effects associated with traditional paclitaxel treatments (Green et al., 2006).

These protein-based nanoparticles are nanoscale structures, typically ranging from 20 to 1000 nm (Verma et al., 2018; Kaltbeitzel and Wich, 2023; Herrera Estrada and Champion, 2015). The size of the protein-based nanoparticles significantly impacts their cellular uptake and ultimately their therapeutic efficacy. The protein-based nanoparticles can also be engineered to target specific cells, tissues, and organs by modification on their surface to achieve targeted drug delivery (Jain et al., 2018; Kianfar, 2021). Unlike nanoparticles from conventional synthetic nanoparticles, metallic and inorganic sources, protein-based nanoparticles do not have limitations such as toxicity, rapid clearance from the body, large size, or aggregation (Verma et al., 2018; Green et al., 2006). Furthermore, the abundance of hydroxyl, amino, and carboxyl groups in the side chains of proteins enables efficient chemical modification. As a result, protein-based nanoparticles can bind covalently or noncovalently to various ligands and drug molecules (Jain et al., 2018; Sripriyalakshmi et al., 2014). They demonstrate a range of potential drug loading mechanisms, such as hydrophobic interactions, covalent binding, and electrostatic attractions.

The choice of protein source and type used to prepare the protein-based nanoparticles depends on the properties of the encapsulated drug and the desired application of the nanoparticles. Protein-based nanoparticles can be virus like nanoparticles (VLN) that do not contain genetic material or nanoparticle systems obtained from animal or plant proteins. VLNs form nanoparticle systems that can transport drugs in a controlled and targeted manner due to their size and well-defined geometry, which provide ideal endocytosis after the genetic material is removed. VLNs also have low toxicity and can be functionalized on their internal or external surfaces (Kim et al., 2023a). Besides albumin, many fibrous proteins such as keratin, collagen, elastin, and silk proteins like fibroin are the most widely employed animal based protein sources and are abundant in plasma, making them a biocompatible, biodegradable, and low immunogenicity carrier for drug delivery applications (Gu and Jiang, 2014; Zaher et al., 2023). The hydrophobic character of plant proteins such as gliadin, whey protein isolates, zein, and casein makes them more advantageous than animal proteins for avoiding toxic chemical crosslinkers and lower production costs (Zaher et al., 2023; Ezpeleta et al., 1996; Tarhini et al., 2017). Apart from these, heat shock proteins, chaperones, and ferritin, particularly amenable to genetic or chemical modification, have been favored to encapsulate various cargo molecules (Tarhini et al., 2017; Aljabali et al., 2022; Yin et al., 2022). Since proteins have similar properties, the choice of protein in the application depends on the characteristics of the molecule to be delivered, such as its hydrophobic or hydrophilic nature (Tarhini et al., 2017).

Each of the self-assembly, chemical, and physical methods used in preparing protein nanoparticles offers unique benefits that can be leveraged depending on the desired application and the properties of the protein being used (Hong et al., 2020). The choice of method will depend on factors such as particle size requirements, stability, drug loading capacity, and the nature of the protein and drug involved. Among these techniques, one of the most widely utilized fabrication techniques is desolvation, with its simplicity, scalability, and low manufacturing costs, and the other is self-assembly, which ensures precise and highly conserved protein clusters (Kaplan et al., 2024; Habibi et al., 2022).

Studying the protein nanoparticle interactions is of crucial significance, especially in drug delivery. Challenges such as protein corona formation (Kopac, 2021; Ahsan et al., 2018), production scalability (Fuchs and Coester, 2010), and extensive characterization methods (He et al., 2024) need to be addressed to better understand the behavior of these protein-based nanoparticles in complex biological environments before their widespread use for clinical use. Especially the formation of this corona can significantly affect the protein nanoparticle's originally designed properties, such as its targeting, cellular uptake, in vivo clearance, toxicity, and overall efficacy (Rahman et al., 2013). This book chapter discusses interaction mechanisms of protein-based nanoparticles with biological systems, protein corona formation, cellular uptake mechanisms and targeting strategies, and drug loading and release mechanisms in detail.

## 2. Environmental, physical, and biological interaction mechanisms of protein-based nanoparticles

Understanding the interactions of protein-based nanoparticles with biological systems is crucial for their design and efficacy. This section provides a detailed examination of the interaction processes between protein-based nanoparticles and biological systems, including stages such as cellular uptake and cargo molecule release, and the various barriers they encounter. Protein-based nanoparticles encounter numerous biological barriers upon entering the body, such as the circulatory system, cell membranes, and endosomal/lysosomal systems (Fig. 6.1) (Meng et al., 2018). Initially, a layer known as the "protein corona" may form on the surface of the nanoparticles. This corona affects the colloidal stability and biodistribution of the nanoparticles, determining their interactions with cells (Kim et al., 2023b). Furthermore, enzymes and other biomolecules present in the body can bind to or alter the surface of nanoparticles, influencing the formation of the corona and the stability of the nanoparticles. Enzymatic degradation may increase the biodegradability of protein nanoparticles, but it can also lead to premature cargo release and reduced efficacy (Habibi et al., 2022).

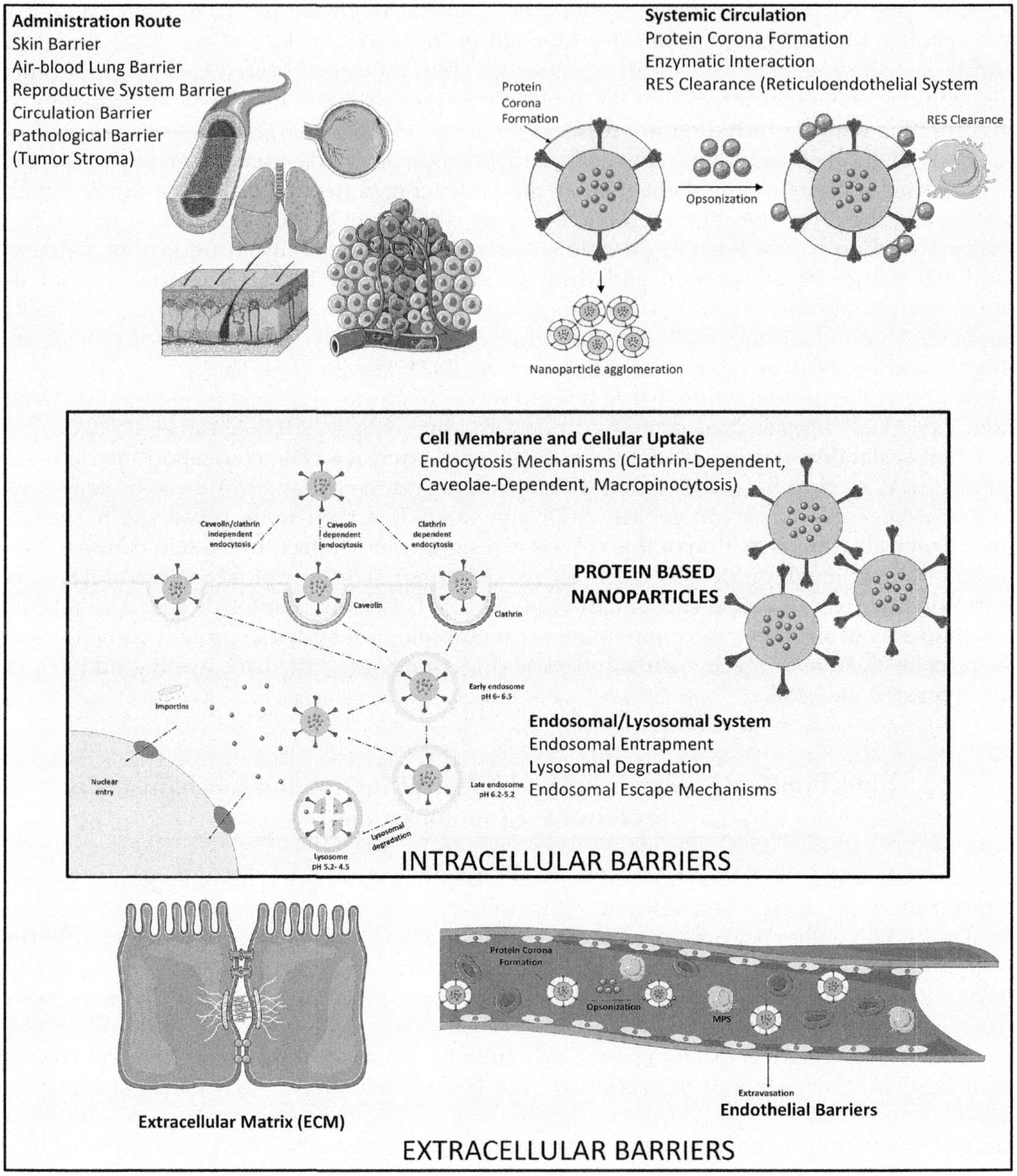


**FIGURE 6.1** Biological barriers for protein-based nanoparticle delivery system.

In the circulatory system, protein nanoparticles need to remain stable in the blood plasma and avoid rapid clearance by the reticuloendothelial system (RES) to reach their target. While circulating in the blood, nanoparticles can be captured by the RES, hindering their ability to reach their target (Roh et al., 2019). Throughout the circulatory system, nanoparticles face challenges such as endothelial barriers. Tight junctions between endothelial cells make it difficult for nanoparticles to pass into tissues, making their transit through endothelial cells and reaching the target tissue a critical step (Mitchell et al., 2021). Upon reaching the target tissue, nanoparticles must overcome the extracellular matrix (ECM), which fills the intercellular spaces. The ECM consists of proteins and polysaccharides in an extracellular network structure, complicating the spread of nanoparticles between tissues. To cross the ECM barrier, nanoparticles must have an appropriate size and surface properties. Enzymatic modification of the ECM or the addition of ligands that can bind to ECM components on the nanoparticles' surface can effectively overcome this barrier (Engin et al., 2017).

Finally, nanoparticles that have crossed the ECM must penetrate the cell membrane to enter the cells. The cell membrane plays a crucial role in nanoparticle uptake and intracellular transport. Nanoparticles can utilize various endocytosis mechanisms, such as clathrin-dependent endocytosis, caveolae-dependent endocytosis, and macropinocytosis while passing through the cell membrane. Once internalized, nanoparticles risk being captured and degraded by the endosomal/lysosomal system. In this case, endosomal escape mechanisms must be activated to ensure the effective release of the cargo molecule (Sousa de Almeida et al., 2021).

Nanoparticles can enter the body through various routes, including injection, ocular penetration, oral, dermal, and inhalation. When nanoparticles come into contact with physical barriers via various administration routes, they can aggregate and/or dissolve. Additionally, physiological fluids such as tears, gastrointestinal and respiratory mucus, and blood can affect the properties of nanoparticles and, thereby, their interactions with cells (Meng et al., 2018). Inhalation is used to treat lung diseases or the systemic distribution of nanoparticles. With their large surface area, the lungs allow nanoparticles to accumulate in alveoli, which is advantageous for pulmonary distribution (Anderson et al., 2020). When administered intravenously, nanoparticles are largely retained in RES organs such as the spleen, kidneys, and liver (Desai, 2012). Topical ocular medication administration, often in the form of eye drops, treats ocular illnesses and necessitates contact with various tissues of the sclera and anterior segment. Precorneal and anatomical obstacles such as nasolacrimal drainage, tear turnover, and blinking can all impact drug absorption (Mofidfar et al., 2021). Nanoparticles usually stay on the skin's surface in dermal applications, but in transdermal applications, they can permeate the stratum corneum via intercellular channels (Liu et al., 2023).

Moreover, the tumor microenvironment (TME) is another significant barrier to consider. Protein-based nanoparticles encounter a complex and heterogeneous structure after passing from blood vessels into the TME. The TME contains both cellular and noncellular components and has distinct physiological circumstances such as proteases, high interstitial fluid pressure, hypoxia, and acidic pH (Weinberg, 2022). The tumor stroma supports the cells in solid tumors, and this stroma contains a variety of components, including tumor associated macrophages, new blood vessels, connective tissue cells, and ECM (Li et al., 2007). Connective tissue cells in the tumor are extremely active, producing cytokines, proteases, growth factors, and chemokines. These cells, known as "cancer associated fibroblasts," promote ECM remodeling, tumor angiogenesis, and cell proliferation. When ECM is remodeled, it becomes denser, stiffer, and more fibrotic, increasing stress in solid tumors and compressing the vascular structure. This situation becomes a considerable physical barrier restricting nanoparticle mobility, penetration, and dispersion inside the tumor parenchyma (Belhabib et al., 2021). As the size of nanoparticles decreases, their ability to travel and spread in the tumor interstitial space increases. The size, shape, and surface of protein-based nanoparticle charges all significantly impact their tumor penetration. Because of the small size, simple diffusion allows nanoparticles to travel through the TME's extracellular area (Yang et al., 2021). Overcoming all these biological barriers is crucial for successfully delivering protein nanoparticles to their targets. Many factors are involved in these processes. A detailed examination of the factors influencing the interactions of protein-based nanoparticles with biological systems is required to overcome these barriers. The following sections detail the mechanisms of interactions between protein nanoparticles and biological systems.

## 2.1 Protein corona

When nanoparticles interact with biological systems, a protein corona forms around them due to the high protein concentration and the abundance of freely circulating proteins in the body. This corona is typically divided into two layers: the hard and the soft corona. The hard corona is the innermost layer, consisting of more tightly bound proteins, while the soft corona comprises proteins loosely associated with the hard corona (García-Álvarez and Vallet-Regí, 2021). The shape, size, and molecular structure of nanoparticles greatly influence the composition of a protein corona (Pinals et al., 2020). For example, big hydrophobic nanoparticles create distinct protein coronas from tiny positively charged nanoparticles. The protein corona substantially influences the stability and biodistribution of nanoparticles (Rampado et al., 2020). The precise role of proteins within the protein corona and the mechanisms involved in determining the fate of nanoparticles are still under investigation. Recent studies have revealed that not only the identity but also the conformations of the proteins in the protein corona are crucial. The conformation of the proteins in the corona affects the nanoparticles' aggregation behavior, overall toxicity, and delivery to target cells. These conformational changes may arise from interactions with nanoparticles and neighboring proteins within the corona. Thus, a dynamic system forms with proteins continuously adsorbing and desorbing from the corona (Bashiri et al., 2023). Protein secondary structures, such as α-helices and β-sheets, depend on hydrogen bonding and hydrophobic interactions for their stability. The tertiary structure of many proteins is formed through electrostatic interactions and hydrogen bonding between side-chain amino acid residues within hydrophobic cores. Additionally, van der Waals interactions maintain protein folding (Caporale et al., 2021). When proteins come into proximity with a surface, the adsorption forces governing protein–surface interactions can disrupt these noncovalent bonds, leading to conformational changes or denaturation of the protein structure. Protein side chains can be hydrophilic, hydrophobic, or carry positive or negative charges. Upon interaction with a hydrophilic surface, a protein undergoes structural and orientational changes, exposing its hydrophilic regions. When exposed to a hydrophobic surface, the protein reveals its hidden hydrophobic regions, while on charged surfaces, it exhibits regions of opposite charge to the surface (Zhou and Pang, 2018). Conformational changes in proteins can have dual effects. Additionally, conformational changes in adsorbed proteins may impair protein functionality and affect the interaction of nanoparticles with cells or expose hidden binding sites on the proteins, potentially triggering an immune response. These modifications can be used to elicit the appropriate cell signaling for therapeutic purposes. The structure of the protein corona on protein-based nanoparticles is governed by various factors, including the adsorption and binding of proteins to the nanoparticle, as well as the size, shape, surface area, and surface charge of the nanoparticles (Bashiri et al., 2023). For example, Pitek and colleagues demonstrated that a protein corona forms on the surface of tobacco mosaic virus (TMV) after exposure to blood plasma. The amount of protein adsorbed onto TMV was approximately six times lower than that absorbed by synthetic silica nanoparticles. The heterogeneous surface properties of TMV, compared to the smooth surfaces and uniform surface charges of synthetic silica nanoparticles, supported a more enriched formation of the protein corona (Pitek et al., 2016b). Furthermore, the same study found that opsonins were the most abundant components of TMVs' protein corona, facilitating their clearance by the mononuclear phagocyte system (MPS) (Pitek et al., 2016b). Opsonin proteins in the protein corona trigger recognition by the MPS, leading to rapid phagocytosis and clearance of opsonin coated protein-based nanoparticles from the bloodstream. This rapid innate immune response reduces the concentration of protein-based nanoparticles, preventing therapeutic doses from reaching their target areas and posing a significant barrier for many drug delivery systems (Panico et al., 2022). Interestingly, heat induced changes in TMV shape from rod like to spherical, as well as the addition of lysine residues to improve surface charge positivity, had negligible effects on TMV's protein corona profile (Pitek et al., 2016b).

### *2.1.1 Modifications for protein corona*

The composition of a protein corona can vary significantly depending on the route of administration, underscoring the importance of exposure sequence in the development of the protein corona. Nanoparticles injected into the bloodstream initially encounter plasma proteins such as globulins, fibrinogen, plasma fibronectin, and albumin before interacting with ECM proteins like fibronectin and collagen. On the other hand, nanoparticles injected outside the bloodstream pass through the skin and muscles before absorption. Nanoparticles interact with the ECM surrounding tumor tissue before reaching the cellular target location. For protein-based nanoparticles to be considered suitable drug delivery vehicles in clinical applications, they must exhibit favorable pharmacokinetic and biodistribution profiles. Protein-based nanoparticles must resist breakdown and metabolism, identification and clearance of the immune system, and nonspecific cellular uptake. To overcome these challenges, various "stealth" coatings have been developed and applied to protein-based nanoparticles (Sandra et al., 2019).

PEGylation is one of the most well-known and widely used strategies to help drug delivery systems evade the immune system and increase their circulation time in the bloodstream. PEGylation promotes the formation of protein coronas enriched with dysopsonins while reducing serum protein adsorption and opsonization (Suk et al., 2016). Dysopsonin proteins prevent phagocytic uptake by macrophages. Studies have shown that pegylated nanoparticles exhibit reduced opsonization. However, PEGylation has been shown to induce the production of PEG specific antibodies upon repeated administrations, leading to the clearance of PEGylated nanoparticles from the bloodstream (Fang et al., 2017). This has prompted the exploration of alternative "stealth" coatings. In addition to PEG, various polymers such as poloxamers (Khaliq et al., 2017), polypyrrole (Vaitkuviene et al., 2013), and polybornene (Gulati et al., 2018) have also been reported as potential stealth coatings for drug delivery. Another strategy involves the use of repeating, highly hydrophilic peptides that mimic the physicochemical and "stealth" properties of PEG.

For example, X-TEN is a random sequence of hydrophilic amino acids. Genetic fusion of X-TEN to ferritin resulted in long-circulating ferritin nanocages (LCFNs) (Lee et al., 2017a). In another study, Falco and colleagues used the "PASylation" approach, which involves genetically fusing PAS (Pro-Ala-Ser) polypeptides to the N-termini of ferritin subunits (up to 75 residues). PASylation has been used to inhibit ferritin from interacting with its native receptor TfR-1, decrease absorption by healthy cells, and increase circulation time. PASylated ferritin showed reduced binding to TfR-1 compared to wild-type ferritin. PASylated ferritin also provided a longer duration of action by extending the half-life of DOX compared to wild-type ferritin (Fracasso et al., 2016). A repeating "PASE" sequence formed by adding glutamate residues resulted in negatively charged residues on ferritin, leading to a longer circulation lifetime and reduced liver accumulation (Falvo et al., 2018).

Additionally, biomimicry strategies such as CD47 have been applied to nanoparticles to prevent clearance by the immune system. A fragment of the CD47 protein has been employed as an antiphagocytosis ligand in drug delivery mechanisms (Wang et al., 2019). Another peptide that extends the half-life of protein-based nanoparticles is the circulation-extended peptide 1 (BCP1) derived from the MS13 bacteriophage. BCP1 was genetically added to DOX-loaded ferritin. DOX-loaded BCP1-ferritin showed a longer half-life in mice than wild-type ferritin. BCP1 delayed macrophage-mediated clearance due to platelet binding interactions and increased ferritin retention in the bloodstream. Due to the prolonged circulation time, DOX-loaded BCP1-ferritin demonstrated enhanced antitumor activity (Jin et al., 2019).

To avoid detection by PEG-specific antibodies, albumin is used as an alternate surface coating method for PEGylated protein-based nanoparticles. As the most abundant plasma protein, albumin is a typical de-opsonin. Coating protein nanoparticles with albumin or directly conjugating therapeutic molecules to albumin greatly minimizes opsonin adsorption, inhibits macrophage phagocytosis, reduces nanoparticle cytotoxicity, and increases bloodstream circulation duration. Albumin binding can inhibit other adsorption of plasma proteins onto nanoparticles. Nanoparticles coated with maleimide groups can bind exclusively to endogenous albumin in vivo, and an albumin-rich corona can reduce the adsorption of other plasma proteins on nanoparticles (Singh et al., 2021). Pitek and colleagues found that conjugating serum albumin to TMV-based nanoparticles provided a more effective "camouflage" effect than PEG coatings. In mice, serum albumin-coated TMV particles inhibited antibody recognition while improving pharmacokinetics (Pitek et al., 2016a).

## 2.2 Cell membrane and cellular uptake mechanisms

As discussed in earlier sections, nanoparticles come into contact with the outer cell membrane after interacting with human chemical and physical barriers. They can interact with components of the outer plasma membrane before being absorbed. Endocytosis is the fundamental biological process of nanoparticle internalization, which involves the infolding of the cell membrane followed by the production of intracellular/endocytic vesicles. When nanoparticles come into contact with mammalian cells, they interact with the ECM, cell membrane, cytoplasmic proteins, nucleus, and other cellular organelles. This interaction leads to the internalization of nanoparticles and triggers various physiological responses. Multiple factors, such as size, size distribution, shape, net charge, and hydrophobicity/hydrophilicity, can influence the interactions between nanoparticles and cell membranes, their subsequent internalization, and interactions with intracellular components (Augustine et al., 2020).

### 2.2.1 Size and size distribution of nanoparticles

Particle size and distribution are important determinants of cell–nanoparticle interactions. The size of particles significantly affects their cellular uptake, drug release kinetics, biodistribution, and toxicity. The phagocytosis of nanoparticles by macrophages is size-dependent, as these cells can generally detect and ingest only larger nanoparticles. Cellular uptake kinetics and intracellular distribution of nanoparticles are also affected by their size (Hoshyar et al., 2016). For nanoparticles to effectively interact with cells and trigger a biological response, they must pass through the ECM. With its porous, mesh-like structure, the ECM tightly controls the movement of nanoparticles within it. The mechanical properties of the ECM are determined primarily by the organization of its macromolecular components: nanoparticles smaller than the ECM pore size are permeated, while larger nanoparticles are blocked. Collagen fibrils within the ECM have interfibrillar spaces of 20–40 nm, which permits the passage of smaller nanoparticles. Although the ECM presents multiple barriers that impede the diffusion of nanomaterials, factors such as hydrodynamic diameter and surface charge can significantly improve their mobility in the ECM. After passing through the ECM, nanoparticles must cross the cell membrane to enter cells. Smaller nanoparticles with a larger surface area relative to their volume can more easily penetrate cells (Augustine et al., 2020). Particle size is also crucial in determining the uptake mechanism; for example, smaller nanoparticles are typically internalized via clathrin-coated pits, while larger ones are taken up via caveolae-mediated endocytosis (Rejman et al., 2004). Furthermore, the size of nanoparticles affects the activation of cell membrane receptors and subsequent protein expression (Albanese et al., 2012). The effect of nanoparticle size on nanoparticle–cell interactions should consider their hydrodynamic dimensions. Hydrodynamic size is an indicator of how the particle behaves in a liquid and represents the most realistic size of nanoparticles in cell culture systems or in vivo conditions. It is also important to consider that the shape of the protein corona formed around the nanoparticles can significantly change the size and affect cellular uptake (Augustine et al., 2020).

### 2.2.2 Shapes of nanoparticles

The form of nanoparticles influences their absorption, distribution, interactions with cellular components, and subsequent cellular activities. Elongated nanomaterials, for example, have a greater absorption than spherical ones because they can stick more effectively to cell membranes. Because of their curved surface, spherical nanoparticles have fewer binding sites to interact with and conform to the cell membrane and are less likely to be internalized. For example, studies have found that nanostructures such as rods and cylinders are more successfully absorbed by cells than spherical particles. Furthermore, nanoparticles with sharp edges can pass through cell membranes and be properly absorbed (Dasgupta et al., 2014; Li et al., 2020).

### 2.2.3 *Surface charge of nanoparticles*

The negative charge of the ECM is largely due to the presence of glycosaminoglycan chains, which contain numerous negatively charged functional groups. Besides size filtration, charge-dependent mechanisms also influence the movement of nanoparticles through the ECM. Under physiological conditions, forming a protein corona on nanoparticles can alter their original surface charge and interaction patterns (Engin et al., 2017). Typically, positively charged nanoparticles are more readily internalized by cells than negatively charged ones. This preference can be attributed to the electrostatic interactions between the positively charged nanoparticles and the negatively charged cell membranes (Zhang et al., 2021).

When in contact with cells, nanoparticles may induce deformation of lipid membranes, disrupt the phospholipid bilayer, or create "holes" in the cell membranes (Behzadi et al., 2017). Positively charged nanoparticles can cause more significant membrane disruption than those with neutral or negative charges. Such disruptions can lead to leakage of intracellular components and cell death. Cationic nanoparticles interact strongly with negatively charged cell membranes, facilitating rapid internalization. In contrast, anionic nanoparticles, which carry a similar charge to cell membranes, are generally less disruptive (Nangia and Sureshkumar, 2012). Despite the general trend, experimental studies have shown that negatively charged nanomaterials can also penetrate negatively charged cell membranes and enter cells. In contrast, neutral nanoparticles exhibit low affinity for cells and thus are internalized less efficiently. Hydrophobicity is another factor that can play a crucial role in the uptake of charged nanoparticles, leading to varying outcomes regarding the effect of charge on cellular uptake (Augustine et al., 2020).

### 2.2.4 *Functional groups of nanoparticles*

The surface functional groups on nanoparticles can significantly alter their interactions with cells. The presence of functional groups determines specific interactions between the nanoparticles and cell surface ligands. Proper functionalization of the surface can facilitate strong interactions with cell membranes and enable safe entry into the cells. Additionally, functionalization can reduce the cytotoxic effects of nanoparticles. Functionalization with ligands such as nucleic acids, small molecules, antibodies, and peptides is an effective strategy for targeting specific cells or cellular components (Kianfar, 2021). It can also prevent the formation of a protein corona during contact with serum proteins. For instance, positively charged peptides often bind to negatively charged proteoglycans on cell surfaces through electrostatic interactions. These peptides can be used in multifunctional proteins when specific targeting is not required. Cell penetrating peptides (CPPs) are known for their nonspecific cellular binding and internalization. However, for therapeutic effects requiring specific cell or tissue targeting, receptor ligands can be used to achieve more precise interactions (Zorko et al., 2022). Ligand–receptor interactions can promote the uptake of ligand–receptor complexes into cells. Many peptides are identified as receptor-specific ligands in the literature, and they can be added to multifunctional proteins to enhance cellular specificity. Furthermore, functionalization with specific biomolecules like antibodies is an important approach in nanomedicine to target and facilitate internalization (Domingo-Espín et al., 2011).

### 2.2.5 *Hydrophobicity/hydrophilicity of nanoparticles*

The interaction between nanoparticles and cells is significantly influenced by the hydrophobic or hydrophilic properties of the nanoparticles. Studies have shown that nanoparticles with moderately hydrophilic surfaces have higher cell adhesion and proliferation rates (Mager et al., 2011). Proteins are zwitterionic molecules containing both hydrophobic and hydrophilic regions. This differentiation within their structure arises from the diverse sequences of amino acids they possess. Additionally, the conformational structure of proteins is a crucial factor influencing their surface properties. This aspect affects the characteristics of all protein-based nanoparticles, directly influencing the formation of self-assembled protein nanoparticle structures through secondary forces such as van der Waals forces, electrostatic interactions, and hydrogen bonds. Moreover, the hydrophilicity/hydrophobicity groups of the nanoparticle play a significant role in its interaction with biological systems. In a study conducted by Pustulka et al., protein nanoparticles with different charges, hydrophobicities, and sequences were examined for corona formation, revealing that these characteristics result in distinct differences in the recognition of protein-based nanoparticles by the corona and macrophages (Champion et al., 2020). Hydrophilic surface groups generally make nanoparticles more resistant to phagocytosis, allowing them to remain in circulation for longer periods. In another study by Vannucci et al., ferritin nanoparticles were PEGylated. The results indicated that controlled modification with PEG molecules of appropriate length significantly reduced nonspecific recognition and uptake by the reticuloendothelial and mononuclear phagocytic systems (Vannucci et al., 2012).

## 2.3 Cellular uptake mechanisms of nanoparticles

Various endocytosis pathways for cellular uptake of nanoparticles have been identified (Fig. 6.2). Among these, clathrin-mediated endocytosis is a significant route for the internalization of nanoparticles by cells. Inhibition of clathrin-mediated endocytosis reduces the intracellular uptake of nanoparticles. Other studies have demonstrated that nanoparticles can be taken up through caveola-mediated endocytosis, interacting with caveolin-1 proteins found in caveolae and caveosomes. Caveolin-mediated endocytosis is typically responsible for the uptake of nanoparticles in the range of 20–100 nm, while clathrin-mediated endocytosis is more associated with particles in the range of 100–350 nm (Gustafson et al., 2015). Depending on the properties of nanoparticles, multiple internalization pathways may be possible, including clathrin/caveola-mediated endocytosis, clathrin/caveola-independent endocytosis, and macropinocytosis. It is known that multiple internalization pathways can be utilized simultaneously, although peptide-based nanoparticles generally favor specific endocytosis routes (Sousa de Almeida et al., 2021). Furthermore, it has been observed that proteins interacting with specific cellular receptors are internalized through clathrin-mediated endocytosis. Most endosomal vesicles eventually fuse with cellular lysosomes.

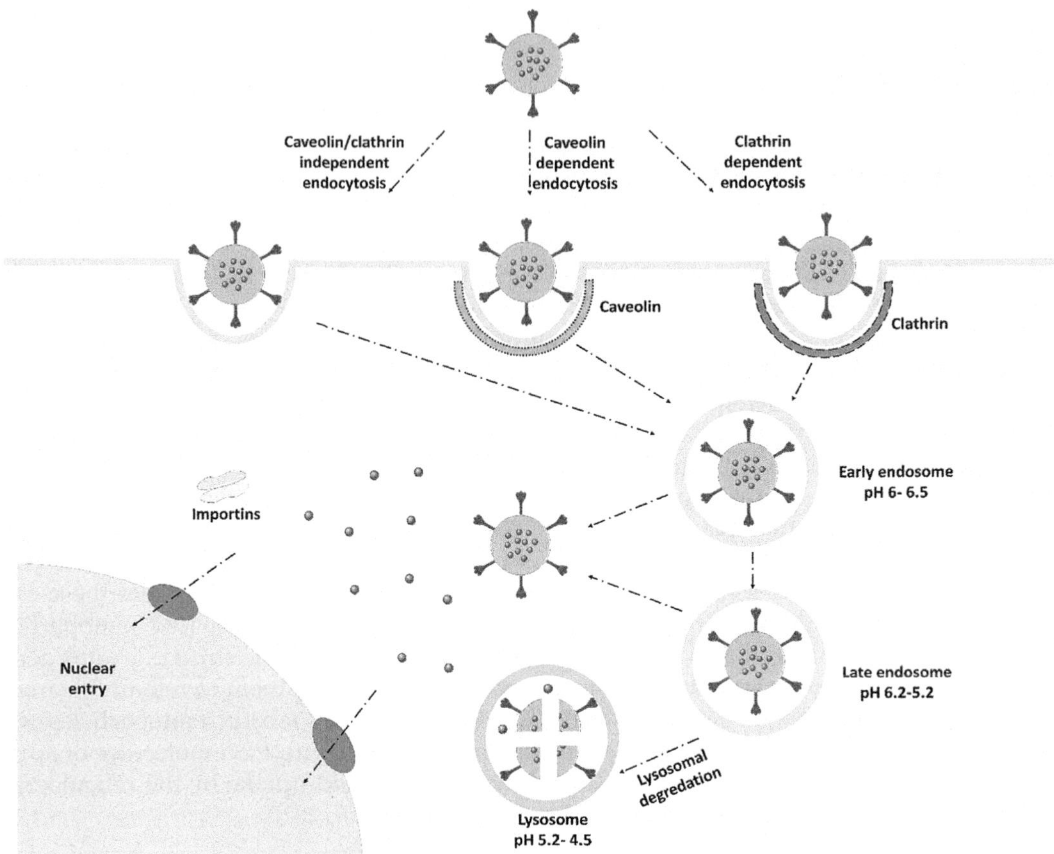


FIGURE 6.2 Cellular uptake mechanisms of nanoparticles.

Multifunctional proteins remaining in cellular endosomes may be degraded, necessitating their escape from degradation and release into the cytoplasm. Studies have identified fusogenic peptides and histidine-rich peptides that support endosomal escape (Voltà-Durán et al., 2023). Fusogenic peptides are small peptides composed of hydrophobic amino acids interspersed with negatively charged amino acids. As endosomes transition from early to late stages, the acidic environment triggers a conformational change in these peptides, allowing them to form an amphipathic structure. This structural shift enables the peptides to fuse with the endosomal membrane, resulting in pore formation and the release of the endosomal contents into the cytoplasm (Sánchez-García et al., 2017).

Histidine-rich peptides operate through the proton sponge effect to reduce the pH of endosomes. These peptides are characterized by their high histidine content. As the endosomal pH decreases, the imidazole groups in histidine residues become protonated, attracting $Cl^-$ ions and buffering the proton pump. This action causes osmotic swelling of the endosomes, which eventually leads to the release of their contents into the cytoplasm (Ferrer-Miralles et al., 2011). López-Laguna et al., in their study, found that histidine-rich peptides could specifically bind to and be internalized by target cells. They demonstrated that the peptide H5E (HEHEHEHEH) effectively promotes the endosomal escape of associated full-length proteins upon endosomal internalization. Their numerical modeling also revealed a negative relationship between the amount of protein internalized into target cells and the efficiency of cytoplasmic release, highlighting a saturation point in the His-mediated proton sponge-based endosomal escape mechanism (López-Laguna et al., 2020).

## 2.4 Intracellular traffic of nanoparticles

During the process of nanoparticles reaching the cellular cytoplasm, these particles can be degraded by cellular proteases or the proteasome system. To ensure that proteins can reach the nucleus without degradation, avoiding such breakdown is crucial. Once the nanoparticle is targeted to the cytoplasm, it must remain there long enough to exert its therapeutic effect. To achieve this, proteasome-inhibitory peptides can be utilized. These peptides can protect nanoparticles, enhancing their cytoplasmic stability. For instance, Epstein–Barr virus nuclear antigen one contains a peptide made up of glycine–alanine repeats that can inhibit proteasomal proteolysis. It has been determined that at least a four-amino acid Gly–Ala repeat is necessary for protective activity (Frappier, 2012). If the protein vector carries DNA or RNA, it is also important to preserve the integrity of the nucleic acids to prevent degradation by cytosolic endonucleases (Torres-Vanegas et al., 2021). Some DNA/RNA-binding peptides, like protamines, shield DNA from cytoplasmic endonucleases, enhancing its stability (Liu et al., 2015). The cellular cytoplasm is a complex environment filled with macromolecules such as organelles and the cytoskeleton, which makes free diffusion of macromolecules challenging. However, cytoskeletal elements like microtubules, as well as endosomes and other cytosolic macromolecules, facilitate intracellular mobility. Dyneins can transport these macromolecules retrogradely along microtubules toward the nucleus. Several small peptides that can bind to dyneins have been identified, and these peptides can be incorporated into multifunctional protein nanoparticles to promote intracellular transport toward the nucleus. Additionally, some viruses exploit transport systems by using dynein-binding proteins. Through the study of these protein sequences, a peptide sequence (KSTQT) that binds to dynein LC8 light chain has been identified (Vázquez et al., 2009). Molecules smaller than 45 kDa/10–30 nm can often reach the nucleus by passive diffusion. However, macromolecules bigger than 45 kDa/10–30 nm require active transport via the nuclear pore system (Glover et al., 2009). This transport pathway usually needs a peptide signal known as a nuclear localization signal (NLS). Cellular importins sense these signals, and they actively carry them via the nuclear pore. Both monopartite and bipartite NLS sequences have been identified. As a result, if DNA has to be delivered to the cell nucleus, these peptide sequences can be included in the final protein vector (Lu et al., 2021). One of the most often utilized NLS peptides is generated from the SV40 monkey virus large tumor antigen amino acids 111–135. Other NLS sequences include GAL4, protamines, or Tat (Drescher et al., 2021).

## 3. Modifications and targeting strategies for protein-based nanoparticles

Improving the pharmacokinetic and pharmacodynamic profiles of protein nanoparticles is crucial for achieving an effective therapeutic response. For this reason, the in vivo applications of protein-based nanoparticles necessitate the effective design or modification of the nanoparticle's surface chemistry. In this context, protein-based nanoparticles can be modified using various techniques. These modifications can be achieved through genetic reprogramming (Balke and Zeltins, 2019), covalent bioconjugation (Park et al., 2020; Liu et al., 2020), or by coating the nanoparticle surface, which involves only secondary interactions without covalent bonding (Wang et al., 2015; Pham et al., 2018). Covalent bioconjugation can be performed using the functional groups of amino acids such as lysine, glutamic acid, aspartic acid, cysteine, or tyrosine, which have amine, carboxylic acid, thiol, or phenol groups, respectively. This modification can alter the surface properties of protein nanoparticles by conjugating small molecules (Xu et al., 2011), ligands (Mishra et al., 2006), peptides (Mottaghitalab et al., 2017), large proteins (Zensi et al., 2009; Kreuter et al., 2007), or polymers (Mehtala et al., 2015) to the inner or outer surfaces of protein cages, aiming for targeted delivery to cell surface receptors or for developing them as drug or imaging agent carriers.

In a study by Zhao et al., the major rotavirus protein VP6 was first chemically conjugated with doxorubicin (DOX) using 1-Ethyl-3-(3-dimethylaminopropyl)carbodiimide (EDC)/N-hydroxysuccinimide (NHS) activators, and after conjugation, the DOX-VP6 conjugates spontaneously formed virus-like particles (VLP) under appropriate protein concentration and ionic strength. Secondly, chemical conjugation with the targeting ligand lactobionic acid (LA) was performed using EDC/NHS activators (DVLPLA). Simulated 72-hour release profiles showed that under lysosomal conditions, DVLPLAs hydrolyzed and released DOX or DOX derivatives in a controlled manner into the nucleus. Additionally, in a control experiment with pH 7.4 and no protease, the DOX release from DVLPLAs remained very low, indicating the nanoparticle's safety for blood circulation. To verify the ASGPR-mediated endocytosis of DVLPLAs, it was shown that the endocytosis of DVLPLAs in HepG2 cells was dose-dependently inhibited by free LA. The specific targeting of DVLPLAs to HepG2 cells was also examined in ASGPR-negative A549, MCF-7, and HeLa cells, and immunofluorescence results confirmed that nanoparticles with galactose groups could specifically interact with HepG2 cells, which highly express ASGPR. In cytotoxicity studies, while free DOX rapidly internalized into cells and affected their function, DOX-loaded DVLPLAs showed controlled release behavior dependent on protease degradation and DOX release. Time-dependent measurements showed that the fluorescence from DOX release by DVLPLAs was mostly at the cell membrane at the first hour, in the cytoplasm after 2 hours, both in the cytoplasm and nucleus at the third hour, and predominantly in the nucleus after 4 hours of incubation. Cytotoxicity data supported this, showing that DVLPLAs did not exhibit significant cytotoxicity against HepG2 cells at the first hour, whereas free DOX reduced cell viability to 45%. At the end of the third hour, cell viability was 50% for DVLPLAs and 25% for DOX; after 4 hours of incubation, both DVLPLAs and DOX killed all cells. The study results demonstrated that DOX- and LA-conjugated VLPs are suitable nanoparticles for the targeted and controlled delivery of DOX (Zhao et al., 2011).

In a different study by Ren et al., they investigated the targeted delivery of DOX to ovarian cancer cells (OVCAR-3) by modifying the Hibiscus chlorotic ringspot virus

(HCRSV) with folic acid. Firstly, for folic acid modification on the HCRSV surface, activation was performed using EDC/NHS activators to form a stable NHS ester-based amide bond. Then, to achieve the required size and charge for the reformation of the protein cage structure after removing the genetic material, DOX and polystyrene sulfonic acid were loaded simultaneously, a process referred to as the "polyanion association." Sucrose gradient analysis and agarose gel electrophoresis results of drug loading studies showed that DOX was encapsulated within the HCRSV capsids. The nanoparticle structure confirmed by Transmission Electron Microscopy (TEM) results proved the effectiveness of the "polyanion association" method for capsid reassembly and drug loading. The release profile behavior showed that HCRSV protein cages provide controlled release drug delivery with almost complete release of the loaded drug. In cytotoxicity analyses on the OVCAR-3 cell line, free DOX and nonmodified HCRSV capsids showed similar cellular internalization, indicating that encapsulation of DOX alone is insufficient for intracellular drug accumulation, while folic acid-modified HCRSV capsids achieved twice the cellular uptake of DOX. In control experiments on the human diploid fibroblast cell line CCL-186, neither free DOX nor DOX-HCRSV capsids with or without folic acid modification showed specific behavior. Confocal micrograph analysis on OVCAR-3 cells indicated that DOX-loaded folic acid-conjugated HCRSV capsids exhibited more intense fluorescence compared to free DOX or nontargeted capsids. The fluorescence emissions observed in the cytoplasm during the cellular uptake of folic acid-conjugated HCRSV capsids were consistent with the endocytosis pathway through folate receptor-mediated cellular uptake (Ren et al., 2007).

In a study by Lee et al., VLPs derived from the icosahedral virus bacteriophage Qβ were conjugated with biocompatible and hydrophilic mPEG, poly(oligo(ethylene glycol) methyl ether acrylate) (POEGMEA), and anhydride-end-capped poly(norbornene–(oligo(ethylene glycol) ester)) (PNB). Qβ conjugates were synthesized using an amine-reactive polymer grafting approach by functionalizing the terminal groups. The stealth properties of different polymers against carrier specific antibodies showed that POEGMEA conjugation reduced antibody recognition by 16% compared to unmodified Qβ, while mPEG and PNB conjugations reduced antigenicity by 42% and 49%, respectively. The antibody shielding efficiency of PEG- and PNB-conjugated Qβ indicated two different escape mechanisms, suggesting that PNB conjugation prevents contact with IgG and reduces antibody binding (Lee et al., 2017b).

Various modifications, modification mechanisms, and cell interactions of protein-based nanoparticles are summarized in Table 6.1.

## 4. Drug loading and release mechanisms for protein-based nanoparticles

### 4.1 Mechanisms of drug loading in protein-based nanoparticles

Drug loading in protein-based systems refers to the process of loading therapeutic agents onto protein carriers, and this step is crucial for determining the loading capacity of the delivery system, release kinetics, and targeting strategies (Hong et al., 2020). Drug loading mechanisms into protein-based systems can be generally examined under two headings. The first of these is the conjugation of the drug with protein-based systems, through

**TABLE 6.1** Modifications and targeting of protein-based nanoparticles.

| Protein-based nanoparticle | Location | Modification | Drug | Reaction mechanism steps | Results | References |
|---|---|---|---|---|---|---|
| Gelatin | NP surface modification | NeutrAvidin$^{FITC}$-biotinylated epidermal growth factor (bEGF) | Cisplatin | Gelatin amino groups thiolated with 2-iminothiolane and activated with sulfo-MBS for thiol group conjugation. | • Effective formulation for inducing cell apoptosis.<br>• Rapid interaction attributed to bEGF surface modification. | Tseng et al. (2009) |
| Albumin | NP surface modification | Apolipoprotein E (Apo E) | - | Amino group on nanoparticle surface reacted with thiol group on Apo E via bifunctional Mal-PEG-NHS crosslinker | • Apo E-bound nanoparticles endocytosed by cerebral endothelium.<br>• Transported to brain parenchyma through transcytosis.<br>• An effective brain-targeted system | Zwain et al. (2022) |
| Collagen | Conjugation | Poli (3-akrilamidofenilboronik asit) | DOX | Collagen interacts with boronic groups via reversible boronic acid-diol reaction | • High stability across wide pH and temperature ranges.<br>• Very low cytotoxicity against A2780 cells.<br>• Controlled release | Jiang et al. (2020) |
| Keratin | Conjugation | Chlorin e6 | Paclitaxel | Activation via NHS/EDC | • Novel nanoformulation combining chemotherapy and photodynamic therapy.<br>• Enhanced intracellular internalization.<br>• Prolonged efficacy under physiological conditions due to sustained release | Martella et al. (2018) |
| Sericin | Conjugation | Folic acid | DOX | Activation via NHS/EDC | • Controlled release<br>• Effective cell internalization | Huang et al. (2016) |

| | | | | | | |
|---|---|---|---|---|---|---|
| Ferritin | Genetic modification + Conjugation | Melanoma-targeting hormone (α-MSH) and stabilizing PEG | Rhodamine | Genetically linked to α-MSH Conjugation with PEG | • Cell surface receptor-targeted delivery | Al-Suhaimi et al. (2019) |
| VP6-ferritin | Genetic modification | VP6 | | Via modifying the coding sequence of nucleotides | • Boosting the defense mechanism of the immune system<br>• Effective antigenicity | Li et al. (2019) |
| Bluetongue virus (BTV) structural proteins, VP3 and VP7 | Conjugation | Cy5 | | Using N-succinimidyl (NHS) ester for conjugation of Cy5 | • Cell surface receptor-targeted delivery<br>• Maintenance of self-assembly VLP structure after modification | Brillault et al. (2017) |
| Cowpea mosaic virus (CPMV) | Conjugation | A folic acid–PEG conjugate | | Using the copper-catalyzed azide-alkyne cycloaddition reaction | • Cell surface receptor-targeted delivery<br>• Avoiding nonspecific uptake into healthy cells | Destito et al. (2007) |
| MS2 bacteriophage capsid | Conjugation | HIV-1 Tat47–57 peptide | microRNA | Using sulfosuccinimidyl 4-(p-maleimidophenyl) butyrate (sulfo-SMPB) | • Cell surface receptor-targeted delivery<br>• Ability to enhance miRNA expression in vitro and in vivo | Champion et al. (2020) |

noncovalent interactions and through covalent interactions; the second is the placement of the drug in a polymer matrix by encapsulation techniques and entrapment techniques (Tarhini et al., 2017). These loading mechanisms not only minimize the side effects of the drug and maximize bioavailability, but also provide the stability required to maximize therapeutic efficacy and the related controlled and sustained release (Aljabali et al., 2022).

### 4.1.1 *Drug loading mechanism via noncovalent interactions*

Drug loading via noncovalent interactions is a mechanism widely used by researchers that enables reversible binding of drugs to protein-based carriers without changing the chemical structure of any component by utilizing noncovalent interactions such as hydrogen bonding, electrostatic interactions, van der Waals forces, and hydrophobic effects (Hong et al., 2020). For instance, such conjugates can be effectively loaded by interacting with hydrophobic groups of drugs with protein-based nanoparticles containing hydrophobic groups, while at the same time, they can be obtained by the interaction of oppositely charged groups in the drug and protein-based nanoparticles (Ezpeleta et al., 1999). Similarly, the interaction of the hydrophobic groups on paclitaxel with the hydrophobic groups on human serum albumin, which was selected as the carrier, resulted in efficient loading of the drug onto the carrier, thus increasing the solubility and delivery of the drug. The conjugate obtained in this way led to the development of Abraxane, a clinically approved formulation (Green et al., 2006). As another example, in the study conducted by Mishra et al., the azidothymidine was loaded onto the transferrin protein functionalized pegylated albumin nanoparticles via electrostatic interactions, which were used to target cancer cells overexpressing transferrin receptors, facilitating targeted delivery of DOX and reducing its toxicity (Mishra et al., 2006). Similarly, Montalbán et al.'s study on loading curcumin onto silk fibroin via hydrogen bonding highlights the adaptability of noncovalent interactions in building drug–protein complexes that provide sustained release and better drug stability (Montalbán et al., 2018). In conclusion, as a result of these interactions, the bioactivity of the drug is preserved, and its bioavailability is increased, while drug–protein complexes that can circulate in the bloodstream for a long time can be formed.

The noncovalent loading mechanism also enables the design of protein-based drug delivery nanoparticles that can respond to specific physiological conditions (triggered by environmental changes such as pH, temperature, or the presence of certain enzymes), allowing targeted and controlled release of drugs for the treatment of localized diseases where the drug must be released in a specific tissue or cellular environment (Hassanin and Elzoghby, 2020). In addition, the noncovalent approach allows multiple drug molecules to be loaded onto a single protein carrier without the need for any complex chemical modifications. This feature allows the desired variety of drugs to be loaded at the desired capacity according to the therapeutic dose, enabling the development of versatile and effective protein-based drug delivery nanoparticles (Zou et al., 2020). However, noncovalent loading mechanisms also have limitations, such as reducing the stability of the drug–protein complex and being affected by changes in the physiological environment, which may lead to premature drug release or reduced targeting efficiency. Furthermore, the consistency and predictability of drug delivery can be affected by the strength and specificity of noncovalent interactions, which may vary depending on the nature of the drug and protein (Lo and

Wang, 2010). Despite all these limitations, noncovalent drug loading is nevertheless a potent and adaptable method in the development of advanced drug delivery systems.

### 4.1.2 Drug loading mechanism via covalent interactions

Drug loading via covalent conjugation involves the formation of stable chemical bonds between therapeutic agents and protein-based carriers, which creates a safer and more controlled drug delivery system. Covalent conjugation is usually achieved by forming bonds such as amide or disulfide bonds or chemical reactions such as click chemistry between structures such as cysteine, lysine, or tyrosine on protein carriers and the drug (Park et al., 2020). Trastuzumab emtansine (Kadcyla) is one of the most important examples of this mechanism, which is an antibody–drug conjugate containing trastuzumab, a humanized IgG1 monoclonal antibody produced from mammalian cell suspension culture, and covalently linked to DM1, a microtubule inhibitor, via a stable thioether linker MCC (4-[N-maleimidomethyl] cyclohexane-1-carboxylate) (Lambert and Chari, 2014). Due to this reaction mechanism, the sensitivity of the drug to reach the target tissue or organ is increased, while the risk of premature release is minimized. This makes covalent conjugation particularly advantageous for the sustained and precise release of potent drugs, where uncontrolled release can lead to serious side effects (chemotherapeutic agents or biologics), since it can only be degraded under certain conditions, such as enzymatic cleavage (Behzadipour and Hemmati, 2024).

However, certain difficulties and limitations exist in the use of covalent conjugation in drug loading, especially the potential change in the drug's bioactivity as a result of existing chemical reactions, affecting the drug's efficacy, or the loss of functionality of the protein carrier along with the drug's bioactivity due to the complexity of the reaction process (Behzadipour and Hemmati, 2024). In addition, the possibility that immunogenicity potential may occur due to this negative change in protein structures, that is, immune responses may occur in some patients, should be considered. For this reason, the pharmacokinetics of drugs such as PEG-interferon and PEG-asparaginase have been improved and immunogenicity reduced through the approach known as PEGylation, which increases the stability and half-life of therapeutic proteins in the bloodstream (Suk et al., 2016; Fang et al., 2017) Despite these challenges, advances in efficiency and specificity in covalent conjugation (especially in critical areas such as stability and controlled release) have made it a powerful tool in designing protein-based drug delivery nanoparticles for various therapeutic applications.

### 4.1.3 Drug loading mechanism via encapsulation and entrapment

The mechanism of drug loading via encapsulation and entrapment in protein-based carriers involves physical enclosure within protein matrices or nanostructures that offer a protective environment for sensitive drugs such as proteins, peptides, or hydrophobic compounds that may be degraded or inactivated under physiological conditions. The encapsulation technique increases the bioavailability of the drug, helps protect it from enzymatic degradation, prolongs its residence time in the bloodstream, and also allows multiple drug combinations required for the treatment of complex diseases such as cancer to be contained in a single protein-based carrier (Vedakumari et al., 2019). In addition, the surface of protein-based carriers can be designed differently after this process by making modifications with various groups to provide targeting groups according to the region where the drug will act and/or to provide sensitivity to enzymes or changes in pH during drug release, thus providing controlled and targeted drug release. The most commonly used proteins in the literature for this method are albumin, silk fibroin, and casein due to their biocompatibility and ability to form stable structures (Kudarha and Sawant, 2017; Liu et al., 2017; Elzoghby et al., 2011). As mentioned above, human serum albumin nanoparticles used in the FDA-approved Abraxane formulation have attracted intense interest from researchers in recent years. Similarly, in addition to casein micelles used to encapsulate hydrophobic drugs such as curcumin (Barick et al., 2021), increase their stability, and improve their release kinetics, silk fibroin-based carriers prepared to improve the controlled and sustained release of various antibiotics or cancer drugs by encapsulating them, and also by taking advantage of the robust structure and biodegradability properties of silk, have recently been considered quite remarkable by researchers (Harishchandra Yadav et al., 2024). As seen in this and similar studies in the literature, the preference for encapsulation and confinement mechanisms increases the versatility and effectiveness of protein-based carrier systems because they improve the pharmacokinetics and therapeutic potential of drugs.

While encapsulation and entrapment mechanisms offer significant advantages, they also have some difficulties and limitations, such as the fact that drug efficiency can be significantly reduced due to the inability to encapsulate the entire drug homogeneously, which can reduce dosage accuracy. In addition, the release profiles of drugs, especially those with hydrophobic and large structures, may not be at the desired level after encapsulation, or the size, polydispersity, and zeta values of protein–drug complexes may vary depending on the nanoparticle technique used, which may prevent them from passing certain biological barriers (Tarhini et al., 2017). Despite all these challenges, advanced developments in protein engineering and nanotechnology make encapsulation and confinement mechanisms a promising approach to enhance drug stability, bioavailability, and targeted delivery in protein-based drug delivery nanoparticles.

## 4.2 Mechanisms of drug release from protein-based systems

Protein-based carrier systems provide various mechanisms to deliver controlled and sustained release treatments of therapeutic agents loaded into their structures, considering critical issues such as efficacy, safety, and timing. The release profiles of therapeutic agents from these structures can be tailored through the design of the protein carrier and its interaction with the drug. In this way, these structures offer advantages such as targeting a specific area, being biocompatible, providing better patient compliance, and showing less toxicity. The basic mechanisms of release of therapeutic agents from protein-based nanoparticles can be examined in four groups based on where, when, and how the drug will be released in the body: environmental stimuli (pH, temperature, etc.), degradation, diffusion, and enzymatic activity (Tarhini et al., 2017).

### 4.2.1 *Stimuli-responsive release*

Protein-based stimuli-responsive delivery nanoparticles are sophisticated mechanisms that can provide sensitive responses to specific environmental triggers, such as pH, temperature, or the presence of certain enzymes, to efficiently deliver therapeutic agents by targeting specific tissues or disease sites (Shah et al., 2018). For instance, the TME is typically more acidic than healthy tissue, which can be utilized by creating protein-based carriers that release their payload exclusively in acidic conditions (Kaltbeitzel and Wich, 2023). Gelatin and casein are two examples of proteins that have been utilized in the development of pH-sensitive drug delivery systems. These systems involve the protein carrier changing shape or solubility in response to an acidic environment, ultimately releasing the drug (Gandhi and Roy, 2019; Curcio et al., 2013). Similarly, in response to targeted heating, a method used in treating hyperthermia in cancer diseases, it can release drugs in its structure at the relevant efficiency using temperature-sensitive protein carriers (Ferraro et al., 2024).

### 4.2.2 *Degradation-mediated release*

Another critical mechanism based on the biodegradability of protein nanoparticles, such as silk fibroin, collagen, and casein, is degradation-mediated release. In this mechanism, the protein nanoparticles are broken down over time by natural processes in the body, resulting in the release of the loaded therapeutic agent. Protein-based nanoparticles with a degradation mechanism via hydrolysis or enzymatic activity are particularly advantageous for long-term therapies where the encapsulated or conjugated drug must be released gradually over weeks or months (Hawkins et al., 2008). The enzymatic activity approach is particularly useful for targeting areas where certain enzymes are overexpressed, such as inflamed tissues or cancerous tumors. Enzyme-responsive protein nanoparticles are designed to release drugs through degradation upon exposure to these enzymes, with the aim of increasing the precision of drug targeting and reducing off-target effects (Yu et al., 2018). Similarly, protein-based nanoparticles can be degraded under physiological conditions through hydrolysis, a process in which water molecules break bonds in the protein structure. Again, this degradation is usually enzyme-mediated, with proteases targeting specific peptide bonds in the protein. This method minimizes the need for frequent dosing, especially for drugs that require controlled release over time, by using cross-linking agents to slow the rate of hydrolysis or degradation of protein structure (Gong et al., 2024). For this reason, protein-based nanosystems with a degradation-mediated release mechanism are quite advantageous compared to other systems due to their biocompatibility and ability to degrade into nontoxic by-products.

### 4.2.3 *Diffusion-controlled release*

One of the most common protein nanoparticle drug release mechanisms is diffusion-controlled release, where the drug slowly passes from the carrier to the biological environment (Fathi et al., 2018). The protein nanoparticle, which acts as a reservoir, releases drug molecules from its surface over time. This mechanism is affected by factors such as the diffusion rate of the drug, the size of the drug molecules, the porosity of the protein nanostructure, and the interaction between the drug and the protein nanoparticle (Fathi et al., 2018). For example, in albumin-based nanoparticles, hydrophobic drugs such as paclitaxel are usually loaded within the hydrophobic structures and are slowly released as they diffuse through the albumin structure, providing a sustained release profile that provides long-term therapeutic effects (Bansal et al., 2011).

## 5. Conclusion

In conclusion, protein-based nanoparticles offer significant advantages in the development of a new generation of therapeutics. One of the most important advantages of these is their inherent biocompatibility and biodegradability after administration, which minimizes toxicity and eliminates the risk of adverse immune reactions. Moreover, protein-based nanoparticles can provide targeted drug delivery, which allows them to reach specific diseased sites or tissues with high precision. These delivery systems can be designed to release drugs in response to specific stimuli such as pH, temperature, or the presence of specific enzymes, providing controlled and sustained release profiles to suit the therapeutic needs of different diseases. In summary, protein-based nanoparticles offer a versatile and promising perspective for drug delivery due to their unique properties and the ability to be designed for targeted applications. However, understanding their interactions with biological systems, especially protein corona formation and cellular uptake mechanisms, as well as drug loading and release mechanisms, is important to optimize their therapeutic potential. Future research should focus on increasing nanoparticle scalability for large-scale production, improving in vivo stability to extend circulation time and reduce premature degradation, and improving surface modifications to ensure consistent performance in various biological environments.

## References

Ahsan, S.M., Rao, C.M., Ahmad, MdF., 2018. Nanoparticle-protein interaction: the significance and role of protein corona. Science and Business Media LLC 1048, 175–198. https://doi.org/10.1007/978-3-319-72041-8_11.

Albanese, A., Tang, P.S., Chan, W.C.W., 2012. The effect of nanoparticle size, shape, and surface chemistry on biological systems. Annu. Rev. Biomed. Eng. 14, 1–16. https://doi.org/10.1146/annurev-bioeng-071811-150124.

Aljabali, A.A.A., Rezigue, M., Alsharedeh, R.H., Obeid, M.A., Mishra, V., Serrano-Aroca, Á., El-Tanani, M., Tambuwala, M.M., 2022. Protein-based nanomaterials: a new tool for targeted drug delivery. Ther. Deliv. 13 (6), 321–338. https://doi.org/10.4155/tde-2021-0091.

Al-Suhaimi, E., Ravinayagam, V., Jermy, B.R., Mohamad, T., Elaissari, A., 2019. Protein/hormone based nanoparticles as carriers for drugs targeting- protein-protein interactions. Curr. Top. Med. Chem. 19 (6), 444–456. https://doi.org/10.2174/1568026619666190304152320.

Anderson, C.F., Grimmett, M.E., Domalewski, C.J., Cui, H., 2020. Inhalable nanotherapeutics to improve treatment efficacy for common lung diseases. WIREs Nanomedicine and Nanobiotechnology 12 (1). https://doi.org/10.1002/wnan.1586.

Archakov, A.I., Govorun, V.M., Dubanov, A.V., Ivanov, Y.D., Veselovsky, A.V., Lewi, P., Janssen, P., 2003. Protein-protein interactions as a target for drugs in proteomics. Proteomics 3 (4), 380–391. https://doi.org/10.1002/pmic.200390053.

Augustine, R., Hasan, A., Primavera, R., Wilson, R.J., Thakor, A.S., Kevadiya, B.D., 2020. Cellular uptake and retention of nanoparticles: Insights on particle properties and interaction with cellular components. Mater. Today Commun. 25, 101692. https://doi.org/10.1016/j.mtcomm.2020.101692.

Baimanov, D., Cai, R., Chen, C., 2019. Understanding the Chemical nature of nanoparticle–protein interactions. Bioconjug. Chem. 30 (7), 1923–1937. https://doi.org/10.1021/acs.bioconjchem.9b00348.

Balke, I., Zeltins, A., 2019. Use of plant viruses and virus-like particles for the creation of novel vaccines. Adv. Drug Deliv. Rev. 145, 119–129. https://doi.org/10.1016/j.addr.2018.08.007.

Bansal, A., Kapoor, D., Kapil, R., Chhabra, N., Dhawan, S., 2011. Design and development of paclitaxel-loaded bovine serum albumin nanoparticles for brain targeting. Acta Pharm. 61 (2), 141–156. https://doi.org/10.2478/v10007-011-0012-8.

Barick, K.C., Tripathi, A., Dutta, B., Shelar, S.B., Hassan, P.A., 2021. Curcumin encapsulated casein nanoparticles: Enhanced bioavailability and anticancer efficacy. J. Pharmaceut. Sci. 110 (5), 2114–2120. https://doi.org/10.1016/j.xphs.2020.12.011.

Bashiri, G., Padilla, M.S., Swingle, K.L., Shepherd, S.J., Mitchell, M.J., Wang, K., 2023. Nanoparticle protein corona: from structure and function to therapeutic targeting. Lab Chip 23 (6), 1432–1466. https://doi.org/10.1039/d2lc00799a.

Behzadi, S., Serpooshan, V., Tao, W., Hamaly, M.A., Alkawareek, M.Y., Dreaden, E.C., Brown, D., Alkilany, A.M., Farokhzad, O.C., Mahmoudi, M., 2017. Cellular uptake of nanoparticles: Journey inside the cell. Chem. Soc. Rev. 46 (14), 4218–4244. https://doi.org/10.1039/c6cs00636a.

Behzadipour, Y., Hemmati, S., 2024. Covalent conjugation and non-covalent complexation strategies for intracellular delivery of proteins using cell-penetrating peptides. Biomed. Pharmacother. 176, 116910. https://doi.org/10.1016/j.biopha.2024.116910.

Belhabib, I., Zaghdoudi, S., Lac, C., Bousquet, C., Jean, C., 2021. Extracellular matrices and cancer-associated fibroblasts: Targets for cancer diagnosis and therapy? Cancers 13 (14), 3466. https://doi.org/10.3390/cancers13143466.

Brillault, L., Jutras, P.V., Dashti, N., Thuenemann, E.C., Morgan, G., Lomonossoff, G.P., Landsberg, M.J., Sainsbury, F., 2017. Engineering recombinant virus-like nanoparticles from plants for cellular delivery. ACS Nano 11 (4), 3476–3484. https://doi.org/10.1021/acsnano.6b07747.

Caporale, A., Adorinni, S., Lamba, D., Saviano, M., 2021. Peptide-protein interactions: from drug design to supramolecular biomaterials. Molecules 26 (5). https://doi.org/10.3390/molecules26051219.

Champion, J.A., Pustulka, S.M., Ling, K., Pish, S.L., 2020. Protein nanoparticle charge and hydrophobicity govern protein corona and macrophage uptake. ACS Appl. Mater. Interfaces 12 (43), 48284–48295. https://doi.org/10.1021/acsami.0c12341.

Curcio, M., Altimari, I., Spizzirri, U.G., Cirillo, G., Vittorio, O., Puoci, F., Picci, N., Iemma, F., 2013. Biodegradable gelatin-based nanospheres as pH-responsive drug delivery systems. J. Nanoparticle Res. 15 (4). https://doi.org/10.1007/s11051-013-1581-x.

Dasgupta, S., Auth, T., Gompper, G., 2014. Shape and orientation matter for the cellular uptake of nonspherical particles. Nano Lett. 14 (2), 687–693. https://doi.org/10.1021/nl403949h.

Desai, N., 2012. Challenges in development of nanoparticle-based therapeutics. AAPS J. 14 (2), 282–295. https://doi.org/10.1208/s12248-012-9339-4.

Destito, G., Yeh, R., Rae, C.S., Finn, M.G., Manchester, M., 2007. Folic acid-mediated targeting of cowpea mosaic virus particles to tumor cells. Chem. Biol. 14 (10), 1152–1162. https://doi.org/10.1016/j.chembiol.2007.08.015.

Domingo-Espín, J., Unzueta, U., Saccardo, P., Rodríguez-Carmona, E., Corchero, J.L., Vázquez, E., Ferrer-Miralles, N., 2011. Engineered biological entities for drug delivery and gene therapy: Protein nanoparticles. Mol. Biol. Trans. Sci. 104, 247–298. https://doi.org/10.1016/B978-0-12-416020-0.00006-1.

Drescher, D., Büchner, T., Schrade, P., Traub, H., Werner, S., Guttmann, P., Bachmann, S., Kneipp, J., 2021. Influence of nuclear localization sequences on the intracellular fate of gold nanoparticles. ACS Nano 15 (9), 14838–14849. https://doi.org/10.1021/acsnano.1c04925.

Du, X., Li, Y., Xia, Y.-L., Liang, A.S.-M., Sang, J., et al., 2016. Insights into protein–ligand interactions: mechanisms, models, and methods. Int. J. Mol. Sci. 17 (2).

Elzoghby, A.O., Abo El-Fotoh, W.S., Elgindy, N.A., 2011. Casein-based formulations as promising controlled release drug delivery systems. J. Contr. Release 153 (3), 206–216. https://doi.org/10.1016/j.jconrel.2011.02.010.

Engin, A.B., Nikitovic, D., Neagu, M., Henrich-Noack, P., Oana Docea, A., Shtilman, M.I., Golokhvast, K., Tsatsakis, A.M., 2017. Mechanistic understanding of nanoparticles' interactions with extracellular matrix: the cell and immune system. Part. Fibre Toxicol. 14 (1). https://doi.org/10.1186/s12989-017-0199-z.

Ezpeleta, I., Irache, J.M., Stainmesse, S., Chabenat, C., Gueguen, J., Popineau, Y., Orecchioni, A.M., 1996. Gliadin nanoparticles for the controlled release of all-trans-retinoic acid. Int. J. Pharm. 131 (2), 191–200. https://doi.org/10.1016/0378-5173(95)04338-1.

Ezpeleta, I., Arangoa, M.A., Irache, J.M., Stainmesse, S., Chabenat, C., Popineau, Y., Orecchioni, A.M., 1999. Preparation of Ulex europaeus lectin-gliadin nanoparticle conjugates and their interaction with gastrointestinal mucus. Int. J. Pharm. 191 (1), 25–32. https://doi.org/10.1016/S0378-5173(99)00232-X.

Falvo, E., Malagrinò, F., Arcovito, A., Fazi, F., Colotti, G., Tremante, E., Micco, P.Di, Braca, A., Opri, R., Giuffrè, A., Fracasso, G., Ceci, P., 2018. The presence of glutamate residues on the PAS sequence of the stimuli-sensitive nano-ferritin improves in vivo biodistribution and mitoxantrone encapsulation homogeneity. J. Contr. Release 275, 177–185. https://doi.org/10.1016/j.jconrel.2018.02.025.

Fang, Y., Xue, J., Gao, S., Lu, A., Yang, D., Jiang, H., He, Y., Shi, K., Pegylation, C., 2017. A strategy for overcoming the "PEG dilemma" in efficient drug delivery. Drug Deliv. 24 (2), 22–32. https://doi.org/10.1080/10717544.2017.1388451.

Fathi, M., Donsi, F., McClements, D.J., 2018. Protein-based delivery systems for the nanoencapsulation of food ingredients. Compr. Rev. Food Sci. Food Saf. 17 (4), 920–936. https://doi.org/10.1111/1541-4337.12360.

Ferraro, C., Dattilo, M., Patitucci, F., Prete, S., Scopelliti, G., Parisi, O., Puoci, F., 2024. Exploring protein-based carriers in drug delivery: a review. Pharmaceutics 16 (9), 1172. https://doi.org/10.3390/pharmaceutics16091172.

Ferrer-Miralles, N., Corchero, J.L., Kumar, P., Cedano, J.A., Gupta, K.C., Villaverde, A., Vazquez, E., 2011. Biological activities of histidine-rich peptides; merging biotechnology and nanomedicine. Microb. Cell Fact. 10. https://doi.org/10.1186/1475-2859-10-101Spain.

Fracasso, G., Falvo, E., Colotti, G., Fazi, F., Ingegnere, T., Amalfitano, A., Battista Doglietto, G., Alfieri, S., Boffi, A., Morea, V., Conti, G., Tremante, E., Giacomini, P., Arcovito, A., Ceci, P., 2016. Selective delivery of doxorubicin by novel stimuli-sensitive nano-ferritins overcomes tumor refractoriness. J. Contr. Release 239, 10–18. https://doi.org/10.1016/j.jconrel.2016.08.010.

Frappier, L., 2012. The Epstein-Barr virus EBNA1 protein. Sci. Tech. Rep. 2012, 1–15. https://doi.org/10.6064/2012/438204.

Fuchs, S., Coester, C., 2010. Protein-based nanoparticles as a drug delivery system: chances, risks, perspectives. J. Drug Deliv. Sci. Technol. 20 (5), 331–342. https://doi.org/10.1016/s1773-2247(10)50056-x.

Gandhi, S., Roy, I., 2019. Doxorubicin-loaded casein nanoparticles for drug delivery: Preparation, characterization and in vitro evaluation. Int. J. Biol. Macromol. 121, 6–12. https://doi.org/10.1016/j.ijbiomac.2018.10.005.

García-Álvarez, R., Vallet-Regí, M., 2021. Hard and soft protein corona of nanomaterials: Analysis and relevance. Nanomaterials 11 (4), 888. https://doi.org/10.3390/nano11040888.

Glover, D.J., May Ng, S., Mechler, A., Martin, L.L., Jans, D.A., 2009. Multifunctional protein nanocarriers for targeted nuclear gene delivery in nondividing cells. FASEB J. 23 (9), 2996–3006. https://doi.org/10.1096/fj.09-131425.

Gong, H., Fu, H., Zhang, J., Zhang, Q., Wang, Y., Wang, Di, Cai, L., Chen, J., Yu, H., Lyu, B., 2024. Preparation of soybean protein-based nanoparticles and its application as encapsulation carriers of bioactive substances. LWT 191, 115680. https://doi.org/10.1016/j.lwt.2023.115680.

Green, M.R., Manikhas, G.M., Orlov, S., Afanasyev, B., Makhson, A.M., Bhar, P., Hawkins, M.J., 2006. Abraxane®, a novel Cremophor®-free, albumin-bound particle form of paclitaxel for the treatment of advanced non-small-cell lung cancer. Ann. Oncol. 17 (8), 1263–1268. https://doi.org/10.1093/annonc/mdl104.

Gu, Z., Jiang, X., 2014. Drug delivery from protein-based nanoparticles. Bioinspired and Biomimetic Polymer Systems for Drug and Gene Delivery 12, 149–170. https://doi.org/10.1002/9783527672752.ch6.

Gulati, N.M., Stewart, P.L., Steinmetz, N.F., 2018. Bioinspired shielding strategies for nanoparticle drug delivery applications. Mol. Pharm. 15 (8), 2900–2909. https://doi.org/10.1021/acs.molpharmaceut.8b00292.

Gustafson, H.H., Holt-Casper, D., Grainger, D.W., Ghandehari, H., 2015. Nanoparticle uptake: the phagocyte problem. Nano Today 10 (4), 487–510. https://doi.org/10.1016/j.nantod.2015.06.006.

Habibi, N., Mauser, A., Ko, Y., Lahann, J., 2022. Protein nanoparticles: Uniting the power of proteins with engineering design approaches. Adv. Sci. 9 (8). https://doi.org/10.1002/advs.202104012.

Harishchandra Yadav, R., Kenchegowda, M., Angolkar, M., Meghana, T.S., Osmani, R.A.M., Palaksha, S., Veerabhadrappa Gangadharappa, H., 2024. A review of silk fibroin-based drug delivery systems and their applications. Eur. Polym. J. 216, 113286. https://doi.org/10.1016/j.eurpolymj.2024.113286.

Hassanin, I.A., Elzoghby, A.O., 2020. Self-assembled non-covalent protein-drug nanoparticles: an emerging delivery platform for anti-cancer drugs. Expet Opin. Drug Deliv. 17 (10), 1437–1458. https://doi.org/10.1080/17425247.2020.1813713.

Hawkins, M.J., Soon-Shiong, P., Desai, N., 2008. Protein nanoparticles as drug carriers in clinical medicine. Adv. Drug Deliv. Rev. 60 (8), 876–885. https://doi.org/10.1016/j.addr.2007.08.044.

He, Z., Qu, S., Shang, L., 2024. Perspectives on protein–nanoparticle interactions at the in vivo level. Langmuir 40 (15), 7781–7790. https://doi.org/10.1021/acs.langmuir.4c00181.

Herrera Estrada, L.P., Champion, J.A., 2015. Protein nanoparticles for therapeutic protein delivery. Biomater. Sci. 3 (6), 787–799. https://doi.org/10.1039/C5BM00052A.

Hong, S., Choi, D.W., Kim, H.N., Park, C.G., Lee, W., Park, H.H., 2020. Protein-based nanoparticles as drug delivery systems. Pharmaceutics 12 (7), 1–28. https://doi.org/10.3390/pharmaceutics12070604.

Hoshyar, N., Gray, S., Han, H., Bao, G., 2016. The effect of nanoparticle size on in vivo pharmacokinetics and cellular interaction. Nanomedicine 11 (6), 673–692. https://doi.org/10.2217/nnm.16.5.

Huang, L., Tao, K., Liu, J., Qi, C., Xu, L., Chang, P., Gao, J., Shuai, X., Wang, G., Wang, Z., Wang, L., 2016. Design and fabrication of multifunctional sericin nanoparticles for tumor targeting and pH-responsive subcellular delivery of cancer chemotherapy drugs. ACS Appl. Mater. Interfaces 8 (10), 6577–6585. https://doi.org/10.1021/acsami.5b11617.

Huang, P.S., Boyken, S.E., Baker, D., 2016. The coming of age of de novo protein design. Nature 537 (7620), 320–327. https://doi.org/10.1038/nature19946.

Huang, S.-M., Zhao, H., Lee, J.-I., Reynolds, K., Zhang, L., Temple, R., Lesko, L.J., 2010. Therapeutic protein–drug interactions and implications for drug development. Clin. Pharmacol. Therapeut. 87 (4), 497–503. https://doi.org/10.1038/clpt.2009.308.

Jain, A., Singh, S.K., Arya, S.K., Kundu, S.C., Kapoor, S., 2018. Protein nanoparticles: promising platforms for drug delivery applications. ACS Biomater. Sci. Eng. 4 (12), 3939–3961. https://doi.org/10.1021/acsbiomaterials.8b01098.

Jiang, H., Liang, G., Dai, M., Dong, Y., Wu, Y., Zhang, L., Xi, Q., Qi, L., 2020. Preparation of doxorubicin-loaded collagen-PAPBA nanoparticles and their anticancer efficacy in ovarian cancer. Ann. Transl. Med. 8 (14). https://doi.org/10.21037/atm-20-5028, 880–880.

Jin, P., Sha, R., Zhang, Y., Liu, L., Bian, Y., Qian, J., Qian, J., Lin, J., Ishimwe, N., Hu, Y., Zhang, W., Liu, Y., Yin, S., Ren, L., Wen, L.P., 2019. Blood circulation-prolonging peptides for engineered nanoparticles identified via phage display. Nano Lett. 19 (3), 1467–1478. https://doi.org/10.1021/acs.nanolett.8b04007.

Kaltbeitzel, J., Wich, P.R., 2023. Protein-based nanoparticles: from drug delivery to imaging, nanocatalysis and protein therapy. Angew. Chem., Int. Ed. 62 (44). https://doi.org/10.1002/anie.202216097.

Kaplan, Ö., Gök, M.K., Pekmez, M., Tayhan, S.E., Özgümüş, S., Gökçe, İ., Arda, N., 2024. Development of recombinant protein-based nanoparticle systems for inducing tumor cell apoptosis: in vitro evaluation of their cytotoxic and apoptotic effects on cancer cells. J. Drug Deliv. Sci. Technol. 95, 105565. https://doi.org/10.1016/j.jddst.2024.105565.

Khaliq, N.U., Oh, K.S., Sandra, F.C., Joo, Y., Lee, J., Byun, Y., Kim, I.S., Kwon, I.C., Seo, J.H., Kim, S.Y., Yuk, S.H., 2017. Assembly of polymer micelles through the sol-gel transition for effective cancer therapy. J. Contr. Release 255, 258–269. https://doi.org/10.1016/j.jconrel.2017.04.039.

Kianfar, E., 2021. Protein nanoparticles in drug delivery: animal protein, plant proteins and protein cages, albumin nanoparticles. J. Nanobiotechnol. 19 (1). https://doi.org/10.1186/s12951-021-00896-3.

Kim, K.R., Lee, A.S., Kim, S.M., Heo, H.R., Kim, C.S., 2023a. Virus-like nanoparticles as a theranostic platform for cancer. Front. Bioeng. Biotechnol. 10. https://doi.org/10.3389/fbioe.2022.1106767.

Kim, W., Ly, N.Ky, He, Y., Li, Y., Yuan, Z., Yeo, Y., 2023b. Protein corona: Friend or foe? Co-opting serum proteins for nanoparticle delivery. Adv. Drug Deliv. Rev. 192, 114635. https://doi.org/10.1016/j.addr.2022.114635.

Kopac, T., 2021. Protein corona, understanding the nanoparticle–protein interactions and future perspectives: a critical review. Int. J. Biol. Macromol. 169, 290–301. https://doi.org/10.1016/j.ijbiomac.2020.12.108.

Kreuter, J., Hekmatara, T., Dreis, S., Vogel, T., Gelperina, S., Langer, K., 2007. Covalent attachment of apolipoprotein A-I and apolipoprotein B-100 to albumin nanoparticles enables drug transport into the brain. J. Contr. Release 118 (1), 54–58. https://doi.org/10.1016/j.jconrel.2006.12.012.

Kudarha, R.R., Sawant, K.K., 2017. Albumin based versatile multifunctional nanocarriers for cancer therapy: Fabrication, surface modification, multimodal therapeutics and imaging approaches. Mater. Sci. Eng. C 81, 607–626. https://doi.org/10.1016/j.msec.2017.08.004.

Lambert, J.M., Chari, R.V.J., 2014. Ado-trastuzumab emtansine (T-DM1): An antibody-drug conjugate (ADC) for HER2-positive breast cancer. J. Med. Chem. 57 (16), 6949–6964. https://doi.org/10.1021/jm500766w.

Lee, N.K., Lee, E.J., Kim, S., Nam, G.h., Kih, M., Hong, Y., Jeong, C., Yang, Y., Byun, Y., Kim, I.S., 2017a. Ferritin nanocage with intrinsically disordered proteins and affibody: a platform for tumor targeting with extended pharmacokinetics. J. Contr. Release 267, 172–180. https://doi.org/10.1016/j.jconrel.2017.08.014.

Lee, P.W., Isarov, S.A., Wallat, J.D., Molugu, S.K., Shukla, S., Sun, J.E.P., Zhang, J., Zheng, Y., Lucius Dougherty, M., Konkolewicz, D., Stewart, P.L., Steinmetz, N.F., Hore, M.J.A., Pokorski, J.K., 2017b. Polymer structure and conformation alter the antigenicity of virus-like particle-polymer conjugates. J. Am. Chem. Soc. 139 (9), 3312–3315. https://doi.org/10.1021/jacs.6b11643.

Li, H., Fan, X., Houghton, J.M., 2007. Tumor microenvironment: the role of the tumor stroma in cancer. J. Cell. Biochem. 101 (4), 805–815. https://doi.org/10.1002/jcb.21159.

Li, J., Wang, J., Yao, Q., Li, T., Yan, Y., Li, Z., Zhang, J., 2020. Why synthetic virus-like nanoparticles can achieve higher cellular uptake efficiency? Nanoscale 12 (27), 14911–14918. https://doi.org/10.1039/d0nr03234d.

Li, Z., Cui, K., Wang, H., Liu, F., Huang, K., Duan, Z., Wang, F., Shi, D., Liu, Q., 2019. A milk-based self-assemble rotavirus VP6–ferritin nanoparticle vaccine elicited protection against the viral infection. J. Nanobiotechnol. 17 (1). https://doi.org/10.1186/s12951-019-0446-6.

Liu, L., Zhao, W., Ma, Q., Gao, Y., Wang, W., Zhang, X., Dong, Y., Zhang, T., Liang, Y., Han, S., Cao, J., Wang, X., Sun, W., Ma, H., Sun, Y., 2023. Functional nano-systems for transdermal drug delivery and skin therapy. Nanoscale Adv. 5 (6), 1527–1558. https://doi.org/10.1039/d2na00530a.

Liu, M., Feng, B., Shi, Y., Su, C., Song, H., Cheng, W., Zhao, L., 2015. Protamine nanoparticles for improving shRNA-mediated anti-cancer effects. Nanoscale Res. Lett. 10 (1). https://doi.org/10.1186/s11671-015-0845-z.

Liu, Q., Liu, H., Fan, Y., 2017. Preparation of silk fibroin carriers for controlled release. Microsc. Res. Tech. 80 (3), 312–320. https://doi.org/10.1002/jemt.22606.

Liu, X., Mohanty, R.P., Maier, E.Y., Peng, X., Wulfe, S., Looney, A.P., Aung, K.L., Ghosh, D., 2020. Controlled loading of albumin-drug conjugates ex vivo for enhanced drug delivery and antitumor efficacy. J. Contr. Release 328, 1–12. https://doi.org/10.1016/j.jconrel.2020.08.015.

Lo, S.L., Wang, S., 2010. Intracellular protein delivery systems formed by noncovalent bonding interactions between amphipathic peptide carriers and protein cargos. Macromol. Rapid Commun. 31 (13), 1134–1141. https://doi.org/10.1002/marc.200900934.

Lohcharoenkal, W., Wang, L., Chen, Y.C., Rojanasakul, Y., 2014. Protein nanoparticles as drug delivery carriers for cancer therapy. BioMed Res. Int. 2014, 1–12. https://doi.org/10.1155/2014/180549.

López-Laguna, H., Cubarsi, R., Unzueta, U., Mangues, R., Vázquez, E., Villaverde, A., 2020. Endosomal escape of protein nanoparticles engineered through humanized histidine-rich peptides. Sci. China Mater. 63 (4), 644–653. https://doi.org/10.1007/s40843-019-1231-y.

Lu, J., Wu, T., Zhang, B., Liu, S., Song, W., Qiao, J., Ruan, H., 2021. Types of nuclear localization signals and mechanisms of protein import into the nucleus. Cell Commun. Signal. 19 (1). https://doi.org/10.1186/s12964-021-00741-y.

Mager, M.D., Lapointe, V., Stevens, M.M., 2011. Exploring and exploiting chemistry at the cell surface. Nat. Chem. 3 (8), 582–589. https://doi.org/10.1038/nchem.1090.

Martella, E., Ferroni, C., Guerrini, A., Ballestri, M., Columbaro, M., Santi, S., Sotgiu, G., Serra, M., Donati, D.M., Lucarelli, E., Varchi, G., Duchi, S., 2018. Functionalized keratin as nanotechnology-based drug delivery system for the pharmacological treatment of osteosarcoma. Int. J. Mol. Sci. 19 (11), 3670. https://doi.org/10.3390/ijms19113670.

Martínez-López, A.L., Pangua, C., Reboredo, C., Campión, R., Morales-Gracia, J., Irache, J.M., 2020. Protein-based nanoparticles for drug delivery purposes. Int. J. Pharm. 581, 119289. https://doi.org/10.1016/j.ijpharm.2020.119289.

Mehtala, J.G., Kulczar, C., Lavan, M., Knipp, G., Wei, A., 2015. Cys34-PEGylated human serum albumin for drug binding and delivery. Bioconjug. Chem. 26 (5), 941–949. https://doi.org/10.1021/acs.bioconjchem.5b00143.

Meng, H., Leong, W., Leong, K.W., Chen, C., Zhao, Y., 2018. Walking the line: the fate of nanomaterials at biological barriers. Biomaterials 174, 41–53. https://doi.org/10.1016/j.biomaterials.2018.04.056.

Mishra, V., Mahor, S., Rawat, A., Gupta, P.N., Dubey, P., Khatri, K., Vyas, S.P., 2006. Targeted brain delivery of AZT via transferrin anchored pegylated albumin nanoparticles. J. Drug Target. 14 (1), 45–53. https://doi.org/10.1080/10611860600612953.

Mitchell, M.J., Billingsley, M.M., Haley, R.M., Wechsler, M.E., Peppas, N.A., Langer, R., 2021. Engineering precision nanoparticles for drug delivery. Nat. Rev. Drug Discov. 20 (2), 101–124. https://doi.org/10.1038/s41573-020-0090-8.

Mofidfar, M., Abdi, B., Ahadian, S., Mostafavi, E., Desai, T.A., Abbasi, F., Sun, Y., Manche, E.E., Ta, C.N., Flowers, C.W., 2021. Drug delivery to the anterior segment of the eye: a review of current and future treatment strategies. Int. J. Pharm. 607, 120924. https://doi.org/10.1016/j.ijpharm.2021.120924.

Montalbán, M.G., Coburn, J.M., Lozano-Pérez, A.A., Cenis, J.L., Víllora, G., Kaplan, D.L., 2018. Production of curcumin-loaded silk fibroin nanoparticles for cancer therapy. Nanomaterials 8 (2). https://doi.org/10.3390/nano8020126.

Mottaghitalab, F., Kiani, M., Farokhi, M., Kundu, S.C., Reis, R.L., Gholami, M., Bardania, H., Dinarvand, R., Geramifar, P., Beiki, D., Atyabi, F., 2017. Targeted delivery system based on gemcitabine-loaded silk fibroin nanoparticles for lung cancer therapy. ACS Appl. Mater. Interfaces 9 (37), 31600–31611. https://doi.org/10.1021/acsami.7b10408.

Nangia, S., Sureshkumar, R., 2012. Effects of nanoparticle charge and shape anisotropy on translocation through cell membranes. Langmuir 28 (51), 17666–17671. https://doi.org/10.1021/la303449d.

Panico, S., Capolla, S., Bozzer, S., Toffoli, G., Dal Bo, M., Macor, P., 2022. Biological features of nanoparticles: protein corona formation and interaction with the immune system. Pharmaceutics 14 (12), 2605. https://doi.org/10.3390/pharmaceutics14122605.

Park, J., Chariou, P.L., Steinmetz, N.F., 2020. Site-specific antibody conjugation strategy to functionalize virus-based nanoparticles. Bioconjug. Chem. 31 (5), 1408–1416. https://doi.org/10.1021/acs.bioconjchem.0c00118.

Pham, D.T., Saelim, N., Tiyaboonchai, W., 2018. Crosslinked fibroin nanoparticles using EDC or PEI for drug delivery: physicochemical properties, crystallinity and structure. J. Mater. Sci. 53 (20), 14087–14103. https://doi.org/10.1007/s10853-018-2635-3.

Pinals, R.L., Chio, L., Ledesma, F., Landry, M.P., 2020. Engineering at the nano-bio interface: Harnessing the protein corona towards nanoparticle design and function. Analyst 145 (15), 5090–5112. https://doi.org/10.1039/d0an00633e.

Pitek, A.S., Jameson, S.A., Veliz, F.A., Shukla, S., Steinmetz, N.F., 2016a. Serum albumin 'camouflage' of plant virus based nanoparticles prevents their antibody recognition and enhances pharmacokinetics. Biomaterials 89, 89–97. https://doi.org/10.1016/j.biomaterials.2016.02.032.

Pitek, A.S., Wen, A.M., Shukla, S., Steinmetz, N.F., 2016b. The protein corona of plant virus nanoparticles influences their dispersion properties, cellular interactions, and in vivo fates. Small 12 (13), 1758–1769. https://doi.org/10.1002/smll.201502458.

Rahman, M., Laurent, S., Tawil, N., Yahia, L'Hocine, Mahmoudi, M., 2013. Protein Corona: Applications and Challenges. Springer Science and Business Media LLC, Berlin, pp. 45–63. https://doi.org/10.1007/978-3-642-37555-2_3.

Rampado, R., Crotti, S., Caliceti, P., Pucciarelli, S., Agostini, M., 2020. Recent advances in understanding the protein corona of nanoparticles and in the formulation of "stealthy" nanomaterials. Front. Bioeng. Biotechnol. 8. https://doi.org/10.3389/fbioe.2020.00166.

Rejman, J., Oberle, V., Zuhorn, I.S., Hoekstra, D., 2004. Size-dependent internalization of particles via the pathways of clathrin- and caveolae-mediated endocytosis. Biochem. J. 377 (1), 159–169. https://doi.org/10.1042/bj20031253.

Ren, Y., Wong, S.M., Lim, L.-Y., 2007. Folic acid-conjugated protein cages of a plant virus: a novel delivery platform for doxorubicin. Bioconjug. Chem. 18 (3), 836–843. https://doi.org/10.1021/bc060361p.

Roh, Y.G., Shin, S.W., Kim, S.Y., Kim, S., Lim, Y.T., Byung-Keun, Um, S.H., 2019. Protein nanoparticle fabrication for optimized reticuloendothelial system evasion and tumor accumulation. Langmuir 35 (11), 3992–3998. https://doi.org/10.1021/acs.langmuir.8b03776.

Sánchez-García, L., Serna, N., Mattanovich, M., Cazzanelli, P., Sánchez-Chardi, A., Conchillo-Solé, O., Cortés, F., Daura, X., Unzueta, U., Mangues, R., Villaverde, A., Vázquez, E., 2017. The fusogenic peptide HA2 impairs selectivity of CXCR4-targeted protein nanoparticles. Chem. Commun. 53 (33), 4565–4568. https://doi.org/10.1039/C6CC09900A.

Sandra, F., Khaliq, N.U., Sunna, A., Care, A., 2019. Developing protein-based nanoparticles as versatile delivery systems for cancer therapy and imaging. Nanomaterials 9 (9). https://doi.org/10.3390/nano9091329.

Shah, A., Malik, M.S., Khan, G.S., Nosheen, E., Iftikhar, F.J., Khan, F.A., Shukla, S.S., Akhter, M.S., Kraatz, H.B., Aminabhavi, T.M., 2018. Stimuli-responsive peptide-based biomaterials as drug delivery systems. Chem. Eng. J. 353, 559–583. https://doi.org/10.1016/j.cej.2018.07.126.

Singh, N., Marets, C., Boudon, J., Millot, N., Saviot, L., Maurizi, L., 2021. In vivo protein corona on nanoparticles: does the control of all material parameters orient the biological behavior? Nanoscale Adv. 3 (5), 1209–1229. https://doi.org/10.1039/d0na00863j.

Sousa de Almeida, M., Susnik, E., Drasler, B., Taladriz-Blanco, P., Petri-Fink, A., Rothen-Rutishauser, B., 2021. Understanding nanoparticle endocytosis to improve targeting strategies in nanomedicine. Chem. Soc. Rev. 50 (9), 5397–5434. https://doi.org/10.1039/d0cs01127d.

Sripriyalakshmi, S., Jose, P., Ravindran, A., Anjali, C.H., 2014. Recent trends in drug delivery system using protein nanoparticles. Cell Biochem. Biophys. 70 (1), 17–26. https://doi.org/10.1007/s12013-014-9896-5.

Suk, J.S., Xu, Q., Kim, N., Hanes, J., Ensign, L.M., 2016. PEGylation as a strategy for improving nanoparticle-based drug and gene delivery. Adv. Drug Deliv. Rev. 99, 28–51. https://doi.org/10.1016/j.addr.2015.09.012.

Tarhini, M., Greige-Gerges, H., Elaissari, A., 2017. Protein-based nanoparticles: from preparation to encapsulation of active molecules. Int. J. Pharm. 522 (1–2), 172–197. https://doi.org/10.1016/j.ijpharm.2017.01.067, 03785173.

Torres-Vanegas, J.D., Cruz, J.C., Reyes, L.H., 2021. Delivery systems for nucleic acids and proteins: Barriers, cell capture pathways and nanocarriers. Pharmaceutics 13 (3). https://doi.org/10.3390/pharmaceutics13030428.

Tseng, C.L., Su, W.Y., Yen, K.C., Yang, K.C., Lin, F.H., 2009. The use of biotinylated-EGF-modified gelatin nanoparticle carrier to enhance cisplatin accumulation in cancerous lungs via inhalation. Biomaterials 30 (20), 3476–3485. https://doi.org/10.1016/j.biomaterials.2009.03.010.

Vaitkuviene, A., Kaseta, V., Voronovic, J., Ramanauskaite, G., Biziuleviciene, G., Ramanaviciene, A., Ramanavicius, A., 2013. Evaluation of cytotoxicity of polypyrrole nanoparticles synthesized by oxidative polymerization. J. Hazard Mater. 250–251, 167–174. https://doi.org/10.1016/j.jhazmat.2013.01.038.

Vannucci, L., Falvo, E., Fornara, M., Di Micco, P., Benada, O., Krizan, J., Svoboda, J., Hulikova-Capkova, K., Morea, V., Boffi, A., Ceci, P., 2012. Selective targeting of melanoma by PEG-masked protein-based multifunctional nanoparticles. Int. J. Nanomed. 7, 1489–1509. https://doi.org/10.2147/IJN.S28242.

Vázquez, E., Ferrer-Miralles, N., Mangues, R., Corchero, J.L., Schwartz, S., Villaverde, A., 2009. Modular protein engineering in emerging cancer therapies. Curr. Pharm. Des. 15 (8), 893–916. https://doi.org/10.2174/138161209787582084.

Vedakumari, S.W., Senthil, R., Sekar, S., Babu, C.S., Sastry, T.P., 2019. Enhancing anti-cancer activity of erlotinib by antibody conjugated nanofibrin - In vitro studies on lung adenocarcinoma cell lines. Mater. Chem. Phys. 224, 328–333. https://doi.org/10.1016/j.matchemphys.2018.11.061.

Verma, D., Gulati, N., Kaul, S., Mukherjee, S., Nagaich, U., 2018. Protein based nanostructures for drug delivery. Journal of Pharmaceutics 2018, 1–18. https://doi.org/10.1155/2018/9285854.

Voltà-Durán, E., Parladé, E., Serna, N., Villaverde, A., Vazquez, E., Unzueta, U., 2023. Endosomal escape for cell-targeted proteins. Going out after going in. Biotechnol. Adv. 63, 108103. https://doi.org/10.1016/j.biotechadv.2023.108103.

Wang, S., Xu, T., Yang, Y., Shao, Z., 2015. Colloidal stability of silk fibroin nanoparticles coated with cationic polymer for effective drug delivery. ACS Appl. Mater. Interfaces 7 (38), 21254–21262. https://doi.org/10.1021/acsami.5b05335.

Wang, Y., Wang, Z., Qian, Y., Fan, L., Yue, C., Jia, F., Sun, J., Hu, Z., Wang, W., 2019. Synergetic estrogen receptor-targeting liposome nanocarriers with anti-phagocytic properties for enhanced tumor theranostics. J. Mater. Chem. B 7 (7), 1056–1063. https://doi.org/10.1039/c8tb03351j.

Wei, Q., Becherer, T., Angioletti-Uberti, S., Dzubiella, J., Wischke, C., Neffe, A.T., Lendlein, A., Ballauff, M., Haag, R., 2014. Protein interactions with polymer coatings and biomaterials. Angew. Chem., Int. Ed. 53 (31), 8004–8031. https://doi.org/10.1002/anie.201400546.

Weinberg, R.A., 2022. Biomaterial Based Approaches to Study the Tumour Microenvironment. Royal Society of Chemistry, London.

Xu, R., Fisher, M., Juliano, R.L., 2011. Targeted albumin-based nanoparticles for delivery of amphipathic drugs. Bioconjug. Chem. 22 (5), 870–878. https://doi.org/10.1021/bc1002295.

Yang, M., Li, J., Gu, P., Fan, X., 2021. The application of nanoparticles in cancer immunotherapy: Targeting tumor microenvironment. Bioact. Mater. 6 (7), 1973–1987. https://doi.org/10.1016/j.bioactmat.2020.12.010.

Yang, S.T., Liu, Y., Wang, Y.W., Cao, A., 2013. Biosafety and bioapplication of nanomaterials by designing protein-nanoparticle interactions. Small 9 (9–10), 1635–1653. https://doi.org/10.1002/smll.201201492.

Yin, S., Davey, K., Dai, S., Liu, Y., Bi, J., 2022. A critical review of ferritin as a drug nanocarrier: Structure, properties, comparative advantages and challenges. Particuology 64, 65–84. https://doi.org/10.1016/j.partic.2021.04.020.

Yu, X., Gou, X., Wu, P., Han, L., Tian, D., Du, F., Chen, Z., Liu, F., Deng, G., Chen, A.T., Ma, C., Liu, J., Hashmi, S.M., Guo, X., Wang, X., Zhao, H., Liu, X., Zhu, X., Sheth, K., Chen, Q., Fan, L., Zhou, J., 2018. Activatable protein nanoparticles for targeted delivery of therapeutic peptides. Adv. Mater. 30 (7). https://doi.org/10.1002/adma.201705383.

Zaher, S., Soliman, M.E., Elsabahy, M., Hathout, R.M., 2023. Protein nanoparticles as natural drugs carriers for cancer therapy. Advances in Traditional Medicine 23 (4), 1035–1064. https://doi.org/10.1007/s13596-022-00668-w.

Zensi, A., Begley, D., Pontikis, C., Legros, C., Mihoreanu, L., Wagner, S., Büchel, C., von Briesen, H., Kreuter, J., 2009. Albumin nanoparticles targeted with Apo E enter the CNS by transcytosis and are delivered to neurones. J. Contr. Release 137 (1), 78–86. https://doi.org/10.1016/j.jconrel.2009.03.002.

Zhang, M., Gao, S., Yang, D., Fang, Y., Lin, X., Jin, X., Liu, Y., Liu, X., Su, K., Shi, K., 2021. Influencing factors and strategies of enhancing nanoparticles into tumors in vivo. Acta Pharm. Sin. B 11 (8), 2265–2285. https://doi.org/10.1016/j.apsb.2021.03.033.

Zhao, Q., Chen, W., Chen, Y., Zhang, L., Zhang, J., Zhang, Z., 2011. Self-assembled virus-like particles from rotavirus structural protein VP6 for targeted drug delivery. Bioconjug. Chem. 22 (3), 346–352. https://doi.org/10.1021/bc1002532.

Zhou, H.-X., Pang, X., 2018. Electrostatic interactions in protein structure, folding, binding, and condensation. Chem. Rev. 118 (4), 1691–1741. https://doi.org/10.1021/acs.chemrev.7b00305.

Zorko, M., Jones, S., Langel, Ü., 2022. Cell-penetrating peptides in protein mimicry and cancer therapeutics. Adv. Drug Deliv. Rev. 180, 114044. https://doi.org/10.1016/j.addr.2021.114044.

Zou, Q., Chang, R., Yan, X., 2020. Self-assembling proteins for design of anticancer nanodrugs. Chem. Asian J. 15 (9), 1405–1419. https://doi.org/10.1002/asia.202000135.

Zwain, T., Zwayen, S., Palshetkar, K.K., 2022. Chapter 9 - albumin nanoparticles—a versatile and a safe platform for drug delivery applications. Nanoparticle Therapeutics 13, 327–358.

# PART II

# Applications of protein-based nanoparticles in drug delivery

CHAPTER

# 7

# Protein nanoparticles in cancer therapy

*Soodabeh Shafiee*[1], *Mitra Samadi*[2,3], *Marzieh Peyman*[4,5] *and Zahra Mohammadpour*[4]

**[1]Recombinant Proteins in Cancer Department, Breast Cancer Research Center, National Cancer Institute, ACECR, Tehran, Iran; [2]Department of Molecular Genetics, Faculty of Biological Sciences, Tarbiat Modares University, Tehran, Iran; [3]Genetics Department, Breast Cancer Research Center, National Cancer Institute, ACECR, Tehran, Iran; [4]Medical Nanotechnology Department, Breast Cancer Research Center, National Cancer Institute, ACECR, Tehran, Iran; [5]Department of Nanotechnology, Faculty of Advanced Sciences and Technology, Tehran Medical Sciences Islamic Azad University, Tehran, Iran**

## 1. Introduction

Supported by cancer incidence and mortality data from population-based cancer registries (PBCR) and the World Health Organization (WHO) mortality database, cancer remains the leading cause of death worldwide. This trend is further exacerbated by the magnifying global burden of the disease. It is anticipated that by the year 2050, the worldwide incidence of cancer will reach 35.3 million cases, showing a 76.6% enhancement from the 20 million diagnoses recorded in 2022. A similar tendency is expected for cancer-associated mortalities, which are projected to increase by 89.7%, reaching 18.5 million compared to 9.7 million deaths documented in 2022 (Bray et al., 2024). Chemotherapy, surgical intervention, radiotherapy (Arruebo et al., 2011), and biological therapy constitute the main therapeutic modalities routinely implemented alone or in combination for cancer treatment in clinics (Cheng et al., 2021). However, these therapies still face a significant treatment failure rate. The reasons for this outcome are often attributed to multiple factors, such as adverse side effects along with chemoresistance, in vivo instability, and rapid clearance of biological therapies (Gou et al., 2018).

Proteins are highly valued carriers for drug delivery due to their low cytotoxicity, reduced potential for immunogenicity, inherent biocompatibility, biodegradability, and capability to serve as efficient delivery platforms for both hydrophobic and hydrophilic

*Protein-Based Nanoparticles in Drug Delivery*
https://doi.org/10.1016/B978-0-443-33639-3.00004-0

drugs. These properties contribute to their classification as generally recognized as safe (GRAS) for use in drug delivery. Additionally, the hydrophilic steric barrier helps minimize the chances of proteins being opsonized and removed by the reticuloendothelial system (RES) (Hassanin and Elzoghby, 2020). Other unique characteristics of proteins that enhance their suitability for drug delivery applications include the following: (1) Proteins are easily soluble, uniformly distributed, and maintain their stability under various conditions. (2) They feature three distinct interfaces that can be tailored to introduce new functionalities. (3) With extensive data available on the crystal structure, genetics, and molecular details of many protein-based nanoparticles (PNPs), rational modifications can be applied. (4) Owning a consistent and repetitive nature, these structures support the homogeneously integrated multiple copies of a specific portion or portions. The variability of PNPs that encapsulate various molecular cargoes, including catalytic, therapeutic, and imaging agents, in combination with their easy scalability, has made them invaluable across a wide range of practical applications (Diaz et al., 2018). Multiple proteins such as albumin, ferritin, gelatine, transferrin, casein, silk fibroin (SF), zein, lactoferrin, lipoprotein, lectin, virus-like polypeptides (VLP), elastin-like polypeptides (ELP), and gliadin have been adopted as the foundation of nanoparticles (NPs) utilized in drug delivery systems (DDSs).

The tumor microenvironment (TME) represents a significant barrier to the effectiveness of protein-based nanomedicines and cancer therapeutic modalities. Beyond impeding the delivery of therapeutic agents, it can undermine their potency, even when they successfully localize within the TME. In addition to hindering the delivery of protein nanomaterials, this critical obstacle is also responsible for inducing immunosuppression (Martin et al., 2020). Therefore, alternative TME normalization strategies that target, modulate, and even interrupt this milieu are needed to further enhance the delivery of tumor-targeted NPs and, as a result, treatment efficiency (Yang and Gao, 2017). In this chapter, we discuss the integration of various PNPs with different cancer treatment strategies and how these NPs can be specifically delivered to cancer cells. Additionally, we discuss their application in targeting and modulating the TME. Furthermore, we outline the use of protein-based NPs for anticancer drug delivery purposes.

## 2. Utilization of PNPs in cancer therapeutic modalities

### 2.1 Chemotherapy

Chemotherapy, beyond its utility in neoadjuvant, adjuvant, and combination therapy regimens, has demonstrated efficacy in managing certain forms of metastatic malignancies (Arruebo et al., 2011). Although chemotherapy exhibits considerable therapeutic efficacy, it is accompanied by several major drawbacks that may hinder its clinical applicability. Systemic administration of conventional chemotherapeutic agents allows them to circulate throughout the body. However, the nonspecific distribution of these molecules contributes to adverse effects on healthy tissues and multiplying normal cells, as the drugs often induce off-target toxicity resulting from a lack of tissue selectivity. Consequently, the therapeutic dose attainable within the solid tumor remains constrained, leading to suboptimal efficacy due to pronounced systemic toxicities (Danhier et al., 2010). The concept of exploiting the vascular abnormalities inherent in tumors to prevent penetration of chemotherapy drugs into noncancerous tissue matrices while enabling targeted access to tumor sites is particularly appealing (Park et al., 2008). Moreover, chemotherapy drugs exhibit low aqueous solubility and accelerated systemic elimination, which further complicates their therapeutic efficacy. Additional hurdles associated with chemotherapy include the emergence of acquired chemoresistance, alongside the proliferation of cancer stem-like cell population (Dai et al., 2016). In this regard, the tumor-targeted nanomedicine-based therapeutics address the poor specificity seen with traditional chemotherapeutics and provide greater efficacy. Multidrug resistance (MDR) is a major obstacle to the failure of chemotherapy in clinical practice, and finding new ways to tackle it is of crucial importance for improving treatment outcomes. Li et al. reported a chemotherapy approach that combined multiple agents to effectively overcome MDR synergistically via hypoxia-inducible factor (HIF) function blockade and drug efflux "stop." These multiresponsive SF nanoparticles (SFNs), coloaded with the chemotherapeutic drug doxorubicin (DOX) and PX478 (a HIF inhibitor), were functionalized with tumor-targeting ligand folic acid (FA). PX478 release effectively suppressed the HIF gene, thereby blocking its related downstream genes, HIF-1α, MDR1, VEGF, GLUT-1, and P-gp, which are correlated with drug efflux pump and drug resistance (Li et al., 2022).

## 2.2 Immunotherapy

Generally, cancer-targeted immunotherapies elicit their therapeutic effects by stimulating and reinforcing the patient's innate immune system, along with reestablishing and maintaining the antitumor immune response cycle. This targeted mechanism guarantees that immune effector functions are specifically directed to the tumor site, thereby minimizing damage to healthy tissues (Wang et al., 2023b). In the usual course of events, solid tumors recruit tumor-infiltrating immune cells, contributing to the establishment of an immunosuppressive microenvironment that supports tumor progression. This so-called immunosuppressive tumor immune microenvironment is typically driven by the accumulation of regulatory T cells (Tregs) and myeloid-derived suppressor cells (MDSCs), accompanied by the secretion of immunomodulatory factors, including vascular endothelial growth factor (VEGF) and transforming growth factor β (TGF-β). Furthermore, the aberrant vasculature of the TME in conjunction with the fast proliferation of tumor cells induces hypoxia, which in turn exacerbates immunosuppression in the TME (Yang et al., 2021). Cancer immunotherapy predominantly involves immune checkpoint inhibitors (ICIs), adoptive cell transfer therapy, cytokines, tumor-specific vaccines, and small-molecule immunomodulatory compounds. At present, ICIs stand at the forefront of cancer immunotherapy, driving significant advancements in therapeutic approaches. Two main types of ICIs target cytotoxic T-lymphocyte-associated protein 4 (CTLA-4) and programmed death 1/programmed death ligand 1 (PD-1/PD-L1) and have received Food and Drug Administration (FDA) approval for treating a wide range of cancers (Wang et al., 2023b). To improve the therapeutic outcomes of cancer immunotherapy, it is crucial to create novel strategies that manipulate the TME and convert the tumor's phenotype from immunologically "cold" to "hot," relieving immunosuppression and boosting immunotherapeutic efficiency. Integrating antiimmunosuppression mechanisms with NP-based delivery platforms can enhance therapeutic efficacy

(Jia et al., 2021) and potentially reverse therapy resistance. Disrupting the indoleamine 2,3-dioxygenase (IDO) pathway and downregulating this immunosuppressive molecule promotes immunogenic cell death (ICD) in tumor cells and, therefore, potentiates immunotherapy (Musetti and Huang, 2018). In the process of ICD, tumor cells discharge danger-associated molecular patterns (DAMPs), tumor-associated antigens (TAAs), and proinflammatory cytokines. Among IDO1 inhibitors showing promising outcomes in clinical trials, nanomedicines incorporating navoximod and indoximod have undergone preclinical in vivo investigations (Shen et al., 2020). Recent studies have shown that the immuno-photodynamic therapy (PDT) combination approach, for example, by using PDT-induced antitumor immunity using the ICD mechanism, can lead to the release of DAMPs and improved tumor immunogenicity (Ng et al., 2018). PNPs tailored to selectively engage with key components of the TME exhibit substantial efficacy in reshaping its immunosuppressive characteristics into an immunostimulatory phenotype, thereby boosting the therapeutic outcomes of anticancer immunotherapy. Additionally, NP-based delivery platforms can improve the therapeutic efficiency of tumor immunotherapy by improving the ICI therapy, the cytotoxic activity of natural killer cells, and the activity of dendritic cells (DCs) (Qi et al., 2020). Tumor immunotherapy using ICIs requires TME remodeling. Therefore, various nanodrug delivery platforms have been employed to hinder tumor progression by codelivering ICIs with other agents to optimize the therapeutic outcomes of ICIs via modulating the TME (Ou et al., 2018). The combination of PDT with checkpoint-blockade immunotherapy has shown superior efficacy in eradicating primary tumors, hindering metastasis, and averting recurrence. To simultaneously improve PDT-driven intracellular reactive oxygen species (ROS) generation and ICD induction, NP-based physical ICD inducers were utilized in combination with ICIs. A serum albumin (SA)-coated boehmite organic–inorganic scaffold was loaded with Ce6 photosensitizer and a honey bee venom melittin (MLT) cytolytic peptide (Fig. 7.1A). The multifunctional Ce6/MLT@SAB platform showed MLT-enhanced PDT antitumor effects in vitro. Following phototreatment and intracellular ROS generation, cells treated with Ce6/MLT@SAB exhibited significantly enhanced levels of ICD and an improved capacity to activate DCs. Combining anti-PD1 with Ce6/MLT@SAB phototreatment amplified antitumor efficacy and resulted in elevated levels of tumor-infiltrating $CD4^+$ and $CD8^+$ T-cell populations alongside a decreased presence of MDSCs (Fig. 7.1C–D) (Liu et al., 2019).

Chemo-PDT combination therapy through integration of PDT with agents capable of boosting tumor immunogenicity and strengthening immune responses is another strategy that has gained attention in cancer nanomedicine. A versatile nanoplatform was designed to codeliver the IR780 small molecule, an NLG919 dimer, alongside tirapazamine (TPZ), a hypoxia-activated prodrug. NLG919 is an antagonist of the IDO1 enzyme. TPZ-based chemotherapy synergistically enhanced PDT-triggered ICD. The glutathione (GSH)-rich TME activated NLG919 and could effectively reverse the immunosuppressive TME phenotype through selective inhibition of the IDO1 enzyme (Wang et al., 2023c).

## 2.3 Phototherapy

PDT is a common oxidative therapeutic strategy featuring spatiotemporal selectivity and noninvasive nature. This treatment modality harnesses the cytotoxic potential of ROS,

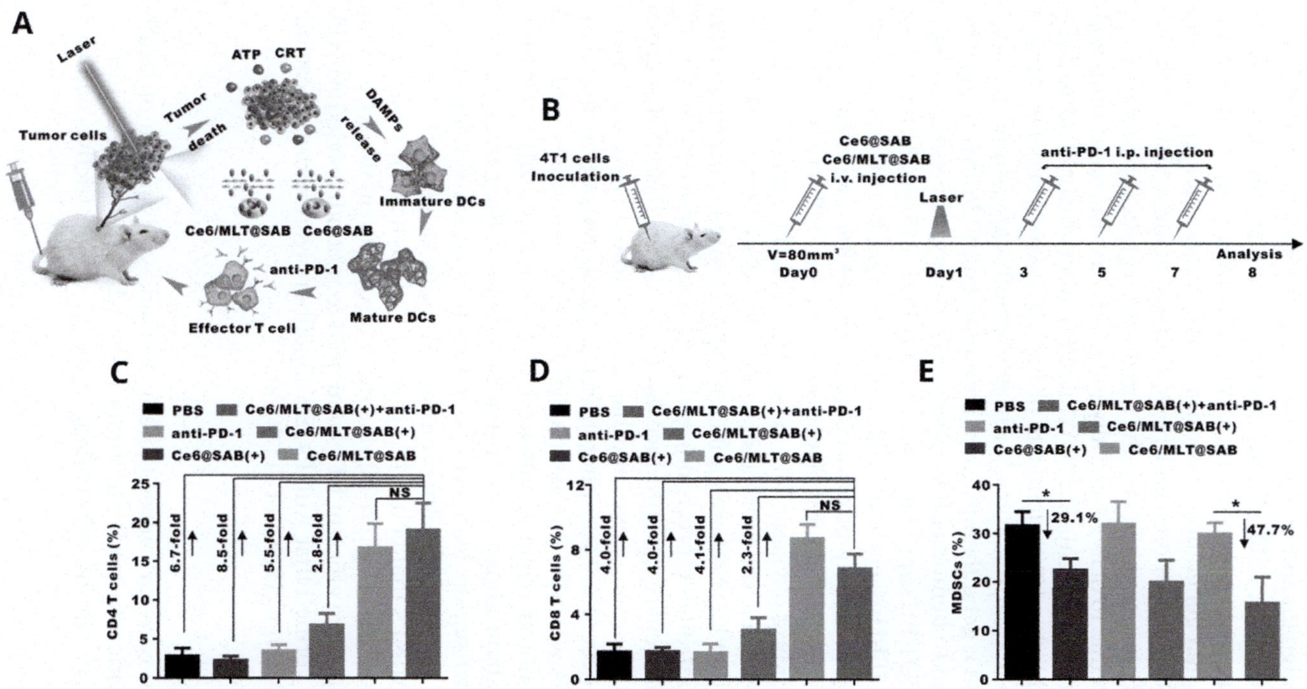


FIGURE 7.1 MLT-mediated immunogenic PDT leads to the in vivo activation of immune responses. (A) A schematic illustration of an organic–inorganic hybrid nanocarrier coloaded with the bee venom-derived melittin (MLT) peptide and Ce6 photosensitizer for combinational immuno-PDT. (B) Schematic representation showing the experimental setup for Ce6/MLT@SAB-mediated immunotherapy. (C, D) Flow cytometric evaluation of $CD4^+$ and $CD8^+$ T-cell percentages under different treatment conditions. (E) Flow cytometric evaluation of MDSCs in tumors under different treatment conditions. *Adapted from: H. Liu, Y. Hu, Y. Sun, C. Wan, Z. Zhang, X. Dai, Z. Lin, Q. He, Z. Yang, P. Huang, Y. Xiong, J. Cao, X. Chen, Q. Chen, J.F. Lovell, Z. Xu, H. Jin, K. Yang, Co-Delivery of bee venom melittin and a photosensitizer with an organic-inorganic hybrid nanocarrier for photodynamic therapy and immunotherapy. ACS Nano. 13 (11) (2019), 12638–12652, https://doi.org/10.1021/acsnano.9b04181; Adapted with permission from Liu et al. Copyright 2019 American Chemical Society.*

produced from molecular oxygen in the presence of light at a defined wavelength (650–850 nm) and photoactivatable agents (photosensitizers). Upon light activation, this mechanism induces phototoxicity, targeting both premalignant and malignant cells, thereby serving as an effective approach to cancer treatment (Yang et al., 2018). Photosensitizers are typically hydrophobic and prone to aggregation in aqueous environments, which adversely impacts their photophysical properties (reduced singlet oxygen generation), chemical stability, and biological efficacy (suboptimal tumor localization). To rise to these challenges, PNPs provide a viable solution by enabling the selective delivery of photosensitizers to the tumor site, significantly minimizing damage to healthy tissues and systemic toxicity, especially when utilized in conjunction with spatially controlled light irradiation (Duan et al., 2019). While PDT offers distinct advantages per se, several studies have also highlighted its potential to provide numerous benefits through combinatorial application with traditional therapies, such as chemotherapy, surgery, radiotherapy, photothermal therapy (PTT), gene therapy, and immunotherapy. In this regard, for instance, a DSS combining PDT and chemotherapy can exert a synergistic effect, wherein chemotherapeutic drugs enhance PDT by supplying oxygen, and PDT, in turn, facilitates the release of chemotherapeutic agents (El-Hussein et al., 2021). Nevertheless, the therapeutic efficacy of PDT can be significantly impeded by hypoxia, a consequence of the abnormal vasculature typically found in solid tumors. To address this challenge, numerous NP-based strategies aimed at tumor hypoxia relief, including oxygenic NPs (Prasad et al., 2014; Fang et al., 2019), have been recently introduced to optimize the therapeutic outcomes of standard PDT.

PTT is an innovative approach that has become an increasingly favored cancer treatment because of its merits, including controllable precision, great efficiency, and lack of side effects. PTT modality harnesses photoenergy to produce heat and cause localized thermal ablation of tumor cells using photothermal agents and has demonstrated significant therapeutic potential. PNPs can be engineered to carry photothermal agents for use in efficacious in vivo PTT. Gold NPs (AuNPs), $Fe_3O_4$ NPs, graphene oxide, carbon nanotubes, and black phosphorus are commonly used photothermal agents for PTT (Wang et al., 2019). Of these photosensitizers, spherical AuNPs have shown great promise; however, their poor light absorption in the near-infrared (NIR) region leads to low photothermal conversion, which negatively affects PTT efficiency. To overcome this hurdle, Wang et al. used SF as a biotemplate to generate aggregated AuNPs that could improve PTT efficiency for tumor therapy. AuNPs/SF nanofibers could successfully redshift the light absorption in the NIR region and, in consequence, demonstrate a more efficient PTT compared to monodispersed AuNPs. In vivo evaluations following PTT verified that AuNPs/SF nanofibers were more efficacious at inhibiting tumor growth than AuNPs (Wang et al., 2019).

## 2.4 Radiotherapy

Radiotherapy is the standard of care for cancer therapy and takes advantage of locally applied high-energy ionizing radiation to eradicate tumor cells. NPs administered intravenously for glioblastoma therapy face significant challenges due to the restrictive nature of the blood–brain barrier, which greatly impedes their delivery. To study whether some specifically engineered PNPs can overcome this barrier, a synthetic protein nanoparticle (SPNP) based on human serum albumin (HSA) modified with the cell-penetrating peptide iRGD was generated by Gregory et al. The in vitro and in vivo assessments indicated that SPNPs loaded with siRNA against signal transducer and activator of transcription 3 (STAT3i) resulted in downregulation of STAT3. It has been reported that there is a direct correlation between STAT3 overexpression and cancer radioresistance. Regarding this, a combination of STAT3i SPNP therapy with focused radiotherapy demonstrated that seven mice out of the eight studied reached the 90-day postinoculation threshold for long-term survival. Also, mice showed no evidence of tumors following this period (Gregory et al., 2020).

## 3. Tumor-targeting strategies for PNP delivery

Unlike conventionally used free drugs, nanodrug formulations (ranging from 10 to 200 nm) exhibit an extended plasma half-life and increased tumor accumulation by exploiting passive and/or active targeting mechanisms. Extensive research has been conducted to optimize the targeting design of NP-based therapeutics. The selective targeting of tumors by NPs enhances the pharmacokinetic and pharmacodynamic profiles, provides controlled and sustained drug release, improves specificity, increases cellular uptake, enables more effective subcellular delivery, and substantially reduces systemic toxicity. PNPs offer various possibilities for chemical surface modification due to the presence of functional carboxylic, amino, and thiol groups on their surface. Mechanisms aimed at enhancing the tumor-targeting capabilities of nanocarriers are generally classified into two primary categories: passive and active targeting (Bae, 2009).

### 3.1 Passive targeting

NPs commonly used for chemotherapeutic agent delivery typically rely on passive targeting to tumors. Systemically administered NPs can passively localize and accumulate in tumoral tissue through the aberrant vasculature of the tumor and defective lymphatic drainage in tumors via the enhanced permeability and retention (EPR) effect. In passive targeting, the drug carriers exhibit prolonged blood circulation with reduced accumulation in normal organs (Peer et al., 2020). The size of NPs affects their ability to be passively targeted to tumors through the EPR effect. Despite high EPR, less than 1% of passively targeted NPs accumulate in tumors (Wilhelm et al., 2016). The common method to protect nanocarriers from the RES consists of chemical coupling of polyethylene glycol (PEG) chains to the surface of the proteins or particles. PEGylation results in a prolonged blood circulation half-life by several orders of magnitude (greater than 50-fold), reducing their immunogenicity, and also promoting their accumulation in tumors due to the EPR effect. PEGylation increases the hydrodynamic size of the particles, decreasing their clearance through the kidney and extending their circulation time. Furthermore, by creating a dense hydrophilic shell of long PEG chains as a protective layer around the NPs, steric repulsion forces repel the nonspecific hydrophobic absorption of serum opsonin proteins, thereby blocking and delaying the opsonization process, resulting in reduced uptake by RES (Danhier et al., 2010; Elzoghby et al., 2015).

### 3.2 Active targeting

Various tumor types show an overexpression of specific receptors, which can be targeted selectively by different therapeutic agents. Among them, proteins offer the distinct advantage of binding specifically to receptors and nutrient transporters on the surface of tumor cells. To enhance the tumor-targeting ability of PNPs and facilitate their selective accumulation at tumor sites, these NPs are efficiently functionalized with a variety of tumor-targeting ligands. These ligands are typically covalently attached to the functional groups on the NP surface through chemical conjugation reactions (Elzoghby et al., 2015; Rosenblum et al., 2018). The majority of these ligands specifically bind to receptors that are consistently overexpressed on cancer cells, while being either negligibly expressed or completely absent on normal cells. This strategy is anticipated to enhance tumor accumulation, but none of the actively targeted NPs for cancer drug delivery have yet advanced beyond clinical trials. One of the factors contributing to the failure of active targeting strategies is the development of a serum protein corona on NPs during their circulation in the bloodstream. The formation of a protein corona impairs the interaction of actively targeted NPs with cancer cell surface receptors. The adsorbed serum proteins contribute to immune recognition and rapid clearance from the bloodstream, ultimately resulting in suboptimal tumor accumulation (Zhao et al., 2016; Oh et al., 2018). Numerous integrin receptors, including integrin αvβ3, are abundantly expressed in the cellular membrane of multiple cancer cell types, where they can drive tumor cell invasion and metastatic processes through interactions with their extracellular matrix (ECM) ligands. Targeting αvβ3 integrin receptors using cyclic peptide Arg-Gly-Asp (cRGD) ligand conjugated to bovine serum albumin (BSA), used as a precoating protein corona, revealed that chitosan-based NPs encapsulating small interfering RNA (siRNA) directed against VEGF (siVEGF) could intensify blockade of endothelial cell-attributed activities such as proliferation, migration, invasion, and tube formation, inhibiting tumor growth and angiogenesis (Wu et al., 2024). The stromal component often predominates in the TME of most solid tumors, with cancer-associated fibroblasts (CAFs) forming a substantial portion of the stromal matrix. This stroma can be responsible for limited tumor-targeting capability and attenuated antitumor efficacy of conventional NPs. One such example is the presence of a dense stroma with high interstitial fluid pressure in a pancreatic tumor that can impair drug penetration, preventing it from reaching the tumor (He et al., 2024a). To surmount this formidable physical barrier and to attain both optimal tumor accumulation and penetration alongside sustained blood retention in pancreatic tumors, size-adjustable PNPs were developed in a study. These dual-responsive NPs were composed of small-sized albumin NPs of paclitaxel (HSA-PTX) with superior tumor penetration capability that were encapsulated into the CAP (a fibroblast-activated protein-α (FAP-α) responsive cleavable amphiphilic peptide) modified thermosensitive liposomes (CAP-TSL). These NPs were responsive to FAP-α, a membrane-bound serine protease uniquely overexpressed on the surface of CAFs. Through the application of PTT, CAP enhanced deep tumor accumulation of PTX and activated the enzymatic reaction with FAP-α, facilitating the release of HSA-PTX (Yu et al., 2020a).

## 4. TME-responsive PNPs for cancer therapy

TME refers to the sophisticated and dynamic network of extracellular and intracellular elements, defined by an array of cellular subsets and noncellular components. Given its close connection to metastasis and recurrence, combined with its role in orchestrating key events in tumor initiation, progression, and therapeutic response, the TME represents a critical target for innovative cancer treatment strategies (Li et al., 2020). Since the emergence of cancer nanotherapeutics, this field has consistently encountered obstacles requiring innovative solutions. One major challenge lies in the ability of NPs to surmount the body's biophysical barriers, including the blood–brain barrier and the gastrointestinal tract. Another hurdle arises from the TME's distinct physiological barriers, characterized by hallmark features, including hypoxia, acidosis, elevated ROS levels, heightened protease activity, and aberrant vascular architecture (Fig. 7.2). NPs need to first overcome these barriers to achieve efficient delivery to their site of action (de Lázaro and Mooney, 2021). Consequently, the design of innovative nanoengineered strategies that are more reliable, precisely controlled, and finely customizable is of paramount importance. These attributes will promote their effective accumulation within the TME, enhance their active targeting capabilities for TME modulation, and minimize off-target effects and systemic toxicities. Although encouraging achievements have been made in nanotechnology-based cancer therapy, a gap remains between in vitro findings and their clinical translation, likely due to insufficient consideration of TME hallmarks in research settings. This has significantly contributed to the failure of tumor-targeting drug-delivery nanomedicines to achieve their expected efficacy in cancer treatment. Numerous nano-delivery platforms with stimuli-responsive behavior have been

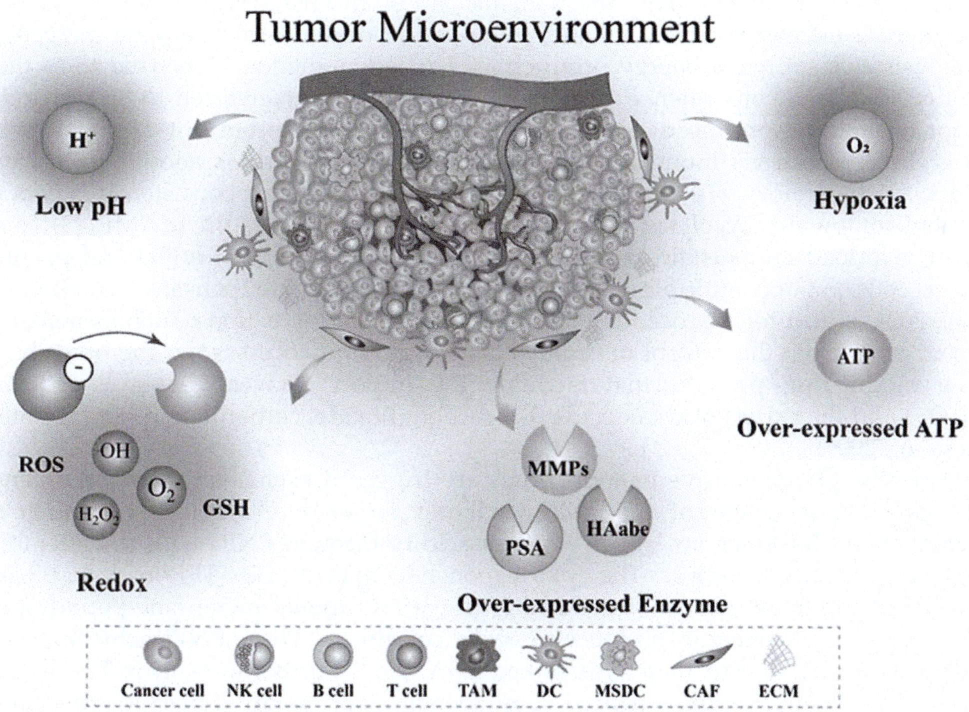


FIGURE 7.2 Schematic representation of TME hallmarks. *Adapted from: S. Peng, F. Xiao, M. Chen, H. Gao, Tumor-microenvironment-responsive nanomedicine for enhanced cancer immunotherapy. Adv. Sci.. 9 (1) (2022), https://doi.org/10.1002/advs.202103836 under the terms of Creative Commons CC BY license.*

designed to sense changes within the TME and then activate targeted drug release in a precisely controlled spatiotemporal fashion in response to particular cancer-related conditions. In contrast, other distinct types of nano-delivery systems are able to modulate and reestablish normal conditions in the biochemical microenvironments (Wang et al., 2016a). In this section, we discuss PNP-based delivery systems that have been specifically designed to respond to or modulate the hallmarks of TME and enhance anticancer therapeutic efficiency. In this regard, these PNP-based platforms can be exploited either as monotherapy or in combination with traditional cancer therapeutic modalities.

## 4.1 Acidity-responsive PNPs

The intracellular pH in healthy tissues and tumors remains largely comparable; however, the extracellular pH in tumors is notably lower than in normal tissues. On average, the extracellular tumor pH ranges from 6.0 to 7.0, whereas the extracellular pH in normal tissues and blood is consistently around 7.4 (Danhier et al., 2010). The acidic extracellular pH of the TME is the outcome of a combination of multiple contributing factors. Regions of TME with inadequate perfusion are often characterized by low pH arising from excess metabolic activity and alterations in metabolic pathways (Neri and Supuran, 2011). The acidic extracellular pH in tumors is primarily caused by multiple intricate processes and molecular abnormalities. These mechanisms can be discussed as follows: (1) Cancer cells rewire their metabolic pathways and, even in the presence of adequate oxygen, exploit glycolysis as a source of energy production. This phenomenon is referred to as the "Warburg effect." As a consequence, glucose is predominantly converted to lactate and H+ in tumor tissue. The produced lactate is subsequently transported out of the cells into the extracellular space via monocarboxylate transporters and brings about further reduction in pH. (2) In tumors, HIF-1α protein is aberrantly stable and consistently steers cellular metabolism toward glycolysis, further aggravating the acidic nature of TME. (3) To manage proton overload and sustain an intracellular pH conducive to survival and proliferation, cancer cells engage multiple short-term and long-term compensatory pathways (Han et al., 2024). Short-term procedures involve rapid buffering actions, such as instant relocation of acids from the cytosol to organelles. Long-term processes, on the other hand, rely upon modulating proteins that facilitate the import of weak bases like bicarbonate ($HCO_3^-$) and the export of weak acids like carbon dioxide, carbonic acid, and lactate (Ebbesen et al., 2009).

Typically, pH-responsive nanomaterials are triggered exclusively when they encounter the acidic environment of the TME, enabling targeted and selective content release. Numerous studies have investigated tumor acidity through PNPs with considerable acid/pH-responsive capabilities. The pH-responsive hybrid Dox-TPP-loaded BSA-grafted PLGA PNPs took advantage of the acidity-triggered rational membrane peptide to release their content exclusively in response to acidic conditions. These PNPs achieved robust circulation stability due to their crosslinked BSA shell. Furthermore, Dox-TPP-loaded NPs demonstrated significantly enhanced cytotoxic effects on mouse cancer cell lines, including neuroblastoma Neuro-2a and breast cancer 4T1, under acidic conditions (pH 6.5) compared to neutral pH (7.4) (Palanikumar et al., 2020).

## 4.2 Hypoxia-responsive PNPs

Regional hypoxia is a prominent attribute of many solid tumors and significantly contributes to tumor angiogenesis, metastasis, and the development of drug resistance. Hypoxia arises due to the rapid proliferation of tumor cells and the dysfunctional architecture of tumor vasculature. The oxygen partial pressure in tumor tissue is normally between 30 and 40 mm Hg, but in certain local zones it can be diminished to 0–2.5 mm Hg and consequently leads to the development of an oxygen-deficient TME (Vaupel et al., 1991). This hypoxic condition intervenes in the metabolic functions of cells and forces them to adapt to hypoxia-triggered stress through the activation of multiple HIFs, with HIF-1 being the most prominent factor involved in this process (Wilson and Hay, 2011). HIF-1 serves as a critical regulator of oxygen homeostasis and triggers angiogenesis along with anaerobic glycolysis processes. This mechanism will improve oxygen availability and, meanwhile, deplete oxygen utilization. This adaptation to hypoxia alters the overall biochemical milieu surrounding the cells. Given the pronounced differences between cancerous and noncancerous tissues, hypoxia has become a crucial target for therapeutic purposes. Hence, hypoxia can be exploited as an intrinsic stimulus for tumor therapeutic interventions (Kiyose et al., 2010). NP-based approaches that are currently employed for hypoxia relief and immunosuppression reversion act to reoxygenate the tumor tissue, achieved either by delivering oxygen directly to the tumor site or by stimulating the breakdown of hydrogen peroxide (Oguntade et al., 2021). To modulate the TME through synchronous alleviation of the levels of TME-associated hallmarks, hypoxia, ROS, and acidosis, Prasad P. et al. designed multifunctional, colloidally stable bioinorganic A-$MnO_2$ NPs comprising a polyelectrolyte–albumin complex combined with $MnO_2$ NPs. A-$MnO_2$ NPs could react with $H_2O_2$ produced by cancer cells under hypoxic conditions and increase tumor oxygenation by 45% and the pH from 6.7 to 7.2. Consequently, the A-$MnO_2$ NPs not only suppressed tumor progression markers HIF-1α and VEGF but also significantly enhanced the effectiveness of radiotherapy (Prasad et al., 2014). In a study by Luo Z. et al., hybrid protein oxygen carriers (HPOCs) were developed by hybridizing hemoglobin and albumin through disulfide reconfiguration. They showed that their developed tumor-targeted nanomedicines enhanced oxygen delivery to tumors, overcoming hypoxia-induced resistance to chemotherapy and PDT. By encapsulating DOX and Ce6, the resulting ODC-HPOCs demonstrated significant therapeutic efficacy in oxygen-enhanced chemo-PDT. The study revealed that reversing hypoxia-driven chemoresistance was achieved through a dramatic alteration in tumor hypoxia, which exerted its impact via suppressing the expression of HIF-1α, MDR1, and P-gp. Concurrently, the elevated oxygen levels amplified ROS production during PDT. This augmented chemo-PDT approach enabled a single-dose treatment, significantly reducing the required dosages of DOX and Ce6 (Fig. 7.3) (Luo et al., 2018). In a similar study, smart multifunctional HSA-$MnO_2$-Ce6&Pt NPs with pH/$H_2O_2$-sensitive properties and capability for TME-responsive size changes were designed through the albumin-based biomineralization of $Mn^{2+}$. These NPs generated oxygen to overcome hypoxia-associated PDT resistance and degraded into albumin-drug complexes with sizes below 10 nm in the acidic TME, enhancing permeability and efficacy in combined PDT and chemotherapy (Chen et al., 2016).

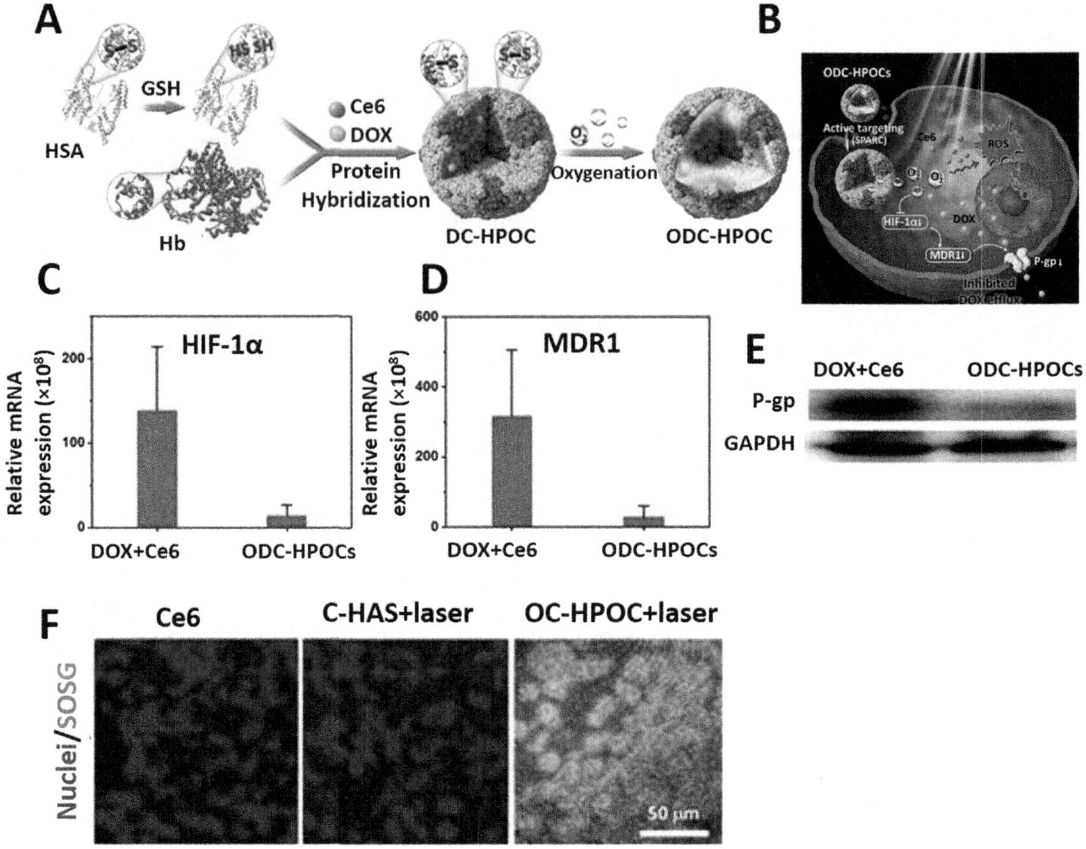


FIGURE 7.3 Combined chemo-PDT utilizing tumor-targeted ODC-HPOCs. (A) A detailed diagram depicting the fabrication steps of the ODC-HPOCs. (B) A schematic representation illustrating the $O_2$-augmented chemo-PDT utilizing ODC-HPOCs. (C–E) Quantification of mRNA expression levels of HIF-1α (C) and MDR1 gene (D) via qRT-PCR, and assessment of P-gp (E) protein levels by western blot analysis following treatment of tumor-bearing mice with DOX + Ce6 and ODC-HPOCs. (F) In vivo measurement of singlet oxygen generation following the administration of C-HSA and OC-HPOCs under laser irradiation. Adapted from Luo et al. (2018). *Adapted from: Adapted from: Z. Luo, H. Tian, L. Liu, Z. Chen, R. Liang, Z. Chen, Z. Wu, A. Ma, M. Zheng, L. Cai, Tumor-targeted hybrid protein oxygen carrier to simultaneously enhance hypoxia-dampened chemotherapy and photodynamic therapy at a single dose. Theranostics. 8 (13) (2018), 3584–3596, https://doi.org/10.7150/thno.25409 under the terms of Creative Commons Attribution (CC BY-NC) license.*

## 4.3 ROS-responsive PNPs

Various biological and environmental factors in the TME often undergo simultaneous fluctuations. Consequently, NPs that respond to a single stimulus often fail to deliver drugs effectively in real-world applications. Hence, combining multiple functions into a single NP would be a more efficient approach. To suppress breast cancer growth locally and hinder its lung metastasis, Zhang et al. utilized regenerated SF (RSF), an FDA-approved naturally occurring bioactive compound, to be functionalized with LyP-1 and then serve as a delivery carrier for quercetin (QR). LyP-1-QU-NPs. RSF-based NPs have shown multibioresponsive behavior, that is to say, they respond to changes in pH, ROS, and GSH changes of the TME. Ligand-mediated active targeting was achieved by employing LyP-1 (CGNKRTRGC), a cyclic nonapeptide, to direct the PNPs to the cancer cell mitochondria (Zhang et al., 2020).

## 4.4 GSH-responsive PNPs

GSH is a tripeptide consisting of glutamate, cysteine, and glycine. It is the dominant intracellular scavenger of ROS and is typically found in millimolar concentrations. GSH is oxidized upon reaction with most of the ROS, such as $H_2O_2$, superoxide, and hydroxyl radicals. Subsequently, GSH undergoes reduction through reduced NADPH-derived electrons and establishes a redox buffering cycle (Park and Jeong, 2024). In the TME, GSH is present at higher concentrations than in normal tissue. Different DDSs with disulfide bonds profit from the GSH gradient between the extracellular and intracellular spaces of the TME, allowing for GSH-responsive release of their cargo inside the target cells. Moreover, GSH is critical in maintaining redox homeostasis and hampering oxidative stress in cancer cells. GSH depletion is responsible for increased ROS levels in cancer cells and apoptosis induction. Therefore, reducing the GSH content in cancer cells is considered a promising strategy in cancer therapy. Dual redox potential and matrix metalloproteinase 2 (MMP-2) concentration-sensitive PNPs were fabricated with BSA as the ligand for tumor targeting and gelatin as an MMP-2-sensitive reagent. while the disulfide bond provides a redox-responsive mechanism for targeted tumor therapy. To create a redox-sensitive amphiphilic polymer, a prodrug (PTX-SS-COOH) incorporating disulfide bond was attached to sulfhydryl-modified gelatin. Due to the EPR effect and BSA-based active targeting, the NPs targeted the tumor tissue and were disintegrated into smaller particles upon MMP-2 activation. The in vitro and in vivo evaluations also supported the substantial anticancer efficacy and safety of these PNPs (Wu et al., 2017).

## 4.5 Enzyme-responsive PNPs

An overabundance of multiple families of active enzymes, namely hyaluronidase (HAdase), MMPs, γ-glutamyl transpeptidase, and esterase, has been identified in TME. These enzymes play a key role in coordinating the turnover of the ECM in the TME. Aberrantly dysregulated matrix turnover accelerates the degradation of the normal matrix and promotes its replacement by tumor-associated matrix that supports aggressive traits. Enhanced MMP9 release facilitates the liberation of trapped VEGF from the matrix, thereby initiating active angiogenesis from vascular quiescence. Moreover, MMPs are the dominant group of matrix-degrading proteinases, and their dysregulation in various cancer types contributes to tumor development and progression (Cox, 2021). Also, normal hyaluronan turnover is of crucial importance for health and its dysregulation, commonly observed in cancer, often results in the accumulation of excessive levels of enzyme. Thus, enzyme-responsive nanomedicine has become a hotspot issue and has gained significant attention as a promising approach to improving cancer therapy (Peng et al., 2022). The ability of intelligent DDSs to target tumors and respond to stimuli allows for efficient therapeutic delivery while reducing the off-target toxicity of conventional chemotherapy drugs. Various methods have been utilized to design nanocarriers with stimulus-responsive capabilities for targeted drug release. A smart inhalable delivery system was designed using MMP-2 responsive gelatin NPs that targeted mannose receptors. Gelatin NPs (GeNPs), laden with concanavalin A (con-A) as a ligand targeting mannose residues on cell surface glycoproteins, were loaded with cisplatin (CCG-NP). Then, NPs were evaluated for their receptor-specific targeting and "on-demand" controlled drug release in lung cancer treatment. Enzyme-induced drug release and enhanced endocytosis were observed with CCG-NP after an incubation period of 12 hours. Under the influence of MMP-2, the therapeutic potential of CCG-NP was significantly enhanced in lung cancer cells (Vaghasiya et al., 2021).

## 5. Protein nanoparticle platforms

### 5.1 Albumin

Albumin is a family of globular proteins with unique properties, including acidity, high solubility due to the predominance of ionized residues, and remarkable stability, as it can tolerate temperatures of 60°C for up to 10 h (Belinskaia et al., 2021b). HSA consists of 585 amino acids (approximately 66.5 kD) and plays a critical role in various vertebrate species. Albumin contains both hydrophilic and hydrophobic domains, along with charged amino acids. Its surface features amino and carboxyl groups that serve as binding sites for polymers or ligands, facilitating its role in drug delivery (Shen et al., 2021). Three naturally derived albumins—ovalbumin (OVA), BSA, and HSA—have been extensively studied for the delivery of various small-molecule drugs. However, the preference for HSA is primarily due to the potential immunological responses associated with using OVA and BSA in vivo, which can restrict their clinical applications (Mogues et al., 2005). HSA, the predominant protein in blood plasma or serum, plays a crucial role in determining oncotic pressure and regulating fluid distribution between body compartments. It also carries a wide range of endogenous and exogenous compounds, including drugs, fatty acids, nucleic acids, hormones, metals, toxins, and thyroxine (Belinskaia et al., 2021a). Recombinant albumin offers an alternative to animal- or human-derived albumin. Direct genetic fusion with recombinant albumin enables the one-step production of therapeutic proteins.

Albumin NPs are widely utilized in various disease therapies due to their modifiable chemical groups, cell-binding sites that promote adhesion, and strong affinity for protein drugs, enabling the formation of nanocomplexes (Qu et al., 2024). A nanosized protein-based DSS was developed using BSA as a drug carrier, combining two compounds, Dox and betulinic acid (BeA) (which exhibit significant cytotoxic activity against various cancer types). This NP has the competence to synergistically enhance the therapeutic effect of Dox while reducing chemoresistance induced by epidermal growth factor receptor (EGFR) expression, using natural BeA against nonsmall cell lung cancer (NSCLC) cells (Torres-Martinez et al., 2023). In another study, HSA-based NPs were created by covalently attaching trastuzumab to the surface of HSA using a bifunctional PEG linker. These HSA-based NPs effectively targeted human EGFR 2 (HER2)/neu-positive cells and exhibited high selectivity for the HER2/neu-positive SKBR3 cell line (Tran et al., 2024).

Active targeting of NPs plays a crucial role in enhancing drug delivery to cancer cells, and albumin NPs can be functionalized with various ligands to improve their targeting capabilities. In one study, sorafenib (SRF) was coated with HSA and conjugated with FA on the NP surface (FA-HSA-SRF-NPs) to enhance tumor targeting (Gao et al., 2019). In vitro results demonstrated that FA-HSA-SRF-NPs exhibited enhanced cytotoxicity against hepatocellular BEL-7402 cells compared to SRF alone and HSA-SRF-NPs. The study demonstrated that FA-HSA-SRF-NPs significantly enhanced antitumor activity compared to HSA-SRF-NPs and SRF alone, with tumor volumes notably smaller in the FA-HSA-SRF-NP group. The addition of FA improved the active targeting and therapeutic efficacy of the NPs, showing stronger antitumor effects without increasing systemic toxicity, as indicated by consistent body weights across all groups. Safety evaluations, including hematological and histological analyses, revealed no significant abnormalities in blood parameters or major organ tissues. While SRF treatment commonly causes issues like elevated amylase and liver dysfunction, these NPs did not exacerbate these effects. The observed safety and efficacy of FA-HSA-SRF-NPs were attributed to the biocompatibility of albumin and FA, along with their superior tumor-targeting capabilities. Furthermore, FA-HSA-SRF-NPs showed antiproliferative effects and suppression of tumor angiogenesis in nude mouse tumors.

Currently, a major challenge in cancer therapy is the insufficient delivery of therapeutic agents into solid tumors through systemic administration. SA accumulates in tumor tissues due to its effective interaction with the gp60 receptor (Desai et al., 2006) and an ECM glycoprotein known as secreted protein acidic and rich in cysteine (SPARC) (Desai et al., 2009), which is overexpressed in various tumors. This interaction actively enhances the uptake of NPs, enabling albumin-based NPs to bypass drug efflux mechanisms in tumor cells. In this context, research on combined anticancer drug delivery has concentrated on enhancing cellular uptake via gp60- and SPARC-mediated transcytosis, increasing drug accumulation, and ensuring the effective delivery of unstable therapeutics. Zheng et al. developed albumin NPs encapsulating an NF-κB-controllable CRISPR activation system, which enables tumor-selective SPARC upregulation by responding to the highly activated NF-κB in tumor cells (Zheng et al., 2024a; 2024b). SPARC exhibits a strong binding affinity for albumin and has been demonstrated to facilitate the penetration and uptake of albumin-based DDSs in tumors. In vitro studies on organoids demonstrated that the administration of SP-NPs created a positive feedback loop, leading to progressive increases in SPARC expression, as well as enhanced tumor cell uptake and tumor penetration of the NPs. In vivo studies with subcutaneous tumors produced similar results. In another study, the SPARC-based codelivery of trichosanthin (TCS) and albendazole (ABZ) by albumin-coated silver NPs for overcoming MDR and metastasis was addressed. A combination therapy was undertaken through a self-assembled nanosystem (Tang et al., 2017). TCS, a ribosome-inactivating protein known for its potent antitumor activity, and ABZ, an antihelmintic drug that also exhibits potential antitumor effects, were used in combination. Figure 7.4 shows the internalization and mechanism of action of the self-assembled nanosystem based on SPARC. The negatively charged ABZ@BSA/Ag NP was bound to cationic TCS that was modified with a cell-penetrating peptide and formed a self-assembled nanosystem. The nanosystem was shown to inhibit the proliferation of drug-resistant tumor cells by disrupting the cytoskeleton, arresting the cell cycle, and promoting apoptosis. Additionally, it demonstrated the ability to impede tumor cell migration and invasion. In vivo studies further validated the system's efficacy in overcoming drug resistance and inhibiting metastasis in a subcutaneous tumor mouse model.

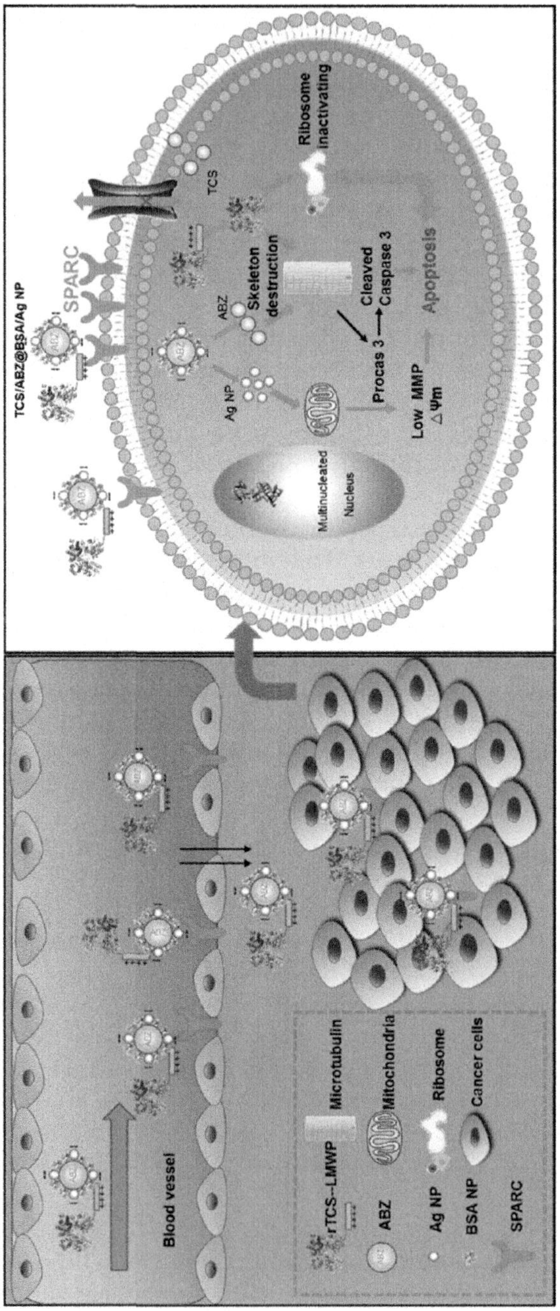


**FIGURE 7.4** Internalization and mechanism of action of TCS- and ABZ-loaded silver NPs. *Adapted from (Y. Tang, J. Liang, A. Wu, Y. Chen, P. Zhao, T. Lin, M. Zhang, Q. Xu, J. Wang, Y. Huang, Co-delivery of trichosanthin and albendazole by nano-self-assembly for overcoming tumor multidrug-resistance and metastasis. ACS Appl. Mater. Interfaces. 9 (32) (2017), 26648–26664, https://doi.org/10.1021/acsami.7b05292); Adapted with permission from Tang et al. Copyright 2017 American Chemical Society.*

Nanotheranostics, an emerging field combining diagnostics and therapeutics in a single nanoplatform, offers promising solutions for personalized cancer treatment. In this context, a novel multifunctional probe, Gd-EB-ICG (gadolinium–Evans blue–indocyanine green), for fluorescence/magnetic resonance (FL/MR) dual-modal imaging-guided PTT of cancer was designed and synthesized (Yu et al., 2023). Gd-EB-ICG (GIs) can self-assemble with endogenous albumin to form drug-albumin complexes (GIAs). Albumin protects GIAs from recognition and clearance by the mononuclear phagocytic system. Its high plasma concentration and prolonged half-life facilitate the continuous accumulation of GIAs in tumor regions through the EPR effect and specific tumor uptake mechanisms. In vitro experiments on 4T1 cells demonstrated that the probe significantly enhanced fluorescence emission, MR contrast, and photothermal efficiency in a synergistic manner. The results indicate that the high photothermal conversion efficiency of GIAs can effectively kill tumor cells in vitro. In vivo experiments demonstrated that the imaging and PTT performance on 4T1-tumor-bearing nude mice was highly effective for cancer theranostics. To evaluate the therapeutic efficacy of GIAs, mice were divided into four groups: phosphate buffered saline (PBS) only, laser only, GIAs only, and GIAs combined with laser. Tumor volumes and body weights were monitored postlaser treatment. Tumor growth was similar in the control groups, indicating minimal effects from laser or GIAs alone. In contrast, the combined GIAs and laser treatment led to complete tumor ablation without relapse, attributed to enhanced photothermal conversion and tumor targeting. Body weight remained stable across all groups, indicating low systemic toxicity. Table 7.1 demonstrates some recent studies on albumin-based nanoplatforms for cancer therapy.

As shown in Table 7.2, albumin-based NPs have emerged as a significant area of interest in clinical trials, particularly due to their potential in DDSs for cancer treatment.

**TABLE 7.1** Albumin-based NPs.

| Type of albumin | Formulation | Type of cancer | Key outcomes of in vivo/in vitro study | Ref. |
|---|---|---|---|---|
| BSA | BSA-siRNA-NPs | Lung cancer | BSA NPs/siRNA had an equal antitumor effect as Lipo/siRNA by downregulating the expression of survivin mRNA and survivin protein<br>The tumor inhibition rate of BSA NPs/siRNA was much higher than that of naked siRNA in vivo. | Wang et al. (2021) |
| BSA | BSA-$MnO_2$@ HMSNs-DOX-Ce6 (mesoporous silica nanospheres) | Cervical cancer | The nanoplatform could suppress cervical carcinomas and be employed for efficient chemo-PDT even in the hypoxic TME in HeLa cells and mice. | Fang et al. (2019) |
| BSA | rTL/ABZ@ BSA/Ag NPs | Lung cancer | Inhibition of the proliferation of the tumor cells (A549/T and HCT8/ADR) and inhibition of metastases and drug resistance in the mouse model. | Tang et al. (2017) |

(*Continued*)

**TABLE 7.1** Albumin-based NPs.—cont'd

| Type of albumin | Formulation | Type of cancer | Key outcomes of in vivo/in vitro study | Ref. |
|---|---|---|---|---|
| BSA | Au@BSA-siRNA-FAM | Pancreatic cancer | Effectively enhanced the intracellular delivery of siRNA and simultaneously inhibited survivin activity and subsequently led to cancer cell apoptosis. | Wang et al. (2016a, 2016b) |
| BSA | Gal-BSA-Cur NPs | hepatocellular carcinoma | Gal-BSA-Cur NPs had higher release rates, improved curcumin solubility, and could selectively recognize receptors on the surface of HCC (HepG2) cells, improving the drug's internalization ability. | Huang et al. (2018) |
| BSA | ICG-BSA NCs (nanocomplex) | Breast cancer (TNBC) | Tumor accumulation, growth suppression, and efficient PDT on a triple-negative breast tumor mouse model. | Sarkar et al. (2020) |
| BSA | BSA-siRNA NPs (siRNA (anti-Kras G125 mutation) | Lung adenocarcinoma | Encapsulating the siRNA in the NPs could mediate significant sequence-specific KRAS knockdown, resulting in reduced cell growth of siRNA-transfected lung cancer cells. | Mehta et al. (2019) |
| BSA | FA-RLX-BSA-NPs | Breast cancer | Sustained release of FA-RLX-BSA-NPs in vitro with a superior cell inhibition against MCF-7 and MDA-MB-231 cells at lower $IC_{50}$ values compared to RLX and RLX-BSA-NPs. | Sinai Kunde and Wairkar (2022) |
| BSA | FA-Rg5-BSA NPs | Breast cancer | Enhanced cellular uptake of FA-Rg5-BSA NPs compared to Rg5 and Rg5-BSA, with a superior antitumor efficacy and tumor growth inhibition. | Dong et al. (2019) |
| HSA | DOX@FNPs (cysHSA-HA NPs) | Breast cancer (TNBC) | Compared to free DOX, DOX@FNPs exhibited a superior ability to reduce cellular viability and motility. | Cirillo et al. (2024) |
| HSA | HSA-DOX NPs | Neuroblastoma | Enhanced DOX sensitivity and anticancer activity against resistant cancer cells. | Onafuye et al. (2019) |
| HSA | HAS-curcumin NPs | Breast cancer | Anticancer effects of NPs on the cancer cells were much greater compared to curcumin alone. | Matloubi and Hassan (2020) |
| HSA | Apt-NP-FEXO | Immune checkpoint blockade (ICB) for cancer treatment | Apt-modified NPs could selectively bind with CTLA-4-positive cells and improve lymphocyte-mediated antitumor cytotoxicity in vitro. Compared with the free CTLA-4 aptamer, Apt-NP significantly enhanced antitumor immunity in a mouse model. | Yao et al. (2023) |
| HSA | HAlbNPs (redox responsive) | Breast cancer | The efficient uptake of NPs by cancer cells through CD44 receptors with improved intracellular drug release and decreased $IC_{50}$ values. | Brindisi et al. (2022) |

DOX: doxorubicin; PTX: paclitaxel; Cur: curcumin; TNBC: triple negative breast cancer; PDT: photodynamic therapy; GAL: galactosylated; cys: cystamine; ICG: indocyanine green; ABZ: albendazole; FEXO: fexofenadine; Apt: CTLA-4 aptamer; ERT: erlotinib/RLX: raloxifene hydrochloride; FA: folic acid; Rg5: ginsenoside Rg5.

**TABLE 7.2** Albumin-based nanomedicine in clinic and clinical trials.

| Drug name | Molecular type | Indication | Status |
|---|---|---|---|
| Abraxane® (ABI-007) | Nanoparticle albumin-bound paclitaxel | Breast/lung/prostate cancer | Approved |
| Fyarro (ABI-009) | Nanoparticle albumin-bound rapamycin | Solid tumors | Approved |
| Nanocoll | $^{99m}$Tc-labeled HSA | SPECT scan for sentinel node localization in breast cancer | Approved |
| Optison | Injectable suspension of perflutren protein-type A microsphere | Contrast agent for ultrasound imaging | Approved |
| ABI-008 | Nanoparticle albumin-bound docetaxel | Prostate cancer | Phase I/II |
| Aldoxorubicin | Doxorubicin–maleimide conjugate | Soft tissue sarcomas, small cell lung cancer | Phase III |
| ABI-009 | Rapamycin-albumin NP | Cancer | Phase I |
| ABI-010 | Nanoparticle albumin-bound 17-AAG | Solid tumors | Phase I |
| ABI-011 | Nanoparticle albumin-binding thiocolchicine dimer | Solid tumors | Phase I |
| BTP-114 | Albumin-binding cisplatin | Pancreatic/ovarian/breast/prostatic neoplasms | Phase I |
| MTX-HSA | Methotrexate albumin conjugate | Metastatic renal cell carcinoma | Phase II |
| INNO-206 | Albumin-binding prodrug of doxorubicin | Malignant solid tumor | Phase III |
| Neugranin | Fusion protein/GCSF | Breast cancer | Phase III |
| Balugrastim | Fusion protein | Breast cancer | Phase III |

## 5.2 Gelatin

Collagen is a structural protein found in the connective tissues of all vertebrates, with particularly high expression in the skin, tendons, and ligaments (Ahmad et al., 2024). Gelatin is derived from collagen, and its primary structure closely resembles that of collagen. It is obtained through the partial hydrolysis of collagen using acid-, alkaline-, or heat-based processes (Milano et al., 2023). Generally, two types of natural gelatin are available: cationic Type A and anionic Type B. Their differences arise from the specific collagen hydrolysis processes used during manufacturing (Varanko et al., 2020a). Gelatin is widely used in the pharmaceutical industry, particularly in the biomedical field, due to its numerous advantageous properties, including biocompatibility, solubility, low immunogenicity, low cytotoxicity, and availability, making it highly suitable for biomedical applications. It plays an important role as a biomaterial for the creation of DDSs, structures for tissue engineering, and regenerative medicine. Its strong compatibility with various production methods and potential as a carrier for a wide range of bioactive substances, as well as its capacity to regulate the release rate of specific medications, make it a selected option for drug delivery (Zhang and Wang, 2024).

Gelatin nanoparticles (GeNPs) have been extensively employed as carriers for drugs and genes, with a focus on various diseases, including cancer. Their low cytotoxicity, coupled with a straightforward and reliable production process, makes them promising candidates for therapeutic applications (Thakur et al., 2023). In addition, numerous integrin-binding sites, including arginine–glycine–aspartic acid (RGD) sequences, are present in the gelatin chain, which can be recognized by integrin αV, particularly αVβ3. This kind of integrin is abundantly present in endothelial and tumor cells but is minimally expressed in resting endothelial cells and most normal tissues (Morán et al., 2018). With the advancement of nanomaterials, gelatin-based drug delivery carriers have evolved into various forms, including gelatin-based nanospheres, hydrogels, nanogels, and nanofibers (Jiang et al., 2023).

Both in vitro and in vivo studies demonstrated the enhanced effectiveness of gelatin NPs loaded with anticancer drugs compared to unbound drugs. In a study, cisplatin was complexed with a gelatin matrix (CG-NP) to evaluate its stimuli responsiveness in lung cancer cells and analyze its release profile (Vaghasiya et al., 2021). The surface of these gelatin NPs was modified with con-A, which enhances their ability to bind to mannose residues of overexpressed glycoproteins on the surface of tumor cells. This modification significantly enhances the cancer cell-specific uptake of the NPs. MMPs, which are protease enzymes overexpressed in tumorous tissues at all stages of cancer, play a key role in the release of cisplatin. The elevated levels of MMPs in tumor tissues facilitate controlled drug release. The efficacy of the NP was significantly increased in the presence of the MMP-2 enzyme in the A549 lung cancer cell line. Additionally, they significantly enhanced ROS generation, induced cell cycle arrest in the S and G2/M phases, and promoted apoptosis in cancer cells.

Some studies emphasize the promising role of siRNA in cancer therapy, particularly when delivered using nanocarriers like gelatin NPs. A study introduced cancer cell membrane-camouflaged gelatin NPs (CSG@B16F10), designed for the codelivery of catalase (CAT) to generate oxygen and CD73 siRNA to silence the CD73 gene, a key player in T-cell immunosuppression (Yuan et al., 2022). These NPs employ an MMP-responsive design for controlled payload release, optimizing tumor targeting and immune evasion. In melanoma-bearing mice, CSG@B16F10 demonstrated significant tumor suppression (~83%) when combined with PD-L1 checkpoint blockade therapy. The treatment increased cytotoxic T-cell activity, reduced Tregs, and elevated antitumor cytokine levels, indicating an enhanced immune response. This research presented a strategy for synergistically addressing tumor hypoxia and immune suppression, potentially improving the efficacy of PD-1/PD-L1 checkpoint therapies in clinical applications.

Recent studies underscore the potential of combining chemotherapy with PTT as a promising strategy for breast cancer treatment. This approach seeks to improve therapeutic outcomes while reducing the side effects commonly associated with conventional chemotherapy. Chen et al. designed GeNPs to encapsulate ICG and DOX (Chen et al., 2021). The GNP-DOX/ICG exhibited size reduction and enhanced drug release upon degradation by overexpressed MMP-2 in tumors. In vitro experiments confirmed that GNP-DOX/ICG provided an improved and synergistic therapeutic effect. In vivo experiments demonstrated that GNP-DOX/ICG effectively suppresses 4T1 tumor growth in BALB/c mice. In another study, a nanosystem was developed by combining gene therapy and PTT, utilizing a polypyrrole-polyethyleneimine-siILK nanocomplex (PPRILK) for papillary thyroid cancer (PTC) (Xu et al., 2022a). The gelatin-stabilized polypyrrole exhibited charge reversal properties, enabling strong binding of the siILK gene at physiological pH (7.35–7.45) and its release in acidic lysosomal environments (pH 4.0–5.5). This release was facilitated by the proton sponge effect, which enhanced the escape of siILK from lysosomes into the cytoplasm, where it effectively inhibited PTC cell proliferation and lymphatic spread. In vivo results in BALB/c nude mice revealed that the combined PTT eradicated tumors completely and significantly reduced recurrence and metastasis through the therapeutic effects of siILK. Table 7.3 presents some of the nanoformulations based on gelatin used for cancer treatment.

**TABLE 7.3** Gelatin-based NPs.

| Protein | Formulation | Type of cancer | Key outcomes of in vivo/in vitro study | Ref. |
|---|---|---|---|---|
| Gelatin type A | BSA/Gel-SS-PTX/PTX-SS-COOH NPs | Breast cancer | Increased chemotherapy drugs at the tumor site and reduced toxicity of PTX, high anticancer effect, and safety of BSA/Gel-SS-PTX/PTX-SS-COOH NPs in vivo | Zhou et al. (2020) |
| Gelatin type A | Curcumin-gelatin-polyethylene glycol-methyl (mPEG) nanogels | Epithelial carcinoma | Controlled and prolonged (96 hours) release of CUR in vitro | Tran et al. (2019) |
| Gelatin type A | PEOT/PBT-gelatin-DK and CTC | Solid soft tumors | Effective release of chemotherapeutics and the nontoxicity of the scaffolds | Liguori et al. (2022) |
| Gelatin type A | AuNPs/AuNRs-gelatin-MTX | Breast cancer | Higher cytotoxic effect of MTX-loaded AuNR2-gelatin on the MCF-7 cells compared to the free drug | Khodashenas et al. (2021) |
| Gelatin type A | GelMA-PEDOT/PSS hydrogels | Skin cancer | Higher drug release when voltage was applied to the hydrogels<br>Controlled drug release in response to electric stimulus | Oktay and Alemdar (2019) |
| Gelatin type B | Gelatin type B 5-fluorouracil-protamine sulfate NPs) | Human breast adenocarcinoma and epithelial carcinoma | Effective cellular internalization<br>Enhanced uptake, internalization, and apoptosis in tumor cells compared to free drug | Morán et al. (2018) |
| Gelatin type B | $Fe_3O_4$/CuS/Cur@GeNPs-FA | Lung adenocarcinoma-breast cancer | Higher killing efficiency of MCF-7 cells<br>Time-dependent cellular uptake | Xia et al. (2023) |
| Gelatin | CUR-Gel-MNPs | Lung and breast cancer | The developed nanocarrier showed good colloidal stability of NPs and pH-dependent release of CUR-Gel-MNPs and enhanced long-term toxicity toward cancer cells | Dutta et al. (2022) |
| Gelatin | Oxidized alginate/gelatin/chitosan/AuNPs/DOX | Breast cancer | pH-dependent drug release<br>Cytocompatible hydrogel on MCF-7 cells with cytotoxic effect when containing DOX | Alioghli Ziaei et al. (2023) |

PTX: paclitaxel; CuS: copper sulfide; Fe3O4: iron oxide; CUR: curcumin; GeNP: gelatin NP; FA: folic acid; BSA: bovine serum albumin; DOX: doxorubicin; PEOT/PBT: poly(ethylene oxide)/poly(butylene terephthalate); DK: diclofenac; CTC: chlortetracycline hydrochloride; MTX: methotrexate; AuNRs: gold nanorods; AuNPs: gold NPs; MNPs: magnetic NPs.

## 5.3 Gliadin

Wheat is one of the most widely cultivated cereal grains and is primarily composed of two protein fractions: gliadin and glutenin. Gliadins are further classified into three subtypes—α/β-, γ-, and ω-gliadins—and are recognized for their surface-active properties. These properties have expanded their application in both food and nonfood industries. Gliadin has found widespread applications in both the food and pharmaceutical industries due to its low cost, ease of extraction, high foaming capacity, wide availability, and significant surface hydrophobicity (Rani et al., 2023). Zein in corn and gliadin in wheat are prolamins, a group of storage proteins found in the endosperm of cereal grains. These proteins exhibit tunable self-assembly behaviors, enabling the construction of nano- and microarchitectures. Researchers have utilized prolamins as green building materials for delivery vehicles, including nanoarchitectures and Pickering emulsions. These materials are entirely natural, biocompatible, and biodegradable, offering promising applications across various fields (Li et al., 2023).

Effective lung cancer treatments with minimal side effects have increasingly focused on gliadin-based NPs. In a study, procyanidolic oligomers (PCOs), a natural antioxidant, were used to treat cancer-linked oxidative stress (Lal et al., 2024). The study aimed to synthesize a highly stable gliadin-encapsulated PCO nanoformulation (PCO-NF). Results showed that PCO-NF significantly inhibited lung cancer cells at all tested concentrations, reducing cell viability to 31.54%, which was even lower than that of the standard anticancer drug. The nanoencapsulation enhanced the antimicrobial, antioxidant, and anticancer potential of PCOs, demonstrating the promise of this approach for improved cancer therapy.

In another study, gliadin/sodium caseinate NPs were developed via the pH cycle method (Xu et al., 2022b). These nanogels were used as a carrier for the antitumor agent, methotrexate (MTX). MTT assay indicated that the MTX-Gli/CAS nanogels effectively killed cancer cells, while cytotoxicity analysis revealed that the Gli/CAS NPs demonstrated good biocompatibility. Overall, the results demonstrated that MTX-loaded nanogels were effectively endocytosed by HepG2 cells, significantly enhancing cancer cell apoptosis. Figure 7.5 confirms the endocytosis of MTX-Gli/CAS NPs.

In another study, DOX hydrochloride-loaded gliadin NPs (DOX-GNPs) were developed for breast cancer treatment (Voci et al., 2023). These nanosystems exhibited excellent stability and a high drug-loading capacity with a prolonged and sustained release for up to a week. An in vitro viability assay demonstrated that the nanocarrier modulated the cytotoxicity of the DOX compound as a function of the incubation time, compared to the free form of the drug. Specifically, the authors observed that DOX encapsulation in gliadin NPs showed the same cytotoxicity after 72 h as free DOX did after 24 h. Table 7.4 shows other examples of drug-loaded gliadin nanoformulations for tumor therapy.

## 5.4 Lysozyme

Lysozyme, a key bacteriostatic protein, is found in various body fluids and tissues of numerous living organisms. In its native state, this enzyme exists as a monomer. However, when modified into its dimeric form, it acquires entirely new and valuable properties, including enhanced medical applications (Leśnierowski and Yang, 2021). Lysozyme can

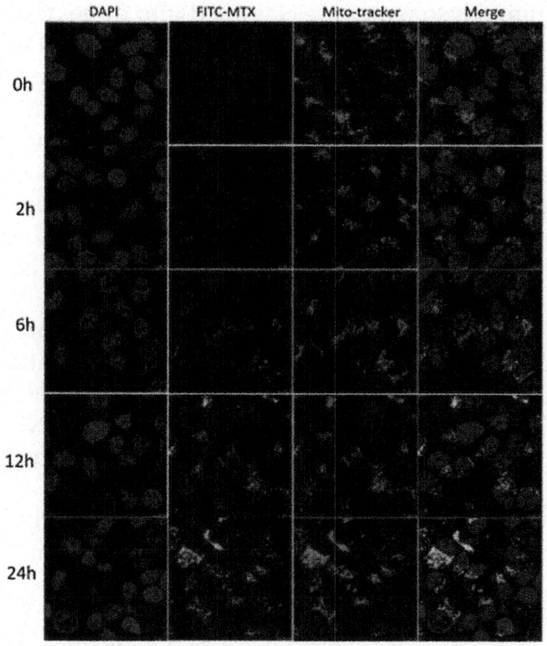


**FIGURE 7.5** FITC-MTX NPs phagocytosis in HepG2 cells. The cell nuclei are blue (DAPI), and the lysosome is red (Lyso Tracker Red). The green spots show the internalization of FITC-MTX NPs into cells, which was time-dependent. The NPs were distributed within the cytoplasm and exhibited significant overlap with the red fluorescence of lysosomes, indicating their accumulation in lysosomes following endocytosis. *Adapted from W. Xu, S. Zheng, H. Sun, Z. Li, R. Xi, D. Luo, Y. Li, B.R. Shah, Green-step fabrication of gliadin/sodium caseinate nanogels for methotrexate release, cytotoxicity and cell phagocytosis. J. Drug Deliv. Sci. Technol. 67 (2022b), 103028, https://doi.org/10.1016/j.jddst.2021.103028. Copyright 2022 Elsevier.*

**TABLE 7.4** Gliadin-based NPs.

| Protein Formulation | Type of cancer | Key outcomes of in vivo/in vitro study | Ref. |
|---|---|---|---|
| Gliadin HA-UA-GNP | Breast cancer | Significantly high cytotoxic effect and cellular uptake in the 4T1 cell<br>Higher tumor growth suppression and necrosis in mice compared to UA-GNP or free UA | Farzan et al. (2023) |
| Gliadin Curcumin-loaded gliadin nanofibers | Various types of cancer | Controlled release of curcumin<br>Antibacterial activities against Staphylococcus aureus and Escherichia coli<br>Enhanced the antioxidant and antibacterial activities of curcumin | Akman et al. (2019) |
| Gliadin Gliadin/SSPSNPs | Various types of cancer | Improved stability and bioaccessibility of curcumin | Guo et al. (2022) |
| Gliadin Cur-G-P | Breast and osteosarcoma | pH-sensitive nanocomposite with a high curcumin release under acidic pH<br>Cytotoxic effects against MCF7 and Saos2 cell lines | Banaee et al. (2022) |

GNPs: gliadin nanoparticles; HA: hyaluronic acid; UA: usnic acid; SSPS: soluble soybean polysaccharide; G: gliadin; P: pectin.

be obtained from animal and plant sources. Animal lysozymes are classified into three dominant families: chicken-type (c-type), goose-type (g-type), and invertebrate-type (i-type) (Wu et al., 2019). Plant lysozymes are categorized into two groups, namely, family 18 (h-type) or family 19 (b-type), based on their structure. Lysozyme can be commercially sourced from chicken egg white, while native lysozyme is obtained from hen egg white (HEWL) (Zhang et al., 2024). Recombinant lysozyme exhibits high properties in some areas, such as medicine and pharmacology. One method of obtaining recombinant lysozyme is through the expression of protein production in the yeast *Pichia pastoris*. This approach is particularly useful for producing human lysozyme, which holds significant potential as a safe human drug and food additive in the future (He et al., 2020).

Lysozyme has also been utilized in the fabrication of nanocomposites, including protein NPs and protein-conjugated NPs. Its interactions with various NPs have been investigated, owing to lysozyme's stability across broad ranges of pH and temperature, its small molecular weight, and its ease of crystallization. In lysozyme NPs, lysozyme itself forms the NPs, whereas lysozyme-conjugated NPs involve lysozyme being conjugated to NPs made from other organic or inorganic sources (Sarkar et al., 2020).

In a study, lysozyme was combined with hydrophobic drugs such as curcumin, ellipticine, and dasatinib, along with fructose, to create stable NPs approximately 150 nm in size (Cao et al., 2024). The process began by mixing lysozyme with selected hydrophobic drugs and fructose, which served as a template for NP formation. The results demonstrated that lysozyme significantly stabilized curcumin-fructose particles for up to 7 days. Furthermore, dual-drug formulations (lysozyme combined with both ellipticine and dasatinib) were shown to enhance cytotoxicity and cellular uptake in cancer cell lines, including MCF-7, RAW 264.7, and U-87 MG. These findings suggest that lysozyme combined with fructose and hydrophobic drugs can effectively form stable protein-based NPs suitable for drug delivery.

NP targeting using ligands like hyaluronic acid (HA) is crucial for enhancing the specificity and efficacy of DDSs in cancer therapy. By exploiting the overexpression of receptors like CD44 on cancer cells, ligand-conjugated NPs can increase cellular uptake through receptor-mediated endocytosis, leading to improved drug accumulation in tumor tissues while minimizing systemic toxicity. In one study, researchers developed targeted, pH-responsive lysozyme-hyaluronan NPs for the codelivery of 5-fluorouracil (5-FU) and curcumin, aiming to enhance therapeutic outcomes in colorectal cancer (CRC) treatment (Li et al., 2024a). The NPs were composed of lysozyme and hyaluronan, a biopolymer known for its biocompatibility and its ability to target cancer cells due to its affinity for CD44 receptors, which are overexpressed in many tumors. These NPs were designed to respond to the acidic microenvironment, typical of tumor tissues. At lower pH levels, the NPs underwent structural changes that facilitated the release of the encapsulated drugs, thereby enhancing their therapeutic efficacy. This targeting mechanism increased cellular uptake and minimized systemic side effects associated with conventional chemotherapy. In vitro studies showed that the codelivery system significantly enhanced the cytotoxic effects of both 5-FU and curcumin on CRC cell lines compared to free drug treatments.

Cancer nano-theranostics offer a promising multifunctional approach for both diagnosis and treatment of cancer. The development of lysozyme-templated biocompatible fluorescent nanocomposites presents a significant advancement in nanotechnology, especially for cell

**TABLE 7.5** Lysozyme-based NPs.

| Formulation | Type of cancer | Key outcomes of in vivo/in vitro study | Ref. |
|---|---|---|---|
| $SN_{LYZ}$-Cur | Multiple cancer types | Enhancement of the stability and solubility of curcumin in physiological environments<br>pH-dependent drug release | Somu and Paul (2021) |
| LyMs-NRs-5-FU | Leukemia | An ultrasound-responsive drug delivery system<br>Enhanced anticancer activity of 5-FU | Bhargawa et al. (2022) |
| AuNPs-C6H4-4-COOH-lysozyme | Osteosarcoma cancer | No efficient internalization to MG-63 cells | Hameed et al. (2020) |
| EGCG-LYS siRNA | Gastric cancer | Demonstrated superior siRNA delivery efficiency compared to Lipofectamine 2000, resulting in highly effective silencing of the circMAP2K2 gene | Dong et al. (2023) |
| CUR-LYS-CRG | Multiple cancer types | Increased thermal, photo-, and storage stability of CUR with high antioxidant activity | Huang et al. (2020) |

SNLYZ: egg-white lysozyme; LyMs: lysozyme microspheres; NRs: gold nanorods; 5-FU: 5-fluorouracil; AuNPs–$C_6H_4$–4-COOH: gold-aryl nanoparticles; EGCG-LYS: epigallocatechin-3-gallate-lysozyme; CRG: κ-carrageenan.

imaging, hydrogen peroxide sensing, and cancer therapy. Das et al. synthesized fluorescent bimetallic nanocomposites (NCs) of silver-gold (Ag@Au NC) and silver-platinum (Ag@Pt NC) by reducing silver nitrate ($AgNO_3$) on gold NPs and platinum NPs (AuNPs, PtNPs), with lysozyme that acts as a capping agent (Das et al., 2023). In vitro studies, conducted in normal cells including Chinese hamster ovary (CHO) and human umbilical vein endothelial (HUVEC), as well as in vivo studies using the mouse and chicken egg chorioallantoic membrane models, demonstrated the biocompatibility of these nanocomposites. These NCs inhibited cancer cell proliferation when administered to various cancer cell lines, including MCF-7, MDA-MB-231, and B16F10. Intraperitoneal injection of these NCs led to the regression of melanoma tumors in the C57BL/6J mouse model. In another study, Xie et al. synthesized a light-induced, self-assembled nanoplatform system of lysozyme for active tumor targeting, imaging, and chemotherapy (Xie et al., 2019). This system encapsulated quantum dots (QDs) and the anticancer drug PTX within lysozyme. The nanohybrid was further functionalized with the cyclic tripeptide cRGD, containing ligands specifically designed to recognize the overexpressed αvβ3 integrin on cancer cells. They compared LYS-PTX-QDs/NPs, LYS-PTXQDs-RGD/NPs, and free PTX. LYS-PTXQDs-RGD/NPs demonstrated a more significant tumor accumulation, exceptional tumor imaging, and effective tumor inhibition in both in vivo and in vitro experiments. Table 7.5 demonstrates some studies on lysozyme NPs used for cancer therapy.

## 5.5 Silk

Silks are a class of proteins naturally produced by different insects, including silkworms (Bombyx mori), spiders, scorpions, mites, wasps, flies, and bees. The protein extracted from silkworm cocoons (Bombyx mori) comprises a filament core protein called fibroin and a glue-like coating substance made up of sericin (SER) (Saad et al., 2023).

Silk, produced by the glands of lepidopteran insects, is known for its rapid production cycle and exceptional biological properties. These include biodegradability, biocompatibility, nontoxicity, and the ability to induce only a mild immune response. Additionally, silk offers the versatility to form various morphological structures. These qualities have established silk as a highly regarded biomaterial in numerous biomedical applications, including tissue engineering and drug or gene delivery (Hassan et al., 2024).

The unique physicochemical properties of silk arise from the primary and secondary structures of silk proteins. The structure comprises highly repetitive hydrophobic crystalline regions interspersed with hydrophilic noncrystalline blocks. These features enable silk proteins to self-assemble, resulting in strong physical interactions and mechanically robust biomaterials. The crystalline domains in silk enhance hydrophobic carrier–drug interactions, allowing precise control over drug loading and release. Silk NPs, in particular, hold significant potential for systemic cancer drug delivery applications (Florczak et al., 2021).

### 5.5.1 Silk fibroin

SF consists of heavy (~325 kDa) and light chains (~26 kDa) linked by a disulfide bond. The heavy chain features extensive internal repetitive sequences with shorter N- and C-terminal domains, while the light chain contains nonrepetitive amino acid sequences, making it more hydrophilic and elastic. This characteristic enhances the fiber's mobility. Silk's exceptional mechanical properties arise from the interplay of strong crystalline regions and flexible amorphous regions, providing an ideal balance of rigidity and elasticity (Asakura and Williamson, 2023).

Yu Tang et al. developed inhalable Pluronic F127-modified SF NPs loaded with QR (referred to as QR-SF (PF127) NPs). These NPs were designed to overcome the airway mucus barrier and enhance the therapeutic efficacy of QR in cancer treatment. The Pluronic F127 modification reduced interactions between the NPs and mucin proteins, facilitating the diffusion of NPs through the mucus layer. A substantial number of NPs were distributed uniformly across the airway sections in mice, demonstrating excellent retention in the respiratory tract. The therapeutic efficacy of QR-SF (PF127) NPs was evaluated using a mouse melanoma lung metastasis model. The results indicated that a higher concentration of PF127 enhanced the ability to penetrate mucus. After 14 days of pulmonary administration, lungs were analyzed, revealing that QR-SF(PF127) NPs significantly reduced tumor nodules ($10.6 \pm 3.0$) compared to QR-SF NPs, which showed a weaker antitumor effect with $24.6 \pm 6.5$ tumor nodules (Tang et al., 2023).

For the treatment of solid tumors with the anticancer drug ibrutinib (IB), FA-conjugated silk NPs were employed to deliver IB specifically to cancer cell lines HeLa, BT-474, and SKBR3 (Fuster et al., 2023). These cell lines overexpress folate receptors on their surfaces. Cellular uptake studies confirmed that NPs functionalized with FA were effectively internalized by the cancer cells, in contrast to nonfunctionalized NPs. This finding suggests that the cellular uptake was mediated by the overexpressed folate receptors on the cancer cells. In another study, an Acacia gum (AG)-SF hydrogel/polyvinyl alcohol (PVA)/$Fe_3O_4$ magnetic nanobiocomposite was developed (Pajoum et al., 2024). The MTT assay indicated that the synthesized nanobiocomposite was nontoxic to the healthy HEK293T cell line while reducing the viability of BT549 breast cancer cells by 22% at 1.75 mg/mL concentration after 72 hours.

Multimodal cancer therapy has emerged as a powerful approach in oncology, combining different treatment modalities to enhance therapeutic efficacy and overcome the limitations of single-modality treatments. By integrating various strategies such as chemotherapy, radiotherapy, immunotherapy, and targeted therapies, multimodal approaches can address the complex nature of cancer and improve patient outcomes. SF-based nanocarriers have been widely investigated for tumor treatment and suppression. In one study, copper sulfide (CuS) NPs were coated with SF, while PD-L1 siRNA was loaded into the NPs (Zheng et al., 2024a). This approach was combined with immunotherapy to enhance antitumor efficacy. The resulting CuS-PEI-siRNA-SF NPs were evaluated for anticancer activity. The findings revealed that these NPs induced cuproptosis (a type of cell death induced by the buildup of copper in the mitochondria) and exhibited antitumor effects through multiple mechanisms, including PTT, chemodynamic therapy (CDT), and immune activation. In vivo experiments demonstrated that the NPs efficiently accumulated in the tumor tissues of a breast cancer mouse model, effectively inhibited primary tumor growth and lung metastasis, and exhibited excellent biosafety and antitumor activity.

### 5.5.2 Silk sericin

Silk sericins (SSs) are coating proteins that make up approximately 15%–35% of the total cocoon weight. These proteins are rich in polar side chains, comprising hydroxyl, carboxyl, and amino groups, which confer high chemical reactivity to sericins. The amino acids that constitute SSs are predominantly hydrophilic, such as serine and aspartic acid. Structurally, silk sericins feature a combination of β-sheets and random coil domains (Yuan et al., 2024). Sericins have gained increasing attention in biomedicine due to their valuable properties, including enhanced biodegradability, biocompatibility, and cell adhesion. However, the potential of sericins for the development of nanomedicines has not been thoroughly explored (Jia et al., 2022). Despite their advantages, silk sericins exhibit limitations such as high water solubility and physicochemical instability under varying pH levels and temperatures, which restrict their broader application (Crivelli et al., 2018). To address these challenges, sericins can be combined with other polymers to develop DDSs (Deng et al., 2019).

Numerous studies have explored the use of silk sericin-based nanocarriers for tumor treatment and suppression. Sericin's solubility and high hydrophilic amino acid content make it capable of forming stable NPs that encapsulate various compounds. In one study focused on drug delivery for breast cancer, researchers developed protein-coated nanocapsules composed of magnetic silica NPs, phosphotungstate, and sericin (MSN-PTA-SER) (Jalilian et al., 2024). In vitro studies demonstrated that MSN-PTA-SER effectively inhibited cell viability in MCF-7 and ZR-75-1 breast cancer cell lines. The release kinetics of MSN-PTA-SER were pH-dependent, with release percentages of 32% at pH 7% and 65% at pH 6 after 24 h. By the end of a 50-hour period, the release of MSN-PTA-SER reached maximum levels of 40% at pH 7% and 71% at pH 6. This pH-sensitive behavior is attributed to the charge reversal property of sericin at lower pH levels. At a pH of approximately 6, aligning with the isoelectric point (pI) of sericin, the surface charge of these nanocarriers became positive. This transformation enhances their affinity for cell membranes, facilitating the internalization of MSN-PTA-SER by MCF-7 and ZR-75-1 cells (charge reversal effect). Specifically, these pH-sensitive properties enhance the nanocarriers' interaction with cancer cells, enabling more efficient drug delivery directly to tumor sites.

Researchers investigated the potential of sericin-conjugated silver NPs (S-$AgNO_3$ NPs) to combat toxicity induced by 7,12-dimethylbenzanthracene (DMBA), a harmful polycyclic aromatic hydrocarbon (Mumtaz et al., 2024). Silk sericin, extracted from silkworm cocoons, was used to create these NPs due to its antioxidant properties. The study involved administering DMBA to female albino mice over 8–10 weeks, followed by treatment with S-$AgNO_3$ NPs. After 60 days, blood samples were analyzed to assess the NPs' effectiveness in mitigating DMBA-induced toxicity. The treatment led to improved hematological parameters, including increased levels of red blood cells, platelets, lymphocytes, and hemoglobin, while decreasing white blood cells, neutrophils, eosinophils, and monocytes. Biochemical markers such as GSH, lactate dehydrogenase, alkaline phosphatase, and immunoglobulins (IgA, IgG, and IgM) were significantly reduced compared to the DMBA-induced group. Lower levels of these markers indicate a potential decrease in oxidative stress and inflammation, suggesting that the treatment with sericin-conjugated silver NPs (S-$AgNO_3$ NPs) may have effectively mitigated the toxic effects caused by DMBA exposure. Histopathological examinations revealed that S-$AgNO_3$ NPs, particularly at the highest concentration of 200 mg/kg body weight, effectively mitigated DMBA-induced cytotoxic effects in the liver, kidneys, and brain. These results collectively indicate that silk S-$AgNO_3$ NPs possess substantial pharmacological potential in combating cancer-inducing toxicity. In another example, sericin-$AgNO_3$ NP was designed and developed for the treatment of human breast cancer (Mumtaz et al., 2023). Sericin and sericin-$AgNO_3$ NPs exhibited significant time- and dose-dependent antiproliferative effects on MCF-7 and MDA-MB-231 cancer cell lines. After 72 h, MCF-7 cells showed a higher sensitivity to sericin and sericin-$AgNO_3$ NPs (41% inhibition) compared to 24 and 48 h. Similarly, MDA-MB-231 cells demonstrated growth inhibition, though at a lower rate (20%) compared to MCF-7 cells. To confirm the apoptotic effects of sericin and sericin-$AgNO_3$ NPs, qRT-PCR analysis was performed on MDA-MB-231 and MCF-7 breast cancer cells treated with various doses of $AgNO_3$, sericin, sericin-$AgNO_3$ NPs, and tamoxifen. The analysis revealed significant upregulation of growth arrest and cyclin-dependent kinase inhibitor (CDKN1A, CDKN1B) genes and DNA damage (GADD) family gene. These findings revealed that sericin and sericin-$AgNO_3$ NPs exhibited anticancer activity and cytotoxic effects on selected human breast cancer cells by inducing apoptosis and triggering genetic modifications related to the cell cycle arrest gene.

In another study, sericin/propolis/fluorouracil NPs were developed for the treatment of CRC (Diab et al., 2024). These NPs inhibited the PI3K/AKT/mTOR signaling pathway, effectively halting cancer cell growth. The NPs also increased the production of thiobarbituric acid reactive substances (TBARS), which triggered cell apoptosis. In vivo, the nanoformulation induced autophagy and apoptosis while reducing ROS generation. Histopathological analysis confirmed that this nanoformulation exhibits both preventive and therapeutic effects against CRC. Table 7.6 represents some of the nanoformulations based on SF and silk sericin for cancer therapy.

## 5.6 Zein

Zein, a storage protein derived from corn, is known for its versatile properties, including biocompatibility, biodegradability, self-assembly, amphiphilic nature, flexibility, high surface area, low cytotoxicity, and film-forming ability (Sun et al., 2023). It

TABLE 7.6 Silk-based NPs.

| Protein | Formulation | Type of cancer | Key outcomes of in vivo/in vitro study | Ref. |
|---|---|---|---|---|
| Silk fibroin | CUR-HA-PLLA-SF | Various types of cancer | Excellent pH stability in physiological and acidic environments, with inhibition of cell growth and differentiation in cancer cells while showing minimal impact on normal cells. | Lin et al. (2024) |
| Silk fibroin | Ce6/R837@ $Lp_{127}$NPs | Colorectal cancer | Maintained stability during passage through the gastrointestinal tract and achieved efficient colonic mucus infiltration and specific tumor penetration.<br>Induction of immunogenic death of colorectal tumor cells by sonodynamic treatment,<br>Served as a potent in situ vaccine in the presence of R837. | Zu et al. (2024) |
| Silk fibroin | DOX/survivin siRNA/PEI-SFNPs | Breast cancer | Induction of apoptosis with a significant decrease in the expression of survivin mRNA in the 4T1 cell line<br>High accumulation of SFNPs in the tumor in vivo<br>Remarkably reduced growth rate of breast tumors in the mouse model. | Norouzi et al. (2021) |
| Silk fibroin | CS hydrogel/ SF/CN/$Fe_3O_4$ | Breast cancer | Reduction in cell viability of BT549 cells and nontoxicity to the human embryonic kidney cell line (HEK293T). | Sadat et al. (2024) |
| Silk fibroin | TG hydrogel/ SF/$Fe_3O_4$ | Breast cancer | Hemocompatible NPs with low cytotoxicity effect<br>Candidate for hyperthermia cancer therapy and in vivo application. | Eivazzadeh-Keihan et al. (2024) |
| Silk fibroin | cRGD-SFNs-NDI-1 | Human glioma | A significantly higher cytotoxicity effect of NDI-1 delivered by cRGD-SFN on U373 cells compared to D384 cells. | Pirota et al. (2023) |
| Silk fibroin | RSA-DOX-Ato NPs | Breast cancer | very low cytotoxicity of NPs alone to 4T1 cell lines, with high cell growth inhibition of RSA-DOX-Ato NPs<br>enhancement of ROS levels in TME. | Bin et al. (2022) |
| Silk fibroin | SF-FA-Leva TKI | Hepatocellular carcinoma | Tumor-targeted accumulation and potent inhibition of HCC cell survival and angiogenesis<br>Low immunogenicity and high reproducibility of SF. | Yu et al. (2024) |
| Silk fibroin | SFN-AF | Colorectal cancer | SFN enhanced the cytotoxicity of AF in CRC lines. | Pérez-Lloret et al. (2024) |
| Silk fibroin | SMPF-NPs | Breast cancer | High drug-loading capability and selective release of drugs in acidic TME<br>Generate high levels of oxygen under $H_2O_2$ with more reactive oxygen after loading Ce6<br>In vitro and in vivo accumulation in breast tumor tissues,<br>Efficiently killing cancer cells and destroying | Wang et al. (2023a) |

(*Continued*)

**TABLE 7.6** Silk-based NPs.—cont'd

| Protein | Formulation | Type of cancer | Key outcomes of in vivo/in vitro study | Ref. |
|---|---|---|---|---|
| | | | breast cancer tumors through a combination of chemotherapy and photodynamic therapy (PDT). Moreover, providing fluorescence and magnetic resonance (MR) imaging for guiding cancer therapy. | |
| Silk sericin | MR-SNC | Breast cancer | Significant toxicity of NC in MCF-7 cells. The efficient cellular uptake of NC, induction of DNA fragmentation, chromatin condensation, and cell apoptosis at pH 6. | Aghaz et al. (2023) |
| Silk sericin | SF-SS-SMC-α CD47 | Various types of cancer | Enhancement of in vivo retention time to over 21 days and sustained release of αCD47<br>Reprogramming the tumor microenvironment from an immunosuppressive state to an antitumoral one by shifting macrophages from the M2 (antiinflammatory) phenotype to the M1 (proinflammatory) phenotype without requiring additional drugs<br>Strong immunotherapeutic efficacy against local, metastatic, and recurrent tumors. | Gou et al. (2023) |
| Silk sericin | SPIONs-SS-ROR1 siRNA, | TNBC | Significant death of cancer cells and an almost complete shutdown of ROR1 expression<br>Enhanced accumulation of NPs in breast tumors induced by 4T1 cells in BALB/c mice<br>Necrosis occurred 14 days after treatment with the siRNA-loaded NPs and decreased the tumor growth rate in a mouse model. | Shirangi et al. (2022) |
| Silk sericin | AgNPs-sericin-chitosan-ethosome | Nonmelanoma skin carcinoma (NMSC) | Induction of apoptosis and necrosis due to overproduction of superoxide ($O_2$) and nitric oxide (NO) radicals<br>Stimulation of IgM secretion with T-cell-mediated immune response. | Nayak et al. (2021) |
| Silk sericin | SS-Ce6 | Breast cancer | Improved intracellular uptake and tumor sphere penetration compared to free Ce6<br>Minimal cytotoxicity in darkness but significant anticancer effects under low-power laser irradiation<br>Suppressing tumor growth more than free Ce6 without causing noticeable side effects<br>Higher tumor accumulation compared to free Ce6. | Gao et al. (2021) |

TC: tamoxifen citrate; SF: silk fibroin; PEI: polyethylenimine; CS: chitosan; CN: carbon nitride; TG: tragacanth hydrogel; NDI: naphthalene diimide; cRGD: cyclopentapeptides Arg-Gly-Asp; RSA: Arg-Gly-Asp–SF–polylactic acid; Ato: atovaquone; FA: folic acid; Leva: Lenvatinib/TKI: tyrosine kinase inhibitor; SFN: silk fibroin nanoparticles; AF: auranofin; PLLA: poly(l-lactic acid); HA: hypocrellin A; Ce6: chlorin e6; R837: imiquimod; $Lp_{127}$: lipids and pluronic F127; SMPF: silk fibroin-$MnO_2$-PEG-folic acid; MR-SNC: sericin-based nanocarrier to codeliver resveratrol and melatonin; SS: silk sericin; SMC: supramolecular nanocomplex; α CD47: anti-CD47 antibody; SPIONs: superparamagnetic iron oxide nanoparticles; DOX: doxorubicin; Ce6: chlorin e6; PEI: polyethyleneimine.

belongs to a class of proteins known as prolamins, composed primarily of hydrophobic and nonpolar amino acids. It includes four types: α-, β-, γ-, and δ-zein prolamins. Among these, α-zein is particularly suitable for biodegradable film formation and the production of protein-based nanocarriers. These nanocarriers are effectively employed for the coencapsulation of both hydrophobic and hydrophilic active compounds (Yan et al., 2022). Zein contains a high proportion of hydrophobic amino acids in its structure, providing excellent capability for loading hydrophobic drugs and preserving the loaded compounds even in the harsh gastrointestinal environment. The use of zein nanoparticles (ZNPs) as drug carriers shows great promise in the prevention and treatment of cancer (Rahman et al., 2023).

The coencapsulation of multiple bioactive compounds within zein-based systems enables their beneficial interaction within a single delivery system. For instance, incorporating resveratrol (RSV) and QR into zein-based carriers has demonstrated enhanced efficacy in therapeutic applications, including antiinflammatory and anticancer effects (Liu et al., 2022a). In another investigation, Jayalakshmi et al. used gum arabic (GA) as the optimal stabilizer, with GA-stabilized curcumin-loaded ZNPs (GA-Cur-ZNPs) (Jayalakshmi et al., 2025). This NP demonstrated sustained release of Cur over 72 hours and lower $IC_{50}$ values and higher antiproliferative effects on three different cancer cell lines. Additionally, the NP also exhibited superior intracellular uptake and negligible toxicity to human dermal fibroblast cells. Similar uptake results were obtained by Srivastav et al. They developed glycyrrhizic acid-encapsulated zein NPs to target the MCF-7 cell line. In vitro studies demonstrated that glycyrrhizic acid-loaded ZNPs exhibit superior cellular uptake in MCF-7 cells compared to free glycyrrhizic acid, indicating their potential for improved drug delivery. Computational studies complemented the in vitro findings, providing insights into the interactions between glycyrrhizic acid-loaded ZNPs and cellular components, further supporting their targeted delivery mechanism (Srivastav et al., 2024).

To improve breast cancer treatment, silymarin-loaded ZNPs (SLNPs), stabilized by beta-cyclodextrin, were developed (Jaiswal et al., 2024). The study aimed to enhance the solubility and bioavailability of silymarin, a compound recognized for its anticancer properties but limited by poor bioavailability. The SLNPs exhibited a uniform size and spherical shape, with an encapsulation efficiency of 84.32% and a loading efficiency of 15.25%. The NPs demonstrated dose- and time-dependent cytotoxicity, with mechanisms involving the upregulation of the proapoptotic protein Bax and the downregulation of the antiapoptotic protein Bcl-2, indicating that SLNPs promote apoptosis in cancer cells. These findings suggest that SLNPs are more effective than pure silymarin in enhancing bioavailability and therapeutic potential against breast cancer.

Lai et al. developed HA-modified PEG-conjugated ZNPs (zein-PEG/HA NPs) to enhance the cytotoxicity of PTX in SKOV3 ovarian cancer cells (Lai and Lin, 2024). PTX@zein-PEG micelles were complexed with HA, forming PTX@zein-PEG/HA NPs. Cellular uptake was high in CD44-overexpressing SKOV3 cells, and NPs demonstrated significantly greater cytotoxicity than free PTX and PTX@zein-PEG micelles. PTX@zein-PEG/HA NPs induced the highest expression levels of apoptotic proteins, particularly poly(ADP-ribose) polymerase (PARP), in SKOV3 cells. Table 7.7 demonstrates some other examples of zeinNPs application in cancer therapy.

TABLE 7.7 Zein-based NPs.

| Protein | Formulation | Type of cancer | Key outcomes of in vivo/in vitro study | Ref. |
|---|---|---|---|---|
| Zein | Cel/Zein@HA NPs | Hepatocellular carcinoma | Efficient inhibitory effect on tumor proliferation and low systemic toxicity<br>Bax- and Bcl-2-dependent apoptosis in hepatocellular carcinoma cells | He et al. (2024a) |
| Zein | Zein-metformin (ZN8) | Ehrlich carcinoma | Significant reduction in tumor volume in mice-bearing solid<br>Enhancement of the anticancer effects of metformin through sustained release and improved bioavailability | Elmahboub et al. (2024) |
| Zein | Zein-docetaxel-chondroitin sulfate | Prostate cancer | Lower $IC_{50}$ values than free docetaxel<br>Enhanced tumor accumulation of the NPs<br>9.5-fold longer terminal half-life, versus free docetaxel | Lee et al. (2021a, 2021b) |
| Zein | Zein-sodium deoxycholate paclitaxel | Various types of cancer | Significantly increased cytotoxicity compared to free paclitaxel in different cancer cell lines | Gagliardi et al. (2019) |
| Zein | SZBC-NCs | Colon cancer | Significant antioxidant activity and selective cytotoxic effects on HT-29 cells<br>Enhancement of the bioavailability and therapeutic efficacy of the drug | al Alabdullah et al. (2024) |
| Zein | Maytansine/ZNPs | Nonsmall cell lung cancer | A strong inhibitory effect on A549 cells<br>Enhanced cellular uptake<br>No toxic effects | Yu et al. (2020b) |
| Zein | PSA-Zein-HNK-NPs | Breast cancer | Improved colloid stability of zein nanoparticles via PSA coating<br>2.58-fold higher cellular uptake of PSA-Zein-Cou6 nanoparticles in 4T1 cells with higher $IC_{50}$ value and higher growth inhibition compared to nontargeting Zein-Cou6 | Zhang et al. (2022) |
| Zein | Cur-Z/TSNPs | Colon cancer | Good physical and chemical stability with excellent redispersibility<br>Improved the solubilization and bioaccessibility of curcumin | Yuan et al. (2021) |
| Zein | Zein-Doxorubicin Pectin NPs | Cervical cancer | Sustained release of drugs<br>Increased storability and a suitable environment for drugs | Kaushik et al. (2020) |
| Zein | ICG-Z/PC-NP | Various types of cancer | Inhibition of ICG aggregation and degradation in storage resulted in two-fold higher phototoxicity on cancer cells, not in PC-NP, and maintained its photocytotoxicity after | Lee et al. (2021a) |

ZNPs: zein nanoparticles; PSA: polysialic acid; HNK: honokiol; Cur: curcumin; Z: zein; TS: tea saponin; Cel: celastrol; HA: hyaluronic acid; SZBC-NCs: silibinin-loaded zein-β cyclodextrin nanocarriers; PTX: paclitaxel; FA: folate; LVS: lovastatin; ICG: indocyanine green; PC: phosphatidylcholine.

## 5.7 Milk proteins

Milk proteins perform a variety of functions in the body, serving as carriers for micronutrients such as calcium and phosphate, building blocks for various macromolecules, and contributors to passive immunity as elements of the immune system. Casein, which constitutes 80% of the total protein content in cow's milk, is the predominant protein, while the remaining 20% is comprised of whey proteins. It is important to note that these proportions can vary significantly across different species, and in some cases, whey protein may be more abundant than casein (Tavakoli et al., 2021).

### *5.7.1 Casein*

Caseins have evolved from a group of secreted phosphoproteins capable of binding calcium phosphate. They are categorized into four distinct types: αs1, αs2, β-, and κ-caseins. While these types share common characteristics such as being amphiphilic and rich in proline, they differ in their amino acid composition, phosphorus content, and carbohydrate profiles. Notably, caseins lack a well-defined structure, which grants them the flexibility necessary for intermolecular associations (Varanko et al., 2020a). As a result, caseins form micelles ranging in size from 50 to 500 nm, characterized by negatively charged surfaces. The size distribution of these micelles can be readily influenced by environmental factors such as pH, ionic strength, and hydrostatic pressure, owing to their amphiphilic nature and lack of a tertiary structure. While caseins are stable at high temperatures up to approximately 71°C, they are quickly destabilized in acidic environments, making them ideal candidates for oral drug delivery. Leveraging their natural micellar structure, caseins have been successfully employed as drug nanocarriers (Kianfar, 2021).

Khatun and colleagues developed casein nanoparticles (CN NPs) modified with GSH and encapsulated with camptothecin and the NIR dye IR 797 (CCN NPs) for a combinatorial approach to treating triple-negative breast cancer (TNBC) (Khatun et al., 2024b). The interaction of CCN NPs with cell surface receptors altered their anionic charge to catanionic, facilitating the internalization of the NPs by the targeted cells. These "Casein Nano-Trojans" effectively delivered their therapeutic payload into target cells, inhibiting cell proliferation and significantly increasing cell death. Disruption of the mitochondrial membrane potential, along with inhibition of cell migration and regrowth, was observed. Further validation of substantial DNA damage was provided by immunofluorescence, acridine orange/ethidium bromide staining, and nuclear fragmentation assays, which showed elevated expression of γH2AX and p53. Remarkable therapeutic efficacy was demonstrated in 3D spheroids of 4T1 cells and an in vivo mouse model of breast cancer.

In a study, nano-assemblies of bovine casein hydrolyzed peptides (HP) modified with fatty acids containing alkyl chains (C8, C10, C12, and C14) were synthesized to assess the potential activity of the casein peptide and its fatty acid modification in enhancing cytotoxicity against cancer cells (Song et al., 2024). HP-C12 exhibited a flower-shaped morphology with droplet sizes around ~20 nm. HP-C12 demonstrated the highest cytotoxicity, inhibiting MCF-7 cell growth by 66.03% with an $IC_{50}$ value of 7.4 μM. The in vitro cytotoxicity of these NPs against human breast cancer MCF-7 cells was evaluated using the CCK-8 assay and flow cytometry analysis. The NPs significantly impacted the migration, invasion, and apoptosis of MCF-7 cells.

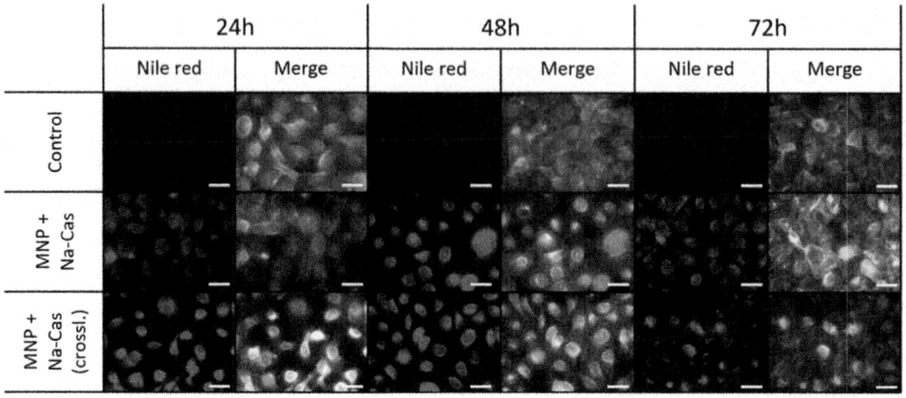


**FIGURE 7.6** Internalization of the model drug (hydrophobic Nile red) into the cells using casein-coated MNPs as the drug carrier adapted from (Wenck et al., 2024). *Adapted from C. Wenck, N. Meier, E. Heinrich, V. Grützner, F. Wiekhorst, R. Bleul, Design and characterisation of casein coated and drug loaded magnetic nanoparticles for theranostic applications. RSC Adv.. 14 (36) (2024), 26388–26399, https://doi.org/10.1039/d4ra02626h under a Creative Commons Attribution 3.0 Unported License.*

In a study, casein NPs were used as a delivery system to evaluate the cytotoxic effects of encapsulated SRF on human hepatocarcinoma cells in vitro. Treatment-induced changes in cell morphology and DNA fragmentation indicated the occurrence of apoptosis. Flow cytometry analysis revealed a G1 phase cell cycle arrest and a 26% increase in the apoptotic cell population compared to the control group (Mittal et al., 2024). SRF-loaded casein NPs induced a 6-fold increase in ROS production in HepG2 cells, compared to a 4-fold increase observed with the free drug. Gene and protein expression analyses through qPCR and western blotting revealed upregulation of the tumor suppressor gene p53, proapoptotic Bax, and caspase-3, alongside downregulation of the antiapoptotic Bcl-2 gene and protein expression, further supporting apoptosis as the mechanism of cell death.

In a nano theranostic platform, Na-caseinate-coated magnetic nanoparticles (MNPs) were prepared to evaluate their potential as a theranostic system (magnetic particle imaging, drug delivery, and magnetic hyperthermia). The MNPs were synthesized continuously, coated with Na-caseinate, and enzymatically crosslinked with transglutaminase (crossl.) to enhance colloidal stability and facilitate drug loading. The results demonstrated effective Nile red loading as a model drug, with efficiency reaching approximately 75%, as well as favorable release kinetics, including successful delivery into cutaneous squamous cell carcinoma cells (Wenck et al., 2024). Fig. 7.6 demonstrates a perinuclear accumulation of the Nile Red fluorescence signal, indicating cellular internalization of MNP + Na-Cas and MNP + Na-Cas (crosslinked) through endocytosis or direct cellular entry mechanisms such as translocation or lipid fusion. Notably, after 24 h, a strong Nile Red signal is visible, suggesting that an uptake process has occurred.

### 5.7.2 *Whey proteins*

β-Lactoglobulin (β-LG) is a globular protein belonging to the lipocalin family, which consists of transport proteins. Increasingly, studies have explored the potential of β-LG as a nanotransporter for various compounds and medications. Oral DDSs have recently gained popularity over intravenous methods; however, developing an effective oral medication requires careful consideration of its stability and absorption within the gastrointestinal tract. Due to its physicochemical properties, β-LG is regarded as a reliable nanotransporter, capable of delivering drugs directly to the intestines while protecting them from the acidic conditions of the stomach that often degrade medications (Varlamova and Zaripov, 2020).

α-Lactalbumin (α-LA) is a whey protein distinguished by its tightly packed, single-chain globular structure and calcium-binding properties, with a relatively low molecular weight of approximately 14.2 kDa. Its exceptional techno-functional properties make it highly versatile for various applications. Complex formation with α-LA, along with the development of NPs, fibrils, nanotubes (NTs), and micelle encapsulation, has shown great promise for nutraceutical delivery. Notably, in its partially unfolded apo-form, α-LA can interact with oleic acid to form a complex that exhibits cytotoxic effects on tumor cells, offering potential benefits for cancer prevention and treatment (Bhutto et al., 2024).

A nanocarrier based on cationic protein, the AS1411 aptamer-conjugated poly-L-lysine/β-LG nanoparticles (BNP/PLL/Apt), was developed in a study (Mohammed and Taheri-Kafrani, 2023). To assess the therapeutic efficacy of BNP/PLL/Apt, DOX was loaded into the nanocarriers with the encapsulation efficiency of 92%. The DOX-encapsulated BNP/PLL/Apt (BNP@DOX/PLL/Apt) exhibited a controlled drug release profile under mildly acidic physiological conditions, which may enhance therapeutic effectiveness in cancer cells. Moreover, BNP@DOX/PLL/Apt demonstrated superior efficacy against MCF-7 tumor cells compared to free DOX. The increased cellular uptake of BNP/PLL/Apt NPs in MCF-7 cells, attributed to the specific interaction between the AS1411 aptamer and its receptor overexpressed on cancer cells, was also observed, in contrast to BNPs lacking aptamer modification.

In a study, an NT-based delivery system/nanocarrier was developed using α-LA (Hou et al., 2024). During the loading process of the antitumor agents, Dox and siRNA, NTs were conjugated with the tLyp-1 peptide to specifically target the neuropilin-1 receptor, which is present on the surface of MDA-MB-231 cancer cells. The efficiency of cellular uptake and the tumor accumulation of NTs in MDA-MB-231 breast cancer cells were significantly enhanced following tLyp-1 modification. In vitro, the relative viability of MDA-MB-231 cells was reduced by 70.1% after treatment with tLyp-1/NTs/Dox/siRNA. Ultimately, a combined anticancer effect of Dox and siRNA loaded in tLyp-1/NTs was observed in the treatment of MDA-MB-231 tumor-bearing mice.

In another study, α-LA mRNA-lipid nanoparticles (α-LNP) were developed for the treatment of TNBC (He et al., 2024b). The α-LNPs induced the production of specific IgG antibodies and stimulated IFN-γ-secreting T cells in vivo. Additionally, the safety of α-LNPs was verified in vivo. When administered before tumor implantation, α-LNPs demonstrated a preventive effect against the growth of 4T1 tumors and improved survival in the tumor model by stimulating memory immune responses. Furthermore, α-LNP treatment, when combined with surgical removal of the tumor, effectively slowed tumor progression and metastasis in the TNBC model.

Lactoferrin (Lf) is a glycoprotein known for its remarkable properties, including antimicrobial, antioxidant, antiinflammatory, and anticancer effects. It functions widely throughout the human body, with Lf receptors present in various tissues. Lf is used in NP technology as a coating material, encapsulated biomolecule, and even as an NP itself. Due to the widespread presence of Lf receptors, Lf can be employed as a surface material in NPs for targeted delivery, particularly for certain types of cancer. Additionally, Lf can be synthesized in NP form. Beyond its effects on cytokine production, Lf can inhibit the growth and spread of cancer cells, indirectly trigger apoptosis by promoting caspase activation, and may also modulate gene expression (Akdaşçi et al., 2024).

Lactoferrin shows promise in the treatment of CRC; however, its oral delivery presents challenges that hinder its clinical use. In a study, dual-responsive engineered lactoferrin nanostructured microbeads were developed to address these delivery challenges (Abd Elhamid et al., 2024). Mesalazine (MSZ) was conjugated with lactoferrin to create amphiphilic conjugate NPs, and RSV was subsequently encapsulated within the hydrophobic core of the LF-MSZ NPs. A thermoresponsive poly N-isopropylacrylamide shell was added, and the particles were further encapsulated in pectin–alginate beads for gastrointestinal resistance and pH responsiveness. These NPs demonstrated internalization and cytotoxic effects against HCT colon cancer cells through LF receptor-mediated endocytosis. Thermal triggering and controlled drug release were achieved, while the coatings protected the drugs from degradation. When orally administered, the microbeads significantly reduced tumor burden in a mouse model of colon cancer, leading to decreased carcinoembryonic antigen (CEA) levels and increased antioxidant enzyme activity.

Zayed et al. developed a multiparticulate system responsive to ligand and pH for the oral delivery of drugs to the colon (Zayed et al., 2024). Calcium alginate/hydroxyethyl cellulose microbeads (CA/HEC-MBs) were designed for the combined delivery of indomethacin and QR to target colon cancer treatment. To enhance tumor targeting, both NPs were coated with Lf, facilitating interaction with Lf receptors found on cancerous HCT-116 cells. Among various simulated gastrointestinal fluids, the developed CA/HEC-MBs containing the NPs selectively released the drugs exclusively in the colon (pH 6.8). When administered orally to mice bearing colorectal tumors, the Lf-targeted nanostructured microbeads demonstrated enhanced antitumor efficacy in vivo. The microbeads effectively reduced the levels of CEA and proliferating cell nuclear antigen, as well as serum concentrations of IL-6, IL-1, and TNF-$\alpha$. Apoptosis was enhanced, as evidenced by an increased Bax/Bcl2 ratio and heightened activation of caspase-3 and caspase-9.

A study developed lactoferrin-functionalized carboxymethyl dextran-coated egg albumin nanoconjugates (LF-CMD@CAP-EGA-NCs) for the targeted delivery of capsaicin (an anticancer compound) to enhance its efficacy in treating CRC (Rajput et al., 2024). The nanoconjugate exhibited increased cytotoxicity in HCT-116 and LoVo cell lines, attributed to the overexpression of LF receptors in colorectal HCT-116 cells. Furthermore, LF-CMD@CAP-EGA-NCs displayed excellent biocompatibility.

In another study, biosynthesized selenium nanocomposites (Se NPs) were successfully conjugated to apo-lactoferrin (ALF), forming the ALF-Se NPs drug conjugate. This conjugate was extensively investigated for its in vitro properties and anticancer mechanism. LF-CMD@CAP-EGA-NCs exhibited a sustained release of CAP ($76.52 \pm 1.01\%$ in 24 h) in a pH 5.8 buffer, with anomalous transport due to the CMD and EGA matrix shell. The nanoconjugate showed enhanced cytotoxicity in HCT-116 and LoVo cell lines, attributed to the overexpression of LF receptors in colorectal HCT-116 cells. Additionally, LF-CMD@CAP-EGA-NCs demonstrated excellent biocompatibility, as evidenced by the FHC-CRL-1831 cell line. Table 7.8 shows the therapeutic outcomes of some milk protein NPs in cancer therapy.

TABLE 7.8 Milk protein-based NPs.

| Protein | Formulation | Type of cancer | Key outcomes of in vivo/in vitro study | Ref. |
|---|---|---|---|---|
| Casein | CCS NPs | Breast cancer | Excellent biocompatibility in fibroblast cell lines L929, NIH-3T3, and zebrafish embryos<br>Enhanced uptake of CCS NPs in zebrafish embryos and 4T1 cells, cancer cell toxicity of nearly 80%–85%, subcellular mitochondrial localization, alterations of mitochondrial membrane potential, lysosomal localization, and ROS generation that cause cancer cell apoptosis<br>Growth inhibition of 4T1 cells' colony and antimetastatic activity<br>Upregulation of γ-H2AX causes DNA damage, downregulation of the PARP protein related to DNA repair, and increased level of the CHOP protein marker for the endoplasmic reticulum stress-mediated cell death<br>Deep tumor penetration with significant therapeutic efficacy for CCS NP in 3D model of 4T1 cells | Khatun et al. (2023) |
| Casein | DRB-loaded casein NPs | Acute lymphocytic leukemia | pH-responsive and sustained drug release<br>Modification of the metrics of mitochondrial respiration and ATP generation, and significant cytotoxic effects on lymphoblastic cell lines | Zahariev et al. (2023) |
| Casein | MSNs-CN-VTD | Colorectal cancer (CRC) | Significant affinity of negatively surface-charged MSNs toward positively charged cancer cells in the presence of MMP-7<br>A dramatic increase in drug release efficiency<br>Confirmed the effectiveness of the enzyme-triggered mechanism | Wijewantha et al. (2021) |
| Casein | CCM@PTX | Cervical and prostate cancer | Greater cytotoxic effects of CCM@PTX compared to the free drug<br>Promising candidate for parenteral delivery, allowing for subsequent accumulation in the TME through passive targeting and facilitating the enzyme-triggered release of PTX | Cuggino et al. (2021) |
| Casein | CAAT NPs | TNBC | Successful internalization in 4T1 cells with minimal toxicity to healthy cell lines and organisms<br>Subcellular distribution, changes in | Khatun et al. (2024a) |

(Continued)

**TABLE 7.8** Milk protein-based NPs.—cont'd

| Protein | Formulation | Type of cancer | Key outcomes of in vivo/in vitro study | Ref. |
|---|---|---|---|---|
| | | | mitochondrial membrane potential, nuclear fragmentation, reduced migration, and growth inhibition in 4T1 cells<br>Considerable therapeutic effectiveness in a three-dimensional model of 4T1 cells | |
| β-Lactoglobulin | FBZ-MCM-BLG | Prostate cancer | Improve the solubility and bioavailability of fenbendazole (FBZ)<br>Higher cytotoxicity effects of FBZ-MCM-BLG against PC-3 cells when compared to FBZ and FBZ-MCM NPs<br>Increased production of ROS and inhibition of the migration of PC-3 cells compared to the FBZ and FBZ-MCM NPs | (Koohi Moftakhari Esfahani et al., 2022) |
| α-Lactalbumin | MSN-BAMLET/DTX | Cervical and breast cancer | A sustained and pH-responsive drug release with good biocompatibility enhanced the cytotoxic effect against cancer cells<br>Enhanced the dispersibility of the composite in solution and reduced cancer cell migration due to the incorporation of the lipoprotein complex in MSN-BAMLET<br>Successful cancer eradication and extended survival in vivo | Pei et al. (2022) |
| α-Lactalbumin | AuQCs-α-Lactalbumin | Breast cancer | Safe and biodegradable NPs<br>Extended circulation times, minimal accumulation within the RESs, prolonged retention in tumors, negligible toxicity, and effective renal clearance<br>Inhibition of the MAPK and PI3K-AKT pathways due to the formation of an anticancer lipoprotein complex with oleic acid, facilitated by the partially unfolded structure of alpha-lactalbumin within the nanoprobe | Yang et al. (2020) |
| Lactoferrin | LF-IONPs | Gastric cancer | Improved cytotoxic effects after hyperthermia treatment (cell death of 67.75 ± 5.2%) with a reduction in cell migration and the highest inhibition after 36 h of treatment<br>These results imply that LF-IONPs have potential utility in the targeted hyperthermia therapy for gastric cancer | Attri et al. (2023) |
| Lactoferrin | CNM/NAR-loaded LF/ | Breast and lung cancer | A slow release of CNM and NAR of dual drug-loaded LF/NaCAS-coated zein NPs in simulated gastric fluid (SGF) with an | Mohamed et al. (2024) |

**TABLE 7.8** Milk protein-based NPs.—cont'd

| Protein | Formulation | Type of cancer | Key outcomes of in vivo/in vitro study | Ref. |
|---|---|---|---|---|
| | NaCAS-coated zein NPs | | enhancement of bioavailability compared to NaCAS-coated NPs, free CNM, and free NAR<br>Good physical stability and hemocompatibility<br>Improved liver architecture, reduced inflammation, and enhanced antioxidant potential, without signs of toxicity in DOX-induced oxidative stress mice, suggesting a reduction in ROS-mediated damage | |
| Lactoferrin | DTX-LfNPs | Prostate cancer | Greater (2.5 times) antiproliferative activity than free DTX and doubled drug bioavailability in the prostate<br>In an orthotopic prostate cancer model, DTX-LfNPs<br>Significantly improved anticancer activity of DTX and reduction of prostate tissue weight and volume<br>Enhancement of the synergistic effect of DTX in inhibiting metastasis, evidenced by a decrease in lactate dehydrogenase, alkaline phosphatase, TNF alpha, and IFNγ levels | Muj et al. (2023) |
| Lactoferrin | DTX-ATR-LF | Colon cancer | Prolonged release of the NPs from the nanocarrier-loaded microdoses in the rat cecum<br>Inhibition of p-AKT, p-ERK1/2, and NF-κB in vivo, suggesting microdoses are superior to NPs in colorectal cancer treatment | Elmorshedy et al. (2023) |
| Lactoferrin | LF-FNPs-LP-CNPs | Colorectal adenocarcinoma, breast cancer, hepatocellular carcinoma | The combination of LPCNPs and LFFNPs showed the most significant growth inhibition against Caco2, HepG2, and MCF7 cells when LPCNPs and LFFNPs were combined, lowering the half-maximal inhibitory concentration ($IC_{50}$) compared to nanometals, LP, LF, and individual nanoproteins<br>Induction of the highest apoptosis in the combination of LPCNPs and LFFNPs with increased annexin-stained apoptotic cells, a higher G0 population, and notable changes in the expression of apoptosis regulators (p53 and Bcl2), along with a strong reduction in the proliferation marker (Ki67)<br>In silico enhancement of AMP-activated | El-Fakharany et al. (2022) |

(*Continued*)

TABLE 7.8 Milk protein-based NPs.—cont'd

| Protein | Formulation | Type of cancer | Key outcomes of in vivo/in vitro study | Ref. |
|---|---|---|---|---|
| | | | protein kinase (AMPK) activity and inhibition of migration-related proteases, such as cathepsin B and MMP9 | |
| Lactoferrin | CS/Lf/PTS-SLNs | Breast cancer | In vitro investigations conducted on demonstrated<br>Significant cytotoxic effects of CS/Lf/PTS-SLNs on triple-negative MDA-MB-231 cells with an enhancement of antimigratory impact and cellular uptake compared to the PTS solution<br>Tumor growth reduction (2.4-fold) in an orthotopic cancer model compared to the PTS solution. | Aly et al. (2023) |
| Lactoferrin | LF-C2 NPs | Glioma | Effective elimination of glioma cells by triggering both apoptosis and autophagic cell death<br>Traversing of the BBB, inhibition of the growth of glioma, and preferential accumulation within the tumor tissue<br>Significant reduction OF the side effects associated with C2 | Zhang et al. (2023) |

CCS NPs: camptothecin casein nanoparticles; DRB: daunorubicin hydrochloride; MSNs: mesoporous silica nanoparticles; CN: casein; VTD: veratridine; CCM: crosslinked casein micelles; PTX: paclitaxel; CAAT: 7-amino-6H-anthra[9,1-cd] isothiazol-6-one casein; FBZ-MCM-BLG: fenbendazole-Mobil Composition of Matter-β-lactoglobulin; MSN-BAMLET-DTX: mesoporous silica nanoparticles-bovine α-lactalbumin made lethal against tumor cell-docetaxel; LF-IONPs: lactoferrin-iron oxide nanoparticles; DTX: docetaxel; C2: Au complex; ATR: atorvastatin; CS/Lf/PTS-SLNs: chondroitin-sulfate-lactoferrin-solid lipid nanoparticles; LF-FNPs-LP-CNPs: lactoferrin-Fe NPs-lactoperoxidase-Cu NPs/CNM/NAR-loaded LF/NaCAS-coated zein NPs: cinnamaldehyde-naringin-loaded lactoferrin sodium caseinate-coated zein NPs.

## 5.8 Virus-like polypeptides

Viral protein nanoparticles (ViP NPs), including VLPs and virosomes, are biocompatible, biodegradable, and functional structures. The absence of a viral genome eliminates the safety concerns associated with viruses. VLPs, which mimic the structure of viruses but lack genetic material, are noninfective. They can be prepared by expressing complete viruses and removing the viral genome or by directly expressing viral capsid proteins from a vector. Therapeutic agents can be incorporated into the cavity of the viral NP, where they are protected from degradation, or into the coating layers, which can be functionalized with targeting moieties for specific cell types. Both VLPs and virosomes have intrinsic targeting properties. For example, the hepatitis E virus (HEV) has a selective tropism for the liver, so HEV-VLPs can be used as vehicles for targeted liver delivery. This ability allows them to overcome the limitations of targeted delivery that other NPs face (Mellid-Carballal et al., 2023).

Despite numerous efforts, only a limited number of liposomes and protein-based NPs, such as Abraxane and Doxil, have received approval for the administration of cancer therapies. Furthermore, many of these nanomaterials exhibit instability and are quickly eliminated, a process facilitated by DCs and phagocytes. Recently, virus-like particles, a new type of nanocarrier, have gained attention as a potential delivery method (Yuan et al., 2023).

For the treatment of metastatic castration-resistant prostate cancer, VLPs carrying a suicide gene, thymidine kinase, driven by the PSA promoter (PSAtk-VLPs), were used. This gene can inhibit tumor growth in animal models of human prostate cancer. The PSAtk-VLPs were systemically administered via the tail vein of mice-bearing castration-resistant prostate cancer (CRPC) orthotopic tumors, along with the prodrug ganciclovir. The results demonstrated that systemic administration of PSAtk-VLPs effectively suppressed growth in mouse CRPC orthotopic tumors and significantly reduced metastasis (Chou et al., 2024).

The effectiveness of therapeutic cancer vaccines is limited by the low antigenicity of soluble antigens and the presence of immunosuppressive tumor-associated macrophages (TAMs) that facilitate tumor growth. In a recent study, a dual-targeting nano-vaccine (NV) based on virus-like particles (VLPs) derived from hepatitis B core antigen, known as N-M2T-gp100 HBc NV, was developed with the capability to target both specific intercellular adhesion molecule grabbing nonintegrin (SIGNR+), DCs, and TAMs, as well as a high-density display of TAAs. In a melanoma model, VLPs significantly inhibited tumor progression and enhanced long-term immune protection. This impressive antitumor response was accomplished by effectively stimulating T cells and transforming M2-like TAMs (Wang et al., 2024). Table 7.9 presents some of the nanoformulations based on VLP NPs in cancer therapy.

**TABLE 7.9** VLP-based NPs.

| Protein | Formulation | Type of cancer | Key outcomes of in vivo/in vitro study | Ref. |
|---|---|---|---|---|
| VLP | 1V209 or poly(I:C) + VNPs/VLPs | Various types of cancer | Significant activation of immune cells and promotion of the production of the proinflammatory cytokine interleukin 6 by the conjugation of 1V209 to CPMV, CCMV, and Qβ virus-like particles<br>Reduction of tumor growth and prolonged survival in mice compared to those treated with free 1V209 or a simple mixture of 1V209 and viral particles | Jung et al. (2023) |
| VLP | LNPs/VLPs + anti-CD3/anti-NKp46/anti-CD14 | Ovarian cancer | A 2 to 7 times increase in the immune cells' capacity to kill ovarian cancer cells | Beltran-Garcia et al. (2023) |
| VLP | VLP-GOx@HSA | Breast cancer | Significant cytotoxic effects on breast cancer cell cultures<br>Production of oxygen due to the CAT antioxidant enzyme, triggered by the substantial generation of hydrogen peroxide from the activity of GOx. | Gama et al. (2023) |
| VLP | DOX-VLDP | Melanoma tumor | A delayed and endocytosis-dependent DOX-VLDP internalization in melanoma tumor cells<br>Enhanced and selective cytotoxicity against | Gonçalves et al. (2023) |

*(Continued)*

**TABLE 7.9** VLP-based NPs.—cont'd

| Protein | Formulation | Type of cancer | Key outcomes of in vivo/in vitro study | Ref. |
|---|---|---|---|---|
| | | | tumor cells<br>Induction of apoptosis and autophagy | |
| VLP | HBc VLPs | Colorectal cancer | Elevation of the survival rate of mice with MC-38 tumors by pairing of PDT and HBc VLPs<br>Inhibition of tumor recurrence in vivo by boosting immune memory T cells following treatment | Hao et al. (2022) |
| VLP | GE11-MrNV-VLP | Colorectal cancer | The findings indicated that both chimeric R-MrNV and E-MrNV are capable of encapsulating cargo like exogenous DNA and effectively delivering it to cells that express EGFR. This research highlights the potential application of surface-modified virus-like particles derived from shrimp viruses as nanocarriers for targeted delivery of cancer therapeutics. | Grataitong et al. (2021) |
| VLP | VLP-OVAB and VLP-OVAT | Lymphoma | Promotion of the production of antibodies against the peptide antigen by VLP-OVAB<br>Robust activation of a CTL response specific to the T epitope by VLP-OVAT<br>Restriction of tumor growth in vivo by VLP-OVAT | Li et al. (2021) |
| VLP | ES2B-C001 cVLP Vaccine | Breast cancer | Induction of robust antibody responses against HER-2, involving all Ig isotypes, that lasted for several months<br>Effective suppression of the three-dimensional growth of both trastuzumab-sensitive and trastuzumab-resistant human HER-2+ breast cancer cells | Ruzzi et al. (2022) |
| VLP | DARPinEGFR-HBVSpyTag (yCD2, GFP) VLPs | Breast cancer | Improved absorption and toxicity in EGFR-overexpressing triple-negative breast cancer (TNBC) cells compared to noncancerous breast epithelial cells | Yur et al. (2023) |

1V209: TLR7 agonist; VNPs: virus nanoparticles; VLPs: virus-like particles; GOX: glucose oxidase; HSA: human serum albumin; VLDP: virus-like DNA particles; DOX: doxorubicin; HBc: hepatitis B core; MrNV: *Macrobrachium rosenbergii* nodavirus; GE11: chimeric peptide, which have been shown to target the EGFR in several human cancer cells; OVAB peptide and OVAT peptide: the B and T epitopes of ovalbumin; DARPin: EGFR-binding designed ankyrin repeat protein; yCD2: yeast cytosine deaminase.

## 5.9 Elastin

Elastin is a crucial protein found in the ECM and connective tissues, particularly in organs requiring elasticity and resilience, such as the skin, ligaments, lungs, and blood vessels. Its distinctive properties influence its recombinant production, purification, drug-loading capacity, and in vivo behavior. The soluble precursor of elastin, tropoelastin, features alternating hydrophobic and hydrophilic regions that undergo enzymatic crosslinking through lysine residues in the extracellular environment. While elastin fibrils are durable and insoluble, their properties posed challenges in early efforts to utilize elastin as a biomaterial. However, ELPs, soluble recombinant forms of elastin, have been widely adopted for drug delivery applications (Varanko et al., 2020a).

### 5.9.1 *Elastin-like polypeptides*

ELPs exhibit nonimmunogenicity, biocompatibility, and biodegradability, making them ideal for transporting and releasing biologically active substances. As a result, ELPs have been effectively employed in a wide range of biomedical applications, including drug and vaccine delivery. Their straightforward manufacturing process, thermal responsiveness, and capacity for self-assembly into nanostructures position them as promising materials for NP development. Self-assembling ELP-based NPs have been designed to deliver therapeutic agents for treating various diseases (Varanko et al., 2020b).

The CD99 protein is highly expressed in acute myeloid leukemia. In a recent study, a dual-function construct, anti-CD99-A192 scFv-ELP, was developed to target leukemic cells while simultaneously activating T cells. Treatment of T cells with anti-CD99-A192 significantly promoted their proliferation. Cytokine analysis revealed substantial increases in IL-1β/IL-1F2 and TNF-α levels, along with a notable reduction in IL-8 levels. Additionally, elevated concentrations of granulocyte-macrophage colony-stimulating factor (GM-CSF) and IL-16 were observed. Enhanced apoptosis was detected in MV4-11 cells, accompanied by a reduction in the number of viable leukemic cells. These findings indicate that the anti-CD99-A192 scFv-ELP NP effectively promotes T-cell proliferation, enhances activation markers, and boosts the production of proinflammatory cytokines (Kadam et al., 2024).

The downregulation or loss of miR-34a expression is associated with various cancers, as this microRNA exhibits tumor-suppressing properties. Low levels of miR-34a are correlated with larger tumor sizes. Jisan Hong et al. demonstrated that ELP-based NPs can efficiently deliver miRNA to cancer cells, potentially regulating gene expression and inhibiting tumor growth. After successfully synthesizing the miRNA-34a/Tat-A86 nanoformulation, its effects on LLC cells were extensively evaluated both in vitro and in vivo. The miRNA-34a/Tat-A86 nanoformulation demonstrated exceptional potential for delivering miRNA-34a to tumor sites by specifically targeting IL-4R, a receptor predominantly expressed in various solid tumors. The nanocomplexes exhibited strong affinity for cellular membranes, facilitating efficient cellular uptake and maximizing apoptosis induction. In 3D LLC spheroids, the Tat-A86 delivery system showcased impressive penetration capabilities. In vivo tumor inhibition studies revealed that Tat-A86 NPs were significantly more effective in suppressing tumor growth. These findings support the potential of the Tat-A86 delivery system for broader applications across diverse cancer types and various miRNAs (Hong et al., 2024).

In another study, the cowpea chlorotic mottle virus (CCMV) was selected as a nanodelivery platform due to its uniform and consistent size and natural capacity for regulated self-assembly. Leveraging these attributes, CCMV-based NPs were engineered and modified with ELPs at their N-terminal region. The resulting EVLP@DOX NPs exhibited a consistent size distribution, enhancing their uptake by tumor cells and facilitating efficient drug release, thereby improving antitumor efficacy. In vivo studies demonstrated that these NPs could stimulate an immune response within the TME, further suppressing tumor growth. Moreover, they exhibited significant therapeutic efficacy and favorable safety profiles in murine melanoma and CRC models (Shen et al., 2024).

A multifunctional ELP carrier system was developed and synthesized by Aayush et al. This system utilized a layer-by-layer (LbL) formulation method designed to deliver nucleic acid (NA) cargo, including siRNA and plasmids. The physical properties and biological efficacy of the LbL ELP nucleic acid nanoparticles (LENNs) were evaluated in murine and human bladder tumor cell lines. LENN complexes adhered to bladder tumor cells within 30 min and were rapidly internalized, releasing their NA cargo within 60 min. The findings highlight the development of a highly adaptable NA delivery system, notable for its versatile targeting capability, compatibility with various cargo sizes, and customizable disassembly kinetics. This innovative approach offers a promising alternative to traditional lipid NP formulations, which often suffer from inefficiency and physicochemical instability, as well as viral vectors, which are challenged by manufacturing complexities and immune rejection issues. The flexible ELP-based nanocarrier provides a biomanufacturable, biodegradable, biocompatible, and highly customizable solution for nucleic acid delivery. It is designed to effectively target cells by interacting with overexpressed surface receptors, paving the way for more efficient and reliable therapeutic applications (Aayush et al., 2024).

A fusion protein combining a HER2-targeted affibody with an ELP was developed and synthesized. This construct was subsequently conjugated with monomethyl auristatin E to form a protein-drug conjugate named Z-ELP-M. Leveraging its temperature-responsive properties, Z-ELP-M rapidly self-assembles into nanomicelles at body temperature. With its active targeting capability and distinctive nanostructure, Z-ELP-M demonstrates enhanced cellular uptake and deeper tumor penetration in vitro. Additionally, Z-ELP-M exhibited superior tumor-targeting efficiency and significant antitumor activity against HER2-positive ovarian cancer, effectively inhibiting tumor growth (Li et al., 2024b).

In a study, elastin-like peptides were engineered to create NPs responsive to NIR light. This innovative design enables the NPs to undergo substantial size reduction, enhancing their ability to penetrate dense tumor structures. Specifically, the formulation was tailored to respond to NIR light, facilitating a rapid size decrease from approximately 120–25 nm upon exposure, which allowed deeper penetration into three-dimensional (3D) cancer spheroids. Additionally, the NPs were equipped with targeting ligands to improve their specificity for cancer cells. The study demonstrated that the light-responsive properties of these ELP-based NPs significantly enhanced their penetration capabilities in 3D cancer spheroids. This effectiveness was further validated through in vitro studies on epidermoid carcinoma cell lines (Le et al., 2023). Table 7.10 presents some examples of ELP-based NPs used in cancer therapy.

## 6. Protein nanoparticles marketed and under clinical trial

The search for FDA-approved PNPs and those undergoing clinical trials for cancer therapy was conducted by using "protein nanoparticles" and "protein nanoparticle" in the "Other terms" field, along with "cancer" in the "Condition or disease" field. Overall, as of 1990, 40 clinical trials were listed as "completed," and another 38 were "active" or "recruiting" on ClinicalTrials.gov. In 1999, denileukin diftitox (DAB-IL-2, Ontak (Eisai Inc.)), a diphtheria toxin-based fusion protein that depletes CD25-positive cells, including Tregs, was approved by the FDA for the treatment of persistent cutaneous T-cell lymphoma (Cheung et al., 2019; Foss, 2006). Abraxane/ABI-007 (Celgene Pharmaceuticals, Inc.), an albumin-

**TABLE 7.10** ELP-based NPs.

| Protein | Formulation | Type of cancer | Key outcomes of in vivo/in vitro study | Ref. |
|---|---|---|---|---|
| ELP | ELP-AuNPs | Various types of cancer | A shift to longer wavelengths of the localized surface plasmon resonance peak of embedded gold NPs following cluster size increase<br>The construction of NPs aggregates below the ELP transition temperature, enabling near-quantitative cargo delivery | Cai et al. (2024) |
| ELP | aPD-L1/GEM-encapsulated ELP hydrogel | Melanoma | Sustained release of chemotherapeutics<br>Effective killing of melanoma cells and enhancement of the upregulation of PD-L1 in tumor cells<br>A 3.0-fold increase in tumor-infiltrating $CD8^+$ T cells and a 60% reduction in Tregs compared to the PBS group | Yu et al. (2023) |
| ELP | ELP-Rapa | Breast cancer | Nonhemolytic NPs<br>No interference with plasma coagulation or platelet function, and no activation of the complement system<br>Significant cellular uptake in HepG2 cells and trafficked to acidic organelles, likely lysosomes<br>Enhancement of oxidative stress four-fold compared to free drug or ELP controls<br>No hepatotoxicity in a mouse model with orthotopic hormone receptor-positive BT-474 breast tumors after high-dose ELP-Rapa administration (about 10 times the therapeutic dose) over 1 month<br>Effectively suppressed tumor growth and mTOR signaling without affecting body weight | Peddi et al. (2020) |
| ELP | GE11&PCK-ELPs-mCherry | Colon adenocarcinoma | A 2-fold increase in apoptotic cell death in vitro<br>Significant suppression of tumor growth in mice-bearing colon cancer xenograft | (Liu et al., 2022b) |
| ELP | ELP/MMP/CPP/Dox | Breast cancer | A 4-fold enhancement in cell penetration and increased death in breast cancer cells, including doxorubicin-resistant ones | Ryu et al. (2021) |
| ELP | Tat-$A_1E_{28}$ or Tat-$A_4V_{48}$/siRNA | Breast cancer | Enhancement of transfection efficiency and stability<br>Targeted polypeptides (TatA1E28 or TatA4V48)<br>Selective delivery of siRNA to tumor cells via receptor-specific interactions followed by facilitated endosomal and lysosomal escape, and release of the gene into the cytosol<br>Validated results in a murine breast carcinoma 4T1 allograft mouse model | Yi et al. (2020) |

(*Continued*)

TABLE 7.10 ELP-based NPs.—cont'd

| Protein | Formulation | Type of cancer | Key outcomes of in vivo/in vitro study | Ref. |
|---|---|---|---|---|
| ELP | ELP-Dox | Glioma | Enhancement of drug release rates at lower pH levels<br>Reduction of the survival and proliferation of GBM cells. | Dragojevic et al. (2022) |
| ELP | Azurin-ELPNPs | Prostate cancer | Size-dependent cytotoxicity of azurin-ELP d-bc<br>Six times higher killing of LNCaP cells by azurin-ELP d-bc in the cross-linked micelles than the unimeric form of azurin-ELP at 5 μM concentration. | Bhardwaj and Mishra (2024) |
| ELP | AP1-ELP-KLAK | Glioblastoma | A 2- to 3-fold increase in cell death in D54/efflux and U97MG/efflux cells compared to the control<br>A time-dependent increase in caspase-3 activity in D54/C cells and tumor-bearing mice with AP1-ELP-KLAK treatment<br>Reduced tumor growth by inducing apoptosis in D54/efflux tumor-bearing mice. | Sarangthem et al. (2021) |
| ELP | $^{131}$Iodine-ELP-PTX-NPs | Pancreatic tumor | Significant reduction of tumor growth and improved survival rates by combination therapy compared to either treatment modality alone. | Schaal et al. (2022) |
| ELP | AP1-ELPs | Breast cancer | Superior binding, faster entry, and more efficient processing via the IL-4R-dependent endocytic pathway of high-molecular-weight AP1-ELP compared to low-molecular-weight polypeptides<br>Better tumor penetration, prolonged retention in tumor tissue, and reduced nonspecific accumulation in vital organs by high molecular weight micelle-forming AP1-ELPs. | Sarangthem et al. (2020) |

GEM: gemcitabine; aPD-L1: antibody PD-1; Dox: doxorubicin; CPP: cell-penetrating peptide; MMP: matrix metalloproteinase; KLAK: proapoptotic peptide; PTX: paclitaxel; AP1: IL-4 receptor-targeting ligand.

bound NP formulation of PTX, is another FDA-approved protein nanotechnology-based chemotherapeutic agent. This NP formulation has been approved for the treatment of multiple indications in oncology, including metastatic breast cancer (2005), locally advanced or metastatic NSCLC (2012), metastatic adenocarcinoma of the pancreas (2013), and advanced gastric cancer (in Japan, 2013; Desai, 2016). Moreover, FYARRO (a sirolimus albumin-bound nanoformulation) has recently received FDA approval for intravenous administration in adult patients with locally advanced, unresectable, or metastatic malignant perivascular epithelioid cell tumors (PEComa). This treatment is currently the first and only FDA-approved therapy for advanced malignant PEComa in adults (Hua et al., 2024).

# 7. Concluding remarks

Protein-based nanosystems have increasingly come to the forefront, gaining far more attention than other types of NPs. Although protein nanoformulations constitute only a small fraction, their remarkable biocompatibility, full degradability, easy and cheap production, proper uptake by cells, and binding of the drug to specific sites render them a compelling option for the development of next-generation NP DDSs. At present, a number of protein-based nanotherapeutics, including Abraxane and virus-like particles, have either been approved or are approaching the final phases of clinical trials. Naturally occurring PNPs, such as albumin, animal-derived proteins, and plant-based proteins, offer promising platforms for drug delivery in cancer therapy. These PNPs enhance the delivery of therapeutic agents and improve antigen targeting capabilities. Some of the PNPs, such as gelatin VLP and ELP, have reactive groups that allow for a wide range of chemical or genetic modifications for the development of targeted anticancer DDSs. Albumin possesses a variety of functional groups, enabling it to bind to considerable amounts of anticancer drugs such as ganciclovir, oligonucleotides, and dual compounds. The potential to design and produce ELPs through genetic engineering offers numerous advantages for these proteins and their NPs, including the attainment of optimal pharmacokinetic properties, precise control over molecular weight, and the creation of uniform-sized polymers. The unique brick-like structure of zein facilitates the encapsulation of hydrophilic compounds such as 5-FU and DOX, allowing for controlled release and enhanced therapeutic efficacy. VLPs can be altered through chemical or genetic engineering techniques without affecting the integrity of the cage structure, enabling their application in cancer therapies. Their nanometer size prevents them from traversing the endothelial layer of normal blood vessels, resulting in an extended half-life in circulation. However, these cages are sufficiently small to penetrate the pores of tumor vasculature, facilitating effective adhesion to tumor cells and enabling the targeted delivery of substantial amounts of chemotherapy agents. In the evolving landscape of cancer-targeting nanomaterials, substantial emphasis has been placed on the TME. The complexity inherent in TME requires the implementation of a combination of multidimensional therapeutic strategies for enhanced outcomes. Converging protein-based nanoplatforms with modalities such as immunotherapy, phototherapy, and radiotherapy, while considering tumor biology, opens new frontiers in addressing the complexities of current therapeutic limitations. Codelivering diverse therapeutic agents, such as drugs, genes, or immune modulators, by protein nanotherapeutics provides complex therapeutic benefits and significantly improves treatment effectiveness. Although the physical and chemical properties of the TME hinder the effectiveness of conventional anticancer treatments, they also serve as targets for the development of more potent therapies. PNPs offer substantial potential to drive future progress in biomedical and therapeutic innovations and deliver efficient and tailored solutions for patients. Progress in this field has been impressive, but there are still several unresolved issues. Despite the existing challenges, such as minimizing off-target effects, it is essential to develop functionalized PNPs that can specifically target designated regions within the body. The design and properties of PNPs must evolve in tandem with the advancement of new pharmaceuticals to ensure they serve as effective carriers for drug delivery. As additional research findings are released and the functionality of these protein materials is enhanced, interest in them is likely to grow.

## References

Aayush, A., Darji, S., Estes, K.M., Yeh, E., Thompson, D.H., 2024. Development of an elastin-like polypeptide-based nucleic acid delivery system targeted to EGFR+ bladder cancer cells using a layer-by-layer approach. Biomacromolecules 25 (9), 5729–5744. https://doi.org/10.1021/acs.biomac.4c00165.

Abd Elhamid, A.S., Heikal, L., Ghareeb, D.A., Abdulmalek, S.A., Mady, O., Teleb, M., Khattab, S.N., El-Gizawy, S. A., 2024. Engineering thermo/pH-responsive lactoferrin nanostructured microbeads for oral targeting of colorectal cancer. ACS Biomater. Sci. Eng. 10 (8), 4985–5000. https://doi.org/10.1021/acsbiomaterials.4c00666.

Aghaz, F., Asadi, Z., Sajadimajd, S., Kashfi, K., Arkan, E., Rahimi, Z., 2023. Codelivery of resveratrol melatonin utilizing pH responsive sericin based nanocarriers inhibits the proliferation of breast cancer cell line at the different pH. Sci. Rep. 13 (1). https://doi.org/10.1038/s41598-023-37668-y. https://www.nature.com/srep/.

Ahmad, M.I., Li, Y., Pan, J., Liu, F., Dai, H., Fu, Y., Huang, T., Farooq, S., Zhang, H., 2024. Collagen and gelatin: structure, properties, and applications in food industry. Int. J. Biol. Macromol. 254 (Pt 3), 128037. https://doi.org/10.1016/j.ijbiomac.2023.128037.

Akdaşçi, E., Eker, F., Duman, H., Singh, P., Bechelany, M., Karav, S., 2024. Lactoferrin as a versatile agent in nanoparticle applications: from therapeutics to agriculture. Nanomaterials 14 (24), 2018. https://doi.org/10.3390/nano14242018.

Akman, P.K., Bozkurt, F., Balubaid, M., Yilmaz, M.T., 2019. Fabrication of curcumin-loaded gliadin electrospun nanofibrous structures and bioactive properties. Korean fiber society. Fibers Polym. 20 (6), 1187–1199. https://doi.org/10.1007/s12221-019-8950-8.

al Alabdullah, M.A.A., Goodarzi, M.T., Homayouni Tabrizi, M., 2024. The silibinin-loaded Zein-β cyclodextrin nano-carriers (SZBC-NCs) as a novel selective cancer cell drug delivery system in HT-29 cell line. Sci. Rep. 14 (1). https://doi.org/10.1038/s41598-024-65881-w. https://www.nature.com/srep/.

Alioghli Ziaei, A., Erfan-Niya, H., Fathi, M., Amiryaghoubi, N., 2023. In situ forming alginate/gelatin hybrid hydrogels containing doxorubicin loaded chitosan/AuNPs nanogels for the local therapy of breast cancer. Int. J. Biol. Macromol. 246, 125640. https://doi.org/10.1016/j.ijbiomac.2023.125640.

Aly, S., El-Kamel, A.H., Sheta, E., El-Habashy, S.E., 2023. Chondroitin/Lactoferrin-dual functionalized pterostilbene-solid lipid nanoparticles as targeted breast cancer therapy. Int. J. Pharm. 642. https://doi.org/10.1016/j.ijpharm.2023.123163.

Arruebo, M., Vilaboa, N., Sáez-Gutierrez, B., Lambea, J., Tres, A., Valladares, M., González-Fernández, A., 2011. Assessment of the evolution of cancer treatment therapies. Cancers 3 (3), 3279–3330. https://doi.org/10.3390/cancers3033279Spain.

Asakura, T., Williamson, M.P., 2023. A review on the structure of Bombyx mori silk fibroin fiber studied using solid-state NMR: An antipolar lamella with an 8-residue repeat. Int. J. Biol. Macromol. 245, 125537. https://doi.org/10.1016/j.ijbiomac.2023.125537.

Attri, K., Chudasama, B., Mahajan, R.L., Choudhury, D., 2023. Therapeutic potential of lactoferrin-coated iron oxide nanospheres for targeted hyperthermia in gastric cancer. Sci. Rep. 13 (1). https://doi.org/10.1038/s41598-023-43725-3.

Bae, Y.H., 2009. Drug targeting and tumor heterogeneity. J. Contr. Release 133 (1), 2–3. https://doi.org/10.1016/j.jconrel.2008.09.074.

Banaee, F., Poureini, F., Mohammadi, M., Najafpour, G.D., Moghadamnia, A.A., 2022. Encapsulation of curcumin in gliadin-pectin in a core–shell nanostructure for efficient delivery of curcumin to cancer cells in vitro. Colloid Polym. Sci. 300 (9), 1063–1073. https://doi.org/10.1007/s00396-022-04998-8.

Belinskaia, D.A., Voronina, P.A., Shmurak, V.I., Jenkins, R.O., Goncharov, N.V., 2021a. Serum albumin in health and disease: esterase, antioxidant, transporting and signaling properties. Int. J. Mol. Sci. 22 (19). https://doi.org/10.3390/ijms221910318. https://www.mdpi.com/1422-0067/22/19/10318/pdf.

Belinskaia, D.A., Voronina, P.A., Batalova, A.A., Goncharov, N.V., 2021b. Serum albumin. Encyclopedia 1 (1), 65–75. https://doi.org/10.3390/encyclopedia1010009.

Beltran-Garcia, J., Han, S., Perez, B.S., Gunn, J., Kwon, E., Kaufman, D., 2023. Development of novel lipid nanoparticles and virus-like particles for in vivo engineering of immune cells for targeted cancer therapy. Blood 142 (Suppl. 1). https://doi.org/10.1182/blood-2023-184312.

Bhardwaj, R., Mishra, P., 2024. Multiresponsive nanoscale self-assembly of azurin-elastin-like polypeptide fusion protein for enhanced prostate cancer therapy. Biomacromolecules 25 (1), 508–521. https://doi.org/10.1021/acs.biomac.3c01125.

Bhargawa, B., Sharma, V., Ganesh, M.R., Cavalieri, F., Ashokkumar, M., Neppolian, B., Sundaramurthy, A., 2022. Lysozyme microspheres incorporated with anisotropic gold nanorods for ultrasound activated drug delivery. Ultrason. Sonochem. 86. https://doi.org/10.1016/j.ultsonch.2022.106016.

Bhutto, R.A., Bhutto, N.H., Fan, Y., Kang, L., Wang, M., Iqbal, S., Yi, J., 2024. Bovine α-lactalbumin: Source, extraction, techno-functional properties, and applications as a (nano-) delivery system for nutraceuticals. Trends Food Sci. Technol. 146, 104381. https://doi.org/10.1016/j.tifs.2024.104381.

Bin, L., Yang, Y., Wang, F., Wang, R., Fei, H., Duan, S., Huang, L., Liao, N., Zhao, S., Ma, X., 2022. Biodegradable silk fibroin nanocarriers to modulate hypoxia tumor microenvironment favoring enhanced chemotherapy. Front. Bioeng. Biotechnol. 10. https://doi.org/10.3389/fbioe.2022.960501.

Bray, F., Laversanne, M., Sung, H., Ferlay, J., Siegel, R.L., Soerjomataram, I., Jemal, A., 2024. Global cancer statistics 2022: GLOBOCAN estimates of incidence and mortality worldwide for 36 cancers in 185 countries. CA Cancer J. Clin. 74 (3), 229–263. https://doi.org/10.3322/caac.21834. http://onlinelibrary.wiley.com/journal/10.3322/(ISSN)1542-4863.

Brindisi, M., Curcio, M., Frattaruolo, L., Cirillo, G., Leggio, A., Rago, V., Nicoletta, F.P., Cappello, A.R., Iemma, F., 2022. CD44-targeted nanoparticles with GSH-responsive activity as powerful therapeutic agents against breast cancer. Int. J. Biol. Macromol. 221, 1491–1503. https://doi.org/10.1016/j.ijbiomac.2022.09.157.

Cai, Y., Naser, N.Y., Ma, J., Baneyx, F., 2024. Precision loading and delivery of molecular cargo by size-controlled coacervation of gold nanoparticles functionalized with elastin-like peptides. Biomacromolecules 25 (4), 2390–2398. http://pubs.acs.org/journal/bomaf6. doi: 10.1021/acs.biomac.3c01312.

Cao, C., Tian, L., Li, J., Raveendran, R., Stenzel, M.H., 2024. Mix and shake: A mild way to drug-loaded lysozyme nanoparticles. ACS Appl. Mater. Interfaces 16 (21), 27177–27186. https://doi.org/10.1021/acsami.4c05497.

Chen, Q., Feng, L., Liu, J., Zhu, W., Dong, Z., Wu, Y., Liu, Z., 2016. Intelligent albumin–$MnO_2$ nanoparticles as pH-/$H_2O_2$-responsive dissociable nanocarriers to modulate tumor hypoxia for effective combination therapy. Adv. Mater. 28 (33), 7129–7136. https://doi.org/10.1002/adma.201601902.

Chen, X., Zou, J., Zhang, K., Zhu, J., Zhang, Y., Zhu, Z., Zheng, H., Li, F., Piao, J.G., 2021. Photothermal/matrix metalloproteinase-2 dual-responsive gelatin nanoparticles for breast cancer treatment. Acta Pharm. Sin. B 11 (1), 271–282. https://doi.org/10.1016/j.apsb.2020.08.009.

Cheng, Z., Li, M., Dey, R., Chen, Y., 2021. Nanomaterials for cancer therapy: Current progress and perspectives. J. Hematol. Oncol. (1), 14. https://doi.org/10.1186/s13045-021-01096-0.

Cheung, L.S., Fu, J., Kumar, P., Kumar, A., Urbanowski, M.E., Ihms, E.A., Parveen, S., Bullen, C.K., Patrick, G.J., Harrison, R., Murphy, J.R., Pardoll, D.M., Bishai, W.R., 2019. Second-generation IL-2 receptor-targeted diphtheria fusion toxin exhibits antitumor activity and synergy with anti–PD-1 in melanoma. Proc. Natl. Acad. Sci. U. S. A 116 (8), 3100–3105. https://doi.org/10.1073/pnas.1815087116.

Chou, C.C., Tseng, C.E., Lin, Y.S., Wang, M., Chen, P.L., Chang, D., Shen, C.H., Fang, C.Y., 2024. Inhibition of orthotopic castration-resistant prostate cancer growth and metastasis in mice by JC VLPs carrying a suicide gene driven by the PSA promoter. Cancer Gene Ther. 31 (2), 250–258. https://doi.org/10.1038/s41417-023-00699-8.

Cirillo, G., Cappello, A.R., Curcio, M., Fiorillo, M., Frattaruolo, L., Avena, P., Scorzafave, L., Dolce, V., Nicoletta, F. P., Iemma, F., 2024. Novel CD44-targeted albumin nanoparticles: An innovative approach to improve breast cancer treatment. Int. J. Mol. Sci. 25 (19). https://doi.org/10.3390/ijms251910560. http://www.mdpi.com/journal/ijms.

Cox, T.R., 2021. The matrix in cancer. Nat. Rev. Cancer 21 (4), 217–238. https://doi.org/10.1038/s41568-020-00329-7.

Crivelli, B., Perteghella, S., Bari, E., Sorrenti, M., Tripodo, G., Chlapanidas, T., Torre, M.L., 2018. Silk nanoparticles: from inert supports to bioactive natural carriers for drug delivery. Soft Matter 14 (4), 546–557. https://doi.org/10.1039/c7sm01631j.

Cuggino, J.C., Picchio, M.L., Gugliotta, A., Bürgi, M., Ronco, L.I., Calderón, M., Etcheverrigaray, M., Alvarez Igarzabal, C.I., Minari, R.J., Gugliotta, L.M., 2021. Crosslinked casein micelles bound paclitaxel as enzyme activated intracellular drug delivery systems for cancer therapy. Eur. Polym. J. 145. https://doi.org/10.1016/j.eurpolymj.2020.110237. https://www.journals.elsevier.com/european-polymer-journal.

Dai, L., Liu, J., Luo, Z., Li, M., Cai, K., 2016. Tumor therapy: Targeted drug delivery systems. J. Mater. Chem. B 4 (42), 6758–6772. https://doi.org/10.1039/c6tb01743f.

Danhier, F., Feron, O., Préat, V., 2010. To exploit the tumor microenvironment: Passive and active tumor targeting of nanocarriers for anti-cancer drug delivery. J. Contr. Release 148 (2), 135–146. https://doi.org/10.1016/j.jconrel.2010.08.027.

Das, S., Tripathy, S., Sreedhar, B., Mukherjee, S., Patra, C.R., 2023. Design of lysozyme-templated biocompatible fluorescent nanocomposites and their potential applications for cell imaging, hydrogen peroxide sensing, and cancer therapy. Adv. Therapeut. 6 (6). https://doi.org/10.1002/adtp.202200293. http://onlinelibrary.wiley.com/journal/10.1002/(ISSN)2366-3987.

de Lázaro, I., Mooney, D.J., 2021. Obstacles and opportunities in a forward vision for cancer nanomedicine. Nat. Mater. 20 (11), 1469–1479. https://doi.org/10.1038/s41563-021-01047-7.

Deng, L., Guo, W., Li, G., Hu, Y., Zhang, L.M., 2019. Hydrophobic IR780 loaded sericin nanomicelles for phototherapy with enhanced antitumor efficiency. Int. J. Pharm. 566, 549–556. https://doi.org/10.1016/j.ijpharm.2019.05.075.

Desai, N., 2016. Nanoparticle albumin-bound paclitaxel (abraxane®). Albumin in Medicine: Pathological and Clinical Applications. Springer Singapore, United States, pp. 101–119. https://doi.org/10.1007/978-981-10-2116-9_6.

Desai, N., Trieu, V., Damascelli, B., Soon-Shiong, P., 2009. SPARC expression correlates with tumor response to albumin-bound paclitaxel in head and neck cancer patients. Trans. Oncol. 2 (2), 59–64. https://doi.org/10.1593/tlo.09109.

Desai, N., Trieu, V., Yao, Z., Leslie, L., Ci, S., Yang, A., Tao, C., De, T., Beals, B., Dykes, D., Noker, P., Yao, R., Labao, E., Hawkins, M., Soon-Shiong, P., 2006. Increased antitumor activity, intratumor paclitaxel concentrations, and endothelial cell transport of cremophor-free, albumin-bound paclitaxel, ABI-007, compared with cremophor-based paclitaxel. Clin. Cancer Res. 12 (4), 1317–1324. https://doi.org/10.1158/1078-0432.ccr-05-1634.

Diab, S.E., Tayea, N.A., Elwakil, B.H., Elshewemi, S.S., Gad, A.A.E.M., Abdulmalek, S.A., Ghareeb, D.A., Olama, Z. A., 2024. In vitro and in vivo anti-colorectal cancer effect of the newly synthesized sericin/propolis/fluorouracil nanoplatform through modulation of PI3K/AKT/mTOR pathway. Sci. Rep. 14 (1). https://doi.org/10.1038/s41598-024-52722-z. https://www.nature.com/srep/.

Diaz, D., Care, A., Sunna, A., 2018. Bioengineering strategies for protein-based nanoparticles. Genes 9 (7). https://doi.org/10.3390/genes9070370. http://www.mdpi.com/2073-4425/9/7/370/pdf.

Dong, Y., Fu, R., Yang, J., Ma, P., Liang, L., Mi, Y., Fan, D., 2019. Folic acid-modified ginsenoside Rg5-loaded bovine serum albumin nanoparticles for targeted cancer therapy in vitro and in vivo. Int. J. Nanomed. 14, 6971–6988. https://doi.org/10.2147/IJN.S210882.

Dong, J., Zheng, Z., Zhou, M., Wang, Y., Chen, J., Cen, J., Cao, T., Yang, T., Xu, Y., Shu, G., Lu, X., Liang, Y., 2023. EGCG-LYS fibrils-mediated CircMAP2K2 silencing decreases the proliferation and metastasis ability of gastric cancer cells in vitro and in vivo. Adv. Sci. 10 (32). https://doi.org/10.1002/advs.202304075. http://onlinelibrary.wiley.com/journal/10.1002/(ISSN)2198-3844.

Dragojevic, S., Turner, L., Pal, P., Janorkar, A.V., Raucher, D., 2022. Elastin-like polypeptide hydrogels for tunable, sustained local chemotherapy in malignant glioma. Pharmaceutics 14 (10). https://doi.org/10.3390/pharmaceutics14102072. http://www.mdpi.com/journal/pharmaceutics.

Duan, X., Chan, C., Lin, W., 2019. Nanoparticle-mediated immunogenic cell death enables and potentiates cancer immunotherapy. Angew. Chem. - Inter. Ed. 58 (3), 670–680. https://doi.org/10.1002/anie.201804882. http://onlinelibrary.wiley.com/journal/10.1002/(ISSN)1521-3773.

Dutta, B., Shelar, S.B., Rajan, V., Checker, S., Barick, K.C., Pandey, B.N., Kumar, S., Hassan, P.A., 2022. Gelatin grafted $Fe_3O_4$ based curcumin nanoformulation for cancer therapy. J. Drug Deliv. Sci. Technol. 67, 102974. https://doi.org/10.1016/j.jddst.2021.102974.

Ebbesen, P., Pettersen, E.O., Gorr, T.A., Jobst, G., Williams, K., Kieninger, J., Wenger, R.H., Pastorekova, S., Dubois, L., Lambin, P., Wouters, B.G., Van Den Beucken, T., Supuran, C.T., Poellinger, L., Ratcliffe, P., Kanopka, A., Grlach, A., Gasmann, M., Harris, A.L., Maxwell, P., Scozzafava, A., 2009. Taking advantage of tumor cell adaptations to hypoxia for developing new tumor markers and treatment strategies. J. Enzym. Inhib. Med. Chem. 24 (1), 1–39. https://doi.org/10.1080/14756360902784425.

Eivazzadeh-Keihan, R., Mohammadi, A., Aghamirza Moghim Aliabadi, H., Kashtiaray, A., Bani, M.S., Karimi, A.H., Maleki, A., Mahdavi, M., 2024. A novel ternary magnetic nanobiocomposite based on tragacanth-silk fibroin hydrogel for hyperthermia and biological properties. Sci. Rep. 14 (1). https://doi.org/10.1038/s41598-024-58770-9. https://www.nature.com/srep/.

El-Fakharany, E.M., Abu-Serie, M.M., Habashy, N.H., Eltarahony, M., 2022. Augmenting apoptosis-mediated anticancer activity of lactoperoxidase and lactoferrin by nanocombination with copper and iron hybrid nanometals. Sci. Rep. 12 (1). https://doi.org/10.1038/s41598-022-17357-y. www.nature.com/srep/index.html.

El-Hussein, A., Manoto, S.L., Ombinda-Lemboumba, S., Alrowaili, Z.A., Mthunzi-Kufa, P., 2021. A review of chemotherapy and photodynamic therapy for lung cancer treatment. Anti Cancer Agents Med. Chem. 21 (2), 149–161. https://doi.org/10.2174/1871520620666200403144945.

Elmahboub, Y., Albash, R., Magdy William, M., Rayan, A.H., Hamed, N.O., Ousman, M.S., Raslan, N.A., Mosallam, S., 2024. Metformin loaded zein polymeric nanoparticles to augment antitumor activity against ehrlich carcinoma via activation of AMPK pathway: D-optimal design optimization, in vitro characterization, and in vivo study. Molecules 29 (7). https://doi.org/10.3390/molecules29071614. http://www.mdpi.com/journal/molecules.

Elmorshedy, Y.M., Teleb, M., Sallam, M.A., Elkhodairy, K.A., Bahey-El-Din, M., Ghareeb, D.A., Abdulmalek, S.A., Abdel Monaim, S.A.H., Bekhit, A.A., Elzoghby, A.O., Albericio, F., Khattab, S.N., 2023. Engineered microencapsulated lactoferrin nanoconjugates for oral targeted treatment of colon cancer. Biomacromolecules 24 (5), 2149–2163. https://doi.org/10.1021/acs.biomac.3c00037.

Elzoghby, A.O., Elgohary, M.M., Kamel, N.M., 2015. Implications of protein- and peptide-based nanoparticles as potential vehicles for anticancer drugs. Adv. Protein Chem. Struct. Biol. 98, 169–221. https://doi.org/10.1016/bs.apcsb.2014.12.002.

Fang, J., Wang, Q., Yang, G., Xiao, X., Li, L., Yu, T., 2019. Albumin-MnO 2 gated hollow mesoporous silica nanosystem for modulating tumor hypoxia and synergetic therapy of cervical carcinoma. Colloids Surf. B Biointerfaces 179, 250–259. https://doi.org/10.1016/j.colsurfb.2019.03.070.

Farzan, M., Varshosaz, J., Mirian, M., Minaiyan, M., Pezeshki, A., 2023. Hyaluronic acid-conjugated gliadin nanoparticles for targeted delivery of usnic acid in breast cancer: an in vitro/in vivo translational study. J. Drug Deliv. Sci. Technol. 84, 104459. https://doi.org/10.1016/j.jddst.2023.104459.

Florczak, A., Deptuch, T., Kucharczyk, K., 2021. Dams-Kozlowska, Systemic and local silk-based drug delivery systems for cancer therapy. Cancers 13 (21). https://doi.org/10.3390/cancers13215389.

Foss, F., 2006. Clinical experience with denileukin diftitox (ONTAK). Semin. Oncol. 33 (3), 11–16. https://doi.org/10.1053/j.seminoncol.2005.12.017.

Fuster, M.G., Montalbán, M.G., Moulefera, I., Víllora, G., Kaplan, D.L., 2023. Folic acid-modified ibrutinib-loaded silk fibroin nanoparticles for cancer cell therapy with over-expressed folate receptor. Pharmaceutics 15 (4). https://doi.org/10.3390/pharmaceutics15041186. http://www.mdpi.com/journal/pharmaceutics.

Gagliardi, A., Bonacci, S., Paolino, D., Celia, C., Procopio, A., Fresta, M., Cosco, D., 2019. Paclitaxel-loaded sodium deoxycholate-stabilized zein nanoparticles: characterization and in vitro cytotoxicity. Heliyon 5 (9). https://doi.org/10.1016/j.heliyon.2019.e02422. http://www.journals.elsevier.com/heliyon/.

Gama, P., Juárez, P., Rodríguez-Hernández, A.G., Vazquez-Duhalt, R., 2023. Glucose oxidase virus-based nanoreactors for smart breast cancer therapy. Biotechnol. J. 18 (10). https://doi.org/10.1002/biot.202300199. http://onlinelibrary.wiley.com/journal/10.1002/(ISSN)1860-7314.

Gao, W., Jia, X., Wu, J., Song, Y., Yin, J., Zhang, M., Qiu, N., Li, X., Wu, P., Qi, X., Liu, Z., 2019. Preparation and evaluation of folate-decorated human serum albumin nanoparticles for the targeted delivery of sorafenib to enhance antihepatocarcinoma efficacy. J. Drug Deliv. Sci. Technol. 54, 101349. https://doi.org/10.1016/j.jddst.2019.101349.

Gao, Y.E., Hou, S., Cheng, J., Li, X., Wu, Y., Tang, Y., Li, Y., Xue, P., Kang, Y., Xu, Z., Guo, M., 2021. Silk Sericin-Based Nanoparticle as the Photosensitizer Chlorin e6 Carrier for Enhanced Cancer Photodynamic Therapy. ACS Sustain. Chem. Eng. 9 (8), 3213–3222. http://pubs.acs.org/journal/ascecg. doi: 10.1021/acssuschemeng.0c08326.

Gonçalves, A.P., Ramos, J.É.B., Madureira, K.H., Martins, M.L., Santos, A.A., de Vries, R., 2023. Virus-like particle-encapsulated doxorubicin enters and kills murine tumor cells differently from free doxorubicin. Macromol. Biosci. 23 (6). https://doi.org/10.1002/mabi.202200530. http://onlinelibrary.wiley.com/journal/10.1002/(ISSN)1616-5195.

Gou, Y., Miao, D., Zhou, M., Wang, L., Zhou, H., Su, G., 2018. Bio-inspired protein-based nanoformulations for cancer theranostics. Front. Pharmacol. 9. https://doi.org/10.3389/fphar.2018.00421. https://www.frontiersin.org/articles/10.3389/fphar.2018.00421/full.

Gou, S., Meng, W., Panayi, A.C., Wang, R., Zhang, R., Gao, P., He, T., Geng, W., Hu, S., Yu, Y., Feng, Q., Cai, K., 2023. Bioresponsive self-reinforcing sericin/silk fibroin hydrogel for relieving the immune-related adverse events in tumor immunotherapy. Adv. Funct. Mater. 33 (15). https://doi.org/10.1002/adfm.202213867. http://onlinelibrary.wiley.com/journal/10.1002/(ISSN)1616-3028.

Grataitong, K., Huault, S., Chotwiwatthanakun, C., Jariyapong, P., Thongsum, O., Chawiwithaya, C., Chakrabandhu, K., Hueber, A.O., Weerachatyanukul, W., 2021. Chimeric virus-like particles (VLPs) designed from shrimp nodavirus (MrNV) capsid protein specifically target EGFR-positive human colorectal cancer cells. Sci. Rep. 11 (1). https://doi.org/10.1038/s41598-021-95891-x. www.nature.com/srep/index.html.

Gregory, J.V., Kadiyala, P., Doherty, R., Cadena, M., Habeel, S., Ruoslahti, E., Lowenstein, P.R., Castro, M.G., Lahann, J., 2020. Systemic brain tumor delivery of synthetic protein nanoparticles for glioblastoma therapy. Nat. Commun. 11 (1). https://doi.org/10.1038/s41467-020-19225-7. http://www.nature.com/ncomms/index.html.

Guo, S., Zhao, Y., Luo, S., Mu, D., Li, X., Zhong, X., Jiang, S., Zheng, Z., 2022. Encapsulation of curcumin in soluble soybean polysaccharide-coated gliadin nanoparticles: interaction, stability, antioxidant capacity, and bioaccessibility. J. Sci. Food Agric. 102 (12), 5121–5131. https://doi.org/10.1002/jsfa.11862. http://onlinelibrary.wiley.com/journal/10.1002/(ISSN)1097-0010.

Hameed, M., Panicker, S., Abdallah, S.H., Khan, A.A., Han, C., Chehimi, M.M., Mohamed, A.A., 2020. Protein-coated aryl modified gold nanoparticles for cellular uptake study by osteosarcoma cancer cells. Langmuir 36 (40), 11765–11775. http://pubs.acs.org/journal/langd5. doi: 10.1021/acs.langmuir.0c01443.

Han, J., Dong, H., Zhu, T., Wei, Q., Wang, Y., Wang, Y., Lv, Y., Mu, H., Huang, S., Zeng, K., Xu, J., Ding, J., 2024. Biochemical hallmarks-targeting antineoplastic nanotherapeutics. Bioact. Mater. 36, 427–454. https://doi.org/10.1016/j.bioactmat.2024.05.042.

Hao, Y., Gu, Z., Yu, Z., Schomann, T., Sayedipour, S., Aguilar, J.C., Ten Dijke, P., Cruz, L.J., 2022. Photodynamic therapy in combination with the Hepatitis B core virus-like particles (HBc VLPs) to prime anticancer immunity for colorectal cancer treatment. Cancers 14 (11), 2724. https://doi.org/10.3390/cancers14112724.

Hassan, M.A., Basha, A.A., Eraky, M., Abbas, E., El-Samad, L.M., 2024. Advancements in silk fibroin and silk sericin-based biomaterial applications for cancer therapy and wound dressing formulation: A comprehensive review. Int. J. Pharm. 662. https://doi.org/10.1016/j.ijpharm.2024.124494. A. https://www.sciencedirect.com/science/journal/03785173.

Hassanin, I.A., Elzoghby, A.O., 2020. Self-assembled non-covalent protein-drug nanoparticles: An emerging delivery platform for anti-cancer drugs. Expet Opin. Drug Deliv. 17 (10), 1437–1458. https://doi.org/10.1080/17425247.2020.1813713.

He, H., Wu, S., Mei, M., Ning, J., Li, C., Ma, L., Zhang, G., Yi, L., 2020. A combinational strategy for effective heterologous production of functional human lysozyme in Pichia pastoris. Front. Bioeng. Biotechnol. 8. https://doi.org/10.3389/fbioe.2020.00118.

He, C., Zhou, J., Wu, X., Zhou, Y., Wang, S., Liu, B., Luo, T., Chen, Y., Jia, Y., Wang, Di, Zhang, C., Shi, J., 2024a. Hyaluronic acid-zein shell-core biopolymer nanoparticles enhance hepatocellular carcinoma therapy of celastrol via CD44-mediated cellular uptake. Int. J. Biol. Macromol. 281 (Pt 1), 136096. https://doi.org/10.1016/j.ijbiomac.2024.136096.

He, Y.R., Xia, H., Yun, P., Xu, Y., Ma, W.M.J., Xiao, Z.X., Zha, G.F., 2024b. α-Lactalbumin mRNA-LNP evokes an anti-tumor effect combined with surgery in triple-negative breast cancer. Pharmaceutics 16 (7). https://doi.org/10.3390/pharmaceutics16070940. http://www.mdpi.com/journal/pharmaceutics.

Hong, J., Sim, D., Lee, B.H., Sarangthem, V., Park, R.W., 2024. Multifunctional elastin-like polypeptide nanocarriers for efficient miRNA delivery in cancer therapy. J. Nanobiotechnol. 22 (1). https://doi.org/10.1186/s12951-024-02559-5.

Hou, G., Wu, D., Li, X., Liu, B., 2024. Tumor targeted and GSH stimuli-response α-lactalbumin nanotubes co-delivering doxorubicin and siRNA for cancer therapy. J. Future Foods 4 (4), 300–308. https://doi.org/10.1016/j.jfutfo.2023.11.002.

Hua, Y., Qin, Z., Gao, L., Zhou, M., Xue, Y., Li, Y., Xie, J., 2024. Protein nanoparticles as drug delivery systems for cancer theranostics. J. Contr. Release 371, 429–444. https://doi.org/10.1016/j.jconrel.2024.06.004.

Huang, Y., Hu, L., Huang, S., Xu, W., Wan, J., Wang, D., Zheng, G., Xia, Z., 2018. Curcumin-loaded galactosylated BSA nanoparticles as targeted drug delivery carriers inhibit hepatocellular carcinoma cell proliferation and migration. Int. J. Nanomed. 13, 8309–8323. https://doi.org/10.2147/IJN.S184379.

Huang, W., Wang, L., Wei, Y., Cao, M., Xie, H., Wu, D., 2020. Fabrication of lysozyme/κ-carrageenan complex nanoparticles as a novel carrier to enhance the stability and in vitro release of curcumin. Journal of Biological Macromolecules 146, 444–452. https://doi.org/10.1016/j.ijbiomac.2020.01.004.

Jaiswal, J., Rajput, P.K., Srivastav, A.K., Rao, M.J., Yadav, U.C.S., Kumar, U., 2024. Synthesis, physiochemical characterization, molecular docking study, and anti-breast cancer activity of silymarin loaded zein nanoparticles. Int. J. Biol. Macromol. 264. https://doi.org/10.1016/j.ijbiomac.2024.130679. https://www.sciencedirect.com/science/journal/01418130.

Jalilian, S., Bahremand, K., Arkan, E., Jaymand, M., Aghaz, F., 2024. A comparative study of sericin and gluten for magnetic nanoparticle-mediated drug delivery to breast cancer cell lines. Sci. Rep. 14 (1). https://doi.org/10.1038/s41598-024-69009-y. https://www.nature.com/srep/.

Jayalakshmi, C.S., Mohamed, H., Rawas-Qalaji, M., Sanpui, P., 2025. Curcumin-loaded zein nanoparticles: A quality by design approach for enhanced drug delivery and cytotoxicity against cancer cells. Colloids Surf. B Biointerfaces 245, 114319. https://doi.org/10.1016/j.colsurfb.2024.114319.

Jia, M., Zhang, D., Zhang, C., Li, C., 2021. Nanoparticle-based delivery systems modulate the tumor microenvironment in pancreatic cancer for enhanced therapy. J. Nanobiotechnol. 19 (1). https://doi.org/10.1186/s12951-021-01134-6.

Jia, L., Lin, S., Deng, Y., Zou, M., Cai, B., Song, Y., Wang, Z., Wang, L., 2022. Silk sericin-based materials for biomedical applications. Biomaterials 287, 121638. https://doi.org/10.1016/j.biomaterials.2022.121638.

Jiang, X., Du, Z., Zhang, X., Zaman, F., Song, Z., Guan, Y., Yu, T., Huang, Y., 2023. Gelatin-based anticancer drug delivery nanosystems: A mini review. Front. Bioeng. Biotechnol. 11. https://doi.org/10.3389/fbioe.2023.1158749.

Jung, E., Chung, Y.H., Steinmetz, N.F., 2023. TLR agonists delivered by plant virus and bacteriophage nanoparticles for cancer immunotherapy. Bioconjug. Chem. 34 (9), 1596–1605. http://pubs.acs.org/journal/bcches. doi: 10.1021/acs.bioconjchem.3c00271.

Kadam, S., Ali, A., Pospiech, M., Onyemaechi, S., Meng, Y., Dhuri, K., MacKay, J.A., Alachkar, H., 2024. Enhanced T cell activation and cytotoxicity against AML via targeted anti-CD99 nanoparticle treatment. Biomed. Pharmacother. 179. https://doi.org/10.1016/j.biopha.2024.117265. https://www.sciencedirect.com/science/journal/07533322.

Kaushik, P., Priyadarshini, E., Rawat, K., Rajamani, P., Bohidar, H.B., 2020. pH responsive doxorubucin loaded zein nanoparticle crosslinked pectin hydrogel as effective site-specific anticancer substrates. Int. J. Biol. Macromol. 152, 1027–1037. https://doi.org/10.1016/j.ijbiomac.2019.10.190.

Khatun, S., Pebam, M., Putta, C.L., Rengan, A.K., 2023. Camptothecin loaded casein nanosystem for tuning the therapeutic efficacy against highly metastatic triple-negative breast cancer cells. Biomater. Sci. 11 (7), 2518–2530. https://doi.org/10.1039/d2bm01814d.

Khatun, S., Kshtriya, V., Gour, N., Murugaiyan, K., Rengan, A.K., 2024a. 7-Amino-6H-anthra[9,1-cd] isothiazol-6-one-casein nanosystem for live cell staining and augmenting therapeutic effectiveness in triple negative breast cancer. ACS Appl. Nano Mater. 7 (7), 8022–8034. https://doi.org/10.1021/acsanm.4c00594.

Khatun, S., Pebam, M., Sankaranarayanan, S.A., Pogu, S.V., Bantal, V.S., Rengan, A.K., 2024b. Glutathione-IR 797 coupled Casein Nano-Trojan for augmenting the therapeutic efficacy of camptothecin in highly invasive triple negative breast cancer. Biomater. Adv. 159.

Khodashenas, B., Ardjmand, M., Rad, A.S., Esfahani, M.R., 2021. Gelatin-coated gold nanoparticles as an effective pH-sensitive methotrexate drug delivery system for breast cancer treatment. Mater. Today Chem. 20, 100474. https://doi.org/10.1016/j.mtchem.2021.100474.

Kianfar, E., 2021. Protein nanoparticles in drug delivery: animal protein, plant proteins and protein cages, albumin nanoparticles. J. Nanobiotechnol. 19 (1). https://doi.org/10.1186/s12951-021-00896-3.

Kiyose, K., Hanaoka, K., Oushiki, D., Nakamura, T., Kajimura, M., Suematsu, M., Nishimatsu, H., Yamane, T., Terai, T., Hirata, Y., Nagano, T., 2010. Hypoxia-sensitive fluorescent probes for in vivo real-time fluorescence imaging of acute ischemia. J. Am. Chem. Soc. 132 (45), 15846–15848. https://doi.org/10.1021/ja105937q.

Koohi Moftakhari Esfahani, M., Alavi, S.E., Cabot, P.J., Islam, N., Izake, E.L., 2022. β-Lactoglobulin-modified mesoporous silica nanoparticles: a promising carrier for the targeted delivery of fenbendazole into prostate cancer cells. Pharmaceutics 14 (4), 884. https://doi.org/10.3390/pharmaceutics14040884.

Lai, M.H., Lin, W.J., 2024. Zein-PEG nanoparticles modified with hyaluronic acid for paclitaxel delivery in SKOV3 ovarian cancer cells. Int. J. Biol. Macromol. 281. https://doi.org/10.1016/j.ijbiomac.2024.136651.

Lal, S., Kataria, M., Rani, R., Dilbaghi, N., 2024. Gliadin encapsulated procyanidolic oligomers nanoformulation: Aggrandized antimicrobial, antioxidant as well as anticancer potential makes it an effective therapeutic modality for lung carcinoma. Springer, India Indian Journal of Microbiology. https://doi.org/10.1007/s12088-024-01380-w. https://www.springer.com/journal/12088.

Le, D.H.T., Ibrahimova, V., van den Wildenberg, S.A.H., Wu, H., Fonseca, A., Torres, T., Garanger, E., Leenders, W. P.J., Brock, R., Lecommandoux, S., van Hest, J.C.M., 2023. Light-responsive elastin-like peptide-based targeted nanoparticles for enhanced spheroid penetration. Angew. Chem. - Int. Ed. 62 (24). https://doi.org/10.1002/anie.202300511. http://onlinelibrary.wiley.com/journal/10.1002/(ISSN)1521-3773.

Lee, E.H., Lee, M.K., Lim, S.J., 2021a. Enhanced stability of indocyanine green by encapsulation in zein-phosphatidylcholine hybrid nanoparticles for use in the phototherapy of cancer. Pharmaceutics 13 (3), 1–10. https://doi.org/10.3390/pharmaceutics13030305. https://www.mdpi.com/1999-4923/13/3/305/pdf.

Lee, H.S., Kang, N.W., Kim, H., Kim, D.H., Chae, J.w., Lee, W., Song, G.Y., Cho, C.W., Kim, D.D., Lee, J.Y., 2021b. Chondroitin sulfate-hybridized zein nanoparticles for tumor-targeted delivery of docetaxel. Carbohydr. Polym. 253. https://doi.org/10.1016/j.carbpol.2020.117187. http://www.elsevier.com/wps/find/journaldescription.cws_home/405871/description#description.

Leśnierowski, G., Yang, T., 2021. Lysozyme and its modified forms: A critical appraisal of selected properties and potential. Trends Food Sci. Technol. 107, 333–342. https://doi.org/10.1016/j.tifs.2020.11.004.

Li, C., Jiang, P., Wei, S., Xu, X., Wang, J., 2020. Regulatory T cells in tumor microenvironment: New mechanisms, potential therapeutic strategies and future prospects. Mol. Cancer 19 (1). https://doi.org/10.1186/s12943-020-01234-1.

Li, W., Jing, Z., Wang, S., Li, Q., Xing, Y., Shi, H., Li, S., Hong, Z., 2021. P22 virus-like particles as an effective antigen delivery nanoplatform for cancer immunotherapy. Biomaterials 271, 120726. https://doi.org/10.1016/j.biomaterials.2021.120726.

Li, Z., Cheng, G., Zhang, Q., Wu, W., Zhang, Y., Wu, B., Liu, Z., Tong, X., Xiao, B., Cheng, L., Dai, F., 2022. PX478-loaded silk fibroin nanoparticles reverse multidrug resistance by inhibiting the hypoxia-inducible factor. Int. J. Biol. Macromol. 222, 2309–2317. https://doi.org/10.1016/j.ijbiomac.2022.10.018.

Li, S.Q., Huang, X.N., Wei, S.H., Yu, X.H., Yang, X.Q., Zhu, J.H., Yin, S.W., 2023. Gliadin-based nanoparticles used for Pickering stabilization: Current status and future perspective. Food Hydrocoll. 145. https://doi.org/10.1016/j.foodhyd.2023.109020.

Li, M., Liu, Y., Liu, Y., Lin, J., Ding, L., Wu, S., Gong, J., 2024a. Fabrication of targeted and pH responsive lysozyme-hyaluronan nanoparticles for 5-fluorouracil and curcumin co-delivery in colorectal cancer therapy. Int. J. Biol. Macromol. 254 (Pt 2), 127836. https://doi.org/10.1016/j.ijbiomac.2023.127836.

Li, Q., Yang, X., Xia, X., Xia, X.X., Yan, D., 2024b. Affibody-functionalized elastin-like peptide-drug conjugate nanomicelle for targeted ovarian cancer therapy. Biomacromolecules 25 (10), 6474–6484. https://doi.org/10.1021/acs.biomac.4c00640.

Liguori, A., De Vita, A., Rossi, G., Dolci, L.S., Panzavolta, S., Gualandi, C., Mercatali, L., Ibrahim, T., Focarete, M.L., 2022. A modular composite device of poly(ethylene oxide)/poly(butylene terephthalate) (PEOT/PBT) nanofibers and gelatin as a dual drug delivery system for local therapy of soft tissue tumors. Int. J. Mol. Sci. 23 (6). https://doi.org/10.3390/ijms23063239. https://www.mdpi.com/1422-0067/23/6/3239/pdf.

Lin, P., Gu, H., Zhuang, X., Wang, F., Hu, X., 2024. Controlled release of curcumin and hypocrellin A from electrospun poly(l-lactic acid)/silk fibroin nanofibers for enhanced cancer cell inhibition. ACS Appl. Bio Mater. 7 (8), 5423–5436. https://doi.org/10.1021/acsabm.4c00582.

Liu, H., Hu, Y., Sun, Y., Wan, C., Zhang, Z., Dai, X., Lin, Z., He, Q., Yang, Z., Huang, P., Xiong, Y., Cao, J., Chen, X., Chen, Q., Lovell, J.F., Xu, Z., Jin, H., Yang, K., 2019. Co-Delivery of bee venom melittin and a photosensitizer with an organic-inorganic hybrid nanocarrier for photodynamic therapy and immunotherapy. ACS Nano 13 (11), 12638–12652. https://doi.org/10.1021/acsnano.9b04181.

Liu, K., Chen, Y.Y., Pan, L.H., Li, Q.M., Luo, J.P., Zha, X.Q., 2022a. Co-encapsulation systems for delivery of bioactive ingredients. China Food Res. Int. 155. https://doi.org/10.1016/j.foodres.2022.111073.

Liu, N., Cui, M., Hu, N., Yang, F., Mu, Y., Guo, C., Guan, X., Xie, Z., 2022b. An engineered three-in-one hybrid nanosystem from elastin-like polypeptides for enhanced cancer suppression. Colloids Surf. B Biointerfaces 220, 112976. https://doi.org/10.1016/j.colsurfb.2022.112976.

Luo, Z., Tian, H., Liu, L., Chen, Z., Liang, R., Chen, Z., Wu, Z., Ma, A., Zheng, M., Cai, L., 2018. Tumor-targeted hybrid protein oxygen carrier to simultaneously enhance hypoxia-dampened chemotherapy and photodynamic therapy at a single dose. Theranostics 8 (13), 3584–3596. https://doi.org/10.7150/thno.25409.

Martin, J.D., Cabral, H., Stylianopoulos, T., Jain, R.K., 2020. Improving cancer immunotherapy using nanomedicines: Progress, opportunities and challenges. Nat. Rev. Clin. Oncol. 17 (4), 251–266. https://doi.org/10.1038/s41571-019-0308-z.

Matloubi, Z., Hassan, Z., 2020. HSA-curcumin nanoparticles: a promising substitution for curcumin as a Cancer chemoprevention and therapy. Daru 28 (1), 209–219. https://doi.org/10.1007/s40199-020-00331-2.

Mehta, A., Dalle Vedove, E., Isert, L., Merkel, O.M., 2019. Targeting KRAS mutant lung cancer cells with siRNA-loaded bovine serum albumin nanoparticles. Pharm. Res. 36 (9). https://doi.org/10.1007/s11095-019-2665-9. www.wkap.nl/journalhome.htm/0724-8741.

Mellid-Carballal, R., Gutierrez-Gutierrez, S., Rivas, C., Garcia-Fuentes, M., 2023. Viral protein-based nanoparticles (part 2): Pharmaceutical applications. Eur. J. Pharmaceut. Sci. 189, 106558. https://doi.org/10.1016/j.ejps.2023.106558.

Milano, F., Masi, A., Madaghiele, M., Sannino, A., Salvatore, L., Gallo, N., 2023. Current trends in gelatin-based drug delivery systems. Pharmaceutics 15 (5), 1499. https://doi.org/10.3390/pharmaceutics15051499.

Mittal, A., Mahala, N., Dhanawade, N.H., Dubey, S.K., Dubey, U.S., 2024. Evaluation of the cytotoxic activity of sorafenib-loaded camel milk casein nanoparticles against hepatocarcinoma cells. Biotechnol. J. 19 (3). https://doi.org/10.1002/biot.202300449. http://onlinelibrary.wiley.com/journal/10.1002/(ISSN)1860-7314.

Mogues, T., Li, J., Coburn, J., Kuter, D.J., 2005. IgG antibodies against bovine serum albumin in humans - their prevalence and response to exposure to bovine serum albumin. J. Immunol. Methods 300 (1–2), 1–11. https://doi.org/10.1016/j.jim.2005.01.022.

Mohamed, S.A., Helmy, M.W., Mahmoud, H.E., Embaby, A.M., Haroun, M., Sabra, S.A., 2024. Cinnamaldehyde/naringin co-loaded into lactoferrin/casienate-coated zein nanoparticles as a gastric resistance oral carrier for mitigating doxorubicin-induced hepatotoxicity. J. Drug Deliv. Sci. Technol. 96. https://doi.org/10.1016/j.jddst.2024.105688.

Mohammed, L.J., Taheri-Kafrani, A., 2023. Fabrication of doxorubicin loaded aptamer-functionalized cationic β-lactoglobulin nanocomplex: A biocompatible multifunctional nanoplatform for encapsulation and controlled release of anticancer drugs. J. Drug Deliv. Sci. Technol. 81, 104254. https://doi.org/10.1016/j.jddst.2023.104254.

Morán, M.C., Carazo, J., Busquets, M.A., 2018. Dual responsive gelatin-based nanoparticles for enhanced 5-fluorouracil efficiency. Colloids Surf. B Biointerfaces 172, 646–654. https://doi.org/10.1016/j.colsurfb.2018.09.027.

Muj, C., Mukhopadhyay, S., Jana, P., Kondapi, A.K., 2023. Synergistic action of lactoferrin in enhancing the safety and effectiveness of docetaxel treatment against prostate cancer. Cancer Chemother. Pharmacol. 91 (5), 375–387. https://doi.org/10.1007/s00280-023-04524-9.

Mumtaz, S., Ali, S., Pervaiz, A., Qureshi, M.Z., Kanwal, K., Saleem, T., 2023. Apoptotic and antiproliferative effects of silk protein sericin conjugated-AgNO3 nanoparticles in human breast cancer cells. Saudi J. Biol. Sci. 30 (2), 103551. https://doi.org/10.1016/j.sjbs.2022.103551.

Mumtaz, S., Ali, S., Pervaiz, A., Awan, U.A., Nauroze, T., Kanwal, L., Summer, M., Mumtaz, S., Mughal, T.A., Tahir, H.M., 2024. Toxicological effects of dimethlybenzeneanthracene in Balb C mice and pharmacological intervention by silk sericin–conjugated silver nanoparticles. Sci. Prog. 107 (1). https://doi.org/10.1177/00368504231221670. https://journals.sagepub.com/home/SCI.

Musetti, S., Huang, L., 2018. Nanoparticle-mediated remodeling of the tumor microenvironment to enhance immunotherapy. ACS Nano 12 (12), 11740–11755. https://doi.org/10.1021/acsnano.8b05893.

Nayak, D., Thathapudi, N.C., Ashe, S., Nayak, B., 2021. Bioengineered ethosomes encapsulating AgNPs and Tasar silk sericin proteins for non melanoma skin carcinoma (NMSC) as an alternative therapeutics. Int. J. Pharm. 596, 120265. https://doi.org/10.1016/j.ijpharm.2021.120265.

Neri, D., Supuran, C.T., 2011. Interfering with pH regulation in tumours as a therapeutic strategy. Nat. Rev. Drug Discov. 10 (10), 767–777. https://doi.org/10.1038/nrd3554.

Ng, C.W., Li, J., Pu, K., 2018. Recent progresses in phototherapy-synergized cancer immunotherapy. Adv. Funct. Mater. 28 (46), 1804688. https://doi.org/10.1002/adfm.201804688, 1804688.

Norouzi, P., Motasadizadeh, H., Atyabi, F., Dinarvand, R., Gholami, M., Farokhi, M., Shokrgozar, M.A., Mottaghitalab, F., 2021. Combination therapy of breast cancer by codelivery of doxorubicin and survivin siRNA using polyethylenimine modified silk fibroin nanoparticles. ACS Biomater. Sci. Eng. 7 (3), 1074–1087. http://pubs.acs.org/journal/abseba. doi: 10.1021/acsbiomaterials.0c01511.

Oguntade, A.S., Al-Amodi, F., Alrumayh, A., Alobaida, M., Bwalya, M., 2021. Anti-angiogenesis in cancer therapeutics: The magic bullet. J. Egypt. Natl. Cancer Inst. 33 (1). https://jenci.springeropen.com/. doi: 10.1186/s43046-021-00072-6.

Oh, J.Y., Kim, H.S., Palanikumar, L., Go, E.M., Jana, B., Park, S.A., Kim, H.Y., Kim, K., Seo, J.K., Kwak, S.K., Kim, C., Kang, S., Ryu, J.H., 2018. Cloaking nanoparticles with protein corona shield for targeted drug delivery. Nat. Commun. 9 (1). https://doi.org/10.1038/s41467-018-06979-4. http://www.nature.com/ncomms/index.html.

Oktay, S., Alemdar, N., 2019. Electrically controlled release of 5-fluorouracil from conductive gelatin methacryloyl-based hydrogels. J. Appl. Polym. Sci. 136 (1). https://doi.org/10.1002/app.46914. http://onlinelibrary.wiley.com/journal/10.1002/(ISSN)1097-4628.

Onafuye, H., Pieper, S., Mulac, D., Cinatl, J., Wass, M.N., Langer, K., Michaelis, M., 2019. Doxorubicin-loaded human serum albumin nanoparticles overcome transporter-mediated drug resistance in drug-adapted cancer cells. J. Nanotechnol. 10, 1707–1715. https://doi.org/10.3762/bjnano.10.166.

Ou, W., Thapa, R.K., Jiang, L., Soe, Z.C., Gautam, M., Chang, J.H., Jeong, J.H., Ku, S.K., Choi, H.G., Yong, C.S., Kim, J.O., 2018. Regulatory T cell-targeted hybrid nanoparticles combined with immuno-checkpoint blockage for cancer immunotherapy. J. Contr. Release 281, 84–96. https://doi.org/10.1016/j.jconrel.2018.05.018.

Pajoum, Z., Aliabadi, H.A.M., Mohammadi, A., Sadat, Z., Kashtiaray, A., Bani, M.S., Shahiri, M., Mahdavi, M., Eivazzadeh-Keihan, R., Maleki, A., Heravi, M.M., 2024. Hyperthermia and biological investigation of a novel magnetic nanobiocomposite based on acacia gum-silk fibroin hydrogel embedded with poly vinyl alcohol. Heliyon 10 (20). https://doi.org/10.1016/j.heliyon.2024.e39073. https://www.sciencedirect.com/science/journal/24058440.

Palanikumar, L., Al-Hosani, S., Kalmouni, M., Nguyen, V.P., Ali, L., Pasricha, R., Barrera, F.N., Magzoub, M., 2020. pH-responsive high stability polymeric nanoparticles for targeted delivery of anticancer therapeutics. Commun. Biol. 3 (1). https://doi.org/10.1038/s42003-020-0817-4.

Park, Y., Jeong, E.M., 2024. Glutathione dynamics in the tumor microenvironment: A potential target of cancer stem cells and T cells. Int. J. Stem Cells 17 (3), 270–283. https://doi.org/10.15283/ijsc24060.

Park, J.H., Lee, S., Kim, J.-H., Park, K., Kim, K., Kwon, I.C., 2008. Polymeric nanomedicine for cancer therapy. Prog. Polym. Sci. 33 (1), 113–137. https://doi.org/10.1016/j.progpolymsci.2007.09.003.

Peddi, S., Roberts, S.K., Mackay, J.A., 2020. Nanotoxicology of an elastin-like polypeptide rapamycin formulation for breast cancer. Biomacromolecules 21 (3), 1091–1102. https://doi.org/10.1021/acs.biomac.9b01431.

Peer, D., Karp, J.M., Hong, S., Farokhzad, O.C., Margalit, R., Langer, R., 2020. Nanocarriers as an Emerging Platform for Cancer Therapy. Informa UK Limited, Informa UK Limited, pp. 61–91. https://doi.org/10.1201/9780429399039-2.

Pei, W., Cai, L., Gong, X., Zhang, L., Zhang, J., Zhu, P., Jiang, H., Wang, C., Wang, S., Chen, J., 2022. Drug-loaded oleic-acid grafted mesoporous silica nanoparticles conjugated with α-lactalbumin resembling BAMLET-like anticancer agent with improved biocompatibility and therapeutic efficacy. Mater. Today Bio 15, 100272. https://doi.org/10.1016/j.mtbio.2022.100272.

Peng, S., Xiao, F., Chen, M., Gao, H., 2022. Tumor-microenvironment-responsive nanomedicine for enhanced cancer immunotherapy. Adv. Sci. 9 (1). https://doi.org/10.1002/advs.202103836. http://onlinelibrary.wiley.com/journal/10.1002/(ISSN)2198-3844.

Pérez-Lloret, M., Reidy, E., Lozano-Pérez, A.A., Marchal, J.A., Lens, P.N.L., Ryan, A.E., Erxleben, A., 2024. Auranofin loaded silk fibroin nanoparticles for colorectal cancer treatment. Drug Deliv. Transl. Res. https://doi.org/10.1007/s13346-024-01719-2. https://www.springer.com/journal/13346.

Pirota, V., Bisbano, G., Serra, M., Torre, M.L., Doria, F., Bari, E., Paolillo, M., 2023. cRGD-functionalized silk fibroin nanoparticles: A strategy for cancer treatment with a potent unselective naphthalene diimide derivative. Cancers 15 (6). https://doi.org/10.3390/cancers15061725. http://www.mdpi.com/journal/cancers/.

Prasad, P., Gordijo, C.R., Abbasi, A.Z., Maeda, A., Ip, A., Rauth, A.M., Dacosta, R.S., Wu, X.Y., 2014. Multifunctional albumin-MnO2 nanoparticles modulate solid tumor microenvironment by attenuating hypoxia, acidosis, vascular endothelial growth factor and enhance radiation response. ACS Nano 8 (4), 3202–3212. https://doi.org/10.1021/nn405773r.

Qi, F.l., Wang, M.f., Li, B.z., Lu, Z.f., Nie, G.j., Li, S.p., 2020. Reversal of the immunosuppressive tumor microenvironment by nanoparticle-based activation of immune-associated cells. Acta Pharmacol. Sin. 41 (7), 895–901. https://doi.org/10.1038/s41401-020-0423-5.

Qu, N., Song, K., Ji, Y., Liu, M., Chen, L., Lee, R.J., Teng, L., 2024. Albumin nanoparticle-based drug delivery systems. Int. J. Nanomed. 19, 6945–6980. https://doi.org/10.2147/IJN.S467876.

Rahman, M., Dip, T.M., Haase, T., Truong, Y.B., Le, T.C., Houshyar, S., 2023. Fabrication of zein-based fibrous scaffolds for biomedical applications—a review. Macromol. Mater. Eng. https://doi.org/10.1002/mame.202300175. http://onlinelibrary.wiley.com/journal/10.1002/(ISSN)1439-2054.

Rajput, H., Nangare, S., Khan, Z., Patil, A., Bari, S., Patil, P., 2024. Design of lactoferrin functionalized carboxymethyl dextran coated egg albumin nanoconjugate for targeted delivery of capsaicin: spectroscopic and cytotoxicity studies. Int. J. Biol. Macromol. 256 (Pt 1), 128392. https://doi.org/10.1016/j.ijbiomac.2023.128392.

Rani, M., Siddiqi, R.A., Sharma, R., Gill, B.S., Sogi, D.S., 2023. Functional and structural properties of gliadin as influenced by pH, extraction protocols, and wheat cultivars. Int. J. Biol. Macromol. 234. https://doi.org/10.1016/j.ijbiomac.2023.123484. www.elsevier.com/locate/ijbiomac.

Rosenblum, D., Joshi, N., Tao, W., Karp, J.M., Peer, D., 2018. Progress and challenges towards targeted delivery of cancer therapeutics. Nat. Commun. 9 (1). https://doi.org/10.1038/s41467-018-03705-y. http://www.nature.com/ncomms/index.html.

Ruzzi, F., Palladini, A., Clemmensen, S., Strøbæk, A., Buijs, N., Domeyer, T., Dorosz, J., Soroka, V., Grzadziela, D., Rasmussen, C.J., Nielsen, I.B., Soegaard, M., Semprini, M.S., Scalambra, L., Angelicola, S., Landuzzi, L., Lollini, P.-L., Thorn, M., 2022. Prevention and therapy of metastatic HER-2+ mammary carcinoma with a human candidate HER-2 virus-like particle vaccine. Biomedicines 10 (10), 2654. https://doi.org/10.3390/biomedicines10102654.

Ryu, J.S., Kratz, F., Raucher, D., 2021. Cell-penetrating doxorubicin released from elastin-like polypeptide kills doxorubicin-resistant cancer cells in in vitro study. Int. J. Mol. Sci. 22 (3), 1–11. https://doi.org/10.3390/ijms22031126.

Saad, M., El-Samad, L.M., Gomaa, R.A., Augustyniak, M., Hassan, M.A., 2023. A comprehensive review of recent advances in silk sericin: extraction approaches, structure, biochemical characterization, and biomedical applications. Int. J. Biol. Macromol. 250. https://doi.org/10.1016/j.ijbiomac.2023.126067. https://www.sciencedirect.com/journal/international-journal-of-biological-macromolecules.

Sadat, Z., Kashtiaray, A., Ganjali, F., Aliabadi, H.A.M., Naderi, N., Bani, M.S., Shojaei, S., Eivazzadeh-Keihan, R., Maleki, A., Mahdavi, M., 2024. Production of a magnetic nanocomposite for biological and hyperthermia applications based on chitosan-silk fibroin hydrogel incorporated with carbon nitride. Int. J. Biol. Macromol. 279. https://doi.org/10.1016/j.ijbiomac.2024.135052. https://www.sciencedirect.com/science/journal/01418130.

Sarangthem, V., Seo, B.Y., Yi, A., Lee, Y.J., Cheon, S.H., Kim, S.K., Singh, T.D., Lee, B.H., Park, R.W., 2020. Effects of molecular weight and structural conformation of multivalent-based elastin-like polypeptides on tumor accumulation and tissue biodistribution. Nanotheranostics 4 (2), 57–70. https://doi.org/10.7150/ntno.39804.

Sarangthem, V., Yi, A., Kim, Y., Rehemtulla, A., Lee, B.H., Jeon, Y.H., Singh, T.D., Park, R.W., 2021. Therapeutic effect of IL-4 receptor-targeting pro-apoptotic peptide (Ap1-elp-klak) in glioblastoma tumor model. Int. J. Nanomed. 16, 5039–5052. https://doi.org/10.2147/IJN.S316388.

Sarkar, S., Gulati, K., Mishra, A., Poluri, K.M., 2020. Protein nanocomposites: Special inferences to lysozyme based nanomaterials. Int. J. Biol. Macromol. 151, 467–482. https://doi.org/10.1016/j.ijbiomac.2020.02.179.

Schaal, J.L., Bhattacharyya, J., Brownstein, J., Strickland, K.C., Kelly, G., Saha, S., Milligan, J., Banskota, S., Li, X., Liu, W., 2022. I-ELP brachytherapy synergizes with nanoparticle paclitaxel to overcome resistance to radiochemotherapy in multiple pancreatic tumors. Nat. Biomed. Eng. 131 (10). https://doi.org/10.1038/s41551-022-00949-4.

Shen, F., Feng, L., Zhu, Y., Tao, D., Xu, J., Peng, R., Liu, Z., 2020. Oxaliplatin-/NLG919 prodrugs-constructed liposomes for effective chemo-immunotherapy of colorectal cancer. Biomaterials 255, 120190. https://doi.org/10.1016/j.biomaterials.2020.120190.

Shen, X., Liu, X., Li, T., Chen, Y., Chen, Y., Wang, P., Zheng, L., Yang, H., Wu, C., Deng, S., Liu, Y., 2021. Recent advancements in serum albumin-based nanovehicles toward potential cancer diagnosis and therapy. Front. Chem. 9. https://doi.org/10.3389/fchem.2021.746646. http://journal.frontiersin.org/journal/chemistry.

Shen, L., Zhou, P., Wang, Y.M., Zhu, Z., Yuan, Q., Cao, S., Li, J., 2024. Supramolecular nanoparticles based on elastin-like peptides modified capsid protein as drug delivery platform with enhanced cancer chemotherapy efficacy. Int. J. Biol. Macromol. 256 (Pt 2), 128107. https://doi.org/10.1016/j.ijbiomac.2023.128107.

Shirangi, A., Mottaghitalab, F., Dinarvand, S., Atyabi, F., 2022. Theranostic silk sericin/SPION nanoparticles for targeted delivery of ROR1 siRNA: Synthesis, characterization, diagnosis and anticancer effect on triple-negative breast cancer. Int. J. Biol. Macromol. 221, 604–612. https://doi.org/10.1016/j.ijbiomac.2022.09.020.

Sinai Kunde, S., Wairkar, S., 2022. Folic acid anchored urchin-like raloxifene nanoparticles for receptor targeting in breast cancer: Synthesis, optimisation and in vitro biological evaluation. Int. J. Pharm. 623, 121926. https://doi.org/10.1016/j.ijpharm.2022.121926.

Somu, P., Paul, S., 2021. Surface conjugation of curcumin with self-assembled lysozyme nanoparticle enhanced its bioavailability and therapeutic efficacy in multiple cancer cells. J. Mol. Liq. 338, 116623. https://doi.org/10.1016/j.molliq.2021.116623.

Song, Y., Wang, Z., Ji, H., Jiang, Z., Li, X., Du, Z., Song, W., Sun, Y., 2024. Fatty acid modification of casein bioactive peptides nano-assemblies, synthesis, characterization and anticarcinogenic effect. Int. J. Biol. Macromol. 254 (Pt 1), 127718. https://doi.org/10.1016/j.ijbiomac.2023.127718.

Srivastav, A.K., Rajput, P.K., Jaiswal, J., Yadav, U.C.S., Kumar, U., 2024. In vitro and in silico investigation of glycyrrhizic acid encapsulated zein nanoparticles: A synergistic targeted drug delivery approach for breast cancer. Int. J. Biol. Macromol. 266. https://doi.org/10.1016/j.ijbiomac.2024.131368. https://www.sciencedirect.com/science/journal/01418130.

Sun, Y., Wei, Z., Xue, C., 2023. Development of zein-based nutraceutical delivery systems: A systematic overview based on recent researches. Food Hydrocoll. 137, 108368. https://doi.org/10.1016/j.foodhyd.2022.108368.

Tang, Y., Liang, J., Wu, A., Chen, Y., Zhao, P., Lin, T., Zhang, M., Xu, Q., Wang, J., Huang, Y., 2017. Co-delivery of trichosanthin and albendazole by nano-self-assembly for overcoming tumor multidrug-resistance and metastasis. ACS Appl. Mater. Interfaces 9 (32), 26648–26664. http://pubs.acs.org/journal/aamick. doi: 10.1021/acsami.7b05292.

Tang, Y., Zhang, L., Sun, R., Luo, B., Zhou, Y., Zhang, Y., Liang, Y., Xiao, B., Wang, C., 2023. Pulmonary delivery of mucus-traversing PF127-modified silk fibroin nanoparticles loading with quercetin for lung cancer therapy. Asian J. Pharm. Sci. 18 (4), 100833. https://doi.org/10.1016/j.ajps.2023.100833.

Tavakoli, N., Divsalar, A., Haertlé, T., Sawyer, L., Saboury, A.A., Muronetz, V., 2021. Milk protein-based nanodelivery systems for the cancer treatment. J. Nanostruct. Chem. 11 (4), 483–500. https://doi.org/10.1007/s40097-021-00399-5.

Thakur, S., Shahtaghi, N.R., Kaur, M., Shivgotra, R., Jain, S.K., 2023. Gelatin in drug delivery system for treatment of lung diseases. In: Natural polymeric materials based drug delivery systems in lung diseases. Springer Nature, India, India, pp. 235–244. https://doi.org/10.1007/978-981-19-7656-8_13. https://link.springer.com/book/10.1007/978-981-19-7656-8.

Torres-Martinez, Z., Pérez, D., Grace, T., Sthephanie, E., Correa, C., Mederos, N., Velazquez, K., Castillo, B., Griebenow, K., Delgado, Y., 2023. A synergistic pH-responsive serum albumin-based drug delivery system loaded with doxorubicin and pentacyclic triterpene betulinic acid for potential treatment of NSCLC. BioTech 12 (1), 13. https://doi.org/10.3390/biotech12010013.

Tran, D.H.N., Nguyen, T.H., Vo, T.N.N., Pham, L.P.T., Vo, D.M.H., Nguyen, C.K., Bach, L.G., Nguyen, D.H., 2019. Self-assembled poly (ethylene glycol) methyl ether-grafted gelatin nanogels for efficient delivery of curcumin in cancer treatment. J. Appl. Polym. Sci. 136 (20). https://doi.org/10.1002/app.47544.

Tran, X., Mulac, D., Langer, K., 2024. Investigating the selectivity of the targeting properties of trastuzumab-bound nanoparticles to HER2/neu positive cells in co-culture. J. Drug Deliv. Sci. Technol. 100, 106040. https://doi.org/10.1016/j.jddst.2024.106040.

Vaghasiya, K., Ray, E., Singh, R., Jadhav, K., Sharma, A., Khan, R., Katare, O.P., Verma, R.K., 2021. Efficient, enzyme responsive and tumor receptor targeting gelatin nanoparticles decorated with concanavalin-A for site-specific and controlled drug delivery for cancer therapy. Mater. Sci. Eng. C 123. https://doi.org/10.1016/j.msec.2021.112027. https://www.journals.elsevier.com/materials-science-and-engineering-c.

Varanko, A., Saha, S., Chilkoti, A., 2020a. Recent trends in protein and peptide-based biomaterials for advanced drug delivery. Adv. Drug Deliv. Rev. 156, 133–187. https://doi.org/10.1016/j.addr.2020.08.008.

Varanko, A.K., Su, J.C., Chilkoti, A., 2020b. Elastin-like polypeptides for biomedical applications. Annu. Rev. Biomed. Eng. 22, 343–369. http://www.annualreviews.org/journal/bioeng. doi: 10.1146/annurev-bioeng-092419-061127.

Varlamova, E.G., Zaripov, O.G., 2020. Beta–lactoglobulin–nutrition allergen and nanotransporter of different nature ligands therapy with therapeutic action. Res. Vet. Sci. 133, 17–25. https://doi.org/10.1016/j.rvsc.2020.08.014.

Vaupel, P., Schlenger, K., Knoop, C., Höckel, M., 1991. Oxygenation of human tumors: evaluation of tissue oxygen distribution in breast cancers by computerized O2 tension measurements. Cancer Res. 51 (12), 3316–3322.

Voci, S., Gagliardi, A., Ambrosio, N., Salvatici, M.C., Fresta, M., Cosco, D., 2023. Gliadin nanoparticles containing doxorubicin hydrochloride: Characterization and cytotoxicity. Pharmaceutics 15 (1). https://doi.org/10.3390/pharmaceutics15010180. http://www.mdpi.com/journal/pharmaceutics.

Wang, S., Huang, P., Chen, X.Y., 2016a. Hierarchical targeting strategy for enhanced tumor tissue accumulation/retention and cellular internalization. Adv. Mater. 28 (34), 7340–7364. https://doi.org/10.1002/adma.201601498. http://onlinelibrary.wiley.com/journal/10.1002/(ISSN)1521-4095.

Wang, Z., Wu, H., Shi, H., Wang, M., Huang, C., Jia, N., 2016b. A novel multifunctional biomimetic Au@BSA nanocarrier as a potential siRNA theranostic nanoplatform. J. Mater. Chem. B 4 (14), 2519–2526. https://doi.org/10.1039/c5tb02326b.

Wang, J., Zhang, Y., Jin, N., Mao, C., Yang, M., 2019. Protein-induced gold nanoparticle assembly for improving the photothermal effect in cancer therapy. ACS Appl. Mater. Interfaces 11 (12), 11136–11143. http://pubs.acs.org/journal/aamick. doi: 10.1021/acsami.8b21488.

Wang, Y., Chen, S., Yang, X., Zhang, S., Cui, C., 2021. Preparation optimization of bovine serum albumin nanoparticles and its application for siRNA delivery. Drug Des. Dev. Ther. 15, 1531–1547. https://doi.org/10.2147/DDDT.S299479.

Wang, J., Wang, Y., Chen, Y., Lv, R., Yu, Y., Wang, J., Cheng, Q., Shuai, Y., Chen, Y., Mao, C., Yang, M., 2023a. Biomimetic nucleation of manganese oxide on silk fibroin nanoparticles for designing raspberry-structured tumor environment-responsive anticancer nanocarriers. Advanced NanoBiomed Research 3 (11). https://doi.org/10.1002/anbr.202300056. https://onlinelibrary.wiley.com/journal/26999307.

Wang, L., Geng, H., Liu, Y., Liu, L., Chen, Y., Wu, F., Liu, Z., Ling, S., Wang, Y., Zhou, L., 2023b. Hot and cold tumors: Immunological features and the therapeutic strategies. MedComm 4 (5). https://doi.org/10.1002/mco2.343.

Wang, M., He, M., Zhang, M., Xue, S., Xu, T., Zhao, Y., Li, D., Zhi, F., Ding, D., 2023c. Controllable hypoxia-activated chemotherapy as a dual enhancer for synergistic cancer photodynamic immunotherapy. Biomaterials 301, 122257. https://doi.org/10.1016/j.biomaterials.2023.122257.

Wang, C., Zhao, J., Duan, Y., Lin, L., Zhang, Q., Zheng, H., Shan, W., Wang, X., Ren, L., 2024. Tumor-associated myeloid cells selective delivery of a therapeutic tumor nano-vaccine for overcoming immune barriers for effective and long-term cancer immunotherapy. Adv. Healthcare Mater. 13 (26). https://doi.org/10.1002/adhm.202401416. http://onlinelibrary.wiley.com/journal/10.1002/(ISSN)2192-2659.

Wenck, C., Meier, N., Heinrich, E., Grützner, V., Wiekhorst, F., Bleul, R., 2024. Design and characterisation of casein coated and drug loaded magnetic nanoparticles for theranostic applications. RSC Adv. 14 (36), 26388–26399. https://doi.org/10.1039/d4ra02626h.

Wilhelm, S., Tavares, A.J., Dai, Q., Ohta, S., Audet, J., Dvorak, H.F., Chan, W.C.W., 2016. Analysis of nanoparticle delivery to tumours. Nat. Rev. Mater. 1. https://doi.org/10.1038/natrevmats.2016.14.

Wijewantha, N., Eikanger, M.M., Antony, R.M., Potts, R.A., Rezvani, K., Sereda, G., 2021. Targeting colon cancer cells with enzyme-triggered casein-gated release of cargo from mesoporous silica-based nanoparticles. Bioconjug. Chem. 32 (11), 2353–2365. https://doi.org/10.1021/acs.bioconjchem.1c00416.

Wilson, W.R., Hay, M.P., 2011. Targeting hypoxia in cancer therapy. Nat. Rev. Cancer 11 (6), 393–410. https://doi.org/10.1038/nrc3064.

Wu, J., Zhang, J., Deng, C., Meng, F., Cheng, R., Zhong, Z., 2017. Robust, responsive, and targeted PLGA anticancer nanomedicines by combination of reductively cleavable surfactant and covalent hyaluronic acid coating. ACS Appl. Mater. Interfaces 9 (4), 3985–3994. https://doi.org/10.1021/acsami.6b15105.

Wu, T., Jiang, Q., Wu, D., Hu, Y., Chen, S., Ding, T., Ye, X., Liu, D., Chen, J., 2019. What is new in lysozyme research and its application in food industry? A review. Food Chem. 274, 698–709. https://doi.org/10.1016/j.foodchem.2018.09.017.

Wu, Z., Chen, Y., Xia, Q., Qu, Y., Yang, H., Du, Q., Xu, B., 2024. Pre-coating cRGD-modified bovine serum albumin enhanced the anti-tumor angiogenesis of siVEGF-loaded chitosan-based nanoparticles by manipulating the protein corona composition. Int. J. Biol. Macromol. 267 (Pt 2), 131546. https://doi.org/10.1016/j.ijbiomac.2024.131546.

Xia, Y., Xu, R., Ye, S., Yan, J., Kumar, P., Zhang, P., Zhao, X., 2023. Microfluidic formulation of curcumin-loaded multiresponsive gelatin nanoparticles for anticancer therapy. ACS Biomater. Sci. Eng. 9 (6), 3402–3413. https://doi.org/10.1021/acsbiomaterials.3c00318.

Xie, J., Mei, L., Huang, K., Sun, Y., Iris, A., Ma, B., Qiu, Y., Li, J., Han, G., 2019. A photo-inducible protein-inorganic nanoparticle assembly for active targeted tumour theranostics. Nanoscale 11 (13), 6136–6144. https://doi.org/10.1039/C9NR01120J.

Xu, M., Zhao, D., Chen, Y., Chen, C., Zhang, L., Sun, L., Chen, J., Tang, Q., Sun, S., Ma, C., Liang, X., Wang, S., 2022a. Charge reversal polypyrrole nanocomplex-mediated gene delivery and photothermal therapy for effectively treating papillary thyroid cancer and inhibiting lymphatic metastasis. ACS Appl. Mater. Interfaces 14 (12), 14072–14086. https://doi.org/10.1021/acsami.1c25179.

Xu, W., Zheng, S., Sun, H., Li, Z., Xi, R., Luo, D., Li, Y., Shah, B.R., 2022b. Green-step fabrication of gliadin/sodium caseinate nanogels for methotrexate release, cytotoxicity and cell phagocytosis. J. Drug Deliv. Sci. Technol. 67, 103028. https://doi.org/10.1016/j.jddst.2021.103028.

Yan, X., Li, M., Xu, X., Liu, X., Liu, F., 2022. Zein-based nano-delivery systems for encapsulation and protection of hydrophobic bioactives: A review. Front. Nutr. 9. https://doi.org/10.3389/fnut.2022.999373.

Yang, S., Gao, H., 2017. Nanoparticles for modulating tumor microenvironment to improve drug delivery and tumor therapy. Pharmacol. Res. 126, 97–108. https://doi.org/10.1016/j.phrs.2017.05.004.

Yang, C., Chen, D., Zhang, L., Liu, J., 2018. Tumor-pH-Responsive dissociable albumin-tamoxifen nanocomplexes enabling efficient tumor penetration and hypoxia relief for enhanced cancer photodynamic therapy. Small 14 (49). https://doi.org/10.1002/smll.201803262.

Yang, J., Wang, T., Zhao, L., Rajasekhar, V.K., Joshi, S., Andreou, C., Pal, S., Hsu, H.t., Zhang, H., Cohen, I.J., Huang, R., Hendrickson, R.C., Miele, M.M., Pei, W., Brendel, M.B., Healey, J.H., Chiosis, G., Kircher, M.F., 2020. Gold/alpha-lactalbumin nanoprobes for the imaging and treatment of breast cancer. Nat. Biomed. Eng. 4 (7), 686–703. https://doi.org/10.1038/s41551-020-0584-z.

Yang, M., Li, J., Gu, P., Fan, X., 2021. The application of nanoparticles in cancer immunotherapy: Targeting tumor microenvironment. Bioact. Mater. 6 (7), 1973–1987. https://doi.org/10.1016/j.bioactmat.2020.12.010.

Yao, F., An, Y., Lai, X., Li, X., Yu, Z., Yang, X.D., 2023. Novel nanotherapeutics for cancer immunotherapy by CTLA-4 aptamer-functionalized albumin nanoparticle loaded with antihistamine. J. Cancer Res. Clin. Oncol. 149 (10), 7515–7527. https://doi.org/10.1007/s00432-023-04698-y.

Yi, A., Sim, D., Lee, Y.J., Sarangthem, V., Park, R.W., 2020. Development of elastin-like polypeptide for targeted specific gene delivery in vivo. J. Nanobiotechnology 18 (1). https://doi.org/10.1186/s12951-020-0574-z.

Yu, Q., Qiu, Y., Li, J., Tang, X., Wang, X., Cun, X., Xu, S., Liu, Y., Li, M., Zhang, Z., He, Q., 2020a. Targeting cancer-associated fibroblasts by dual-responsive lipid-albumin nanoparticles to enhance drug perfusion for pancreatic tumor therapy. J. Contr. Release 321, 564–575. https://doi.org/10.1016/j.jconrel.2020.02.040.

Yu, X., Wu, H., Hu, H., Dong, Z., Dang, Y., Qi, Q., Wang, Y., Du, S., Lu, Y., 2020b. Zein nanoparticles as nontoxic delivery system for maytansine in the treatment of non-small cell lung cancer. Drug Deliv. 27 (1), 100–109. https://doi.org/10.1080/10717544.2019.1704942.

Yu, C., Ding, Z., Liu, H., Ren, Y., Zhang, M., Liao, Q., Luo, T., Gao, L., Lyu, S., Tan, H., Hu, L., Chen, Z., Xu, P., Xiao, E., 2023. Novel albumin-binding multifunctional probe for synergistic enhancement of FL/MR dual-modal imaging and photothermal therapy. Front. Chem. 11. https://doi.org/10.3389/fchem.2023.1253379. http://journal.frontiersin.org/journal/chemistry.

Yu, K., Wang, Y., Sun, H., Lou, Y., Bao, H., Wang, X., Zhang, J., Shi, J., Tang, G., Wang, Q., Bai, H., 2024. Silk fibroin-based Lenvatinib nanomedicine with conformation tunability for systemic treatment of hepatocellular carcinoma. ACS Appl. Mater. Interfaces 16 (44), 60070–60083. http://pubs.acs.org/journal/aamick. doi: 10.1021/acsami.4c16424.

Yuan, Y., Xiao, J., Zhang, P., Ma, M., Wang, D., Xu, Y., 2021. Development of pH-driven zein/tea saponin composite nanoparticles for encapsulation and oral delivery of curcumin. Food Chem. 364, 130401. https://doi.org/10.1016/j.foodchem.2021.130401.

Yuan, C.S., Teng, Z., Yang, S., He, Z., Meng, L.Y., Chen, X.G., Liu, Y., 2022. Reshaping hypoxia and silencing CD73 via biomimetic gelatin nanotherapeutics to boost immunotherapy. J. Contr. Release 351, 255–271. https://doi.org/10.1016/j.jconrel.2022.09.029.

Yuan, B., Liu, Y., Lv, M., Sui, Y., Hou, S., Yang, T., Belhadj, Z., Zhou, Y., Chang, N., Ren, Y., Sun, C., 2023. Virus-like particle-based nanocarriers as an emerging platform for drug delivery. J. Drug Target. 31 (5), 433–455. https://doi.org/10.1080/1061186X.2023.2193358.

Yuan, Y., Nasri, M., Manayi, A., Zhang, J., Wu, C., Jeon, T.J., Kang, L., 2024. Sericin coats of silk fibres, a degumming waste or future material? Mater. Today Bio 29. https://doi.org/10.1016/j.mtbio.2024.101306. https://www.sciencedirect.com/science/journal/25900064.

Yur, D., Sullivan, M.O., Chen, W., 2023. Highly modular hepatitis B virus-like nanocarriers for therapeutic protein encapsulation and targeted delivery to triple negative breast cancer cells. J. Mater. Chem. B 11 (18), 3985–3993. https://doi.org/10.1039/d3tb00445g.

Zahariev, N., Draganova, M., Zagorchev, P., Pilicheva, B., 2023. Casein-based nanoparticles: A potential tool for the delivery of Daunorubicin in acute lymphocytic leukemia. Pharmaceutics 15 (2), 471. https://doi.org/10.3390/pharmaceutics15020471.

Zayed, D.G., Khattab, S.N., Heikal, L., Teleb, M., Ghareeb, D.A., Abdulmalek, S.A., Mady, O.Y., Salem, N.M.H., Elgizawy, S.A., 2024. Tailored design of pH-responsive microbeads for oral delivery of lactoferrin nanotherapeutics of colon cancer. J. Drug Deliv. Sci. Technol. 97. https://doi.org/10.1016/j.jddst.2024.105791. https://www.sciencedirect.com/science/journal/17732247.

Zhang, Y., Wang, J., 2024. Current status and prospects of gelatin and its derivatives in oncological applications: Review. Int. J. Biol. Macromol. 274 (Pt 1), 133590. https://doi.org/10.1016/j.ijbiomac.2024.133590.

Zhang, X., Huang, Y., Song, H., Canup, B.S.B., Gou, S., She, Z., Dai, F., Ke, B., Xiao, B., 2020. Inhibition of growth and lung metastasis of breast cancer by tumor-homing triple-bioresponsive nanotherapeutics. J. Contr. Release 328, 454–469. https://doi.org/10.1016/j.jconrel.2020.08.066.

Zhang, Q., Li, D., Guan, S., Liu, D., Wang, J., Xing, G., Yue, L., Cai, D., 2022. Tumor-targeted delivery of honokiol via polysialic acid modified zein nanoparticles prevents breast cancer progression and metastasis. Int. J. Biol. Macromol. 203, 280–291. https://doi.org/10.1016/j.ijbiomac.2022.01.148.

Zhang, J., Fang, R., Li, Y., Jin, J., Yang, F., Chen, J., 2023. Encapsulation of Au(III) complex using lactoferrin nanoparticles to combat glioma. Mol. Pharm. 20 (7), 3632–3644. http://pubs.acs.org/journal/mpohbp. doi: 10.1021/acs.molpharmaceut.3c00239.

Zhang, Q., Zhao, Y., Yao, Y., Wu, N., Chen, S., Xu, L., Tu, Y., 2024. Characteristics of hen egg white lysozyme, strategies to break through antibacterial limitation, and its application in food preservation: A review. Food Res. Int. 181. https://doi.org/10.1016/j.foodres.2024.114114. https://www.sciencedirect.com/science/journal/09639969.

Zhao, Y., Fay, F., Hak, S., Manuel Perez-Aguilar, J., Sanchez-Gaytan, B.L., Goode, B., Duivenvoorden, R., De Lange Davies, C., Bjørkøy, A., Weinstein, H., Fayad, Z.A., Pérez-Medina, C., Mulder, W.J.M., 2016. Augmenting drug-carrier compatibility improves tumour nanotherapy efficacy. Nat. Commun. 7. https://doi.org/10.1038/ncomms11221. http://www.nature.com/ncomms/index.html.

Zheng, L., Cheng, L., Xiang, X., Jia, R., Zhu, S., Zhang, Q., Cheng, G., Wu, B., Liu, Z., Tong, X., Xiao, B., Dai, F., 2024a. Cuproptosis-based layer-by-layer silk fibroin nanoplatform-loaded PD-L1 siRNA combining photothermal and chemodynamic therapy against metastatic breast cancer. Mater. Today Bio 29, 101298. https://doi.org/10.1016/j.mtbio.2024.101298.

Zheng, B., Chen, Y., Niu, L., Zhang, X., Yang, Y., Wang, S., Chen, W., Cai, Z., Huang, W., Huang, W., 2024b. Modulating the tumoral SPARC content to enhance albumin-based drug delivery for cancer therapy. J. Contr. Release 366, 596–610. https://doi.org/10.1016/j.jconrel.2023.12.057.

Zhou, K., Zhu, Y., Chen, X., Li, L., Xu, W., 2020. Redox-and MMP-2-sensitive drug delivery nanoparticles based on gelatin and albumin for tumor targeted delivery of paclitaxel. Mater. Sci. Eng. C 114. https://doi.org/10.1016/j.msec.2020.111006.

Zu, M., Ma, Y., Zhang, J., Sun, J., Shahbazi, M.A., Pan, G., Reis, R.L., Kundu, S.C., Liu, J., Xiao, B., 2024. An oral nanomedicine elicits in situ vaccination effect against colorectal cancer. ACS Nano 18 (4), 3651–3668. https://doi.org/10.1021/acsnano.3c11436.

CHAPTER

# 8

# Protein nanoparticles in cancer imaging

*Swagat Ranjan Maharana*[1], *Kiran Mahapatra*[1], *Aiswarya Pati*[1], *Sheary Somam Tete*[1], *Archana Padhiary*[1], *Binata Nayak*[1], *Safdar Ali*[2], *Showkat Ahmad Mir*[1] *and Mehboob Hoque*[3]

[1]**School of Life Sciences, Sambalpur University, Jyotivihar, Odisha, India;** [2]**Applied Biochemistry Lab, Department of Biological Sciences, Aliah University, Kolkata, West Bengal, India;** [3]**Clinical and Applied Genomics Lab, Department of Biological Sciences, Aliah University, Kolkata, West Bengal, India**

## 1. Introduction

Spectroscopy and optical imaging have attracted a lot of interest in the domain of medical science and biomedical research due to their compact design, low cost, and ability to offer detailed molecular and functional insights (Hebden et al., 1997). Absorption, scattering, and light emission are some of the photophysical processes that occur when light interacts with biological tissues during optical imaging. These procedures are helpful for gathering structural and biochemical data regarding specific cells or tissues. Several imaging platforms, such as planar, diffuse, spectroscopic, and hybrid biomedical optics, rely on the numerous contrast mechanisms made possible by these optical approaches. The range of imaging platforms highlights the versatility and efficacy of optical technology in cancer monitoring and detection (Solomon et al., 2011). Optical imaging can be classified into three types, e.g., fluorescence, near-infrared (NIR), and photoacoustic imaging (PAI) (Liu et al., 2017).

Fluorescence has become the favored technique for live cell imaging, especially when aiming for fine cellular resolution and multiplex imaging. This approach enables the simultaneous visualization of various targets, each labeled with distinct fluorescent colors, allowing for detailed and dynamic cellular studies. These advancements are proving invaluable for both preoperative cancer diagnostics and fluorescence-guided surgery, offering real-

*Protein-Based Nanoparticles in Drug Delivery*
https://doi.org/10.1016/B978-0-443-33639-3.00019-2

time, enhanced visual guidance for surgeons (Liu et al., 2017; Wang et al., 2018). Numerous fluorescent probes can be used for in vivo tumor imaging. These include biologically marked macromolecules such as antibodies, fluorescent proteins, fluorescent polymer compounds, upconversion nanoparticles, and quantum dots (QDs) (Lv et al., 2016; Chan et al., 2018). Fluorescent proteins are often used to identify native proteins in biomedical research. These applications help us to study about small molecules, the activities of enzymes, and the presence of different proteins and ions in the cells (Chan et al., 2018).

NIR has low absorption and autofluorescence from biological tissues within the 700–1000 nm wavelength range, which has attracted a lot of interest among the scientists. This enables sensitive, noninvasive imaging, improves tissue penetration, and lowers the background noise (Hilderbrand and Weissleder, 2010). Cancer imaging using NIR fluorescence depends on high-performance NIR probes with superior chemical and photophysical properties.

Along with excellent chemical stability and photostability, they also have high molar absorptivity and quantum yield to enhance fluorescence. In addition, they should have functional groups for bioconjugation with targeted ligands and are water-soluble to avoid aggregation. In general, NIR probes have two categories: organic or inorganic compounds (Frangioni, 2003).

Although metal nanoparticles and QDs, which are examples of inorganic NIR agents, have become popular as fluorescent probes in the biological imaging field, they have drawbacks such as cytotoxicity, expensive and small-scale manufacture, and repeatability problems (Wang and Chen, 2011; Nurunnabi et al., 2010). On the other hand, organic NIR dyes show greater promise because of their improved photophysical characteristics, easy conjugation with biomolecules such as proteins, DNA, and antibodies, and scalable production, which makes them perfect for molecular imaging applications (Tromberg et al., 2008; Xu et al., 2009).

An advanced development in ultrasonic technology, PAI exploits the absorption of optical radiation to produce acoustic waves. When a short, noninvasive laser pulse is applied to tissues, the absorbed light changes into heat, which expands thermally with detectable waves. Some of the strengths of this technology include high contrast, high signal-to-noise ratios, and the capability to image large amounts of biological tissue without the use of ionizing radiation or tissue damage. This is a bioengineering advance because of its deep tissue penetration with improved resolution and optical contrast. In PAI, it uses endogenous as well as exogenous contrast molecules. Naturally occurring molecules like hemoglobin and melanin are endogenous agents, which have strong optical absorption in the visible and NIR regions. This high absorption allows them to produce a notable photoacoustic contrast relative to the surrounding tissues. However, imaging early-stage tumors using only endogenous contrast agents often provides insufficient information. To address this, biocompatible exogenous contrast agents are employed, offering improved signal contrast and enhanced image quality (Zhang et al., 2011).

Clinical and preclinical research can greatly benefit from in vivo structural imaging, but in order to learn about the actual structures of the physiological time-varying processes that underlie disease manifestations, morphological data and in vivo molecular imaging need to be combined (Vaquero and Kinahan, 2015). Positron emission tomography (PET) is rapidly gaining popularity due to its unmistakable status as a distinct imaging technique that has demonstrated clinical utility in the treatment of cancer patients (Vaquero and Kinahan, 2015). Relative to other cross-sectional imaging modalities like computed tomography

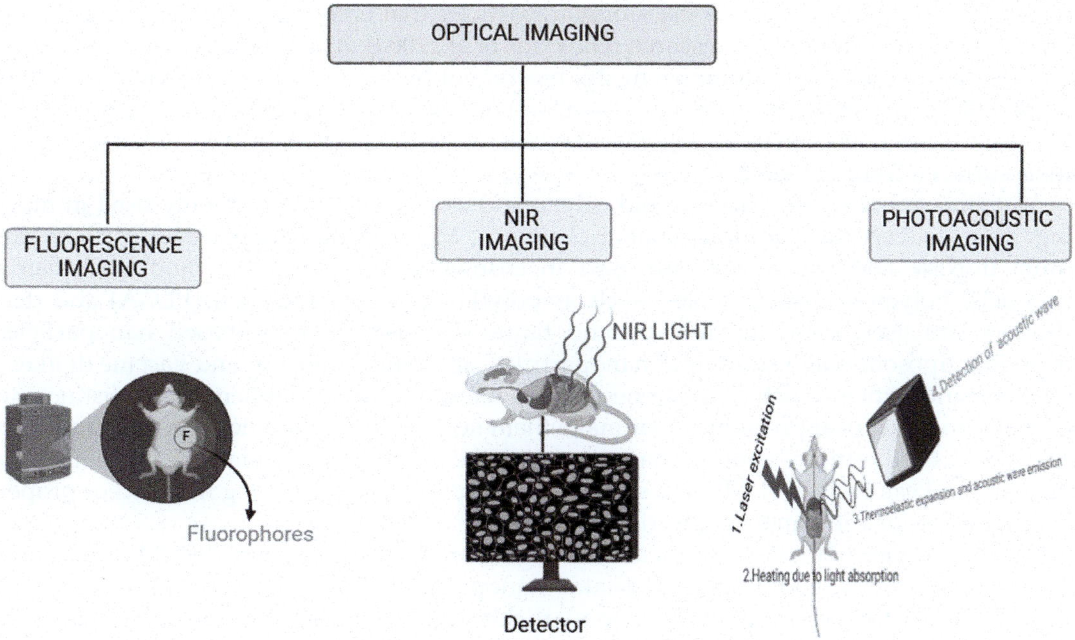


**FIGURE 8.1** Types of optical imaging.

(CT), PET provides a clear advantage because, unlike other imaging modalities, it quantitatively demonstrates the scintigraphy representation of both tumor physiology and architecture (Jiang et al., 2019). PET is a noninvasive imaging tool that provides physiological information by injecting radioactive compounds called radiotracer. Initially, PET imaging was used for research, but nowadays it is often employed for cancer detection and stage identification. Also, it helps to treat certain heart and brain disorders (Neupane et al., 2018). The primary basis for its growing popularity is that PET imaging, when combined with specific imaging agents, can provide necessary knowledge regarding the functioning of tissues and organs. Depending on the agent and the disease, PET imaging might be used to detect and identify diseases (Tai and Piccini, 2004), determine the type and stage of diseases, plan and predict treatment outcomes (Tai and Piccini, 2004), evaluate the efficacy of therapy (Slough et al., 2016), and monitor alterations over time (Suridjan et al., 2019). The accuracy of diagnoses and the efficiency of therapeutic strategies are enhanced by the utilization of functional and anatomical imaging, which eventually improves patient outcomes. The various optical imaging methods are shown in Fig. 8.1.

## 2. Protein nanoparticles used in cancer optical imaging

Protein nanotechnology is a rapidly developing field of study that combines nanoscale technology with the various physicochemical characteristics of proteins. Protein nanoparticles (PNPs) are a new class of nanoparticles that emerged from the integration of this field into pharmaceutical research (Hawkins et al., 2008). Among nanocarriers, PNPs are unique due to their low immunogenicity, biocompatibility, and biodegradability. Furthermore, mild preparation conditions are used, and no toxic solvents are required (Lohcharoenkal et al., 2014). PNPs can be readily modified thanks to the presence of functional groups on their surface (Weber et al., 2000).

Metallic nanoparticles, such as gold, silver, and iron oxide, are commonly used in imaging, drug delivery, and antimicrobial applications. Metal oxide nanoparticles, such as titanium dioxide and zinc oxide, are used in cosmetics, UV protection, and antibacterial products. Polymeric nanoparticles, such as poly(lactic-co-glycolic acid) (PLGA) and dendrimers, are used for drug delivery and tissue engineering. Lipid-based nanoparticles, including liposomes and solid lipid nanoparticles, are critical for drug and vaccine delivery. Carbon nanoparticles, such as fullerenes, carbon nanotubes, and graphene, have distinct mechanical and electrical properties that make them suitable for biomedical and electronic applications. Furthermore, ceramic nanoparticles like silica and alumina are used in drug delivery and catalysis, and QDs are semiconductor particles with strong fluorescent properties, ideal for imaging and diagnostics.

Some examples of PNPs used in cancer imaging are ferritin nanoparticles (FNs), albumin-based nanoparticles, apolipoprotein-related nanoparticles, transferrin nanoparticles, virus-like PNPs, elastin-like polypeptide nanoparticles, and antibody-based nanoparticles (Fig. 8.2).

## 2.1 Ferritin nanoparticles

Ferritin has a hollow cavity and the ability to store iron. It is composed of a hydrated iron oxide core ($5Fe_2O_3\sqrt{9H_2O}$) with 6 nm diameter, covered by a spherical polypeptide shell (apoferritin) (Meldrum et al., 1992). It has two subunits: a heavy chain (21 kDa) and a light chain (19 kDa). Ferritin and FNs are highly stable in biological fluids and resistant to denaturation, even at high temperatures above 80°C (Arosio et al., 2009). Ferritin's cavity can bond with metals with high affinity, and its surface groups, such as amino, carboxyl, and sulfhydryl groups, are chemically linked with ligands to create a multifunctional nanocarrier for successful drug administration (Wang et al., 2017). And also, it is capable of encapsulating various substances, including PET tracers, which is labeled with radioisotopes like zirconium-89 ($^{89}Zr$) for PET imaging.

## 2.2 Albumin-based nanoparticles

One of the most prevalent proteins in the blood is albumin, which includes ovalbumin (OVA), human serum albumin (HSA), and bovine serum albumin (BSA). The half-life period for albumin protein is nearly 18–19 days (Yurt et al., 2023). Albumin possesses a large number of drug-binding sites and excellent water solubility, making it an ideal drug carrier (Sleep et al., 2013). NIR fluorescent HSA nanoparticles are developed by encapsulating an NIR fluorescent dye within the HSA matrix, which enhances the dye's photostability. Tumor-targeting molecules such as peanut agglutinin (PNA) and anticarcinoembryonic antigen (anti-CEA) antibodies are chemically linked to the NIR fluorescent albumin nanoparticles. This modification increases the fluorescent signal in tumors that overexpress the corresponding receptors, aiding in tumor detection (Cohen et al., 2013).

Any medical condition that leads to aberrant alveolar-capillary membrane permeability, including inflammatory lung disorders, may be detected in real time using PET imaging of tagged albumin. Serum albumin is a common carrier protein that is used to form nanoparticles, often loaded with PET tracers like gallium-68 ($^{68}$Ga) or fluorine-18 ($^{18}$F), which gives another opportunity to evaluate tumor angiogenesis and response to antiangiogenic treatment (Almer et al., 2015).

## 2.3 Apolipoprotein-related nanoparticles

In nanomedicine, apolipoprotein-related nanoparticles can be employed as drug delivery systems. They can be utilized for brain targeting, cardiovascular research, gene delivery, and cancer treatment. Bacteriochlorin e6 bisoleate serves as a versatile theranostic agent that integrates seamlessly into high density lipoprotein (HDL). This fluorescent photosensitizer can be visualized in living systems through NIR fluorescence imaging. When exposed to light, it generates singlet oxygen, enabling its use in photodynamic therapy. By utilizing fluorophore-loaded HDL, the uptake of this fluorescent agent was monitored over time using the dorsal skinfold window chamber technique. This method provides high-resolution insights into how nanoparticles penetrate tumors, both spatially and temporally (Cao et al., 2009).

It has been reported that a PET radiotracer based on apolipoprotein A1 (ApoA1) is Zr-mA1 that binds to lipoproteins and accumulates in phagocytes. It can be used to monitor macrophage burden in mouse models of cardiovascular disease and cancer. Apolipoprotein E is also used for brain imaging in PET. They can cross the blood–brain barrier, making them suitable for imaging of neurodegenerative diseases (Almer et al., 2015).

## 2.4 Transferrin nanoparticles

Transferrin is crucial in cancer imaging because of its unique interaction with the transferrin receptor, a glycoprotein that is widely expressed on the surface of cancer cells to support their heightened iron requirements for fast proliferation. Nanoparticles connected to transferrin utilize this receptor upregulation, enabling the targeted delivery of imaging agents to malignant cells. This receptor-driven method leads to increased accumulation of transferrin-bound nanoparticles in tumor cells compared to normal cells. Consequently, transferrin is employed as a tumor marker to enhance the precision of cancer imaging and improve the effectiveness of detection methods (Li et al., 2009). Transferrin is a protein that binds to the transferrin receptor, which is overexpressed in many cancer cells. Transferrin nanoparticles labeled with PET isotopes (e.g., $^{68}$Ga or $^{18}$F) have been explored for tumor imaging (Kumar et al., 2011).

## 2.5 Virus-like protein nanoparticles

Virus-like particles (VLPs) serve as adaptable platforms in cancer imaging, resembling viruses in structure but lacking genetic material, making them noninfectious (Shahrivarkevishahi et al., 2022). Their function in optical imaging stems from their ability to carry various imaging agents, such as fluorescent dyes or magnetic contrast materials. VLPs are particularly useful due to their consistent structure, biocompatibility, and ease of customization. This allows them to be engineered to target cancer cells with high precision, enhancing the accuracy and effectiveness of imaging. VLPs can encapsulate imaging agents such as QDs, cyanine dyes (e.g., Cy5 and Cy5.5), or magnetic nanoparticles, enabling their application in imaging modalities like fluorescence imaging and MRI. These particles can be chemically or genetically modified to attach cancer-targeting molecules, such as peptides, ensuring they home in on tumor sites, thus improving tissue contrast during imaging. For example, Physalis mottle virus (PhMV) VLPs have been chemically linked to Cy5.5 to boost fluorescent imaging of cancer cells (Kim et al., 2023). VLPs are uniform in shape and easy to functionalize, giving them a huge advantage in drug loading and cancer therapy (Jeevanandam et al., 2019). They are ideal carriers of therapeutic nucleic acids. Additionally, due to their hollow structure, they can also carry other kinds of molecules like medicines, siRNA, antibodies, and nanoparticles. These nanoparticles are also used as carriers for PET tracers. They can be functionalized with PET isotopes like $^{68}Ga$ or $^{18}F$ and help in the imaging of tumors.

## 2.6 Elastin-like polypeptide nanoparticles

Elastin-like polypeptides (ELPs) are particularly valuable in cancer optical imaging because of their distinctive biophysical features, such as heat sensitivity and biocompatibility (Guo et al., 2023). Due to their high structural similarities to the body's natural elastin, the immune system also fails to recognize them, and they can avoid the immune system (Kianfar, 2021). Comprised of repeating pentapeptide sequences (Val–Pro–Gly–Xaa–Gly), where X can be any amino acid except proline, these polypeptides are soluble at lower temperatures but become insoluble when heated. This thermal responsiveness enables precise control over the release of imaging agents. In the context of cancer imaging, ELPs can be tailored to target specific tumor receptors by introducing targeting ligands, which facilitate the selective delivery of imaging agents to malignant areas. This increases the visibility of malignancies. Additionally, ELPs are capable of encapsulating other compounds, such as fluorescent dyes, preserving them from degradation and ensuring sustained imaging signals. Their unique phase transition property also enables the controlled release of diagnostic chemicals in the tumor microenvironment, boosting contrast and making them highly effective in delivering imaging agents and enhancing imaging clarity (Yi et al., 2020).

ELPs have been used in ocular drug delivery systems and are also used as a modulator in protein trafficking. They can also be labeled with radioisotopes like copper-64 ($^{64}Cu$) for PET imaging for the identification of tumors.

## 2.7 Antibody-based nanoparticles

Antibody-conjugated nanoparticles are pivotal in advancing cancer optical imaging, primarily through their ability to target specific antigens that are overexpressed on the surface of tumor cells. These nanoparticles are often functionalized with various imaging agents, such as fluorescent dyes or radionuclides, to provide clear and enhanced visualization of malignant tissues. The inherent specificity of antibodies allows these nanoparticles to bind selectively to cancer cells, significantly improving the contrast and precision of imaging while reducing interference from healthy tissues. Leveraging FDA-approved antibodies or engineering novel ones enables these nanoparticle systems to efficiently deliver imaging agents directly to the tumor microenvironment. This targeted approach enhances early cancer detection, facilitates precise tumor localization, and allows for real-time visualization during surgical procedures. By minimizing off-target accumulation, antibody-based nanoparticles not only improve imaging accuracy but also reduce potential side effects. This targeted delivery system holds great potential in enhancing optical imaging modalities, such as fluorescence-guided surgery or molecular imaging, and represents a promising strategy for achieving high-resolution, tumor-specific visualization in clinical oncology settings (Warram et al., 2014).

Ab-NPs can be directed toward tumor-specific markers, enabling early detection and monitoring of cancer. For instance, these nanoparticles target human epidermal growth factor receptor 2 (HER2) or epidermal growth factor receptor (EGFR) receptors in breast or lung cancer, which can improve PET signal specificity, and target inflammatory markers like VCAM-1, which are used to visualize atherosclerotic plaques (Fig. 8.2).

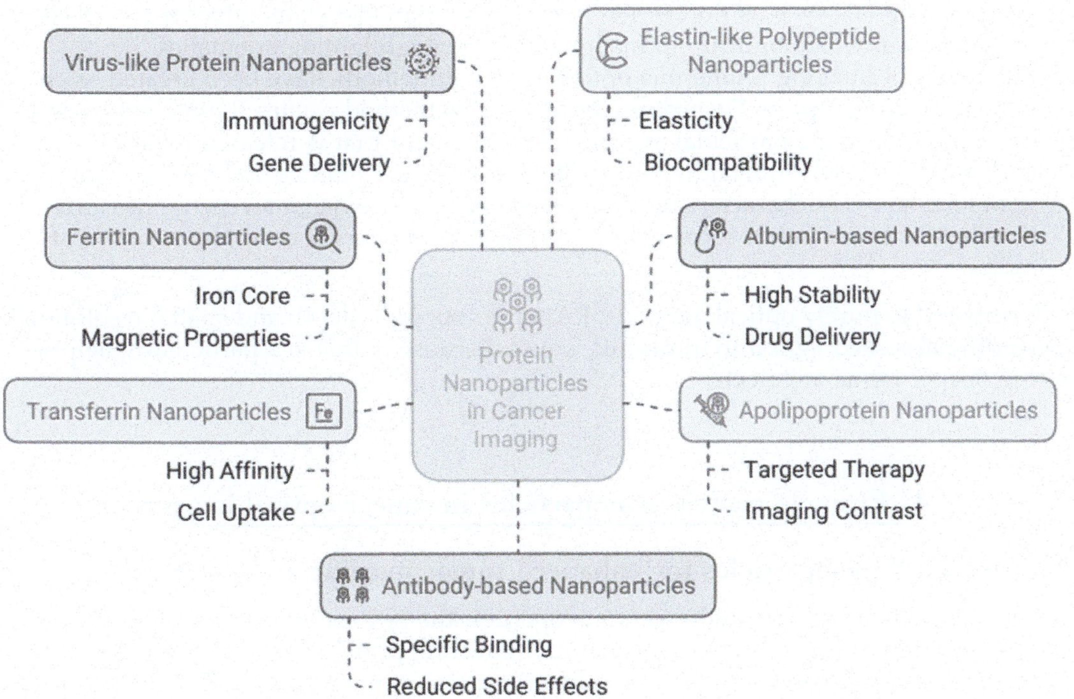


FIGURE 8.2 Different types of nanoparticles used in cancer optical imaging.

## 3. Mechanism of optical imaging for the detection of cancer

The optical imaging method for cancer detection is supported by a few basic principles based on the interaction of light with biological tissues (Zhang et al., 2011; Solomon et al., 2011).

1. Interaction of Light with Tissue

Biological tissue responds to light in a variety of ways, highlighting significant distinctions between malignant and healthy regions:
*Absorption*: Light is absorbed by certain tissue molecules called chromophores, such as hemoglobin or melanin. This produces contrast, which aids in identifying aberrant cells. *Emission*: Absorbing light can occasionally be reemitted at a longer, different wavelength. In the presence of certain dyes or molecular probes, this may manifest as fluorescence or natural autofluorescence. *Scattering*: Information about the structure of the tissue can be gleaned from the way light scatters within it. Scattering patterns make it simpler to identify morphological changes, including those brought on by cancer.

2. Mechanisms of Contrast Contrast—the ability of malignant tissue to be distinguished from healthy tissue—is crucial to the effectiveness of optical imaging. This can be accomplished in two primary ways: *Endogenous Contrast:* This technique makes use of the body's own chemicals. Tumors can be identified, for instance, because substances like hemoglobin and nicotinamide adenine dinucleotide hydride (NADH) absorb particular wavelengths or produce autofluorescence. *Exogenous Contrast Agents:* These include materials such as fluorescent dyes or nanoparticles (like indocyanine green). These substances are built up in malignant tissue, highlighting anomalies.
3. Modalities of Imaging Numerous optical imaging methods have been created, each with a specific purpose: *Fluorescence Imaging:* This method excites fluorescent molecules (fluorophores) using particular wavelengths. The light that is released makes it easier to distinguish between healthy and malignant tissues. *Diffuse optical imaging:* This technique analyzes characteristics like blood content or oxygen levels by measuring how light scatters and absorbs within tissues. It is frequently used to detect breast cancer.

Compared to purely optical methods, PAI offers superior depth and spatial resolution by converting absorbed light into ultrasonic waves. Because of this, it's particularly helpful for seeing deeper tissue architecture.

## 4. Example protein nanoparticles in cancer optical imaging

### 4.1 smURFP nanoparticles for enhanced tumor imaging and diagnostics

Because of its improved fluorescence properties, the newest generation of ultrared fluorescent protein, known as miniature ultrared fluorescent protein (smURFP), has been shown to be especially well-suited for cancer imaging using optical probes. The cyanobacterial origin of smURFP (phycoerythrocyanin) makes it similar to previously reported reporter genes. This allows it to produce radiation with peak emission throughout the far-red/NIR spectrum of 650–900 nm, which is perfect for greater tissue penetration. Because light in the NIR region is less absorbed and scattered by biological tissues, it is highly effective for noninvasive tumor imaging or biosensing of biomolecules, enabling crisper imaging of interior structures like tumors (Rodriguez et al., 2016; RSC - Page load error, 2025).

One of the difficulties with cancer molecular imaging has been the creation of imaging probes that can collect preferentially in tumors rather than healthy tissues. This enables smURFP to bind with BSA and transform into a nanoparticle. These 12–14 nm nanoparticles selectively aggregate in tumors by taking advantage of the enhanced permeation and retention (EPR) effect. Because the EPR effect leverages passive targeting strategies based on selective drug accumulation in target tissues, which are preferred by more permeable microvasculature (such as tumors), this trait is especially significant in tumor-targeted drug delivery (An et al., 2014a,b). After injection, the smURFP nanoparticles exhibit a high signal-to-noise ratio for fluorescence imaging that lasts for several hours, despite gradually self-quenching (An et al., 2020).

Additionally, smURFP nanoparticles are nontoxic and biocompatible, which makes them great options for both preclinical and clinical research (Shu et al., 2009). SmURFP aids in their application for detection in acidic tumor environments where conventional cancer measurement materials cannot remain stable. These nanoparticles are a very powerful reusable diagnostic and therapeutic tool since in vivo tests in mice show that they can scan tumors for 24 h after injection. Due to its potential applications in real-time intraoperative visualization and even as a dual-function theragnostic agent, these characteristics collectively make smURFP a promising candidate for cancer optical imaging with improved tumor specificity, possibly acting as a better substitute for previously described UPR-based tools (An et al., 2020).

## 4.2 Optical imaging of cancer using self-stabilized silk sericin-based nanoparticles (SSC@NPs)

Self-stabilizing silk sericin-based nanoparticles (SSC@NPs) have demonstrated great promise in the field of optical imaging for cancer in recent years. Their distinct qualities, namely their exceptional hydrophilia and biocompatibility, make them a viable option for drug delivery and medical imaging, especially in the context of cancer diagnostics (Hu et al., 2018). SSC@NPs, which are made from silk sericin, a protein found naturally in silkworms, have the unique capacity to stabilize without the use of outside agents. When introducing nanoparticles into the bloodstream, this inherent stability is essential, as it reduces frequent problems like aggregation. Preventing aggregation is essential because it minimizes the possibility of provoking harmful reactions or unintended immunological responses. SSC@NPs reduce these dangers by maintaining stability in biological contexts (Nel et al., 2009).

These nanoparticles greatly increase the visibility of tumor locations in imaging applications when paired with contrast agents like indocyanine green (ICG). Better diagnostic tools are made available to medical professionals by their increased capacity to accumulate within malignant tissues, which enables sharper and more comprehensive imaging (Hu et al., 2018). The pH sensitivity of these nanoparticles is an intriguing feature. SSC@NPs experience a shift in surface charge in the acidic milieu commonly present in tumors, which promotes increased uptake by cancer cells. In addition to increasing imaging precision, this pH-triggered behavior also boosts therapeutic potential by guaranteeing that more medication efficiently reaches the tumor location (Wang et al., 2015).

Additionally, even in complex biological fluids like blood plasma, SSC@NPs retain their colloidal stability due to their resistance to protein adsorption. This property, which is essential for long-term cancer imaging and treatment, makes them perfect for recurrent usage without diminishing functionality (Serda, 2013).

The nontoxic and biodegradable nature of SSC@NPs is one of their most alluring features. They are a dependable choice for continuing cancer therapies because clinical research has shown that they are safe, even at increased dosages. Crucially, they have also demonstrated the ability to lessen the cardiotoxic side effects linked to conventional chemotherapy medications such as doxorubicin (Xiao et al., 2011).

Lastly, the nanoparticles have outstanding cryoprotective properties. SSC@NPs maintain their stability and functional qualities even after undergoing freeze-drying, a procedure necessary for long-term preservation. They remain useful in both clinical and research settings because they reconstitute with consistent particle size and dispersion (Tsujimoto et al., 2001).

SC@NPs provide a very effective, safe, and adaptable platform for optical imaging of cancer. They are a promising option for enhancing the accuracy and results of cancer tests and treatments due to their exceptional stability, targeted action within tumors, and nontoxic nature. These nanoparticles may play a key role in cancer treatment and medical imaging in the future as research into them progresses.

### *4.2.1 Luc-linker@HFn in cancer optical imaging*

A luciferin-loaded ferritin nanocage called Luc-linker@HFn has become a very effective tool for optical imaging of malignancy. This bioluminescent nanoparticle approach combines the potent imaging properties of luciferin, which is triggered in the presence of luciferase inside tumor cells, with the natural tumor-targeting properties of human ferritin (HFn) (Truffi et al., 2016). Ferritin nanocages are perfect for medical applications since they are naturally nontoxic and biocompatible. In particular, HFn binds to transferrin receptor 1 (TfR1), a protein that is often overexpressed in many malignancies, giving it the amazing ability to target cancer cells. Receptor-mediated endocytosis attracts the nanoparticles into the cancer cells once they have bound to these receptors. By limiting off-target effects and increasing imaging accuracy, our natural targeting strategy guarantees that Luc-linker@HFn nanoparticles concentrate primarily in tumor tissues (Fan et al., 2012).

The smart way that Luc-linker@HFn takes advantage of the elevated glutathione levels present in cancer cells is what makes it so effective. Once inside the tumor cell, glutathione breaks down the disulfide bonds in the luciferin-linker system, allowing free luciferin to enter the cytoplasm. This is where the true magic takes place: the enzyme luciferase, which is present in tumor cells, interacts with this liberated luciferin to produce a bioluminescent signal that is detectable in real time. By limiting background noise from surrounding tissues, this special process makes sure that the light signal is only produced once the nanoparticles have penetrated the cancer cells (Bellini et al., 2020).

The capacity of Luc-linker@HFn to provide a persistent bioluminescent signal distinguishes it from conventional imaging agents. As long as luciferin is available, bioluminescence imaging (BLI) provides a continuous, steady signal in contrast to fluorescence techniques, which have problems including photobleaching and restricted tissue penetration. Longer imaging windows are made possible by the gradual and steady release of luciferin into cancer cells by Luc-linker@HFn nanoparticles. This is especially helpful in preclinical research, where monitoring the transport of nanoparticles in real time is crucial (Sadikot and Blackwell, 2005).

The direct reflection of intracellular uptake provided by BLI with Luc-linker@HFn is a major benefit over fluorescence imaging. Signals from nanoparticles in the tumor environment, rather than necessarily within cancer cells, may be seen using fluorescence-based techniques. On the other hand, BLI provides a clear image of whether the nanoparticles have penetrated the cells effectively. Since successful treatments rely on getting the medications into the cancer cells, this difference is essential for evaluating the effectiveness of drug delivery systems. Furthermore, BLI circumvents typical issues such as endosome-trapped nanoparticles, which might reduce the effectiveness of medications. The luciferin-luciferase reaction occurs in the cytoplasm using Luc-linker@HFn, providing a precise measurement of nanoparticle diffusion (Berger et al., 2008). Luc-linker@HFn has already shown remarkable outcomes in both in vivo and in vitro investigations. The nanoparticles were quickly absorbed in laboratory experiments using TfR1-overexpressing cancer cells, such as murine 4T1 breast cancer cells, and robust bioluminescent signals were seen shortly after exposure (Truffi et al., 2016). In vivo studies in animal models of breast cancer provided further evidence for these conclusions, since the nanoparticles effectively targeted tumor locations and generated bioluminescent signals that persisted for many hours after injection (Bellini et al., 2020).

An important development in cancer optical imaging is Luc-linker@HFn. It is a vital tool for preclinical research because of its capacity to target tumor cells precisely and provide a sustained bioluminescent signal. This method opens the door to more efficient cancer therapies and more intelligent nanodrug delivery systems by advancing our knowledge of intracellular absorption and nanoparticle dispersion.

## 4.3 CuS-ferritin nanocages' function in cancer treatment and imaging

Because of their adaptable characteristics, which are essential for both diagnosis and therapy, copper sulfide-ferritin nanocages (CuS-Fn NCs) provide exciting advancements in cancer imaging. Ferritin, a naturally occurring protein with a hollow shape, is used in the creation of these nanoparticles. CuS nanoparticle size and shape may be precisely controlled thanks to its cage-like architecture, which functions as an ideal nanoreactor. Notably, this technique guarantees that the nanoparticles will continue to be biocompatible, allowing for their safe use in living patients (Yu et al., 2007).

CuS-Fn NCs' significant absorption in the NIR spectrum is one of their primary characteristics. This characteristic is essential for improving optical imaging methods, especially PAI. The nanoparticles provide high-quality contrast in PAI by absorbing NIR light and turning it into heat, enabling precise, real-time pictures of deep tissues. This noninvasive method provides a good image of tumors, increasing the precision of cancer surveillance and diagnosis (Huang et al., 2013).

Furthermore, these nanoparticles may be labeled with radionuclides, such as 64Cu, to facilitate PET imaging. The sensitivity and specificity of cancer diagnosis are improved when PET and PAI are used together. Compared to conventional treatments, CuS-Fn NCs provide a much stronger tumor-to-background contrast because they have a tendency to concentrate in tumor tissues. Clinicians have a more complete tool to effectively diagnose and treat cancer thanks to this dual-imaging technique (Hu et al., 2014).

Additionally, the CuS-Fn NCs exhibit outstanding photothermal conversion efficiency, which is a characteristic that makes them very useful in photothermal treatment (PTT). The nanoparticles provide a targeted therapy alternative by producing heat when exposed to NIR laser light, which may kill cancer cells while preserving healthy tissue. The potential of CuS-Fn NCs as a major actor in cancer theranostics is highlighted by this combination of precision therapy and enhanced imaging (Sun et al., 2014).

To put it simply, CuS-Fn nanoparticles improve cancer optical imaging by improving contrast in PAI, PET precision, and PTT. Their multifunctionality and biocompatibility provide a bright future in clinical cancer therapy.

## 5. Advantages of protein nanoparticles in cancer optical imaging

*Biocompatibility*: Albumin, ferritin, and VLPs are examples of PNPs that originate from natural or biocompatible sources. They are thus safer to employ for cancer imaging in the human body since they are less likely to elicit an immune reaction.

*Biodegradability*: One of PNPs' main advantages is that, after their function is completed, they spontaneously decompose into innocuous components. This dispels worries about long-term toxicity, which is a problem often connected to inorganic nanoparticles like iron or gold.

*Functional Flexibility:* PNPs allow for a great deal of personalization. It is simple to attach different agents to them because of their reactive sites, which include amine, thiol, and carboxyl groups. These surface alterations improve the selectivity and multifunctionality of therapeutic medications, imaging agents, and targeting ligands.

*Controlled Drug Delivery:* Some PNPs, such as ferritin and silk fibroin, contain a hollow core that may hold therapeutic medications or imaging agents. This makes regulated, prolonged release possible, which is advantageous for imaging as well as therapy.

*Multifunctionality*: Imaging agents like fluorescent dyes or radioactive markers may be included in PNPs to provide multimodal imaging (e.g., combining optical imaging with MRI or PET). Additionally, their surfaces may be altered to target certain cancer cells, enhancing the contrast and accuracy of imaging.

*Eco-Friendly Synthesis:* Toxic chemicals are generally avoided in the processes used to create PNPs, such as emulsification and desolvation. As a result, the production method is more environmentally friendly and safer for clinical usage.

## 6. Disadvantages of PNPs in cancer optical imaging

*Stability Problems:* Enzymatic degradation, temperature, and pH may all have a significant impact on PNP stability. These environmental factors may lead to their early decomposition or loss of efficacy.
*Limited Circulation Time:* Albumin and ferritin are two examples of PNPs that may not remain in the circulation long enough to optimize their imaging capabilities. Their circulation duration can be increased by modifications like PEGylation, but the design of the nanoparticle becomes more difficult.
*Immunogenicity Potential:* Some PNPs, especially those that resemble viruses, may nevertheless cause an immunological reaction in some people even if they are biocompatible. This restricts their use for those who could have negative side effects.
*Difficult Production Process:* To guarantee stability and uniformity, producing PNPs often requires exact control over solvent ratios and pH levels. In contrast to simpler nanoparticle systems, this results in a more costly and intricate manufacturing procedure.
*Limited Tumor Penetration:* PNPs may effectively target cancer cells, but they may not be able to fully penetrate tumor tissues due to their comparatively large size in comparison to tiny molecules. This might limit their usefulness for imaging and medication administration.

## 7. Future prospects of protein nanoparticles in cancer optical imaging

*Improved Specificity and Targeting:* Going forward, developments are probably going to concentrate on raising the precision of PNP targeting. Advanced targeting ligands, such as peptides or antibodies, may help detect cancer more accurately while minimizing off-target effects.
*Multimodal Imaging Platforms:* Multifunctional PNPs that support many imaging modalities at once, including combining optical, MRI, and PET, are probably going to be developed in the future. This will provide physicians with more detailed information regarding the location, size, and molecular composition of tumors.
*Integration with Phototherapy:* A potential new area is the combination of protein-based imaging agents with therapeutic properties like photothermal or photodynamic therapy. These "theranostic" nanoparticles would administer tailored therapy straight to malignancies while enabling real-time treatment monitoring.
*Nanocarrier Innovations:* PNPs with enhanced stability, adaptable release mechanisms, and superior tumor penetration will be made possible by developments in protein engineering and nanotechnology. These developments will increase the efficiency of PNPs in the delivery of therapeutics and imaging agents.
*Biodegradable and environmentally safe nanoparticles:* To further lower the risks of long-term toxicity, future research is anticipated to concentrate on improving the biodegradability of PNPs. This will be especially crucial for creating nanoparticles that can be used for long-term cancer therapy or recurrent imaging.

The emerging development of PNPs has shown enormous potential to transform cancer diagnosis and therapy by offering safer, more accurate instruments for future individualized care.

## 8. Protein nanoparticles in positron emission tomography

When compared to both macroscopic materials and molecular systems, nanoscopic materials can be designed to offer a special advantage over them (Welch et al., 2009). Nanoparticles are particles having diameters that vary from 1 to 1000 nanometers, or nearly 1000 times smaller than the typical human cell. As they seem to lack overt toxicity and have unique physicochemical features, such as better mechanical performance, the potential for surface functionalization, a large surface area, and adjustable porosity, nanoparticles are highly beneficial as imaging probes (Abdel-Haleem et al., 2021). Currently, there is a lot of interest in using nanoparticles for molecular imaging. As a consequence, radionuclides, targeting ligands, and polyethylene glycol have been allowed to be coupled to both organic and inorganic nanoparticles to functionalize the particles and also modify their pharmacokinetics to produce an imaging signal (Welch et al., 2009).

Nanoparticles come in various types, including metallic nanoparticles like gold, silver, and iron oxide, used in imaging, drug delivery, and antimicrobial applications. Metal oxide nanoparticles, such as titanium dioxide and zinc oxide, find use in cosmetics, UV protection, and antibacterial treatments. Polymeric nanoparticles, like PLGA and dendrimers, are employed in drug delivery and tissue engineering. Lipid-based nanoparticles, such as liposomes and solid lipid nanoparticles, are essential for drug and vaccine delivery. Carbon-based nanoparticles, including fullerenes, carbon nanotubes, and graphene, offer unique mechanical and electrical properties for biomedical and electronic applications. Additionally, ceramic nanoparticles like silica and alumina are used in drug delivery and catalysis, while QDs are semiconductor particles with strong fluorescent properties, ideal for imaging and diagnostics (Frates, 2018).

Due to diverse applications, PNPs are the most prominent of all these varieties (Ghai et al., 2015). PNPs are a distinct form of biodegradable and biocompatible nanoparticles which are generated from several types of natural proteins (Kianfar, 2021). These nanoparticles offer a sustainable and nontoxic platform for biological applications (Barhoum et al., 2019; Gaur et al., 2021), including medication delivery (Mehrotra, 2016), vaccine carriers, and imaging agents, and their ability to self-assemble, together with surface modification potential, allows for precise targeting and regulated release of types of medicinal agents (Patra et al., 2018).

The coupling of nanotechnology and PET is an attractive cooperation that promises advantages for both parties. PNPs also serve a promising function in PET by serving as adaptable carriers for radiolabeled molecules and boosting the imaging process. PNPs can be functionalized with targeting ligands, such as antibodies or peptides, to transport PET tracers specifically to disease sites like tumors or areas of inflammation for enhancing imaging precision. Additionally, these nanoparticles can incorporate PET isotopes (e.g., $^{18}F$, $^{68}Ga$), allowing for better radiolabeling efficiency and extended circulation in the body. Their natural protein composition can also ensure better interaction with biological systems, reducing unwanted side effects. By enabling targeted delivery, higher stability, and controlled release. PNPs improve the sensitivity, accuracy, and safety of PET imaging,

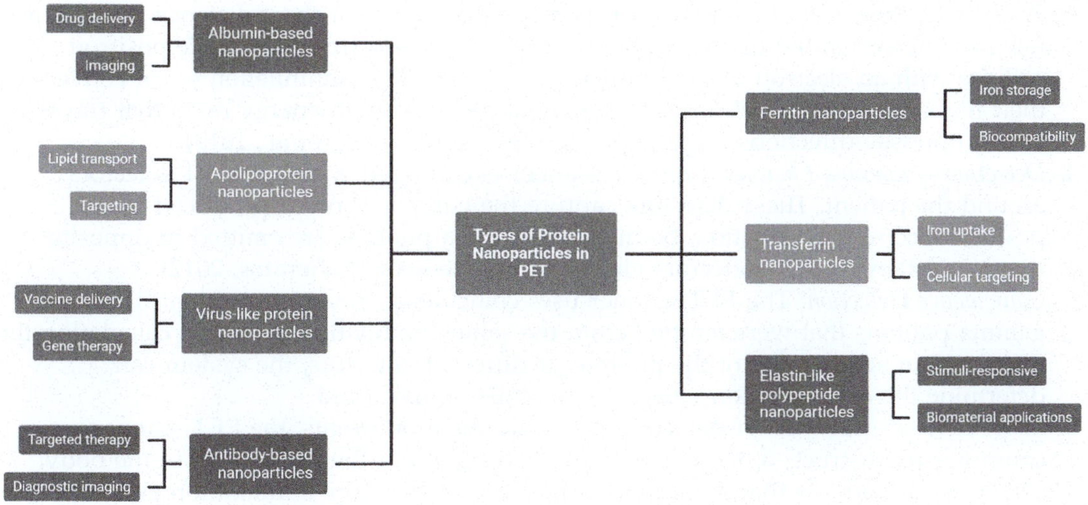


FIGURE 8.3 Types of protein nanoparticles used in PET.

particularly in oncology and cardiovascular disease diagnosis. Some examples of PNPs used in PET imaging are FNs, albumin-based nanoparticles, apolipoprotein-related nanoparticles, transferrin nanoparticles, virus-like PNPs, ELP nanoparticles, and antibody-based nanoparticles (Fig. 8.3).

## 8.1 Basic principles of PET

The basic principle of PET imaging involves mainly seven steps, which include (Fig. 8.4)

1. *Radiotracer Injection:* A radiotracer is a molecule labeled with a positron-emitting radionuclide (such as $^{18}F$, $^{68}Ga$, or carbon-11). The radiotracer is typically designed to target specific tissues or biological processes, such as glucose metabolism or cancer cells.
2. *Positron Emission:* Once the radiotracer is injected, it travels through the bloodstream and accumulates in the target tissues based on the biochemical properties of the radiotracer. The radionuclide in the radiotracer decays, emitting a positron ($\beta+$) (Jiang et al., 2019).

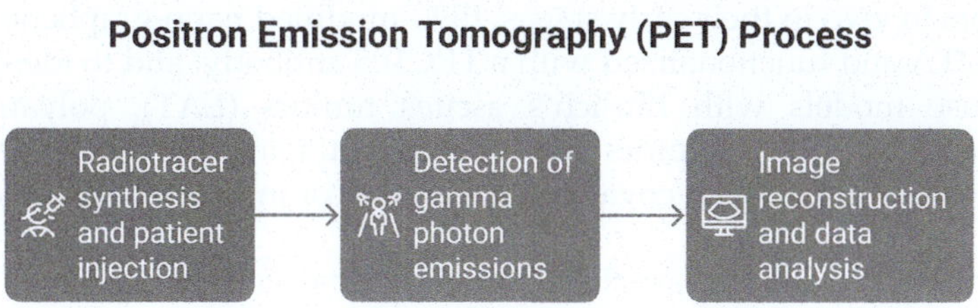


FIGURE 8.4 Image acquisition in PET.

3. *Positron-Electron Annihilation:* The emitted positron travels a short distance (usually a few millimeters) in the tissue before encountering an electron. When the positron collides with an electron, they annihilate each other. This annihilation event converts their mass into energy, releasing two gamma photons (high-energy rays) that travel in nearly opposite directions (approximately 180° apart) (Jiang et al., 2019).
4. *Detection of Gamma Photons:* The PET scanner is equipped with a ring of detectors around the patient. These detectors capture the gamma photons produced by the positron-electron annihilation. Because the gamma photons are emitted in opposite directions, they hit two detectors almost simultaneously (Livieratos, 2012).
5. *Coincidence Detection:* The PET scanner uses coincidence detection to identify pairs of gamma photons that were emitted from the same annihilation event. By calculating the difference in arrival time of the photons at different detectors, the system can determine the exact location where the annihilation occurred.
6. *Image Reconstruction:* After detecting many annihilation events, the PET scanner's computer reconstructs a 3D image of the distribution of the radiotracer in the body. The more radiotracer that accumulates in a region, the more annihilation events occur, which translates to higher signals in that area of the image (Disselhorst et al., 2014).
7. *Interpretation of the Image:* The 3D image shows regions of the body where the radiotracer has accumulated. High levels of accumulation can indicate areas of increased biological activity, such as cancer cells, inflammation, or brain activity. The image is then used by doctors to diagnose or monitor diseases (Disselhorst et al., 2014).

## 8.2 Mechanism of action

The mechanism of action of PNPs in PET imaging involves a sequence of phases, commencing with nanoparticle manufacturing and design. PNPs, manufactured from biocompatible proteins like albumin or antibodies, are tailored for biodegradability and surface functionalization, allowing them to target specific tissues or cells. These PNPs are functionalized with targeting ligands that bind to overexpressed markers on sick tissues, such as cancer cells, and their surface characteristics can be changed to promote circulation and biodistribution. For detection in PET imaging, PNPs are tagged with positron-emitting radionuclides. The choice of radionuclides, such as $^{18}F$, $^{68}Ga$, $^{64}Cu$, and $^{89}Zr$, depends on characteristics including half-life and decay mode (Brandt et al., 2018).

Radionuclides are commonly attached via chelating agents, including DOTA (1,4,7,10-tetraazacyclododecane-1,4,7,10-tetraacetic acid) or NOTA (1,4,7-triazacyclononane-1,4,7-triacetic acid), which form strong complexes to prevent premature release. For example, to target numerous tumors in vivo in their early stages, PEG-modified nano-graphene sheets were conjugated with NOTA and functionalized with a TRC105 antibody. and to identify tumor angiogenesis in mouse models with Ehrlich's ascites tumors (EAT), polyamide dendrimers (PAMAM) linked with αϋβ receptors were tagged utilizing the BFC DOTA (Ghai et al., 2015). Labeling can be direct, with covalent attachment, or indirect, utilizing chelators (Brandt et al., 2018).

Functionalization of the nanoparticle surface is critical, comprising chemical changes that provide binding sites for the radionuclide or chelator, ensuring targeted delivery (Brandt et al., 2018). Bioconjugation procedures, such as amide bond formation or click chemistry, connect the radionuclide to the nanoparticle (Hong et al., 2012). Stability is crucial, as unstable labeling can lead to free radionuclides, background noise, or toxicity. Efficient labeling ensures that a large percentage of radionuclide attaches successfully, enhancing imaging while minimizing background signal. The biodistribution and clearance of labeled PNPs rely on their size, shape, and surface features, while modifications such as PEGylation lengthen their circulation time.

After administration, radiolabeled PNPs circulate in the bloodstream and aggregate in target tissues through active or passive targeting processes. As the connected radionuclides decay, they release positrons that undergo annihilation with electrons, generating gamma rays, which are detected by the PET scanner. Coincidence detection of these photons permits the production of a 3D picture, displaying the distribution of PNPs within the body. The positron-electron annihilation mechanism producing antiparallel 511 keV photons is shown in Fig. 8.5.

The selectivity of PNPs boosts the signal-to-noise ratio, enabling precise imaging of tiny lesions or early-stage disease. Following imaging, the nanoparticles are metabolized or removed from the body, depending on their design. The generated images are used for diagnostic and therapeutic applications, providing insights into disease processes and therapy efficacy.

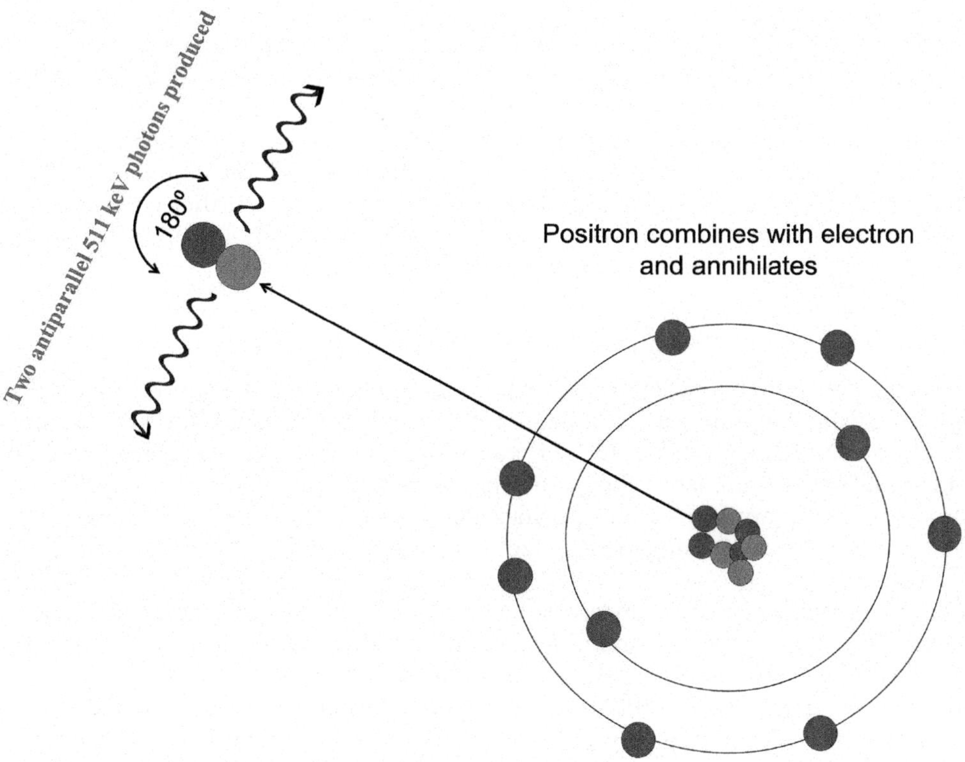


**FIGURE 8.5** Annihilation mechanism in positron emission tomography.

## 8.3 Advantages of using PNPs in PET

PNPs offer numerous advantages when applied in PET imaging, positioning them as a highly effective tool for medical diagnostics. One of the primary benefits is their inherent biocompatibility and biodegradability, which makes them safer for in vivo use compared to synthetic nanoparticles, reducing the risk of toxicity or long-term side effects (Sandra et al., 2019). As natural or bio-derived materials, PNPs are more likely to be metabolized by the body, minimizing any adverse immune responses that can compromise patient safety or the accuracy of imaging results (Debbage and Jaschke, 2008). Moreover, PNPs can be readily functionalized with various targeting ligands, such as antibodies, peptides, or small molecules. This capability allows them to selectively bind to specific biomarkers, tissues, or tumor cells, thereby increasing the precision of PET imaging. By honing in on particular biological targets, PNPs ensure that the radioactive tracers are delivered to the intended sites, enhancing the sensitivity and resolution of the imaging process (Wilhelm et al., 2016). This targeted approach reduces background noise, allowing clinicians to obtain clearer, more detailed images, which can aid in early diagnosis or in monitoring disease progression. Another critical advantage is their ability to encapsulate and deliver radioactive tracers in a controlled manner. Unlike conventional delivery systems, PNPs can sustain the release of tracers over extended periods, which improves the quality and duration of the imaging signal. This sustained release ensures that the imaging window is prolonged, providing clinicians with more time to conduct thorough scans and capture dynamic biological processes. In addition, the small size of PNPs enhances their pharmacokinetics. They can more easily penetrate biological barriers, such as blood vessels and cell membranes, enabling efficient distribution within tissues and organs. This improves not only the delivery of imaging agents to hard-to-reach areas but also ensures uniform tracer distribution throughout the target region, leading to higher-quality imaging. The ability of PNPs to circulate for longer periods without rapid clearance from the body further contributes to their effectiveness in PET imaging (Bhaskar and Lim, 2017), ultimately leading to more accurate, detailed, and informative diagnostic outcomes (Hahn et al., 2011).

## 8.4 Disadvantages of using protein nanoparticles in PET

Although PNPs offer a variety of benefits for PET applications, including specialized targeting and biocompatibility, their utilization has major limitations. One key concern is stability, since PNPs are subject to pH variations, temperature changes, and protease degradation, which diminishes their efficiency during in vivo PET imaging. Furthermore, the procedures of manufacture and purification are sophisticated and expensive. It can be challenging to produce homogeneous size and structure, which could explain differences in PET values.

Immunogenicity is another concern; when PNPs are injected, they may activate immune reactions that speed up their clearance and result in inflammatory reactions, which limit imaging window duration and skew scan accuracy (Saif et al., 2023).

Additionally, the capacity of PNPs to aggregate in target tissues is limited since they usually have a shorter circulation length than other types, such as synthetic or inorganic nanoparticles (Saif et al., 2023).

The difficulties in radiolabeling are particularly noteworthy; it can be tricky to affix radionuclides without compromising the performance of the nanoparticles, which could have an impact on the precision of PET imaging (Saif et al., 2023). Another concern is regulatory hurdles, since protein-based nanoparticles must go through tougher licensing processes than other kinds of nanoparticles or traditional radiotracers. Lastly, the synthesis of PNPs for therapeutic utilization can be prohibitively expensive and scalable, and their propensity to collect nonspecifically in organs like the liver or kidneys makes it more difficult to interpret PET scans by adding undesirable signals.

## 9. Future perspectives

The future prospects of PNPs in PET imaging are highly promising, with advancements in nanotechnology, molecular biology, and radiopharmaceuticals poised to further enhance their capabilities. As research progresses, PNPs are expected to be engineered with even greater precision for targeted delivery, incorporating advanced ligand design and genetic engineering techniques to improve specificity toward disease biomarkers. This could enable more personalized PET imaging, where nanoparticles are tailored to individual patient profiles, improving diagnosis, treatment planning, and monitoring of diseases like cancer and neurological disorders. Furthermore, integrating novel radiotracers with PNPs could enhance signal sensitivity and image resolution, potentially reducing the dose of radioactive material required, which would minimize patient exposure to radiation. In addition, the development of multifunctional PNPs capable of combining diagnostic and therapeutic (theragnostic) functions holds great potential, allowing simultaneous imaging and treatment on a single platform. As protein-based nanoparticles continue to evolve, they may also play a key role in noninvasive imaging of previously inaccessible tissues, improving early detection and expanding the use of PET imaging in a wider range of diseases.

## References

Abdel-Haleem, F.M., Mahmoud, S., Abdel-Ghani, N.E.T., El Nashar, R.M., Bechelany, M., Barhoum, A., 2021. Polyvinyl chloride modified carbon paste electrodes for sensitive determination of levofloxacin drug in serum, urine, and pharmaceutical formulations. Sensors 21 (9). https://doi.org/10.3390/s21093150.

Almer, G., Mangge, H., Zimmer, A., Prassl, R., 2015. Lipoprotein-related and apolipoprotein-mediated delivery systems for drug targeting and imaging. Curr. Med. Chem. 22 (31), 3631–3651. https://doi.org/10.2174/0929867322666150716114625.

An, F., Chen, N., Conlon, W.J., Hachey, J.S., Xin, J., Aras, O., Rodriguez, E.A., Ting, R., 2020. Small ultra-red fluorescent protein nanoparticles as exogenous probes for noninvasive tumor imaging in vivo. Int. J. Biol. Macromol. 153, 100–106. https://doi.org/10.1016/j.ijbiomac.2020.02.253.

An, F.F., Yang, Y.L., Liu, J., Ye, J., Zhang, J.F., Zhou, M.J., Zhang, X.J., Zheng, C.J., Liang, X.J., Zhang, X.H., 2014a. A reticuloendothelial system-stealthy dye-albumin nanocomplex as a highly biocompatible and highly luminescent nanoprobe for targeted in vivo tumor imaging. RSC Adv. 4 (12), 6120–6126. https://doi.org/10.1039/c3ra47058j.

An, F.F., Deng, Z.J., Ye, J., Zhang, J.F., Yang, Y.L., Li, C.H., Zheng, C.J., Zhang, X.H., 2014b. Aggregation-induced near-infrared absorption of squaraine dye in an albumin nanocomplex for photoacoustic tomography in vivo. ACS Appl. Mater. Interfaces 6 (20), 17985–17992. https://doi.org/10.1021/am504816h.

Arosio, P., Ingrassia, R., Cavadini, P., 2009. Ferritins: A family of molecules for iron storage, antioxidation and more. Biochim. Biophys. Acta Gen. Subj. 1790 (7), 589–599. https://doi.org/10.1016/j.bbagen.2008.09.004.

Barhoum, A., Pal, K., Rahier, H., Uludag, H., Kim, I.S., Bechelany, M., 2019. Nanofibers as new-generation materials: From spinning and nano-spinning fabrication techniques to emerging applications. Appl. Mater. Today 17, 1–35. https://doi.org/10.1016/j.apmt.2019.06.015.

Bellini, M., Riva, B., Tinelli, V., Rizzuto, M.A., Salvioni, L., Colombo, M., Mingozzi, F., Visioli, A., Marongiu, L., Frascotti, G., Christodoulou, M.S., Passarella, D., Prosperi, D., Fiandra, L., 2020. Engineered ferritin nanoparticles for the bioluminescence tracking of nanodrug delivery in cancer. Small 16 (39). https://doi.org/10.1002/smll.202001450.

Berger, F., Paulmurugan, R., Bhaumik, S., Gambhir, S.S., 2008. Uptake kinetics and biodistribution of 14C-d-luciferin-a radiolabeled substrate for the firefly luciferase catalyzed bioluminescence reaction: Impact on bioluminescence based reporter gene imaging. Eur. J. Nucl. Med. Mol. Imag. 35 (12), 2275–2285. https://doi.org/10.1007/s00259-008-0870-6.

Bhaskar, S., Lim, S., 2017. Engineering protein nanocages as carriers for biomedical applications. NPG Asia Mater. 9 (4). https://doi.org/10.1038/am.2016.128.

Brandt, M., Cardinale, J., Aulsebrook, M.L., Gasser, G., Mindt, T.L., 2018. An overview of PET radiochemistry, part 2: Radiometals. J. Nucl. Med. 59 (10), 1500–1506. https://doi.org/10.2967/jnumed.117.190801.

Cao, W., Ng, K.K., Corbin, I., Zhang, Z., Ding, L., Chen, J., Zheng, G., 2009. Synthesis and evaluation of a stable bacteriochlorophyll-analog and its incorporation into high-density lipoprotein nanoparticles for tumor imaging. Bioconjug. Chem. 20 (11), 2023–2031. https://doi.org/10.1021/bc900404y.

Chan, M.H., Pan, Y.T., Chan, Y.C., Hsiao, M., Chen, C.H., Sun, L., Liu, R.S., 2018. Nanobubble-embedded inorganic 808 nm excited upconversion nanocomposites for tumor multiple imaging and treatment. Chem. Sci. 9 (12), 3141–3151. https://doi.org/10.1039/c8sc00108a.

Cohen, S., Pellach, M., Kam, Y., Grinberg, I., Corem-Salkmon, E., Rubinstein, A., Margel, S., 2013. Synthesis and characterization of near IR fluorescent albumin nanoparticles for optical detection of colon cancer. Mater. Sci. Eng. C 33 (2), 923–931. https://doi.org/10.1016/j.msec.2012.11.022.

Debbage, P., Jaschke, W., 2008. Molecular imaging with nanoparticles: Giant roles for dwarf actors. Histochem. Cell Biol. 130 (5), 845–875. https://doi.org/10.1007/s00418-008-0511-y.

Disselhorst, J.A., Bezrukov, I., Kolb, A., Parl, C., Pichler, B.J., 2014. Principles of PET/MR imaging. J. Nucl. Med. 55 (6). https://doi.org/10.2967/jnumed.113.129098.

Fan, K., Cao, C., Pan, Y., Lu, D., Yang, D., Feng, J., Song, L., Liang, M., Yan, X., 2012. Magnetoferritin nanoparticles for targeting and visualizing tumour tissues. Nat. Nanotechnol. 7 (7), 459–464. https://doi.org/10.1038/nnano.2012.90.

Frangioni, J., 2003. In vivo near-infrared fluorescence imaging. Curr. Opin. Chem. Biol. 7 (5), 626–634. https://doi.org/10.1016/j.cbpa.2003.08.007.

Frates, K.De, 2018. Protein polymer-based nanoparticles: Fabrication and medical applications. Int. J. Mol. Sci. 19. https://doi.org/10.3390/IJMS19061717.

Gaur, M., Misra, C., Yadav, A.B., Swaroop, S., Maolmhuaidh, F., Bechelany, M., Barhoum, A., 2021. Biomedical applications of carbon nanomaterials: Fullerenes, quantum dots, nanotubes, nanofibers, and graphene. Materials 14 (20). https://doi.org/10.3390/ma14205978.

Ghai, A., Singh, B., Panwar Hazari, P., Schultz, M.K., Parmar, A., Kumar, P., Sharma, S., Dhawan, D., Kumar Mishra, A., 2015. Radiolabeling optimization and characterization of 68Ga labeled DOTA-polyamido-amine dendrimer conjugate - animal biodistribution and PET imaging results. Appl. Radiat. Isot. 105, 40–46. https://doi.org/10.1016/j.apradiso.2015.07.021.

Guo, Y., Liu, S., Jing, D., Liu, N., Luo, X., 2023. The construction of elastin-like polypeptides and their applications in drug delivery system and tissue repair. J. Nanobiotechnol. 21 (1). https://doi.org/10.1186/s12951-023-02184-8.

Hahn, M.A., Singh, A.K., Sharma, P., Brown, S.C., Moudgil, B.M., 2011. Nanoparticles as contrast agents for in-vivo bioimaging: Current status and future perspectives. Anal. Bioanal. Chem. 399 (1), 3–27. https://doi.org/10.1007/s00216-010-4207-5.

Hawkins, M.J., Soon-Shiong, P., Desai, N., 2008. Protein nanoparticles as drug carriers in clinical medicine. Adv. Drug Deliv. Rev. 60 (8), 876–885. https://doi.org/10.1016/j.addr.2007.08.044.

Hebden, J.C., Arridge, S.R., Delpy, D.T., 1997. Optical imaging in medicine: I. Experimental techniques. Phys. Med. Biol. 42 (5), 825–840. https://doi.org/10.1088/0031-9155/42/5/007.

Hilderbrand, S.A., Weissleder, R., 2010. Near-infrared fluorescence: Application to in vivo molecular imaging. Curr. Opin. Chem. Biol. 14 (1), 71–79. https://doi.org/10.1016/j.cbpa.2009.09.029.

Hong, H., Zhang, Y., Engle, J.W., Nayak, T.R., Theuer, C.P., Nickles, R.J., Barnhart, T.E., Cai, W., 2012. In vivo targeting and positron emission tomography imaging of tumor vasculature with 66Ga-labeled nano-graphene. Biomaterials 33 (16), 4147–4156. https://doi.org/10.1016/j.biomaterials.2012.02.031.

Hu, D., Li, T., Xu, Z., Liu, D., Yang, M., Zhu, L., 2018. Self-stabilized silk sericin-based nanoparticles: In vivo biocompatibility and reduced doxorubicin-induced toxicity. Acta Biomater. 74, 385–396. https://doi.org/10.1016/j.actbio.2018.05.024.

Hu, H., Huang, P., Weiss, O.J., Yan, X., Yue, X., Zhang, M.G., Tang, Y., Nie, L., Ma, Y., Niu, G., Wu, K., Chen, X., 2014. PET and NIR optical imaging using self-illuminating 64Cu-doped chelator-free gold nanoclusters. Biomaterials 35 (37), 9868–9876. https://doi.org/10.1016/j.biomaterials.2014.08.038.

Huang, P., Lin, J., Li, W., Rong, P., Wang, Z., Wang, S., Wang, X., Sun, X., Aronova, M., Niu, G., Leapman, R.D., Nie, Z., Chen, X., 2013. Biodegradable gold nanovesicles with an ultrastrong plasmonic coupling effect for photoacoustic imaging and photothermal therapy. Angew. Chem. 125 (52), 14208–14214. https://doi.org/10.1002/ange.201308986.

Jeevanandam, J., Pal, K., Danquah, M.K., 2019. Virus-like nanoparticles as a novel delivery tool in gene therapy. Biochimie 157, 38–47. https://doi.org/10.1016/j.biochi.2018.11.001.

Jiang, W., Chalich, Y., Deen, M.J., 2019. Sensors for positron emission tomography applications. Sensors (Switzerland) 19 (22). https://doi.org/10.3390/s19225019.

Kianfar, E., 2021. Protein nanoparticles in drug delivery: Animal protein, plant proteins and protein cages, albumin nanoparticles. J. Nanobiotechnol. 19 (1). https://doi.org/10.1186/s12951-021-00896-3.

Kim, K.R., Lee, A.S., Kim, S.M., Heo, H.R., Kim, C.S., 2023. Virus-like nanoparticles as a theranostic platform for cancer. Front. Bioeng. Biotechnol. 10. https://doi.org/10.3389/fbioe.2022.1106767.

Kumar, V., Boddeti, D.K., Evans, S.G., Roesch, F., Howman-Giles, R., 2011. Potential use of 68Ga-apo-transferrin as a PET imaging agent for detecting Staphylococcus aureus infection. Nucl. Med. Biol. 38 (3), 393–398. https://doi.org/10.1016/j.nucmedbio.2010.09.011.

Li, J.L., Wang, L., Liu, X.Y., Zhang, Z.P., Guo, H.C., Liu, W.M., Tang, S.H., 2009. In vitro cancer cell imaging and therapy using transferrin-conjugated gold nanoparticles. Cancer Lett. 274 (2), 319–326. https://doi.org/10.1016/j.canlet.2008.09.024.

Liu, J.N., Bu, W., Shi, J., 2017. Chemical design and synthesis of functionalized probes for imaging and treating tumor hypoxia. Chem. Rev. 117 (9), 6160–6224. https://doi.org/10.1021/acs.chemrev.6b00525.

Livieratos, L., 2012. Basic principles of SPECT and PET imaging. Radionuclide and Hybrid Bone Imaging 345–359. https://doi.org/10.1007/978-3-642-02400-9_12.

Lohcharoenkal, W., Wang, L., Chen, Y.C., Rojanasakul, Y., 2014. Protein nanoparticles as drug delivery carriers for cancer therapy. BioMed Res. Int. 2014. https://doi.org/10.1155/2014/180549.

Lv, G., Guo, W., Zhang, W., Zhang, T., Li, S., Chen, S., Eltahan, A.S., Wang, D., Wang, Y., Zhang, J., Wang, P.C., Chang, J., Liang, X.J., 2016. Near-Infrared Emission CuInS/ZnS quantum dots: All-in-One theranostic nanomedicines with intrinsic fluorescence/photoacoustic imaging for tumor phototherapy. ACS Nano 10 (10), 9637–9645. https://doi.org/10.1021/acsnano.6b05419.

Mehrotra, P., 2016. Biosensors and their applications - A review. J. Oral Biol. Craniofac. Res. 6 (2), 153–159. https://doi.org/10.1016/j.jobcr.2015.12.002.

Meldrum, F.C., Heywood, B.R., Mann, S., 1992. Magnetoferritin: In vitro synthesis of a novel magnetic protein. Science 257 (5069), 522–523. https://doi.org/10.1126/science.1636086.

Nel, A.E., Mädler, L., Velegol, D., Xia, T., Hoek, E.M.V., Somasundaran, P., Klaessig, F., Castranova, V., Thompson, M., 2009. Understanding biophysicochemical interactions at the nano-bio interface. Nat. Mater. 8 (7), 543–557. https://doi.org/10.1038/nmat2442.

Neupane, R., Gaudana, R., Boddu, S.H.S., 2018. Imaging techniques in the diagnosis and management of ocular tumors: Prospects and Challenges. AAPS J. 20 (6). https://doi.org/10.1208/s12248-018-0259-9.

Nurunnabi, M., Cho, K.J., Choi, J.S., Huh, K.M., Lee, Y.k., 2010. Targeted near-IR QDs-loaded micelles for cancer therapy and imaging. Biomaterials 31 (20), 5436–5444. https://doi.org/10.1016/j.biomaterials.2010.03.057.

Patra, J.K., Das, G., Fraceto, L.F., Campos, E.V.R., Rodriguez-Torres, M.D.P., Acosta-Torres, L.S., Diaz-Torres, L.A., Grillo, R., Swamy, M.K., Sharma, S., Habtemariam, S., Shin, H.S., 2018. Nano based drug delivery systems: Recent developments and future prospects. J. Nanobiotechnol. 16 (1). https://doi.org/10.1186/s12951-018-0392-8.

Rodriguez, E.A., Tran, G.N., Gross, L.A., Crisp, J.L., Shu, X., Lin, J.Y., Tsien, R.Y., 2016. A far-red fluorescent protein evolved from a cyanobacterial phycobiliprotein. Nat. Methods 13 (9), 763–769. https://doi.org/10.1038/nmeth.3935.

RSC - Page Load Error . (2025).

Sadikot, R.T., Blackwell, T.S., 2005. Bioluminescence imaging, 6. In: Proceedings of the American Thoracic Society, 2, pp. 537–540. https://doi.org/10.1513/pats.200507-067DS.

Saif, A., Anjum, L., Faisal, Z., Akram, N., Shah, Y.A., Irfan, R., Saeed, F., Afzaal, M., Asif Shah, M., 2023. Recent advances in protein-based nanoparticles and their applications in the delivery of bioactive compounds. Int. J. Food Prop. 26 (2), 2881–2895. https://doi.org/10.1080/10942912.2023.2261662.

Sandra, F., Khaliq, N.U., Sunna, A., Care, A., 2019. Developing protein-based nanoparticles as versatile delivery systems for cancer therapy and imaging. Nanomaterials 9 (9). https://doi.org/10.3390/nano9091329.

Serda, M., 2013. Synteza i aktywność biologiczna nowych analogów tiosemikarbazonowych chelatorów żelaza. Uniwersytet śląski. 7, 343–354.

Shahrivarkevishahi, A., Hagge, L.M., Brohlin, O.R., Kumari, S., Ehrman, R., Benjamin, C., Gassensmith, J.J., 2022. Virus-like particles: a self-assembled toolbox for cancer therapy. Mater. Today Chem. 24, 100808. https://doi.org/10.1016/j.mtchem.2022.100808.

Shu, X., Royant, A., Lin, M.Z., Aguilera, T.A., Lev-Ram, V., Steinbach, P.A., Tsien, R.Y., 2009. Mammalian expression of infrared fluorescent proteins engineered from a bacterial phytochrome. Science 324 (5928), 804–807. https://doi.org/10.1126/science.1168683.

Sleep, D., Cameron, J., Evans, L.R., 2013. Albumin as a versatile platform for drug half-life extension. Biochim. Biophys. Acta Gen. Subj. 1830 (12), 5526–5534. https://doi.org/10.1016/j.bbagen.2013.04.023.

Slough, C., Masters, S.C., Hurley, R.A., Taber, K.H., 2016. Clinical positron emission tomography (PET) neuroimaging: Advantages and limitations as a diagnostic tool. J. Neuropsychiatry Clin. Neurosci. 28 (2), 66–71. https://doi.org/10.1176/appi.neuropsych.16030044.

Solomon, M., Liu, Y., Berezin, M.Y., Achilefu, S., 2011. Optical imaging in cancer research: Basic principles, tumor detection, and therapeutic monitoring. Med. Princ. Pract. 20 (5), 397–415. https://doi.org/10.1159/000327655.

Sun, X., Huang, X., Yan, X., Wang, Y., Guo, J., Jacobson, O., Liu, D., Szajek, L.P., Zhu, W., Niu, G., Kiesewetter, D.O., Sun, S., Chen, X., 2014. Chelator-free 64Cu-integrated gold nanomaterials for positron emission tomography imaging guided photothermal cancer therapy. ACS Nano 8 (8), 8438–8446. https://doi.org/10.1021/nn502950t.

Suridjan, I., Comley, R.A., Rabiner, E.A., 2019. The application of positron emission tomography (PET) imaging in CNS drug development. Brain Imaging and Behavior 13 (2), 354–365. https://doi.org/10.1007/s11682-018-9967-0.

Tai, Y.F., Piccini, P., 2004. Applications of positron emission tomography (PET) in neurology. J. Neurol. Neurosurg. Psychiatry 75 (5), 669–676. https://doi.org/10.1136/jnnp.2003.028175.

Tromberg, B.J., Pogue, B.W., Paulsen, K.D., Yodh, A.G., Boas, D.A., Cerussi, A.E., 2008. Assessing the future of diffuse optical imaging technologies for breast cancer management. Med. Phys. 35 (6), 2443–2451. https://doi.org/10.1118/1.2919078.

Truffi, M., Fiandra, L., Sorrentino, L., Monieri, M., Corsi, F., Mazzucchelli, S., 2016. Ferritin nanocages: A biological platform for drug delivery, imaging and theranostics in cancer. Pharmacol. Res. 107, 57–65. https://doi.org/10.1016/j.phrs.2016.03.002.

Tsujimoto, K., Takagi, H., Takahashi, M., Yamada, H., Nakamori, S., 2001. Cryoprotective effect of the serine-rich repetitive sequence in silk protein sericin. J. Biochem. 129 (6), 979–986. https://doi.org/10.1093/oxfordjournals.jbchem.a002946.

Vaquero, J.J., Kinahan, P., 2015. Positron emission tomography: Current challenges and opportunities for technological advances in clinical and preclinical imaging systems. Annu. Rev. Biomed. Eng. 17, 385–414. https://doi.org/10.1146/annurev-bioeng-071114-040723.

Wang, C., Wang, Z., Zhao, T., Li, Y., Huang, G., Sumer, B.D., Gao, J., 2018. Optical molecular imaging for tumor detection and image-guided surgery. Biomaterials 157, 62–75. https://doi.org/10.1016/j.biomaterials.2017.12.002.

Wang, Y., Chen, L., 2011. Quantum dots, lighting up the research and development of nanomedicine. Nanomed. Nanotechnol. Biol. Med. 7 (4), 385–402. https://doi.org/10.1016/j.nano.2010.12.006.

Wang, Z., Gao, H., Zhang, Y., Liu, G., Niu, G., Chen, X., 2017. Functional ferritin nanoparticles for biomedical applications. Front. Chem. Sci. Eng. 11 (4), 633–646. https://doi.org/10.1007/s11705-017-1620-8.

Wang, Z., Ma, G., Zhang, J., Yuan, Z., Wang, L., Bernards, M., Chen, S., 2015. Surface protonation/deprotonation controlled instant affinity switch of nano drug vehicle (NDV) for pH triggered tumor cell targeting. Biomaterials 62, 116–127. https://doi.org/10.1016/j.biomaterials.2015.05.020.

Warram, J.M., De Boer, E., Sorace, A.G., Chung, T.K., Kim, H., Pleijhuis, R.G., Van Dam, G.M., Rosenthal, E.L., 2014. Antibody-based imaging strategies for cancer. Cancer Metastasis Rev. 33 (2–3), 809–822. https://doi.org/10.1007/s10555-014-9505-5.

Weber, C., Coester, C., Kreuter, J., Langer, K., 2000. Desolvation process and surface characterisation of protein nanoparticles. Int. J. Pharm. 194 (1), 91–102. https://doi.org/10.1016/S0378-5173(99)00370-1.

Welch, M.J., Hawker, C.J., Wooley, K.L., 2009. The advantages of nanoparticles for PET. J. Nucl. Med. 50 (11), 1743–1746. https://doi.org/10.2967/jnumed.109.061846.

Wilhelm, S., Tavares, A.J., Dai, Q., Ohta, S., Audet, J., Dvorak, H.F., Chan, W.C.W., 2016. Analysis of nanoparticle delivery to tumours. Nat. Rev. Mater. 1. https://doi.org/10.1038/natrevmats.2016.14.

Xiao, K., Li, Y., Luo, J., Lee, J.S., Xiao, W., Gonik, A.M., Agarwal, R.G., Lam, K.S., 2011. The effect of surface charge on in vivo biodistribution of PEG-oligocholic acid based micellar nanoparticles. Biomaterials 32 (13), 3435–3446. https://doi.org/10.1016/j.biomaterials.2011.01.021.

Xu, H., Eck, P.K., Baidoo, K.E., Choyke, P.L., Brechbiel, M.W., 2009. Toward preparation of antibody-based imaging probe libraries for dual-modality positron emission tomography and fluorescence imaging. Bioorg. Med. Chem. 17 (14), 5176–5181. https://doi.org/10.1016/j.bmc.2009.05.048.

Yi, A., Sim, D., Lee, Y.J., Sarangthem, V., Park, R.W., 2020. Development of elastin-like polypeptide for targeted specific gene delivery in vivo. J. Nanobiotechnol. 18 (1). https://doi.org/10.1186/s12951-020-0574-z.

Yu, X., Cao, C., Zhu, H., Li, Q., Liu, C., Gong, Q., 2007. Nanometer-sized copper sulfide hollow spheres with strong optical-limiting properties. Adv. Funct. Mater. 17 (8), 1397–1401. https://doi.org/10.1002/adfm.200600245.

Yurt, F., Özel, D., Tunçel, A., Gokbayrak, O., Aktas, S., 2023. Synthesis and optimization of the docetaxel-loaded and durvalumab-targeted human serum albumin nanoparticles, in vitro characterization on triple-negative breast cancer cells. ACS Omega 8 (29), 26287–26300. https://doi.org/10.1021/acsomega.3c02682.

Zhang, Y., Hong, H., Cai, W., 2011. Photoacoustic imaging. Cold Spring Harb. Protoc. 2011 (9). https://doi.org/10.1101/pdb.top065508 pdb.top.065508.

CHAPTER

# 9

# Protein-based nanotechnologies as cancer theranostics

*Anamika Verma, Abhishesh Kumar Mehata, Kavipriya Murugaiyan and Aravind Kumar Rengan*

**Department of Biomedical Engineering, Indian Institute of Technology, Hyderabad, Telangana, India**

## 1. Introduction

Cancer is the most significant health condition that causes major death in the human population (Khan et al., 2021). The burden of cancer is expected to increase by 60% in the coming 2 decades. The mortality of cancer affects the older population, urging the need for improving healthcare systems in a population with most elderly people and lower health expenditures. Prevalence of cancer is influenced by conditions such as aging and development and other habits such as smoking, sedentary lifestyle, and food. Acidogenic diet and exposure to chemicals, radiation, and toxins are other associated risk factors (Ramadan et al., 2025; Bahrami and Tafrihi, 2023). The disability-adjusted life years (DALY) caused by cancer has profound impact on the economy in healthcare systems, impacting around 1.16 trillion, which represents 1.5% of the world's gross domestic product (Garlasco et al., 2022).

Resection of tumors is employed in clinics as the most common procedure to treat cancers. But this is applicable to tumors that are diagnosed in early stages. Chemotherapy, radiotherapy, or their combination is currently being advised in clinics for tumors in advanced stages. High doses and nonselectivity are the major adverse reactions associated with these treatment options. Drug resistance is also a drawback associated with chemotherapy, which is caused either by decreased absorption or efflux of these drugs (Kaur et al., 2023; Shapira et al., 2011).

Tumor growth and recurrence are mainly controlled by genetic and epigenetic factors (Ghazal et al., 2024). The progression and metastatic potential of cancer is mediated by the cancer stem cells, or otherwise called as cancer progenitor stem cells. Epigenetic changes

*Protein-Based Nanoparticles in Drug Delivery*
**https://doi.org/10.1016/B978-0-443-33639-3.00001-5**

allow for the development of cancer progenitor stem cells and are critical for epithelial–mesenchymal transition (EMT). Epigenetic changes such as hypomethylation of oncogenes, hypermethylation of suppressor genes, diminishing hydroxymethylation, alterations associated with acetylation and methylation, miRNA expression, etc., are frequently associated with many cancers (Sarkar et al., 2013). With the evolving understanding of metastasis, the genes responsible for metastasis are being classified into metastasis-initiation genes, progression genes, and virulence genes. For example, three genes, EREG, COX-2, and MMP-1, potentiate angiogenesis and intravasation in tumors via vascular remodeling, significantly contributing to progression in breast tumors (Nguyen and Massagué, 2007). Along with the genetic and epigenetic factors, environmental factors (external carcinogens), which often stem from human behavior, contribute to 80%–90% of malignancy (Lewandowska et al., 2019). For example, consumption of alcohol and cigarette smoking played a key role in the progression of head and neck cancer, showing at least 70%–80% association (Jethwa and Khariwala, 2017).

The advent of nanotechnology has influenced numerous applications in science, especially in biomedical applications (Mahendra Kumar et al., 2023). With the unique properties attributed to the particles in nanoscale, it aims to overcome the challenges put forward by the tumor microenvironment (TME). Nanomedicines can be engineered to improve bioavailability, promote drug release, and improve the pharmacokinetics for better patient compliance. Through enhanced permeation and retention effect, the nanoparticles reduce the dosage, off-target effects, and spare healthy tissues (Miao and Huang, 2015; Kanapathipillai et al., 2014). Many organic, inorganic, and hybrid nanosystems are available for targeted therapy of cancer (Mohajer et al., 2023).

Among them, protein-based nanoparticles have gained popularity because of the commercial success of Abraxane, which is a paclitaxel–albumin conjugate. More than 200 proteins have been approved for the treatment of cancers, protein deficiencies, and genetic disorders (Zhang et al., 2020). The formation of protein nanoparticles often relies on self-assembly or interaction with other nanomaterials. Protein-based nanosystems (Fig. 9.1)

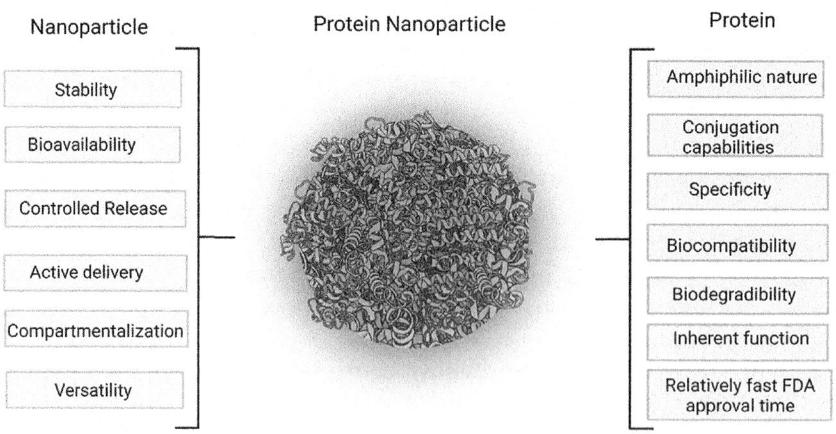


**FIGURE 9.1** Protein nanoparticles: Uniting the power of proteins with engineering design approaches.

are found to have significance in different areas such as biosensing, bioimaging, and drug delivery due to their excellent biocompatibility (Ding et al., 2021). Cancer theranostics (or theragnostics) represent a combinatorial approach to both diagnosis and treatment, thereby reducing delays in treatment and improving patient compliance. There are different platforms that utilize this concept of theranostics, which include photothermal therapy (PTT), photodynamic therapy (PDT), high-intensity focused ultrasound, etc. (Chen and Wong, 2014). The theranostic approach also advances the concept of personalized nanomedicine, allowing for simultaneous detection and diagnosis (Gobbo et al., 2015). Protein-based nanosystems have potential in theranostics due to their superior tunability for enhanced imaging and therapeutics (Hua et al., 2024). In this chapter, we will further discuss in detail the different protein-based nanosystems available, their theranostic applications, current advancements, and insights, which will further our understanding of the above systems.

## 2. Protein-based nanomaterials in cancer theranostics

Protein nanoparticles are often used as successful candidates to deliver drugs and growth factors. The loading of these agents commonly requires techniques such as diffusion or surface modification using covalent or noncovalent binding (Kundu et al., 2010; Wang et al., 2013). The size of the protein nanoparticles typically ranges between 100 and 1000 nm, with some methods reporting sizes less than 100 nm. Selection of preparation conditions plays an important role in tuning their size, improving drug entrapment, and achieving required pharmacological action (Jain et al., 2018). Based on their source, protein nanoparticles can be classified as animal proteins, plant proteins, protein cages, and protein conjugates.

### 2.1 Animal protein-based nanoparticles

Examples of these nanoparticles include gelatin, collagen, casein, and fibroin. Albumin is the most abundant protein found in blood plasma and is responsible for maintaining oncotic pressure and for the transportation of certain biomolecules. Both human and bovine serum albumin have been exploited for anticancer and drug delivery applications. Collagen is an abundant protein source found in bone, tendons, muscles, etc., and exhibits properties such as biodegradability, tensile strength, biomimetic nature, and lower antigenicity. Collagen nanoparticles can be useful in fighting cancer due to their ability to mimic the tumor microenvironment (Arun et al., 2021). Gelatin is a denatured protein form of collagen obtained by acid or alkaline hydrolysis. The chains of gelatin contain Arg-Gly-Asp (RGD) sequences, which modify cell behavior. Drugs loaded in gelatin nanoparticles showed higher toxicity, which might be attributed to the increased endocytotoxic uptake in cancer cells (Sahoo et al., 2015). Casein is a milk protein that contains a rich source of proline. They are amphiphilic proteins that are generally heat-stable and can form stable micelles. The proline content causes these nanoparticles to undergo proteolytic cleavage (Elzoghby et al., 2011). Owing to their biocompatibility, casein nanoparticles are being used for the oral delivery of drugs and also against anticancer activity. Silk fibroin is obtained from *Bombyx mori*, which contains hydrophobic domains of Β-pleated sheets in antiparallel direction. It exhibits excellent biocompatibility, biodegradability, and very low immunogenicity.

Silk fibroin nanoparticles were found to exhibit optical entrapment, improved therapeutic index, and maximum toxicity against breast cancer cells (Elahi et al., 2021).

## 2.2 Plant protein-based nanoparticles

Examples include zein, gliadin, and soy proteins. Zein is a biocompatible and biodegradable plant protein obtained from corn. Heterogeneous types exist with different molecular weights (α-zein, β-zein, γ-zein, δ-zein). Zein is usually dissolved in ethanol, but it is also recommended to use propylene glycol and later stabilize it in gum arabic. Encapsulation of zein in other nanoparticles is also a preferred way to obtain stability and also to increase bioavailability. Zein can facilitate the delivery of hydrophobic compounds due to the presence of nonpolar and uncharged amino acids such as glutamine, proline, leucine, and alanine. Gliadin is distinct because of its glutamine- and proline-rich central parts. They are gluten proteins obtained from wheat that are soluble in 70% ethanol. Coating of these nanoparticles with polysaccharides or pectin improved their stability. Deamidation could also improve gliadin stability through hydrophobic interactions and hydrogen bonding. Soy proteins are one of the commonly available proteins that are dissolved in ethanol or calcium-induced cold gelation process. They have been conjugated with various biomolecules to obtain specificity or modified with enzymes to increase the payload. Nanoparticles were also obtained from pea protein isolates for the protection and delivery of resveratrol. Other miscellaneous proteins, such as legumins, walnut proteins, and rice bran albumin, are also being explored for their properties and drug delivery applications (Reddy and Rapisarda, 2021; Joye et al., 2015).

## 2.3 Viral and nonviral protein cages

Protein cages are macromolecular aggregates obtained from self-assembly or repeated protein units. They range from small plant viruses (25–30 nm), large protein shells (80–100 nm), and filamentous particles of various bacteriophages. The interaction between these particles and the immune system is opening arenas for interactions between the cellular receptors mediated by uptake. The immunogenicity of these cages also varies, which needs to be considered while engineering nanoparticles. Caged proteins like ferritin are a major storage site of iron in the body, with 450 kDa. The smaller size and nonimmunogenicity make them ideal candidates as photosensitizers and also for drug delivery purposes (Ding et al., 2021).

## 2.4 Protein drug conjugates

Protein and peptide conjugates are emerging nanoplatforms for effective drug delivery against cancer. Protein–antibody and drug conjugates have emerged as beneficial tools to serve multifunctional purposes in a single construct (Spicer et al., 2018).

## 2.5 Protein polymer conjugates

Covalent modification of proteins with hydrophobic polymers leads to self-aggregation of the conjugates, with the polymer forming the hydrophobic core. With various preparation

TABLE 9.1 Different preparation techniques of protein nanoparticles (Kundu et al., 2010; Jain et al., 2018; Tanhaei et al., 2021; Patel and Haemmerich, 2024).

| Type of preparation | Emulsion/solvent extraction | Desolvation/ coacervation | Salt precipitation | Polyelectrolyte complexation |
|---|---|---|---|---|
| **Principle** | Emulsion systems (W/O or O/W) | Reduce the solubility of protein by using a nonsolvent, leading to precipitation | Similar to desolvation, hydrophobic–hydrophobic protein interactions are prepared in high salt concentration | pH-dependent interaction between protein and other macromolecules |
| **Size** | Generally, larger particles than those obtained in desolvation | Smaller size | Depends on pH, sizes can range between 100 and 1000 nm | Smaller sizes |
| **Factors affecting the size** | Crosslinkers, temperature, and surfactants | pH | pH | pH, polymer–protein and polymer–polymer interactions |
| **Stabilization** | Chemical or physical crosslinking | Chemical crosslinking | Chemical crosslinking | Complex formation depends on the electrostatic interactions |
| **Advantages** | Higher encapsulation efficiency | Mild conditions required | Simple method | Higher encapsulation efficiency |
| **Disadvantages** | Difficulty in controlling the size of the nanoparticle | Promotes aggregation | Loss of bioactivity, increased heterogeneity | Influenced by strong pH |
| **Others** | Simplest method—generally used for preparing polymer nanoparticles | Method of choice for preparing protein nanoparticles | Can affect the conformation of protein | Depending on the isoelectric point of the protein, the polycations or polyanions are selected |

methods available, denaturation of protein can occur due to the lack of a common solvent. This could be overcome by using lower critical solution temperature (LCST) polymers, such as PNIPAM (poly (N-isopropylacrylamide)), where the polymer and the protein are water soluble, and upon heating, crosslinking of proteins occurs, forming nanoparticles (Kaltbeitzel and Wich, 2023). Thus, different protein nanoparticles exist that can be effectively manipulated according to the loading or targeting agent against cancer. The preparation of these nanoparticles, as mentioned in Table 9.1 also plays a crucial role in engineering effective nanoparticles for cancer therapeutics.

# 3. Therapeutic applications of protein-based nanoparticles

## 3.1 Drug delivery systems

Protein-based nanoparticles offer significant potential in drug delivery due to their biocompatibility, biodegradability, and ability to be tailored for specific therapeutic targets. These nanoparticles can be fabricated from various proteins such as albumin, gelatin, and silk, among others. Their natural origin makes them safer for biological systems and enhances their interaction with cellular components.

### *3.1.1 Controlled release and targeting*

Protein-based nanoparticles can be engineered to provide controlled and sustained drug release over time. This is achieved by manipulating the protein matrix's degradation rate. In 2018, Bourbon et al. developed chitosan-coated lactoferrin-glycomacropeptide nanohydrogels to enhance the stability and bio-accessibility of encapsulated drugs. In vitro studies showed that these nanohydrogels reduced enzymatic degradation and improved the bioaccessibility of both hydrophobic (curcumin) and hydrophilic (caffeine) drugs, indicating a sustained-release profile (Bourbon et al., 2018). During in vitro digestion, approximately $10.2 \pm 0.2\%$ of free curcumin underwent degradation, compared to only $8.1 \pm 0.1\%$ when encapsulated within the nanohydrogel. Additionally, the absorption efficiency of free curcumin was limited to $57.2 \pm 0.4\%$ (measured in the jejunal and ileal filtrates), whereas the encapsulated curcumin demonstrated significantly higher absorption, reaching $72 \pm 1.2\%$ (Fig. 9.2).

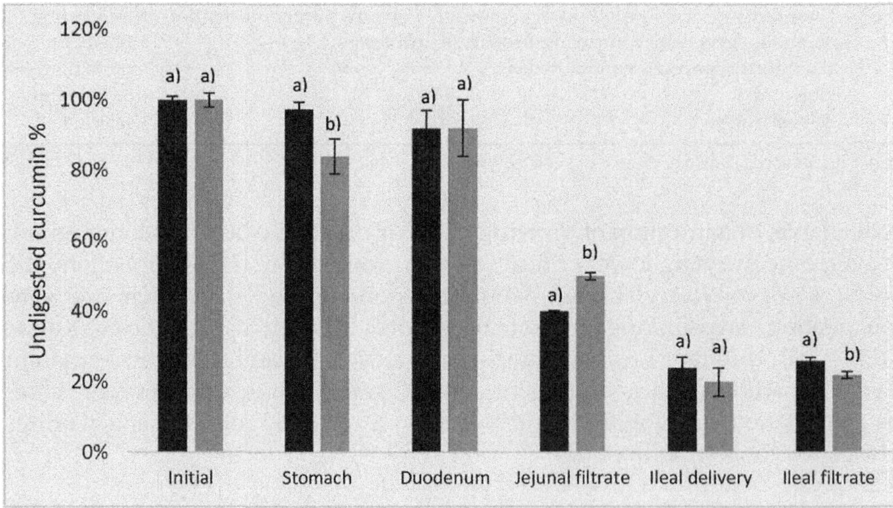


FIGURE 9.2 Undigested percentage of curcumin in various compartments of the dynamic gastrointestinal system during in vitro digestion for the free curcumin (gray bar) and curcumin encapsulated in coated nanohydrogels (black bar). Data are expressed as mean ± 95% confidence interval; values with different superscript letters indicate statistically significant differences ($P < .05$).

Another example involves the use of TAT-modified human serum albumin (HSA) nanoparticles for the sustained release of tetramethylpyrazine (TMP) targeting spinal cord injury. These nanoparticles exhibited a spherical structure with uniform particle size, and in vitro studies demonstrated a sustained-release function, prolonging the therapeutic action of TMP in vivo (Lin et al., 2021). Additionally, albumin nanoparticles are often used in cancer therapy to deliver chemotherapeutics specifically to tumor sites. Multifunctional protein-based drug delivery systems, such as cRGD-conjugated bovine serum albumin loaded with curcumin and complexed with protamine sulfate, have been constructed by Qin et al. (2020) to improve the bioavailability of hydrophobic drugs and achieve tumor-targeted therapy. These nanoparticles showed enhanced intracellular drug accumulation in tumor cells and a sustained inhibitory effect on malignant cells (Qin et al., 2020). The nanoparticles can exploit the enhanced permeability and retention (EPR) effect, a phenomenon in which large molecules tend to accumulate in tumor tissues more than in normal tissues due to leaky vasculature. A recent study by Yang et al. (2020) demonstrated that nanocapsules encapsulating therapeutic antibodies (tAbs), such as cetuximab, can enhance the EPR effect for improved tumor accumulation. These nanocapsules accumulated in tumor tissues via the EPR effect and released cetuximab, which targeted vascular endothelial cells, disrupting the blood–tumor barrier. This disruption led to a self-augmentation of the EPR effect, facilitating further tumor accumulation of the long-circulating nanocapsules. Compared to native cetuximab, the nanocapsules exhibited an effective tumor suppressive effect for up to 3 weeks following a single dose administration (Yang et al., 2020).

### 3.1.2 *Surface modification for targeting*

Surface functionalization of protein nanoparticles allows for targeted delivery. By attaching ligands like antibodies or peptides, the nanoparticles can specifically bind to receptors overexpressed on diseased cells (e.g., folate receptors on cancer cells). This selective targeting improves therapeutic efficacy while minimizing side effects. Peng et al. (2013) investigated the use of a preformed albumin corona as a protective coating for nanoparticles in drug delivery systems. This approach leverages the natural affinity of albumin for certain cell receptors, facilitating targeted delivery and improving biocompatibility (Peng et al., 2013). Zensi et al. (2009) demonstrated that albumin nanoparticles functionalized with apolipoprotein E (Apo E) could cross the blood–brain barrier via transcytosis and deliver drugs to neurons. This method shows promise for targeting central nervous system disorders (Zensi et al., 2009).

### 3.1.3 *Reduction of toxicity*

Protein-based nanoparticles encapsulate hydrophobic drugs, enhancing their solubility and reducing their systemic toxicity. They also protect sensitive drugs from premature degradation in the bloodstream, ensuring they reach the target tissues intact. Pullulan (~67 kDa) derivatives modified with hydrophobic groups, such as cholesterol, can self-assemble into nanoparticles suitable for drug delivery. Cholesteryl-pullulan (CHP) nanoparticles (Nagatomo et al., 2015), for example, have been utilized to deliver anticancer drugs effectively.

Kicková et al. (2021) developed pullulan-dexamethasone-cyanine3 (PDC) nanoparticles for targeted ocular drug delivery, focusing on retinal pigment epithelium (ARPE-19) cells.

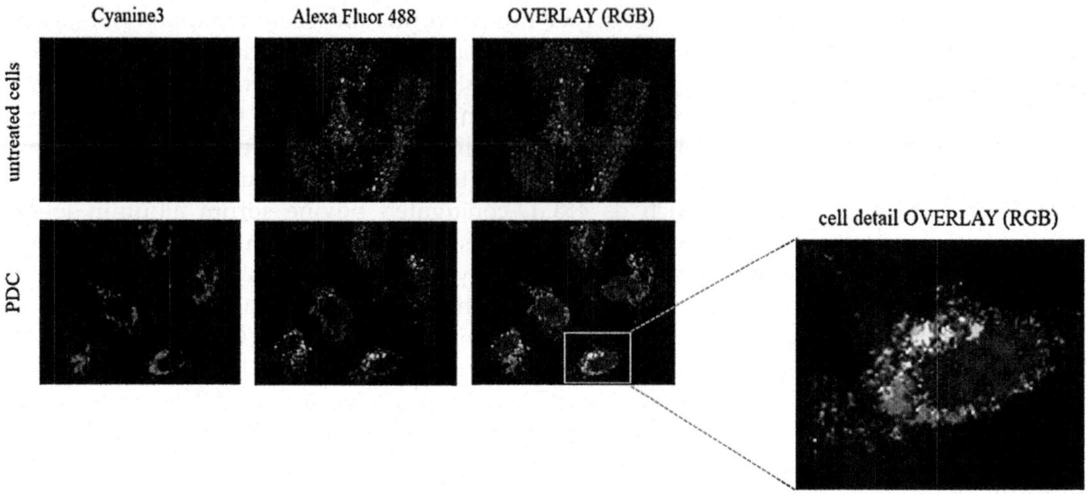


**FIGURE 9.3** Confocal microscopy images of ARPE-19 cells incubated with 0.2 mg/mL PDC nanoparticles, shown in red. (A) Endosomes are stained green using rabbit anti-EEA1 primary antibody and Alexa Fluor 488-labeled goat antirabbit IgG H&L secondary antibody. The magnified view of the region highlighted by the white square displays the overlay of endosomes and nanoparticles (RGB). Scale bar: 20 μm.

The nanoparticles showed controlled release, with ~50% of dexamethasone released over 2 weeks in the vitreous and faster release (50% in 2 days) under acidic lysosomal conditions, i.e., pH 5.0. Preclinical studies in mice, rats, and rabbits confirmed their safety and effective targeting of ganglion and Müller cells showed prolonged ocular retention for over 16 days. Pharmacokinetic simulations demonstrated a balance between ocular retention and sustained drug release. The nanoparticles' negative zeta potential enabled efficient cellular uptake with minimal cytotoxicity, highlighting their promise for safe and sustained intravitreal drug delivery (Kicková et al., 2021, 2022). Fig. 9.3 demonstrates that PDC nanoparticles exhibit strong cellular association and predominantly localize within endosomes, as indicated by the fluorescence overlap between the cyanine3-labeled conjugate and the Alexa Fluor 488-labeled endosomal marker antibody.

## 3.2 Gene therapy

Gene therapy in cancer focuses on the delivery of therapeutic genes into tumor cells or surrounding tissues to silence oncogenes through RNA interference (RNAi), deliver tumor suppressor genes (like *p53*), induce apoptosis (programmed cell death), and enhance immune system recognition (cancer vaccines) (Table 9.2). The success of gene therapy hinges on the delivery system (vector), which ensures the genetic material reaches the target cells safely and efficiently without degradation. Protein-based vectors are natural or engineered proteins used to bind, protect, and deliver nucleic acids to target cells. They offer several advantages over viral vectors, such as lower risk of immunogenicity and toxicity, the ability to escape the endosomal/lysosomal degradation pathway, and tunable properties for targeted delivery and controlled release. Protein-based vectors represent an exciting frontier in

**TABLE 9.2** Applications and therapeutic genes.

| Gene therapy strategy | Protein vector | Target Gene/Application |
|---|---|---|
| Enhanced transfection | Silk fibroin | Plasmid DNA, RGD (Kundu et al., 2010) |
| Oncogene silencing (iRNA) | Gelatin | siRNA against KRAS (Srikar et al., 2016) |
| Antiangiogenesis | Gelatin | siRNA targeting vasculo-endothelial growth factor (VEGF) (Matsumoto et al., 2006) |
| Apoptosis induction | CPP protein conjugates | Bax, Bcl-2, caspase-3 (Hong et al., 2019) |
| Immunotherapy | Protamine, albumin | PD-L1 (Jiang et al., 2023), antigen presentation, and potent T-cell response (Zhu et al., 2017) |

anticancer gene therapy, offering safer and more targeted alternatives to viral systems. Their biocompatibility, flexibility for modification, and ability to deliver a variety of therapeutic genes make them highly attractive for future clinical applications.

Numata et al. (2010) explored the potential of bioengineered silk proteins as nonviral gene delivery systems, focusing on silk-based block copolymers that include cationic poly(L-lysine) domains and RGD cell-binding motifs. These modifications are designed to enhance the interaction with plasmid DNA (pDNA) and improve transfection efficiency in HeLa and human embryonic kidney (HEK) cells (Fig. 9.4).

The researchers found that specific formulations, particularly those with 30 lysine residues and 11 RGD sequences at an N/P ratio of 2, achieved the highest transfection efficiency. This research underscores the promise of these customized silk proteins as effective gene delivery vehicles, offering a solution to the limitations of traditional viral vectors (Numata et al., 2010).

Srikar et al. (2016) developed triblock nanoparticles (TBNs) to enhance siRNA delivery and efficacy in KRAS mutant nonsmall cell lung cancer (NSCLC) cells. The system features

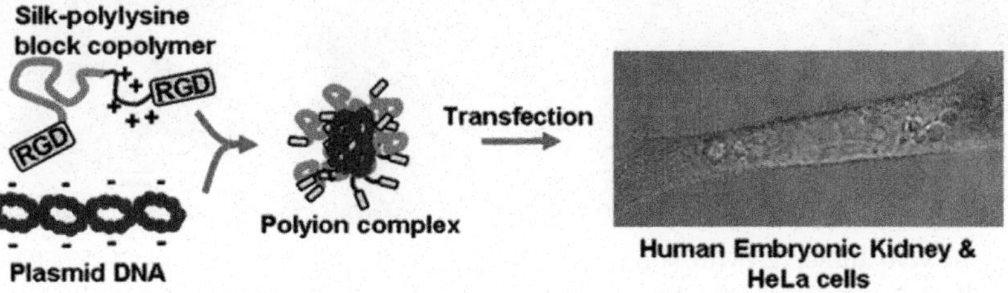


**FIGURE 9.4** Confocal laser scanning microscopy (CLSM) images showing the intracellular distribution of Cy5-labeled pDNA complexes. The Cy5-labeled pDNA was localized near the cell membrane and in the perinuclear region, indicating successful transfer of the pDNA close to the nucleus. *Reprinted with permission from Numata, K., Hamasaki, J., Subramanian, B., Kaplan, D.L., Gene delivery mediated by recombinant silk proteins containing cationic and cell binding motifs. J. Contr. Release. 146 (1) (2010), 136–143.*

a gelatin nanocore encapsulating gefitinib, a tyrosine kinase inhibitor (TKI), and is surface-functionalized with a cetuximab–siRNA conjugate for targeted delivery. Gelatin is utilized in the study as a component serving as a biodegradable carrier, providing controlled drug release and protecting and stabilizing the siRNA from degradation. The resultant TBN demonstrated efficient siRNA delivery and oncogene knockdown, leading to enhanced cytotoxicity and disruption of key cancer signaling pathways (Srikar et al., 2016).

In a study by Matsumoto et al. (2006), gelatin is used in its cationized form by introducing amine residues, giving it a positive charge, causing it to effectively interact with negatively charged pDNA, facilitating its internalization into cells, which is typically challenging due to the DNA's large size and negative charge. In the context of the study, cationized gelatin hydrogels were used to deliver a VEGF vector-based siRNA into tumors, increasing cellular uptake and prolonging the release of the siRNA. This approach was shown to have an anti-angiogenic effect, reducing tumor growth and angiogenesis. The effects of cationized gelatin microspheres on the stability of injected siVEGF-5 were observed through fluorescent micrographs taken 10 days postinjection. Strong fluorescence was observed in tumors following injection with fluorescein-labeled siVEGF-5 carried by cationized gelatin microspheres. In contrast, no fluorescence was detected in tumors injected with fluorescein-labeled siVEGF-5 alone (Fig. 9.5). These findings suggest that the period during which siVEGF-5 exerts its effect in vivo is preserved, and its release is controlled by the cationized gelatin microspheres (Matsumoto et al., 2006).

Hong et al. (2019) discussed a nanoformulation that induces apoptosis in cancer cells. This formulation, known as Afa/LPN-HR, combines afatinib and microRNA-139 (miR-139) encapsulated in lipid polymeric nanoparticles conjugated with dual pH-responsive cell-penetrating peptides (CPP) known as peptide H. It interacts with cells by forming pores and possesses arginine (R)- and histidine (H)-rich residues that respond to the acidic pH

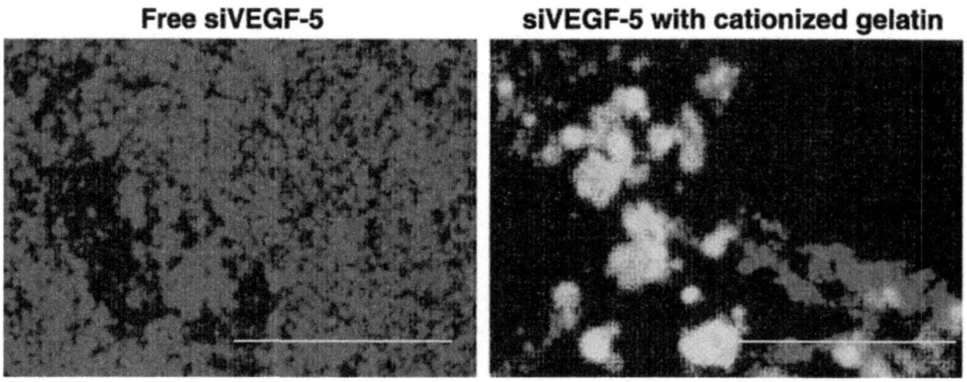


**FIGURE 9.5** In vivo tumor growth suppression following the administration of siVEGF-loaded cationized gelatin microspheres. A significant reduction in tumor vascularity was observed in the siVEGF-transfected tumors. Fluorescence microscopy revealed the sustained presence of siVEGF-cationized gelatin complexes around the tumor site even 10 days postinjection, whereas free siVEGF had completely dissipated by this time. *Reprinted with permission from Matsumoto, G., Kushibiki, T., Kinoshita, Y., Lee, U., Omi, Y., Kubota, E., Tabata, Y., Cationized gelatin delivery of a plasmid DNA expressing small interference RNA for VEGF inhibits murine squamous cell carcinoma. Cancer Sci. 97 (4) (2006), 313–321.*

in the TME responsible for the enhanced uptake of the aforementioned nanoformulation into human colorectal adenocarcinoma Caco-2 cells (Hong et al., 2019). The combined treatment of miR-139/LPN-HR and Afa/LPN-HR significantly increases the apoptotic cell population compared to other formulations, indicating a synergistic effect in promoting cell death. Additionally, the treatment downregulates antiapoptotic proteins (Bcl-2) and upregulates proapoptotic proteins (Bax, cleaved caspase-3, and PARP), further confirming the induction of apoptosis (Fig. 9.6).

Proteins like histones or protamines are naturally involved in gene packaging and regulation, making them ideal candidates for forming complexes with nucleic acids (Mukherjee et al., 2021). Protamine, a natural polycationic macromolecule, is utilized as a carrier in the construction of a nanovaccine for cancer immunotherapy. Combining a protamine-based nanovaccine with a PD-L1 gene silencing nanoparticle in cancer treatment offers several potential benefits. This combination can synergistically enhance the therapeutic efficiency by

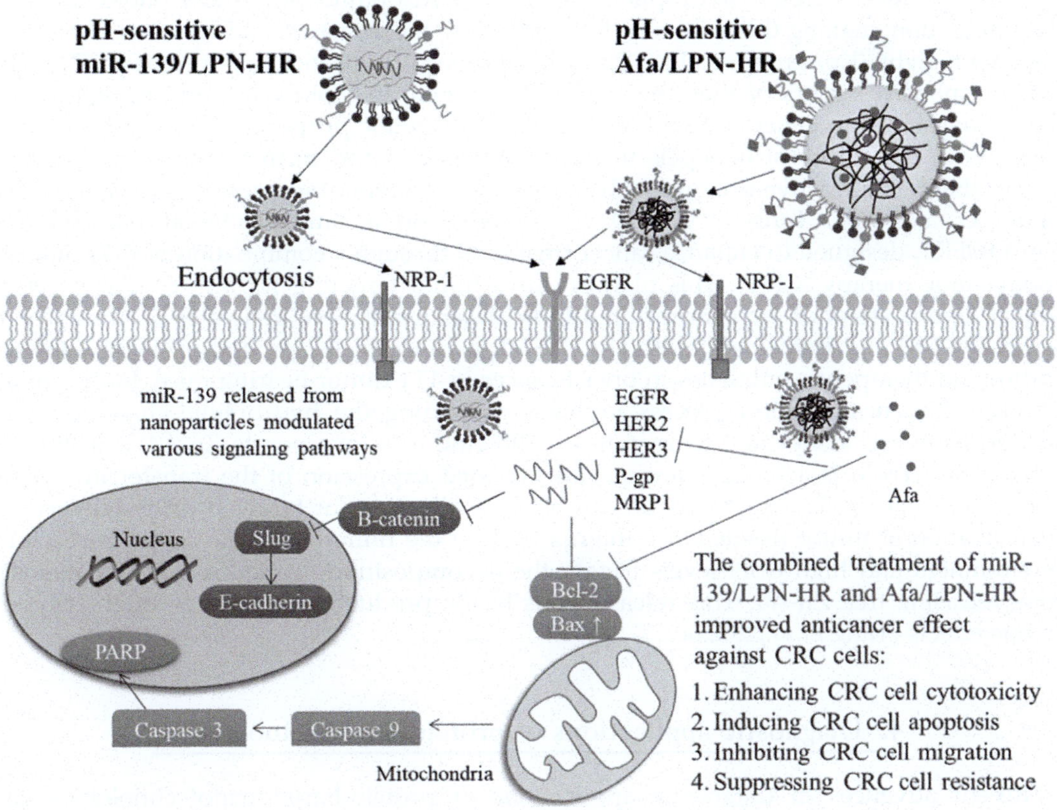


**FIGURE 9.6** Schematic illustration of CPP (peptide H)-functionalized lipid polymeric nanoparticles coloaded with afatinib and miR-139, designed to enhance anticancer efficacy against colorectal cancer (CRC) cells. *Reprinted with permission from Hong, S.-T., Lin, H., Wang, C.-S., Chang, C.-H., Lin, A.M.-Y., Chih-Hsin Yang, J., Lo, Y.-L., Improving the anticancer effect of afatinib and microRNA by using lipid polymeric nanoparticles conjugated with dual pH-responsive and targeting peptides. J. Nanobiotechnol. 17 (1) (2019).*

stimulating antitumor immune responses while simultaneously reducing tumor immune escape. The protamine-based nanovaccine facilitates the uptake by antigen-presenting cells and enhances antigen cross-presentation, optimizing in vivo delivery. Meanwhile, the PD-L1 gene silencing nanoparticle downregulates PD-L1 expression, which helps to cripple the tumor's ability to evade the immune system (Jiang et al., 2023).

### 3.3 Photothermal and photodynamic therapy

Protein-based nanoparticles are also utilized in cancer treatments like PTT and PDT, which are minimally invasive approaches that use light to target cancer cells.

Hirakura et al. (2004) studied the combination of pullulan and spiropyrane in the formation of photoresponsive nanogels for applications in PTT. These nanogels are synthesized by the self-assembly of spiropyrane-bearing pullulan (SpP), achieved via the isomerization between hydrophobic spiropyrane and hydrophilic merocyanine. Spiropyrane molecules are known to isomerize from a hydrophobic form to a hydrophilic form under photo- and thermostimulation, making them suitable for controlling the structure and function of biomaterials with light (Kozlenko et al., 2023). This property is particularly useful in PTT. The photoresponsive nature of these nanogels allows them to rapidly respond to light, which can be harnessed to generate localized heat for therapeutic purposes. This capability, combined with the ability of nanogels to trap biomolecules and form hierarchical structures, makes them an attractive option for drug delivery and other biomedical applications (Hirakura et al., 2004; Tang et al., 2025). A study on a multifunctional nanoplatform, Zn-A4@FRT, designed to enhance cancer treatment through a combination of PDT and chemodynamic therapy (CDT). This platform uses tumor-targeting ferritin to deliver Zn-A4, which, upon activation by near-infrared (NIR) laser irradiation, generates reactive oxygen species (ROS) and depletes glutathione (GSH) in cancer cells, promoting ferroptosis and improving therapeutic outcomes in breast cancer in 4T1 tumor-bearing mice. In the context of PDT, the encapsulation process involves expanding the hydrophilic channels of the ferritin nanocage at elevated temperatures, allowing it to incorporate Zn-A4. Selective targeting via ferritin is achieved through the elevated expression of the transferrin receptor (TfR1) on tumor cells, which ferritin can bind to, allowing for targeted drug delivery and visualization of tumor tissue. Once internalized by the tumor cells, the acidic intracellular environment and high GSH levels trigger the decomposition of the Zn-A4@FRT nanosystem, releasing free Zn-A4. This release leads to the production of ROS through photodynamic effects (Tang et al., 2025).

## 4. Diagnostic applications of protein-based nanoparticles

Recent advances in diagnostic applications of protein-based nanotechnologies have unlocked exciting possibilities for earlier, more accurate cancer detection, as well as improved real-time monitoring of treatment progress. By enabling noninvasive imaging and precise biomarker detection, protein-based nanomaterials are redefining how clinicians approach cancer diagnosis and therapy monitoring.

## 4.1 Molecular beacons: Imaging agents and real-time monitoring capabilities

One of the most promising trends in protein-based nanotechnology for diagnostics is the development of molecular imaging agents that enhance the visibility of tumors under imaging techniques like magnetic resonance imaging (MRI), positron emission tomography (PET), and fluorescence imaging. Protein nanoparticles, especially those functionalized with targeting ligands, have shown great potential to act as "molecular beacons" that selectively bind to cancer cells and highlight them in imaging scans. Recent studies have utilized ferritin nanocages, which naturally accumulate in high concentrations in tumor tissues, as a vehicle to carry imaging agents to cancerous cells. When loaded with paramagnetic ions, such as gadolinium, these nanocages produce strong contrast in MRI images, allowing for the visualization of even small tumors and early metastases that would otherwise go undetected (Zhang et al., 2024). Additionally, albumin-based nanoparticles have gained traction as versatile imaging agents. Albumin, due to its compatibility with the human body and ability to bind various imaging compounds, has been engineered to carry NIR fluorescent dyes and other contrast agents. This enables detailed imaging of tumor progression and response to treatments in real time. The use of protein-based nanomaterials in imaging holds particular promise for precision medicine, as these nanoparticles can be customized to bind to specific tumor markers or receptors, offering highly personalized and accurate diagnostics.

## 4.2 Cancer detectives: Biomarker detection

Another vital trend in diagnostic applications involves using protein-based nanoparticles for biomarker detection. Biomarkers, which are molecules that signify disease presence or progression, are invaluable for early cancer diagnosis and treatment planning. Protein-based nanomaterials have demonstrated exceptional sensitivity in detecting these biomarkers, even at low concentrations, which is essential for identifying cancer at its earliest stages. For instance, recent innovations have employed enzyme-conjugated protein nanoparticles to amplify signals from cancer biomarkers, making them easier to detect in blood tests or biopsies. Ferritin-based nanoparticles have been utilized to bind to specific cancer markers and signal their presence through colorimetric or fluorescent changes, providing a clear and immediate indication of the marker's presence. Additionally, researchers have designed nanocages derived from viral capsids to detect DNA and RNA mutations associated with specific cancers. These viral nanocages bind to the mutated genetic material, which can then be easily identified through advanced sequencing technologies. This trend of using protein nanomaterials for biomarker detection aligns with the broader goal of creating noninvasive, highly accurate tests for early cancer screening. In the future, these protein-based sensors could be integrated into portable diagnostic devices, making it possible to conduct routine cancer screenings with minimal invasiveness and cost.

## 4.3 Real-time monitoring: Spying on treatment progress

A key challenge in cancer therapy is assessing treatment efficacy in real time, especially when it comes to determining if a tumor is responding to chemotherapy or immunotherapy. Protein-based nanoparticles are increasingly being used to monitor treatment responses by carrying imaging agents that can be tracked throughout the treatment period. For example, researchers are now engineering albumin nanoparticles to carry not only therapeutic agents but also fluorophores that emit light under certain wavelengths. As these nanoparticles accumulate in or around the tumor, changes in the fluorescence signal can indicate whether the tumor is shrinking or proliferating.

Moreover, protein nanocages like ferritin have been adapted to carry both chemotherapeutic drugs and imaging agents. These multifunctional nanoparticles provide a "spy" on the cancer cells, allowing clinicians to monitor how effectively the drug is attacking the tumor and if any adjustments in treatment are needed. The ability to visualize the treatment effect without invasive procedures is invaluable, particularly in assessing highly aggressive cancers that may require rapid therapeutic adjustments.

## 4.4 Multifunctional potential: The future of diagnostics in protein nanotechnology

One of the most exciting future directions for protein-based nanotechnology in cancer diagnostics lies in developing multifunctional platforms that can perform both diagnostic and therapeutic roles simultaneously. For example, recent studies are exploring protein–polymer conjugates that combine imaging agents, therapeutic drugs, and targeting ligands in a single nanoparticle. Such "all-in-one" platforms not only help in identifying and visualizing cancer cells but also initiate treatment immediately after diagnosis, thereby shortening the time to therapy and reducing the potential for cancer spread.

In conclusion, recent advancements in protein-based nanotechnologies are driving remarkable improvements in cancer diagnostics. From enhanced imaging agents and ultrasensitive biomarker detection to real-time treatment monitoring and multifunctional theranostic platforms, these protein-based technologies are poised to transform the landscape of cancer diagnosis and therapy. The continued evolution of these diagnostic applications promises to make cancer treatment more precise, timely, and personalized, ultimately improving outcomes for patients around the world.

# 5. Protein-based nanoparticles aided multifunctional platforms

In the rapidly advancing field of cancer theranostics, multifunctional protein-based nanotechnologies are emerging as transformative tools, capable of integrating diagnostic and therapeutic functions within a single platform. These multifunctional "all-in-one" solutions not only streamline treatment processes but also offer more precise, efficient, and personalized approaches to cancer care. Recent trends in multifunctional protein-based nanomaterials are focused on enhancing specificity, optimizing delivery, and developing real-time, adaptable systems that can diagnose, monitor, and treat cancer cells all in one go.

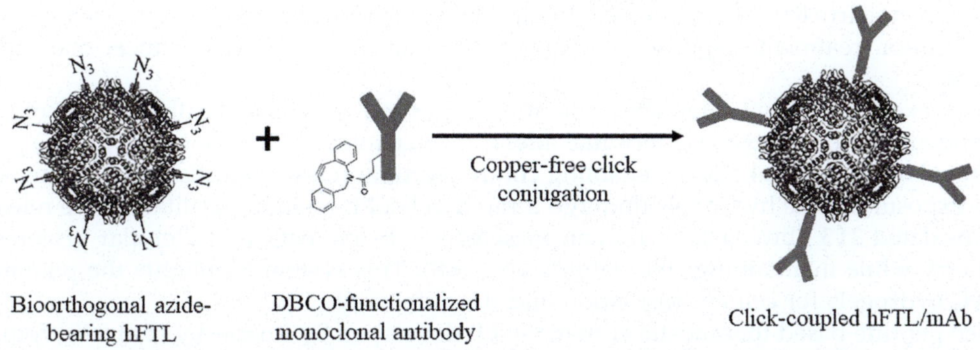


**FIGURE 9.7** Schematic representation of bioorthogonal click chemistry variant of hFTL. *Reprinted with permission from Khoshnejad, M., Greineder, C.F., Pulsipher, K.W., Villa, C.H., Altun, B., Pan, D.C., Tsourkas, A., Dmochowski, I.J., Muzykantov, V.R., Ferritin nanocages with biologically orthogonal conjugation for vascular targeting and imaging. Bioconjug. Chem. 29 (4) (2018), 1209–1218.*

## 5.1 Bioorthogonal alchemy: Precision functionalization with click chemistry

Bioorthogonal chemistry, particularly click chemistry, has emerged as a critical tool in the development of multifunctional protein-based nanotechnologies. Click chemistry, a chemical approach that enables molecules to "click" together under mild conditions, allows researchers to precisely attach various functional groups to protein nanostructures without interfering with the proteins' natural biological activities. This method is revolutionizing the functionalization of protein nanomaterials, making it possible to combine imaging agents, therapeutic molecules, and targeting ligands within a single nanoparticle. For example, recent advances have shown that click chemistry can be used to attach both fluorescent markers and chemotherapeutic drugs to ferritin nanocages. A study by Khoshnejad et al. (2018) (Fig. 9.7) highlights the potential of ferritin nanocages by incorporating 4-azidophenylalanine into the human ferritin light chain (hFTL); site-specific conjugation of small molecules and antibodies is enabled. The engineered hFTL-5X variant efficiently couples with fluorophores and antibodies, targeting markers like ICAM-1, particularly under inflammatory conditions. This precise conjugation optimizes selective uptake and controlled drug release (Khoshnejad et al., 2018). These modified ferritin cages can then seek out specific tumor cells, illuminating them for diagnostic imaging while simultaneously delivering a targeted therapeutic dose. This precision not only improves drug delivery but also enhances the ability to visualize the tumor and track the response to treatment over time. Bioorthogonal functionalization is also allowing for the customization of protein-based nanoparticles to match unique tumor characteristics, paving the way for highly personalized theranostic approaches.

## 5.2 Swiss army nanoparticles: Integrated theranostic systems

One of the most exciting recent trends is the development of integrated theranostic platforms—nanoparticles that perform diagnostic and therapeutic roles in one. These "Swiss

Army" nanoparticles are engineered to simultaneously detect cancer cells, deliver drugs, and monitor treatment responses, creating a streamlined and effective cancer management system.

One example of an integrated theranostic system is a genetically engineered B12-dependent photoresponsive C-terminal adenosylcobalamin binding domain ($CarH_C$) protein hydrogel by Wang et al. (2017), enabling controlled dual release of cells and proteins. Upon light exposure, these hydrogels undergo a rapid gel-sol transition, facilitating the release of encapsulated 3T3 fibroblasts or human mesenchymal stem cells and globular proteins like mCherry while maintaining cell viability (Fig. 9.8). This system highlights the potential of $CarH_C$ hydrogels for cell encapsulation and drug delivery.

The peptide-based theranostic system 5-CLB developed by Rozovsky et al. (2019) utilizes the specificity of peptides for targeted drug delivery in cancer therapy. It integrates chlorambucil (CLB), the somatostatin receptor-targeting peptide octreotide amide (OctA), and a dual fluorescent cyanine dye (IRD) for real-time drug tracking. The system employs ratiometric fluorescence to enhance monitoring accuracy, overcoming challenges like light scattering and photobleaching. Synthesized via solid-phase peptide synthesis, 5-CLB features a biodegradable ester linker that enables controlled drug release in the TME. Tested on PANC-1 (pancreatic cancer cells), it demonstrated superior cytotoxicity compared to free CLB or OctA alone (Fig. 9.9), highlighting its potential for precision oncology (Rozovsky et al., 2019).

A popular approach involves the use of albumin-bound nanoparticles, such as those used in Abraxane, which are now being modified to carry both therapeutic agents and imaging markers. These multifunctional particles allow clinicians to observe the drug delivery process and assess how the tumor is responding in real time. Another approach uses viral capsid-derived nanocages to encapsulate both therapeutic agents and imaging molecules. For example, viral capsids can be loaded with radionuclides for PET imaging and combined with cytotoxic agents to form a single nanoparticle capable of both diagnosing and treating

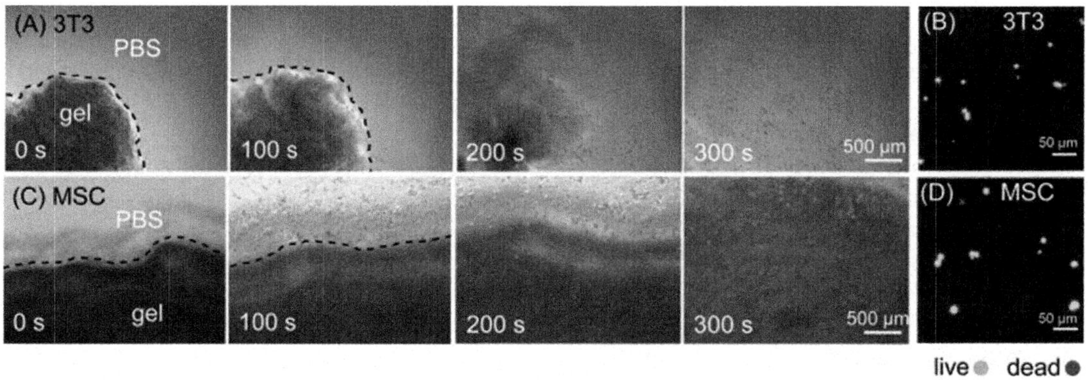


**FIGURE 9.8** Light-triggered release of encapsulated cells via gel-sol transition: (A) 3T3 fibroblasts and (C) hMSCs were encapsulated in $CarH_C$ hydrogels (red) and released upon white light exposure (22 klux). Bright-field images (0–300 seconds) show gel dissolution, with dashed lines marking gel boundaries. (B, D) Live/dead staining confirms cell viability postrelease. *Reprinted with permission from Wang, R., Yang, Z., Luo, J., Hsing, I.M., Sun, F., B12-dependent photoresponsive protein hydrogels for controlled stem cell/protein release. Proceedings of the National Academy of Sciences of the United States of America. 114 (23) (2017), 5912–5917.*

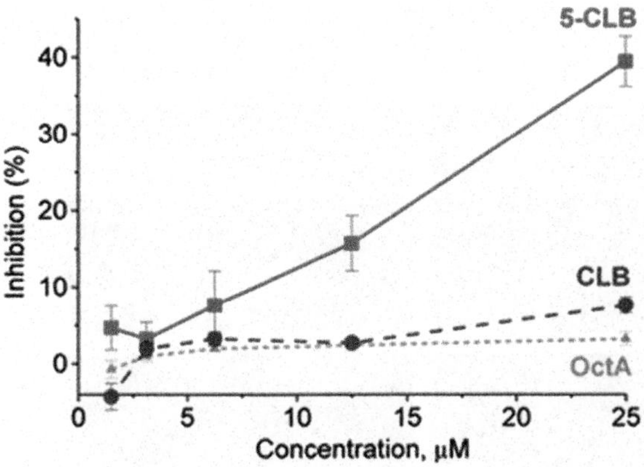


FIGURE 9.9 Evaluation of PANC-1 growth inhibition by 5-CLB, CLB, and OctA using the XTT assay after 24 h. Growth inhibition at each concentration is expressed as the mean ± standard error from independent experiments performed in triplicate. *Reprinted with permission from Rozovsky, A., Ebaston, T.M., Zaporozhets, A., Bazylevich, A., Tuchinsky, H., Patsenker, L., Gellerman, G., Theranostic system for ratiometric fluorescence monitoring of peptide-guided targeted drug delivery. RSC Adv. 9 (56) (2019), 32656–32664.*

tumors. Researchers have demonstrated the effectiveness of such platforms in preclinical models, where viral nanocages have provided both a highly visible image of tumor sites and a localized release of therapeutic agents. The ability to detect and target tumors with this level of precision reduces the risk of damaging healthy tissues and minimizes the likelihood of side effects.

## 5.3 Tumor microenvironment-sensitive platforms: Smarter drug release

Protein-based nanotechnologies are also being developed to respond to specific conditions in the TME, such as low pH, elevated temperatures, or high enzyme levels. These “smart” nanoparticles are programmed to release their payload only when they encounter the unique environment within a tumor, ensuring that therapeutic agents are delivered exactly where they are needed. This is especially useful in cancers where the TME plays a crucial role in tumor growth and spread, as in pancreatic and brain cancers. Recent advancements have led to the creation of pH-sensitive ferritin nanoparticles, which release their drug payload only under the acidic conditions of the TME. This approach minimizes drug release in the bloodstream or healthy tissues, reducing systemic toxicity.

Engineered hypoxia-responsive albumin nanoparticles have been developed by Wang et al. (2025) for targeted cancer therapy by codelivering hydroxychloroquine (HCQ) and a mitochondrial-targeting type-I photosensitizer (SMNB) to enhance oxidative stress and disrupt mitophagy in hypoxic tumors (Wang et al., 2025). These stimuli-responsive nanoparticles release their payload under hypoxic conditions (Fig. 9.10), where HCQ weakens tumor resilience, and SMNB generates ROS upon laser irradiation, further damaging mitochondria (Chen et al., 2023). Their spherical morphology (~20 nm), negative charge, and long-term stability ensure effective drug delivery, while HSA enhances biocompatibility and circulation time (Liu et al., 2017). The nanoparticles, SHC4H, induce apoptosis and necroptosis, offering a promising platform for treating hypoxic tumors with enhanced antitumor efficacy. Additionally, enzyme-sensitive viral capsids that degrade upon contact with enzymes commonly found in tumors have been developed for targeted delivery. These smart systems

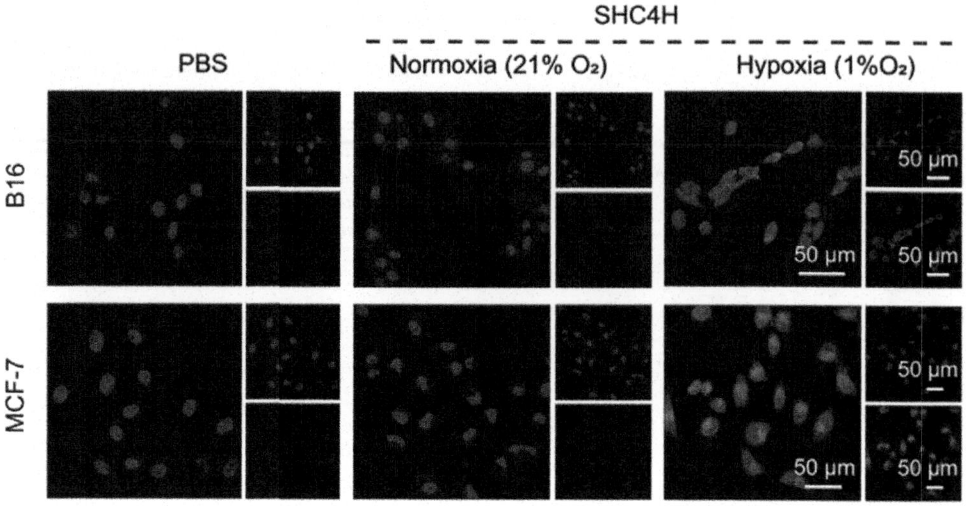


**FIGURE 9.10** Hypoxia imaging in B16 and MCF-7 cells treated with SHC4H under normoxic (21% $O_2$) and hypoxic (1% $O_2$) conditions. Weak red fluorescence was observed in normoxia after 12 hours, whereas bright fluorescence appeared in hypoxia at 6 hours, intensifying by 12 hours, indicating SMNB release and fluorescence restoration. *Reprinted with permission from Wang, W., Yao, S.Y., Luo, J., Ding, C., Huang, Q., Yang, Y., Shi, Z., Lin, J., Pan, Y.C., Zeng, X., Guo, D.S., Chen, H., Engineered hypoxia-responsive albumin nanoparticles mediating mitophagy regulation for cancer therapy. Nat. Commun. 16 (1) (2025).*

hold immense potential for maximizing treatment efficacy while minimizing side effects, and they represent a promising direction for personalized, on-demand cancer therapy.

## 5.4 Real-time feedback: Monitoring treatment efficacy in action

Another cutting-edge trend in multifunctional protein-based nanotechnologies is the incorporation of real-time monitoring capabilities that allow clinicians to observe treatment efficacy as it happens. This capability is crucial for tracking how a patient's tumor responds to therapy, particularly in cases where cancer is aggressive and may require rapid treatment adjustments. Multifunctional nanocarriers that combine imaging agents with therapeutic payloads offer an opportunity to visualize drug delivery and therapeutic response over time without invasive procedures. For example, recent studies have used albumin-bound nanoparticles that carry both chemotherapy agents and fluorescent markers. As the nanoparticles circulate, they not only deliver the drug but also emit a fluorescent signal that clinicians can observe through noninvasive imaging techniques. Changes in fluorescence intensity can indicate whether the tumor is absorbing the therapeutic agent or if adjustments are needed. Such real-time feedback enables more adaptable treatment plans and reduces the risk of overtreatment or undertreatment.

## 5.5 Future potential: Customizable platforms for precision oncology

Looking ahead, the ultimate goal of multifunctional protein-based nanotechnologies is to create fully customizable platforms that can be tailored to the unique genetic and molecular profile of each patient's cancer. Personalized approaches, enabled by advances in bioorthogonal chemistry, smart-release mechanisms, and real-time monitoring, promise to optimize treatment outcomes while minimizing side effects. Researchers are exploring combinations of protein nanocages and polymer conjugates that can simultaneously carry a range of agents—chemotherapeutics, genetic therapies, imaging compounds, and immune modulators—within a single platform. By targeting specific mutations or markers, these next-generation platforms could provide individualized treatments for each patient's cancer, maximizing efficacy and minimizing adverse effects.

In conclusion, multifunctional protein-based nanotechnologies are at the forefront of a new era in cancer theranostics. Through precision functionalization, integrated theranostic capabilities, tumor-responsive delivery, and real-time monitoring, these multifunctional platforms offer an unprecedented level of control and adaptability in cancer treatment. As research progresses, these "all-in-one" solutions are expected to become increasingly sophisticated and versatile, transforming cancer care by making it more personalized, effective, and less invasive.

# 6. Case studies and recent advances

## 6.1 Albumin-bound paclitaxel (Abraxane)

Albumin is the predominant circulating protein present in plasma. It constitutes 50 percent of the plasma's total protein content (3.5 g/dL to 5 g/dL) in healthy human individuals. Liver hepatocytes produce albumin and promptly release it into the circulatory system at a rate of approximately 10–15 g daily. Albumin, the predominant protein in blood, binds and transports both hydrophobic and hydrophilic and lipophilic substances essential for cellular and tissue development and proliferation. The surface positioning of charged groups and the inside hydrophobic region facilitates the transport of proteins, peptides, amino acids, fatty acids, nutrients, and other macromolecules. It is a multidomain protein that plays a role in several blood activities, including its contribution to oncotic pressure. Due to its distinctive sequence and structure, albumin can be effectively employed to create medication delivery systems for numerous disorders, including cancer. This protein, characterized by a surface rich in both negative and positive charges, garners significant interest in the field of drug administration. Inner hydrophobic locations have been demonstrated to be effective for the delivery of hydrophobic and lipophilic pharmaceuticals. Albumin binding domains, broadly dispersed among receptors and matricellular molecules, enable its entry into cells. A high ratio of cysteine offers stability to the molecule and promotes thiol-disulfide interactions, which play a key role in drug discharge (Asrorov et al., 2024).

Paclitaxel, originally known as Taxol, was first discovered in nature as a diterpenoid molecule derived from the Pacific yew tree, *Taxus brevifolia*. Its discovery is credited to the research efforts of the National Cancer Institute (NCI) during the late 1960s and early 1970s. While screening plant extracts for potential anticancer agents, scientists found that paclitaxel exhibited unique cytotoxic properties against cancer cells. What particularly captured their interest was its ability to inhibit microtubule depolymerization, leading to cell cycle arrest and apoptosis. This discovery prompted further investigation. In the mid-1980s, early-phase clinical trials were conducted to assess the safety, dosage, and pharmacokinetics of paclitaxel in cancer patients. Encouraging results from these trials paved the way for its progression into later stages of clinical development. By the late 1980s and early 1990s, phase 2 trials demonstrated paclitaxel's promising anticancer activity across a range of solid tumors, including lung, breast, and ovarian cancers. Subsequently, numerous large-scale randomized phase 3 trials compared standard chemotherapy or best supportive care with paclitaxel-based treatment regimens. The results revealed significant improvements in response rates, progression-free survival, and overall survival in patients receiving paclitaxel-based therapies (Hoyer, 2000).

In 1992, the U.S. Food and Drug Administration (FDA) approved paclitaxel for the treatment of ovarian cancer that was resistant to standard therapies. Shortly thereafter, paclitaxel received full approval as a primary therapeutic option for ovarian cancer. Over time, the FDA expanded its indications to include additional conditions such as Kaposi's sarcoma, NSCLC, and breast cancer, further solidifying paclitaxel's role as a versatile and effective anticancer agent (Kohler and Goldspiel, 1994; Alqahtani et al., 2019).

Abraxane, a chemotherapy drug also known as paclitaxel bound to albumin, is used to treat several cancers, including pancreatic, nonsmall cell lung, and breast cancer. This patented nanoparticle-based formulation binds paclitaxel to HSA, improving the drug's transport to cancer cells. Compared to conventional paclitaxel formulations, this albumin-protein complex enhances efficacy and reduces toxicity. The improved delivery mechanism allows for better targeting of cancer cells, which leads to a more favorable safety profile. Abraxane has been approved by the FDA and is also frequently used off-label for the treatment of other cancer types (Hama et al., 2021).

A new 130-nm albumin-bound formulation of paclitaxel, known as Abraxane (ABI-007), was developed to enhance drug delivery in NSCLC. A phase II trial evaluated the safety and efficacy of Abraxane at a dosage of 260 $mg/m^2$ administered every 3 weeks in patients with detectable NSCLC. Among the 43 enrolled patients, the overall response rate was 16%, with a disease control rate of 49%. The overall survival rate was recorded at 11 months, while the median progression-free survival was 6 months. Notably, after 1 year, the overall survival rate increased to 45%, and the progression-free survival rate reached 13%. Importantly, 95% of patients received treatment without any dose reductions, and the medication was well tolerated, with no serious hypersensitivity reactions reported. Only 5% of patients discontinued treatment due to toxicities, such as fatigue and neuropathy, and no grade 4 toxicities were observed. These findings suggest that further research is warranted to explore higher dosages and combination therapies (Green et al., 2006).

## 6.2 Ferritin and viral capsid nanocages

In biomedical research, protein nanocages have emerged as promising carriers for therapeutic and diagnostic agents. These nanocages are formed through the self-assembly of protein subunits, resulting in a caged structure with customizable interior, exterior, and intersubunit surfaces. By filling these nanocages with various therapeutic and diagnostic compounds, researchers can enhance their utility in targeted drug delivery and imaging. Additionally, modifications to the exterior surfaces of the nanocages have been developed to improve biocompatibility and facilitate specific targeting to desired tissues or cells. Importantly, alterations to the intersubunit contacts can influence the self-assembly process, which has significant implications for controlling the release profiles of the encapsulated molecules. This tunability allows for the design of nanocages tailored to meet specific therapeutic needs, making them a versatile platform in the field of nanomedicine (Kim et al., 2023).

Years of research into viral assembly, replication, and infection pathways have led to a comprehensive understanding of the stability and activity of viruses. Central to this understanding is the role of self-assembling protein structures known as capsids, which interact with host cells and facilitate the transfer of viral DNA into target cell compartments. The exterior surface of viral capsids offers numerous opportunities for site-specific modifications and various chemical functionalizations, allowing for the attachment of targeted moieties and the integration of organic and inorganic materials. Viruses possess an inherent ability to protect their genomes, transport them to the extracellular environment, evade the immune response by engaging with receptors on target cells, and deliver nucleic acids into the appropriate cellular compartments. This intrinsic capability provides viruses with advantages over artificial delivery vehicles, making them effective carriers for targeted distribution. As a result, viruses are classified as one of the most common forms of bionanoparticles, typically ranging in size from 10 to 100 nm. These protein-based systems not only exhibit highly ordered spatial configurations but also possess the ability to target cells and deliver genes efficiently. Extensive research has established the stability and functionality of these materials, further enhancing our understanding of viral infection, replication, and assembly processes (Bhaskar and Lim, 2017).

The cowpea mosaic virus (CPMV) (PDB ID 2BFU) was the first virus known to be successfully conjugated to a variety of functional chemicals. As a well-characterized plant virus, CPMV can be produced in large quantities, making it an attractive candidate for bioconjugation applications. The amino acid residue composition of CPMV is extensively characterized, facilitating its use in the attachment of functional molecules. Notably, CPMV demonstrates remarkable stability across a wide range of temperatures, organic solvents, and pH levels. This stability enhances its potential for assembling additional inorganic nanoparticles, thereby broadening its applications in nanotechnology and drug delivery systems. The ability to modify CPMV and integrate it with various functional components underscores its significance as a versatile nanocage in biomedical research and nanomedicine (Fontana et al., 2014). Gold nanospheres can be covalently linked to genetically modified CPMV that possesses thiol groups. This innovative approach results in a tenfold increase in local electromagnetic fields, as the nanospheres self-assemble into icosahedral plasmonic nanoclusters, following the spatial arrangement of the thiol groups on the CPMV. The unique optical properties of these plasmonic nanoclusters make them particularly valuable for applications in spectroscopy and cancer therapy. Furthermore, through genetic engineering techniques, it is feasible to create multiple orthogonal reactive sites on viral nanocages, enabling bioconjugation with signaling moieties and biological recognition patterns. This versatility not only enhances the functionality of the nanocages but also expands their potential use in targeted drug delivery and diagnostic applications in the field of nanomedicine (Barnhill et al., 2007).

The protein structure ferritin was identified in 1937 and is in charge of storing and transferring iron throughout biological systems in order to preserve iron homeostasis (Knovich et al., 2009). Ferritin was first isolated from horse spleen and contains approximately 20% natural iron. While the first X-ray diffraction measurements of ferritin were published in 1943, the crystal structure of human ferritin was determined later, in 1991. With an interior chamber measuring 8 nm and an external diameter of 12 nm, ferritin resembles a caged, spherical structure composed of 24 subunits, allowing it to store iron in a form that is both bioavailable and insoluble. The quaternary structure of the protein is stable across various environments, and metal ions regulate its self-assembly and disassembly, facilitating the absorption and release of active compounds. These structural and biochemical characteristics have made ferritin suitable for biomedical applications, including vaccine development and nanoparticle production (Tesarova et al., 2020).

Cai et al. (2020) designed a recombinant human heavy chain (H-chain) ferritin with Gadolinium (Gd) labeling, HFn-Gd nanoparticles, to offer significant advantages over traditional Gd-DTPA agents in MRI, particularly for tumor imaging. Their higher R1 relaxivity, due to the large molecular weight of HFn, enhances MRI signal strength even at lower doses. Additionally, they provide prolonged signal duration, lasting up to 60 min compared to just 10 min with Gd-DTPA, improving diagnostic accuracy. A key advantage of HFn-Gd nanoparticles is their active targeting of TfR1-positive cancer cells. Fluorescence colocalization studies confirm their specificity, showing strong colocalization with TfR1 in cancer cells like CFPAC-1 and MDA-MB-231. Competition experiments further validate this targeting, as blocking TfR1 significantly reduces HFn-Gd accumulation. Moreover, these nanoparticles require a lower dosage than conventional Gd-DTPA, minimizing the risks of Gd deposition. Their excellent biocompatibility and stability make them well-suited for in vivo applications, hence, a safer and more effective alternative for MRI contrast enhancement, particularly in oncological imaging (Cai et al., 2020).

## 6.3 PEGylated proteins and other conjugates

PEGylation is an increasingly popular technique for enhancing the medicinal and biotechnological potential of peptides and proteins. When poly-(ethylene glycol) (PEG) is properly attached to a polypeptide, it alters many of the polypeptide's characteristics while preserving its primary physiological functions, such as enzyme activity and receptor recognition. PEG coupling reduces kidney ultrafiltration, inhibits the action of antibodies or antigen-processing cells, and lessens degradation by proteolytic enzymes by masking the protein's outermost layer and increasing the molecular size of the polypeptide. Additionally, PEG modifies the biodistribution and solubility of both peptide and nonpeptide medications by imparting its physicochemical properties to these molecules. PEGylation is particularly valuable in modern bioengineering, as it enhances the solubility and activity of enzymes in organic solvents. This property allows for the solubilization of several insoluble drugs through PEG conjugation, facilitating easier administration. Consequently, PEGylation opens new avenues in biocatalysis and pharmaceutical research (Suk et al., 2016).

PEGylation is the process of attaching PEG chains to proteins to enhance their solubility, biological compatibility, and pharmacokinetics. However, PEG's polydispersity presents challenges, as it leads to molecular weight fluctuations even in high-purity PEGs. Typically,

PEGylation targets nucleophilic groups, such as thiols and amino groups, under mild conditions; however, achieving selectivity and control in these reactions can be problematic. To improve conjugation and provide greater versatility, amino acid or peptide arms can be introduced between PEG and proteins. Despite these advancements, characterizing PEG conjugates remains difficult, particularly due to PEG's opacity and lack of fluorescence, necessitating the precise quantification of PEG chains linked to proteins through various analytical techniques. Site-specific PEGylation at cysteine residues using thiol-reactive PEGs has emerged as a more precise approach, while targeting rarer amino acids, such as arginine or carboxyl groups, can be more complex. It is important to note that PEGylation can inhibit protein activity or block active sites, especially in enzymes or receptor-binding proteins, making nonspecific binding a potential risk. The hydrophilicity and flexibility of bifunctional PEGs have led to their use as cross-linking agents, and PEGylation enhances solubility in organic solvents. Reversible PEGylation enables selective PEG removal, improving control over modifications. The field continues to evolve, with the development of monofunctional PEG polymers and innovative PEGylation techniques, such as dendrimer PEG, enhancing their medicinal applications (Veronese, 2001).

## 7. Challenges and limitations

Protein nanoparticles have garnered significant attention in drug delivery due to their ability to enhance the solubility and bioavailability of poorly water-soluble drugs, leading to improved therapeutic outcomes. Functionalization (Richards et al., 2024) with ligands or antibodies enables targeted delivery to diseased cells, such as cancer cells, thereby minimizing damage to healthy tissues and reducing systemic toxicity. The natural biocompatibility and biodegradability of proteins like albumin, casein, and gelatin further contribute to their appeal, as they reduce the likelihood of adverse immune responses (Yadav et al., 2025) and allow for controlled drug release, maintaining optimal drug levels without causing toxic spikes. Additionally, encapsulating drugs within protein nanoparticles can enhance intracellular uptake, decreasing the chance of efflux by drug-resistant cells and preventing the development of resistance. However, challenges (Verma et al., 2018) such as controlling nanoparticle size, stability issues due to high surface energy leading to aggregation, slow biodegradability causing unintended accumulation, limited chemical reactivity necessitating additional modifications, unpredictable biological behavior, and reduced flexibility in dosage adjustments pose significant hurdles (Fig. 9.11). Addressing these challenges through advanced formulation techniques and a thorough understanding of protein nanoparticle interactions within biological systems is crucial for their successful application in clinical settings.

### 7.1 Scalability: Production methods and challenges

Scalability is a big challenge for protein-based nanotechnology due to the intricacy of its manufacture. These nanoparticles are generally generated using techniques including self-assembly, chemical conjugation, or genetic modification, which can be extremely susceptible to external factors such as pH and temperature. Establishing these specific settings at a

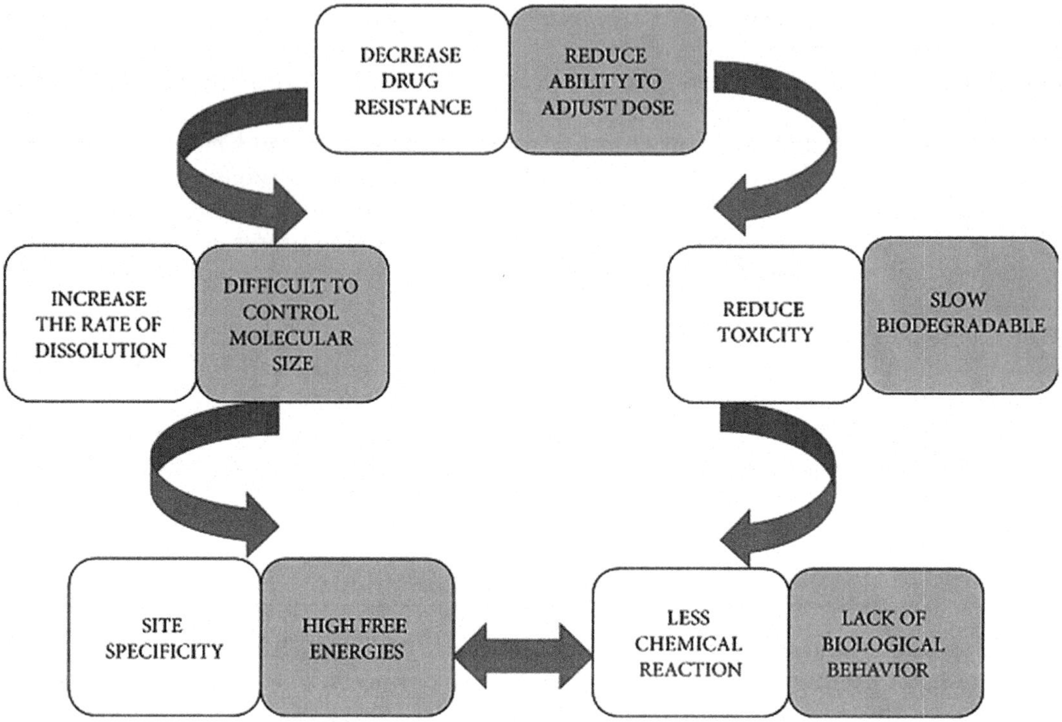


**FIGURE 9.11** Pictorial presentation of positive and negative aspects of protein nanoparticles. *Reprinted with permission from Verma, D., Gulati, N., Kaul, S., Mukherjee, S., Nagaich, U., Protein based nanostructures for drug delivery. J. Pharm. 2018 (2018), 1–18.*

bigger manufacturing scale is tough and sometimes leads to issues. Additionally, producing high-purity proteins suited for nanoparticle production is labor-intensive and expensive. During manufacture, proteins may clump or misfold, affecting both the output and overall quality of the final product. This further complicates massive manufacturing and drives up production costs. Consistency across multiple production batches can also be challenging to maintain, since even modest variations during production circumstances might result in variability in the size, shape, or surface features of the nanoparticles, possibly compromising their therapeutic effectiveness (Herdiana et al., 2022).

Another significant difficulty linked to scaling is the stability of protein-based nanoparticles. Proteins are intrinsically prone to deterioration, particularly when in storage and handling. They may suffer enzymatic hydrolysis or denaturation, which reduces their shelf life and restricts the practicality of long-term, large-scale manufacture. This makes it challenging to build protein-based nanotechnologies that can be generated in bulk and kept for lengthy periods while preserving their biological viability (Moleirinho et al., 2020).

## 7.2 Characterization: Need for standardized techniques

The characterization of protein-based nanoparticles remains a problem due to the intrinsic complexity and diversity of proteins. In contrast to synthetic components, proteins display heterogeneity in size, shape, and charge, which can lead to discrepancies in how they behave when utilized in nanotechnologies. Standardizing characterization procedures to ensure repeatability across laboratories is vital, but currently, there is no globally approved approach for characterizing protein-based nanoparticles. This lack of homogeneity makes it difficult to verify that therapeutic nanoparticles act consistently in biological systems, which is crucial for their clinical application (Sapsford et al., 2011).

Additionally, based on proteins, nanoparticles typically undergo surface changes to increase their targeting or drug delivery capabilities. These adjustments need to be extensively defined to ensure that they work as intended, but standardized methods to precisely measure and analyze these surface changes are currently missing. This generates uncertainties regarding the repeatability and efficiency of the modified nanoparticles. Biological interactions, such as the creation of a protein corona—where proteins from the circulation attach onto its nanoparticle surface—can further complicate the characterization process. Forecasting how nanoparticles will act in vivo needs accurate tests, but the existing methodologies are not adequately evolved to produce precise and uniform forecasts of these relationships (McClements and McClements, 2016).

## 7.3 Safety and efficacy: Long-term evaluation in clinical settings

When it comes to protein-based products, the use of nanotechnology, safety, and effectiveness are major considerations, especially when contemplating long-term usage in clinical settings. The possible immunogenicity of the proteins included in these nanoparticles is one of the main concerns about safety. Even small changes in the structure of proteins can trigger an immune response and have negative consequences like inflammation or allergic responses. It is challenging to guarantee the safety of protein-based nanoparticles because of their unpredictable nature, particularly when using them often or in large quantities. Furthermore, even though a lot of protein-based nanoparticles are intended to be benign and biodegradable, the products of their breakdown often result in harmful or unexpected immunological responses. To properly comprehend these consequences, long-term research is needed, but for many protein-based systems, these studies are still in their early phases (Singh and Tripathi, 2023).

Concerns about the effectiveness also stem from the nanoparticles' capacity to enter tumors and gather there. To successfully transport therapeutic medicines, protein-based nanocarriers must negotiate complicated biological settings such as the aberrant vasculature of tumors and the thick extracellular matrix. These nanoparticles frequently experience fast bloodstream clearance or absorption by nontarget tissues, which limits their capacity to accumulate to high enough concentrations within the tumor. This restricts their potential for therapeutic use and calls for more design optimization. Lastly, a major obstacle still stands in the way of protein-based nanotechnologies receiving regulatory approval. The regulatory landscape around these technologies is still developing, and in order to meet the strict standards for clinical usage, extensive safety and effectiveness data—especially from long-term clinical trials—are required (Singh and Tripathi, 2023; Yu et al., 2016).

# 8. Summary and future directives

Protein-based nanomaterials' biocompatibility, biodegradability, and multifunctionality make them highly promising for use in cancer theranostics. However, before their clinical translation can be widely implemented, several issues need to be addressed. Novel strategies, such as the creation of fusion proteins, genetically modified proteins, and hybrid nanostructures, are essential for resolving scalability and stability concerns. These developments, in conjunction with stimuli-responsive nanomaterials, may lead to more potent and successful cancer treatments. To overcome the existing lack of standardized characterization methodologies, which impedes repeatability and uniformity across investigations, the creation of standardized methods for evaluating the characteristics of protein nanoparticles is necessary. Additionally, clearer regulatory frameworks emphasizing clinical effectiveness, pharmacokinetics, and long-term safety are needed to expedite the licensing process. Ethical issues related to genetic modifications and biosafety must also be carefully addressed. As protein-based nanoparticles continue to advance, they are playing an increasingly significant role in personalized medicine, enabling treatments that are more precisely targeted, less invasive, and less likely to cause adverse effects. The future of this research lies in developing multifunctional nanomaterials that can be used for simultaneous diagnosis, therapy, and real-time monitoring, as well as incorporating cutting-edge technologies like artificial intelligence for nanoparticle creation. Unlocking the full potential of protein-based nanotechnologies will require close collaboration among scientists, physicians, regulatory bodies, and industry stakeholders to pave the way for safer, more effective, and customized cancer treatments.

## Acknowledgments

The authors would like to acknowledge the project grants ICMR (IIRPIG/2024/01), IITH/BME/SOCH3, SUPRA (SPR/2022/230), SPARC (SPARC/2019-2020/P2082/SL), and MoE STARS (MoE STARS-2/2023-640) for funding the laboratory activities. A.V. would like to thank the University Grants Commission (UGC), Government of India, for the UGC-JRF fellowship. A.K.M. would like to acknowledge the Indian Institute of Technology for funding his fellowship through the institute's Postdoctoral Fellowship Program. K.M. would like to acknowledge the Anusandhan National Research Foundation, Government of India (SPR/2022/230) for funding her fellowship.

## References

Alqahtani, F.Y., Aleanizy, F.S., El Tahir, E., Alkahtani, H.M., AlQuadeib, B.T., 2019. Paclitaxel. Profiles Drug Subst. Excipients Relat. Methodol. 44, 205–238. https://doi.org/10.1016/bs.podrm.2018.11.001.

Arun, A., Malrautu, P., Laha, A., Luo, H., Ramakrishna, S., 2021. Collagen nanoparticles in drug delivery systems and tissue engineering. Appl. Sci. (Switzerland) 11 (23). https://doi.org/10.3390/app112311369.

Asrorov, A.M., Mukhamedov, N., Kayumov, M., Yashinov, A.S., Wali, A., Yili, A., Mirzaakhmedov, S.Y., Huang, Y., 2024. Albumin is a reliable drug-delivering molecule: Highlighting points in cancer therapy. Medicine in Drug Discovery 22, 100186. https://doi.org/10.1016/j.medidd.2024.100186.

Bahrami, H., Tafrihi, M., 2023. Global trends of cancer: The role of diet, lifestyle, and environmental factors. Cancer Innovation 2 (4), 290–301. https://doi.org/10.1002/cai2.76.

Barnhill, H.N., Claudel-Gillet, S., Ziessel, R., Charbonnière, L.J., Wang, Q., 2007. Prototype protein assembly as scaffold for time-resolved fluoroimmuno assays. J. Am. Chem. Soc. 129 (25), 7799–7806. https://doi.org/10.1021/ja069148u.

Bhaskar, S., Lim, S., 2017. Engineering protein nanocages as carriers for biomedical applications. NPG Asia Mater. 9 (4), e371. https://doi.org/10.1038/am.2016.128.

Bourbon, A.I., Pinheiro, A.C., Cerqueira, M.A., Vicente, A.A., 2018. In vitro digestion of lactoferrin-glycomacropeptide nanohydrogels incorporating bioactive compounds: Effect of a chitosan coating. Food Hydrocoll. 84, 267–275. https://doi.org/10.1016/j.foodhyd.2018.06.015.

Cai, Y., Wang, Y., Zhang, T., Pan, Y., 2020. Gadolinium-labeled ferritin nanoparticles as T1Contrast agents for magnetic resonance imaging of tumors. ACS Appl. Nano Mater. 3 (9), 8771–8783. https://doi.org/10.1021/acsanm.0c01563.

Chen, X., Wong, S.T.C., 2014. Cancer Theranostics: An Introduction Cancer Theranostics. Elsevier Inc., United States, pp. 3–8. https://doi.org/10.1016/B978-0-12-407722-5.00001-3.

Chen, Z., Han, F., Du, Y., Shi, H., Zhou, W., 2023. Hypoxic microenvironment in cancer: Molecular mechanisms and therapeutic interventions. Signal Transduct. Targeted Ther. 8 (1). https://doi.org/10.1038/s41392-023-01332-8.

Ding, S., Zhang, N., Lyu, Z., Zhu, W., Chang, Y.C., Hu, X., Du, D., Lin, Y., 2021. Protein-based nanomaterials and nanosystems for biomedical applications: A review. Mater. Today 43, 166–184. https://doi.org/10.1016/j.mattod.2020.11.015.

Elahi, M., Ali, S., Tahir, H.M., Mushtaq, R., Bhatti, M.F., 2021. Sericin and fibroin nanoparticles—natural product for cancer therapy: a comprehensive review. International Journal of Polymeric Materials and Polymeric Biomaterials 70 (4), 256–269. https://doi.org/10.1080/00914037.2019.1706515.

Elzoghby, A.O., Abo El-Fotoh, W.S., Elgindy, N.A., 2011. Casein-based formulations as promising controlled release drug delivery systems. J. Contr. Release 153 (3), 206–216. https://doi.org/10.1016/j.jconrel.2011.02.010.

Fontana, J., Dressick, W.J., Phelps, J., Johnson, J.E., Rendell, R.W., Sampson, T., Ratna, B.R., Soto, C.M., 2014. Virus-templated plasmonic nanoclusters with icosahedral symmetry via directed self-assembly. Small 10 (15), 3058–3063. https://doi.org/10.1002/smll.201400470.

Garlasco, J., Cesare Nurchis, M., Bordino, V., Sapienza, M., Altamura, G., Damiani, G., Gianino, M.M., 2022. Cancers: What are the costs in relation to disability-adjusted life years? A systematic review and meta-analysis. Int. J. Environ. Res. Publ. Health 19 (8), 4862. https://doi.org/10.3390/ijerph19084862.

Ghazal, H., Waqar, A., Yaseen, F., Shahid, M., Sultana, M., Tariq, M., Bashir, M.K., Tahseen, H., Raza, T., Ahmad, F., 2024. Role of nanoparticles in enhancing chemotherapy efficacy for cancer treatment. Next Mater. 2, 100128. https://doi.org/10.1016/j.nxmate.2024.100128.

Gobbo, O.L., Sjaastad, K., Radomski, M.W., Volkov, Y., Prina-Mello, A., 2015. Magnetic nanoparticles in cancer theranostics. Theranostics 5 (11), 1249–1263. https://doi.org/10.7150/thno.11544.

Green, M.R., Manikhas, G.M., Orlov, S., Afanasyev, B., Makhson, A.M., Bhar, P., Hawkins, M.J., 2006. Abraxane®, a novel Cremophor®-free, albumin-bound particle form of paclitaxel for the treatment of advanced non-small-cell lung cancer. Ann. Oncol. 17 (8), 1263–1268. https://doi.org/10.1093/annonc/mdl104.

Hama, M., Ishima, Y., Chuang, V.T.G., Ando, H., Shimizu, T., Ishida, T., 2021. Evidence for delivery of abraxane via a denatured-albumin transport system. ACS Appl. Mater. Interfaces 13 (17), 19736–19744. https://doi.org/10.1021/acsami.1c03065.

Herdiana, Y., Wathoni, N., Shamsuddin, S., Muchtaridi, M., 2022. Scale-up polymeric-based nanoparticles drug delivery systems: Development and challenges. OpenNano 7. https://doi.org/10.1016/j.onano.2022.100048.

Hirakura, T., Nomura, Y., Aoyama, Y., Akiyoshi, K., 2004. Photoresponsive nanogels formed by the self-assembly of spiropyrane-bearing pullulan that act as artificial molecular chaperones. Biomacromolecules 5 (5), 1804–1809. https://doi.org/10.1021/bm049860o.

Hong, S.-T., Lin, H., Wang, C.-S., Chang, C.-H., Lin, A.M.-Y., Chih-Hsin Yang, J., Lo, Y.-L., 2019. Improving the anti-cancer effect of afatinib and microRNA by using lipid polymeric nanoparticles conjugated with dual pH-responsive and targeting peptides. J. Nanobiotechnol. 17 (1). https://doi.org/10.1186/s12951-019-0519-6.

Hoyer, K.A., 2000. Paclitaxel. Clin. J. Oncol. Nurs. 4 (1), 51–52.

Hua, Y., Qin, Z., Gao, L., Zhou, M., Xue, Y., Li, Y., Xie, J., 2024. Protein nanoparticles as drug delivery systems for cancer theranostics. J. Contr. Release 371, 429–444. https://doi.org/10.1016/j.jconrel.2024.06.004.

Jain, A., Singh, S.K., Arya, S.K., Kundu, S.C., Kapoor, S., 2018. Protein nanoparticles: Promising platforms for drug delivery applications. ACS Biomater. Sci. Eng. 4 (12), 3939–3961. https://doi.org/10.1021/acsbiomaterials.8b01098.

Jethwa, A.R., Khariwala, S.S., 2017. Tobacco-related carcinogenesis in head and neck cancer. Cancer Metastasis Rev. 36 (3), 411–423. https://doi.org/10.1007/s10555-017-9689-6.

Jiang, M., Chen, W., Sun, Y., Zeng, J., Ma, L., Gong, J., Guan, X., Lu, K., Zhang, W., 2023. Synergistically enhanced cancer immunotherapy by combining protamine-based nanovaccine with PD-L1 gene silence nanoparticle. Int. J. Biol. Macromol. 242 (Pt 4), 125223. https://doi.org/10.1016/j.ijbiomac.2023.125223.

Joye, I.J., Nelis, V.A., McClements, D.J., 2015. Gliadin-based nanoparticles: Fabrication and stability of food-grade colloidal delivery systems. Food Hydrocoll. 44, 86–93. https://doi.org/10.1016/j.foodhyd.2014.09.008.

Kaltbeitzel, J., Wich, P.R., 2023. Protein-based nanoparticles: From drug delivery to imaging, nanocatalysis and protein therapy. Angewandte Chemie - International Edition 62 (44). https://doi.org/10.1002/anie.202216097.

Kanapathipillai, M., Brock, A., Ingber, D.E., 2014. Nanoparticle targeting of anti-cancer drugs that alter intracellular signaling or influence the tumor microenvironment. Adv. Drug Deliv. Rev. 79, 107–118. https://doi.org/10.1016/j.addr.2014.05.005.

Kaur, R., Bhardwaj, A., Gupta, S., 2023. Cancer treatment therapies: Traditional to modern approaches to combat cancers. Mol. Biol. Rep. 50 (11), 9663–9676. https://doi.org/10.1007/s11033-023-08809-3.

Khan, H., Ullah, H., Martorell, M., Valdes, S.E., Belwal, T., Tejada, S., Sureda, A., Kamal, M.A., 2021. Flavonoids nanoparticles in cancer: Treatment, prevention and clinical prospects. Semin. Cancer Biol. 69, 200–211. https://doi.org/10.1016/j.semcancer.2019.07.023.

Khoshnejad, M., Greineder, C.F., Pulsipher, K.W., Villa, C.H., Altun, B., Pan, D.C., Tsourkas, A., Dmochowski, I.J., Muzykantov, V.R., 2018. Ferritin nanocages with biologically orthogonal conjugation for vascular targeting and imaging. Bioconjug. Chem. 29 (4), 1209–1218. https://doi.org/10.1021/acs.bioconjchem.8b00004.

Kicková, E., Salmaso, S., Mastrotto, F., Caliceti, P., Urtti, A., 2021. Pullulan based bioconjugates for ocular dexamethasone delivery. Pharmaceutics 13 (6), 791. https://doi.org/10.3390/pharmaceutics13060791.

Kicková, E., Sadeghi, A., Puranen, J., Tavakoli, S., Sen, M., Ranta, V.-P., Arango-Gonzalez, B., Bolz, S., Ueffing, M., Salmaso, S., Caliceti, P., Toropainen, E., Ruponen, M., Urtti, A., 2022. Pharmacokinetics of pullulan–dexamethasone conjugates in retinal drug delivery. Pharmaceutics 14 (1), 12. https://doi.org/10.3390/pharmaceutics14010012.

Kim, S.A., Lee, Y., Ko, Y., Kim, S., Kim, G.B., Lee, N.K., Ahn, W., Kim, N., Nam, G.H., Lee, E.J., Kim, I.S., 2023. Protein-based nanocages for vaccine development. J. Contr. Release 353, 767–791. https://doi.org/10.1016/j.jconrel.2022.12.022.

Knovich, M.A., Storey, J.A., Coffman, L.G., Torti, S.V., Torti, F.M., 2009. Ferritin for the clinician. Blood Rev. 23 (3), 95–104. https://doi.org/10.1016/j.blre.2008.08.001.

Kohler, D.R., Goldspiel, B.R., 1994. Paclitaxel (Taxol). Pharmacotherapy 14 (1), 3–34. https://doi.org/10.1002/j.1875-9114.1994.tb02785.x.

Kozlenko, A.S., Ozhogin, I.V., Pugachev, A.D., Lukyanova, M.B., El-Sewify, I.M., Lukyanov, B.S., 2023. A modern look at spiropyrans: From single molecules to smart materials. Top. Curr. Chem. 381 (1). https://doi.org/10.1007/s41061-022-00417-2.

Kundu, J., Chung, Y.I., Kim, Y.H., Tae, G., Kundu, S.C., 2010. Silk fibroin nanoparticles for cellular uptake and control release. Int. J. Pharm. 388 (1–2), 242–250. https://doi.org/10.1016/j.ijpharm.2009.12.052.

Lewandowska, A.M., Rudzki, M., Rudzki, S., Lewandowski, T., Laskowska, B., 2019. Environmental risk factors for cancer - review paper. Ann. Agric. Environ. Med. 26 (1), 1–7. https://doi.org/10.26444/aaem/94299.

Lin, Y., Wan, Y., Du, X., Li, J., Wei, J., Li, T., Li, C., Liu, Z., Zhou, M., Zhong, Z., 2021. TAT-modified serum albumin nanoparticles for sustained-release of tetramethylpyrazine and improved targeting to spinal cord injury. J. Nanobiotechnol. 19 (1). https://doi.org/10.1186/s12951-020-00766-4.

Liu, J.N., Bu, W., Shi, J., 2017. Chemical design and synthesis of functionalized probes for imaging and treating tumor hypoxia. Chem. Rev. 117 (9), 6160–6224. https://doi.org/10.1021/acs.chemrev.6b00525.

Mahendra Kumar, S., Rajni, Y., Prasad, T.S., 2023. Recent advances in nanotechnology. Int. J. Nanomater. Nanotechnol. Nanomed. 9 (2), 015–023. https://doi.org/10.17352/2455-3492.000053.

Matsumoto, G., Kushibiki, T., Kinoshita, Y., Lee, U., Omi, Y., Kubota, E., Tabata, Y., 2006. Cationized gelatin delivery of a plasmid DNA expressing small interference RNA for VEGF inhibits murine squamous cell carcinoma. Cancer Sci. 97 (4), 313–321. https://doi.org/10.1111/j.1349-7006.2006.00174.x.

McClements, J., McClements, D.J., 2016. Standardization of nanoparticle characterization: Methods for testing properties, stability, and functionality of edible nanoparticles. Crit. Rev. Food Sci. Nutr. 56 (8), 1334–1362. https://doi.org/10.1080/10408398.2014.970267.

Miao, L., Huang, L., 2015. Exploring the tumor microenvironment with nanoparticles. Cancer Treat Res. 166, 193–226. https://doi.org/10.1007/978-3-319-16555-4_9.

Mohajer, F., Mirhosseini-Eshkevari, B., Ahmadi, S., Ghasemzadeh, M.A., Mohammadi Ziarani, G., Badiei, A., Farshidfar, N., Varma, R.S., Rabiee, N., Iravani, S., 2023. Advanced nanosystems for cancer therapeutics: A review. ACS Appl. Nano Mater. 6 (9), 7123–7149. https://doi.org/10.1021/acsanm.3c00859.

Moleirinho, M.G., Silva, R.J.S., Alves, P.M., Carrondo, M.J.T., Peixoto, C., 2020. Current challenges in biotherapeutic particles manufacturing. Expet Opin. Biol. Ther. 20 (5), 451–465. https://doi.org/10.1080/14712598.2020.1693541.

Mukherjee, A., De Izarra, A., Degrouard, J., Olive, E., Maiti, P.K., Jang, Y.H., Lansac, Y., 2021. Protamine-controlled reversible DNA packaging: A molecular glue. ACS Nano 15 (8), 13094–13104. https://doi.org/10.1021/acsnano.1c02337.

Nagatomo, D., Taniai, M., Ariyasu, H., Taniguchi, M., Aga, M., Ariyasu, T., Ohta, T., Fukuda, S., 2015. Cholesteryl pullulan encapsulated TNF-α nanoparticles are an effective mucosal vaccine adjuvant against influenza virus. BioMed Res. Int. 2015, 1–15. https://doi.org/10.1155/2015/471468.

Nguyen, D.X., Massagué, J., 2007. Genetic determinants of cancer metastasis. Nat. Rev. Genet. 8 (5), 341–352. https://doi.org/10.1038/nrg2101.

Numata, K., Hamasaki, J., Subramanian, B., Kaplan, D.L., 2010. Gene delivery mediated by recombinant silk proteins containing cationic and cell binding motifs. J. Contr. Release 146 (1), 136–143. https://doi.org/10.1016/j.jconrel.2010.05.006.

Patel, P.R., Haemmerich, D., 2024. Review on electrospray nanoparticles for drug delivery: Exploring applications. Polym. Adv. Technol. 35 (7). https://doi.org/10.1002/pat.6507.

Peng, Q., Zhang, S., Yang, Q., Zhang, T., Wei, X.Q., Jiang, L., Zhang, C.L., Chen, Q.M., Zhang, Z.R., Lin, Y.F., 2013. Preformed albumin corona, a protective coating for nanoparticles based drug delivery system. Biomaterials 34 (33), 8521–8530. https://doi.org/10.1016/j.biomaterials.2013.07.102.

Qin, Y., Xu, L., Guan, Y.Y., Liu, H., 2020. Multifunctionalized protein-based drug delivery system for inhibition of tumor growth and progression. ACS Appl. Bio Mater. 3 (5), 3196–3202. https://doi.org/10.1021/acsabm.0c00190.

Ramadan, M., AlGhamdi, S., Alsiary, R., 2025. Analyzing the cancer mortality-to-incidence ratios and health expenditures in the aging population: a 20-year comparative study across high-income countries. Frontiers in Aging 6. https://doi.org/10.3389/fragi.2025.1506897.

Reddy, N., Rapisarda, M., 2021. Properties and applications of nanoparticles from plant proteins. Materials 14 (13), 3607. https://doi.org/10.3390/ma14133607.

Richards, B.A., Goncalves, A.G., Sullivan, M.O., Chen, W., 2024. Engineering protein nanoparticles for drug delivery. Curr. Opin. Biotechnol. 86. https://doi.org/10.1016/j.copbio.2024.103070.

Rozovsky, A., Ebaston, T.M., Zaporozhets, A., Bazylevich, A., Tuchinsky, H., Patsenker, L., Gellerman, G., 2019. Theranostic system for ratiometric fluorescence monitoring of peptide-guided targeted drug delivery. RSC Adv. 9 (56), 32656–32664. https://doi.org/10.1039/c9ra06334j.

Sahoo, N., Sahoo, R.K., Biswas, N., Guha, A., Kuotsu, K., 2015. Recent advancement of gelatin nanoparticles in drug and vaccine delivery. Int. J. Biol. Macromol. 81, 317–331. https://doi.org/10.1016/j.ijbiomac.2015.08.006.

Sapsford, K.E., Tyner, K.M., Dair, B.J., Deschamps, J.R., Medintz, I.L., 2011. Analyzing nanomaterial bioconjugates: A review of current and emerging purification and characterization techniques. Anal. Chem. 83 (12), 4453–4488. https://doi.org/10.1021/ac200853a.

Sarkar, S., Horn, G., Moulton, K., Oza, A., Byler, S., Kokolus, S., Longacre, M., 2013. Cancer development, progression, and therapy: An epigenetic overview. Int. J. Mol. Sci. 14 (10), 21087–21113. https://doi.org/10.3390/ijms141021087 (United States).

Shapira, A., Livney, Y.D., Broxterman, H.J., Assaraf, Y.G., 2011. Nanomedicine for targeted cancer therapy: Towards the overcoming of drug resistance. Drug Resist. Updates 14 (3), 150–163. https://doi.org/10.1016/j.drup.2011.01.003.

Singh, D.B., Tripathi, T., 2023. Protein-based Therapeutics. Springer Nature Singapore. https://doi.org/10.1007/978-981-19-8249-1.

Spicer, C.D., Jumeaux, C., Gupta, B., Stevens, M.M., 2018. Peptide and protein nanoparticle conjugates: Versatile platforms for biomedical applications. Chem. Soc. Rev. 47 (10), 3574–3620. https://doi.org/10.1039/c7cs00877e.

Srikar, R., Suresh, D., Zambre, A., Taylor, K., Chapman, S., Leevy, M., Upendran, A., Kannan, R., 2016. Targeted nanoconjugate co-delivering siRNA and tyrosine kinase inhibitor to KRAS mutant NSCLC dissociates GAB1-SHP2 post oncogene knockdown. Sci. Rep. 6. https://doi.org/10.1038/srep30245.

Suk, J.S., Xu, Q., Kim, N., Hanes, J., Ensign, L.M., 2016. PEGylation as a strategy for improving nanoparticle-based drug and gene delivery. Adv. Drug Deliv. Rev. 99, 28–51. https://doi.org/10.1016/j.addr.2015.09.012.

Tang, Y., Zhang, Q., Chen, H., Chen, G., Li, Z., Chen, G., Lin, L., Yu, Z., Su, M., Zhang, B., 2025. A integrated molecule based on ferritin nanoplatforms for inducing tumor ferroptosis with the synergistic photo/chemodynamic treatment. ACS Appl. Mater. Interfaces 17 (4), 5909–5920. https://doi.org/10.1021/acsami.4c18072.

Tanhaei, A., Mohammadi, M., Hamishehkar, H., Hamblin, M.R., 2021. Electrospraying as a novel method of particle engineering for drug delivery vehicles. J. Contr. Release 330, 851–865. https://doi.org/10.1016/j.jconrel.2020.10.059.

Tesarova, B., Musilek, K., Rex, S., Heger, Z., 2020. Taking advantage of cellular uptake of ferritin nanocages for targeted drug delivery. J. Contr. Release 325, 176–190. https://doi.org/10.1016/j.jconrel.2020.06.026.

Verma, D., Gulati, N., Kaul, S., Mukherjee, S., Nagaich, U., 2018. Protein based nanostructures for drug delivery. J. Pharm. 2018, 1–18. https://doi.org/10.1155/2018/9285854.

Veronese, F.M., 2001. Peptide and protein PEGylation. Biomaterials 22 (5), 405–417. https://doi.org/10.1016/s0142-9612(00)00193-9.

Wang, H., Zou, Q., Boerman, O.C., Nijhuis, A.W.G., Jansen, J.A., Li, Y., Leeuwenburgh, S.C.G., 2013. Combined delivery of BMP-2 and bFGF from nanostructured colloidal gelatin gels and its effect on bone regeneration in vivo. J. Contr. Release 166 (2), 172–181. https://doi.org/10.1016/j.jconrel.2012.12.015.

Wang, R., Yang, Z., Luo, J., Hsing, I.M., Sun, F., 2017. B12-dependent photoresponsive protein hydrogels for controlled stem cell/protein release. In: Proceedings of the National Academy of Sciences of the United States of America, 114, pp. 5912–5917. https://doi.org/10.1073/pnas.1621350114.

Wang, W., Yao, S.Y., Luo, J., Ding, C., Huang, Q., Yang, Y., Shi, Z., Lin, J., Pan, Y.C., Zeng, X., Guo, D.S., Chen, H., 2025. Engineered hypoxia-responsive albumin nanoparticles mediating mitophagy regulation for cancer therapy. Nat. Commun. 16 (1). https://doi.org/10.1038/s41467-025-55905-y.

Yadav, K., Princely Ebenezer Gnanakani, S., Kumar Sahu, K., Sucheta, A.D., Minz, S., Raza, W., Pradhan, M., 2025. Unleashing the potential of natural protein based nanoparticles for the delivery of therapeutic nucleic acid: A comprehensive review. Int. J. Pharm. 669, 125049. https://doi.org/10.1016/j.ijpharm.2024.125049.

Yang, C., Tan, Y., Qi, H., Zhou, J., Long, L., Zhan, Q., Wang, Y., Yuan, X., Kang, C., 2020. Boosting of the enhanced permeability and retention effect with nanocapsules improves the therapeutic effects of cetuximab. Cancer Biol. Med. 17 (2), 433–443. https://doi.org/10.20892/j.issn.2095-3941.2019.0292.

Yu, M., Wu, J., Shi, J., Farokhzad, O.C., 2016. Nanotechnology for protein delivery: Overview and perspectives. J. Contr. Release 240, 24–37. https://doi.org/10.1016/j.jconrel.2015.10.012.

Zensi, A., Begley, D., Pontikis, C., Legros, C., Mihoreanu, L., Wagner, S., Büchel, C., von Briesen, H., Kreuter, J., 2009. Albumin nanoparticles targeted with Apo E enter the CNS by transcytosis and are delivered to neurones. J. Contr. Release 137 (1), 78–86. https://doi.org/10.1016/j.jconrel.2009.03.002.

Zhang, N., Mei, K., Guan, P., Hu, X., Zhao, Y., 2020. Protein-based artificial nanosystems in cancer therapy. Small 16 (23). https://doi.org/10.1002/smll.201907256.

Zhang, J., Yuan, C., Kong, L., Zhu, F., Yuan, W., Zhang, J., Hong, J., Deng, F., Chen, Q., Chen, C., Wang, T., Zuo, Z., Liang, M., 2024. H-ferritin-nanocaged gadolinium nanoparticles for ultra-sensitive MR molecular imaging. Theranostics 14 (5), 1956–1965. https://doi.org/10.7150/thno.93856.

Zhu, G., Lynn, G.M., Jacobson, O., Chen, K., Liu, Y., Zhang, H., Ma, Y., Zhang, F., Tian, R., Ni, Q., Cheng, S., Wang, Z., Lu, N., Yung, B.C., Wang, Z., Lang, L., Fu, X., Jin, A., Weiss, I.D., Vishwasrao, H., Niu, G., Shroff, H., Klinman, D.M., Seder, R.A., Chen, X., 2017. Albumin/vaccine nanocomplexes that assemble in vivo for combination cancer immunotherapy. Nat. Commun. 8 (1). https://doi.org/10.1038/s41467-017-02191-y.

CHAPTER

# 10

# Protein-based nanoparticles for the delivery of genetic materials

*Ahmad Vaez*[1, 2, 3], *Majid Salehi*[4, 5], *Ali Mohammad Amani*[6] *and Hadi Samadian*[7]

[1]Biotechnology Research Center, Shiraz University of Medical Sciences, Shiraz, Iran; [2]Department of Tissue Engineering, School of Advanced Medical Sciences and Technologies, Shiraz University of Medical Sciences, Shiraz, Iran; [3]Histomorphometry and Stereology Research Center, Shiraz University of Medical Sciences, Shiraz, Iran; [4]Tissue Engineering and Stem Cells Research Center, Shahroud University of Medical Sciences, Shahroud, Iran; [5]Department of Tissue Engineering, School of Medicine, Shahroud University of Medical Sciences, Shahroud, Iran; [6]Department of Medical Nanotechnology, School of Advanced Medical Sciences and Technologies, Shiraz University of Medical Sciences, Shiraz, Iran; [7]Research Center for Molecular Medicine, Hamadan University of Medical Sciences, Hamadan, Iran

## 1. Introduction

### 1.1 Genetic material delivery systems

Systems for delivering genetic material are important for improving gene therapy, creating vaccines, and other scientific uses. These systems are made to safely and effectively carry nucleic acids, such as DNA, RNA, or oligonucleotides, into specific cells. The type of delivery method used can greatly affect how well genetic treatments work and their safety. Here is a summary of different ways to send genetic material, including how they work, their benefits, and their difficulties.

*Protein-Based Nanoparticles in Drug Delivery*
https://doi.org/10.1016/B978-0-443-33639-3.00018-0

### 1.1.1 Viral vectors

Viral vectors are one of the best ways to deliver genetic material into cells. They use viruses, which naturally attack cells and add their genetic material. Common viral vectors are adenoviruses, lentiviruses, adeno-associated viruses (AAV), and retroviruses. Each type has special features. For example, AAVs are known for causing fewer immune reactions and can enter cells that are not growing, which makes them good for gene therapy. Viral vectors can effectively transfer genes and can carry a lot of genetic material. They work very well for keeping genes active at a steady level. However, the use of viral vectors raises worries about safety, including possible immunogenic reactions and insertional mutagenesis. Making viral vectors can be complicated and expensive (Fig. 10.1) (Chen et al., 2018).

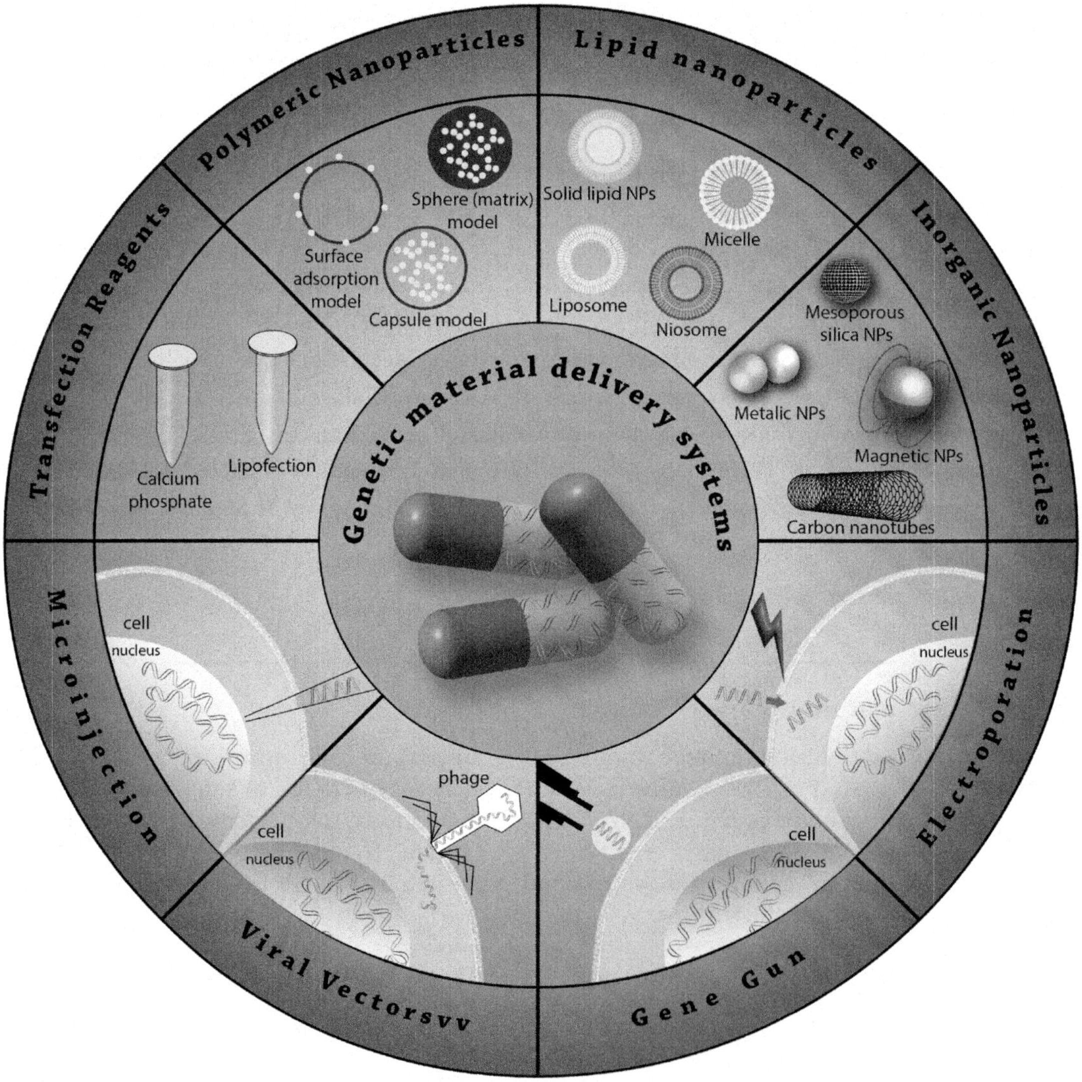


FIGURE 10.1 Various genetic material delivery systems.

### 1.1.2 *Lipid nanoparticles*

Liposomes are circular spheres made of lipid bilayers that can encapsulate nucleic acids. They can be made to be cationic, anionic, or neutral, based on the intended contact with the genetic material and target cells. Cationic liposomes work well to deliver negatively charged nucleic acids because of their electrical attraction. Liposomes are safe to use in the body and can shield nucleic acids from breaking down. They can also be changed with targeted molecules to improve selectivity for certain cell types. The effectiveness of using liposomes to deliver substances can vary, and they may not always release genetic material inside the target cell effectively. Also, there can be concerns about how stable liposomes are in body fluids (Fig. 10.1) (Cuomo, no date; Shueng et al., 2022).

### 1.1.3 *Polymeric nanoparticles*

Polymeric nanoparticles (NPs) are made from recyclable materials and can hold nucleic acids. These NPs can be designed to manage how genetic material is released and improve cellular uptake. Polymeric NPs can be designed in many ways, making it easy to control how they release their contents and targeted delivery. They are usually biocompatible and can be designed for special uses. Developing polymeric NPs can be complicated, and it can be difficult to get them to be the same size, and drug loading can be challenging. Also, how quickly nucleic acids are released from these carriers can vary (Fig. 10.1) (Lee et al., 2022; Oyaghire et al., 2020).

### 1.1.4 *Inorganic nanoparticles*

Inorganic NPs, such as gold and silica NPs, can be used to deliver genetic material. These NPs can carry nucleic acids and targeted molecules to enhance cellular uptake. Inorganic NPs can help keep nucleic acids stable and protected. They can be easily changed for targeted delivery and imaging applications. However, biocompatibility and potential toxicity of these NPs are major issues. Also, the way these carriers release nucleic acids can be less effective than in organic systems (Fig. 10.1) (Bagheri et al., 2018; Sowmiya et al., 2023).

### 1.1.5 *Electroporation technique*

Electroporation is a physical method that uses electrical pulses to form temporary holes in the cell membrane, allowing for the uptake of nucleic acids. This method can be applied to different cell kinds, including hard-to-transfect cells. Electroporation can achieve a high transfer rate and is useful to a wide range of cell types. It does not need chemicals, which reduces potential toxicity. However, the method needs special tools and can harm cells if not used correctly. Also, the efficiency can change based on the type of cell and the settings used (Fig. 10.1) (Ho et al., 2017; Ulgekar et al., 2022).

### 1.1.6 *Microinjection method*

Microinjection involves the direct injection of nucleic acids into the cytoplasm or nucleus of a cell using a fine glass needle. This method is commonly used to create transgenic animals and some types of cell lines. Microinjection allows for accurate transport of genetic material and can achieve high transfection efficiency. It is particularly useful for large nucleic acids that may not be effectively delivered by other methods. Although the technique is labor-intensive and necessitates the expertise of professional personnel. Furthermore, it is constrained to processing a limited number of cells simultaneously, making it less appropriate for high-throughput applications (Fig. 10.1) (Alegria et al., 2024; Takahashi et al., 2015).

### 1.1.7 *Gene gun technique*

High-velocity microprojectiles coated with DNA are used by the gene gun, also known as the biolistic particle delivery device, to introduce genetic material into cells. When it comes to transferring DNA to plant cells and tissues, this technique is very helpful. Numerous cell types, even those that are challenging to transfect with traditional techniques, may deliver DNA from the gene gun. Large DNA constructions may likewise be delivered by this method. However, there are differences in the effectiveness of gene delivery, and the technique may harm the target cells. Furthermore, the apparatus needs meticulous calibration and might be expensive (Fig. 10.1) (Belyantseva, 2016; Gotesman et al., 2022).

### 1.1.8 *Transfection reagents*

Chemical techniques called transfection reagents, such as lipofection and calcium phosphate, let cells absorb nucleic acids more easily. By forming compounds with nucleic acids, these chemicals may improve the delivery of those molecules into cells. Transfection reagents may be used on a variety of cell types and are very simple to use. Additionally, they may be tailored for certain uses. However, the effectiveness of transfection might fluctuate greatly depending on the reagent and cell type. Furthermore, some chemicals may cause immunological reactions or cytotoxicity (Kumar et al., 2019).

### 1.1.9 *Ultrasound-assisted (sonoporation) methods*

Using ultrasonic waves to permeabilize the cell membrane and enable DNA absorption makes sonoporation a noninvasive technique. Microbubbles are used to first transfer genetic elements of interest into the bloodstream, and subsequently, ultrasonic waves are used to follow (Fig. 10.2). By causing cavitation and disrupting microbubbles inside the target tissue's blood vessels, the ultrasonic vibrations weaken nearby cell membranes, allowing the therapeutic gene to be transfected specifically. Safety, noninvasiveness, and the ability to reach inside organs are just a few of the many advantages of sonoporation (Jangjou et al., 2021).

## 1.2 Methods for producing protein NPs

With uses ranging from drug delivery to vaccine development, the production of protein NPs is an important field of study in nanotechnology and biomedicine. Protein NPs may be made using a variety of techniques, each with unique benefits and drawbacks. In the following, we provide several important techniques for producing protein NPs.

### 1.2.1 *Self-assembly techniques*

Self-assembly is a common technique for making protein NPs. Under certain conditions, this mechanism depends on the innate ability of proteins to spontaneously rearrange into

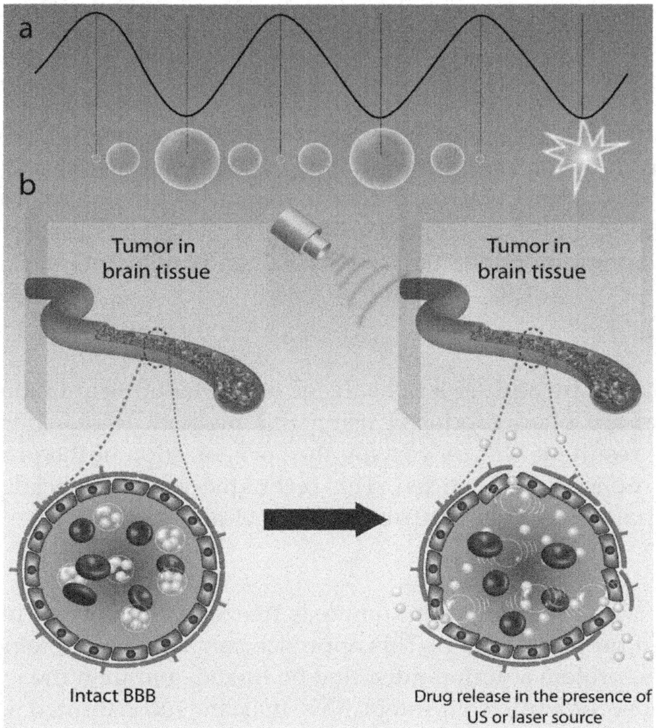


**FIGURE 10.2** (A) The physical mechanism by which activated ultrasound-induced microbubbles affect physiological functions. (B): Diagram illustrating the process by which microbubbles created by ultrasound-induced the gap in the blood–brain barrier (BBB). *Adapted with permission from ref. (Jangjou et al., 2021). Licensed under CC BY-NC 4.0. https://creativecommons.org/licenses/by-nc/4.0/.*

structured NPs to encapsulate genetic materials. To encourage self-assembly in aquatic conditions, proteins may be modified to have both hydrophilic and hydrophobic areas. Commonly used methods include coacervation, in which proteins aggregate in a liquid phase. The simplicity of this process and its capacity to generate NPs without the use of harsh chemicals make it valuable (Ma et al., 2017).

### 1.2.2 *Chemical cross-linking*

Chemical cross-linking uses cross-linking agents to stabilize protein structures and create NPs. The size and shape of the NPs may be precisely controlled using this technique. Carbodiimides and glutaraldehyde are common cross-linking agents. The technique typically involves combining proteins with the cross-linker under carefully monitored circumstances to create stable NPs. When making NPs with certain functional groups for targeted gene delivery, this technique can be extremely helpful (Inostroza-Brito et al., 2017).

### 1.2.3 *Electrostatic assembly*

Electrostatic assembly uses the charge characteristics of proteins to create NPs. Proteins may be assembled via electrostatic interactions by adjusting the pH and ionic strength of the solution. This technique works very well when making NPs from oppositely charged proteins or polymers. For some uses, such as drug and gene delivery systems that need regulated release profiles, the resultant NPs may be customized (Jacobs et al., 2022).

### 1.2.4 *Solvent evaporation*

The solvent evaporation method involves dissolving proteins in a volatile organic solvent, followed by the gradual evaporation of the solvent to form NPs. This technique allows for the encapsulation of genetic materials within the protein matrix, enhancing the solubility and bioavailability of the drugs. The size and morphology of the NPs can be controlled by adjusting the solvent type and evaporation rate (Shankar Raman, Narayanan and Durai, 2021; Sharma and Saroha, 2024).

### 1.2.5 *Nanoprecipitation*

Proteins are separated from a solution by adding a nonsolvent using nanoprecipitation. NPs with a limited size distribution are often produced using this method. Researchers may adjust the size and shape of the resultant NPs by varying the concentration of the protein solution and the pace at which nonsolvent is added. This technique works especially well for encapsulating genetic materials in protein matrices (Tarhini et al., 2018).

### 1.2.6 *Lyophilization*

Protein NPs can be produced via lyophilization, also known as freeze-drying, which involves extracting water from a frozen protein solution. This approach can stabilize proteins and aid in the production of NPs. The protein solution must first be frozen, and then the ice must sublimate in a vacuum. Because lyophilized protein NPs may be reconstituted in aqueous solutions, they can be used for several purposes, such as gene delivery (Vesely, 2024).

### 1.2.7 *Microfluidic technique*

Microfluidic methods provide a new method for creating protein NPs with great accuracy and control over size and shape. Researchers may establish situations that encourage the creation of NPs by adjusting fluid flow at the microscale. This process makes it possible to produce NPs continuously and is readily scalable for use in industrial settings. Additionally, regulated gene encapsulation into protein NPs is made possible by microfluidics (Fig. 10.3) (Dortaj et al., 2024).

### 1.2.8 *High-pressure homogenization*

By applying high pressure to protein solutions, a mechanical process known as "high-pressure homogenization" generates shear stresses that result in the formation of NP. This method works well for creating NPs with a consistent size distribution. Control over the final NP properties may be achieved by optimizing the process by varying the pressure and number of passes through the homogenizer (Wu et al., 2015).

### 1.2.9 *Electrospray technique*

Electrospraying may create submicron particles from liquid solutions. By adding high voltage to the solution, a nozzle ejects a thin jet of liquid, generating an aerosol of charged droplets. Solid particles develop from aerosolized droplet solvent evaporation and contain

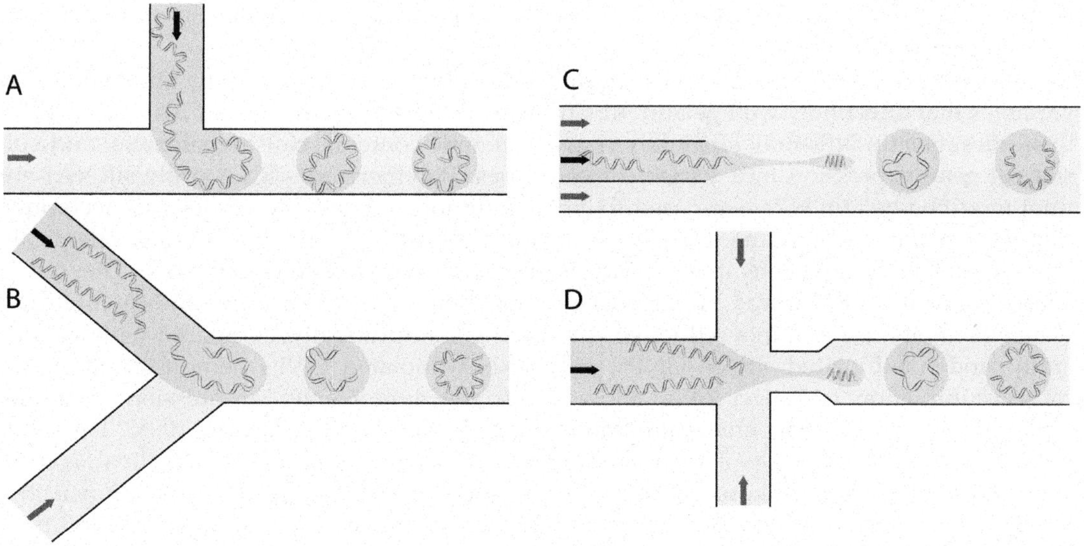


**FIGURE 10.3** T-shaped (A) and Y-shaped (B) connections of cross-flowing, coflowing (C), and flow-focusing (D) droplet generation methods. Black and red arrows indicate genetic material suspension and typically cross-linker or oil flows, respectively.

proteins that envelope nucleic acids. Electrospraying creates a charged jet that breaks down into small droplets by applying high voltage to a polymer solution. This technology resembles nanostructure synthesis via electrical radiation (Hong et al., 2020).

# 2. Protein NPs potentials in gene therapy

## 2.1 Animal proteins

### *2.1.1 Gelatin NPs*

The most prevalent protein in the human body, collagen, gives tissues and organs their structural integrity. Collagen is hydrolyzed to produce gelatin, which is more soluble in water and nevertheless has many of the same advantageous qualities as collagen. Gelatin may be processed to create NPs, which are capable of encasing biomolecules, particularly genetic material such as plasmids, DNA, or RNA. They are interesting candidates for gene delivery systems due to their natural origin and advantageous biological characteristics (Echave et al., 2017; Monfared et al., 2019). The uptake mechanism is strongly influenced by the NPs' size and surface charge. Eighteen unevenly distributed amino acids with both positive and negative charges form gelatin. The main method for creating cationic gelatin is to utilize polyethyleneimine, cholamine, ethylenediamine (EDA), putrescine, spermidine, or spermine to attach amine residues to the carboxyl groups of gelatin (Madkhali et al., 2019). Because of their electrostatic interactions with the negatively charged cell membrane, cationic NPs have a tendency to increase cellular absorption (Ahn et al., 2015). Furthermore, adjustments such as adding targeted ligands might enhance the cellular uptake's efficiency and specificity even further (Echave et al., 2017).

The kind of nucleic acid, the NPs' composition, and the target cell type are some of the variables that affect how well gelatin NPs transfer genes (Aldawsari et al., 2019). According to studies, gelatin NPs may efficiently transfer genetic contents, causing silencing and substantial gene expression in a variety of cell types. Polymerized siRNA (poly-siRNA) and thiol-modified gelatin NPs were used to create a tumor-targeted siRNA delivery technique. The thiol group self-polymerized to create the poly-siRNA, which was then chemically cross-linked to encapsulate it inside the self-assembled thiolated gold NPs. The results showed that the siRNA was protected from enzymatic breakdown; the siRNA molecules were effectively released in a reductive environment. Additionally, compared with lipofectamine and nonthiolated siRNA-GNPs, poly-siRNA-thiolated GNPs demonstrated significant accumulation in cancer cells, allowed effective target gene suppression in tumors after intravenous injection, and maintained high cell viability, approaching 100%. The stability of the NPs, which results in improved gene expression and higher cell survival, is probably tied to the disulfide bonds formed by the thiol group (Lee et al., 2013). Transfection efficiency may be increased by optimizing NP formulations, for example, by modifying the gelatin-to-nucleic acid ratio (Ahn et al., 2015; Attarwala et al., 2017; Liu, no date). Researchers have investigated several targeting techniques using gelatin NPs in an effort to increase the specificity of gene delivery. This may include attaching targeting ligands such as peptides, antibodies, or small molecules to the NPs' surface (Dabbadie et al., 2022; San et al., 2016). These ligands can facilitate receptor-mediated endocytosis, enhancing the uptake of NPs by specific cell types, such as cancer cells or immune cells (Dabbadie et al., 2022; San et al., 2016; Atabakhshi-Kashi et al., 2021; Yoo et al., 2019). For example, EGFR-targeted GNPs with plasmid DNA expressing EGFp-N1 exhibited the best transfection efficiency in Panc-1 pancreatic cancer cells compared with other controls, especially 48 h posttransfection (Magadala and Amiji, 2008).

Gelatin NPs have shown significant promise in cancer gene therapy. These NPs have the ability to target tumor cells and inhibit tumor development by encapsulating therapeutic genes or RNA interference (RNAi) molecules (Magadala and Amiji, 2008; Madkhali et al., 2019). Gelatin NPs loaded with siRNA have been shown to efficiently silence oncogenes in cancer cell lines, resulting in decreased cell proliferation and increased apoptosis (Madkhali et al., 2019; Du et al., 2015; Abozeid et al., 2016). Also, gelatin NPs are being explored for vaccine delivery (Sahoo et al., 2015). The immune response may be improved by their capacity to encapsulate adjuvants and antigens. For example, messenger RNA (mRNA) vaccines have been delivered using gelatin NPs (NPs), which provide a safe environment for the mRNA and facilitate its absorption by dendritic cells, which are essential for triggering immunological responses (Zeng et al., 2023).

### 2.1.2 *Chitosan*

Chitosan is a biopolymer produced from chitin, a natural carbohydrate found in crustaceans' shells. It is a desirable option for many biological applications, including drug and gene delivery, due to its exceptional biocompatibility, biodegradability, and nontoxicity. Because of their capacity to encapsulate nucleic acids, enhance stability, and promote cellular absorption, chitosan NPs have drawn interest as an efficient gene delivery carrier

(Pradhan et al., 2019). The most common methods for producing chitosan NPs are solvent evaporation, coacervation, and ionic gelation. When subjected to polyanions or cross-linking agents, the chitosan molecules that make up the basic structure may self-assemble into NPs (Raj et al., 2018; Al-Absi et al., 2023; Zhang et al., 2016). Chitosan's physicochemical characteristics, such as its positive charge at physiological pH, improve its ability to interact with cell membranes that are negatively charged. When compared with other carriers, this electrostatic contact improves transport efficiency by encouraging cellular absorption via endocytosis. Additionally, chitosan may be modified by adding copolymers or functional groups to improve its stability and solubility (Jadidi-Niaragh et al., 2016; Qi et al., 2016).

The molecular weight, genetic material type, and chitosan concentration all have a significant impact on the encapsulation effectiveness of chitosan NPs. After encapsulation, the complex shields the DNA or RNA from bloodstream nucleases that may break it down (Ahmadi and Barisic, 2019). Chitosan NPs are mostly absorbed by cells by endocytosis after injection. The NPs and the encapsulating genetic material may degrade because the endosomes carrying the NPs merge with lysosomes once they are inside the cell. Nevertheless, chitosan NPs may promote endosomal escape, presumably because of chitosan's buffering ability, therefore releasing the genetic material into the cytosol (Zhang et al., 2024; Joris et al., 2018).

Furthermore, a certain amount of modification is possible to fine-tune biocompatibility due to the intrinsic features of chitosan. For example, the degree of chitosan's deacetylation might affect how well it functions biologically; higher degrees of deacetylation usually lead to better solubility and cellular absorption (Dmour and Islam, 2022; Iacob et al., 2021; El-Araby et al., 2023). Because of its flexibility, chitosan may be functionalized, which enhances its effectiveness as a matrix for gene delivery. It is possible to attach ligands, peptides, or other polymers, among other chemical alterations. Improving the precise targeting of tissues or cells may enhance gene delivery efficiency while minimizing off-target effects (Hozumi and Nomizu, 2018).

Stimuli-sensitive drug/gene transfer systems can release drugs or genes in response to external factors (such as magnetic fields, mechanical forces, ultrasound waves, or light exposure) or intrinsic factors (including enzymes, ATP, glutathione, variations in biomolecular activities such as hormones, temperature changes, and shifts in extracellular or intracellular pH levels) (Naghib et al., 2024). Also, research indicates that PEGylation of chitosan improves the stability of chitosan formulations in human plasma. H. Ragelle et al. used fluorescence fluctuation spectroscopy and single particle tracking (SPT) to examine the stability of siRNA-chitosan carriers in human plasma (Ragelle et al., 2014). Chitosan-siRNA formulations that did not include PEGylated chitosan released 70% of their original siRNA levels in human plasma after 30 min. The findings suggested that these formulations were unstable as siRNA carriers in vivo and could have broken down during plasma incubation (Ragelle et al., 2014). The deprotonation of some chitosan amino groups at physiological pH, which results in a decreased binding affinity for siRNA, might be the cause of the instability. Furthermore, siRNA and anionic plasma proteins fight for chitosan binding, which may cause disintegration. However, after 2 hours of incubation, PEGylated NPs showed no dissociation in human plasma, indicating that using PEGylated chitosan in siRNA delivery formulations enhances plasma stability (Ragelle et al., 2013).

Chitosan NPs may be delivered to certain cells that overexpress particular receptors more precisely by coupling them with targeting ligands such as folic acid or antibodies (Hamrang et al., 2023). This focused strategy may be especially helpful in cancer treatment, where minimizing harm to healthy tissues and optimizing the therapeutic impact on tumor cells are critical (Cheraghi et al., 2020; Khan, 2024; Song et al., 2017). Chitosan NPs are showing promise in cancer gene therapy because of their capacity to transfer therapeutic genes that may stop tumor cell development and promote apoptosis (Karayianni et al., 2023). For example, chitosan NPs have been investigated for delivering siRNAs that target oncogenes, thereby inhibiting the expression of proteins critical for tumor growth (Al-Absi et al., 2023). Research has shown that chitosan NP-containing formulations may increase the genetic material's bioavailability, improving therapy results for a variety of cancer types (Dang et al., 2024; Sethi et al., 2019). Additionally, to create a synergistic impact on tumors, researchers are looking into combination treatments in which chitosan NPs codeliver genes and chemotherapeutic drugs (Zhang et al., 2021). Additionally, chitosan NPs are being investigated for vaccine development. They may be used as carriers for DNA vaccines because of their inherent adjuvant qualities, which may strengthen the immune response to encapsulated antigens (Gong et al., 2022). The positive charge of chitosan facilitates interactions with negatively charged DNA plasmids, creating stable vaccine formulations suitable for administration (Gong et al., 2022; Sinani et al., 2019). It has been shown that chitosan NPs may preserve DNA vaccines against degradation and increase their absorption by antigen-presenting cells, resulting in enhanced immune responses. Customizing chitosan NPs with particular antigens might boost their efficiency in triggering tailored immune responses against infectious diseases (Pan et al., 2023).

### 2.1.3 *Alginate*

Alginate is a naturally occurring polysaccharide generated from brown seaweed that is well known for its biocompatibility, biodegradability, and hydrogel-forming properties. Because of its advantageous features, alginate has emerged as a critical material in the area of drug delivery, notably for gene delivery applications. Alginate NPs have various benefits, including the encapsulation of nucleic acids, controlled release profiles, and improved cellular absorption, making them particularly useful in therapeutic situations (Islam and Raikwar, 2024; Venkatesan et al., 2016).

Alginate is made up of linear chains of guluronic acid (G) and mannuronic acid (M) monomers, which may form a gel-like consistency when exposed to divalent cations (such as calcium ions). This feature is critical in the creation of alginate NPs, which may be generated via a variety of processes, including ionotropic gelation, coacervation, and emulsification (Fernando et al., 2022). At physiological pH, alginate NPs have a negative charge, which may impact their interaction with positively charged ions and polymers, allowing them to form complexes with cationic carriers for gene delivery. In this approach, Zhan et al. created a straightforward sodium alginate (SA)–doped cationic NP SA@GP/DNA for dual gene delivery. Sodium alginate, polycation, and plasmid DNA may produce NPs electrostatically (Zhan et al., 2022). Furthermore, the inherent ability of alginate to interact with biological tissues and their nontoxic nature enhances their potential for in vivo applications (Hecht and Srebnik, 2016; Follit et al., 2017).

Encapsulation, nucleic acid protection from degradation, cellular uptake, endosomal escape, and subsequent release into the cytoplasm are all key processes in the gene delivery process using alginate NPs. Alginate efficiently encapsulates numerous forms of nucleic acids, therefore preserving them from enzymatic breakdown in body fluids (Tariq et al., 2019). After delivery, alginate NPs tend to interact with cell membranes, resulting in cellular uptake. Negatively charged alginate may occasionally interfere with electrostatic interactions with cell membranes; hence, it is often used in conjunction with cationic polymers (such as chitosan or polyethyleneimine) to improve cell absorption (Azuma et al., 2018; Jin et al., 2018).

Functionalization of alginate NPs is an important step toward increasing their effectiveness as gene delivery vehicles. Alginate's surface characteristics may be modified in a variety of ways, including the addition of targeted ligands, peptides, and other polymers. This may improve selectivity for cells or tissues, improving the likelihood of successful gene transfer. For example, conjugating alginate NPs with targeting ligands such as folic acid or antibodies that target particular receptors on cancer cells may greatly increase absorption. This focused technique allows for more efficient gene delivery while minimizing side effects, which is an important concern in minimizing harm to healthy tissues in therapeutic applications (Yoo et al., 2019; Kashani et al., 2024; Junyaprasert and Thummarati, 2023). Alginate's unique gel-forming properties enable it to encapsulate not only genetic components but also growth factors and other bioactive compounds. This feature is crucial for boosting tissue regeneration and repair, especially when combined with gene therapy (Chu et al., 2024; Sonaye, no date).

Recent advances in formulation processes have improved the efficacy of alginate NPs in gene delivery. For example, using microfluidic devices to generate alginate NPs provides more control over particle size, shape, and dispersity, which may affect biological performance. Furthermore, these methods may lead to the development of more consistent and repeatable formulations. Encapsulation efficiency may be improved by exploring various cross-linking agents and procedures. Adjusting the cross-linker ratio during the synthesis of alginate NPs may dramatically boost the stability and release patterns of encapsulated nucleic acids, therefore increasing the overall gene delivery efficiency (Kamat et al., 2023; Joshy et al., 2018).

Alginate NPs are being studied as vaccine carriers, notably for DNA vaccines. Their natural capacity to improve the stability and transport of genetic materials makes them ideal candidates for delivering DNA vaccines, which have shown considerable promise in activating immune responses against infectious diseases (Vijayan et al., 2019). Alginate NPs may increase the immunogenicity of vaccines by encapsulating plasmid DNA encoding for antigens of interest and boosting their absorption by antigen-presenting cells. This capacity may lead to larger and more effective immune responses, as well as increased vaccine efficacy (Tiptiri-Kourpeti et al., 2016).

### 2.1.4 *Albumin*

Albumin, a globular protein found in human plasma, is a prominent choice for drug and gene delivery systems because of its biocompatibility, stability, and capacity to bind diverse molecules (Paul et al., 2022; Kunjiappan et al., 2020). Albumin's unusual tertiary structure allows it to encapsulate a variety of therapeutic substances, including nucleic acids (Wang et al., 2021). Albumin NPs' hydrophilic surface characteristics improve solubility and stability in aqueous settings, making them appropriate for intravenous administration. Negative pH influences the interaction with positively charged cellular membranes (Kanwa et al., 2020). Researchers may improve the selectivity of NPs by altering their surface with ligands or targeted moieties, such as conjugating albumin NPs with folic acid (Wang et al., 2023), polyethylenimine (Rhaese et al., 2003), and chitosan (Karimi et al., 2013). Incorporating imaging compounds into albumin NPs permits real-time monitoring of gene delivery, enhancing pharmacokinetics and biodistribution, and assisting in preclinical and clinical research (Wang et al., 2020).

Albumin NPs are being investigated as carriers for gene vaccination because they have the potential to boost immunogenicity, improve stability, shield nucleic acids from degradation, and enhance systemic administration, making them a viable delivery mechanism for DNA and RNA vaccines (Zhu et al., 2017). Novel tactics are being used to enhance this aspect of delivery, such as adding disulfide links that can be broken in the reducing environment of the cytosol, encouraging the release of nucleic acids (Elzoghby et al., 2012). Furthermore, hybrid systems that mix albumin NPs with other materials, such as cationic polymers, might improve cellular uptake and guarantee that nucleic acids reach their intended targets (Cai et al., 2023).

### 2.1.5 *Silk fibroin*

Silk fibroin, a natural protein generated from silkworms and spiders, has received substantial interest in biotechnology and healthcare applications, notably in drug and gene delivery systems (Li et al., 2023). Silk fibroin is known for its high mechanical strength, biocompatibility, and biodegradability. It offers a unique platform for producing NPs that may successfully encapsulate and transfer genetic material to target cells (Ji et al., 2015). Silk fibroin is becoming more popular as a gene delivery vehicle due to its capacity to generate stable NPs that preserve nucleic acids from degradation while enabling cellular uptake. Silk fibroin NPs may be synthesized utilizing a variety of processes, including solvent evaporation, electrospinning, and self-assembly processes (Fan et al., 2023). Their distinctive features include their capacity to preserve structural integrity under varied environmental conditions, which is enabled by hydrophobic and hydrophilic areas found in silk fibroin (Tadepalli et al., 2016). Furthermore, the amphiphilic characteristic of silk fibroin allows for the modification and functionalization of NPs, increasing their potential for targeted gene delivery applications (Ma et al., 2020). Silk fibroin's inherent properties stimulate interactions with cell membranes, hence enabling cellular entrance. After absorption, the problem is to release encapsulated nucleic acids from endosomes into the cytoplasm (Liu et al., 2022).

Silk fibroin NPs' surfaces may be changed with ligands, peptides, or polymers to increase cell or tissue selection. For example, adding tumor-targeting ligands may increase the absorption of silk fibroin NPs by cancer cells while minimizing exposure to healthy organs (Hama and Nakazawa, 2024). In addition to passive targeting, active targeting strategies can also be employed by conjugating antibodies or receptor ligands onto the silk fibroin NP surface (Bi et al., 2016).

Silk fibroin NPs may act as carriers for genetic vaccines, increasing their stability, protecting them from degradation, and encouraging absorption by antigen-presenting cells

(Vijayan et al., 2019). Because of their particular features, silk fibroin NPs have the potential to improve immunogenic responses and lead to more effective vaccinations against infectious diseases (Vijayan et al., 2019; Guo et al., 2024; Stinson et al., 2017).

#### 2.1.6 Elastin

Elastin, a natural protein with distinct structural features, has received attention in biological applications, including drug delivery and gene therapy (Ye, no date). Elastin-based NPs have emerged as a viable approach for systemic gene delivery, enabling the targeted transfer of genetic materials to specific cells and organs (Pina, 2015; Monfort and Koria, 2017). Functionalizing elastin NPs can enhance their efficacy in targeted gene delivery by modifying surface properties and using stimuli-responsive materials for controlled release mechanisms (Bahniuk et al., 2020). Elastin NPs can be used in cancer gene therapy, addressing genetic disorders caused by defective or absent genes, and in vaccine development (Santos et al., 2019). Elastin NPs can also stimulate robust immune responses, particularly in infectious diseases such as COVID-19 (Arora et al., 2023).

### 2.2 Milk proteins

#### 2.2.1 Casein

Casein NPs, a type of phosphoproteins present in mammalian milk, have received interest as a drug and gene delivery vehicle because of their biocompatibility, biodegradability, and structural features (Elzoghby et al., 2011). These NPs serve as effective encapsulating agents for various therapeutic agents, including nucleic (Elzoghby et al., 2011). Developing casein-based NPs for gene delivery offers significant prospects for targeted treatment, increased cellular uptake, and enhanced safety profiles (Elzoghby et al., 2011; Xv et al., 2020). Codelivery techniques using casein NPs may contain numerous therapeutic agents, allowing for combination treatment regimens that exploit both gene therapy and traditional chemotherapy (Purushothaman and Maheswari, 2021; Spicer et al., 2018; Shiri et al., 2022). Casein NPs have the potential to revolutionize gene delivery by encapsulating genetic materials (Khatun, 2024). In this regard, chitosan-casein (ChiCas) NPs have been optimized for gene delivery (Costa, 2017, 2019). The particles were used to entrap or adsorb DNA, forming NPs-DNA complexes (Costa, 2019). DNA delivery into plant cells was achieved using casein NPs, which encapsulated a plasmid containing the red fluorescent protein DsRed. The zeta potential of CNPs is adjusted to ensure successful delivery into the plant model (Ben-Haim et al., 2024).

### 2.3 Plant proteins

#### 2.3.1 Zein

Zein NPs, a class of prolamine proteins derived from corn, are being recognized as an innovative material for gene delivery applications (Campos, 2023). These NPs offer unique properties such as biocompatibility, biodegradability, and a naturally hydrophobic nature, making them potential carriers for gene therapies against many disorders (Luo et al., 2023). Zein NPs have shown significant promise in cancer gene therapy since they may transport therapeutic genes targeted at suppressing tumor development or leading to apoptosis in cancer cells (Elzoghby et al., 2017). By encapsulating genetic materials targeting specific oncogenes, zein

NPs provide targeted gene therapy that addresses the genetic basis of cancer (El Sharkawi et al., 2017). The capacity to distribute both nucleic acids and chemotherapeutic drugs concurrently offers up prospects for combination therapy, in which zein NPs may boost the effectiveness of standard treatments while minimizing systemic adverse effects (El Sharkawi et al., 2017). Zein NPs also extend to vaccine development, particularly with the rise of DNA and RNA vaccines (Corteggio et al., 2024). Zein NPs may stabilize and ease the transfer of genetic elements to antigen-presenting cells, hence enhancing vaccine efficacy (Farris and Development, 2019). The incorporation of adjuvants into zein NP formulations can further enhance immune responses by promoting the activation of immune cells (Hassan et al., 2022).

### 2.3.2 *Lectin*

Lectins are carbohydrate-binding proteins that play an important role in several biological processes, including cell–cell interactions, immunological response, and pathogen identification (Raposo et al., 2021). Lectin NPs may be extracted from a variety of sources and have a broad range of structural and binding properties. They may be coupled with NPs formed of biocompatible polymers, lipids, or inorganic components, optimizing them for cellular uptake (Alavi et al., 2020). They have received attention in drug and gene delivery because of their unique capacity to identify and bind particular carbohydrates on the surface of cells (Yin et al., 2006). Researchers may employ lectin NPs to create tailored gene delivery systems that improve the effectiveness and specificity of gene therapies (Gajbhiye and Gong, 2013).

## 2.4 Protein cages

### 2.4.1 *Viral protein cages*

Viral protein cages, also known as viral capsids, constitute a unique type of NPs produced from viral structural proteins that naturally encapsulate viral genetic material (Aumiller et al., 2018). They may be modified to deliver therapeutic genes or RNA-based therapies, making use of their innate features for effective cellular uptake and targeted delivery (Rother et al., 2016). Because of their origins in viruses, these protein cages feature unique structural, biochemical, and biophysical properties, making them great candidates for drug and gene delivery applications (Ma et al., 2012). The most common kinds of viral protein cages that may be utilized in gene delivery are produced from plant viruses (such as tobacco mosaic virus), bacteriophages (such as MS2), and animal viruses (such as adenoviruses and retroviruses) (Lam and Steinmetz, 2018). These protein cages are made up of one or more kinds of proteins that self-assemble into well-defined structures, providing stability and protection for their cargo (Wang and Douglas, 2022). One of the primary benefits of utilizing viral protein cages is their capacity to encapsulate nucleic acids with great loading efficiency (Liu et al., 2021). They may also be manipulated to display certain surface features, such as charge and hydrophobicity, allowing for targeted interactions with target cells (Daniel et al., 2010). Surface alterations may include the attachment of targeting ligands such as peptides, antibodies, or carbohydrates that are recognized by particular receptors on target cells (Steinmetz et al., 2020). One of the most promising applications of viral protein cages is cancer gene therapy. Preclinical investigations have demonstrated that viral protein cages may limit tumor growth and cause apoptosis in several cancer types (Steinmetz et al., 2020). Furthermore, the ability to integrate gene therapy with standard chemotherapy inside a single viral protein cage might generate synergistic benefits, boosting overall therapeutic effectiveness and possibly overcoming resistance to conventional therapies (Schoonen and Van Hest, 2014).

## 3. Challenges and future prospects

Protein-based NPs are biocompatible, biodegradable, and functionalized for targeted delivery, making them ideal for genetic material transfer. However, the researcher must overcome several obstacles to reach their potential. Protein-based NP stability under physiological conditions is a major issue. Proteins may be desaturated, degraded, and aggregated, reducing their delivery potential. The immune system may also see these NPs as foreign bodies, limiting their therapeutic use. Designing and modifying proteins with higher breakdown resistance or changing their surface to prevent immune identification are needed to overcome stability and immunogenicity issues. Protein-based NPs' cellular uptake and endosomal escape are also issues. These NPs may target specific cells or tissues, but internalizing and releasing genetic material into the cytoplasm is difficult. Protein-based NPs for genetic delivery must be scalable, repeatable, and standardized for therapeutic use. Temperature, pH, and ionic strength affect protein folding and self-assembly, making it challenging to mass-produce NPs with uniform size, shape, and function. Biomanufacturing approaches such as recombinant protein expression and precision engineering must improve to make protein-based NPs reliable for clinical usage. These new delivery techniques also need significant characterization and quality control for regulatory approval, which delays their laboratory-to-clinic transfer. NPs with enhanced stability, targeted specificity, and controlled release are made possible via computer modeling and protein engineering. For instance, applying AI to predict protein shapes and interactions speeds up delivery system design. Finally, functionalizing protein-based NPs with ligands, antibodies, or other targeting moieties allows personalized medicine to tailor treatments to individuals' genetic profiles.

## Conflicts of interest

The authors declare no conflict of interest.

## AI disclosure

During the preparation of this work, the author(s) used ChatGPT to improve grammar and writing structure. After using this tool/service, the author(s) reviewed and edited the content as needed and take(s) full responsibility for the content of the publication.

## References

Abozeid, S.M., Hathout, R.M., Abou-Aisha, K., 2016. Silencing of the metastasis-linked gene, AEG-1, using siRNA-loaded cholamine surface-modified gelatin nanoparticles in the breast carcinoma cell line MCF-7. Colloids Surf. B Biointerfaces 145, 607–616. https://doi.org/10.1016/j.colsurfb.2016.05.066.

Ahmadi, Y., Barisic, I., 2019. Gene-therapy inspired polycation coating for protection of DNA origami nanostructures. J. Vis. Exp. 10 (143).

Ahn, S., Seo, E., Kim, K.H., Lee, S.J., 2015. Physical property control on the cellular uptake pathway and spatial distribution of nanoparticles in cells. J. Biomed. Nanotechnol. 11 (6), 1051–1070. https://doi.org/10.1166/jbn.2015.2037.

Al-Absi, M.Y., Caprifico, A.E., Calabrese, G., 2023. Chitosan and its structural modifications for siRNA delivery. Adv. Pharmaceut. Bull. 13 (2), 275–282. https://doi.org/10.34172/apb.2023.030.

Alavi, M., Asare-Addo, K., Nokhodchi, A., 2020. Lectin protein as a promising component to functionalize micelles, liposomes and lipid nps against coronavirus. Biomedicines 8 (12), 1–16. https://doi.org/10.3390/biomedicines8120580.

Aldawsari, H.M., Dhaliwal, H.K., Aljaeid, B.M., Alhakamy, N.A., Banjar, Z.M., Amiji, M.M., 2019. Optimization of the conditions for plasmid DNA delivery and transfection with self-assembled hyaluronic acid-based nanoparticles. Mol. Pharm. 16 (1), 128–140. https://doi.org/10.1021/acs.molpharmaceut.8b00904.

Alegria, A.D., Joshi, A.S., Mendana, J.B., Khosla, K., Smith, K.T., Auch, B., Donovan, M., Bischof, J., Gohl, D.M., Kodandaramaiah, S.B., 2024. High-throughput genetic manipulation of multicellular organisms using a machine-vision guided embryonic microinjection robot. Genetics 226 (4). https://doi.org/10.1093/genetics/iyae025.

Arora, S., Vyavahare, N., Mukhopadhyay, P., 2023. Elastin-targeted nanoparticles delivering doxycycline mitigate cytokine storm and reduce immune cell infiltration in LPS-mediated lung inflammation. PLoS One 18 (6), e0286211. https://doi.org/10.1371/journal.pone.0286211.

Atabakhshi-Kashi, M., Carril, M., Mahdavi, H., Parak, W.J., Carrillo-Carrion, C., Khajeh, K., 2021. In vitro cellular uptake studies of self-assembled fluorinated nanoparticles labelled with antibodies. Nanomaterials 11 (8), 1906. https://doi.org/10.3390/nano11081906.

Attarwala, H., Clausen, V., Chaturvedi, P., Amiji, M.M., 2017. Cosilencing intestinal transglutaminase-2 and interleukin-15 using gelatin-based nanoparticles in an in vitro model of celiac disease. Mol. Pharm. 14 (9), 3036–3044. https://doi.org/10.1021/acs.molpharmaceut.7b00233.

Aumiller, W.M., Uchida, M., Douglas, T., 2018. Protein cage assembly across multiple length scales. Chem. Soc. Rev. 47 (10), 3433–3469. https://doi.org/10.1039/c7cs00818j.

Azuma, Y., Imai, H., Kawaguchi, Y., Nakase, I., Kimura, H., Futaki, S., 2018. Modular redesign of a cationic lytic peptide to promote the endosomal escape of biomacromolecules. Angew. Chem. Int. Ed. 57 (39), 12771–12774. https://doi.org/10.1002/anie.201807534.

Bagheri, E., Ansari, L., Abnous, K., Taghdisi, S.M., Charbgoo, F., Ramezani, M., Alibolandi, M., 2018. Silica based hybrid materials for drug delivery and bioimaging. J. Contr. Release 277, 57–76. https://doi.org/10.1016/j.jconrel.2018.03.014.

Bahniuk, M.S., Alshememry, A.K., Unsworth, L.D., 2020. Human plasma protein adsorption to elastinlike polypeptide nanoparticles. Biointerphases 15 (2). https://doi.org/10.1116/6.0000027.

Belyantseva, I.A., 2016. Helios® gene gun-mediated transfection of the inner ear sensory epithelium: Recent updates. Methods Mol. Biol. 1427, 3–26. https://doi.org/10.1007/978-1-4939-3615-1_1.

Ben-Haim, A.E., Feldbaum, R.A., Belausov, E., Zelinger, E., Maria, R., Nativ-Roth, E., Mani, K.A., Barda, O., Sionov, E., Mechrez, G., 2024. DNA delivery to intact plant cells by casein nanoparticles with confirmed gene expression. Adv. Funct. Mater. 34 (16). https://doi.org/10.1002/adfm.202314756.

Bi, Y., Hao, F., Yan, G., Teng, L., Lee, R.J., Xie, J., 2016. Actively targeted nanoparticles for drug delivery to tumor. Curr. Drug Metabol. 17 (8), 763–782. https://doi.org/10.2174/1389200217666160619191853.

Cai, X., Dou, R., Guo, C., Tang, J., Li, X., Chen, J., Zhang, J., 2023. Cationic polymers as transfection reagents for nucleic acid delivery. Pharmaceutics 15 (5), 1502. https://doi.org/10.3390/pharmaceutics15051502.

Campos, Z., 2023. Nanoparticles for drug delivery: preparation methods and biological applications. Int. J. Pharm. 635.

Chen, Y.H., Keiser, M.S., Davidson, B.L., 2018. Viral vectors for gene transfer. Current protocols in mouse biology 8 (4), e58. https://doi.org/10.1002/cpmo.58.

Cheraghi, R., Nazari, M., Alipour, M., Hosseinkhani, S., 2020. Stepwise development of biomimetic chimeric peptides for gene delivery. Protein Pept. Lett. 27 (8), 698–710. https://doi.org/10.2174/0929866527666200206153328.

Chu, X., Xiong, Y., Lu, L., Wang, Y., Wang, J., Zeng, R., Hu, L., Yan, C., Zhao, Z., Lin, S., Mi, B., Liu, G., 2024. Research progress of gene therapy combined with tissue engineering to promote bone regeneration. APL Bioeng. 8 (3). https://doi.org/10.1063/5.0200551.

Corteggio, A., Heinzl, T., Boraschi, D., Voci, S., Gagliardi, A., Cosco, D., Italiani, P., 2024. Safety of zein nanoparticles on human innate immunity and inflammation. Int. J. Mol. Sci. 25 (21), 11630. https://doi.org/10.3390/ijms252111630.

Costa, Chitosan-based nanoparticles for gene delivery internship reports and monograph titled. (2017),

Costa, P., 2019. Optimization of chitosan-α-casein nanoparticles for improved gene delivery: characterization, stability, and transfection efficiency. AAPS PharmSciTech 20, 1–12.

Cuomo, F., Oral delivery of all-trans retinoic acid mediated by liposome carriers . Colloids Surf. B Biointerfaces. 201.

Dabbadie, A., Salerno, A., Perriman, A., Lian, L.-Y., Hollander, A.P., 2022. Development of chimeric forms of the matrix metalloproteinase 2 collagen binding domain as artificial membrane binding proteins for targeting stem cells to cartilage lesions in osteoarthritic joints. Biomaterials 285, 121547. https://doi.org/10.1016/j.biomaterials.2022.121547.

Dang, M.N., Suri, S., Li, K., Gomez Casas, C., Stigliano, G., Riley, R.S., Scully, M.A., Hoover, E.C., Aboeleneen, S.B., Kramarenko, G.C., Day, E.S., 2024. Antibody and siRNA nanocarriers to suppress wnt signaling, tumor growth, and lung metastasis in triple-negative breast cancer. Adv. Therapeut. 7 (6). https://doi.org/10.1002/adtp.202300426.

Daniel, M.C., Tsvetkova, I.B., Quinkert, Z.T., Murali, A., De, M., Rotello, V.M., Kao, C.C., Dragnea, B., 2010. Role of surface charge density in nanoparticle-templated assembly of bromovirus protein cages. ACS Nano 4 (7), 3853–3860. https://doi.org/10.1021/nn1005073.

Dmour, I., Islam, N., 2022. Recent advances on chitosan as an adjuvant for vaccine delivery. Int. J. Biol. Macromol. 200, 498–519. https://doi.org/10.1016/j.ijbiomac.2021.12.129.

Dortaj, H., Amani, A.M., Tayebi, L., Azarpira, N., Toudeshkchouei, M.G., Hassanpour-Dehnavi, A., Karami, N., Abbasi, M., Najafian-Najafabadi, A., Behjani, Z.Z., Vaez, A., 2024. Droplet-based microfluidics: an efficient high-throughput portable system for cell encapsulation. J. Microencapsul. 41 (6), 479–501. https://doi.org/10.1080/02652048.2024.2382744.

Du, Q., Ma, T., Fu, C., Liu, T., Huang, Z., Ren, J., Shao, H., Xu, K., Tang, F., Meng, X., 2015. Encapsulating ionic liquid ANd Fe 3 O 4 nanoparticles in gelatin microcapsules as microwave susceptible agent for MR imaging-guided tumor thermotherapy. ACS Appl. Mater. Interfaces 7 (24), 13612–13619. https://doi.org/10.1021/acsami.5b03230.

Echave, M.C., Burgo, L.S., Pedraz, J.L., Orive, G., 2017. Gelatin as biomaterial for tissue engineering. Curr. Pharm. Des. 23 (24), 3567–3584. https://doi.org/10.2174/0929867324666170511123101.

El Sharkawi, F.Z., Ewais, S.M., Fahmy, R.H., Rashed, L.A., 2017. PTEN and TRAIL genes loaded zein nanoparticles as potential therapy for hepatocellular carcinoma. J. Drug Target. 25 (6), 513–522. https://doi.org/10.1080/1061186X.2017.1289536.

El-Araby, A., Janati, W., Ullah, R., Ercisli, S., Errachidi, F., 2023. Chitosan, chitosan derivatives, and chitosan-based nanocomposites: eco-friendly materials for advanced applications (a review). Front. Chem. 11. https://doi.org/10.3389/fchem.2023.1327426.

Elzoghby, A., Freag, M., Mamdouh, H., Elkhodairy, K., 2017. Zein-based nanocarriers as potential natural alternatives for drug and gene delivery: Focus on cancer therapy. Curr. Pharm. Des. 23 (35), 5261–5271. https://doi.org/10.2174/1381612823666170622111250.

Elzoghby, A.O., Abo El-Fotoh, W.S., Elgindy, N.A., 2011. Casein-based formulations as promising controlled release drug delivery systems. J. Contr. Release 153 (3), 206–216. https://doi.org/10.1016/j.jconrel.2011.02.010.

Elzoghby, A.O., Samy, W.M., Elgindy, N.A., 2012. Albumin-based nanoparticles as potential controlled release drug delivery systems. J. Contr. Release 157 (2), 168–182. https://doi.org/10.1016/j.jconrel.2011.07.031.

Fan, X., Peng, X., Wang, T., Gu, Y., Sun, G., Shou, Q., Song, H., Nian, R., Liu, W., 2023. Optimized silk fibroin nanoparticle functionalization with anti-CEA nanobody enhancing active targeting of colorectal cancer cells. Biomedical Materials 18 (4), 045027. https://doi.org/10.1088/1748-605x/acdeba.

Farris, E., 2019. Development, optimization and validation of a chitosan-zein dual-material non viral gene delivery system for applications in oral gene delivery.

Fernando, I.P.S., Kirindage, K.G.I.S., Jayasinghe, A.M.K., Han, E.J., Lee, C.M., Heo, S.J., Ahn, G., 2022. Alginate nanocapsules by water-in-oil emulsification and external gelation for drug delivery to fine dust stimulated keratinocytes. Int. J. Biol. Macromol. 218, 102–114. https://doi.org/10.1016/j.ijbiomac.2022.07.097.

Follit, C.A., Woodruff, S.R., Vogel, P.D., Wise, J.G., Tsarevsky, N.V., 2017. Cationic branched polymers for cellular delivery of negatively charged cargo. J. Drug Deliv. Sci. Technol. 39, 324–333. https://doi.org/10.1016/j.jddst.2017.04.013.

Gajbhiye, V., Gong, S., 2013. Lectin functionalized nanocarriers for gene delivery. Biotechnol. Adv. 31 (5), 552–562. https://doi.org/10.1016/j.biotechadv.2013.01.005.

Gong, X., Gao, Y., Shu, J., Zhang, C., Zhao, K., 2022. Chitosan-based nanomaterial as immune adjuvant and delivery carrier for vaccines. Vaccines 10 (11), 1906. https://doi.org/10.3390/vaccines10111906.

Gotesman, M., Hosein, R.E., Williams, S.A., 2022. Using a hand-held gene gun for genetic transformation of tetrahymena thermophila. Methods Mol. Biol. 2364, 349–361. https://doi.org/10.1007/978-1-0716-1661-1_18.

Guo, Y., Muhammad Awais, M., Fei, S., Xia, J., Sun, J., Feng, M., 2024. Applications and potentials of a silk fibroin nanoparticle delivery system in animal husbandry. Animals 14 (4), 655. https://doi.org/10.3390/ani14040655.

Hama, R., Nakazawa, Y., 2024. Evaluation of the modification effects of heparin/dalteparin on silk fibroin structure and physical properties for skin wound healing. Polymers 16 (3). https://doi.org/10.3390/polym16030321.

Hamrang, R., Moniri, E., Heydarinasab, A., Safaeijavan, R., 2023. In vitro evaluation of copper sulfide nanoparticles decorated with folic acid/chitosan as a novel pH-sensitive nanocarrier for the efficient controlled targeted delivery of cytarabine as an anticancer drug. Biotechnol. Appl. Biochem. 70 (1), 330–343. https://doi.org/10.1002/bab.2355.

Hassan, E.A., Hathout, R.M., Gad, H.A., Sammour, O.A., 2022. A holistic review on zein nanoparticles and their use in phytochemicals delivery. J. Drug Deliv. Sci. Technol. 73, 103460. https://doi.org/10.1016/j.jddst.2022.103460.

Hecht, H., Srebnik, S., 2016. Structural characterization of sodium alginate and calcium alginate. Biomacromolecules 17 (6), 2160–2167. https://doi.org/10.1021/acs.biomac.6b00378.

Ho, Y.K., Zhou, L.H., Tam, K.C., Too, H.P., 2017. Enhanced non-viral gene delivery by coordinated endosomal release and inhibition of β-tubulin deactylase. Nucleic Acids Res. 45 (6). https://doi.org/10.1093/nar/gkw1143.

Hong, S., Choi, D.W., Kim, H.N., Park, C.G., Lee, W., Park, H.H., 2020. Protein-based nanoparticles as drug delivery systems. Pharmaceutics 12 (7), 604. https://doi.org/10.3390/pharmaceutics12070604.

Hozumi, K., Nomizu, M., 2018. Mixed peptide-conjugated chitosan matrices as multi-receptor targeted cell-adhesive scaffolds. Int. J. Mol. Sci. 19 (9). https://doi.org/10.3390/ijms19092713.

Iacob, A.T., Lupascu, F.G., Apotrosoaei, M., Vasincu, I.M., Tauser, R.G., Lupascu, D., Giusca, S.E., Caruntu, I.D., Profire, L., 2021. Recent biomedical approaches for chitosan based materials as drug delivery nanocarriers. Pharmaceutics 13 (4). https://doi.org/10.3390/pharmaceutics13040587.

Inostroza-Brito, K.E., Collin, E.C., Majkowska, A., Elsharkawy, S., Rice, A., del Río Hernández, A.E., Xiao, X., Rodríguez-Cabello, J., Mata, A., 2017. Cross-linking of a biopolymer-peptide co-assembling system. Acta Biomater. 58, 80–89. https://doi.org/10.1016/j.actbio.2017.05.043.

Islam, M.M., Raikwar, S., 2024. Enhancement of oral bioavailability of protein and peptide by polysaccharide-based nanoparticles. Protein Pept. Lett. 31 (3), 209–228. https://doi.org/10.2174/0109298665292469240228064739.

Jacobs, M.I., Bansal, P., Shukla, D., Schroeder, C.M., 2022. Understanding supramolecular assembly of supercharged proteins. ACS Cent. Sci. 8 (9), 1350–1361. https://doi.org/10.1021/acscentsci.2c00730.

Jadidi-Niaragh, F., Atyabi, F., Ali, R., Mollarazi, E., Kiani, M., Razavi, A., Yousefi, M., Kheshtchin, N., Hassannia, H., Hadjati, J., Shokri, F., 2016. Downregulation of CD73 in 4T1 breast cancer cells through siRNA-loaded chitosan-lactate nanoparticles. Tumor Biol. 37 (6), 8403–8412. https://doi.org/10.1007/s13277-015-4732-0.

Jangjou, A., Meisami, A.H., Jamali, K., Hadi Niakan, M., Abbasi, M., Shafiee, M., Salehi, M., Hosseinzadeh, A., Ali, M.A., Vaez, A., 2021. The promising shadow of microbubble over medical sciences: from fighting wide scope of prevalence disease to cancer eradication. J. Biomed. Sci. 28 (1). https://doi.org/10.1186/s12929-021-00744-4.

Ji, L., Ke, J., Jia, L., Guo, L., Zhu, J., 2015. Research progress of silk fibroin as a drug delivery materials. Sheng wu yi xue gong cheng xue za zhi = Journal of biomedical engineering = Shengwu yixue gongchengxue zazhi 32 (6), 1364–1368.

Jin, M., Jin, G., Kang, L., Chen, L., Gao, Z., Huang, W., 2018. Smart polymeric nanoparticles with pH-responsive and PEG-detachable properties for co-delivering paclitaxel and survivin siRNA to enhance antitumor outcomes. Int. J. Nanomed. 13, 2405–2426. https://doi.org/10.2147/IJN.S161426.

Joris, F., De Backer, L., Vyver, T.Van de, Bastiancich, C., De Smedt, S.C., Raemdonck, K., 2018. Repurposing cationic amphiphilic drugs as adjuvants to induce lysosomal siRNA escape in nanogel transfected cells. J. Contr. Release 269, 266–276. https://doi.org/10.1016/j.jconrel.2017.11.019.

Joshy, K.S., Alex Susan, M., Snigdha, S., Nandakumar, K., Pothen Laly, A., Sabu, T., 2018. Encapsulation of zidovudine in PF-68 coated alginate conjugate nanoparticles for anti-HIV drug delivery. Int. J. Biol. Macromol. 107 (Pt A), 929–937. https://doi.org/10.1016/j.ijbiomac.2017.09.078.

Junyaprasert, V.B., Thummarati, P., 2023. Innovative design of targeted nanoparticles: polymer–drug conjugates for enhanced cancer therapy. Pharmaceutics 15 (9). https://doi.org/10.3390/pharmaceutics15092216.

Kamat, V., Dey, P., Bodas, D., Kaushik, A., Boymelgreen, A., Bhansali, S., 2023. Active microfluidic reactor-assisted controlled synthesis of nanoparticles and related potential biomedical applications. J. Mater. Chem. B 11 (25), 5650–5667. https://doi.org/10.1039/d3tb00057e.

Kanwa, N., Kanti De, S., Maity, A., Chakraborty, A., 2020. Interaction of aliphatic amino acids with zwitterionic and charged lipid membranes: hydration and dehydration phenomena. Phys. Chem. Chem. Phys. 22 (6), 3234–3244. https://doi.org/10.1039/c9cp06188f.

Karayianni, M., Sentoukas, T., Skandalis, A., Pippa, N., Pispas, S., 2023. Chitosan-based nanoparticles for nucleic acid delivery: Technological aspects, applications, and future perspectives. Pharmaceutics 15 (7), 1849. https://doi.org/10.3390/pharmaceutics15071849.

Karimi, M., Avci, P., Mobasseri, R., Hamblin, M.R., Naderi-Manesh, H., 2013. The novel albumin-chitosan core-shell nanoparticles for gene delivery: preparation, optimization and cell uptake investigation. J. Nanoparticle Res. 15 (5). https://doi.org/10.1007/s11051-013-1651-0.

Kashani, G.K., Morteza Naghib, S., Soleymani, S., Mozafari, M.R., 2024. A review of DNA nanoparticles-encapsulated drug/gene/protein for advanced controlled drug release: current status and future perspective over emerging therapy approaches. Int. J. Biol. Macromol. 268 (Pt 1), 131694. https://doi.org/10.1016/j.ijbiomac.2024.131694.

Khan, M., 2024. Polymers as efficient non-viral gene delivery vectors: the role of the chemical and physical architecture of macromolecules. Polymers 16 (18), 2629. https://doi.org/10.3390/polym16182629.

Khatun, S., 2024. Glutathione-IR 797 coupled casein nano-trojan for augmenting the therapeutic efficacy of camptothecin in highly invasive triple negative breast cancer. Biomater. Adv. 159.

Kumar, P., Nagarajan, A., Uchil, P.D., 2019. Lipofection. Cold Spring Harb Protoc.

Kunjiappan, S., Govindaraj, S., Parasuraman, P., Sankaranarayanan, M., Arunachalam, S., Palanisamy, P., Priya Mohan, U., Babkiewicz, E., Maszczyk, P., Vellaisamy, S., Panneerselvam, T., 2020. Design, in silico modelling and functionality theory of folate-receptor-targeted myricetin-loaded bovine serum albumin nanoparticle formulation for cancer treatment. Nanotechnology 31 (15), 155102. https://doi.org/10.1088/1361-6528/ab5c56.

Lam, P., Steinmetz, N.F., 2018. Plant viral and bacteriophage delivery of nucleic acid therapeutics. Wiley Interdiscip. Rev. Nanomed. Nanobiotechnol. 10 (1). https://doi.org/10.1002/wnan.1487.

Lee, S.J., Yhee, J.Y., Kim, S.H., Kwon, I.C., Kim, K., 2013. Biocompatible gelatin nanoparticles for tumor-targeted delivery of polymerized siRNA in tumor-bearing mice. J. Contr. Release 172 (1), 358–366. https://doi.org/10.1016/j.jconrel.2013.09.002.

Lee, S.Y., Kim, S.Y., Ku, S.H., Park, E.J., Jang, D.J., Kim, S.T., Kim, S.B., 2022. Polyhydroxyalkanoate decelerates the release of paclitaxel from poly(lactic-co-glycolic acid) nanoparticles. Pharmaceutics 14 (8). https://doi.org/10.3390/pharmaceutics14081618.

Li, Y., Wei, Y., Zhang, G., Zhang, Y., 2023. Sericin from fibroin-deficient silkworms served as a promising resource for biomedicine. Polymers 15 (13), 2941. https://doi.org/10.3390/polym15132941.

Liu, C.H., Multifunctional magnetic nanocarriers for delivery of siRNA and shRNA plasmid to mammalian cells: characterization, adsorption and release behaviors . Colloids Surf. B Biointerfaces. 219.

Liu, J., Sun, H., Peng, Y., Chen, L., Xu, W., Shao, R., 2022. Preparation and characterization of natural silk fibroin hydrogel for protein drug delivery. Molecules 27 (11), 3418. https://doi.org/10.3390/molecules27113418.

Liu, Q., Ahmed, S., Kyllönen, D., Kostiainen, M.A., 2021. Polyelectrolyte encapsulation and confinement within protein cage-inspired nanocompartments. Pharmaceutics 13 (10), 1551. https://doi.org/10.3390/pharmaceutics13101551.

Luo, X., Wu, S., Xiao, M., Gu, H., Zhang, H., Chen, J., Liu, Y., Zhang, C., Zhang, J., 2023. Advances and prospects of prolamine corn protein zein as promising multifunctional drug delivery system for cancer treatment. Int. J. Nanomed. 18, 2589–2621. https://doi.org/10.2147/IJN.S402891.

Ma, C., Liu, X., Wu, G., Zhou, P., Zhou, Y., Wang, L., Huang, X., 2017. Efficient way to generate protein-based nanoparticles by in-situ photoinitiated polymerization-induced self-assembly. ACS Macro Lett. 6 (7), 689–694. https://doi.org/10.1021/acsmacrolett.7b00422.

Ma, Y., Nolte, R.J.M., Cornelissen, J.J.L.M., 2012. Virus-based nanocarriers for drug delivery. Adv. Drug Deliv. Rev. 64 (9), 811–825. https://doi.org/10.1016/j.addr.2012.01.005.

Ma, Y., Canup, B.S.B., Tong, X., Dai, F., Xiao, B., 2020. Multi-responsive silk fibroin-based nanoparticles for drug delivery. Front. Chem. 8. https://doi.org/10.3389/fchem.2020.585077.

Madkhali, O., Mekhail, G., Wettig, S.D., 2019. Modified gelatin nanoparticles for gene delivery. Int. J. Pharm. 554, 224–234. https://doi.org/10.1016/j.ijpharm.2018.11.001.

Magadala, P., Amiji, M., 2008. Epidermal growth factor receptor-targeted gelatin-based engineered nanocarriers for DNA delivery and transfection in human pancreatic cancer cells. AAPS J. 10 (4), 565–576. https://doi.org/10.1208/s12248-008-9065-0.

Monfared, M., Taghizadeh, S., Zare-Hoseinabadi, A., Mousavi, S.M., Hashemi, S.A., Ranjbar, S., Amani, A.M., 2019. Emerging frontiers in drug release control by core–shell nanofibers: a review. Drug Metab. Rev. 51 (4), 589–611. https://doi.org/10.1080/03602532.2019.1642912.

Monfort, D.A., Koria, P., 2017. Recombinant elastin-based nanoparticles for targeted gene therapy. Gene Ther. 24 (10), 610–620. https://doi.org/10.1038/gt.2017.54.

Naghib, S.M., Ahmadi, B., Mikaeeli Kangarshahi, B., Mozafari, M.R., 2024. Chitosan-based smart stimuli-responsive nanoparticles for gene delivery and gene therapy: Recent progresses on cancer therapy. Int. J. Biol. Macromol. 278 (Pt 3), 134542. https://doi.org/10.1016/j.ijbiomac.2024.134542.

Oyaghire, S.N., Quijano, E., Piotrowski-Daspit, A.S., Saltzman, W.M., Glazer, P.M., 2020. Poly(lactic-co-glycolic acid) nanoparticle delivery of peptide nucleic acids in vivo. Methods Mol. Biol. 2105, 261–281. https://doi.org/10.1007/978-1-0716-0243-0_17.

Pan, C., Wang, L., Zhang, M., Li, J., Liu, J., Liu, J., 2023. In situ polymerization-mediated antigen presentation. J. Am. Chem. Soc. 145 (24), 13261–13272. https://doi.org/10.1021/jacs.3c02682.

Paul, M., Itoo, A.M., Ghosh, B., Biswas, S., 2022. Current trends in the use of human serum albumin for drug delivery in cancer. Expet Opin. Drug Deliv. 19 (11), 1449–1470. https://doi.org/10.1080/17425247.2022.2134341.

Pina, M.J., 2015. Elastin-like recombinamers with acquired functionalities for gene-delivery applications. J. Biomed. Mater. Res. 103 (10).

Pradhan, S., Moore, K.M., Ainslie, K.M., Yadavalli, V.K., 2019. Flexible, microstructured surfaces using chitin-derived biopolymers. J. Mater. Chem. B 7 (35), 5328–5335. https://doi.org/10.1039/c9tb00965e.

Purushothaman, B.K., Maheswari, U., Sheriffa Begum, K.M., 2021. pH and magnetic field responsive protein-inorganic nanohybrid conjugated with biotin: a biocompatible carrier system targeting lung cancer cells. J. Appl. Polym. Sci. 138 (10).

Qi, X., Qin, J., Fan, Y., Qin, X., Jiang, Y., Wu, Z., 2016. Carboxymethyl chitosan-modified polyamidoamine dendrimer enables progressive drug targeting of tumors via ph-sensitive charge inversion. J. Biomed. Nanotechnol. 12 (4), 667–678. https://doi.org/10.1166/jbn.2016.2206.

Ragelle, H., Riva, R., Vandermeulen, G., Naeye, B., Pourcelle, V., Le Duff, C.S., D'Haese, C., Nysten, B., Braeckmans, K., De Smedt, S.C., Jérôme, C., Préat, V., 2014. Chitosan nanoparticles for siRNA delivery: optimizing formulation to increase stability and efficiency. J. Contr. Release 176 (1), 54–63. https://doi.org/10.1016/j.jconrel.2013.12.026.

Ragelle, H., Vandermeulen, G., Préat, V., 2013. Chitosan-based siRNA delivery systems. J. Contr. Release 172 (1), 207–218. https://doi.org/10.1016/j.jconrel.2013.08.005.

Raj, P.M., Raj, R., Kaul, A., Mishra, A.K., Ram, A., 2018. Biodistribution and targeting potential assessment of mucoadhesive chitosan nanoparticles designed for ulcerative colitis: via scintigraphy. RSC Adv. 8 (37), 20809–20821. https://doi.org/10.1039/c8ra01898g.

Raposo, C.D., Canelas, A.B., Barros, M.T., 2021. Human lectins, their carbohydrate affinities and where to find them. Biomolecules 11 (2), 1–22. https://doi.org/10.3390/biom11020188.

Rhaese, S., von Briesen, H., Rübsamen-Waigmann, H., Kreuter, J., Langer, K., 2003. Human serum albumin–polyethylenimine nanoparticles for gene delivery. J. Contr. Release 92 (1–2), 199–208. https://doi.org/10.1016/s0168-3659(03)00302-x.

Rother, M., Nussbaumer, M.G., Renggli, K., Bruns, N., 2016. Protein cages and synthetic polymers: a fruitful symbiosis for drug delivery applications, bionanotechnology and materials science. Chem. Soc. Rev. 45 (22), 6213–6249. https://doi.org/10.1039/c6cs00177g.

Sahoo, N., Sahoo, R.K., Biswas, N., Guha, A., Kuotsu, K., 2015. Recent advancement of gelatin nanoparticles in drug and vaccine delivery. Int. J. Biol. Macromol. 81, 317–331. https://doi.org/10.1016/j.ijbiomac.2015.08.006.

San, B.H., Li, Y., Tarbet, E.B., Yu, S.M., 2016. Nanoparticle assembly and gelatin binding mediated by triple helical collagen mimetic peptide. ACS Appl. Mater. Interfaces 8 (31), 19907–19915. https://doi.org/10.1021/acsami.6b05707.

Santos, M., Serrano-Dúcar, S., González-Valdivieso, J., Vallejo, R., Girotti, A., Cuadrado, P., Arias, F.J., 2019. Genetically engineered elastin-based biomaterials for biomedical applications. Curr. Med. Chem. 26 (40), 7117–7146. https://doi.org/10.2174/0929867325666180508094637.

Schoonen, L., Van Hest, J.C.M., 2014. Functionalization of protein-based nanocages for drug delivery applications. Nanoscale 6 (13), 7124–7141. https://doi.org/10.1039/c4nr00915k.

Sethi, A., Ahmad, M., Khan, W.S., 2019. High molecular weight cross linked chitosan nanoparticles for controlled release of 5-Fluorouracil; Enhances its bioavailability. Pak. J. Pharm. Sci. 32 (3), 1137–1143.

Shankar Raman, S., Narayanan, V.H.B., Durai, R., 2021. Lamotrigine nanoparticle laden polymer composite oral dissolving films for improving therapeutic potential of the hydrophobic antiepileptic molecule. Assay Drug Dev. Technol. 19 (1), 2–16. https://doi.org/10.1089/adt.2020.992.

Sharma, U., Saroha, K., 2024. A review of hydrotropic solubilization techniques for enhancing the bioavailability of poorly soluble drugs. Int. J. Toxicol. 43 (1), 63–71. https://doi.org/10.1177/10915818231216414.

Shiri, P., Ramezanpour, S., Amani, A.M., Dehaen, W., 2022. A patent review on efficient strategies for the total synthesis of pazopanib, regorafenib and lenvatinib as novel anti-angiogenesis receptor tyrosine kinase inhibitors for cancer therapy. Mol. Divers. 26 (5), 2981–3002. https://doi.org/10.1007/s11030-022-10406-8.

Shueng, et al., 2022. Charge conversion polymer-liposome complexes to overcome the limitations of cationic liposomes in mitochondrial-targeting drug delivery. Int. J. Mol. Sci. 23 (6).

Sinani, G., Sessevmez, M., Koray Gök, M., Özgümüş, S., Oya Alpar, H., Cevher, E., 2019. Modified chitosan-based nanoadjuvants enhance immunogenicity of protein antigens after mucosal vaccination. Int. J. Pharm. 569, 118592. https://doi.org/10.1016/j.ijpharm.2019.118592.

Sonaye, S.Y., Extrusion-based 3d bioprinting of bioactive and piezoelectric scaffolds as potential therapy for treating critical soft tissue wounds. Adv. Wound Care. 301.

Song, L., Pan, Z., Zhang, H., Li, Y., Zhang, Y., Lin, J., Su, G., Ye, S., Xie, L., Yang, L., Hou, Z., 2017. Dually folate/CD44 receptor-targeted self-assembled hyaluronic acid nanoparticles for dual-drug delivery and combination cancer therapy. J. Mater. Chem. B 5 (33), 6835–6846. https://doi.org/10.1039/C7TB01548H.

Sowmiya, P., Stalin Dhas, T., Inbakandan, D., Anandakumar, N., Nalini, S., Uma Suganya, K.S., Remya, R.R., Karthick, V., Vineeth Kumar, C.M., 2023. Optically active organic and inorganic nanomaterials for biological imaging applications: a review. Micron 172, 103486. https://doi.org/10.1016/j.micron.2023.103486.

Spicer, C.D., Jumeaux, C., Gupta, B., Stevens, M.M., 2018. Peptide and protein nanoparticle conjugates: Versatile platforms for biomedical applications. Chem. Soc. Rev. 47 (10), 3574–3620. https://doi.org/10.1039/c7cs00877e.

Steinmetz, N.F., Lim, S., Sainsbury, F., 2020. Protein cages and virus-like particles: from fundamental insight to biomimetic therapeutics. Biomater. Sci. 8 (10), 2771–2777. https://doi.org/10.1039/d0bm00159g.

Stinson, J.A., Raja, W.K., Lee, S., Kim, H.B., Diwan, I., Tutunjian, S., Panilaitis, B., Omenetto, F.G., Tzipori, S., Kaplan, D.L., 2017. Silk fibroin microneedles for transdermal vaccine delivery. ACS Biomater. Sci. Eng. 3 (3), 360–369. https://doi.org/10.1021/acsbiomaterials.6b00515.

Tadepalli, S., Henry, H., Sang, H.P., Cao, S., Naik, R.R., 2016. Srikanth singamaneni, adsorption behavior of silk fibroin on amphiphilic graphene oxide. ACS Biomater. Sci. Eng. 2 (7), 1084–1092. https://doi.org/10.1021/acsbiomaterials.6b00232.

Takahashi, G., Channabasavaiah, B.G., Wada, K., Miura, H., Sato, M., Ohtsuka, M., 2015. GONAD: Genome-editing via oviductal nucleic acids delivery system: a novel microinjection independent genome engineering method in mice. Sci. Rep. 5 (1). https://doi.org/10.1038/srep11406.

Tarhini, M., Benlyamani, I., Hamdani, S., Agusti, G., Fessi, H., Greige-Gerges, H., Bentaher, A., Elaissari, A., 2018. Protein-based nanoparticle preparation via nanoprecipitation method. Materials 11 (3), 394. https://doi.org/10.3390/ma11030394.

Tariq, I., Reddy Pinnapireddy, S., Duse, L., Ali, M.Y., Ali, S., Amin, M.U., Goergen, N., Jedelská, J., Schäfer, J., Bakowsky, U., 2019. Lipodendriplexes: a promising nanocarrier for enhanced gene delivery with minimal cytotoxicity. Eur. J. Pharm. Biopharm. 135, 72–82. https://doi.org/10.1016/j.ejpb.2018.12.013.

Tiptiri-Kourpeti, A., Spyridopoulou, K., Pappa, A., Chlichlia, K., 2016. DNA vaccines to attack cancer: strategies for improving immunogenicity and efficacy. Pharmacology & Therapeutics 165, 32–49. https://doi.org/10.1016/j.pharmthera.2016.05.004.

Ulgekar, G., Kaur, D., Ganesan, V., Sharma, S.S., Ganguli, N., Majumdar, S.S., 2022. Anhydride chemistry-based hexanoylation of polyethylenimine increases transfection efficiency and expression of tagged DNA for therapeutic proteins in cultured cells. Biotechnol. Bioeng. 119 (11), 3275–3283. https://doi.org/10.1002/bit.28196.

Venkatesan, J., Anil, S., Kim, S.-K., Shim, M., 2016. Seaweed polysaccharide-based nanoparticles: preparation and applications for drug delivery. Polymers 8 (2), 30. https://doi.org/10.3390/polym8020030.

Vesely, L., 2024. Impact of secondary ice in a frozen NaCl freeze-concentrated solution on the extent of methylene blue aggregation. Int J Pharm 650.

Vijayan, V., Mohapatra, A., Uthaman, S., Park, I.-K., 2019. Recent advances in nanovaccines using biomimetic immunomodulatory materials. Pharmaceutics 11 (10), 534. https://doi.org/10.3390/pharmaceutics11100534.

Wang, H., Wu, Di, Wang, P., Gao, C., Teng, H., Liu, D., Zhao, Y., Du, R., 2023. Albumin nanoparticles and their folate modified counterparts for delivery of a lupine derivative to hepatocellular carcinoma. Biomed. Pharmacother. 167, 115485. https://doi.org/10.1016/j.biopha.2023.115485.

Wang, M., Tsukamoto, M., Sergeyev, V.G., Zinchenko, A., 2021. Fluorescent nanoparticles synthesized from DNA, RNA, and nucleotides. Nanomaterials 11 (9), 2265. https://doi.org/10.3390/nano11092265.

Wang, M., Zhang, M., Fu, L., Lin, J., Zhou, X., Zhou, P., Huang, P., Hu, H., Han, Y., 2020. Liver-targeted delivery of TSG-6 by calcium phosphate nanoparticles for the management of liver fibrosis. Theranostics 10 (1), 36–49. https://doi.org/10.7150/thno.37301.

Wang, Y., Douglas, T., 2022. Bioinspired approaches to self-assembly of virus-like particles: from molecules to materials. Accounts of Chemical Research 55 (10), 1349–1359. https://doi.org/10.1021/acs.accounts.2c00056.

Wu, S., Ding, Y., Zhang, G., 2015. Mechanic insight into aggregation of lysozyme by ultrasensitive differential scanning calorimetry and sedimentation velocity. J. Phys. Chem. B 119 (52), 15789–15795. https://doi.org/10.1021/acs.jpcb.5b08190.

Xv, L., Qian, X., Wang, Y., Yu, C., Qin, D., Zhang, Y., Jin, P., Du, Q., 2020. Structural modification of nanomicelles through phosphatidylcholine: the enhanced drug-loading capacity and anticancer activity of celecoxib-casein nanoparticles for the intravenous delivery of celecoxib. Nanomaterials 10 (3), 451. https://doi.org/10.3390/nano10030451.

Ye, X., Mechanism of silk secretion revealed by proteomic analysis of silkworm cocoons with fibroin light chain mutations . J Proteomics. 265.

Yin, Y.S., Chen, D.W., Qiao, M.X., Lu, Z., Hu, H.Y., 2006. Preparation and evaluation of lectin-conjugated PLGA nanoparticles for oral delivery of thymopentin. J. Contr. Release 116 (3), 337–345. https://doi.org/10.1016/j.jconrel.2006.09.015.

Yoo, J., Park, C., Yi, G., Lee, D., Koo, H., 2019. Active targeting strategies using biological ligands for nanoparticle drug delivery systems. Cancers 11 (5), 640. https://doi.org/10.3390/cancers11050640.

Zeng, Y., Zou, F., Xia, N., Li, S., 2023. In-depth review of delivery carriers associated with vaccine adjuvants: current status and future perspectives. Expet Rev. Vaccine 22 (1), 681–695. https://doi.org/10.1080/14760584.2023.2238807.

Zhan, Y.R., Chen, P., He, X., Hei, M.W., Zhang, J., Yu, X.Q., 2022. Sodium alginate-doping cationic nanoparticle as dual gene delivery system for genetically bimodal therapy. Biomacromolecules 23 (12), 5312–5321. https://doi.org/10.1021/acs.biomac.2c01119.

Zhang, D., Song, Y., Wang, Y., Liu, X., Yu, W., Ma, X., 2016. Insight of in vitro small-interfering RNA Release from chitosan nanoparticles under enzymolysis with förster resonance energy transfer analysis. J. Pharmaceut. Sci. 105 (1), 301–307. https://doi.org/10.1002/jps.24698.

Zhang, L., Li, Q., Chen, J., Tang, C., Yin, C., 2021. Enhanced antitumor efficacy of glutathione-responsive chitosan based nanoparticles through co-delivery of chemotherapeutics, genes, and immune agents. Carbohydr. Polym. 270, 118384. https://doi.org/10.1016/j.carbpol.2021.118384.

Zhang, Y., Qin, L.-M., Feng, M.-F., Yu, X., Wu, Y., 2024. RNA-binding peptide and endosomal escape-assisting peptide (L2) improved siRNA delivery by the hexahistidine–metal assembly. J. Mater. Chem. B 12 (40), 10309–10319. https://doi.org/10.1039/d4tb01433b.

Zhu, P., et al., 2017. Progress in biophysics and molecular biology. 1–15.

CHAPTER

# 11

# Human serum albumin–based nanocarriers for drug delivery

*Ali Nematollahzadeh and Navid Ahadi-Jomairan*
**Chemical Engineering Department, University of Mohaghegh Ardabili, Ardabil, Iran**

## 1. Properties and significance of human serum albumin

Human serum albumin (HSA) is the most abundant extracellular protein in plasma, composed of 585 amino acids (Kragh-Hansen, 1990; Neault and Tajmir-Riahi, 1998), and synthesized in the liver at a rate of 0.7 mg per gram of liver tissue per hour. Its natural role includes maintaining pH and osmotic balance and transporting both metabolic and exogenous compounds (Yang et al., 2007). Due to its endogenous origin, HSA exhibits excellent biocompatibility and biodegradability, making it a preferred choice for drug delivery carriers. HSA has a remarkable ability to bind a variety of compounds, including fatty acids, drugs, and cations (Naik et al., 2010). It contains two primary binding sites, allowing for diverse ligand docking. Its role as a natural transporter in the bloodstream provides it with high affinity and specificity for various therapeutic agents, enabling efficient drug delivery mechanisms. HSA has an extended half-life of approximately 19 days in the human body (Kratz, 2008). This long circulation time enhances its ability to serve as a prolonged drug carrier, ensuring sustained therapeutic effects and reducing the need for frequent dosing (Nematollahzadeh et al., 2023). As a naturally occurring protein in humans, HSA is nonimmunogenic, which minimizes the risk of adverse immune responses. This feature is particularly important for repeated or long-term therapeutic applications, where immunogenicity could compromise treatment efficacy (Divsalar et al., 2012). Additionally, tumors rely on albumin for nutrition, and this specificity can be exploited for selective targeting and accumulation in tumor tissues. Albumin can also be transported effectively to tumors via overexpressed glycoprotein receptors such as albondin (Vogel et al., 2001). This functionality allows albumin-based nanocarriers (ANCs) to serve as efficient tools for delivering chemotherapeutics to tumor sites, enhancing specificity, reducing cytotoxicity, and maintaining therapeutic agent concentration for longer durations (Zeeshan et al., 2021).

*Protein-Based Nanoparticles in Drug Delivery*
https://doi.org/10.1016/B978-0-443-33639-3.00022-2

### 1.1 Advantages of HSA nanocarriers

HSA nanocarriers possess numerous characteristics that make them a promising platform for drug delivery systems. HSA is a natural, endogenous protein that is nontoxic, nonimmunogenic, and biodegradable. These properties make HSA nanocarriers highly biocompatible, reducing the risk of adverse immune responses. This high safety profile makes them suitable for use in sensitive drug delivery routes, such as nose-to-brain systems. Additionally, the structural features of HSA enable it to effectively bind to a wide range of hydrophilic and hydrophobic drugs, resulting in a high drug-loading capacity. This enhances the bioavailability and therapeutic efficacy of various compounds, while controlled drug release minimizes toxicity and adverse effects, particularly for potent drugs like anticancer agents (Jithan et al., 2011; Wilson et al., 2014).

HSA nanoparticles also show excellent stability in both liquid suspension and freeze-dried forms, maintaining their physical and chemical characteristics over long periods. Their mucoadhesive properties, particularly when combined with chitosan coatings, improve residence time in mucosal environments such as the nasal cavity, further enhancing their performance as drug carriers. Furthermore, HSA nanoparticles can improve permeability and cellular uptake, facilitating drug delivery across complex barriers such as the blood–brain barrier (BBB). Their surface can be easily functionalized with ligands, polymers, or other molecules for precise targeting and controlled release profiles. This versatility allows for the development of personalized drug delivery systems tailored to the specific needs of different therapeutic applications. Additionally, scalable and cost-effective production methods for HSA-based systems, such as nanoemulsions, make them suitable for large-scale pharmaceutical use, while their resistance to destabilization processes ensures drug stability during storage and use (Anhorn et al., 2008).

## 2. Fabrication methods of HSA-based nanocarriers

### 2.1 Desolvation

The desolvation and coacervation methods are widely employed to fabricate HSA nanoparticles due to their efficiency and reproducibility (Weber et al., 2000; Langer et al., 2003). Both the techniques are employed for nanoparticle synthesis and encapsulation, but they differ significantly in their mechanisms, processes, and specific applications. In the desolvation method, the addition of a nonsolvent results in sedimentation, while in coacervation, meaning “crowding together,” polymer dissolution leads to phase separation and coating of the polymer on a support surface. However, in the desolvation/coacervation approach, HSA is initially dissolved in an aqueous sodium chloride solution, and the pH is carefully adjusted to between 8 and 9, as higher pH levels facilitate the formation of smaller nanoparticles. Ethanol is then gradually introduced to the solution, acting as a desolvating agent. Ethanol’s properties, including its dielectric constant and solubility parameters, disrupt the hydrophilic shell of HSA, leading to protein denaturation and subsequent nanoparticle formation (Mohammad-Beigi et al., 2016). Among potential desolvating agents such as acetone and methanol, ethanol is preferred due to its lower toxicity (Likhodii et al., 2003).

To stabilize the nanoparticles, glutaraldehyde is added as a cross-linking agent. It reacts with the amino groups of HSA, ensuring structural integrity and enhancing the stability. For optimal results, the amount of glutaraldehyde is calculated to match 100% of the amino groups available in HSA, striking a balance between particle size, homogeneity, and stability. The resulting nanoparticles are spherical and exhibit a hydrodynamic diameter typically ranging from 230 to 250 nm. However, to reach particles in the nanoscale range less than 100 nm, the research group led by Nematollahzadeh introduced two distinct methodologies, which include mixing the protein solution under high shear rate in the presence of a cross-linker (Hassanzadeh et al., 2021) and decorating the protein molecules around a support nanoparticles as a hard template, cross-linking of the proteins and subsequently removing the template by acid wash (Lotfalian et al., 2021).

The serum albumin particles negatively charged surface, attributed to the terminal carboxyl groups of HSA, imparts a high zeta potential, which prevents aggregation and enhances suspension stability. Moreover, the nanoparticles demonstrate a high yield, indicating efficient transformation of HSA into nanoparticles (Likhodii et al., 2003). The desolvation method has also been adapted for drug loading, such as incorporating sulforhodamine B, a hydrophilic fluorescent dye, as a model compound. This loading process minimally affects the nanoparticles' size and distribution, making the desolvation method an effective technique for developing HSA-based nanocarriers with potential applications in drug delivery systems (Guccione et al., 2017; Piazzini, Landucci, et al., 2019a). The preparation process is shown in Fig. 11.1.

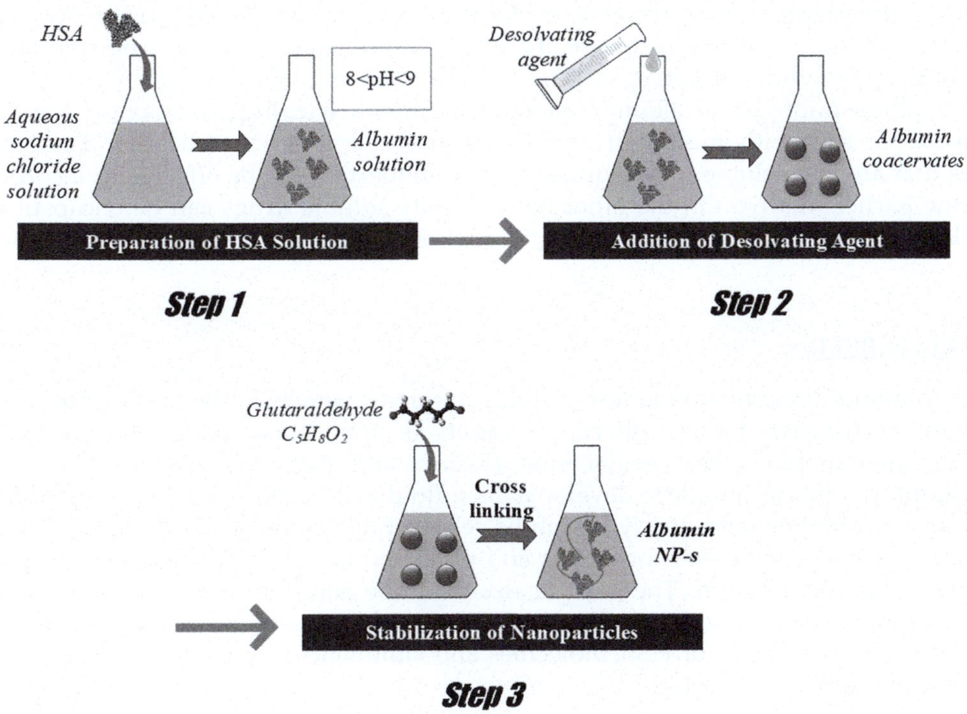


FIGURE 11.1 Schematic of the desolvation–coacervation method for HSA nanoparticle synthesis.

Several factors affect the process of preparing human serum albumin (HSA) nanoparticles by the desolvation method. These factors include the type of desolvating agent (such as methanol, ethanol, acetone, and their mixtures), the stirring rate of the solution, and the method of continuous or dropwise addition of the desolvating agent. In addition, the dielectric constant of the solvents and the concentration and composition of the starting materials can also affect the size and properties of the nanoparticles (Von Storp et al., 2012). The use of methanol and mixtures of methanol and ethanol results in particle sizes that remain significantly smaller than 100 nm, while ethanol and acetone produce larger particles, between 140 and 300 nm. These differences indicate the influence of the chemical properties and dielectric constant of the solvents on the desolvation process. The rate of stirring the solution is also very effective in determining the particle size. Increasing the stirring speed to at least 500 rpm produces smaller and more uniform particles, as faster stirring leads to a more uniform distribution of the desolvating agent and improves the precipitation process. Conversely, decreasing the stirring rate leads to the formation of larger particles, as the precipitation process becomes more gradual and irregular (Von Storp et al., 2012).

The method of continuous addition of the desolvating agent is another influential factor. This method allows for more uniform changes in the concentration of the desolvating agent and prevents uncontrolled particle growth, which helps produce smaller nanoparticles. These properties and parameters can be used to precisely produce albumin nanoparticles of desired and specific sizes. This is crucial for therapeutic applications, as particle size has a significant impact on drug performance, absorption in the body, and distribution in tissues. Furthermore, tuning the type of desolvating agent allows researchers to tailor the properties of the nanoparticles to specific drug requirements, such as drug solubility and type of therapy (Von Storp et al., 2012).

Using these findings, the albumin nanoparticle manufacturing process can be optimized to create particles with specific properties for each therapeutic application. For example, drugs that are less soluble may require larger nanoparticles to be effectively incorporated into the particle matrix. On the other hand, highly soluble drugs can be encapsulated in smaller nanoparticles that have better absorption in the target tissue (Von Storp et al., 2012).

## 2.2 Microfluidics

Microfluidics uses small volumes of fluids in microchannels in the range of tens to hundreds of micrometers in size, offering a variety of applications as an efficient and cost-effective tool in biomedical engineering (Razavi and Nematollahzadeh, 2025). Hakala et al. employed this technique to develop a microfluidic device that used a coflow of ethanol, HSA protein solution, and highly lipophilic celastrol (Hakala et al., 2020) as a model drug into microchannels with tee-connections and produced HSA-loaded celastrol nanoparticles of narrow size distribution. The particle size could be adjusted in the range of 100 nm to 1 μm by tuning the feed flow rate. In a similar study, Sun et al. utilized the microfluidic device for the self-assembly of HSA molecules and simultaneously loaded the particles with cabazitaxel (Sun et al., 2020).

## 2.3 nab technology

The nanoparticle albumin-bound (nab) technology is an advanced platform designed to encapsulate poorly water-soluble active pharmaceutical ingredients (APIs) within an HSA shell (Desai et al., 1999). This encapsulation results in albumin-stabilized nanosuspensions, primarily tailored for intravenous administration. One of the key features of nab technology is its ability to eliminate the need for synthetic solubilizers and cross-linking agents, which often pose toxicity concerns (Adick et al., 2024).

The standard nab process involves three critical steps, including emulsification, high-pressure homogenization, and solvent evaporation. Initially, the API is dissolved in an appropriate organic solvent, such as dichloromethane, ethyl acetate, or their mixtures with ethanol. This organic phase is emulsified with an aqueous albumin solution to form a primary emulsion. High-pressure homogenization follows, inducing hydrodynamic cavitation, which generates intense shear forces. This step leads to partial cross-linking of the albumin at the particle surface and within the surrounding solution. The final step involves solvent evaporation, resulting in nanoparticles comprising an amorphous drug core encapsulated within an albumin shell (Adick et al., 2024). The schematic of this method is presented in Fig. 11.2.

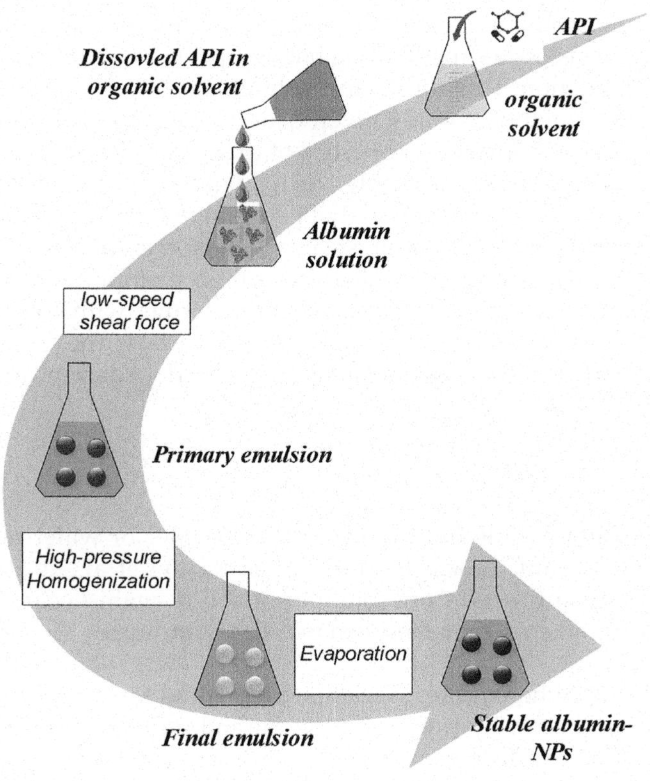


FIGURE 11.2 Schematic of the nab technology.

HSA in these nanosuspensions interacts with the API primarily through hydrophobic forces, enabling stabilization and controlled release. FDA-approved formulations such as Abraxane and Fyarro exemplify the clinical success of nab technology. For instance, Abraxane, a paclitaxel nanosuspension stabilized by HSA, demonstrated superior tumor uptake and reduced hypersensitivity compared to conventional formulations such as Taxol. Similarly, Fyarro, a rapamycin-based nanosuspension, underscores the adaptability of nab technology to diverse APIs (Adick et al., 2024; Meredith et al., 2023; Harshita et al., 2019).

Despite its versatility, nab technology is not universally applicable to all hydrophobic drugs. The success of API encapsulation often depends on specific physicochemical properties such as solubility, molecular weight, and melting point. Nevertheless, nab technology remains a robust and scalable approach for producing albumin-stabilized nanocarriers, facilitating the effective delivery of hydrophobic drugs via intravenous routes (Adick et al., 2024). One of the main challenges of nab technology is that some drugs, despite being hydrophobic, form unstable nanosuspensions. For example, drugs such as fenofibrate and lapatinib produce nanoparticles that lack long-term stability and may aggregate or degrade over time. On the other hand, certain drugs such as carbamazepine and nimodipine fail to form small and uniform nanoparticles; instead, they generate larger or micron-sized structures, which limits their use in injectable formulations (Adick et al., 2024).

Another major limitation of this technology is its dependence on the pH sensitivity of certain drugs. Drugs containing carboxyl groups, such as indomethacin and valsartan, exhibit increased solubility at neutral pH and completely dissolve in the albumin solution. As a result, they fail to create a solid core necessary for forming nanosuspensions, rendering nab technology ineffective for their formulation. This constraint highlights the need for careful chemical analysis before selecting this method for any given drug (Adick et al., 2024).

Moreover, research has shown that specific physical properties of drugs can significantly influence the success or failure of this technology. Notably, drugs with high molecular weights, such as paclitaxel and rapamycin, which have already been commercialized using nab technology, demonstrate better stability in forming nanosuspensions due to their larger molecular structures and higher polar surface areas. Additionally, a high melting point is another factor that contributes to the formation of stable solid cores. Drugs with lower melting points may remain in solution rather than forming solid particles during the nanosuspension process, making them unsuitable for this formulation method (Adick et al., 2024).

## 2.4 Emulsification

Nanoemulsions are mixtures of two immiscible liquid phases (oil-in-water or water-in-oil) with droplet sizes typically below 500 nm (Lewinski et al., 2008; Razavi et al., 2022). They possess unique properties, including improved drug solubility, stability against coalescence, and ease of production. These characteristics make them excellent candidates for targeted drug delivery.

Divsalar et al. (2012) conducted a study wherein they developed a method for preparing and characterizing nanoemulsions. They began by preparing the oil and aqueous phases. The oil phase was created by blending a cosurfactant with an oil under magnetic stirring,

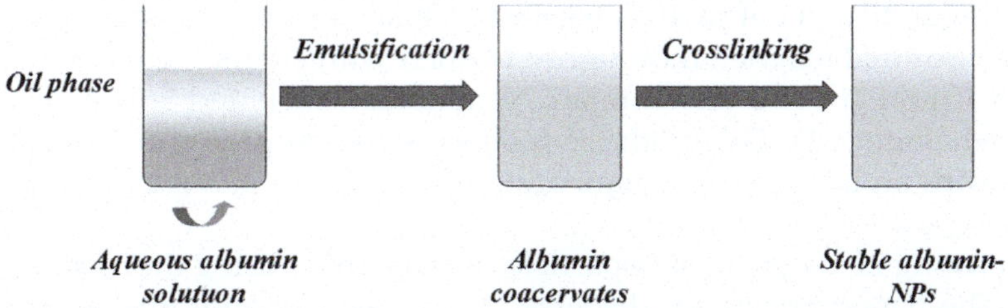


**FIGURE 11.3** Schematic of the emulsification method. *Regenerated from H.-y. Tao, R.-q. Wang, W.-j. Sheng, Y.-s. Zhen, The development of human serum albumin-based drugs and relevant fusion proteins for cancer therapy, Int. J. Biol. Macromol. 187 (2021) 24-34.*

while heating at 70 °C for 15 min. Simultaneously, the aqueous phase was prepared by dissolving a surfactant in deionized water. Water was gradually added to the oil phase, resulting in the formation of an emulsion. The final nanoemulsion was produced by mixing the oil and aqueous phases using a high-shear mixer (Ultra-Turrax T25) at 10,000 rpm for 5 min. To characterize the nanoemulsion, they used dynamic light scattering (DLS) and scanning electron microscopy (SEM). DLS analysis showed that the average particle size was around 227 nm, with a polydispersity index (PDI) of 0.134, indicating a uniform particle size distribution. SEM analysis confirmed these results, revealing that the nanoemulsion droplets were spherical and monodisperse, with diameters consistent with the DLS findings. The method introduced by Divsalar et al. offers several advantages. The high-shear mixing technique allows for scalability in industrial applications. Additionally, the small droplet sizes and uniformity improve drug loading efficiency and stability. The process is adaptable, enabling the production of either oil-in-water or water-in-oil nanoemulsions, depending on the solubility of the drug. In the context of HSA-based nanocarriers, their nanoemulsion approach has significant advantages, such as enhancing the solubilization of hydrophobic drugs, improving bioavailability, and increasing stability against degradation. When integrated with HSA, these nanoemulsions become efficient carriers for drug delivery, ensuring prolonged circulation and targeted therapeutic effects.

Fig. 11.3 illustrates the preparation of albumin-based nanosuspensions. It depicts the combination of an albumin aqueous solution with an oil phase containing drugs and emulsifiers, followed by the formation of an oil-in-water (W/O) emulsion using techniques such as stirring, ultrasonication, or high-pressure homogenization. The emulsion is stabilized through either chemical or physical cross-linking methods. Lastly, any remaining chemical cross-linking agents and organic solvents are thoroughly removed (Tao et al., 2021).

## 2.5 Surface modification

Magnetic iron oxide nanoparticles ($Fe_3O_4$ or $\gamma$-$Fe_2O_3$) are synthesized using the chemical coprecipitation method. In this process, $FeCl_3{\cdot}6H_2O$ and $FeCl_2{\cdot}4H_2O$ are dissolved in deionized water with a molar ratio of 2:1. For the synthesis of magnetite ($Fe_3O_4$), the solution is purged with an inert gas to remove any dissolved oxygen. Then the solution is heated to 80 °C, and ammonium hydroxide (25%) is added dropwise to the mixture while maintaining vigorous stirring until a pH of *ca.* 10 is reached. A black precipitate is formed, which is separated using an external magnet, thoroughly washed with ethanol and deionized water, and dried under vacuum at 40 °C (Saleh Iman, Nematollahzadeh and Soltani Toularoud, 2024). Similarly, maghemite (γ-$Fe_2O_3$) synthesis follows the same procedure except that the solution purging with an inert gas for eliminating dissolved oxygen is not performed (Mirzayi et al., 2015).

The silica coating of magnetic nanoparticles is performed using the Stöber method (Stöber et al., 1968). The nanoparticles are dispersed in a water–ethanol mixture and subjected to sonication. Tetraethyl orthosilicate (TEOS) is then added to the mixture, which is stirred to achieve a uniform coating. The silica-coated nanoparticles ($Fe_3O_4$@$SiO_2$) are subsequently separated and dried at 50 °C under vacuum conditions (Haji-Khorasani and Safajou-Jahankhanemlou, 2025; Hosseinpour Moghadam et al., 2019).

Surface modification of the silica-coated nanoparticles is carried out using (3-chloropropyl)-trimethoxysilane (CPTMS) in dry xylene under a nitrogen atmosphere. During this process, reactive functional groups are introduced onto the surface of the nanoparticles, enhancing their compatibility for drug loading and further functionalization. Controlled reaction conditions are maintained to ensure uniform surface modification. Drug loading is achieved by dissolving drugs such as oseltamivir, tenofovir, and nevirapine in ethanol and mixing the solution with the modified nanoparticles. The mixture is stirred for 6 hours to facilitate effective drug adsorption, and unbound drugs are removed by repeated washing with ethanol. The resulting drug-loaded nanoparticles ($Fe_3O_4$@$SiO_2$@Drug) are prepared for subsequent functionalization. In the final step, HSA is immobilized onto the surface of the drug-loaded nanoparticles. The nanoparticles are dispersed in an HSA solution containing triethylamine, enabling covalent bonding between HSA and the nanoparticle surface. The HSA-coated nanoparticles ($Fe_3O_4$@$SiO_2$@-Drug@HSA) are then separated magnetically, washed, and purified for applications such as DNA-binding studies and controlled drug release assays (Hosseinpour Moghadam et al., 2019). Fig. 11.4 illustrates the process of surface modification in nanoparticles (Hosseinpour Moghadam et al., 2019).

## 2.6 Mechanisms of drug loading and release

### *2.6.1 Interaction between nanoemulsion and HSA*

The interaction between a nanoemulsion and HSA was studied using spectroscopic techniques such as intrinsic fluorescence, extrinsic fluorescence, and circular dichroism (CD). The interactions alter the protein's structure, influencing its drug-binding and release capabilities (Lewinski et al., 2008). In the fabrication of albumin-stabilized nanosuspensions using nab technology, HSA plays a crucial role in stabilizing the nanoemulsion. The process begins with the dissolution of the drug in an organic solvent, followed by emulsification with an aqueous HSA solution. During high-energy methods such as high-pressure homogenization or ultrasonic treatment, the hydrophobic domains of HSA interact with the dispersed drug phase. This interaction results in the formation of a primary emulsion, where HSA encapsulates the drug molecules, creating a stabilized nanoemulsion suitable for further processing (Adick et al., 2024).

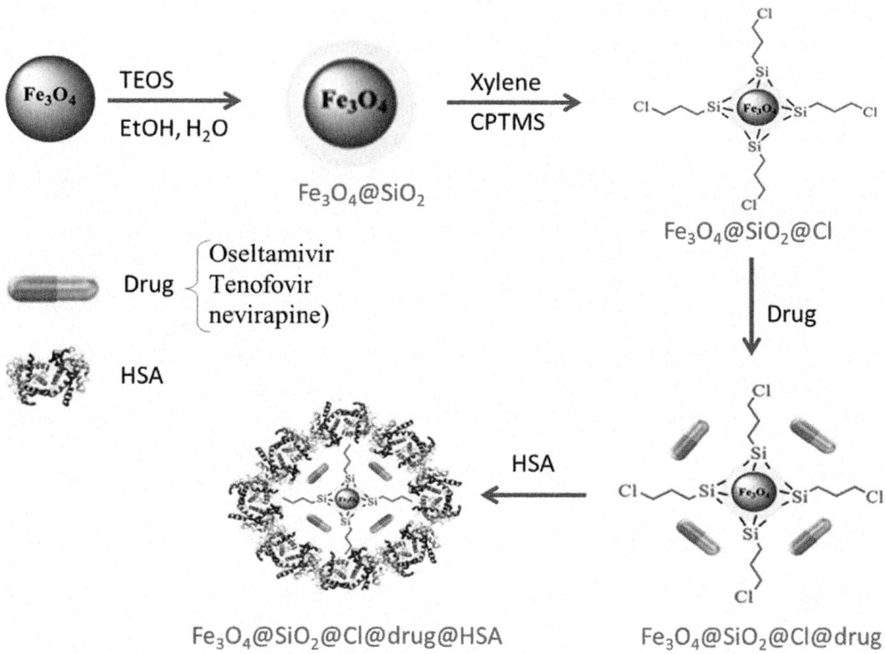


**FIGURE 11.4** Process of surface modification in nanoparticles (Hosseinpour Moghadam et al., 2019). *Reprinted from N.H. Moghadam, S. Salehzadeh, J. Rakhtshah, A.H. Moghadam, H. Tanzadehpanah, M. Saidijam, Preparation of a highly stable drug carrier by efficient immobilization of human serum albumin (HSA) on drug-loaded magnetic iron oxide nanoparticles, Int. J. Biol. Macromol. 125 (2019) 931-940.*

## 3. Drug loading mechanisms

### 3.1 Hydrophobic interactions

HSA nanoparticles exhibit a hydrophobic core that allows the binding of hydrophobic drugs. These interactions occur naturally as drugs are encapsulated or adsorbed into the nanoparticle matrix, driven by the protein's inherent hydrophobic pockets (Piazzini, Landucci, et al., 2019a). HSA contains hydrophobic binding pockets, particularly near the single tryptophan residue (Trp-214), which are crucial for drug binding. When the nanoemulsion interacts with HSA, it causes the hydrophobic core of the protein to become exposed, thereby enhancing its ability to bind hydrophobic drugs more effectively. This interaction plays a key role in improving the drug-binding efficiency of HSA-based nanocarriers (Matulis et al., 1999). Hydrophobic interactions between the API and the binding domains of HSA are the primary drivers of drug loading in nab formulations. These interactions ensure the stabilization of poorly water-soluble drugs by encapsulating them within the albumin shell during the nanoparticle formation process (Adick et al., 2024). HSA contains specific binding sites, such as the warfarin-binding site (site I) and diazepam-binding site (site II), which allow reversible interactions with drug molecules. Additionally, albumin molecules possess amino and carboxyl groups that facilitate covalent or noncovalent interactions, enabling

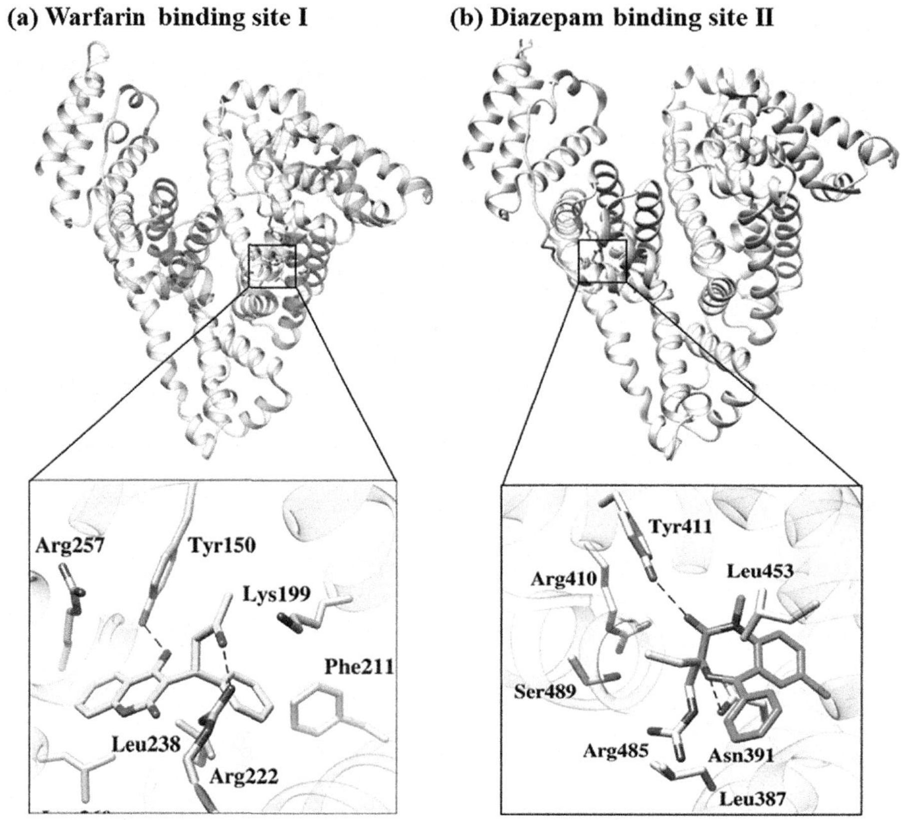


FIGURE 11.5 Crystal structure of HSA bound to warfarin (a) and diazepam (b). *Reprinted from S. Ashraf, H. Qaiser, S. Tariq, A. Khalid, H.A. Makeen, H.A. Alhazmi, Z. Ul-Haq, Unraveling the versatility of human serum albumin–A comprehensive review of its biological significance and therapeutic potential, Current Research in* Structural Biology (2023) *100114.*

high drug-loading capacities. The structural flexibility of HSA further supports the accommodation of a diverse range of therapeutic agents, including small molecules, peptides, and hydrophobic drugs (Yang et al., 2014). In Fig. 11.5, the crystal structure of HSA is depicted in complex with warfarin (a) and diazepam (b). Amino acid residues and drug molecules are represented using stick models and are color-coded based on atom type. Carbon atoms in diazepam are shown in orange, while those in amino acid residues are gray; carbon in warfarin is yellow. Oxygen atoms are marked in red, nitrogen in blue, and chlorine in green (Ashraf et al., 2023; Ghuman et al., 2005; Curry, 2009).

## 3.2 Structural alterations to facilitate binding

Interaction with nanoemulsions causes partial unfolding or loosening of HSA's native structure. This conformational change increases the accessibility of binding sites,

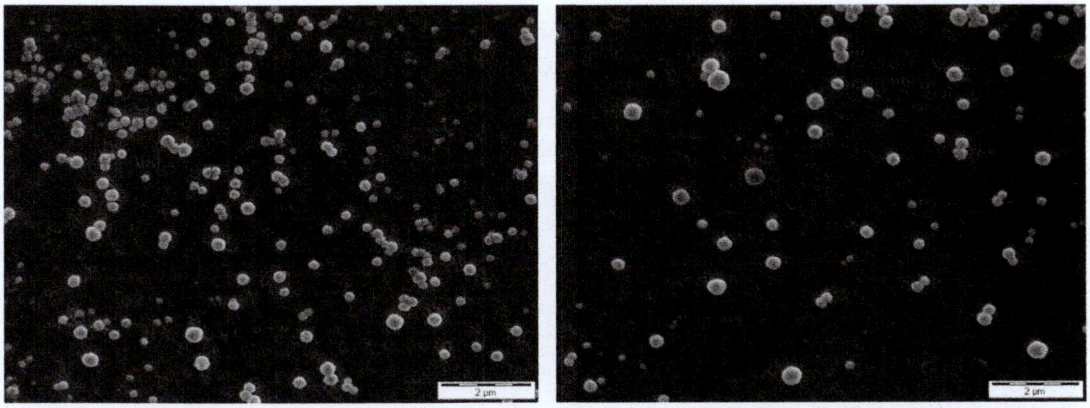

**FIGURE 11.6** Shows SEM images of an itraconazole nanosuspension stabilized with HSA, prepared using ultrasonic treatment under the central point conditions of the experimental design (40% amplitude, 70% pulse-pause ratio, and 8000 Ws energy output).The images reveal spherical itraconazole nanoparticles approximately 200 nm in size, deposited on a polycarbonate membrane with 100 nm pores (Adick et al., 2024).

particularly the hydrophobic regions, which are critical for drug loading (Divsalar et al., 2012; Kaboli et al., 2021). HSA demonstrates conformational flexibility, enabling it to accommodate various APIs by altering its structure. During high-energy processes such as high-pressure homogenization or ultrasonic treatment, these structural adjustments enhance drug binding and nanoparticle stability (Adick et al., 2024). Structural modifications, such as the introduction of silica coatings and functional linkers such as organosilanes, play a significant role in facilitating drug binding. These alterations create additional active sites for drug attachment, enhancing the drug-loading capacity of the nanoparticles. Moreover, the immobilization of HSA further optimizes the structural compatibility of the carrier for binding with specific drugs (Hosseinpour Moghadam et al., 2019).

Fig. 11.6 shows SEM images of HSA-stabilized itraconazole nanoparticles (~200 nm) on a polycarbonate membrane with 100 nm pores, prepared by ultrasonic treatment, scale bar: 2 μm. Reprinted from A. Adick, W. Hoheisel, S. Schneid, S. Hester, K. Langer, Development of a screening platform for the formulation of poorly water-soluble drugs as albumin-stabilized nanosuspensions using nab technology, Int. J. Pharm. 662 (2024) 124,491.

The SEM image of $Fe_3O_4$@$SiO_2$@Osel@HSA nanoparticles, shown in Fig. 11.7, illustrates that the nanoparticles are predominantly spherical in shape. The majority of the nanoparticles exhibit a uniform size distribution, with their diameters ranging from approximately 9–14 nm. This consistency in size suggests well-controlled synthesis conditions and a stable nanoparticle formation (Hosseinpour Moghadam et al., 2019).

The binding of a hydrophobic dye, 1-anilino-8-naphthalene sulfonic acid (ANS), to HSA is used to monitor changes in the protein's tertiary structure. Increasing concentrations of the nanoemulsion lead to a rise in ANS fluorescence intensity, indicating greater exposure of hydrophobic regions, thus suggesting enhanced drug loading capacity (Divsalar et al., 2012; Chamani et al., 2010).

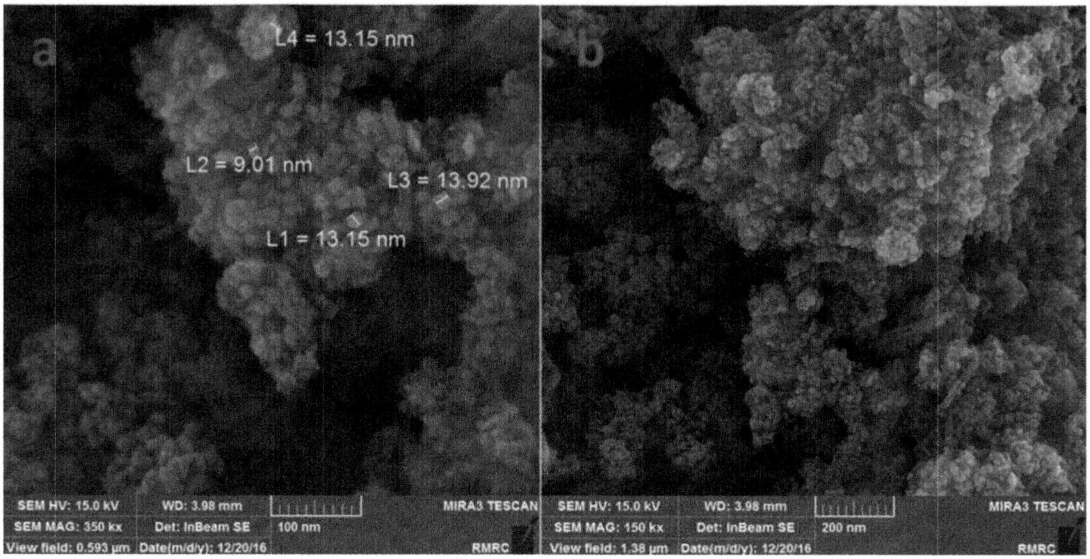


**FIGURE 11.7** FE-SEM images of $Fe_3O_4@SiO_2@Osel@HSA$ nanoparticles are shown with scale bars of 100 nm (a) and 200 nm (b). *Reprinted from N.H. Moghadam, S. Salehzadeh, J. Rakhtshah, A.H. Moghadam, H. Tanzadehpanah, M. Saidijam, Preparation of a highly stable drug carrier by efficient immobilization of human serum albumin (HSA) on drug-loaded magnetic iron oxide nanoparticles, Int. J. Biol. Macromol. 125 (2019) 931-940.*

## 3.3 Electrostatic and chemical bonding

Drugs with charged functional groups interact electrostatically with oppositely charged regions of the HSA structure. Additionally, chemical cross-linking agents, such as glutaraldehyde, can enhance drug stability by covalently linking the drug molecules to the nanoparticle (Piazzini, Landucci, et al., 2019a). The interaction between the functionalized silica surface of the nanoparticles and the drug molecules ensures that they are securely attached, minimizing premature release. HSA, as a capping agent, forms additional bonds with the drugs, stabilizing the overall structure (Hosseinpour Moghadam et al., 2019). In this method, the charges of albumin are reversed by the drugs, allowing drug-loaded albumin with positive charges to directly absorb hyaluronic acid (HA) and create further modifications on the nanoparticle surface. This strategy serves as a means to enhance the stability and improve the performance of HSA nanoparticles in drug delivery, especially for positively charged drugs (Fig. 11.8) (Lei et al., 2021).

## 3.4 Encapsulation efficiency and diffusion

Encapsulation efficiency depends on drug solubility and affinity for HSA. Hydrophobic drugs often achieve higher loading efficiency, while hydrophilic drugs rely on diffusion into preformed nanoparticles (Piazzini, Landucci, et al., 2019a). High-energy processes such as ultrasonic treatment play a crucial role in ensuring efficient encapsulation of APIs. Parameters such as energy output, amplitude, and pulse–pause ratio significantly influence the size and stability of the resulting nanoparticles. Increased energy output during

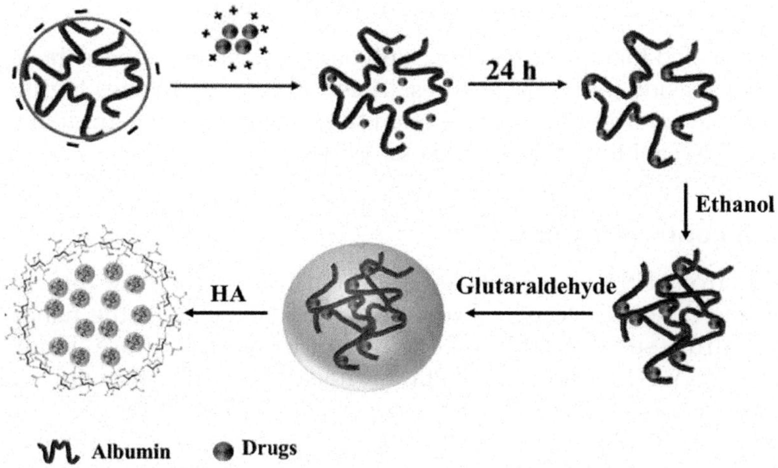


FIGURE 11.8 Common preparation methods of hyaluronic acid (HA) and albumin-based nanoparticles through desolvation and electrostatic interactions. *Reprinted from C. Lei, X.-R. Liu, Q.-B. Chen, Y. Li, J.-L. Zhou, L.-Y. Zhou, T. Zou, Hyaluronic acid and albumin-based nanoparticles for drug delivery, Journal of Controlled Release 331 (2021) 416-433.*

ultrasonic homogenization results in reduced particle size and more uniform distribution, which enhances encapsulation efficiency (Adick et al., 2024). The silica coating of the nanoparticles provides a porous matrix that supports high drug encapsulation efficiency. The diffusion of drugs from this matrix is influenced by the surface chemistry and structural design, ensuring a controlled and gradual release. The study highlights the successful encapsulation of drugs such as oseltamivir, nevirapine, and tenofovir, with consistent diffusion profiles observed during in vitro experiments (Hosseinpour Moghadam et al., 2019).

## 4. Mechanisms of drug release

### 4.1 Stimuli-responsive behavior

The structural flexibility of HSA allows it to adapt to environmental changes such as pH, temperature, and the presence of other molecules. The interaction with nanoemulsions causes a shift in HSA's fluorescence spectrum (red shift), reflecting structural changes that facilitate controlled drug release (Divsalar et al., 2012).

### 4.2 Temperature dependency

Fluorescence studies at two temperatures (25°C and 37°C) showed that HSA undergoes different levels of quenching at varying nanoemulsion concentrations. At higher temperatures, the structural flexibility of HSA increases, promoting faster drug release (Divsalar et al., 2012; Jayasree et al., 2011).

## 4.3 Role of circular dichroism in release monitoring

CD studies revealed that the interaction with nanoemulsions reduces the α-helical content of HSA while increasing β-sheet structures. These structural changes highlight the mechanism by which HSA transitions to a more open state, facilitating the gradual release of drugs (Divsalar et al., 2012; Schippers and Dekkers, 1981).

## 4.4 Diffusion-controlled release

Drug release from HSA nanoparticles is primarily governed by diffusion. The rate is influenced by the drug's molecular size and its interaction with the nanoparticle matrix. A hydrophilic drug such as sulforhodamine B tends to diffuse more rapidly from chitosan-coated HSA NPs, resulting in faster release profiles (Piazzini, Landucci, et al., 2019a). Models such as Higuchi and Korsmeyer-Peppas are employed to understand the release mechanisms. These models often indicate diffusion as the primary mode of drug release, with non-Fickian behavior reflecting complex interactions within the protein matrix (Piazzini, Landucci, et al., 2019a). This controlled release mechanism ensures a steady supply of therapeutic agents over an extended period, maintaining efficacy (Hosseinpour Moghadam et al., 2019). A couple of the mathematical models that could represent the drug release from the HSA-based nanocarriers are outlined in Table 11.1.

**TABLE 11.1** Common applicable models on the drug release from HSA-based carriers and the underlying mechanisms.

| No. | Model | Equation | Mechanisms |
|---|---|---|---|
| (1) | Zero-order | $Q_t = Q_0 + k_0 t$ | • Diffusion-controlled release<br>• Reservoir systems<br>• Hydrophilic and hydrophobic matrices |
| (2) | First-order | $Q_t = Q_0(1 - e^{-k_1 t})$ | • Concentration-dependent release<br>• Diffusion control |
| (3) | Higuchi | $Q_t = k_H t^{0.5}$ | • Diffusion-controlled release<br>• Perfect sink conditions<br>• Sustained release<br>• Negligible swelling and erosion |
| (4) | Korsmeyer–Peppas | $Q_t = Kt^n, (Q_t \leq 60\%)$ | • Fickian diffusion (n < 0.45)<br>• Non-Fickian transport (0.45 < n < 0.89)<br>• Case II transport (n = 0.89)<br>• Super case II transport (n > 0.89) |
| (5) | Hopfenberg | $Q_t = Q_0(1 - (1 - \kappa t)^3)$ | Constant surface area |
| (6) | Hixson–Crowell | $W_t^{1/3} = W_0^{1/3} - k_w t$ | • Surface erosion and dissolution control |
| (7) | Gallagher–Corrigan | $Q_t = Q_0(1 - e^{-k_1 t}) + (Q_0 - Q_B)\frac{e^{k_2(t - t_{max})}}{1 + e^{k_2(t - t_{max})}}$ | • Initial burst release followed by gradual release |

In Table 11.1, $Q_t$ and $Q_0$ are the released drug percentages at time $t$ and the maximum released drug percentage, respectively, $W_t$ is the residual amount of drug in the carrier at time $t$, $k_w$ is a constant related to the surface to volume ratio of the carrier, $W_0$ is the initial amount of the drug in the carrier, $t_{max}$ is the time at which the maximum drug release rate is achieved, $Q_B$ is the fraction of the released drug in the first stage or the burst release fraction, $k_0$ and $k_1$ are the zero- and first-order rate constants, $k_H$ is the Higuchi dissolution constant, and $\kappa$ is the constant associated with polymer degradation or surface erosion process, initial drug loading, and geometry of the carrier (Fan et al., 2019; Dolinina et al., 2017).

As an example, the in vitro study of paclitaxel release from bovine serum albumin showed that the Gallagher-Corrigan model has the highest compatibility with experimental data. Interestingly, the model exhibited a three-phase release of the drug, including the burst release, lag phase, and final release of the drug (Lotfalian et al., 2021). Curve fitting of the kinetic models given in Table 11.1 is shown in Fig. 11.9.

## 4.5 Matrix degradation and cross-linking

The degradation of the HSA matrix, mediated by enzymatic or environmental factors, also contributes to drug release. Cross-linking with agents such as glutaraldehyde slows matrix breakdown, enabling sustained release (Sonvico et al., 2018). High-energy inputs during fabrication, such as ultrasonic or high-pressure homogenization, influence the degree of cross-linking in the albumin shell. The extent of this cross-linking impacts the rate of matrix degradation and drug release. A higher energy output typically results in a more stable shell, enabling slower and more controlled drug release (Adick et al., 2024).

## 4.6 Surface coatings for controlled release

Modifications with biopolymers such as chitosan coating enhance mucoadhesion and add a secondary barrier to diffusion, ensuring a slower and more controlled drug release. This is particularly beneficial for nasal or brain-targeted delivery systems (Bonferoni et al., 2010). The term "mucoadhesion" refers to the interaction between polymeric carriers and mucosal tissues. This property is observed in certain polymers that develop adhesive characteristics upon absorbing moisture (Ponchel et al., 1997). The silica coating acts as a critical element for controlled release, providing a biocompatible barrier that regulates the diffusion of drugs. This coating enhances the stability of the nanoparticles and ensures the gradual release of encapsulated agents, reducing the risk of drug burst release (Hosseinpour Moghadam et al., 2019).

Another surface modifications of HSA nanocarriers, such as PEGylation or functionalization with targeting ligands such as folic acid and antibodies, provide steric stability and prolongs circulation time by evading immune system recognition. These coatings enhance the biocompatibility of the nanocarriers and prevent premature drug release. Additionally, ligands facilitate specific interactions with overexpressed receptors on target cells, enabling active targeting to diseased tissues such as tumors. Advanced surface coatings, including biodegradable polymers and molecules such as chitosan or hyaluronic acid, contribute to better control of drug release. These materials not only stabilize the nanocarrier structure but also allow environmental responsiveness, such as pH-triggered drug release in acidic tumor microenvironments. Furthermore, the interaction between the coatings and the

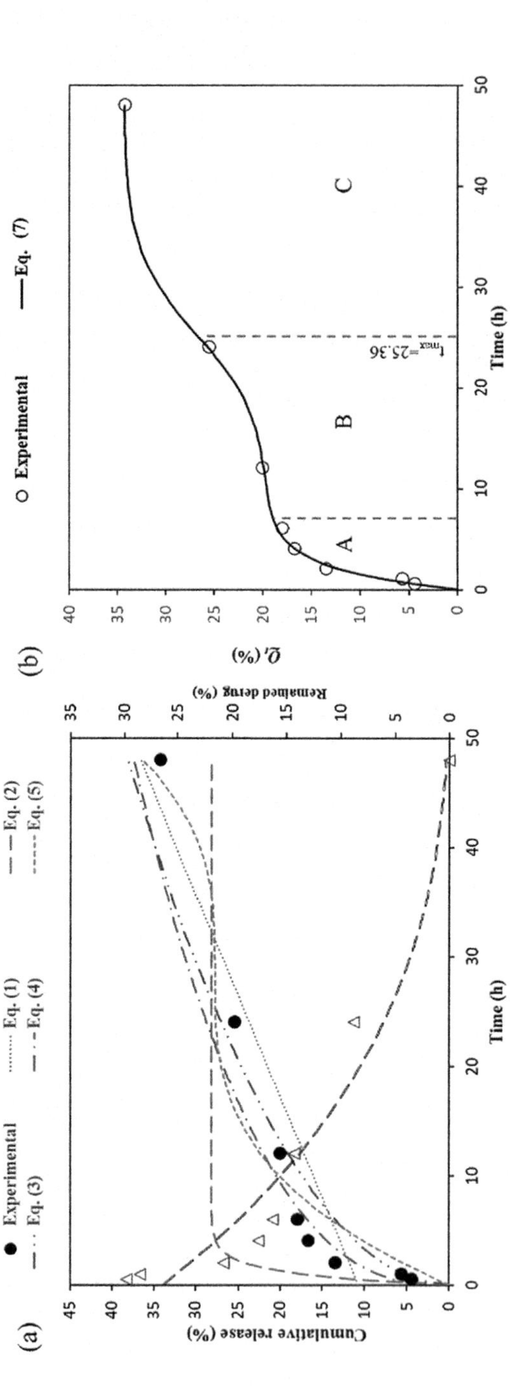


FIGURE 11.9 Experimental cumulative drug release and curve fitting of the kinetic models given in Table 1, (a) Eqs. (1)–(6), (b) Eq. (7) with the superiors regression coefficient of 0.992 (region A: Initial burst release, region B: Lag time, and region C: Final release). Reprinted from S. Lotfalian, A. Nematollahzadeh, S. Ghasemi, Hierarchically structured protein-based hollow-nanospheres for drug delivery, Reactive and Functional Polymers 160 (2021) 104821.

biological environment can enhance cellular uptake and endosomal escape, improving therapeutic efficacy (Zeeshan et al., 2021).

## 4.7 Conformational dynamics of HSA for drug delivery

The unique conformational plasticity of HSA, induced by interaction with nanoemulsions, plays a critical role in both drug loading and release. Key observations include a red shift in fluorescence emission maxima (approximately 3 nm), indicating that the hydrophobic Trp residue becomes more exposed to a hydrophilic environment. This exposure is linked to the gradual release of hydrophobic drugs from the HSA-bound nanoemulsion system, highlighting the potential of HSA-based nanocarriers for controlled and efficient drug delivery (Divsalar et al., 2012).

## 4.8 Applications in drug delivery

Nanoemulsions significantly improve the solubility of hydrophobic drugs, which often have poor water solubility (Lewinski et al., 2008). By encapsulating these drugs within the nanoemulsion droplets, their bioavailability and therapeutic efficiency are enhanced. Nanoemulsions, when combined with HSA, enhance the retention time of drugs within the circulatory system. This reduces the required dosage and frequency of drug administration, improving patient compliance. HSA is a natural carrier that binds to a variety of endogenous and exogenous compounds. When integrated with nanoemulsions, it can facilitate targeted delivery to specific tissues or cells. This is particularly useful for delivering anticancer or antiviral drugs where precise targeting is critical. Nanoemulsions can be adapted for various drug delivery routes, including oral, transdermal, and intravenous administration. Their small size and stability make them suitable for a wide range of applications.

## 4.9 Cancer therapy

Nanoemulsions can serve as carriers for hydrophobic chemotherapeutic agents, improving their solubility and reducing systemic toxicity. HSA's natural affinity for cancer cells due to increased albumin uptake ensures that the drug-carrier system is concentrated at tumor sites (Divsalar et al., 2012). HSA-based nanoparticles have been widely used in oncology for delivering chemotherapeutic agents to tumors. Functionalizing these nanoparticles with ligands such as antibodies or peptides enables active targeting of tumor cells, reducing systemic toxicity. For example, HSA nanoparticles loaded with paclitaxel have been developed to improve the efficacy and specificity of breast cancer treatment (Piazzini, Landucci, et al., 2019a).

The most prominent application of nab technology is in anticancer therapy, where it is used to deliver hydrophobic chemotherapeutic agents more effectively. Abraxane, an HSA-stabilized paclitaxel nanosuspension, exemplifies the success of this technology in oncology. By utilizing natural albumin transport pathways, such as gp60 receptor-mediated transcytosis and SPARC-mediated targeting, Abraxane achieves enhanced drug delivery to tumor tissues. These mechanisms improve drug accumulation at the tumor site, reduce systemic toxicity, and eliminate the need for toxic solubilizers, which are common in traditional formulations such as Taxol(Adick et al., 2024; Desai, 2007; Loureiro et al., 2016).

As shown in Fig. 11.10a, albumin is initially internalized by tumor cells through the glycoprotein receptor gp60, which facilitates its uptake as a nutrient. Once inside the tumor cells, albumin interacts with the secreted protein acidic and rich in cysteine (SPARC), an extracellular matrix (ECM) glycoprotein that is overexpressed in various tumor cells. This interaction between albumin and SPARC enhances the targeting and accumulation of albumin within the tumor stroma, promoting efficient drug delivery to tumor sites (Lei et al., 2021).

Similarly, HSA nanoparticles can bind specifically to receptors such as CD44 that are commonly overexpressed on cancer cells. This interaction facilitates the selective targeting of HSA-NPs to these cancer cells. When HSA-NPs attach to cancer cells, they can deliver therapeutic agents directly to the targeted cells, inhibiting their growth and preventing metastasis. This feature makes HSA NPs a promising drug delivery system for cancer therapy, as they leverage the specific binding properties of CD44 to enhance drug uptake and treatment efficacy (Fig. 11.10b) (Lei et al., 2021).

## 4.10 Antimicrobial and antiviral applications

Encapsulating antibiotics or antiviral agents within nanoemulsions protects them from enzymatic degradation in the bloodstream, enhancing their efficacy. The slow and controlled release ensures sustained therapeutic effects against infections (Divsalar et al., 2012). Studies indicate that nanoparticles modified with biocompatible coatings, such as silica and HSA, are capable of delivering antiviral drugs effectively. Drugs such as nevirapine, oseltamivir, and tenofovir, when loaded onto these carriers, maintain their therapeutic properties and exhibit controlled release profiles. This approach has been shown to improve the bioavailability and stability of antiviral agents, making them more effective in combating viral infections such as HIV and influenza (Hosseinpour Moghadam et al., 2019).

## 4.11 Drug delivery in chronic diseases

For chronic conditions requiring long-term treatment, such as diabetes or autoimmune diseases, HSA-based nanoemulsions ensure prolonged drug action and fewer side effects by maintaining a steady drug concentration (Divsalar et al., 2012). Recently, HSA-based drug cargo was developed to induce apoptosis in chronic lymphocytic leukemia patient cells by biomimetic cross-linking of CD20 and/or CD38 receptors on malignant B cells without the need for low-molecular-weight drugs (Li et al., 2024).

## 4.12 Applications in protein and gene delivery

Nanoemulsions combined with HSA can also be functionalized for the delivery of biomolecules such as proteins, peptides, or nucleic acids, broadening their use in emerging therapeutic modalities (Divsalar et al., 2012). Recently, a cationic HSA-based gene-delivery system containing plasmid DNA was proposed to overcome the drawbacks such as toxicity, immunogenicity, and low transfection efficiency of the traditional drug carriers.

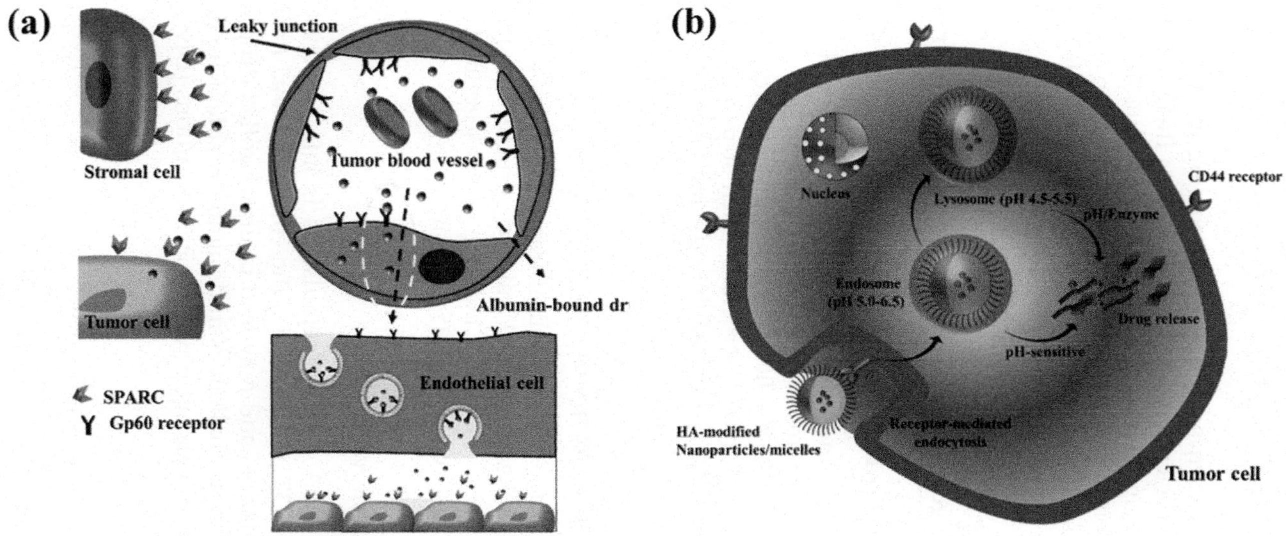


FIGURE 11.10 (a) Schematic of albumin uptake by tumor cells via gp60 and its interaction with SPARC for targeted drug delivery, and (b) interaction of HSA nanoparticles with CD44 receptors on cancer cells, promoting targeted drug delivery and inhibition of tumor growth and metastasis. *Reprinted from C. Lei, X.-R. Liu, Q.-B. Chen, Y. Li, J.-L. Zhou, L.-Y. Zhou, T. Zou, Hyaluronic acid and albumin-based nanoparticles for drug delivery, Journal of Controlled Release 331 (2021) 416-433.*

The drug carrier exhibited a desired antitumor effect in vivo, demonstrating a superior inhibition rate of 57.3% and significant upregulation in p53 protein (Guan et al., 2019).

### 4.13 Nose-to-brain drug delivery

HSA nanoparticles have shown potential in overcoming the BBB by utilizing the nasal route. Coating these nanoparticles with chitosan enhances their mucoadhesive properties, increasing the residence time in the nasal cavity and facilitating drug delivery to the brain through olfactory and trigeminal pathways. This strategy has been explored for the delivery of anti-Alzheimer's drugs such as tacrine and R-flurbiprofen, demonstrating improved bioavailability and targeted action (Mistry et al., 2009).

## 5. Challenges and limitations of HSA nanocarriers

### 5.1 Structural alterations in HSA

The interaction between HSA and nanoemulsions induces significant structural changes in the protein, as studies using fluorescence and circular dichroism (CD) have shown. These changes include a decrease in the α-helical content and an increase in β-sheet structures, indicating a partial loss of HSA's native structure. Such structural disruptions may affect the stability and functionality of HSA, potentially reducing its effectiveness as a drug carrier (Divsalar et al., 2012).

### 5.2 Protein unfolding and hydrophobic exposure

Nanoemulsions induce "inside-out" structural transformations in HSA, exposing its hydrophobic core to the external environment. While this structural change enhances the protein's drug-binding capacity, it may also increase its susceptibility to aggregation or degradation under physiological conditions (Sun et al., 2010).

### 5.3 Temperature-dependent variability

The interaction between HSA and nanoemulsions is influenced by temperature, with higher temperatures, such as 37 °C, increasing the conformational flexibility of HSA. This results in faster structural changes and may lead to uncontrolled drug release. The temperature sensitivity of HSA presents challenges in designing stable drug delivery systems that can perform consistently under varying physiological conditions (Divsalar et al., 2012; Lieberman et al., 2020).

### 5.4 Risk of saturation in drug binding

As nanoemulsion concentration increases, HSA's drug-binding sites become saturated. Beyond a certain threshold, no further drug molecules can bind to the carrier, which limits its loading capacity and efficiency in high-dose therapies (Divsalar et al., 2012).

## 5.5 Potential immunogenicity of modified systems

Although HSA is naturally nonimmunogenic, structural modifications resulting from its interaction with nanoemulsions could potentially alter its immunogenic profile. The exposure of hydrophobic regions or changes in its structure might trigger unintended immune responses, especially in sensitive individuals.

## 5.6 Complexity of nanoemulsion design

The preparation of nanoemulsions with precise size and uniformity demands specialized equipment and strict control over parameters such as surfactant concentration, temperature, and mixing speed. Variability in these factors can result in inconsistencies in particle size and drug loading efficiency, posing challenges for large-scale production (Solans et al., 2005).

## 5.7 Environmental sensitivity

The efficacy of HSA-based nanocarriers is influenced by factors such as pH and ionic strength, which can vary across different biological environments. For instance, in acidic tumor microenvironments or inflamed tissues, the structural integrity of HSA may be compromised, potentially impacting its performance as a drug carrier (Divsalar et al., 2012; Solans et al., 2005).

## 5.8 Challenges in nose-to-brain drug delivery

While nose-to-brain drug delivery route is potentially for treating neurological disorders, various critical challenges are encountered in drug delivery through the nose-to-brain strategy, which restrict its success in clinical practice, including:

- **Blood–brain barrier (BBB):** The BBB is a selective permeability barrier that prevents most hydrophilic molecules and high-molecular-weight compounds from entering the brain. This characteristic presents a fundamental obstacle for effective drug delivery (Piazzini, Cinci, et al., 2019b).
- **Anatomical barriers:** The small volume of the nasal cavity restricts the amount of drug that can be delivered at one time (Sonvico et al., 2018).
- **Mucociliary clearance:** This natural defense mechanism reduces drug retention time, impacting the efficacy of NTB delivery systems (Agrawal et al., 2018).
- **Enzymatic degradation:** Enzymes present in the nasal cavity can degrade drugs before they reach their target (Feng et al., 2018).
- **Nasomucosal toxicity:** Prolonged exposure to certain nanoparticles may induce toxicity, necessitating careful material selection (Sonvico et al., 2018).
- **Device dependency:** Effective NTB delivery often requires specialized administration devices to ensure accurate drug deposition (Piazzini, Landucci, et al., 2019a).

# 6. Future perspectives of HSA-based nanoemulsions

## 6.1 Optimizing nanoemulsion–HSA interactions

The interaction between nanoemulsions and HSA causes structural transformations in the protein, such as exposure of hydrophobic regions and partial unfolding. While these changes enhance drug loading, future research can focus on refining the interaction to balance stability and binding efficiency. Engineering nanoemulsions to minimize undesirable structural disruptions in HSA could improve the overall performance of these drug delivery systems. Future research is focused on enhancing the interactions between nanoemulsions and HSA by optimizing surface modifications such as chitosan coating. These modifications improve drug retention, mucoadhesion, and permeability, making the delivery systems more effective for applications such as NTB drug delivery (Piazzini, Landucci, et al., 2019a).

## 6.2 Enhancing stability in biological systems

Nanoemulsions often face stability challenges in the bloodstream due to enzymatic activity and interactions with other biomolecules. Future studies could explore innovative surface modifications or encapsulation techniques to improve the stability and circulation time of HSA-based carriers. Freeze-drying with cryoprotectants such as sucrose has been shown to improve the stability of HSA-based systems. This approach ensures that nanoemulsions retain their physical and chemical properties in complex biological environments and during storage (Piazzini, Landucci, et al., 2019a). Strategies such as advanced cross-linking techniques, incorporation of stabilizing agents, and surface modifications can be used to reduce aggregation, maintain particle size, and prevent premature drug release (Zeeshan et al., 2021).

## 6.3 Development of stimuli-responsive systems

HSA's structural flexibility makes it a suitable platform for stimuli-responsive drug delivery systems. Researchers could design HSA-nanoemulsion systems that release drugs in response to specific environmental triggers such as pH, temperature, or enzymatic activity, ensuring precise targeting of diseased tissues such as tumors. This approach not only enhances therapeutic efficacy but also minimizes off-target effects, making the delivery systems more efficient and safer (Zeeshan et al., 2021).

## 6.4 Functionalization for targeted delivery

Functionalizing HSA-based nanoemulsions with ligands such as peptides, antibodies, or aptamers could enhance their targeting capabilities. For example, targeted delivery to cancer cells or inflamed tissues could be improved by incorporating surface markers that interact specifically with receptors on these cells.

## 6.5 Expanding applications beyond drug delivery

Beyond traditional drug delivery, HSA–nanoemulsion systems could find applications in gene therapy, vaccine delivery, and diagnostic imaging. Combining HSA carriers with diagnostic agents could enable theranostic platforms, where the system simultaneously delivers therapeutic agents and monitors disease progression.

### 6.6 Scale-up and manufacturing challenges

While the preparation methods described in the article are effective for lab-scale production, future efforts could focus on scaling up these processes for industrial applications. Developing cost-effective and reproducible techniques for nanoemulsion synthesis could make these systems commercially viable. Scalability remains a significant challenge. Improvements in manufacturing processes, including the use of cryoprotectants and optimization of freeze-drying techniques, are essential for large-scale production (Piazzini, Landucci, et al., 2019a).

### 6.7 Reducing side effects and immunogenicity

The structural modifications in HSA caused by nanoemulsions may potentially alter its immunogenicity. Future studies should investigate how to mitigate immune responses while preserving drug delivery efficiency, ensuring safer clinical applications.

### 6.8 Combining HSA nanocarriers with emerging technologies

Integrating HSA-based nanocarriers with artificial intelligence (AI) and machine learning could optimize their design, predicting ideal particle sizes, drug release profiles, and targeting strategies. AI can contribute to HSA nanocarriers design, synthesis, and applications through several ways, including providing data-driven insights by analyzing extensive datasets from previous studies on HSA formulations. It can also facilitate the development of predictive models for HSA-based drug carriers according their composition and structure, identifying the best combination of formulation parameters such as pH, ionic strength, concentration, and temperature, and improve molecular dynamics (MD) simulations and design of experiments (DOE) to model the interactions between HSA and drugs. Employing AI can enable researchers to implement real-time monitoring of synthesis procedures, and integrate the processes with omics data. These advancements may also accelerate the development of personalized medicine by tailoring HSA–nanoemulsion systems to individual patient needs (Gholap et al., 2024).

## 7. Conclusion

HSA-based nanocarriers have attracted attention as one of the leading platforms in targeted drug delivery due to their high biocompatibility, long half-life, and ability to bind to a variety of drugs. In this chapter, by collecting and analyzing the research conducted, various synthesis methods of these nanocarriers, including separation, nab technology, emulsification, and surface modification, were investigated, each of which offers its own advantages and limitations in optimizing the size, stability, and drug loading. According to previous studies, the drug loading and release mechanisms in these nanocarriers are affected by hydrophobic interactions, ionic bonds, and structural changes in HSA, which can significantly affect the efficiency of drug delivery. The findings have shown that these nanocarriers are particularly effective in anticancer drug delivery, because albumin accumulates in tumors through the gp60 receptor and SPARC protein, increasing the effectiveness of treatment. In addition, studies have shown that these systems also perform well in delivering antiviral drugs and treating chronic diseases such as diabetes and Alzheimer's. Also, the high potential of albumin nanoparticles to cross the BBB via the nose–brain route has attracted attention for their use in the treatment of neurological diseases.

Despite these advantages, previous studies have pointed out challenges such as structural changes in HSA, saturable drug binding sites, limited stability in biological conditions, and difficulties in industrial-scale production. In addition, the possibility of immune responses due to structural changes in albumin protein is an issue that requires more detailed preclinical research. Based on the analysis of the studies conducted, optimization of these nanocarriers can be achieved through the development of environmentally sensitive systems, surface modifications for active targeting, and improved stability in biological environments. Also, combining this technology with AI-based methods can improve the design of nanomedicines and enable the development of personalized therapies. Overall, the summary of the research shows that HSA nanocarriers, with appropriate modifications, have a high potential for transformation into targeted drug delivery systems and can be considered as one of the new solutions in the treatment of complex diseases in the future.

## References

Adick, A., Werner, H., Schneid, S., Hester, S., Langer, K., 2024. Development of a screening platform for the formulation of poorly water-soluble drugs as albumin-stabilized nanosuspensions using nab™ technology. Int. J. Pharm. 662, 124491. https://doi.org/10.1016/j.ijpharm.2024.124491.

Agrawal, M., Saraf, S., Saraf, S., Antimisiaris, S.G., Chougule, M.B., Shoyele, S.A., Alexander, A., 2018. Nose-to-brain drug delivery: an update on clinical challenges and progress towards approval of anti-Alzheimer drugs. J. Contr. Release 281, 139–177. https://doi.org/10.1016/j.jconrel.2018.05.011.

Anhorn, M.G., Mahler, H.C., Langer, K., 2008. Freeze drying of human serum albumin (HSA) nanoparticles with different excipients. Int. J. Pharm. 363 (1–2), 162–169. https://doi.org/10.1016/j.ijpharm.2008.07.004.

Ashraf, S., Qaiser, H., Tariq, S., Khalid, A., Makeen, H.A., Alhazmi, H.A., Ul-Haq, Z., 2023. Unraveling the versatility of human serum albumin – a comprehensive review of its biological significance and therapeutic potential. Current Research in Structural Biology 6. https://doi.org/10.1016/j.crstbi.2023.100114.

Bonferoni, M.C., Sandri, G., Ferrari, F., Rossi, S., Larghi, V., Zambito, Y., Caramella, C., 2010. Comparison of different in vitro and ex vivo methods to evaluate mucoadhesion of glycol-palmitoyl chitosan micelles. J. Drug Deliv. Sci. Technol. 20 (6), 419–424. https://doi.org/10.1016/s1773-2247(10)50073-x.

Chamani, J., Asoodeh, A., Homayoni-Tabrizi, M., Amiri Tehranizadeh, Z., Baratian, A., Saberi, M.R., Gharanfoli, M., 2010. Spectroscopic and nano-molecular modeling investigation on the binary and ternary bindings of colchicine and lomefloxacin to Human serum albumin with the viewpoint of multi-drug therapy. J. Lumin. 130 (12), 2476–2486. https://doi.org/10.1016/j.jlumin.2010.08.016.

Curry, S., 2009. Japanese society for the study of xenobiotics United Kingdom lessons from the crystallographic analysis of small molecule binding to human serum albumin. Drug Metabol. Pharmacokinet. 4, 342–357. https://doi.org/10.2133/dmpk.24.342.

Desai, N., 2007. Nab technology: a drug delivery platform utilising endothelial gp60 receptor-based transport and tumour-derived SPARC for targeting. Drug Delivery Report 16, 37–41.

N.P. Desai, C. Tao, A. Yang, L. Louie, T. Zheng, Z. Yao, P. Soon-Shiong, S. Magdassi, Protein stabilized pharmacologically active agents, methods for the preparation thereof and methods for the use thereof. Google Patents, Google Patents, (1999).

Divsalar, A., Saboury, A.A., Nabiuni, M., Zare, Z., Kefayati, M.E., Seyedarabi, A., 2012. Characterization and side effect analysis of a newly designed nanoemulsion targeting human serum albumin for drug delivery. Colloids Surf. B Biointerfaces 98, 80–84. https://doi.org/10.1016/j.colsurfb.2012.04.036.

Dolinina, E.S., Vlasenkova, M.I., Parfenyuk, E.V., 2017. Effect of trehalose on structural state of bovine serum albumin adsorbed onto mesoporous silica and the protein release kinetics in vitro. Colloids Surf. A Physicochem. Eng. Asp. 527, 101–108. https://doi.org/10.1016/j.colsurfa.2017.05.014.

Fan, Y., Zheng, X., Ali, Y., Berggren, P.O., Loo, S.C.J., 2019. Local release of rapamycin by microparticles delays islet rejection within the anterior chamber of the eye. Sci. Rep. 9 (1). https://doi.org/10.1038/s41598-019-40404-0.

Feng, Y., He, H., Li, F., Lu, Y., Qi, J., Wu, W., 2018. An update on the role of nanovehicles in nose-to-brain drug delivery. Drug Discov. Today 23 (5), 1079–1088. https://doi.org/10.1016/j.drudis.2018.01.005.

Gholap, A.D., Uddin, M.J., Faiyazuddin, M., Omri, A., Gowri, S., Khalid, M., 2024. Advances in artificial intelligence for drug delivery and development: a comprehensive review. Comput. Biol. Med. 178. https://doi.org/10.1016/j.compbiomed.2024.108702.

Ghuman, J., Zunszain, P.A., Petitpas, I., Bhattacharya, A.A., Otagiri, M., Curry, S., 2005. Structural basis of the drug-binding specificity of human serum albumin. J. Mol. Biol. 353 (1), 38–52. https://doi.org/10.1016/j.jmb.2005.07.075.

Guan, G., Song, B., Zhang, J., Chen, K., Hu, H., Wang, M., Chen, D., 2019. An effective cationic human serum albumin-based gene-delivery carrier containing the nuclear localization signal. Pharmaceutics 11 (11), 608. https://doi.org/10.3390/pharmaceutics11110608.

Guccione, C., Oufir, M., Piazzini, V., Eigenmann, D.E., Jähne, E.A., Zabela, V., Faleschini, M.T., Bergonzi, M.C., Smiesko, M., Hamburger, M., Bilia, A.R., 2017. Andrographolide-loaded nanoparticles for brain delivery: Formulation, characterisation and in vitro permeability using hCMEC/D3 cell line. Eur. J. Pharm. Biopharm. 119, 253–263. https://doi.org/10.1016/j.ejpb.2017.06.018.

Haji-Khorasani, A.N.P., Safajou-Jahankhanemlou, M., 2025. Competitive separation of mixed antibiotics from aqueous solutions via polyvinylpyridine-modified magnetic adsorbent. Separ. Sci. Technol. 60 (8), 956–975.

Hakala, T.A., Davies, S., Toprakcioglu, Z., Bernardim, B., Bernardes, G.J.L., Knowles, T.P.J., 2020. A microfluidic co-flow route for human serum albumin-drug–nanoparticle assembly. Chem. Eur J. 26 (27), 5965–5969. https://doi.org/10.1002/chem.202001146.

Harshita, Barkat, M.A., Beg, S., Pottoo, F.H., Ahmad, F.J., 2019. Nanopaclitaxel therapy: an evidence based review on the battle for next-generation formulation challenges. Nanomedicine 14 (10), 1323–1341. https://doi.org/10.2217/nnm-2018-0313.

Hassanzadeh, S., Ali, N., Mirzayi, B., Fatemeh Kaboli, S., 2021. Protein-based nanoparticles synthesized at a high shear rate and optimized for drug delivery applications. J. Mol. Liq. 335, 116133. https://doi.org/10.1016/j.molliq.2021.116133.

Hosseinpour Moghadam, N., Salehzadeh, S., Rakhtshah, J., Hosseinpour Moghadam, A., Tanzadehpanah, H., Saidijam, M., 2019. Preparation of a highly stable drug carrier by efficient immobilization of human serum albumin (HSA) on drug-loaded magnetic iron oxide nanoparticles. Int. J. Biol. Macromol. 125, 931–940. https://doi.org/10.1016/j.ijbiomac.2018.12.143.

Jayasree, A., Sasidharan, S., Koyakutty, M., Nair, S., Menon, D., 2011. Mannosylated chitosan-zinc sulphide nanocrystals as fluorescent bioprobes for targeted cancer imaging. Carbohydr. Polym. 85 (1), 37–43. https://doi.org/10.1016/j.carbpol.2011.01.034.

Jithan, A.V., Madhavi, K., Madhavi, M., Prabhakar, K., 2011. Preparation and characterization of albumin nanoparticles encapsulating curcumin intended for the treatment of breast cancer. International Journal of Pharmaceutical Investigation 1 (2), 119. https://doi.org/10.4103/2230-973x.82432.

Kaboli, S.F., Mehrnejad, F., Ali, N., 2021. Molecular modeling prediction of albumin-based nanoparticles and experimental preparation, characterization, and in-vitro release kinetics of prednisolone from the nanoparticles. J. Drug Deliv. Sci. Technol. 64, 102588. https://doi.org/10.1016/j.jddst.2021.102588.

Kragh-Hansen, U., 1990. Structure and ligand binding properties of human serum albumin. Dan. Med. Bull. 37 (1), 57–84.

Kratz, F., 2008. Albumin as a drug carrier: Design of prodrugs, drug conjugates and nanoparticles. J. Contr. Release 132 (3), 171–183. https://doi.org/10.1016/j.jconrel.2008.05.010.

Langer, K., Balthasar, S., Vogel, V., Dinauer, N., von Briesen, H., Schubert, D., 2003. Optimization of the preparation process for human serum albumin (HSA) nanoparticles. Int. J. Pharm. 257 (1–2), 169–180. https://doi.org/10.1016/s0378-5173(03)00134-0.

Lei, C., Liu, X.R., Chen, Q.B., Li, Y., Zhou, J.L., Zhou, L.Y., Zou, T., 2021. Hyaluronic acid and albumin based nanoparticles for drug delivery. J. Contr. Release 331, 416–433. https://doi.org/10.1016/j.jconrel.2021.01.033.

Lewinski, N., Colvin, V., Drezek, R., 2008. Cytotoxicity of nanopartides. Small 4 (1), 26–49. https://doi.org/10.1002/smll.200700595.

Li, J., Gambles, M.T., Jones, B., Williams, J.A., Camp, N.J., Shami, P.J., Yang, J., Kopeček, J., 2024. Human serum albumin-based drug-free macromolecular therapeutics induce apoptosis in chronic lymphocytic leukemia patient cells by crosslinking of CD20 and/or CD38 receptors. Drug Deliv. Transl. Res. 14 (8), 2203–2215. https://doi.org/10.1007/s13346-024-01629-3.

Lieberman, H., Rieger, M., Banker, G.S., 2020. Pharmaceutical Dosage Forms: Disperse Systems. CRC Press, USA.

Likhodii, S.S., Serbanescu, I., Cortez, M.A., Murphy, P., Snead, O.C., Burnham, W.M.I., 2003. Anticonvulsant properties of acetone, a brain ketone elevated by the ketogenic diet. Ann. Neurol. 54 (2), 219–226. https://doi.org/10.1002/ana.10634.

Lotfalian, S., Ali, N., Ghasemi, S., 2021. Hierarchically structured protein-based hollow-nanospheres for drug delivery. React. Funct. Polym. 160, 104821. https://doi.org/10.1016/j.reactfunctpolym.2021.104821.

Loureiro, A., Azoia, N.G., Gomes, A.C., Cavaco-Paulo, A., 2016. Albumin-based nanodevices as drug carriers. Curr. Pharm. Des. 22 (10), 1371–1390. https://doi.org/10.2174/1381612822666160125114900.

Matulis, D., Baumann, C.G., Bloomfield, V.A., Lovrien, R.E., 1999. 1-Anilino-8-naphthalene sulfonate as a protein conformational tightening agent. Biopolymers 49 (6), 451–458. https://doi.org/10.1002/(SICI)1097-0282(199905)49:6<451::AID-BIP3>3.0.CO;2-6.

Meredith, L., Chao, T., Nevler, A., Basu Mallick, A., Singla, R.K., McCue, P.A., Bowne, W.B., Jiang, W., 2023. A rare metastatic mesenteric malignant PEComa with TSC2 mutation treated with palliative surgical resection and nab-sirolimus: a case report. Diagn. Pathol. 18 (1). https://doi.org/10.1186/s13000-023-01323-x.

Mirzayi, B., Nematollahzadeh, A., Seraj, S., 2015. Synthesis and characterization of magnetic maghemite/catecholamine core/shell nanoparticles. Powder Technol. 270, 185–191. https://doi.org/10.1016/j.powtec.2014.10.022.

Mistry, A., Stolnik, S., Illum, L., 2009. Nanoparticles for direct nose-to-brain delivery of drugs. Int. J. Pharm. 379 (1–2), 146–157. https://doi.org/10.1016/j.ijpharm.2009.06.019.

Mohammad-Beigi, H., Shojaosadati, S.A., Morshedi, D., Mirzazadeh, N., Arpanaei, A., 2016. The effects of organic solvents on the physicochemical properties of human serum albumin nanoparticles. Iran. J. Biotechnol. 14 (1), 45–50. https://doi.org/10.15171/ijb.1168.

Naik, P.N., Chimatadar, S.A., Nandibewoor, S.T., 2010. Interaction between a potent corticosteroid drug – dexamethasone with bovine serum albumin and human serum albumin: a fluorescence quenching and fourier transformation infrared spectroscopy study. J. Photochem. Photobiol. B Biol. 100 (3), 147–159. https://doi.org/10.1016/j.jphotobiol.2010.05.014.

Neault, J.F., Tajmir-Riahi, H.A., 1998. Interaction of cisplatin with human serum albumin. Drug binding mode and protein secondary structure. Biochim. Biophys. Acta Protein Struct. Mol. Enzymol. 1384 (1), 153–159. https://doi.org/10.1016/s0167-4838(98)00011-9.

Nematollahzadeh, A., Harzand, F.V., Vaseghi, Z., 2023. Sustained Drug Delivery—The Nano Advantage Materials Horizons: from Nature to Nanomaterials. Springer Nature, Iran, pp. 93–110. https://doi.org/10.1007/978-981-19-8718-2_5.

Piazzini, V., Landucci, E., D'Ambrosio, M., Tiozzo Fasiolo, L., Cinci, L., Colombo, G., Pellegrini-Giampietro, D.E., Bilia, A.R., Luceri, C., Bergonzi, M.C., 2019a. Chitosan coated human serum albumin nanoparticles: a promising strategy for nose-to-brain drug delivery. Int. J. Biol. Macromol. 129, 267–280. https://doi.org/10.1016/j.ijbiomac.2019.02.005.

Piazzini, V., Cinci, L., D'ambrosio, M., Luceri, C., Bilia, A.R., Bergonzi, M.C., 2019b. Solid lipid nanoparticles and chitosan-coated solid lipid nanoparticles as promising tool for silybin delivery: Formulation, characterization, and in vitro evaluation. Curr. Drug Deliv. 16 (2), 142–152. https://doi.org/10.2174/1567201815666181008153602.

Ponchel, G., Montisci, M.J., Dembri, A., Durrer, C., Duchêne, D., 1997. France Mucoadhesion of colloidal particulate systems in the gastro-intestinal tract. Eur. J. Pharm. Biopharm. 44 (1), 25–31. https://doi.org/10.1016/S0939-6411(97)00098-2.

Razavi, M.S., Nematollahzadeh, A., 2025. Advances in Microfluidics for Biomedical Engineering Applications. Elsevier BV, pp. 301–327. https://doi.org/10.1016/b978-0-323-95292-7.00028-1.

Razavi, M.S., Golmohammadi, A., Nematollahzadeh, A., Rovera, C., Farris, S., 2022. Cinnamon essential oil encapsulated into a fish gelatin-bacterial cellulose nanocrystals complex and active films thereof. Food Biophys. 17 (1), 38–46. https://doi.org/10.1007/s11483-021-09696-6.

Saleh Iman, S.P., Nematollahzadeh, A., Soltani Toularoud, A.A., 2024. Bioinspired catecholamine-based polymer coating stability and biodegradation in living soil. J. Polym. Environ. 32 (1), 81–93. https://doi.org/10.1007/s10924-023-02950-7.

Schippers, P.H., Dekkers, H.P.J.M., 1981. Direct determination of absolute circular dichroism data and calibration of commercial instruments. Anal. Chem. 53 (6), 778–782. https://doi.org/10.1021/ac00229a008.

Solans, C., Izquierdo, P., Nolla, J., Azemar, N., Garcia-Celma, M.J., 2005. Nano-emulsions. Curr. Opin. Colloid Interface Sci. 10 (3–4), 102–110. https://doi.org/10.1016/j.cocis.2005.06.004.

Sonvico, F., Clementino, A., Buttini, F., Colombo, G., Pescina, S., Stanisçuaski Guterres, S., Raffin Pohlmann, A., Nicoli, S., 2018. Surface-modified nanocarriers for nose-to-brain delivery: from bioadhesion to targeting. Pharmaceutics 10 (1), 34. https://doi.org/10.3390/pharmaceutics10010034.

Stöber, W., Fink, A., Bohn, E., 1968. Controlled growth of monodisperse silica spheres in the micron size range. J. Colloid Interface Sci. 26 (1), 62–69. https://doi.org/10.1016/0021-9797(68)90272-5.

Sun, Q., Gu, H., Zeng, Y., Xia, Y., Wang, Y., Jing, Y., Yang, L., Wang, B., 2010. Hsa-mir-27a genetic variant contributes to gastric cancer susceptibility through affecting miR-27a and target gene expression. Cancer Sci. 101 (10), 2241–2247. https://doi.org/10.1111/j.1349-7006.2010.01667.x.

Sun, Y., Lee, R.J., Meng, F., Wang, G., Zheng, X., Dong, S., Teng, L., 2020. Microfluidic self-assembly of high cabazitaxel loading albumin nanoparticles. Nanoscale 12 (32), 16928–16933. https://doi.org/10.1039/c9nr10941b.

Tao, H.Y., Wang, R.Q., Sheng, W.J., Zhen, Y.S., 2021. The development of human serum albumin-based drugs and relevant fusion proteins for cancer therapy. Int. J. Biol. Macromol. 187, 24–34. https://doi.org/10.1016/j.ijbiomac.2021.07.080.

Vogel, S.M., Minshall, R.D., Pilipović, M., Tiruppathi, C., Malik, A.B., 2001. Albumin uptake and transcytosis in endothelial cells in vivo induced by albumin-binding protein. Am. J. Physiol. Lung Cell. Mol. Physiol. 281 (6), L1512. https://doi.org/10.1152/ajplung.2001.281.6.l1512.

Von Storp, B., Engel, A., Boeker, A., Ploeger, M., Langer, K., 2012. Albumin nanoparticles with predictable size by desolvation procedure. J. Microencapsul. 29 (2), 138–146. https://doi.org/10.3109/02652048.2011.635218.

Weber, C., Coester, C., Kreuter, J., Langer, K., 2000. Desolvation process and surface characterisation of protein nanoparticles. Int. J. Pharm. 194 (1), 91–102. https://doi.org/10.1016/s0378-5173(99)00370-1.

Wilson, B., Lavanya, Y., Priyadarshini, S.R.B., Ramasamy, M., Jenita, J.L., 2014. Albumin nanoparticles for the delivery of gabapentin: Preparation, characterization and pharmacodynamic studies. Int. J. Pharm. 473 (1–2), 73–79. https://doi.org/10.1016/j.ijpharm.2014.05.056.

Yang, F., Bian, C., Zhu, L., Zhao, G., Huang, Z., Huang, M., 2007. Effect of human serum albumin on drug metabolism: Structural evidence of esterase activity of human serum albumin. J. Struct. Biol. 157 (2), 348–355. https://doi.org/10.1016/j.jsb.2006.08.015.

Yang, F., Zhang, Y., Liang, H., 2014. Interactive association of drugs binding to human serum albumin. Int. J. Mol. Sci. 15 (3), 3580–3595. https://doi.org/10.3390/ijms15033580.

Zeeshan, F., Madheswaran, T., Panneerselvam, J., Taliyan, R., Kesharwani, P., 2021. Human serum albumin as multifunctional nanocarrier for cancer therapy. J. Pharmaceut. Sci. 110 (9), 3111–3117. https://doi.org/10.1016/j.xphs.2021.05.001.

CHAPTER

# 12

# Bovine serum albumin-based nanocarriers for drug delivery

*Davi Siqueira da Silva de Souza*[1], *Giovana Cristina Zambuzi*[2], *Gabriela Bevilaqua*[3], *Rafael César Russo Chagas*[4], *Lucimara Lopes Da Silva*[5] and *Kelly Roberta Francisco*[1, 2]

**[1]Center for Science and Technologies for Sustainability, Federal University of São Carlos, Sorocaba, SP, Brazil; [2]Center for Natural and Human Sciences, Federal University of ABC, Santo André, SP, Brazil; [3]Department of Physical Chemistry, Institute of Chemistry, State University of Campinas (UNICAMP), Campinas, SP, Brazil; [4]Laboratory of Biosorption and Chemical Synthesis - Labiosin, Federal University of São João del Rei (UFSJ), Divinópolis, MG, Brazil; [5]Department of Chemical Engineering, Federal University of Technology - Paraná, Londrina, PR, Brazil**

## 1. Introduction

Controlled drug release refers to delivering pharmaceutical agents at a predetermined rate over a specified period, enhancing therapeutic efficacy while minimizing side effects. This approach contrasts with traditional drug delivery systems, which often result in fluctuating plasma drug levels. Various technologies can be utilized, including matrix tablets and osmotic systems, to maintain consistent drug concentrations, making it easier for patients to adhere to medication schedules and, thus, improving therapeutic outcomes (Shinde et al., 2024). By maintaining drug levels within the therapeutic range, these systems also minimize side effects, reducing the risk of adverse reactions (Swarnalatha et al., 2024). Furthermore, controlled release systems enhance drug stability by protecting the active ingredients from degradation, ensuring their effectiveness over time (Shinde et al., 2024).

Despite these advantages, challenges remain, particularly in achieving targeted delivery and managing complex pharmacokinetics, which add to the difficulty in developing

*Protein-Based Nanoparticles in Drug Delivery*
**https://doi.org/10.1016/B978-0-443-33639-3.00014-3**

effective controlled drug release systems (Palakurthi et al., 2024). To overcome such challenges, nanocarriers have been used as advanced drug delivery systems that utilize nanotechnology to enhance the efficacy and targeting of therapeutic agents, addressing limitations of traditional delivery methods and making them suitable for various medical applications. The advanced mechanism of nanocarriers' action is enhanced targeting, where they can be engineered to bind specifically to target cells. This targeted approach increases the precision of drug delivery, improving therapeutic outcomes by ensuring that drugs interact with the intended cells and tissues. Additionally, nanocarriers can overcome biological barriers, making them suitable for various routes of administration, including transdermal, injectable, and oral applications. Examples of successful transport across barriers are in the stratum corneum in transdermal applications and blood–brain barrier, which facilitates deeper penetration and improved absorption of drugs through the skin (Abdoh et al., 2024) and across the brain for treating neurological conditions. In this last example, nanocarriers enhance therapeutic efficacy while minimizing side effects, playing a crucial role in developing nano-assisted therapies for brain disorders like tumors, stroke, and neurodegeneration (Liu et al., 2024a).

Nanocarriers are typically sized in nanometers, including organic and inorganic structures (Cao et al., 2024), which facilitate improved solubility, bioavailability, high binding capacity, biodegradability, low cytotoxicity, and controlled release of drugs. Their unique properties allow for better penetration through biological barriers, making them suitable for various routes of administration, including transdermal, injectable, and oral applications. We can mention micelles, dendrimers, liposomes, solid lipid nanoparticles, nanogels, nanoemulsions, polymeric micelles, nanofibers, and proteins as organic release structures. Among all these, proteins have gained significant attention in nanomedicine as nanocarriers due to their biocompatibility, biodegradability, low cytotoxicity, and ability to enhance the delivery of various therapeutic agents (Solanki and Patel, 2023). Protein nanocarriers can also effectively encapsulate drugs, improve stability, and facilitate targeted delivery, making them suitable for applications in vaccine development, transdermal delivery, and phytoconstituent transport. Also, they enhance the stability of encapsulated proteins and phytoconstituents, addressing issues like poor solubility and rapid clearance (Solanki and Patel, 2023). Some examples are the silk protein fibroin, known for its biocompatibility and mechanical strength, widely used in drug delivery systems (Hong et al., 2020); the soy globulins (7 and 11S), which can be complexed with folic acid to form nanocarriers with high binding affinity and potential applications in nutraceuticals (Ochnio et al., 2018); and albumin, frequently employed due to its effective drug encapsulation capabilities and nontoxic nature, providing a stable and safe medium for therapeutic delivery (Verma et al., 2018).

The use of bovine serum albumin (BSA) as a nanocarrier will be emphasized in this chapter. This protein has emerged as a versatile nanocarrier in drug delivery systems due to its biocompatibility, ease of modification, and ability to encapsulate various therapeutic agents. BSA nanoparticles (BSA-NPs) can be engineered for specific applications, enhancing the efficacy of drug delivery while minimizing side effects. One of the primary applications of BSA-NPs is to deliver antituberculosis drugs. BSA-NPs have been successfully synthesized to immobilize isoniazid and rifampicin, with an encapsulation efficiency of 89% for rifampicin. These nanoparticles demonstrated a controlled release profile, making them particularly suitable for tuberculosis treatment (Yessentayeva et al., 2024). Another key application is in nasal drug administration, where BSA-NPs have been optimized to exhibit high mucoadhesive properties, with a 67% mucin binding efficiency, and rapid drug release (88.15%–95.47% within 4 h) (Mardikasari et al., 2023b).

Albumin also stands out as a possibility for overcoming challenges in the development of antitumor drugs, such as low water solubility, weak targeting of most antitumor drugs, poor bioavailability, and major adverse reactions. Overcoming such challenges means reducing systemic side effects, tumor resistance, and hyperprogression during drug treatment, which limits the effective use of these drugs (Li et al., 2024). Due to their numerous advantages, albumin-based nanodelivery systems have attracted significant attention from researchers, particularly in the field of oncology. Albumin is the most abundant protein in plasma, accounting for roughly 50% of the total plasma proteins. In the physiological environment, it functions as a natural transport carrier in the bloodstream, exhibiting multifunctionality by reversibly binding to a wide range of endogenous and exogenous molecules, such as long-chain fatty acids, bilirubin, iron, calcium, taxanes, sulfonamides, and various drugs, which are subsequently delivered to different tissues (Kouchakzadeh et al., 2015).

BSA-based nanocarriers have been designed to respond to tumor microenvironments, delivering drugs such as doxorubicin and copper ions for combined chemotherapy and chemodynamic therapy. This approach leverages the unique conditions of tumors to enhance therapeutic efficacy. Furthermore, BSA nanohydrogels, created via inverse nanoemulsion, have shown potential for encapsulating a variety of cargos, including drugs and nucleic acids, for diverse biomedical applications (Sihler et al., 2023).

Given the relevance of the theme described in this introductory section, this chapter aims to provide a concise overview of the global panorama of scientific research related to the use of BSA as a nanocarrier in drug release and the relevant BSA characteristics to its use as a nanocarrier, indicating the synthesis routes and describing the drug delivery systems using BSA protein as a nanocarrier in pharmacology, cell imaging, and theranostics (therapy + diagnostics) in the health field. Finally, the knowledge gaps, challenges, trends, and future perspectives on using these systems will be addressed.

## 1.1 Global panorama of scientific research related to the use of BSA as a nanocarrier

To compile results found in the literature and determine the relevance of the documents focusing on the applications of BSA to obtain nanocarriers for drug delivery systems, the Smart Bibliometrics systematic review methodology (Pessin et al., 2022) was applied. The keyword combinations and Boolean operators used were: ("bovine serum albumin" OR BSA) and nanocarrier* AND "drug delivery." Scopus (426 results) and Web of Science (294 results) databases were used, totaling 562 articles about the thematic, after removing duplicate work or work outside the review area of interest.

Figure 12.1 shows that research on using BSA as a nanocarrier has been increasing since 2007, when four papers were published. Since then, the number of publications has been increasing until 2019 (the most prevalent year) with 60 publications. The growth in the number of publications in this period is probably due to a result of the success of the first drug synthesized with albumin nanoparticles drug delivery technology (Abraxane), approved by the FDA in January 2005, for the treatment of metastatic breast cancer (Shi et al., 2017). After

2019, publications began to decrease. However, a new albumin nanoparticle (Fyarro) was introduced in November 2021 to treat locally advanced unresectable or metastatic malignant perivascular epithelioid cell tumor (PEComa). The launch of this drug succeeded and provided a boost to the field of albumin nanoparticle drug delivery technology (Liu et al., 2024b). So far, in 2024, 38 publications were made (Fig. 12.1), evidencing a decrease in interest in this area, probably due to the emergence of new cancer treatment techniques such as photothermal therapy (Dong et al., 2023).

Articles related to the application of BSA nanocarriers for drug delivery were published in 49 countries (Fig. 12.2). China was the most productive country, with 183 articles, followed by India with 70 articles and Iran with 49 articles. These three countries accounted for 53.73% of the articles published in this field.

The journal with the highest impact factor (IF = 21) is Nano Today (Fig. 12.3) with only one publication and 17 citations, while the journal with the highest number of citations is *Colloids and Surfaces B: Biointerfaces*, with 4110 citations. Next, in terms of citations, we have two journals focused on controlled drug release, which are the *Journal of Controlled Release* (21 records, 2455 citations, IF = 10) and *Advanced Drug Delivery Reviews* (7 records, 1883 citations, IF = 15).

Figure 12.4 shows that records of journal publications were highest for the *Journal of Drug Delivery Science and Technology* at 29 (5.16% of records), followed by the *International Journal of Pharmaceutics* and the *Journal of Controlled Release*. Across all 214 journals, records ranged from 1 to 29.

When analyzing the word cloud (Fig. 12.5), it is observed that the words that stand out in decreasing order are: "delivery," "nanoparticles," "drug," and "albumin," and after, in

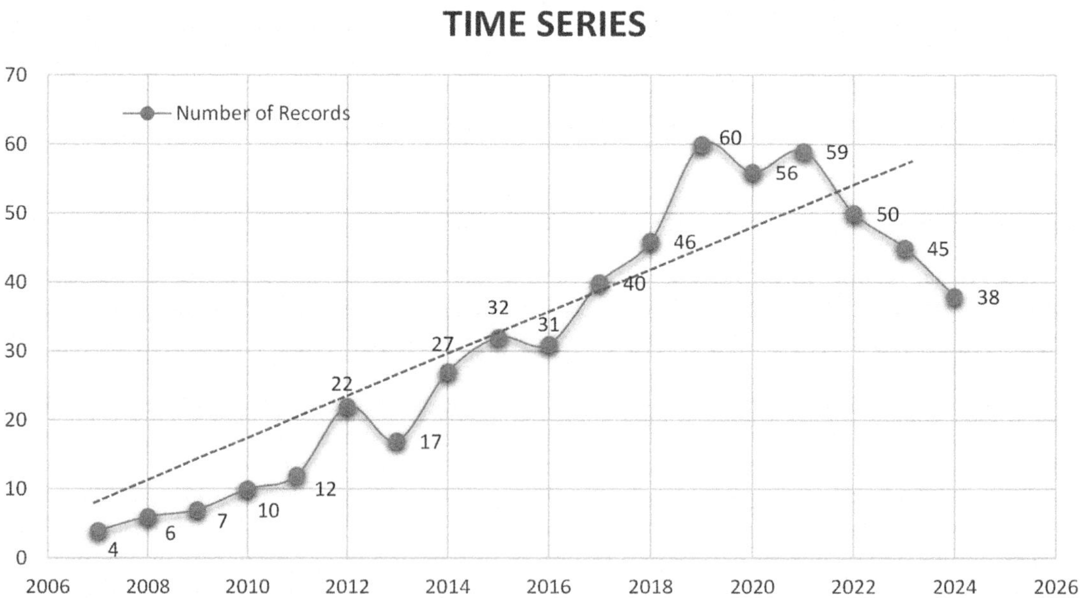


**FIGURE 12.1** Time series of papers with the abovementioned keywords according to the Smart Bibliometrics systematic review methodology. *Source: https://app.powerbi.com/.*

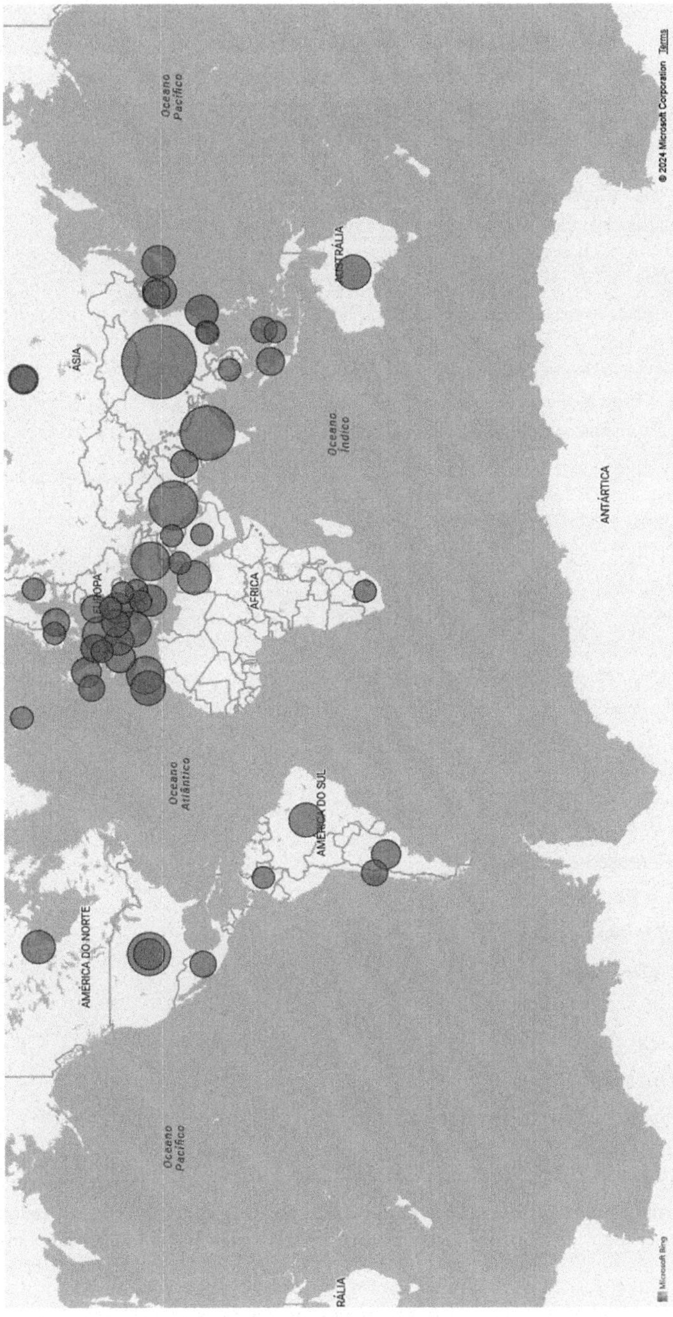


**FIGURE 12.2** Countries related to research on BSA nanocarriers in drug delivery, according to the Smart Bibliometrics systematic review methodology. *Source: https://app.powerbi.com/.*

(a)

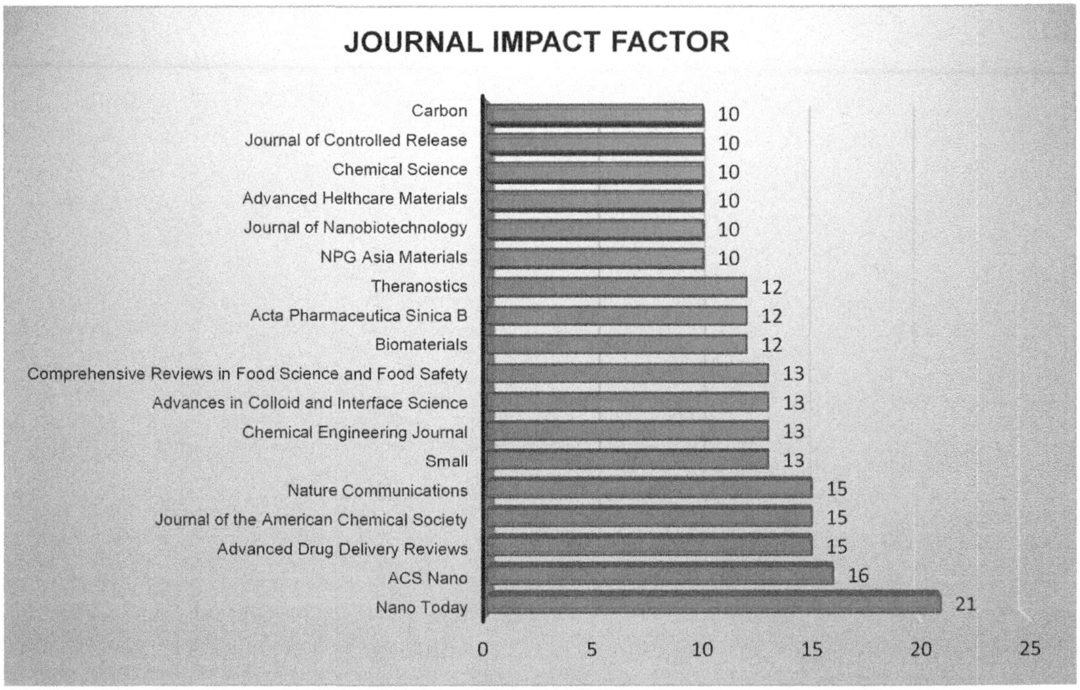


(b)

| Journal | Citations | Records |
|---|---|---|
| *Colloids and Surfaces B: Biointerfaces* | 4,110 | 14 |
| *Journal of Controlled Release* | 2,455 | 21 |
| *Advanced Drug Delivery Reviews* | 1,883 | 7 |
| *International Journal of Pharmaceutics* | 1,039 | 25 |
| *Expert Opinion on Drug Delivery* | 876 | 8 |
| *Biomaterials* | 592 | 8 |
| *Molecular Pharmaceutics* | 589 | 8 |
| *BioMed Research International* | 588 | 2 |
| *Journal of Drug Delivery Science and Technology* | 460 | 29 |
| *Theranostics* | 456 | 3 |

FIGURE 12.3 (a) Journal impact factor of BSA nanocarriers in drug delivery and (b) records and citations of BSA nanocarriers in drug delivery, according to the Smart Bibliometrics systematic review methodology. *Source: https://app.powerbi.com/.*

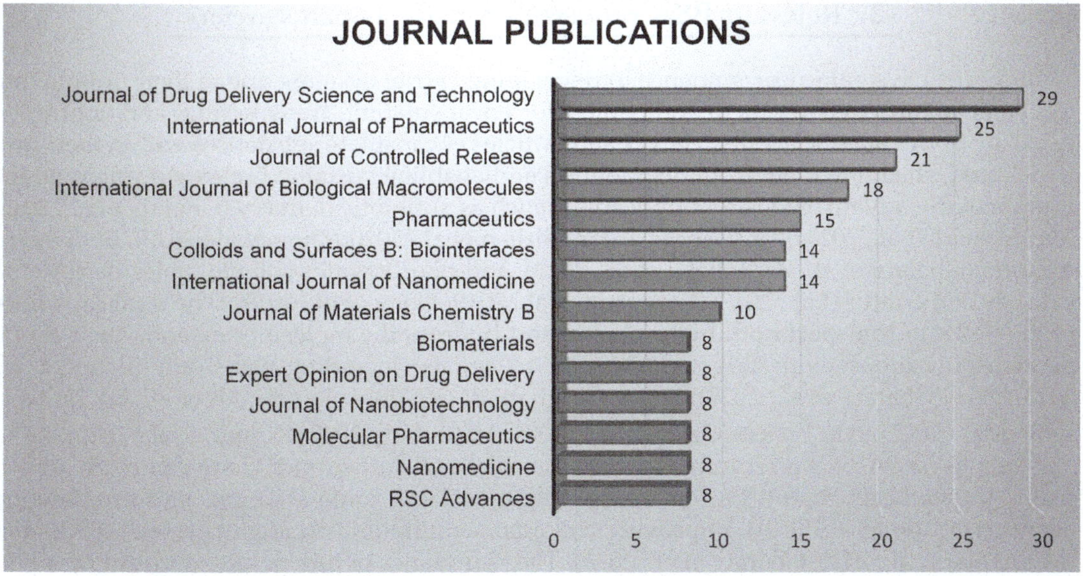


**FIGURE 12.4** The top 14 journals in number of publications. *Source: https://app.powerbi.com/.*

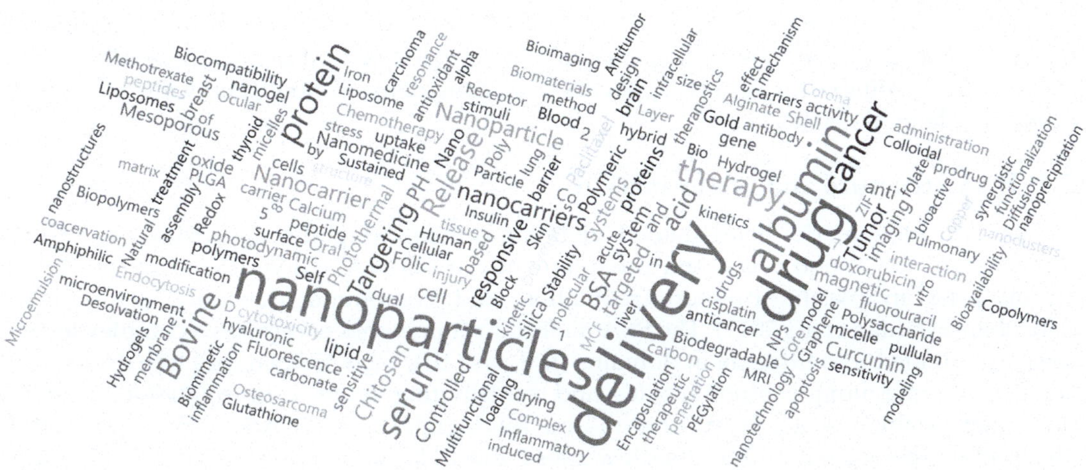


**FIGURE 12.5** Word cloud containing the most cited words in the articles obtained according to the Smart Bibliometrics systematic review methodology. *Source: https://app.powerbi.com/.*

similar proportions, the words "cancer," "bovine," "serum," "protein," and "therapy," which indicates that the controlled release systems of nanocarriers containing albumin are mainly for cancer treatment therapy. The characteristics of this biomolecule that make it so efficient as a drug nanocarrier will be addressed in the next topics.

## 2. Relevant BSA properties for use as nanocarriers

BSA-NPs have gained prominence in developing carrier systems due to their unique molecular structure, making them well-suited for encapsulating, transporting, and controlled releasing of therapeutic agents. These nanoparticles encapsulate substances within their protein matrix, shielding them from degradation and enabling sustained release profiles, which is particularly advantageous for applications such as antibiotic delivery (Ghataty et al., 2023; Mardikasari et al., 2023*a*), anticancer drugs (Birhan et al., 2020; Zhou et al., 2020), fluorescent markers (Ghataty et al., 2023; Patel et al., 2013), and poorly water-soluble molecules (Mehta et al., 2019; Ferrado et al., 2019; Arriagada et al., 2019; Dong et al., 2019). The dual capability of BSA-NPs to transport both hydrophobic and hydrophilic molecules extends their therapeutic applications, with targeted delivery to organs including the brain (Patel et al., 2013), skin (Ghataty et al., 2023), lungs (Singh et al., 2017*b*), colon (Singh et al., 2017*b*; Hosseini et al., 2021), and breast (Özsoy et al., 2021; Hsu et al., 2023; Kumar et al., 2020).

Moreover, BSA-NPs offer tunable properties like size and surface charge through adjustments in synthesis conditions such as pH, temperature, ionic strength, and crosslinking agents (Ferrado et al., 2019), improving colloidal stability and tuning drug release kinetics (Muthappa et al., 2020; Ghataty et al., 2023). The abundance of functional groups in BSA permits chemical modifications that improve solubility, binding specificity, and drug-loading efficiency. Chemical modifications on BSA-NPs reduce nonspecific protein adsorption and cytotoxicity while maintaining encapsulation and release efficiency (Yogasundaram et al., 2012). Such modifications optimize BSA-NPs' biological properties, with promising applications in oncology treatments (Nosrati et al., 2018; Choi and Meghani, 2016). Additionally, BSA-NPs' nontoxicity, nonimmunogenicity, biodegradability, and high drug-binding capacity make them suitable for various applications in drug delivery, food, and veterinary industries (Solanki et al., 2021).

### 2.1 BSA structure and conformation

BSA is a monomeric, heart-shaped globular protein weighing approximately 66 kDa, composed of 583 amino acids, and predominantly produced by liver hepatocytes, serving crucial roles in plasma pressure regulation and compound transport in the blood (Jahanban-Esfahlan et al., 2019). The BSA molecular framework comprises a complex tertiary structure divided into three main domains (I, II, and III), each divided into two domains (A and B), offering unique binding sites and contributing to its conformational flexibility (Jahanban-Esfahlan et al., 2015; Khatun and Riyazuddeen, 2018; Adamczyk et al., 2024). The binding regions within BSA, Sudlow sites I and II, located in domains II and III, respectively, enable selective interactions, allowing the protein to act as a versatile nanocarrier for various sizes of bioactive molecules, including both hydrophilic and hydrophobic compounds, enhancing drug encapsulation and release properties (Khatun and Riyazuddeen, 2018; Adamczyk et al., 2023; Adamczyk et al., 2024). For instance, the partially unfolded tertiary BSA structure enables binding of hydrophobic drugs, supporting its potential as a delivery system (Rout et al., 2023). Figure 12.6 presents a schematic model of the BSA structure.

Environmental factors like pH, ionic strength, and temperature influence BSA's conformation, inducing structural changes, such as exposing hydrophobic regions that improve

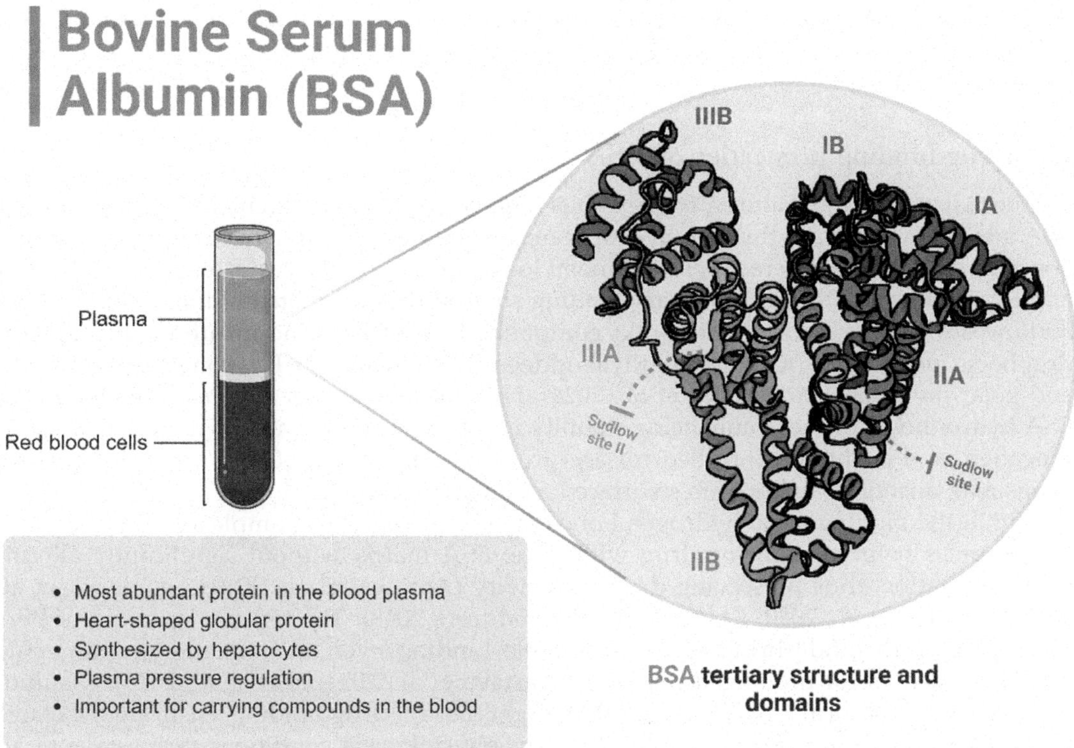


**FIGURE 12.6** BSA structure, indicating its domains (I, II, and III) and subdomains (A and B), as well as the Sudlow I and II sites, present in domains II and III, respectively. *Source: Prepared by the authors from a template on Biorender.com, adapted from: Adamczyk, O.; Szota, M.; Rakowski, K.; Prochownik, M. et al. (2024). Bovine serum albumin as a platform for designing biologically active nanocarriers – experimental and computational studies. Int. J. Mol. Sci., 25, 37. https://doi.org/10.3390/ijms25010037 and Asrorov et al. (2024).*

drug binding (Rout et al., 2023; Srivastav et al., 2020). BSA is structurally stable between pH 4.5 and 7.4 (Srivastav et al., 2020), and controlled denaturation at acidic pH conditions facilitates drug encapsulation and release (Singh et al., 2017*b*). The structure is further stabilized by 17 disulfide bridges that confer stability and enable BSA to maintain its configuration under physiological and acidic conditions, offering high resistance to thermal and chemical denaturation—an important feature for targeted drug release across diverse environments (Jahanban-Esfahlan et al., 2015; Singh et al., 2017*b*). Disulfide bridges impart redox-responsive properties, making BSA nanocarriers sensitive to reducing agents in specific cellular environments, such as tumors (Zhou et al., 2020; Birhan et al., 2020; Can Egil et al., 2022; Hsu et al., 2023).

Additionally, BSA hydrophilic surface regions contribute to its high solubility in water, a beneficial characteristic for in vivo applications (Ghataty et al., 2023; El Tokhy et al., 2022). Encapsulation within polymers like poly(lactic-co-glycolic) acid (PLGA) or polypeptide complex coacervates allows BSA to maintain its secondary structure, presenting systems with great stability (Chang et al., 2012; Zhang et al., 2014; Black et al., 2014; Guedj et al.,

2015), while binding with polyelectrolyte brushes and reversible conformational changes underscore its potential for controlled drug encapsulation and release (Jackler et al., 2004; Varga et al., 2016).

## 2.2 Drug-binding properties of BSA

Due to its structural features, BSA exhibits high versatility and specificity in drug binding. BSA interacts with drugs through hydrophobic interactions, van der Waals forces, hydrogen bonding, electrostatic interactions, and metal ion coordination (Srivastav et al., 2020; Khatun and Riyazuddeen, 2018). The primary binding sites on BSA facilitate binding diverse drugs: Sudlow site I favors hydrophobic, bulky compounds and strong binding affinity through hydrophobic interactions (Khatun and Riyazuddeen, 2018), while site II accommodates smaller and polar molecules (Adamczyk et al., 2024). Hydrophobic drugs are encapsulated within BSA hydrophobic pockets, enhancing stability in aqueous environments, reducing drug aggregation, and enabling controlled release profiles (Singh et al., 2017*b*), while hydrophilic drugs may anchor to the protein's surface (Adamczyk et al., 2024).

Within the binding sites, hydrogen bonds stabilize drug–BSA complexes, while van der Waals forces help position the drug within the BSA matrix without significantly altering its conformation, thus preserving drug bioactivity (Agrawal et al., 2019; Adamczyk et al., 2024; Srivastav et al., 2020; Khatun and Riyazuddeen, 2018). The tertiary structure of BSA, reinforced by disulfide bridges, enables stable binding even in dynamic environments, which is essential for prolonged release (Srivastava et al., 2021; Hsu et al., 2023). Disulfide bonds prevent conformational changes that might disrupt drug binding, ensuring the stability of the nanocarrier structure under different physiological conditions (Srivastava et al., 2021; Hsu et al., 2023; Ghataty et al., 2023).

BSA has successfully encapsulated curcuminoids (Fattahian Kalhor et al., 2020; Amani et al., 2019; Khodashenashenas et al., 2020), polysaccharides (Mardikasari et al., 2023a; Amani et al., 2019; Kovács et al., 2021), and anticancer drugs, such as doxorubicin (Birhan et al., 2020; Baneshi et al., 2019) and paclitaxel (Zhou et al., 2020), allowing controlled release in tumor microenvironments to enhance treatment efficacy while minimizing toxicity (Solanki et al., 2021; Rout et al., 2023). Furthermore, BSA's stable conformation in both aqueous and ethanol environments supports efficient drug loading, preserving the protein's structural integrity (Singh et al., 2017*b*; Srivastava et al., 2021; Ghataty et al., 2023). Additionally, BSA-NPs transport drugs such as prednisolone (Kaboli et al., 2021), dexamethasone (El Tokhy et al., 2022), and ibuprofen (Rout et al., 2023), primarily through hydrogen bonding and hydrophobic and ionic interactions. BSA's binding capacity also extends to metal-organic frameworks, offering pH-responsive drug delivery options for breast cancer treatment (Özsoy et al., 2021). Notably, BSA can also bind drugs in a partially unfolded state, a property supporting models like the "necklace and bead structure," potentially expanding its drug-loading capabilities (Rout et al., 2023).

Furthermore, these protein NPs can bind to glycans, enhancing targeted drug delivery, and interact with gold nanoparticles (AuNPs) via electrostatic forces, including salt bridges formed between citrate and lysine on the protein surface (Hosseini et al., 2021) (Khodashenashenas et al., 2020; Kumari et al., 2019; Adamczyk et al., 2024). Naphthyl-based hydroxamic acids also bind to BSA via hydrogen bonding and van der Waals interactions, affecting drug transport and metabolism (Agrawal et al., 2019). BSA demonstrates the binding and transport of the antitumor drug hydroxyurea through adsorption and inclusion mechanisms (Tazhbayev et al., 2020). These properties, alongside BSA's nontoxicity, nonimmunogenicity, and biodegradability, make it a highly suitable platform for targeted and efficient drug delivery across diverse therapeutic areas (Solanki et al., 2021).

## 2.3 Chemical modifications of BSA to enhance drug nanodelivery

Chemical modifications on BSA-NPs enhance their functionality as nanocarriers by improving stability, delivery specificity, and encapsulation efficiency. Ligands such as glycans and polymers facilitate active targeting, reduce premature degradation, and enable precise targeting of cancer cells, directly impacting encapsulation efficiency and drug bioavailability (Xie *et al.*, 2012; Jiang et al., 2016; Dong et al., 2019). PEGylation involves conjugating polyethylene glycol (PEG) to BSA-NPs, preventing aggregation, enhancing suspension stability, and improving pharmacokinetics (Xie *et al.*, 2012). This process leverages four key interactions: hydrogen bonding, hydrophobic interactions, steric hindrance, and electrostatic interactions. Hydrogen bonds stabilize the PEGylated structure, hydrophobic interactions enhance stability, steric hindrance from PEG chains reduces immune recognition, and electrostatic interactions lower the zeta potential, preventing aggregation (Xie *et al.*, 2012). Together, these interactions improve PEGylated BSA-NPs' drug delivery performance by increasing their circulation half-life and reducing immune clearance (Xie *et al.*, 2012; Zhang et al., 2013).

Crosslinking with glutaraldehyde strengthens BSA-NPs by forming covalent bonds between amino groups, enhancing their stability against enzymatic degradation and reinforcing structural integrity for controlled drug release at target sites (Srivastava et al., 2021; Patel et al., 2013; Fattahian Kalhor et al., 2020). Crosslinked BSA-NPs exhibit resistance to pH fluctuations, with stable zeta potentials below −30 mV and diameters within the optimal 100–300 nm range, making them suitable for systemic circulation and targeted tumor delivery (Baneshi et al., 2019; Patel et al., 2013). Additionally, modifications have shown benefits for intranasal drug delivery (Mardikasari et al., 2023*a*) and endothelial cell targeting through specific glycan conjugation for consistent drug distribution (Yuana et al., 2020; Patel et al., 2013).

Coating BSA-NPs with metal oxides (Baneshi et al., 2019; Uma Maheswari et al., 2021; Aghaei et al., 2023; Amani et al., 2019) and metal nanoparticles like AuNPs (Hosseini et al., 2021; Hong et al., 2021; Khodashenashenas et al., 2020) further increases colloidal stability, allowing controlled drug release through adjustable dissolution rates in biological environments.

Incorporating targeting folic acid moieties is frequently used as a functionalization strategy, because it enhances BSA specificity for cancer cells that overexpress folate receptors, facilitating receptor-mediated endocytosis and boosting drug accumulation at tumor sites. Folic acid-conjugated BSA nanohybrids, including BSA–calcium ferrite and BSA–silica composites, serve as pH-responsive and magnetic field-sensitive carriers for targeted drug delivery to folate receptor-overexpressing cancer cells, particularly in breast cancer (Uma Maheswari et al., 2021; Lu et al., 2019). For example, nanohybrids effectively encapsulate hydrophobic anticancer agents like hesperidin (62.94% efficiency) and eugenol (85.58%), with controlled, pH-responsive drug release under acidic tumor conditions, enhancing site-specific delivery (Uma Maheswari et al., 2021). The calcium ferrite's magnetic properties facilitate further drug release acceleration when exposed to an external magnetic field. Similarly, folic acid-modified BSA carriers loaded with ginsenoside Rg5 improve solubility, stability, and bioavailability, enabling increased tumor targeting, cellular uptake, cytotoxicity, and apoptosis in cancer cells, as evidenced by enhanced efficacy in MCF-7 cells and superior in vivo tumor accumulation (Dong et al., 2019).

Silica-based nanocarriers modified with folic acid–BSA (FA-BSA) exhibit effective targeting, biodegradability, and dual pH/glutathione responsiveness, supporting controlled drug release in the tumor microenvironment (Lu et al., 2019). For example, FA-BSA modifications enable pH-sensitive release for agents like quercetin and curcumin under acidic cancerous conditions (Niazi and Ashjari, 2023; Muthappa et al., 2020). Additionally, folate-targeted hybrid nanoparticles incorporating bioactive compounds, such as anethole and fisetin, leverage BSA's stability to induce apoptosis, enhance cellular uptake, and improve therapeutic efficacy with minimal in vivo side effects (Sadeghzadeh et al., 2023; Solanki et al., 2024). This targeted approach also supports receptor-mediated endocytosis and a multifunctional theranostic potential, demonstrated by folic acid-conjugated BSA core-shell nanocarriers loaded with multiple drugs like doxorubicin and cisplatin, which achieve potent anticancer effects and controlled, stimulus-responsive release (Song et al., 2019). This combination of functionalization, crosslinking, and pH-sensitive release makes chemically modified BSA-NPs versatile and effective carriers for cancer therapeutics.

## 3. BSA-based nanocarrier synthesis methods

Many procedures can be set up to obtain BSA and BSA-based nanoparticles with controllable size, charge, morphology, porosity, roughness, and intermolecular interactions to encapsulate and release different drugs in specific regions.

For instance, the desolvation technique is widely used to obtain nanoparticles by reducing their high solubility in a given solvent by adding another solvent (nonsolvent) under stirring in the system, in which these particles have low affinity. Generally, ethanol or acetone is the nonsolvent used to produce BSA-NPs from an aqueous phase. Thus, colloidal particles can be obtained due to the coacervation process or structural changes of nanoaggregates (Jahanban-Esfahlan et al., 2016).

Li et al. (2013) studied the release of oridonin (ORI) molecules from nanoparticles of galactosylated bovine serum albumin (GBSA) and BSA. The first step was to prepare GB by attaching lactobionic acid to the amino groups of the protein via an amidation reaction. Then, BSA and GB nanoparticles were obtained using the desolvation technique by adding ethanol under stirring to an aqueous system containing GB or BSA in the presence of ORI molecules. Nanoparticles of ORI-BSA and ORI-GB were finally obtained after crosslinking with glutaraldehyde (Li et al., 2015). also obtained chitosan-stabilized BSA-NPs to encapsulate bone morphogenetic protein-2 (BMP-2) by desolvation using ethanol as a nonsolvent. In their work, nanofibers of poly(ε-caprolactone) formed by electrospinning with chitosan–BSA–BMP-2-loaded nanoparticles and dexamethasone were obtained to be applied in bone tissue engineering. Many researchers have successfully produced BSA and BSA-based nanoparticles from the desolvation process, generally using water as a solvent and ethanol as a nonsolvent, and a good number of works used glutaraldehyde to stabilize and act as a cross-linker of the particles (Ji et al., 2024; Hsu et al., 2023; Esim et al., 2021; Alkulabi et al., 2024). Nonetheless, Sozer et al. (2020) verified that acetonitrile was a better nonsolvent than ethanol for obtaining cationic BSA-NPs for salicylic acid loading. Table 12.1 shows some preparation methods to obtain BSA-based nanoparticles.

BSA-NPs can also be produced by other techniques, such as (i) desolvation process combined with gamma ray irradiation using a $^{60}Co$ source as a cross-linker for emolin encapsulation (Siri et al., 2020); (ii) thermal treatment at 70 °C or 85 °C for BSA solutions at pH 9 or

**TABLE 12.1** Different preparation methods of BSA and BSA-based nanocarriers for drug delivery.

| Nanoparticles | Drug | Preparation method | Reference |
|---|---|---|---|
| Galactosylated-BSA and<br>BSA<br>Chitosan-stabilized BSA<br>BSA<br>Glycated BSA<br>BSA-Ag<br>BSA | Oridonin<br>BMP-2 and dexamethasone<br>Resveratrol<br>Doxorubicin<br>Piperine<br>Carboplatin | Desolvation (water as a solvent and ethanol as a nonsolvent) | Li et al. (2013)<br>Li et al. (2015)<br>Ji et al. (2024)<br>Hsu et al. (2023)<br>Alkulabi et al. (2024)<br>Esim et al. (2021) |
| Cationic-BSA | Salicylic acid | Desolvation (water as a solvent and acetonitrile as a nonsolvent) | Sozer et al. (2020) |
| BSA | Emolin | Desolvation (water as a solvent and ethanol as a nonsolvent) combined with gamma rays | (Siri et al., 2020) |
| BSA | Chrysin | Thermal treatment at 70 and 85°C | Ferrado et al. (2019) |
| BSA-$MnO_2$ | Chlorine e6 and doxorubicin coloaded hollow mesoporous silica nanospheres | Biomineralization at 37 °C, 2 h vigorous stirring | Fang et al. (2019) |
| BSA-golden | Cisplatin | Adsorption of BSA on gold nanoparticles | Jaiswal et al. (2023) |
| Maltose-BSA | Doxorubicin | Maillard reaction at 65°C in darkness | Wang et al. (2024) |
| BSA-SH | Magnolol (Mag) and hyaluronic acid (AH) | BSA particles modified with 2-thiamine hydrochloride (BSA-SH), then thiol-ene click reaction with magnolol, followed by HA dehydration condensation | Li et al. (2024) |
| BSA | Camptothecin | Ultrasonic emulsification | Song et al. (2024) |
| BSA-ferrocene and purpurin | Ferrocene and purpurin | Coassembly | Xu et al. (2021) |

11 over 5 minutes, followed by cooling in an ice bath and loading with chrysin molecules (Ferrado et al., 2019); and (iii) the biomineralization method to obtain BSA-$MnO_2$, which consisted of vigorous stirring of BSA in the presence of $Mn^{2+}$ at 37 °C for 2 h for chlorine e6 and doxorubicin coloaded hollow mesoporous silica nanospheres (Fang et al., 2019). Other approaches to obtaining BSA-NPs for drug delivery have also been effectively achieved.

Jaiswal et al. (2023) also reported the syntheses of BSA-golden nanoparticles by adsorption of BSA chains on the golden nanoparticle surfaces at 25 °C for 30 minutes to be used as a platform for cisplatin delivery. In fact, many metal–BSA-based nanoparticles can be obtained by adsorption methods (Hu et al., 2018; Thilagam and Gnanamani, 2020; Wang et al., 2024), and synthesized maltose–BSA-NPs in the proportion of amino:maltose of 1:1.5 via the Maillard reaction at 65°C in darkness. After the reaction, nanoparticles were dissolved in water, and glutathione was added, resulting in sulfhydryl protein. Then, doxorubicin was loaded into maltose–BSA-NPs at pH 8.5 and stirred for 6 hours in the dark (Li et al., 2024). also obtained BSA particles for treating ulcerative colitis by incorporating magnolol (Mag) molecules. BSA surfaces were modified with 2-thiamine hydrochloride to form BSA-SH particles in this case. Then, magnolol reacted with BSA-SH particles by thiol-ene click reaction under UV light at 365 nm for 48 hours, followed by dehydration condensations with hyaluronic acid (HA), giving HA–BSA–SH–Mag nanoparticles. Other techniques have also been developed to obtain BSA and BSA-based nanoparticles, such as BSA-NPs efficiently with camptothecin by ultrasonic emulsification and BSA-based NPs via coassembly with ferrocene and purpurin in an aqueous phase for cancer treatment (Song et al., 2024; Xu et al., 2021). To sum up, due to the structure of BSA, many methods of obtaining BSA-NPs have been used successfully, showing that BSA-NPs are good candidates to use as platforms for drug delivery.

## 4. Applications of BSA nanocarriers in drug delivery

The challenge to minimize the side effects of drugs and ensure that they reach difficult targets for treating various diseases has led to increased studies related to drug carrier systems. Drug delivery systems have the advantage of exploiting structural engineering, almost always at the nanometric scale, which can be customized according to the need for the required therapeutic action (Guindani et al., 2020). Thus, many systems have been developed using various synthesis and modification techniques for carrier systems and functionalized nanoparticles. In this context, BSA emerges as a biomolecule that can interact with a relevant number of drugs and perform different functions in conjugated systems due to the variety of functional groups on its surface. In addition, it has positively and negatively charged sites and hydrophobic domains, capable of promoting versatility to bind with different species (Ondreas et al., 2022).

The activation of microemulsion surfaces, especially oil-in-water, is one of the applications of BSA in carrier systems. In a recent study, BSA and PEG nanoparticles present in the aqueous phase of triacetin microemulsion were able to activate the surface of the nanostructures, with potential application for drug carrier systems. The evident stabilization promoted by the presence of BSA in the hybrid system could be proven by the zeta potential of the nanoparticles, in which the particles without serum albumin presented a value equal to −4.98 mV and the particles with serum albumin presented a value equal to −8.47 mV, showing the stabilizing effect of BSA (Gharbavi et al., 2019). The same effect was observed in nanoparticles formed from a poly(methyl methacrylate) (PMMA) miniemulsion conjugated with BSA. The addition of bovine serum protein was theoretically configured to cover the surface of all nanoparticles. The addition of BSA to the polymeric miniemulsion promoted a change in the zeta potential from −40 mV to −52 mV, which the authors also attribute to the effect of the negative charge of the BSA contribution. The evident stabilization of the system presents itself as an advantage for its potential application, which is to serve as a structure to encapsulate anticancer drugs, which almost always present hydrophobic properties (Guindani et al., 2020). Chitosan and BSA particles presented negative zeta potential, and the addition of an additional layer of bovine serum protein did not signal a change in this value, although the authors state that extra layers can decrease the zeta potential to affect the mobility of the particles. The stability of BSA, as well as its characteristics of non-immunoreactivity and biocompatibility, was a factor pointed out as relevant in the synthesis of a hybrid system of bovine serum albumin-poly(2-(diisopropylamino)ethyl methacrylate) (BSA-poly(DPA)). Proposed as a nanoconjugated nanocarrier, this system was able to prevent the early release of the model compound carried in specific cell organelles, with the release being sensitive to the pH of the medium (Papadimitriou et al., 2022).

It is interesting to note that the concentration of BSA in hybrid systems affects the predominant type of interaction between their components, probably due to the influence of the functional groups on the surface of the serum protein and its electrical charge properties. This can be observed in the combination of oleic HA and BSA as a controlled release system for curcumin for dermal use. The nanostructures with charge density on the surface of oleic HA allow that at lower molar ratios (less than 0.25) of BSA:oleic HA in phosphate solution (pH = 7.4) the predominant interactions are hydrogen bonds and electrostatic interactions, whereas in the molar ratio range of BSA:oleic HA between 0.25 and 0.5 there is a considerable increase in hydrophobic interactions between the components, probably between the bovine serum protein and the oleic groups of the HA. At higher BSA concentrations, there is a return to the prevalence of exothermic interactions, as observed at lower molar ratios. This difference in the predominance of interactions appears to affect the efficiency of the carrier system in penetrating the skin, so lower molar ratios seem to be more promising for this purpose. The presence of BSA promoted changes in the internal structure; however, this change did not alter the system's ability to promote a controlled release of curcumin for a prolonged period in the tissues analyzed (Ondreas et al., 2022). On the other hand, Joshi and Kishore (2023) observed conformational changes in BSA, reporting changes in protein helices and a reduction in secondary structure, when associated with micelles of a nonionic surfactant used in the composition of a release system. According to the authors, these changes are positive since they can promote the emergence of sites that are conveniently occupied by drug molecules. In addition, conformational changes of proteins adsorbed on nanoparticles can influence the recognition of nanostructures by the cell, so that the formulation of carriers is extremely important for the interaction between BSA-NPs and the cell (Guindani et al., 2020).

The size and size distribution of the carrier structures are a crucial factor for their use in sustained drug release (Ondreas et al., 2022). Nanocomposites based on BSA and oxidized gum arabic were produced with an average size suitable for sustained drug release, reaching a value equal to 219 nm (Jalali et al., 2023), since smaller particles have a pharmacotechnical profile suitable for prolonged release (Guindani et al., 2020). Hollow mesoporous silica nanoparticles coated with BSA modified with folic acid had an average size of 241.4 nm and can be used in the encapsulation of drugs with therapeutic action in tumor cells of the gastric system (Zhang and Liang, 2024). In fact, the modification of BSA with folic acid can increase the efficiency in the delivery of anticancer drugs, with greater precision in targeting the target cells (Lei et al., 2024). A hybrid carrier of BSA with $CaFe_2O_4$, also with folic acid, presented a size of 152 nm when in the presence of hesperidin and 145 nm when in the presence of eugenol, two bioactive agents for application in fighting cancer cells. The release of the drugs could be modulated by pH, and the presence of a magnetic species in the carrier allows a more efficient loading of the drug in the hybridized system (Uma Maheswari et al., 2021). For drug application by the inhalation route, the particles may, however, have a larger size for pulmonary release, so particles of 1.1–5.2 μm were synthesized through sequential addition of layers of chitosan, which acts as a polycation, and BSA, which acts as a polyanion, to a polymeric core. The particles were stable, probably due to interactions between the polyelectrolyte layers, and the tests showed that they behave appropriately for deep lung deposition when inhaled (Chauhan et al., 2024).

Nanocarriers have been suggested as an alternative to chemotherapy for tumor treatment since the use of chemotherapeutics presents high toxicity, especially for structures that act on cell replication, such as DNA and RNA (Hsu et al., 2023). In this line, the presence of BSA in nanostructures developed to act on tumor and metastatic cells has been observed to overcome problems such as low solubility of oncological drugs and their low bioavailability in the body. Doxorubicin is a drug used to treat breast cancer and has low specificity, among other drawbacks that interfere with its therapeutic action. To minimize these problems, nanoparticles composed of the drug with glycated BSA were synthesized; that is, they were chemically modified so that the conjugated structure formed could interact more efficiently with cancer cells. The particle population was homogeneous, with spherical morphology, and the average size (60.74 nm) of the nanoparticles is adequate to increase the retention time in the bloodstream. Fourier transform infrared spectroscopy (FTIR) did not indicate any structural change in the drug and glycated BSA when associated in the conjugate, unlike what was indicated by Ondreas et al. (2022), in which there was a reorganization of the hybrid structures and an increase in the hydrodynamic size of the particles. Still, doxorubicin in the presence of the vehicle was able to reach tumor cells with less pronounced effects on normal cells, also showing that the release of the transported drug presents a different behavior than the free drug (Hsu et al., 2023; Lei et al., 2024). They also explore the application of drugs for the treatment of lung cancer through a nanocomposite consisting of BSA as the core and a zeolitic imidazolate structure on the outside. The nanocomposites were used to encapsulate kaempferol, a flavonoid with anticancer and antitumor activity, with 77.5% efficiency, giving rise to organic structures associated with metals with potential use in the sustained release of drugs. Still in applications in anticancer therapies, the inhibitory effect of curcumin nanoparticles in BSA on cancer cells was evaluated. The cytotoxicity of the nanoparticles was shown to be analogous to that of free curcumin up to a period of 72 hours of incubation. After a limit of 96 hours, the inhibitory effect of the nanoparticles was more pronounced due to the sustained release behavior of the drug (Salehiabar et al., 2018).

The stabilizing action of BSA has also been explored in the synthesis of implants. The use of these devices ensures that the drug is released in the body at sustained levels, maintaining its therapeutic action and reducing the frequency of dose ingestion. For an implant to perform properly, it is necessary to ensure the stability of the drug in the release system, and, in this context, a 0.1% w/v BSA solution was able to retain 90% of the synthetic hormone levothyroxine, used to treat hypothyroidism, for at least 14 days. This behavior enabled the synthesis of a polycaprolactone implant, and in vitro tests showed effusive release in the first few days and subsequent slow release in the linear phase, proving to be suitable for patients who require lower doses of the drug (Stewart et al., 2021). When the drug is directly bound to BSA, release control can also be influenced by the binding of the drug to serum protein. If the interaction between the two is too strong, the therapeutic action may be compromised, since the drug will not be able to reach its target. The opposite, in turn, compromises the therapeutic action, so that the drug may not present adequate plasma concentration and will not perform its role correctly (Oliveira et al., 2017). Devices with potential applications in bone repair were also studied with a focus on the controlled release of baicalein, a natural flavonoid, for bone repair. The bioactive compound used was loaded into BSA and subsequently coated with tannic acid, so that the osteogenic action was optimized, ensuring the delivery of baicalein, a hydrophobic drug, with 99% encapsulation efficiency. The devices showed antioxidant action, in addition to good biocompatibility, characteristics that make them viable for use in implants for bone tissue (Yang et al., 2023).

That said, there have been many applications of BSA in controlled drug release systems, exploring its versatility in complexation with different bioactive compounds, improving the efficiency of drug loading in biodevices and the ability to direct drugs to specific targets and functionalization, acting in the control of early drug release, and ensuring good stability in the physiological environment, in addition to presenting an economic advantage due to its low cost and accessibility.

Table 12.2 presents a summary of the main BSA-based systems listed for the delivery of different drugs. Information on nanoparticle size, zeta potential, and the main therapeutic application is presented.

## 5. Unresolved questions and emerging challenges

### 5.1 Different pH values

BSA is a globular protein, made up of a variety of amino acids. Due to their structures, several factors can influence their stability, including pH. Several studies were carried out to evaluate the behavior of BSA at different pH values, observing the impact that protonation/deprotonation causes on the structure, conformation, stability, and surface charge of these compounds. It was observed that at pH 4.5 to 9, BSA remains in its normal form (N form); however, at pH below 4, its form changes to the fast form (F form). Both forms coexist in the pH range of 4 and 4.5, and at pH below 3.5, the structure has a flattened

**TABLE 12.2** Size and zeta potential of BSA-based systems for drug delivery and therapeutic application.

| Drug delivery system | Size and zeta potential | Drug | Therapeutic application | Reference |
|---|---|---|---|---|
| Triacetin-microemulsion hybridized with BSA | 46.4 nm<br>−8.47 mV | – | Anticancer activity | Gharbavi et al. (2019) |
| Poly(methyl methacrylate) (PMMA) conjugated with BSA | 151–179 nm<br>−52 mV | – | | Guindani et al. (2020) |
| Glycated BSA-NPs | 60.74 nm<br>−42.20 mV | Doxorubicin | | Hsu et al. (2023) |
| BSA/oxidized gum Arabic nanocomposite | 219–378 nm<br>−24.4 mV | Piperine | | Jalali et al. (2023) |
| Folic acid-modified BSA cloaked mesoporous silica NPs | 241.4 nm<br>~ −27 mV | Paclitaxel | | Zhang and Liang (2024) |
| Folic acid conjugated BSA-calcium ferrite nanohybrid | 152 and 145 nm<br>−27.3 mV and −29.5 mV | Hesperidin<br>Eugenol | | Uma Maheswari et al. (2021) |
| BSA | 92.59 nm<br>−9.19 mV | Curcumin | | Salehiabar et al. (2018) |
| BSA/zeolitic imidazolate framework-8 | 350–450 nm<br>−33.85 mV and −31.45 mV | Kaempferol<br>Sorafenib | | Lei et al. (2024) |
| BSA-oleyl-hyaluronan | 5–1000 nm | Curcumin | Skin diseases | Ondreas et al. (2022) |
| BSA/poly-ε-caprolactone | – | Levothyroxine | Hypothyroidism | Stewart et al. (2021) |
| BSA | ~400 nm<br>−15 mV/−20 mV | Baicalein | Bone repair | Yang et al. (2023) |
| BSA-poly(2-(diisopropylamino)ethyl methacrylate | 80–200 nm<br>−24.32 mV | Metachromatic dye acridine orange | Lysosomal diseases | Papadimitriou et al. (2022) |
| Polystyrene coated with chitosan/BSA | 0.5–5.2 nm<br>−2 mV | – | Lung diseases | Chauhan et al. (2024) |

spheroid shape (E form) (Carter and Ho, 1994; Cao et al., 2013). Figure 12.7 shows the BSA conformational changes as the variation of the medium pH value.

Xu and Grassian (2017) investigated how pH and the presence of phosphate affected the adsorption of BSA on the surface of $TiO_2$ nanoparticles. Thus, they sought to understand the interaction of BSA with $TiO_2$, and how phosphate adsorption influences the secondary structure of BSA and provide information to prevent BSA denaturation. Their studies were

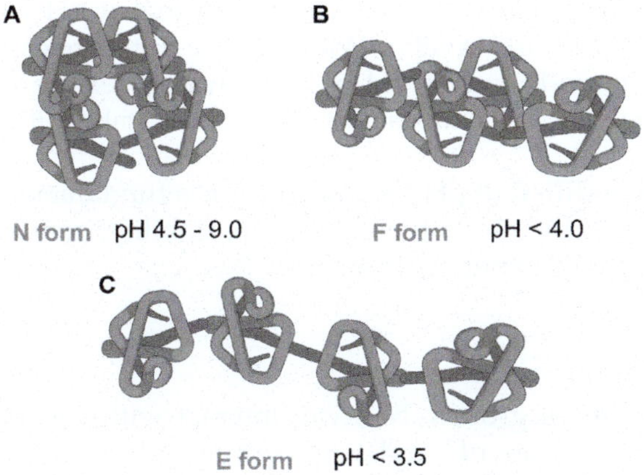


**FIGURE 12.7** Schematic of BSA conformational changes as a function of different pH values. *Source: Prepared by the authors from a template on Biorender.com, adapted from TaS. Ji, W. Wang, Y. Huang, Q. Xia, Tamarind seed polysaccharide-guar gum buccal films loaded with resveratrol-bovine serum albumin nanoparticles: Preparation, characterization, and mucoadhesiveness assessment. Int. J. Biol. Macromol. 262 (2024), 130078, https://doi.org/10.1016/j.ijbiomac.2024.130078; Tadjine, M., Bouzidi, F., Berbri, A., Nehmar, H., Bouhekka, A., 2024. In situ Fourier transform infrared-attenuated total reflection spectroscopy and modeling investigation of protein adsorption: Case of expanded bovine serum albumin on titanium dioxide anatase. Biointerphases 19 (1). doi:10.1116/6.0003020.*

carried out with the ATR-FTIR technique, and the pH used was 7.4 (similar to the pH of blood), 4.5 (similar to the pH of lung fluid), and 2 (similar to the pH of the stomach). In their conclusions, it was observed that at pH 2, BSA lost approximately 50% of its α-helix content and a greater amount of protonated amine groups, indicating the denaturation process. At this pH, phosphate was essential to protect the BSA structures, preventing complete denaturation. At pH 4.5, close to the isoelectric point of BSA, adsorption was maximum, with electrostatic interactions being minimized, increasing the adsorption density on the surface. At pH 7.4, BSA showed a stable structure, with less conformational change when adsorbed on TiO2 and with a large α-helix content.

Wishnia and Pinder (1964) were pioneers in studying the behavior of BSA in acidic media (pH below 5). In their study, they sought to understand the stability and behavior of BSA at different pH levels and how this affects its functionality. In this context, they observed that at pH 4, the transformation to the F form impacts the electrophoretic mobility and viscosity of BSA. At pH below 3, there is the transformation to form E, characterized by the expansion of the molecule, which interacts with the solvent and indicates the denaturation of BSA. Another point studied was its interaction with alkanes. The N form has hydrophobic regions that interact strongly with these solvents, while the F form has a very limited binding capacity. The transition from the N form to the F form occurs in internal hydrophobic regions, where small rearrangements occur, leading to a decrease in the binding capacity with hydrophobic solvents.

Singh et al. (2017a) investigated the preparation of BSA and ginsenoside Rh2 nanoparticles at pH 7.4 and 5 for antitumor release. The nanoparticles obtained were stable, and the connection between BSA and Rh2 was through the amino groups. At pH 7.4, the nanoparticles remained stable for 8 days, thus allowing them to remain in the blood for a longer period. The studies at pH 5 were to determine the applicability of these nanoparticles in tumor cells. It was observed that there was the formation of aggregates, indicating the possible release of Rh2 in tumor cells.

Chen et al. (2015) developed nanocarriers from BSA modified with folic acid to release paclitaxel in tumor cells. The systems developed are sensitive to pH due to the incorporation of 1,2-dioleoyl-sn-glycero-3-phosphoethanolamine (DOPE), aiming at selective release to cancer cells with a pH between 5 and 6. The release tests of paclitaxel showed that at pH 7.4, there was a slow release, with less than 37% release in 48 h. While at pH 6, the release reached approximately 58.9% in the same period, and at pH 5, there was a release of 68.5% in 48 h. Thus, the addition of BSA allows the nanocarriers to remain stable until they reach cancer cells.

Therefore, the behavior of BSA is different at different pH values, which is a fundamental factor for the design of nanocarriers, as pH directly affects their structure, stability, conformation, surface charge, and ability to interact with other substances.

## 5.2 Enzyme activity and stability

Due to the hydrophobic regions and functional groups, BSA can interact with several molecules, including enzymes. Some factors, such as pH and temperature, can influence this type of interaction. BSA can act to stabilize enzymes through hydrophobic interactions and increase viscosity. However, a very pronounced increase in viscosity and an increase in BSA concentration can generate the formation of aggregates that result in an asymmetric formation of nanoparticles, as well as a decrease in the availability of enzymes (Duskey et al., 2020; Hong et al., 2018).

In addition to being used in association with enzymes, BSA can act as a protection against the enzymatic degradation of nanocarriers, as shown by studies by Arnedo et al. (2002). In his work, he evaluated the effectiveness of BSA-NPs as delivery systems for antisense oligonucleotides. It was observed that pH plays an important role in the association of BSA with oligonucleotides due to electrostatic forces and that BSA increases the stability and protection of oligonucleotides, ensuring their intracellular delivery.

Another aspect studied by Lomova et al. (2015) is the development of BSA and tannic acid capsules to release substances due to enzymatic degradation. These capsules would encapsulate hydrophilic and hydrophobic drugs and be degraded by specific enzymes, such as α-chymotrypsin.

Pan et al. (2016) investigated the formation of nanocarriers with BSA as the main matrix for assembling iron oxide nanoparticles, nanoclusters, and gold nanorods. The objective is to apply these nanocarriers in bioimaging, photothermal therapy, and drug delivery. The challenges were related to the interaction between BSA and other inorganic components and the formation of a hydration layer on BSA, increasing the hydrodynamic diameter. Furthermore, BSA proved to be effective in stabilizing inorganic components, without affecting their properties and fulfilling the objective of drug delivery.

## 5.3 Size control

For the large-scale production of BSA nanocarriers, the distribution and sizes of these particles must be strictly controlled, thus being a challenge. When there is a large variation between the sizes of the nanocarriers, there may be an interference in their efficiency, generating an impact on the stability and bioavailability of the nanocarriers. BSA-NPs can be synthesized in different ways, such as desolvation (Zhu et al., 2008; Li et al., 2008) and emulsification (Ko and Gunasekaran, 2006). In this sense, Queiroz et al. (2016) developed

BSA-NPs using high-energy irradiation, combined with different concentrations of cosolvents such as methanol and ethanol. This methodology can control the size of these nanoparticles without the need for binding agents. As challenges were faced, size control was carried out by adjusting the concentration of cosolvents, and the bond formation was carried out with 10 kGγ irradiation.

Using the desolvation technique, Paik et al. (2013) established a methodology with intermittent addition of ethanol in this process. The idea was to avoid uneven aggregation of BSA molecules. It was observed that pH also influences sizes, generating aggregation due to the charge generated. Furthermore, the intermittent method contributed to improving the limitations regarding particle size control formed by BSA.

The stability of BSA-based nanocarriers can be a major challenge, especially in intracellular environments. Studies carried out by Zhang et al. (2019) developed nanocarriers based on BSA and green tea polyphenol to release doxorubicin (DOX) in tumor cells. In this work, the nanocarriers developed showed drug release in response to the presence of glutathione (GSH) and the enzyme trypsin, which are found in tumor cells. However, the release of DOX was only carried out through the breaking of disulfide bonds that occur in environments with high concentrations of GSH. Furthermore, modifications with folic acid were performed to enhance the specificity of the nanocarriers and thus improve treatment efficiency. Therefore, nanocarriers based on BSA and green tea polyphenol require specific conditions for drug release.

Jaiswal et al. (2022) investigated nanocarriers formed by BSA modified with folic acid and gold nanorods for the release of therapeutic proteins in colon cancer cells. The challenge of stabilization and aggregate formation of nanocarriers was addressed again. Folic acid was used to allow a more targeted delivery of proteins, reducing nonspecific interactions and preventing the formation of protein corona. This brief review demonstrated that BSA is a widely used matrix because it is versatile and can be modulated according to the need for release. Its behavior is dependent on pH, which can influence its structure, stability, and drug-release capacity. Its stable form is obtained at neutral pH (7.4), and it may present better results as nanocarriers, while at acidic pH, the conformational changes that occur impact its functionality. Furthermore, during the synthesis of nanocarriers, challenges may be encountered, such as nanocarrier aggregation, stability, and size control. These factors indicate that the parameters during synthesis must be controlled and that modifications of BSA with folic acid (Zhang et al., 2019; Jaiswal et al., 2022) can increase its stability and expand its applications and use.

## 6. Recent advances and future perspectives

Theranostics represents a significant advancement in personalized medicine, combining diagnostic and therapeutic capabilities in a single platform (Shetty et al., 2019). This approach enables real-time monitoring of disease progression and treatment efficacy, particularly in oncology and other critical areas (Degrauwe et al., 2019). Beyond oncology applications, combining diagnosis and treatment in a single platform is expanding the use of theranostics in various medical fields. Nanotheranostics are being developed to detect and treat conditions like atherosclerosis and myocardial infarction (Pala et al., 2021). For neurodegenerative disorders such as Alzheimer's and Parkinson's disease, nanocarriers designed to cross the blood–brain barrier can deliver targeted therapies while providing diagnostic feedback through imaging techniques like Magnetic Resonance Imaging (MRI) and Positron Emission Tomography (PET) (Joshi et al., 2023). Additionally, theranostics is being explored for infectious diseases, with the development of antimicrobial nanomaterials that can diagnose infections and deliver targeted therapy (Shetty et al., 2019).

BSA has emerged as a promising carrier for theranostic applications in cancer treatment as an anticancer drug delivery due to its nontoxicity, biodegradability, and high drug-binding capacity (Solanki et al., 2021). BSA-NPs can be functionalized with carbon quantum dots for enhanced drug delivery and diagnostic capabilities (Yazdani et al., 2022). These nanoparticles can be tailored for targeted delivery, as demonstrated by the development of glutathione-sensitive, doxorubicin-coupled glycated BSA-NPs for breast cancer therapy (Hsu et al., 2023). BSA also serves as a template for synthesizing bimetallic oxide nanotheranostics, enabling MR/CT imaging-guided photothermal and photodynamic therapies (Cai et al., 2023). Similarly, Ding et al. (2018) utilized BSA to synthesize multifunctional nanostructures with Au nanoclusters, which enabled cell fluorescence imaging and targeted delivery of doxorubicin to various tumor cell lineages.

Controlled nanocarriers have also emerged as a promising innovation in targeted drug delivery, offering enhanced therapeutic efficacy and reduced side effects (Majumder et al., 2019). These nanocarriers can respond to internal stimuli, such as pH and redox potential, and external stimuli, including light and magnetic fields, enabling controlled release of therapeutic cargo (Mi, 2020; Zhu et al., 2019). The development of multifunctional and stimuli-sensitive nanocarriers has shown tremendous potential for site-specific drug delivery, improving bioavailability and intracellular delivery (Majumder et al., 2019).

BSA has emerged as a versatile nanocarrier for controlled and stimulus-responsive drug delivery. BSA-NPs can encapsulate hydrophilic and hydrophobic drugs, offering high loading capacity and colloidal stability (Arriagada et al., 2019; Yang et al., 2020). These nanocarriers exhibit pH-sensitive behavior, enabling controlled release in acidic tumor microenvironments (Yang et al., 2020; Gooneh-Farahani et al., 2021). BSA-based nanocomposites, such as BSA-stabilized graphene/chitosan, have shown prolonged and sustained drug release profiles, reducing burst release and enhancing anticancer efficacy (Gooneh-Farahani et al., 2021). The stimuli-responsive nature of these nanocarriers allows for on-demand drug delivery, overcoming multidrug resistance, and improving therapeutic outcomes (Mi, 2020). Furthermore, a graphene oxide@zeolitic imidazolidate framework-8 was engineered with folic acid-conjugated BSA to enhance tumor cell recognition, thereby improving nanoparticle efficiency (Liu et al., 2022).

Another approach is that protein engineering has emerged as a powerful tool for developing advanced drug delivery systems. As previously mentioned, BSA-NPs are nontoxic, biocompatible, and have a high drug-binding capacity, making them promising candidates for cancer therapy (Solanki et al., 2021). Similarly, human serum albumin (HSA) offers multiple binding sites and enzymatic activities, making it suitable for drug discovery and development (Rabbani and Ahn, 2019). Protein-based nanoparticles provide advantages such as biocompatibility, biodegradability, and mild preparation conditions (Hong et al., 2020). These biomolecules can be engineered to create various drug delivery platforms, including peptide- and protein–drug conjugates, injectable particles, and drug depots for delivering small-molecule drugs, therapeutic proteins, and nucleic acids (Varanko et al., 2020). The ability to tailor proteins for specific functionalities through genetic and chemical modifications has significantly enhanced their potential in therapeutic applications.

BSA's structure allows for surface and internal drug immobilization, with two active sites (Sudlow I and II) confirmed for binding (Adamczyk et al., 2023). Researchers have developed fatty-amine-conjugated cationic BSA-NPs, which exhibit high stability against various stresses and improved drug delivery potential (Saha et al., 2019). Studies have shown that BSA-NPs can effectively encapsulate anticancer drugs like oxaliplatin, providing sustained release and improved efficacy while reducing cytotoxicity to normal cells (Ziaaddini et al., 2020). The ability to optimize BSA through genetic modifications and chemical conjugations offers opportunities to enhance drug-loading capacity, increase stability, and improve targeted delivery, making BSA-NPs a versatile platform for developing advanced anticancer therapies (Solanki et al., 2021; Adamczyk et al., 2023).

Lastly, multicompartment nanocarriers are innovative drug delivery systems, mimic cellular architecture, and enable the encapsulation of multiple therapeutic agents (Nayanathara et al., 2020). These nanocarriers allow for codelivery of chemo-, immuno-, and gene therapies (Hopkins *et al.*, 2022). By facilitating synergistic delivery approaches, nanocarriers can enhance tumor targeting, overcome multidrug resistance, and improve therapeutic efficacy compared to single-agent treatments (Chen *et al.*, 2023). Various types of nanocarriers, including lipid-based, polymeric, and inorganic carriers, have been developed to achieve controlled and targeted drug delivery (Khizar et al., 2022). These systems protect drugs from metabolic modifications, increase bioavailability, and minimize adverse effects (Khizar et al., 2022). The ability to fine-tune drug release profiles and deliver multiple therapeutic agents simultaneously positions multicompartment nanocarriers as a promising platform for improving treatment strategies (Hopkins *et al.*, 2022; Chen *et al.*, 2023).

Numerous studies have recently investigated the use of BSA in various nanocarrier systems to enhance drug delivery. Kumar et al. (2020) developed BSA-conjugated lipid nanocarriers for quercetin, demonstrating improved cytotoxicity against drug-resistant breast cancer cells (Prange et al., 2019). utilized cubosome nanocarriers loaded with BSA, achieving a two-fold increase in cellular uptake, particularly in renal tubular cells, thus addressing endocytosis deficiencies (Kovács et al., 2021). characterized a novel protein-polysaccharide nanocarrier system formed by BSA and HA, revealing a pH-dependent relationship influencing encapsulation efficiency. Also, Nayanathara et al. (2020) reviewed multicompartment polymeric nanocarriers, emphasizing their potential to mimic cellular architecture for biomedical applications, including drug delivery.

## 7. Conclusions

BSA has emerged as a versatile and effective drug carrier due to its biocompatibility, biodegradability, and ability to encapsulate and modify drugs chemically. The increasing number of publications and diversity studies indicate a strong scientific interest and potential for innovations in the area of nanomedicine, highlighting the importance of BSA as a versatile nanocarrier. Key properties include high binding capacity, structural stability, and improved solubility and bioavailability of hydrophobic drugs, enabling controlled release. Advances in nanoparticle synthesis methods like desolvation, emulsification, gamma irradiation, and thermal treatment hold promise for enhancing treatment safety and efficacy. Chemical modifications, such as folic acid conjugation, enable precise targeting of cancer cells, reducing systemic toxicity. BSA's responsiveness to pH also enhances its application in tumor environments, where acidic conditions promote drug release while maintaining stability in neutral pH. Another important factor is that modifying BSA with groups such as folic acid increases the specificity of release, targeting drugs to cancer cells and improving treatment efficacy. Drug interactions with BSA occur through hydrophobic pockets, van der Waals forces, hydrogen bonding, and electrostatic interactions, ensuring stable complexes. However, challenges like interactions with cellular inorganic components and increased hydrodynamic size limiting cell penetration must be addressed. Future research should focus on improving nanoparticle stability and size control to optimize the clinical potential of BSA-based therapies.

## Acknowledgments

The authors thank the financial support of FAPESP (grant 2024/00851-5), INCT/CNPq (grant 406925/2022-4), and Centro de Ciências Agrárias/UFSCar (FAI RTI-CCA). This study was partly financed by CAPES (Finance Code 001). D.S.S.S. and G.C.Z. hold fellowships from CNPq (grant 141298/2024-3) and FAPESP (grant 2024/00825-4), respectively. Figures 12.6 and 12.7 were created with Biorender.com.

## Conflicts of interest

The authors declare no conflict of interest.

## References

Abdoh, A., Liu, D., Mohammed, Y., 2024. Enhancement of drug permeation across skin through stratum corneum ablation. RSC Pharmaceutics 1 (2), 151–160. https://doi.org/10.1039/d4pm00089g.

Adamczyk, O., Szota, M., Rakowski, K., Prochownik, M., Doveiko, D., Chen, Y., Jachimska, B., 2023. Bovine serum albumin as a platform for designing biologically active nanocarriers—experimental and computational studies. Int. J. Mol. Sci. 25 (1), 37. https://doi.org/10.3390/ijms25010037.

Adamczyk, O., Szota, M., Rakowski, K., Prochownik, M., et al., 2024. Bovine serum albumin as a platform for designing biologically active nanocarriers – experimental and computational studies. Int. J. Mol. Sci. 25, 37. https://doi.org/10.3390/ijms25010037.

Aghaei, A., Sadiqi, H., Khwaja Mohammad, A.A., Gulmohammad, A.w., Likozar, B., Nosrati, H., Danafar, H., Shaterian, M., 2023. Magnetic ferrite nanoparticles coated with bovine serum albumin and glycine polymers for controlled release of curcumin as a model. J. Biomater. Sci. Polym. Ed. 34 (18), 2537–2550. https://doi.org/10.1080/09205063.2023.2265181.

Agrawal, R., Siddiqi, M.K., Thakur, Y., Tripathi, M., Asatkar, A.K., Khan, R.H., Pande, R., 2019. Explication of bovine serum albumin binding with naphthyl hydroxamic acids using a multispectroscopic and molecular docking approach along with its antioxidant activity. Luminescence 34 (6), 628–643. https://doi.org/10.1002/bio.3645. http://onlinelibrary.wiley.com/journal/10.1002/(ISSN)1522-7243.

Alkulabi, H.M.M., Ghobeh, M., Homayouni Tabrizi, M., 2024. A study of bioengineered piperine-loaded silver-bovine serum albumin nanoparticles and determining anticancer effects, anti-inflammatory and anti-oxidant properties against cancer cells. J. Mol. Liq. 393 (123559), 123559. https://doi.org/10.1016/j.molliq.2023.123559.

Amani, S., Mohamadnia, Z., Mahdavi, A., 2019. pH-responsive hybrid magnetic polyelectrolyte complex based on alginate/BSA as efficient nanocarrier for curcumin encapsulation and delivery. Int. J. Biol. Macromol. 141, 1258–1270. https://doi.org/10.1016/j.ijbiomac.2019.09.048.

Arnedo, A., Espuelas, S., Irache, J.M., 2002. Albumin nanoparticles as carriers for a phosphodiester oligonucleotide. Int. J. Pharm. 244 (1–2), 59–72. https://doi.org/10.1016/s0378-5173(02)00300-9.

Arriagada, F., Günther, G., Zabala, I., Rubio-Retama, J., Morales, J., 2019. Development and characterization of florfenicol-loaded BSA nanoparticles as controlled release carrier. AAPS PharmSciTech 20 (5). https://doi.org/10.1208/s12249-019-1419-7.

Asrorov, A.M., Mukhamedov, N., Kayumov, M., Yashinov, A.S., Wali, A., Yili, A., Mirzaakhmedov, S.Y., Huang, Y., 2024. Albumin is a reliable drug-delivering molecule: Highlighting points in cancer therapy. Medicine in Drug Discovery 22. https://doi.org/10.1016/j.medidd.2024.100186. https://www.sciencedirect.com/science/journal/25900986.

Baneshi, M., Dadfarnia, S., Shabani, A.M.H., Sabbagh, S.K., Haghgoo, S., Bardania, H., 2019. A novel theranostic system of AS1411 aptamer-functionalized albumin nanoparticles loaded on iron oxide and gold nanoparticles for doxorubicin delivery. Int. J. Pharm. 564, 145–152. https://doi.org/10.1016/j.ijpharm.2019.04.025.

Birhan, Y.S., Darge, H.F., Hanurry, E.Y., Andrgie, A.T., Mekonnen, T.W., Chou, H.Y., Lai, J.Y., Tsai, H.C., 2020. Fabrication of core crosslinked polymeric micelles as nanocarriers for doxorubicin delivery: Self-assembly, in situ diselenide metathesis and redox-responsive drug release. Pharmaceutics 12 (6), 1–22. https://doi.org/10.3390/pharmaceutics12060580.

Black, K.A., Priftis, D., Perry, S.L., Yip, J., Byun, W.Y., Tirrell, M., 2014. Protein encapsulation via polypeptide complex coacervation. ACS Macro Letters 3 (10), 1088–1091. https://doi.org/10.1021/mz500529v.

Cai, C., Tian, F., Ma, J., Yu, Z., Yang, Mo, Yi, C., 2023. BSA-templated synthesis of Ir/Gd bimetallic oxide nanotheranostics for MR/CT imaging-guided photothermal and photodynamic synergistic therapy. Nanoscale 15 (9), 4457–4468. https://doi.org/10.1039/d2nr06306a.

Can Egil, A., Kesim, H., Ustunkaya, B., Kutlu, Ö., Ozaydin Ince, G., 2022. Self-assembled albumin nanoparticles for redox responsive release of curcumin. J. Drug Deliv. Sci. Technol. 76, 103831. https://doi.org/10.1016/j.jddst.2022.103831.

Cao, X.L., Li, H.W., Yue, Y., Wu, Y., 2013. PH-Induced conformational changes of BSA in fluorescent AuNCs@BSA and its effects on NCs emission. Vib. Spectrosc. 65, 186–192. https://doi.org/10.1016/j.vibspec.2013.01.004.

Cao, Z., Liu, J., Yang, X., 2024. Deformable nanocarriers for enhanced drug delivery and cancer therapy. Exploration (Beijing, China) 4 (5), 20230037. https://doi.org/10.1002/EXP.20230037.

Carter, D.C., Ho, J.X., 1994. Structure of serum albumin. Adv. Protein Chem. 45, 153–203.

Chang, J., Paillard, A., Passirani, C., Morille, M., Benoit, J.P., Betbeder, D., Garcion, E., 2012. Transferrin adsorption onto PLGA nanoparticles governs their interaction with biological systems from blood circulation to brain cancer cells. Pharm. Res. 29 (6), 1495–1505. https://doi.org/10.1007/s11095-011-0624-1.

Chauhan, G., Wang, X., Quadros, M., Vats, M., Gupta, V., 2024. Chitosan/bovine serum albumin layer-by-layer assembled particles for non-invasive inhaled drug delivery to the lungs. Int. J. Biol. Macromol. 271, 132526. https://doi.org/10.1016/j.ijbiomac.2024.132526.

Chen, Z., Han, F., Du, Y., Shi, H., Zhou, W., 2023. Hypoxic microenvironment in cancer: molecular mechanisms and therapeutic interventions. Signal Transduct. Targeted Ther. 8 (1). https://doi.org/10.1038/s41392-023-01332-8.

Chen, C., Hu, H., Qiao, M., Zhao, X., Wang, Y., Chen, K., Guo, X., Chen, D., 2015. Tumor-targeting and pH-sensitive lipoprotein-mimic nanocarrier for targeted intracellular delivery of paclitaxel. Int. J. Pharm. 480 (1–2), 116–127. https://doi.org/10.1016/j.ijpharm.2015.01.036.

Choi, J.-S., Meghani, N., 2016. Impact of surface modification in BSA nanoparticles for uptake in cancer cells. Colloids Surfaces. B Biointerfaces 145, 653–661. https://doi.org/10.1016/j.colsurfb.2016.05.050.

Degrauwe, N., Hocquelet, A., Digklia, A., Schaefer, N., Denys, A., Duran, R., 2019. Theranostics in interventional oncology: Versatile carriers for diagnosis and targeted image-guided minimally invasive procedures. Front. Pharmacol. 10 (MAY). https://doi.org/10.3389/fphar.2019.00450. http://www.frontiersin.org/Pharmacology.

Ding, C., Xu, Y., Zhao, Y., Zhong, H., Luo, X., 2018. Fabrication of BSA@AuNC-based nanostructures for cell fluoresce imaging and target drug delivery. ACS Appl. Mater. Interfaces 10 (10), 8947–8954. https://doi.org/10.1021/acsami.7b18493.

Dong, Y., Fu, R., Yang, J., Ma, P., Liang, L., Mi, Y., Fan, D., 2019. Folic acid-modified ginsenoside Rg5-loaded bovine serum albumin nanoparticles for targeted cancer therapy in vitro and in vivo. Int. J. Nanomed. 14, 6971–6988. https://doi.org/10.2147/IJN.S210882.

Dong, Y., Xia, P., Xu, X., Shen, J., Ding, Y., Jiang, Y., Wang, H., Xie, X., Zhang, X., Li, W., Li, Z., Wang, J., Zhao, S.C., 2023. Targeted delivery of organic small-molecule photothermal materials with engineered extracellular vesicles for imaging-guided tumor photothermal therapy. J. Nanobiotechnol. 21 (1). https://doi.org/10.1186/s12951-023-02133-5.

Duskey, J.T., da Ros, F., Ottonelli, I., Zambelli, B., Vandelli, M.A., Tosi, G., Ruozi, B., 2020. Enzyme stability in nanoparticle preparations part 1: Bovine serum albumin improves enzyme function. Molecules 25 (20). https://doi.org/10.3390/molecules25204593. https://www.mdpi.com/1420-3049/25/20/4593.

El Tokhy, S.S., Elgizawy, S.A., Osman, M.A., Goda, A.E., Unsworth, L.D., 2022. Tailoring dexamethasone loaded albumin nanoparticles: A full factorial design with enhanced anti-inflammatory activity In vivo. J. Drug Deliv. Sci. Technol. 72. https://doi.org/10.1016/j.jddst.2022.103411. http://www.editionsdesante.fr/category.php?id_category=48.

Esim, O., Gedik, M.E., Dogan, A.L., Gunaydin, G., Hascicek, C., 2021. Development of carboplatin loaded bovine serum albumin nanoparticles and evaluation of its effect on an ovarian cancer cell line . Editions de Sante. J. Drug Deliv. Sci. Technol. 64. https://doi.org/10.1016/j.jddst.2021.102655. http://www.editionsdesante.fr/category.php?id_category=48.

Fang, J., Wang, Q., Yang, G., Xiao, X., Li, L., Yu, T., 2019. Albumin-MnO 2 gated hollow mesoporous silica nanosystem for modulating tumor hypoxia and synergetic therapy of cervical carcinoma. Colloids Surfaces B Biointerfaces 179, 250–259. https://doi.org/10.1016/j.colsurfb.2019.03.070.

Fattahian Kalhor, N., Saeidifar, M., Ramshini, H., Saboury, A.A., 2020. Interaction, cytotoxicity and sustained release assessment of a novel anti-tumor agent using bovine serum albumin nanocarrier. J. Biomol. Struct. Dynam. 38 (9), 2546–2558. https://doi.org/10.1080/07391102.2019.1638303.

Ferrado, J.B., Perez, A.A., Visentini, F.F., Islan, G.A., Castro, G.R., Santiago, L.G., 2019. Formation and characterization of self-assembled bovine serum albumin nanoparticles as chrysin delivery systems. Colloids Surfaces B Biointerfaces 173, 43–51. https://doi.org/10.1016/j.colsurfb.2018.09.046.

Gharbavi, M., Manjili, H.K., Amani, J., Ali, S., Danafar, H., 2019. In vivo and in vitro biocompatibility study of novel microemulsion hybridized with bovine serum albumin as nanocarrier for drug delivery. Heliyon 5 (6), e01858. https://doi.org/10.1016/j.heliyon.2019.e01858.

Ghataty, D.S., Amer, R.I., Amer, M.A., Abdel Rahman, M.F., Shamma, R.N., 2023. Green synthesis of highly fluorescent carbon dots from bovine serum albumin for linezolid drug delivery as potential wound healing biomaterial: Bio-synergistic approach, antibacterial activity, and in vitro and ex vivo evaluation. Pharmaceutics 15 (1). https://doi.org/10.3390/pharmaceutics15010234. http://www.mdpi.com/journal/pharmaceutics.

Gooneh-Farahani, S., Naghib, S.M., Naimi-Jamal, M.R., Seyfoori, A., 2021. A pH-sensitive nanocarrier based on BSA-stabilized graphene-chitosan nanocomposite for sustained and prolonged release of anticancer agents. Scientific Reports 11 (1). https://doi.org/10.1038/s41598-021-97081-1. www.nature.com/srep/index.html.

Guedj, A.S., Kell, A.J., Barnes, M., Stals, S., Gonçalves, D., Girard, D., Lavigne, C., 2015. Preparation, characterization, and safety evaluation of poly(lactide-co-glycolide) nanoparticles for protein delivery into macrophages. Int. J. Nanomed. 10, 5965–5979. https://doi.org/10.2147/IJN.S82205.

Guindani, C., Feuser, P.E., Cordeiro, A.P., de Meneses, A.C., Possato, J.C., da Silva Abel, J., Machado-de-Ávila, R.A., Sayer, C., de Araújo, P.H.H., 2020. Bovine serum albumin conjugation on poly(methyl methacrylate) nanoparticles for targeted drug delivery applications . Editions de Sante. J. Drug Deliv. Sci. Technol. 56. https://doi.org/10.1016/j.jddst.2019.101490. http://www.editionsdesante.fr/category.php?id_category=48.

Hong, S., Choi, D.W., Kim, H.N., Park, C.G., Lee, W., Park, H.H., 2020. Protein-based nanoparticles as drug delivery systems. Pharmaceutics 12 (7), 1–28. https://doi.org/10.3390/pharmaceutics12070604.

Hong, T., Iwashita, K., Shiraki, K., 2018. Viscosity control of protein solution by small solutes: A review. Curr. Protein Pept. Sci. 19, 746–758. https://doi.org/10.2174/1389203719666171213114919.

Hong, Y., Ju, Y., Chen, W., Liu, Y., Zhang, M., Zhao, H., 2021. Fabrication of PεCL–AuNP–BSA core–shell–corona nanoparticles for flexible spatiotemporal drug delivery and SERS detection. Biomater. Sci. 9 (12), 4440–4447. https://doi.org/10.1039/d1bm00388g.

Hopkins, C., Javius-Jones, K., Wang, Y., Hong, H., Hu, Q., Hong, S., 2022. Combinations of chemo-, immuno-, and gene therapies using nanocarriers as a multifunctional drug platform. Expet Opin. Drug Deliv. 19 (10), 1337–1349. https://doi.org/10.1080/17425247.2022.2112569.

Hosseini, S., Wetzel, O., Kostka, K., Heggen, M., Loza, K., Epple, M., 2021. Pathways for oral and rectal delivery of gold nanoparticles (1.7 nm) and gold nanoclusters into the colon: Enteric-coated capsules and suppositories. Molecules 26 (16), 5069. https://doi.org/10.3390/molecules26165069.

Hsu, W.H., Ku, C.L., Lai, Y.R., Wang, S.S.S., Chou, S.H., Lin, T.H., 2023. Developing targeted drug delivery carriers for breast cancer using glutathione-sensitive doxorubicin-coupled glycated bovine serum albumin nanoparticles. Int. J. Biol. Macromol. 249. https://doi.org/10.1016/j.ijbiomac.2023.126114. https://www.sciencedirect.com/journal/international-journal-of-biological-macromolecules.

Hu, D., Xu, H., Xiao, B., Li, D., Zhou, Z., Liu, X., Tang, J., Shen, Y., 2018. Albumin-stabilized metal–organic nanoparticles for effective delivery of metal complex anticancer drugs. ACS Appl. Mater. Interfaces 10 (41), 34974–34982. https://doi.org/10.1021/acsami.8b12812.

Jackler, G., Wittemann, A., Ballauff, M., Czeslik, C., 2004. Spherical polyelectrolyte brushes as carrier particles for proteins: An investigation of the structure of adsorbed and desorbed bovine serum albumin. J. Spectrosc. 18 (2), 289–299. https://doi.org/10.1155/2004/526159.

Jahanban-Esfahlan, A., Panahi-Azar, V., Sajedi, S., 2015. Spectroscopic and molecular docking studies on the interaction between N-acetyl cysteine and bovine serum albumin: Interaction of NAC with BSA. Biopolymers 103 (11), 638–645. https://doi.org/10.1002/bip.22697.

Jahanban-Esfahlan, A., Dastmalchi, S., Davaran, S., 2016. A simple improved desolvation method for the rapid preparation of albumin nanoparticles. Int. J. Biol. Macromol. 91, 703–709. https://doi.org/10.1016/j.ijbiomac.2016.05.032.

Jahanban-Esfahlan, A., Ostadrahimi, A., Jahanban-Esfahlan, R., Roufegarinejad, L., Tabibiazar, M., Amarowicz, R., 2019. Recent developments in the detection of bovine serum albumin. Int. J. Biol. Macromol. 138, 602–617. https://doi.org/10.1016/j.ijbiomac.2019.07.096.

Jaiswal, N., Halder, S., Mahata, N., Chanda, N., 2022. Bi-functional gold nanorod–protein conjugates with biomimetic BSA@folic acid corona for improved tumor targeting and intracellular delivery of therapeutic proteins in colon cancer 3D spheroids. ACS Appl. Bio Mater. 5 (4), 1476–1488. https://doi.org/10.1021/acsabm.1c01216.

Jaiswal, V.D., Pangam, D.S., Dongre, P.M., 2023. Biophysical study of cisplatin loaded albumin-gold nanoparticle and its interaction with glycans of gp60 receptor. Int. J. Biol. Macromol. 231 (123368), 123368. https://doi.org/10.1016/j.ijbiomac.2023.123368.

Jalali, E.S., Shojaosadati, S.A., Hamedi, S., 2023. Green synthesis of bovine serum albumin/oxidized gum Arabic nanocomposite as pH-responsive carrier for controlled release of piperine and the molecular docking study. Int. J. Biol. Macromol. 225, 51–62. https://doi.org/10.1016/j.ijbiomac.2022.11.283.

Ji, S., Wang, W., Huang, Y., Xia, Q., 2024. Tamarind seed polysaccharide-guar gum buccal films loaded with resveratrol-bovine serum albumin nanoparticles: Preparation, characterization, and mucoadhesiveness assessment. Int. J. Biol. Macromol. 262, 130078. https://doi.org/10.1016/j.ijbiomac.2024.130078.

Jiang, Y., Lu, H., Chen, F., Callari, M., Pourgholami, M., Morris, D.L., Stenzel, M.H., 2016. PEGylated albumin-based polyion complex micelles for protein delivery. Biomacromolecules 17 (3), 808–817. https://doi.org/10.1021/acs.biomac.5b01537.

Joshi, A., Kishore, N., 2023. Non-ionic surfactants in drug delivery vehicles: Physicochemical insights with systems of drugs, Igepal CA-630, bovine serum albumin and hen egg-white lysozyme. Colloids Surf. A Physicochem. Eng. Asp. 656, 130433. https://doi.org/10.1016/j.colsurfa.2022.130433.

Joshi, R., Missong, H., Mishra, J., Kaur, S., Saini, S., Kandimalla, R., Reddy, P.H., Babu, A., Bhatti, G.K., Bhatti, J.S., 2023. Nanotheranostics revolutionizing neurodegenerative diseases: From precision diagnosis to targeted therapies. J. Drug Deliv. Sci. Technol. 89. https://doi.org/10.1016/j.jddst.2023.105067. https://www.sciencedirect.com/science/journal/17732247.

Kaboli, S.F., Mehrnejad, F., Nematollahzadeh, A., 2021. Molecular modeling prediction of albumin-based nanoparticles and experimental preparation, characterization, and *in-vitro* kinetics of prednisolone from nanoparticles. J. Drug Deliv. Sci. Technol. 64, 102588. https://doi.org/10.1016/j.jddst.2021.102588.

Khatun, S., Riyazuddeen, 2018. Interaction of colchicine with BSA: spectroscopic, calorimetric and molecular modeling approaches. J. Biomol. Struct. Dynam. 36 (12), 3122–3129. https://doi.org/10.1080/07391102.2017.1384397.

Khodashenas, B., Ardjmand, M., Sharifzadeh Baei, M., Shokuhi Rad, A., Akbarzadeh Khiyavi, A., 2020. Bovine serum albumin/gold nanoparticles as a drug delivery system for Curcumin: Experimental and computational studies. J. Biomol. Struct. Dynam. 38 (15), 4644–4654. https://doi.org/10.1080/07391102.2019.1683073.

Khizar, S., Elaissari, A., Al-Dossary, A.A., Zine, N., Jaffrezic-Renault, N., Errachid, A., 2022. Advancement in nanoparticle-based biosensors for point-of-care in vitro diagnostics. Curr. Top. Med. Chem. 22 (10), 807–833. https://doi.org/10.2174/1568026622666220401160121.

Ko, S., Gunasekaran, S., 2006. Preparation of sub-100-nm β-lactoglobulin (BLG) nanoparticles. J. Microencapsul. 23 (8), 887–898. https://doi.org/10.1080/02652040601035143.

Kouchakzadeh, H., Safavi, M.S., Shojaosadati, S.A., 2015. Efficient delivery of therapeutic agents by using targeted albumin nanoparticles. Adv. Protein Chem. Struct. Biol. 98, 121–143. https://doi.org/10.1016/bs.apcsb.2014.11.002.

Kovács, A.N., Varga, N., Juhász, Á., Csapó, E., 2021. Serum protein-hyaluronic acid complex nanocarriers: Structural characterisation and encapsulation possibilities. Carbohydr. Polym. 251. https://doi.org/10.1016/j.carbpol.2020.117047. http://www.elsevier.com/wps/find/journaldescription.cws_home/405871/description#description.

Kumar, R., Choudhary, D.K., Debnath, M., 2020. Development of BSA conjugated on modified surface of quercetin-loaded lipid nanocarriers for breast cancer treatment. Mater. Res. Express 7 (1), 015411. https://doi.org/10.1088/2053-1591/ab6774.

Kumari, N., Mathe, V.L., Dongre, P.M., 2019. Albumin nanoparticles conjugates binding with glycan - A strategic approach for targeted drug delivery. Int. J. Biol. Macromol. 126, 74–90. https://doi.org/10.1016/j.ijbiomac.2018.12.184.

Lei, C., Liu, Di, Zhou, Q., Ma, S., Qian, H., 2024. Engineering of dopamine conjugated with bovine serum albumin and zeolite imidazole framework: A promising drug delivery nanocarrier on lung cancer cells. Heliyon 10 (17), e36580. https://doi.org/10.1016/j.heliyon.2024.e36580.

Li, F.Q., Su, H., Wang, J., Liu, J.Y., Zhu, Q.G., Fei, Y.B., Pan, Y.H., Hu, J.H., 2008. Preparation and characterization of sodium ferulate entrapped bovine serum albumin nanoparticles for liver targeting. Int. J. Pharm. 349 (1–2), 274–282. https://doi.org/10.1016/j.ijpharm.2007.08.001.

Li, C., Zhang, D., Guo, H., Leilei, H., Zheng, D., Liu, G., Shen, J., Tian, X., Zhang, Q., 2013. Preparation and characterization of galactosylated bovine serum albumin nanoparticles for liver-targeted delivery of oridonin. Int. J. Pharm. 448 (1), 79–86. https://doi.org/10.1016/j.ijpharm.2013.03.019.

Li, L., Zhou, G., Wang, Y., Yang, G., Ding, S., Zhou, S., 2015. Controlled dual delivery of BMP-2 and dexamethasone by nanoparticle-embedded electrospun nanofibers for the efficient repair of critical-sized rat calvarial defect. Biomaterials 37, 218–229. https://doi.org/10.1016/j.biomaterials.2014.10.015.

Li, Y., Chen, T., Chen, L., Wu, Di, Hu, J., 2024. Construction of hyaluronic acid-functionalized magnolol nanoparticles for ulcerative colitis treatment. Int. J. Biol. Macromol. 268, 131920. https://doi.org/10.1016/j.ijbiomac.2024.131920.

Liu, W., Semcheddine, F., Guo, Z., Jiang, H., Wang, X., 2022. Glucose-responsive ZIF-8 nanocomposites for targeted cancer therapy through combining starvation with stimulus-responsive nitric oxide synergistic treatment. ACS Appl. Bio Mater. 5 (6), 2902–2912. https://doi.org/10.1021/acsabm.2c00262.

Liu, W., Liu, L., Li, H., Xie, Y., Bai, J., Guan, J., Qi, H., Sun, J., 2024a. Targeted pathophysiological treatment of ischemic stroke using nanoparticle-based drug delivery system. J. Nanobiotechnol. 22 (1), 499. https://doi.org/10.1186/s12951-024-02772-2.

Liu, Y., Li, Y., Shen, W., Li, M., Wang, W., Jin, X., 2024b. Trend of albumin nanoparticles in oncology: A bibliometric analysis of research progress and prospects. Front. Pharmacol. 15, 1409163. https://doi.org/10.3389/fphar.2024.1409163.

Lomova, M.V., Brichkina, A.I., Kiryukhin, M.V., Vasina, E.N., Pavlov, A.M., Gorin, D.A., Sukhorukov, G.B., Antipina, M.N., 2015. Multilayer capsules of bovine serum albumin and tannic acid for controlled release by enzymatic degradation. ACS Appl. Mater. Interfaces 7 (22), 11732–11740. https://doi.org/10.1021/acsami.5b03263.

Lu, J., Chen, Q., Ding, X., Wen, J., Zhang, Y., Li, H., Xu, Y., Liu, F., Chen, S.S., Sun, S., 2019. BSA modified, disulfide-bridged mesoporous silica with low biotoxicity for dual-responsive drug delivery. Microporous Mesoporous Materials 278, 257–266. https://doi.org/10.1016/j.micromeso.2018.12.001.

Majumder, J., Taratula, O., Minko, T., 2019. Nanocarrier-based systems for targeted and site specific therapeutic delivery. Adv. Drug Deliv. Rev. 144, 57–77. https://doi.org/10.1016/j.addr.2019.07.010.

Mardikasari, S.A., Katona, G., Sipos, B., Ambrus, R., Csóka, I., 2023b. Preparation and optimization of bovine serum albumin nanoparticles as a promising gelling system for enhanced nasal drug administration. Gels 9 (11). https://doi.org/10.3390/gels9110896. www.mdpi.com/journal/gels.

Mardikasari, S.A., Katona, G., Budai-Szűcs, M., Sipos, B., Orosz, L., Burián, K., Rovó, L., Csóka, I., 2023a. Quality by design-based optimization of in situ ionic-sensitive gels of amoxicillin-loaded bovine serum albumin nanoparticles for enhanced local nasal delivery. Int. J. Pharm. 645 (123435), 123435. https://doi.org/10.1016/j.ijpharm.2023.123435.

Mehta, A., Dalle Vedove, E., Isert, L., Merkel, O.M., 2019. Targeting KRAS mutant lung cancer cells with siRNA-loaded bovine serum albumin nanoparticles. Pharm. Res. 36 (9). https://doi.org/10.1007/s11095-019-2665-9. www.wkap.nl/journalhome.htm/0724-8741.

Muthappa, R., Purushothaman, B.K., Meera Sheriffa Begum, K.M., Maheswari, P.U., 2020. Kinetic modeling and optimization of the release mechanism of curcumin from folate conjugated hybrid BSA nanocarrier. Chem. Prod. Process Model. 15 (1). https://doi.org/10.1515/cppm-2019-0026. www.degruyter.com/view/j/cppm.

Nayanathara, U., Kermaniyan, S.S., Such, G.K., 2020. Multicompartment polymeric nanocarriers for biomedical applications. Macromol. Rapid Commun. 41 (18), 1–28. https://doi.org/10.1002/marc.202000298.

Niazi, Z., Ashjari, M., 2023. Formulation of silica-chitosan hybrid modified by BSA-folate as a drug nanocarrier. J. Nanostructures 13 (2), 382–389. https://doi.org/10.22052/JNS.2023.02.008.

Nosrati, H., Sefidi, N., Ali, S., Danafar, H., Manjili, H.K., 2018. Bovine Serum Albumin (BSA) coated iron oxide magnetic nanoparticles as biocompatible carriers for curcumin-anticancer drug. Bioorg. Chem. 76, 501–509. https://doi.org/10.1016/j.bioorg.2017.12.033.

Ochnio, M.E., Martínez, J.H., Allievi, M.C., Palavecino, M., Martínez, K.D., Pérez, O.E., 2018. Proteins as nanocarriers for bioactive compounds. The case of 7S and 11S soy globulins and folic acid complexation. Polymers 10 (2). https://doi.org/10.3390/polym10020149. http://www.mdpi.com/2073-4360/10/2/149/pdf.

Oliveira, L.T., de Paula, M.A., Roatt, B.M., Garcia, G.M., Silva, L.S.B., Reis, A.B., de Paula, C.S., Vilela, J.M.C., Andrade, M.S., Pound-Lana, G., Mosqueira, V.C.F., 2017. Impact of dose and surface features on plasmatic and liver concentrations of biodegradable polymeric nanocapsules. J. Pharm. Sci. 105, 19–32. https://doi.org/10.1016/j.ejps.2017.04.017.

Ondreas, F., Sita, J., Cepa, M., Svecova, E., Velebny, V., 2022. Interactions of hydrophobically modified hyaluronan carrier with bovine serum albumin. Appl. Surf. Sci. 593, 153440. https://doi.org/10.1016/j.apsusc.2022.153440.

Özsoy, M., Atiroğlu, V., Guney Eskiler, G., Atiroğlu, A., Deveci Ozkan, A., Özacar, M., 2021. A protein-sulfosalicylic acid/boswellic acids @metal–organic framework nanocomposite as anticancer drug delivery system. Colloids Surf. B Biointerfaces 204, 111788. https://doi.org/10.1016/j.colsurfb.2021.111788.

Paik, S.Y.R., Nguyen, H.H., Ryu, J., Che, J.H., Kang, T.S., Lee, J.K., Song, C.W., Ko, S., 2013. Robust size control of bovine serum albumin (BSA) nanoparticles by intermittent addition of a desolvating agent and the particle formation mechanism. Food Chem. 141 (2), 695–701. https://doi.org/10.1016/j.foodchem.2013.04.059.

Pala, R., Pattnaik, S., Busi, S., Nauli, S.M., 2021. Nanomaterials as novel cardiovascular theranostics. Pharmaceutics 13 (3). https://doi.org/10.3390/pharmaceutics13030348. https://www.mdpi.com/1999-4923/13/3/348/pdf.

Palakurthi, S.S., Shah, B., Kapre, S., Charbe, N., Immanuel, S., Pasham, S., Thalla, M., Jain, A., Palakurthi, S., 2024. A comprehensive review of challenges and advances in exosome-based drug delivery systems. Nanoscale Adv. https://doi.org/10.1039/d4na00501e.

Pan, U.N., Khandelia, R., Sanpui, P., Das, S., Paul, A., Chattopadhyay, A., 2016. Protein-based multifunctional nanocarriers for imaging, photothermal therapy, and anticancer drug delivery. ACS Appl. Mater. Interfaces 9, 19495–19501. https://doi.org/10.1021/acsami.6b06099.

Papadimitriou, L., Theodorou, A., Papageorgiou, M., Voutyritsa, E., Papagiannaki, A., Kelly, V., Ranella, A., 2022. pH responsive biohybrid BSA-poly(DPA) nanoparticles for interlysosomal drug delivery. J. Drug Deliv. Sci. Technol. 75, 103591. https://doi.org/10.1016/j.jddst.2022.103591.

Patel, P.J., Acharya, N.S., Acharya, S.R., 2013. Development and characterization of glutathione-conjugated albumin nanoparticles for improved brain delivery of hydrophilic fluorescent marker. Drug Deliv. 20 (3–4), 143–155. https://doi.org/10.3109/10717544.2013.801050.

Pessin, V.Z., Yamane, L.H., Siman, R.R., 2022. Smart bibliometrics: an integrated method of science mapping and bibliometric analysis. Scientometrics 127 (6), 3695–3718. https://doi.org/10.1007/s11192-022-04406-6.

Prange, J.A., Aleandri, S., Komisarski, M., Luciani, A., Käch, A., Schuh, C.D., Hall, A.M., Mezzenga, R., Devuyst, O., Landau, E.M., 2019. Overcoming endocytosis deficiency by cubosome nanocarriers. ACS Appl. Bio Mater. 2 (6), 2490–2499. https://doi.org/10.1021/acsabm.9b00187.

Queiroz, R.G., Varca, G.H.C., Kadlubowski, S., Ulanski, P., Lugão, A.B., 2016. Radiation-synthesized protein-based drug carriers: size-controlled BSA nanoparticles. Int. J. Biol. Macromol. 85, 82–91. https://doi.org/10.1016/j.ijbiomac.2015.12.074.

Rabbani, G., Ahn, S.N., 2019. Structure, enzymatic activities, glycation and therapeutic potential of human serum albumin: A natural cargo. Int. J. Biol. Macromol. 123, 979–990. https://doi.org/10.1016/j.ijbiomac.2018.11.053.

Rout, D., Sharma, S., Agarwala, P., Upadhyaya, A.K., Sharma, A., Sasmal, D.K., 2023. Interaction of ibuprofen with partially unfolded bovine serum albumin in the presence of ionic micelles and oligosaccharides at different λex and pH: A spectroscopic analysis. ACS Omega 8 (3), 3114–3128. https://doi.org/10.1021/acsomega.2c06447.

Sadeghzadeh, F., Nasiraei Haghighi, H., Ghiyamati, M., Hajizadenadaf, F., Tabrizi, M.H., 2023. In vitro and in vivo study on the anticancer effects of anethole-loaded bovine serum albumin nanoparticles surface decorated with chitosan and folic acid. Cancer Nanotechnology 14 (1). https://doi.org/10.1186/s12645-023-00181-y.

Saha, A., Pradhan, N., Chatterjee, S., Singh, R.K., Trivedi, V., Bhattacharyya, A., Manna, D., 2019. Fatty-amine-conjugated cationic bovine serum albumin nanoparticles for target-specific hydrophobic drug delivery. ACS Appl. Nano Mater. 2 (6), 3671–3683. https://doi.org/10.1021/acsanm.9b00607.

Salehiabar, M., Nosrati, H., Javani, E., Aliakbarzadeh, F., Kheiri Manjili, H., Davaran, S., Danafar, H., 2018. Production of biological nanoparticles from bovine serum albumin as controlled release carrier for curcumin delivery. Int. J. Biol. Macromol. 115, 83–89. https://doi.org/10.1016/j.ijbiomac.2018.04.043.

Shetty, Y., Prabhu, P., Prabhakar, B., 2019. Emerging vistas in theranostic medicine. Int. J. Pharm. 558 (December 2018), 29–42. https://doi.org/10.1016/j.ijpharm.2018.12.068.

Shi, J., Kantoff, P.W., Wooster, R., Farokhzad, O.C., 2017. Cancer nanomedicine: Progress, challenges and opportunities. Nat. Rev. Cancer 17 (1), 20–37. https://doi.org/10.1038/nrc.2016.108.

Shinde, S.R., Jadhav, R.V., Devale, T.L., Vanshiv, S., 2024. Formulation and evaluation of taste masked oral disintegrating tablet of lacosamide. Int. J. Pharma. Sci. Res. 15 (5), 1405–1420. https://doi.org/10.13040/IJPSR.0975-8232.15(5).1405-20.

Sihler, S., Krämer, M., Schmitt, F., Favella, P., Mützel, L., Baatz, J., Frank, R., Ulrich, Z., 2023. Robust protocol for the synthesis of BSA nanohydrogels by inverse nanoemulsion for drug delivery. Langmuir 39 (23), 8176–8185. https://doi.org/10.1021/acs.langmuir.3c00635.

Singh, P., Kim, Y.J., Singh, H., Ahn, S., Castro-Aceituno, V., Yang, D.C., 2017a. In situ preparation of water-soluble ginsenoside Rh2-entrapped bovine serum albumin nanoparticles: In vitro cytocompatibility studies. Int. J. Nanomed. 12, 4073–4084. https://doi.org/10.2147/IJN.S125154.

Singh, P., Singh, H., Castro-Aceituno, V., Ahn, S., Kim, Y.J., Yang, D.C., 2017b. Bovine serum albumin as a nanocarrier for the efficient delivery of ginsenoside compound K: Preparation, physicochemical characterizations and in vitro biological studies. RSC Advances 7 (25), 15397–15407. https://doi.org/10.1039/c6ra25264h.

Siri, M., Grasselli, M., Alonso, S.del V., 2020. Correlation between assembly structure of a gamma irradiated albumin nanoparticle and its function as a drug delivery system. Colloids Surf. A Physicochem. Eng. Asp. 603, 125176. https://doi.org/10.1016/j.colsurfa.2020.125176.

Solanki, R., Rostamabadi, H., Patel, S., Jafari, S.M., 2021. Anticancer nano-delivery systems based on bovine serum albumin nanoparticles: A critical review. Int. J. Biol. Macromol. 193, 528–540. https://doi.org/10.1016/j.ijbiomac.2021.10.040.

Solanki, R., Srivastav, A.K., Patel, S., Singh, S.K., Jodha, B., Kumar, U., Patel, S., 2024. Folate conjugated albumin as a targeted nanocarrier for the delivery of fisetin: in silico and in vitro biological studies. RSC Advances 14 (11), 7338–7349. https://doi.org/10.1039/d3ra08434e.

Solanki, Raghu, Patel, S., 2023. Preparation, characterization and in vitro anticancer efficacy of biotin-conjugated, silibinin loaded bovine serum albumin nanoparticles. Food Biosci. 56, 103150. https://doi.org/10.1016/j.fbio.2023.103150.

Song, F., Li, Y., Wang, S., Zhang, L., Chen, Q.L., 2019. Multifunctional dual-mesoporous silica nanoparticles loaded with a protein and dual antitumor drugs as a targeted delivery system. New J. Chem. 43 (44), 17284–17297. https://doi.org/10.1039/c9nj03001h.

Song, Y., Liu, H., Zhao, N., Chen, J., Zhang, X., Zhang, H., Wu, T., Ruan, H., Qu, G., 2024. Bovine serum albumin-Camptothecin nanoparticles for RNAs packaging to improve the prognosis of Cancer. Int. J. Biol. Macromol. 282, 136997. https://doi.org/10.1016/j.ijbiomac.2024.136997.

Sozer, S.C., Egesoy, T.O., Basol, M., Cakan-Akdogan, G., Akdogan, Y., 2020. A simple desolvation method for production of cationic albumin nanoparticles with improved drug loading and cell uptake. J. Drug Deliv. Sci. Technol. 60. https://doi.org/10.1016/j.jddst.2020.101931. http://www.editionsdesante.fr/category.php?id_category=48.

Srivastav, A.K., Gupta, S.K., Kumar, U., 2020. A molecular simulation approach towards the development of universal nanocarriers by studying the pH- and electrostatic-driven changes in the dynamic structure of albumin. RSC Adv. 10 (23), 13451–13459. https://doi.org/10.1039/d0ra00803f.

Srivastava, A., Prajapati, A., Pramanik, P., Singh, V.K., 2021. A modified method for the production of stable surface-functionalized bovine serum albumin nanoparticles. Biomed. Biotechnol. Res. J. (BBRJ) 5 (3), 335–341. https://doi.org/10.4103/bbrj.bbrj_125_21.

Stewart, S.A., Waite, D., Domínguez-Robles, J., McAlister, E., Permana, A.D., Donnelly, R.F., Larrañeta, E., 2021. HPLC method for levothyroxine quantification in long-acting drug delivery systems. Validation and evaluation of bovine serum albumin as levothyroxine stabilizer. J. Pharm. Biomed. Anal. 203. https://doi.org/10.1016/j.jpba.2021.114182. www.elsevier.com/locate/jpba.

Swarnalatha, K.M., Iswariya, V.T., Akash, B., Bhandari, S., Shirisha, R., Ramarao, T., 2024. A comprehensive review of controlled drug release delivery systems: Current status and future directions. Int. J. Pharm. Phytopharmacol. Res. 14 (2), 24–30. https://doi.org/10.51847/d6pncgcouf.

Tazhbayev, Y., Mukashev, O., Burkeyev, M., Lozinsky, V.I., 2020. synthesis and comparative study of nanoparticles derived from bovine and human serum albumins. Polymers 12 (6), 1301. https://doi.org/10.3390/polym12061301.

Thilagam, R., Gnanamani, A., 2020. Preparation, characterization and stability assessment of keratin and albumin functionalized gold nanoparticles for biomedical applications. Appl. Nanosci. 10 (6), 1879–1892. https://doi.org/10.1007/s13204-020-01250-z.

Uma Maheswari, P., Muthappa, R., Purushothaman Bindhya, K., Meera Sheriffa Begum, K.M., 2021. Evaluation of folic acid functionalized BSA-CaFe2O4 nanohybrid carrier for the controlled delivery of natural cytotoxic drugs hesperidin and eugenol. J. Drug Deliv. Sci. Technol. 61, 102105. https://doi.org/10.1016/j.jddst.2020.102105.

Varanko, A., Saha, S., Chilkoti, A., 2020. Recent trends in protein and peptide-based biomaterials for advanced drug delivery. Adv. Drug Deliv. Rev. 156, 133–187. https://doi.org/10.1016/j.addr.2020.08.008.

Varga, N., Hornok, V., Sebők, D., Dékány, I., 2016. Comprehensive study on the structure of the BSA from extended-to aged form in wide (2–12) pH range. Int. J. Biol. Macromol. 88, 51–58. https://doi.org/10.1016/j.ijbiomac.2016.03.030.

Verma, R., Mittal, V., Kaushik, D., 2018. Quality based design approach for improving oral bioavailability of valsartan loaded smedds and study of impact of lipolysis on the drug diffusion. Drug Deliv. Lett. 8 (2), 130–139. https://doi.org/10.2174/2210303108666180313141956.

Wang, L., Wu, Y., Yang, N., Yin, W., Yang, H., Li, C., Zhuang, Y., Song, Z., Cheng, X., Shi, S., Wu, Y., 2024. Self-assembly of maltose-albumin nanoparticles for efficient targeting delivery and therapy in liver cancer. Int. J. Biol. Macromol. 258, 128691. https://doi.org/10.1016/j.ijbiomac.2023.128691.

Wishnia, A., Pinder, T., 1964. Hydrophobic interactions in proteins: Conformation changes in bovine serum albumin below pH 5. Biochemistry 3 (9), 1377–1384. https://doi.org/10.1021/bi00897a031.

Xie, L., Tong, W., Yu, D., Xu, J., Jun, L., Gao, C., 2012. Bovine serum albumin nanoparticles modified with multilayers and aptamers for pH-responsive and targeted anti-cancer drug delivery. J. Mater. Chem. 22 (13), 6053. https://doi.org/10.1039/c2jm16831f.

Xu, Z., Grassian, V.H., 2017. Bovine serum albumin adsorption on TiO2 nanoparticle surfaces: Effects of ph and coadsorption of phosphate on protein-surface interactions and protein structure. J. Phys. Chem. C 121 (39), 21763–21771. http://pubs.acs.org/journal/jpccck. doi: 10.1021/acs.jpcc.7b07525.

Xu, L., Xu, R., Saw, P.E., Wu, J., Cheng, S.X., Xu, X., 2021. Nanoparticle-mediated inhibition of mitochondrial glutaminolysis to amplify oxidative stress for combination cancer therapy. Nano Lett. 21 (18), 7569–7578. http://pubs.acs.org/journal/nalefd. doi: 10.1021/acs.nanolett.1c02073.

Yang, Z., Zhang, N., Ma, T., Liu, L., Zhao, L., Xie, H., 2020. Engineered bovine serum albumin-based nanoparticles with pH-sensitivity for doxorubicin delivery and controlled release. Drug Deliv. 27 (1), 1156–1164. https://doi.org/10.1080/10717544.2020.1797243.

Yang, S., Ni, G., Xia, M., Li, H., Gao, Z., 2023. Mussel inspired multifunctional bovine serum albumin (BSA) coatings loaded with Baicalein (BAI) to enhance osteogenesis and resist oxidative stress for potential application on implant. Int. J. Biol. Macromol. 229, 752–765. https://doi.org/10.1016/j.ijbiomac.2022.12.285.

Yazdani, M., Rahmandoust, M., Kouchakzadeh, H., 2022. Development of various carbon nanoparticles and albumin complexes for potential theranostics applications. J. Drug Deliv. Sci. Technol. 77 (June), 103901. https://doi.org/10.1016/j.jddst.2022.103901.

Yessentayeva, N.A., Galiyeva, A.R., Daribay, A.T., Sadyrbekov, D.T., Zhumagalieva, T.S., Marsel, D.T., Buketov, E. A., 2024. Synthesis and optimization of bovine serum albumin nanoparticles immobilized with antituberculosis drugs. Eurasian J. Chem. 29 (1), 33–42. https://doi.org/10.31489/2959-0663/1-24-6.

Yogasundaram, H., Bahniuk, M.S., Singh, H.D., Aliabadi, H.M., Uludağ, H., Unsworth, L.D., 2012. BSA nanoparticles for siRNA delivery: Coating effects on nanoparticle properties, plasma protein adsorption, and in vitro siRNA delivery. Int. J. Biomat. https://doi.org/10.1155/2012/584060.

Yuana, Y., Balachandran, B., van der Wurff-Jacobs, K.M.G., Schiffelers, R.M., Moonen, C.T., 2020. Potential use of extracellular vesicles generated by microbubble-assisted ultrasound as drug nanocarriers for cancer treatment. Int. J. Mol. Sci. 21 (8). https://doi.org/10.3390/ijms21083024. https://www.mdpi.com/1422-0067/21/8/3024/pdf.

Zhang, Y., Liang, Y., 2024. Fabrication of folic acid-modified bovine serum albumin cloaked dual-drug loaded hollow mesoporous silica nanoparticles for pH-responsive and targeted delivery of gastric cancer therapy. Heliyon 10 (8), e29274. https://doi.org/10.1016/j.heliyon.2024.e29274.

Zhang, L., Lu, Z., Bai, Y., Wang, T., Wang, Z., Chen, J., Ding, Y., Yang, F., Xiao, Z., Ju, S., Zhu, J., He, N., 2013. PEGylated denatured bovine serum albumin modified water-soluble inorganic nanocrystals as multifunctional drug delivery platforms. J. Mater. Chem. B 1 (9), 1289–1295. https://doi.org/10.1039/c2tb00380e.

Zhang, J., Li, Y., Fang, X., Zhou, D., Wang, Y., Chen, M., 2014. TPGS-g-PLGA/Pluronic F68 mixed micelles for tanshinone IIA delivery in cancer therapy. Int. J. Pharm. 476 (1–2), 185–198. https://doi.org/10.1016/j.ijpharm.2014.09.017.

Zhang, J., Ren, X., Tian, X., Zhang, P., Chen, Z., Hu, X., Mei, X., 2019. GSH and enzyme responsive nanospheres based on self-assembly of green tea polyphenols and BSA used for target cancer chemotherapy. Colloids Surf. B Biointerfaces 173, 654–661. https://doi.org/10.1016/j.colsurfb.2018.10.037.

Zhou, K., Zhu, Y., Chen, X., Li, L., Xu, W., 2020. Redox- and MMP-2-sensitive drug delivery nanoparticles based on gelatin and albumin for tumor targeted delivery of paclitaxel. Mater. Sci. Eng. C 114, 111006. https://doi.org/10.1016/j.msec.2020.111006.

Zhu, Y., Tong, W., Gao, C., Möhwald, H., 2008. Fabrication of bovine serum albumin microcapsules by desolvation and destroyable cross-linking. J. Mater. Chem. 18 (10), 1153–1158. https://doi.org/10.1039/b714647g.

Zhu, D., Roy, S., Liu, Z., Weller, H., Parak, W.J., Feliu, N., 2019. Remotely controlled opening of delivery vehicles and release of cargo by external triggers. Adv. Drug Deliv. Rev. 138, 117–132. https://doi.org/10.1016/j.addr.2018.10.003.

Ziaaddini, V., Saeidifar, M., Eslami-Moghadam, M., Saberi, M., Mozafari, M., 2020. Improvement of efficacy and decrement cytotoxicity of oxaliplatin anticancer drug using bovine serum albumin nanoparticles: synthesis, characterisation and release behaviour. IET Nanobiotechnol. 14 (1), 105–111. https://doi.org/10.1049/iet-nbt.2019.0086.

CHAPTER

# 13

# Milk protein/casein-based nanocarriers for drug delivery

*Mona M. Agwa*[1], *Hesham S.M. Soliman*[2, 3], *Heba Elmotasem*[4], *Hossam M. El-Masry*[1] *and Sally Sabra*[5]

[1]**Department of Chemistry of Natural and Microbial Products, Pharmaceutical and Drug Industries Research Institute, National Research Centre, Giza, Cairo, Egypt;** [2]**Pharmacognosy Department, Faculty of Pharmacy, Capital University (Previously Helwan University), Cairo, Egypt;** [3]**Faculty of Pharmacy, Egypt-Japan University of Science and Technology, New Borg El Arab, Alexandria, Egypt;** [4]**Pharmaceutical Technology Department, Pharmaceutical and Drug Industries Research Institute, National Research Centre, Giza, Cairo, Egypt;** [5]**Department of Biotechnology, Institute of Graduate Studies and Research, Alexandria University, Alexandria, Egypt**

## 1. Introduction

Over the past decade, the application of biodegradable polymers as potential delivery agents with a controlled release manner for many pharmaceuticals has dramatically increased (Hamza et al., 2023; El-Sayed et al., 2024). Biodegradable polymers can be categorized into natural or synthetic (Agwa et al., 2024a; 2024b; 2024c). Synthetic polymers exhibit superior advantages over natural polymers, as they can be easily tailored to give a broad range of characteristics, but they display high toxicity (Agwa et al., 2022). On the other hand, natural polymers are prioritized over synthetic ones and are generally deemed more safer and highly biocompatible when being harnessed as nano-delivery systems (Amer et al., 2023). Among all the natural polymers, food proteins possess many characteristics when being employed as a nanocarrier for therapeutics (Sabra and Agwa, 2020; Agwa and Sabra, 2021). First, they exhibit high feeding value and do not liberate any dangerous materials when administered orally and digested into smaller fractions in vivo, which implies they are already valuable for the body (Tavakoli et al., 2021). Second, they possess multiple functional groups on their surface, which facilitates binding with many drugs and

*Protein-Based Nanoparticles in Drug Delivery*
**https://doi.org/10.1016/B978-0-443-33639-3.00025-8**

receptors at the aimed site (Agwa et al., 2023a, 2023b, 2024b). Third, they offer superior functional characteristics, involving foaming, gelation, emulsification, and water-binding capacity (Agwa et al., 2020). Therapeutic materials can be encapsulated into these natural polymers with high capacity through multiple mechanisms involving hydrophobic interactions, electrostatic attractions, and covalent bonding (Agwa et al., 2024b). Popular natural proteins that have been successfully applied for drug delivery are gelatin, albumin, collagen, and milk proteins (Shalaby et al., 2020). Among these natural proteins, casein has acquired great interest recently. Casein is the highly plentiful protein in milk, constituting more than 80% of overall milk proteins (Aboras et al., 2021). It is economically inexpensive, highly stable, nontoxic, nonantigenic, easily digestible, biocompatible, biodegradable, and readily available. As a unique natural food product, this GRAS (generally recognized as safe) casein protein is a suitable carrier for the construction of smart nutraceutical and drug delivery vehicles with improved therapeutic potential (Mittal et al., 2022). The amphiphilic nature of this protein was assigned to the existence of both hydrophilic and lipophilic amino acids. Thus, they can be self-assembled in the aqueous phase to form stable core/shell structure nano-micelles with excellent emulsifying strength in which the inside is constructed from the hydrophobic section, while the external shell is constructed from the hydrophilic section (Agwa et al., 2021). So, casein nano-micelles are very suitable for delivering both hydrophobic and hydrophilic cargoes (Agwa et al., 2018). Additionally, the pH-dependent manner of casein nano-micelles renders it ideal for the controlled release of orally administered therapeutics. Furthermore, the unfolded framework of casein nano-micelles renders them readily attainable for proteolysis by proteolytic enzymes, guaranteeing good drug release. Interestingly, casein nano-micelles can permeate intracellularly in an energy-independent manner, which can reinforce cellular uptake (Mittal et al., 2022; Milenkova et al., 2022). In this chapter, we aim to present some recent examples of casein nanocarrier-encapsulated drugs and feature their potential for treating various diseases.

## 2. Structural manifestation

Casein comprises low molecular weight colloidal calcium phosphate (6%), which is fundamental to keeping the architecture of casein together. It is a protein with high phosphate content constructed from four subunits involving αS1, αS2, β-, and κ-casein, having a molecular weight between 19 and 25 kDa and occurring approximately in ratios of 4:14:1 by weight, respectively (Gandhi and Roy, 2021). Their isoelectric point (pI) ranges between 4.6 and 4.8. All casein subunits display ill-defined frameworks and don't have a determined secondary or tertiary architecture. The cause is that casein is rich in proline and devoid of disulfide bonds, which hinders the generation of alpha helices and beta sheets, thus caseins are far more heat resistant. Besides, the open structure of the caseins renders them readily attainable for proteolytic digestion (Elzoghby et al., 2011). Caseins are amphiphilic and have the feature of self-assembling into stable nano-micelles in aqueous media. These nano-micellar frameworks are constructed from the formerly mentioned four subunits linked together by hydrophobic attraction and via the bridging of colloidal calcium phosphate, which is linked to the serine residues through their phosphate moiety (Milenkova et al., 2022). The interior part of the nano-micelles is mostly hydrophobic and constructed from αS1, αS2, and β-casein. The external surface of the nano-micelles is primarily constructed from the hydrophilic κ-casein that makes the micellar surfaces highly charged and stable against agglomeration (Wenck et al., 2024). All of these merits render casein an interesting vehicle for drug delivery implementation.

## 3. Methods of preparation

Casein nano-micelles were successfully formulated via multiple techniques for the delivery of various drugs (Fig. 13.1).

### 3.1 Desolvation

In the desolvation technique, nanoparticles (NPs) are acquired upon dropwise addition of a desolvating material (e.g., acetone or alcohol) to an aqueous casein solution under continuous stirring to dehydrate the protein and generate conformational modification from stretched to coil architecture. Afterward, coacervates were strengthened by cross-linking the amino groups in the casein protein (Langer et al., 2003).

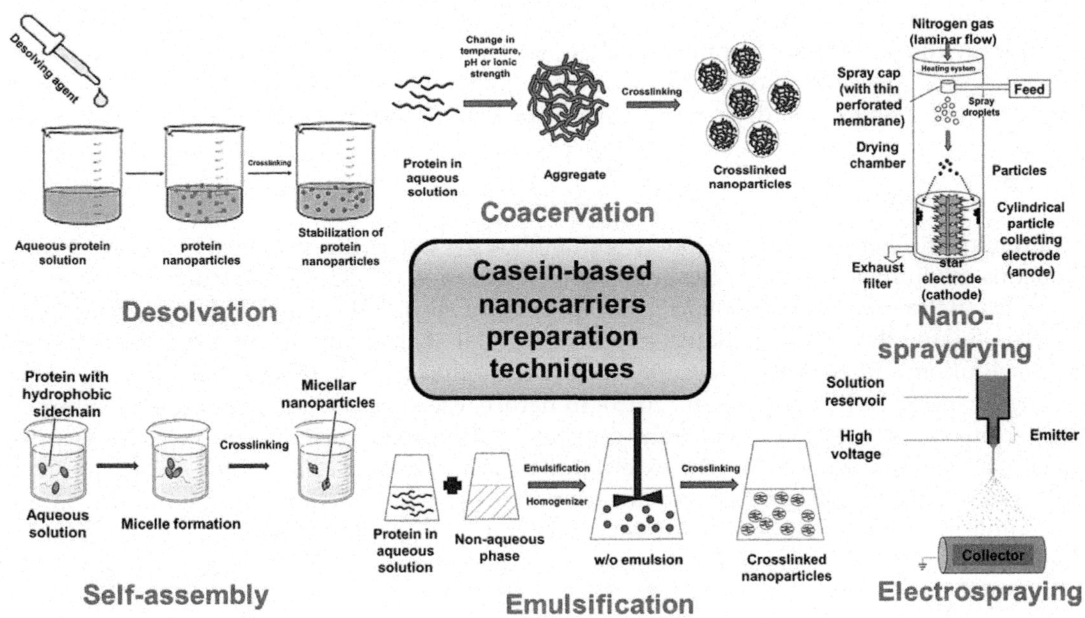


FIGURE 13.1 Different techniques utilized for the preparation of diverse casein nanocarriers.

## 3.2 Coacervation

Coacervation relies on the differential solubility of proteins in solvents that depends on the solvent's ionic strength, pH, polarity, or involvement of electrolytes. It minimizes the solubility of the protein, causing phase separation. In the coacervation technique, the addition of salt to the protein solution causes liquid–liquid phase disconnection and gives rise to a lower polymer-rich layer and an upper transparent solution layer, resulting in the demanded NPs (Lu et al., 2004).

## 3.3 Emulsification

There are two prime strategies regarding emulsification via harnessing the solvent evaporation technique. The first relies on the formulation of a single emulsion or oil-in-water (o/w) emulsion, and the other relies on the formulation of double emulsions or water-in-oil-in-water (w/o/w) emulsion. These techniques exploit ultrasonication or high-speed homogenization, followed by solvent evaporation under continuous stirring at ambient temperature or reduced pressure. Next, the solid NPs can be assembled by ultracentrifugation (Krishna Sailaja et al., 2011).

## 3.4 Nano spray drying

Spray drying is a well-settled technique generally employed in the pharmaceutical industry to generate a dry powder from a liquid medium. It is very convenient when treating heat-labile ingredients like proteins, preventing their degradation. In contrast to traditional spray dryers that utilize pressure nozzles and rotary atomizers for designing the sprayed droplets, the nano spray dryer utilizes a vibrating mesh technology for tiny droplet production. Nano spray drying process presents a novel, easy, and alternative tactic for the generation of NPs with the advantage of a single-step drying and scalable process (Rehman et al., 2021).

## 3.5 Self-assembly

Protein micelles can be generated spontaneously when the protein is dissolved in an aqueous medium above the critical micelle concentration (CMC) to construct nano-sized aggregates (Batrakova et al., 2006). Micellar architectures could be stabilized and strengthened by crosslinking the polymer chains, and the formulated crosslinked nano-micelles are stable upon dilution and tolerate alterations in experimental circumstances (e.g., solvents, ionic strength, and pH) (Elzoghby et al., 2015). In nature, casein possessed the shape of submicellar architectures loaded with calcium phosphate. The inner core of the micelles comprises αs1-, αs2-, and β-caseins, while the external shell comprises κ-casein, which creates a powerful steric repulsion that provides stabilization to the structure. In aqueous media, casein protein molecules were self-assembled into nano-micellar structures where the hydrophobic inner core of micelles serves as a micro-reservoir for hydrophobic drugs (Davidov-Pardo et al., 2015).

### 3.6 Electrospraying

Protein-based nanofibers or nano-capsules can be constructed using the electrospinning technique, where an electrical field is harnessed to drag a protein solution through a thin nozzle (Hamza et al., 2023; El-Aassar et al., 2024). Briefly, protein and drug are solubilized in a mutually adequate solvent and inserted into a capillary syringe. After providing a high-voltage electrical field, the protein solution is dragged out of the syringe, forming a lean jet followed by the generation of either capsules or fibers on the collection plate according to the nature of the protein solution and the electric field intensity. The complete volatilization of the solvent occurs when the electrosprayed jet rushes to the collector plate, thus the space must be quite long to fully evaporate the solvent; otherwise, proteins will merge (Agwa et al., 2024a; 2024b; 2024c; Tarhini et al., 2017).

## 4. Drug delivery applications of casein nanocarriers

### 4.1 Casein-based nanocarriers for delivery of anticancer drugs

Most anticancer drugs are sparingly soluble in water with very low bioavailability, resulting in the administration of frequent doses with high concentrations to be therapeutically effective (Madan et al., 2020). In addition, many of the anticancer drugs have diverse side effects, which is a fundamental concern for both patients and clinicians (Agwa et al., 2024c). Biocompatible natural polymers such as casein can be used to further encapsulate these drugs so as to minimize their toxicity, increase their bioavailability, and afford improved uptake by tumor cells due to the small size of these NPs (Jahangirian et al., 2017).

In this light, celecoxib (antiinflammatory COX-2 inhibitor) and prodigiosin (microbial red pigment) were coloaded into zein (shell)/sodium caseinate (core) NPs in order to improve their aqueous solubility (Mohamed et al., 2024). Dual drug-loaded zein/sodium caseinate NPs were prepared by the antisolvent technique, in which sodium caseinate was included in the preparation in order to form a shell to stabilize the prepared zein NPs due to the good emulsifying properties of caseinate. Results revealed the formation of homogenous spherical NPs with good encapsulation efficiency for both drugs and low hemolytic potential. In vitro studies conducted on MDA-MB-231 breast cancer cells showed lower $IC_{50}$ for the nanoformulation in comparison to the combination of free drugs. Furthermore, scratch assay revealed reduced cellular migration for treated cells, associated with reduced inflammation and angiogenesis.

In another study, sodium caseinate micelles were utilized to simultaneously encapsulate celecoxib and dasatinib (tyrosine kinase inhibitor) into their hydrophobic core via the solvent evaporation technique (Lamey et al., 2023). Physicochemical characterization showed a formation of spherical micelles with hydrodynamic particle size of about 160 nm with encapsulation efficiencies of about 80% and 92% for celecoxib and dasatinib, respectively. In vitro cytotoxic study on MCF-7 and MDA-MB-231 cells displayed improved effect with good synergy. In vivo studies in Ehrlich ascites tumor-bearing Swiss CD1 female mice showed that intravenous administration of dual drug-loaded micelles resulted in a significant reduction in angiogenesis, proliferation, and migration markers, besides improvement in the apoptosis level. In addition, the prepared formulation was found to reduce the systemic toxicity of the drugs when compared to the free drug combination.

In another approach, 10-hydroxy camptothecin (which causes cellular DNA damage) and Nile red were coencapsulated into casein NPs using calcium chloride as a crosslinker (Khatun et al., 2023). Synthesized NPs exhibited hydrodynamic particle sizes of about 120–160 nm with a sustained in vitro drug release profile. In addition, drug-loaded casein NPs showed superior biocompatibility when examined with L929 fibroblast cells, NIH-3T3, and zebrafish embryos, associated with enhanced cellular uptake for both 10-hydroxy camptothecin (which causes cellular DNA damage) and Nile red, with potent cancer cell toxicity (>80% cell death) and deep penetration in a 3D model of 4T1 cells. Furthermore, prepared drug-loaded NPs revealed excessive reactive oxygen species (ROS) production with alterations in the membrane potential of the mitochondria, leading to cancer cell apoptosis. Moreover, some proteins related to DNA damage, such as γ-H2AX, were overexpressed, and proteins related to DNA repair, such as Poly (ADP ribose) polymerase (PARP) protein, were downregulated, confirming the potent anticancer effect of the prepared NPs.

A smart enzyme-responsive nanocarrier encapsulating eugenol (a phenolic compound in clove oil and honey) was prepared from casein protein and mesoporous silica NPs (MSNs) (Wijewantha et al., 2023). MSNs were synthesized and then carboxylated in a two-step reaction. First, MSNs were aminated by reaction with (3-aminopropyl) triethoxysilane (APTES). In the second step, aminated MSNs were further treated with succinic anhydride. Eugenol was then loaded into carboxylated MSNs, followed by casein conjugation onto the surface of the nano-assembly via EDC/sulfo-NHS reaction. The resultant nanoplatform showed a particle size of about 245 nm and a polydispersity index (PDI) of about 0.3. In vitro studies on colorectal cancer cells indicated a prominent decrease in cancer cell population, migration, and invasion due to higher affinity and internalization into cancer cells, with no toxicity observed on normal cells. This enhanced effect in cancer cells could be attributed to the digestion of casein, "the gatekeeper," by the released matrix metalloproteinases from the edges of migratory tumor cells and local exposure of the cells to high concentrations of eugenol, which is not the case in normal cells. These results suggest that this smart casein-based nanocarrier can serve as a promising antimetastatic approach.

Daunorubicin (an anthracycline antibiotic widely used to treat leukemia) was loaded into casein NPs using a coacervation technique, followed by spray drying (Zahariev et al., 2023). Results indicated that the encapsulation efficiency depended on the casein-to-drug ratio and the particle size was between 127 and 167 nm. In addition, in vitro drug release was found to be pH-dependent due to possible alterations in the structure and size of the NPs, as casein NPs' swelling properties are pH-dependent, suggesting the suitability of these NPs for sustained drug release. When drug-loaded NPs were examined on Reh lymphoblastic cells, there was a notable alteration in the mitochondrial respiration and ATP production, causing a potent cytotoxic effect compared to free drug.

Sorafenib (a multikinase inhibitor with low oral bioavailability) was encapsulated into camel milk casein NPs to be used in managing hepatocellular carcinoma (Mittal et al., 2022). Sorafenib-loaded casein NPs were synthesized using $CaCl_2$ (10 mM) as a crosslinker, followed by centrifugation at low speed to remove microparticles. Drug-loaded casein NPs showed a spherical shape with a particle size (PS) of about 212 nm, with encapsulation efficiency of about 51.5 ± 3.2% and a negative zeta potential (−20 mV). In vitro cellular studies conducted on HepG2 cell lines revealed more cytotoxic effect for sorafenib-loaded casein NPs in comparison to the free drug, which might be related to better cellular internalization.

In another study, paclitaxel was loaded into casein NPs using the solvent evaporation technique, and then the surface of drug-loaded casein NPs was further functionalized with specific molecular weight hyaluronic acid oligosaccharides using the carbodiimide conjugation reaction (Wang et al., 2022). These hyaluronic acid oligosaccharides were prepared by hydrolysis of high molecular weight hyaluronic acid using leech hyaluronidase as previously reported (Jin et al., 2014). The molecular weight of the hydrolyzed hyaluronic acid was estimated using size exclusion chromatography. Hyaluronic acid oligosaccharides were used instead of high molecular weight hyaluronic acid owing to their unique contribution in cell motility, inflammation, and cancer metastasis, besides their potential to bind to CD44 receptors overexpressed on the surface of tumor cells (Agwa et al., 2023b). Results manifested that hyaluronic acid conjugated paclitaxel-casein NPs at a mass ratio of 3:1 were the optimum formulation with PS of 235.5 nm, encapsulation efficiency of about 93.1%, and stability at 4°C for more than 10 days with more than 80% drug retention. Moreover, functionalized drug-loaded casein NPs revealed a high in vitro cytotoxic effect (61.3%) on human melanoma A375 cells, which was comparable to the effect of cisplatin (64.9%). More importantly, in vivo studies in a tumor animal model showed that intravenous administration of the prepared functionalized drug-loaded casein NPs twice a week exhibited superior tumor inhibition up to 74.6% in comparison to drug-loaded casein NPs, which displayed only 39.8% tumor inhibition.

Aptamers are short sequences of DNA or RNA that can fold into a specific three-dimensional structure with high affinity to bind to certain receptors on the cell surface, so as to improve cellular internalization to a specific cell type. Like antibodies, aptamers are highly selective for certain cancer cell receptors. However, they have several advantages over antibodies: they are easy to synthesize and modify; cost-effective; small enough to effectively penetrate tumors; thermostable; and they have minimal immunogenic effects (Agwa et al., 2023a). In this regard, sodium caseinate was first prepared from casein using NaOH (1M), followed by dialysis and freeze-drying. BODIPY (lipophilic dye)-loaded casein NPs were then prepared using 1 M $CaCl_2$ as a crosslinker, and then drug-loaded casein NPs were further functionalized with either amino-terminated CL4 or amino-terminated CL4-scrambled (SCR) aptamers using the EDC/NHS carbodiimide conjugation reaction (Franchini, 2022). CL4 RNA aptamer was selected for functionalization as it can efficiently bind to domain IV in the epidermal growth factor receptor (EGFR) extracellular region. These receptors are overexpressed on the surface of triple-negative breast cancer cell lines such as MDA-MB-231 and BT-549 cells, and hence they can be used for active targeting of this cancer subtype (Camorani et al., 2015). Prepared CL4-conjugated dye-loaded caseinate NPs showed PS of about 194 nm with a zeta potential value of about −12 mV and encapsulation efficiency in the range of 44%. In vitro cellular studies showed that conjugation of the CL4 aptamer to casein NPs revealed improved cellular uptake in MDA-MB-231 and BT-549 cells in comparison to scrambled CL4-conjugated NPs, confirming that the enhanced internalization is due to the CL4 aptamer.

In another study, chemically stable crosslinked casein micelles were prepared in a two-step technique in which casein micelles were first re-assembled via dialysis in the presence of $CaCl_2$, and then an intra-micellar crosslinking reaction was conducted between NH2 and COOH groups present in the casein molecule using the EDC/NHS conjugation reaction to increase the structural stability. Afterward, paclitaxel was loaded into crosslinked micelles using the dialysis technique, depending on hydrophobic interactions, with a drug loading percentage ranging from 10% to 20% (Cuggino et al., 2021). Results revealed that crosslinking was able to maintain the stability of the micelles at pH 13 without any significant change in the PS, which was about 180 nm. In addition, in vitro cellular uptake studies using Rhodamine B as a fluorescent dye in the presence of some uptake inhibitors, such as sucrose and sodium azide, confirmed that the main internalization mechanism is clathrin-mediated endocytosis. Meanwhile, in vitro cytotoxicity studies performed on HeLa and PC3 cancer cells revealed that paclitaxel-crosslinked casein micelles were more toxic in comparison to free drug, suggesting that these micelles can accumulate in the tumor microenvironment (TME) by passive targeting depending on the enhanced permeation and retention effect (EPR), and the payload can be precisely released due to overexpressed proteases such as trypsin in TME.

Superparamagnetic calcium ferrite NPs were synthesized using the sol-gel method, and subsequently, the prepared magnetic NPs were hybridized with casein via the desolvation technique. Afterward, thymoquinone (a plant-derived compound) was encapsulated via the coacervation technique. Finally, drug-loaded hybrid NPs were functionalized by glutamic acid using carbodiimide conjugation reaction through the formation of CO–NH Schiff base bonding (Purushothaman et al., 2021). This multifunctional platform showed improved drug targetability based on the pH sensitivity of casein in response to the acidic tumor environment and magnetic response in the presence of an external magnetic field, besides the active targeting potential of glutamate. Moreover, there was a notable sustainability in the in vitro drug release profile, at which after 4 hours only about 16% of the drug was released at pH 7.4, while the release increased up to 67% at pH 5.4 and 70% under application of an external magnetic field at the same time interval. In addition, an *in vitro* cytotoxicity study performed on glioblastoma U87 cells revealed a better anticancer effect due to increased internalization based on the overexpressed glutamate receptors, suggesting that multiresponsive nanocarriers can be a good therapeutic choice.

Triptolide is an epoxy diterpene lactone extracted from different parts of *Tripterygium wilfordii.* It possesses antiinflammatory, immunosuppressive, and broad-spectrum antitumor effects, especially for oral cancer. However, its clinical use is hampered due to poor aqueous solubility, low bioavailability, and very high toxicity (Li et al., 2014). In this regard, casein-based NPs encapsulating triptolide were prepared depending on the self-assembly properties of casein using the ultrasonication/freeze-drying technique (Liu et al., 2020). Results indicated that the prepared drug-loaded casein NPs were spherical with PS of about 128 nm and encapsulation efficiency of about 72% and sustained an in vitro drug release profile at pH 7.4. More importantly, oral administration of triptolide-casein NPs in healthy rats showed improved in vivo pharmacokinetics compared to oral administration of the oral drug suspension in terms of higher mean plasma concentration, $C_{max,}$ and area under the curve (Table 13.1).

**TABLE 13.1** Recent information of casein-based nanostructures in drug delivery applications and their associated profits and perspectives.

| Nano-system | Active drug | Preparation method | Highlights | Ref |
|---|---|---|---|---|
| Sodium caseinate (shell)/zein NPs (core) | Celecoxib and prodigiosin | Antisolvent technique | Reduced IC50 for the prepared NPs in comparison to the free drug combination with reduced cellular migration, inflammation, and angiogenesis. | Mohamed et al. (2024) |
| Sodium caseinate micelles | Celecoxib and dasatinib | Solvent evaporation | Improved in vivo antitumor effect in an animal model upon intravenous administration in terms of reduced tumor volume, decreased angiogenesis, and proliferation levels. | Lamey et al. (2023) |
| Casein NPs | 10-Hydroxy camptothecin and Nile red | Nanoprecipitation with $CaCl_2$ as crosslinker | Deep penetration in a 3D model of 4T1 cells with increased ROS production and alterations in the membrane potential of the mitochondria. | Khatun et al. (2023) |
| Mesoporous silica NPs conjugated to casein | Eugenol | Amination, EDC/NHS conjugation | Better in vitro anticancer effect with reduced metastasis due to selective casein digestion by matrix metalloproteinases of migratory tumor cells. | Wijewantha et al. (2023) |
| Casein NPs | Daunorubicin | Coacervation, spray drying. | Potent in vitro cytotoxic effect due to notable alteration in the mitochondrial respiration and ATP production in Reh lymphoblastic cells. | Zahariev et al. (2023) |
| Casein NPs | Sorafenib | Nanoprecipitation with $CaCl_2$ as crosslinker | More cytotoxic effect on HepG2 cells due to better internalization. | Mittal et al. (2022) |
| Casein NPs functionalized with hyaluronic acid oligosaccharides | Paclitaxel | Solvent evaporation, EDC/NHS conjugation | Superior in vivo tumor growth inhibition (74.6%) in comparison to drug-loaded casein NPs without hyaluronic acid oligosaccharides (39.8%). | Wang et al. (2022) |

*(Continued)*

**TABLE 13.1** Recent information of casein-based nanostructures in drug delivery applications and their associated profits and perspectives.—cont'd

| Nano-system | Active drug | Preparation method | Highlights | Ref |
|---|---|---|---|---|
| Sodium caseinate functionalized with CL4 aptamer | BODIPY | Nanoprecipitation with $CaCl_2$ as crosslinker, EDC/NHS conjugation | Improved in vitro cellular uptake in MDA-MB-231 and BT-549 cells due to efficient binding between the CL4 aptamer and domain IV in the overexpressed epidermal growth factor receptor (EGFR) extracellular region. | Franchini (2022) |
| Crosslinked casein micelles | Paclitaxel | Re-assembly in the presence of $CaCl_2$, then intracrosslinking with EDC/NHS conjugation, dialysis | Better in vitro accumulation in TME of HeLa and PC3 cells by passive targeting and precise payload release due to overexpressed proteases such as trypsin. | Cuggino et al. (2021) |
| Calcium ferrite NPs hybridized with casein and functionalized with glutamic acid | Thymoquinone | Sol-gel/desolvation, coacervation, carbodiimide conjugation | Increased in vitro drug release in response to low pH (5.4) and external magnetic field, associated with increased uptake in U87 cells due to overexpressed glutamate receptors | Purushothaman et al. (2021) |
| Vitamin D3-coated casein micelles | Vitamin D3, etoposide | Solvent evaporation, thin film hydration | Enhanced in vivo biodistribution and antitumor effect due to increased targeting by the aid of overexpressed vitamin D3 receptors on cancer cells. | Agwa et al. (2021) |
| Casein NPs | Triptolide | Ultrasonication/freeze drying | Improved pharmacokinetic profile in healthy rats upon oral administration compared to the free drug form | Liu et al. (2020) |
| Casein | Chrysin. | Solvent evaporation method | Powerful antibacterial efficiency against lung infection in vivo owing to improved oral bioavailability. | Tang et al. (2024) |
| Sodium caseinate | Thymol and lauric acid | Emulsification method | Powerful antibacterial efficiency against *Listeria monocytogenes* owing to improved solubility, prolonging the shelf life of meat products | Ge et al. (2023) |
| Casein | Apigenin | Hydrogen bond formation | Superior in vivo hypoglycemic activity owing to improved solubility, bioavailability, and pharmacokinetics. | (Li Wang et al., 2024) |

**TABLE 13.1** Recent information of casein-based nanostructures in drug delivery applications and their associated profits and perspectives.—cont'd

| Nano-system | Active drug | Preparation method | Highlights | Ref |
|---|---|---|---|---|
| Sodium caseinate/ gum arabic | Orange oil, allyl caproate, linalool, isoamyl acetate, and linalool | Emulsification method | Enhanced biochemical parameters and superior hypoglycemic activity accompanied by lowered oral glucose tolerance without any health risks in vivo. | Mohammed et al. (2023) |
| Sodium caseinate | Curcumin | Ultrasound treatment | Powerful in vitro antiinflammatory owing to perfect uptake | Li et al. (2022) |
| Chitosan/casein | Ophiopogon japonicus polysaccharides | Electrostatic Coassembly | Efficient uptake by macrophages and powerful in vitro antiinflammatory impact via suppressing nickel-provoked toxicity to macrophages and minimizing the ability of LPS to trigger nitric oxide generation. | Lin et al. (2022) |
| Casein | Ferulic acid, resveratrol, and rhein | Hydrogen bonding and hydrophobic interactions | Augmented antioxidant impact for polyphenol-loaded casein nanoparticles owing to improved solubility and stability. | (Wang et al., 2024b) |
| Casein | Curcumin | Controllable pH-shifting mechanism and hydrophobic interaction. | Augmented antioxidant impact for curcumin-loaded casein nanoparticles owing to improved solubility and stability. | Du et al. (2022) |
| Casein | AuNPs and AuNCs | Self-assembly in aqueous solution | Powerful in vitro and in vivo anticancer and photodynamic performance after light irradiation. | Zhang et al. (2022) |
| Casein-functionalized glutathione | IR 797 dye and cytotoxic camptothecin | Nanoprecipitation using $CaCl_2$ as crosslinker | Powerful reduction in tumor size and volume in vivo after laser irradiation owing to enhanced uptake of the chemo/phototherapy by tumor cells. | Khatun et al. (2024) |
| Sodium caseinate | Pheophorbide a (Pba) | Ultracentrifugation using $CaCl_2$ as crosslinker | Complete tumor eradication in vivo without noticeable side effects following laser exposure owing to enhanced uptake of the PDT by tumor cells. | Kim et al. (2024) |

*(Continued)*

**TABLE 13.1** Recent information of casein-based nanostructures in drug delivery applications and their associated profits and perspectives.—cont'd

| Nano-system | Active drug | Preparation method | Highlights | Ref |
|---|---|---|---|---|
| Sodium caseinate | Magnetic nanoparticles | Self-assembly in aqueous solution | Efficient in vitro cellular uptake accompanied by intratumoral localization near the nucleus, which in turn signalizes and improves therapeutic and theranostic impact at the aimed site. | Wenck et al. (2024) |
| Casein/polyvinyl alcohol | Ag NPs | Electrospinning | Maximum cell viability against 3T3 mouse fibroblast cells accompanied by superior scratch wound closure via increasing the migration and proliferation. | George et al. (2024) |
| Sodium caseinate/ polyvinyl alcohol | ZnO NPs | Electrospinning | Improved antibacterial activity and cell viability when incubated with the mouse L929 fibroblast. | Şendil et al. (2023) |
| Casein/ polycaprolactone | Green tea essential oil | Electrospinning | Efficient antioxidant and antimicrobial performance accompanied by powerful cell viability and proliferation for NIH-3T3 fibroblast cells. | (Yavari Maroufi et al., 2022) |
| Sodium caseinate/ gelatin | MgO NPs and menthol essential oil | Electrospinning | Efficient in vitro suppression of *L. monocytogenes* and *S. aureus* growth, which in turn prolongs the shelf life of trout fillets over cold preservation for 13 days. | Eghbalian et al. (2021) |
| Casein/polyethylene oxide | Thymol/β-CD | Electrospinning | Long-term antimicrobial activity with a good potential for expanding the shelf life of stored chilled beef for 7 days. | Dai et al. (2022) |
| Casein/Chitosan | | Self-assembly through polyelectrolyte complexation | High ability to stop bleeding and provoke blood coagulation within seconds, accompanied by no re-bleeding after removal from the injured site. | Mishra et al. (2021) |
| Casein/Polyvinyl alcohol | Zinc-based metal organic framework (MOF) | Electrospinning | High ability to stop bleeding and provoke blood coagulation, accompanied by efficient antimicrobial | Lamei and Hasanzadeh (2024) |

## 4.2 Casein-based nanocarriers for delivery of antimicrobial drugs

Respiratory tract infection is one of the most common diseases that causes significant morbidity worldwide. Antibiotic prescriptions are the principal treatment strategy for managing lung infection (Fayez et al., 2021; Abdelsattar et al., 2023). However, bacterial resistance to many antibiotics has become a challenging health issue globally. Therefore, extensive surveys to discover new natural supplements should be performed to defeat such issues and present alternative natural antimicrobials with minimal hazards to humans (Makky et al., 2023; Rezk et al., 2022). Chrysin is a natural flavonoid that exhibits multiple pharmacological actions, such as antimicrobial. Its weak aqueous solubility, bad intestinal absorption, reduced oral bioavailability, rapid systemic clearance, and powerless in vivo potential extremely restrict its wider clinical implementation (Ting et al., 2021). The low oral bioavailability of chrysin was successfully addressed by Tang et al. via encapsulation into casein NPs using the solvent evaporation method (Tang et al., 2024). The formulated chrysin-loaded casein displayed high loading efficiency (79.84%), particle size in the nanorange (225.3 nm), high negative zeta potential (−33 mV), and a preferable release pattern for chrysin. The in vivo investigations revealed that chrysin-loaded casein can successfully alleviate pulmonary infections induced by *Acinetobacter baumannii* compared to free chrysin in terms of lowering cytokine levels and attenuating the generated oxidative stress owing to improved oral bioavailability. These outcomes emphasize the advantage of casein as a nanodelivery vehicle to improve the therapeutic performance of chrysin against lung infection.

Food-borne pathogenic bacteria that contaminate food during processing, storage, and transportation can induce serious economic losses and pose a fundamental burden on public health after food consumption. The widely used antimicrobial chemical preservatives are potentially harmful to humans. Therefore, for better safety, preservatives based on natural ingredients have become in demand (Savary et al., 2019). Thymol, the major ingredient of thyme oil, has been categorized as safe natural preservative due to its widespread antimicrobial efficiencies. However, the weak aqueous solubility and high volatility limited its application as a natural preservative (Cai et al., 2022). Recently, the harnessing of nanoencapsulation utilizing colloidal delivery systems, like casein protein, has significantly modulated its physicochemical stability, water solubility, and antimicrobial efficiencies (Xue et al., 2019). In this regard, a smart formulated casein/thymol-lauric acid NP was constructed by Ge et al. to estimate the synergistic antibacterial efficiency against gram-positive *Listeria monocytogenes* pathogens (Ge et al., 2023). The NPs loaded with thymol-lauric acid were prepared via the emulsification method, at which the homogenous thymol-lauric acid eutectic solvents were added to the aqueous casein solution under stirring, followed by homogenization. The examined properties of these NPs showed a satisfactory long-term release manner, excellent storage stability, and superior antibacterial activity against *L. monocytogenes* compared to thymol oil-loaded casein NPs. Additionally, the meat preservation test revealed that casein/thymol-lauric acid NPs displayed higher efficiency in suppressing bacterial growth and lipid oxidation than casein/thymol NPs, which prolongs the shelf life of meat products. These findings may encourage the implementation of thymol in the food industry to upgrade food quality and safety.

Vitamin D3-functionalized casein micelles were utilized for anticancer active targeting combinational therapy by exploiting vitamin D3 receptors overexpressed on the surface of cancer cells. Casein micelles were first coloaded with vitamin D3 and etoposide (anticancer drug) using the solvent evaporation technique, then a coat comprised of vitamin D3/phospholipid complex was used to functionalize the surface of dual drug-loaded micelles via the thin film hydration technique (Agwa et al., 2021). The prepared formulation displayed very low hemolytic potential and improved in vitro cytotoxic effect on cancer cell lines. In addition, an in vivo biodistribution study in Ehrlich ascites cells-bearing female Albino Swiss CD1 mice showed that intravenous administration of rhodamine B-loaded vitamin D3-casein micelles resulted in increased accumulation of the micelles in the tumor when compared to the free dye, which might be related to better targeting and internalization into the cancer cells. Moreover, a better in vivo antitumor effect was observed in the casein micelles-treated group, which was confirmed by reduced tumor volume with a pronounced decline in the expression levels of angiogenesis, invasion, and autophagy markers, with almost no signs of systemic toxicity (Table 13.1).

## 4.3 Casein-based nanocarriers for delivery of antidiabetic drugs

Apigenin (AP) is a natural flavonoid that has successfully gained the awareness of the pharmaceutical and food industries recently due to its broad range of health benefits involving anticancer, antiviral, antiinflammatory, antioxidant, and hypoglycemic activities. However, the minimal water solubility and low bioavailability limited its clinical application (Kassem et al., 2021). To conquer these issues, AP-loaded casein nanoparticles (AP/Cas-NPs) were formulated by Wang et al. for mending the bioavailability and aqueous solubility of AP (Wang et al., 2024a). The particle size, zeta potential, and encapsulation efficiency of AP/Cas-NPs were $238.7 \pm 2.1$ nm, $7.48 \pm 0.24$ mV, and 48.56%, respectively. Additionally, the formulated AP/Cas-NPs displayed a preferable release pattern for AP and prolonged plasma residence time after oral administration compared to free AP. The in vivo experiment conducted on diabetic mice showed that AP/Cas-NPs displayed superior hypoglycemic activity compared to free AP, owing to improved solubility accompanied by negligible toxicity. These results proposed that AP/Cas-NPs are a promising strategy for mending the therapeutic potential of AP via improving the bioavailability.

In another interesting study, the potential antidiabetic therapeutic impact of some food flavors involving orange oil, allyl caproate, linalool, isoamyl acetate, and linalool after encapsulation into sodium caseinate (SC)/gum arabic (GA) via emulsification method was investigated by Mohammed et al. (2023). Nanoencapsulation appears hopeful in evading the poor aqueous dispersibility and can overcome inadequate absorption and imperfect bioavailability. All constructed NPs displayed a monomodal size distribution manner, with the smallest size recorded for citral-SC/GA (277.3 nm) and isoamyl acetate-SC/GA (287.1 nm), while the largest size was recorded for orange oil-SC/GA (628.8 nm). Additionally, they all displayed high encapsulation efficiency. The in vivo test performed in diabetic rats revealed that rats treated with encapsulated SC/GA flavors offered enhanced biochemical parameters and superior hypoglycemic activity, accompanied by lowered oral glucose tolerance compared to free flavors. Interestingly, encapsulated SC/GA flavors had no pronounced hypoglycemic effects in normal rats. These findings emphasize the antidiabetic therapeutic potential of encapsulated SC/GA flavors in diabetic rats without any health risks (Table 13.1).

## 4.4 Casein-based nanocarriers for delivery of antiinflammatory drugs

Curcumin is a polyphenol that holds valuable biological roles, involving antidiabetic, anticancer, antiinflammatory, antioxidant, and antibacterial properties. However, owing to its minimal aqueous dispersibility, low stability, and inadequate bioavailability, its applications are restricted. Thereby, nanoencapsulation of curcumin into water-soluble polymer may overcome all these issues (Mehanny et al., 2016). For this purpose, Li et al. encapsulated curcumin (CUR) into SC nano-micelles via ultrasound treatment to form CUR/SC nano-micelles with a favorable size (100–120 nm) for enhanced cellular endocytosis and excellent storage stability (Li et al., 2022). The formulated CUR/SC nano-micelles offered powerful in vitro inhibitory performance against the propagation and pro-inflammatory cytokines of human fibroblast (HFLS) like HFLS-rheumatoid (RA) cells and synoviocyte-osteoarthritis (HFLS-OA) cells compared to free CUR, owing to perfect uptake. The results emphasize the higher potential of the formulated CUR/SC nano-micelles for treating arthritis than free CUR.

Ophiopogon japonicus polysaccharides (OJPs) have great potential in the treatment of chronic inflammatory diseases. However, the weak bioavailability owing to inadequate absorption after oral intake and short half-life limit its applicability in pharmaceutical and biomedical fields (Zheng et al., 2019). Therefore, Lin and his colleagues successfully fabricated a novel nano-delivery system constructed from chitosan (CHI) and casein hydrolysate (Cas) loaded with antiinflammatory and antioxidant OJPs via electrostatic coassembly to form Cas/OJPs/CHI NPs intended for oral administration (Lin et al., 2022). The designed optimized OJP-loaded NPs displayed a 198 nm particle size and high encapsulation efficiency (88.1%). The in vitro release experiment elucidated that the formulated NPs were capable of controlling OJPs release in media having pH simulating the digestive tract, and that release pattern was enhanced by enzymatic degradation. Interestingly, in contrast to free OJPs, the formulated OJP-loaded NPs showed powerful in vitro suppressing strength against nickel-provoked toxicity to macrophages, accompanied by more than 30% inhibition of the ability of lipopolysaccharide (LPS) to trigger nitric oxide generation owing to efficient uptake by macrophages. These findings elucidate the potential antiinflammatory impact of the constructed OJP-loaded NPs (Table 13.1).

## 4.5 Casein-based nanocarriers for delivery of antioxidant drugs

Phenolic compounds symbolize natural ingredients having multiple biological roles. However, their broader applications have been restricted owing to weak aqueous solubility and inadequate oral bioavailability (Araújo et al., 2021). To ameliorate these issues, Wang and his colleagues successfully customized pH-driven tactic to encapsulate three different polyphenols involving ferulic acid, resveratrol, and rhein into casein NPs via hydrophobic interactions and construct three different formulae with improved solubility and storage stability for the loaded phenolic compound (Wang et al., 2024b). The encapsulation efficiency for the three formulated NPs was 95% for ferulic acid and 94% for resveratrol and rhein. The in vitro antioxidant activity disclosed that the casein NPs loaded with polyphenols could effectively heighten the antioxidant impact of phenolic compounds assessed by the

2,2′-azino-bis (3-ethylbenzothiazoline-6-sulphonic acid) (ABTS) and 2,2-diphenyl-1-picrylhydrazyl (DPPH) free radical-scavenging techniques.

In another study, conducted by Du et al., novel goat milk casein NPs were successfully formulated via a controllable pH-shifting mechanism to encapsulate hydrophobic CUR (Du et al., 2022). The mean particle size and zeta potential of the formulated CUR-loaded goat casein NPs were 104.6 nm and −26.62 mV, respectively. Moreover, it exhibited enhanced solubility and good stability during storage and high encapsulation efficiency (81.80%). The results of the in vitro release showed that the NPs have a preferable sustained release manner and small intestine targeting. The in vitro antioxidant activity assessed by the ABTS and DPPH-free radical-scavenging techniques disclosed that the casein NPs loaded with CUR could effectively heighten the antioxidant impact of CUR compared to free CUR (Table 13.1).

## 4.6 Casein-based nanocarriers for delivery of phototherapeutic and nanotheranostic agents

Phototherapy is a laser- or light-based noninvasive treatment style that is used in the treatment of multiple diseases, such as cancer. Photodynamic therapy (PDT) is one notable mechanism in phototherapy that produces cytotoxic ROS after exposing the photosensitizer (PS) to certain laser light wavelengths in the presence of oxygen, leading to severe oxidative stress that can harm cellular components such as lipids, proteins, and DNA and cause cell death in the irradiated tissues (Agwa et al., 2023a). Additionally, some PSs have been harnessed in photothermal therapy, as they can transform the absorbed light into heat, causing thermal damage to the irradiated tissues and provoking apoptosis. However, the inadequate water dispersibility of various PSs is a critical issue in phototherapy that hinders their efficient delivery to the targeted tissue. For this objective, multiple NPs have been constructed and used to mend the solubility and cellular targeting ability of the PSs (Agwa et al., 2023b). In this regard, Zhang and his colleagues formulated a core/shell nanocomposite comprising gold nanoparticles (AuNPs) as the core and casein gold nanoclusters (Cas-AuNCs) as the shell, having higher photodynamic efficiency than AuNCs and AuNPs (Zhang et al., 2022). Casein was utilized as a template for AuNCs preparation owing to its reducing and antifouling properties. The constructed Cas-AuNCs/AuNPs demonstrated higher in vitro photodynamic performance than AuNCs and AuNPs, evidenced by high ROS generation following 390 nm light irradiation. The in vitro and in vivo results demonstrated powerful anticancer and photodynamic performance for the constructed Cas-AuNCs/AuNPs after light irradiation compared to those not irradiated and other treated groups.

In another study, Khatun and his colleagues constructed SC NPs functionalized with glutathione and encapsulated with PS IR 797 dye and cytotoxic camptothecin (CPT) to form G/SC-CPT-IR NPs against triple-negative breast cancer overexpressing γ-glutamyl transpeptidase (GGT) receptors (Khatun et al., 2024). The hydrodynamic diameter and zeta potential of the constructed G/SC-CPT-IR NPs were 160 nm and −2.53 mV, respectively. The drug release from the constructed targeted NPs was high (93.56%) in an acidic environment in contrast to the physiological pH (31.72%), suggesting a successful delivery into acidic TME. The constructed G/SC-CPT-IR NPs demonstrated a considerably enhanced photothermal effect (more than 43°C) and ROS generation after continuous near-infrared (NIR) laser beam exposure for 3 minutes compared to free IR 797. The appropriate biocompatibility of the formulated NPs in normal fibroblast cell lines (NIH-3T3 and L929) and hemocompatibility proved the safety of the formulated nanosystem. The quantitative and qualitative analyses showed the powerful cell-killing capacity of G/SC-CPT-IR NPs when incubated with 2D and 3D spheroids of 4T1 cells upon NIR laser irradiation owing to improved uptake into deep tumors. Additionally, massive DNA damage arose from γH2AX and p53 overexpression as revealed by the immunofluorescence check. The cells also displayed fragmented nuclei and apoptotic cell death. The in vivo findings signalize the therapeutic potential of the formulated G/SC-CPT-IR NPs + 808 nm laser irradiation in reducing the size and volume of the tumor after injection into the primary and highly metastatic 4T1 BALB/c mice tumor model compared to other treatments via spending long-lasting chemo/photothermal influence.

In another recent study implemented by Kim et al., SC NPs encapsulated a PS hydrophobic pheophorbide a (Pba) via hydrophobic interaction to form SC/Pba NPs for PDT application (Kim et al., 2024). The mean size distribution, zeta potential, and encapsulation efficiency of the formulated SC/Pba NPs were 220.03 nm, −14.57 mV, and 54.7%, respectively. Additionally, a higher colloidal stability for 4 months and a very slow release pattern were detected. The formulated SC/Pba NPs manifested high intracellular singlet oxygen and ROS generation after 671 nm laser irradiation compared to free Pba when incubated with SCC7 tumor cells. Also, they display fast cellular uptake and powerful in vitro tumor-killing efficiency against SCC7 tumor cells following laser irradiation by photodynamic action. After systemic injection into the SCC7 tumor mouse model, the formulated SC/Pba NPs offer about 2-fold higher intratumoral accumulation of Pba compared to free Pba. The in vivo results reveal that after 671 nm laser exposure to the tumor area, the formulated SC/Pba NPs showed complete tumor eradication without noticeable side effects. These findings signalize the potential of the formulated Pba-loaded NPs for in vivo PDT application.

Recently, theranostic systems showed great promise and fast expansion in nanomedicine research scope, as they can merge various imbricated functionalities for imaging, diagnostic, and therapeutic purposes. Theragnostic systems in early cancer diagnosis and treatment exhibit tremendous possibilities to save and upgrade the lives of many patients worldwide (Farinha et al., 2021). In this regard, novel SC NPs functionalized with iron oxide magnetic nanoparticles (MNPs) have been designed by Wenck et al. to be harnessed as a promising nanohybrid theranostic system in a physiological environment (Wenck et al., 2024). This system authorizes tracking by magnetic imaging, drug delivery, and treatment through magnetic hyperthermia. Firstly, MNPs were constructed and then functionalized with SC to protect the surface from degradation or oxidation and stabilize the magnetic performance against dynamic signal absence in the existence of salts. After that, the SC layer was crosslinked via transglutaminase to mend its colloidal stability and enhance MNP loading. The constructed MNP-functionalized SC NPs were tested before and after functionalization in terms of their magnetic performance. The results demonstrated that SC coating has a negligible impact on the magnetic performance of the loaded MNP, indicating their suitability for magnetic imaging and hyperthermia. The constructed SC/MNP NPs were further loaded with a hydrophobic Nile red (NR) as a model drug to permit cellular uptake investigation and intratumoral localization via harnessing its fluorescence features. The efficient cellular uptake in squamous cell carcinoma (SCL-1) cells, accompanied by intratumoral localization of the Nile red near the nucleus, signalizes an efficient aggregation at the aimed site for various antitumor therapies (Table 13.1).

## 5. Application of casein-based nanofibers

Nanofibers possess magnificent potential in multiple pharmaceutical and biomedical scopes, involving drug delivery, wound healing, and tissue engineering. They are generally realized as solid fibers having a submicrometer dimension with high porosity and surface-to-volume proportion, besides the better and easier handleability (El-Shanshory et al., 2022). Multiple fiber-formulation methods have been developed, involving phase separation, force spinning, solution blowing, and electrospinning. Amongst these methods, electrospinning, which prompts the generation of solid nanofibers via providing a high-voltage electrical field to the polymer solution, exhibits several merits like low cost, versatility, scalability, and simplicity (Hamza et al., 2023). Furthermore, electrospun nanofibers can be readily enriched with unique and particular functionalities to fulfill certain demands for the required application. Fortunately, because NPs, drugs, and other diverse ingredients can be successfully incorporated within the constructed nanofibers, the electrospun nanofibers have huge applicability in several delivery applications (Elsherbini and Sabra, 2022). Based on this evidence, George and his colleagues constructed casein/polyvinyl alcohol (Cas/PVA) nanofiber scaffolds that incorporated silver nanoparticles (Ag NPs) via the electrospinning method for the management of diabetic wound healing (George et al., 2024). The scanning electron microscope (SEM) analysis of the constructed Cas/PVA-Ag nanofibers displays a continuous smooth homogenous architecture, which emphasizes the proper miscibility of the utilized polymers and better integration of Ag NPs into the nanofibrous blend. The constructed Cas/PVA-Ag nanofibers offered significant antibacterial activity against the Gram-negative bacteria *Escherichia coli*. The constructed nanofibers displayed maximum cell viability against 3T3 mouse fibroblast cells, accompanied by superior scratch wound closure via increasing migration and proliferation. Considering these findings, the constructed nanofibers incorporating Ag NPs hold promise for preventing infection and treating diabetic wounds.

Another sodium caseinate and polyvinyl alcohol (SC/PVA) nanofibers encapsulated zinc oxide nanoparticles (ZnO NPs) as antibacterial agents were designed by Sendil and his colleagues for antibacterial applications (Şendil et al., 2023). The designed SC/PVA-ZnO nanofibers offered powerful antibacterial activity against *E. coli* and *Staphylococcus aureus*. According to the in vitro cytotoxicity results, the antibacterial nanofiber showed high cell viability when incubated with the mouse L929 fibroblast cell line and thus could be harnessed as a fibroblast tissue scaffold. All in vitro results emphasize the utility of the designed nanofibers as an effective antibacterial wound dressing.

In an attempt to design smart food packaging that aims to abolish the hazards of nondegradable oil-based packaging ingredients, extend the shelf life, and improve the safety and quality of the food products, Maroufi et al. designed an active food packaging material comprising casein/polycaprolactone (Cas/PCL) nanofibers encapsulated green tea (GT) to restrain food loss via spoilage (Yavari Maroufi et al., 2022). The SEM analysis of the constructed Cas/PCL-GT nanofibers displays a continuous, smooth, homogenous architecture with a mean diameter of 203 nm and excellent mechanical properties. The constructed Cas/PCL-GT nanofibers exhibited a long-term slow release behavior for GT with efficient antioxidant and antimicrobial performance against *S. aureus* and *E. coli* bacteria. The in vitro cytotoxicity results offered powerful cell viability and proliferation for NIH-3T3 fibroblast cells in the existence of fiber with and without GT. These in vitro findings emphasize the promising potential of the constructed nanofibers for active food packaging.

In another study, implemented by Eghbalian and his colleagues, active antimicrobial food packaging nanofibers comprising sodium caseinate/gelatin (SC/GEL) blend dually loaded with MgO NPs and menthol essential oil (MEO) were designed via electrospinning to expand the shelf life of fresh trout fillets over cold preservation (Eghbalian et al., 2021). The constructed SC/GEL-MEO-MGO nanofibers displayed higher encapsulation efficiency and in vitro controlled release for the loaded antimicrobial compounds. The morphological characteristics of the constructed nanofibers showed smooth, regular, uniform, and bead-free architectures, emphasizing that the integration of MgO NPs and MEO didn't deteriorate the installation of the nanofibers. The average diameters of the constructed nanofibers were 472.842 and 462.264 nm. The constructed SC/GEL-MEO-MgO nanofibers greatly suppressed the in vitro growth of *L. monocytogenes* and *S. aureus*. Additionally, the integration of MgO NPs and MEO into the constructed nanofibers could successfully prolong the shelf life of trout fillets over cold preservation for 13 days.

As there are many restrictions in the harnessing of natural compounds in fresh meat preservation for long period, Dai and his colleagues fabricated a bio-based controlled release nanofibrous packing system by electrospinning comprising casein and polyethylene oxide (Cas/PEO) blend incorporated with thymol as an efficient antibacterial after complexation with β-cyclodextrin (β-CD) to form Cas/PEO-THY/β-CD nanofibers (Dai et al., 2022). The constructed Cas/PEO-THY/β-CD nanofibers exhibited a broad-spectrum antibacterial efficiency against numerous harmful bacteria. Interestingly, the casein-based nanofibers could fulfill the controlled release behavior following exposure to bacterial protease, which hydrolyzes the casein and reinforces the antibacterial efficiency during the application. Finally, the preservative application test indicated that the constructed Cas/PEO-THY/β-CD nanofibers showed long-term antimicrobial activity with a good potential for expanding the shelf life of stored chilled beef for 7 days.

Mishra et al. have developed a novel self-assembled casein/chitosan (Cas/CHI) nanofibrous material aimed to enhance blood clotting and address the critical issues of uncontrollable bleeding from major arteries, which poses a significant risk of mortality globally. This innovative hemostat is designed to stop bleeding immediately and safely. The self-assembled Cas/CHI nanofibers were constructed via polyelectrolyte complexation (Mishra et al., 2021). Their diameters were less than 100 nm with a high surface area. Under in vitro conditions, the constructed Cas/CHI nanofibers provoke platelet coalescence and absorb blood to generate stable blood clots within 9 s via activation of the extrinsic coagulation mechanism. The in vivo application showed that Cas/CHI nanofibers were nontoxic, hemocompatible, and able to stop bleeding and provoke blood coagulation during 37 s in a large wounded artery (1 cm) in a rabbit model. Interestingly, no re-bleeding was noticed in the injured area after 120 s of pressure application. Additionally, the nanofibers were nontoxic and safe, as no toxic clinical symptoms or mortalities were noticed in the treated animals.

In another recent study, a novel casein-based wound dressing nanofibrous mat incorporating zinc-based metal organic framework (MOF) particles with improved hemostatic and antibacterial features was designed by Lamei et al. via the electrospinning technique (Lamei and Hasanzadeh, 2024). The constructed Cas/PVA-MOF nanofibrous mat displayed uniform, smooth, and beadless morphology with an average size between 80 and 150 nm. The hemostasis potential of the constructed Cas/PVA-MOF nanofibers was checked utilizing a blood clotting time assay, and the results signalize that the constructed nanofibers showed shorter clotting time that is attributed to the porous architecture of MOF particles as well as the hydrophilic nature of the constructed nanofibers. Furthermore, the nanofiber mat showed lower prothrombin time (PT) and partial thromboplastin time (PTT) values, indicating the superiority of the nanofibers in triggering blood coagulation and hemostasis. The antibacterial screening tests manifested an outstanding suppression against *S. aureus* and *E. coli*. The outcomes propose a promising strategy to design a highly efficacious wound dressing nanofibrous mat with enhanced antibacterial and hemostatic effects (Table 13.1).

## 6. Conclusion

In conclusion, protein-based nanocarriers like casein present significant advancements in drug delivery systems for the pharmaceutical and nutraceutical industries. Their ability to protect loaded drug cargoes from degradation and enhance bioavailability and therapeutic performance through improved solubilization and reduced toxicity makes them highly valuable. Casein, being abundant, cost-effective, biodegradable, and biocompatible, has shown great promise in encapsulating various compounds. Its amphiphilicity and unique self-assembling capabilities allow for the formation of stable nano-micelles in a core/shell nanostructure, making it suitable for delivering hydrophobic and hydrophilic drugs with controlled release properties. The ongoing research into casein's applications in biomedicine suggests a bright future for its use in developing more effective formulations.

## References

Abdelsattar, A.S., Kamel, A.G., Hussein, A.H., Azzam, M., Makky, S., Rezk, N., Essam, K., Agwa, M.M., El-Shibiny, A., 2023. The promising antibacterial and anticancer activity of green synthesized zinc nanoparticles in combination with silver and gold nanoparticles. J. Inorg. Organomet. Polym. Mater. 33 (7), 1868–1881. https://doi.org/10.1007/s10904-023-02614-y.

Aboras, S.I., Korany, M.A., Abdine, H.H., Ragab, M.A.A., Ahmed, El D., Agwa, M.M., 2021. HPLC with fluorescence detection for the bioanalysis and pharmacokinetic study of Doxorubicin and Prodigiosin loaded on eco-friendly casein nanomicelles in rat plasma. J. Chromatogr. B 1187, 123043. https://doi.org/10.1016/j.jchromb.2021.123043.

Agwa, M.M., Sabra, S., 2021. Lactoferrin coated or conjugated nanomaterials as an active targeting approach in nanomedicine. Int. J. Biol. Macromol. 167, 1527–1543. https://doi.org/10.1016/j.ijbiomac.2020.11.107.

Agwa, M.M., Elessawy, F.M., Hussein, A., El Demellawy, M.A., Elzoghby, A.O., Abd El-Salam, M.H., Eldiwany, A.I., 2018. Development and validation of a robust analytical method to quantify both etoposide and prodigiosin in polymeric nanoparticles by reverse-phase high-performance liquid chromatography. Anal. Methods 10 (19), 2272–2280. https://doi.org/10.1039/c8ay00030a.

Agwa, M.M., Abdelmonsif, D.A., Khattab, S.N., Sabra, S., 2020. Self-assembled lactoferrin-conjugated linoleic acid micelles as an orally active targeted nanoplatform for Alzheimer's disease. Int. J. Biol. Macromol. 162.

Agwa, M.M., Abu-Serie, M.M., Abdelmonsif, D.A., Moussa, N., Elsayed, H., Khattab, S.N., Sabra, S., 2021. Vitamin D3/phospholipid complex decorated caseinate nanomicelles for targeted delivery of synergistic combination therapy in breast cancer. Int. J. Pharm. 607. https://doi.org/10.1016/j.ijpharm.2021.120965.

Agwa, M.M., Sabra, S., Atwa, N.A., Dahdooh, H.A., Lithy, R.M., Elmotasem, H., 2022. Potential of frankincense essential oil-loaded whey protein nanoparticles embedded in frankincense resin as a wound healing film based on green technology. J. Drug Deliv. Sci. Technol. 71. https://doi.org/10.1016/j.jddst.2022.103291. http://www.editionsdesante.fr/category.php?id_category=48.

Agwa, M.M., Elmotasem, H., Moustafa, R.I., Abdelsattar, A.S., Mohy-Eldin, M.S., Fouda, M.M.G., 2023a. Advent in proteins, nucleic acids, and biological cell membranes functionalized nanocarriers to accomplish active or homologous tumor targeting for smart amalgamated chemotherapy/photo-therapy: A review. Int. J. Biol. Macromol. 253. https://doi.org/10.1016/j.ijbiomac.2023.127460. https://www.sciencedirect.com/journal/international-journal-of-biological-macromolecules.

Agwa, M.M., Elmotasem, H., Elsayed, H., Abdelsattar, A.S., Omer, A.M., Gebreel, D.T., Mohy-Eldin, M.S., Fouda, M.M.G., 2023b. Carbohydrate ligands-directed active tumor targeting of combinatorial chemotherapy/phototherapy-based nanomedicine: A review. Int. J. Biol. Macromol. 239. https://doi.org/10.1016/j.ijbiomac.2023.124294. www.elsevier.com/locate/ijbiomac.

Agwa, M.M., El-Aassar, M.R., Moustafa, R.I., Elsayed, H., El-Beheri, N.G., 2024a. Rapid RP-HPLC detection method for quantification of gentamicin sulfate loaded wound dressing nanofiber formulation with accelerated in vivo wound healing. National information and documentation centre. J. Chem. 67 (6), 445–456. https://doi.org/10.21608/EJCHEM.2024.252585.8939.

Agwa, M.M., Marzouk, R.E., Sabra, S.A., 2024b. Advances in active targeting of ligand-directed polymeric nanomicelles via exploiting overexpressed cellular receptors for precise nanomedicine. RSC Adv. 14 (32), 23520–23542. https://doi.org/10.1039/d4ra04069d.

Agwa, M.M., Elmotasem, H., El-Lakany, S.A., 2024c. Small molecules and peptide ligands directed nanotherapeutics for precise oncological phototherapy: Emphasis towards enhancing chemotherapeutic active tumor targeting efficacy. J. Drug Deliv. Sci. Technol. 101, 106313. https://doi.org/10.1016/j.jddst.2024.106313.

Amer, E.I., Allam, S.R., Hassan, A.Y., El-Fakharany, E.M., Agwa, M.M., Khattab, S.N., Sheta, E., El-Faham, M.H., 2023. Can antibody conjugated nanomicelles alter the prospect of antibody targeted therapy against schistosomiasis mansoni? . Public Library of Science. PLoS Neglected Trop. Dis. 17 (12). https://doi.org/10.1371/journal.pntd.0011776. https://journals.plos.org/plosntds/article/file?id=10.1371/journal.pntd.0011776&type=printable.

Araújo, F.F., de, P., Farias, D., Neri-Numa, I.A., Gm, 2021. Pastore, Polyphenols and their applications: an approach in food chemistry and innovation potential. Food Chem. 338.

Batrakova, E.V., Bronich, T.K., Vetro, J.A., Kabanov, A.V., 2006. Polymer micelles as drug carriers. In Nanoparticulates as Drug Carriers, pp. 57–93.

Cai, Q., Zhang, Y., Fang, X., Lin, S., He, Z., Peng, S., Liu, W., 2022. Improving anti-Listeria activity of thymol emulsions by adding lauric acid. Front. Nutr. 9. https://doi.org/10.3389/fnut.2022.859293.

Camorani, S., Crescenzi, E., Colecchia, D., Carpentieri, A., Amoresano, A., Fedele, M., Chiariello, M., Cerchia, L., 2015. Aptamer targeting EGFRvIII mutant hampers its constitutive autophosphorylation and affects migration, invasion and proliferation of glioblastoma cells. Oncotarget 6 (35), 37570–37587. https://doi.org/10.18632/oncotarget.6066.

Cuggino, J.C., Picchio, M.L., Gugliotta, A., Bürgi, M., Ronco, L.I., Calderón, M., Etcheverrigaray, M., Alvarez Igarzabal, C.I., Minari, R.J., Gugliotta, L.M., 2021. Crosslinked casein micelles bound paclitaxel as enzyme activated intracellular drug delivery systems for cancer therapy. Eur. Polym. J. 145. https://doi.org/10.1016/j.eurpolymj.2020.110237. https://www.journals.elsevier.com/european-polymer-journal.

Dai, J., Hu, W., Yang, H., Li, C., Cui, H., Li, X., Lin, L., 2022. Controlled release and antibacterial properties of PEO/casein nanofibers loaded with Thymol/β-cyclodextrin inclusion complexes in beef preservation. Food Chem. 382, 132369. https://doi.org/10.1016/j.foodchem.2022.132369.

Davidov-Pardo, G., Joye, I.J., Mcclements, D.J., 2015. Food-grade protein-based nanoparticles and microparticles for bioactive delivery: Fabrication, characterization, and utilization. Adv. Protein Chem. Struct. Biol. 98, 293–325. https://doi.org/10.1016/bs.apcsb.2014.11.004.

Du, X., Jing, H., Wang, L., Huang, X., Mo, L., Bai, X., Wang, H., 2022. pH-shifting formation of goat milk casein nanoparticles from insoluble peptide aggregates and encapsulation of curcumin for enhanced dispersibility and bioactivity. LWT 154, 112753. https://doi.org/10.1016/j.lwt.2021.112753.

Eghbalian, M., Shavisi, N., Shahbazi, Y., Dabirian, F., 2021. Active packaging based on sodium caseinate-gelatin nanofiber mats encapsulated with Mentha spicata L. essential oil and MgO nanoparticles: preparation, properties, and food application. Food Packag. Shelf Life 29, 100737. https://doi.org/10.1016/j.fpsl.2021.100737.

El-Aassar, M.R., Ibrahim, O.M., Albogmi, R.G., Hussein, M.F., Alsirhani, A.M., Rafea, M.A., Zaki, M.E.A., Hassan, H.M.A., Agwa, M.M., 2024. Capsaicin/silica-infused polygalacturonic acid/polyvinyl alcohol nanomatrix for enhanced wound healing in skin injuries. Int. J. Biol. Macromol. 282. https://doi.org/10.1016/j.ijbiomac.2024.137319. https://www.sciencedirect.com/science/journal/01418130.

El-Sayed, G.M., Agwa, M.M., Emam, M.T.H., Kandil, H., Abdelhamid, A.E., Nour, S.A., 2024. Utilizing immobilized recombinant serine alkaline protease from Bacillus safensis lab418 in wound healing: Gene cloning, heterologous expression, optimization, and characterization. Int. J. Biol. Macromol. 270 (Pt 1), 132286. https://doi.org/10.1016/j.ijbiomac.2024.132286.

El-Shanshory, A.A., Agwa, M.M., Abd-Elhamid, A.I., Soliman, H.M.A., Mo, X., Kenawy, E.R., 2022. Metronidazole topically immobilized electrospun nanofibrous scaffold: novel secondary intention wound healing accelerator. Polymers 14 (3). https://doi.org/10.3390/polym14030454. https://www.mdpi.com/2073-4360/14/3/454/pdf.

Elsherbini, A.M., Sabra, S.A., 2022. Nanoparticles-in-nanofibers composites: Emphasis on some recent biomedical applications. J. Contr. Release 348, 57–83. https://doi.org/10.1016/j.jconrel.2022.05.037.

Elzoghby, A.O., Abo El-Fotoh, W.S., Elgindy, N.A., 2011. Casein-based formulations as promising controlled release drug delivery systems. J. Contr. Release 153 (3), 206–216. https://doi.org/10.1016/j.jconrel.2011.02.010.

Elzoghby, A.O., Elgohary, M.M., Kamel, N.M., 2015. Implications of protein- and peptide-based nanoparticles as potential vehicles for anticancer drugs. Adv. Protein Chem. Struct. Biol. 98, 169–221. https://doi.org/10.1016/bs.apcsb.2014.12.002.

Farinha, P., Coelho, J.M.P., Reis, C.P., Gaspar, M.M., 2021. A comprehensive updated review on magnetic nanoparticles in diagnostics. Nanomaterials 11 (12), 3432. https://doi.org/10.3390/nano11123432.

Fayez, M.S., Hakim, T.A., Agwa, M.M., Abdelmoteleb, M., Aly, R.G., Montaser, N.N., Abdelsattar, A.S., Rezk, N., El-Shibiny, A., 2021. Topically applied bacteriophage to control multi-drug resistant Klebsiella pneumoniae infected wound in a rat model. Antibiotics 10 (9). https://doi.org/10.3390/antibiotics10091048. https://www.mdpi.com/2079-6382/10/9/1048/pdf.

Franchini, M., 2022. Synthesis and functionalization of casein nanoparticles with aptamers for triple-negative breast cancer targeting. New J. Chem. 46.

Gandhi, S., Roy, I., 2021. Drug delivery applications of casein nanostructures: A minireview. J. Drug Deliv. Sci. Technol. 66, 102843. https://doi.org/10.1016/j.jddst.2021.102843.

Ge, Y., Fang, X., Zhang, Y., Peng, S., Lin, S., Zhou, L., McClements, D.J., Liu, W., 2023. Improving the stability and anti-L. monocytogenes activity of thymol casein nanoparticles by forming eutectic solvent with lauric acid. LWT 189, 115493. https://doi.org/10.1016/j.lwt.2023.115493.

George, N., Chakraborty, S., Mary, N.L., Suguna, L., 2024. Incorporating silver nanoparticles into electrospun nanofibers of casein/polyvinyl alcohol to develop scaffolds for tissue engineering. Int. J. Biol. Macromol. 267 (Pt 2), 131501. https://doi.org/10.1016/j.ijbiomac.2024.131501.

Hamza, K.H., El-Shanshory, A.A., Agwa, M.M., Abo-Alkasem, M.I., El-Fakharany, E.M., Abdelsattar, A.S., El-Bardan, A.A., Kassem, T.S., Mo, X., Soliman, H.M.A., 2023. Topically applied biopolymer-based tri-layered hierarchically structured nanofibrous scaffold with a self-pumping effect for accelerated full-thickness wound healing in a rat model. Pharmaceutics 15 (5). https://doi.org/10.3390/pharmaceutics15051518. http://www.mdpi.com/journal/pharmaceutics.

Jahangirian, H., Lemraski, E.G., Webster, T.J., Rafiee-Moghaddam, R., Abdollahi, Y., 2017. A review of drug delivery systems based on nanotechnology and green chemistry. Int. J. Nanomed. 12, 2957–2978. https://doi.org/10.2147/IJN.S127683. https://www.dovepress.com/getfile.php?fileID=35980.

Jin, P., Kang, Z., Zhang, N., Du, G., Chen, J., 2014. High-yield novel leech hyaluronidase to expedite the preparation of specific hyaluronan oligomers. Sci. Rep. 4 (1). https://doi.org/10.1038/srep04471.

Kassem, F.A., Abdelaziz, A.E., El Maghraby, G.M., 2021. Ethanol-assisted kneading of apigenin with arginine for enhanced dissolution rate of apigenin: development of rapidly disintegrating tablets. Pharmaceut. Dev. Technol. 26 (6), 693–700. https://doi.org/10.1080/10837450.2021.1922441.

Khatun, S., Pebam, M., Putta, C.L., Rengan, A.K., 2023. Camptothecin loaded casein nanosystem for tuning the therapeutic efficacy against highly metastatic triple-negative breast cancer cells. Biomater. Sci. 11 (7), 2518–2530. https://doi.org/10.1039/d2bm01814d.

Khatun, S., Pebam, M., Sankaranarayanan, S.V.P., Bantal, V.S., Rengan, A.K., 2024. Glutathione-IR 797 coupled Casein Nano-Trojan for augmenting the therapeutic efficacy of camptothecin in highly invasive triple negative breast cancer. Biomater. Adv. 159.

Kim, S.H., Lee, Y., Lim, S.G., Lee, C., Park, J.S., Koo, H., 2024. Pheophorbide a-loaded casein micelle for in vivo drug delivery and efficient photodynamic therapy. J. Drug Deliv. Sci. Technol. 95, 105598. https://doi.org/10.1016/j.jddst.2024.105598.

Krishna Sailaja, A., Amareshwar, P., Chakravarty, P., 2011. Different techniques used for the preparation of nanoparticles using natural polymers and their application. Int. J. Pharm. Pharmaceut. Sci. 3 (2), 45–50.

Lamei, E., Hasanzadeh, M., 2024. Concurrent electrospinning of microporous metal-organic framework-laden casein/PVA nanofibrous composites for potential antibacterial wound dressing applications. Int. J. Polym. Mater. Polym. Biomater. 73 (8), 637–645. https://doi.org/10.1080/00914037.2023.2191199.

Lamey, C.A., Moussa, N., Helmy, M.W., Haroun, M., Sabra, S.A., 2023. Simultaneous encapsulation of dasatinib and celecoxib into caseinate micelles towards improved in vivo anti-breast cancer efficacy with reduced drug toxicity. J. Drug Deliv. Sci. Technol. 87, 104807. https://doi.org/10.1016/j.jddst.2023.104807.

Langer, K., Balthasar, S., Vogel, V., Dinauer, N., von Briesen, H., Schubert, D., 2003. Optimization of the preparation process for human serum albumin (HSA) nanoparticles. Int. J. Pharm. 257 (1–2), 169–180. https://doi.org/10.1016/s0378-5173(03)00134-0.

Li, X.J., Jiang, Z.Z., Zhang, L.Y., 2014. Triptolide: Progress on research in pharmacodynamics and toxicology. J. Ethnopharmacol. 155 (1), 67–79. https://doi.org/10.1016/j.jep.2014.06.006.

Li, K., Zhang, Y., Hao, X., Xie, D., Wang, C., Zhang, H., Jin, P., Du, Q., 2022. Improved stability and in vitro anti-arthritis bioactivity of curcumin–casein nanoparticles by ultrasound-driven encapsulation. Nutrients 14 (23), 5192. https://doi.org/10.3390/nu14235192.

Lin, C., Hsu, F.Y., Lin, W.T., Cha, C.Y., Ho, Y.C., Mi, F.L., 2022. Biodegradable nanoparticles prepared from chitosan and casein for delivery of bioactive polysaccharides. Polymers 14 (14). https://doi.org/10.3390/polym14142966. http://www.mdpi.com/journal/polymers.

Liu, C., Jiang, T.T., Yuan, Z.X., Lu, Y., 2020. Self-assembled casein nanoparticles loading triptolide for the enhancement of oral bioavailability. Nat. Prod. Commun. 15 (8). https://doi.org/10.1177/1934578X20948352. https://journals.sagepub.com/loi/npx?year=2018.

Lu, Z., Yeh, T.K., Tsai, M., Au, J.L.S., Wientjes, M.G., 2004. Paclitaxel-loaded gelatin nanoparticles for intravesical bladder cancer therapy. Clin. Cancer Res. 10 (22), 7677–7684. https://doi.org/10.1158/1078-0432.CCR-04-1443.

Madan, J.R., Ansari, I.N., Dua, K., Awasthi, R., 2020. Formulation and in vitro evaluation of casein nanoparticles as carrier for celecoxib. Adv. Pharm. Bull. 10 (3), 408–417. https://doi.org/10.34172/apb.2020.049. http://apb.tbzmed.ac.ir/.

Makky, S., Rezk, N., Abdelsattar, A.S., Hussein, A.H., Eid, A., Essam, K., Kamel, A.G., Fayez, M.S., Azzam, M., Agwa, M.M., El-Shibiny, A., 2023. Characterization of the biosynthesized Syzygium aromaticum-mediated silver nanoparticles and its antibacterial and antibiofilm activity in combination with bacteriophage. Results Chem. 5, 100686. https://doi.org/10.1016/j.rechem.2022.100686.

Mehanny, M., Hathout, R.M., Geneidi, A.S., Mansour, S., 2016. Exploring the use of nanocarrier systems to deliver the magical molecule; Curcumin and its derivatives. J. Contr. Release 225, 1–30. https://doi.org/10.1016/j.jconrel.2016.01.018.

Milenkova, S., Pilicheva, B., Uzunova, Y., Yovcheva, T., Marudova, M., 2022. Casein microgels as benzydamine hydrochloride carriers for prolonged release. Materials 15 (4), 1333. https://doi.org/10.3390/ma15041333.

Mishra, B., Hossain, S., Mohanty, S., Gupta, M.K., Verma, D., 2021. Fast acting hemostatic agent based on self-assembled hybrid nanofibers from chitosan and casein. Int. J. Biol. Macromol. 185, 525–534. https://doi.org/10.1016/j.ijbiomac.2021.06.116.

Mittal, A., Mahala, N., Krishna, K.V., Dubey, U.S., Dubey, S.K., 2022. Calcium chloride linked camel milk derived casein nanoparticles for the delivery of sorafenib in hepatocarcinoma cells. Biocell 46 (1), 127–136. https://doi.org/10.32604/biocell.2022.015932.

Mohamed, W.A., El-Nekhily, N.A., Mahmoud, H.E., Hussein, A.A., Sabra, S.A., 2024. Prodigiosin/celecoxib-loaded into zein/sodium caseinate nanoparticles as a potential therapy for triple negative breast cancer. Sci. Rep. 14 (1). https://doi.org/10.1038/s41598-023-50531-4. https://www.nature.com/srep/.

Mohammed, D.M., Abdelgawad, M.A., Ghoneim, M.M., El-Sherbiny, M., Mahdi, W.A., Alshehri, S., Ebrahim, H.A., Farouk, A., 2023. Effect of nano-encapsulated food flavorings on streptozotocin-induced diabetic rats. Food Funct. 14 (19), 8814–8828. https://doi.org/10.1039/d3fo01299a.

Purushothaman, B.K., Maheswari, P.U., Begum, K.M.S., 2021. Glutamic acid functionalized casein-calcium ferrite magnetic nanosystem based on paired targeting effect for synergistic anticancer therapy. Mater. Lett. 303.

Rehman, A., Tong, Q., Jafari, S.M., Korma, S.A., Khan, I.M., Mohsin, A., Manzoor, M.F., Ashraf, W., Mushtaq, B.S., Zainab, S., Cacciotti, I., 2021. Spray dried nanoemulsions loaded with curcumin, resveratrol, and borage seed oil: the role of two different modified starches as encapsulating materials. Int. J. Biol. Macromol. 186, 820–828. https://doi.org/10.1016/j.ijbiomac.2021.07.076.

Rezk, N., Abdelsattar, A.S., Elzoghby, D., Agwa, M.M., Abdelmoteleb, M., Aly, R.G., Fayez, M.S., Essam, K., Zaki, B. M., El-Shibiny, A., 2022. Bacteriophage as a potential therapy to control antibiotic-resistant Pseudomonas aeruginosa infection through topical application onto a full-thickness wound in a rat model. J. Genet. Eng. Biotechnol. 20 (1). https://jgeb.springeropen.com/. doi: 10.1186/s43141-022-00409-1.

Sabra, S., Agwa, M.M., 2020. Lactoferrin, a unique molecule with diverse therapeutical and nanotechnological applications. Int. J. Biol. Macromol. 164, 1046–1060. https://doi.org/10.1016/j.ijbiomac.2020.07.167.

Savary, S., Willocquet, L., Jane Pethybridge, S., Paul, E., McRoberts, N., Nelson, A., 2019. The global burden of pathogens and pests on major food crops. Nat. Ecol. Evol. 3 (3), 430–439. https://doi.org/10.1038/s41559-018-0793-y.

Şendil, Ö., Samatya Yilmaz, S., Yazici Ozcelik, E., Uzuner, H., Aytac, A., 2023. Cross-linked electrospun polyvinyl alcohol/sodium caseinate nanofibers for antibacterial applications. J. Vinyl Addit. Technol. 29 (1), 48–65. https://doi.org/10.1002/vnl.21942.

Shalaby, M., Agwa, M., Saeed, H., Khedr, S.M., Morsy, O., El-Demellawy, M.A., 2020. Fish scale collagen preparation, characterization and its application in wound healing. J. Polym. Environ. 28 (1), 166–178. https://doi.org/10.1007/s10924-019-01594-w.

Tang, H., Dong, L., Xia, X., Chen, X., Ren, M., Shu, G., Fu, H., Lin, J., Zhao, L., Zhang, L., Cheng, G., Wang, X., Zhang, W., 2024. Preparation, optimization, and anti-pulmonary infection activity of casein-based chrysin nanoparticles. Int. J. Nanomed. 19, 5511–5522. https://doi.org/10.2147/IJN.S457643.

Tarhini, M., Greige-Gerges, H., Elaissari, A., 2017. Protein-based nanoparticles: from preparation to encapsulation of active molecules. Int. J. Pharm. 522 (1–2), 172–197. https://doi.org/10.1016/j.ijpharm.2017.01.067.

Tavakoli, N., Divsalar, A., Haertlé, T., Sawyer, L., Saboury, A.A., Muronetz, V., 2021. Milk protein-based nanodelivery systems for the cancer treatment . Springer Medizin. J. Nanostruct. Chem. 11 (4), 483–500. https://doi.org/10.1007/s40097-021-00399-5.

Ting, P., Srinuanchai, W., Suttisansanee, U., Tuntipopipat, S., Charoenkiatkul, S., Praengam, K., Chantong, B., Temviriyanukul, P., Nuchuchua, O., 2021. Development of chrysin loaded oil-in-water nanoemulsion for improving bioaccessibility. Foods 10 (8), 1912. https://doi.org/10.3390/foods10081912.

Wang, M., Zhang, Y., Fei, Z., Xie, D., Zhang, H., Du, Q., Jin, P., 2022. Hyaluronan oligosaccharides-coated paclitaxel-casein nanoparticles with enhanced stability and antitumor activity. Nutrients 14 (19), 3888. https://doi.org/10.3390/nu14193888.

Wang, L., Jia, W., Yang, Q., Cai, H., Zhao, X., 2024a. Casein nanoparticles as oral delivery carriers for improved bioavailability and hypoglycemic activity of apigenin. Food Hydrocoll. 146, 109194. https://doi.org/10.1016/j.foodhyd.2023.109194.

Wang, X., Chen, C., Bao, Y., Wang, Y., Leonidovna Strakh, Y., 2024b. Encapsulation of three different types of polyphenols in casein using a customized pH-driven method: Preparation and characterization. Food Res. Int. 189, 114547. https://doi.org/10.1016/j.foodres.2024.114547.

Wenck, C., Meier, N., Heinrich, E., Grützner, V., Wiekhorst, F., Bleul, R., 2024. Design and characterisation of casein coated and drug loaded magnetic nanoparticles for theranostic applications. RSC Adv. 14 (36), 26388–26399. https://doi.org/10.1039/d4ra02626h.

Wijewantha, N., Sane, S., Morgan, E., Antony, R.M., Potts, R.A., Lang, L., Rezvani, K., Sereda, G., 2023. Enhancing anti-tumorigenic efficacy of eugenol in human colon cancer cells using enzyme-responsive nanoparticles. Cancers 15 (4), 1145. https://doi.org/10.3390/cancers15041145.

Xue, Y., Zhou, S., Fan, C., Du, Q., Jin, P., 2019. Enhanced antifungal activities of eugenol-entrapped casein nanoparticles against anthracnose in postharvest fruits. Nanomaterials 9 (12), 1777.

Yavari Maroufi, L., PourvatanDoust, S., Naeijian, F., Ghorbani, M., 2022. Fabrication of electrospun polycaprolactone/casein nanofibers containing green tea essential oils: Applicable for active food packaging. Food Bioprocess Technol. 15 (11), 2601–2615. https://doi.org/10.1007/s11947-022-02905-1.

Zahariev, N., Draganova, M., Zagorchev, P., Pilicheva, B., 2023. Casein-based nanoparticles: a potential tool for the delivery of daunorubicin in acute lymphocytic leukemia. Pharmaceutics 15 (2), 471. https://doi.org/10.3390/pharmaceutics15020471.

Zhang, Y., Huang, Y., Chen, H., Luo, X., Zhang, J., Wang, H., Zou, Q., Wang, S., 2022. Design of a nanocomposite with gold nanoparticles as the core and casein-templated gold nanoclusters as the shell with ultra-low protein corona for enhanced photodynamic therapy. Mater. Adv. 3 (23), 8438–8448.

Zheng, Y., Bai, L., Zhou, Y., Tong, R., Zeng, M., Li, X., Shi, J., 2019. Polysaccharides from Chinese herbal medicine for anti-diabetes recent advances. Int. J. Biol. Macromol. 121, 1240–1253. https://doi.org/10.1016/j.ijbiomac.2018.10.072.

CHAPTER

# 14

# Silk-based nanocarriers for drug delivery

*Panoraia I. Siafaka[1], Androulla N. Miliotou[2], Ioannis D. Karantas[3], Emre Şefik Çağlar[4], Mehmet Evren Okur[5] and Neslihan Üstündağ Okur[6]*

[1]Department of Life Sciences, School of Sciences, Program of Pharmacy, European University Cyprus, Nicosia, Cyprus; [2]Department of Health Sciences, School of Life & Health Sciences, University of Nicosia, Nicosia, Cyprus; [3]Apostolos Loukas Medical Centre, Nicosia, Cyprus; [4]Department of Pharmaceutical Biotechnology, Faculty of Pharmacy, University of Health Sciences, Istanbul, Turkey; [5]Department of Pharmacology, Faculty of Pharmacy, University of Health Sciences, Istanbul, Turkey; [6]Department of Pharmaceutical Technology, Faculty of Pharmacy, University of Health Sciences, Istanbul, Turkey

## 1. Introduction

Over the last few decades, the drug delivery field has expanded,resulting in the development of various drug dosage forms that focus on rare diseases or common disorders. The incorporation of nanocarriers (NCs) into drug dosage forms, whether liquid or solid, seems to improve parameters such as instability, toxicity, inefficient targeting, low release rate, and bioavailability (Siafaka et al., 2016a,b; Danaei et al., 2018). Nanotechnology-based carriers can be formulated using various polymers, either natural or synthetic, as well as proteins, lipids, and inorganic nanoparticles (NPs), such as gold, silver, and graphene (Siafaka et al., 2016a,b; Wen et al., 2017). Natural polymers have been reported as potent biomaterials for drug delivery and tissue engineering since they can provide an artificial matrix mimicking the cell microenvironment and promote cell proliferation (Puertas-Bartolomé et al., 2021). They can be derived from plants, i.e., cellulose (Gupta et al., 2021); animals, i.e., silk (Polat et al., 2024); and microorganisms, i.e., alginate (ter Horst et al., 2019). The features identifying natural polymers as promising biomaterials are high biocompatibility, improved water retention, and mechanical potency (ter Horst et al., 2019).

*Protein-Based Nanoparticles in Drug Delivery*
https://doi.org/10.1016/B978-0-443-33639-3.00008-8

NCs based on natural polymers, such as silk NCs, are widely used for drug delivery, and various drug delivery systems have been produced for ocular (Upadhayay et al., 2016), dermal (Bernardes et al., 2024), oral and nasal (Chung et al., 2022), and other administration routes (Yu et al., 2023). Silk as a drug carrier has a growing interest for biomedical applications since it presents biocompatibility, biodegradability, and mechanical activity and is safe to use (Yu et al., 2023). Considering this, drug-loaded NPs based on silk fibroin (SF) possess various biological functions (Qu et al., 2014). Silk is comprised of two proteins: fibroin (65%–85%) and sericin (SER, 15%–35%). Besides, SF derived from the silkworm *Bombyx mori* has been approved by the Food and Drug Administration (FDA) as a safe material (Kundu et al., 2013) for biomedical applications. SF forms the inner core of silk, while silk sericin (SS), which forms the external shell of silk, is under investigation for its potential. SF represents a gum-like product being insoluble in water, while SS possesses aqueous solubility and adhesiveness (Das et al., 2021). SF-based NCs can be thoroughly found in literature, while SS-based NCs are mostly developed through blending with other polymers (Das et al., 2021; Crivelli et al., 2018). Consequently, silk-based NCs demonstrate excellent biocompatibility and desirable biodegradability while demonstrating multiresponsive features. Moreover, due to their efficacy in entrapping drugs, proteins, and genes via various techniques such as physical entrapment, surface adsorption, and chemical conjugations, silk-based NCs can be applied against drug degradation, enhancing pharmacokinetics, and increasing cellular drug uptake (Zhao et al., 2015; Ma et al., 2020). NCs include NPs (Tang et al., 2023), nanocapsules, and nanofibers (NFs); nanofibrous systems based on SF are widely developed since NFs present high surface area and porosity, which are important for wound healing (Radulescu et al., 2024), tissue engineering (Niu et al., 2017) or transdermal delivery (Yoon et al., 2013; Siafaka et al., 2016a, 2016b).

In this chapter, an examination of silk-based NCs for drug delivery is carried out, elucidating the structure and types of silk and various applications in the biomedical field. The NCs were categorized based on their administration route, i.e., ocular, oral, dermal, and other routes. Moreover, silk-based NCs for gene and protein delivery are being discussed, revealing their significance in the biotechnology field.

## 2. Silk: Structure, types, properties, and preparation methods

Silk is a natural fibrous polymer derived from glands of arthropods, such as spiders (*Nephila clavipes*; Babb et al., 2017), silkworm (*Bombyx mori*; Rockwood et al., 2011), *Antheraea mylitta* (Darshan et al., 2017), bees (*Apis mellifera*; Weisman et al., 2010), scorpions (Li et al., 2023), etc. As it is rational, silk, due to its different origin, presents diversity in its structure and properties. For example, Fig. 14.1 depicts the structures of silk fibers from silk and *B. mori*; although both consist of a protein core of nanofibrils within a protein matrix, silk from *B. mori* has a further cover from sericin.

From the above, the most well-known and used silk type is the *B. mori* silk (also called mulberry silk), which belongs to the Bombycidae family. On the other hand, *Antheraea mylitta* silk is a nonmulberry silk. Moreover, spider-based silk is rarely utilized since the spiders can only produce small quantities of silk and are harder to domesticate (Crivelli et al., 2018).

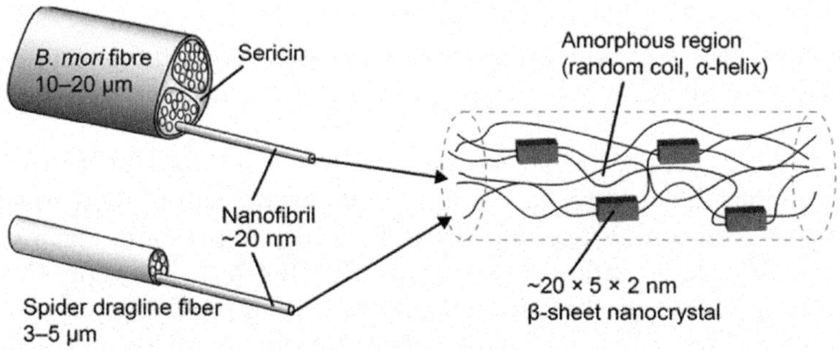


**FIGURE 14.1** The structures of silk types derived from *Bombyx mori* and spiders. *Obtained from Blamires, S.J., Rawal, A., Edwards, A.D., Yarger, J.L., Oberst, S., Allardyce, B.J., Rajkhowa, R., 2023. Methods for silk property analyses across structural hierarchies and scales. Molecules 28 (5), 14203049. https://doi.org/10.3390/molecules28052120, ©2023 by License, Basel, Switzerland. This article is an open access article distributed under the terms and conditions of the Creative Commons Attribution (CC BY) license.*

Herein, the structure of silk from *B. mori* is analyzed due to its extensive utilization. The cocoons of *B. mori* consist of two primary proteins: the SF and SS, which despite their relation, have different structures and properties. SF makes up 60%–80% of the silk, while SS constitutes 15%–35% of the silk. Furthermore, the silk also contains 1%–5% of wax, pigments, sugar, and mineral salts, as well as other impurities (Cao and Zhang, 2016).

Sericin is responsible for encasing two fibroin filaments, binding them together into silk fibers, which creates the cocoon. This cocoon is like a shelter to the silkworm during its progression from larva to adult, protecting it from the environmental changes (Cao and Zhang, 2016).

The fibrous core of fibroin consists of a heavy chain and a light chain. The heavy chain weighs between 350 and 390 kDa, while the light chain weighs between 25 and 26 kDa. The chains are linked together through a single disulfide bond at the C-terminus of the H-chain and a 25 kDa glycoprotein-P25 and further covered by sericin (Moreno-Tortolero et al., 2024). The light chain is composed of nonrepetitive sequences and therefore is more hydrophilic and relatively elastic, while the heavy chain is composed of glycine (46%), alanine (29%), serine (12%), and tyrosine (5%), forming characteristic repetitive hexapeptide sequences (Gly–Ala–Gly–Ala–Gly–Ser) or dipeptide sequences (Gly–Ala/Ser/Tyr), which

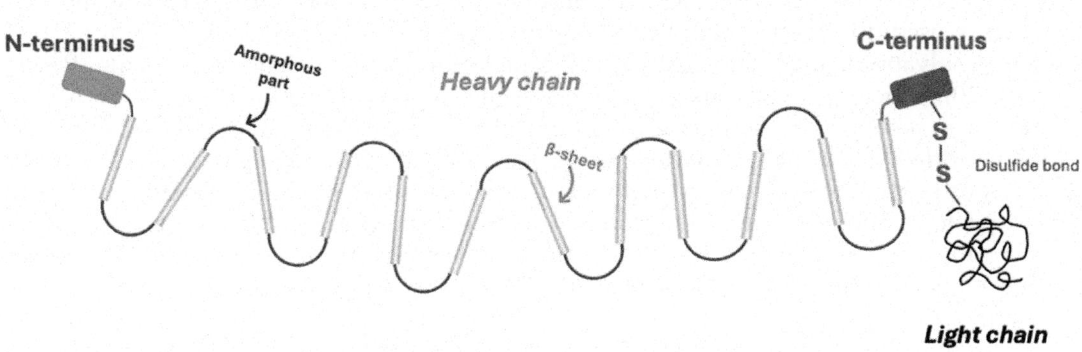


**FIGURE 14.2** The structure of silk fibroin.

are related to its secondary structure (Qi et al., 2017). Additionally, small amounts of charged amino acids like arginine, glutamate, lysine, and aspartate are present. Figure 14.2 shows the structure of SF, clearly demonstrating the bonding between the heavy and light chains.

Furthermore, two main crystal structures of silkworm-based SF have been identified: Type I, which is metastable and reveals a dominant conformation of β-turns (a controversial topic, according to Asakura, 2021), and Type II, which represents an antiparallel β-sheet structure with a monoclinic lattice. The rigidity and the tensile strength of SF are due to the hydrogen bonding between the segments. It has been reported that type I could be transformed to type II by treating the silk I with potassium phosphate or methanol. Additionally, α-helices, random coils, and turns have been reported as amorphous and less stable SF structures (Jaramillo-Quiceno et al., 2017; Wen et al., 2023).

Compared to SF, SS is a globular macromolecular protein that covers SF and facilitates the flow of SF during the spinning of the silkworms. SS is comprised of 18 amino acids, with the most abundant being serine as well as aspartic acid, accounting for approximately 16.7% and 33.4%, respectively (Wen et al., 2023; Suryawanshi et al., 2020).

SF demonstrates great mechanical and physicochemical as well as biological properties that cannot be found in other materials. For example, although silk evokes an impression of softness, it is a very tough material with high tensile strength and elongation at breakage (Koh et al., 2015), simulating Kevlar synthetic fiber but lacking biodegradability. Moreover, SF presents excellent stability, as well as good oxygen and water vapor permeability. Furthermore, SF demonstrates biocompatibility and antiinflammatory activity (Mazurek et al., 2022), while any safety concerns are due to SS residues (Crivelli et al., 2018). SS also provides good mechanical, physicochemical, and biological properties, while any limitations can be overcome by producing hybrid materials (Kumar Dan et al., 2022; Kunz et al., 2016).

## 2.1 Preparation methods for silk NCs

Various methodologies have been applied for the preparation of silk-based NPs, including self-assembly, emulsification, spray drying, and freeze-drying. Other methods include desolvation (Subia and Kundu, 2013), microemulsification, mechanical comminution, and supercritical fluid methodology (Zhao et al., 2015). The selection of the appropriate method is based on the advantages of desolvation and salting-out, which are the most frequently used due to their simplicity.

The desolvation-nanoprecipitation method incorporates a desolvating molecule (Pandey et al., 2020), which decreases silk solubility, leading to phase separation. Firstly, SF is being dissolved in a solvent, and afterward, an antisolvent (always miscible with the initial solvent) is added, inducing phase separation (Zhao et al., 2015; Kundu et al., 2010). The salting-out method involves the development of SF NPs by enhancing the interactions between proteins and removing the water barriers between them, further leading to protein aggregation and precipitation. The factors influencing the morphology of the NCs are the salting agent (e.g., LiBr, Sun et al., 2016; $CaCl_2$, Pham and Tiyaboonchai, 2020), pH, and ionic strength (Lammel et al., 2010). Moreover, silk NPs can be derived through the electrospraying technique; this method utilizes electrical forces to scatter liquid out of a capillary nozzle

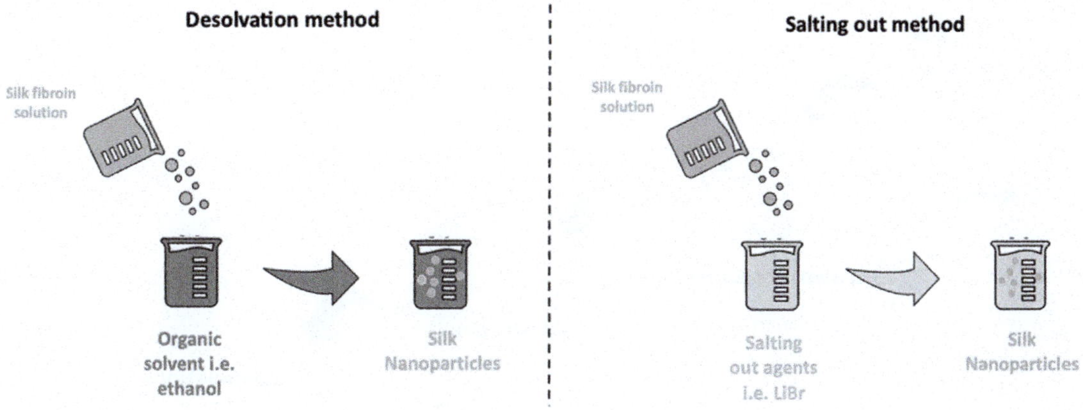


**FIGURE 14.3** Representation scheme of desolvation and salting-out methods for silk nanoparticles.

into tiny droplets via an electric field (Cao et al., 2017). Figure 14.3 depicts the two most common preparation methods for SF NCs: salting-out and desolvation techniques.

## 3. Silk-based nanocarriers

NP-based delivery systems comprised of SF are reported to enhance drug delivery and therapeutic efficiency; NPs, nanogels, hydrogels, nanosponges, scaffolds of nanodiameter, and films developed by SF have been identified as potent NCs with improved therapeutic efficacy. Figure 14.4 represents some nanoformulations that can be fabricated by SF.

### 3.1 Silk NCs for oral delivery

SF has garnered increasing interest as a natural biomaterial for drug delivery applications, particularly in the field of oral delivery systems (Harishchandra Yadav et al., 2024). This protein polymer has a unique combination of properties such as biocompatibility, biodegradability, and exceptional mechanical strength, which render it suitable for drug encapsulation and delivery (Wang et al., 2007; Gianak et al., 2018). The structure of SF is composed of two chains, the heavy and light chains, linked by disulfide bonds. The primary sequence consists predominantly of amino acids like glycine, alanine, and serine, which contribute to its amphiphilic nature, allowing self-assembly into diverse nanostructures suitable for drug delivery (Du et al., 2022).

Oral drug delivery remains one of the most preferred routes for drug administration due to its convenience, noninvasiveness, and patient compliance. However, the gastrointestinal tract presents a challenging environment due to its varying pH, enzymatic degradation, and mucus barriers that hinder effective drug absorption (Tallian et al., 2018). SF NCs have shown great potential in overcoming these barriers, primarily because of their stability in acidic conditions, their ability to respond to pH changes, and their tunable degradation profile. Additionally, the mucoadhesive properties of SF facilitate prolonged residence time in

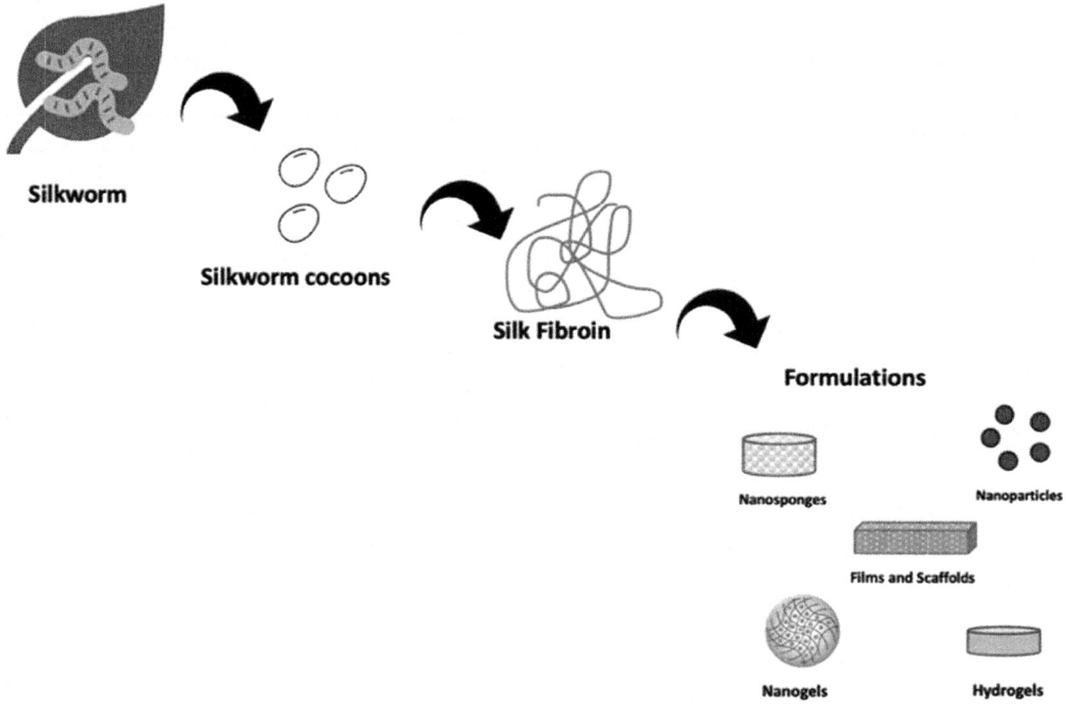


FIGURE 14.4 Schematic diagram of silk fibroin-based nanocarriers.

the gastrointestinal tract, enhancing drug absorption and bioavailability (Harishchandra Yadav et al., 2024).

For instance, Thi Phuong Thao et al. (2024) developed SF NPs modified with poly(vinyl alcohol) (PVA) so as to enhance zwitterionic ciprofloxacin delivery. These fibroin NPs exhibited controlled release properties, with 80% of the drug residing on the surface of the NPs via electrostatic interactions. The conjugation of SF and PVA helped stabilize the fibroin NPs under gastric conditions (pH 1.2) while promoting efficient drug release in the intestines (pH 6.8), ensuring targeted and sustained drug delivery to the lower parts of the gastrointestinal tract (Thi Phuong Thao et al., 2024). This highlights the potential of SF to encapsulate and deliver drugs that are sensitive to environmental conditions in the stomach and require precise delivery to the intestines for therapeutic efficacy.

SF's enzymatic degradation profile is particularly advantageous for oral drug delivery. It is selectively degraded by intestinal enzymes such as chymotrypsin and trypsin but remains stable in the acidic environment of the stomach, where pepsin is the predominant enzyme (Navamajiti et al., 2024). This selective degradation allows for tailored drug release in the small intestine, improving the bioavailability of the drug and ensuring delivery to the site of action. Such enzyme-responsive coatings made of SF can be combined with other polymers like polymethacrylates to enhance protection against premature drug degradation and facilitate site-specific release in the intestine. To enhance control over drug release in response to the pH conditions of the gastrointestinal tract, SF has been functionalized with pH-responsive polymers. Eudragit S100, a pH-sensitive copolymer, has been utilized to coat SF NPs (ES100-FNPs), making them highly responsive to the pH transitions within the gastrointestinal tract (Rai et al., 2016; Cardoso et al., 2023; Yoo et al., 2011). The ES100 coating provides protection to the encapsulated drug in the acidic stomach environment and facilitates controlled drug release in the more neutral conditions of the intestines (Alghurabi et al., 2022). Such pH-sensitive systems are beneficial for delivering drugs that are prone to degradation in acidic conditions or require targeted release in the intestines for therapeutic efficacy. Pham et al. (2024) demonstrated the application of ES100-FNPs loaded with furosemide, a model zwitterionic drug, to achieve controlled and sustained drug release depending on the pH environment (Pham et al., 2024). These spherical NPs with or without a smooth surface (Fig. 14.5) protected the active molecule from the gastric environment and

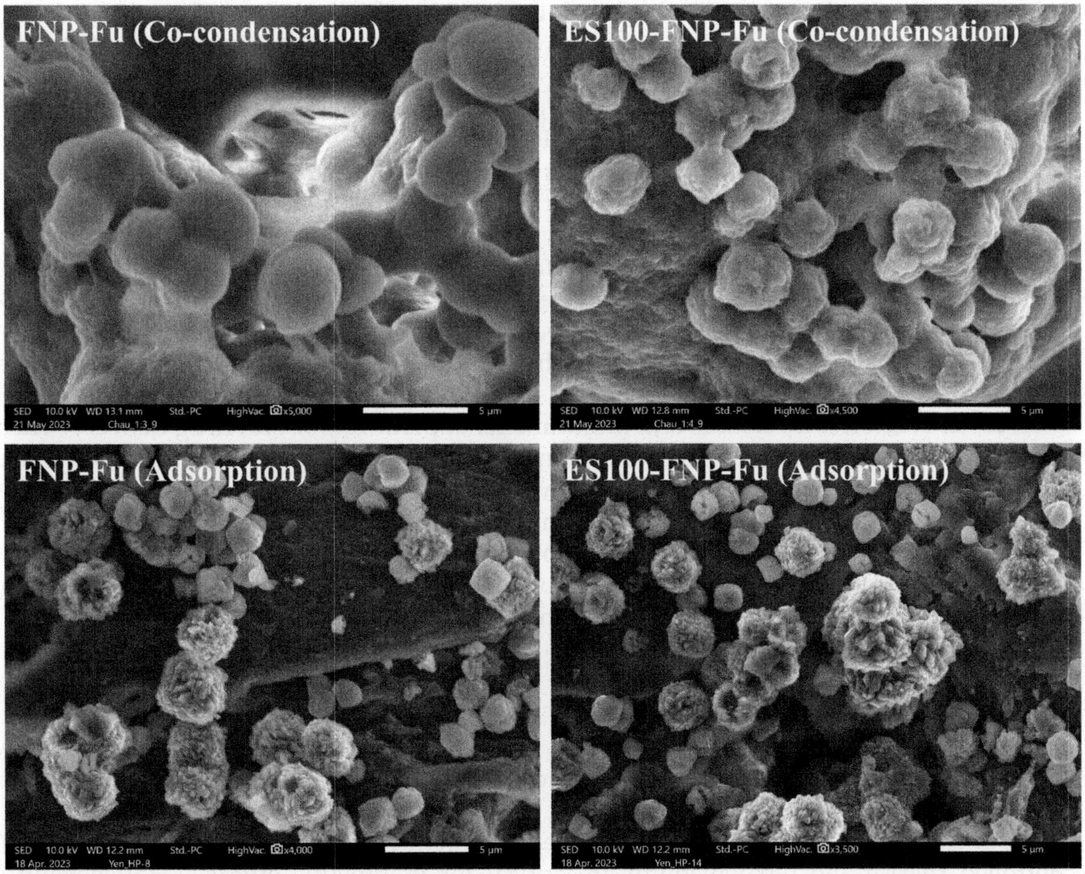


**FIGURE 14.5** Scanning electron microscopy micrographs of FNP-furosemide and ES100-FNP-furosemide using the cocondensation and adsorption methods. Reprinted under open access article distributed under the terms of the Creative Commons Attribution License, © 2024 Pham et al. (Pham et al., 2024). *Reprinted under open access article distributed under the terms of the Creative Commons Attribution License, © 2024 Pham et al. (D.T. Pham, D.X.T. Nguyen, N. Y. Nguyen, T.T.L. Nguyen, T.Q.C. Nguyen, A.V.T. Tu, N.H. Nguyen, B.T.P. Thuy, Development of pH-responsive Eudragit S100-functionalized silk fibroin nanoparticles as a prospective drug delivery system. PLoS One. 19326203. 19 (5) (2024), https://doi.org/10.1371/journal.pone.0303177).*

released it in the intestines at pH 6.8. The method of NP preparation, either by cocondensation or adsorption, influenced the release profile, providing a versatile platform for tuning drug delivery based on the desired therapeutic outcome.

The ability to fine-tune SF's properties, such as its crystallinity and β-sheet content, plays a critical role in controlling the stability and release profile of the encapsulated drug. Increased β-sheet content enhances the mechanical strength and stability of SF while reducing its solubility, thus enabling a more sustained and controlled drug release. Modulating factors such as temperature, solvent exposure, and SF concentration allow for tailored drug delivery systems suited to the desired pharmacokinetic and pharmacodynamic properties of the encapsulated therapeutic agent (Johnston et al., 2018; Drnovšek et al., 2016; Sun et al., 2021). Dyakonov et al. (2012) explored the use of SF films and spray-dried microparticles for controlled oral drug delivery of naproxen sodium, demonstrating that the degree of β-sheet crystallinity directly influenced the release kinetics of the drug. Such findings underscore the versatility of SF in creating oral delivery systems with tunable release profiles, mechanical strength, and degradation rates (Dyakonov et al., 2012).

SF NPs are not only limited to single-drug delivery but can also be designed to deliver combination therapies (Norouzi et al., 2021). For example, SF NPs can encapsulate both anti-inflammatory agents and immunomodulatory compounds to target inflammatory diseases like ulcerative colitis (Xie et al., 2022; Gou et al., 2019). Du et al. (2022) designed patchouli alcohol-loaded SF NPs functionalized with cyclic RGD peptides to target inflammatory sites in colitis (Gou et al., 2019). The resulting system provided targeted delivery to inflamed colon tissues, demonstrated antiinflammatory effects, and improved the integrity of the intestinal barrier. This multifunctional approach offers potential for the treatment of inflammatory bowel diseases and other gastrointestinal conditions requiring targeted and controlled drug delivery.

SF-based NCs offer a versatile and multifunctional platform for oral drug delivery. Their stability in varying gastrointestinal conditions, ability to provide controlled and sustained drug release, and potential for targeted delivery through enzymatic or pH responsiveness make them ideal candidates for enhancing the bioavailability and efficacy of oral therapeutics. The adaptability of SF NPs, coatings, and microneedle systems paves the way for advancements in oral drug delivery technologies that can cater to a wide array of therapeutic needs and disease conditions (Pham and Tiyaboonchai, 2020).

## 3.2 Silk NCs for ocular delivery

SF-based NCs have gained prominence as a promising strategy for ocular drug delivery because they present various advantages such as cytocompatibility, biodegradability, mechanical strength, and capacity for sustained drug release. These features make SF particularly suited for use in drug delivery systems targeting sensitive ocular tissues, where controlled release and bioavailability are critical for therapeutic efficacy (Harishchandra Yadav et al., 2024; Wenk et al., 2011).

Because of SF's mechanical properties and tunability, it can be modified or crosslinked with other polymers, enhancing stability and allowing controlled, sustained release profiles, which are particularly beneficial in ocular delivery where prolonged drug retention and minimal dosing frequency are required (Pham and Tiyaboonchai, 2020).

SF-based scaffolds have demonstrated significant potential in corneal repair and regeneration. Gavrilova et al. investigated scaffolds based on SF that incorporated glial cell line-derived neurotrophic factor to enhance corneal healing and restoration in cases of epithelial-stromal damage. The scaffolds, particularly at glial cell line-derived neurotrophic factor concentrations of 250 and 500 ng/mL, significantly improved keratocyte proliferation and reduced the area of corneal epithelial defects. The inclusion of glial cell line-derived neurotrophic factor was associated with enhanced epithelialization, increased proliferative activity of both epithelial cells and keratocytes, and expedited formation of the stromal nerve plexus. These findings underscore the importance of SF scaffolds in supporting corneal healing processes, reducing scarring, and promoting tissue regeneration (Gavrilova et al., 2021).

Similarly, SF films have been used as drug carriers for the treatment of corneal wounds. Insulin-loaded SF films have demonstrated the ability to stabilize and sustain the release of bioactive insulin, which is beneficial for corneal wound healing. In vivo studies in diabetic rats showed that the films effectively released insulin in a controlled manner over time, reducing glycemia and facilitating epithelial recovery (Cubayachi et al., 2019). The SF films' transparent nature, mechanical resilience, and capacity to maintain their native conformation make them suitable for ocular applications.

The development of SF-coated liposomes has also been a breakthrough in ocular drug delivery. Dong et al. explored SF-coated liposomes for topical ocular delivery, aiming to improve the bioavailability of encapsulated drugs, particularly through enhancing corneal permeability and prolonging residence time. SF-coated liposomes were able to sustain drug release and demonstrated better permeation through the corneal membrane compared to conventional drug solutions and noncoated liposomes. The mucoadhesive properties of SF contributed to a longer retention time on the ocular surface, enhancing the therapeutic efficacy of drugs for conditions such as dry eye syndrome, conjunctivitis, and other anterior segment disorders (Dong et al., 2015).

Another significant application of SF in ocular therapy is its use in hydrogel formulations for sustained release of antivascular endothelial growth factor (anti-VEGF). SF hydrogels have been developed to prolong the delivery of anti-VEGF agents for conditions such as diabetic retinopathy, age-related macular degeneration, and retinal vein occlusion, where repeated intravitreal injections are the standard of care. Lovett et al. demonstrated that SF hydrogels could deliver anti-VEGF therapeutics like bevacizumab over a period of 3 months in vitro and in vivo, significantly reducing the need for frequent intravitreal injections. The biodegradability and biocompatibility of SF ensure that the gels degrade over time, allowing for the possibility of repeated treatments (Lovett et al., 2015).

Recent advancements have focused on the development of SF NPs and microparticles for the delivery of therapeutics to ocular tissues. Polat et al. formulated metformin-loaded SF microparticles to treat corneal neovascularization, a condition associated with inflammation and vascular growth on the cornea. These SF microparticles, loaded with metformin, showed promising results in reducing corneal neovascularization, demonstrating improved entrapment efficacy, controlled release for 14 days, and desirable therapeutic efficacy comparable to standard treatments like dexamethasone (Polat et al., 2024). The sustained release mechanism followed Peppas-Sahlin kinetics, which underscores the potential of SF microparticles for prolonged treatment with reduced dosing frequency.

Additionally, the development of thermosensitive poloxamer-based in situ hydrogels containing moxifloxacin-loaded SF NPs has been explored for improving the treatment of bacterial keratitis (Chomchalao et al., 2024). This hybrid system exhibited a prolonged residence time on the ocular surface, effective antibacterial activity against pathogens like *Staphylococcus aureus* and *Pseudomonas aeruginosa*, and was nontoxic to corneal cells, suggesting a safe and efficient approach to treating bacterial infections. The thermosensitive properties of the hydrogels allow for easy application as a liquid that gels upon contact with the ocular surface, providing sustained drug release and minimizing the need for frequent administration.

The structural versatility of SF and its ability to be engineered into a range of material formats, such as films, scaffolds, NPs, and hydrogels, make it an exceptional candidate for ocular drug delivery applications. By tailoring the physical and chemical properties of SF, researchers have been able to achieve controlled and sustained drug release profiles, improved corneal penetration, and longer residence times on the ocular surface—all of which are essential for enhancing therapeutic outcomes in ocular diseases.

## 3.3 Silk NCs for dermal/transdermal delivery

Transdermal delivery is a quite interesting administration route with fewer side effects than the others, i.e., compared to oral, hepatic first-pass metabolism is avoided; therefore, it is a desirable administration pathway of drugs with low bioavailability (N'Da, 2014). Despite the advantages, the transdermal route might limit drug absorption since the skin acts as a barrier for the drugs. In addition, not all drugs can permeate the deeper tissues of the skin. The molecule should present a balance between lipophilicity and hydrophilicity, i.e., logP: 1–3, a molar mass less than 500 Da (Souto et al., 2022). There are limited studies employing silk-based NPs for transdermal delivery, despite the fact that drug NCs improve skin permeability. Moreover, SF's crystalline and amorphous structure due to hydrophobic and hydrophilic amino acids can be useful as a transdermal system due to the balance between hydrophilicity and hydrophobicity. Takeuchi et al. developed SF NPs of a size around 40 nm, which were able to penetrate deeper into the skin. According to storage stability studies and in vivo skin permeability, the SF NPs are stable, and they can penetrate the stratum corneum, being delivered deep into the skin (Takeuchi et al., 2019). Electrospun composites between SF and poly(lactic acid) showed cell attachment and proliferation efficiently while simultaneously influencing cell growth. Moreover, when SF concentration increased, hydrophilicity and enzymatic degradation also enhanced. According to the obtained data, electrospinning of SF and poly(lactic acid) (PLA) can be used to provide scaffolds and dressings for the biomedicine field (Gu et al., 2022). For example, scaffolds should possess significant mechanical and structural properties. They should also be able to control drug release and be biocompatible and biodegradable. Scaffolds based on SF and poly(ε-caprolactone) (PCL) core-shell NFs developed via emulsion electrospinning and show improved mechanical properties. The NFs were able to release the drug in a sustainable manner and can be useful for biomedical applications (Wang et al., 2021).

The wound healing journey is quite challenging since bacterial infection can. Hinder the healing process; innovative wound dressings can improve the wound healing, especially when they incorporate antimicrobial substances. In an interesting study, PLA and SF were used to develop electrospun nanofibrous membranes that incorporate silver nanoparticles (Ag NPs) as well as silver oxide ($Ag_2O$). The incorporation of SF improved the water vapor permeability and the liquid absorption, while as the SF concentration increased, the degradation rate and surface hydrophilicity also were enhanced. Finally, the nanofibrous mat demonstrated antimicrobial properties against *Pseudomonas aeruginosa* as well as great biocompatibility (Fang et al., 2024). Another nanofibrous mat constituted by SF and gelatin was analyzed for its possible wound healing activity. The NFs loaded with silver and gold NPs showed a significant wound healing rate of around 99% within 21 days and therefore can be used for wound dressings (Arumugam et al., 2023). Sun et al. prepared composite nanofibrous membranes comprised of SF and poly (vinylpyrrolidone) (PVP), which impregnated Chinese herbal extract puerarin (PUE). The incorporation of the extract improved properties such as diameter, porosity, and hydrophilicity, which are useful for better cell adhesion and proliferation. In addition, the fibrous composites showed significant antioxidant activity, cytocompatibility, and alleviation of lipopolysaccharide (LPS)-induced inflammation. Moreover, the NFs could efficiently improve wound healing rate via various pathways (Sun et al., 2022). Another study exploits the use of SF, poly(ethylene oxide) (PEO), and chondroitin sulfate (CS) electrospun dressings loaded with silver sulfadiazine so as to control wound infections. The diameter changed before and after PEO removal; in general, the diameter ranged between 200 and 350 nm. According to the characterization results, the nontoxic fibrous dressings showed improved antimicrobial activity corresponding to the CS addition, while in vivo experiments with Wistar rats demonstrated that the nanofibrous dressing characteristics were the same as those of silver sulfadiazine (SSD) cream treatment (Cestari et al., 2022). Similarly, Li et al. fabricated SF NFs with Ag NPs to improve their antibacterial activity. Tannic acid and PEO were added to the electrospinning solution to improve the process. The antibacterial tests showed that the fibers loaded with a higher concentration of Ag NPs inhibit the greater growth of *S. aureus* and *E. coli* (Fig. 14.6). Despite the fact that there are no studies about wound healing or release, this composite could be beneficial in future applications for dermal delivery (Li et al., 2024).

Additionally, Foroushani et al. developed NFs composed of SF, chitosan, Ag, and curcumin to improve the pH-responsive release of curcumin and accelerate wound healing. It was revealed that the beadless NFs with 600–1100 nm diameter (Fig. 14.7) exhibited significant antibacterial activity. Furthermore, both physical and mechanical properties also depend on CS concentration. Finally, the nontoxic fibers, as tested on NIH 3T3 fibroblasts, could be beneficial as wound dressings. It should also be noted that CS hydrogel impacts the pH-responsive release of curcumin. Additionally, Sheikh et al. aimed to develop artificial skin for use in the treatment of diseases such as wounds, burns, and diabetic ulcers. For this purpose, the researchers obtained NF by the electrospinning method using SF. They have developed a promising formulation in the course of their work (Sheikh et al., 2015).

Diabetic wound healing is quite difficult to treat, given that the skin of diabetic patients is more sensitive, and the healing process takes time. Consequently, the use of wound dressings that can effectively treat wounds is significant; SF and poly-(L-lactide-co-

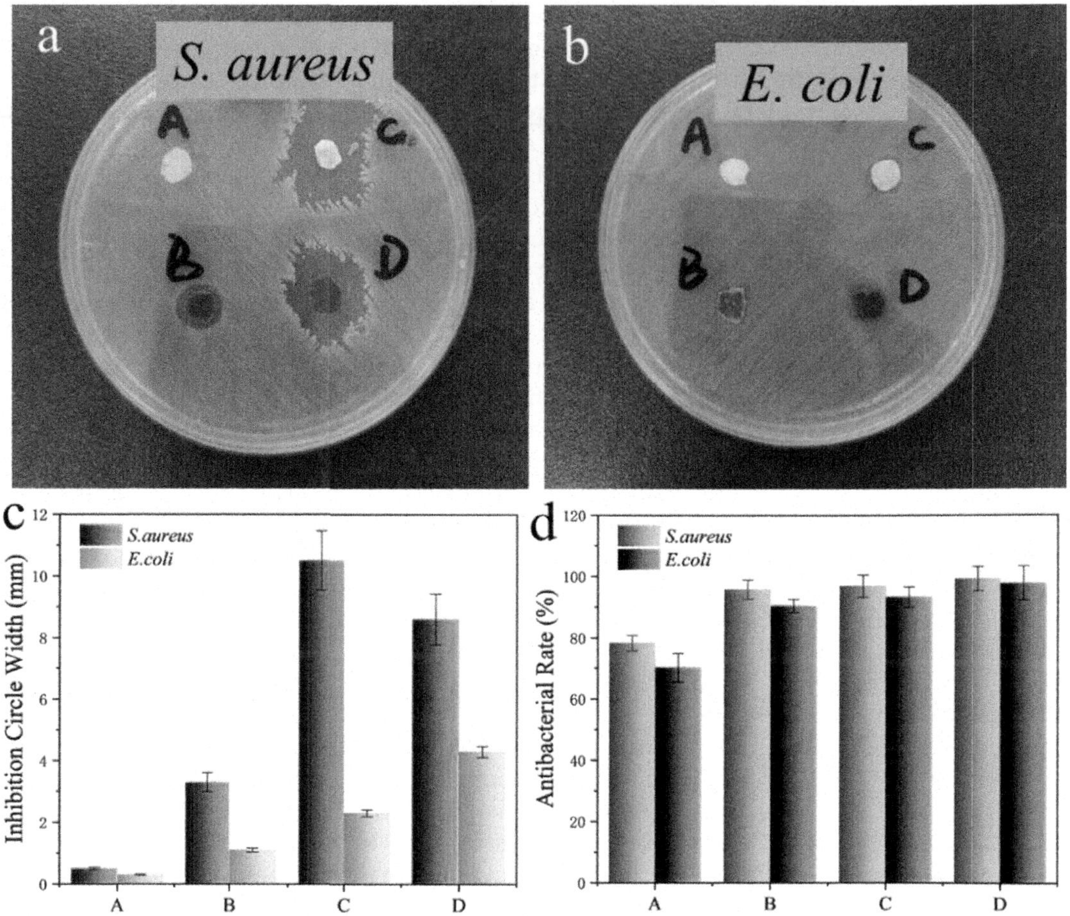


**FIGURE 14.6** Inhibition zones of fibers based on silk fibroin/poly(ethylene oxide)/silver nanoparticles against (a) *S. aureus* and (b) *E. coli*. (c) The width of the inhibition zone of four fibers. (d) The antibacterial rate of A: SF/PEO/AgNPs-1, B: SF/PEO/AgNPs-2, C: SF/PEO/AgNPs-3, and D: SF/PEO/AgNPs-4 fibers. Obtained by Li et al. Under open access license by MDPI (Li et al., 2024). *Obtained by Li et al. under open access license by MDPI (Q. Li, H. Gong, X. Jia, R. Wang, Z. Liu, L. Zhang, J. Li, T. Jiao, Electrospinning silk-fibroin-based fibrous membranes with AgNPs for antimicrobial application. Polymers. 16 (5) (2024), 648, https://doi.org/10.3390/polym16050648).*

caprolactone) (PLCL) NFs loaded with Huangbai Liniment were assessed as possible dressings for diabetic wound healing. The bead-free fibers showed a sustained drug release and activity against *S. aureus* and *E. coli*. In addition, the fibers exerted improved NIH-3T3 cells, while in vivo experiments exhibited that the SF dressings promote wound healing in diabetic mice (Xu et al., 2021).

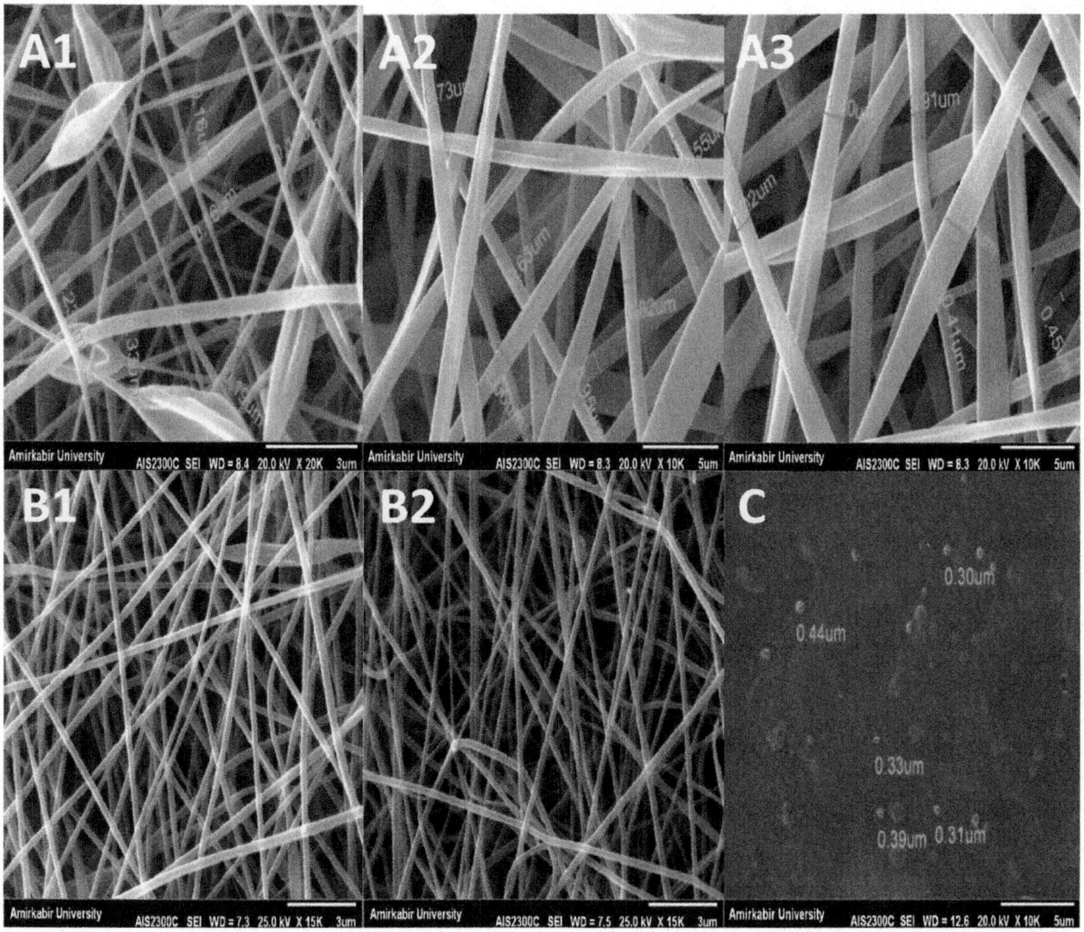


**FIGURE 14.7** SEM micrographs of the nanofibrous mats based on silk fibroin (SF), chitosan (CS), and Ag and curcumin using various CS concentrations of (A1) 5% *w/v*, (A2) 7% *w/v*, and (A3) 9% *w/v*. SEM micrographs of nanofibers before (B1) and after crosslinking (B2) (C) SEM micrographs of reduced Ag nanoparticles in CS solution. Obtained by Foroushani et al. Under open access license by MDPI (Heydari Foroushani et al., 2022). *Obtained by Foroushani et al. under open access license by MDPI (P. Heydari Foroushani, E. Rahmani, I. Alemzadeh, M. Vossoughi, M. Pourmadadi, A. Rahdar, A.M. Díez-Pascual, Curcumin sustained release with a hybrid chitosan-silk fibroin nanofiber containing silver nanoparticles as a novel highly efficient antibacterial wound dressing. Nanomaterials . 12 (19) (2022), https://doi.org/10.3390/nano12193426).*

## 3.4 Silk NCs for other routes

Intravenous (IV) administration is one of the most commonly used methods of drug administration. IV injection is the introduction of a medication into the veins using a needle, and it is used when rapid absorption is called for, when fluid cannot be taken by mouth, or when the medication to be administered is too irritating to be injected into the skin or muscles. The most important advantage is that the active substance of the drug is quickly given to the systemic circulation, and a rapid response is obtained. With IV administration, different formulations can be applied to the patient for the treatment of different diseases (Zhou et al., 2015).

As explained above, SF nanostructures can be applied with different application routes for different treatments. One of these ways is IV application. In the literature search, formulations of SF nanostructures loaded with drug active substances, especially designed for use in cancer treatment, were found.

In one study, researchers used a magnetic nanobiocomposite for the treatment of cancer by using the hyperthermia features of the prepared formulation. For this purpose, they prepared sodium alginate hydrogel and modified it with halloysite nanotubes, SF, and ferrous chloride magnetic NPs. The obtained results showed no important difference in red blood cell hemolysis. In addition to these results, no toxicity was observed in HEK293T cell lines. The researchers claimed that this nanobiocomposite could be effective in the treatment of breast cancer (Eivazzadeh-Keihan et al., 2022). Gangrade et al. prepared injectable doxorubicin loaded in folic acid-modified single-walled carbon nanotube-laden SF hydrogels for the treatment of breast cancer. In this study, the researchers aimed at controlled drug release by loading the active ingredient doxorubicin, which has a high dosing frequency of application, into an injectable silk-fibroin hydrogel. As a result, they observed that the drug was released for 14 days (Gangrade and Mandal, 2019). In another study, researchers aimed to develop a nanozyme by using SF biopolymer. For this purpose, they combined the silk NPs that they developed with cerium oxide NPs. The cerium oxide NPs, on the other hand, were modified with carbon nanotubules. They also introduced sulforaphane, a powerful antioxidant, into the system. This NC has been tested in lung cancer cell lines, and very significant results have been obtained (Passi et al., 2020). Qu et al. prepared cisplatin-loaded SF NPs by electrospray without using any type of organic solvent for the treatment of lung cancer. The size of the prepared formulation was almost 59 nm, and the drug was sustainably released by the formulation. According to cytotoxicity results of the formulation, the prepared formulation was easily internalized by lung cancer cells (Qu et al., 2014). In another study, curcumin-loaded crystalline silk nanodiscs were prepared for the treatment of cervical cancer. Results of the study showed that prepared formulations sustainably released curcumin and were effective against human cervical cancers (Patwa et al., 2018). Xu et al. prepared indocyanine green-loaded SF NPs for the photothermal therapy of glioblastoma. The size of the developed formulation was found to be $209.4 \pm 1.4$ nm and negatively charged. In addition, the prepared formulation showed good stability in a physiological medium. In vivo studies showed that the developed formulation was easily internalized by tumor cells (Xu et al., 2018). Wu et al. prepared dual drugs (paclitaxel and doxorubicin) loaded SF nanospheres for cancer treatment. The size of the formulations ranged between 100 and 600 nm. Drug release was found to be over 7 days. In addition, drug-loaded nanospheres showed high cellular uptake (Wu et al., 2018). Yang et al. developed manganese oxide-modified SF NPs for the diagnosis of cancer. For this reason, researchers used indocyanine green as a photodynamic agent and doxorubicin as an anticancer drug. Results showed that the developed formulation was a promising way of diagnosing and treating cancer disease (Yang et al., 2019). Li et al. prepared 5-fluorouracil and curcumin-loaded SF NPs for the anticancer effect. Prepared formulations were found to be $217.0 \pm 0.4$ nm. Animal studies also showed a significant decrease at the tumor site

(Sun et al., 2016). Nasrine et al. prepared anastrozole-loaded SF NP for the treatment of breast cancer. For the formulation preparation, researchers used factorial design to obtain the NPs. The size of the NPs was 181.70 ± 1.3 nm, and sustained drug release was observed (Nasrine et al., 2022).

SF nanocomposites have been widely used not only in IV administration, but also in vaccination or tissue regeneration. In one study, researchers investigated the inoculation efficacy of outer membrane protein (rOmpA)-loaded SF sodium alginate NPs against pneumonia. In their study, they found the particle size to be 160 nm and the loading efficiency to be 80%. They found that the developed formulation increased the immune response in *in vivo* studies and developed an effective method against pneumonia (Shahbazi et al., 2023). In another study, SF NP was used as a nanoadjuvant in urinary tract infection. The formulations were loaded with FimH-LutA antigen. The size of silk-fibroin NPs was found to be 180 nm, and the encapsulation efficiency was 88%. At the end of 42 days, antigen release from the formulation was found to be 18%. In animal studies, formulations have been found to increase humoral and cellular immunity.

Furthermore, silk-fibroin nanocomposites are widely used in tissue regeneration. Kandhasamy et al. developed vitamin K3-carnosine peptide-loaded silk-fibroin fibers for use in the treatment of bronchopleural fistula. While the fibers they developed were biocompatible with Human Bronchial Epithelial Cells (HBEC), they also showed cytotoxic properties in A549 lung cancer cells. In animal studies, they found that tissue regeneration occurred, and angiogenesis began (Kandhasamy and Zeng, 2022). Wei et al. prepared polycaprolactone/silk-fibroin/collagen-based NF for the urethral reconstruction. For this reason, NFs were prepared by using the electrospinning technique. In addition, several characterization studies were performed. The results showed that nanosized fibers were obtained. Furthermore, cell culture studies on mucosal cells showed that NFs could effectively be used for tissue repair (Wei et al., 2015). Pan et al. prepared kartogenin-loaded liposome-laden SF NF for cartilage tissue regeneration. Developed formulations were characterized and found to be appropriate for use in cartilage implantation (Pan et al., 2023). In one study, researchers developed an SF NF for myringoplasty. In their results, they determined that the NF they developed was biocompatible in both cell culture studies and in vivo studies and increased cell proliferation and tissue regeneration (Rathnakara et al., 2022). Li et al. aimed to develop microRNA-222-loaded chitosan NPs laden with silk-fibroin NFs for neuronal stem cell differentiation for neuronal stem cell transplantation. First, they developed microRNA-222-loaded chitosan NPs, and the encapsulation efficiency was found to be 96.4 ± 0.3%. In addition, silk-fibroin NF was developed and characterized. Results showed that the developed formulation improved the neuronal differentiation (Li et al., 2022). In another study, researchers examined the impact of a bacterial cellulose/gelatin-based NF formulation containing VEGF-loaded silk-fibroin NPs on angiogenesis. In both in vitro and in vivo studies, researchers found that the formulation they developed was effective in increasing angiogenesis (Wang et al., 2017).

## 4. Silk NCs for gene therapy and protein delivery

NCs consisting of silk fibers provide a flexible platform, particularly for drug delivery purposes such as gene therapy and protein therapeutics. Such approaches use SF because of its biocompatible, biodegradable, and tunable properties to solve problems with genetic materials like plasmid DNA (pDNA), small interfering RNA (siRNA), and micro RNA (miRNA), which are intrinsically unstable and have poor cellular uptake. Silk-based delivery systems (i.e., silk elastin-like polymers, silk polysine, etc.) can provide controlled release, high transfection efficiency, and low toxicity. Furthermore, silk NCs have been found to dramatically prolong the half-time of therapeutic proteins while facilitating controlled release of growth factors essential in tissue engineering, vaccine peptides, and anticancer strategies. These innovations are indicative of the feasibility of silk-based NCs in both gene and protein delivery applications, reinforcing their potential in therapeutic interventions.

## 4.1 Silk NCs for gene therapy

Currently, the two main structural categories of drugs approved by the U.S. FDA are the small molecules and the biological molecules, including nucleic acids and recombinant proteins. Small-molecule drugs consist mainly of hydrophobic organic compounds. These drugs mostly work by inactivating or inhibiting target proteins through competitive binding. However, only about 2%–5% of the proteins encoded by the human genome have the properties allowing them to be targeted by these small-molecule drugs. In contrast, biological molecules, like drug proteins (e.g., recombinant proteins, antibodies), can bind with great specificity to a range of targets or can be used to replace mutated or missing proteins (e.g., insulin for the treatment of diabetes) (Verdine and Walensky, 2007) in the context of protein replacement therapy (PRT). However, the size and stability of the therapeutic proteins, as well as their multiple purification steps, reduce their applicability to several potential targets and diseases. Thus, personalized genomics targets therapies beyond those offered by current treatments of small molecular drugs and therapeutic proteins. Protein precursors, messenger RNA (mRNA), and pDNA hold the promise in PRT and represent an alternative route to treating genetic abnormalities, where a protein is produced inefficiently or not produced at all. Furthermore, siRNAs and miRNAs are used to knock down harmful protein expression (Vaidya et al., 2019; Catalanotto et al., 2016).

Nevertheless, as with small molecule-based drugs, biological molecule-based treatments face several drug delivery challenges. Successful intracellular transduction may be prevented due to their large molecular weight and charge and degradation by harmful endonucleases (Wu et al., 2022). Therefore, by offering protection and facilitating delivery across the membrane, novel methods like silk-based delivery systems can be employed to lessen these difficulties (Gonzalez-Obeso et al., 2023). The unique properties of SF NPs, including their biocompatibility, biodegradability, and ability to be tailored for various functions, have positioned them as a promising candidate for gene delivery applications. Silk-based delivery systems can overcome key challenges in gene therapy, such as instability and inefficient cellular uptake of genetic materials, such as pDNA, siRNA, and miRNA (Harishchandra Yadav et al., 2024).

SELPs, which are silk elastin-like polymers, have been designed as good matrices for the steady release of nucleic acids, such as naked DNA and pDNA, which can be combined with nonviral or viral vectors. SELPs help with effective DNA delivery, provide safety from damaging nucleases, and lower toxicity. In a preliminary investigation carried out in 2002, SELP hydrogels were observed to efficiently release pDNA in a controllable manner using an alterable ion-exchange process. The extent of control available with SELP hydrogels was evident as modulation of the release of pDNA was achieved by ionic strength, polymer concentration, and cure time, among other factors (Megeed et al., 2002). Furthermore, the high in vitro and in vivo release of bioactive pDNA and viral vectors entrapped in these biomaterials into cells, which resulted in elevated gene transfection in models of breast cancer, indicated that these hydrogels can also be effective for nucleic acid delivery (Megeed et al., 2004). In addition, the release rates of DNA are influenced by the design of the SELP hydrogel, where more release is noted in hydrogels with less polymer content and when the cure time is shorter. This characteristic allows for precise control over the pDNA delivery efficiency (Hwang et al., 2009). In a study carried out by Dandu et al. in 2008, a murine breast cancer model was treated with adenoviral vector gene therapeutics delivered within SELP hydrogels. Data analyses showed that polymer concentration and design of the SELP properties greatly influenced the transfection efficacy and functionality of the delivered DNA. A more substantial release of the viral vectors was seen at a higher content of elastin in the SELPs, illustrating that the structure of the polymer improves gene delivery efficacy (Dandu et al., 2008). Finally, the use of time-lapse imaging techniques on live cell systems has enabled greater optimization of targeting systems based on SELP polymers. By employing imaging of the whole animal organism, it was found that the content of the polymer and the proportion of silk and elastin polymers influenced viral gene expression in a xenograft model of head and neck cancer (Cresce et al., 2008).

Another innovative strategy is to utilize bioengineered silk–polylysine block copolymers for nonviral gene delivery. Silk polylysine copolymers encompass the biocompatibility provided by SF and the ability of polylysine to ionically interact with condensed DNA. These polymers form self-assembled NPs, which can also incorporate pDNA, thereby preventing its enzymatic degradation and aiding intracellular transduction. In a study with human embryonic kidney (HEK) cells, silk polylysine copolymers offered high transfection efficiency with low toxicity and resistance to DNase degradation, making them preferable nonviral vectors for gene delivery systems, which are essential in minimizing the risks of using viral vectors (Numata et al., 2009). An enhancement of the transfection efficiency of silk-polylysine constructs can be done by including cell membrane-destabilizing peptides, such as ppTG1. These peptides promote pDNA delivery by enhancing the endosomal escape of the plasmid and disrupting the cellular membrane for easier delivery of the genetic cargoes. The silk-polylysine-ppTG1 complexes transfected cells with an efficacy that was similar to that of Lipofectamine (2000), a commonly used commercial transfection reagent, but with a lower toxicity level and better DNA shielding properties. This method is thus a valid alternative for gene delivery that is ideal for use in the clinics, as it is less toxic and highly effective (Numata and Kaplan, 2010).

SF has also been extensively studied as a scaffold material for tissue engineering applications, particularly in bone and dermal tissue engineering. One of the most notable applications is the combination of SF with adenoviruses expressing bone morphogenetic protein 7 (BMP7). Zhang et al. focused on bone tissue regeneration, where silk scaffolds loaded with BMP7 adenovirus were shown to promote osteogenesis by inducing bone-forming osteoblasts. The scaffolds provided sustained release of BMP7 adenovirus for up to 21 days,

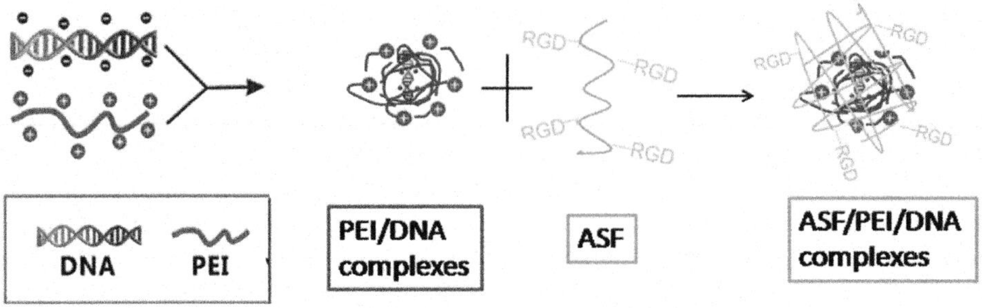


FIGURE 14.8 Schematic diagram of *Antheraea pernyi* silk fibroin/PEI/DNA ternary complexes. *Obtained under open access license from MDPI, Liu et al., (Y. Liu, R. You, G. Liu, X. Li, W. Sheng, J. Yang, M. Li, Antheraea pernyi silk fibroin-coated PEI/DNA complexes for targeted gene delivery in HEK 293 and HCT 116 cells, Int. J. Mol. Sci.. 14220067. 15 (5) (2014), 7049–7063, https://doi.org/10.3390/ijms15057049).*

enhancing new bone formation in a calvarial defect model. This approach not only demonstrated the utility of silk scaffolds in tissue engineering but also highlighted their potential for sustained gene delivery in regenerative medicine (Zhang et al., 2012). In addition, cationized SF from *B. mori* (CBSF) has been used in gene delivery systems for tissue regeneration, particularly in promoting angiogenesis in dermal tissues. A recent study investigated the use of CBSF to deliver a coexpression plasmid encoding VEGF and angiopoietin-1 (Ang-1), both of which are critical for promoting blood vessel formation. The results demonstrated that CBSF scaffolds loaded with this plasmid significantly enhanced neovascularization studied in in vitro and in vivo models, offering a promising tool for dermal tissue regeneration and wound healing applications (Luo et al., 2019).

Finally, the recent focus on innovative approaches to gene therapy highlights the targeted gene delivery. In gene therapy, it is essential to deliver the therapeutic genes to the specific cell types, thus preventing any possible effects arising from other cell types. SF from *Antheraea pernyi,* which is rich in RGD peptides (the tri-amino acid sequence, arginine–glycine––aspartate), was applied to wrap complexes of PEI/DNA to enhance targeting. The complexes (Fig. 14.8) containing *Antheraea pernyi* silk fibroin (ASF) showed higher transfection efficiency than regular PEI complexes in colorectal carcinoma cells, as RGD peptides in ASF bind to the integrins that are overexpressed on tumor cells. This targeting strategy not only facilitated delivering DNA effectively but also decreased the toxicity experienced by the cells in comparison to the normal PEI systems (Liu et al., 2014). Toward another aim of increasing the gene delivery specificity prompted by the tumor cells, magnetic silk-PEI NPs are also investigated in a study on breast cancer cells, whereby significant enhancement in the uptake of antisense oligodeoxynucleotides (ODNs) and suppression of cancer cells was achieved. This approach of magnetic targeting proved to enhance the effect of gene therapy while also lessening the toxic effect as opposed to the traditional delivery systems using PEI (Song et al., 2019). In fact, localized delivery systems define a strong means of restricting the gene delivery to specific tissues and organs. Adhesively assembled SF microcapsules employing a layer-by-layer method have been designed for the targeted delivery of pDNA. These microcapsules managed to provide control of pDNA release for three (3) days without adverse effects, in relation to the traditional values, on cells. Further, microcapsules containing a pDNA construct encoding for enhanced green fluorescent protein (eGFP) were successfully used for gene expression in cell cultures, indicating their usefulness for localized gene delivery (Li et al., 2014).

## 4.2 Silk NCs for protein delivery

Studies have demonstrated the effectiveness of silk-based NC systems in providing drug delivery platforms beyond gene therapy, exploiting peptide and protein therapeutics, and even vaccines. Silk NCs increase the in vivo integrity of proteins, which is a major limitation in protein therapy because of the protein's short half-life, which hinders their therapeutic effect. In addition, silk matrices were shown to be able to attach to the proteins as an additional component by using the process of covalent bonding, which is usually achieved with cross-linking agents such as glutaraldehyde, thereby ensuring protein rigidity and lengthening the period of their activity within the organism (Tomeh et al., 2019).

Silk fibroin-insulin (SF-Ins) bioconjugates were synthesized by Shang et al. in order to formulate stable insulin preparations (Zhang et al., 2006). Bursting folded SF, sanitary insulin was dense-coated onto the surface, providing enhanced cross-linking with SF in human blood serum compared to other insulin-derived polymers. Interestingly, constructs based on SF-Ins bioconjugates showed several times longer circulatory half-life in diabetic rats compared to native insulin. These constructs demonstrated prolonged pharmacological action in insulin-deprived rats for about 21 h, roughly 3.5 times longer than what native insulin is able to achieve (Zhang et al., 2006).

The aim of combining SF matrices and growth factors is focused on tissue regeneration. In particular, interest has been drawn to SF matrix incorporation with the osteoinductive growth factor bone morphogenetic protein-2 (BMP-2). For example, the in vitro calcification rates reported for BMP-2-containing electrospun SF/PEO fibers were higher than rates recorded for BMP-2-free fibers. It was noted that the release of BMP-2 from the scaffold occurred upon dissolution of the PEO component, which made the SF matrix more porous, thus allowing for the amendment of the release and calcification kinetics by blending SF with different ratios of PEO. In addition to electrospun fibers, prefabricated SF scaffolds loaded with BMP-2 also exhibited the possibility of efficient growth factor delivery, which only required the scaffold to be placed in an aqueous solution of BMP-2. The cumulative release rate of BMP-2 came to 75% after 1 week, while of the initial amount of BMP-2 in the scaffolds, 25% was irreversibly bound to the scaffold. This controlled interaction with and release of the growth factors justifies the use of the SF Matrix in tissue engineering, especially in cases where human mesenchymal stem cells (hMSCs) require osteogenic differentiation. In a separate investigation aimed at the restoration of bone tissues, SF matrices were employed to encapsulate BMP-2, which is one of the key growth factors for bone development. Carbodiimide chemistry was used to attach BMP-2 to SF coatings, which were able to stimulate osteogenic differentiation of hMSCs (Wenk et al., 2011). In relation to unmodified SF films, the silk films carrying BMP-2 increased alkaline phosphatase activity, enhanced calcium deposition, and elevated expression of osteogenic markers, further reinforcing the ability of the SF matrices to actively support protein therapy for bone regeneration (Karageorgiou et al., 2004). This substrate-mediated delivery approach—where growth factors are firmly attached to the matrix rather than simply released—mimics the physiological role of the extracellular matrix (ECM), which acts as a reservoir for growth factors like fibroblast growth factor-2 (FGF-2; Wenk et al., 2010), nerve growth factor (NGF; Uebersax et al., 2007), and insulin-like growth factor I (IGF-I; Uebersax et al., 2008). When such growth factors interact with the ECM and bind to cell surface receptors, they are capable of eliciting biological responses, which may trigger other cellular signaling pathways as opposed to soluble factors (Wenk et al., 2011). Also, SF has been assessed for its ability to provide a binding support for antibodies in biosensor development, with positive results being attained. Thanks to the ability of solvent-induced conformational transition of SF, antibodies can be immobilized in a way that maintains their biological activity and does not require a laborious procedure; thus, such silk-based biosensors are more practical than others (Lu et al., 2011).

In the field of cancer therapy, silk NPs have been used for the administration of therapeutic proteins. As an illustration, Eri silk NPs were employed as a carrier of bovine lactoferrin (bLf) for targeted delivery to a breast cancer model in 2016. Significant internalization and cancer-specific cytotoxicity were observed in both apo-bovine lactoferrin (Apo-bLf) and iron-loaded bLf NPs in MDA-MB-231 (EGFR-positive) and MCF-7 (EGFR-negative) breast cancer cellular lines. The study reported that the receptor-mediated endocytosis of these NPs led to apoptosis in a significantly more enhanced manner in the EGFR-overexpressing cells, thus providing a beneficial approach for treating cancer and a promising strategy for exploiting milk proteins in breast cancer therapy (Kanwar et al., 2015).

For the past few years, vaccine development has focused on using particulate platforms to improve their stability and immunogenicity. Silk-based platforms have notable benefits in the case of peptide vaccines and controlled release of antigens. Lucke et al. in 2018 developed particles from spider silk to deliver peptide vaccines. Antigenic peptides were fused with a recombinant spider silk protein known as eADF4(C16), which was later incorporated into dendritic cells for the activation of cytotoxic T lymphocytes. A cathepsin-cleavable linker was added, which improved immune response, allowing for significant levels of antigen-specific T-cell expansion without the use of a vaccine adjuvant. This innovative approach to vaccine development highlighted the usefulness of spider silk particles as an adjustable, long-lasting, and effective delivery system for peptide vaccines (Lucke et al., 2018).

Moreover, the method of vaccine delivery considerably determines the immune response produced by particulate-type vaccines. Mohanan et al. conducted a cross-sectional study that assessed the immune responses elicited by all possible routes of administration—subcutaneous, intradermal, intramuscular, and intralymphatic—using particulate systems of delivery, including liposomal and NP delivery systems. Antibody responses (IgG1 subclass) were found to be fairly robust with respect to any of the administration routes, but in contrast, the Th1 type of immune response (IgG2a subclass) was found to be highly influenced by the delivery route. In particular, the IgG2a response was pronounced with the intralymphatic administration, and this poses an interesting aspect in considering vaccine delivery systems aiming toward cellular immunity (Mohanan et al., 2010). To facilitate further clinical translation of vaccine delivery, intranodal injection of adjuvant-releasing polymer particles was evaluated as a means to improve the effectiveness of vaccines. By using biodegradable microparticles to deliver the Toll-like receptor agonist polyIC, it was shown that while intramuscular injection only resulted in a modest increase in antigen-specific T-cell responses, more than eightfold improvement was achieved when the injection was intranodal. This technique delivers the vesicles to the lymph nodes long term, retaining the adjuvants for an extended period and providing a strong means to enhance the efficacy of therapeutic and preventive vaccines (Jewell et al., 2011). In another direction, design-mounted microneedles for vaccine release were created from a combination of silk and composite implant materials. These microneedles were designed to engage and activate the skin dendritic cells, similar to the action of any invading pathogen. Incorporating SF tips with a base made of poly(acrylic acid) (PAA), the system administered a protein subunit vaccine in two phases: an initial bolus encapsulated within the PAA base and a slow continuous release from the silk reservoir. This system also enhanced the antigen-specific T-cell and antibody responses, showing the advantage of silk microneedles for transcutaneous immunization (Demuth et al., 2014).

## 5. Conclusions

The nanotechnology field offers improved therapeutic efficacy of drugs since NCs can provide tissue targeting through various functionalization methods, such as chemical conjugation or absorption of various agents. Protein-based NCs seem to offer great bioavailability and biocompatibility, which are important features for drug delivery systems. It can be concluded that silk is an important biopolymer in the field of drug delivery. Its properties of biocompatibility, biodegradability, water retention, solubility, and mechanical tunability, as well as its ability to blend with other biomaterials, have made this multifunctional biopolymer one of the most studied materials in the field. Furthermore, it was reported that silk-based NCs can control the drug release rate due to their controlled degradation rate. In the past, drug delivery nanosystems based on SF were produced. However, nowadays, more and more studies evaluate the effectiveness of NCs based on SS since it can develop hybrid biomaterials. Consequently, silk-based NCs for drug delivery will take the lead in clinical practice in the coming years.

Gene therapy development exploiting silk-based NCs is very encouraging, especially for overcoming the shortcomings of the traditional systems of nucleic acid delivery. For example, recent studies support SELPs that facilitate the controlled release of pDNA using an ion-exchange process that can be varied to enhance gene delivery (Griswold et al., 2022). This design variable is related to the polymer concentration as well as the cure time, which indicates that the efficiency of the delivery may be further fine-tuned by making appropriate changes to the carrier structural design. Also, the application of silk-polylysine copolymers, incorporating SF's exceptional biocompatibility along with polylysine's DNA condensing properties, protects the pDNA from enzymatic degradation and ensures low toxicity during intracellular transduction, thereby improving gene delivery (Wang et al., 2019). All these advances suggest that systems based on silk may be wrapped up more safely than all gene therapy viral vectors in use clinically today.

In addition to gene therapy, silk NCs can deliver proteins in a sustainable manner, which is necessary for therapeutic purposes such as tissue regeneration. Observations revealed that it is feasible to fuse SF with hormones such as insulin and growth-promoting proteins like bone morphogenetic protein-2 (BMP-2) to enhance their bioavailability and achieve sustained drug release in vivo. These systems have been found to be especially useful in areas concerning the restoration of bone and dermal tissues due to silk matrices, which provide sustained release and targeted delivery, thereby acting within the ECM (Sun et al., 2021). Furthermore, silk NPs have also been applied in the treatment of cancer, where they help the delivery of proteins, with increased effectiveness only to cancerous cells (Yu et al., 2023). These findings highlight the multifunctionality of silk NCs in the delivery of both nucleic acids and proteins, thus increasing the potential of their exploitation in various treatment strategies.

## References

Alghurabi, H., Tagami, T., Ogawa, K., Ozeki, T., 2022. Preparation, characterization and in vitro evaluation of eudragit S100-coated bile salt-containing liposomes for oral colonic delivery of budesonide. Polymers 14, 2693. https://doi.org/10.3390/polym14132693.

Arumugam, M., Murugesan, B., Balasekar, P., Ponnurengam Malliappan, S., Kumar Chinnalagu, D., Chinniah, K., Cai, Y., Mahalingam, S., 2023. Silk fibroin and gelatin composite nanofiber combined with silver and gold nanoparticles for wound healing accelerated by reducing the inflammatory response. Process Biochem. 134, 1–16. https://doi.org/10.1016/j.procbio.2023.10.017.

Asakura, T., 2021. Structure of silk I (Bombyx mori silk fibroin before spinning) -type II β-turn, not α-helix-. Molecules 26 (12), 3706. https://doi.org/10.3390/molecules26123706.

Babb, P.L., Lahens, N.F., Correa-Garhwal, S.M., Nicholson, D.N., Kim, E.J., Hogenesch, J.B., Kuntner, M., Higgins, L., Hayashi, C.Y., Agnarsson, I., Voight, B.F., 2017. The Nephila clavipes genome highlights the diversity of spider silk genes and their complex expression. Nat. Genet. 49, 895–903. https://doi.org/10.1038/ng.3852.

Bernardes, B.G., Veiga, A., Barros, J., García-González, C.A., Oliveira, A.L., 2024. Sustainable silk-based particulate systems for the controlled release of pharmaceuticals and bioactive agents in wound healing and skin regeneration. Int. J. Mol. Sci. 25 (6). https://doi.org/10.3390/ijms25063133. http://www.mdpi.com/journal/ijms.

Blamires, S.J., Rawal, A., Edwards, A.D., Yarger, J.L., Oberst, S., Allardyce, B.J., Rajkhowa, R., 2023. Methods for silk property analyses across structural hierarchies and scales. Molecules 28 (5). https://doi.org/10.3390/molecules28052120. http://www.mdpi.com/journal/molecules.

Cao, T.T., Zhang, Y.Q., 2016. Processing and characterization of silk sericin from Bombyx mori and its application in biomaterials and biomedicines. Mater. Sci. Eng. C 61, 940–952. https://doi.org/10.1016/j.msec.2015.12.082.

Cao, Y., Liu, F., Chen, Y., Yu, T., Lou, D., Guo, Y., Li, P., Wang, Z., Ran, H., 2017. Drug release from core-shell PVA/silk fibroin nanoparticles fabricated by one-step electrospraying. Sci. Rep. 7 (1). https://doi.org/10.1038/s41598-017-12351-1. www.nature.com/srep/index.html.

Cardoso, A.M.L., Oliveira, E.E., Machado, B.A.S., Marcelino, H.R., 2023. Eudragit®-based nanoparticles for controlled release through topical use. J. Nanoparticle Res. 25 (2). https://doi.org/10.1007/s11051-023-05678-6. https://www.springer.com/journal/11051.

Catalanotto, C., Cogoni, C., Zardo, G., 2016. MicroRNA in control of gene expression: An overview of nuclear functions. Int. J. Mol. Sci. 17 (10), 1712. https://doi.org/10.3390/ijms17101712.

Cestari, M., Caldas, B.S., Fonseca, D.P., Balbinot, R.B., Lazarin-Bidóia, D., Otsuka, I., Nakamura, C.V., Borsali, R., Muniz, E.C., 2022. Silk fibroin nanofibers containing chondroitin sulfate and silver sulfadiazine for wound healing treatment. J. Drug Deliv. Sci. Technol. 70, 17732247. https://doi.org/10.1016/j.jddst.2022.103221.

Chomchalao, P., Saelim, N., Lamlertthon, S., Sisopa, P., Tiyaboonchai, W., 2024. A potential thermosensitive poloxamer 407-based in situ hydrogel containing moxifloxacin-loaded silk fibroin nanoparticles for prolonged ocular delivery. J. Drug Deliv. Sci. Technol. 99, 105988. https://doi.org/10.1016/j.jddst.2024.105988.

Chung, T.-W., Wu, T.-Y., Siah, Z.-Y., Liu, D.-Z., 2022. Antioxidative NAC-loaded silk nanoparticles with opening mucosal tight junctions for nasal drug delivery: an in vitro and in vivo study. Pharmaceutics 14, 1288. https://doi.org/10.3390/pharmaceutics14061288.

Cresce, A.von W., Dandu, R., Burger, A., Cappello, J., Ghandehari, H., 2008. Characterization and real-time imaging of gene expression of adenovirus embedded silk-elastinlike protein polymer hydrogels. Mol. Pharm. 5 (5), 891–897. https://doi.org/10.1021/mp800054w.

Crivelli, B., Perteghella, S., Bari, E., Sorrenti, M., Tripodo, G., Chlapanidas, T., Torre, M.L., 2018. Silk nanoparticles: From inert supports to bioactive natural carriers for drug delivery. Soft Matter 14 (4), 546–557. https://doi.org/10.1039/c7sm01631j.

Cubayachi, C., Lemos, C.N., Pereira, F., Dias, K., Herculano, R.D., de Freitas, O., Lopez, R.F.V., 2019. Silk fibroin films stabilizes and releases bioactive insulin for the treatment of corneal wounds. Eur. Polym. J. 118, 502–513. https://doi.org/10.1016/j.eurpolymj.2019.06.022.

Danaei, M., Dehghankhold, M., Ataei, S., Hasanzadeh Davarani, F., Javanmard, R., Dokhani, A., Khorasani, S., Mozafari, M.R., 2018. Impact of particle size and polydispersity index on the clinical applications of lipidic nanocarrier systems. Pharmaceutics 10 (2), 57. https://doi.org/10.3390/pharmaceutics10020057.

Dandu, R., Ghandehari, H., Cappello, J., 2008. Characterization of structurally related adenovirus-laden silk-elastinlike hydrogels. J. Bioact. Compat Polym. 23 (1), 5–19. https://doi.org/10.1177/0883911507085278.

Darshan, G.H., Kong, D., Gautrot, J., Vootla, S., 2017. Physico-chemical characterization of Antheraea mylitta silk mats for wound healing applications. Sci. Rep. 7 (1). https://doi.org/10.1038/s41598-017-10531-7.

Das, G., Shin, H.S., Campos, E.V.R., Fraceto, L.F., del Pilar Rodriguez-Torres, M., Mariano, K.C.F., de Araujo, D.R., Fernández-Luqueño, F., Grillo, R., Patra, J.K., 2021. Sericin based nanoformulations: a comprehensive review on molecular mechanisms of interaction with organisms to biological applications. J. Nanobiotechnol. 19 (1). https://doi.org/10.1186/s12951-021-00774-y.

Demuth, P.C., Min, Y., Irvine, D.J., Hammond, P.T., 2014. Implantable silk composite microneedles for programmable vaccine release kinetics and enhanced immunogenicity in transcutaneous immunization. Adv. Healthcare Mater. 3 (1), 47–58. https://doi.org/10.1002/adhm.201300139. http://onlinelibrary.wiley.com/journal/10.1002/(ISSN)2192-2659.

Dong, Y., Dong, P., Huang, D., Mei, L., Xia, Y., Wang, Z., Pan, X., Li, G., Wu, C., 2015. Fabrication and characterization of silk fibroin-coated liposomes for ocular drug delivery. Eur. J. Pharm. Biopharm. 91, 82–90. https://doi.org/10.1016/j.ejpb.2015.01.018.

Drnovšek, N., Kocen, R., Gantar, A., Drobnič-Košorok, M., Leonardi, A., Križaj, I., Rečnik, A., Novak, S., 2016. Size of silk fibroin β-sheet domains affected by Ca 2+. J. Mater. Chem. B 4 (40), 6597–6608. https://doi.org/10.1039/C6TB01101B.

Du, Y., Shi, J., Duan, R., Tsim, K.W.K., Shen, L., Zhang, N., Wang, B., 2022. cRGD peptide incorporated with patchouli alcohol loaded silk fibroin nanoparticles for enhanced targeting of inflammatory sites in colitis. Biomater. Adv. 140. https://doi.org/10.1016/j.bioadv.2022.213069. https://www.sciencedirect.com/journal/biomaterials-advances/about/aims-and-scope.

Dyakonov, T., Yang, C.H., Bush, D., Gosangari, S., Majuru, S., Fatmi, A., 2012. Design and characterization of a silk-fibroin-based drug delivery platform using naproxen as a model drug. J. Drug Deliv. 2012, 1–10. https://doi.org/10.1155/2012/490514.

Eivazzadeh-Keihan, R., Sadat, Z., Aghamirza Moghim Aliabadi, H., Ganjali, F., Kashtiaray, A., Salimi Bani, M., Komijani, S., Ahadian, M.M., Salehpour, N., Ahangari Cohan, R., Maleki, A., 2022. Fabrication of a magnetic alginate-silk fibroin hydrogel, containing halloysite nanotubes as a novel nanocomposite for biological and hyperthermia applications. Sci. Rep. 12 (1). https://doi.org/10.1038/s41598-022-19511-y. www.nature.com/srep/index.html.

Fang, Y., Liu, Z., Jin, Y., Huang, Y., Zhou, S., Tian, H., Wu, H., 2024. Electrospun high hydrophilicity antimicrobial poly (lactic acid)/silk fibroin nanofiber membrane for wound dressings. Int. J. Biol. Macromol. 277, 133905. https://doi.org/10.1016/j.ijbiomac.2024.133905, 01418130.

Gangrade, A., Mandal, B.B., 2019. Injectable carbon nanotube impregnated silk based multifunctional hydrogel for localized targeted and on-demand anticancer drug delivery. ACS Biomater. Sci. Eng. 5 (5), 2365–2381. https://doi.org/10.1021/acsbiomaterials.9b00416.

Gavrilova, N.A., Borzenok, S.A., Revishchin, A.V., Tishchenko, O.E., Ostrovkiy, D.S., Bobrova, M.M., Safonova, L. A., Efimov, A.E., Agapova, O.I., Agammedov, M.B., Pavlova, G.V., Agapov, I.I., 2021. The effect of biodegradable silk fibroin-based scaffolds containing glial cell line-derived neurotrophic factor (GDNF) on the corneal regeneration process. Int. J. Biol. Macromol. 185, 264–276. https://doi.org/10.1016/j.ijbiomac.2021.06.040, 01418130.

Gianak, O., Pavlidou, E., Sarafidis, C., Karageorgiou, V., Deliyanni, E., 2018. Silk fibroin nanoparticles for drug delivery: effect of bovine serum albumin and magnetic nanoparticles addition on drug encapsulation and release. Separations. 5 (2). https://doi.org/10.3390/separations5020025. https://www.mdpi.com/2297-8739/5/2/25/pdf.

Gonzalez-Obeso, C., Jane Hartzell, E., Scheel, R.A., Kaplan, D.L., 2023. Delivering on the promise of recombinant silk-inspired proteins for drug delivery. Adv. Drug Deliv. Rev. 192, 114622. https://doi.org/10.1016/j.addr.2022.114622.

Gou, S., Huang, Y., Wan, Y., Ma, Y., Zhou, X., Tong, X., Huang, J., Kang, Y., Pan, G., Dai, F., Xiao, B., 2019. Multi-bioresponsive silk fibroin-based nanoparticles with on-demand cytoplasmic drug release capacity for CD44-targeted alleviation of ulcerative colitis. Biomaterials 212, 39–54. https://doi.org/10.1016/j.biomaterials.2019.05.012.

Griswold, E., Cappello, J., Ghandehari, H., 2022. Silk-elastinlike protein-based hydrogels for drug delivery and embolization. Adv. Drug Deliv. Rev. 191, 114579. https://doi.org/10.1016/j.addr.2022.114579.

Gu, H., Wang, F., Liu, H., Printon, K., Hu, X., 2022. Multifunctional silk fibroin – poly(L-lactic acid) porous nanofibers: Designing adjustable nanopores to control composite properties and biological responses. Mater. Des. 222, 111053. https://doi.org/10.1016/j.matdes.2022.111053.

Gupta, B., Mishra, V., Gharat, S., Momin, M., Omri, A., 2021. Cellulosic polymers for enhancing drug bioavailability in ocular drug delivery systems. Pharmaceuticals 14 (11), 1201. https://doi.org/10.3390/ph14111201.

Harishchandra Yadav, R., Kenchegowda, M., Angolkar, M., Meghana, T.S., Osmani, R.A.M., Palaksha, S., Veerabhadrappa Gangadharappa, H., 2024. A review of silk fibroin-based drug delivery systems and their applications. Eur. Poly. J. 216, 113286. https://doi.org/10.1016/j.eurpolymj.2024.113286.

Heydari Foroushani, P., Rahmani, E., Alemzadeh, I., Vossoughi, M., Pourmadadi, M., Rahdar, A., Díez-Pascual, A. M., 2022. Curcumin sustained release with a hybrid chitosan-silk fibroin nanofiber containing silver nanoparticles as a novel highly efficient antibacterial wound dressing. Nanomaterials 12 (19). https://doi.org/10.3390/nano12193426. http://www.mdpi.com/journal/nanomaterials.

Hwang, D., Moolchandani, V., Dandu, R., Haider, M., Cappello, J., Ghandehari, H., 2009. Influence of polymer structure and biodegradation on DNA release from silk-elastinlike protein polymer hydrogels. Int. J. Pharm. 368 (1–2), 215–219. https://doi.org/10.1016/j.ijpharm.2008.10.021.

Jaramillo-Quiceno, N., Álvarez-López, C., Restrepo-Osorio, A., 2017. Structural and thermal properties of silk fibroin films obtained from cocoon and waste silk fibers as raw materials. Procedia Eng. 200, 384–388. https://doi.org/10.1016/j.proeng.2017.07.054.

Jewell, C.M., Bustamante López, S.C., Irvine, D.J., 2011. In situ engineering of the lymph node microenvironment via intranodal injection of adjuvant-releasing polymer particles. Proc. Nat. Acad. Sci. 108 (38), 15745–15750. https://doi.org/10.1073/pnas.1105200108.

Johnston, E.R., Miyagi, Y., Chuah, J.A., Numata, K., Serban, M.A., 2018. Interplay between silk fibroin's structure and its adhesive properties. ACS Biomater. Sci. Eng. 4 (8), 2815–2824. https://doi.org/10.1021/acsbiomaterials.8b00544.

Kandhasamy, S., Zeng, Y., 2022. Fabrication of vitamin K3-carnosine peptide-loaded spun silk fibroin fibers/collagen bi-layered architecture for bronchopleural fistula tissue repair and regeneration applications. Biomater. Adv. 137, 212817. https://doi.org/10.1016/j.bioadv.2022.212817.

Kanwar, J., Patel, Y., Roy, K., Kanwar, R., Rajkhowa, R., Wang, X., 2015. Biodegradable Eri silk nanoparticles as a delivery vehicle for bovine lactoferrin against MDA-MB-231 and MCF-7 breast cancer cells. Int. J. Nanomed. 11, 25. https://doi.org/10.2147/ijn.s91810.

Karageorgiou, V., Meinel, L., Hofmann, S., Malhotra, A., Volloch, V., Kaplan, D., 2004. Bone morphogenetic protein-2 decorated silk fibroin films induce osteogenic differentiation of human bone marrow stromal cells. J. Biomed. Mater. Res. - Part A 71 (3), 528–537. https://doi.org/10.1002/jbm.a.30186.

Koh, L.-D., Cheng, Y., Teng, C.-P., Khin, Y.-W., Loh, X.-J., Tee, S.-Y., Low, M., Ye, E., Yu, H.-D., Zhang, Y.-W., Han, M.-Y., 2015. Structures, mechanical properties and applications of silk fibroin materials. Prog. Polym. Sci. 46, 86–110. https://doi.org/10.1016/j.progpolymsci.2015.02.001.

Kumar Dan, A., Aamna, B., De, S., Pereira-Silva, M., Sahu, R., Paiva-Santos, A.C., Parida, S., 2022. Sericin nanoparticles: Future nanocarrier for target-specific delivery of chemotherapeutic drugs. J. Mol. Liq. 368, 120717. https://doi.org/10.1016/j.molliq.2022.120717.

Kundu, J., Chung, Y.I., Kim, Y.H., Tae, G., Kundu, S.C., 2010. Silk fibroin nanoparticles for cellular uptake and control release. Int. J. Pharm. 388 (1–2), 242–250. https://doi.org/10.1016/j.ijpharm.2009.12.052, 03785173.

Kundu, B., Rajkhowa, R., Kundu, S.C., Wang, X., 2013. Silk fibroin biomaterials for tissue regenerations. Adv. Drug Deliv. Rev. 65 (4), 457–470. https://doi.org/10.1016/j.addr.2012.09.043.

Kunz, R.I., Brancalhão, R.M.C., Ribeiro, L.D.F.C., Natali, M.R.M., 2016. Silkworm sericin: Properties and biomedical applications. BioMed Res. Int. 2016, 23146141. https://doi.org/10.1155/2016/8175701. http://www.hindawi.com/journals/biomed/.

Lammel, A.S., Hu, X., Park, S.H., Kaplan, D.L., Scheibel, T.R., 2010. Controlling silk fibroin particle features for drug delivery. Biomaterials 31 (16), 4583–4591. https://doi.org/10.1016/j.biomaterials.2010.02.024.

Li, L., Puhl, S., Meinel, L., Germershaus, O., 2014. Silk fibroin layer-by-layer microcapsules for localized gene delivery. Biomaterials 35 (27), 7929–7939. https://doi.org/10.1016/j.biomaterials.2014.05.062.

Li, Z., Meng, Z., Zhao, Z., 2022. Silk fibroin nanofibrous scaffolds incorporated with microRNA-222 loaded chitosan nanoparticles for enhanced neuronal differentiation of neural stem cells. Carbohydr. Polym. 277, 118791. https://doi.org/10.1016/j.carbpol.2021.118791.

Li, M., You, J., Qin, Q., Liu, M., Yang, Y., Jia, K., Zhang, Y., Zhou, Y., 2023. A comprehensive review on silk fibroin as a persuasive biomaterial for bone tissue engineering. Int. J. Mol. Sci. 24 (3), 2660. https://doi.org/10.3390/ijms24032660.

Li, Q., Gong, H., Jia, X., Wang, R., Liu, Z., Zhang, L., Li, J., Jiao, T., 2024. Electrospinning silk-fibroin-based fibrous membranes with AgNPs for antimicrobial application. Polymers 16 (5), 648. https://doi.org/10.3390/polym16050648.

Liu, Y., You, R., Liu, G., Li, X., Sheng, W., Yang, J., Li, M., 2014. Antheraea pernyi silk fibroin-coated PEI/DNA complexes for targeted gene delivery in HEK 293 and HCT 116 cells. Int. J. Mol. Sci. 15 (5), 7049–7063. https://doi.org/10.3390/ijms15057049.

Lovett, M.L., Wang, X., Yucel, T., York, L., Keirstead, M., Haggerty, L., Kaplan, D.L., 2015. Silk hydrogels for sustained ocular delivery of anti-vascular endothelial growth factor (anti-VEGF) therapeutics. Eur. J. Pharm. Biopharm. 95, 271–278. https://doi.org/10.1016/j.ejpb.2014.12.029.

Lu, Q., Wang, X., Zhu, H., Kaplan, D.L., 2011. Surface immobilization of antibody on silk fibroin through conformational transition. Acta Biomater. 7 (7), 2782–2786. https://doi.org/10.1016/j.actbio.2011.03.001.

Lucke, M., Mottas, I., Herbst, T., Hotz, C., Römer, L., Schierling, M., Herold, H.M., Slotta, U., Spinetti, T., Scheibel, T., Winter, G., Bourquin, C., Engert, J., 2018. Engineered hybrid spider silk particles as delivery system for peptide vaccines. Biomaterials 172, 105–115. https://doi.org/10.1016/j.biomaterials.2018.04.008.

Luo, Z., Li, J., Qu, J., Sheng, W., Yang, J., Li, M., 2019. Cationized Bombyx mori silk fibroin as a delivery carrier of the VEGF165–Ang-1 coexpression plasmid for dermal tissue regeneration. J. Mater. Chem. B 7, 80–94. https://doi.org/10.1039/C8TB01424H.

Mazurek, Ł., Szudzik, M., Rybka, M., Konop, M., 2022. Silk fibroin biomaterials and their beneficial role in skin wound healing. Biomolecules 12, 1852. https://doi.org/10.3390/biom12121852.

Ma, Y., Canup, B.S.B., Tong, X., Dai, F., Xiao, B., 2020. Multi-responsive silk fibroin-based nanoparticles for drug delivery. Front. Chem. 8. https://doi.org/10.3389/fchem.2020.585077.

Megeed, Z., Cappello, J., Ghandehari, H., 2002. Controlled release of plasmid DNA from a genetically engineered silk-elastinlike hydrogel. Pharm. Res. 19 (7), 954–959. https://doi.org/10.1023/A:1016406120288.

Megeed, Z., Haider, M., Li, D., O'Malley, B.W., Cappello, J., Ghandehari, H., 2004. In vitro and in vivo evaluation of recombinant silk-elastinlike hydrogels for cancer gene therapy. J. Contr. Release 94 (2–3), 433–445. www.elsevier.com/locate/jconrel. doi: 10.1016/j.jconrel.2003.10.027.

Mohanan, D., Slütter, B., Henriksen-Lacey, M., Jiskoot, W., Bouwstra, J.A., Perrie, Y., Kündig, T.M., Gander, B., Johansen, P., 2010. Administration routes affect the quality of immune responses: A cross-sectional evaluation of particulate antigen-delivery systems. J. Contr. Release 147 (3), 342–349. https://doi.org/10.1016/j.jconrel.2010.08.012.

Moreno-Tortolero, R.O., Luo, Y., Parmeggiani, F., Skaer, N., Walker, R., Serpell, L.C., Holland, C., Davis, S.A., 2024. Molecular organization of fibroin heavy chain and mechanism of fibre formation in Bombyx mori. Commun. Biol. 7 (1). https://doi.org/10.1038/s42003-024-06474-1. https://www.springer.com/journal/42003.

Nasrine, A., Gulzar Ahmed, M., Narayana, S., 2022. Silk fibroin-anastrozole loaded prolonged-release biodegradable nanomedicine: A promising drug delivery system for breast cancer therapy. Mater. Today Proc. 68, 56–65. https://doi.org/10.1016/j.matpr.2022.06.101.

Navamajiti, N., Gardner, A., Cao, R., Sugimoto, Y., Yang, J.W., Lopes, A., Phan, N.V., Collins, J., Hua, T., Damrongsakkul, S., Kanokpanont, S., Steiger, C., Reker, D., Langer, R., Traverso, G., 2024. Silk fibroin-based coatings for pancreatin-dependent drug delivery. J. Pharmaceut. Sci. 113 (3), 718–724. https://doi.org/10.1016/j.xphs.2023.09.001.

Niu, B., Li, B., Gu, Y., Shen, X., Liu, Y., Chen, L., 2017. In vitro evaluation of electrospun silk fibroin/nano-hydroxyapatite/BMP-2 scaffolds for bone regeneration. J. Biomater. Sci. Polym. Ed. 28 (3), 257–270. https://doi.org/10.1080/09205063.2016.1262163.

Norouzi, P., Motasadizadeh, H., Atyabi, F., Dinarvand, R., Gholami, M., Farokhi, M., Shokrgozar, M.A., Mottaghitalab, F., 2021. Combination therapy of breast cancer by codelivery of doxorubicin and survivin siRNA using polyethylenimine modified silk fibroin nanoparticles. ACS Biomater. Sci. Eng. 7 (3), 1074–1087. https://doi.org/10.1021/acsbiomaterials.0c01511.

Numata, K., Kaplan, D.L., 2010. Silk-based gene carriers with cell membrane destabilizing peptides. Biomacromolecules 11 (11), 3189–3195. https://doi.org/10.1021/bm101055m.

Numata, K., Subramanian, B., Currie, H.A., Kaplan, D.L., 2009. Bioengineered silk protein-based gene delivery systems. Biomaterials 30 (29), 5775–5784. https://doi.org/10.1016/j.biomaterials.2009.06.028.

N'Da, D., 2014. Prodrug strategies for enhancing the percutaneous absorption of drugs. Molecules 19, 20780–20807. https://doi.org/10.3390/molecules191220780.

Pan, Z., Hou, M., Zhang, Y., Liu, Y., Tian, X., Hu, X., Ge, X., Zhao, Z., Liu, T., Xu, Y., Yang, H., Liu, H., Zhu, X., He, F., 2023. Incorporation of kartogenin and silk fibroin scaffolds promotes rat articular cartilage regeneration through enhancement of antioxidant functions. Regen. Biomater. 10, 20563426. https://doi.org/10.1093/rb/rbad074. https://academic.oup.com/rb.

Pandey, V., Haider, T., Chandak, A.R., Chakraborty, A., Banerjee, S., Soni, V., 2020. Surface modified silk fibroin nanoparticles for improved delivery of doxorubicin: development, characterization, in-vitro studies. Int. J. Biol. Macromol. 164, 2018–2027. https://doi.org/10.1016/j.ijbiomac.2020.07.326.

Passi, M., Kumar, V., Packirisamy, G., 2020. Theranostic nanozyme: Silk fibroin based multifunctional nanocomposites to combat oxidative stress. Mater. Sci. Eng. C 107, 110255. https://doi.org/10.1016/j.msec.2019.110255.

Patwa, R., Soundararajan, N., Mulchandani, N., Bhasney, S.M., Shah, M., Kumar, S., Kumar, A., Katiyar, V., 2018. Silk nano-discs: A natural material for cancer therapy. Biopolymers 109 (11), 10970282. https://doi.org/10.1002/bip.23231. http://onlinelibrary.wiley.com/journal/10.1002/(ISSN)1097-0282.

Pham, D.T., Tiyaboonchai, W., 2020. Fibroin nanoparticles: a promising drug delivery system. .Drug Deliv. 27 (1), 431–448. https://doi.org/10.1080/10717544.2020.1736208.

Pham, D.T., Nguyen, D.X.T., Nguyen, N.Y., Nguyen, T.T.L., Nguyen, T.Q.C., Tu, A.V.T., Nguyen, N.H., Thuy, B.T.P., 2024. Development of pH-responsive Eudragit S100-functionalized silk fibroin nanoparticles as a prospective drug delivery system. PLoS One 19 (5), 19326203. https://doi.org/10.1371/journal.pone.0303177. https://journals.plos.org//plosone/article?id=10.1371/journal.pone.0303177.

Polat, H.K., Aytekin, E., Karakuyu, N.F., Çaylı, Y.A., Çalamak, S., Demirci, N., Ünal, S., Kurt, N., Çırak, R., Erkan, E., Mokhtare, B., Mendil, A.S., Bozdağ Pehlivan, S., 2024. Harnessing silk fibroin microparticles for metformin delivery: A novel approach to treating corneal neovascularization. J. Drug Deliv. Sci. Technol. 96, 17732247. https://doi.org/10.1016/j.jddst.2024.105625.

Puertas-Bartolomé, M., Mora-Boza, A., García-Fernández, L., 2021. Emerging biofabrication techniques: a review on natural polymers for biomedical applications. Polymers 13, 1209. https://doi.org/10.3390/polym13081209.

Qi, Y., Wang, H., Wei, K., Yang, Y., Zheng, R.Y., Kim, I.S., Zhang, K.Q., 2017. A review of structure construction of silk fibroin biomaterials from single structures to multi-level structures. Int. J. Mol. Sci. 18 (3), 14220067. https://doi.org/10.3390/ijms18030237.

Qu, J., Liu, Y., Yu, Y., Li, J., Luo, J., Li, M., 2014. Silk fibroin nanoparticles prepared by electrospray as controlled release carriers of cisplatin. Mater. Sci. Eng. C 44, 166–174. https://doi.org/10.1016/j.msec.2014.08.034.

Radulescu, D.M., Andronescu, E., Vasile, O.R., Ficai, A., Vasile, B.S., 2024. Silk fibroin-based scaffolds for wound healing applications with metal oxide nanoparticles. J. Drug Deliv. Sci. Technol. 96, 17732247. https://doi.org/10.1016/j.jddst.2024.105689.

Rai, G., Yadav, A.K., Jain, N.K., Agrawal, G.P., 2016. Eudragit-coated dextran microspheres of 5-fluorouracil for site-specific delivery to colon. Drug Deliv. 23 (1), 328–337. https://doi.org/10.3109/10717544.2014.913733.

Rathnakara, S.H., Raju, S.R., Kumar, R., Hegde, G., 2022. Silk fibroin nanofiber scaffold (SFNS) as a graft material for myringoplasty- in vitro and in vivo. Materialia 26, 25891529. https://doi.org/10.1016/j.mtla.2022.101562.

Rockwood, D.N., Preda, R.C., Yücel, T., Wang, X., Lovett, M.L., Kaplan, D.L., 2011. Materials fabrication from Bombyx mori silk fibroin. Nat. Protoc. 6 (10), 1612–1631. https://doi.org/10.1038/nprot.2011.379.

Shahbazi, S., Habibi, M., Badmasti, F., Sabzi, S., Farokhi, M., Karam, M.R.A., 2023. Design and fabrication of a vaccine candidate based on rOmpA from Klebsiella pneumoniae encapsulated in silk fibroin-sodium alginate nanoparticles against pneumonia infection. Int. Immunopharmacol. 125, 111171. https://doi.org/10.1016/j.intimp.2023.111171.

Sheikh, F.A., Ju, H.W., Lee, J.M., Moon, B.M., Park, H.J., Lee, O.J., Kim, J.H., Kim, D.K., Park, C.H., 2015. 3D electrospun silk fibroin nanofibers for fabrication of artificial skin. Nanomed. Nanotechnol. Biol. Med. 11 (3), 681–691. https://doi.org/10.1016/j.nano.2014.11.007.

Siafaka, P.I., Üstündağ Okur, N., Karavas, E., Bikiaris, D.N., 2016a. Surface modified multifunctional and stimuli responsive nanoparticles for drug targeting: Current status and uses. Int. J. Mol. Sci. 17 (9), 14220067. https://doi.org/10.3390/ijms17091440.

Siafaka, P.I., Barmbalexis, P., Bikiaris, D.N., 2016b. Novel electrospun nanofibrous matrices prepared from poly(lactic acid)/poly(butylene adipate) blends for controlled release formulations of an anti-rheumatoid agent. Eur. J. Pharmaceut. Sci. 88, 12–25. https://doi.org/10.1016/j.ejps.2016.03.021.

Song, W., Gregory, D.A., Al-janabi, H., Muthana, M., Cai, Z., Zhao, X., 2019. Magnetic-silk/polyethyleneimine core-shell nanoparticles for targeted gene delivery into human breast cancer cells. Int. J. Pharm. 555, 322–336. www.elsevier.com/locate/ijpharm. doi: 10.1016/j.ijpharm.2018.11.030.

Souto, E.B., Fangueiro, J.F., Fernandes, A.R., Cano, A., Sanchez-Lopez, E., Garcia, M.L., Severino, P., Paganelli, M. O., Chaud, M.V., Silva, A.M., 2022. Physicochemical and biopharmaceutical aspects influencing skin permeation and role of SLN and NLC for skin drug delivery. Heliyon 8 (2). https://doi.org/10.1016/j.heliyon.2022.e08938. http://www.journals.elsevier.com/heliyon/.

Subia, B., Kundu, S.C., 2013. Drug loading and release on tumor cells using silk fibroin–albumin nanoparticles as carriers. Nanotechnology 24 (3), 035103. https://doi.org/10.1088/0957-4484/24/3/035103.

Sun, Z.L., Li, H., Tian, J., Wu, A., Wang, J., Ge, C., 2016. Self-assembled silk fibroin nanoparticles loaded with binary drugs in the treatment of breast carcinoma. Int. J. Nanomed. 11, 4373–4380. https://doi.org/10.2147/ijn.s108633.

Sun, W., Gregory, D.A., Tomeh, M.A., Zhao, X., 2021. Silk fibroin as a functional biomaterial for tissue engineering. Int. J. Mol. Sci. 22 (3), 1–28. https://doi.org/10.3390/ijms22031499.

Sun, S., Ding, C., Liu, X., Zhao, Y., Zhang, J., Ding, Q., Zhang, Y., Zhang, Y., Mingqian, H., Zheng, Y., Liu, W., Yang, M., 2022. Silk protein/polyvinylpyrrolidone nanofiber membranes loaded with puerarin accelerate wound healing in mice by reducing the inflammatory response. Biomater. Adv. 135, 212734. https://doi.org/10.1016/j.bioadv.2022.212734.

Suryawanshi, R., Kanoujia, J., Parashar, P., Saraf, S.A., 2020. Sericin: a versatile protein biopolymer with therapeutic significance. Curr. Pharm. Des. 26 (42), 5414–5429. https://doi.org/10.2174/1381612826666200612165253.

Takeuchi, I., Shimamura, Y., Kakami, Y., Kameda, T., Hattori, K., Miura, S., Shirai, H., Okumura, M., Inagi, T., Terada, H., Makino, K., 2019. Transdermal delivery of 40-nm silk fibroin nanoparticles. Colloids Surf. B Biointerfaces 175, 564–568. https://doi.org/10.1016/j.colsurfb.2018.12.012.

Tallian, C., Herrero-Rollett, A., Stadler, K., Vielnascher, R., Wieland, K., Weihs, A.M., Pellis, A., Teuschl, A.H., Lendl, B., Amenitsch, H., Guebitz, G.M., 2018b. Structural insights into pH-responsive drug release of self-assembling human serum albumin-silk fibroin nanocapsules. Eur. J. Pharm. Biopharm. 133, 176–187. https://doi.org/10.1016/j.ejpb.2018.10.002.

Tang, Y., Zhang, L., Sun, R., Luo, B., Zhou, Y., Zhang, Y., Liang, Y., Xiao, B., Wang, C., 2023. Pulmonary delivery of mucus-traversing PF127-modified silk fibroin nanoparticles loading with quercetin for lung cancer therapy. Asian J. Pharm. Sci. 18 (4), 100833. https://doi.org/10.1016/j.ajps.2023.100833.

ter Horst, B., Moiemen, N.S., Grover, L.M., 2019. Natural Polymers Biomaterials for Skin Repair and Regeneration. Elsevier, United Kingdom, pp. 151–192. https://doi.org/10.1016/B978-0-08-102546-8.00006-6. http://www.sciencedirect.com/science/book/9780081025468.

Thi Phuong Thao, N., Nguyen, N.Y., Ben Co, V., Thanh, L.H.V., Nguyen, M.Q., Pan-On, S., Pham, D.T., 2024. Formulations of poly(vinyl alcohol) functionalized silk fibroin nanoparticles for the oral delivery of zwitterionic ciprofloxacin. PLoS One 19, e0306140. https://doi.org/10.1371/journal.pone.0306140.

Tomeh, M.A., Hadianamrei, R., Zhao, X., 2019. Silk fibroin as a functional biomaterial for drug and gene delivery. Pharmaceutics 11, 494. https://doi.org/10.3390/pharmaceutics11100494.

Uebersax, L., Mattotti, M., Papaloizos, M., Merkle, H., Gander, B., Meinel, L., 2007. Silk fibroin matrices for the controlled release of nerve growth factor (NGF). Biomaterials 28 (30), 4449–4460. https://doi.org/10.1016/j.biomaterials.2007.06.034.

Uebersax, L., Merkle, H.P., Meinel, L., 2008. Insulin-like growth factor I releasing silk fibroin scaffolds induce chondrogenic differentiation of human mesenchymal stem cells. J. Contr. Release 127 (1), 12–21. https://doi.org/10.1016/j.jconrel.2007.11.006, 01683659.

Upadhayay, P., Kumar, M., Pathak, K., 2016. Norfloxacin loaded pH triggered nanoparticulate in-situ gel for extraocular bacterial infections: optimization, ocular irritancy and corneal toxicity. Iran. J. Pharm. Res. IJPR. 15, 3–22.

Vaidya, A.M., Sun, Z., Ayat, N., Schilb, A., Liu, X., Jiang, H., Sun, D., Scheidt, J., Qian, V., He, S., Gilmore, H., Schiemann, W.P., Lu, Z.R., 2019. Systemic delivery of tumor-targeting siRNA nanoparticles against an oncogenic LncRNA facilitates effective triple-negative breast cancer therapy. Bioconjug. Chem. 30 (3), 907–919. https://doi.org/10.1021/acs.bioconjchem.9b00028.

Verdine, G.L., Walensky, L.D., 2007. The challenge of drugging undruggable targets in cancer: lessons learned from targeting BCL-2 family members. Clin. Cancer Res. 13 (24), 7264–7270. https://doi.org/10.1158/1078-0432.CCR-07-2184.

Wang, X., Wenk, E., Matsumoto, A., Meinel, L., Li, C., Kaplan, D.L., 2007. Silk microspheres for encapsulation and controlled release. J. Control. Release 117 (3), 360–370. https://doi.org/10.1016/j.jconrel.2006.11.021.

Wang, B., Lv, X., Chen, S., Li, Z., Yao, J., Peng, X., Feng, C., Xu, Y., Wang, H., 2017. Bacterial cellulose/gelatin scaffold loaded with VEGF-silk fibroin nanoparticles for improving angiogenesis in tissue regeneration. Cellulose 24 (11), 5013–5024. https://doi.org/10.1007/s10570-017-1472-x.

Wang, F., Wu, H., Venkataraman, V., Hu, X., 2019. Silk fibroin-poly(lactic acid) biocomposites: effect of protein-synthetic polymer interactions and miscibility on material properties and biological responses. Mater. Sci. Eng. C 104, 109890. https://doi.org/10.1016/j.msec.2019.109890.

Wang, Z., Song, X., Cui, Y., Cheng, K., Tian, X., Dong, M., Liu, L., 2021. Silk fibroin H-fibroin/poly(ε-caprolactone) core-shell nanofibers with enhanced mechanical property and long-term drug release. J. Colloid Interface Sci. 593, 142–151. https://doi.org/10.1016/j.jcis.2021.02.099.

Wei, G., Li, C., Fu, Q., Xu, Y., Li, H., 2015. Preparation of PCL/silk fibroin/collagen electrospun fiber for urethral reconstruction. Int. Urol. Nephrol. 47 (1), 95–99. https://doi.org/10.1007/s11255-014-0854-3.

Weisman, S., Haritos, V.S., Church, J.S., Huson, M.G., Mudie, S.T., Rodgers, A.J.W., Dumsday, G.J., Sutherland, T. D., 2010. Honeybee silk: Recombinant protein production, assembly and fiber spinning. Biomaterials 31 (9), 2695–2700. https://doi.org/10.1016/j.biomaterials.2009.12.021.

Wen, M.M., El-Salamouni, N.S., El-Refaie, W.M., Hazzah, H.A., Ali, M.M., Tosi, G., Farid, R.M., Blanco-Prieto, M.J., Billa, N., Hanafy, A.S., 2017. Nanotechnology-based drug delivery systems for Alzheimer's disease management: Technical, industrial, and clinical challenges. J. Control. Release. 245, 95–107. https://doi.org/10.1016/j.jconrel.2016.11.025.

Wen, Q., Zhang, L., Chen, Y., Su, Y., Yu, J., Chen, P., Zheng, T., 2023. Novel applications of silk proteins based on their interactions with metal ions. Sustainability 15 (22), 16053. https://doi.org/10.3390/su152216053.

Wenk, E., Murphy, A.R., Kaplan, D.L., Meinel, L., Merkle, H.P., Uebersax, L., 2010. The use of sulfonated silk fibroin derivatives to control binding, delivery and potency of FGF-2 in tissue regeneration. Biomaterials 31 (6), 1403–1413. https://doi.org/10.1016/j.biomaterials.2009.11.006.

Wenk, E., Merkle, H.P., Meinel, L., 2011. Silk fibroin as a vehicle for drug delivery applications. J. Contr. Release 150 (2), 128–141. https://doi.org/10.1016/j.jconrel.2010.11.007.

Wu, M., Yang, W., Chen, S., Yao, J., Shao, Z., Chen, X., 2018. Size-controllable dual drug-loaded silk fibroin nanospheres through a facile formation process. J. Mater. Chem. B 6 (8), 1179–1186. https://doi.org/10.1039/C7TB03113K.

Wu, J., Sahoo, J.K., Li, Y., Xu, Q., Kaplan, D.L., 2022. Challenges in delivering therapeutic peptides and proteins: A silk-based solution. J. Contr. Release 345, 176–189. www.elsevier.com/locate/jconrel. doi: 10.1016/j.jconrel.2022.02.011.

Xie, D., Zhou, X., Xiao, B., Duan, L., Zhu, Z., 2022. Mucus-penetrating silk fibroin-based nanotherapeutics for efficient treatment of ulcerative colitis. Biomolecules 12 (9), 1263. https://doi.org/10.3390/biom12091263.

Xu, H.L., ZhuGe, D.L., Chen, P.P., Tong, M.Q., Lin, M.T., Jiang, X., Zheng, Y.W., Chen, B., Li, X.K., Zhao, Y.Z., 2018. Silk fibroin nanoparticles dyeing indocyanine green for imaging-guided photo-thermal therapy of glioblastoma. Drug Deliv. 25 (1), 364–375. https://doi.org/10.1080/10717544.2018.1428244.

Xu, X., Wang, X., Qin, C., Khan, A.u.R., Zhang, W., Mo, X., 2021. Silk fibroin/poly-(L-lactide-co-caprolactone) nanofiber scaffolds loaded with Huangbai Liniment to accelerate diabetic wound healing. Colloids Surf. B Biointerfaces 199. https://doi.org/10.1016/j.colsurfb.2021.111557. www.elsevier.com/locate/colsurfb.

Yang, R., Hou, M., Gao, Y., Lu, S., Zhang, L., Xu, Z., Li, C.M., Kang, Y., Xue, P., 2019. Biomineralization-inspired crystallization of manganese oxide on silk fibroin nanoparticles for in vivo MR/fluorescence imaging-assisted tri-modal therapy of cancer. Theranostics 9 (21), 6314–6333. https://doi.org/10.7150/thno.36252.

Yoo, J.W., Giri, N., Lee, C.H., 2011. PH-sensitive Eudragit nanoparticles for mucosal drug delivery. Int. J. Pharm. 403 (1–2), 262–267. https://doi.org/10.1016/j.ijpharm.2010.10.032.

Yoon, Y.I., Park, K.E., Lee, S.J., Park, W.H., 2013. Fabrication of microfibrous and nano-/microfibrous scaffolds: Melt and hybrid electrospinning and surface modification of poly(L-lactic acid) with plasticizer. BioMed Res. Int. 2013. https://doi.org/10.1155/2013/309048.

Yu, B., Li, Y., Lin, Y., Zhu, Y., Hao, T., Wu, Y., Sun, Z., Yang, X., Xu, H., 2023. Research progress of natural silk fibroin and the application for drug delivery in chemotherapies. Front. Pharmacol. 13. https://doi.org/10.3389/fphar.2022.1071868. http://www.frontiersin.org/Pharmacology.

Zhang, Y.Q., Ma, Y., Xia, Y.Y., Shen, W.D., Mao, J.P., Zha, X.M., Shirai, K., Kiguchi, K., 2006. Synthesis of silk fibroin-insulin bioconjugates and their characterization and activities in vivo. J. Biomed. Mater. Res. - Part B Appl. Biomater. 79 (2), 275–283. https://doi.org/10.1002/jbm.b.30539.

Zhang, Y., Wu, C., Luo, T., Li, S., Cheng, X., Miron, R.J., 2012. Synthesis and inflammatory response of a novel silk fibroin scaffold containing BMP7 adenovirus for bone regeneration. Bone 51 (4), 704–713. https://doi.org/10.1016/j.bone.2012.06.029.

Zhao, Z., Li, Y., Xie, M.B., 2015. Silk fibroin-based nanoparticles for drug delivery . MDPI AG. China Int. J. Mol. Sci. 16 (3), 4880–4903. https://doi.org/10.3390/ijms16034880.

Zhou, Q., J.-fen Jin, L.-ling Zhu, M. Chen, H.-min Xu, H.-fen Wang, X.-qin Feng, X.-ping Zhu, The optimal choice of medication administration route regarding intravenous, intramuscular, and subcutaneous injection. Patient Prefer. Adherence. 1177–889X. 9 (2015), 923, https://doi.org/10.2147/ppa.s87271.

CHAPTER

# 15

# Zein-based nanocarriers for drug delivery

*Mohammad Hossein Karami and Omid Moini Jazani*

**Department of Chemical Engineering, Faculty of Engineering, University of Isfahan, Isfahan, Iran**

## 1. Introduction

There has been an increasing fascination with the possibilities of nanoparticles for drug delivery, which are created through nanobiotechnology (Sung et al., 2021; Zhang et al., 2022; Qi et al., 2019). Researchers develop nanoparticles enhancing drug effects, addressing bioavailability, stability, solubility, reactions, and delivery challenges. Proteins are preferred for making nanoparticles due to their advantages over lipids, carbohydrates, polymers, and carriers (Bhattacharya, 2022; Qiao et al., 2022; Fang et al., 2021). Various benefits, such as being biodegradable, easily accessible, environmentally friendly, and possessing a strong drug-binding capacity, are present. A diverse array of proteins from animals and plants has been widely used to create nanoparticles (Huang et al., 2023; Chauhan et al., 2018). Plant-based proteins, in particular, tend to be more cost-effective and present a lower risk of disease transmission compared to animal proteins. Zein, the storage protein of corn, has intrigued scientists since its discovery in 1821 (Huang et al., 2021). Zein, a mixture of peptides with varying weights, includes α, β, γ, and δ types. It is rich in nonpolar amino acids such as alanine, leucine, proline, and glutamine. The presence of amino acid groups enhances the solubility of zein and increases its nutritional value. Zein has both amphiphilic and hydrophobic characteristics; it doesn't dissolve in water but can dissolve in alcohol, urea, alkaline conditions, or anionic surfactants because of its unique properties. Zein, unlike hydrophilic proteins, traps hydrophobic substances for sustained drug release (Jiang et al., 2015a). Zein has been designated as Generally Recognized as Safe (GRAS) and is capable of

*Protein-Based Nanoparticles in Drug Delivery*
**https://doi.org/10.1016/B978-0-443-33639-3.00021-0**

forming different types of nanoparticles based on the specific conditions. Consequently, zein has been the subject of extensive research regarding its ability to encapsulate and deliver bioactive ingredients. Over the years, numerous studies have investigated zein-based biomaterials for applications in food and nutrition, phytochemical delivery, oral drug administration, tissue engineering, and other biomedical applications (Gaber et al., 2020). Advanced materials like metal nanomaterials, liposomes, micelles, and proteins offer benefits such as improved drug stability, longer circulation time, controlled release, enhanced bioavailability, lower toxicity, and better cellular uptake. Zein, a natural protein, shows potential as a substitute for synthetic materials, particularly in cancer treatment. In summary, zein's distinctive properties and its GRAS status position it as a promising option for cutting-edge drug delivery systems (DDSs), especially in the realm of cancer treatment, where precise and effective drug delivery is crucial (Chen et al., 2023; Dong et al., 2019; Yu et al., 2022).

This paper aims to provide a comprehensive overview of the preparation, characterization, and therapeutic applications of zein nanoparticles (ZNPs). It will explore the challenges and solutions associated with their use as nanocarriers, highlight advancements in smart and responsive DDSs, and discuss hybrid systems. Furthermore, the paper will examine the various applications of ZNPs in cancer treatment and diabetes management, ultimately offering insights into future perspectives and conclusions regarding their effectiveness and potential in medical applications. **The mechanism of drug release is illustrated in the graphical abstract.**

## 2. Preparation of zein-based nanoparticles

In 1989, Suzuki et al. developed zein particles by crosslinking them with glutaraldehyde and incorporating antitumor drugs such as mitomycin. Zein particles contain carboxyl groups, amino, and hydroxyl groups that facilitate chemical interactions with both hydrophobic and hydrophilic drugs. However, crosslinking can result in the aggregation of nanoparticles, leading to an increase in their size (Jin et al., 2019). The crosslinking process can produce either toxic or inert derivatives of the drugs, and the presence of harmful residues from crosslinking agents and organic solvents raises safety concerns regarding the final products. Therefore, there is an urgent need to investigate alternative methods for formulating ZNPs (Danhier et al., 2010). To date, a variety of techniques have been employed to create zein-based nanoparticles, which can generally be categorized into desolvation, dispersion, and micromixing methods, each with its own drawbacks, as summarized in Table 15.1.

### 2.1 Desolvating strategy

#### *2.1.1 Solvent/nonsolvent method*

Ethanol and water are the most frequently applied solvent and nonsolvent combination for producing ZNPs. The solubility of zein can range from 2% to 60%, depending on the concentration of ethanol (Wang et al., 2017). The process involves mixing zein and the drug in

**TABLE 15.1** Benefits and drawbacks of the methods for producing zein nanoparticles.

| Method | Advantage and disadvantage | References |
|---|---|---|
| pH-guided procedure | Basic zein composite nanoparticles for desalination are eco-friendly, made without solvents, aiding in efficient salt removal. | Bhattacharya (2022) |
| Liquid–liquid emulsion | Small-scale, fast homogenizing machine for nanoparticles. | Huang et al. (2023) |
| Dialysis method | Efficient encapsulation, batch processing, simple separation, effective but laborious. | Chauhan et al. (2018) |
| Atomizing/antisolvent precipitation | Design with core inside shell boosts energy efficiency and enhances performance in applications. | Huang et al. (2021) |
| Supercritical antisolvent process | Organic solvents used in semicontinuous processes at high pressure with specific equipment. | Danhier et al. (2010) |
| Solvent/nonsolvent method | Low cost, easy operation, small particles. Batch process with solvent consumption concerns. Tedious separation. | Fang et al. (2021) |
| Microfluidic technique | Laminar flow in pipelines is disrupted by blockages, impacting efficiency in continuous processes and production. | Huang et al. (2021) |
| Glutaraldehyde-mediated crosslinking reaction | When encapsulating hydrophobic and hydrophilic actives, consider safety risks like chemical exposure and equipment concerns. | Chen et al. (2023) |
| Spray drying | User-friendly, compact, suitable for large production, high temperature. | Wang et al. (2017) |
| Coacervation method | Simple microscale operation with complex coacervation and low efficiency. | Nakamura et al. (2016) |
| Flash nanoprecipitation | Particle size control in continuous process using turbulent microfluidics can cause aggregation. | Hassan et al. (2022) |
| Electrospraying | Continuous, high-energy efficient process using simple equipment at high voltage; undesired structures form with high zein concentration. | Caro and Pozo (2015) |

ethanol, then adding this mixture to water, which causes the zein molecules to self-assemble. After the solvent is eliminated, ZNPs can be gathered. This method has successfully encapsulated a variety of drugs, such as ivermectin, ciprofloxacin, prednisolone, and curcumin (Nakamura et al., 2016). The resulting nanoparticles exhibit uniform size, a high drug loading capacity, and a smooth surface texture. For instance, ZNPs encapsulating 5-fluorouracil were produced with a size of 114.9 nm, an encapsulation efficiency (EE) of 60.7%, and a drug loading of 9.17% (Hassan et al., 2022).

### 2.1.2 Coacervation method

The coacervation method involves dissolving zein and the drug in water or anhydrous ethanol, then slowly adding the other solvent based on a ternary phase diagram. Zein molecules tend to form coacervates when the ethanol concentration is below 40% or above 90% (Caro and Pozo, 2015). Muthuselvi and Dhathathreyan (2006) developed zein coacervates for the encapsulation of gitoxin; however, they experienced low EE due to the formation of micron-sized particles. The use of crosslinking agents can enhance the characteristics and stability of the particles (Nichols and Bae, 2014). Simple zein coacervates often clump together over time because of their hydrophobic characteristics. In contrast, a more intricate coacervation that includes proteins, phospholipids, and polysaccharides can improve stability and minimize aggregation (Caro et al., 2021).

### 2.1.3 pH-driven method

A pH-driven technique leveraging the solubility characteristics of zein has been developed for the fabrication of composite nanoparticles. Zein is soluble under alkaline conditions ($pH \geq 11.0$) but becomes insoluble in neutral or acidic settings. In this method, zein is dispersed in deionized water and solubilized by increasing the pH with NaOH, followed by a decrease in pH using HCl (Li et al., 2023a). This pH shift leads to the formation of nanoparticles through protonation. Various composite nanoparticles have been successfully synthesized utilizing this approach, including carvacrol-loaded zein/sodium caseinate and zein/tea saponin nanoparticles designed for curcumin encapsulation (Hou et al., 2018). These nanoparticles are spherical in shape, with sizes ranging from 50 to 250 nm and EEs between 77.96% and 83.73%. By combining zein with materials such as propylene glycol alginate and whey protein isolate, researchers can tailor the properties of the nanoparticles for applications in the pharmaceutical and other industries. Recent studies have shown advancements in creating surface-coated ZNPs and incorporating bioactive compounds into them (Huang et al., 2019).

### 2.1.4 Dialysis method

ZNPs are created by employing dialysis methods that involve both a solvent and a nonsolvent. In this process, a mixture of zein and the drug is placed inside a dialysis bag, which is then immersed in a dialyzate to facilitate interaction (van Ballegooie et al., 2022). This method differs from conventional techniques that depend on organic solvents and complicated separation procedures; instead, dialysis simultaneously extracts the solvent while introducing a nonsolvent, thereby eliminating the requirement for extra extraction methods (Kaushik et al., 2020). In our research, we enhanced the ultrasonic dialysis process, resulting in the production of smaller and more uniform zein particles than those achieved through traditional techniques. Zein particles created using the dialysis process exhibited a spherical shape, with sizes ranging between 400 and 2500 nm (Fig. 15.1). They demonstrated a high EE of 89.1% for polydopamine-coated zein-indomethacin particles, designed for colon-targeted drug delivery (Wang et al., 2018).

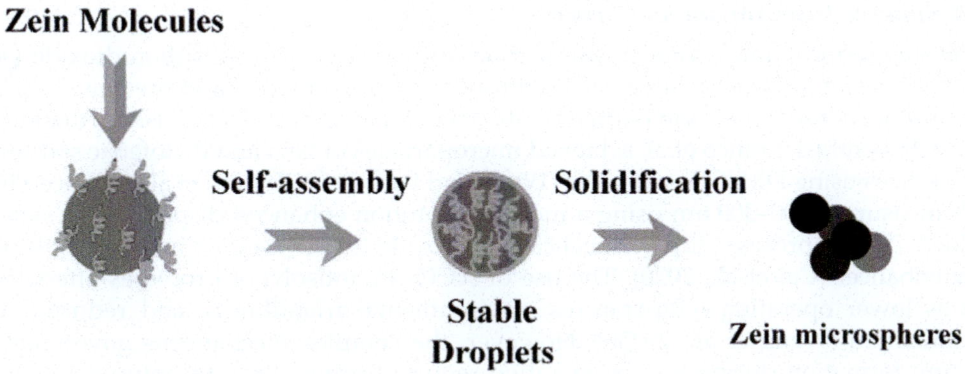


FIGURE 15.1 Self-assembly of zein microspheres using the dialysis technique.

## 2.2 Dispersing strategy

### *2.2.1 Liquid–liquid dispersion*

In this method, the zein stock solution is prepared in a solution of 55%–90% ethanol and then subjected to high-speed homogenization, resulting in the formation of small granules. These beads are subsequently immersed in deionized water, leading to the rapid diffusion of ethanol (Zhu et al., 2020). As the concentration of ethanol within the beads decreases, they tend to aggregate into nanoparticles. Typically, ZNPs range from 100 to 200 nm in size. Smaller particles are produced when higher shear rates, greater ethanol concentrations, or lower zein concentrations are utilized in the stock solution (Zhang et al., 2016a).

### *2.2.2 Spray drying*

Spray drying is a widely used technique in the pharmaceutical industry for converting liquid formulations into powders. The process involves atomizing the liquid to create fine droplets, which then interact with airflow to facilitate drying and shape the resulting particles, with the final product being separated from the drying air (Seok et al., 2018). Atomization is a critical phase, as it generates tiny droplets necessary for achieving specific product characteristics. There are various kinds of atomizers, including sonic nozzles, pressure atomizers, rotary atomizers, and pneumatic atomizers, that serve this function (Elzoghby et al., 2017b). One such application is the encapsulation of lysozyme in zein for controlled antimicrobial release using a mini spray dryer. While spray drying offers advantages such as rapid drying and uniform product dispersion, it may not be suitable for temperature-sensitive ingredients and can produce smaller particle sizes (von Baeckmann et al., 2021).

### 2.2.3 Supercritical antisolvent process

The supercritical antisolvent (SAS) method utilizes supercritical carbon dioxide ($scCO_2$) as an antisolvent to create small particles through solvent diffusion and precipitation. Zhong et al. produced lysozyme/zein particles with irregular shapes and sizes using ethanol–water solvent. In contrast, Franco et al. achieved microparticles of zein and diclofenac sodium with varying sizes using DMSO as a solvent (Wang and Padua, 2012a). Hu et al. produced lutein/ZNPs measuring 200–300 nm using a modified solution enhanced dispersion by supercritical fluids (SEDS) process. Supercritical carbon dioxide ($scCO_2$) served as an antisolvent and spray enhancer (Cai et al., 2020). The use of $scCO_2$ in antisolvent processes offers benefits such as lower operating temperatures, environmental friendliness, and reduced solvent contamination (Wang et al., 2023b). However, the complex mechanisms governing nanostructure formation during SAS preparation require further study to optimize the process for ZNPs. Research on how operating parameters affect nucleation and growth processes is crucial for enhancing the efficiency and effectiveness of the SAS method in nanoparticle production (Song et al., 2021).

### 2.2.4 Electrospraying

In this method, biopolymers are used to create nanoparticles by dispersing a zein solution in charged droplets through an electric field. This process occurs within a gas atmosphere, allowing the solvent to evaporate at the interface between the liquid and air. ZNPs exhibit a significant charge, facilitating the effective incorporation of beneficial molecules (Wang and Padua, 2012b). For instance, ZNPs containing curcumin typically range in size from 175 to 900 nm and achieve an EE of 85%–90%. In contrast, those encapsulating tamoxifen citrate vary in size from 0.68 to 1.54 μm (Kawabata et al., 2011). Additionally, β-carotene can be efficiently encapsulated within ZNPs. The electrospraying process is characterized by its simple equipment, high throughput, and small particle sizes, which eliminates the need for complex separation techniques. Raising the concentration of zein leads to larger particle sizes, which can result in the creation of undesirable particles (Loftsson and Brewster, 2010).

### 2.2.5 Atomizing/antisolvent precipitation process (AAP)

In this approach, folate-conjugated zein core-shell nanoparticles (Fa-zein) were used to deliver docetaxel (DTX). This method combined atomization and antisolvent self-assembly techniques to produce ZNPs (Aucamp and Milne, 2019). The resulting core-shell nanoparticles consisted of Fa-zein, a surfactant, and carboxymethyl chitosan (CMC), aimed at enabling targeted delivery of DTX. In this procedure, a mixture of zein, soy lecithin (SL), and DTX dissolved in ethanol–water was sprayed into droplets and added to a CMC antisolvent phase, resulting in the self-assembly of nanoparticles (Masimirembwa et al., 2003). This transition shifted the solution from a hydrophobic to a hydrophilic state, as illustrated in Fig. 15.2. The technique successfully demonstrated its capability in fabricating these nanoparticles for drug delivery applications (Zhang et al., 2016b).

Core-shell DTX/FZLC nanoparticles exhibit an EE of $79.22\% \pm 0.37\%$, a size of $206.9 \pm 48.73$ nm, and a zeta potential of $-41.8 \pm 3.97$ mV. These characteristics improve solubility, enable sustained release, and enhance cytotoxicity, highlighting the effectiveness of the AAP method. Further research is recommended (Chauhan et al., 2018).

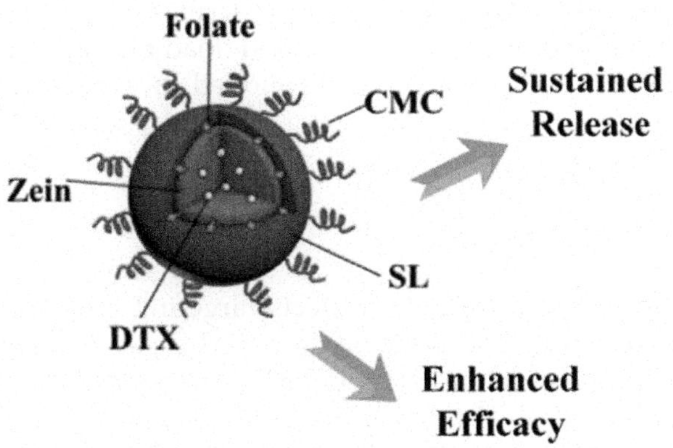


FIGURE 15.2 Creation of DTX/FZLC nanoparticles using the AAP process for targeted drug delivery.

## 2.3 Micromixing

### 2.3.1 *Flash nanoprecipitation*

Researchers prepare nanoparticles in a controlled chamber by mixing a solution stream with a nonsolvent stream, which leads to rapid mixing and the formation of nanoparticles (Huang et al., 2021). They successfully developed resveratrol-loaded ZNPs with adjustable sizes ranging from 50 to 108 nm and a consistent distribution. Additionally, they created polysaccharide-stabilized ZNPs for sustained release of doxorubicin and PEG-b-PLA/ZNPs for paclitaxel delivery (Jiang et al., 2015b).

### 2.3.2 *Microfluidic technique*

Microfluidic methods for creating ZNPs offer advantages over traditional techniques by utilizing smaller channel diameters, which reduce turbulence and ensure consistent mixing. Studies using Y-junction and T-junction designs have successfully produced small, uniform ZNPs, demonstrating the potential for continuous and reproducible production (Gaber et al., 2020).

# 3. Characterization of zein-based nanoparticles

## 3.1 Particle morphology

Microscopy techniques such as scanning electron microscopy (SEM), atomic force microscopy (AFM), and transmission electron microscopy (TEM) are used to study zein's amphiphilic molecules, revealing structures such as spheres, microcapsules, films, and rods (Aljabali et al., 2022).

ZNPs are typically nanospheres with smooth surfaces, formed through a process that involves the transformation from alpha-helix to beta-sheet, ribbon organization, coiling into rings, and stabilization of these rings (Oleandro et al., 2024). Some ZNPs are hollow, which enhances their loading capacity and provides prolonged release characteristics. These hollow ZNPs can be created using a two-step process that incorporates sacrificial templates with sodium carbonate, resulting in smaller diameters and increased loading capacity compared to solid counterparts. Furthermore, researchers have developed crocin-loaded hollow ZNPs that are coated with dextran sulfate and chitosan using a layer-by-layer self-assembly technique (Marco, 2022).

### 3.2 Particle size and surface charge

The size of nanoparticles is critical in pharmaceuticals, as it affects targeting and drug release. Dynamic light scattering measures Brownian motion to analyze particle size, which is useful for various types of particles. Techniques such as SEM and TEM are employed to determine the size of irregularly shaped particles (Van Hung, 2016). Controlling particle size is essential for effective drug delivery using ZNPs. Additionally, monitoring size changes during self-assembly with TEM is vital (Li and Song, 2020). Larger particles may encounter challenges related to efficiency and drug release. Therefore, understanding and controlling particle size is crucial for pharmaceutical applications. Assessing the dispersibility and stability of nanoparticles depends on their surface charge, which is commonly evaluated through zeta potential measurements (Kikushima and Kamiya, 2008). A zeta potential value above 30 mV prevents aggregation, while the isoelectric point results in a zero zeta potential, affecting clustering in water. Methods for modifying surface charge include adding surfactants, coatings, or biopolymers such as sodium caseinate, which can shift the isoelectric point and promote stability in complex nanoparticles (Salvador-Reyes et al., 2021).

### 3.3 Intermolecular interactions and loading of the drug

Interactions of ZNPs can be analyzed using circular dichroism and fluorescence spectroscopy. Fourier transform infrared (FTIR) spectrophotometry detects hydrogen bond peaks. Molecular dynamics simulations investigate interactions with compounds such as epigallocatechin-3-gallate, revealing van der Waals forces (Sousa et al., 2013). Ferulic acid binds more stably to zein under alkaline conditions. These methods provide insights into ZNP interactions for diverse applications. The structure of the zein molecule enables the efficient encapsulation of hydrophobic drugs, with a higher capacity than that of hydrophilic and amphiphilic drugs. Drug concentration can be analyzed using HPLC or UV spectrophotometry, while X-ray diffraction and differential scanning calorimetry (DSC) techniques can be employed to examine the crystalline structure of the nanoparticles (Paliwal and Palakurthi, 2014).

## 4. Treatment of zein nanoparticles

### 4.1 Sodium caseinate

Casein, a key protein found in milk, is utilized in various forms, such as sodium caseinate, due to its solubility and emulsifying properties. It is particularly effective in stabilizing ZNPs. Sodium caseinate modifies the isoelectric point of the particles, preventing aggregation around zein's native isoelectric point (Aytac et al., 2021). Additionally, it enhances the stability and redispersibility of ZNPs. Studies indicate that the interaction between sodium caseinate and ZNPs occurs through electrostatic adsorption, without any chemical reactions taking place (Lan et al., 2023). Composite nanoparticles made from zein, caseinate, and pectin demonstrate small size, uniform distribution, and a negative charge. Nanoparticles that contain curcumin show stability in a broad range of pH levels and can withstand high salt concentrations. Furthermore, zein/sodium caseinate nanoparticles loaded with anticancer drugs show increased cytotoxicity, likely due to enhanced stability and cellular absorption (Monteiro et al., 2021).

Overall, sodium caseinate is a versatile and effective ingredient in various applications, ranging from emulsions to DDSs, where it enhances the properties and performance of ZNPs (Xu et al., 2013).

## 4.2 Chitosan

Chitosan is a special type of cationic and water-attracting polysaccharide polymer that is obtained from chitin through a process called acid hydrolysis. It is recognized for its nontoxic nature and high biocompatibility (Fabrikov et al., 2015). Studies have indicated that unmodified ZNPs have a short release time, prompting the use of polysaccharides as stabilizers to enhance ZNPs. Chitosan, which contains hydroxyl and amine functional groups, allows for chemical crosslinking with crosslinking agents in situ. Chitosan-modified ZNPs have demonstrated promise in various applications, including liver-targeted delivery, prolonged antibacterial effects, and enhanced stability under high-strength conditions (Forato et al., 2004). Overall, chitosan plays a significant role in improving the stability and properties of ZNPs for a wide range of potential uses (Cabra et al., 2006).

## 4.3 Lactoferrin

Lactoferrin, a supplement found in mammalian milk, possesses antibacterial and antiviral properties. It interacts with receptors such as CD14, intestinal epithelial cells, lymphocytes, and low-density lipoprotein (LDL) receptor-related protein-1. Lactoferrin can bind to heparan sulfate proteoglycans located on cell surfaces (Forato et al., 2003). This characteristic can be utilized for targeted delivery methods, as it enhances the receptor-mediated absorption of nanoparticles, thereby improving the delivery of various substances. Glycosylated lactoferrin helps to stabilize ZNPs in environments with high salt concentrations, allowing them to encapsulate 7,8-dihydroxyflavone (7,8-DHF) (Bugs et al., 2004).

This bioaccessibility is higher than that of free 7,8-DHF in gastrointestinal digestion tests. Targeted nanoparticles using lactoferrin contribute to anticancer properties and improve uptake in breast cancer cells (Cabra et al., 2005). Additionally, lactoferrin enhances nanoparticle uptake in intestinal epithelial cells, increasing brain permeability. Overall, lactoferrin significantly modifies ZNPs through hydrogen bond formation (Yan et al., 2022).

## 4.4 Folate

Folate, or vitamin B9, is essential for cell division and the health of cells that divide quickly. In many cancerous tissues, folate receptors, which attach to folate, are often found in higher amounts. Research indicates that folate can facilitate the accumulation of nanoparticles in tumors for both diagnostic and therapeutic purposes (Erickson et al., 2020). By linking folic acid (FA) to ZNPs, targeted cancer therapy options can be developed. Instead of using chemical coupling, folate-modified ZNPs have been created to improve drug retention and reduce tumor growth. The modification with folate enhances the targeting capabilities of these nanoparticles, as evidenced by studies focusing on inflammatory sites (Wang and Padua, 2010). This makes folate-modified ZNPs a promising approach for targeted drug delivery in the treatment of cancer and inflammation (Wang and Padua, 2012c).

## 4.5 Hyaluronic acid

Hyaluronic acid is a type of glycosaminoglycan that does not contain sulfate and is present in various tissues. It is believed to be important for the extracellular matrix, as it can attach to receptors such as GHAP, CD44, and TSG6. CD44, a glycoprotein, is found in higher amounts in cancer stem cells and is considered a significant target for cancer treatment (Sturgeon et al., 1973). Researchers have successfully developed ZNPs that are cross-linked with hyaluronic acid to deliver anticancer drugs, such as curcumin and honokiol, specifically to CD44-expressing cancer cells. This focused method could enhance the effectiveness of breast cancer treatment by promoting cell growth, attachment, movement, and spread (Dong et al., 2017). The bonding between zein and hyaluronic acid molecules within the nanoparticles is facilitated by hydrogen bonds, hydrophobic interactions, and electrostatic forces (Chen et al., 1997).

## 4.6 Smart nanoparticles

### *4.6.1 pH-responsive nanoparticles*

Tumor tissue growth can lead to hypoxia and the production of acidic metabolites, resulting in lower pH levels. Kaushik developed pH-responsive ZNPs for the release of adriamycin in HeLa cells. These nanoparticles are also significant for cancer targeting and gastrointestinal delivery (Hughes and Olson, 2001). Li proposed modifying curcumin-loaded ZNPs with glycyrrhizic acid, enabling controlled drug release based on pH levels. pH-responsive ZNPs have applications in diabetes treatment, food preservation, and increasing pesticide solubility. In general, pH-sensitive nanoparticles are utilized in a variety of fields because they can release drugs when there are changes in pH levels (Fernández-Carneado et al., 2004).

### *4.6.2 Magneto-responsive particles*

Magnetic nanoparticles (MNPs) are made from metallic or composite materials and can be manipulated with an external magnetic field to gather in specific locations. These nanoparticles typically consist of modified surfaces and magnetic substances (Reddy and Yang, 2011). Throb and his team developed MNPs by enclosing superparamagnetic iron oxide and gefitinib within folate-conjugated zein. The study demonstrated an increased uptake of gefitinib by cancer cells due to the nanoparticles' magnetic response and active targeting capabilities. In addition to cancer research, magnetically responsive ZNPs have potential applications in environmental protection and food safety testing (Hurtado-López and Murdan, 2006).

#### 4.6.3 *Photo-responsive nanoparticles*

Research on photodynamic and photothermal therapy is progressing, with a particular emphasis on photosensitizers (Park and Nahm, 1997). Lee et al. developed zein-phosphatidylcholine nanoparticles loaded with indocyanine green (ICG), which enhanced phototoxicity in cancer cells. Abdulsalam et al. used light-responsive ZNPs containing hypericin to target HepG2 cells, observing increased apoptosis compared to the control group (Pasini et al., 2002).

These findings underscore the potential of targeted, light-sensitive nanoparticles in cancer treatment, demonstrating their effectiveness in inducing cancer cell death (Lee et al., 2005).

## 5. The difficulties and solutions of using zein-based nanocarriers for targeted cancer treatment

### 5.1 Stable zein-based DDSs

The effectiveness of DDSs is essential for the administration of cancer medications. Zein-based nanoparticles, nanohydrogels, and micelles, despite their small size and large surface area, can easily aggregate during storage ("American Association of Cereal Chemists, Maize endosperm proteins compared by sodium dodecyl sulfate gel electrophoresis and isoelectric focusing," 1981). Enhancing stability can be achieved by increasing the zeta potential; for instance, lowering the pH can raise the surface charge of zein particles to 40 mV, thereby improving stability. Modifying zein with substances like lecithin or casein can enhance its properties, but it complicates the preparation process (Perumal et al., 2009). Since zein formulations are not ideal for long-term use, producing a freeze-dried powder from them is a more viable option. Research into the freeze-drying of zein is critical, despite the limited existing documentation (Boraschi et al., 2017).

### 5.2 Targeting zein-based DDSs

DDSs offer advantages over traditional methods by reducing drug toxicity, minimizing side effects, and limiting damage to healthy cells, while simultaneously improving drug concentration at tumor sites (Esmaeili et al., 2008). It is essential to explore various delivery systems to effectively administer cancer medications. The enhanced permeability and retention (EPR) effect in tumors, which makes the walls of blood vessels more permeable, plays a crucial role in how effective nanocarriers are in DDSs. PEGylation is commonly employed in zein-based DDSs to improve tumor targeting (Williams, 1987). Active targeting in DDSs achieves specificity by binding to surface receptors on tumor cells. The interaction between targeting molecules and cancer cell receptors is critical for effective treatment (Fournier et al., 2003). Various approaches, including the conjugation of sugar molecules, FA, transferrin, and peptides, are used to develop zein-based nanocarriers, as shown in Fig. 15.3.

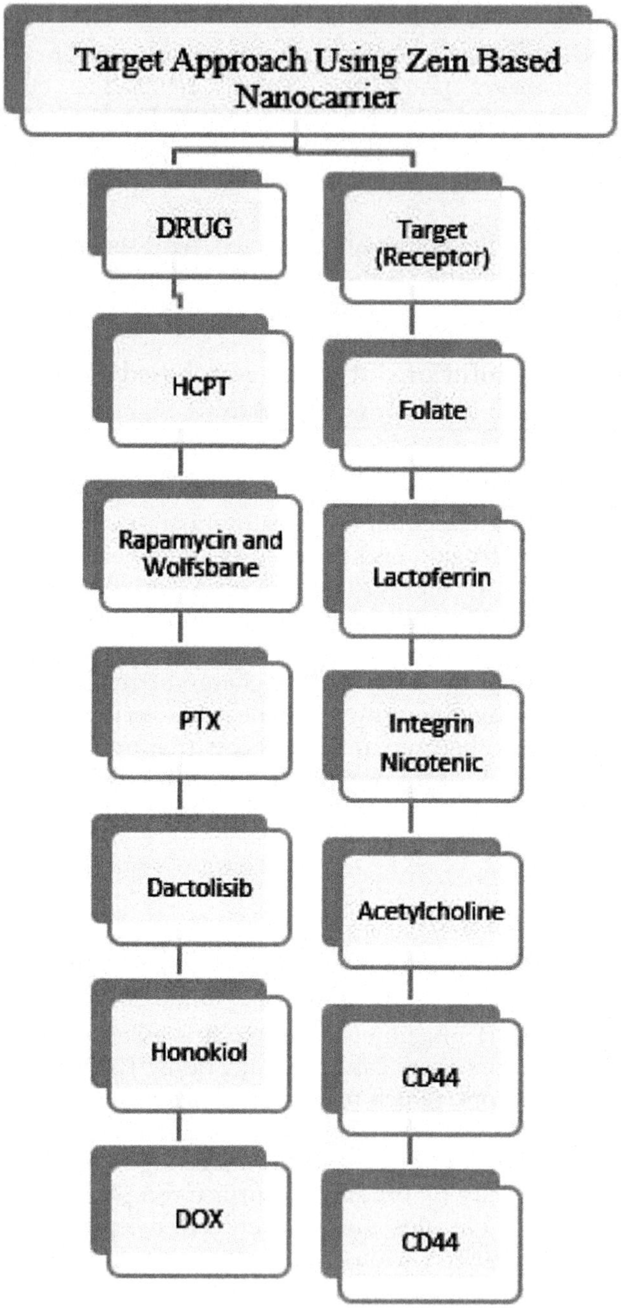


FIGURE 15.3 Targeted approach using zein-based nanocarriers.

## 5.3 Using folic acid

Cancer cells have much higher levels of folate receptors than healthy cells, which is why nanocarriers are often modified with FA to enable targeted drug delivery (Williams, 2008). Liu et al. enhanced the delivery of hydroxycamptothecin (HCPT) using FA-modified ZNPs, showing increased binding levels with higher FA content. Their cytotoxicity studies demonstrated specific targeting of cancer cells with minimal harm to healthy cells (Middleton and Tipton, 2000). Wang et al. effectively delivered HCPT by utilizing gold nanoparticles in combination with zein and polydopamine, which led to significant light emissions at the tumor location (Crawford et al., 2021). Soe et al. developed small, uniform FA-modified ZNPs for improved drug dispersion in tumor-bearing mice, with Paclitaxel (PTX) showing promising results. Wu et al. linked zein with FA to enhance the cancer-fighting effectiveness of DTX in laboratory tests (Demir et al., 2017).

## 5.4 Grafting with peptides

Peptides offer advantages for targeted cancer treatment because they have a low risk of triggering immune reactions, produce safe breakdown products, and maintain prolonged efficacy at tumor sites (Dong et al., 2004). Previous research developed a safe delivery method utilizing zein for combined chemotherapy and heat therapy. A unique peptide, cRGD, was attached to nanoparticles that carried the drug PTX, which were coated with silica and gold (Liu et al., 2022c). Tests demonstrated that these nanoparticles effectively targeted and were better absorbed by cancer cells, proving to be highly efficient against tumors. Furthermore, new ZNPs were created to deliver dactolisib alongside a brain-targeting peptide, RVG29, which enhances the absorption of the drug by tumor cells at the boundary of brain tumors (Liu et al., 2015).

## 5.5 Modifying with sugar residues

CD44 is highly present in various cancers and primarily interacts with sugar substances such as hyaluronic acid (Gong et al., 2006). Zhang and colleagues used core-shell nanoparticles composed of zein and hyaluronic acid to deliver honokiol to targeted areas, which improved cellular absorption and triggered cell death (Wang et al., 2007). Li et al. introduced zein-based nanoparticles with chondroitin sulfate to selectively deliver dactolisib, improving stability and cellular absorption, which led to nanoparticle accumulation in tumor tissues. Both studies highlight the potential of targeting CD44 to enhance antitumor effects in cancer treatment through innovative DDSs (Kim et al., 2021).

## 5.6 Others

Cell film coating is an innovative method for enhancing the accuracy of drug delivery by mimicking the functions of cell membranes (Song et al., 2021; Chacon et al., 2023). This advancement improves drug retention, targeting capabilities, and absorption within the body. In a recent study, cancer cells were layered onto ZNPs to create a safe and effective DDS that specifically targets cancer cells. Lactoferrin, a protein that binds to receptors on cancer cells and blood–brain barrier cells, is commonly used to enhance targeted DDSs (Lepeltier et al., 2014). Sabra and colleagues developed a unique micelle with a lactoferrin outer layer and a zein core, which improves tumor targeting, reduces interactions with blood proteins, and prolongs retention in the body (Jiang et al., 2015a; Gaber et al., 2020; Chen et al., 2023; Dong et al., 2019; Yu et al., 2022; Jin et al., 2019; Danhier et al., 2010; Wang et al., 2017; Nakamura et al., 2016; Hassan et al., 2022; Caro and Pozo, 2015; Nichols and Bae, 2014; Caro et al., 2021; Li et al., 2023a; Hou et al., 2018; Huang et al., 2019; van Ballegooie et al., 2022; Kaushik et al., 2020; Wang et al., 2018; Zhu et al., 2020; Zhang et al., 2016a; Seok et al., 2018; Elzoghby et al., 2017b; von Baeckmann et al., 2021; Wang and Padua, 2012a; Cai et al., 2020; Wang et al., 2023b; Song et al., 2021; Wang and Padua, 2012b; Kawabata et al., 2011; Loftsson and Brewster, 2010; Aucamp and Milne, 2019; Masimirembwa et al., 2003; Zhang et al., 2016b; Chauhan et al., 2018; Huang et al., 2021; Jiang et al., 2015b; Gaber et al., 2020; Aljabali et al., 2022; Oleandro et al., 2024; Marco, 2022; Van Hung, 2016; Li and Song, 2020; Kikushima and Kamiya, 2008; Salvador-Reyes et al., 2021; Sousa et al., 2013; Paliwal and Palakurthi, 2014; Aytac et al., 2021; Lan et al., 2023; Monteiro et al., 2021; Xu et al., 2013; Fabrikov et al., 2015; Forato et al., 2004; Cabra et al., 2006; Forato et al., 2003; Bugs et al., 2004; Cabra et al., 2005; Yan et al., 2022; Erickson et al., 2020; Wang and Padua, 2010, 2012c; Sturgeon et al., 1973; Dong et al., 2017; Chen et al., 1997; Hughes and Olson, 2001; Fernández-Carneado et al., 2004; Reddy and Yang, 2011; Hurtado-López and Murdan, 2006; Park and Nahm, 1997; Pasini et al., 2002; Lee et al., 2005; "American Association of Cereal Chemists, Maize endosperm proteins compared by sodium dodecyl sulfate gel electrophoresis and isoelectric focusing," 1981; Perumal et al., 2009; Boraschi et al., 2017; Esmaeili et al., 2008; Williams, 1987; Fournier et al., 2003; Williams, 2008; Middleton and Tipton, 2000; Crawford et al., 2021; Demir et al., 2017; Dong et al., 2004; Liu et al., 2022c; Liu et al., 2015; Gong et al., 2006; Wang et al., 2007; Kim et al., 2021; Song et al., 2021; Chacon et al., 2023; Lepeltier et al., 2014; Cai et al., 2022; Liu et al., 2022a; Li et al., 2024).

## 6. Responsive zein-based DDSs

### 6.1 pH response

Tumors exhibit unique physical characteristics due to their unpredictable growth and abnormal structures (Kell et al., 2020). Their rapid growth leads to a deficiency of nutrients and oxygen, resulting in the accumulation of acidic waste within the tumor area. Research has shown that tumors typically have a pH level ranging from 6.5 to 7.0, in contrast to normal tissues, which maintain a pH of around 7.4. Scientists have developed specialized delivery systems that respond to pH changes in tumors to effectively transport chemotherapy drugs (Rawat et al., 2012; Jiang et al., 2011; Fillebeen et al., 1999). These systems include metal and plant compound carriers, pH-sensitive nanocarriers, and pH-responsive gels (Milewska et al., 2014). By leveraging these innovative technologies, researchers aim to enhance the targeted delivery of drugs to cancerous tissues while minimizing harmful effects on healthy cells, ultimately improving cancer treatment outcomes (Ando et al., 2010).

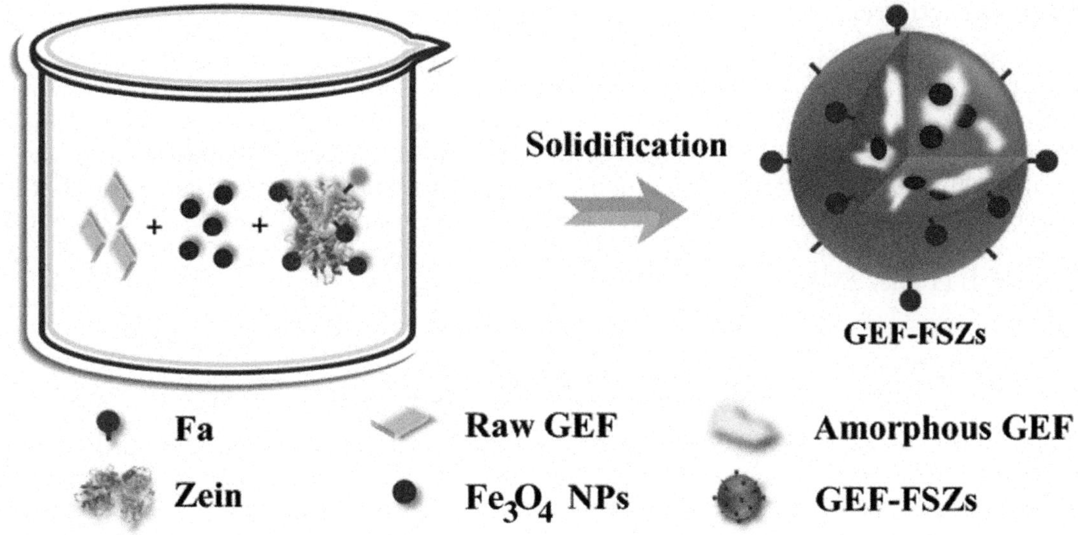


FIGURE 15.4 The process of preparing a magnetic zein-based nanocore.

## 6.2 Redox response

Differences in redox potential between healthy cells and tumor cells can be utilized to develop DDSs that respond to specific stimuli (Chen et al., 2020c). Glutathione (GSH) is a crucial antioxidant in cells, helping to maintain chemical balance. Disulfide bonds, which are common connections in proteins, can change through oxidation (El-Lakany et al., 2018).

GSH regulates the cellular environment by using reactive oxygen species (ROS) to form or disrupt disulfide bonds (Wang et al., 2023a). Tumor cells have elevated levels of GSH, which makes redox-responsive DDSs, such as the zein-based system that releases paclitaxel in the presence of GSH, promising for cancer treatment. This targeted treatment has shown effectiveness in both laboratory tests and in living organisms, specifically favoring cancer cells (Xu et al., 2000).

## 6.3 Photo response

Photodynamic therapy (PDT) employs photosensitizers to specifically target and eliminate cancer cells without the need for surgery. ICG is an encouraging near-infrared dye used in this treatment, as it produces ROS that can destroy tumor cells when activated by light (Paulos et al., 2004). Li and colleagues studied ICG-encapsulated zein-phosphatidylcholine nanoparticles for cancer treatment, finding enhanced cell killing with light exposure (Turk et al., 2004). Yu et al. developed heat-absorbing nanoparticles loaded with DTX, coated with green tea compounds and iron (GTP/FeIII), showing a 37.82% thermal response to near-infrared laser. Both laboratory (in vitro) and live organism (in vivo) studies show that these nanoparticles are effective in slowing down tumor growth by using a combination of chemical, safe, and heat-based techniques (Parker et al., 2005; Handali et al., 2019; Wusigale et al., 2021). Overall, these studies highlight the potential of light-sensitive compounds and nanoparticle delivery systems in enhancing cancer treatment outcomes (Hou et al., 2019).

### 6.4 Magnetic response

MNPs utilized in biomedical applications exhibit unique properties and biophysical characteristics (Wu et al., 2022). They can be categorized as pure metals, metal oxides, or composites and are specifically engineered to target tumors using an external magnetic field. When integrated into zein-based DDSs, their transport efficiency is improved (Vasvani et al., 2020). Pang et al. developed a magnetic zein-based nanocomplex (nanocore) that incorporates $Fe_3O_4$, which showed over 95.6% fluorescence signal uptake in cells within 10 min when exposed to an external magnetic field, significantly enhancing uptake in vitro (Fig. 15.4) (Toole, 2004).

## 7. Hybrid zein-based DDSs

Enhancing zein-based nanocarriers for cancer treatment involves addressing challenges related to stability, targeting, and hydrophobicity. An efficient nanocarrier design is essential for optimizing therapeutic effects (Gupta et al., 2019). Hybrid zein-based DDSs provide various anticancer benefits by combining different components, such as polysaccharides, proteins, surfactants, and inorganic materials. These hybrid nanoparticles are assembled through electrostatic interactions, hydrophobic effects, and hydrogen bonding, enabling the integration of advantages for targeted cancer treatment (Tsuji et al., 2022; McKee et al., 1996; Gronthos et al., 2001).

### 7.1 Zein–protein hybrid nanoparticles

Combining zein-based nanoparticles with hydrophilic proteins such as silk fibroin or bovine serum albumin enhances drug delivery, improving the inhibition of tumor cell growth with drugs like paclitaxel and curcumin (Ponta et al., 2003). Additionally, the inclusion of lipids further enhances performance, resulting in significant anticancer efficacy in vivo with all-trans retinoic acid and genistein-loaded nanoparticles (Zöller, 2011).

### 7.2 Zein–surfactant hybrid nanoparticles

Surfactants play a vital role in improving DDSs by enhancing solubility (Li et al., 2014). In their research, Gagliardi et al. evaluated Tween 80, Poloxamer 188, and sodium deoxycholate as stabilizers for zein-based nanocarriers (Liu et al., 2022b). They found that ZNPs stabilized with sodium deoxycholate displayed the best physicochemical characteristics for drug formulation. These sodium deoxycholate-stabilized ZNPs, when loaded with paclitaxel, effectively encapsulated the drug and increased its cytotoxic effects on cancer cells (Seok et al., no date). Additionally, Ye et al. created pluronic-zein-curcumin DDSs that improved the hydrophilicity, stability, and transport efficiency of zein. After the pluronic modification, the surface angle decreased by 33.1%–62.8%, and the system maintained stability across different pH and salinity levels (Zhang et al., 2020).

### 7.3 Zein–inorganic hybrid nanoparticles

Inorganic nanoparticles possess unique properties that are beneficial for DDSs. Researchers are focusing on combining zein with inorganic nanoparticles to enhance drug delivery capabilities (Zhang et al., 2019). For example, Chauhan synthesized gold-deposited zein nanoshells for photothermal cancer treatment, successfully reducing the viability of cancer cells. Anirudhan utilized zein to encapsulate mesoporous silica, enabling sustained drug release (Lee et al., 2008). Bahmani developed zein-based multiwalled carbon nanotubes loaded with anticancer drugs, which exhibited high biocompatibility and significantly reduced cancer cell viability. These innovative approaches highlight the potential of combining zein with inorganic nanoparticles to create improved DDSs with enhanced performance (Li et al., 2023).

## 8. Applications of zein nanoparticles

### 8.1 Antiinflammatory

Disturbance is a crucial bodily response that helps combat harmful germs and maintain health. It is important to manage excessive inflammation to prevent tissue damage and long-term consequences caused by ROS (Razavi et al., 2021). Long-term inflammation can lead to serious health issues, including tumors, heart disease, and arthritis. Problems with the immune system and damaged cells can exacerbate inflammatory conditions. Research is ongoing into substances that can reduce inflammation, with natural alternatives gaining increasing interest (Kong et al., 2023). ZNPs may effectively encapsulate common but unstable compounds, improving their solubility and safety (Ahmed et al., 2015). In Fig. 15.5, the zein nanostructures demonstrate their method and potential in reducing inflammation.

Penalva and colleagues discovered that ZNPs can effectively release resveratrol regardless of pH levels, increasing medication absorption by 50% and reducing side effects in mice (Anderson and Lamsa, 2011). They also found that encapsulating quercetin in ZNPs enhanced absorption by 60% and alleviated symptoms of endotoxic shock. Ruan et al. demonstrated that

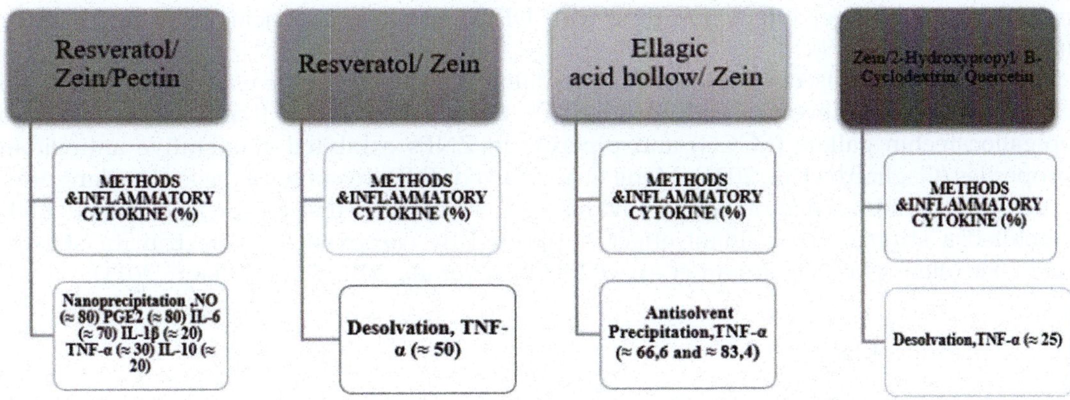


FIGURE 15.5 Zein nanostructures: method and potential in reducing inflammation.

ellagic acid in ZNPs exhibited superior stability and increased retention in the body, while Liu and his team showed that ZNPs facilitated four times more resveratrol absorption in Caco-2 cells, resulting in higher levels in the bloodstream (Arora et al., 2012; Arunkumar et al., 2017; Asrorov et al., 2020; Bao et al., 2020). This increase led to enhanced antiinflammatory activity, reduced levels of certain proteins, and improved oral administration and retention within the body. These findings suggest that technology-based medicines such as ZNPs could help reduce inflammation, protect against toxins, prevent infections, and promote overall health in various applications (Cantó et al., 2020; Chang et al., 2017; Chen et al., 2018; 2020a,b).

## 8.2 Antioxidant

Antioxidant compounds protect the body from diseases related to oxidative stress, such as atherosclerosis and cancer. Nanocarriers encapsulate unstable antioxidants to enhance their stability (Chen et al., 2020c; Cheng and Jones, 2017; Cheng et al., 2016, 2020). Research on ZNPs that incorporate antioxidant properties shows promising results. Studies demonstrate their effectiveness against free radicals, such as 2,2-diphenyl-1-picrylhydrazyl (DPPH) and 2,2′-azino-bis(3-ethylbenzothiazoline-6-sulfonic acid) (ABTS). Quercetin-loaded nanoparticles maintain antioxidant activity under heat and UV exposure. ZNPs containing quercetin exhibit good stability and antioxidant activity in simulated stomach fluids (Chuacharoen and Sabliov, 2017; Dai et al., 2018; Araújo et al., 2020). Additionally, nanoparticles with quercetin and resveratrol display enhanced antioxidant properties in liver cancer cells. Various studies highlight the potential of nanoparticle delivery systems for antioxidants (Dong et al., 2016). In 2021, research found that ZNPs combined with low-molecular-weight sodium hyaluronate (SHA) and resveratrol exhibited strong antioxidant properties. The ZNPs demonstrated 4.5 times greater antioxidant activity than zein-SHA with resveratrol and were more effective than the free compound. These nanoparticles were small, water-dispersible, and stable, which improved the effectiveness of resveratrol in combating oxidation and cancer (El-Lakany et al., 2020; Elzoghby et al., 2017a; Feng et al., 2020). Nanocarriers made from zein are effective in delivering hydrophobic nutrients and protective agents to combat cancer (Foerg et al., 2005).

In 2015, it was discovered that ZNPs containing thyme oil exhibited increasing antioxidant effects with higher dosages, leading to reduced levels of DPPH. Encapsulated compounds have a longer interaction time with DPPH radicals, enhancing their effectiveness (Gagliardi et al., 2019).

Zhang and Han discovered that ZNPs containing rutin, which have a circular shape, efficiently reduced the levels of DPPH and ABTS. Dahiya et al. found that the combination of epigallocatechin gallate (EGCG) and piperine in ZNPs exhibited cooperative antioxidant properties (Gagliardi et al., 2021). Meng et al. utilized ZNPs to enhance the antioxidant properties of curcumin, while de Souza Tavares et al. discovered that ellagic acid-loaded ZNPs exhibited a stronger antioxidant effect, supported by carboxymethyl dextrin for stability and controlled release (Gautam et al., 2020; Ghalei et al., 2018; Lai and Guo, 2011).

## 8.3 Antimicrobial

Microbes cause infections such as urinary tract infections, pneumonia, and bacteremia, resulting in high morbidity and mortality due to resistance. Nanoparticles are being used to deliver antimicrobial agents for treatment (Li et al., 2018a). Research is being conducted on ZNPs for their antibacterial potential (Li et al., 2018b). The encapsulation of thymol and carvacrol enhances effectiveness against both Gram-positive and Gram-negative bacteria. Anacardic acid-loaded ZNPs have proven effective against *Streptococcus mutans* and exhibit prolonged antibacterial effects against *Pseudomonas aeruginosa* (Li et al., 2009). Overall, ZNPs show promise for various applications, including dental care and food preservation (Liang et al., 2015).

### 8.4 Anticancer

Cancer arises from uncontrolled cell growth and genetic changes, presenting a significant global health challenge (Liang et al., 2004). Encapsulating anticancer agents in nanoparticles allows for targeted delivery to tumor cells based on specific characteristics and has shown promising results in various cancer cell lines (Liang et al., 2018a). ZNPs enhance the properties and effectiveness of cancer treatments, with studies demonstrating increased anticancer activity and stability. The development of novel formulations using ZNPs holds great potential for improving chemotherapy outcomes (Liang et al., 2018b).

### 8.5 Antidiabetic

Diabetes mellitus is a metabolic disorder characterized by elevated blood sugar levels, which can significantly impact both health and the economy. Treatments for diabetes often require injections due to patients' sensitivity to certain medications (Liu and Rubenstein, 1992). ZNPs enhance oral drug delivery by improving stability and efficacy while reducing side effects. Research has combined ZNPs with PEG-Gantrez AN and Gantrez AN-PEG for the oral delivery of antidiabetic drugs in animal studies, effectively reducing ROS, fat accumulation, and blood glucose levels (Liu et al., 2020a,b; Patel et al., 2012; Peñalva et al., 2015). Overall, ZNPs represent a promising method for oral drug delivery (Penalva et al., 2015, 2017; Raza et al., 2020; Rivera et al., 2021; Ruan et al., 2018).

## 9. Zein-based nanotechnology applications in cancer therapy

In recent years, zein has been extensively researched for its potential in developing nanoscale DDSs for cancer treatment. ZNPs, particularly when combined with anticancer drugs, have shown promising results in enhancing cytotoxicity against cancer cells (Sabra et al., 2018; Seok et al., 2018; Maviah et al., 2020). Additionally, zein-based nanoparticles have been investigated for delivering various anticancer agents, suggesting their potential for new cancer treatment strategies (Patel and Velikov, 2011). Studies have demonstrated that ZNPs modified with FA can effectively target cancer cells, while encapsulating gambogenic acid within ZNPs leads to pH-sensitive drug release and enhanced anticancer effects (Tan and McClements, 2021). The liver-targeting capabilities of ZNPs have also been confirmed in in vivo studies (Table 15.2).

In their study from 2013, Luo et al. discovered that enhancing the redispersibility of ZNPs using caseinate in saline solutions resulted in enhanced cellular uptake and epithelial

**TABLE 15.2** Zein nanoparticles for cancer treatment and their physical and chemical properties.

| Loaded compound | Encapsulation efficiency (%) | Loading efficiency (%) | Size (nm) | Results | References |
|---|---|---|---|---|---|
| PTX | 40 | 3.84 | 105 | Stable structure at 50°C. | Li et al. (2018b) |
| Carvacrol | 78 | 13 | 240–260 | Zein-lecithin (5:1) yielded optimal physicochemical parameters. | Liang et al. (2004) |
| Vorinostat Bortezomib | 62 | 2.8 | 150–160 | Increased toxicity and reduced migration. | Liang et al. (2018a) |
| Hydroxycamptothecin | 93.62 | 8.76 | 190–199 | Improved cell survival with PFA. | Liu and Rubenstein (1992) |
| β-Carotene | 55–69 | — | 81–32 | Strong combined effect with methotrexate. | Liu et al. (2020b) |
| 5-Fluorouracil | 59–62 | 9.17 | 55–174 | Targeting highest liver tissue accumulation. | Peñalva et al. (2015) |
| Terpinen-4-ol | 79–93.5 | — | 182–196 | Stable, monodisperse agent for drug release. | Penalva et al. (2017) |
| Gambogenic acid | 72–77 | 24–30 | 309–316 | Low pH triggers uncrosslinked drug release. | Raza et al. (2020) |
| Maytansine | 83 | 3.32 | 112.3 | Release under 40% in 24 h. | Hu and McClements (2015) |

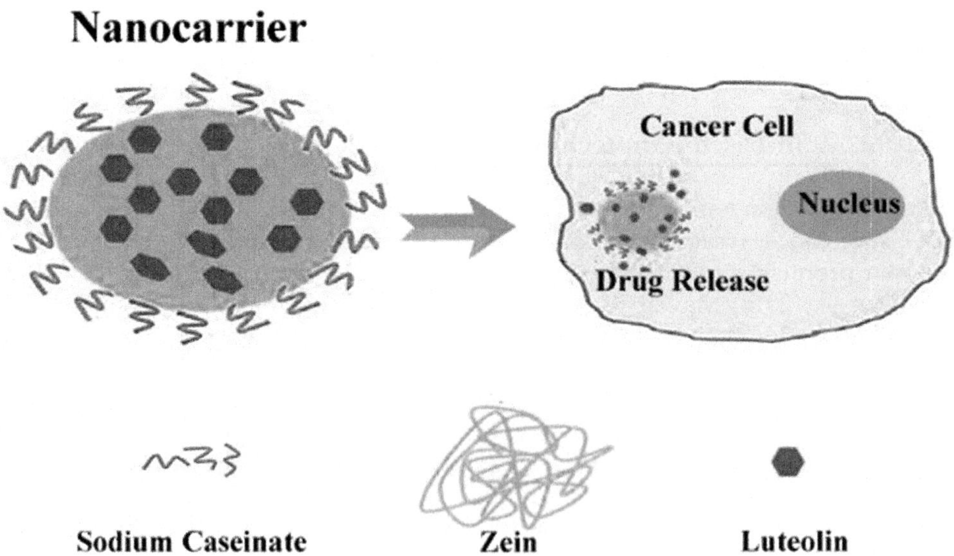


FIGURE 15.6 Focusing on colon cancer cells using sodium caseinate.

transport. The nanoparticles, ranging from 120 to 140 nm in size, exhibited no harmful effects on Caco-2 cells (Hu and McClements, 2015). Sodium caseinate reduced the particle size, with larger proportions resulting in smaller sizes. Cell uptake efficiency was increased in a manner that depended on both time and concentration. Zein/casein nanoparticles in a 1:1 ratio exhibited no significant size change after 4 h (Gagliardi et al., 2020). Additionally, zein/casein nanoparticles in a 1:1 or 1:2 ratio demonstrated 2.5 times higher cell uptake effectiveness compared to a 2:1 ratio. Furthermore, luteolin in zein nanoparticles specifically targeted SW-480 colon cancer cells (Fig. 15.6) (Gomez-Estaca et al., 2012).

## 10. Zein-based delivery system for active substances targeting type II diabetes

Zein, which has gained recognition in drug delivery, is used to transport bioactive substances for type II diabetes. Research over the past decade has demonstrated that zein-coated drugs with both higher and lower molecular weights are effective in enhancing drug delivery efficiency (Sun et al., 2020). Zein-lysine nanoparticles coated with poly (anhydride)-thiamine exhibit optimal physicochemical properties. These nanoparticles have shown a significant reduction in fat accumulation in Caenorhabditis elegans and lower blood glucose levels in diabetic rats when compared to traditional drug delivery methods (Yuan et al., 2021). CSA usually refers to Chondroitin Sulfate A, which is often used as a coating or stabilizing material for nanoparticle formulations, including insulin-loaded zein nanoparticles (ZNPs) and increases the production of epitomes, as shown in Fig. 15.7.

The FTIR analysis indicated that higher concentrations of CSA exhibited hydrogen bonding, electrostatic interactions, and hydrophobic interactions (Feng et al., 2018).

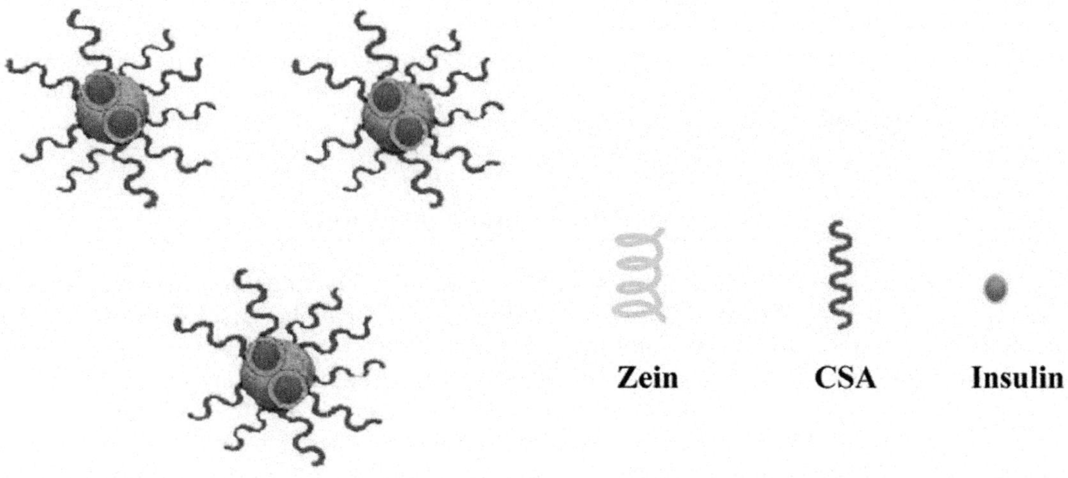


FIGURE 15.7 Encapsulating insulin using zein nanoparticles.

TABLE 15.3 Delivering active compounds in zein nanoparticles for diabetes.

| Bioactive substances | Loading efficiency (%) | Encapsulation efficiency (%) | References |
|---|---|---|---|
| Exenatide | <1 | — | Li et al. (2018b) |
| Insulin | 84 | >80 | Raza et al. (2020) |
| Glibenclamide | 3.8–4.6 | 38–48 | Ruan et al. (2018) |
| Barjie Essential oil | 19–21 | 91–98 | Patel and Velikov (2011) |
| Insulin | 6.4–7.2 | 88.5–90.5 | Yuan et al. (2021) |
| Insulin | 8.7–9.2 | 83.6–90.5 | Chen et al. (2019) |

Both zein and zein-CSA nanoparticles exhibited similar drug release patterns in phosphate-buffered saline (PBS), although the release was slower for the zein-CSA coating. Coating with chitosan further decreased drug release rates. Chitosan-coated nanoparticles did not affect the time to reach maximum concentration ($T_{max}$) after oral administration in mice, but they significantly improved blood glucose and serum insulin levels for up to 6 hours (Brotons-Canto et al., 2020). Zein-based delivery systems, such as I/zein-CSA/chitosan and zein-cholic acid-phosphatidylcholine, showed promise in controlling drug release and enhancing bioavailability. The nanoparticle structure with a lysine surface in zein was studied and revealed a high discharge of GB in simulated intestinal fluid (SIF) (Hu and McClements, 2014). ZNPs increased the fat content in *Caenorhabditis elegans* without causing toxicity. Zein electrospun nanofibers demonstrated promising drug delivery properties for essential oils. Another nanofiber incorporating Cu-GZS and graphene oxide displayed optimized copper release for diabetic wound healing and also stimulated new blood vessel formation (Patel et al., 2010; Chen et al., 2014; Hu et al., 2015). These studies illustrate the potential therapeutic effects of zein-based nanofibers in various applications. The physicochemical characteristics of zein-based antidiabetic nanoformulations can be found in Table 15.3.

## 11. Perspectives and conclusions

Zein, a protein known for its ability to form nanocarriers, is valuable across various sectors, including textiles, food, and pharmaceuticals. ZNPs can be easily produced using methods such as antisolvent precipitation, pH-driven processes, and electrospraying, offering advantages like cost-effectiveness, consistency, and scalability (Yuan et al., 2021; Feng et al., 2018; Brotons-Canto et al., 2020; Hu and McClements, 2014). These nanoparticles can encapsulate bioactive ingredients, including antiinflammatory, antioxidant, and antimicrobial agents, thereby enhancing their efficacy and stability. The production methods also influence characteristics such as size, surface charge, and ease of manufacturing. These nanoparticles have the potential for oral administration to treat a variety of diseases, including infections, cancer, diabetes, and neurological disorders (Patel et al., 2010; Chen et al., 2014, 2019; Hu et al., 2015). Laboratory studies have shown promising results, underscoring the need for further testing in living organisms and clinical trials to fully understand the capabilities of these nano-based products. The ongoing research into the applications of ZNPs in different fields is crucial, given their versatility and potential to improve drug delivery and biological activity (Ghobadi-Oghaz et al., 2022). Encapsulating bioactives in ZNPs has demonstrated several benefits, including controlled release, improved solubility, and protection against degradation, making them a promising option for future oral therapies. Overall, the manufacturing techniques and properties of ZNPs have the potential to revolutionize drug delivery and treatment methods (McClements, 2020; Chen et al., 2020a,b; Carrasco-Sandoval et al., 2021; Tchuenbou-Magaia et al., 2022).

## CRediT authorship contribution statement

**Dr. Mohammad Hossein Karami (first corresponding author):** Writing—review & editing, Writing—original draft, Visualization, Validation, Supervision, Software, Resources, Project administration, Methodology, Investigation, Formal analysis, Data curation, Conceptualization. **Dr. Omid Moini Jazani (second corresponding author):** Writing—review, Validation, Supervision.

## Declaration of competing interest

The authors declare that they have no known competing financial interests or personal relationships that could have appeared to influence the work reported in this paper.

## References


Ahmed, O.A.A., Hosny, K.M., Al-Sawahli, M.M., Fahmy, U.A., 2015. Optimization of caseinate-coated simvastatin-zein nanoparticles: improved bioavailability and modified release characteristics. Drug Des. Dev. Ther. 9, 655–662. https://doi.org/10.2147/DDDT.S76194.

Aljabali, A.A.A., Rezigue, M., Alsharedeh, R.H., Obeid, M.A., Mishra, V., Serrano-Aroca, Á., El-Tanani, M., Tambuwala, M.M., 2022. Protein-based nanomaterials: a new tool for targeted drug delivery. Ther. Deliv. 13 (6), 321–338. https://doi.org/10.4155/tde-2021-0091.

American Association of Cereal Chemists, Maize endosperm proteins compared by sodium dodecyl sulfate gel electrophoresis and isoelectric focusing. Cereal Chem. 58 (1981), 275–281.

Anderson, T.J., Lamsa, B.P., 2011. Zein extraction from corn, corn products, and coproducts and modifications for various applications: a review. Cereal Chem. 88 (2), 159–173. https://doi.org/10.1094/CCHEM-06-10-0091.

Ando, K., Hasegawa, K., Shindo, K.-ichi, Furusawa, T., Fujino, T., Kikugawa, K., Nakano, H., Takeuchi, O., Akira, S., Akiyama, T., Gohda, J., Inoue, J.-ichiro, Hayakawa, M., 2010. Human lactoferrin activates NF-κB through the Toll-like receptor 4 pathway while it interferes with the lipopolysaccharide-stimulated TLR4 signaling. FEBS J. 277 (9), 2051–2066. https://doi.org/10.1111/j.1742-4658.2010.07620.x.

Araújo, J.T.C.d., Lima, L.A., Vale, E.P., Martin-Pastor, M., Lima, R.A., Silva, P.G.d.B., Sousa, F.F.O.d., 2020. Toxicological and genotoxic evaluation of anacardic acid loaded-zein nanoparticles in mice. Toxicol. Rep. 7, 1207–1215. https://doi.org/10.1016/j.toxrep.2020.08.024.

Arora, S., Singh, S., Piazza, G.A., Contreras, C.M., Panyam, J., Singh, A.P., 2012. Honokiol: a novel natural agent for cancer prevention and therapy. Curr. Mol. Med. 12 (10), 1244–1252. https://doi.org/10.2174/156652412803833508.

Arunkumar, P., Indulekha, S., Vijayalakshmi, S., Srivastava, R., 2017. In vitro comparative studies of zein nanoparticles and composite chitosan thermogels based injectable formulation of doxorubicin. J. Drug Deliv. Sci. Technol. 40, 116–124. https://doi.org/10.1016/j.jddst.2017.05.015.

Asrorov, A.M., Gu, Z., Min, K.A., Shin, M.C., Huang, Y., 2020. Advances on tumor-targeting delivery of cytotoxic proteins. ACS Pharmacol. Transl. Sci. 3 (1), 107–118. https://doi.org/10.1021/acsptsci.9b00087.

Aucamp, M., Milne, M., 2019. The physical stability of drugs linked to quality-by-design (QbD) and in-process technology (PAT) perspectives. Eur. J. Pharmaceut. Sci. 139, 105057. https://doi.org/10.1016/j.ejps.2019.105057.

Aytac, Z., Xu, J., Raman Pillai, S.K., Eitzer, B.D., Xu, T., Vaze, N., Ng, K.W., White, J.C., Chan-Park, M.B., Luo, Y., Demokritou, P., 2021. Enzyme- and relative humidity-responsive antimicrobial fibers for active food packaging. ACS Appl. Mater. Interfaces 13 (42), 50298–50308. https://doi.org/10.1021/acsami.1c12319.

von Baeckmann, C., Rubio, G.M.D.M., Kählig, H., Kurzbach, D., Reithofer, M.R., Kleitz, F., 2021. Evaporation-induced self-assembly of small peptide-conjugated silica nanoparticles. Angewandte Chemie - International Edition 60 (42), 22700–22705. https://doi.org/10.1002/anie.202108378.

van Ballegooie, C., Wretham, N., Ren, T., Popescu, I.M., Yapp, D.T., Bally, M.B., 2022. PEG conjugated zein nanoparticles for in vivo use. Pharmaceutics 14 (9). https://doi.org/10.3390/pharmaceutics14091831.

Bao, X., Qian, K., Yao, P., 2020. Oral delivery of exenatide-loaded hybrid zein nanoparticles for stable blood glucose control and β-cell repair of type 2 diabetes mice. J. Nanobiotechnol. 18 (1). https://doi.org/10.1186/s12951-020-00619-0.

Bhattacharya, S., 2022. Genotoxicity and in vitro investigation of gefitinib-loaded polycaprolactone fabricated nanoparticles for anticancer activity against NCI-H460 cell lines. J. Exp. Nanosci. 17 (1), 214–246. https://doi.org/10.1080/17458080.2022.2060501.

Boraschi, D., Italiani, P., Palomba, R., Decuzzi, P., Duschl, A., Fadeel, B., Moein Moghimi, S., 2017. Nanoparticles and innate immunity: new perspectives on host defence. Semin. Immunol. 34, 33–51. https://doi.org/10.1016/j.smim.2017.08.013.

Brotons-Canto, A., Gonzalez-Navarro, C.J., Gurrea, J., González-Ferrero, C., Manuel Irache, J., 2020. Zein nanoparticles improve the oral bioavailability of resveratrol in humans. J. Drug Deliv. Sci. Technol. 57, 101704. https://doi.org/10.1016/j.jddst.2020.101704.

Bugs, M.R., Forato, L.A., Bortoleto-Bugs, R.K., Fischer, H., Mascarenhas, Y.P., Ward, R.J., Colnago, L.A., 2004. Spectroscopic characterization and structural modeling of prolamin from maize and pearl millet. Eur. Biophys. J. 33 (4), 335–343. https://doi.org/10.1007/s00249-003-0354-3.

Cabra, V., Arreguin, R., Galvez, A., Quirasco, M., Vazquez-duhalt, R., Farres, A., 2005. Characterization of a 19 kDa α-Zein of high purity. J. Agric. Food Chem. 53 (3), 725–729. https://doi.org/10.1021/jf048530s.

Cabra, V., Arreguin, R., Vazquez-Duhalt, R., Farres, A., 2006. Effect of temperature and pH on the secondary structure and processes of oligomerization of 19 kDa alpha-zein. Biochimica et Biophysica Acta (BBA) - Proteins and Proteomics 1764 (6), 1110–1118. https://doi.org/10.1016/j.bbapap.2006.04.002.

Cai, T., Xiao, P., Yu, N., Zhou, Y., Mao, J., Peng, H., Deng, S., 2020. A novel pectin from Akebia trifoliata var. australis fruit peel and its use as a wall-material to coat curcumin-loaded zein nanoparticle. Int. J. Biol. Macromol. 152, 40–49. https://doi.org/10.1016/j.ijbiomac.2020.02.234.

Cai, Z., Chen, L., Yu, X., Yagoub, A.E.G.A., Okonkwo, C.E., Zhou, C., 2022. Effect of molecular weight of chitosan on the formation and properties of zein-nisin-chitosan nanocomplexes. Carbohydr. Polym. 292, 119664. https://doi.org/10.1016/j.carbpol.2022.119664.

Cantó, A.B., Navarro, C.J.G., Javier, G., González-Ferrero, C., Irache, J.M., 2020. Zein nanoparticles improve the oral bioavailability of resveratrol in humans. J. Drug Deliv. Sci. Technol. 57.

Caro, C., Pozo, D., 2015. Polysaccharide colloids as smart vehicles in cancer therapy. Curr. Pharm. Des. 21 (33), 4822–4836. https://doi.org/10.2174/1381612821666150820100812.

Caro, C., Avasthi, A., Paez-Muñoz, J.M., Pernia Leal, M., Garcia-Martin, M.L., 2021. Passive targeting of high-grade gliomas: via the EPR effect: a closed path for metallic nanoparticles? Biomater. Sci. 9 (23), 7984–7995. https://doi.org/10.1039/d1bm01398j.

Carrasco-Sandoval, J., Aranda-Bustos, M., Henríquez-Aedo, K., López-Rubio, A., Fabra, M.J., 2021. Bioaccessibility of different types of phenolic compounds co-encapsulated in alginate/chitosan-coated zein nanoparticles. LWT 149, 112024. https://doi.org/10.1016/j.lwt.2021.112024.

Chacon, C., Verruck, W.D., Monteiro, S., Valencia, G.A., 2023. The mechanism biopolymers and active compounds for the production of nanoparticles by anti-solvent precipitation: a review. Food Res. Int. 168.

Chang, C., Wang, T., Hu, Q., Zhou, M., Xue, J., Luo, Y., 2017. Pectin coating improves physicochemical properties of caseinate/zein nanoparticles as oral delivery vehicles for curcumin. Food Hydrocoll. 70, 143–151. https://doi.org/10.1016/j.foodhyd.2017.03.033.

Chauhan, D.S., Arunkumar, P., Prasad, R., Mishra, S.K., Reddy, B.P.K., De, A., Srivastava, R., 2018. Facile synthesis of plasmonic zein nanoshells for imaging-guided photothermal cancer therapy. Mater. Sci. Eng. C 90, 539–548. https://doi.org/10.1016/j.msec.2018.04.081.

Chen, H.I., Einbond, A., Kwak, S.J., Linn, H., Koepf, E., Peterson, S., Kelly, J.W., Sudol, M., 1997. Characterization of the WW domain of human Yes-associated protein and its polyproline-containing ligands. J. Biol. Chem. 272 (27), 17070–17077. https://doi.org/10.1074/jbc.272.27.17070.

Chen, J., Zheng, J., McClements, D.J., Xiao, H., 2014. Tangeretin-loaded protein nanoparticles fabricated from zein/β-lactoglobulin: preparation, characterization, and functional performance. Food Chem. 158, 466–472. https://doi.org/10.1016/j.foodchem.2014.03.003.

Chen, S., Han, Y., Sun, C., Dai, L., Yang, S., Wei, Y., Mao, L., Fang, Y., Gao, Y., 2018. Effect of molecular weight of hyaluronan on zein-based nanoparticles: fabrication, structural characterization and delivery of curcumin. Carbohydr. Polym. 201, 599–607. https://doi.org/10.1016/j.carbpol.2018.08.116.

Chen, G., Fu, Y., Niu, F., Zhang, H., Li, X., Li, X., 2019. Evaluation of the colloidal/chemical performance of core-shell nanoparticle formed by zein and gum Arabic. Colloids Surf. A Physicochem. Eng. Asp. 560, 130–135. https://doi.org/10.1016/j.colsurfa.2018.10.006.

Chen, S., Li, Q., McClements, D.J., Han, Y., Dai, L., Mao, L., Gao, Y., 2020a. Co-delivery of curcumin and piperine in zein-carrageenan core-shell nanoparticles: formation, structure, stability and in vitro gastrointestinal digestion. Food Hydrocoll. 99, 105334. https://doi.org/10.1016/j.foodhyd.2019.105334.

Chen, S., Ma, X., Han, Y., Yang, W., Guo, Q., Yang, S., Zhang, Y., Liao, W., Gao, Y., 2020b. Effect of chitosan molecular weight on zein-chitosan nanocomplexes: formation, characterization, and the delivery of quercetagetin. Int. J. Biol. Macromol. 164, 2215–2223. https://doi.org/10.1016/j.ijbiomac.2020.07.245.

Chen, Y., Zhao, Z., Xia, G., Xue, F., Chen, C., Zhang, Y., 2020c. Fabrication and characterization of zein/lactoferrin composite nanoparticles for encapsulating 7,8-dihydroxyflavone: enhancement of stability, water solubility and bioaccessibility. Int. J. Biol. Macromol. 146, 179–192. https://doi.org/10.1016/j.ijbiomac.2019.12.251.

Chen, X., Yu, C., Zhang, Y., Wu, Y.C., Ma, Y., Li, H.J., 2023. Co-encapsulation of curcumin and resveratrol in zein-bovine serum albumin nanoparticles using a pH-driven method. Food Funct. 14 (7), 3169–3178. https://doi.org/10.1039/d2fo03929j.

Cheng, C.J., Jones, O.G., 2017. Stabilizing zein nanoparticle dispersions with ι-carrageenan. Food Hydrocoll. 69, 28–35. https://doi.org/10.1016/j.foodhyd.2017.01.022.

Cheng, H.T., Hsieh, S.Y., Chen, T.H., Hung, P.F., Pan, S.H., 2016. Sorafenib-fortified zein-chondroitin sulphate biopolymer nanoparticles as a novel therapeutic system in gastric cancer treatment. RSC Adv. 6 (62), 57266–57274. https://doi.org/10.1039/c6ra06775a.

Cheng, H., Khan, M.A., Xie, Z., Tao, S., Li, Y., Liang, L., 2020. A peppermint oil emulsion stabilized by resveratrol-zein-pectin complex particles: enhancing the chemical stability and antimicrobial activity in combination with the synergistic effect. Food Hydrocoll. 103, 105675. https://doi.org/10.1016/j.foodhyd.2020.105675.

Chuacharoen, T., Sabliov, C.M., 2017. Zein nanoparticles as delivery systems for covalently linked and physically entrapped folic acid. J. Nanoparticle Res. 19 (2). https://doi.org/10.1007/s11051-017-3763-4.

Crawford, L., Wyatt, M., Bryers, J., Ratner, B., 2021. Biocompatibility evolves: Phenomenology to toxicology to regeneration. Adv. Healthcare Mater. (11), 10. https://doi.org/10.1002/adhm.202002153.

Dai, L., Li, R., Wei, Y., Sun, C., Mao, L., Gao, Y., 2018. Fabrication of zein and rhamnolipid complex nanoparticles to enhance the stability and in vitro release of curcumin. Food Hydrocoll. (77), 617–628. https://doi.org/10.1016/j.foodhyd.2017.11.003.

Danhier, F., Feron, O., Préat, V., 2010. To exploit the tumor microenvironment: Passive and active tumor targeting of nanocarriers for anti-cancer drug delivery. J. Contr. Release 148 (2), 135–146. https://doi.org/10.1016/j.jconrel.2010.08.027.

Demir, M., Rivera, L.R.-, Silva, R., Nazhat, S.N., Boccaccini, A.R., 2017. Zein-based composites in biomedical applications. J. Biomed. Mater. Res. 105 (6), 1656–1665. https://doi.org/10.1002/jbm.a.36040.

Dong, J., Sun, Q., Wang, J.Y., 2004. Basic study of corn protein, zein, as a biomaterial in tissue engineering, surface morphology and biocompatibility. Biomaterials 25 (19), 4691–4697. https://doi.org/10.1016/j.biomaterials.2003.10.084.

Dong, F., Dong, X., Zhou, L., Xiao, H., Ho, P.-Y., Wong, M.-S., Wang, Y., 2016. Doxorubicin-loaded biodegradable self-assembly zein nanoparticle and its anti-cancer effect: preparation, in vitro evaluation, and cellular uptake. Colloids Surf. B Biointerfaces 140, 324–331. https://doi.org/10.1016/j.colsurfb.2015.12.048.

Dong, S.R., Xu, H.H., Tan, J.Y., Xie, M.M., Yu, G.P., 2017. The structure and amphipathy characteristics of modified γ-zeins by SDS or alkali in conjunction with heating treatment. Food Chem. 233, 361–368. https://doi.org/10.1016/j.foodchem.2017.04.128.

Dong, P., Rakesh, K.P., Manukumar, H.M., Mohammed, Y.H.E., Karthik, C.S., Sumathi, S., Mallu, P., Qin, H.L., 2019. Innovative nano-carriers in anticancer drug delivery—a comprehensive review. Bioorg. Chem. 85, 325–336. https://doi.org/10.1016/j.bioorg.2019.01.019.

El-Lakany, S.A., Elgindy, N.A., Helmy, M.W., Abu-Serie, M.M., Elzoghby, A.O., 2018. Lactoferrin-decorated vs PEGylated zein nanospheres for combined aromatase inhibitor and herbal therapy of breast cancer. Expet Opin. Drug Deliv. 15 (9), 835–850. https://doi.org/10.1080/17425247.2018.1505858.

El-Lakany, S.A., Kamoun, E.A., Abd-Elhamid, A.I., Aly, R.G., Samy, W.M., Elgindy, N.A., 2020. Graphene oxide crosslinked-zein nanofibrous scaffolds for prominent Cu-adsorption as tissue regeneration promoters in diabetic rats: nanofibers optimization and in vivo assessment. Int. J. Pharm. 590. https://doi.org/10.1016/j.ijpharm.2020.119919.

Elzoghby, A., Freag, M., Mamdouh, H., Elkhodairy, K., 2017a. Zein-based nanocarriers as potential natural alternatives for drug and gene delivery: Focus on cancer therapy. Curr. Pharm. Des. 23 (35), 5261–5271. https://doi.org/10.2174/1381612823666170622111250.

Elzoghby, A.O., El-Lakany, S.A., Helmy, M.W., Abu-Serie, M.M., Elgindy, N.A., 2017b. Shell-crosslinked zein nanocapsules for oral codelivery of exemestane and resveratrol in breast cancer therapy. Nanomedicine 12 (24), 2785–2805. https://doi.org/10.2217/nnm-2017-0247.

Erickson, D.P., Ozturk, O.K., Selling, G., Chen, F., Campanella, O.H., Hamaker, B.R., 2020. Corn zein undergoes conformational changes to higher β-sheet content during its self-assembly in an increasingly hydrophilic solvent. Int. J. Biol. Macromol. 157, 232–239. https://doi.org/10.1016/j.ijbiomac.2020.04.169.

Esmaeili, F., Hossein Ghahremani, M., Esmaeili, B., Reza Khoshayand, M., Atyabi, F., Dinarvand, R., 2008. PLGA nanoparticles of different surface properties: preparation and evaluation of their body distribution. Int. J. Pharm. 349 (1–2), 249–255. https://doi.org/10.1016/j.ijpharm.2007.07.038.

Fabrikov, D., Varga, Á.T., García, M.C.V., Bélteky, P., Kozma, G., Kónya, Z., et al., 2015. Antimicrobial and antioxidant activity of encapsulated tea polyphenols in chitosan/alginate-coated Zein nanoparticles: a possible supplement against fish pathogens in aquaculture. Environ. Sci. Pollut. Res. Int. 25, 47–55.

Fang, C.y., Lou, D.y., Zhou, L.q., Wang, J.c., Yang, B., He, Q.j., Wang, J.j., Weng, Q.j., 2021. Natural products: potential treatments for cisplatin-induced nephrotoxicity. Acta Pharmacol. Sin. 42 (12), 1951–1969. https://doi.org/10.1038/s41401-021-00620-9.

Feng, Z., Khan, M.A., Hao, C., Li, L., 2018. Co-encapsulation of α-tocopherol and resveratrol within zein nanoparticles: impact on antioxidant activity and stability. J. Food Eng. 247, 9–18.

Feng, S., Sun, Y., Wang, D., Sun, P., Shao, P., 2020. Effect of adjusting pH and chondroitin sulfate on the formation of curcumin-zein nanoparticles: synthesis, characterization and morphology. Carbohydr. Polym. 250, 116970. https://doi.org/10.1016/j.carbpol.2020.116970.

Fernández-Carneado, J., Kogan, M.J., Castel, S., Giralt, E., 2004. Potential peptide carriers: Amphipathic proline-rich peptides derived from the n-terminal domain of γ-zein. Angew. Chem. Int. Ed. 43 (14), 1811–1814. https://doi.org/10.1002/anie.200352540.

Fillebeen, C., Descamps, L., Dehouck, M.-P., Fenart, L., Benaissa, M., Spik, G., Cecchelli, R., Pierce, A., 1999. Receptor-mediated transcytosis of lactoferrin through the blood-brain barrier. J. Biol. Chem. 274 (11), 7011–7017. https://doi.org/10.1074/jbc.274.11.7011.

Foerg, C., Ziegler, U., Fernandez-Carneado, J., Giralt, E., Rennert, R., Beck-Sickinger, A.G., Merkle, H.P., 2005. Decoding the entry of two novel cell-penetrating peptides in HeLa cells: Lipid raft-mediated endocytosis and endosomal escape. Biochemistry 44 (1), 72–81. https://doi.org/10.1021/bi048330+.

Forato, L.A., Bicudo, T.De C., Colnago, L.A., 2003. Conformation of α zeins in solid state by Fourier transform IR. Biopolymers 72 (6), 421–426. https://doi.org/10.1002/bip.10481.

Forato, L.A., Doriguetto, A.C., Fischer, H., Mascarenhas, Y.P., Craievich, A.F., Colnago, L.A., 2004. Conformation of the Z19 prolamin by FTIR, NMR, and SAXS. J. Agric. Food Chem. 52 (8), 2382–2385. https://doi.org/10.1021/jf035020+.

Fournier, E., Passirani, C., Montero-Menei, C.N., Benoit, J.P., 2003. Biocompatibility of implantable synthetic polymeric drug carriers: Focus on brain biocompatibility. Biomaterials 24 (19), 3311–3331. https://doi.org/10.1016/s0142-9612(03)00161-3.

Gaber, M., Elhasany, K.A., Sabra, S., Helmy, M.W., Fang, J.Y., Khattab, S.N., Bekhit, A.A., Teleb, M., Elkodairy, K. A., Elzoghby, A.O., 2020. Co-administration of tretinoin enhances the anti-cancer efficacy of etoposide via tumor-targeted green nano-micelles. Colloids Surf. B Biointerfaces 192. https://doi.org/10.1016/j.colsurfb.2020.110997.

Gagliardi, A., Bonacci, S., Paolino, D., Celia, C., Procopio, A., Fresta, M., Cosco, D., 2019. Paclitaxel-loaded sodium deoxycholate-stabilized zein nanoparticles: characterization and in vitro cytotoxicity. Heliyon 5 (9), e02422. https://doi.org/10.1016/j.heliyon.2019.e02422.

Gagliardi, A., Froiio, F., Salvatici, M.C., Paolino, D., Fresta, M., Cosco, D., 2020. Characterization and refinement of zein-based gels. Food Hydrocoll. 101, 105555. https://doi.org/10.1016/j.foodhyd.2019.105555.

Gagliardi, A., Paolino, D., Costa, N., Fresta, M., Cosco, D., 2021. Zein- vs PLGA-based nanoparticles containing rutin: a comparative investigation. Mater. Sci. Eng. C 118, 111538. https://doi.org/10.1016/j.msec.2020.111538.

Gautam, M., Santhiya, D., Dey, N., 2020. Zein coated calcium carbonate nanoparticles for the targeted controlled release of model antibiotic and nutrient across the intestine. Mater. Today Commun. 25, 101394. https://doi.org/10.1016/j.mtcomm.2020.101394.

Ghalei, S., Asadi, H., Ghalei, B., 2018. Zein nanoparticle-embedded electrospun PVA nanofibers as wound dressing for topical delivery of anti-inflammatory diclofenac. J. Appl. Polym. Sci. 135 (33). https://doi.org/10.1002/app.46643.

Ghobadi-Oghaz, N., Asoodeh, A., Mohammadi, M., 2022. Fabrication, characterization and in vitro cell exposure study of zein-chitosan nanoparticles for co-delivery of curcumin and berberine. Int. J. Biol. Macromol. 204, 576–586. https://doi.org/10.1016/j.ijbiomac.2022.02.041.

Gomez-Estaca, J., Balaguer, M.P., Gavara, R., Hernandez-Munoz, P., 2012. Formation of zein nanoparticles by electrohydrodynamic atomization: effect of the main processing variables and suitability for encapsulating the food coloring and active ingredient curcumin. Food Hydrocoll. 28 (1), 82–91. https://doi.org/10.1016/j.foodhyd.2011.11.013.

Gong, S., Wang, H., Sun, Q., Xue, S., Wang, J., 2006. Mechanical properties and in vitro biocompatibility of porous zein scaffolds. Biomaterials 27 (20), 3793–3799. https://doi.org/10.1016/j.biomaterials.2006.02.019.

Gronthos, S., Franklin, D.M., Leddy, H.A., Robey, P.G., Storms, R.W., Gimble, J.M., 2001. Surface protein characterization of human adipose tissue-derived stromal cells. J. Cell. Physiol. 189 (1), 54–63. https://doi.org/10.1002/jcp.1138.

Gupta, R.C., Lall, R., Srivastava, A., Sinha, A., 2019. Hyaluronic acid: molecular mechanisms and therapeutic trajectory. Front. Vet. Sci. 6. https://doi.org/10.3389/fvets.2019.00192.

Handali, S., Moghimipour, E., Kouchak, M., Ramezani, Z., Amini, M., Angali, K.A., Saremy, S., Dorkoosh, F.A., Rezaei, M., 2019. New folate receptor targeted nano liposomes for delivery of 5-fluorouracil to cancer cells: strong implication for enhanced potency and safety. Life Sci. 227, 39–50. https://doi.org/10.1016/j.lfs.2019.04.030.

Hassan, E.A., Hathout, R.M., Gad, H.A., Sammour, O.A., 2022. Multi-purpose zein nanoparticles for battling hepatocellular carcinoma: a Green approach. Eur. Polym. J. 176. https://doi.org/10.1016/j.eurpolymj.2022.111396.

Hou, H., Zhang, D., Lin, J., Zhang, Y., Li, C., Wang, Z., Ren, J., Yao, M., Wong, K.H., Wang, Y., 2018. Zein-paclitaxel prodrug nanoparticles for redox-triggered drug delivery and enhanced therapeutic efficiency. J. Agric. Food Chem. 66 (44), 11812–11822. https://doi.org/10.1021/acs.jafc.8b04627.

Hou, H., Zhang, D., Zeng, J., Zhou, L., Wang, Z., Yao, M., Ren, J., Hu, N., Wang, Y., 2019. Bilayer nanocarriers with protein–acid conjugation for prolonged release and enhanced anticancer effects. Langmuir 35 (10), 3710–3716. https://doi.org/10.1021/acs.langmuir.8b02882.

Hu, K., McClements, D.J., 2014. Fabrication of surfactant-stabilized zein nanoparticles: a pH modulated antisolvent precipitation method. Food Res. Int. 64, 329–335. https://doi.org/10.1016/j.foodres.2014.07.004.

Hu, K., McClements, D.J., 2015. Fabrication of biopolymer nanoparticles by antisolvent precipitation and electrostatic deposition: zein-alginate core/shell nanoparticles. Food Hydrocoll. 44, 101–108. https://doi.org/10.1016/j.foodhyd.2014.09.015.

Hu, K., Huang, X., Gao, Y., Huang, X., Xiao, H., McClements, D.J., 2015. Core-shell biopolymer nanoparticle delivery systems: synthesis and characterization of curcumin fortified zein-pectin nanoparticles. Food Chem. 182, 275–281. https://doi.org/10.1016/j.foodchem.2015.03.009.

Huang, W., Li, S., Li, Z., Zhu, W., Lu, S., Jiang, Y., 2019. Development of a resveratrol–zein–dopamine–lecithin delivery system with enhanced stability and mucus permeation. J. Mater. Sci. 54 (11), 8591–8601. https://doi.org/10.1007/s10853-019-03465-0.

Huang, W., Deng, Y., Ye, L., Xie, Q., Jiang, Y., 2021. Enhancing hemocompatibility and the performance of Au@silica nanoparticles by coating with cRGD functionalized zein. Mater. Sci. Eng. C 125, 112064. https://doi.org/10.1016/j.msec.2021.112064.

Huang, W., Li, Z., Liu, W., Liu, S., Zhou, R., Jiang, Y., 2023. Preparation of B16 cancer cell membrane coated α-zein biomimetic drug delivery system for the enhancement of homotypic target ability. Ind. Crop. Prod. 194. https://doi.org/10.1016/j.indcrop.2023.116301.

Hughes, R.E., Olson, J.M., 2001. Therapeutic opportunities in polyglutamine disease. Nat. Med. 7 (4), 419–423. https://doi.org/10.1038/86486.

Van Hung, P., 2016. Phenolic compounds of cereals and their antioxidant capacity. Crit. Rev. Food Sci. Nutr. 56 (1), 25–35. https://doi.org/10.1080/10408398.2012.708909.

Hurtado-López, P., Murdan, S., 2006. An investigation into the adjuvanticity and immunogenicity of zein microspheres being researched as drug and vaccine carriers. J. Pharm. Pharmacol. 58 (6), 769–774. https://doi.org/10.1211/jpp.58.6.0007.

Jiang, R., Lopez, V., Kelleher, S.L., Lönnerdal, B., 2011. Apo- and holo-lactoferrin are both internalized by lactoferrin receptor via clathrin-mediated endocytosis but differentially affect ERK-signaling and cell proliferation in Caco-2 cells. J. Cell. Physiol. 226 (11), 3022–3031. https://doi.org/10.1002/jcp.22650.

Jiang, L., Li, L., He, X., Yi, Q., He, B., Cao, J., Pan, W., Gu, Z., 2015. Overcoming drug-resistant lung cancer by paclitaxel loaded dual-functional liposomes with mitochondria targeting and pH-response. Biomaterials 52 (1), 126–139. https://doi.org/10.1016/j.biomaterials.2015.02.004.

Jin, J., Krishnamachary, B., Barnett, J.D., Chatterjee, S., Chang, D., Mironchik, Y., Wildes, F., Jaffee, E.M., Nimmagadda, S., Bhujwalla, Z.M., 2019. Human cancer cell membrane-coated biomimetic nanoparticles reduce fibroblast-mediated invasion and metastasis and induce t-cells. ACS Appl. Mater. Interfaces 11 (8), 7850–7861. https://doi.org/10.1021/acsami.8b22309.

Kaushik, P., Priyadarshini, E., Rawat, K., Rajamani, P., Bohidar, H.B., 2020. pH responsive doxorubucin loaded zein nanoparticle crosslinked pectin hydrogel as effective site-specific anticancer substrates. Int. J. Biol. Macromol. 152, 1027–1037. https://doi.org/10.1016/j.ijbiomac.2019.10.190.

Kawabata, Y., Wada, K., Nakatani, M., Yamada, S., Onoue, S., 2011. Formulation design for poorly water-soluble drugs based on biopharmaceutics classification system: Basic approaches and practical applications. Int. J. Pharm. 420 (1), 1–10. https://doi.org/10.1016/j.ijpharm.2011.08.032.

Kell, D.B., Heyden, E.L., Pretorius, E., 2020. The biology of lactoferrin, an iron-binding protein that can help defend against viruses and bacteria. Front. Immunol. 11. https://doi.org/10.3389/fimmu.2020.01221.

Kikushima, K., Kamiya, R., 2008. Clockwise translocation of microtubules by flagellar inner-arm dyneins in vitro. Biophys. J. 94 (10), 4014–4019. https://doi.org/10.1529/biophysj.107.123083.

Kim, Y., Park, C.H., An, J.S., Choi, S.H., Kim, T.W., 2021. Biocompatible artificial synapses based on a zein active layer obtained from maize for neuromorphic computing. Sci. Rep. 11 (1). https://doi.org/10.1038/s41598-021-00076-1.

Kong, J., Ge, X., Sun, Y., Mao, M., Yu, H., Chu, R., Wang, Y., 2023. Multi-functional pH-sensitive active and intelligent packaging based on highly cross-linked zein for the monitoring of pork freshness. Food Chem. 404, 134754. https://doi.org/10.1016/j.foodchem.2022.134754.

Lai, L.F., Guo, H.X., 2011. Preparation of new 5-fluorouracil-loaded zein nanoparticles for liver targeting. Int. J. Pharm. 404 (1–2), 317–323. https://doi.org/10.1016/j.ijpharm.2010.11.025.

Lan, X., Zhang, X., Wang, L., Wang, H., Hu, Z., Ju, X., Yuan, Y., 2023. A review of food preservation based on zein: the perspective from application types of coating and film. Food Chem. 424, 136403. https://doi.org/10.1016/j.foodchem.2023.136403.

Lee, S.H., Benmoussa, M., Sathe, S.K., Roux, K.H., Teuber, S.S., Hamaker, B.R., 2005. A 50 kDa maize γ-zein has marked cross-reactivity with the almond major protein. J. Agric. Food Chem. 53 (20), 7965–7970. https://doi.org/10.1021/jf0479618.

Lee, E.S., Gao, Z., Han Bae, Y., 2008. Recent progress in tumor pH targeting nanotechnology. J. Contr. Release 132 (3), 164–170. https://doi.org/10.1016/j.jconrel.2008.05.003.

Lepeltier, E., Bourgaux, C., Couvreur, P., 2014. Nanoprecipitation and the "Ouzo effect": application to drug delivery devices. Adv. Drug Deliv. Rev. 71, 86–97. https://doi.org/10.1016/j.addr.2013.12.009.

Li, C., Song, R., 2020. The regulation of zein biosynthesis in maize endosperm. Theoretical and Applied Genetics 133 (5), 1443–1453. https://doi.org/10.1007/s00122-019-03520-z.

Li, Y., Lim, L.-T., Kakuda, Y., 2009. Electrospun zein fibers as carriers to stabilize (−)-Epigallocatechin gallate. J. Food Sci. 74 (3), C233. https://doi.org/10.1111/j.1750-3841.2009.01093.x.

Li, L., Xinbao, H., Qin, J., Tang, W., He, F., Smith, A., Zhang, M., Simeone, D.M., Qiao, X.T., Chen, Z.-N., Lawrence, T.S., Xu, L., 2014. Antibody against CD44s inhibits pancreatic tumor initiation and postradiation recurrence in mice. Gastroenterology 146 (4), 1108. https://doi.org/10.1053/j.gastro.2013.12.035.

Li, J., Xu, X., Chen, Z., Wang, T., Lu, Z., Hu, W., Wang, L., 2018a. Zein/gum Arabic nanoparticle-stabilized pickering emulsion with thymol as an antibacterial delivery system. Carbohydr. Polym. 200, 416–426. https://doi.org/10.1016/j.carbpol.2018.08.025.

Li, M.F., Chen, L., Xu, M.Z., Zhang, J.L., Wang, Q., Zeng, Q.Z., Wei, X.C., Yuan, Y., 2018b. The formation of zein-chitosan complex coacervated particles: Relationship to encapsulation and controlled release properties. Int. J. Biol. Macromol. 116, 1232–1239. https://doi.org/10.1016/j.ijbiomac.2018.05.107.

Li, Z., Liu, W., Sun, C., Wei, X., Liu, S., Jiang, Y., 2023. Gastrointestinal pH-sensitive pickering emulsions stabilized by zein nanoparticles coated with bioactive glycyrrhizic acid for improving oral bioaccessibility of curcumin. ACS Appl. Mater. Interfaces. https://doi.org/10.1021/acsami.2c21549.

Li, S., Liu, X., Zhang, X., Fan, L., Wang, F., Zhou, J., Zhang, H., 2024. Preparation and characterization of zein-tannic acid nanoparticles/chitosan composite films and application in the preservation of sugar oranges. Food Chem. 437, 137673. https://doi.org/10.1016/j.foodchem.2023.137673.

Liang, Q., Chalamaiah, M., Liao, W., Ren, X., Wu, J., 2004. Zein hydrolysate and its peptides exert anti-inflammatory activity on endothelial cells by preventing TNF-α-induced NF-κB activation. Ann. N. Y. Acad. Sci. 64, 195–203.

Liang, H., Zhou, B., Li, J., Xu, W., Liu, S., Li, Y., Chen, Y., Li, B., 2015. Supramolecular design of coordination bonding architecture on zein nanoparticles for pH-responsive anticancer drug delivery. Colloids Surf. B Biointerfaces 136, 1224–1233. https://doi.org/10.1016/j.colsurfb.2015.09.037.

Liang, Q., Ren, X., Zhang, X., Hou, T., Chalamaiah, M., Ma, H., Xu, B., 2018a. Effect of ultrasound on the preparation of resveratrol-loaded zein particles. J. Food Eng. 221, 88–94. https://doi.org/10.1016/j.jfoodeng.2017.10.002.

Liang, Q., Chalamaiah, M., Ren, X., Ma, H., Wu, J., 2018b. Identification of new anti-inflammatory peptides from zein hydrolysate after simulated gastrointestinal digestion and transport in Caco-2 cells. J. Agric. Food Chem. 66 (5), 1114–1120. https://doi.org/10.1021/acs.jafc.7b04562.

Liu, C.N., Rubenstein, I., 1992. Genomic organization of an α-zein gene cluster in maize. MGG Molecular & General Genetics 231 (2), 304–312. https://doi.org/10.1007/BF00279804.

Liu, X., Xie, Y., Li, W., Wen, S., Li, Y., Tong, Z., Ni, H., Huselstein, C., Wang, X., Chen, Y., 2015. Structure, physical properties, hemocompatibility and cytocompatibility of starch/zein composites. Bio Med. Mater. Eng. 25 (s1), 47–55. https://doi.org/10.3233/bme-141227.

Liu, Q., Han, C., Tian, Y., Liu, T., 2020a. Fabrication of curcumin-loaded zein nanoparticles stabilized by sodium caseinate/sodium alginate: curcumin solubility, thermal properties, rheology, and stability. Process Biochemistry 94, 30–38. https://doi.org/10.1016/j.procbio.2020.03.017.

Liu, Y., Liang, X., Zou, Y., Peng, Y., McClements, D.J., Hu, K., 2020b. Resveratrol-loaded biopolymer core-shell nanoparticles: bioavailability and anti-inflammatory effects. Food Funct. 11 (5), 4014–4025. https://doi.org/10.1039/d0fo00195c.

Liu, J., Li, Y., Zhang, H., Liu, S., Yang, M., Cui, M., Zhang, T., Yu, Y., Xiao, H., Du, Z., 2022a. Fabrication, characterization and functional attributes of zein-egg white derived peptides (EWDP)-chitosan ternary nanoparticles for encapsulation of curcumin: role of EWDP. Food Chem. 372, 131266. https://doi.org/10.1016/j.foodchem.2021.131266.

Liu, L., Yang, S., Chen, F., Cheng, K.W., 2022b. Hyaluronic acid-zein core-shell nanoparticles improve the anticancer effect of curcumin alone or in combination with oxaliplatin against colorectal cancer via Cd44-mediated cellular uptake. Molecules 27.

Liu, Q., Qin, Y., Jiang, B., Chen, J., Zhang, T., 2022c. Development of self-assembled zein-fucoidan complex nanoparticles as a delivery system for resveratrol. Colloids Surf. B Biointerfaces 216, 112529. https://doi.org/10.1016/j.colsurfb.2022.112529.

Loftsson, T., Brewster, M.E., 2010. Pharmaceutical applications of cyclodextrins: Basic science and product development. J. Pharm. Pharmacol. 62 (11), 1607–1621. https://doi.org/10.1111/j.2042-7158.2010.01030.x.

Marco, I.De, 2022. Zein microparticles and nanoparticles as drug delivery systems. Polymers 14.

Masimirembwa, C.M., Bredberg, U., Andersson, T.B., 2003. Metabolic stability for drug discovery and development: Pharmacokinetic and biochemical challenges. Clin. Pharmacokinet. 42 (6), 515–528. https://doi.org/10.2165/00003088-200342060-00002.

Maviah, M.B.J., Farooq, M.A., Mavlyanova, R., Veroniaina, H., Filli, M.S., Aquib, M., Kesse, S., Boakye-Yiadom, K. O., Wang, B., 2020. Food protein-based nanodelivery systems for hydrophobic and poorly soluble compounds. AAPS PharmSciTech 21 (3). https://doi.org/10.1208/s12249-020-01641-z.

McClements, D.J., 2020. Nano-enabled personalized nutrition: developing multicomponent-bioactive colloidal delivery systems. Adv. Colloid Interface Sci. 282, 102211. https://doi.org/10.1016/j.cis.2020.102211.

McKee, C.M., Penno, M.B., Cowman, M., Burdick, M.D., Strieter, R.M., Bao, C., Noble, P.W., 1996. Hyaluronan (HA) fragments induce chemokine gene expression in alveolar macrophages: the role of HA size and CD44. J. Clin. Investig. 98 (10), 2403–2413. https://doi.org/10.1172/JCI119054.

Middleton, J.C., Tipton, A.J., 2000. Synthetic biodegradable polymers as orthopedic devices. Biomaterials 21 (23), 2335–2346. https://doi.org/10.1016/S0142-9612(00)00101-0.

Milewska, A., Zarebski, M., Nowak, P., Stozek, K., Potempa, J., Pyrc, K., Perlman, S., 2014. Human coronavirus NL63 utilizes heparan sulfate proteoglycans for attachment to target cells. J. Virol. 88 (22), 13221–13230. https://doi.org/10.1128/jvi.02078-14.

Monteiro, R.A., Camara, M.C., de Oliveira, J.L., Campos, E.V.R., Carvalho, L.B., Proença, P.L.d.F., Guilger-Casagrande, M., Lima, R., do Nascimento, J., Gonçalves, K.C., Polanczyk, R.A., Fraceto, L.F., 2021. Zein based-nanoparticles loaded botanical pesticides in pest control: an enzyme stimuli-responsive approach aiming sustainable agriculture. J. Hazard Mater. 417. https://doi.org/10.1016/j.jhazmat.2021.126004.

Muthuselvi, L., Dhathathreyan, A., 2006. Simple coacervates of zein to encapsulate Gitoxin. Colloids Surf. B Biointerfaces 51 (1), 39–43. https://doi.org/10.1016/j.colsurfb.2006.05.012. ISSN 0927-7765.

Nakamura, Y., Mochida, A., Choyke, P.L., Kobayashi, H., 2016. Nanodrug delivery: is the enhanced permeability and retention effect sufficient for curing cancer? Bioconjug. Chem. 27 (10), 2225–2238. https://doi.org/10.1021/acs.bioconjchem.6b00437.

Nichols, J.W., Bae, Y.H., 2014. EPR: Evidence and fallacy. J. Contr. Release 190, 451–464. https://doi.org/10.1016/j.jconrel.2014.03.057.

Oleandro, E., Stanzione, M., Buonocore, G.G., Lavorgna, M., 2024. Zein-based nanoparticles as active platforms for sustainable applications: recent advances and perspectives. Nanomaterials 14 (5). https://doi.org/10.3390/nano14050414.

Paliwal, R., Palakurthi, S., 2014. Zein in controlled drug delivery and tissue engineering. J. Contr. Release 189, 108–122. https://doi.org/10.1016/j.jconrel.2014.06.036.

Park, H.S., Nahm, D.H., 1997. Identification of IgE - binding components in occupational asthma caused by corn dust. Ann. Allergy Asthma Immunol. 79 (1), 75–79. https://doi.org/10.1016/S1081-1206(10)63089-X.

Parker, N., Turk, M.J., Westrick, E., Lewis, J.D., Low, P.S., Leamon, C.P., 2005. Folate receptor expression in carcinomas and normal tissues determined by a quantitative radioligand binding assay. Anal. Biochem. 338 (2), 284–293. https://doi.org/10.1016/j.ab.2004.12.026.

Pasini, G., Simonato, B., Curioni, A., Vincenzi, S., Cristaudo, A., Santucci, B., Dal Belin Peruffo, A., Giannattasio, M., 2002. IgE-mediated allergy to corn: a 50 kDa protein, belonging to the reduced soluble proteins, is a major allergen. Allergy 57 (2), 98–106. https://doi.org/10.1034/j.1398-9995.2002.1o3413.x.

Patel, A.R., Velikov, K.P., 2011. Colloidal delivery systems in foods: a general comparison with oral drug delivery. LWT - Food Sci. Technol. (Lebensmittel-Wissenschaft -Technol.) 44 (9), 1958–1964. https://doi.org/10.1016/j.lwt.2011.04.005.

Patel, A., Hu, Y., Tiwari, J.K., Velikov, K.P., 2010. Synthesis and characterisation of zein-curcumin colloidal particles. Soft Matter 6 (24), 6192–6199. https://doi.org/10.1039/c0sm00800a.

Patel, A.R., Heussen, P.C.M., Hazekamp, J., Drost, E., Velikov, K.P., 2012. Quercetin loaded biopolymeric colloidal particles prepared by simultaneous precipitation of quercetin with hydrophobic protein in aqueous medium. Food Chem. 133 (2), 423–429. https://doi.org/10.1016/j.foodchem.2012.01.054.

Paulos, C.M., Turk, M.J., Breur, G.J., Low, P.S., 2004. Folate receptor-mediated targeting of therapeutic and imaging agents to activated macrophages in rheumatoid arthritis. Adv. Drug Deliv. Rev. 56 (8), 1205–1217. https://doi.org/10.1016/j.addr.2004.01.012.

Peñalva, R., Esparza, I., González-Navarro, C.J., Quincoces, G., Peñuelas, I., Irache, J.M., 2015. Zein nanoparticles for oral folic acid delivery. J. Drug Deliv. Sci. Technol. 30, 450–457. https://doi.org/10.1016/j.jddst.2015.06.012.

Penalva, R., Esparza, I., Larraneta, E., González-Navarro, C.J., Gamazo, C., Irache, J.M., 2015. Zein-based nanoparticles improve the oral bioavailability of resveratrol and its anti-inflammatory effects in a mouse model of endotoxic shock. J. Agric. Food Chem. 63 (23), 5603–5611. https://doi.org/10.1021/jf505694e.

Penalva, R., González-Navarro, C.J., Gamazo, C., Esparza, I., Irache, J.M., 2017. Zein nanoparticles for oral delivery of quercetin: Pharmacokinetic studies and preventive anti-inflammatory effects in a mouse model of endotoxemia. Nanomed. Nanotechnol. Biol. Med. 13 (1), 103–110. https://doi.org/10.1016/j.nano.2016.08.033.

O.P. Perumal, Podaralla, R.S. Kaushik, Method of forming non-immunogenic hydrophobic protein nanoparticles and uses therefor. (2009).

Ponta, H., Sherman, L., Herrlich, P.A., 2003. CD44: from adhesion molecules to signalling regulators. Nat. Rev. Mol. Cell Biol. 4 (1), 33–45. https://doi.org/10.1038/nrm1004.

Qi, L., Luo, Q., Zhang, Y., Jia, F., Zhao, Y., Wang, F., 2019. Advances in toxicological research of the anticancer drug cisplatin. Chem. Res. Toxicol. 32 (8), 1469–1486. https://doi.org/10.1021/acs.chemrestox.9b00204.

Qiao, H., Chen, Z., Fu, S., Yu, X., Sun, M., Zhai, Y., Sun, J., 2022. Emerging platinum(0) nanotherapeutics for efficient cancer therapy. J. Contr. Release 352, 276–287. https://doi.org/10.1016/j.jconrel.2022.10.021.

Rawat, P., Kumar, S., Sheokand, N., Raje, C.I., Raje, M., 2012. The multifunctional glycolytic protein glyceraldehyde-3-phosphate dehydrogenase (GAPDH) is a novel macrophage lactoferrin receptor. Biochem. Cell. Biol. 90 (3), 329–338. https://doi.org/10.1139/o11-058.

Raza, A., Hayat, U., Bilal, M., Iqbal, H.M.N., Wang, J.-Y., 2020. Zein-based micro- and nano-constructs and biologically therapeutic cues with multi-functionalities for oral drug delivery systems. J. Drug Deliv. Sci. Technol. 58, 101818. https://doi.org/10.1016/j.jddst.2020.101818.

Razavi, R., Esmaeilzadeh Kenari, R., Farmani, J., Jahanshahi, M., 2021. Preparation of double-layer nanoemulsions with controlled release of glucose as prevention of hypoglycemia in diabetic patients. Biomed. Pharmacother. 138, 111464. https://doi.org/10.1016/j.biopha.2021.111464.

Reddy, N., Yang, Y., 2011. Potential of plant proteins for medical applications. Trends Biotechnol. 29 (10), 490–498. https://doi.org/10.1016/j.tibtech.2011.05.003.

Rivera, L.R., Cochis, A., Biser, S., Canciani, E., Ferraris, S., Rimondini, L., Boccaccini, A.R., 2021. Antibacterial, pro-angiogenic and pro-osteointegrative zein-bioactive glass/copper based coatings for implantable stainless steel aimed at bone healing. Bioact. Mater. 6 (5), 1479–1490. https://doi.org/10.1016/j.bioactmat.2020.11.001.

Ruan, J., Yang, Y., Yang, F., Wan, K., Fan, D., Wang, D., 2018. Novel oral administrated ellagic acid nanoparticles for enhancing oral bioavailability and anti-inflammatory efficacy. J. Drug Deliv. Sci. Technol. 46, 215–222. https://doi.org/10.1016/j.jddst.2018.05.021.

Sabra, S.A., Elzoghby, A.O., Sheweita, S.A., Haroun, M., Helmy, M.W., Eldemellawy, M.A., Xia, Y., Goodale, D., Allan, A.L., Rohani, S., 2018. Self-assembled amphiphilic zein-lactoferrin micelles for tumor targeted co-delivery of rapamycin and wogonin to breast cancer. Eur. J. Pharm. Biopharm. 128, 156–169. https://doi.org/10.1016/j.ejpb.2018.04.023.

Salvador-Reyes, R., Rebellato, A.P., Lima Pallone, J.A., Ferrari, R.A., Clerici, M.T.P.S., 2021. Kernel characterization and starch morphology in five varieties of Peruvian Andean maize. Food Res. Int. 140. https://doi.org/10.1016/j.foodres.2020.110044.

m Y Seok, Rejinold, KM Lekshmi, K Cherukula, Park, Cd44 targeting biocompatible and biodegradable hyaluronic acid cross-linked Zein Nanogels for curcumin delivery to Cancer cells: in vitro and in vivo evaluation . J Control Release.

Seok, H.Y., Sanoj Rejinold, N., Lekshmi, K.M., Cherukula, K., Park, I.K., Kim, Y.C., 2018. CD44 targeting biocompatible and biodegradable hyaluronic acid cross-linked zein nanogels for curcumin delivery to cancer cells: in vitro and in vivo evaluation. J. Contr. Release 280, 20–30. https://doi.org/10.1016/j.jconrel.2018.04.050.

Song, J., Sun, C., Gul, K., Mata, A., Fang, Y., 2021. Prolamin-based complexes: structure design and food-related applications. Compr. Rev. Food Sci. Food Saf. 20 (2), 1120–1149. https://doi.org/10.1111/1541-4337.12713.

Sousa, F.F.O., Luzardo-Álvarez, A., Blanco-Méndez, J., Otero-Espinar, F.J., Martín-Pastor, M., Sández Macho, I., 2013. Use of 1H NMR STD, WaterLOGSY, and Langmuir monolayer techniques for characterization of drug–zein protein complexes. Eur. J. Pharm. Biopharm. 85 (3), 790–798. https://doi.org/10.1016/j.ejpb.2013.07.008.

S.R. Sturgeon, Brinton, S.S. Devesa, Kurman, situ and invasive vulvar cancer incidence trends. 166 (1973).

Sun, X., Pan, C., Ying, Z., Yu, D., Duan, X., Huang, F., Ling, J., Ouyang, X.k., 2020. Stabilization of zein nanoparticles with k-carrageenan and tween 80 for encapsulation of curcumin. Int. J. Biol. Macromol. 146, 549–559. https://doi.org/10.1016/j.ijbiomac.2020.01.053.

Sung, H., Ferlay, J., Siegel, R.L., Laversanne, M., Soerjomataram, I., Jemal, A., Bray, F., 2021. Global cancer statistics 2020: GLOBOCAN estimates of incidence and mortality worldwide for 36 cancers in 185 Countries. CA Cancer J. Clin. 71 (3), 209–249. https://doi.org/10.3322/caac.21660.

Tan, Y., McClements, D.J., 2021. Plant-based colloidal delivery systems for bioactives. Molecules 26 (22), 6895. https://doi.org/10.3390/molecules26226895.

Tchuenbou-Magaia, F.L., Tolve, R., Anyadike, U., Giarola, M., Favati, F., 2022. Co-encapsulation of vitamin D and rutin in chitosan-zein microparticles. J. Food Meas. Char. 16 (3), 2060–2070. https://doi.org/10.1007/s11694-022-01340-2.

Toole, B.P., 2004. Hyaluronan: from extracellular glue to pericellular cue. Nat. Rev. Cancer 4 (7), 528–539. https://doi.org/10.1038/nrc1391.

Tsuji, R., Ogata, S., Mochizuki, S., 2022. Interaction between CD44 and highly condensed hyaluronic acid through crosslinking with proteins. Bioorg. Chem. 121, 105666. https://doi.org/10.1016/j.bioorg.2022.105666.

Turk, M.J., Waters, D.J., Low, P.S., 2004. Folate-conjugated liposomes preferentially target macrophages associated with ovarian carcinoma. Cancer Lett. 213 (2), 165–172. https://doi.org/10.1016/j.canlet.2003.12.028.

Vasvani, S., Kulkarni, P., Rawtani, D., 2020. Hyaluronic acid: a review on its biology, aspects of drug delivery, route of administrations and a special emphasis on its approved marketed products and recent clinical studies. Int. J. Biol. Macromol. 151, 1012–1029. https://doi.org/10.1016/j.ijbiomac.2019.11.066.

Wang, Y., Padua, G.W., 2010. Formation of zein microphases in ethanol-water. Langmuir 26 (15), 12897–12901. https://doi.org/10.1021/la101688v.

Wang, Y., Padua, G.W., 2012. Nanoscale characterization of zein self-assembly. Langmuir 28 (5), 2429–2435. https://doi.org/10.1021/la204204j.

Wang, H., Gong, S., Lin, Z., Fu, J., Xue, S., Huang, J., Wang, J., 2007. In vivo biocompatibility and mechanical properties of porous zein scaffolds. Biomaterials 28 (27), 3952–3964. https://doi.org/10.1016/j.biomaterials.2007.05.017.

Wang, H., Zhu, W., Huang, Y., Li, Z., Jiang, Y., Xie, Q., 2017. Facile encapsulation of hydroxycamptothecin nanocrystals into zein-based nanocomplexes for active targeting in drug delivery and cell imaging. Acta Biomater. 61, 88–100. https://doi.org/10.1016/j.actbio.2017.04.017.

Wang, H., Zhang, X., Zhu, W., Jiang, Y., Zhang, Z., 2018. Self-assembly of zein-based microcarrier system for colon-targeted oral drug delivery. Ind. Eng. Chem. Res. 57 (38), 12689–12699. https://doi.org/10.1021/acs.iecr.8b02092.

Wang, G., Han, J., Meng, X., Kang, S.S., Liu, X., Sun, Y.E., Luo, Q., Ye, K., 2023a. Zein-based nanoparticles improve the therapeutic efficacy of a TrkB agonist toward alzheimer's disease. ACS Chem. Neurosci. 14 (17), 3249–3264. https://doi.org/10.1021/acschemneuro.3c00401.

Wang, Y., Zhang, C., Xiao, M., Ganesan, K., Gao, F., Liu, Q., Ye, Z., Sui, Y., Zhang, F., Wei, K., Wu, Y., Wu, J., Du, B., Xu, C., Li, Y., Peng, L., Zhang, J., Chen, J., 2023b. A tumor-targeted delivery of oral isoliquiritigenin through encapsulated zein phosphatidylcholine hybrid nanoparticles prevents triple-negative breast cancer. J. Drug Deliv. Sci. Technol. 79, 103922. https://doi.org/10.1016/j.jddst.2022.103922.

Williams, D., 1987. Proceedings of a Consensus Conference of the European Society for Biomaterials; Proceedings.

Williams, D.F., 2008. On the mechanisms of biocompatibility. Biomaterials 29 (20), 2941–2953. https://doi.org/10.1016/j.biomaterials.2008.04.023.

Wu, A., Chen, C., Lu, J., Sun, J., Xiao, M., Yue, X., Zhou, P., Zhao, S., Zhong, G., Huang, C., Qu, Y., Zhang, C., 2022. Preparation of oral core–shell zein nanoparticles to improve the bioavailability of glycyrrhizic acid for the treatment of ulcerative colitis. Biomacromolecules 23 (1), 210–225. https://doi.org/10.1021/acs.biomac.1c01233.

Wusigale, T.W., Hu, Q., Xue, J., Khan, M.A., Liang, L., Luo, Y., 2021. Partition and stability of folic acid and caffeic acid in hollow zein particles coated with chitosan. Int. J. Biol. Macromol. 183, 2282–2292. https://doi.org/10.1016/j.ijbiomac.2021.05.216.

Xu, Q.B., Zhang, X., Yang, 2000. Folate-mediated chemotherapy and diagnostics: an updated review and outlook. J Control Release 252, 129–132.

Xu, H., Zhang, Y., Jiang, Q., Reddy, N., Yang, Y., 2013. Biodegradable hollow zein nanoparticles for removal of reactive dyes from wastewater. J. Environ. Manag. 125, 33–40. https://doi.org/10.1016/j.jenvman.2013.03.050.

Yan, X., Li, M., Xu, X., Liu, X., Liu, F., 2022. Zein-based nano-delivery systems for encapsulation and protection of hydrophobic bioactives: a review. Front. Nutr. 9. https://doi.org/10.3389/fnut.2022.999373.

Yu, X., Han, N., Dong, Z., Dang, Y., Zhang, Q., Hu, W., Wang, C., Du, S., Lu, Y., 2022. Combined chemo-immuno-photothermal therapy for effective cancer treatment via an all-in-one and one-for-all nanoplatform. ACS Appl. Mater. Interfaces 14 (38), 42988–43009. https://doi.org/10.1021/acsami.2c12969.

Yuan, Y., Ma, M., Zhang, S., Liu, C., Chen, P., Li, H., Wang, D., Xu, Y., 2021. Effect of sophorolipid on the curcumin-loaded ternary composite nanoparticles self-assembled from zein and chondroitin sulfate. Food Hydrocoll. (113), 106493. https://doi.org/10.1016/j.foodhyd.2020.106493.

Zhang, H., Zhai, Y., Wang, J., Zhai, G., 2016a. New progress and prospects: the application of nanogel in drug delivery. Mater. Sci. Eng. C 60, 560–568. https://doi.org/10.1016/j.msec.2015.11.041.

Zhang, Y., Cui, L., Li, F., Shi, N., Li, C., Yu, X., Chen, Y., Kong, W., 2016b. Design, fabrication and biomedical applications of zein-based nano/micro-carrier systems. Int. J. Pharm. 513 (1–2), 191–210. https://doi.org/10.1016/j.ijpharm.2016.09.023.

Zhang, Y.R., Lin, R., Li, H.J., He, W.l., Du, J.Z., Wang, J., 2019. Strategies to improve tumor penetration of nanomedicines through nanoparticle design. Wiley Interdiscip. Rev. Nanomed. Nanobiotechnol. 11 (1). https://doi.org/10.1002/wnan.1519.

Zhang, Q., Wang, J., Liu, D., Zhu, W., Guan, S., Fan, L., Cai, D., 2020. Targeted delivery of honokiol by zein/hyaluronic acid core-shell nanoparticles to suppress breast cancer growth and metastasis. Carbohydr. Polym. 240, 116325. https://doi.org/10.1016/j.carbpol.2020.116325.

Zhang, T., Tai, Z., Cui, Z., Chai, R., Zhu, Q., Chen, Z., 2022. Nano-engineered immune cells as "guided missiles" for cancer therapy. J. Contr. Release 341, 60–79. https://doi.org/10.1016/j.jconrel.2021.11.016.

Zhu, W., Huang, W., Ye, L., Deng, Y., Xie, Q., Jiang, Y., 2020. Facile preparation of succinylated-zein-ZIF-8 hybrid for enhanced stability and pH-responsive drug delivery. Chem. Eng. Sci. 228, 115981. https://doi.org/10.1016/j.ces.2020.115981.

Zöller, M., 2011. CD44: can a cancer-initiating cell profit from an abundantly expressed molecule? Nat. Rev. Cancer 11 (4), 254–267. https://doi.org/10.1038/nrc3023.

CHAPTER

# 16

# Gliadin-based nanocarriers for drug delivery

*Joseph D. Tanfani, Harsh Anchan, Mahima Singh and Kamal Jonnalagadda*

**Department of Pharmaceutical Sciences, Philadelphia College of Pharmacy, Saint Joseph's University, Philadelphia, PA, United States**

## 1. Brief overview of nanocarriers in drug delivery

Nanocarrier drug delivery systems continue to evolve rapidly, with clinical implications in fields ranging from vaccine delivery to oncology (Joseph et al., 2023). Nanocarriers are even being explored as delivery vehicles to alter the fabric of the human genome through the CRISPR-Cas9 mechanism (Duan et al., 2021). Among the wide range of materials suited for nanocarrier fabrication, plant-based proteins offer several critical advantages: wide availability, low cost, high biocompatibility, and high biodegradability (Reddy and Rapisarda, 2021; Voci et al., 2021; Rani et al., 2023; Mehanna and Mneimneh, 2020).

Gliadins are a collection of prolamin proteins derived from wheat grain sources (Table 16.1) (Prakash et al., 2022). Along with glutenins, they make up the polymeric gluten network within wheat (Barak et al., 2015). Prolamins have a high concentration of proline and glutamine residues, facilitating hydrophobic interactions with tissues such as gastrointestinal mucosa (Prakash

**TABLE 16.1** Types of gliadins (Voci et al., 2021).

| Gliadin type | Molecular weight (kDa) |
|---|---|
| α-Gliadin | 25–35 |
| β-Gliadin | 30–35 |
| γ-Gliadin | 35–40 |
| ω-Gliadin | 55–70 |

*Protein-Based Nanoparticles in Drug Delivery*
https://doi.org/10.1016/B978-0-443-33639-3.00007-6

et al., 2022; Holding and Messing, 2013; Chen et al., 2024). Similar to other prolamins, gliadins have low water solubility and are soluble in aqueous ethanol, allowing for a straightforward nanocarrier manufacturing process via nanoprecipitation (Voci et al., 2021; Song et al., 2021).

Gliadin nanocarriers have been explored as drug delivery systems for targeted delivery of antibiotics, chemotherapeutics, and nutraceuticals (Ramteke et al., 2008; Umamaheshwari et al., 2004; Voci et al., 2023). The strong mucoadhesive properties of these nanocarriers have enabled exploration in their use for conditions that require gastrointestinal delivery and targeting, such as *Helicobacter pylori* infection (Voci et al., 2021; Prakash et al., 2022; Ramteke et al., 2008). Gliadin has also been explored as a nanocarrier material for the delivery of chemotherapeutics such as doxorubicin and usnic acid (Voci et al., 2023; Farzan et al., 2023). In patients with celiac disease, the breakdown of gliadin-like proteins results in inflammation and gastric distress (Londei et al., 2005).

## 2. Chemical structure and composition

Gliadins consist of a central domain composed mainly of proline and glutamine residues (Voci et al., 2021). Two terminal domains encompass the central domain and consist of an amino terminal (N-TD) and a carboxy terminal (C-TD). Further distinguishing characteristics vary by gliadin subtype: α/β, ω, and γ. The central and N-TD domains are large in α/β and γ gliadins, while the C-TD domains are comparatively small. A very large central domain flanked by small N-TD and C-TD domains is characteristic of ω gliadins. In the α/β and γ gliadins, β-sheet and α-fold secondary structures are particularly abundant. In contrast, ω-gliadins are devoid of these secondary structures and instead contain numerous β-turns (Fig. 16.1). The amino terminals in α/β gliadins are plentiful in glutamine, proline, phenylalanine, and tyrosine residues.

α-gliadin and β-gliadin share a similar DNA sequence, and thus they can be categorized together (Shewry et al., 1986; Kasarda et al., 1987). α/β-gliadins have a distinctive structure comprising several key regions: a signal peptide, an N-TD segment, a repetitive domain, and a C-TD region. The signal peptide, consisting of 20 amino acids, is followed by a short

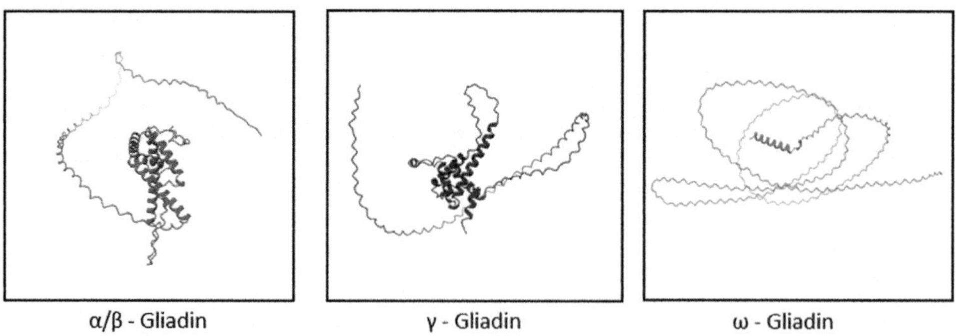


**FIGURE 16.1** Gliadin structure predictions by AlphaFold 3 (Abramson et al., 2024). Structural representation of gliadin subtype structure generated by AlphaFold 3.

N-terminal region. The repetitive domain, which spans 110–130 residues, features a specific repeat motif P(F/Y)PQ$_{3\text{-}5}$ (Urade et al., 2018). Further, the C-TD ranges from 140 to 160 residues and is notable for its cysteine-rich segment of six cysteine residues forming three intermolecular disulfide bonds (Khan and Shewry, 2009). This region also includes two stretches of glutamine. The mass of α/β-gliadins varies between 28 and 35 kDa, primarily due to differences in the lengths of the repetitive domain and the polyglutamine sequences (Fig. 16.2) (Voci et al., 2021; Kasarda, 1980).

γ-gliadins begin with a 19-amino acid signal peptide, leading into distinct regions including a brief N-terminal segment, a repetitive domain spanning 80–160 residues, and a C-TD region. Their most notable feature is the presence of eight cysteine residues that form four important intermolecular disulfide bonds, primarily located in the C-TD region. They also contain characteristic glutamine-rich segments (Muller and Wieser, 1997). These proteins show molecular mass variation between 35 and 40 kDa (Voci et al., 2021). In contrast, ω-gliadins are structurally simpler, characterized by a longer repetitive domain (238 residues), a very short C-TD region, and notably, a complete absence of cysteine residues. Both γ-gliadins and ω-gliadins contain specific motifs in their repetitive domains, though these patterns are distinct for each type (Hsia and Anderson, 2001). The variations in repetitive domain lengths and polyglutamine sequences contribute to the mass differences among the gliadin subtypes, while their distinct cysteine content and distribution patterns influence their structural properties and functionality (Table 16.2).

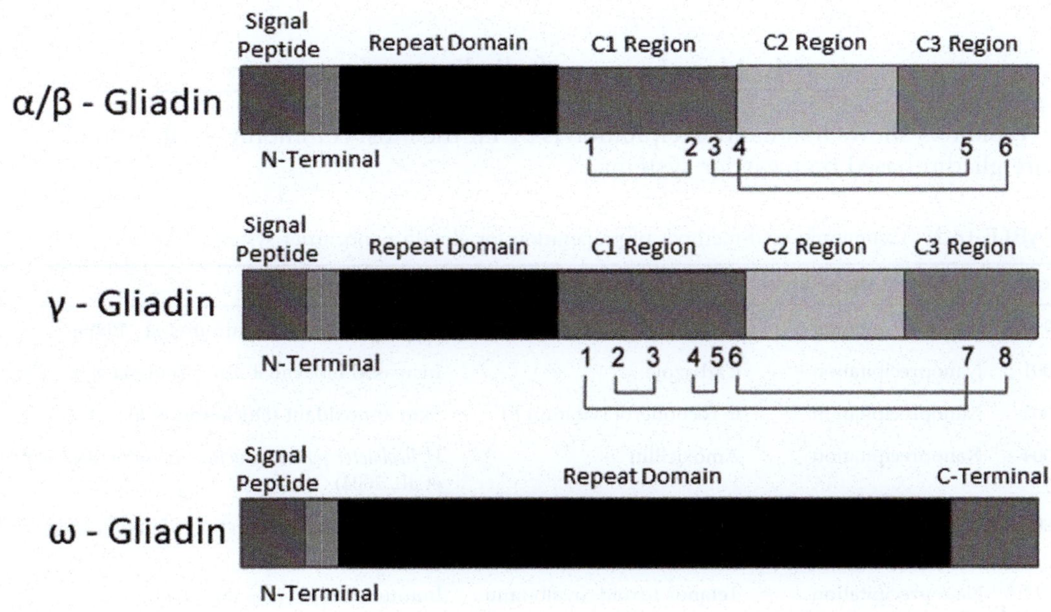


FIGURE 16.2 Gliadin primary structure by subtype. Variation in gliadin primary structure by subtype.

**TABLE 16.2** Gliadin structural content by subtype.

| Feature | α/β-gliadin | γ-gliadin | ω-gliadin |
|---|---|---|---|
| Signal peptide | 20 aa | 19 aa | 19 aa |
| N-terminal region | 5 residues | 12 residues | 11 residues |
| Repetitive domain | 110–130 residues | 80–160 residues | Approx. 238 residues |
| Repeat motif | $P(F/Y)PQ_{3\text{-}5}$ | $PFPQQ_{0\text{-}1}(PQQ)_{1\text{-}2}$ | $PFPQ_{1\text{-}2}PQ_{1\text{-}2}$ |
| C-terminal region | 140–160 residues | 140–150 residues | 12 residues |
| Cysteine residues | 6 | 8 | 0 |
| Intermolecular disulfide bonds | 3 | 4 | 0 |
| Molecular Mass | 28–35 kDa | 35–40 kDa | 55–70 kDa |

## 3. Role in celiac disease

Gliadin is highly biodegradable and largely biocompatible, though it can provoke inflammation and gastrointestinal distress in patients with celiac disease (Reddy and Rapisarda, 2021; Voci et al., 2021; Rani et al., 2023; Mehanna and Mneimneh, 2020; Prakash et al., 2022). Celiac disease is aggravated by prolamins such as gliadin/gluten, so future clinical applications of gliadin nanocarriers in drug delivery must take this into consideration (Prakash et al., 2022).

## 4. Manufacture of gliadin nanocarriers

Table 16.3 shows that nanoprecipitation is by far the most commonly used method to prepare gliadin-based nanocarrier systems.

**TABLE 16.3** Commonly used methods of preparation for gliadin nanocarrier systems.

| Year | Method of preparation | Entrapped compound | Clinical application |
|---|---|---|---|
| 1999 | Nanoprecipitation | *All-trans* retinoic acid | Skin treatment (Duclairoir et al., 1999) |
| 2001 | Nanoprecipitation | Carbazole | Increased bioavailability (Arangoa et al., 2001) |
| 2002 | Nanoprecipitation | α-Tocopherol (vitamin E) | Skin antioxidant (Duclairoir et al., 2002) |
| 2004 | Nanoprecipitation | Amoxicillin | *Helicobacter pylori* infection (Umamaheshwari et al., 2004) |
| 2008 | Nanoprecipitation | Amoxicillin, clarithromycin, omeprazole | *Helicobacter pylori* infection (Ramteke et al., 2008) |
| 2011 | Nanoprecipitation | Tetanus toxoid, ovalbumin | Immunization (Kajal and Misra, 2011) |
| 2012 | Electrospraying | Cyclophosphamide | Cancer (Gulfam et al., 2012) |
| 2014 | Lipid film hydration | Paclitaxel | Cancer (Sharma et al., 2014) |

**TABLE 16.3** Commonly used methods of preparation for gliadin nanocarrier systems.—cont'd

| Year | Method of preparation | Entrapped compound | Clinical application |
|---|---|---|---|
| 2016 | Nanoprecipitation | Curcumin | Colon cancer (Sonekar et al., 2016) |
| 2016 | Electrospraying | Meletin | Nutraceutical (Yang et al., 2018) |
| 2020 | Nanoprecipitation | Resveratrol | Nutraceutical (Wu et al., 2020) |
| 2022 | Nanoprecipitation | Fucoxanthin | Colon health (Wang et al., 2022) |
| 2022 | Electrospraying | γ-Oryzanol | Nutraceutical (Sharif et al., 2022) |
| 2023 | Nanoprecipitation | Doxorubicin | Cancer (Voci et al., 2023) |
| 2023 | Nanoprecipitation | Lutein | Nutraceutical (Tong et al., 2023) |
| 2023 | Nanoprecipitation | Usnic acid | Cancer (Farzan et al., 2023) |
| 2023 | Nanoprecipitation | Resveratrol | Nutraceutical (Li et al., 2023) |
| 2024 | Enzymatic hydrolysis | Naringin | Nutraceutical (Wang et al., 2024) |
| 2024 | Nanoprecipitation | Thiamine HCl | Supplement (Voci et al., 2024) |

## 5. Gliadin extraction

Gliadin may be extracted from bulk wheat material by a variety of methods. The Osborne method involves adding ethanol to wheat flour and subsequently shaking this mixture overnight (Osborne, 1924). Once the mixture is centrifuged at 4°C, the resulting supernatant containing gliadin is then evaporated on an apparatus such as a rotary evaporator to precipitate the protein. Weiss modified Osborne's method to produce a new protocol for gliadin extraction (Weiss et al., 1993). Ground wheat was vortexed at 4°C in Tris-HCl buffer for 1 h in 15 min intervals. The mixture was then centrifuged for 20 min at 20,000 *g*; the resulting supernatant (containing globulins and albumin) was discarded (Weiss et al., 1993). Several Tris buffer extractions were performed on the pellet, and the supernatant was discarded. Then, the pellet was stirred at 25°C with 75% v/v ethanol for 2 h and centrifuged. This supernatant, containing extracted gliadin, was preserved at −80°C.

The Wallace method involves a modification of the Landry-Morineux fractionation method (Wallace et al., 1990; Landry, Moureaux, and Moureaux, no date). The 70% ethanol-insoluble pellet obtained at the end of the Landry-Morineux protocol is dissolved in a 0.0125 M sodium borate buffer at pH 10.0 containing 2% 2-mercaptoethanol and 1% sodium dodecyl sulfate (SDS). Ethanol 70% is then added to precipitate nongliadin proteins. Centrifugation of this mixture produces a supernatant containing the desired gliadins, which are then extracted and stored for further use. The method used to extract gliadin used by DuPont et al. makes use of an extraction solution containing 0.3 M sodium iodide and 7.5% 1-propanol (DuPont et al., 2005). Wheat flour is mixed with the extraction solution, shaken, and then centrifuged. The supernatant is then incubated at −20°C with ammonium acetate in a methanol solution to precipitate the gliadin proteins (Rani et al., 2023; DuPont et al., 2005).

## 6. Preparation of gliadin nanocarriers

Gliadin nanocarriers may be prepared by a variety of methods, as outlined below (Fig. 16.3).

***Nanoprecipitation***: Nanoprecipitation, also known as antisolvent precipitation, is a straightforward technique that makes use of gliadins' limited aqueous solubility to prepare drug-loaded nanoparticles. Gliadin is typically first dissolved in aqueous solutions of 60%–80% ethanol (Ramteke et al., 2008; Voci et al., 2023; Tong et al., 2023). This polymer solution is then filtered through pores on the micron scale. The compound to be entrapped is added to the filtered solution (Kajal and Misra, 2011). This mixture is then poured into the "antisolvent," such as low-concentration sodium chloride solution or purified water. The resulting solution is then centrifuged at high speeds (15,000 to 40,000 rpm) (Kajal and Misra, 2011). Supernatant containing the gliadin nanoparticles is then removed, filtered, and processed for storage and future use.

***Electrospraying***: Electrospraying is a versatile technique that has been utilized by numerous researchers for gliadin nanoparticle fabrication (Gulfam et al., 2012; Yang et al., 2018). A high-voltage electrical device is used to apply an electrical field to a polymeric solution contained within a syringe (Patel and Haemmerich, 2024). A syringe pump expels the charged solution through a needle with a designated pore size. The resulting propulsion, known as the Taylor cone, contains particles that are further disintegrated by an increasingly higher voltage (Patel and Haemmerich, 2024; Rosell-Llompart et al., 2018). This disintegration results in the formation of nanoparticles, which are deposited onto a collection vessel. After the solvent evaporates, the resulting nanoparticles are collected.

Nanoparticles of varying morphologies can be prepared by electrospraying: spherical, hollow, porous, Janus, etc. (Patel and Haemmerich, 2024). Polymer solution parameters such as concentration, conductivity, density, and viscosity can greatly influence the size and morphology of nanoparticles fabricated by electrospraying. Critical process parameters that influence the size and morphology of resulting nanoparticles include the flow rate set by the syringe pump, the voltage applied to the polymer solution, the syringe needle pore size, the distance for particle deposition, and the type of collection vessel utilized (stationary or rotating). Environmental factors such as the ambient relative humidity during the process can also influence the resulting nanoparticle size and morphology (Patel and Haemmerich, 2024).

Gulfam et al. synthesized gliadin loaded with cyclophosphamide for breast cancer treatment. They used polymer solutions containing 7% gliadin in 70% ethanol, with cyclophosphamide present at a concentration of 1 mg/1 mL polymer solution (Gulfam et al., 2012). A 12–14 kV electric field was applied, and a stainless steel syringe tip with a 32-gauge diameter was utilized (Gulfam et al., 2012). The resulting gliadin nanoparticles had a mean diameter of $\approx$219 nm and a zeta potential of +18.5 mV (Gulfam et al., 2012). Sharif et al. prepared an 8% (w/v) gliadin solution in glacial acetic acid and loaded the solution with 10% (w/w) oryzanol relative to gliadin concentration. An 18 kV electrical field was applied, with a flow rate of 0.8 mL/hour and a collection distance of 100 mm. The resulting oryzanol-loaded gliadin nanoparticles had a mean diameter of $\approx$482 nm (Sharif et al., 2022).

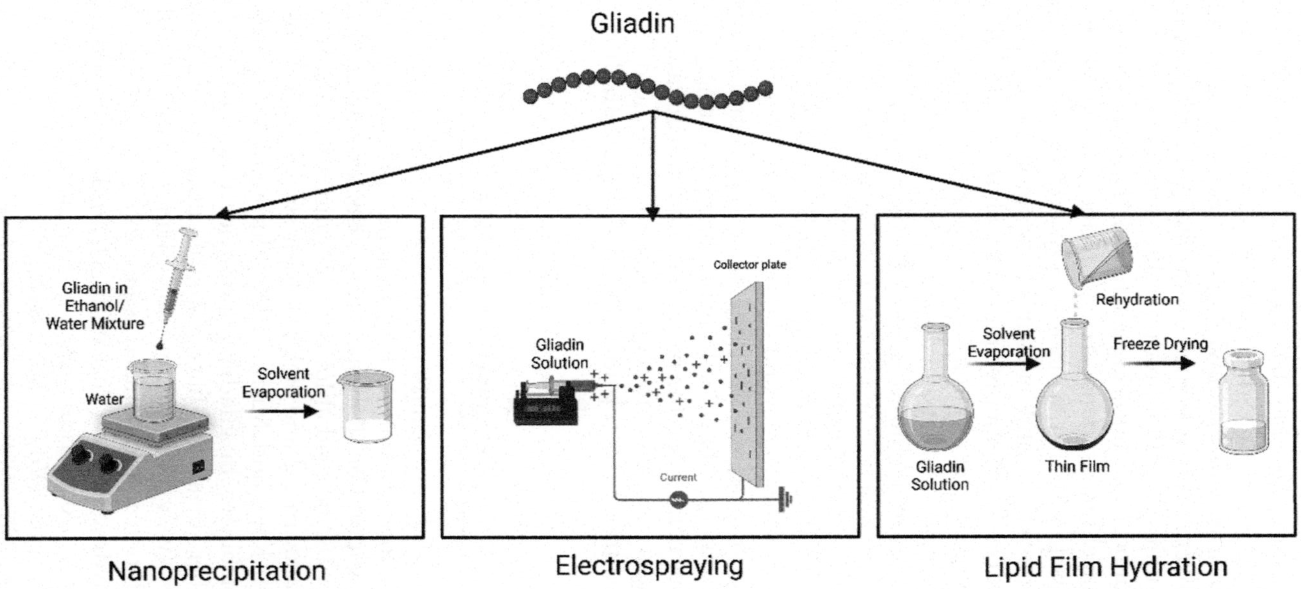


FIGURE 16.3 Methods of preparation for gliadin nanocarriers. Created with BioRender. Gliadin nanocarriers can be prepared using several methods: nanoprecipitation, electrospraying, and lipid film hydration.

***Lipid film hydration***: Sharma et al. prepared paclitaxel-loaded gliadin nanocarriers by an alternative technique described as lipid film hydration (Sharma et al., 2014). As in nanoprecipitation, gliadin was first dissolved in 70% aqueous ethanol solution. Separately, paclitaxel and Pluronic F127 were dissolved in a small volume of chloroform. The aqueous ethanol solution containing gliadin was added dropwise to the chloroform solution over the course of 1 hour while mixing. This mixture was then evaporated under high vacuum to remove the organic solvent. The resulting thin film produced after evaporation was reconstituted in water to obtain gliadin nanocarriers encasing paclitaxel. These nanocarriers were compared side-by-side with paclitaxel gliadin nanocarriers produced using the traditional nanoprecipitation method. It was found that nanocarriers produced by the lipid film hydration method were smaller, more stable, and had superior surface characteristics for targeting cancer cells than those produced by nanoprecipitation (Sharma et al., 2014).

***Enzymatic hydrolysis***: Wang et al. prepared gliadin nanocarriers encasing the nutraceutical naringin by a process of enzymatic hydrolysis (Wang et al., 2024). Gliadin from wheat was extracted and dissolved in deionized water at 1% (w/v) at 55°C, with the pH adjusted to 8.5. The enzyme alcalase was then added to the solution to facilitate hydrolysis, with NaOH addition used to maintain the pH of the solution as the reaction progressed. After 1 h, the solution was heated to 95 °C to inactivate the enzyme and halt the hydrolysis process. The resulting solution was centrifuged, and the supernatant containing amphiphilic gliadin polypeptides was extracted. After freeze-drying, these polypeptides were dissolved in pure water and added to an aqueous ethanol solution containing naringin to facilitate the formation of nanoscale micelles entrapping the nutraceutical. Centrifugation was performed, and subsequently, dialysis was performed to remove ethanol present in the solution. The nanocarrier solution was then freeze-dried prior to further characterization and analysis (Wang et al., 2024).

## 7. Nanocarrier stabilization

***Gliadin nanocarrier stabilization with surfactants***: In the precipitation step, researchers often choose to include a low concentration of nonionic surfactant to stabilize gliadin nanocarriers during solvent evaporation (Ramteke et al., 2008; Voci et al., 2023, 2024). Commonly, Pluronic F68 (poloxamer 188) is used at low concentrations (≈0.5% (w/v)) to prevent larger aggregates of gliadin nanocarriers and stabilize their structure (Ramteke et al., 2008; Umamaheshwari et al., 2004; Kajal and Misra, 2011). Pluronic F127 (poloxamer 407) has also been employed as a stabilizer in gliadin nanocarrier manufacture (Farzan et al., 2023; Sharma et al., 2014). Other surfactants have also been used. Voci et al. added polyoxyethylene (2) oleyl ether 0.1% (w/v) to their aqueous ethanol mixture (2 ethanol:1 water, v/v) prior to adding this solution into deionized water and precipitating gliadin nanoparticles encasing doxorubicin hydrochloride (Voci et al., 2023). In a separate work involving the entrapment of thiamine hydrochloride within gliadin nanocarriers, Voci et al. utilized Brij O 2.1% (w/v) for this purpose (Voci et al., 2024).

***Gliadin nanocarrier stabilization with gum arabic***: Gum arabic is a food-grade polysaccharide with protein-rich regions that is often used as a stabilizing agent for protein-based emulsions (Evans et al., 2013). Wu et al. investigated the effects of gum arabic addition on the subsequent formation of gliadin nanocarriers by the nanoprecipitation method (Wu et al., 2018). Gum arabic's effect on gliadin nanocarrier stability was investigated by exposing the nanoparticles to a range of pH, ionic environments, and temperature conditions. It was found that gum arabic helped to prevent aggregation of the gliadin nanocarriers at pH 6–7 when compared to gliadin nanocarriers prepared without gum arabic. However, an increase in particle size was observed in gum arabic gliadin nanoparticles compared to gliadin nanoparticles prepared without the polysaccharide. Particle size measurements at pH 4 to 5 were similar between the two formulations.

The effect of salt ion (NaCl) concentration and high temperature (80°C) on the stability of the nanocarriers was also assessed. Plain gliadin particle size showed a substantial increase in the presence of 20–80 mM NaCl at pH 5.0. Nanocarriers prepared with gum arabic showed a drastically lower particle size increase in the presence of NaCl at the 20–80 mM concentration range studied, indicating that the presence of gum arabic inhibited aggregation of the nanocarriers in the ion-rich environment. Similar results were observed for temperature stability studies. At 1 h postincubation at 80°C (pH 5.0), plain gliadin nanocarriers showed a significant increase in particle size, indicating aggregation, while the particle size of gliadin nanocarriers prepared with gum arabic remained roughly unchanged through 2 h postincubation at 80°C (pH 5.0) (Wu et al., 2018).

In a later work, Wu et al. investigated the stabilizing effect of gum arabic on gliadin nanocarriers encasing the nutraceutical polyphenol resveratrol. It was found that resveratrol encapsulated in gum arabic gliadin nanocarriers better retained its ability to scavenge the free radical 2,2-diphenyl-1-picrylhydrazyl (DPPH). In addition, resveratrol encased in gum arabic gliadin nanocarriers, also stabilized by chitosan hydrochloride, had increased antioxidant activity (measured by the ability to reduce $Fe^{3+}$ to $Fe^{2+}$) when compared with resveratrol released by nonstabilized gliadin nanocarriers (Wu et al., 2020).

***Impact of pH on nanocarrier morphology*:** Tong et al. conducted an investigation studying the effects of a wide range of pH values on the formation of gliadin nanocarriers formed by a nanoprecipitation method. Gliadin nanoparticles were formed with and without lutein, a carotenoid compound with numerous health benefits (Mitra et al., 2021). Nanoparticles were formed at pH 3–10. Particle characterization was performed by dynamic light scattering (DLS), X-ray diffraction (XRD), Fourier transform infrared spectroscopy (FTIR), and circular dichroism (CD). Particle size of lutein-loaded gliadin nanocarriers fell over the pH range of 3–5 and also over the pH range of 8–10 (Tong et al., 2023). CD analysis revealed that alpha-coil content in lutein-loaded gliadin nanocarriers increased in acidic pH, inferred by the researchers to indicate a conversion of random-coil conformations to α-helices in an acidic environment. In alkaline environments, the authors noticed conformational trends that indicated a transition of β-sheets to α-helices and β-turns (Tong et al., 2023). FTIR revealed changes in the amide I and amide II bond characteristic peaks of gliadin over the pH range, indicating changes in hydrogen bonding in gliadin nanocarriers with and without lutein (Tong et al., 2023). Incorporation of lutein was found to lower the surface hydrophobicity of the nanoparticles significantly in the pH range studied, signaling the role an active pharmaceutical ingredient (API) may play in determining final gliadin nanocarrier morphology. Additionally, while unloaded gliadin carriers were amorphous, XRD showed a shift in crystallinity from 0.92% to 3% and back down to 1.91% over a pH range of 3–10 (Tong et al., 2023).

*Drug Loading and Encapsulation*

***Methods for drug incorporation***: Incorporation of the API during preparation of gliadin nanoparticles is achieved by dissolving the API in the aqueous ethanol solution containing gliadin prior to desolvation (nanoprecipitation) or by incorporating the API into the polymer solution (electrospraying). Ramteke et al. dissolved amoxicillin, omeprazole, and clarithromycin into the aqueous ethanol/water mixture containing gliadin. This solution was then poured into a 0.9% (w/v) NaCl solution containing 0.5% (w/v) Pluronic F68 for stabilization for nanocarrier formation (Ramteke et al., 2008). Glutaraldehyde was then added to the solution to increase the hardness of the nanoparticles before the solvent evaporation step (Ramteke et al., 2008). Voci et al. incorporated doxorubicin hydrochloride at a concentration of 0.6–0.8 mg/mL in their aqueous ethanol solution containing dissolved gliadin prior to desolvation, homogenization, and subsequent solvent evaporation to form doxorubicin-encased gliadin nanocarriers (Voci et al., 2023). Gulfam et al. incorporated cyclophosphamide into 70% ethanol solution containing dissolved gliadin prior to aging of the polymer solution in preparation for nanocarrier formation via electrospraying (Gulfam et al., 2012).

***Encapsulation efficiency***: Encapsulation of doxorubicin hydrochloride by gliadin nanocarriers was evaluated by Voci et al. using UV-Vis spectroscopy. Encapsulation efficiency (EE) %'s of these nanocarriers formed by nanoprecipitation varied between ≈60% and ≈90% depending on the concentration of doxorubicin dissolved during nanocarrier formation (Voci et al., 2023). However, it was found that a higher initial concentration of doxorubicin increased the size and particle size distribution (PDI) of the resultant nanocarriers beyond an acceptable level. Thus, the optimum formulation achieved an EE of 74% with doxorubicin hydrochloride present at a concentration of ≈0.6 mg/mL during gliadin nanocarrier formation (Voci et al., 2023).

***Factors influencing drug-loading capacity***: Gulfam et al. noted a higher drug-loading capacity of cyclophosphamide in pure gliadin nanoparticles (72%) compared to gliadin/gelatin composite nanoparticles (53%–64%), which they attributed to the inherent adherence properties of gliadin (Gulfam et al., 2012). Voci et al. saw an increase in the loading of doxorubicin hydrochloride into gliadin nanoparticles with a higher drug concentration initially present during nanocarrier precipitation over the 0.2–0.8 mg/mL concentration range. They attributed this to noncovalent interactions between negatively charged gliadin carboxyl groups and positively charged amine groups of doxorubicin hydrochloride, which allowed more drug to be incorporated into nanocarriers' polymeric matrices at higher drug concentrations (Voci et al., 2023).

## 8. Characterization of gliadin nanocarriers

a) ***Size and morphology analysis***: Gliadin nanocarrier size can be quantified using techniques such as DLS. Polydispersity Index (PDI) is an indicator used to benchmark the quality of the preparation of gliadin nanocarriers, with a PDI less than 0.3 usually considered ideal (Voci et al., 2023; Danaei et al., 2018). Nanocarriers with a lower PDI have a more uniform size distribution, which lends itself to more meaningful insights in further experiments (Danaei et al., 2018). Morphology of gliadin nanocarriers is often investigated using scanning electron microscopy (SEM) and transmission electron microscopy (TEM) (Sonekar et al., 2016; Yang et al., 2018). SEM and TEM analysis can reveal important particle morphology characteristics that may affect the in vitro and in vivo utility of the nanocarriers (Falsafi et al., 2020).

**b)** ***Nanoparticle charge analysis***: Sharma et al. measured zeta potential for gliadin nanocarriers incorporating paclitaxel. Nanocarriers were prepared by two methods: nanoprecipitation and lipid film hydration (Sharma et al., 2014). Nanoprecipitated gliadin nanocarriers were formed in the presence of Pluronic F127: these nanocarriers had a zeta potential of −3.75 mV. Nanocarriers formed by lipid film hydration were made in the presence of various surfactant combinations of Pluronic F127, Tween 80, and Triton X100. Paclitaxel gliadin nanocarriers formed with Pluronic F127 alone had a zeta potential of −21 mV, those formed with Pluronic F127/Tween 80 had a zeta potential of −10.8 mV, and those formed with Pluronic F127/Triton ×100 had a zeta potential of −11.6 mV.

**c)** ***Drug release kinetics***

***Diffusion-controlled release***: Cyclophosphamide release from gliadin and gliadin/gelatin nanocarriers was characterized by Gulfam et al. to be biphasic: an initial burst release (25% for gliadin, 30%–45% for gliadin/gelatin) within the first hour followed by a diffusion-controlled release over the next 48 h (80% release by gliadin, 90%–95% release for gliadin/gelatin) (Gulfam et al., 2012). Yang et al. characterized meletin release from gliadin nanocarriers prepared by electrospraying. Release data was fit using the Korsmeyer–Peppas formation, and release exponent values (n) were found to be lower than 0.45, indicating a Fickian release mechanism for meletin from the nanoparticles (Yang et al., 2018).

***Stimuli-responsive release:*** Tong et al. studied the release of lutein from gliadin nanocarriers manufactured at pH in the range of 3–10, 3, 4, 5, 6, 7, 8, 9, and 10 in simulated gastric fluid (SGF) and simulated intestinal fluid (SIF). No significant differences were observed in the release rates of lutein between the nanocarriers formed at different pH values (Tong et al., 2023). The release rate of lutein over 120 min was significantly higher in SIF than SGF (Tong et al., 2023).

## 9. Clinical applications

***Cancer therapy***: Gulfam et al. prepared cyclophosphamide-loaded gliadin nanoparticles via electrospraying for the treatment of breast cancer (Gulfam et al., 2012). Drug-loading percentage was approximately 72% (Gulfam et al., 2012). Release of cyclophosphamide was characterized as a rapid burst (25% drug release) within the first hour and a slower, steady release thereafter for 48 h (80% drug release) (Gulfam et al., 2012). In vitro testing was performed on MCF-7 cells. After 24 h, western blot analysis confirmed the presence of apoptotic cells that were incubated in the presence of cyclophosphamide-loaded gliadin nanocarriers (Gulfam et al., 2012).

Gliadin nanocarriers encasing paclitaxel were prepared by Sharma et al. with the lipid film hydration method (Sharma et al., 2014). The cancerous cell lines MDA-MB-231 and MCF-7 were incubated in the presence of paclitaxel gliadin nanocarriers to investigate the in vitro cytotoxic effect exhibited by the nanocarriers. The MTT assay was used to assess cell viability. Cells were exposed to gliadin nanocarrier concentrations ranging from 0.782 to 6.5 μM. Viability of the cell lines was measured after 48 h of incubation. The gliadin nanocarriers encasing paclitaxel exhibited an IC50 value of 6.3 μM in comparison to a value of 1.75 μM for the free drug (Sharma et al., 2014).

One of the most widely used chemotherapeutic drugs, doxorubicin, exhibits toxic effects on parts of the body other than the therapeutic site of action (Pugazhendhi et al., 2018). Voci et al. prepared gliadin nanocarriers encasing doxorubicin hydrochloride via the nanoprecipitation method. Characterization of the particles revealed an average diameter of roughly 180 nm, a polydispersity index of 0.1–0.2, and zeta potentials ranging from ≈35 to 50 mV (Voci et al., 2023). Doxorubicin release in simulated physiological and tumor fluid environments showed a biphasic drug release: an initial burst release followed by a slower controlled release. In vitro viability tests were conducted on the MCF-7 cell line. Doxorubicin-loaded gliadin nanocarriers took longer to achieve a cytotoxic effect than the free drug, which was attributed to doxorubicin entrapment within the gliadin polymer matrix (Voci et al., 2024).

Usnic acid is limited in its pharmacotherapeutic use due to its severe hepatotoxicity (Kwong and Wang, 2020). Farzan et al. sought to overcome this limitation by preparing usnic acid-encased gliadin nanoparticles through nanoprecipitation. The nanocarriers were then conjugated with hyaluronic acid to target CD44 cell receptors, typically overexpressed in malignant tumors (Farzan et al., 2023). In vivo experiments were conducted in mice infected with the cancerous 4T1 cell line, characterized by an overexpression of CD44 receptors (Zhang et al., 2020). Usnic acid-encased gliadin nanoparticles functionalized for CD44 targeting with conjugated hyaluronic acid suppressed tumor growth to a greater extent than both nonconjugated gliadin nanoparticles with usnic acid and free drug. This demonstrated the potential of the conjugated gliadin nanocarriers to possibly circumvent the inherent toxicity associated with usnic acid.

***Gastrointestinal delivery***: Ramteke et al. prepared gliadin nanoparticles via nanoprecipitation and conjugated the lectin Concavalin A (CON A) to the nanocarriers in an effort to further improve mucoadhesive properties (Ramteke et al., 2008). The conjugated nanoparticles were loaded with a triple antibiotic ensemble consisting of amoxicillin, clarithromycin, and omeprazole in an effort to study the ability of the gliadin nanocarriers to treat *Helicobacter pylori* infection. High adhesion of the nanoparticles to mucin was found in vitro, with ≈93% and ≈87% adhesion measured for gliadin nanoparticles with and without conjugated lectin, respectively. Lectin-conjugated gliadin nanoparticles loaded with the triple antibiotic therapy showed a 94% eradication rate in vitro compared to a 78% eradication rate for plain triple therapy. In vivo studies in mice revealed a superior clearance of *H. pylori* in mice treated with lectin-conjugated gliadin nanoparticles loaded with the triple therapy, with only a few bacteria visible at the conclusion of the study (Ramteke et al., 2008).

***Skin delivery***: Gliadin nanoparticles also have potential applications in drug delivery to the skin, with the high concentration of proline residues within gliadin facilitating interactions with epidermal keratin (Teglia and Secchi, 1994). Duclaroir et al. prepared gliadin nanocarriers encasing all-*trans* retinoic acid, a drug with lipophilic tendencies in aqueous environments (Duclairoir et al., 1999). Retinoic acid has been shown to aid differentiation in epithelial cells, but clinical applications have been hampered due to drawbacks such as teratogenicity (Szymański et al., 2020; Piersma et al., 2017). Gliadin nanoparticles encasing retinoic acid were shown to have an initial burst release of 20% in physiological media, followed by a slower diffusion-controlled 20% release over the course of 3 h (Duclairoir et al., 1999). A more controlled release of all-*trans* retinoic acid in this fashion may have more clinical utility for skin treatments while avoiding potential drawbacks. In a separate work, Duclaroir et al. prepared gliadin nanocarriers encapsulating α-tocopherol, Vitamin E, for therapeutic skin applications. Vitamin E is easily degraded by oxygen and UV light. Encasing it in a nanoparticle system allows a controlled release to make use of its potent free radical scavenging ability while avoiding degradation. An initial burst release was observed for α-tocopherol gliadin nanocarriers, followed by a more measured controlled release over a time period exceeding 20 h (Duclairoir et al., 2002).

## 10. Challenges and future perspectives

**(a)** ***Scalability and manufacturing considerations***: Though gliadin nanoparticles developed by independent researchers have shown promise for applications in drug delivery, the feasibility of using these manufacturing methods on a larger scale must be considered for future clinical applications. Current techniques, such as nanoprecipitation and electrospraying, while effective, have limitations that need to be addressed for large-scale production. For instance, the nanoprecipitation method, though versatile, requires precise control over solvent ratios and stirring conditions to achieve uniform particle sizes and high EE (Martínez Rivas et al., 2017). Therefore, there is a need for more streamlined and automated processes that can ensure consistency and reproducibility at larger scales. This could involve the integration of continuous flow systems, advanced automation, and real-time monitoring to control critical parameters such as particle size, zeta potential, and EE. Spray drying can be a highly effective method for producing gliadin nanocarriers, offering several advantages in terms of scalability, consistency, and controlled particle formation (Lee et al., 2011; Dobry et al., 2015). Microfluidics offers a robust and scalable approach that can be leveraged to transition the production of gliadin nanocarriers from preclinical to industrial volumes, mirroring the successful scaling of lipid nanoparticles (LNPs) (Yu et al., 2024).

Flash nanoprecipitation has also been discussed in the context of manufacturing gliadin nanocarriers on a larger scale. It was originally described by Johnson and Prudhomme to exploit the use of an amphiphilic block copolymer and hydrophobic active ingredient dissolved in an organic phase (Johnson and Prud'homme, 2003). When mixed using a confined impinging jet (CIJ) device in the presence of an antisolvent (such as water), nanoparticles containing the active and coated by polymer were rapidly obtained with a narrow PDI. Flash nanoprecipitation has been used in the production of zein nanoparticles entrapping sodium caseinate (Li et al., 2014). Zein is a prolamin, like gliadin, and is derived from corn. The use of flash nanoprecipitation to produce gliadin nanocarriers may be an efficient way to scale up manufacture, potentially producing nanocarriers with a narrow PDI and consistent morphology more appropriate for clinical applications.

**(b)** ***Regulatory aspects and clinical translation***: There are numerous challenges that hamper a more widespread use of protein-based nanoparticles for drug delivery, such as gliadin nanocarriers. Particles on the nanoscale exhibit an extremely high surface area compared to their relative volume, encouraging interactions between nanoparticles that encourage phenomena such as aggregation (Zhang, 2014; Shrestha et al., 2020). Therapeutic protein aggregate complexes have been found in some cases to provoke an immunogenic response, presenting in patients as a multitude of symptoms ranging from mild (allergic responses) to severe (anaphylaxis) (Lundahl et al., 2021; Corona et al., 1999; Henney and Ellis, 1968; Orbach et al., 2005). The unique nature of nanocarrier-based delivery systems sometimes translates to very specific and resource-intensive storage conditions, such as continuous incubation in temperatures as low as −80°C to preserve the stability and condition of the formulation (Schoenmaker et al., 2021).

## 11. Outlook for future research and development

***Expanding into nutraceutical delivery:*** Gliadin nanocarriers offer promising avenues for the delivery of nutraceuticals—bioactive compounds that provide health benefits (Yang et al., 2018; Wu et al., 2020; Sharif et al., 2022; Tong et al., 2023). Their bioadhesive properties can allow for targeted delivery within the gastrointestinal tract, which can improve the bioavailability and effectiveness of nutrients that might be unstable or poorly absorbed in their free form, such as resveratrol (Ramteke et al., 2008; Li et al., 2023). Encapsulating antioxidants, vitamins, or omega-3 fatty acids in gliadin nanoparticles could protect these compounds from degradation during digestion and ensure their release at optimal sites for absorption.

***Application in cosmeceuticals:*** In the cosmeceutical industry, gliadin nanocarriers can be used to enhance the penetration and efficacy of skin-care ingredients. Gliadin has been found to bind to keratin in the skin (Teglia and Secchi, 1994). Antiaging compounds, moisturizers, or antiinflammatory agents could be delivered more effectively into deeper layers of the skin. The bioadhesive nature of gliadin also means that these carriers could form films that provide prolonged action of the active compounds, reducing the frequency of application needed and improving user convenience (Mehanna and Mneimneh, 2020; Da Costa Ribeiro et al., 2017).

***Utilization in food technology:*** Gliadin nanocarriers can be applied in food technology for the encapsulation and delivery of flavors, supplements, preservatives, or even probiotics. Their ability to protect encapsulated materials from harsh processing conditions and improve controlled release can enhance the stability and effectiveness of food additives (Assadpour and Mahdi Jafari, 2019). For instance, encapsulating probiotics in gliadin nanoparticles could help in safeguarding the bacteria from the acidic environment of the stomach, thereby enhancing their survival and activity in the intestines (Gómez-Guillén and Montero, 2021).

## 12. Conclusion

Gliadin is a protein material derived from wheat, which is biodegradable, largely biocompatible, cost-effective, and widely available (Reddy and Rapisarda, 2021; Voci et al., 2021; Rani et al., 2023; Mehanna and Mneimneh, 2020). As a nanocarrier material, it possesses numerous advantages. Gliadin is soluble in aqueous ethanol, making nanocarrier manufacture straightforward using the nanoprecipitation technique (Voci et al., 2021; Song et al., 2021). Being a prolamin, its amino acid content facilitates mucoadhesive interactions, allowing for targeted drug delivery to the gastrointestinal tract (Prakash et al., 2022). This also allows for gliadin to bind to epidermal keratin, giving it potential as a material for therapeutic nanocarrier delivery to the skin (Teglia and Secchi, 1994). Research has shown that gliadin nanocarriers also have applications in oncology (Voci et al., 2023; Farzan et al., 2023; Gulfam et al., 2012). As with many protein-based nanocarrier systems, the scalability of manufacture using gliadin must be considered for future clinical applications. Flash nanoprecipitation is a technique that may allow for the formulation of gliadin nanocarriers with a uniform size distribution on a clinical scale (Johnson and Prud'homme, 2003; Li et al., 2014). The breakdown of prolamins in the gastrointestinal tract triggers symptoms in patients with celiac disease, and so future applications of gliadin nanocarriers must take this into consideration (Prakash et al., 2022). Overall, independent researchers have shown that gliadin nanocarriers have a wide range of applications: delivery of nutraceuticals, cosmetic applications, targeted gastrointestinal delivery, and the treatment of cancer (Ramteke et al., 2008; Voci et al., 2023; Duclairoir et al., 2002; Wu et al., 2020). The use of gliadin as a protein-based material for nanocarrier delivery should continue to be refined for future clinical translation.

## References

Abramson, J., Adler, J., Dunger, J., Evans, R., Green, T., Pritzel, A., Ronneberger, O., Willmore, L., Ballard, A.J., Bambrick, J., Bodenstein, S.W., Evans, D.A., Hung, C.C., O'Neill, M., Reiman, D., Tunyasuvunakool, K., Wu, Z., Žemgulytė, A., Arvaniti, E., Beattie, C., Bertolli, O., Bridgland, A., Cherepanov, A., Congreve, M., Cowen-Rivers, A.I., Cowie, A., Figurnov, M., Fuchs, F.B., Gladman, H., Jain, R., Khan, Y.A., Low, C.M.R., Perlin, K., Potapenko, A., Savy, P., Singh, S., Stecula, A., Thillaisundaram, A., Tong, C., Yakneen, S., Zhong, E.D., Zielinski, M., Žídek, A., Bapst, V., Kohli, P., Jaderberg, M., Hassabis, D., Jumper, J.M., 2024. Accurate structure prediction of biomolecular interactions with AlphaFold 3. Nature 630 (8016), 493–500. https://doi.org/10.1038/s41586-024-07487-w.

Arangoa, M.A., Campanero, M.A., Renedo, M.J., Ponchel, G., Irache, J.M., 2001. Gliadin nanoparticles as carriers for the oral administration of lipophilic drugs. Relationships between bioadhesion and pharmacokinetics. Pharm. Res. 18 (11), 1521–1527. https://doi.org/10.1023/A:1013018111829.

Assadpour, E., Mahdi Jafari, S., 2019. A systematic review on nanoencapsulation of food bioactive ingredients and nutraceuticals by various nanocarriers. Crit. Rev. Food Sci. Nutr. 59 (19), 3129–3151. https://doi.org/10.1080/10408398.2018.1484687, 1040-8398.

Barak, S., Mudgil, D., Khatkar, B.S., 2015. Biochemical and functional properties of wheat gliadins: A review. Crit. Rev. Food Sci. Nutr. 55 (3), 357–368. https://doi.org/10.1080/10408398.2012.654863.

Chen, X., Wang, Z.X., Liu, W., Wu, Y.C., Li, H.J., 2024. Understanding the nanostructures of prolamin-based oral carrier to deliver functional compounds: A review. Trends Food Sci. Technol. 150. https://doi.org/10.1016/j.tifs.2024.104571.

Corona, T., Leon, C., Ostrosky-Zeichner, L., 1999. Severe anaphylaxis with recombinant interferon beta. Neurology 52 (2), 425. https://doi.org/10.1212/wnl.52.2.425-a, 0028-3878.

Da Costa Ribeiro, A., Leite, D.C., Soares, R.M.D., Da Silveira, N.P., 2017. Recent advances and development of gliadin-based drug delivery system. Adv. Chem. Res. 35, 1–18.

Danaei, M., Dehghankhold, M., Ataei, S., Hasanzadeh Davarani, F., Javanmard, R., Dokhani, A., Khorasani, S., Mozafari, M.R., 2018. Impact of particle size and polydispersity index on the clinical applications of lipidic nanocarrier systems. Pharmaceutics 10 (2), 57. https://doi.org/10.3390/pharmaceutics10020057, 1999-4923.

Dobry, D.E., Settell, D.M., Baumann, J.M., 2015. Spray drying and scale-up. pharmaceutical amorphous solid dispersions.

Duan, L., Ouyang, Kan, Xu, X., Xu, L., Wen, C., Zhou, X., Qin, Z., Xu, Z., Sun, W., Liang, Y., 2021. Nanoparticle delivery of CRISPR/Cas9 for genome editing. Front. Genet. 12. https://doi.org/10.3389/fgene.2021.673286, 1664-8021.

Duclairoir, C., Irache, J.M., Nakache, E., Orecchioni, A.M., Chabenat, C., Popineau, Y., 1999. Gliadin nanoparticles: Formation, all-trans-retinoic acid entrapment and release, size optimization. Polym. Int. 48 (4), 327–333. https://doi.org/10.1002/(sici)1097-0126(199904)48:4<327::aid-pi165>3.0.co;2-y.

Duclairoir, C., Orecchioni, A.M., Depraetere, P., Nakache, E., 2002. α-Tocopherol encapsulation and in vitro release from wheat gliadin nanoparticles. J. Microencapsul. 19 (1), 53–60. https://doi.org/10.1080/02652040110055207.

DuPont, F.M., Chan, R., Lopez, R., Vensel, W.H., 2005. Sequential extraction and quantitative recovery of gliadins, glutenins, and other proteins from small samples of wheat flour. J. Agric. Food Chem. 53 (5), 1575–1584. https://doi.org/10.1021/jf048697l, 00218561.

Evans, M., Ratcliffe, I., Williams, P.A., 2013. Emulsion stabilisation using polysaccharide–protein complexes. Curr. Opin. Colloid Interface Sci. 18 (4), 272–282. https://doi.org/10.1016/j.cocis.2013.04.004, 13590294.

Falsafi, S.R., Rostamabadi, H., Assadpour, E., Jafari, S.M., 2020. Morphology and microstructural analysis of bioactive-loaded micro/nanocarriers via microscopy techniques; CLSM/SEM/TEM/AFM. Adv. Colloid Interface Sci. 280. https://doi.org/10.1016/j.cis.2020.102166.

Farzan, M., Varshosaz, J., Mirian, M., Minaiyan, M., Pezeshki, A., 2023. Hyaluronic acid-conjugated gliadin nanoparticles for targeted delivery of usnic acid in breast cancer: An in vitro/in vivo translational study. J. Drug Deliv. Sci. Technol. 84, 104459. https://doi.org/10.1016/j.jddst.2023.104459, 17732247.

Gómez-Guillén, M.C., Montero, M.P., 2021. Enhancement of oral bioavailability of natural compounds and probiotics by mucoadhesive tailored biopolymer-based nanoparticles: A review. Food Hydrocoll. 118. https://doi.org/10.1016/j.foodhyd.2021.106772.

Gulfam, M., Kim, J.E., Lee, J.M., Ku, B., Chung, B.H., Chung, B.G., 2012. Anticancer drug-loaded gliadin nanoparticles induce apoptosis in breast cancer cells. Langmuir 28 (21), 8216–8223. https://doi.org/10.1021/la300691n, 15205827.

Henney, C.S., Ellis, E.F., 1968. Antibody production to aggregated human gamma-G-globulin in acquired hypogammaglobulinemia. N. Engl. J. Med. 278 (21), 1144–1146. https://doi.org/10.1056/NEJM196805232782104, 00284793.

Holding, D., Messing, J., 2013. Evolution, structure, and function of prolamin storage proteins seed genomics. Wiley-Blackwell, United States, pp. 138–158. https://doi.org/10.1002/9781118525524.ch8.

Hsia, C.C., Anderson, O.D., 2001. Isolation and characterization of wheat ω-gliadin genes. Theor. Appl. Genet. 103 (1), 37–44. https://doi.org/10.1007/s00122-001-0552-2, 0040-5752.

Johnson, B.K., Prud'homme, R.K., 2003 10. Flash NanoPrecipitation of organic actives and block copolymers using a confined impinging jets mixer. J. Chem. 56. https://doi.org/10.1071/CH03115.

Joseph, T.M., Kar Mahapatra, D., Esmaeili, A., Piszczyk, Ł., Hasanin, M.S., Kattali, M., Haponiuk, J., Thomas, S., 2023. Nanoparticles: Taking a unique position in medicine. Nanomaterials 13 (3). https://doi.org/10.3390/nano13030574.

Kajal, H., Misra, A., 2011. Preparation of tetanus toxoid and ovalbumin loaded gliadin nanoparticles for oral immunization. J. Biomed. Nanotechnol. 7 (1), 211–212. https://doi.org/10.1166/jbn.2011.1273, 1550-7033.

Kasarda, D., Adalstein, A., Lásztity, R., Békés, F., 1987. Proc. 3rd int. workshop on gluten proteins.

Kasarda, D., 1980. Structure and properties of alpha-gliadins.

Khan, K., Shewry, P., 2009. Wheat, chemistry and technology.

Kwong, S.P., Wang, C., 2020. Review: Usnic acid-induced hepatotoxicity and cell death. Environ. Toxicol. Pharmacol. 80, 103493. https://doi.org/10.1016/j.etap.2020.103493, 13826689.

Lee, S.H., Heng, D., Ng, W.K., Chan, H.K., Tan, R.B.H., 2011. Nano spray drying: A novel method for preparing protein nanoparticles for protein therapy. Int. J. Pharm. 403 (1–2), 192–200. https://doi.org/10.1016/j.ijpharm.2010.10.012, 03785173.

Li, D., Wei, Z., Li, X., 2023. Development, characterization and resveratrol delivery of hollow gliadin nanoparticles: advantages over solid gliadin nanoparticles. Foods 12 (13), 2436. https://doi.org/10.3390/foods12132436, 2304-8158.

Li, K.K., Zhang, X., Huang, Q., Yin, S.W., Yang, X.Q., Wen, Q.B., Tang, C.H., Lai, F.R., 2014. Continuous preparation of zein colloidal particles by Flash NanoPrecipitation (FNP). J. Food Eng. 127, 103–110. https://doi.org/10.1016/j.jfoodeng.2013.12.001, 02608774.

Londei, M., Ciacci, C., Ricciardelli, I., Vacca, L., Quaratino, S., Maiuri, L., 2005. Gliadin as a stimulator of innate responses in celiac disease. Mol. Immunol. 42 (8), 913–918. https://doi.org/10.1016/j.molimm.2004.12.005, 01615890.

Lundahl, M.L.E., Fogli, S., Colavita, P.E., Scanlan, E.M., 2021. Aggregation of protein therapeutics enhances their immunogenicity: causes and mitigation strategies. RSC Chem. Biol. 2 (4), 1004–1020. https://doi.org/10.1039/d1cb00067e.

Martínez Rivas, C.J., Tarhini, M., Badri, W., Miladi, K., Greige-Gerges, H., Nazari, Q.A., Galindo Rodríguez, S.A., Román, R.Á., Fessi, H., Elaissari, A., 2017. Nanoprecipitation process: From encapsulation to drug delivery. Int. J. Pharm. 532 (1), 66–81. https://doi.org/10.1016/j.ijpharm.2017.08.064.

Mehanna, M.M., Mneimneh, A.T., 2020. Updated but not outdated "Gliadin": A plant protein in advanced pharmaceutical nanotechnologies. Int. J. Pharm. 587. https://doi.org/10.1016/j.ijpharm.2020.119672.

Mitra, S., Rauf, A., Tareq, A.M., Jahan, S., Emran, T.B., Shahriar, T.G., Dhama, K., Alhumaydhi, F.A., Aljohani, A.S.M., Rebezov, M., Uddin, M.S., Jeandet, P., Shah, Z.A., Shariati, M.A., Rengasamy, K.R., 2021. Potential health benefits of carotenoid lutein: An updated review. Food Chem. Toxicol. 154. https://doi.org/10.1016/j.fct.2021.112328.

Muller, S., Wieser, H., 1997. The location of disulphide bonds in monomeric y-type gliadins. J. Cereal. Sci. 26 (2), 169–176. https://doi.org/10.1006/s0733-5210(97)90100-4, 07335210.

Orbach, H., Katz, U., Sherer, Y., Shoenfeld, Y., 2005. Intravenous immunoglobulin: Adverse effects and safe administration. Clin. Rev. Allergy Immunol. 29 (3), 173–184. https://doi.org/10.1385/CRIAI:29:3:173, 10800549.

Osborne, T.B., 1924. The vegetable proteins. Longmans, Green and Company.

Patel, P.R., Haemmerich, D., 2024. Review on electrospray nanoparticles for drug delivery: exploring applications. Polym. Adv. Technol. 35 (7). https://doi.org/10.1002/pat.6507.

Piersma, A.H., Hessel, E.V., Staal, Y.C., 2017. Retinoic acid in developmental toxicology: Teratogen, morphogen and biomarker. Reprod. Toxicol. 72, 53–61. https://doi.org/10.1016/j.reprotox.2017.05.014.

Prakash, S., Manish, Bansal, P., Kumar, A., Saxena, V., Kumar, V., Katiyar, D., 2022. Overview and in-silico pharmacological profiling of Gliadin: A potential biomaterial. Mater. Today Proc. 62, 276–282. https://doi.org/10.1016/j.matpr.2022.03.259, 22147853.

Pugazhendhi, A., Edison, T.N.J.I., Velmurugan, B.K., Jacob, J.A., Karuppusamy, I., 2018. Toxicity of Doxorubicin (Dox) to different experimental organ systems. Life Sci. 200, 26–30. https://doi.org/10.1016/j.lfs.2018.03.023.

Ramteke, S., Ganesh, N., Bhattacharya, S., Jain, N.K., 2008. Triple therapy-based targeted nanoparticles for the treatment of Helicobacter pylori. J. Drug Target. 16 (9), 694–705. https://doi.org/10.1080/10611860802295839, 1061-186X.

Rani, M., Siddiqi, R.A., Sharma, R., Gill, B.S., Sogi, D.S., 2023. Functional and structural properties of gliadin as influenced by pH, extraction protocols, and wheat cultivars. Int. J. Biol. Macromol. 234. https://doi.org/10.1016/j.ijbiomac.2023.123484.

Reddy, N., Rapisarda, M., 2021. Properties and Applications of nanoparticles from plant proteins. Materials 14 (13), 3607. https://doi.org/10.3390/ma14133607, 1996-1944.

Rosell-Llompart, J., Grifoll, J., Loscertales, I.G., 2018. Electrosprays in the cone-jet mode: From Taylor cone formation to spray development. J. Aerosol Sci. 125, 2–31. https://doi.org/10.1016/j.jaerosci.2018.04.008.

Schoenmaker, L., Witzigmann, D., Kulkarni, J.A., Verbeke, R., Kersten, G., Jiskoot, W., Crommelin, D.J.A., 2021. mRNA-lipid nanoparticle COVID-19 vaccines: Structure and stability. Int. J. Pharm. 601. https://doi.org/10.1016/j.ijpharm.2021.120586.

Sharif, N., Golmakani, M.T., Hajjari, M.M., 2022. Integration of physicochemical, molecular dynamics, and in vitro evaluation of electrosprayed γ-oryzanol-loaded gliadin nanoparticles. Food Chem. 395. https://doi.org/10.1016/j.foodchem.2022.133589.

Sharma, K., Deevenapalli, M., Singh, D., Chourasia, M.K., Bathula, S.R., 2014. Preparation and characterization of paclitaxel-loaded gliadin nanoparticles. J. Biomater. Tissue Eng. 4 (5), 399–404. https://doi.org/10.1166/jbt.2014.1182.

Shewry, P.R., Tatham, A.S., Forde, J., Kreis, M., Miflin, B.J., 1986. The classification and nomenclature of wheat gluten proteins: A reassessment. J. Cereal. Sci. 4 (2), 97–106. https://doi.org/10.1016/S0733-5210(86)80012-1, 07335210.

Shrestha, S., Wang, B., Dutta, P., 2020. Nanoparticle processing: Understanding and controlling aggregation. Adv. Colloid Interface Sci. 279, 102162. https://doi.org/10.1016/j.cis.2020.102162, 00018686.

Sonekar, S., Mishra, M., Patel, A., Nair, S., Singh, C., Singh, A., 2016. Formulation and evaluation of Folic acid conjugated gliadin nanoparticles of curcumin for targeting colon cancer cells. J. Appl. Pharmaceut. Sci. 6 (10), 068–074. https://doi.org/10.7324/JAPS.2016.601009, 2231-3354.

Song, J., Sun, C., Gul, K., Mata, A., Fang, Y., 2021. Prolamin-based complexes: Structure design and food-related applications. Compr. Rev. Food Sci. Food Saf. 20 (2), 1120–1149. https://doi.org/10.1111/1541-4337.12713, 1541-4337.

Szymański, Ł., Skopek, R., Palusińska, M., Schenk, T., Stengel, S., Lewicki, S., Kraj, L., Kamiński, P., Zelent, A., 2020. Retinoic acid and its derivatives in skin. Cells 9.

Teglia, A., Secchi, G., 1994. New protein ingredients for skin detergency: Native wheat protein–surfactant complexes. Int. J. Cosmet. Sci. 16 (6), 235–246. https://doi.org/10.1111/j.1467-2494.1994.tb00100.x, 0142-5463.

Tong, Z., Zhang, L., Liao, W., Wang, Y., Gao, Y., 2023. Extraction, identification and application of gliadin from gluten: Impact of pH on physicochemical properties of unloaded- and lutein-loaded gliadin nanoparticles. Int. J. Biol. Macromol. 253 (Pt 3), 126638. https://doi.org/10.1016/j.ijbiomac.2023.126638, 01418130.

Umamaheshwari, R.B., Ramteke, S., Jain, N.K., 2004. Anti-Helicobacter pylori effect of mucoadhesive nanoparticles bearing amoxicillin in experimental gerbils model. AAPS PharmSciTech 5 (2), 60–68. https://doi.org/10.1208/pt.050232, 1530-9932.

Urade, R., Sato, N., Sugiyama, M., 2018. Gliadins from wheat grain: An overview, from primary structure to nanostructures of aggregates. Biophys. Rev. 10 (2), 435–443. https://doi.org/10.1007/s12551-017-0367-2, 1867-2450.

Voci, S., Gagliardi, A., Ambrosio, N., Salvatici, M.C., Fresta, M., Cosco, D., 2023. Gliadin nanoparticles containing doxorubicin hydrochloride: characterization and cytotoxicity. Pharmaceutics 15 (1). https://doi.org/10.3390/pharmaceutics15010180.

Voci, S., Gagliardi, A., Giuliano, E., Salvatici, M.C., Procopio, A., Cosco, D., 2024. In vitro mucoadhesive features of gliadin nanoparticles containing thiamine hydrochloride. Pharmaceutics 16 (10). https://doi.org/10.3390/pharmaceutics16101296.

Voci, S., Fresta, M., Cosco, D., 2021. Gliadins as versatile biomaterials for drug delivery applications. J. Contr. Release 329, 385–400. https://doi.org/10.1016/j.jconrel.2020.11.048, 01683659.

Wallace, J.C., Lopes, M.A., Paiva, E., Larkins, B.A., 1990. New methods for extraction and quantitation of zeins reveal a high content of γ-zein in modified opaque-2 maize. Plant Physiol. 92 (1), 191–196. https://doi.org/10.1104/pp.92.1.191.

Wang, L., Wei, Z., Xue, C., Tang, Q., Zhang, T., Chang, Y., Wang, Y., 2022. Fucoxanthin-loaded nanoparticles composed of gliadin and chondroitin sulfate: Synthesis, characterization and stability. Food Chem. 379, 132163. https://doi.org/10.1016/j.foodchem.2022.132163, 03088146.

Wang, Z., Cheng, X., Meng, F., Guo, H., Liu, Z., Wang, H., Xu, J., Jin, H., Jiang, L., 2024. Wheat gliadin hydrolysates based nano-micelles for hydrophobic naringin: structure characterization, interaction, and in vivo digestion. Food Chem. X 21, 101136. https://doi.org/10.1016/j.fochx.2024.101136, 25901575.

Weiss, W., Vogelmeier, C., Görg, A., 1993. Electrophoretic characterization of wheat grain allergens from different cultivars involved in bakers' asthma. Electrophoresis 14 (1), 805–816. https://doi.org/10.1002/elps.11501401126, 0173-0835.

Wu, W., Kong, X., Zhang, C., Hua, Y., Chen, Y., Li, X., 2020. Fabrication and characterization of resveratrol-loaded gliadin nanoparticles stabilized by gum Arabic and chitosan hydrochloride. LWT 129, 109532. https://doi.org/10.1016/j.lwt.2020.109532, 00236438.

Wu, W., Kong, X., Zhang, C., Hua, Y., Chen, Y., 2018. Improving the stability of wheat gliadin nanoparticles – effect of gum Arabic addition. Food Hydrocoll. 80, 78–87. https://doi.org/10.1016/j.foodhyd.2018.01.042, 0268005X.

Yang, Y.Y., Zhang, M., Liu, Z.P., Wang, K., Yu, D.G., 2018. Meletin sustained-release gliadin nanoparticles prepared via solvent surface modification on blending electrospraying. Appl. Surf. Sci. 434, 1040–1047. https://doi.org/10.1016/j.apsusc.2017.11.024.

Yu, M., Mathew, A., Liu, D., Chen, Y., Wu, J., Zhang, Y., Zhang, N., 2024. Microfluidics for Formulation and Scale-Up Production of Nanoparticles for Biopharma Industry. Springer Science and Business Media LLC, pp. 395–420. https://doi.org/10.1007/978-3-031-60717-2_16.

Zhang, W., 2014. Nanomaterial: Impacts on Cell Biology and Medicine. Springer, pp. 19–43.

Zhang, W., Wang, F., Hu, C., Zhou, Y., Gao, H., Hu, J., 2020. The progress and perspective of nanoparticle-enabled tumor metastasis treatment. Acta Pharm. Sin. B 10 (11), 2037–2053. https://doi.org/10.1016/j.apsb.2020.07.013, 22113835.

# Further reading

J Landry, Moureaux, T. M., *Heterogeneity of Corn Seed Glutelin: selective Extraction and Amino Acid Composition of the 3* .

CHAPTER

# 17

# Lectin based nanocarriers for drug delivery

*Engin Kaptan*

**Istanbul University Faculty of Science, Department of Biology, Section of Molecular Biology, Istanbul, Turkey**

## 1. Overview of lectins

Lectins are a diverse group of carbohydrate-binding proteins that are found in various organisms, ranging from viruses to animals (Bektas and Kaptan, 2024). They are characterized by their ability to recognize and bind specific carbohydrates or glycan structures with no catalytic activity (Hamid et al., 2013). Lectins possess distinct carbohydrate recognition domains (CRDs), which are regions of the protein specially evolved to recognize and bind carbohydrates. The CRDs can vary substantially in size, shape, and sequence, determining their specificity for certain carbohydrate structures. The binding process is highly selective, reflecting that each lectin is often designed to bind to specific patterns or sugar moieties. CRDs are often located in loops or cavities formed by the polypeptide backbone. The structural configuration allows for specific recognition of carbohydrate structures. This specificity is usually conferred by amino acid residues in the binding pocket that interact with functional groups on the sugar moieties (Chettri et al., 2021). The key chemical interactions of lectin–carbohydrate binding include hydrogen bonds, hydrophobic interactions, and ionic interactions (Ambrosi et al., 2005). The hydroxyl groups (-OH) present in sugars are crucial for hydrogen bonding, forming weak interactions with polar amino acids like serine and threonine located within the CRD. These hydrogen bonds stabilize the lectin–carbohydrate complex. Additionally, hydrophobic regions of both the lectin and the carbohydrate can engage in van der Waals interactions, further promoting binding affinity (André et al., 2015). The orientation of the carbohydrate also plays an essential role in the binding specificity. The specific anomeric configuration (α or β) and the stereochemistry of the sugar can affect how well the sugar fits into the binding pocket of the lectin (Roy et al., 2016). Many lectins exhibit a preference for certain sugar residues, such as mannose, galactose, or fucose, due to the unique three-dimensional arrangement of their CRDs. Many lectins interact with

*Protein-Based Nanoparticles in Drug Delivery*
https://doi.org/10.1016/B978-0-443-33639-3.00005-2

complex oligosaccharides or glycoproteins. Modifications such as branch points and the presence of additional sugar moieties can dramatically influence binding characteristics (Wu et al., 2009). This complexity allows lectins to participate in various biological processes, including cell adhesion, signal transduction, and pathogen recognition. Additionally, some lectins require divalent metal ions to stabilize their structure or enhance binding interactions. For instance, calcium ions ($Ca^{2+}$) are often essential for the structural integrity of certain lectins, allowing for more effective carbohydrate recognition (Cecioni et al., 2015). Lectins can be monomeric (single polypeptide chain) or oligomeric (multiple polypeptide chains, such as dimers or tetramers) (Tobola and Wiltschi, 2022).

Lectins have distinct characteristics, structures, and biological functions, which originate from their evolutionary adaptations. Plant lectins constitute one of the largest and most diverse groups. These proteins are widely distributed in various plant species and serve critical roles in growth, defense, and storage (De Souza Cândido et al., 2011; Vandenborre et al., 2011). Many plant lectins have been studied for their potential use in agriculture and medicine due to their ability to bind to specific carbohydrates and modulate biological processes (Pusztai et al., 2008). Notably, lectins such as phytohemagglutinin from red kidney beans and concanavalin-A (Con-A) from jack beans are well characterized for their ability to agglutinate cells (Pusam et al., 2022). Animal lectins are typically more complex in structure than their plant counterparts, often containing multiple CRDs that enhance their binding capabilities. This complexity allows them to participate in signaling pathways and interact with various cell types and play key roles in cell recognition, immune responses, and developmental biology (Ghazarian et al., 2011). Lectins are located in various compartments of the animal cells, including the cytoplasm, cytoplasmic organelles, cell membranes, and even in the bloodstream (Ahmed et al., 2011; Dan and Ng, 2013). In these locations, they play a crucial role in recognizing and binding to glycoproteins and glycolipids within the cellular milieu, facilitating important cellular interactions and processes. One prominent example is selectins (one of the animal lectin family), which are crucial for mediating leukocyte adhesion during inflammation (León and Ardavín, 2008). The tetrasaccharide $sLe^x$ (sialyl Lewis X), which includes sialic acid and fucose, is an important glycan recognized by selectins. These sugar structures are synthesized by enzymes known as glycosyltransferases in leukocytes. The most prominent function of selectins occurs during the initial stage of the leukocyte adhesion cascade, where their binding facilitates the tethering and rolling of leukocytes on the endothelium (Tvaroška et al., 2020). Microbial lectins encompass a diverse group of lectins produced by bacteria, fungi, and viruses, and also known as adhesins, are crucial in the processes of microbial colonization, disease-causing capability, and interactions between microorganisms. These functions take place by recognizing and binding to specific carbohydrate structures on the microorganisms and/or host cells, facilitating colonization or invasion. For instance, viral lectins, such as hemagglutinins, are essential for recognizing and binding to sialic acids on the surface of host cells, which is a critical step in the viral internalization process (Bektas and Kaptan, 2024). Fungal lectins often play roles in nutrient acquisition by symbiotic interactions and interactions with host organisms. They are located intracellularly and on the surface of the fungal wall (Singh et al., 2011; Lebreton et al., 2021).

Lectins have gained significant interest in various fields: biotechnology, cell biology, medical applications, and agriculture. Lectins are vital tools in studying glycan structures and functions, helping to elucidate the roles of carbohydrates in biological systems (Dan et al., 2016). They can be used as probes to detect the composition of cell surface glycans and to understand cell signaling and adhesion. Lectins can also be utilized in the development of diagnostic assays for detecting specific glycans associated with diseases. Certain lectins have been investigated for their potential use in cancer therapies due to their ability to target specific cancer cell glycoproteins (Hashim et al., 2017; Kaptan et al., 2018; Silva, 2019). Besides, lectins have been used as natural pesticides against certain pests and pathogens, benefiting from their ability to affect cell membranes in insects (Vandenborre et al., 2011; Sadek et al., 2023). Lectins are multifunctional proteins with crucial roles in biological systems. Their ability to bind carbohydrates with specificity makes them invaluable in various research, medical, and industrial applications. Ongoing research continues to explore their potential, particularly in understanding disease mechanisms and developing therapeutic interventions.

## 2. Targeted delivery of drugs using lectins

By attaching drugs to lectins, these nanocarriers can selectively bind to specific cells (e.g., cancer cells, inflammatory cells) that express particular carbohydrate structures. This targeting helps to improve the therapeutic index of drugs, reducing systemic side effects. Lectin-targeted drug delivery is an innovative approach that takes advantage of the unique properties of lectins, which are carbohydrate-binding proteins, to create more effective therapeutic systems. In recent years, this method has gained attention due to its ability to improve the selectivity and efficacy of drug delivery, particularly for cancer therapies, while minimizing side effects. This approach leverages the inherent specificity of lectins for particular sugar moieties, allowing for the targeted delivery of drugs to cells expressing specific glycan markers. At the core of lectin-targeted drug delivery is the understanding of the interaction between lectins and their carbohydrate ligands. By conjugating drugs or nanoparticles with lectins, researchers can enhance the affinity of these therapeutic agents for target cells. For example, many cancers display distinct carbohydrate markers on their surfaces, which differ from those found on normal cells. Cancer-associated glycan antigens are carbohydrate structures present on the surface of cancer cells, playing a crucial role in cancer progression and metastasis. These glycans are often expressed differently on tumor cells compared to normal cells, making them valuable biomarkers for cancer diagnosis and potential targets for therapy.

Sialyl Lewis A ($sLe^a$) and sialyl Lewis X ($sLe^x$) are two glycans frequently overexpressed in cancers such as urothelial, colorectal, pancreatic, and gastric cancers, and also nonsmall cell lung cancer (Trinchera et al., 2017; Munkley, 2019; Ferreira et al., 2019). These glycans contribute to cell adhesion and metastasis by binding to selectins on endothelial cells, helping circulating tumor cells adhere to blood vessel walls and form metastases (Liang et al., 2016). Thomsen nouvelle (α-O-GalNAc, Tn) and Sialyl-Tn (Neu5Acα2-6GalNAcα1) antigens are other notable glycans differentially found in cancer cells (Loureiro et al., 2015). The Tn antigen, a precursor in normal O-glycosylation of proteins, is often incompletely glycosylated in tumor cells. Neo- or overexpression of this antigen in cancer cells derives from functional loss of Cosmc chaperone, which has an important role in O-GalNAc glycan synthesis (Ju et al., 2014). Its sialylated form, Sialyl-Tn, is linked with many types of epithelial cancer, including prostate, gastric, ovarian, breast, lung, colon, esophageal, and endometrial cancers, and serves as a marker of abnormal glycosylation, making it a potential target for cancer immunotherapy (Munkley, 2016). The Thomsen–Friedenreich Antigen (Galβ1,3-GalNAc-α, TF) is another crucial glycan. Typically masked in normal cells, it becomes exposed in cancer cells due to glycosylation changes, and it's associated with about 90% of all human cancers, including breast, colon, bladder, ovary, stomach, and prostate cancers (Yu, 2007). Glycosphingolipids like GM2, GD2, and GD3 are expressed in various tumors, including melanoma, neuroblastoma, and breast cancer, and serve as targets for cancer vaccines and monoclonal antibody therapies (Groux-Degroote and Delannoy, 2021; Jin and Yang, 2023).

It is important to note that disease-associated glycans are not only found in cancers but also in many autoimmune diseases, including immunoglobulin A (IgA) nephropathy, systemic lupus erythematosus, and inflammatory bowel disease, which are also characterized by abnormal glycosylation processes affecting one or more glycoproteins. Diabetes, which is one of the serious metabolic diseases, also involves abnormal O-linked N-acetylglucosamine-mediated signaling and enhanced glycation of multiple proteins (Reily et al., 2019). Additionally, there are important relationships between Alzheimer's disease and protein glycosylation. The glycosylation patterns of the two key proteins, APP and tau, and their metabolites, involved in the disease's pathological lesions, are abnormally glycosylated. Both N- and O-glycosylation patterns of these proteins have been shown to be affected. Therefore, understanding and investigating these glycosylation processes are essential for developing better diagnostic and treatment methods for Alzheimer's disease (Schedin-Weiss et al., 2014). Research into disease-associated glycans is pivotal, not just for understanding molecular changes of diseases, but also for developing targeted diagnostic and therapeutic strategies. Efforts to employ these glycans clinically include creating glycan-based vaccines, developing monoclonal antibodies, and designing glycan-targeted drug delivery systems.

Lectins can be engineered to bind specifically to cancer-associated glycans, thereby facilitating the uptake of attached drugs directly by tumor cells. This specificity improves the targeting of drugs to diseased tissues, enhancing therapeutic efficacy while reducing systemic toxicity (Saad, 2022). One common method to implement lectin-targeted drug delivery involves the formation of lectin–drug conjugates. In this approach, the therapeutic agent or drug is chemically linked to a lectin molecule (Kitaguchi et al., 2020). Lectin rBC2LCN isolated from *Burkholderia* was used as a targeted drug carrier for colorectal cancer (CRC) therapy, utilizing its affinity for fucosylated glycans on cancer cells. The rBC2LCN-PE38 (conjugated form of the lectin with Pseudomonas exotoxin A) significantly reduced tumor growth in CRC mouse models, particularly in cell lines with strong lectin binding affinity, without significant toxicity. These findings indicate that lectin–drug conjugates may offer a novel, targeted treatment approach for CRC (Kitaguchi et al., 2020). In another study, the researchers identified that bladder cancer cells exhibit abnormal glycosylation patterns, particularly an overexpression of mannose. Considering this, they developed a targeted drug delivery system by conjugating epirubicin (EPI) with Con-A, a lectin with a specific affinity for mannose. This conjugation was facilitated by a pH-sensitive linker, allowing the drug to be released in the acidic tumor microenvironment. The Con-A–EPI conjugate demonstrated mannose-targeting abilities, selectively internalizing into cancer cells in vitro without affecting normal cells. In an orthotopic mouse model of bladder cancer, the conjugate showed enhanced antitumor activity compared to conventional EPI, underlining its potential for targeted therapy (Huo et al., 2022). The results of these studies highlight the promising potential of utilizing lectin–drug conjugates as a strategy for targeted drug delivery, particularly in the context of cancer treatment. The specificity of lectins allows for more precise targeting of therapeutic agents to cancerous tissues, minimizing the impact on healthy cells and reducing side effects.

Some lectins, upon binding to specific glycans on the cell surface, can undergo a process known as internalization (Plattner et al., 2008; Žurga et al., 2017). Once bound, the lectin–-glycan complex can trigger receptor-mediated endocytosis. This is a cellular process by which specific molecules are ingested into the cell. The cell membrane invaginates, forming a pocket around the lectin–glycan complex. This pocket then pinches off to form a vesicle inside the cell (Johannes et al., 2016). This method is particularly advantageous for delivering chemotherapy agents, as it can reduce the adverse effects often associated with non-targeted therapies. In addition to direct drug conjugation, lectin-targeted drug delivery can also involve the use of nanoparticles (Yin et al., 2006). Nanoparticles are carriers that can encapsulate therapeutic agents, offering protection from degradation and controlled release (Yetisgin et al., 2020). By functionalizing the surface of nanoparticles with lectins, researchers can facilitate selective binding and uptake by target cells (Gao et al., 2008). For instance, nanoparticles made from biodegradable materials, such as lipids or polymers, can be coated with lectins that specifically recognize carbohydrate structures present on cancer cells (De Oliveira Figueirôa et al., 2017). This approach not only enhances the internalization of nanoparticles into the target cells but also can improve the pharmacokinetics and bioavailability of the encapsulated drugs. The use of lectin-targeted delivery platforms is being actively explored for various therapeutic applications beyond oncology. These strategies are also being investigated for the targeted delivery of vaccines, gene therapies, and antiinflammatory agents (Lavín de Juan et al., 2017). For vaccines, lectins can stimulate an immune response by directing vaccine components to antigen-presenting cells that express specific glycan patterns, thereby enhancing the effectiveness of vaccination strategies. A good example of this strategy is to use LTL (*Lotus tetragonolobus* Lectin), an α-L-fucose-specific lectin, as a targeting agent for poly(lactic-co-glycolic acid) (PLGA) nanoparticles carrying the hepatitis B surface antigen (HBsAg). These nanoparticles aim to target M cells using α-L-fucose receptors, which are found on the surface of M cells, to strengthen the immune response. Testing in mice indicated strong mucosal and systemic immune responses, including increased levels of secretory immunoglobulin A and cytokines, suggesting that these nanoparticles could effectively enhance oral mucosal immunization against hepatitis B (Mishra et al., 2011). It is important to note that lectins are used both as powerful tools for drug delivery systems and as significant targets. For instance, researchers developed a novel adjuvant-free nanoglycoantigen delivery system using PLGA nanoparticles for targeting MUC16-expressing tumors. The engrafting of MUC16-Tn glycoepitopes onto nanoparticles enhanced immune response without needing protein carriers. The nanoparticles specifically targeted macrophage galactose-type lectin (MGL) receptors on immune cells, activating dendritic cells and producing specific IgG against cancer-associated glycoproteoforms. This strategy has shown promise for precise cancer targeting and immunotherapy with minimal toxicity (Freitas et al., 2024).

Ultimately, the successful endocytosis of lectin nanocarriers and their ability to release therapeutic agents within target cells offer a promising approach for enhancing drug delivery systems. By exploiting the natural affinity of lectins for specific carbohydrate structures, researchers aim to create highly selective and effective drug delivery platforms that minimize off-target effects while maximizing therapeutic impact. Ongoing research will continue to refine these systems, address potential challenges, and develop new strategies to optimize lectin-mediated delivery mechanisms for various therapeutic applications, particularly in the field of cancer treatment and other chronic diseases. Research also indicates that the choice of lectin is critical in the formulation of lectin-targeted drug delivery systems. Different lectins exhibit varying degrees of specificity, binding affinity, and internalization mechanisms, which can all impact the overall effectiveness of the drug delivery system. Rigorous determination of the appropriate lectin, as well as the engineering of the drug or nanoparticle platform, is essential to ensure optimal targeting and therapeutic outcomes.

## 3. Lectin-based nanocarrier systems

Lectin-based nanocarriers represent a promising strategy for targeted drug delivery systems owing to their ability to utilize the natural specificity of lectins for carbohydrate recognition. These nanocarriers can be designed using various materials and structures, each possessing distinct properties that influence their performance in drug delivery applications. Understanding the types and materials used in lectin-based nanocarriers is essential for developing effective therapeutic strategies. Various nanocarriers, including liposomes, polymeric nanoparticles, inorganic nanoparticles, hydrogels, and nanodiamonds, can be incorporated into lectins. Each type of nanocarrier takes advantage of the unique properties of lectins to enhance both targeting and therapeutic efficacy (Fig. 17.1).

Liposomes are spherical vesicles composed primarily of phospholipids, forming a bilayer structure that can encapsulate hydrophilic or hydrophobic drugs. The surface of liposomes can be functionalized with specific lectins to engage with glycan structures present on target cells. This targeted approach can significantly improve the selectivity of the drug delivery system, as liposomes tagged with lectins may preferentially accumulate in tissues that express specific carbohydrate profiles. Additionally, liposomes are biocompatible and can be designed to release their cargo in response to environmental stimuli, such as pH changes or temperature variations, which can be beneficial for controlled drug release. In an in vitro study, researchers examined the use of LTL to enhance the targeting of doxorubicin-loaded liposomes to cancer cells. LTL specifically bound to glycoepitopes on highly proliferative cells and penetrated these cells through an unconventional mechanism. Using confocal microscopy, researchers verified LTL's specific binding and uptake in cancer cell lines. LTL-functionalized liposomes significantly increased doxorubicin delivery inside cells compared to unmodified liposomes, entering via unique tubules that avoid lysosomes. In mice with melanoma, these liposomes specifically delivered doxorubicin to tumor cells, suggesting

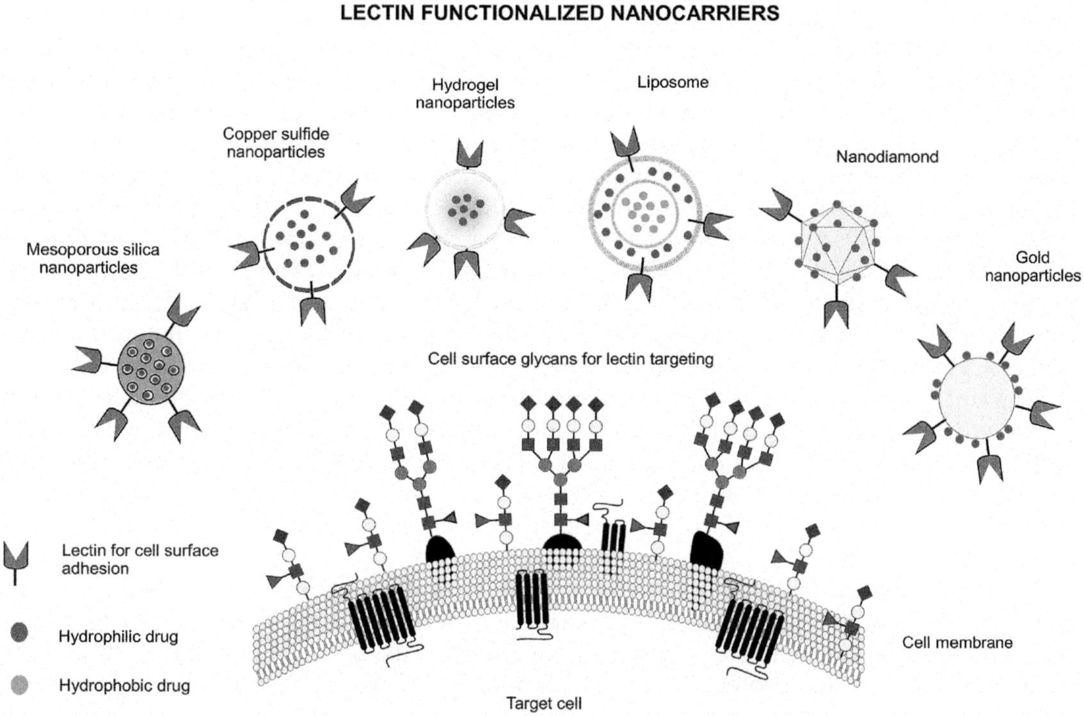


**FIGURE 17.1** **Lectin-based nanocarrier systems.** Lectin-based nanocarriers can be incorporated into different types of nanocarriers, including liposomes, polymeric nanoparticles, inorganic nanoparticles, hydrogels, and nanodiamonds. The specificity of lectins used in nanocarrier systems varies depending on the type of target cell.

that LTL functionalization could reduce nonspecific toxicity and improve treatment efficacy (Della Giovampaola et al., 2017). However, lectin-functionalized liposomes produced using avidin/biotin technology demonstrated that primary human alveolar epithelial cells both bound to and internalized the liposomes, while A549 tumor-derived cells bound to the modified liposomes but did not internalize them (Brück et al., 2001). This affirmed utilization of the right lectin and designing the drug or nanoparticle system is crucial for achieving precise targeting and effective therapy.

Polymeric nanoparticles are another widely studied class of lectin-based nanocarriers. These nanoparticles are often constructed from biodegradable polymers, such as PLGA, chitosan, or polycaprolactone (Vega et al., 2024). The choice of polymer affects the degradation rates and release profiles of the encapsulated drug. Polymeric nanoparticles can be easily modified and functionalized with lectins, enhancing their ability to target specific cancer cells or tissue types (Rekha Mol and Mohamed Hatha, 2023). The size and surface characteristics of these nanoparticles can be tailored to optimize cellular uptake and ultimately improve the therapeutic effects of the loaded drug. It was demonstrated that wheat germ agglutinin (WGA) was integrated into PLGA microparticles with stearoyl gemcitabine to enhance its effectiveness against bladder cancer cells. The diffusion-based uptake of gemcitabine and its efficient activation within cells were shown to be independent of carrier proteins (Neutsch et al., 2013). Inorganic nanoparticles, including those made from metals such as gold, silver, or iron oxides, also serve as effective lectin-based nanocarriers. These nanoparticles can be engineered at the nanoscale, permitting unique optical, magnetic, and electronic properties. The surface of inorganic nanoparticles can be coated or functionalized with lectins to promote selective internalization by target cells expressing the appropriate glycan ligands. In addition to enabling targeted drug delivery, inorganic nanoparticles can also serve additional functions, such as imaging or photothermal therapy, which can enhance the overall efficacy of cancer treatments (Yang et al., 2021). Lectin protein-loaded chitosan-TPP (sodium tripolyphosphate) nanoparticles for their potential use were investigated as anticancer agents against HepG2 cells, a model for human liver cancer. Cytotoxicity tests revealed that the nanoparticles had a significantly lower $IC_{50}$ value (105 μg/mL) compared to the lectin protein alone (265 μg/mL), indicating enhanced anticancer efficacy due to improved delivery and uptake by cancer cells. Mechanistic studies further demonstrated a reduction in the proliferation marker GPC3 and an increase in apoptosis markers such as Caspase 3, p53, and Bax, while antiapoptotic markers like Bcl2 and AFP were downregulated, confirming the potential for inducing cancer cell death (Yasin et al., 2020).

Hydrogels are another type of material used in lectin-based drug delivery systems. These three-dimensional polymer networks are capable of retaining large amounts of water while providing a supportive environment for therapeutic agents. Lectins can be incorporated into hydrogels either as free proteins or as part of a polymeric matrix. This incorporation offers the potential for targeted release, as the hydrogel network can respond to physiological conditions, such as changes in pH or enzymatic activity. Hydrogels can encapsulate a variety of drug types, including peptides, proteins, and small molecules, allowing for versatility in therapeutic applications (Li and Mooney, 2016). Lectin B (LecB/PA-LII), a lectin from *Pseudomonas aeruginosa*, specifically binds to the sugars galactose and fucose and plays a crucial role in the bacterium's pathogenicity, adhesion, and biofilm formation (Gajdos et al., 2022). By attaching lectin B to the surface of a protein-based hydrogel, the hydrogel gains the ability to capture pathogens upon contact. Additionally, the hydrogel includes another layer designed to prevent biofilm development and release a powerful antimicrobial peptide to eliminate microorganisms. This composite hydrogel exhibits strong antimicrobial effects against both the standard *P. aeruginosa* strain and a carbapenem-resistant clinical isolate, which is a challenging Gram-negative class 4 pathogen. Consequently, this hydrogel could be used to create a new type of antimicrobial wound dressing to help prevent infections in burn victims or patients with large wounds (Bodenberger et al., 2018).

A study by Ghanimi Fard et al. (2022) demonstrated the altered glycosylation patterns associated with neurological diseases and brain cancers to enhance the delivery of fluorescent nanodiamonds (FND) into specific brain cell types. Researchers developed a method using carbohydrate-binding lectins to target glycans on brain cells, leveraging the unique properties of FNDs, such as low toxicity and modifiable surfaces. The study targeted three types of brain cells: U87-MG astrocytes, PC12 neurons, and BV-2 microglia. Lectins used for targeting included WGA for sialic acid glycans, tomato lectin (LEL, *Lycopersicon esculentum* lectin) for high mannose glycans, and *Aleuria aurantia* lectin (AAL) for core fucosylated glycans. The experiments showed differential uptake of these lectin-conjugated nanodiamonds by the various cell types. AAL/FND complexes were preferentially absorbed by U87-MG astrocytes, WGA/FND complexes were predominantly taken up by PC12 neurons, and TL/FND complexes were most effectively internalized by BV-2 microglia. These findings highlight the potential of lectin-bioconjugated nanodiamonds to selectively target brain cells based on glycan expression, providing a promising strategy for addressing diseases characterized by glycosylation changes. The study suggests that these nanodiamonds could be developed for theranostic applications, serving both diagnostic and therapeutic roles, thus paving the way for targeted treatments using these multifunctional nanosystems (Ghanimi Fard et al., 2022).

Furthermore, the determination of lectins used in these nanocarriers plays a significant role in determining their binding specificity and targeting efficiency. Different lectins exhibit varying affinities for specific carbohydrates, so selecting the appropriate lectin is critical in developing effective nanocarrier systems. For instance, certain lectins, like Con-A, preferentially bind to mannose and glucose, while others, like WGA, exhibit a preference for N-acetylglucosamine and sialic acid (Hendrickson and Zherdev, 2018). The specificity of the chosen lectin can guide the design of nanocarriers aimed at particular cell types, especially in cancer therapy, where tumor cells often express unique glycan structures. In addition to their targeting capabilities, the materials used in lectin-based nanocarriers can influence several aspects of drug delivery, including stability, biocompatibility, and release kinetics. Biodegradable materials are often preferred, as they minimize long-term toxicity and enable the gradual release of drugs in biological environments. Moreover, the size of the nanocarriers plays a critical role in dictating the route of administration, biodistribution, and cellular uptake, with smaller nanoparticles typically exhibiting enhanced cellular internalization compared to larger counterparts (Ravindran et al., 2018). Table 17.1 provides an overview of lectins utilized in various nanocarrier systems, highlighting their affinities, targeted cell types, and developed applications.

## 4. Advantages of lectin-based nanocarriers

The use of lectin-based nanocarriers as drug delivery systems presents numerous advantages that enhance the effectiveness and specificity of therapeutic interventions. These advantages stem primarily from the unique properties of lectins, which exhibit a high degree of specificity for certain glycan structures present on the surfaces of cells. As a result, lectin-based nanocarriers have the potential to revolutionize drug delivery, particularly in fields such as oncology, gene therapy, immunotherapy, and also antimicrobial therapy (Acosta and Cramer, 2020; Bloise et al., 2021; Elumalai et al., 2021; Choi et al., 2022).

One of the most significant advantages of lectin-based nanocarriers is their ability to achieve targeted delivery of therapeutic agents. By functionalizing nanocarriers with specific lectins, it becomes possible to direct drugs precisely toward cells that express particular carbohydrate markers. This specificity minimizes off-target effects, which are common in traditional drug administration methods. For instance, conventional chemotherapy often leads to systemic toxicity because these drugs indiscriminately affect both cancerous and healthy tissues (Rekha Mol and Mohamed Hatha, 2023). In contrast, lectin-targeted therapies can

**TABLE 17.1** Overview of lectins utilized in various nanocarrier systems, detailing their affinities, targeted cell types, and developed applications.

| Lectin | Source | Specificity | Nanocarrier | Applications | Targeted cells | Ref. |
|---|---|---|---|---|---|---|
| rBC2LCN | *Burkholderia cenocepacia* | α1-2fucosylated trisaccharide | Direct drug conjugation | Anticancer therapy | Colorectal cancer cells | (Kitaguchi et al., 2020) |
| | | | Liposome | Anticancer therapy | Pancreatic cancer cells | (Kimura et al., 2021) |
| Con-A | *Canavalia ensiformis* | D-mannose, D-glucose, D-fructose, GlcNAc | Direct drug conjugation | Anticancer therapy | Bladder cancer cells | (Huo et al., 2022) |
| | | | Nanostructured lipid carriers | Antihypertensive drug delivery | Intestinal lining cells | (Beg et al., 2018) |
| | | | Gliadin nanoparticles | Antimicrobial therapy | *Helicobacter pylori* | (Umamaheshwari and Jain, 2003) |
| | | | PLGA nanoparticles | Antimicrobial therapy | *Helicobacter pylori* | (Jain et al., 2016) |
| | | | FU (fucoidan) nanoparticles | Oral insulin delivery | Mucosal cells | (Zhou et al., 2024) |
| LTL | *Lotus tetragonolobus* | α-L-fucose | PLGA nanoparticles | Vaccination against hepatitis B | M (microfold) cells | (Mishra et al., 2011) |
| | | | Liposome | Anticancer therapy | Prostate cancer cells | (Della Giovampaola et al., 2017) |
| WGA | *Triticum vulgaris* | GlcNAc, NeuAcα2-3Gal NeuAcα2-6Gal | PLGA microparticles | Anticancer therapy | Bladder cancer cells | (Neutsch et al., 2013) |
| | | | Solid lipid nanoparticles | Anticancer therapy | Lung cancer cells | (Pooja et al., 2016) |
| | | | Nanodiamonds | Neurological disorders | PC12 neurons | (Ghanimi Fard et al., 2022) |
| | | | Lipid nanocarriers | Tuberculosis therapy | Alveolar cells | (Hädrich et al., 2022) |
| | | | PLGA nanoparticles | Immunostimulant drug delivery | Intestinal lining cells | (Yin et al., 2006) |
| | | | Liposome | Antimicrobial therapy | Oral mucosal cells | (Wijetunge et al., 2018) |

| | | | | | | |
|---|---|---|---|---|---|---|
| | | | PLGA nanoparticles | Aerosolized drug carriers | Alveolar cells | (Sharma et al., 2004) |
| | | | PLGA nanoparticles | Anticolitis activity | Inflamed tissue cells | (Moulari et al., 2014) |
| | | | NGPE nanoparticles | Oral insulin delivery | Mucosal cells | (Zhang et al., 2006) |
| LecB | *Pseudomonas aeruginosa* | α-L-fucose | Hydrogel nanoparticles | Antimicrobial therapy | *Pseudomonas aeruginosa* | (Bodenberger et al., 2018) |
| STL | *Solanum tuberosum* | β-GlcNAc | PLGA nanoparticles | Brain tissue-specific drug delivery | Nasal epithelial cells | (Chen et al., 2017) |
| | | | PEG-PLGA nanoparticles | Antipsychotic therapy | Dopamine receptor-containing cells | (Piazza et al., 2014) |
| UEA-1 | *Ulex europaeus* | α-L-fucose | PLGA nanoparticles | Vaccination | M (microfold) cells | (Ann Clark et al., 2001; Du et al., 2018) |
| | | | Silica nanoparticles | Early cancer detection | Colorectal polyp cells | (Chen et al., 2012) |
| | | | Gliadin nanoparticles | Antimicrobial therapy | *Helicobacter pylori* | (Umamaheshwari and Jain, 2003) |
| ABL | *Agaricus bisporus* | TF antigen (Galβ1-3GalNAc) | Gold nanoparticles | Anticancer therapy | Leukemic cells | (Akram et al., 2022) |
| Jakalin | *Artocarpus heterophyllus* | TF antigen (Galβ1-3GalNAc) | Copper sulfide nanoparticles | Antimicrobial therapy | *Acinetobacter baumannii* | (Singaravelu et al., 2022) |
| PNA | *Arachis hypogaea* | TF antigen (Galβ1-3GalNAc) | PLGA nanoparticles | Anticolitis therapy | Inflamed tissue cells | (Moulari et al., 2014) |
| LEA | *Lycopersicon esculentum* | Poly-LacNAc | Nanodiamonds | Brain cell-specific drug delivery | BV-2 microglia | (Ghanimi Fard et al., 2022) |
| AAL | *Aleuria aurantia* | Core fucose (α1-6fucose) | Nanodiamonds | Brain cell-specific drug delivery | U87-MG astrocytes | (Ghanimi Fard et al., 2022) |

concentrate the drug at the tumor site, thereby enhancing therapeutic efficacy while reducing adverse side effects (Bloise et al., 2021). Another advantage of lectin-based nanocarriers lies in their potential to enhance cellular uptake (Liu et al., 2010). Lectins not only facilitate the internalization of drugs into targeted cells via endocytic pathways but also the uptake of nanovectors such as small interfering RNA (siRNA) or plasmid DNA. There are two main strategies: direct lectin targeting, where carbohydrates on nanovectors bind to cell surface lectins, and reverse lectin targeting, where lectins on nanovectors bind to carbohydrates on target cells. These interactions facilitate cellular uptake and can assist in delivering genetic material to specific intracellular compartments (Gajbhiye and Gong, 2013).

The ability of lectin-based nanocarriers to improve the pharmacokinetics of drugs is another compelling advantage. By influencing the circulation time and biodistribution of therapeutics, lectin functionalization can potentially prolong the half-life of the drug in the bloodstream. This characteristic is crucial for maintaining effective drug concentrations over time and may lead to less frequent dosing schedules for patients. When comparing the pharmacokinetic profiles of paclitaxel (PTX), which is a hydrophobic anticancer drug, PSN (PTX-loaded solid lipid nanoparticles), and LPSN (WGA-conjugated and drug-loaded nanoparticles) in Wistar rats after oral administration, the results demonstrated that LPSN significantly enhances the oral bioavailability of PTX. LPSN increased the peak plasma concentration and extended the detection of PTX in the bloodstream up to 24 h, whereas free PTX becomes undetectable after 8 h. The absorption and retention of LPSN were notably higher than those of PSN or PTX. Additionally, the mean residence time of LPSN doubles compared to PTX, suggesting prolonged circulation and sustained release, which enhances PTX's therapeutic potential when delivered via LPSN (Pooja et al., 2016). The behavior and distributions of coumarin-6 encapsulated *Solanum tuberosum* lectin-conjugated PLGA nanoparticles (STL-NP) and PLGA were examined in Calu-3 cells (a nasal epithelium model). At pH 4.0 and 7.4, both nanoparticles showed less than 5% coumarin-6 release at 37°C over 24 h, indicating stable encapsulation. STL-NP demonstrated enhanced endocytic capacity in Calu-3 cells at different concentrations and temperatures, showing more extensive distribution with prolonged incubation. After intranasal administration, STL-NP exhibited better brain accumulation, with fluorescence signals lasting in the brainstem, cerebrum, and cerebellum. Ex vivo imaging showed major distribution in the liver, kidney, and spleen, with STL-NP displaying less systemic absorption, suggesting targeted delivery. The safety assessment showed STL-NP as a safe carrier, given the mild toxicity profile under testing conditions (Chen et al., 2012). In another study, researchers also focused on enhancing the delivery and efficacy of the drug olmesartan medoxomil using Con-A-conjugated nanostructured lipid carriers (NLCs). It was reported that Con-A facilitates targeted delivery through its specific binding to glucose and mannose residues on cell surfaces. In the study, excipients were selected based on the drug's solubility in solid and liquid lipids, ensuring effective encapsulation within the NLCs. The formulation process considered various factors affecting particle size, stability, and drug release. The NLCs achieved a particle size of 273.6 nm suitable for cellular uptake, with a stable zeta potential of −30.2 mV and an encapsulation efficiency of 73.3%, which ensures a significant amount of drug loading. The NLCs demonstrated a sustained drug release profile, promoting prolonged therapeutic effects. Comparatively, the NLCs provided a 4.2-fold increase in cellular uptake and a four- to eightfold increase in both maximum concentration ($C_{max}$) and the area under the curve (AUC), indicating enhanced bioavailability. Importantly, the NLCs achieved a 37% reduction in blood pressure, exhibiting exquisite therapeutic potential over the pure drug. Overall, the results underscore the potential of Con-A-conjugated NLCs to significantly enhance the targeted delivery and efficacy of olmesartan medoxomil, representing a promising solution for improving drug therapies needing precision targeting and sustained release (Beg et al., 2018).

Moreover, lectin-based nanocarriers are versatile and adaptable platforms that can be engineered to incorporate various types of therapeutic agents. Whether they are delivering small molecules, peptides, proteins, or nucleic acids, lectin-functionalized nanoparticles can effectively accommodate a wide range of therapeutics. This versatility extends to the development of combination therapies, whereby multiple drugs can be encapsulated within the same nanocarrier. Such approaches can tackle complex diseases like cancer, where multiple pathways are involved, allowing for synergistic effects and improved treatment outcomes. In addition to these therapeutic advantages, the biocompatibility of lectin-based nanocarriers contributes to their appeal as drug delivery systems. Many lectins are derived from natural sources and are generally recognized as safe for medical applications. This biocompatibility minimizes the potential for immunogenic responses that can occur with synthetic materials, allowing for safer long-term administration of therapies. Furthermore, biodegradable materials used in the construction of polymeric or liposomal nanocarriers can ensure that these systems break down into nontoxic byproducts, reducing the risk of cumulative toxicity and enabling the body to eliminate them more efficiently.

Additionally, lectin-based nanocarriers can facilitate the development of more effective vaccines. By incorporating antigens and targeting them with lectins toward dendritic cells, it becomes feasible to enhance the immune response against specific pathogens or cancer tumors. This targeted approach can lead to the production of stronger antibodies and the activation of T cells, which are pivotal in developing long-lasting immunity. Consequently, lectins not only serve as tools for drug delivery but also play an active role in modulating immune responses, ultimately contributing to vaccine efficacy. It has been reported that plant lectins are potential agonists for Toll-like receptors (TLRs) due to their ability to bind specifically to glycans on cell surfaces and TLRs. Lectins can mimic pathogen-associated molecular patterns (PAMPs) in activating TLRs, leading to immune responses. They interact with TLRs and coreceptors, promoting receptor activation and signaling, similar to canonical PAMPs. Various studies show that different lectins can activate multiple TLRs, demonstrating their potential as modulators of immune responses by leveraging their carbohydrate-binding properties (Gupta et al., 2022). This suggests that lectins have the potential to enhance antigen presentation and strengthen immune responses. For instance, the activation of TLRs can lead to the release of proinflammatory cytokines, contributing to the development of adaptive immune responses. Through these mechanisms, lectins might help facilitate the recognition and uptake of vaccine antigens by the immune system. On the other hand, plant lectins are also useful tools for potential mucosal adjuvants in oral vaccines. Oral immunization can activate systemic and mucosal immune responses through the gut-associated lymphoid tissue via M (microfold) cells (Gebert, 1997). However, antigens are vulnerable to acidic and enzymatic degradation, and there's limited M cell availability and uptake. M cells help transcytose antigens to dendritic cells, which then interact with

T and B cells to generate immune responses (Sakhon et al., 2015). Plant lectins are stable in low pH and resistant to digestion, making them suitable for targeting specific gut locations. Using nanocarrier systems by encapsulating antigens and coating them with lectins can protect vaccines from degradation and enhance their targeted delivery to M cells (Jepson et al., 2004; Majee and Biswas, 2013). Studies have shown that covalently coupling lectins, like UEA-1 (*Ulex europaeus* agglutinin-1), to carriers enhances adherence and uptake by M cells more effectively than traditional carriers (Ann Clark et al., 2001). Recently, UEA-1-modified PLGA nanoparticles (UEA-1/PLGA NPs) as an oral vaccine delivery system were tested to improve mucosal immunity. These nanoparticles safeguard the enclosed DNA vaccine (PRRSV DNA vaccine/pcDNA3.1-SynORF5) or protein subunit (ORF5-encoded glycoprotein) from gastrointestinal degradation and release them in a controlled manner. The addition of UEA-1 enhances the targeting and transport by M cells, crucial for initiating a strong immune response. In experimental trials with mice and piglets, the UEA-1/PLGA NPs significantly boosted immune responses, as indicated by higher serum IgG and intestinal IgA levels compared to nonmodified nanoparticles. This enhancement underscores the effectiveness of the UEA-1 modification in stimulating a more robust mucosal and systemic immune response. Thus, these findings highlight the potential of UEA-1/PLGA NPs as a versatile and efficient oral vaccine delivery platform (Du et al., 2018).

Lastly, the incorporation of diagnostic capabilities into lectin-based nanocarriers presents an innovative advantage in combined therapeutic and diagnostic applications, also known as theranostics. By attaching imaging agents to these nanocarriers, it becomes possible to visualize specific tissues or monitor the therapeutic outcomes in real time. This dual functionality enables clinicians to track drug distribution and efficacy, paving the way for adjustments in therapy based on patient responses. The researchers developed mPLGA/IR775 nanoparticles, integrating magnetite and the IR775 dye. Magnetite facilitates quantitative tracking and magnetic-assisted delivery, while IR775 enables fluorescent imaging and light-activated photodynamic therapy (PDT), encapsulating the theranostics concept. Lectins, particularly Con-A, were used to target specific cancer cell glycosylation patterns. In vivo experiments demonstrated that these nanoparticles efficiently targeted and accumulated in tumor sites under a magnetic field, provided clear imaging signals, and achieved complete tumor growth inhibition in mice after a single PDT session. These findings highlight the potential of mPLGA/IR775 as a powerful tool for cancer diagnosis and treatment (Kovalenko et al., 2023). Additionally, a previous study demonstrated that fluorescently labeled mesoporous silica nanoparticles (MSNs) were designed to target and detect early-stage colorectal adenomatous polyps before they transform into cancer. These nanoparticles specifically bound to aberrant α-L-fucose on pathological lesions, enhancing their visibility during endoscopic procedures. The PEGylated UEA1-labeled fluorescent mesoporous silica nanoparticles (FMSNs) were confirmed to specifically target colorectal polyps and early adenomas through imaging and histological analysis. Tests conducted *in vitro*, ex vivo, and in murine models show that these lectin-functionalized MSNs could significantly improve the early detection of colorectal polyps, representing a promising tool for in situ diagnostic imaging (Chen et al., 2017).

In summary, lectin-based nanocarriers offer a remarkable array of advantages as drug delivery systems, characterized by their ability to provide targeted therapy, enhance cellular uptake, improve pharmacokinetics, and enable versatile therapeutic applications. Their biocompatibility, potential for controlled release, and capacity for incorporating diagnostic features further augment their utility in clinical settings. As research progresses, these advantages highlight the transformative potential of lectin-based nanocarriers in developing more effective, personalized therapeutic strategies for a range of diseases, particularly those that have traditionally posed significant treatment challenges.

## 5. Challenges and considerations

One of the primary challenges associated with lectin-based nanocarriers is the complexity of glycan expression on the surfaces of target cells. Different cell types, including cancer cells, often exhibit heterogeneous glycosylation patterns (Pinho and Reis, 2015), which can vary not only between tissues but also among individual patients. Aberrant glycosylation can enhance tumor heterogeneity, significantly contributing to the recurrence and treatment resistance of cancers (Sun et al., 2023). This variability can complicate the targeting strategy, as a lectin that binds specifically to a particular carbohydrate moiety may not be effective across a broader population or for all instances of a disease. This heterogeneity increases the risk of suboptimal targeting, potentially leading to inadequate therapeutic responses or unintended side effects. Therefore, researchers must carefully select optimal lectins for specific therapeutic applications and consider potential variations in glycan expression among different patient populations. Another challenge is that the cross-specificity of lectins, which can bind to multiple glycan structures, may affect the selectivity and cause off-target effects (Silva, 2019). This is due to the ability of lectins to bind various glycans, making it crucial to study their selectivity in the intended biological context. Additionally, the formation of a protein corona when nanoparticles are introduced into the bloodstream can mask lectins and impede targeting efforts (Panico et al., 2022). Moreover, lectin-based nanocarriers can bind to glycoproteins on the surfaces of circulating cells or in the bloodstream. This issue arises because lectins have the ability to bind and agglutinate blood cells (Zubcevic et al., 2016). This binding can hinder the nanocarriers' ability to reach their intended targets, as the lectins may become saturated or blocked, preventing effective interaction with the target cells. This interference can reduce the efficiency of the drug delivery system, highlighting the importance of addressing such interactions during the development of lectin-coated nanocarriers. To address these issues, precoating nanoparticles with proteins like bovine serum albumin can reduce protein corona effects but doesn't fully prevent off-target binding (Mirshafiee et al., 2016). Therefore, alternative strategies and thorough testing are needed to improve the effectiveness of lectin-modified nanocarrier systems.

Additionally, the immunogenicity of lectins is a critical consideration. While many lectins are derived from natural sources and are relatively biocompatible, introducing exogenous lectins into the human body could provoke immune reactions (Mbae et al., 2018). Such reactions can manifest in various ways, including the production of antibodies against the lectin, which may neutralize its therapeutic effects or trigger allergic responses. The risk of immunogenicity can be further heightened if the lectin is derived from a species that the immune system of the patient may recognize as foreign (He et al., 2018). Therefore, thorough safety assessments are paramount in evaluating lectin-based nanocarrier systems before clinical applications. Lectins are found in many fruits and vegetables, and if undigested, they can penetrate gut barriers and provoke immune responses, resulting in antibody production. Using an enzyme-linked immunosorbent assay, researchers found that WGA-specific antibodies reacted with 37 out of 62 tissue antigens, followed by antibodies specific to red kidney bean, soybean, and peanut agglutinins. This suggests possible molecular mimicry and cross-reactivity. Further analysis of 500 nominally healthy donors revealed varying prevalence of lectin-specific antibodies, with significant correlations found between IgM antilectin antibodies and rheumatoid factor (RF), but not with antinuclear antibodies (ANA). These findings highlight a mechanism by which antibodies against undigested lectins may play a role in the pathogenesis of certain autoimmune diseases due to their reaction with human tissue components (Vojdani et al., 2020). On the other hand, kidney beans (*Phaseolus vulgaris* L.), commonly consumed worldwide, have been associated with an increase in allergic reactions characterized by elevated specific IgE levels (Wang et al., 2021).

Therapeutic interventions often require precise dosing and predictable pharmacokinetics to achieve the desired therapeutic effects. The complexity involved in pharmacodynamics and pharmacokinetics must be well understood and modeled when using lectin-based systems. The interplay of the drug with its target, the rate of receptor-mediated endocytosis, and further intracellular trafficking must be accounted for to ensure that therapeutic levels are achieved at the target site while minimizing off-target toxicity. Finally, regulatory hurdles are a significant consideration for the clinical application of lectin-based nanocarriers. The development and approval of new drug delivery systems necessitate compliance with strict regulatory frameworks, which can include comprehensive toxicological assessments and extensive clinical trials. Given the dual nature of lectins as both therapeutic agents and targeted delivery systems, regulatory pathways may be complex and require detailed documentation of safety, efficacy, and manufacturing processes. While lectin-based nanocarriers offer numerous advantages for targeted drug delivery systems, various challenges and considerations need to be addressed. The heterogeneity of glycan expression, potential immunogenicity, and the intricate balance of size and surface properties of nanocarriers necessitate careful design and evaluation. Furthermore, the complexities involved in manufacturing, drug compatibility, pharmacokinetics, and regulatory compliance must be navigated to ensure that lectin-based nanocarriers translate successfully into effective therapeutic applications. Continued research and innovation in this field can help overcome these challenges, enabling the successful implementation of lectin-based strategies in modern medicine.

## 6. Overview of current research

Curcumin, a bioactive compound found in turmeric, is renowned for its potent antiinflammatory and antioxidant properties, making it a promising candidate for treating a variety of health conditions, including arthritis and metabolic syndrome. Additionally, curcumin has shown potential in cancer therapy due to its ability to modulate multiple cellular signaling pathways, thereby inhibiting tumor growth and metastasis (Deguchi, 2015; Pourhabibi-Zarandi et al., 2022). A nasal delivery system for curcumin (Cur) using odorranalectin (OL), which is a small nonimmunogenic lectin-like peptide, and modified nanoparticles (Cur–OL–NPs) was developed to enhance delivery to the brain. Cur shows promise for treating neurological diseases (Adami and Bottai, 2022), but its effectiveness is limited by its difficulty in penetrating the blood–brain barrier (BBB). Using OL, the smallest lectin, the system increased curcumin's residence time in the nasal mucosa and enhanced cellular uptake without severe toxicity. Compared to unmodified nanoparticles, Cur–OL–NPs displayed improved stability, bioavailability, and targeting efficiency. In vivo studies confirmed higher bioavailability, suggesting Cur–OL–NPs are promising for the noninvasive nasal delivery of curcumin to bypass the BBB (Li et al., 2020). Besides, the potential of OL was explored as a carrier for delivering siRNA across the BBB. OL was conjugated with 5-carboxyfluorescein (Roy et al., 2016) and compared to a scrambled peptide in terms of cellular uptake, stability, and intracellular trafficking using hCMEC/D3 cells as a BBB model. Results showed that OL had significantly higher uptake than the scrambled peptide, with uptake being temperature-dependent but unaffected by pH. OL was found to be nontoxic, and its cellular internalization involved colocalization with endosomal markers, suggesting receptor-mediated transcytosis. However, further in vivo studies are needed to evaluate OL's capacity to carry siRNA and transport it across the BBB for targeted brain delivery (Sajja et al., 2019).

In a study addressing the challenge of treating infections caused by intracellular pathogens that escape conventional drug therapies because they reside within host cells, the researchers focused on developing lipid nanocarriers to overcome this obstacle. These nanocarriers are advantageous because they protect the encapsulated drug from degradation, enhance its bioavailability, and allow for targeted release into the intracellular environment. A key component of this strategy is the use of WGA lectin, which binds to specific receptors on alveolar epithelial cells, promoting increased uptake of the nanocarriers by these cells. This enhanced uptake is crucial for delivering the therapeutic compounds directly to the intracellular pathogens. By attaching WGA to their surfaces using novel glycosylated amphiphilic compounds, the researchers designed nanocarriers that can effectively engage with cell membranes. The study utilized in vitro high-content analysis and flow cytometry assays to confirm that macrophages, responsible for engulfing pathogens, efficiently internalized these WGA-functionalized nanocarriers. The carriers, approximately 200 nm in size, were loaded with the lipophilic compound quercetin, which was shown to be released in a controlled manner. The findings revealed that WGA attachment substantially improved the uptake of nanocarriers by macrophages, underlining their potential to enhance intracellular drug delivery (Hädrich et al., 2022).

A novel drug targeting system for leukemia was performed utilizing gold nanoparticles (Au NPs) conjugated with poly(ethylene glycol) (PEG) and lectin to specifically target the Thomsen-Friedenreich antigen (TF-Ag) on leukemic cells. In leukemia cells, the Au NPs-PEG-lectin (PNA, peanut agglutinin) conjugate exhibited significant cytotoxic activity. Cytotoxicity tests on cell lines HL-60 and K562 demonstrated effective $IC_{50}$ values of 132.5 μg/mL and 314.8 μg/mL, respectively. In HL-60 cells, flow cytometry revealed dose-dependent apoptosis rates up to 51.03% without necrosis, alongside G0/G1 phase cell cycle arrest, confirmed through DNA fragmentation and phospho-histone/BrdU dual staining. The responsiveness of the conjugate to acidic environments and interaction with TF-Ag was confirmed via molecular docking. The findings suggest that the Au NPs–PEG–lectin conjugate holds promise as a therapeutic agent for leukemia by specifically targeting and delivering cytotoxic effects to leukemic cells, thereby enhancing treatment specificity (Akram et al., 2022). A glycan-targeting nanoparticle, Lec-Doxosome, is designed to enhance the specificity and effectiveness of cancer treatment by targeting unique glycan patterns on pancreatic cancer cells. Utilizing rBC2LCN lectin, which binds specifically to fucosylated glycans expressed on pancreatic cancer cells, the researchers modified doxorubicin-loaded liposomes to optimize drug delivery. In vitro experiments using the Capan-1 pancreatic cancer cell line revealed that Lec-Doxosome achieved 1.2- to 1.6-fold higher doxorubicin accumulation and a 1.5-fold increase in cytotoxicity compared to unmodified liposomes, indicating improved drug uptake and effectiveness. In vivo studies involved administering Lec-Doxosome intravenously to mice with subcutaneous tumors over 3 weeks. The results showed a significant reduction in mean tumor weight (368 mg) compared to unmodified liposomes (456 mg), without causing additional adverse effects (Kimura et al., 2021).

Lectin-conjugated PLGA nanoparticles (TP5–NPs) were developed for the oral delivery of thymopentin, a therapeutic peptide. WGA was the conjugated lectin to enhance mucosal adhesion and drug delivery. The study showed that WGA–TP5–NPs significantly increased adherence to mucosal surfaces by 1.8–4.2 times compared to nonconjugated nanoparticles and retained sugar-specific binding capabilities. In vitro experiments demonstrated enhanced interaction with pig mucin, indicating strong adhesion to gastrointestinal tract surfaces. Pharmacodynamic studies revealed that oral administration of WGA–TP5–NPs leads to a significant increase in $CD4^+/CD8^+$ ratios, reflecting enhanced immune modulation, which was attributed to the mucoadhesive properties of WGA. This facilitated better interaction with intestinal lining cells and improved thymopentin absorption. Overall, the findings confirm that WGA-conjugated PLGA nanoparticles improve the intestinal uptake and therapeutic effects of thymopentin by increasing specific bioadhesion (Yin et al., 2006).

The use of lectin-conjugated gliadin nanoparticles was carried out as a targeted drug delivery system aimed at neutralizing *Helicobacter pylori* (*H. pylori*). These nanoparticles, loaded with acetohydroxamic acid (AHA), an antimicrobial agent, were tailored to bind specifically to the carbohydrate receptors of *H. pylori*, which is responsible for stomach infections such as ulcers and gastritis. The researchers enhanced targeting specificity by conjugating UEA-I and Con-A to the gliadin nanoparticles and using a two-stage carbodiimide coupling method. The effectiveness of these modifications was confirmed through lectin-agglutination assays, which showed strong binding efficiencies for both Con-A- and UEA-I-modified nanoparticles to the bacterial receptors. Further analysis through in situ adherence assays demonstrated that these formulations could completely inhibit *H. pylori* from adhering to human gastric cells, indicating a potential to prevent infection. The antimicrobial efficacy was further validated by growth inhibition studies, which revealed that the UEA-GNP and ConA-GNP formulations offered approximately twice the inhibitory effect on *H. pylori* compared to nonmodified gliadin nanoparticles. These findings underline the potential of lectin-conjugated gliadin nanoparticles as effective targeted drug delivery systems for treating *H. pylori* infections. By specifically targeting and adhering to *H. pylori*, these nanoparticles enhance the therapeutic effect while minimizing side effects, thereby offering a promising strategy for managing such infections (Umamaheshwari and Jain, 2003). In another study, gastro-retentive nanoparticles were developed using PLGA conjugated with Con-A to deliver AHA and clarithromycin. In vitro tests revealed sustained drug release over 8 h in simulated gastric fluid, showing predominant performance compared to nanoparticles without Con-A. The study also demonstrated that Con-A-conjugated nanoparticles exhibited significant anti-*H. pylori* activity, achieving the largest zone of inhibition among tested formulations. These results suggest that Con-A-conjugated PLGA nanoparticles provide an effective dual-drug delivery system, improving bioadhesion and sustained release. This strategy offers a promising solution for better therapeutic outcomes in treating *H. pylori* infections, addressing a persistent clinical challenge with enhanced antibacterial activity (Jain et al., 2016).

The use of jacalin-fortified cationic copper sulfide (cCuS) nanoparticles, called JcCuS, was investigated for targeted drug delivery against drug-resistant pathogens, focusing on carbapenem-resistant *Acinetobacter baumannii* (*A. baumannii*). Jacalin, a lectin from jackfruit seeds, recognizes bacterial cell surface glycans and enhances pathogen adhesion. JcCuS demonstrated significantly improved antibacterial activity, lowering the minimum inhibitory concentration (MIC) to 15.63 μM, markedly better than cCuS alone and ciprofloxacin. Mechanistically, JcCuS disrupts bacterial membranes, induces reactive oxygen species production, and displays potent antibiofilm activity at 3.91 μM, effectively preventing and disrupting biofilms without affecting bacterial viability. The nanoparticles also inhibited biofilm-related virulence factors like pellicle formation and motility behaviors. In vivo, JcCuS nanoparticles successfully treated *A. baumannii*-infected zebrafish, reducing pathogen proliferation and leading to full recovery within 12 h (Singaravelu et al., 2022).

WGA-functionalized poly(lactide-co-glycolide) nanoparticles (PLGA-NPs) were used as bioadhesive carriers to enhance the delivery of antitubercular drugs. These nanoparticles were tested to reduce dosing frequency in tuberculosis (TB) treatment and improve patient compliance. WGA was successfully conjugated to PLGA-NPs using a two-step carbodiimide process, creating particles that adhered well to biological tissues. When administered to guinea pigs via oral and aerosol routes, the WGA-coated nanoparticles revealed significant improvements in pharmacokinetics. The presence of rifampicin was detectable in plasma for 6–7 days and isoniazid and pyrazinamide for 13–14 days, compared to shorter durations for uncoated nanoparticles. Additionally, all drugs were retained in the lungs, liver, and spleen for up to 15 days. The study demonstrated that WGA-coated PLGA-NPs significantly increased the relative bioavailability of the drugs. Notably, only three doses of the lectin-coated nanoparticles, administered fortnightly, were sufficient to reduce mycobacterial colony-forming units to undetectable levels, compared to 45 doses required for free drugs (Sharma et al., 2004).

Current nanotechnology-based systems lack sufficient targeting in inflammatory bowel disease, leading to drug elimination before reaching therapeutic levels. To combat this, researchers utilized lectin-decorated nanoparticles for selective targeting and adhesion to inflamed tissues in an experimental colitis model. The nanoparticles (PLGA-NPs) were decorated with peanut (PNA) and WGA lectins, which enhanced their bioadhesion and stability. In vivo tests using murine colitis models showed that these lectin-coated nanoparticles, especially those with PNA, bound significantly more to inflamed tissues than uncoated nanoparticles, demonstrating distinguished selectivity and binding percentages—52.2% for PNA 22.0% for WGA, against 18.6% for uncoated NPs. This increased targeting resulted in markedly improved therapeutic outcomes. Notably, inflammatory markers showed significant reductions: PNA-conjugated NPs exhibited lower myeloperoxidase levels (55 ± 37

U/g) compared to uncoated NPs (145 ± 98 U/g), and TNF-α levels were also reduced (3880 ± 380 U/g for PNA-NP vs. 6971 ± 1157 U/g for uncoated NPs) (Moulari et al., 2014).

Lectin-modified solid lipid nanoparticles (SLNs) were developed to enhance the oral delivery of insulin, which has low bioavailability because of its gastrointestinal degradation. In vitro tests showed that both unmodified and WGA-N-glutaryl-phosphatidylethanolamine (WGA-NGPE)-modified SLNs protected insulin from enzymatic breakdown. Importantly, WGA-modified SLNs provided additional stability and possibly improved mucosal adhesion, enhancing retention and absorption. In vivo, oral administration of these SLNs to rats demonstrated improved pharmacological bioavailability of insulin, with 4.46% for SLNs and 6.08% for WGA-modified SLNs. Overall, the study highlights the potential of lectin-modified SLNs in improving oral bioavailability and stability of insulin, suggesting that such modifications could provide a more effective, noninvasive alternative to injection, enhancing patient compliance and quality of life (Zhang et al., 2006). A more recent study presents the development of a smart oral insulin delivery system using vitamin B12-fucoidan-Con-A nanoparticles (VB12-FU-ConA NPs) to improve glycemic management in diabetes. The system benefits from the glucose sensitivity of Con-A and Fucoidan's antiinflammatory and hypoglycemic effects. During conditions of increased glucose concentration, free glucose competes to bind with Con A, which causes the nanocarrier to swell and facilitates insulin release. Vitamin B12 further promotes uptake by binding to intestinal factors, improving transit and insulin absorption. In vitro tests demonstrated that the nanosystem released significantly more insulin in hyperglycemic conditions compared to normoglycemic conditions. In vivo studies in type 1 diabetic mice displayed that oral administration of the nanosystem significantly decreased blood glucose levels and reduced inflammatory markers like TNF-α and IL-6. Blood glucose levels dropped to a minimum of 8.1 ± 0.4 mmol/L after 8 h, indicating effective glucose control with reduced hypoglycemia risk. Additionally, the biodegradability and biosafety of the system were confirmed, showing VB12-FU-ConA nanocarriers as a promising approach for managing blood glucose levels in diabetic patients (Zhou et al., 2024).

The management of oral ulcerative lesions is particularly important for immunosuppressed patients treated with chemotherapy. To improve traditional therapies, which often require frequent dosing and lead to poor compliance, researchers developed WGA-conjugated liposomes to serve as bioadhesive drug carriers. These WGA liposomes were engineered for strong adherence to oral epithelial cells and enable sustained drug release over a span of several days. In vitro experiments revealed that these liposomes, loaded with amoxicillin, maintained prolonged drug release, thus improving therapeutic efficacy. In tests against *Streptococcus* mutans, a common oral pathogen, the WGA liposomes showed potent antimicrobial activity. Exocytosis studies confirmed that the liposomes remained in oral cells for up to 48 h before being expelled, preventing cytotoxicity due to accumulation. Additionally, cell viability tests showed that WGA liposomes reduced damage to bacterially infected oral cells compared to untreated ones, demonstrating effective drug delivery and providing additional protection for host cells (Wijetunge et al., 2018).

The effectiveness of nanoparticles made from polyethylene glycol–block-poly-(D,L)-lactic-co-glycolic acid (PEG-PLGA) and functionalized with STL was tested for haloperidol, which is used to manage the positive symptoms of schizophrenia. This system aimed to enhance brain delivery of haloperidol by targeting specific carbohydrate receptors. These nanoparticles demonstrated high efficiency in STL conjugation and drug encapsulation, ensuring effective delivery of haloperidol with minimal systemic side effects. In vitro studies showed a controlled release, with only 6%–8% of haloperidol released over 96 h, indicating the potential for sustained delivery directly to brain tissue. In vivo efficacy was demonstrated as haloperidol from the nanoparticles successfully targeted dopamine D2 receptors, crucial for antipsychotic effects. Catalepsy tests confirmed the effectiveness of nanoparticles. Notably, intranasal administration resulted in a 1.5 to 3 times increase in brain concentration of haloperidol compared to nonfunctionalized methods, highlighting STL's role in enhancing targeting efficiency (Piazza et al., 2014). Moreover, the nasal mucoadhesive microspheres were examined for direct delivery of rivastigmine, which is the drug to manage and treat neurodegenerative disease in patients with Alzheimer's and Parkinson's disease, to the brain. The surface modification of the microspheres with lectin significantly enhanced the bioadhesion strength of the microspheres, increasing adhesion on goat nasal mucosa from 29% to 64%. This enhancement facilitated improved retention and absorption in the nasal passage, crucial for effective delivery. In vivo studies in rats demonstrated significantly better memory retention in those treated with the lectin-functionalized microspheres compared to a pure drug solution, indicating improved therapeutic efficacy (Gao et al., 2021).

## 7. Conclusion

Currently, specific drug targeting with lectin-based nanocarriers represents a rapidly evolving field with significant outputs for advancing drug delivery systems. These nanocarriers benefit from the unique ability of lectins to selectively bind to specific glycan patterns, which are often distinct on the surface of various cell types. The binding specificity of lectins to certain glycan motifs allows for targeted delivery of therapeutic agents, including many drugs, nucleic acids, and vaccines, potentially enhancing efficacy while minimizing side effects. Additionally, most nanocarrier platforms have been successfully integrated with lectins. One of the major focuses of research in lectin-based nanosystems is optimizing the targeting capabilities of these nanocarriers. Therefore, it is important to identify specific carbohydrate patterns expressed on cancer cells or cells playing a role in disease processes and the lectins with high specificity to them. Besides, researchers are also exploring recombinant lectins and synthetic analogs to improve binding characteristics and reduce immunogenicity. In addition to targeting, optimizing the physicochemical properties of lectin-based nanocarriers is crucial. Adjustments in size, surface charge, and hydrophobicity are being studied to enhance cellular uptake and systemic circulation. Among the innovative applications, one promising area is the delivery of nucleic acids, which is pivotal for treating genetic disorders and cancers. The development of these systems is supported by ongoing studies aimed at evaluating their safety and efficacy. The potential use of lectin-based nanocarriers in vaccine development is another critical research area. By facilitating the targeted delivery of antigens to immune cells, these systems can enhance immunogenic responses and improve vaccine stability. This capability is particularly valuable for addressing emerging infectious diseases by promoting robust and long-lasting immunity.

## AI disclosure

During the preparation of this work, the author(s) used ChatGPT-40 in order to improve the language and readability of the text. After using this tool/service, the author(s) reviewed and edited the content as needed and take(s) full responsibility for the content of the publication.

## References

Acosta, W., Cramer, C.L., 2020. Targeting macromolecules to CNS and other hard-to-treat organs using lectin-mediated delivery. Int. J. Mol. Sci. 21 (3). https://doi.org/10.3390/ijms21030971.

Adami, R., Bottai, D., 2022. Curcumin and neurological diseases. Nutr. Neurosci. 25 (3), 441–461. https://doi.org/10.1080/1028415X.2020.1760531.

Ahmed, H., Guha, P., Kaptan, E., Bandyopadhyaya, G., 2011. Galectin-3: A potential target for cancer prevention. Trends in Carbohydrate Research 3 (2), 12–21.

Akram, S.M., Al-Saffar, A.Z., Hadi, N.A., Akram, S.M., 2022. Utilization of novel lectin-conjugated Au nanoparticles as Thomsen-Friedenreich onco-antigen target for in vitro cytotoxicity and apoptosis induction in leukemic cell line. Life Sci. 311. https://doi.org/10.1016/j.lfs.2022.121163.

Ambrosi, M., Cameron, N.R., Davis, B.G., 2005. Lectins: Tools for the molecular understanding of the glycocode. Org. Biomol. Chem. 3 (9), 1593–1608. https://doi.org/10.1039/b414350g.

André, S., Kaltner, H., Manning, J.C., Murphy, P.V., Gabius, H.J., 2015. Lectins: Getting familiar with translators of the sugar code. Molecules 20 (2), 1788–1823. https://doi.org/10.3390/molecules20021788.

Ann Clark, M., Blair, H., Liang, L., Brey, R.N., Brayden, D., Hirst, B.H., 2001. Targeting polymerised liposome vaccine carriers to intestinal M cells. Vaccine 20 (1–2), 208–217. https://doi.org/10.1016/S0264-410X(01)00258-4.

Beg, S., Choudhry, H., Zamzami, M.A., Alharbi, K.S., Rahman, M., Singh, B., 2018. Nanocolloidal lipidic carriers of olmesartan medoxomil surface-tailored with Concavalin-A for lectin receptor targeting. Nanomedicine 13 (24), 3107–3128. https://doi.org/10.2217/nnm-2018-0188.

Bektas, S., Kaptan, E., 2024. Microbial lectins as a potential therapeutics for the prevention of certain human diseases. Life Sci. 346, 122643. https://doi.org/10.1016/j.lfs.2024.122643.

Bloise, N., Okkeh, M., Restivo, E., Pina, C.Della, Visai, L., 2021. Targeting the "sweet side" of tumor with glycan-binding molecules conjugated-nanoparticles: Implications in cancer therapy and diagnosis. Nanomaterials 11 (2), 289. https://doi.org/10.3390/nano11020289.

Bodenberger, N., Kubiczek, D., Halbgebauer, D., Rimola, V., Wiese, S., Mayer, D., Rodriguez Alfonso, A.A., Ständker, L., Stenger, S., Rosenau, F., 2018. Lectin-functionalized composite hydrogels for "capture-and-Killing" of carbapenem-resistant pseudomonas aeruginosa. Biomacromolecules 19 (7), 2472–2482. https://doi.org/10.1021/acs.biomac.8b00089.

Brück, A., Abu-Dahab, R., Borchard, G., Schäfer, U.F., Lehr, C.M., 2001. Lectin-functionalized liposomes for pulmonary drug delivery: Interaction with human alveolar epithelial cells. J. Drug Target. 9 (4), 241–251. https://doi.org/10.3109/10611860108997933.

Cecioni, S., Imberty, A., Vidal, S., 2015. Glycomimetics versus multivalent glycoconjugates for the design of high affinity lectin ligands. Chem. Rev. 115 (1), 525–561. https://doi.org/10.1021/cr500303t.

Chen, J., Zhang, C., Liu, Q., Shao, X., Feng, C., Shen, Y., Zhang, Q., Jiang, X., 2012. Solanum tuberosum lectin-conjugated PLGA nanoparticles for nose-to-brain delivery: In vivo and in vitro evaluations. J. Drug Target. 20 (2), 174–184. https://doi.org/10.3109/1061186X.2011.622396.

Chen, N.T., Souris, J.S., Cheng, S.H., Chu, C.H., Wang, Y.C., Konda, V., Dougherty, U., Bissonnette, M., Mou, C.Y., Chen, C.T., Lo, L.W., 2017. Lectin-functionalized mesoporous silica nanoparticles for endoscopic detection of premalignant colonic lesions. Nanomed. Nanotechnol. Biol. Med. 13 (6), 1941–1952. https://doi.org/10.1016/j.nano.2017.03.014.

Chettri, D., Boro, M., Sarkar, L., Verma, A.K., 2021. Lectins: Biological significance to biotechnological application. Carbohydr. Res. 506. https://doi.org/10.1016/j.carres.2021.108367.

Choi, Y., Kim, J., Chae, J., Hong, J., Park, J., Jeong, E., Kim, H., Tanaka, M., Okochi, M., Choi, J., 2022. Surface glycan targeting for cancer nano-immunotherapy. J. Contr. Release 342, 321–336. https://doi.org/10.1016/j.jconrel.2022.01.004.

Dan, X., Liu, W., Ng, T.B., 2016. Development and applications of lectins as biological tools in biomedical research. Med. Res. Rev. 36 (2), 221–247. https://doi.org/10.1002/med.21363.

Dan, X.L., Ng, T.B., 2013. Lectins in human cancer: Both a devil and an angel? Curr. Protein Pept. Sci. 14 (6), 481–491. https://doi.org/10.2174/13892037113149990065.

De Oliveira Figueirôa, E., Da Cunha, C.R.A., Albuquerque, P.B.S., De Paula, R.A., Aranda-Souza, M.Â., Alves, M.S., Zagmignan, A., Carneiro-Da-Cunha, M.G., Da Silva, L.C.N., Dos Santos Correia, M.T., 2017. Lectin-carbohydrate interactions: Implications for the development of new anticancer agents. Curr. Med. Chem. 24 (34), 3667–3680. https://doi.org/10.2174/0929867324666170523110400.

De Souza Cândido, E., Pinto, M.F.S., Pelegrini, P.B., Lima, T.B., Silva, O.N., Pogue, R., Grossi-De-Sá, M.F., Franco, O. L., 2011. Plant storage proteins with antimicrobial activity: Novel insights into plant defense mechanisms. Brazil). FASEB (Fed. Am. Soc. Exp. Biol.) J. 25 (10), 3290–3305. https://doi.org/10.1096/fj.11-184291(.

Deguchi, A., 2015. Curcumin targets in inflammation and cancer. Endocr. Metab. Immune Disord. - Drug Targets 15 (2), 88–96. https://doi.org/10.2174/1871530315666150316120458.

Della Giovampaola, C., Capone, A., Ermini, L., Lupetti, P., Vannuccini, E., Finetti, F., Donnini, S., Ziche, M., Magnani, A., Leone, G., Rossi, C., Rosati, F., Bonechi, C., 2017. Formulation of liposomes functionalized with Lotus lectin and effective in targeting highly proliferative cells. Biochim. Biophys. Acta Gen. Subj. 1861 (4), 860–870. https://doi.org/10.1016/j.bbagen.2017.01.015.

Du, L., Yu, Z., Pang, F., Xu, X., Mao, A., Yuan, W., He, K., Li, B., 2018. Targeted delivery of GP5 antigen of PRRSV to M cells enhances the antigen-specific systemic and mucosal immune responses. Front. Cell. Infect. Microbiol. (8). https://doi.org/10.3389/fcimb.2018.00007.

Elumalai, P., Rubeena, A.S., Lakshmi, S., Anbazhagan, V., Arockiaraj, J., Divya, M., Vijayakumar, S., Vaseeharan, B., 2021. Shrimp lectin–conjugated copper sulfide nanoparticles enhance immune response and gene expression in Etroplus suratensis infected with Aeromonas hydrophila. Aquac. Int. 29 (3), 1103–1120. https://doi.org/10.1007/s10499-021-00679-5.

Ferreira, I.G., Carrascal, M., Mineiro, A.G., Bugalho, A., Borralho, P., Silva, Z., Dall'Olio, F., Videira, P.A., 2019. Carcinoembryonic antigen is a sialyl Lewis x/a carrier and an E-selectin ligand in non-small cell lung cancer. Int. J. Oncol. 55 (5), 1033–1048. https://doi.org/10.3892/ijo.2019.4886.

Freitas, R., Ferreira, E., Miranda, A., Ferreira, D., Relvas-Santos, M., Castro, F., Santos, B., Gonçalves, M., Quintas, S., Peixoto, A., Palmeira, C., Silva, A.M.N., Santos, L.L., Oliveira, M.J., Sarmento, B., Ferreira, J.A., 2024. Targeted and self-adjuvated nanoglycovaccine candidate for cancer immunotherapy. ACS Nano 18 (14), 10088–10103. https://doi.org/10.1021/acsnano.3c12487.

Gajbhiye, V., Gong, S., 2013. Lectin functionalized nanocarriers for gene delivery. Biotechnol. Adv. 31 (5), 552–562. https://doi.org/10.1016/j.biotechadv.2013.01.005.

Gajdos, L., Blakeley, M.P., Haertlein, M., Forsyth, V.T., Devos, J.M., Imberty, A., 2022. Neutron crystallography reveals mechanisms used by Pseudomonas aeruginosa for host-cell binding. Nat. Commun. 13 (1). https://doi.org/10.1038/s41467-021-27871-8.

Gao, X., Wang, T., Wu, B., Chen, J., Chen, J., Yue, Y., Dai, N., Chen, H., Jiang, X., 2008. Quantum dots for tracking cellular transport of lectin-functionalized nanoparticles. Biochem. Biophys. Res. Commun. 377 (1), 35–40. https://doi.org/10.1016/j.bbrc.2008.09.077.

Gao, Y., Almalki, W.H., Afzal, O., Panda, S.K., Kazmi, I., Alrobaian, M., Katouah, H.A., Altamimi, A.S.A., Al-Abbasi, F.A., Alshehri, S., Soni, K., Ibrahim, I.A.A., Rahman, M., Beg, S., 2021. Systematic development of lectin conjugated microspheres for nose-to-brain delivery of rivastigmine for the treatment of Alzheimer's disease. Biomed. Pharmacother. 141. https://doi.org/10.1016/j.biopha.2021.111829.

Gebert, A., 1997. The role of M cells in the protection of mucosal membranes. Histochem. Cell Biol. 108 (6), 455–470. https://doi.org/10.1007/s004180050186.

Ghanimi Fard, M., Khabir, Z., Reineck, P., Cordina, N.M., Abe, H., Ohshima, T., Dalal, S., Gibson, B.C., Packer, N. H., Parker, L.M., 2022. Targeting cell surface glycans with lectin-coated fluorescent nanodiamonds. Nanoscale Adv. 4 (6), 1551–1564. https://doi.org/10.1039/d2na00036a.

Ghazarian, H., Idoni, B., Oppenheimer, S.B., 2011. A glycobiology review: Carbohydrates, lectins and implications in cancer therapeutics. Acta Histochem. 113 (3), 236–247. https://doi.org/10.1016/j.acthis.2010.02.004.

Groux-Degroote, S., Delannoy, P., 2021. Cancer-associated glycosphingolipids as tumor markers and targets for cancer immunotherapy. Int. J. Mol. Sci. 22 (11), 6145. https://doi.org/10.3390/ijms22116145.

Gupta, B., Sadaria, D., Warrier, V.U., Kirtonia, A., Kant, R., Awasthi, A., Baligar, P., Pal, J.K., Yuba, E., Sethi, G., Garg, M., Gupta, R.K., 2022. Plant lectins and their usage in preparing targeted nanovaccines for cancer immunotherapy. Semin. Cancer Biol. 80, 87–106. https://doi.org/10.1016/j.semcancer.2020.02.005.

Hädrich, G., Vaz, G.R., Bidone, J., Yurgel, V.C., Teixeira, H.F., Gonçalves Dal Bó, A., da Silva Pinto, L., Hort, M.A., Ramos, D.F., Junior, A.S.V., Almeida da Silva, P.E., Dora, C.L., 2022. Development of a novel lipid-based nanosystem functionalized with WGA for enhanced intracellular drug delivery. Pharmaceutics 14 (10). https://doi.org/10.3390/pharmaceutics14102022.

Hamid, R., Masood, A., Wani, I.H., Rafiq, S., 2013. Lectins: Proteins with diverse applications. J. Appl. Pharmaceut. Sci. 3 (4), S93. https://doi.org/10.7324/JAPS.2013.34.S18India.

Hashim, O.H., Jayapalan, J.J., Lee, C.S., 2017. Lectins: An effective tool for screening of potential cancer biomarkers. PeerJ 2017 (9). https://doi.org/10.7717/peerj.3784.

He, S., Simpson, B.K., Sun, H., Ngadi, M.O., Ma, Y., Huang, T., 2018. Phaseolus vulgaris lectins: A systematic review of characteristics and health implications. Crit. Rev. Food Sci. Nutr. 58 (1), 70–83. https://doi.org/10.1080/10408398.2015.1096234.

Hendrickson, O.D., Zherdev, A.V., 2018. Analytical application of lectins. Crit. Rev. Anal. Chem. 48 (4), 279–292. https://doi.org/10.1080/10408347.2017.1422965.

Huo, F., Zhang, Y., Li, Y., Bu, H., Zhang, Y., Li, W., et al., 2022. Mannose-targeting concanavalin A-epirubicin conjugate for targeted intravesical chemotherapy of bladder cancer. Chem.-Asian J. 17.

Jain, S.K., Haider, T., Kumar, A., Jain, A., 2016. Lectin-conjugated clarithromycin and acetohydroxamic acid-loaded PLGA nanoparticles: A novel approach for effective treatment of H. pylori. AAPS PharmSciTech 17 (5), 1131–1140. https://doi.org/10.1208/s12249-015-0443-5.

Jepson, M.A., Clark, M.A., Hirst, B.H., 2004. M cell targeting by lectins: A strategy for mucosal vaccination and drug delivery. Adv. Drug Deliv. Rev. 56 (4), 511–525. https://doi.org/10.1016/j.addr.2003.10.018.

Jin, X., Yang, G.-Y., 2023. Pathophysiological roles and applications of glycosphingolipids in the diagnosis and treatment of cancer diseases. Prog. Lipid Res. 91, 101241. https://doi.org/10.1016/j.plipres.2023.101241.

Johannes, L., Wunder, C., Shafaq-Zadah, M., 2016. Glycolipids and lectins in endocytic uptake processes. J. Mol. Biol. 428 (24), 4792–4818. https://doi.org/10.1016/j.jmb.2016.10.027.

Ju, T., Aryal, R.P., Kudelka, M.R., Wang, Y., Cummings, R.D., 2014. The cosmc connection to the Tn antigen in cancer. Cancer Biomarkers 14 (1), 63–81. https://doi.org/10.3233/CBM-130375.

Kaptan, E., Sancar-Bas, S., Sancakli, A., Bektas, S., Bolkent, S., 2018. The effect of plant lectins on the survival and malignant behaviors of thyroid cancer cells. J. Cell. Biochem. 119 (7), 6274–6287. https://doi.org/10.1002/jcb.26875.

Kimura, S., Oda, T., Shimomura, O., Enomoto, T., Hashimoto, S., Kuroda, Y., Yu, Y., Kurimori, K., Furuta, T., Miyazaki, Y., Tateno, H., 2021. Novel pancreatic cancer therapy targeting cell surface glycans by liposomes modified with rBC2LCN lectin. Eur. Surg. Res. 61 (4–5), 113–122. https://doi.org/10.1159/000513430.

Kitaguchi, D., Oda, T., Enomoto, T., Ohara, Y., Owada, Y., Akashi, Y., Furuta, T., Yu, Y., Kimura, S., Kuroda, Y., Kurimori, K., Miyazaki, Y., Furuya, K., Shimomura, O., Tateno, H., 2020. Lectin drug conjugate therapy for colorectal cancer. Cancer Sci. 111 (12), 4548–4557. https://doi.org/10.1111/cas.14687.

Kovalenko, V.L., Komedchikova, E.N., Sogomonyan, A.S., Tereshina, E.D., Kolesnikova, O.A., Mirkasymov, A.B., Iureva, A.M., Zvyagin, A.V., Nikitin, P.I., Shipunova, V.O., 2023. Lectin-modified magnetic nano-PLGA for photodynamic therapy in vivo. Pharmaceutics 15 (1). https://doi.org/10.3390/pharmaceutics15010092.

Lavín de Juan, L., García Recio, V., Jiménez López, P., Girbés Juan, T., Cordoba-Diaz, M., Cordoba-Diaz, D., 2017. Pharmaceutical applications of lectins. J. Drug Deliv. Sci. Technol. 42, 126–133. https://doi.org/10.1016/j.jddst.2017.05.018.

Lebreton, A., Bonnardel, F., Dai, Y.C., Imberty, A., Martin, F.M., Lisacek, F., 2021. A comprehensive phylogenetic and bioinformatics survey of lectins in the fungal kingdom. bioRxiv. https://doi.org/10.1101/2021.04.01.438069.

León, B., Ardavín, C., 2008. Monocyte migration to inflamed skin and lymph nodes is differentially controlled by L-selectin and PSGL-1. Blood 111 (6), 3126–3130. https://doi.org/10.1182/blood-2007-07-100610.

Li, J., Mooney, D.J., 2016. Designing hydrogels for controlled drug delivery. Nat. Rev. Mater. 1 (12). https://doi.org/10.1038/natrevmats.2016.71.

Li, X., Su, J., Kamal, Z., Guo, P., Wu, X., Lu, L., Wu, H., Qiu, M., 2020. Odorranalectin modified PEG–PLGA/PEG–PBLG curcumin-loaded nanoparticle for intranasal administration. Drug Dev. Ind. Pharm. 46 (6), 899–909. https://doi.org/10.1080/03639045.2020.1762202.

Liang, J.X., Liang, Y., Gao, W., 2016. Clinicopathological and prognostic significance of sialyl Lewis X overexpression in patients with cancer: A meta-analysis. OncoTargets Ther. 9, 3113–3125. https://doi.org/10.2147/OTT.S102389.

Liu, Y., Wang, P., Sun, C., Feng, N., Zhou, W., Yang, Y., Tan, R., Chen, Z., Wu, S., Zhao, J., 2010. Wheat germ agglutinin-grafted lipid nanoparticles: Preparation and in vitro evaluation of the association with Caco-2 monolayers. Int. J. Pharm. 397 (1–2), 155–163. https://doi.org/10.1016/j.ijpharm.2010.06.030.

Loureiro, L.R., Carrascal, M.A., Barbas, A., Ramalho, J.S., Novo, C., Delannoy, P., Videira, P.A., 2015. Challenges in antibody development against Tn and sialyl-Tn antigens. Biomolecules 5 (3), 1783–1809. https://doi.org/10.3390/biom5031783.

Majee, S.B., Biswas, G.R., 2013. Exploring plant lectins in diagnosis, prophylaxis and therapy. J. Med. Plants Res. 7, 3444–3451.

Mbae, K.M., Umesha, S., Manukumar, H.M., 2018. Therapeutic properties of lectins in herbal supplements. Phytochem. Rev. 17 (3), 627–643. https://doi.org/10.1007/s11101-018-9572-2.

Mirshafiee, V., Kim, R., Park, S., Mahmoudi, M., Kraft, M.L., 2016. Impact of protein pre-coating on the protein corona composition and nanoparticle cellular uptake. Biomaterials 75, 295–304. https://doi.org/10.1016/j.biomaterials.2015.10.019.

Mishra, N., Tiwari, S., Vaidya, B., Agrawal, G.P., Vyas, S.P., 2011. Lectin anchored PLGA nanoparticles for oral mucosal immunization against hepatitis B. J. Drug Target. 19 (1), 67–78. https://doi.org/10.3109/10611861003733946.

Moulari, B., Béduneau, A., Pellequer, Y., Lamprecht, A., 2014. Lectin-decorated nanoparticles enhance binding to the inflamed tissue in experimental colitis. J. Contr. Release 188, 9–17. https://doi.org/10.1016/j.jconrel.2014.05.046.

Munkley, J., 2019. The glycosylation landscape of pancreatic cancer (Review). Oncol. Lett. 17 (3), 2569–2575. https://doi.org/10.3892/ol.2019.9885.

Munkley, J., 2016. The role of sialyl-Tn in cancer. Int. J. Mol. Sci. 17 (3), 275. https://doi.org/10.3390/ijms17030275.

Neutsch, L., Wirth, E.-M., Spijker, S., Pichl, C., Kählig, H., Gabor, F., Wirth, M., 2013. Synergistic targeting/prodrug strategies for intravesical drug delivery — lectin-modified PLGA microparticles enhance cytotoxicity of stearoyl gemcitabine by contact-dependent transfer. J. Contr. Release 169 (1–2), 62–72. https://doi.org/10.1016/j.jconrel.2013.04.004.

Panico, S., Capolla, S., Bozzer, S., Toffoli, G., Dal Bo, M., Macor, P., 2022. Biological features of nanoparticles: Protein corona formation and interaction with the immune system. Pharmaceutics 14 (12), 2605. https://doi.org/10.3390/pharmaceutics14122605.

Piazza, J., Hoare, T., Molinaro, L., Terpstra, K., Bhandari, J., Selvaganapathy, P.R., Gupta, B., Mishra, R.K., 2014. Haloperidol-loaded intranasally administered lectin functionalized poly(ethylene glycol)-block-poly(D,L)-lactic-co-glycolic acid (PEG-PLGA) nanoparticles for the treatment of schizophrenia. Eur. J. Pharm. Biopharm. 87 (1), 30–39. https://doi.org/10.1016/j.ejpb.2014.02.007.

Pinho, S.S., Reis, C.A., 2015. Glycosylation in cancer: Mechanisms and clinical implications. Nat. Rev. Cancer 15 (9), 540–555. https://doi.org/10.1038/nrc3982.

Plattner, V.E., Wagner, M., Ratzinger, G., Gabor, F., Wirth, M., 2008. Targeted drug delivery: Binding and uptake of plant lectins using human 5637 bladder cancer cells. Eur. J. Pharm. Biopharm. 70 (2), 572–576. https://doi.org/10.1016/j.ejpb.2008.06.004.

Pooja, D., Kulhari, H., Kuncha, M., Rachamalla, S.S., Adams, D.J., Bansal, V., Sistla, R., 2016. Improving efficacy, oral bioavailability, and delivery of paclitaxel using protein-grafted solid lipid nanoparticles. Mol. Pharm. 13 (11), 3903–3912. https://doi.org/10.1021/acs.molpharmaceut.6b00691.

Pourhabibi-Zarandi, F., Rafraf, M., Zayeni, H., Asghari-Jafarabadi, M., Ebrahimi, A.A., 2022. Effects of curcumin supplementation on metabolic parameters, inflammatory factors and obesity values in women with rheumatoid arthritis: A randomized, double-blind, placebo-controlled clinical trial. Phytother Res. 36 (4), 1797–1806. https://doi.org/10.1002/ptr.7422.

Pusam, Y., Jaabir, M., Jeyachandran, S., 2022. Molecular Basis of Lectin-Carbohydrate Interaction Lectins: Innate Immune Defense and Therapeutics. Springer Nature, India, pp. 73–88. https://doi.org/10.1007/978-981-16-7462-4_4.

Pusztai, A., Bardocz, S., Ewen, S.W.B., 2008. Uses of plant lectins in bioscience and biomedicine. Front. Biosci. 13 (3), 1130–1140. https://doi.org/10.2741/2750.

Ravindran, S., Suthar, J.K., Rokade, R., Deshpande, P., Singh, P., Pratinidhi, A., Khambadkhar, R., Utekar, S., 2018. Pharmacokinetics, metabolism, distribution and permeability of nanomedicine. Curr. Drug Metabol. 19 (4), 327–334. https://doi.org/10.2174/1389200219666180305154119.

Reily, C., Stewart, T.J., Renfrow, M.B., Novak, J., 2019. Glycosylation in health and disease. Nat. Rev. Nephrol. 15 (6), 346–366. https://doi.org/10.1038/s41581-019-0129-4.

Rekha Mol, K.R., Mohamed Hatha, A.A., 2023. Use of Lectin-Functionalized and Lectin-Targeted Nanoparticles for Multiple Therapeutic Applications Applications of Multifunctional Nanomaterials. Elsevier, India, pp. 543–566. https://doi.org/10.1016/B978-0-12-820557-0.00023-0.

Roy, R., Murphy, P.V., Gabius, H.J., 2016. Multivalent carbohydrate-lectin interactions: How synthetic chemistry enables insights into nanometric recognition. Molecules 21 (5). https://doi.org/10.3390/molecules21050629.

Saad, A.A., 2022. Targeting cancer-associated glycans as a therapeutic strategy in leukemia. Life 15 (1), 378–433. https://doi.org/10.1080/26895293.2022.2049901.

Sadek, H.E., Ebadah, I.M., Mahmoud, Y.A., 2023. Importance of biotechnology in controlling insect pests. J. Mod. Agric. Biotechnol. 2 (1), 5. https://doi.org/10.53964/jmab.2023005.

Sajja, R.K., Cudic, P., Cucullo, L., 2019. In vitro characterization of odorranalectin for peptide-based drug delivery across the blood-brain barrier. BMC Neurosci. 20 (1). https://doi.org/10.1186/s12868-019-0504-x.

Sakhon, O.S., Ross, B., Gusti, V., Pham, A.J., Vu, K., Lo, D.D., 2015. M cell-derived vesicles suggest a unique pathway for trans-epithelial antigen delivery. Tissue Barriers 3 (1–2), e1004975. https://doi.org/10.1080/21688370.2015.1004975.

Schedin-Weiss, S., Winblad, B., Tjernberg, L.O., 2014. The role of protein glycosylation in Alzheimer disease. FEBS J. 281 (1), 46–62. https://doi.org/10.1111/febs.12590.

Sharma, A., Sharma, S., Khuller, G.K., 2004. Lectin-functionalized poly (lactide-co-glycolide) nanoparticles as oral/aerosolized antitubercular drug carriers for treatment of tuberculosis. J. Antimicrob. Chemother. 54 (4), 761–766. https://doi.org/10.1093/jac/dkh411.

Silva, M.L.S., 2019. Lectin biosensors in cancer glycan biomarker detection. Adv. Clin. Chem. 93, 1–61. https://doi.org/10.1016/bs.acc.2019.07.001.

Singaravelu, D.K., Binjawhar, D.N., Ameen, F., Veerappan, A., 2022. Lectin-fortified cationic copper sulfide nanoparticles gain dual targeting capabilities to treat carbapenem-resistant Acinetobacter baumannii infection. ACS Omega 7 (48), 43934–43944. https://doi.org/10.1021/acsomega.2c05252.

Singh, R.S., Bhari, R., Kaur, H.P., 2011. Current trends of lectins from microfungi. Crit. Rev. Biotechnol. 31 (3), 193–210. https://doi.org/10.3109/07388551.2010.505911.

Sun, K., Feng, Z., Fan, C., Min, X., Zhang, P., Xia, L., 2023. A glycosylation signature for predicting the progression and immunotherapeutic response of prostate cancer. J. Gene Med. 25 (6). https://doi.org/10.1002/jgm.3489.

Tobola, F., Wiltschi, B., 2022. One, two, many: strategies to alter the number of carbohydrate binding sites of lectins. Biotechnol. Adv. 60, 108020. https://doi.org/10.1016/j.biotechadv.2022.108020.

Trinchera, M., Aronica, A., Dall'Olio, F., 2017. Selectin ligands sialyl-Lewis A and sialyl-Lewis X in gastrointestinal cancers. Biology 6 (1), 16. https://doi.org/10.3390/biology6010016.

Tvaroška, I., Selvaraj, C., Koča, J., 2020. Selectins-the two Dr. Jekyll and Mr. Hyde faces of adhesion molecules-A review. Molecules 25 (12). https://doi.org/10.3390/molecules25122835.

Umamaheshwari, R.B., Jain, N.K., 2003. Receptor mediated targeting of lectin conjugated gliadin nanoparticles in the treatment of Helicobacter pylori. J. Drug Target. 11 (7), 415–424. https://doi.org/10.1080/10611860310001647771.

Vandenborre, G., Smagghe, G., Van Damme, E.J.M., 2011. Plant lectins as defense proteins against phytophagous insects. Phytochemistry 72 (13), 1538–1550. https://doi.org/10.1016/j.phytochem.2011.02.024.

Vega, E., Burgos, J.M., Souto, E.B., García, M.L., Pujol, M., Sánchez-López, E., 2024. Biodegradable nanoplatforms for antigen delivery: part I–state of the art review of polymeric nanoparticles for cancer immunotherapy. Expet Opin. Drug Deliv. 21 (8), 1251–1262. https://doi.org/10.1080/17425247.2024.2400293.

Vojdani, A., Afar, D., Vojdani, E., 2020. Reaction of lectin-specific antibody with human tissue: Possible contributions to autoimmunity. J. Immunol. Res. 2020. https://doi.org/10.1155/2020/1438957.

Wang, Y., He, S., Zhou, F., Sun, H., Cao, X., Ye, Y., Li, J., 2021. Detection of lectin protein allergen of kidney beans (Phaseolus vulgaris L.) and desensitization food processing technology. J. Agric. Food Chem. 69 (49), 14723–14741. https://doi.org/10.1021/acs.jafc.1c02801.

Wijetunge, S.S., Wen, J., Yeh, C.K., Sun, Y., 2018. Lectin-conjugated liposomes as biocompatible, bioadhesive drug carriers for the management of oral ulcerative lesions. ACS Appl. Bio Mater. 1 (5), 1487–1495. https://doi.org/10.1021/acsabm.8b00425.

Wu, A.M., Lisowska, E., Duk, M., Yang, Z., 2009. Lectins as tools in glycoconjugate research. Glycoconj. J. 26 (8), 899–913. https://doi.org/10.1007/s10719-008-9119-7.

Yang, K., Zhang, S., He, J., Nie, Z., 2021. Polymers and inorganic nanoparticles: A winning combination towards assembled nanostructures for cancer imaging and therapy. Nano Today 36, 101046. https://doi.org/10.1016/j.nantod.2020.101046.

Yasin, U., Bilal, M., Bashir, H., Amirzada, M.I., Sumrin, A., Bin Asad, M.H.H., 2020. Preparation and nanoencapsulation of lectin from lepidium sativum on chitosan-tripolyphosphate nanoparticle and their cytotoxicity against hepatocellular carcinoma cells (HepG2). BioMed Res. Int. 2020. https://doi.org/10.1155/2020/7251346.

Yetisgin, A.A., Cetinel, S., Zuvin, M., Ali, K., Kutlu, O., 2020. Therapeutic nanoparticles and their targeted delivery applications. Molecules 25 (9), 2193. https://doi.org/10.3390/molecules25092193.

Yin, Y.S., Chen, D.W., Qiao, M.X., Lu, Z., Hu, H.Y., 2006. Preparation and evaluation of lectin-conjugated PLGA nanoparticles for oral delivery of thymopentin. J. Contr. Release 116 (3), 337–345. https://doi.org/10.1016/j.jconrel.2006.09.015.

Yu, L.G., 2007. The oncofetal Thomsen-Friedenreich carbohydrate antigen in cancer progression. Glycoconj. J. 24 (8), 411–420. https://doi.org/10.1007/s10719-007-9034-3.

Zhang, N., Ping, Q., Huang, G., Xu, W., Cheng, Y., Han, X., 2006. Lectin-modified solid lipid nanoparticles as carriers for oral administration of insulin. Int. J. Pharm. 327 (1–2), 153–159. https://doi.org/10.1016/j.ijpharm.2006.07.026.

Zhou, J., Ma, H., Guan, M., Feng, J., Dong, X., Wei, Y., Tong, Z., 2024. Anti-inflammatory fucoidan-ConA oral insulin nanosystems for smart blood glucose regulation. Int. J. Pharm. 659, 124250. https://doi.org/10.1016/j.ijpharm.2024.124250.

Zubcevic, N., Damir, S., Focak, M., Rukavina, D., 2016. Effects of plant lectins on human erythrocyte agglutination. Serbian J. Exp. Clin. Res. 17 (3), 207–214. https://doi.org/10.1515/sjecr-2016-0031.

Žurga, S., Nanut, M.P., Kos, J., Sabotič, J., 2017. Fungal lectin MpL enables entry of protein drugs into cancer cells and their subcellular targeting. Oncotarget 8 (16), 26896–26910. https://doi.org/10.18632/oncotarget.15849.

CHAPTER

# 18

# Elastin like polypeptides (ELPs) based nanocarriers for drug delivery

*Ridhima Goel*[1] *and Vijaya Sarangthem*[2]

[1]**Department of Medical Oncology Laboratory, All India Institute of Medical Sciences, New Delhi, India;** [2]**Department of Biochemistry and Cell Biology, Cell and Matrix Research Institute, Kyungpook National University, School of Medicine, Daegu, Republic of Korea**

## 1. Introduction

Elastin-like polypeptides (ELPs) are a class of recombinant biopolymers derived from the repetitive motifs found in tropoelastin, the precursor to lastin, a key protein in the extracellular matrix. Elastin confers strength and extensibility to the underlying connective tissues supporting indefinite cycles of stress and relaxation (Mecham, 1991). Mature elastin is formed by the hierarchical assembly of its spring-like monomer, tropoelastin (Wise et al., 2014; Vrhovski and Weiss, 1998). At the molecular level, tropoelastin is made of repetitive sequences organized into two main regions: "hydrophobic" and "cross-linking" domains. The cross-linking domains, rich in KP or KA motifs, enable the monomers to link together at K residues through lysyl oxidase, forming higher-order structures during elastogenesis (Ozsvar et al., 2021). The hydrophobic domains, which consist of repeating "VPGVG" motifs, drive self-assembly through a reversible process called coacervation. In this process, at temperatures above a certain threshold (Tt), the hydrophobic domains make the monomers to aggregate, while below this temperature, water prevents their association (López Barreiro et al., 2023). Despite the unique mechanical and self-assembling properties of the elastin molecule, the adaptation of this naturally occurring marvel remained underexplored for the longest time due to the inherent insolubility of the fibers, making any manipulation challenging. Interestingly, in 1974, Urry et al. pioneered synthetic elastin-derived sequences (ELPs), showing that the polypentapeptide (VPGVG)n could undergo reversible phase separation in water, mimicking native elastin's behavior (Urry et al., 1974).

*Protein-Based Nanoparticles in Drug Delivery*
**https://doi.org/10.1016/B978-0-443-33639-3.00020-9**

Later on, advances in genetic engineering have led to the development of a wide variety of functional ELP polymers that inherit the remarkable temperature-responsive phase transitions and mechanical properties of their biological counterparts. Through genetic synthesis, researchers can precisely control parameters such as molecular weight, hydrophobicity, and transition temperature of ELPs. This level of customization allows for the design of ELPs tailored to the specific demands of various applications, such as optimizing structures for efficient drug loading, regulating release profiles, or enhancing tissue compatibility. Such flexibility is often unmatched by synthetic polymers, which generally have more rigid structures.

ELPs are characterized by their pentapeptide repeat sequence (VPGXG)n, where X can be any amino acid except proline. This sequence confers unique phase transition behavior, whereby ELPs undergo reversible aggregation in response to temperature changes. Specifically, ELPs are soluble below their inverse transition temperature (Tt) but aggregate into coacervates when the temperature exceeds Tt, a property that is exploited in drug delivery applications for controlled release and targeted delivery (Amiram et al., 2011). The inherent biocompatibility, biodegradability, and tunability of ELPs make them attractive candidates for the development of nanoparticle-based drug delivery systems (DDSs). By adjusting the molecular weight, hydrophobicity, and sequence composition, ELPs can be engineered to self-assemble into nanoparticles capable of encapsulating a wide range of therapeutic agents, including small molecules, peptides, and nucleic acids (Daniels et al., 2009). Furthermore, ELP nanoparticles can be modified with targeting ligands or cell-penetrating peptides (CPPs), enabling selective delivery to specific tissues or cells, thereby enhancing therapeutic efficacy while minimizing off-target effects (García-Arévalo et al., 2014).

One of the key advantages of ELP-based nanoparticles is their ability to respond to external stimuli such as temperature, pH, or enzymatic activity, enabling site-specific drug release. This feature is particularly advantageous in cancer therapy, where the tumor microenvironment presents distinct physiological characteristics such as acidic pH and elevated temperature that can be exploited for controlled drug release (MacEwan and Chilkoti, 2010). In addition, ELP nanoparticles can leverage the enhanced permeability and retention (EPR) effect, a phenomenon by which nanoparticles preferentially accumulate in tumor tissue due to the leaky vasculature and poor lymphatic drainage commonly associated with tumors (Macewan and Chilkoti, 2012). Recent advances in the design and functionalization of ELP nanoparticles have expanded their application beyond oncology to areas such as gene delivery, regenerative medicine, and immunotherapy (Meyer and Chilkoti, 2004). For instance, ELPs have been conjugated with nucleic acids for gene delivery, where their tunable phase transition properties allow for controlled intracellular release (Ruan et al., 2020). This versatility, coupled with their excellent safety profile, positions ELP-based nanoparticles as a promising platform for the development of next-generation DDSs. In this chapter, we discuss the molecular design, functionalization, and biomedical applications of ELP-based nanoparticles, highlighting their potential to enhance drug delivery outcomes in various therapeutic contexts.

# 2. Design and synthesis of ELP-based nanocarriers

## 2.1 Genetic synthesis of ELPs by RDL method

The genetic synthesis of ELPs represents a critical advancement in the creation of biopolymers with customizable properties for biomedical applications. ELP synthesis relies on several gene assembly techniques, including recursive directional ligation (RDL) and tandem repeat cloning, to create long polypeptide sequences without introducing sequence errors (Meyer and Chilkoti, 2002). RDL, for example, enables the construction of long ELP genes by combining smaller gene fragments in a controlled sequence, which ensures that the repeat units remain intact (Fig. 18.1A). This method is particularly effective for generating high-molecular-weight ELPs. The process of RDL generally involves the following steps.

### 2.1.1 *Designing and synthesizing the initial DNA oligomers*

The RDL process begins with the design of small DNA oligonucleotides, or gene cassettes, that encode the repeating unit of the target sequence (e.g., the pentapeptide sequence Val–Pro–Gly–X–Gly for ELPs). These initial sequences are designed with specific restriction sites at their ends, allowing for easy and efficient ligation. In ELP cloning, for instance, flanking the repetitive DNA sequences with two different restriction enzyme recognition sites, often nonpalindromic, ensures directional assembly and prevents self-ligation.

### 2.1.2 *Ligation and amplification of initial cassettes*

Once synthesized, these initial cassettes are amplified through PCR or another suitable cloning technique. Two copies of the gene cassettes are then ligated using compatible overhangs created by the restriction enzymes, resulting in a doubled sequence. For example, two monomer units (encoding a five-peptide ELP sequence) ligate to form a dimer (10 amino acids), and then dimeric units can be joined to form a tetramer, and so on. This process is recursive because it involves repeating these ligation steps to build progressively larger DNA fragments.

### 2.1.3 *Iterative assembly of repeats via alternating restriction enzymes*

RDL requires the use of two unique restriction enzymes, which recognize distinct overhangs on the cassettes. By alternating between these enzymes in sequential ligation steps, researchers can prevent the unwanted insertion of misaligned sequences. After each round of ligation, the joined sequence is treated with one of the enzymes to create a new sticky end for the next sequence, maintaining the orientation of each insert. Through this iterative process, the gene's length doubles in each cycle, allowing for rapid construction of long, highly repetitive sequences (Hassouneh et al., 2010).

### 2.1.4 *Cloning into expression vectors*

Once the desired number of repeats has been reached, the full-length gene encoding the ELP is inserted into an expression vector for protein production. The constructed sequence is typically inserted into a plasmid and then introduced into a host organism, such as

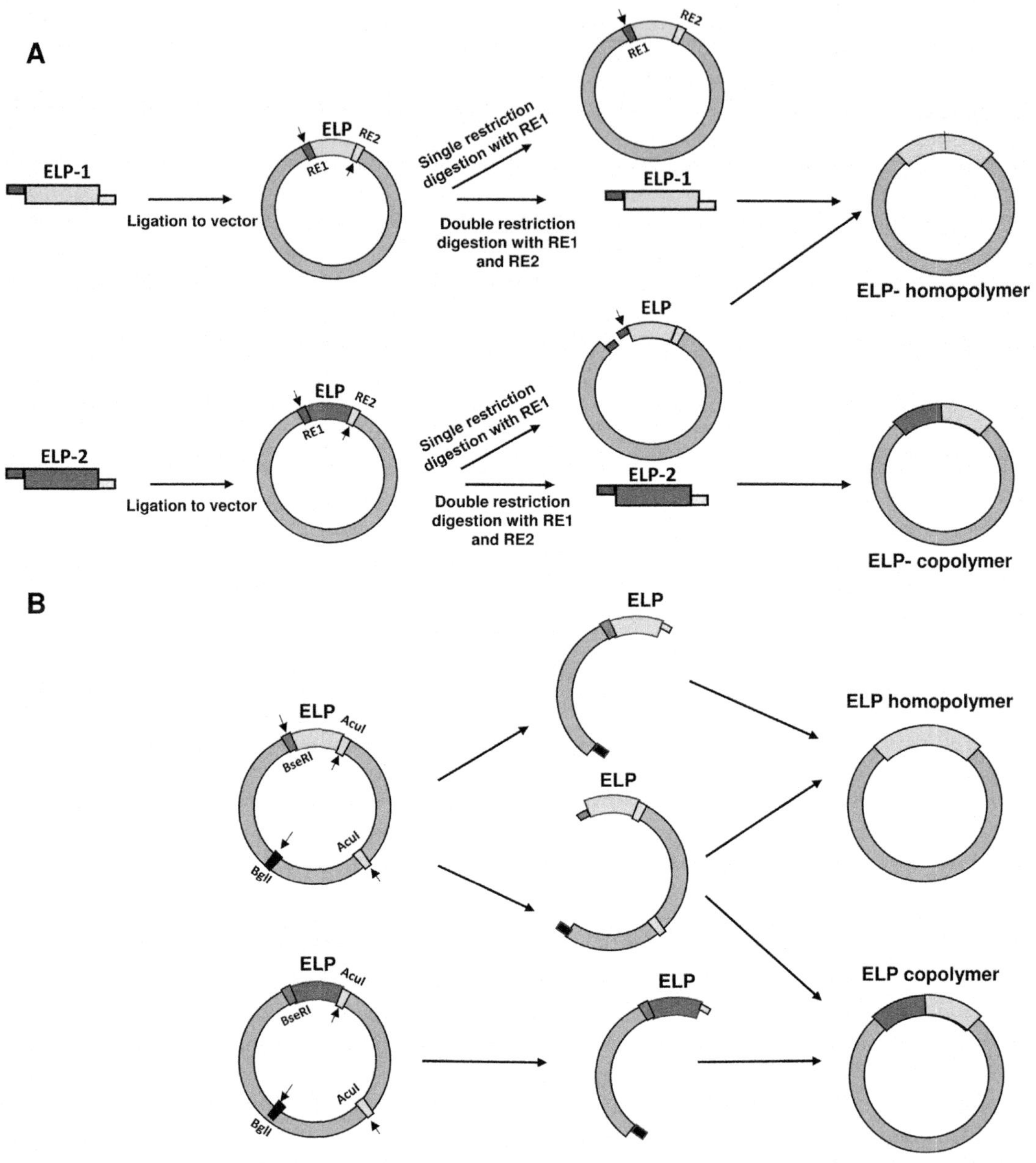


FIGURE 18.1 Genetic synthesis of ELPs by various methods. (A) A schematic illustration of the recursive directional ligation (RDL) method, detailing the stepwise cloning strategy used to assemble ELP repeats. This approach involves inserting ELP monomer units directionally into a vector via specific restriction enzyme (RE) sites, ensuring proper orientation. Each cycle consists of single digestion of the vector with RE1, followed by ligation with ELP fragments that have been double-digested with RE1 and RE2. This process enables controlled and exponential expansion of ELP repeats through repeated cycles of digestion and ligation. Following PRe-RDL, an ELP-1 oligomer or two distinct ELP monomer units, ELP-1 and ELP-2, can be assembled via RDL to create homodimeric or heterodimeric ELPs. (B) The PRe-RDL approach optimizes the RDL process by enabling rapid assembly of extended ELP constructs through initial cloning of an oligomeric unit, instead of individual monomers. This vector is designed with compatible restriction sites flanking the insertion region, allowing for precise ligation and iterative expansion of ELP repeats in subsequent RDL steps. An ELP monomer unit (e.g., ELP-1) can be assembled into an oligomer (e.g., dimer or trimer) using the PRe-RDL method to create a homodimer, or two distinct monomer units, ELP-1 and ELP-2, can be initially cloned separately into oligomeric units to create a heterodimer.

*Escherichia coli*, for recombinant expression of the final protein. This step often involves an additional restriction site outside of the repeating unit to facilitate transfer to expression vectors.

### *2.1.5 Genetic synthesis of ELP by PRe-RDL method*

McDaniel et al. proposed a modified strategy to address the efficiency limitation caused by the use of a single restriction enzyme. The approach referred to as RDL by plasmid reconstruction (PRe-RDL) relies on the generation of a functional plasmid from two independent deconstructed parent plasmid harboring ELP sequences via careful selection of the restriction sites in the two parental plasmids (Fig. 18.1B) (Amiram et al., 2011). The step-wise approach to ELP sequence assembly via RDL and PRe-RDL enables the generation of complex architectures such as block copolymers, as well as the modification of ELP with desirable peptide or protein sequences at the two terminals, providing noble functional attributes to the polymeric sequence. An alternative rather quick approach for the generation of large homopolymeric ELP sequence is overlap extension rolling circle amplification (OERCA) (Amiram et al., 2011). This PCR-based powerful method for multiplexed synthesis uses a circular ssDNA encoding a desired ELP sequence. Initially, rolling circle amplification (RCA) creates a linear ssDNA containing several copies of the circular template. Further, polymerase chain reaction (PCR) with primers complementary to the linear ssDNA product of the RCA reaction yields dsDNA, which lengthens further through overlap extension.

## 2.2 Purification of ELP

The heterologous expression of synthetic ELPs is frequently adapted in *E. coli*, owing to the rapid growth rate, easy scale-up, high yield of product, and cost-effectiveness. However, expression in other model systems such as fungi and plants has also been reported. Purification of ELPs from the lysates of the prokaryote host relies on the polymer's thermal responsive property. Meyer and Chilkoti described a facile method of ELP purification from cellular debris without the need for laborious chromatography. The relatively inexpensive procedure based on the thermoresponsive property of the polymer is referred to as Inverse Transition Cycling (ITC) (Fig. 18.2A) (Meyer and Chilkoti, 1999).

In brief, the method involves three main steps. First, cells expressing the polymer are lysed and centrifuged below the transition temperature of the polymer, such that the ELP is soluble and remains in the supernatant, eliminating cellular debris as a pellet. Further induction of selective aggregation of the polymeric sequences by raising the temperature above the Tt or by depressing the transition temperature to below the solution temperature by the use of kosmotropic salts. This is followed by centrifugation above the Tt to remove the soluble contaminants, recovering ELP in the pellet. The ELP pellet is then solubilized by reversing the phase transition by adding a cold buffer. The solubilized ELP is then centrifuged at a temperature below Tt to further remove additional insoluble contaminants leaving relatively pure ELP in supernatant. Multiple ITC rounds involving repeated cycles of centrifugation above and below the Tt gradually increase the purity of the ELP. This cost- and time-efficient method has been reported to provide yields comparable to those obtained with labor- and time-intensive immobilized metal ion chromatography. Purified ELPs can be

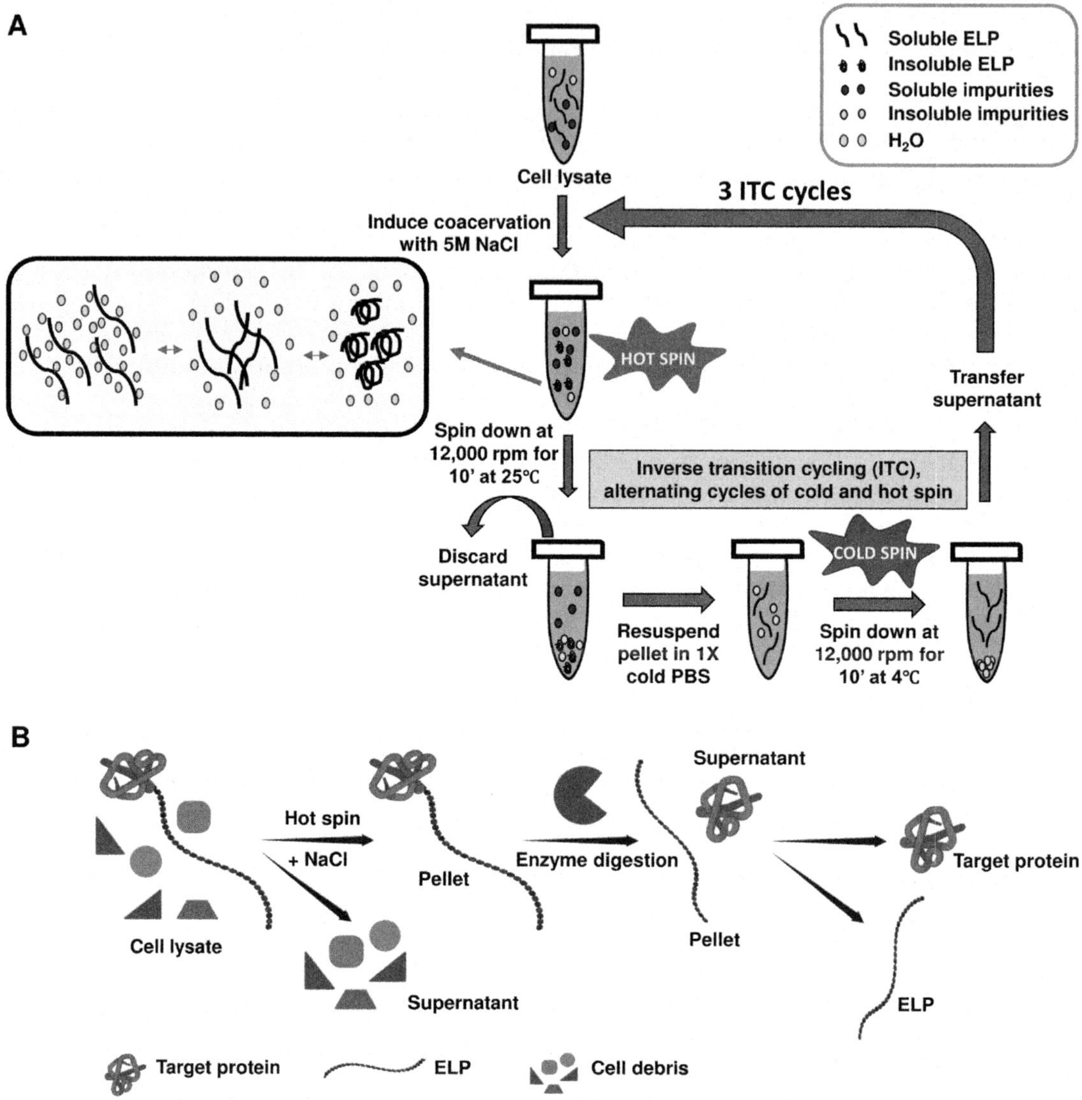


FIGURE 18.2 (A) Purification of elastin-like polymers via facile inverse transition cycling method. ELPs are purified using the inverse transition cycling (ITC) method, a temperature-responsive purification technique. This method involved cyclically altering the solution temperature to promote ELP aggregation and separation from contaminants. At temperatures above the transition threshold, ELPs aggregate and can be easily collected by centrifugation. After removing the supernatant, the temperature is lowered to resolubilize the ELPs in a fresh buffer, facilitating efficient and repeated purification cycles for high-purity ELP recovery. (B) The ELP tag facilitates the purification of fusion proteins expressed in a suitable host system. Initially, the ELP-tagged fusion protein remains soluble. Upon induction of inverse transition cycling (ITC), the ELP tag promotes precipitation of the fusion protein while impurities stay soluble. The fusion protein can then be resuspended in a low-temperature buffer and subjected to enzyme digestion. Further ITC will precipitate the ELP protein, leaving the target protein in the supernatant.

lyophilized for long-term storage. The thermoresponsive property of ELP is retained in a recombinant fusion proteins, making them excellent tags to assist purification of other proteins via ITC(Hassouneh et al., 2010; MacEwan et al., 2014). Several approaches have been reported for cleavage of the ELP tag from its fusion protein. In the first and easiest method, a protease-specific peptide sequence is incorporated between ELP and protein (Fig. 18.2B) (Ge et al., 2005). In the second method, an inducible self-splicing protein intron, called an intein, is inserted between the protein and ELP. The ELP tag is liberated from the fusion partner when a reducing agent, such as dithiothreitol, is added (Ge et al., 2005; Banki et al., 2005). In another approach, a Sortase A (SrtA) recognition site (an LPETG peptide), is introduced between the ELP purification tag and the recombinant protein (Bellucci et al., 2013).

## 2.3 Functionalization via genetic engineering

The sequence of the ELP can be manipulated via genetic engineering to impart added functionality to the polymer without the loss of stimulus responsiveness. The fusion of ELP with CPPs has been shown to bypass cellular barriers, increasing cellular uptake of the payload. Massodi et al. reported that fluorescein-tagged CPP-ELP constructs exhibited improved cellular association in HeLa cells (Massodi et al., 2005). Raucher's group also investigated tumor delivery of an ELP-doxorubicin conjugate using three different CPPs (SynB1, Tat, and Bac). In MCF-7 cells, CPP-tagged ELP-doxorubicin conjugate was shown to be three times more abundant than untagged ELP-doxorubicin (Walker et al., 2012). Additionally, CPP functionalization of diblock copolymer sequence facilitates temperature-controlled interchange of CPP-ELP between the unimer and micelle states. The multivalent presentation of CPP in the micelle state support amplified uptake of the nanopolymer (MacEwan and Chilkoti, 2014). Moreover, the ELP sequence can be modified to present appropriate ligands, promoting active accumulation of the polymer at the pathological site through particular ligand–receptor interactions. Sarangethem et al. cloned IL-4R ligand mimic peptide-AP1 (CRKRLDRN) onto the ELP backbone for active tumor homing of the nanoparticle in IL-4R overexpressing tumors. The functionalized polymer exhibited substantially improved IL-4R binding over the free peptide *ex situ*. Furthermore, compared with the nonfunctionalized polymer, multivalent presentation of the peptide along the polymer backbone considerably improved tumor homing with longer retention in the MDA-MB-231 xenograft mouse model (Sarangthem et al., 2013). Likewise, several independent groups have tried to functionalize ELP using molecules with cell-specific affinities in an effort to improve tumor-directed delivery (Simnick et al., 2010; Simnick et al., 2011; Hassouneh et al., 2012; Sarangthem et al., 2018; Cheon et al., 2020). In summary, the ability to design polypeptides in a modular fashion through genetic encoding of the polymer offers opportunities for unique functionalization and enhanced functionality.

## 2.4 Chemical conjugation

The genetic encoding of ELP sequences gives control over molecular characteristics, allowing for the systematic introduction of synthetic compounds by chemical conjugation.

Drug conjugation to ELPs is a promising approach of drug delivery since it increases bioavailability and pharmacokinetics. The polymer's distinct well-defined pentameric sequence suggests that amino acids such as cysteine, lysine, and other unnatural amino acids can be strategically integrated for targeted conjugation. Dreher et al. reported conjugation of doxorubicin to a rationally placed lysine residue through an acid-labile hydrazone bond (Dreher, 2003). Likewise, cysteine-containing spacer sequences are widely used for small hydrophobic drug conjugation using a maleimide-based Michael addition process (Moktan et al., 2012; Bhattacharyya et al., 2015; Moktan et al., 2012; Bidwell et al., 2007; Dragojevic et al., 2019; McDaniel et al., 2012). The use of chemically reactive lysine and cysteine residues for site-specific attachment of drugs is constrained to instances in which the polypeptide nanoparticle sequence lacks these residues. As a result, a more universal method could involve the use of artificial amino acids. Chilkoti's lab pioneered the co-translational integration of an artificial amino acid (p-acetylphenylalanine) into the ELP sequence, resulting in a unique, bio-orthogonal ketone for the site-specific attachment of small-molecule drugs (Costa et al., 2019). Alternatively, carbodiimide conjugation is utilized to couple a drug via amide bond creation. To this end, amino acid containing carboxylate group in side chains are periodically and precisely placed along the polymer backbone to provide carboxylates convenient for drug attachment. Sinclair et al. chemically modified curcumin to include a reactive primary amine, allowing direct coupling to a thermally responsive glutamate-rich ELP (Sinclair et al., 2013). Therefore, fundamentally, ELP technology allows seamless conjugation of small-molecule drugs via precise modulation of the sequence at the genetic level.

## 3. ELP-based architectures in drug delivery

The recombinant nature of ELPs offers exquisite control over the sequence, providing opportunities to harness the delivery attributes of the polymer into versatile and customizable nanosized architectures. Notably, three broad categories of ELP-based self-assembled biofunctional nanostructures have been widely used for selective delivery to different anatomical sites to treat various diseases such as cancer, type 2 diabetes, neuroinflammation, and ocular diseases.

### 3.1 ELP-based micelles

Precise control over the composition and molecular weight of the ELP sequence can be exploited to create self-assembling spherical micelles. Micellar architectures are typically assembled from ELP sequences consisting of a hydrophobic ELP segment adjoined to a relatively hydrophilic ELP segment (Lee et al., 2000). The guest residue and the length of the two segments of an amphiphilic diblock ELP are designed such that at temperatures between the transition temperatures of the two segments, the relatively hydrophobic ELP block dehydrates and aggregates to form the core of the micelle while the hydrophilic block remains to be hydrated forming the corona of the micelle (Fig. 18.3A).

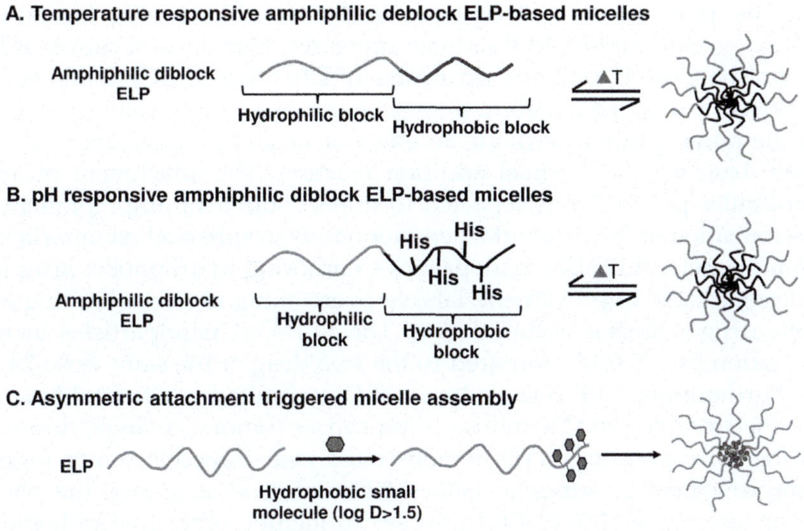


FIGURE 18.3 Amphiphilic deblock elastin-like polypeptide (ELP) micelles. Schematic representation of the synthesis of amphiphilic deblock ELPs, illustrating the polymerization process and the formation of micelles in response to temperature changes (A), pH (B) and upon attachment with drugs counterparts (C).

Further, at temperatures above the higher $T_{t,}$ the more hydrophilic block collapses, and coacervates are formed. The temperature at which soluble diblock ELP monomer sequences transition into micelle is referred to as critical micellization temperature (CMT) (MacEwan and Chilkoti, 2014). Mathematical modeling of the phase transition of the ELP diblock copolymers elucidates the effect of design parameters on CMT. CMT is a function of Tt of the hydrophobic block of the ELP segment whereas the size of the spherical micelle is a function of the length of the $ELP_{BC}$ and the ratio of the hydrophilic-to-hydrophobic block (Janib et al., 2014). Hence, by rational design of the amino acid sequence of the polymer, micelles can be constructed with specific properties with respect to size, surface charge, and temperature-dependent behavior. In general, the diameter of the ELP-based spherical micelles is typically in the range of 40–100 nm. The introduction of local cysteine-dependent cross-linking at the interface between hydrophobic and hydrophilic ELP domains are proposed to increase the stability of the self-assembled micelles (Kim et al., 2010).

Another design strategy for the phase transition of the ELP monomers into micellar architectures involves rational selection of the guest residue of the hydrophobic block. ELPs with histidine at X in the hydrophobic segment form pH-responsive micelle that disassemble upon lowering the pH (Fig. 18.3B). The pH-switchable ELPs are reported to be sensitive to mild acidic environment common for tumors (Callahan et al., 2012). Additionally, asymmetric attachment of hydrophobic moieties such as cholesterol, hydrophobic drugs, and hydrophobic fatty acids via covalent conjugation onto single-segment ELP can induce stable micelle formation (Van Strien et al., 2023). The relatively higher hydrophobicity of these moieties as compared to the hydrophobicity of any natural amino acid supports enhanced stability of these hybrid amphiphiles as compared to the classical fully ELP-based diblock ELP copolymers. The phenomenon of conjugation-driven ELP micelle formation was first observed with a pseudorandom ELP unimer appended with several copies of the small hydrophobic topoisomerase II inhibitor, doxorubicin (Dox) (Fig. 18.3C) (Banki et al., 2005). The authors employed a short conjugation domain harboring eight cysteine residues at the C-terminus of the polypeptide to provide an efficient means for attachment of a maleimide-functionalized drug via the Michael addition reaction. The attachment of approximately five drug molecules per ELP was reported to impart sufficient amphiphilicity driving the spontaneous transition of the drug-attached monomers to spherical nanoparticles of approximately 40 nm diameter. ELP-Dox nanoparticles harboring hydrophobic drug in the micelle core showed remarkable improvement, largely overcoming the dose-limiting adverse effect caused by the drug's cardiac accumulation. The ELP-Dox nanoparticles increased tumor drug concentration by 3.5-fold compared to the free drug at the same dose 24 h after injection in mice. Furthermore, ELP encapsulation of Dox resulted in a fourfold increase in MTD compared to the free drug in C26 mouse colon cancer tumors. A single dosage injection of ELP-Dox at the corresponding MTD demonstrated near-complete tumor regression and a significant improvement in survival. Later McDaniel et al. extended the phenomenon of attachment-triggered assembly of ELP micelles to include other hydrophobic small molecules. The author evaluated the attachment of 14 different small molecules spanning a range of hydrophobicity quantified via their octanol-water distribution coefficient, log D. Mc Daniel et al. reported that a threshold hydrophobicity (log $D > 1.5$) is a prerequisite to trigger self-assembly of conjugated ELP monomers (McDaniel et al., 2013). The attachment of small molecules with a Log D greater than 1.5 was reported to induce spontaneous assembly into particles with diameters between 60 and 120 nm. The extensive study thus established the adaptability of the attachment-triggered assembly across a diverse range of hydrophobic small molecules. Additionally, the study provided a generalized predictive rule that regulates self-assembly by taking into account the hydrophobicity of the conjugating small molecule.

In brief, ELP-based micelles serve as potential DDSs. In general, site-specific conjugation of cargo to the hydrophobic segment results in cargo shielded inside the micelle core, whereas conjugation to the hydrophilic segment causes the cargo to be presented at the corona, where it is available for interactions. The versatility added via functionalization is supported by the unperturbed phase-transition attributes unique to the polymer. Furthermore, the hydrophobicity of the core of the micelle supports passive entrapment of hydrophobic payloads such as small cytotoxic drugs inside the core (Shi et al., 2013). Additionally, genetic encoding of the polymer sequence permits the direct incorporation of an amino-acid-based cargo in the sequence template as a fusion protein/peptide. García-Arévalo et al. inserted the sequence of an immunodominant antigenic peptide from a membrane constituent of *Mycobacterium tuberculosis* at the N-terminus of an amphiphilic diblock ELP polymer sequence (García-Arévalo et al., 2013). The recombinant fusion protein is self-assembles into monodisperse ~55-nm spherical micelles. The subcutaneous administration of the antigen-loaded nanoparticles elicited a pro-chemotactic cytokine response (IL-1β) followed by a pro-Th2/IL-5 response in mice plasma. The biphasic cytokine production was linked with humoral isotype switching from IgM- to IgG-specific antibodies against the antigen.

Furthermore, harnessing the $ELP_{BC}$'s genetic encoding to add CPPs and affinity-based targeting ligands allows for increased uptake and selective targeting capabilities in the micelle. The temperature-triggered transition of a ligand-functionalized $ELP_{BC}$ monomer into a micelle parallels the transition of a monovalent targeting unimer to a multivalent nanoparticle-based targeting system. The increased affinity presented via multivalent expression of the ligand on the micellar architecture facilitates selective targeting, minimizing background uptake of the unimer by normal tissues (Simnick et al., 2010). In 2008, Chilkoti's group published the first report on affinity-modulated active tumor targeting using ligand-functionalized $ELP_{BC}$ (Dreher et al., 2008). The authors instructed tumor vasculature targeting in ELP $_{BC}$ via genetic fusion of the RGD and NGR tripeptides at the hydrophilic terminus of the polymer. Employment of these peptides to $ELP_{BC}$ facilitated the multivalent presentation of the respective peptides upon temperature-guided transition of the functionalized polymer into micelles. Appending NGR peptides to the ELPblock copolymer micelles supported enhanced internalization of the ligand-functionalized micelles compared with nonfunctionalized micelles in the NGR receptor, aminopeptidase N (CD13)-expressing cell line (Simnick et al., 2011). Further, through specific interaction with the tumor vasculature marker CD13, NGR-decorated $ELP_{BC}$ showed greater vascular retention and tumor-dominant accumulation with regard to normal tissue (Simnick et al., 2010). Likewise, RGD-functionalized $ELP_{BC}$ exhibited improved uptake by cells overexpressing $\alpha v\beta 3$ integrin compared with receptor-negative cell line (Simnick et al., 2010). It is noteworthy that ligand functionalization had no bearing on the phase transition of ELP into micelles (Simnick et al., 2011), suggesting the potential for a wide range of multivalent ELP-based nanopolymers with distinct cancer biomarkers for wider use. Sun et al. extended the versatile targeting attribute of $ELP_{BC}$ to larger proteins (>10 kDa). The author incorporated the sequence for the knob domain of adenovirus serotype 5 fiber protein reported to bind the coxsackie and adenovirus receptor (CAR) into $ELP_{BC}$ (Kirby et al., 2000). CAR is a 46 kDa single-pass transmembrane protein expressed in numerous mammalian tissues including brain, heart, and liver (Wehbi et al., 2020). Intriguingly, the large protein appended at the hydrophilic terminus of the $ELP_{BC}$ did not perturb the temperature-guided micelle assembly. Moreover, the knob-functionalized ~40 nm $ELP_{BC}$s displayed greater internalization in CAR overexpressing hepatocytes compared to nonfunctionalized $ELP_{BC}$ micelles (Sun et al., 2011). The study hence provided a proof-of-principal for the versatile temperature-responsive targeted delivery attribute of the ELP vehicle.

## 3.2 ELP polyplexes

Polymeric structures that include condensed or complexed genes or siRNA through electrostatic interactions between the polymer's cationic group and the negatively charged nucleic acids are referred to as polyplexes. Emulating these interactions, the applicability of ELP as a delivery vehicle is extended to gene therapies. Charge separation between the negatively charged DNA and the positively charged ELP polymer directs the spontaneous assembly of ELPs into nanoscale polyplexes that facilitate the delivery of the corresponding DNA inside a cell. Incorporating cationic residues at the guest position within the pentameric repeats of the polymer is a straightforward method for introducing differences in polarity; however, the charge density is insufficient for DNA condensation. Additionally, imposed steric hindrance in the polymer further compromises the assembly of the polymer into a polyplex (Plank et al., 1999). Chen et al. modified ELP via the inclusion of a cationic

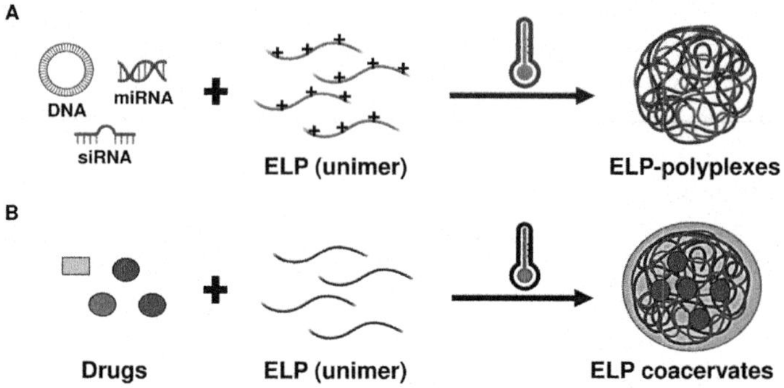


**FIGURE 18.4** Self-assembly of ELPs into different structures. (A) Self-assembly of ELPs into polyplexes in the presence of nucleic acids, highlighting the electrostatic interactions that drive the formation of these complexes. (B) Formation of ELP coacervates under varying pH and ionic conditions highlighting the encapsulation of hydrophobic drugs within the coacervate structures.

domain consisting of an eight-residue oligolysine to facilitate DNA condensation, guiding polyplex formation (Fig. 18.4A).

Electrostatically condensing oligolysine block harboring ELPs were reported to condense plasmid DNA into 32–115 nm radii particles, depending on the N/P ratio between the cationic amine groups of the modified polymer and the anionic phosphate groups of the DNA. The formed polyplexes exhibited stability in the presence of anionic proteins corresponding to physiological conditions, such as heparin. Furthermore, oligolysine-modified ELP was evaluated as a nonviral gene vector employing a plasmid encoding green fluorescent protein (GFP) as a model DNA cargo (Chen et al., 2008). The study demonstrated that the cargo was successfully expressed after transfection in MCF-7 breast cancer cells. However, when using PEI as a vehicle, the transfection efficiency was higher than when using ELP polyplexes. Nevertheless, the significantly lower toxicity of the ELP-based carrier in comparison to PEI indicates that ELP-based polyplexes have potential. Lee et al. exploited ELP-based polyplexes as gene delivery platforms for the delivery of Yamanaka factors to reprogram somatic cells into induced pluripotent stem cells (iPSCs) (Lee et al., 2020). The effective complexation of cationic ELPs with a plasmid containing the four Yamanaka stem cell factors supported the successful reprogramming of mouse embryonic fibroblast cells into iPSCs upon transfection. The resultant iPSCs displayed embryonic stem (ES) cell-like traits, such as the expression of endogenous pluripotency genes, differentiation into three lineages representing the germ layer, and *in vivo* formation of teratomas.

The facile genetic engineering-informed synthesis of ELP has been widely explored to generate a repertoire of ELP sequences with diverse functionalities. Sarangthem et al. rationalized active targeting attribute in ELP via genetic encoding of multiple copies of IL-4R ligand mimic peptide-AP1 (CRKRLDRN). In the MDA-MB-231 xenograft mouse model, the functionalized polymer exhibited significantly enhanced tumor homing with longer retention with respect to the nonfunctionalized polymer. Later Yi et al. harnessed the active targeting attribute of AP1-functionalized ELP and redirected AP1-ELP polymers for gene therapy. The rational was inspired by the unique composition of the AP1 motif, which harbors an abundance of cationic amino acid residues. Intriguingly, the charge density introduced by the inclusion of AP1readily enabled condensation of oppositely charged nucleic acids (Yi et al., 2022). Further, the polyplex exhibited receptor-dependent selective delivery of siRNA *in vitro* and *in vivo* (Yi et al., 2020).

### 3.3 ELP coacervates

The temperature-triggered phase separation of ELP provides an alternative means for the spontaneous assembly of ELP into nanoscale particles. The phenomenon of aggregation is reversible, thus providing an opportunity to exploit the ELP scaffold as a smart temperature-responsive delivery vehicle. Typically, the on/off switch operates in a narrow temperature window of 2–3°C and can be tuned by modulating the Tt of the polymer. Notably, the Tt of the polymer is engineered precisely such that the polymer exists as a soluble unimer in a syringe at room temperature, but spontaneous phase separation occurs in the target tissue, induced by the relatively higher ambient temperature of the body (Fig. 18.4B). The phase-separated ELP provides an insoluble drug reservoir (depot) facilitating increased local drug concentration and sustained release. ELP depots are increasingly being adopted for applications that demand a consistent low-dose drug release over an extended duration, ranging from days to weeks (Despanie et al., 2016). Additionally, these delivery platforms are advantageous for delivery to sites in the body that are not easily accessible via systemic administration (Shamji et al., 2007). Intratumoral delivery of radionuclides for brachytherapy (Liu et al., 2012; Kelly et al., 2022; Liu et al., 2010), intraarticular delivery of anti-inflammatory therapeutics (Shamji et al., 2007), and subcutaneous delivery of bioactive peptides for the treatment of chronic conditions such as diabetes (Amiram et al., 2013; Luginbuhl et al., 2017) are notable examples of drug delivery applications utilizing this strategy.

## 4. Applications of ELP-based nanocarriers

### 4.1 ELP in tumor therapy

Among various DDSs, ELP has attracted considerable attention in cancer therapy as a naturally derived biomaterial system (Jiang et al., 2023). Excellent biocompatibility and biodegradability, low immunogenicity, temperature-responsive property, genetically encoded controlled synthesis, and functional tunability have been instrumental in the favorable reception of the polymer as a vehicle for enhanced cancer therapy in recent years. One of the earlier indications of the potential of ELP as a delivery vehicle based on temperature-dependent coacervation was reported by Chilkoti and colleagues (Fig. 18.5).

The group demonstrated that the development of a thermally sensitive ELP provides a thermally targeted polymer that exhibits enhanced cellular uptake *in vitro* and an approximately two-fold increase in solid tumor targeting *in vivo* upon induction of localized mild hyperthermia compared to the same polypeptide without hyperthermia (Meyer et al., 2001a,b; Liu et al., 2006; Raucher and Chilkoti, 2001). The localized temperature-induced phase separation of ELP unimers into insoluble coacervates provides a nanoscale depot that enables zero-order release kinetics of the appended payload. Locally implanted depot-based drug reservoirs are commonly used for long-term and sustained drug delivery to the therapeutic site while reducing systemic exposure (Magill et al., 2023). Local tumor therapy has been widely explored with ELP depots. Liu et al. evaluated the efficacy of a thermally sensitive ELP conjugated to a therapeutic radionuclide in local cancer radiation

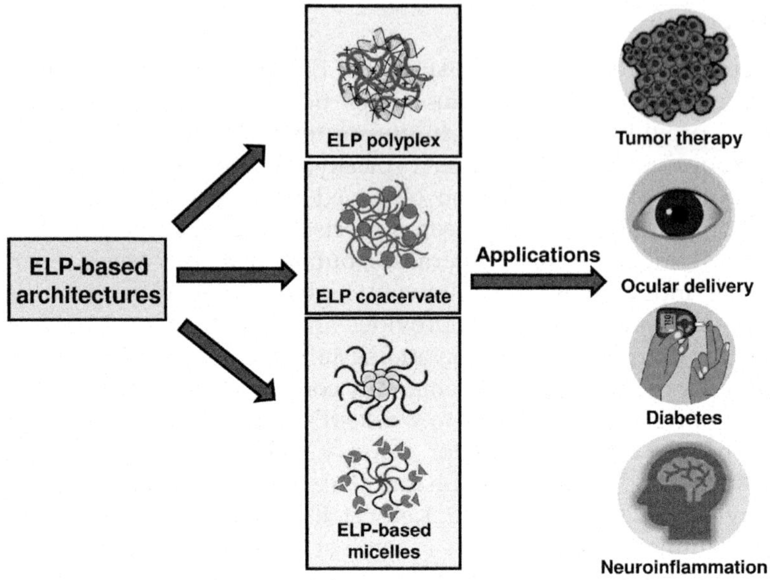


**FIGURE 18.5** Versatile ELP-based architectures for drug delivery in various diseases. The potential of ELP-based architectures in drug delivery systems targeting a range of diseases, including cancer, ocular disorders, diabetes, and neuroinflammation.

therapy (Liu et al., 2010). The authors designed the ELP to have a Tt below 37°C, such that upon intratumoral injection the soluble unimers spontaneously transition into a depot because of their temperature-responsive coacervation property. The radionuclide harboring ELP depots were reported to significantly increase the residence time of the bound radionuclide in murine tumors compared to a soluble, temperature-insensitive ELP control. Furthermore, the conjugated radionuclide was significantly protected from dehalogenation as part of the ELP depot. Additionally, the radionuclide-labeled depots in the mouse xenograft model were reported to cause significant tumor regression and improved survival compared to the soluble ELP control. Later, Liu et al. reported manipulation of radiolabeled ELP injection concentration, composition, and chain length to optimize tumor retention (Liu et al., 2012). The author reported that the temporal stability of the ELP-radionuclide depot can be tuned by controlling the phase transition temperature. Briefly, the work indicated that depression in the ELP's transition temperature is highly correlated with tumor retention. Liang et al. exemplified the utility of ELP-depots in glioblastoma therapy (Liang et al., 2021). The author employed a temperature-sensitive ELP fused to interferon-alpha (IFN) (IFN-ELP(V)). Intracranial injection of the fusion polymer post-GBM resection in a mouse brain orthotopic model of GBM paralleled in situ depot formation. IFN-ELP(V) depots demonstrated dramatically improved pharmacokinetics with a 3-week zero-order sustained release and a 116-fold longer circulatory half-life than IFN. Furthermore, biodistribution studies displayed dramatically improved brain retention of IFN-ELP(V) over IFN, corroborating the benefits of ELP depots. Moreover, due to better brain retention, IFN-ELP(V) groups demonstrated greater efficacy than IFN groups in suppressing GBM recurrence following surgery. Additionally, a combination of IFN-ELP(V) with temozolomide (TMZ) *in vivo* was presented with a remarkably improved efficacy in GBM recurrence inhibition post-surgery (60%) over a combination of surgery + IFN + TMZ (12.5%) with no obvious side effects. A near 1-month zero-order sustained release from the depots in the resection cavity consistently stimulated a strong immunoresponse sustainably polarizing microglias and macrophages from M2-type to M1-type, leading to the alleviation of the GBM immunosuppression. Recently Kelly et al. reported an ELP depot-based combination therapy to control tumor growth and distant metastases in metastatic breast cancer model (Kelly et al., 2022). The author designed a thermally sensitive ELP with an oligolysine tail (ELP-K) to facilitate complexation of a CpG oligodeoxynucleotide immunostimulant. The thermally triggered CpG-ELP depot was shown to dramatically prolong intratumoural retention, reducing the growth of primary tumor and lung metastasis as compared to soluble CpG. Furthermore, a combination of CpG-ELP with radionuclide-labeled ELP depots demonstrated synergistic efficacy in 4T1-breast cancer mouse model inhibiting tumor growth and the development of lung metastasis.

ELP micelles represent yet another exciting class of ELP-based drug delivery platforms in the cancer field. MacKay and coworkers tested the utility of diblock ELPs for the treatment of cancer, with rapamycin (Rapa) as the therapeutic agent (Shi et al., 2013). To this end, the author functionalized $ELP_{BC}$ with cognate protein target of Rapa, FK506 binding protein 12 (FKBP). Specifically, the functionalization promoted the binding of Rapa on the micelle corona, while the hydrophobic core reinforced polymer-drug association via passive encapsulation. Upon administration *in vivo*, Rapa-loaded FKBP-functionalized $ELP_{BC}$ (FSI) exhibited biphasic drug release; Rapa in the micelle core was rapidly released (1.9 hours half-life), followed by a slow release of the corona-bound drug (57.8 hours half-life). The use of FSI was shown to improve antitumor efficacy with reduced gross toxicity compared to free drug treatment in the breast cancer model. Later, the group reported an advanced $ELP_{BC}$-based bifunctional ELP nanoparticle decorated with FKBP and RGD peptide for Rapa delivery (Dhandhukia et al., 2017). The "bifunctional" attribute was conferred on the nanoparticle by inducing the coassembly of two different $ELP_{BC}$ containing drug-loading (FKBP) and tumor-targeting (RGD) domains. The resultant bifunctional ELP nanoparticle demonstrated enhanced potency with superior tumor homing and regression ability compared with the previously described FSI nanoparticle. Recently Wang et al. exploited the delivery attribute of $ELP_{BC}$ to improve pharmacokinetics of therapeutic proteins (Wang et al., 2020). The closely placed therapeutic proteins presented along with ELP chains in the corona of the micelle were hypothesized to exhibit resistance to degradation by proteases due to the steric hindrance. The author rationalized fusion of IFNα to $ELP_{BC}$ to prolong circulation time and reduce renal clearance. The association of IFNα with $ELP_{BC}$ prolonged circulation half-life to as long as 54.7 h with a remarkable increase in antitumor efficacy with no detectable side effects when compared to free IFNα. Pille et al. designed VHH (an EGFR specific heavy chain antibody fragment) decorated $ELP_{BC}$ for specific targeting of EGFR-positive tumors (Pille et al., 2017). To evaluate the selective targeting ability of the above, the VHH-decorated $ELP_{BC}$ were mixed with $ELP_{BC}$ fused with the cytotoxic photosensitizer IRDye700DX, resulting in bifunctional $ELP_{BC}$ that showed specific targeting and light-induced cytotoxicity.

In recent years, noncanonical ELP sequences with unique attributes have been adopted as delivery vehicles by utilizing ELP's genetic encoding feature. One such exemplar described by Banskota et al. is zwitterionic polypeptides (ZIPPs) (Banskota et al., 2019). ZIPP sequence consists of a cation–anion pair within the five-amino acid peptide motif, the repeats of which constitute the polymer backbone. The manipulation imparted "stealth" properties to the polymer facilitating improved pharmacokinetics. Later the author conjugated paclitaxel (PTX) with a log D ~4 to the ZIPPs (Banskota et al., 2020). The amphiphilicity endowed with the conjugation of the hydrophobic drug guided self-assembly of the polymers (ZIPP-PTX) into near-monodisperse sub-100 nm diameter spherical micelles. Encapsulation of the drug in ZIPPs significantly improved the half-life of paclitaxel compared to free PTX and nonstealth control (ELP-PTX). Notably, the drug-loaded polymer retained the "stealth" attribute of the native polymer and exhibited lower liver and spleen uptake compared to ELP-PTX nanoparticles. In addition, tumor regression studies in prostate and colon cancer xenograft models showed a single dose of ZIPP-PTX nanoparticles resulted in near-complete tumor eradication. Additionally, the nanoformulations demonstrated a significantly wider therapeutic window of dose compared with Abraxane, an FDA-approved paclitaxel nanoformulation.

## 4.2 ELP in ocular drug delivery

The avascular corneal epithelium plays a crucial role in maintaining normal vision by refracting light onto the lens and retina. This tissue also serves as a barrier, protecting the inner cornea from environmental infections. This protective function depends on the continuous renewal of the corneal epithelium, which helps maintain a smooth optical surface of the cornea (Lu et al., 2001). The process of renewal requires an integrated balance between proliferation, differentiation, and apoptosis of corneal epithelium guided by myriads of cytokines, growth factors, and chemokines. Though rapid recovery is normally observed in the corneal epithelium, certain clinical conditions such as refractive surgery, diabetic retinopathy, neurotrophic keratopathy, and corneal transplants can delay healing of the corneal epithelium, often precipitating in visual impairment. Therefore, accelerating the corneal wound healing remains a need to facilitate the restoration of the ocular surface. Lacritin (Lacrt), an abundant glycoprotein in tears is a prosecretory mitogen reported to perform cytoprotective roles in ocular homeostasis (Vijmasi et al., 2014). The protein was discovered in an unbiased biochemical secretion screen addressing the biological basis of dry eye (Karnati et al., 2013). Similar to other proteins present at the ocular surface, the durability of its effect is limited by rapid tear turnover. Wang et al. rationalized multivalent presentation of lacritin at the ocular surface via thermoresponsive diblock ELP nanopolymers to augment the bioavailability of the mitogenic protein (Wang et al., 2014). The mitogenic ability of the Lacrt decorated diblock ELP nanopolymers (LSI) was assessed *in vitro* and *in vivo*. A scratch wound healing on human corneal epithelial cells revealed a concentration as low as 10 nM of LS1 exhibited healing of the scratched region similar to a positive control containing epidermal growth factor (EGF) and bovine pituitary extract (BPE). Further, the in vivo efficacy of the LSI nanoparticles was assessed via induction of a circular abrasion wound of around 2 mm diameter on the ocular surface of female NOD mice followed by two rounds of topical administration of LSI nanoparticles within 12 hours after abrasion. Corroborating with the *in vitro* potential, fluorescein staining, and percentage of initial wound area values both confirmed that treatment with LSI outperformed the BPE + EGF co-treatment group. Further, histological analysis of the corneal epithelium after 24 hours reiterated the remarkable recovery of the corneal epithelium with a smooth, reconstituted surface and absence of inflammation with LSI nanoparticles. Moreover, the implication of multivalent presentation with thermoresponsive ELP was assessed *in vivo*. As expected in comparison to thermally insensitive ELP, LSI exhibited pronounced wound healing of the cornea.

Dry eye disease (DED), a prevalent ocular condition associated with disruption of tear film homeostasis affects a significant proportion of the global population (Messmer, 2015). The common ocular symptoms include discomfort, dryness, impaired visual acuity, and potential damage to the cornea. Conventionally topical administration of artificial tears or conservation of the secreted tears with tear plugs and eye shields are implemented in the management of DED. Since many cases of DED are associated with inflammation, anti-inflammatory medications have also been proposed in some cases (Nagai and Novel, 2022). However, these traditional approaches fail to replace the lost regulatory functions of the many components of the normal tears. Inspired by the prosecretory activity of the Lacrt in the lacrimal gland Wang et al. rationalized an ELP-based delivery system for the natural cytoprotective (Wang et al., 2015). The ELP sequence of the Lacrt-ELP fusion protein was designed such that the Tt of the fusion protein is below physiological temperature. The rational was inspired by the thermoresponsive property of ELP guiding the spontaneous assembly of monomers into coacervates that serve as nano-scale depots supporting prolonged exposure of the payload at the pathological site. As reported for ELP fusion proteins Lacrt continued to display its native biological function. The Lacrt-ELP fusion exhibited prosecretory efficacy demonstrated by dose-dependent secretion of β-hexosaminidase from primary rabbit lacrimal gland acinar cells (LGACs). Further evaluation of the efficacy of the fusion protein as a secretagogue in murine model corroborated the potential enhancement in the therapeutics of Lacrt upon association with ELP.

Sjögren's syndrome (SjS) represents a chronic autoimmune disease associated with severe dry eye and compromised visual acuity (Negrini et al., 2022). The disorder is characterized by lymphocytic infiltration and loss of function of the exocrine glands. The MacKay group, in collaboration with the Hamm-Alvarez laboratory, repurposed the FSI rapamycin nanoformulation to address the ocular indications in SjS (Shah et al., 2013). The potent immunomodulatory agent was expected to suppress inflammatory responses directed toward the lacrimal gland restoring the normal physiology of the ocular surface. Nonobese diabetic (NOD) mouse model was selected for the evaluation of the efficacy of the FSI nanoparticles toward inflamed lacrimal gland. The model recapitulates many characteristic symptoms of the autoimmune exocrinopathy, including autoimmune-associated infiltration of lacrimal glands with lymphocytes, a resultant decline in exocrine tissue secretory function, and the development of serum autoantibodies commonly seen in human SjS. Intriguingly, both free Rapa and FSI–Rapa nanoparticles elicited similar therapeutic effects in the lacrimal gland, exhibiting a ~50% reduction in infiltration area; however, FSI encapsulation of Rapa facilitated modulation of renal toxicity. Free Rapa showed significantly enhanced kidney tubule vacuolization in comparison to FSI-Rapa indicating a quantifiable reduction in the nephrotoxicity. Moreover, toxicological studies indicated better tolerance towards FSI-Rapa. Injections with the free Rapa showed 70% edematous tails with 26% becoming bruised and about 4% ending up necrotic. On the contrary, FSI–Rapa-treated mice elicited lower injection site toxicity with only 4% with bruised tails post injection.

## 4.3 ELP in neuroinflammation

Inflammatory responses centralized within the central nervous system in response to diverse insults such as invading pathogens, trauma, aggregated or modified proteins, and stroke are referred to as neuroinflammatory. As an established proinflammatory cytokine, Tumor necrosis factor alpha (TNF-$\alpha$) released from the microglia plays a central role in local neuroinflammatory responses (Gonzalez Caldito, 2023). Thus, targeting TNF-$\alpha$ presents arational approach in the management of neuroinflammation; however, off-target side effects associated with TNF-α-directed drugs limit their therapeutic efficacy. The selective drug delivery attribute of ELP presents a localized delivery platform, overcoming systemic exposure. Shamji et al. encoded the sequence of soluble TNF receptor type II (sTNFRII) to a thermally responsive ELP sequence. The recombinant fusion protein exhibited bivalent functionality, preserving the thermal transitioning of the polymeric vehicle as well as the anti-TNFα activity of the soluble antagonist (Shamji et al., 2008). The polymer-associated TNFα antagonist attenuated inflammatory responses in TNFα-stimulated microglia and astrocyte cultures. Additionally, the ELP-sTNFRII displayed a reversal of artificially stimulated neuroinflammation in rat dorsal root ganglion explants, as monitored by recovery in the balance of pro- and anti-inflammatory cytokines (Shamji et al., 2008). The active component of the herb *Curcuma longa*, curcumin, is an alternative affordable and orally bioavailable immunomodulator with anti-inflammatory activity (Deng et al., 2024). It is reported to block TNFα production and responses in *in vitro* and *in vivo* models (Aggarwal et al., 2013). Sinclair et al. attempted to exploit delivery attributes of the ELP polymer to overcome curcumin's limited bioavailability due to low solubility and poor absorption into the systemic circulation. The natural compound was chemically coupled to a thermally sensitive ELP. The ELP-curcumin conjugates retained bioactivity against TNF-α *in vitro* and *in vivo*. The drug-tethered polymer exhibited a Tt below 37°C facilitating local delivery of the soluble drug-polymer conjugate at $t < Tt$ (room temperature). The sharp and rapid soluble-to-insoluble phase transition into submicron-sized immobile coacervates upon warming at the pathological site provided a sustained delivery depot for the compound. Curcumin ELP depots retained five-fold higher curcumin at 96 h with reduced systemic exposure as evident by a seven-fold lower area under the curve than free drug (Sinclair et al., 2013). Hence, it can be generalized that tethering of therapeutic cargos to temperature-responsive ELP provides a facile means of generating cargo depots. The depots facilitate increased drug longevity owing to slow-release kinetics with reduced serum exposure.

## 4.4 ELP in diabetes

Diabetes mellitus type II is a hyperglycemia-related progressive metabolic condition that is associated with a high prevalence of morbidity and mortality. The chronic disease has an economic impact on individuals, their families, and the healthcare system (Sinclair et al., 2013). A promising alternative therapy for diabetes mellitus type II involves the use of a 30 amino acid incretin hormone, glucagon-like peptide 1 (GLP-1). GLP-1 stimulates insulin secretion and mitosis signaling pathways in pancreatic and insulinoma cells (Castellana et al., 2019). Despite the established physiological effects of the promising therapeutic peptide, its efficacy is limited owing to a short plasma half-life (<2 minutes) (Holst, 2007). To overcome the rapid inactivation associated with clearance of the native multifaceted bioactive peptide, Chilkoti and co-workers designed an ELP-coacervate-based prolong release formulation, which they termed Protease Operated Depot(POD). PODs consisted of an ELP with a Tt below the ambient body temperature fused to six copies of GLP-1 separated by protease cleavage sites. Upon subcutaneous administration, individual GLP-1 monomers were slowly released upon cleavage by extracellular proteases. Notably, a single injection of GLP-1-POD was reported to reduce the levels of glucose in mice's blood for up to 5 days, which was 120 times longer than that with naked peptide. Later, the group assayed the glucose control ability of GLP-1-ELP fusion constructs lacking the proteolytic site. GLP-1 fusion with temperature-sensitive ELP provided a sustained delivery platform for the therapeutic peptide. Intriguingly, GLP-1-ELP fusion preserved the biological activity of the hormone, producing a five times longer effect than that provided by the native peptide (Amiram et al., 2013). Further, the group manipulated molecular features such as ELP Mw and Tt of the fusion polymer to optimize temporal drug release function (Eissa et al., 2021). The study demonstrated that ELPs with a Tt above body temperature exhibit bolus-type release, while ELPs with a Tt below body temperature exhibit minimal release. Specifically, ELPs with a Tt of ~30 °C (just below the subcutaneous temperature of mice) released cargo most efficiently from the depot, controlling blood glucose and effective weight loss for as long as 6 days. Second, the group attempted to optimize Mw for superior efficacy. The study showed that an Mw $\geq$ 35 kDa is needed to prolong circulation and control blood glucose. Moreover, the study demonstrated the superior performance of the optimized construct in three independent mouse models. Subcutaneous administration of optimized peptide-polymer fusion in ob/ob mice reduced hemoglobin A1c relative to control by day 28, and it remained lower at day 56. Likewise, in the diet-induced obesity model, mice gained less weight and had lower hemoglobin A1c after 56 days. Additionally, in cynomolgus monkeys, the depot release resulted in constant GLP-1 plasma levels for 10 days after subcutaneous injection, with levels still detectable for 17–21 days. A long-standing hyperglycemic state in diabetes mellitus is reported to promote the formation and accumulation of advanced glycation end products (AGEs). AGEs are formed through the nonenzymatic glycation of plasma proteins. AGEs are reported to contribute to chronic skin wounds in patients with advanced diabetes (Eissa et al., 2021). The interaction of AGEs with RAGE (receptor for AGEs) triggers pro-inflammatory signals inhibiting the proliferative phase of wound healing (Luginbuhl et al., 2017). Therefore, it is reasonable to reduce glycation-induced tissue damage by competitively inhibiting the binding of circulating AGEs to cellular RAGE. To this end, Kang et al. developed a self-assembled ELP-based coacervate system containing a fusion of vRAGE (binding domain of RAGE) with ELP (vRAGE-ELP) (Chen et al., 2022). vRAGE-ELP was expected to improve diabetic wound healing by blocking AGE-RAGE-mediated signaling. Indeed, the employment of vRAGE-ELP exhibited reversal of several AGE-mediated changes *in vitro* including a decrease in viable cell number, an increase in levels of reactive oxygen species (ROS), and an increased expression of the pro-inflammatory marker, intercellular adhesion molecule-1 (ICAM-1). Additionally, topical application of the construct on full-thickness excisional skin wounds in diabetic mice supported accelerated wound closure.

## 5. Future directions and conclusion

ELPs offer a promising and adaptable platform for nanocarrier development in drug delivery, with distinctive properties that allow for precise customization and controlled release. The ability to tune ELP sequences and structures facilitates targeted delivery of a wide range of therapeutic agents, from small-molecule drugs to peptides and genes. ELP-based systems have demonstrated efficacy in preclinical studies, particularly for cancer therapy, regenerative medicine, and immunomodulation. Future advancements in ELP research should focus on enhancing targeting capabilities, developing multi-functional systems, and optimizing biostability for long-term therapeutic applications. With further research and clinical validation, ELP nanocarriers hold the potential to transform drug delivery, offering safer, more effective treatments for a broad spectrum of diseases.

## References

Aggarwal, B.B., Gupta, S.C., Sung, B., 2013. Curcumin: an orally bioavailable blocker of TNF and other pro-inflammatory biomarkers. Br. J. Pharmacol. 169, 1672–1692.

Amiram, M., Luginbuhl, K.M., Li, X., Feinglos, M.N., Chilkoti, A., 2011. Injectable protease-operated depots of glucagon-like peptide-1 provide extended and tunable glucose control. Proc. Natl. Acad. Sci. 110 (8), 2792–2797.

Amiram, M., Quiroz, Felipe Garcia, Callahan, D.J., Chilkoti, A., 2011. A highly parallel method for synthesizing DNA repeats enables the discovery of "smart" protein polymers. Nat. Mater. 10, 141–148.

Amiram, M., Luginbuhl, K.M., Li, X., Feinglos, M.N., Chilkoti, A., 2013. A depot-forming glucagon-like peptide-1 fusion protein reduces blood glucose for five days with a single injection. J. Contr. Release 172, 144–151.

Amiram, M., Luginbuhl, K.M., Li, X., Feinglos, M.N., Chilkoti, A., 2013. Injectable protease-operated depots of glucagon-like peptide-1 provide extended and tunable glucose control. Proc. Natl. Acad. Sci. U.S.A. 110, 2792–2797.

Banki, M.R., Feng, L., Wood, D.W., 2005. Simple bioseparations using self-cleaving elastin-like polypeptide tags. Nat. Methods 2, 659–662.

Banskota, S., Yousefpour, P., Kirmani, N., Li, X., Chilkoti, A., 2019. Long circulating genetically encoded intrinsically disordered zwitterionic polypeptides for drug delivery. Biomaterials and Biosystems 192, 475–485.

Banskota, S., Saha, S., Bhattacharya, J., Kirmani, N., Yousefpour, P., Dzuricky, M., Zakharov, N., Li, X., Spasojevic, I., Young, K., Chilkoti, A., 2020. Genetically encoded stealth nanoparticles of a zwitterionic polypeptide-paclitaxel conjugate have a wider therapeutic window than Abraxane in multiple tumor models. Nano Lett. 20, 2396–2409.

Bellucci, J.J., Amiram, M., Bhattacharyya, J., McCafferty, D., Chilkoti, A., 2013. Three-in-One chromatography-free purification, tag removal, and site-specific modification of recombinant fusion proteins using Sortase A and elastin-like polypeptides. Angew. Chem. Int. Ed. 52 (13), 3703–3708.

Bhattacharyya, J., Bellucci, J.J., Weitzhandler, I., McDaniel, J.R., Spasojevic, I., Li, X., Lin, C.-C., Chi, J.-T.A., Chilkoti, A., 2015. A paclitaxel-loaded recombinant polypeptide nanoparticle outperforms Abraxane in multiple murine cancer models. Nat. Commun. 6, 7939.

Bidwell, G.L., Fokt, I., Priebe, W., Raucher, D., 2007. Development of elastin-like polypeptide for thermally targeted delivery of doxorubicin. Biochem. Pharmacol. 73, 620–631.

Callahan, D.J., Liu, W., Li, X., Dreher, M.R., Hassouneh, W., Kim, M., Marszalek, P., Chilkoti, A., 2012. Triple stimulus-responsive polypeptide nanoparticles that enhance intratumoral spatial distribution. Nano Lett. 12 (4), 2165–2170.

Castellana, M., Cignarelli, A., Brescia, F., Perrini, S., Natalicchio, A., Laviola, L., Giorgino, F., 2019. Efficacy and safety of GLP-1 receptor agonists as add-on to SGLT2 inhibitors in type 2 diabetes mellitus: A meta-analysis. Sci. Rep. 9, 19351.

Chen, T.-H.H., Bae, Y., Furgeson, D.Y., 2008. Intelligent biosynthetic nanobiomaterials (IBNs) for hyperthermic gene delivery. Pharm. Res. 25, 683–691.

Chen, C., Zhang, J.-Q., Li, L., Guo, M., He, Y., Dong, Y., Meng, H., Yi, F., 2022. Advanced glycation end products in the skin: Molecular mechanisms, methods of measurement, and inhibitory pathways. Front. Med. 9, 837222.

Cheon, S.-H., Seo, B.-Y., Lee, Y.-J., Sim, D., Lee, S.-B., Guruprasath, P., Singh, T.D., Lee, B.-H., Sarangthem, V., Park, R.-W., 2020. Targeting of cisplatin-resistant melanoma using a multivalent ligand presenting an elastin-like polypeptide. ACS Biomater. Sci. Eng. 6, 5024–5031.

Costa, S.A., Mozhdehi, D., Dzuricky, M.J., Isaacs, F.J., Brustad, E.M., Chilkoti, A., 2019. Active targeting of cancer cells by nanobody decorated polypeptide micelle with bio-orthogonally conjugated drug. Nano Lett. 19, 247–254.

Daniels, T.R., Delgado, T., Helguera, G., Penichet, M.L., 2009. The transferrin receptor part II: Targeted delivery of therapeutic agents into cancer cells. Clin. Immunol. 121 (2), 159–176.

Deng, T., Xu, J., Wang, Q., Wang, X., Jiao, Y., Cao, X., Geng, Q., Zhang, M., Zhao, L., Xiao, C., 2024. Immunomodulatory effects of curcumin on macrophage polarization in rheumatoid arthritis. Front. Pharmacol. 15, 1369337.

Despanie, J., Dhandhukia, J.P., Hamm-Alvarez, S.F., MacKay, J.A., 2016. Elastin-like polypeptides: Therapeutic applications for an emerging class of nanomedicines. J. Contr. Release 240, 93–108.

Dhandhukia, J.P., Shi, P., Peddi, S., Li, Z., Aluri, S., Ju, Y., Brill, D., Wang, W., Janib, S.M., Lin, Y.-A., Liu, S., Cui, H., MacKay, J.A., 2017. Bifunctional elastin-like polypeptide nanoparticles bind rapamycin and integrins and suppress tumor growth in vivo. Bioconjug. Chem. 28 (11), 2715–2728.

Dragojevic, S., Mackey, R., Raucher, D., 2019. Evaluation of elastin-like polypeptides for tumor targeted delivery of doxorubicin to glioblastoma. Molecules 24, 3242.

Dreher, M.R., Simnick, A.J., Fischer, K., Smith, R.J., Patel, A., Schmidt, M., Chilkoti, A., 2008. Temperature triggered self-assembly of polypeptides into multivalent spherical micelles. J. Am. Chem. Soc. 130, 687–694.

Dreher, M., 2003. Evaluation of an elastin-like polypeptide–doxorubicin conjugate for cancer therapy. J. Contr. Release 91, 31–43.

Eissa, N.G., Elsabahy, M., Allam, A., 2021. Engineering of smart nanoconstructs for delivery of glucagon-like peptide-1 analogs. Int. J. Pharm. 597, 120317.

García-Arévalo, C., Bermejo-Martín, J.F., Rico, L., Iglesias, V., Martín, L., Rodríguez-Cabello, J.C., Arias, F.J., 2013. Immunomodulatory nanoparticles from elastin-like recombinamers: Single-molecules for tuberculosis vaccine development. Mol. Pharm. 10, 586–597.

García-Arévalo, C.,B.-M.J.F., Rico, L., Chilkoti, A., 2014. Elastin-like polypeptide-based nanoparticles for delivery of therapeutic peptides. J. Contr. Release 189, 75–86.

Ge, X., Yang, D.S.C., Trabbic-Carlson, K., Kim, B., Chilkoti, A., Filipe, C.D.M., 2005. Self-cleavable stimulus responsive tags for protein purification without chromatography. J. Am. Chem. Soc. 127 (32), 11228–11229.

Gonzalez Caldito, N., 2023. Role of tumor necrosis factor-alpha in the central nervous system: a focus on autoimmune disorders. Front. Immunol. 14–1213448.

Hassouneh, W., Christensen, Trine, Chilkoti, A., 2010. Elastin-like polypeptides as a purification tag for recombinant proteins. Curr. Protoc. Protein. Sci.

Hassouneh, W., Fischer, K., MacEwan, S.R., Branscheid, R., Fu, C.L., Liu, R., Schmidt, M., Chilkoti, A., 2012. Unexpected multivalent display of proteins by temperature triggered self-assembly of elastin-like polypeptide block copolymers. Biomacromolecules 13, 1598–1605.

Holst, J.J., 2007. The physiology of glucagon-like peptide 1. Physiol. Rev. 87, 1409–1439.

Janib, S.M., Pastuszka, M.F., Aluri, S., Folchman-Wagner, Z., Hsueh, P.Y., Shi, P., Lin, Y.A., Cui, H., MacKay, J.A., 2014. A quantitative recipe for engineering protein polymer nanoparticles. Polym. Chem. 5, 1614–1625.

Jiang, A., Guan, X., He, L., Guan, X., 2023. Engineered elastin-like polypeptides: An efficient platform for enhanced cancer treatment. Front. Pharmacol. 13, 1113079.

Karnati, R., Laurie, D.E., Laurie, G.W., 2013. Lacritin and the tear proteome as natural replacement therapy for dry eye. Exp. Eye Res. 117, 39–52.

Kelly, G., Milligan, J.J., Mastria, E.M., Kim, S., Zelenetz, S.R., Dobbins, J., Cai, L.Y., Li, X., Nair, S.K., Chilkoti, A., 2022. Intratumoral delivery of brachytherapy and immunotherapy by a thermally triggered polypeptide depot. J. Contr. Release 343, 267–276.

Kim, W., Thévenot, J., Ibarboure, E., Lecommandoux, S., Chaikof, E.L., 2010. Self-assembly of thermally responsive amphiphilic diblock copolypeptides into spherical micellar nanoparticles. Angew. Chem. Int. Ed. 49, 4257–4260.

Kirby, I., Davison, E., Beavil, A.J., Soh, C.P.C., Wickham, T.J., Roelvink, P.W., Kovesdi, I., Sutton, B.J., Santis, G., 2000. Identification of contact residues and definition of the CAR-binding site of adenovirus type 5 fiber protein. J. Virol. 74, 2804–2813.

Lee, T.A.T., Copper, A., Apkarian, R.P., Conticello, V.P., 2000. Thermo-reversible self-assembly of nanoparticles derived from elastin-mimetic polypeptides. Adv. Mater. 12 (15), 1105–1110.

Lee, C.H., Ingrole, R.S.J., Gill, H.S., 2020. Generation of induced pluripotent stem cells using elastin like polypeptides as a non-viral gene delivery system. Biochim. Biophys. Acta, Mol. Basis Dis. 1866 (4), 165405.

Liang, P., Wang, G., Liu, X., Wang, Z., Wang, J., Gao, W., 2021. Spatiotemporal combination of thermosensitive polypeptide fused interferon and temozolomide for post-surgical glioblastoma immunochemotherapy. Biomaterials and Biosystems 264, 120447.

Liu, W., Dreher, M.R., Furgeson, D.Y., Peixoto, K.V., Yuan, H., Zalutsky, M.R., Chilkoti, A., 2006. Tumor accumulation, degradation and pharmacokinetics of elastin-like polypeptides in nude mice. J. Contr. Release 116, 170–178.

Liu, W., MacKay, J.A., Dreher, M.R., Chen, M., McDaniel, J.R., Simnick, A.J., Callahan, D.J., Zalutsky, M.R., Chilkoti, A., 2010. Injectable intratumoral depot of thermally responsive polypeptide–radionuclide conjugates delays tumor progression in a mouse model. J. Contr. Release 144, 2–9.

Liu, W., McDaniel, J., Li, X., Asai, D., Quiroz, F.G., Schaal, J., Park, J.S., Zalutsky, M., Chilkoti, A., 2012. Brachytherapy using injectable seeds that are self-assembled from genetically encoded polypeptides in situ. Cancer Res. 72, 5956–5965.

López Barreiro, D., Minten, I.J., Thies, J.C., Sagt, C.M.J., 2023. Structure–property relationships of elastin-like polypeptides: A review of experimental and computational studies. ACS Biomater. Sci. Eng. 9 (7), 3796–3809.

Lu, L., Reinach, P.S., Kao, W.W.-Y., 2001. Corneal epithelial wound healing. Exp. Biol. Med. 226, 653–664.

Luginbuhl, K.M., Schaal, J.L., Umstead, B., Mastria, E.M., Li, X., Banskota, S., Arnold, S., Feinglos, M., D'Alessio, D., Chilkoti, A., 2017. One-week glucose control via zero-order release kinetics from an injectable depot of glucagon-like peptide-1 fused to a thermosensitive biopolymer. Nat. Biomed. Eng. 1, 0078.

MacEwan, S.R., Chilkoti, A., 2010. Applications of elastin-like polypeptides in drug delivery. J. Contr. Release 148 (2), 190–199.

Macewan, S.R., Chilkoti, A., 2012. Nanoparticle delivery of anti-cancer drugs via ELP block copolymers. J. Contr. Release 164 (2), 314–321.

MacEwan, S.R., Chilkoti, A., 2014. Applications of elastin-like polypeptides in drug delivery. J. Contr. Release 190, 314–330.

MacEwan, S.R., Chilkoti, A., 2014. Controlled apoptosis by a thermally toggled nanoscale amplifier of cellular uptake. Nano Lett. 14, 2058–2064.

MacEwan, S.R., Hassouneh, W., Chilkoti, A., 2014. Non-chromatographic purification of recombinant elastin-like polypeptides and their fusions with peptides and proteins from *Escherichia coli*. J. Vis. Exp. 88, 51583.

Magill, E., Demartis, S., Gavini, E., Permana, A.D., Thakur, R.R.S., Adrianto, M.F., Waite, D., Glover, K., Picco, C.J., Korelidou, A., Detamornrat, U., Vora, L.K., Li, L., Anjani, Q.K., Donnelly, R.F., Domínguez-Robles, J., Larrañeta, E., 2023. Solid implantable devices for sustained drug delivery. Adv. Drug Deliv. Rev. 199, 114950.

Massodi, I., Bidwell, G.L., Raucher, D., 2005. Evaluation of cell penetrating peptides fused to elastin-like polypeptide for drug delivery. J. Contr. Release 108, 396–408.

McDaniel, J.R., Macewan, S.R., Dewhirst, M., Chilkoti, A., 2012. Doxorubicin-conjugated chimeric polypeptide nanoparticles that respond to mild hyperthermia. J. Contr. Release 159, 362–367.

McDaniel, J.R., Bhattacharyya, J., Vargo, K.B., Hassouneh, W., Hammer, D.A., Chilkoti, A., 2013. Self-assembly of thermally responsive nanoparticles of a genetically encoded peptide polymer by drug conjugation. Angew. Chem. Int. Ed. 52, 1683–1687.

Mecham, R.P., 1991. Elastin synthesis and fiber assembly. Ann. N. Y. Acad. Sci. 624, 137–146.

Messmer, E.M., 2015. The pathophysiology, diagnosis, and treatment of dry eye disease. Dtsch. Ärztebl. Int. 112 (5), 71–82.

Meyer, D.E., Chilkoti, A., 1999. Purification of recombinant proteins by fusion with thermally-responsive polypeptides. Nat. Biotechnol. 17, 1112–1115.

Meyer, D.E., Chilkoti, A., 2002. Genetically encoded synthesis of protein-based polymers with precisely specified molecular weight and sequence by recursive directional ligation: Examples from the elastin-like polypeptide system. Biomacromolecules 3 (2), 357–367.

Meyer, D.E., Chilkoti, A., 2004. Purification of recombinant proteins by fusion with thermally-responsive polypeptides. Nat. Biotechnol. 17 (11), 1112–1115.

Meyer, D.E., Shin, B.C., Kong, G.A., Dewhirst, M.W., Chilkoti, A., 2001a. Drug targeting using thermally responsive polymers and local hyperthermia. J. Contr. Release 74, 213–224.

Meyer, D.E., Kong, G.A., Dewhirst, M.W., Zalutsky, M.R., Chilkoti, A., 2001b. Targeting a genetically engineered elastin-like polypeptide to solid tumors by local hyperthermia. Cancer Res. 61, 1548–1554.

Moktan, S., Ryppa, C., Kratz, F., Raucher, D., 2012. A thermally responsive biopolymer conjugated to an acid-sensitive derivative of paclitaxel stabilizes microtubules, arrests cell cycle, and induces apoptosis. Invest New Drugs 30, 236–248.

Moktan, S., Perkins, E., Kratz, F., Raucher, D., 2012. Thermal targeting of an acid-sensitive doxorubicin conjugate of elastin-like polypeptide enhances the therapeutic efficacy compared with the parent compound in vivo. Mol. Cancer Therapeut. 11, 1547–1556.

Nagai, N., Novel, H.O., 2022. Drug delivery systems for the management of dry eye. Adv. Drug Deliv. Rev. 191, 114582.

Negrini, S., Emmi, G., Greco, M., Borro, M., Sardanelli, F., Murdaca, G., Indiveri, F., Puppo, F., 2022. Sjögren's syndrome: a systemic autoimmune disease. Clin. Exp. Med. 22, 9–25.

Ozsvar, J., Cain, S.A., Baldock, C., Tarakanova, A., Weiss, A.S., 2021. Tropoelastin and elastin assembly. Front. Bioeng. Biotechnol. 9, 643110.

Pille, J., Lith, S.A.M.V., Van Hest, J.C.M., Leenders, W.P.J., 2017. Self-assembling VHH-Elastin-Like peptides for photodynamic nanomedicine. Biomacromolecules 18, 1302–1310.

Plank, C., Tang, M.X., Wolfe, A.R., Szoka, F.C., 1999. Branched cationic peptides for gene delivery: Role of type and number of cationic residues in formation and in vitro activity of DNA polyplexes. Hum. Gene Ther. 10 (2), 319–332.

Raucher, D., Chilkoti, A., 2001. Enhanced uptake of a thermally responsive polypeptide by tumor cells in response to its hyperthermia-mediated phase transition. Cancer Res. 61, 7163–7170.

Ruan, Z., Liu, C., Guo, Y., Shen, Y., Zhang, W., Yang, X., 2020. Advances in the application of elastin-like polypeptides for drug delivery and tissue engineering. J. Drug Deliv. Sci. Technol. 55, 101484.

Sarangthem, V., Cho, E.A., Bae, S.M., Singh, T.D., Kim, S.-J., Kim, S., Jeon, W.B., Lee, B.-H., Park, R.-W., 2013. Construction and application of elastin like polypeptide containing IL-4 receptor targeting peptide. PLoS One 8, e81891.

Sarangthem, V., Cho, E.A., Yi, A., Kim, S.K., Lee, B.-H., Park, R.-W., 2018. Application of Bld-1-Embedded elastin-like polypeptides in tumor targeting. Sci. Rep. 8, 3892.

Shah, M., Edman, M.C., Janga, S.R., Shi, P., Dhandhukia, J., Liu, S., Louie, S.G., Rodgers, K., MacKay, J.A., Hamm-Alvarez, S.F., 2013. A rapamycin-binding protein polymer nanoparticle shows potent therapeutic activity in suppressing autoimmune dacryoadenitis in a mouse model of Sjögren's syndrome. J. Contr. Release 171, 269–279.

Shamji, M.F., Betre, H., Kraus, V.B., Chen, J., Chilkoti, A., Pichika, R., Masuda, K., Setton, L.A., 2007. Development and characterization of a fusion protein between thermally responsive elastin-like polypeptide and interleukin-1 receptor antagonist: Sustained release of a local antiinflammatory therapeutic. Arthritis Rheum. 56, 3650–3661.

Shamji, M.F., Chen, J., Friedman, A.H., Richardson, W.J., Chilkoti, A., Setton, L.A., 2008. Synthesis and characterization of a thermally-responsive tumor necrosis factor antagonist. J. Contr. Release 129, 179–186.

Shamji, M.F., Jing, L., Chen, J., Hwang, P., Ghodsizadeh, O., Friedman, A.H., Richardson, W.J., Setton, L.A., 2008. Treatment of neuroinflammation by soluble tumor necrosis factor receptor Type II fused to a thermally responsive carrier. J. Neurosurg. Spine 9 (2), 221–228.

Shi, P., Aluri, S., Lin, Y.-A., Shah, M., Edman, M., Dhandhukia, J., Cui, H., MacKay, J.A., 2013. Elastin-based protein polymer nanoparticles carrying drug at both corona and core suppress tumor growth in vivo. J. Contr. Release 171, 330–338.

Simnick, A.J., Valencia, C.A., Liu, R., Chilkoti, A., 2010. Morphing low-affinity ligands into high-avidity nanoparticles by thermally triggered self-assembly of a genetically encoded polymer. ACS Nano 4, 2217–2227.

Simnick, A.J., Amiram, M., Liu, W., Hanna, G., Dewhirst, M.W., Kontos, C.D., Chilkoti, A., 2011. In vivo tumor targeting by a NGR-decorated micelle of a recombinant diblock copolypeptide. J. Contr. Release 155, 144–151.

Sinclair, S.M., Bhattacharyya, J., McDaniel, J.R., Gooden, D.M., Gopalaswamy, R., Chilkoti, A., Setton, L.A., 2013. A genetically engineered thermally responsive sustained release curcumin depot to treat neuroinflammation. J. Contr. Release 171, 38–47.

Sun, G., Hsueh, P.-Y., Janib, S.M., Hamm-Alvarez, S., MacKay, J.A., 2011. Design and cellular internalization of genetically engineered polypeptide nanoparticles displaying adenovirus knob domain. J. Contr. Release 155 (2), 218–226.

Urry, D.W., Long, M.M., Cox, B.A., Ohnishi, T., Mitchell, L.W., Jacobs, M., 1974. The synthetic polypentapeptide of elastin coacervates and forms filamentous aggregates. Biochim. Biophys. Acta Protein Struct. 371 (2), 597–602.

Van Strien, J., Escalona-Rayo, O., Jiskoot, W., Slütter, B., Kros, A., 2023. Elastin-like polypeptide-based micelles as a promising platform in nanomedicine. J. Contr. Release 353, 713–726.

Vijmasi, T., Chen, F.Y.T., Balasubbu, S., Gallup, M., McKown, R.L., Laurie, G.W., McNamara, N.A., 2014. Topical administration of lacritin is a Novel therapy for aqueous-deficient dry eye disease. Investig. Ophthalmol. Vis. Sci. 55, 5401.

Vrhovski, B., Weiss, A.S., 1998. Biochemistry of tropoelastin. Eur. J. Biochem. 258 (1), 1–18.

Walker, L., Perkins, E., Kratz, F., Raucher, D., 2012. Cell penetrating peptides fused to a thermally targeted biopolymer drug carrier improve the delivery and antitumor efficacy of an acid-sensitive doxorubicin derivative. Int. J. Pharm. 436, 825–832.

Wang, W., Despanie, J., Shi, P., Edman, M.C., Lin, Y.-A., Cui, H., Heur, M., Fini, M.E., Hamm-Alvarez, S.F., MacKay, J.A., 2014. Lacritin-mediated regeneration of the corneal epithelia by protein polymer nanoparticles. J. Mater. Chem. B 2, 8131–8141.

Wang, W., Jashnani, A., Aluri, S.R., Gustafson, J.A., Hsueh, P.-Y., Yarber, F., McKown, R.L., Laurie, G.W., Hamm-Alvarez, S.F., MacKay, J.A., 2015. A thermo-responsive protein treatment for dry eyes. J. Contr. Release 199, 156–167.

Wang, Z., Guo, J., Liu, X., Sun, J., Gao, W., 2020. Temperature-triggered micellization of interferon alpha-diblock copolypeptide conjugate with enhanced stability and pharmacology. J. Contr. Release 328, 444–453.

Wehbi, A., Kremer, E.J., Dopeso-Reyes, I.G., 2020. Location of the cell adhesion molecule "Coxsackievirus and adenovirus receptor" in the adult mouse brain. Front. Neuroanat. 14, 28.

Wise, S.G., Hiob, M.A., Rnjak-Kovacina, J., Kaplan, D.L., Ng, M.K.C., Weiss, A.S., 2014. Tropoelastin: A versatile, bioactive assembly module. Acta Biomater. 10 (4), 1532–1541.

Yi, A., Sim, D., Lee, Y.-J., Sarangthem, V., Park, R.-W., 2020. Development of elastin-like polypeptide for targeted specific gene delivery in vivo. J. Nanobiotechnol. 18, 15.

Yi, A., Sim, D., Lee, S.-B., Sarangthem, V., Park, R.-W., 2022. Application of bioengineered elastin-like polypeptide-based system for targeted gene delivery in tumor cells. Biomaterials and Biosystems 6, 100050.

CHAPTER

# 19

# Virus-like particle (VLP)-based nanocarriers for drug delivery

*Aiswarya Pati*[1], *Sheary Somam Tete*[1], *Archana Padhiary*[1], *Swagat Ranjan Maharana*[1], *Kiran Mahapatra*[1], *Binata Nayak*[1], *Safdar Ali*[2], *Showkat Ahmed Mir*[1] *and Mehboob Hoque*[3]

[1]School of Life Sciences, Sambalpur University, Jyotivihar, Odisha, India; [2]Applied Biochemistry Lab, Department of Biological Sciences, Aliah University, Kolkata, West Bengal, India; [3]Clinical and Applied Genomics Lab, Department of Biological Sciences, Aliah University, Kolkata, West Bengal, India

## 1. Introduction

Nanotechnology has significantly advanced biomedical technology, particularly in the realm of drug delivery. Viral nanoparticles (VLPs), derived from plant viruses, bacteriophages, and mammalian viruses, represent a diverse group of naturally occurring nanomaterials (VNPs). The viral capsid, often referred to as virus-like particle (VLP), is primarily composed of proteins and lacks genetic material. These structures are robust and stable, enabling the encapsulation of drug molecules within confined nanoscale space (Singh et al., 2006a). VLPs serve as efficient nanocarriers for drug delivery applications due to their ability to encapsulate tiny compounds, including nucleic acids and other therapeutic agents (Suffian and Al-Jamal, 2022). Since VLPs do not possess the ability to recombine, replicate, or revert to virulent forms, they are regarded as safer than whole pathogen-based vaccinations (Watanabe et al., 2002; Plummer and Manchester, 2011). They also occur in a variety of unique shapes (mostly icosahedron, spheres, and tubes) and sizes, from roughly about 10 nm to over a micron (Ma et al., 2012). Despite the wide range of sizes and morphologies available, spherical or rod-shaped assemblies have been the foundation for most virus-based nanocarriers (van Kan-Davelaar et al., 2014). VLPs are naturally created as faulty viruses and are observed during normal infection with viruses

*Protein-Based Nanoparticles in Drug Delivery*
https://doi.org/10.1016/B978-0-443-33639-3.00024-6

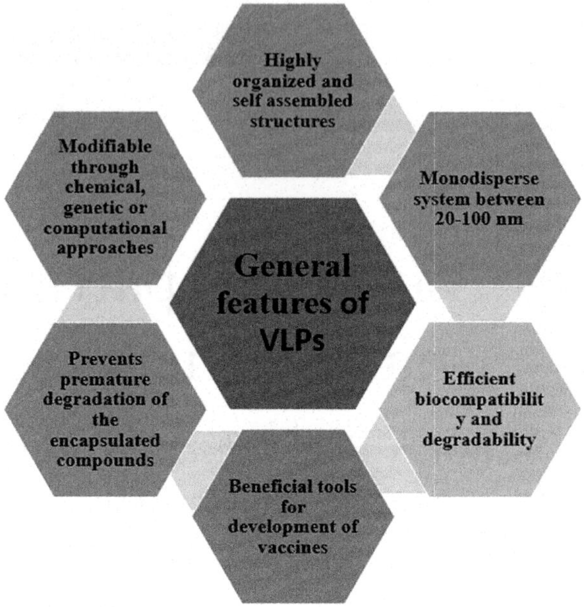


**FIGURE 19.1** General features of VLPs (Mejía-Méndez et al., 2022).

(Pushko et al., 2013). The general features of VLPs are illustrated in Fig. 19.1. The most common and ancient use of VLPs was in the development of vaccinations against viral infection because these vaccines exhibit the natural structure of conformational antigens from viruses, and this elicits the proper immune response without posing an increased risk of infection. Various delivery systems have been developed using physical, chemical, and biological mechanisms for transferring biomolecules into target cells (Ramqvist et al., 2007). However, the immunological responses triggered by viral components are often difficult be predict without *in vivo* evaluation, representing a significant limitation that currently hinders their rapid translation into clinical applications (van Kan-Davelaar et al., 2014). Among the different types of viruses, plant-based viruses and bacteriophages are considered particularly safe, as they are incapable of replicating in humans and are therefore less likely to produce adverse effects compared to mammalian viruses (Costa et al., 2012; Yildiz et al., 2012; Wen et al., 2013).

## 2. Development of nanocarrier

Colloidal nanoparticles, or nanocarriers, are simple systems widely used for transporting drugs and other therapeutic agents to specific target sites (Qian et al., 2012). Based on their high surface-to-volume ratio, nanocarriers are broadly classified into three major categories: organic, inorganic, and hybrid nanocarriers. Solid lipid nanocarriers, dendrimers, liposomes, micelles, polymeric nanocarriers, and viral nanocarriers are examples of organic nanocarriers. Among the inorganic nanocarriers are mesoporous silica, magnetic nanocarriers, quantum dots, and gold based nanostructures. Nanocarriers that combine two or more organic and inorganic nanocarriers, either jointly or separately, are called hybrid nanocarriers. These systems may include organic-inorganic, inorganic-inorgainic, or multifunctional composite structures (Chamundeeswari et al., 2019).

The process of conjugation of viruses with biomolecules—particularly enzymes and antigens—has become increasingly significant recently for modifying viruses into functional nanoparticles (Biabanikhankahdani et al., 2018; Walper et al., 2015). While there is no clinically approved plant or bacteriophage based nanomedicine, several are undergoing preclinical development while some systems are poised to enter transitional development. The plant VLP and VNP-based nanotechnology platform undergoing development for various nanomedical applications are tobacco mosaic virus (TMV), cowpea mosaic virus (CPMV), cowpea chlorotic mottle virus (CCMV), etc. (Chung et al., 2020). Prominent bacteriophages include MS2, P22, Qβ, and M13, all of which are being actively explored for manomedical application.

## 3. Biological nanocarriers

The assembly of protein subunits is the primary mechanism for the formation of bio-nanocarriers (Li et al., 2009; Verma et al., 2018). Different types of nanocarriers and their applications are described in Fig. 19.2. Recent advancements have also enabled the incorporation of whole proteins, protein domains, and hybrid viruses, along with specific protein expression within the viral capsids (Uhde-Holzem et al., 2016; Dickmeis et al., 2015). In recent years, many viruses have been genetically engineered using CRISPR-based systems to create virus-like nanoparticles (Neubi et al., 2018).

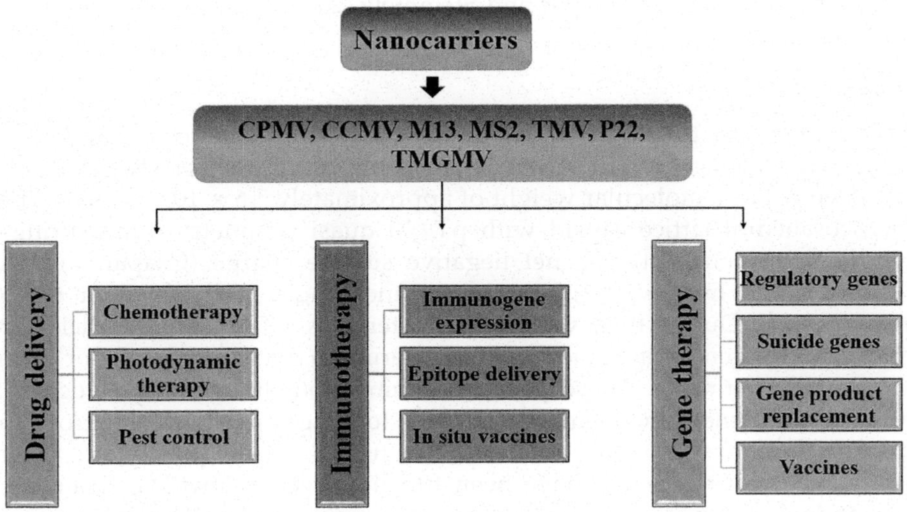


**FIGURE 19.2** Plant viruses and bacteriophages and their application (Czapar and Steinmetz, 2017).

## 4. Virus-based nanocarriers

When used as a framework for "smart" delivery systems, virus-based nanocarriers hold great promise for controlled release of cargo in response to changes in pH, temperature, redox state, or other chemical stimuli (Moghimi et al., 2005). Recent studies show that viruses can be genetically altered to act as catalysts, reactive agents, or as a support system for chemical reactions (Strable and Finn, 2009).

### 4.1 CCMV

CCMV is a small icosahedral plant virus (~28 nm in diameter) composed of 180 identical capsid proteins and is relatively unstable *in vivo* (Dawson and Kuhn, 1974; Speir et al., 1995). The icosahedral CCMV is widely used as a model system for studying the encapsulation and packaging of synthetic and genetic materials (Liepold et al., 2005). It is one of the most commonly used plant virused in nanoscale manufacturing approaches (Flynn et al., 2003).

VLPs originating from the CCMV are an efficient nanocarrier platform for the delivery of nucleic acids due to their high loading capacity, manufacturing efficiency, and functionalization capabilities (Pretto et al., 2021). The distinctive pH-responsive self-assembly activity of CCMV VLPs makes them distinguishable. These nanoparticles break down at neutral pH and assemble impulsively under acidic conditions (pH ~5), despite the absence of viral genome (Lavelle et al., 2007; Garmann et al., 2014). One well-known application of CCMV is in delivering mRNA cargos. Like other VNP-based systems, CCMV may package nonnative RNA of different sequences and lengths. In a study, VLPs comprising a CCMV capsid with heterologous RNA were delivered into cells via lipofectamine; upon cell entry, the nucleic acids were discharged within the cytoplasm of mammalian cells, resulting in the expression of reporter-enhanced yellow fluorescent protein. Encapsulation of these RNAs within VNP carriers prevents genetic material from destruction during transport and storage (Azizgolshani et al., 2013; Czapar and Steinmetz, 2017).

### 4.2 CPMV

The black-eyed pea plant, *Vigna unguiculata*, is naturally infected by the CPMV, a picorna-like virus belonging to the order *Picornavirales*, family *Secoviridae*, and genus *Comoviridae*. This virus has a molecular weight of approximately $5.6 \times 10^6$ g mol$^{-1}$. CPMV is an isometric, icosahedral lattice capsid with pT $= 3$ quasi symmetries, measuring roughly 30 nm in diameter constituting a net negative surface charge (Czapar and Steinmetz, 2017; Steinmetz and Evans, 2007; Manchester and Singh, 2006; Lewis et al., 2006; Lin and Johnson, 2003). Due to their various characteristics, CPMV nanoparticles are promising candidates for genetic and chemical engineering to develop as tools for cancer imaging and various treatments. These particles exhibit nonpathogenicity, biocompatibility, stability, ease of external functionalization, cargo loading capacity, native tropism toward vimentin, and immunostimulatory effect in solid tumor models (Beatty and Lewis, 2019). CPMVs used in cancer research have been functionalized with PEG, ligands, carbohydrates, peptides, epitopes, metal cofactors, photosensitizers, synthetic polymers, and dyes (Steele et al., 2017; Galibert et al., 2011). The CPMVs additionally have been examined for applications other than cancer diagnosis and treatment, including the controlled manufacture of CPMV solid support arrays enabling receptor–ligand binding and recognition, as well as an organometallic moiety of CPMV decorating for nanoscale electricity (Steinmetz et al., 2006a, 2006b). Nanoparticles can also be designed as theranostic agents for use in diagnosis as well as therapy. Such multifunctional CPMV platforms are often known as "smart" tools (Steinmetz et al., 2011). Because CPMV contains the RNA-1 and RNA-2 genomes, which provide genetic code for viral proteins, a genotype–phenotype connection equivalent to the phage display technology is possible (Beatty and Lewis, 2019).

## 4.3 RCNMV

Red Clover Necrotic Mosaic virus (RCNMV) is a bipartite ssRNA virus from the *Tombusviridae* family. It produces particles having icosahedral symmetry with a diameter of about 36 nm (Steinmetz and Evans, 2007). An alternative strategy was explored utilizing the RCNMV, where capsids were infused with doxorubicin (DOX) molecules without causing any structural or native RNA disruption. This approach achieved a high loading efficiency of 1000 DOX molecules per RCNMV virus, comparable to the "polyacid association" method reported in Hibiscus chlorotic ringspot virus Protein cage (HCRSV PC) (Loo et al., 2008). It has been shown that upon exposure to divalent cations, RCNMV may undergo a structural change, leading to the formation of surface pores that extend throughout the capsid. This structural shift in response to the amount of divalent cation levels in the cytoplasm is linked to the bipartite RNA genome's release mechanism *in vivo*. Opening outer pores by altering $Ca^{2+}$ and $Mg^{2+}$ concentrations is highly beneficial for the dense assembly of molecules within the RCNMV capsid (Ma et al., 2012).

## 4.4 TMV

According to Steinmetz and Evans (2007), TMV is a rod-shaped plant virus with helical symmetry from the family *Virgaviridae* (Czapar et al., 2016). In 1999, the use of TMV as a biotemplate for mineralization was first described. This includes the following processes: sol-gel condensation of $SiO_2$, oxidative hydrolysis of iron oxides, and cocrystallization with PbS and CdS (Shenton et al., 1999). TMV has been employed as a scaffold for the selective attachment of fluorescent dyes and small molecules, and it serves as a template for mineralization. The native virions provide carboxylates generated from glutamic acid residues within and accessible exterior tyrosine residues (Schlick et al., 2005). Combining dip-pen nanolithography and coordination chemical processes, it was also feasible to create nanopatterned arrays of single TMV particles by precisely immobilizing and inserting individual virions (Vega et al., 2005). TMV as a model for bionanotechnology is a fast-expanding subject, with applications including the creation of nanostructured electronic devices. Notably, a digital memory device composed of metalized TMV with platinum nanoparticles has already been reported (Tseng et al., 2006).

## 4.5 MS2

RNA-containing bacteriophage (MS2) is an icosahedral RNA bacteriophage with a triangulation number T = 3. The crystalline structure has been determined at 2.8 Å resolution. Bacteriophage MS2's genome is a 3569-nucleotide positive-sense ssRNA molecule that encodes mainly four proteins: main coat protein (CP), maturation protein (A-protein), the replicase (RNA polymerase required for genome multiplication), and lysis protein (Borodavka et al., 2012; Golmohammadi et al., 1993; Valegård et al., 1991a, 1991b; Fu et al., 2016).

Before 2013, more than 110 VLPs had been produced from viruses belonging to 35 families (Zeltins, 2013a). MS2 VLPs, icosahedral capsids that self-assemble from 180 copies of single CP and measure 22–29 nm in diameter, provide a unique delivery platform and have attracted increasing research interest in recent times due to their appealing properties. The clinical uses of MS2 VLPs are possibly their most fascinating feature. Their major applications are in the domain of vaccine development (Fu et al., 2016). In recent times, recombinant MS2 VLPs packaged along with RNA, known as armored RNAs, have been created to be utilized as "controls," "standards," and "calibrators" in the diagnostic process (Stevenson et al., 2008).

MS2 VLP vaccines are additionally effective in preventing human papillomavirus (HPV) infections. Current HPV vaccines, which are developed from the VLPs, encode the HPV main capsid protein L1. For the creation of second-generation HPV vaccines relying on HPV minor capsid protein L2 (Tumban et al., 2012), the technique of genetic recombination was used to insert HPV L2 peptides into the N-terminus of the CP of bacteriophage MS2. These studies demonstrated that L2-based VLP vaccines can induce broadly cross-reactive and cross-protective antibodies against heterologous HPV types. Therefore, using the MS2 VLP platform, recombinant L2-VLPs could form the foundation of a widely protective second-generation HPV vaccine.

Recent studies by Zhang et al. (2015a, 2015b) reported the development of armored hepatitis B virus (HBV) along with HPV DNA constructs for use in nucleic acid-based experiments. These constructs were found to be stable, uniformly distributed, noninfectious, nuclease resistant, and easy to transport. In this work, double-stranded DNA of 1.3, 3.0, 3.5, and 6.5 kb in length was successfully incorporated into MS2 viral capsids with a high reassembly rate. This was the first time Bacteriophage MS2 has been successfully used as a platform for encapsulating double-stranded DNA. This armored DNA could eventually serve as a suitable "control" and "standard" for use in clinical testing and diagnostics, with the potential to serve a variety of applications, particularly as a new platform for producing assay standards for DNA viruses.

Glasgow et al. (2012) described two strategies for protein encapsulation within an MS2 capsids using osmolytes (charged polymers or peptides). In one approach, proteins larger than 1.8 nm were modified with negatively charged polymers, allowing capsid assembly around them. In the second method, negatively charged peptide tags were genetically encoded in the phage capsid, enabling encapsulation of the target protein within the phage particle.

## 4.6 M13

M13 is a filamentous bacteriophage containing a single-stranded DNA genome of 6407 nucleotides, a size of 890 nm, and is surrounded by about 2700 copies of the main CP P8. The morphology of the M13 bacteriophage is well characterized and has been genetically modified to create conductive fibers (Niu et al., 2008). Hajitou et al. (2006) combined adeno-associated virus (AAV) and M13 phage to create a novel hybrid virus with a mammalian virus packaging system and a phage envelope to avoid tropism in the resulting vector. This virus was genetically altered to target cancer cells by displaying the CDCRGDCFC (or RGD-4C) peptide.

Yata et al. (2014) transformed the M13 phage by including the RGD4C ligand (an integrin receptor) and incorporating the luciferase gene. The vector was then covered by two cationic polymers, poly-D-lysine and Diethylaminoethyl-dextran (DEAE-DEX). The polymers generated a positive charge on the phage surface, which increased the particle size and improved phage contracture with the targeted site. Furthermore, recent human clinical studies suggest that bacteriophage M13 is capable of crossing the blood–brain barrier and does not induce significant toxicity or adverse immune responses in humans, highlighting its potential for use in drug delivery applications (Krag et al., 2006).

## 4.7 Turnip yellow mosaic virus (TYMV)

Turnip yellow mosaic virus (TYMV) is a species of the genus *Tymovirus*, family *Tymoviridae* (Dreher, 2004). It is a non-enveloped plant virus measuring approximately 28 nm in diameter. The structure was determined using X-ray crystallography and electron microscopy with negative staining. The genome consists of a single-stranded RNA molecule containing 6318 bases and is enclosed within a protein capsid composed of 180 identical CP molecules of 20,133 Da, organized in a T ¼ three icosahedron (Canady et al., 1996; Brenner and Horne, 1959). TYMV is considered safe for humans and has been successfully used as a template for nanoparticle assembly (Nguyen et al., 2019). This virus also exhibits high structural stability under different conditions (Barnhill et al., 2007).

TYMV capsid can endure a variety of chemical reactions, including the 1-Ethyl-3-(3-dimethylaminopropyl)carbodiimide N-hydroxysuccinimide (EDC/NHS) amidation reaction and Cu(I)-catalyzed “click” chemistry. Indeed, this group can be used to graft fluorescent peptides and molecules to the TYMV surface while leaving the capsid assembly intact (Barnhill et al., 2007; Zeng et al., 2011). Kim et al. (2018) demonstrated that an empty TYMV coupled with a cell-penetrating peptide is capable of being effectively used as transfer cargo for mammalian cells.

## 4.8 Flock house virus (FHV)

The FHV was first identified in the grass grub *Costelytra zealandica* (Coleoptera) in New Zealand. It is a member of the family *Nodaviridae* and the genus *Alphanodavirus* (Scotti et al., 1983). FHV has a viral polymerase that enables autonomous replication of the genome, making it a promising candidate for transgenic expression and directed delivery of RNA into host cells (Maharaj et al., 2014). The FHV genome is relatively simple and consists of two positive-sense single-stranded RNAs packed by a single capsid into a nonenveloped icosahedral virion (Fraenkel-Conrat and Williams, 1955). The FHV RNA1's autonomous replication capabilities, as well as its robust intracellular genome synthesis and protein expression regulated by subgenomic promoters, make FHV a good option for heterologous sequence amplification. The initial synthesis of nodavirus RNA1 and RNA2 transcription plasmids in the T7 promoter-controlled constructs resulted in *in vitro* transcribed RNA, which produced infectious virions in *Drosophila* cells (Dasmahapatra et al., 1986). Further research with nodaviruses resulted in the development of FHV cDNA-based replicon systems, which successfully produced FHV viral proteins *in vitro* in mammalian cells (Ball, 1992). A yeast DNA method was established where the wild-type FHV RNA1 was expressed *in vivo*, and this system was successfully used to express green fluorescent protein (GFP) (Price et al., 2000).

## 4.9 Other virus based nanocarriers

The use of VNPs has emerged as a specialized tool in agricultural pest management. Currently, the Environmental Protection Agency (EPA) has approved tobacco mild green mosaic virus (TMGMV) as one of the biopesticides for controlling the weed tropical soda apple, proving the potential utility of plant virus-based control of pests (Charudattan and Hiebert, 2007).

Qβ VLPs have also been tested with DOX as a potential for cancer cell destruction. A photocleavable nitroveratryl linker was used to conjugate DOX to Qβ VLPs modified with dibromomaleimide chemistry. Light exposure over 15 min resulted in dose-dependent cytotoxic death of MCF-7 cells *in vitro* (Chen et al., 2016).

Another investigation developed a multifunctional nanovehicle employing *Macrobrachium rosenbergii* nodavirus VLPs (MrNVLP) to deliver the anticancer medication DOX for hyperthermia therapy in cancerous cells. MrNVLP was covalently coated with folic acid (FA) for targeting the folate receptor (FR) overexpressing HT29 cancer cells (FA-MrNVLP-DOX). Several studies indicated that FA-MrNVLP-DOX enhanced the cytotoxicity of DOX on HT29 cancer cells, and this drug delivery was enhanced in a sustained manner when subjected to a hyperthermia temperature of 43°C (Thong et al., 2019).

# 5. Packaging drug molecules into VLPs

There are some of the common techniques for delivering biomolecules or compounds that incorporate delivery systems based on physical, chemical, and viral methods (He et al., 2022).

## 5.1 Physical methods

### *5.1.1 Electroporation*

In electroporation, short high-voltage pulses are used to form pores in the cell membrane so that these pores allow foreign DNAs and proteins to enter cells. A cell membrane can reversibly open when exposed to an electric field stronger than its capacitance. During electroporation, first the cell's positive electrode permeabilizes, followed by the breaking of the

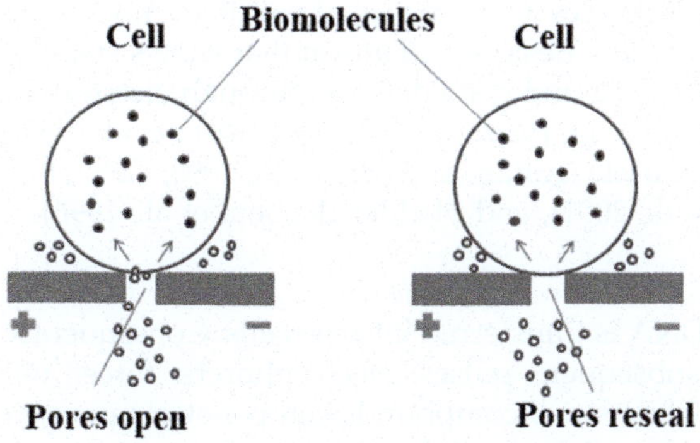


FIGURE 19.3 Single-cell electroporation. Applying an external electric field to the cell membrane can make it permeable, allowing drugs or biomolecules to enter the cell. Once electroporation occurs, the cell membrane will reseal itself.

negative electrode (Kobayashi et al., 2005). It has been shown that there are more failures on the side oriented toward the positive electrode and a larger permeabilized area on the side directed toward the negative electrode (Tekle et al., 1990). Here, the formation of pores occurs within seconds, whereas the resealing of the membrane occurs within a span of minutes. The side oriented toward the positive electrode enables a greater number of molecules to cross the cell membrane, while the side directed toward the negative electrode facilitates the entry of larger molecules more readily (Fig. 19.3).

Both large and small molecules, including DNAs (Furuya et al., 2003), dextrans (Glogauer and McCulloch, 1992), and antibodies, can be delivered using electroporation.

It has been previously demonstrated that electrophoretic forces play a crucial role in the effective transfection of DNA during electroporation (Sukharev et al., 1992). Due to the nature of electroporation, cells can be permeabilized to allow the entry of various types of molecules. Consequently, ions, drugs (Belehradek et al., 1994; Serša et al., 1995; Gehl et al., 1998; Jaroszeski et al., 2000), radiotracers (Engström et al., 1999; Gehl et al., 1999), dyes (Mir et al., 1988; Dinchuk et al., 1992; Gehl et al., 1998), oligonucleotides (Spiller et al., 1998), antibodies, DNA (Neumann et al., 1982; Heller et al., 1996; Rols et al., 1998; Mir et al., 1999) and RNA (Teruel et al., 1999; Saeboe-Larssen et al., 2002) have all been successfully introduced into cells using electroporation.

Electroporation can be of three types.

- *Electroporation in vitro*: In this method, pulsed electric signals are generated to allow precise control over pulse amplitude and duration. Through optimization of the procedure, high level of gene transfection and cell permeabilization can be achieved while maintaining good cell viability. Generally, eight pulsed signals of 100 μs at a rate of one cycle per second using a voltage gradient of 1.2 kV $cm^{-1}$ are utilized to do this.

It is quite easy to optimize the *in vitro* electroporation of suspended cells by using lucifer yellow (Mir et al., 1988; Dinchuk et al., 1992) or propidium iodide (Serša et al., 1995; Gabriel and Teissié, 1997) and by applying, for example, eight 100 μs pulses while gradually increasing the voltage until the ideal value is reached.

- *Electroporation in vivo*

A variety of species have undergone *in vivo* electroporation using either plate or needle electrodes. The plate electrodes are made up of copper plates that are affixed to nonconductive material, whereas the needle electrodes are made up of parallel arrays of hypodermic needles that are implanted into a specially designed platform that shows stability, parallelism, and good electrical contact. *In vivo* drug and gene delivery through electroporation has been demonstrated in tissues such as the brain (Salford et al., 1993; Nishi et al., 1996), liver (Heller et al., 1996; Ramirez et al., 1998), muscle (Aihara and Miyazaki, 1998; Gehl et al., 1999), skin (Prausnitz et al., 1995; Dujardin et al., 2001), and bladder (Kubota et al., 1996).

- *DNA electrotransfer*:

Through the process of permeabilization, DNA is transferred into the cells. Consequently, it has been demonstrated that during the subsequent pulses, electrophoretic forces will transfer DNA and enter the cell cytoplasm, while small compounds can penetrate permeabilized cells minutes prior to membrane resealing (Mir et al., 1999).

- *Gene electrotransfer in vitro*:

Bacterial transfection is one of the most common applications of electroporation-mediated gene transfer *in vitro*.

- *Gene electrotransfer in vivo*:

Utilizing electroporation for gene transfer within living organisms has proven to be highly effective. Specifically, in muscle tissue, where myofibers do not undergo cell division or rapid cell death, gene transfer intended for transient expression may become effectively long-term due to sustained transgene expression (Mir et al., 1999).

### *5.1.2 Sonoporation*

High-intensity ultrasounds and electric pulses both have the capacity to make cell membranes permeable in order to transfer cargo molecules through the development of pores.

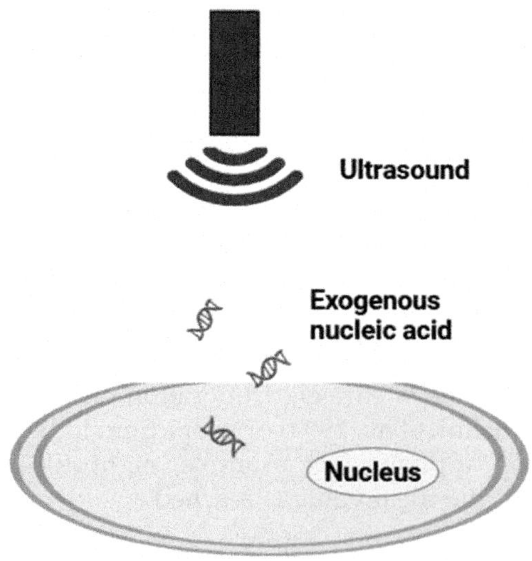


FIGURE 19.4 Pore formation in the cell membrane following ultrasonic exposure. Plasmids and other nucleic acids enter cells through membrane pores formed by ultrasound.

This process is referred to as sonoporation (Fig. 19.4). Sonoporation primarily employs high-frequency ultrasonic waves in the megahertz range (Mehier-Humbert and Guy, 2005). Although the frequency of ultrasound can vary significantly from 20 KHz to 5 MHz in gases, it may reach up to 500 MHz in liquids and solids.

Two categories of physical impacts are generated when ultrasound interacts with the cell membrane: thermal or nonthermal effects (Delalande et al., 2013). Mechanical streaming, radiation forces, and cavitation are examples of nonthermal phenomena that are produced at low ultrasonic intensities. These impacts are used for carrying out ultrasound-assisted delivery. Cavitation bubbles are the activity produced by ultrasonic waves and can occur in a liquid or a similar medium that contains pockets of gas or vapor or bubbles (Zhou et al., 2014). Low-intensity pulses that cause ultrasonic cavitation enhance friction and shear the surrounding tissues. High intensity causes the bubble's oscillations to instantly increase in amplitude, causing a cavitation transition that results in shock waves and microjets (Newman and Bettinger, 2007).

Microbubbles enhance the efficiency of sonoporation transfection. Microbubbles are vesicles filled with gas and enclosed by a stable shell that can be modified with PEG, medicines, antibodies, and targeting ligands (Dasgupta et al., 2016).

Microbubbles can enhance gene delivery and reduce the barrier for sonoporation (Tomizawa et al., 2013). The level of microbubble concentration has a strong correlation with the efficiency of transfection. The effectiveness of transfection via sonoporation can be diminished by microbubble concentrations that are excessively high or too low. The effectiveness of sonoporation for gene delivery, both *in vitro* and *in vivo*, is enhanced by its integration with microbubbles, often used as intravascular ultrasound imaging agents, along with various nanocarriers such as nanoemulsions, polymer nanoparticles, micelles, or liposomal structures (Husseini and Pitt, 2008). Sonoporation is presently used for various tissues, including renal tubules (Kurosaki et al., 2014), endothelial cells (Skachkov et al., 2014), the cardiovascular system (Unger et al., 2014), breast cancer (Bai et al., 2016), liver cancer, and pancreatic cancer (Kotopoulis et al., 2014).

### *5.1.3 Microinjection*

Microinjection is a physical method for gene transfer that employs a small glass needle or micropipette to directly introduce DNA or other genetic components into a cell. This technique allows for the effective transfer and integration of desired genes into the genome of the host cell. It serves as a useful instrument across various study areas, as it allows precise regulation of the distribution of preferred elements.

Microinjection uses an injection needle to physically penetrate the cell membrane and inject materials into specific places within cells, allowing for the direct delivery of cDNAs, peptides, proteins, or nondiffusible large-molecule drugs. Additionally, microinjection delivers into the nucleus or cytoplasm with exact timing and volume (Fig. 19.5). To identify the injected cells, marker dyes such as dextran Texas Red, which cannot diffuse across membranes, may be coinjected, or fluorescently labelled proteins may be used for rapid visualization.

Protein preparation is significantly reduced using microinjection for studies involving less common proteins, synthetic peptides, and high-priced recombinant proteins. Introducing cDNA through injection reduces cellular stress, thereby decreasing the amount of cell death that is frequently seen in liposome-mediated transfections or viral infections (Zhang and Yu, 2008).

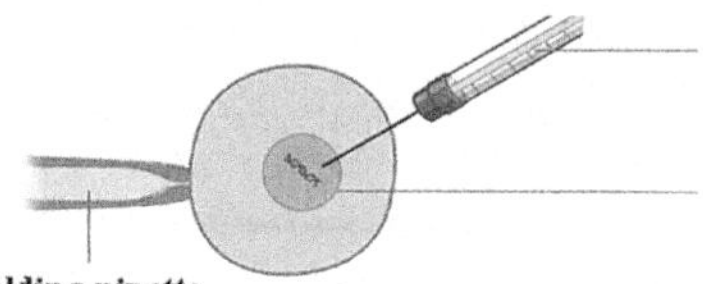


FIGURE 19.5 DNA microinjection. DNA is injected into the cell by puncturing the plasma membrane with a thin glass needle.

Microinjection is rarely used as a single-cell approach to produce overexpressed proteins and transduce a large number of cells for purification, immunoprecipitation, bioluminescence, or western blot. The typical results of microinjection experiments include immunofluorescence, in situ cell death detection (e.g., terminal deoxynucleotidyl transferase-biotin dUTP nick-end labeling), subcellular localization or translocation, and single-cell polymerase chain reaction data (Kacharmina et al., 1999; Zhang et al., 2003, 2004).

The most efficient method for delivering cytosolic and nuclear proteins is by direct microinjection, which can be accomplished by injecting the cDNAs of these membrane-bound proteins. As injecting substances into cells can be physically disruptive, vehicle control is necessary to rule out the potential that injections have a major impact on cell survivability. Both immunohistochemical staining to identify the injected compounds and positive controls are advised to guarantee successful injection. It is not recommended to incubate dividing cell lines for an extended period after injection since cell division continuously dilutes the injected substances.

Numerous studies have used microinjection to analyze human embryos and mitotic cells (Wadsworth, 1998) and also primary cultured human neurons. A variety of cDNA constructs, peptides, and proteins have been introduced into the human neural cytosol, including recombinant caspases, Bax, Hsp70, and neutralizing antibodies (Zhang et al., 2004; Guo et al., 2004). *In vitro* fertilization in clinics, transgenic animal production (Terns and Goldfarb, 1997), and RNA interference transduction (Leonetti et al., 1991) are other common uses for microinjection.

Recently, small interfering RNAs, transgenic Drosophila (Fish et al., 2007), dominant negative mutants (Boström et al., 2007; Broders-Bondon et al., 2007), RNAs (Khanam et al., 2007; Bossi et al., 2007), nanoparticles (Ehrenberg and McGrath, 2005), neutralizing antibodies (Gallego et al., 2008), and sperm (Woodward et al., 2008; Yoshida and Perry, 2007) have all been delivered into cells via microinjecting a single cell. It has also been used to investigate communication at gap junctions and domains of transcription-regulating proteins in viruses. Specifically, a marker dye can identify microinjected cells, and an electrophysiological technique can be used to evaluate the injection material's functionality (Giovannardi et al., 2007).

### *5.1.4 Gene guns/biolistic delivery*

It is a device that functions by bombarding target cells with microparticles coated in DNA at a high speed in order to transfect them with foreign DNA (Fig. 19.6). Many different biological species, including bacteria, fungi, various plant species, and mammalian cells and organs, have had their DNA transferred using this technique.

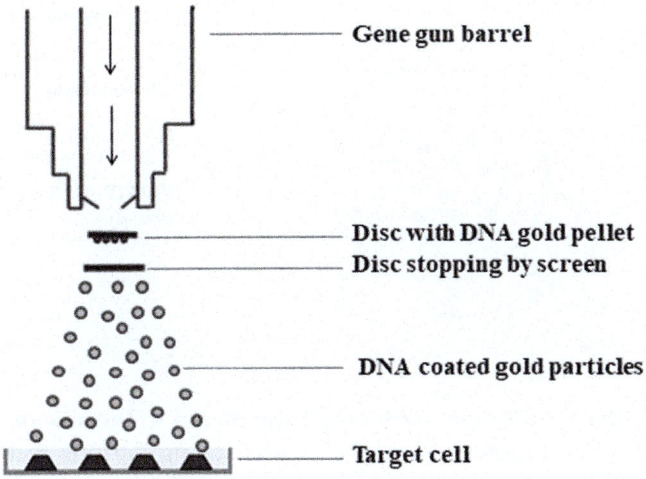


**FIGURE 19.6** Gene gun or biolistic particle delivery system.

Currently, a variety of commercial gene gun devices are available (Powderject, PowderMed, and Iaculor Injection) (Zhang et al., 2014). For the preparation of the particles used in the gene gun process, gold is the most suggested material due to its favorable immunotolerance (Macklin et al., 2000), low toxicity, and high density. Titanium particles have been suggested because of their low cost and strong biocompatibility, which reduces the chance of cell injury (Hou et al., 2014). Tungsten particles have also been used since they are less expensive, but their application is restricted by their toxicity and nonbiocompatibility. Moreover, polymer microparticles or stainless steel have been suggested. However, the diameter size of the microparticles (0.5–100 μm) has a significant impact on their capacity to penetrate through tissue. Therefore, larger particles are predicted to travel an extracellular path, while smaller particles take an intracellular one. In this regard, the smallest particles (0.6 to 6 μm diameter) are ideal for delivering cell DNA (Bryan et al., 2013).

Different types of tissues and organs, such as organotypic slices, have been subjected to biolistic gene transfer in order to maximize usage conditions with the least amount of injury (Arsenault and O'Brien, 2013). DNA vaccines delivered via gene gun primarily induce a Th2 immune response against most antigens, although they are also capable of inducing a mixed Th1/Th2 response, depending on the antigen (Deressa et al., 2014). Human papillomavirus (Kwak et al., 2013), hepatitis C virus in humans (Ahlén et al., 2014), and goose parvovirus (Cai et al., 2013) are only a few of the virus antigens against which effective cellular and humoral responses have been reported. Despite the potential benefits of gene gun over direct intramuscular injection, other studies indicate that gene gun causes less than ideal protection against papilloma and neuroblastoma (Kwak et al., 2013; Berger et al., 2013).

## 5.2 Chemical methods

### *5.2.1 Liposomes*

Liposomes are drug vesicles made from phospholipids that self-assemble to create a bilayer or multiple bilayers surrounding a central water compartment. The dual layer of

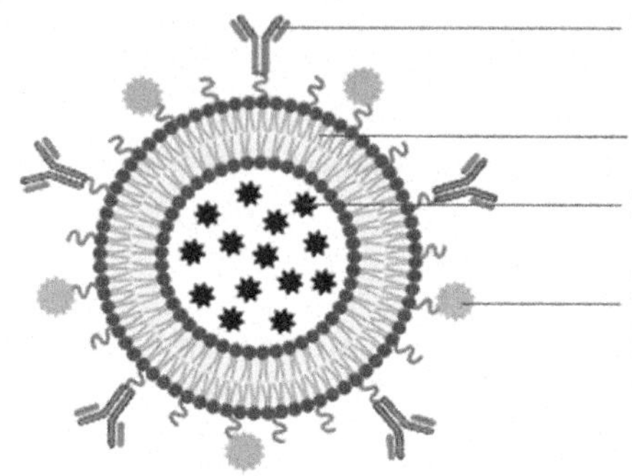


FIGURE 19.7 Schematic diagram of a drug delivery system based on liposomes.

phospholipids in liposomes is 4–5 nm thick, and their sizes vary from 30 nm to the size of a micrometer (Mazur et al., 2017) (Fig. 19.7). Liposomes can be created using various techniques, including the film hydration method, the double-emulsification method, solvent injection techniques, and in situ preparation of liposomes.

Many research studies have been carried out on liposomes as carriers for imaging agents, proteins, nucleic acids, and small molecules (Mirzavi et al., 2021; Wang et al., 2021; Watson et al., 2012). Liposomes have been regarded as a potential and adaptable form of medication delivery system.

They have better qualities than conventional drug delivery systems, such as site-targeting, controlled or prolonged release (Boström et al., 2007), shielding medications from degradation (Niu et al., 2012) and clearance, improved therapeutic benefits, and fewer adverse reactions. In contrast to normal tissue, which has tight intracellular connections between endothelial cells (two to six nm) (Forssen, 1997), aberrant tissues, including solid tumors or inflammatory sites, have capillaries that are extremely porous (100 nm–2 μm, based on the size and composition of the tumor tissue) (Kalyane et al., 2019).

The enhanced permeability and retention (EPR) effect refers to the capability of liposomes to naturally accumulate and remain in abnormal tissues after crossing the discontinuous neovasculature. The ligands and receptors on the surface of tumor cells and liposomes interact in an exclusive manner and are used in active targeting. Certain receptors, including integrin, FA, vascular endothelial growth factor (VEGF), epidermal growth factor (EGF), CD44 (a cell surface glycoprotein), CD13, and prostate-specific membrane antigen, may be overexpressed by tumor cells (Zhang et al., 2021a). Based on these receptors, certain ligands were suggested for liposome surface modification, including antibodies (Dana et al., 2020), nucleic acids (e.g., aptamers) (Hashemi et al., 2020), proteins (e.g., transferrin) (Fernandes et al., 2021), peptides (e.g., iRGD (Danhier et al., 2012), iNGR (Kang et al., 2014), small molecules (e.g., FA) (Liang et al., 2021), and carbohydrates like dextran, mannose, and galactose (Chen et al., 2020), which target macrophages.

### 5.2.2 *Exosomes*

Exosomes, which are phospholipid bilayer vesicles, were initially discovered to be a component of the maturation process of reticulocytes (Johnstone et al., 1987; Pan and Johnstone, 1983).

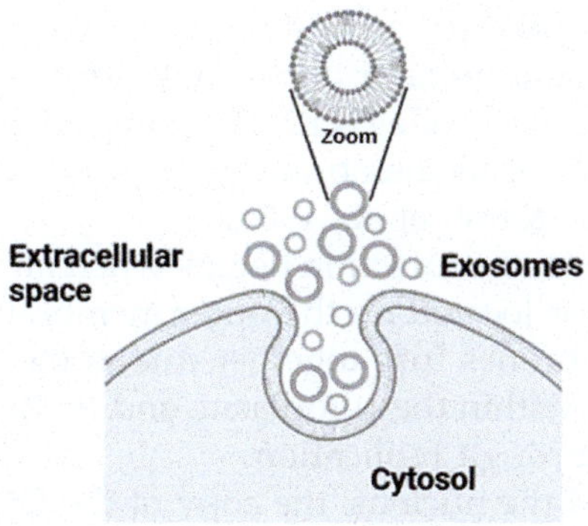


**FIGURE 19.8** Exosome as a drug delivery system.

The ability to produce exosomes is present in a wide variety of cell types, such as neurons, B cells, T cells, macrophages, glial cells, dendritic cells (DCs), the majority of stem cells, and tumor cell lines (Simpson et al., 2008; Van Niel et al., 2006). Exosomes vary in diameter between 40 and 120 nm, and their sucrose density ranges from 1.13 to 1.19 g/mL (Denzer et al., 2000; Liu et al., 2013). Exosomes, the tiniest form of extracellular vesicles, are released from the cell when multiple vascular bodies unite with the plasma membrane (Fig. 19.8). Exosomes can transport valuable cargo between cells in an organic manner, facilitating the transmission of genetic material between living things (Liu et al., 2013). One important step in influencing alterations in cellular behavior is the transfer of exosomes to target cells (Lakhal and Wood, 2011). Additionally, they are crucial for intercellular communication (Zhang and Chopp, 2016). Exosomes are being investigated as ways to transport drugs and genes due to their inherent properties.

## 5.3 Virus-based methods

### *5.3.1 Enveloped virus*

#### 5.3.1.1 Murine leukemia virus (MLV)

MLV is among the most basic retroviruses that have been used as a model (Feher et al., 2006). Only the three polyproteins necessary for generating offspring virus particles are encoded by prototypical gamma retroviruses. These are the structural proteins of retrovirus particles, known as the Gag polyprotein. The Pol protein is made up of three retroviral enzymes: integrase, whose function is to incorporate the DNA into the chromosomes of the host cell; reverse transcriptase, an enzyme changes the viral RNA to DNA during infection of a new host cell; and protease (PR), which catalyzes maturation of the particle. Then infection is started by the Env polyprotein, which causes the virus membrane to merge with the membrane of the new host cell. They have been the subject of extensive research since the 1950s, when it was discovered that a transmissible agent can spread leukemia to young mice (Gross, 1951, 1957; Moloney, 1960). Gene therapy vectors have also been developed using the MLV genome.

The pol open reading frame of retroviruses frequently contains the coding information for retroviral PR. In MLV, the Gag terminator undergoes in-frame suppression (readthrough) to create the PR as a component of the Gag–Pro–Pol polyprotein (Yoshinaka et al., 1985). The PR enzyme also transforms the transmembrane protein Pr15(E) in MLV into p12(E) and p2 (E) (Crawford and Goff, 1985; Katoh et al., 1985).

In the MLV replication cycle, the infection begins when an infectious, fully developed virus particle binds to a receptor located on the outer membrane of the recently infected cell. Then, the viral and cell membranes fuse together due to the virus's Env protein.

The mature core separates within the cytoplasm, and the RNA dimeric virus is converted into double-stranded DNA through replication.

After the DNA has entered the nucleus, the copy of the DNA is integrated into the chromosomal DNA of the cell. Then the transcription of the DNA occurs, and the nucleus exports an RNA product; some molecules present in the cytoplasm get translated into proteins of the virus, while others will be encapsidated into virus particles. The viral components come together to form budding virions, which are premature particles released from the cell. Ultimately, PR (retroviral PR) breaks down the proteins of the virus, transforming premature particles into infectious, mature virions.

#### 5.3.1.2 Human immunodeficiency virus (HIV-1)

The most common form of HIV, a virus that comes from primates and targets the human immune system to result in acquired immunodeficiency syndrome (AIDS), is called HIV-1 (Campbell and Hope, 2008). HIV-1 is an enveloped retrovirus, and the infection process starts when the viral envelope proteins come into contact with T lymphocyte and macrophage surface proteins (Campbell and Hope, 2008).

The HIV-1 genome is composed of three main genes: gag, pol, and env. These genes encode for group-specific antigen, polymerase, and envelope glycoprotein, respectively (Freed, 2001; Cervera et al., 2019). The gag gene codes for Pr55Gag, a polyprotein precursor that is cleaved by the viral PR to generate spacer peptides p2 and p1, along with matrix (MA or p17), capsid (CA or p24), nucleocapsid (NC or p7), and p6 proteins (Freed, 2001; Cervera et al., 2019).

The large polyprotein precursor Pr160GagPol is generated by pol, which is processed by PR to produce the distinct enzymes PR, reverse transcriptase (RT), and integrase encoded by pol (Freed, 2001; Cervera et al., 2019).

A cellular PR processes the polyprotein precursor gp160 to produce two envelope glycoproteins, including the surface Env glycoprotein gp120 and the transmembrane glycoprotein gp4 (Freed, 2001; Cervera et al., 2019).

HIV-1-derived VLPs serve as effective nanoplatforms because of their enclosed surface that makes it easier for them to self-assemble, which only needs the Gag polyprotein for functionalization, as well as their capacity to evoke both natural and immunological reactions (Cervera et al., 2013; Gonelli et al., 2019; Boix-Besora et al., 2022). Several regulatory and auxiliary proteins are also encoded by the HIV-1 genome, including Rev, which facilitates viral RNA movement to the cytoplasm, while Tat is necessary for HIV-1 long terminal repeat transcription (Freed, 2001). Other proteins are Vpu, Vif, Vpr, and Nef (Freed, 2001; Cervera et al., 2019). VLPs based on HIV-1 are robust nanoplatforms with a diameter of approximately 150 nm.

They are made up of glycoproteins, a lipidic envelope that is taken from the host cytoplasmic membrane, and structural internal polyproteins (González-Domínguez et al., 2016; Cervera et al., 2019). These VLPs are attractive recombinant vaccines and delivery systems due to their stability, structure, and functionalization potential (Cervera et al., 2019).

VLPs based on HIV-1 can take two different forms. A juvenile HIV virion-like substance called a Gag-VLP is created when only the gag gene is expressed by the host cell (Fernandes et al., 2020). Next, a Gag-Env VLP will develop, and these enclosed proteins will be apparent on the VLP exterior if the gag gene and the env gene are coexpressed (Zhang et al., 2021b). The ability of HIV-1-based VLPs to self-assemble with just one polyprotein sets them apart from other VLPs (Cervera et al., 2013), displaying HIV-1 epitopes located on the surface that are recognized by antigen-presenting cells (APCs), stimulating both innate and adaptive immune reactions after being cleared into lymph nodes (Gonelli et al., 2019). HIV-1 epitopes are located on the surface and can activate both innate and adaptive immune responses by being absorbed by APCs.

### *5.3.2 Nonenveloped virus*

#### 5.3.2.1 Bluetongue virus (BTV)

An arbovirus known as BTV has been identified as a significant economic threat to cattle and sheep in numerous regions across the globe. On the other hand, prolonged viremia is experienced by infected cattle, and teratogenic abnormalities and miscarriage can result from infection during pregnancy. Although BTV is not communicable, it is spread by competent Culicoides midges biting people (Du Toit, 1944), although a number of newly identified BTV serotypes spread directly through contact with people (Batten et al., 2013; Bréard et al., 2018; Chaignat et al., 2010). The BTV is currently represented by 24 unique serotypes and is the standard prototype of the orbivirus genus within the Reoviridae family.

The genetic material of BTV is surrounded by a protein shell consisting of two capsids, containing 10 segments of double-stranded RNA. There are three smaller (VP1, VP4, VP6) and two larger (VP3, VP7) polypeptides present in the icosahedral inner capsid (Verwoerd et al., 1970, 1972). However, the outer shell is made up of just two polypeptides (VP2, VP5). Then, a double baculovirus expression vector was utilized to construct an empty BTV double capsid particle that lacked the three minor proteins and the dsRNA genome (French et al., 1990).

The only components that create the icosahedral structure of these VLPs are the two primary core proteins, VP3 (from BTV-17) and VP7 (from US BTV-10), that are linked to an external covering composed of VP2 and VP5 (of US BTV-10).

Reverse genetics, which involves transfecting 10 synthetic RNA transcripts from cDNAs in a double transfection process (Boyce et al., 2008), allowed BTV to be recovered from core-derived mRNAs (Boyce and Roy, 2007).

There are countless possibilities to explore viral functions within the cell infected by BTV due to reverse genetics, especially with regard to nonstructural proteins (Ratinier et al., 2011; Van Gennip et al., 2014). The BTV sero group is made up of several neutralization groups with weak cross-protection and infrequent cross-neutralizing antibody expression (Erasmus, 1990; Huismans and Erasmus, 1981).

BTV VLPs are made up of VP3, VP7, VP2, and VP5 that are expressed in insect cells by baculovirus expression (Belyaev and Roy, 1993; French et al., 1990; Stewart et al., 2010,

2012, 2013), the Nicotiana benthamiana plant, and the HyperTrans plant transient expression vector system based on CPMV (Rybicki, 2010). All five serotypes were protected against by a cocktail of VLPs for serotypes 1, 2, 10, 13, and 17, while several other serotypes were partially protected. Marketed inactivated BT vaccinations are probably safer and far less expensive to make. Plant-based protein and VLP production have grown in popularity as a potential cost-effective substitute for synthetic protein production of complex, high-value proteins. It is now feasible to create multiprotein double-shelled VLPs that resemble real virions but lack the genetic material and viral replication machinery due to recent advancements in biotechnology. In addition to having similar biochemical compositions, these double-shelled particles cause guinea pigs to produce strong neutralizing antibodies (French et al., 1990). These particles should therefore have the same immunological potency as "whole" inactivated virus vaccines while being as safe as subunit vaccinations.

## 6. Applications of VLPs

VLPs are viral protein-based nanostructures with a wide range of biological and therapeutic uses, as shown in Fig. 19.9.

### 6.1 VLPs as immunogens

VLPs have been shown to provide greater immunogenicity and antigenicity compared to subunit vaccines, significantly inducing cellular and humoral immunity (McFall-Boegeman and Huang, 2022). When VLPs bind to pattern recognition receptors (PRRs) like Toll-like receptor 2 (TLR2) on DCs, it activates these cells, leading to the expression of maturation markers such as CD40, CD80, and CD86 (Zepeda-Cervantes et al., 2020). VLPs are taken by the cells and presented to cytotoxic T cells ($T_C$) and helper T cells ($T_H$) through MHC I and MHC II (Zepeda-Cervantes et al., 2020; Keikha et al., 2021). The interaction between MHC II and $T_H$ cells (TLR) releases cytokines, which help in the activation of B-cell receptors, further differentiating them into plasma cells and memory cells (Hong et al., 2018) as

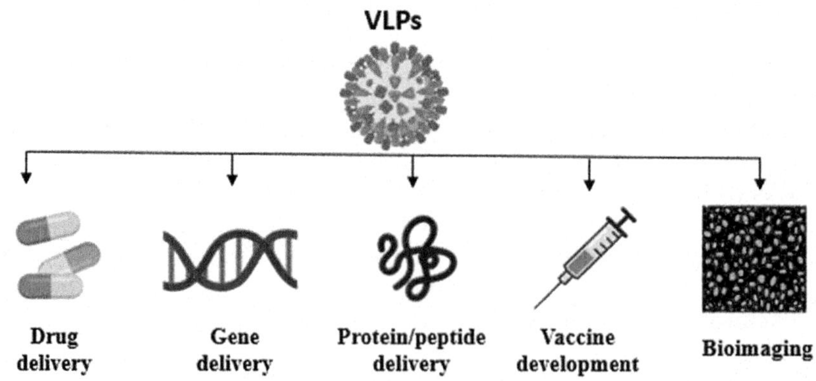


FIGURE 19.9 Applications of VLPs.

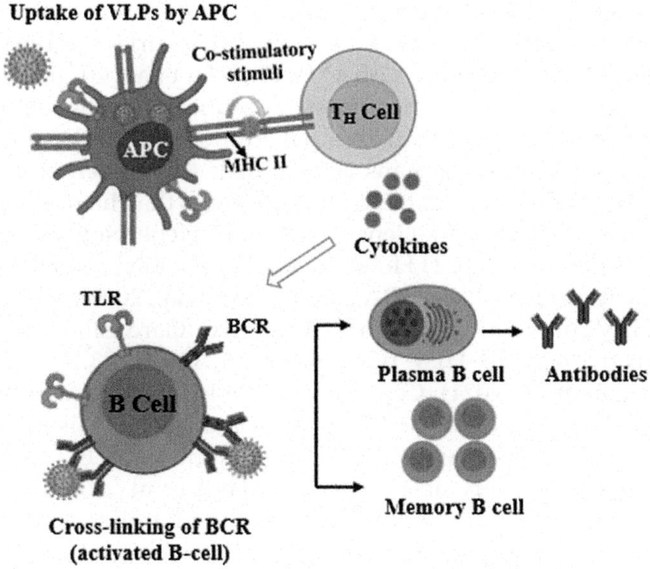


FIGURE 19.10 VLPs get fragmented after being phagocytosed. T helper cells are exposed to these fragments through MHC II, which causes TH cells to release cytokines. Together with the crosslinking of B-cell receptors by VLPs, these cytokines activate B cells, which then divide into memory cells and plasma cells and release more antibodies to neutralize the virus.

shown in Fig. 19.10. The target epitopes can be delivered on the VLP surface by either cross-linking synthetic peptides with the desired epitope or genetically integrating the peptides into the VLPs' specific coding region. The cross-linking approach elicits strong immunogenic reactions, resulting in the development of neutralizing antibodies. It eliminates protein folding issues and can be done enzymatically with Sortase or Spycatcher; however, it is more expensive (Cavelti-Weder et al., 2016; Tang et al., 2016; Janitzek et al., 2019). On the other hand, genetically fusing the peptides into the coding sequence of VLPs causes them to self-assemble into VLPs with the desired peptide on their surface, which has been experimented on with the woodchuck hepatitis virus (WHV) and RNA bacteriophages (Menne et al., 1997; Caldeira et al., 2010, 2020). Although protein folding is a problem, it has been resolved in HBV and RNA phage. In these phages, genetically modified peptide dimers were inserted into the CPs (AB loop), which increased stability (Bolli et al., 2018).

## 6.2 VLP-based vaccines

VLPs are close imitators of viruses. They lack genetic materials, which makes them safe and a feasible alternative to traditional viral vaccines (Teunissen et al., 2013). They are noninfectious and can be eliminated easily from the body without any associated risks or major side effects. VLPs can be generated from enveloped and nonenveloped viruses, and they have proven to be strongly immunogenic, which is a primary criterion that needs to be fulfilled for a vaccine (Nooraei et al., 2021; Qian et al., 2020). VLPs, as a vaccine, do not require an adjuvant, as they are sufficient to elicit all of the responses required by the target. The surface of VLPs is densely packed with repeated epitopes that stimulate the production of huge quantities of effective antibodies and can effectively induce powerful cellular and humoral immune responses (Lim et al., 2020; Marintcheva, 2017) (Fig. 19.11). The first VLPs were developed from CPs of HBV VLPs in yeast using HBV surface antigen (HBsAg) and HBV core antigen (HBcAg) (1980) together with TMV (Vahdat et al., 2021; Zeltins, 2013b). The FDA approved this vaccine in 1986 and commercialized it under the name Recombivax HB (Lagoutte et al., 2016; Monie et al., 2008). This paved the way for the production of VLP vaccines that could be suitable for humans and animals (Teunissen et al., 2013; Suffian and Al-Jamal, 2022; Vuppu et al., 2024). HBV VLP vaccines that have been commercialized include Engerix-B, Euvax B, Hepavax-Gene, GenVac B, Heberbiovac HB, Recombivax HB, and GenHevac B (Vahdat et al., 2021; Ho et al., 2020). Notably, the HPV-preventive VLP vaccine, Gardasil, was approved by the FDA in 2006 (Koutsky, 2009), which led to the introduction of other HPV preventive vaccines, Cervarix, Gardasil-4, and Gardasil-9. Gardasil vaccines are effective against HPV types 6, 11, 16, 18, 31, 33, 45, 52, and 58 (Zhai and Tumban, 2016; Nooraei et al., 2021). Cervarix vaccine is effective against types 16 and 18 (Nooraei et al., 2021). The efficacy of Cervarix and Gardasil-4 persists for a term of 13 years, as compared to Gardasil-9, which is at a minimum of 6 years. Gardasil-9 outperforms Gardasil-4 regarding safety and protection (Huh et al., 2017). As per reports, approximately 110 VLPs have been developed from 35 virus families, with a number of VLP-based vaccines currently undergoing clinical trials (Nooraei et al., 2021; Qian et al., 2020).

VLPs from human viruses have been beneficial for the production of vaccines against other human pathogens. For example, VLP vaccines derived from HBV can target *Helicobacter pylori*, Hepatitis C virus, HPV-associated malignancies, and dengue virus (Boigard et al., 2017). There are several ongoing trials for VLPs targeting the Zika virus (ZIKV). The constant expression of ZIKV-VLPs has been efficiently established by Fowler et al. (2023) in specific cell lines, supporting the importance of these platforms for vaccine development. Such cell lines that produce Zika-VLPs consistently are perfect candidates for the progression of vaccine research. At present, VLPs for the Chikungunya virus are in progress, as there are no traditional vaccines available. Scientists are reconnoitering self-assembled VLPs, produced specifically by expressing the Chikungunya Virus (CHIKV) envelope and capsid proteins, resulting in protection against multiple viral strains (Garg et al., 2020). Arévalo et al. (2019) conducted an experiment on a mouse model that concluded that unadjuvanted CHIKV-VLPs could completely eradicate the infection. The first VLP vaccine

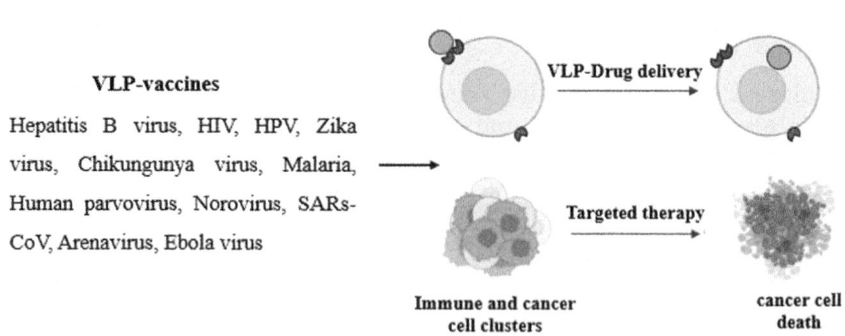


FIGURE 19.11 VLP vaccines deliver drugs, resulting in strong immunity that kills target cells.

developed to eradicate malaria was Mosquirix (RTS, S/AS01), produced by the integration of HBV surface antigen (HBsAg) and malaria parasite circumsporozoite protein (CSP) (Laurens, 2020). This led to a robust immunogenic response (Nadeem et al., 2022). The World Health Organization has approved this vaccine to be taken by children under 5 years in susceptible areas, including sub-Saharan Africa (Sahoo et al., 2021).

The human parvovirus B19 (HPVB19) VLPs are synthesized from the surface proteins VP1 and VP2 in the bacterial or eukaryotic system and have reached clinical trials (Cayetano-Cruz et al., 2019). For Norovirus (NV), the VLPs are composed of VP1 capsid proteins that are expressed in the baculovirus/insect system. VP1-NV VLPs are also produced from transgenic plants. Currently, these vaccines are under clinical trials (Zhang et al., 2021c). Along with these, VLPs for SARS-CoV are expressed by the baculovirus/insect system (Sf21 cells) by expressing Spike Protein, Envelope Protein, and Membrane Protein (Nooraei et al., 2021).

SARS-CoV-2 VLPs synthesized from various mammalian Expression Systems (ESs) produce more effective VLPs than human embryonic kidney (HEK-293T) cells (Xu et al., 2020). A VLP vaccine from the plant *N. benthamiana* has been reported, showing significant development of robust immunogenic responses in individuals. This vaccine is produced by the expression of the spike protein of SARS-CoV-2 in plants. A combination mini spike VLP vaccine showed significant immunity in mice after a single dose, eliciting neutralizing antibodies and protecting them from COVID-19 (Hemmati et al., 2022; Moon et al., 2022).

Severe hemorrhagic fever is caused by the Lassa fever virus (LASV), an arenavirus carried by rodents. Its genome is made up of two RNA segments, S and N, which code for the precursor glycoprotein and virus nucleocapsid protein. Glycoprotein Precursor (GPC) is cleaved posttranslationally to create the GP1 and GP2 glycoproteins, which are the main immunogenic targets. A mammalian cell line may be used to make LASV VLPs, and mice that received an LASV VLP vaccination had notable IgG responses to the viral proteins (Oldstone, 2002; Branco et al., 2010).

In filoviruses, VP40 matrix protein is an essential component for its structure and assembly. However, VLP generation is unfeasible with VP40 expression alone (Warfeld et al., 2007). Thus, Ebola virus (EBOV) VP40 VLPs were produced. It was demonstrated that the resulting VLPs had morphological similarities with virus particles of the wild type. *In vitro*, EBOV VLPs were very immunogenic and successfully stimulated the cytokine production, activation, and maturation of chemokines. Mice given EBOV VLPs demonstrated B-cell activation and strong EBOV-specific antibody production. Additionally, the VLPs protected mice from lethal challenges and activated $CD4^+$ and $CD8^+$ T cells (Warfeld et al., 2003).

## 6.3 VLPs as delivery systems

The delivery of genes, nucleic acids, and proteins into cells or tissues has various applications, including vaccines, gene therapy, and diagnostic imaging (He et al., 2022; Shirbaghaee and Bolhassani, 2016; Yan et al., 2015). VLPs are considered a good option for cargo delivery due to their three-dimensional structure and cell invasion property, making them ideal for intracellular delivery of desired molecules. VLPs protect the cargo from degradation or undesired binding at nontargeted areas while transporting. Genetically engineered VLPs can effectively guide the carrier to the desired cells or organs, attaining targeted cargo delivery (He et al., 2022). VLPs can be designed for their specific application by genetic modification of the CP sequences. This makes them versatile in maintaining stability at blood pH and disassembly in endosomes (low pH) to release cargo (Ghosh and Banerjee, 2021). Specific covalent and noncovalent bonds can also be employed for VLP–antigen fusion.

The heterobifunctional chemical cross-linkers with an amine group at one end and a sulfhydryl-reactive group at the other end are responsible for the most prevalent covalent bond. For example, lysine residues on the exterior of VLPs can be attached to cysteine-containing antigens at a high density (Shirbaghaee and Bolhassani, 2016). Another approach is to use rational or directed evolution approaches to create alternatives to existing VLPs with specific properties to increase the usefulness of VLPs as drug delivery vehicles. Genetic-level point mutations can change their size or shape (Ikwuagwu and Tullman-Ercek, 2022). When larger VLPs are used to target tumors for gene delivery, EPR within the tumor cells is observed (Yang and Gao, 2017).

## 6.4 The loading/unloading and activation of therapeutic agents from VLPs

An optimal drug-delivery scaffold should be flexible enough to load therapeutic agents onto the desired locations (Yuan et al., 2023). To improve the possibility that the particles will reach the intended cell, targeting ligands are affixed to nanoparticles. The targeting groups are attached to specific cell receptors. While active targeting experiments use cell-specific targeting ligands like antibodies on their external surface (Kim et al., 2019), passive targeting investigations frequently use a nonreactive spacer like PEG (Le et al., 2018). VLPs can contain therapeutic agents that are chemically attached to them, placed onto their exterior or interior, or encapsulated (Fig. 19.12). Since changing these areas usually does not affect the VLP or protein structures, protein domains are frequently introduced at the N-terminus, C-terminus, or both (Ikwuagwu and Tullman-Ercek, 2022). There are several ways to load agents onto the scaffold, including osmotic shock, fusion, de novo packing, physical contact, and polymer-mediated adsorption (He et al., 2022).

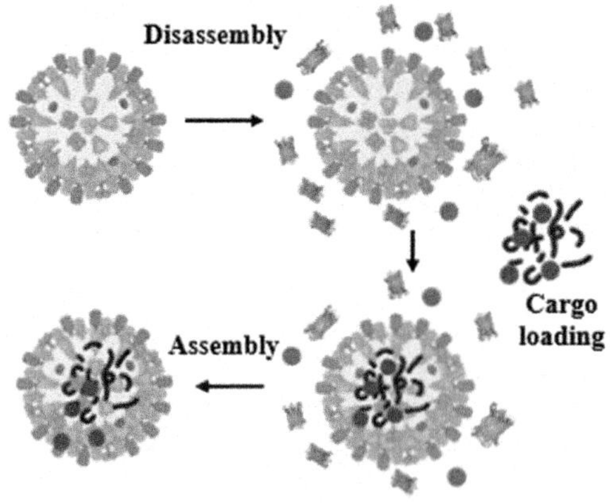


**FIGURE 19.12** Loading of proteins, nucleic acids, and small molecules into the core of VLPs via the disassembly/reassembly mechanism.

The unloading or activation of therapeutic agents is a crucial characteristic of VLPs. Sometimes the agents are altered to make them compatible with different nanoparticle delivery systems, but once they enter the diseased cells, these changes may negatively impact the cargo's therapeutic effect. Furthermore, cargo can effectively kill cells; it is too risky to be widely injected into the body (Rohovie et al., 2017). VLPs resolve both issues because of the cargo association choices, which provide a way to deliver harmful cargo precisely to cells while maintaining therapeutic efficiency. It is possible to tailor VLP–cargo interactions so that pharmacological payloads are released in a particular environment of interest in response to specific pH or the proteolytic enzymes (Tejeda-Rodríguez et al., 2019).

## 6.5 VLP—protein/peptide delivery

The transportation of bulky proteins through the cell membrane is not possible, making conventional delivery systems like liposomes, micelles, and vesicles nonproductive. Considering this issue, VLPs are being explored for protein/peptide delivery due to their nontoxicity, bioavailability, and active cell invasion properties (Xu et al., 2020).

VLPs acquired from both enveloped and nonenveloped viruses have been proficient in targeted protein delivery (Wu and Roth, 2014; Thuenemann et al., 2021; Banskota et al., 2022). Cargo proteins are fused with the VLP with strategies that include PR-cleavable linker, chemical or genetic fusion, and electrostatic interaction between the cargo and the VLP CP (Chung et al., 2023). They are delivered into the target cells or nuclei using viral PR or other alternatives (Chung et al., 2023). Many proteins or peptides are loaded onto VLP via fusion or conjugation. Despite being effective, the approaches have two significant shortcomings: for the VLP subunits or nucleic acids to correct folding. First, the peptide or protein must be responsive to genetic fusion or nucleic acid conjugation and fold into an active state. Second, the protein or peptide should be functional when coupled to the nucleic acid or merged with the CPs. Although free peptides and proteins can be loaded using electrostatic interaction and passive encapsulation procedures, they are less successful. Although electrostatic loading is more efficient than passive loading, it is limited to peptides or proteins, as they are more inclined toward the interior of the VLPs. For example, HBV VLPs load protein by genetic fusion and passive encapsulation (Shan et al., 2018). The only way *Salmonella typhimurium* P22 has been demonstrated to load proteins and peptides is by genetic fusion to the scaffold protein; thus, it does not get removed from the VLP during assembly (Wang and Douglas, 2022). Proteins and peptides have been conjugated to RNA with its stem-loop hairpin structure needed for assembly and then encapsulated using enterobacteria phage MS2 and Qβ VLPs (Palma, 2023). Additionally, MS2 loading was also done using electrostatic interaction between the poly-anionic tag (protein) and the capsid interior (Rohovie et al., 2017; Peabody et al., 2021). CCMV genetic fusions, leucine zippers incorporated into the coat and cargo proteins, and passive encapsulation have all been used to achieve CCMV loading (Pretto et al., 2021).

## 6.6 VLPs—nucleic acid delivery

Nucleic acids cannot be directly delivered through cell membranes, as they are negatively charged and have poor stability. VLPs have gained popularity for intracellular RNA delivery due to their superior biosafety compared to DNA, and variants of RNAs have been successfully delivered by VLPs (Ni et al., 2019). mRNAs can be directly transported into the cytoplasm and interpreted into functional proteins without genome integration risk. However, they are prone to degradation by RNases, hampering the delivery process; thus, enhanced RNA delivery methods are necessary for better therapeutics. Bacteriophage MS2 VLPs are most compatible for RNA loading, which can be achieved via RNA hairpin structure, which further assembles into capsids (Prel et al., 2015). Similarly, bacteriophage Qβ VLPs encapsulate the mRNAs by integrating with the RNA hairpin loop (Fang et al., 2017). Another novel method of VLP production for RNA delivery was utilizing the endogenous gene products in a mouse model. This method was suitable for the introduction of desired mRNA, including Cre and Cas9, into the targeted cells (Segel et al., 2021). This endogenous system might be greatly advantageous for gene delivery. The large size of VLPs makes it easier to load and retain the genes (Rohovie et al., 2017).

Small interfering RNAs (siRNAs) can also be used in gene therapy, autoimmune disorders, and curing malignancies. However, they are associated with risks like degradation by RNase, incompetent delivery, and inability to cross the cell membrane barrier (Hu et al., 2020). To avoid these limitations, VLP nanocarriers have been recognized for siRNA delivery *in vivo* and *in vitro*. The VLPs were derived from the adeno-associated type II virus (AAV) and coated with polyethyleneimine (PEI). Generally, coating VLPs by electrostatic interaction increases the efficacy of systemic siRNA delivery, providing extra protection and enhanced cellular uptake. These PEI-coated AAV-VLPs condense the siRNA, protecting it from enzymatic degradation. They also facilitate cell death in MCF-7 breast cancer cells (Shao et al., 2012).

Some VLPs obtained from PP7 and MS2 bacteriophages transport microRNA (miRNA) into tumor tissues, exhibiting effective delivery by the VLP (Sun et al., 2017). Ribonucleoproteins (RNPs) are composed of protein and RNA complexes involved in processes like genome editing. In the CRISPR-Cas9 system, Cas9 (RNP) acts as a nuclease and is composed of Cas9 protein and single guide RNA (sgRNA) (Singsuksawat et al., 2021). Thus, genetically modified retroviral VLPs were used to package and transport Cas-RNPs; the packaging was done by the direct fusion method. He successfully transported Cas13b-RNPs for treating dengue using pseudotyped VLPs (Singsuksawat et al., 2021). P22-VLPs were also efficient in delivering the RNPs (Cas9 protein and sgRNA), indicating the possibility for RNP delivery through phages (He et al., 2022).

## 6.7 VLPs—drug delivery for cancer monotherapy and combination therapy

Chemical drugs can diffuse into cells randomly, but concentrating them in specific cells is essential for drug efficacy and reducing side effects. VLPs are ideal for targeted intracellular drug delivery, concentrating active molecules within particular tissues, and stimulating further effects. VLPs also envelop drug molecules, preventing their degradation or dilution, allowing controlled release in target tissues or cells. VLPs have higher endosome escape efficiency than liposomes and inorganic nanoparticles, better biocompatibility, and better biodegradability compared to other nanocarriers (Fig. 19.13). VLPs are ideal for tumor therapy, as they can be modified for targeted intracellular distribution and offer better biocompatibility and biodegradability. Due to these benefits, several targeted techniques have been

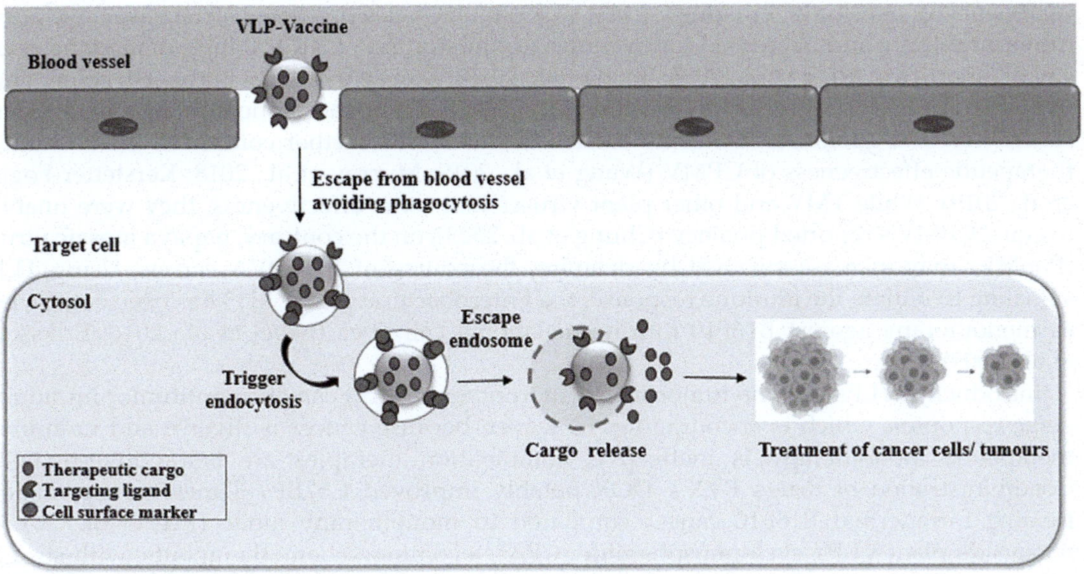


FIGURE 19.13 The cellular uptake of VLPs enables more precise delivery of medications, treatments, and biomaterials to particular cell types, including immune and cancer cells, as well as to specific areas, including tumors.

considered for drug delivery for antibacterial infection and tumor therapy into the cells with VLPs. Despite VLP's inherent tropism, cell targeting is usually accomplished by genetically modifying it to include peptides into the CPs or chemically altering its surface to show ligands or antibodies. Various cancer cell-targeting ligands, including small compounds, antibodies, proteins/peptides, transferrin, and DNA aptamers, have been attached to viral lipoproteins (Lino et al., 2017; Wu et al., 2005; Banerjee et al., 2010). FA is widely used in drug delivery to cancer cells, with uptake mediated by the FR. VLPs represent an attractive system for drug delivery *in vitro*.

To target human hepatocellular carcinoma (HCC) cells, MS2-based viral lipopolymers were altered with a specific peptide (SP94) and encapsulated with a drug, DOX. At $IC_{50}$s of 10–15 nM, it was discovered that DOX-laden VLPs killed HCC cells 20 times more effectively than free DOX (Ashley et al., 2011). Esfandiari et al. (2018) stated that the effect of Herceptin-loaded PVX on cancer cells is greater than that of free Herceptin. Identification of people with breast cancer may be greatly aided by Herceptin's capacity to target the Her-2 receptor on breast carcinoma cells. Herceptin improves disease amelioration, survival rates, and therapeutic response rates when used in conjunction with chemotherapy (Alvandi et al., 2022). DOX is delivered using a variety of VLP techniques, where it is electrostatically attached to the viral capsid's outer layer. As per a study conducted by Singh et al. (2006b), transferrin-conjugated canine parvovirus (CpV) VLPs demonstrated tumor uptake on cancer cell surfaces, whereas cells with minimal transferrin expression did not. Drugs have been delivered via capsids, and tumors have been targeted using chemical, genetic, and noncovalent alterations. Plant virus VLPs have also demonstrated remarkable effectiveness as cancer treatments. In one study, inhaling CPMV VLP nanoparticles produced strong systemic antitumor immunity and decreased intravenous administration of B16F10 lung malignancies in C57BL/6J mice (Chung et al., 2023; Shan et al., 2018). Mouse models with breast, colon, and ovarian tumors were successfully treated with CPMV in situ vaccination. Studies on ovarian cancer, cerebral glioma, and murine cutaneous melanoma further confirmed the immunotherapeutic effectiveness of CPMV (Wang et al., 2019; Murray et al., 2018; Kerstetter-Fogle et al., 2019). While TMV and other plant viruses had some effectiveness, they were unable to equal CPMV's reported potency (Chung et al., 2023); on the contrary, papaya mosaic virus (PapMV) may increase survival by delaying the course of B16-OVA cancer. Using TLR signaling to initiate the immune response, the Enterobacteria phage M13 has been employed as monotherapy against B16F10 murine melanoma cell lines (Lebel et al., 2016; Eriksson et al., 2009).

Introducing VLPs into the tumor microenvironment (TME) can elicit antitumor immunogenic responses, which is encouraging. However, because cancer is diverse and immunotherapeutic monotherapy is ineffective, combination therapies are being investigated. Coadministration of drugs PVX + DOX notably improved C57BL/6J mice's survival for treating intradermal B16F10 cancer compared to monotherapy alone (Lee et al., 2017). Alongside plant VLPs, cyclophosphamide (CPA), a common chemotherapeutic with strong immunomodulatory effects, is employed. CPA causes cell death and releases extracellular TAAs when coupled with CPMV VNPs, whereas CPMV causes immune cell infiltration and facilitates tumor-associated antigen (TAA) detection and processing (Cai et al., 2019). This combination therapy produces synergistic efficacy and systemic antitumor responses in murine models (4T1). Triple-negative breast cancer (TNBC) in Balb/c mice (4T-1) and ovarian cancer have both been treated with CPMV in conjunction with CD47-blocking antibodies. CPMV has also been studied in fusion with radiation therapy, which leads to tumor suppression and apoptosis, releasing many TAAs (Wang et al., 2019; Song et al., 2019). Combining RT with CPMV in situ vaccination noticeably enhanced tumor growth suspension in ID8-Def29/Vegf-A-Luc ovarian tumors compared to their monotherapies (Patel et al., 2018). Along with bacteriophages and plant viruses, mammalian viruses have also been used in combination treatments.

## 6.8 Bioimaging

Bioimaging is crucial for understanding biological structures and cellular dynamics, particularly in tumor progression (Gangadaran et al., 2018). It helps identify tumor location, assess cell morphology, and visualize relevant biological features. Molecular imaging is a budding biomedical research field that allows visualization, characterization, and quantification of biological processes *in vivo*. Imaging technologies, including visual imaging, computed tomography (CT), magnetic resonance imaging (MRI), and positron emission tomography (PET), are used to illustrate cell molecular pathways and mechanisms of disease in living subjects (Steinmetz, 2010). VLPs are more advantageous than synthetic nanoparticles due to their short transmission and retention, reducing complexity. VLPs can also be modified to transfer a series of fluorescent labels and contrast agents and can be altered with aptamers, peptides, or antibodies for better targeting to specified cells and tissues (Chung et al., 2023).

In optical imaging, fluorescent VLPs are utilized to identify particular cells and tissues to evaluate biological connections, pharmacokinetics, and biodistributions. CPMV is a commonly used plant virus for this purpose (Hu et al., 2020). Nevertheless, VLPs deteriorate quickly, which compromises their imaging capabilities. By employing scaffolds, metal-organic frameworks (MOF), and slow-release polymers, VLPs can be made durable to enhance imaging frequency (Luzuriaga et al., 2019). Although optical imaging methods are harmless and do not expose patients to dangerous emissions, they have translational limitations and can only penetrate tissue up to 1–2 mm (Erturk et al., 2009). Clinics frequently use MRI, PET, and CT because they produce incredibly precise imaging of deep tissues. When designed to target certain tissues and cells, VLPs can be loaded with contrast chemicals, enhancing the local concentration and signal-to-noise ratio. In addition to reducing residence time within tissues, protein-based contrast agents significantly lessen the possibility of toxicity in MRI applications (Chung et al., 2020; Chung et al., 2023).

## 7. VLPs—pros and cons

The advantages of VLPs include the following: (a) their repeating (multivalent) and ordered surface structures and (b) their noninfectious and nonreplicating properties, which make them safer than traditional immunizations. Investigations have shown that VLP-based vaccines are safer because they do not include the genomic material necessary for viruses to replicate. Therefore, there is no danger of developing illness in groups immunized with them, as opposed to attenuated viral vaccines. Other advantages include: (c) preventing allergies and the possibility of an anaphylactic reaction, (d) being extremely flexible and stable, (e) being cost-effective and high yield, (f) being stable in challenging environmental circumstances, depending on the VLP's envelope or nonenvelope structure, (g) expressing foreign antigens by acting as carriers through cell/membrane barriers, and (h) enhancing innate and adaptive immune response (Shirbaghaee and Bolhassani, 2016). However, VLP technology faces challenges in scale-up and purification, as well as determining compatibility with VLP assembly and immunogenicity. The chimeric VLP vaccine is effective only for highly preserved B- or T-cell epitopes, as pathogens undergo mutations, rendering it ineffective under host immune defense. The main challenge is developing innovative production platforms to deliver VLP vaccines while minimizing production times and costs.

## 8. Future perspective

Protein engineering and nanotechnology have advanced dramatically, resulting in the creation of medication delivery systems, vaccination carriers, and bioimaging instruments. Because of their antigenicity, particular targeting capabilities, and noninfectious nature, VLPs have become important platforms. They are a desirable substitute for other artificial nanoparticle systems because of these characteristics. VLPs can be designed to confine proteins, peptides, nucleic acids, medications, imaging agents, quantum dots, and other compounds. Through genetic and chemical changes, they can also exhibit targeting moieties on the exterior, enabling adjustable specificity. VLPs have demonstrated significant potential in improving vaccines against transmissible and noninfectious diseases. Various recombinant expression systems have been effectively applied for VLP production, with diverse competence levels. VLPs are considered safe and can act as both adjuvants and antigen delivery systems, increasing antigen uptake by APCs. VLPs have an innate affinity to select host cells, making them useful for cell-targeting applications. Further studies are needed for easy and low-cost purification and *in vivo* delivery systems. Increasing the synthesis of VLPs for clinical use comes with several difficulties. To satisfy the increased demand for large-scale manufacturing, it becomes imperative to optimize VLP production systems, such as cell culture and recombinant protein expression platforms.

## References

Ahlén, G., Holmström, F., Gibbs, A., Alheim, M., Frelin, L., 2014. Long-term functional duration of immune responses to HCV NS3/4A induced by DNA vaccination. Gene Ther. 21 (8), 739–750.

Aihara, H., Miyazaki, J.I., 1998. Gene transfer into muscle by electroporation in vivo. Nat. Biotechnol. 16 (9), 867–870.

Alvandi, N., Rajabnejad, M., Taghvaei, Z., Esfandiari, N., 2022. New generation of viral nanoparticles for targeted drug delivery in cancer therapy. J. Drug Target. 30 (2), 151–165.

Arévalo, M.T., Huang, Y., Jones, C.A., Ross, T.M., 2019. Vaccination with a chikungunya virus-like particle vaccine exacerbates disease in aged mice. PLoS Negl. Trop. Dis. 13, e0007316.

Arsenault, J., O'Brien, J.A., 2013. Optimized heterologous transfection of viable adult organotypic brain slices using an enhanced gene gun. BMC Res. Notes 6, 1–9.

Ashley, C.E., Carnes, E.C., Phillips, G.K., Durfee, P.N., Buley, M.D., Lino, C.A., Peabody, D.S., 2011. Cell-specific delivery of diverse cargos by bacteriophage MS2 virus-like particles. ACS Nano 5 (7), 5729–5745.

Azizgolshani, O., Garmann, R.F., Cadena-Nava, R., Knobler, C.M., Gelbart, W.M., 2013. Reconstituted plant viral capsids can release genes to mammalian cells. Virology 441 (1), 12–17.

Bai, W.K., Zhang, W., Hu, B., Ying, T., 2016. Liposome-mediated transfection of wild-type P53 DNA into human prostate cancer cells is improved by low-frequency ultrasound combined with microbubbles. Oncol. Lett. 11 (6), 3829–3834.

Ball, L.A., 1992. Cellular expression of a functional nodavirus RNA replicon from vaccinia virus vectors. J. Virol. 66 (4), 2335–2345.

Banerjee, D., Liu, A.P., Voss, N.R., Schmid, S.L., Finn, M.G., 2010. Multivalent display and receptor-mediated endocytosis of transferrin on virus-like particles. Chembiochem 11, 1273–1279.

Banskota, S., Raguram, A., Suh, S., Du, S.W., Davis, J.R., Choi, E.H., Wang, X., Nielsen, S.C., Newby, G.A., Randolph, P.B., et al., 2022. Engineered virus-like particles for efficient in vivo delivery of therapeutic proteins. Cell 185, 250–265.e16.

Barnhill, H.N., Reuther, R., Ferguson, P.L., Dreher, T., Wang, Q., 2007. Turnip yellow mosaic virus as a chemoaddressable bionanoparticle. Bioconjug. Chem. 18, 852–859.

Batten, C.A., Henstock, M.R., Steedman, H.M., Waddington, S., Edwards, L., Oura, C.A.L., 2013. Bluetongue virus serotype 26: infection kinetics, pathogenesis and possible contact transmission in goats. Vet. Microbiol. 162 (1), 62–67.

Beatty, P.H., Lewis, J.D., May 2019. Cowpea mosaic virus nanoparticles for cancer imaging and therapy. Adv. Drug Deliv. Rev. 145, 130–144. https://doi.org/10.1016/j.addr.2019.04.005. Epub 2019 Apr 17. PMID: 31004625.

Belehradek, J.J., Orlowski, S., Ramirez, L.H., Pron, G., Poddevin, B., Mir, L.M., 1994. Electropermeabilization of cells in tissues assessed by the qualitative and quantitative electroloading of bleomycin. Biochim. Biophy. Acta (BBA)-Biomembr. 1190 (1), 155–163.

Belyaev, A.S., Roy, P., 1993. Development of baculovirus triple and quadruple expression vectors: co-expression of three or four bluetongue virus proteins and the synthesis of bluetongue virus-like particles in insect cells. Nucleic Acids Res. 21 (5), 1219–1223.

Berger, E., Soldati, R., Huebener, N., Hohn, O., Stermann, A., Durmus, T., Lobitz, S., Zenclussen, A.C., Christiansen, H., Lode, H.N., Fest, S., 2013. Salmonella SL7207 application is the most effective DNA vaccine delivery method for successful tumor eradication in a murine model for neuroblastoma. Cancer Lett. 331 (2), 167–173.

Biabanikhankahdani, R., Ho, K.L., Alitheen, N.B., Tan, W.S., 2018. A dual bioconjugated virus-like nanoparticle as a drug delivery system and comparison with a pHresponsive delivery system. Nanomat 8, 236.

Boigard, H., Alimova, A., Martin, G.R., Katz, A., Gottlieb, P., Galarza, J.M., 2017. Zika virus-like particle (VLP) based vaccine. PLoS Neglected Trop. Dis. 11 (5), e0005608.

Boix-Besora, A., Lorenzo, E., Lavado-García, J., Gòdia, F., Cervera, L., 2022. Optimization, production, purification and characterization of HIV-1 GAG-based virus-like particles functionalized with SARS-CoV-2. Vaccines 10 (2), 250.

Bolli, E., O'Rourke, J.P., Conti, L., Lanzardo, S., Rolih, V., Christen, J.M., Barutello, G., Forni, M., Pericle, F., Cavallo, F.A., 2018. A virus-like-particle immunotherapy targeting epitope-specific anti-xCT expressed on cancer stem cell inhibits the progression of metastatic cancer in vivo. Oncoimmuno 7, e1408746.

Borodavka, A., Tuma, R., Stockley, P.G., 2012. Evidence that viral RNAs have evolved for efficient, two-stage packaging. Proc. Natl. Acad. Sci. U. S. A. 109, 15769–15774.

Bossi, E., Fabbrini, M.S., Ceriotti, A., 2007. Exogenous protein expression in Xenopus oocytes: Basic procedures. In Vitro Transcr. Transl. Protoc. 107–131.

Boström, P., Andersson, L., Rutberg, M., Perman, J., Lidberg, U., Johansson, B.R., Fernandez-Rodriguez, J., Ericson, J., Nilsson, T., Borén, J., Olofsson, S.O., 2007. SNARE proteins mediate fusion between cytosolic lipid droplets and are implicated in insulin sensitivity. Nat. Cell Biol. 9 (11), 1286–1293.

Boyce, M., Roy, P., 2007. Recovery of infectious bluetongue virus from RNA. J. Virol. 81 (5), 2179–2186.

Boyce, M., Celma, C.C., Roy, P., 2008. Development of reverse genetics systems for bluetongue virus: Recovery of infectious virus from synthetic RNA transcripts. J. Virol. 82 (17), 8339–8348.

Branco, L.M., Grove, J.N., Geske, F.J., Boisen, M.L., Muncy, I.J., Magliato, S.A., et al., 2010. Lassa virus-like particles displaying all major immunological determinants as a vaccine candidate for lassa hemorrhagic fever. Virol. J. 7 (1), 1–19.

Bréard, E., Schulz, C., Sailleau, C., Bernelin-Cottet, C., Viarouge, C., Vitour, D., Guillaume, B., Caignard, G., Gorlier, A., Attoui, H., Gallois, M., 2018. Bluetongue virus serotype 27: Experimental infection of goats, sheep and cattle with three BTV-27 variants reveal atypical characteristics and likely direct contact transmission BTV-27 between goats. Transbound. Emerg. Dis. 65 (2), e251–e263.

Brenner, S., Horne, R.W., 1959. A negative staining method for high resolution electron microscopy of viruses. Biochim. Biophys. Acta 34, 103–110.

Broders-Bondon, F., Chesneau, A., Romero-Oliva, F., Mazabraud, A., Mayor, R., Thiery, J.P., 2007. Regulation of XSnail2 expression by rho GTPases. Dev. Dyn.: An Off. Publ. American. Assoc. Anat. 236 (9), 2555–2566.

Bryan, M., Guyach, S., Norris, K.A., 2013. Biolistic DNA vaccination against trypanosoma infection. Biolistic DNA Delivery: Methods Protoc. 305–315.

Cai, M.S., Deng, S.X., Li, M.L., 2013. Comparison of the immune responses in BALB/c mice following immunization with DNA-based and live attenuated vaccines delivered via different routes. Vaccine 31 (9), 1353–1356.

Cai, H., Wang, C., Shukla, S., Steinmetz, N.F., 2019. Cowpea mosaic virus immunotherapy combined with cyclophosphamide reduces breast cancer tumor burden and inhibits lung metastasis. Adv. Sci. 6 (16), 1802281.

Caldeira, J.C., Medford, A., Kines, R.C., Lino, C.A., Schiller, J.T., Chackerian, B., Peabody, D.S., 2010. Immunogenic display of diverse peptides, including a broadly cross-type neutralizing human papillomavirus L2 epitope, on virus-like particles of the RNA bacteriophage. Vaccine 28, 4384–4393.

Caldeira, J.C., Perrine, M., Pericle, F., Cavallo, F., 2020. Virus-like particles as an immunogenic platform for cancer vaccines. Viruses 12 (5), 488.

Campbell, E.M., Hope, T.J., 2008. Live cell imaging of the HIV-1 life cycle. Trends Microbiol. 16 (12), 580–587.

Canady, M.A., Larson, S.B., Day, J., McPherson, A., 1996. Crystal structure of turnip yellow mosaic virus. Nat. Struct. Mol. Biol. 3, 771–781.

Cavelti-Weder, C., Timper, K., Seelig, E., et al., 2016. Development of an interleukin-1beta vaccine in patients with type 2 diabetes. Mol. Ther. 24, 1003–1012.

Cayetano-Cruz, M., Valadez-Garcia, J., Méndez, C., Bustos-Jaimes, I., 2019. Virus-like nanoparticles derived from parvovirus B19 efficiently internalize in human hepatocytes: a biocompatible delivery system for peptides and proteins. ACS Appl. Nano Mater. 2 (10), 6178–6186.

Cervera, L., Gutiérrez-Granados, S., Martínez, M., Blanco, J., Gòdia, F., Segura, M.M., 2013. Generation of HIV-1 Gag VLPs by transient transfection of HEK 293 suspension cell cultures using an optimized animal-derived component free medium. J. Biotechnol. 166 (4), 152–165.

Cervera, L., Gòdia, F., Tarrés-Freixas, F., Aguilar-Gurrieri, F., Carrillo, J., Blanco, J., Gutiérrez-Granados, S., 2019. Production of HIV-1-based virus-like particles for vaccination: Achievements and limits. Appl. Microbiol. Biotechnol. 103, 7367–7384.

Chaignat, V., Schwermer, H., Casati, S., Planzer, J., Worwa, G., Vanzetti, T., Batten, C., Hofmann, M., Thür, B., 2010. Occurrence and spatial distribution of toggenburg orbivirus in Switzerland. Small Rumin. Res. 93 (2–3), 157–164.

Chamundeeswari, M., Jeslin, J., Verma, M.L., 2019. Nanocarriers for drug delivery applications. Env. Chem. Let. 17, 849–865.

Charudattan, R., Hiebert, E., 2007. A plant virus as a bioherbicide for tropical soda apple, Solanum viarum. Outlook. Pest. Man. 18, 167–171.

Chen, Z., Li, N., Chen, L., Lee, J., Gassensmith, J.J., 2016. Dual functionalized bacteriophage Qβ as a photocaged drug carrier. Small 12, 4563–4571. https://doi.org/10.1002/smll.201601053.

Chen, Q., Gao, M., Li, Z., Xiao, Y., Bai, X., Boakye-Yiadom, K.O., Xu, X., Zhang, X.Q., 2020. Biodegradable nanoparticles decorated with different carbohydrates for efficient macrophage-targeted gene therapy. J. Contr. Release 323, 179–190.

Chung, Y.H., Cai, H., Steinmetz, N.F., 2020. Viral nanoparticles for drug delivery, imaging, immunotherapy, and theranostic applications. Adv. Drug Dev. Rev. 156, 214–235. https://doi.org/10.1016/j.addr.2020.06.024.

Chung, Y.H., Ortega-Rivera, O.A., Volckaert, B.A., Jung, E., Zhao, Z., Steinmetz, N.F., 2023. Viral nanoparticle vaccines against S100A9 reduce lung tumor seeding and metastasis. Proc. Nat. Aca. Sci. 120 (43) e2221859120.

Costa, L., Faustino, M.A.F., Neves, M.G.P.M.S., Cunha, Â., 2012. A Almeida Photodynamic inactivation of mammalian viruses and bacteriophages. Viruses 4, 1034–1074.

Crawford, S.A.R.A.H., Goff, S.P., 1985. A deletion mutation in the 5′part of the pol gene of Moloney murine leukemia virus blocks proteolytic processing of the gag and pol polyproteins. J. Virol. 53 (3), 899–907.

Czapar, A.E., Steinmetz, N.F., 2017. Plant viruses and bacteriophages for drug delivery in medicine and biotechnology. Curr. Opin. Chem. Biol. 38, 108–116.

Czapar, A.E., Zheng, Y.-R., Riddell, I.A., Shukla, S., Awuah, S.G., Lippard, S.J., Steinmetz, N.F., 2016. Tobacco mosaic virus delivery of phenanthriplatin for cancer therapy. ACS Nano 10, 4119–4126.

Dana, P., Bunthot, S., Suktham, K., Surassmo, S., Yata, T., Namdee, K., Yingmema, W., Yimsoo, T., Ruktanonchai, U. R., Sathornsumetee, S., Saengkrit, N., 2020. Active targeting liposome-PLGA composite for cisplatin delivery against cervical cancer. Colloids Surf. B Biointerfaces 196, 111270.

Danhier, F., Le Breton, A., Préat, V., 2012. RGD-based strategies to target alpha (v) beta (3) integrin in cancer therapy and diagnosis. Mol. Pharm. 9 (11), 2961–2973.

Dasgupta, A., Liu, M., Ojha, T., Storm, G., Kiessling, F., Lammers, T., 2016. Ultrasound-mediated drug delivery to the brain: principles, progress and prospects. Drug Discov. Today Technol. 20, 41–48.

Dasmahapatra, B., Dasgupta, R., Saunders, K., Selling, B.H., Gallagher, T., Kaesberg, P., 1986. Infectious RNA derived by transcription from cloned cDNA copies of the genomic RNA of an insect virus. Proc. Natl. Acad. Sci. USA 83, 63–66.

Dawson, W.O., Kuhn, C.W., 1974. Of cowpea chlorotic mottle virus in cowpea. Phytopathology 64, 951–957.

Delalande, A., Kotopoulis, S., Postema, M., Midoux, P., Pichon, C., 2013. Sonoporation: mechanistic insights and ongoing challenges for gene transfer. Gene 525 (2), 191–199.

Denzer, K., Kleijmeer, M.J., Heijnen, H.F., Stoorvogel, W., Geuze, H.J., 2000. Exosome: From internal vesicle of the multivesicular body to intercellular signaling device. J. Cell Sci. 113 (19), 3365–3374.

Deressa, T., Stoecklinger, A., Wallner, M., Himly, M., Kofler, S., Hainz, K., Brandstetter, H., Thalhamer, J., Hammerl, P., 2014. Structural integrity of the antigen is a determinant for the induction of T-helper type-1 immunity in mice by gene gun vaccines against E. coli beta-galactosidase. PLoS One 9 (7), e102280.

Dickmeis, C., Honickel, M.M.A., Fischer, R., Commandeur, U., 2015. Production of hybrid chimeric PVX particles using a combination of TMV and PVX-based expression vectors. Front. Bioeng. Biotechnol. 3, 189.

Dinchuk, J.E., Kelley, K.A., Callahan, G.N., 1992. Flow cytometric analysis of transport activity in lymphocytes electroporated with a fluorescent organic anion dye. J. Immunol. Methods 155 (2), 257–265.

Dreher, T.W., 2004. Turnip yellow mosaic virus: transfer RNA mimicry, chloroplasts and a C-rich genome. Mol. Plant. Path. 5 (5), 367–375.

Dujardin, N., Van Deŕ Smissen, P., Préat, V., 2001. Topical gene transfer into rat skin using electroporation. Pharm. Res 18, 61–66.

Ehrenberg, M., McGrath, J.L., 2005. Binding between particles and proteins in extracts: Implications for microrheology and toxicity. Acta Biomater. 1 (3), 305–315.

Engström, P.E., Persson, B.R., Salford, L.G., 1999. Studies of in vivo electropermeabilization by gamma camera measurements of 99mTc-DTPA. Biochim. Biophys. Acta (BBA)-Gen. Subj. 1473 (2–3), 321–328.

Erasmus, B.J., 1990. Bluetongue virus. Virus Infect. Rumin. 3, 227–237.

Eriksson, F., Tsagozis, P., Lundberg, K., Parsa, R., Mangsbo, S.M., Persson, M.A.A., Harris, R.A., Pisa, P., 2009. Tumor-specific bacteriophages induce tumor destruction through activation of tumor-associated macrophages. J. Immunol. 182, 3105–3111.

Erturk, S.M., Johnston, C., Tempany-Afdhal, C., Van den Abbeele, A.D., 2009. Chapter 6 – imaging tools in human research. In: Robertson, D., Williams, G.H. (Eds.), Clinical and Translational Science. Academic Press, San Diego, pp. 87–104.

Esfandiari, N., Arzanani, M.K., Koohi-Habibi, M., 2018. The study of toxicity and pathogenicity risk of potato virus X/herceptin nanoparticles as agents for cancer therapy. Cancer Nanotech. 9, 1–13.

Fang, P.Y., Ramos, L.M.G., Holguin, S.Y., Hsiao, C., Bowman, J.C., Yang, H.W., Williams, L.D., 2017. Functional RNAs: combined assembly and packaging in VLPs. Nucleic Acids Res. 45, 3519–3527.

Feher, A., Boross, P., Sperka, T., Miklossy, G., Kadas, J., Bagossi, P., Oroszlan, S., Weber, I.T., Tözsér, J., 2006. Characterization of the murine leukemia virus protease and its comparison with the human immunodeficiency virus type 1 protease. J. Gen. Virol. 87 (5), 1321–1330.

Fernandes, B., Vidigal, J., Correia, R., Carrondo, M.J., Alves, P.M., Teixeira, A.P., Roldão, A., 2020. Adaptive laboratory evolution of stable insect cell lines for improved HIV-Gag VLPs production. J. Biotechnol. 307, 139–147.

Fernandes, M.A., Eloy, J.O., Luiz, M.T., Junior, S.L.R., Borges, J.C., de la Fuente, L.R., Ortega-de San Luis, C., Marchetti, J.M., Santos-Martinez, M.J., Chorilli, M., 2021. Transferrin-functionalized liposomes for docetaxel delivery to prostate cancer cells. Colloids Surf. A Physicochem. Eng. Asp. 611, 125806.

Fish, M.P., Groth, A.C., Calos, M.P., Nusse, R., 2007. Creating transgenic Drosophila by microinjecting the site-specific φC31 integrase mRNA and a transgene-containing donor plasmid. Nat. Protoc. 2 (10), 2325–2331.

Flynn, C.E., Lee, S.W., Peelle, B.R., Belcher, A.M., 2003. Viruses as vehicles for growth, organization and assembly of materials. Acta Mater. 51, 5867–5880.

Forssen, E.A., 1997. The design and development of DaunoXome® for solid tumor targeting in vivo. Adv. Drug Deliv. Rev. 24 (2–3), 133–150.

Fowler, A., Ye, C., Clarke, E.C., Pascale, J.M., Peabody, D.S., et al., 2023. A method for mapping the linear epitopes targeted by the natural antibody response to Zika virus infection using a VLP platform technology. Virology 579, 101–110.

Fraenkel-Conrat, H., Williams, C.R., 1955. Reconstitution of active *Tobacco Mosaic virus* from its inactive protein and nucleic acid components. Proc. Natl. Acad. Sci. USA 41, 690–698.

Freed, E.O., 2001. HIV-1 replication. Somat. Cell Mol. Genet. 26, 13–33.

French, T.J., Marshall, J.J., Roy, P., 1990. Assembly of double-shelled, viruslike particles of bluetongue virus by the simultaneous expression of four structural proteins. J. Virol. 64 (12), 5695–5700.

Fu, Y., Li, J., 2016. A novel delivery platform based on Bacteriophage MS2 virus-like particles. Virus Res. 211, 9–16.

Furuya, M., Yasuchika, K., Mizutani, K.I., Yoshimura, Y., Nakatsuji, N., Suemori, H., 2003. Electroporation of cynomolgus monkey embryonic stem cells. Genesis 37 (4), 180–187.

Gabriel, B., Teissié, J., 1997. Direct observation in the millisecond time range of fluorescent molecule asymmetrical interaction with the electropermeabilized cell membrane. Biophys. J. 73 (5), 2630–2637.

Galibert, M., et al., 2011. Preparation of peptide and other biomolecular conjugates through chemoselective ligations. Methods Mol. Biol. 751, 67–79.

Gallego, M.A., Ballot, C., Kluza, J., Hajji, N., Martoriati, A., Castera, L., Cuevas, C., Formstecher, P., Joseph, B., Kroemer, G., Bailly, C., 2008. Overcoming chemoresistance of non-small cell lung carcinoma through restoration of an AIF-dependent apoptotic pathway. Oncogene 27 (14), 1981–1992.

Gangadaran, P., Hong, C.M., Ahn, B.C., 2018. An update on in vivo imaging of extracellular vesicles as drug delivery vehicles. Front. Pharma. 9, 169.

Garg, H., Mehmetoglu-Gurbuz, T., Joshi, A., 2020. Virus like particles (VLP) as multivalent vaccine candidate against chikungunya, Japanese encephalitis, yellow fever and Zika virus. Sci. Rep. 10 (1), 4017.

Garmann, R.F., Comas-Garcia, M., Gopal, A., Knobler, C.M., Gelbart, W.M., 2014. J. Mol. Biol. 426, 1050.

Gehl, J., Skovsgaard, T., Mir, L.L., 1998. Enhancement of cytotoxicity by electropermeabilization: an improved method for screening drugs. Anti Cancer Drugs-Int. J. Toxic Non Toxic Anti Cancer Agents 9 (4), 319–326.

Gehl, J., Sørensen, T.H., Nielsen, K., Raskmark, P., Nielsen, S.L., Skovsgaard, T., Mir, L.M., 1999. In vivo electroporation of skeletal muscle: threshold, efficacy and relation to electric field distribution. Biochim. Biophys. Acta (BBA)-Gen. Subj. 1428 (2–3), 233–240.

Van Gennip, R.G., van de Water, S.G., van Rijn, P.A., 2014. Bluetongue virus nonstructural protein NS3/NS3a is not essential for virus replication. PLoS One 9 (1), e85788.

Ghosh, S., Banerjee, M., 2021. A smart viral vector for targeted delivery of hydrophobic drugs. Sci. Rep. 11 (1), 7030.

Giovannardi, S., Soragna, A., Magagnin, S., Faravelli, L., 2007. Functional expression of type 1 rat GABA transporter in microinjected Xenopus laevis oocytes. In Vitro Transcr. Transl. Protoc. 235–255.

Glasgow, J.E., Capehart, S.L., Francis, M.B., Tullman-Ercek, D., 2012. Osmolyte-mediated encapsulation of proteins inside MS2 viral capsids. ACS Nano 6, 8658–8664.

Glogauer, M., McCulloch, C.A.G., 1992. Introduction of large molecules into viable fibroblasts by electroporation: optimization of loading and identification of labeled cellular compartments. Exp. Cell Res. 200 (2), 227–234.

Golmohammadi, R., Valegård, K., Fridborg, K., Liljas, L., 1993. The refined structure of bacteriophage MS2 at 28 A resolution. J. Mol. Biol. 234, 620–639.

Gonelli, C.A., Khoury, G., Center, R.J., Purcell, D.F., 2019. HIV-1-based virus-like particles that morphologically resemble mature, infectious HIV-1 virions. Viruses 11 (6), 507.

González-Domínguez, I., Gutiérrez-Granados, S., Cervera, L., Gòdia, F., Domingo, N., 2016. Identification of HIV-1–based virus-like particles by multifrequency atomic force microscopy. Biophys. J. 111 (6), 1173–1179.

Gross, L., 1951. "Spontaneous" leukemia developing in G3H mice following Inoculation, In Infancy, with AK-Emkemic. Proc. Soc. Exp. Biol. Med. 76 (1), 27–32.

Gross, L., 1957. Development and serial cell-free passage of a highly potent strain of mouse leukemia virus. Proc. Soc. Exp. Biol. Med. 94 (4), 767–771.

Guo, H., Albrecht, S., Bourdeau, M., Petzke, T., Bergeron, C., LeBlanc, A.C., 2004. Active caspase-6 and caspase-6-cleaved tau in neuropil threads, neuritic plaques, and neurofibrillary tangles of Alzheimer's disease. Am. J. Pathol. 165 (2), 523–531.

Hajitou, A., Trepel, M., Lilley, C.E., Soghomonyan, S., Alauddin, M.M., Marini, F.C., Restel, B.H., Ozawa, M.G., Moya, C.A., Rangel, R., 2006. A hybrid vector for ligand-directed tumor targeting and molecular imaging. Cell 125, 385–398.

Hashemi, M., Shamshiri, A., Saeedi, M., Tayebi, L., Yazdian-Robati, R., 2020. Aptamer-conjugated PLGA nanoparticles for delivery and imaging of cancer therapeutic drugs. Arch. Biochem. Biophys. 691, 108485. https://doi.org/10.1016/j.abb.2020.108485.

He, J., Yu, L., Lin, X., Liu, X., Zhang, Y., Yang, F., Deng, W., 2022. Virus-like particles as nanocarriers for intracellular delivery of biomolecules and compounds. Viruses 14 (9), 1905.

Heller, R., Jaroszeski, M., Atkin, A., Moradpour, D., Gilbert, R., Wands, J., Nicolau, C., 1996. In vivo gene electroinjection and expression in rat liver. FEBS Lett. 389 (3), 225–228.

Hemmati, F., Hemmati-Dinarvand, M., Karimzade, M., Rutkowska, D., Eskandari, M.H., Khanizadeh, S., Afsharifar, A., 2022. Plant-derived VLP: a worthy platform to produce vaccine against SARS-CoV-2. Biotech. Lett. 1–13.

Ho, J.K., Jeevan-Raj, B., Netter, H.J., 2020. Hepatitis B virus (HBV) Subviral particles as protective vaccines and vaccine platforms. Viruses 12, 126.

Hong, S., Zhang, Z., Liu, H., Tian, M., Zhu, X., et al., 2018. B cells are the dominant antigen-presenting cells that activate naive CD4+ T cells upon immunization with a virus-derived nanoparticle antigen. Immunity 49 (4), 695–708.

Hou, Y., Lai, M., Chen, X., Li, J., Hu, Y., Luo, Z., Ding, X., Cai, K., 2014. Effects of mesoporous SiO2, Fe3O4, and TiO2 nanoparticles on the biological functions of endothelial cells in vitro. J. Biomed. Mater. Res. Part A102 (6), 1726–1736.

Hu, B., Zhong, L., Weng, Y., Peng, L., Huang, Y., Zhao, Y., Liang, X.J., 2020. Therapeutic siRNA: State of the art. Signal Transduct. Target. Ther. 5 (1), 101.

Huh, W.K., Joura, E.A., Giuliano, A.R., Iversen, O.E., de Andrade, R.P., Ault, K.A., et al., 2017. Final efficacy, immunogenicity, and safety analyses of a nine-valent human papillomavirus vaccine in women aged 16–26 years: A randomised, double-blind trial. Lancet 390 (10108), 2143–2159.

Huismans, H.A.E.B.J., Erasmus, B.J., 1981. Identification of the serotype-specific and group-specific antigens of bluetongue virus. Onderstepoort J. Vet. Res. 48 (2), 51–58.

Husseini, G.A., Pitt, W.G., 2008. Micelles and nanoparticles for ultrasonic drug and gene delivery. Adv. Drug Deliv. Rev. 60 (10), 1137–1152.

Ikwuagwu, B., Tullman-Ercek, D., 2022. Virus-like particles for drug delivery: A review of methods and applications. Curr. Opi. in Biotech. 78, 102785.

Janitzek, C.M., Peabody, J., Thrane, S., Carlsen, P.H.R., et al., 2019. A proof-of-concept study for the design of a VLP-based combinatorial HPV and placental malaria vaccine. Sci. Rep. 9, 5260.

Jaroszeski, M.J., Dang, V., Pottinger, C., Hickey, J., Gilbert, R., Heller, R., 2000. Toxicity of anticancer agents mediated by electroporation in vitro. Anti-Cancer Drugs 11 (3), 201–208.

Johnstone, R.M., Adam, M., Hammond, J.R., Orr, L., Turbide, C., 1987. Vesicle formation during reticulocyte maturation. Association of plasma membrane activities with released vesicles (exosomes). J. Biol. Chem. 262 (19), 9412–9420.

Kacharmina, J.E., Crino, P.B., Eberwine, J., 1999. [1] Preparation of cDNA from single cells and subcellular regions. Methods Enzymol. 303, 3–18.

Kalaiyarasu, S., Karthik, K., Kumar, D.S., Kumar, M., Sankar, P., 2020. Virus-Like Particles: A Future Candidate Vaccine in Livestock and Poultry. Adv Y H Chung RSC Adv H Cai RSC Adv N F Steinmetz RSC Adv ; P Singh RSC Adv M J Gonzalez RSC Adv M Manchester RSC Adv I F Suffian RSC Adv K T Al-Jamal RSC Adv ; T Watanabe RSC Adv S Watanabe RSC Adv G Neumann RSC Adv H Kida RSC Adv Y Kawaoka RSC Adv E M Plummer RSC Adv M Manchester RSC Adv ; Y Ma RSC Adv R J Nolte RSC Adv J J Cornelissen RSC Adv H E Van Kan-Davelaar RSC Adv J C M Van Hest RSC Adv J J L M Cornelissen RSC Adv M S T Koay RSC Adv P Pushko RSC Adv P Pumpens RSC Adv E Grens RSC Adv ; T Ramqvist RSC Adv K Andreasson RSC Adv T Dalianis RSC Adv ; L Costa RSC Adv Faustino RSC Adv Â Neves RSC Adv Cunha RSC Adv ; I Almeida RSC Adv Yildiz RSC Adv Tsvetkova RSC Adv S Wen RSC Adv S Shukla RSC Adv M H Masarapu RSC Adv B Dragnea RSC 1034 1034 Proc. Natl. Acad. Sci. U. S. A. 109 10.1016/j.addr.2020.06.0242 87 104 Academic Press Improving the Intracellular Delivery and Molecular Efficacy of Antisense Oligonucleotides in Chronic Myeloid Leukemia Cells: A Comparison of Streptolysin-O Permeabilization, Electroporation, and Lipophilic Conjugation, Blood 156.

Kalyane, D., Raval, N., Maheshwari, R., Tambe, V., Kalia, K., Tekade, R.K., 2019. Employment of enhanced permeability and retention effect (EPR): Nanoparticle-based precision tools for targeting of therapeutic and diagnostic agent in cancer. Mater. Sci. Eng. C98, 1252–1276.

Kang, T., Gao, X., Hu, Q., Jiang, D., Feng, X., Zhang, X., Song, Q., Yao, L., Huang, M., Jiang, X., Pang, Z., 2014. iNGR-modified PEG-PLGA nanoparticles that recognize tumor vasculature and penetrate gliomas. Biomaterials 35 (14), 4319–4332.

van Kan-Davelaar, H.E., Van Hest, J.C.M., Cornelissen, J.J.L.M., Koay, M.S.T., 2014. Using viruses as nanomedicines. Brt. J. Pharmacol. 171 (17), 4001–4009.

Katoh, I., Yoshinaka, Y., Rein, A., Shibuya, M., Odaka, T., Oroszlan, S., 1985. Murine leukemia virus maturation: protease region required for conversion from "immature" to "mature" core form and for virus infectivity. Virology 145 (2), 280–292.

Keikha, R., Daliri, K., Jebali, A., 2021. The Use of nanobiotechnology in Immunology and vaccination. Vaccines 9, 74.

Kerstetter-Fogle, A., Shukla, S., Wang, C., Beiss, V., Harris, P.L.R., Sloan, A.E., Steinmetz, N.F., 2019. Plant virus-like particle in situ vaccine for intracranial glioma immunotherapy. Cancers (Basel) 11.

Khanam, T., Raabe, C.A., Kiefmann, M., Handel, S., Skryabin, B.V., Brosius, J., 2007. Can ID repetitive elements serve as cis-acting dendritic targeting elements? An in vivo study. PLoS One 2 (9), e961.

Kim, D., Lee, Y., Dreher, T.W., Cho, T.J., 2018. Empty Turnip yellow mosaic virus capsids as delivery vehicles to mammalian cells. Virus Res. 252, 13–21.

Kim, H., Choi, H., Bae, Y., Kang, S., 2019. Development of target-tunable P22 VLP-based delivery nanoplatforms using bacterial superglue. Biotechnol. Bioeng. 116 (11), 2843–2851.

Kobayashi, N., Rivas-Carrillo, J.D., Soto-Gutierrez, A., Fukazawa, T., Chen, Y., Navarro-Alvarez, N., Tanaka, N., 2005. Gene delivery to embryonic stem cells. Birth Defects Res. Part C Embryo Today - Rev. 75 (1), 10–18.

Kotopoulis, S., Delalande, A., Popa, M., Mamaeva, V., Dimcevski, G., Gilja, O.H., Postema, M., Gjertsen, B.T., McCormack, E., 2014. Sonoporation-enhanced chemotherapy significantly reduces primary tumour burden in an orthotopic pancreatic cancer xenograft. Mol. Imag. Biol. 16, 53–62.

Koutsky, L., 2009. The epidemiology behind the HPV vaccine discovery. Ann. Epidemiol. 19 (4), 239–244.

Krag, D.N., Shukla, G.S., Shen, G.P., Pero, S., Ashikaga, T., Fuller, S., Weaver, D.L., Burdette-Radoux, S., Thomas, C., 2006. Selection of tumor-binding ligands in cancer patients with phage display libraries. Cancer Res. 66, 7724–7733.

Kubota, Y., Nakada, T., Yanai, H., Kakizaki, H., Sasagawa, I., Watanabe, M., 1996. Electropermeabilization in bladder cancer chemotherapy. Cancer Chemother. Pharmacol. 39, 67–70.

Kurosaki, T., Kawakami, S., Higuchi, Y., Suzuki, R., Maruyama, K., Sasaki, H., Yamashita, F., Hashida, M., 2014. Development of anionic bubble lipopolyplexes for efficient and safe gene transfection with ultrasound exposure in mice. J. Contr. Release 176, 24–34.

Kwak, K., Jiang, R., Jagu, S., Wang, J.W., Wang, C., Christensen, N.D., Roden, R.B., 2013. Multivalent human papillomavirus l1 DNA vaccination utilizing electroporation. PLoS One 8 (3), e60507.

Lagoutte, P., Mignon, C., Donnat, S., Stadthagen, G., Mast, J., Sodoyer, R., et al., 2016. Scalable chromatography-based purification of virus-like particle carrier for epitope based influenza A vaccine produced in Escherichia coli. J. Virol. Methods 232, 8–11.

Lakhal, S., Wood, M.J., 2011. Exosome nanotechnology: an emerging paradigm shift in drug delivery: Exploitation of exosome nanovesicles for systemic in vivo delivery of RNAi heralds new horizons for drug delivery across biological barriers. Bioessays 33 (10), 737–741.

Laurens, M.B., 2020. RTS, S/AS01 vaccine (Mosquirix™): An overview. Hum. Vaccines Immunother. 16 (3), 480–489.

Lavelle, L., Michel, J.-P., Gingery, M., 2007. J. Virol. Methods 146, 311.

Le, D.H., Méndez-López, E., Wang, C., Commandeur, U., Aranda, M.A., Steinmetz, N.F., 2018. Biodistribution of filamentous plant virus nanoparticles: Pepino mosaic virus versus potato virus X. Biomacromol. 20 (1), 469–477.

Lebel, M.È., Chartrand, K., Tarrab, E., Savard, P., Leclerc, D., Lamarre, A., 2016. Potentiating cancer immunotherapy using papaya mosaic virus-derived nanoparticles. Nano Lett. 16, 1826–1832.

Lee, K.L., Murray, A.A., Le, D.H.T., Sheen, M.R., Shukla, S., Commandeur, U., Fiering, S., Steinmetz, N.F., 2017. Combination of plant virus nanoparticle-based in situ vaccination with chemotherapy potentiates antitumor response. Nano Lett. 17, 4019–4028.

Leonetti, J.P., Mechti, N., Degols, G., Gagnor, C., Lebleu, B., 1991. Intracellular distribution of microinjected antisense oligonucleotides. Proc. Natl. Acad. Sci. 88 (7), 2702–2706.

Lewis, J.D., et al., 2006. Viral nanoparticles as tools for intravital vascular imaging. Nat. Med. 12 (3), 354–360.

Li, L., Liu, J., Diao, Z., Shu, D., Guo, P., Shen, G., 2009. Evaluation of specific delivery of chimeric phi29 pRNA/siRNA nanoparticles to multiple tumor cells. Mol. Biosyst. 5, 1361–1368.

Liang, H., Zou, F., Liu, Q., Wang, B., Fu, L., Liang, X., Liu, J., Liu, Q., 2021. Nanocrystal-loaded liposome for targeted delivery of poorly water-soluble antitumor drugs with high drug loading and stability towards efficient cancer therapy. Int. J. Pharm. 599, 120418.

Liepold, L.O., Revis, J., Allen, M., Oltrogge, L., Young, M., Douglas, T., 2005. Structural transitions in cowpea chlorotic mottle virus (CCMV). Phys. Biol. 2 (4), S166.

Lim, M., Badruddoza, A.Z.M., Firdous, J., Azad, M., Mannan, A., Al-Hilal, T.A., et al., 2020. Engineered nanodelivery systems to improve DNA vaccine technologies. Pharma 12 (1), 30.

Lin, T., Johnson, J.E., 2003. Structures of picorna-like plant viruses: Implications and applications, advances in virus research. Acad Press, pp. 167–239.

Lino, C.A., Caldeira, J.C., Peabody, D.S., 2017. Display of single-chain variable fragments on bacteriophage MS2 virus-like particles. J. Nanobiotechnol. 15, 13.

Liu, R., Liu, J., Ji, X., Liu, Y., 2013. Synthetic nucleic acids delivered by exosomes: A potential therapeutic for generelated metabolic brain diseases. Metab. Brain Dis. 28, 551–562.

Loo, L., Guenther, R.H., Lommel, S.A., Franzen, S., 2008. Infusion of dye molecules into red clover necrotic mosaic virus. Chem. Commun. 7 (1), 88–90.

Luzuriaga, M.A., Welch, R.P., Dharmarwardana, M., Benjamin, C.E., Li, S., Shahrivarkevishahi, A., Popal, S., Tuong, L.H., Creswell, C.T., Gassensmith, J.J., 2019. Enhanced stability and controlled delivery of MOF-encapsulated vaccines and their immunogenic response in vivo. ACS Appl. Mater. Interfaces 11 (10), 9740–9746.

Ma, Y., Nolte, R.J., Cornelissen, J.J., 2012. Virus-based nanocarriers for drug delivery. Adv. Drug Deliv. Rev. 64 (9), 811–825.

Macklin, M.D., Drape, R.J., Swain, W.F., 2000. Preparations for particle-mediated gene transfer using the Accell® gene gun. DNA Vaccines: Methods Protoc. 297–303.

Maharaj, P.D., Mallajosyula, J.K., Thi, P., Lee, G., Zhou, Y., Kearney, C., McCormick, A.A., 2014. Trans-encapsidation of flock house virus with tobacco mosaic virus structural proteins. J. Adv. Biotechnol. Bioeng. 2, 49–59.

Manchester, M., Singh, P., 2006. Virus-based nanoparticles (VNPs): Platform technologies for diagnostic imaging. Adv. Drug Deliv. Rev. 58 (14), 1505–1522.

Marintcheva, B., 2017. Virtual virus, a semester-long interdisciplinary project on the crossroads of creativity and knowledge integration. FEMS Microbiol. Lett. 364, fnx097.

Mazur, F., Bally, M., Städler, B., Chandrawati, R., 2017. Liposomes and lipid bilayers in biosensors. Adv. Colloid Interface Sci. 249, 88–99.

McFall-Boegeman, H., Huang, X., 2022. Mechanisms of cellular and humoral immunity through the lens of VLP-based vaccines. Exp. Rev. of vacc. 21 (4), 453–469.

Mehier-Humbert, S., Guy, R.H., 2005. Physical methods for gene transfer: improving the kinetics of gene delivery into cells. Adv. Drug Deliv. Rev. 57 (5), 733–753.

Mejía-Méndez, J.L., Vazquez-Duhalt, R., Hernández, L.R., Sánchez-Arreola, E., Bach, H., 2022. Virus-like particles: Fundamentals and biomedical applications. Int. J. Mol. Sci. 23, 8579. https://doi.org/10.3390/ijms23158579.

Menne, S., Maschke, J., Tolle, T.K., Lu, M., Roggendorf, M., 1997. Characterization of t-cell response to woodchuck hepatitis virus core protein and protection of woodchucks from infection by immunization with peptides containing a t-cell epitope. J. Virol. 71, 65–74.

Mir, L.M., Banoun, H., Paoletti, C., 1988. Introduction of definite amounts of non permeant molecules into living cells after electropermeabilization: direct access to the cytosol. Exp. Cell Re. 175 (1), 15–25.

Mir, L.M., Bureau, M.F., Gehl, J., Rangara, R., Rouy, D., Caillaud, J.M., Delaere, P., Branellec, D., Schwartz, B., Scherman, D., 1999. High-efficiency gene transfer into skeletal muscle mediated by electric pulses. Proc. Natl. Acad. Sci. 96 (8), 4262–4267.

Mirzavi, F., Barati, M., Soleimani, A., Vakili-Ghartavol, R., Jaafari, M.R., Soukhtanloo, M., 2021. A review on liposome-based therapeutic approaches against malignant melanoma. Int. J. Pharm. 599, 120413. https://doi.org/10.1016/j.ijpharm.2021.120413.

Moghimi, S.M., Hunter, A.C., Murray, J.C., 2005. Nanomedicine: current status and future prospects. FASEB J. 19, 311–330.

Moloney, J.B., 1960. Biological studies on a lymphoid-leukemia virus extracted from sarcoma 37. I. Origin and introductory investigations. J. Nat. Cancer Inst. 24 (4), 933–951.

Monie, A., Hung, C.F., Roden, R., Wu, T.C., 2008. Cervarix™: A vaccine for the prevention of HPV 16, 18-associated cervical cancer. Biol.:Targets Ther 2 (1), 107–113.

Moon, K.B., Jeon, J.H., Choi, H., Park, J.S., Park, S.J., Lee, H.J., Kim, H.S., 2022. Construction of SARS-CoV-2 virus-like particles in plant. Sci. Rep. 12 (1), 1005.

Murray, A.A., Wang, C., Fiering, S., Steinmetz, N.F., 2018. In situ vaccination with cowpea vs tobacco mosaic virus against melanoma. Mol. Pharm. 15, 3700–3716.

Nadeem, A.Y., Shehzad, A., Islam, S.U., Al-Suhaimi, E.A., Lee, Y.S., 2022. Mosquirix™ RTS, S/AS01 vaccine development, immunogenicity, and efficacy. Vaccines 10 (5), 713.

Neubi, G.M.N., Opoku-Damoah, Y., Gu, X., Han, Y., Zhou, J., Ding, Y., 2018. Bio-inspired drug delivery systems: An emerging platform for targeted cancer therapy. Biomater. Sci. 6, 958e973.

Neumann, E., Schaefer-Ridder, M., Wang, Y., Hofschneider, P., 1982. Gene transfer into mouse lyoma cells by electroporation in high electric fields. EMBO J. 1 (7), 841–845.

Newman, C.M.H., Bettinger, T., 2007. Gene therapy progress and prospects: ultrasound for gene transfer. Gene Ther. 14 (6), 465–475.

Nguyen, H.A., Jupin, L., Decorse, P., Lau-Truong, S., Ammar, S., Ha-Duong, N.-T., 2019. Assembly of gold nanoparticles using turnip yellow mosaic virus as an in-solution SERS sensor. RSC Adv. 9, 32296–32307.

Ni, R., Feng, R., Chau, Y., 2019. Synthetic approaches for nucleic acid delivery: choosing the right carriers. Life 9 (3), 59.

Van Niel, G., Porto-Carreiro, I., Simoes, S., Raposo, G., 2006. Exosomes: A common pathway for a specialized function. J. Biochem. 140 (1), 13–21.

Nishi, T., Yoshizato, K., Yamashiro, S., Takeshima, H., Sato, K., Hamada, K., Kitamura, I., Yoshimura, T., Saya, H., Kuratsu, J.I., Ushio, Y., 1996. High-efficiency in vivo gene transfer using intraarterial plasmid DNA injection following in vivo electroporation. Cancer Res. 56 (5), 1050–1055.

Niu, Z., Bruckman, M.A., Harp, B., Mello, C.M., Wang, Q., 2008. Bacteriophage M13 as a scaffold for preparing conductive polymeric composite fibers. Nano Res. 1, 235–241.

Niu, M., Lu, Y., Hovgaard, L., Guan, P., Tan, Y., Lian, R., Qi, J., Wu, W., 2012. Hypoglycemic activity and oral bioavailability of insulin-loaded liposomes containing bile salts in rats: the effect of cholate type, particle size and administered dose. Eur. J. Pharm. Biopharm. 81 (2), 265–272.

Nooraei, S., Bahrulolum, H., Hoseini, Z.S., Katalani, C., Hajizade, A., Easton, A.J., et al., 2021. Virus-like particles: Preparation, immunogenicity and their roles as nanovaccines and drug nanocarriers. J. Nanobiotechnol. 19, 1–27.

Oldstone, M., 2002. Arenaviruses I-The epidemiology, molecular and cell biology of arenaviruses-Preface. Arenaviruses 262, 5–12.

Palma, M., 2023. Aspects of phage-based vaccines for protein and epitope immunization. Vaccines 11 (2), 436.

Pan, B.T., Johnstone, R.M., 1983. Fate of the transferrin receptor during maturation of sheep reticulocytes in vitro: Selective externalization of the receptor. Cell 33 (3), 967–978.

Patel, R., Czapar, A.E., Fiering, S., Oleinick, N.L., Steinmetz, N.F., 2018. Radiation therapy combined with cowpea mosaic virus nanoparticle in situ vaccination initiates immune-mediated tumor regression. ACS Omega 3 (4), 3702–3707.

Peabody, D.S., Peabody, J., Bradfute, S.B., Chackerian, B., 2021. RNA phage VLP-based vaccine platforms. Pharmaceuticals 14 (8), 764.

Plummer, E.M., Manchester, M., 2011. Viral nanoparticles and virus-like particles: Platforms for contemporary vaccine design. Wiley Interdiscip. Rev.: Nanomed. Nanobiotechnol. 3 (2), 174–196.

Prausnitz, M.R., Edelman, E.R., Gimm, J.A., Langer, R., Weaver, J.C., 1995. Transdermal delivery of heparin by skin electroporation. Bio/Technol. 13 (11), 1205–1209.

Prel, A., Caval, V., Gayon, R., Ravassard, P., Duthoit, C., Payen, E., et al., 2015. Highly efficient in vitro and in vivo delivery of functional RNAs using new versatile MS2-chimeric retrovirus-like particles. Mol. Ther. Methods Clin. Dev. 2.

Pretto, C., Tang, M., Chen, M., Xu, H., Subrizi, A., Urtti, A., van Hest, J.C., 2021. Cowpea chlorotic mottle virus-like particles as potential platform for antisense oligonucleotide delivery in posterior segment ocular diseases. Macromol. Biosci. 21 (8), 2100095.

Price, B.D., Roeder, M., Ahlquist, P., 2000. DNA-directed expression of functional flock house virus RNA1 derivatives in *Saccharomyces cerevisiae*, heterologous gene expression, and selective effects on subgenomic mRNA Synthesis. J. Virol. 74 (24), 11724–11733. https://doi.org/10.1128/JVI.74.24.11724-11733.2000.

Pushko, P., Pumpens, P., Grens, E., 2013. Development of virus-like particle technology from small highly symmetric to large complex virus-like particle structures. Intervirology 56, 141–165.

Qian, W., Sun, D., Zhu, R., Du, X., Liu, H., Wang, S., 2012. pH-sensitive strontium carbonate nanoparticles as new anticancer vehicles for controlled etoposide release. Int. J. Nanomed. 7, 5781–5792. https://doi.org/10.2147/IJN.S34773.

Qian, C., Liu, X., Xu, Q., Wang, Z., Chen, J., et al., 2020. Recent progress on the versatility of virus-like particles. Vaccines 8 (1), 139.

Ramirez, L.H., Orlowski, S., An, D., Bindoula, G., Dzodic, R., Ardouin, P., Bognel, C., Belehradek, J., Munck, J.N., Mir, L.M., 1998. Electrochemotherapy on liver tumours in rabbits. Br. J. Cancer 77 (12), 2104–2111.

Ramqvist, T., Andreasson, K., Dalianis, T., 2007. Vaccination, immune and gene therapy based on virus-like particles against viral infections and cancer. Expert Opin. Biol. Ther. 7, 997–1007.

Ratinier, M., Caporale, M., Golder, M., Franzoni, G., Allan, K., Nunes, S.F., Armezzani, A., Bayoumy, A., Rixon, F., Shaw, A., Palmarini, M., 2011. Identification and characterization of a novel non-structural protein of bluetongue virus. PLoS Pathog. 7 (12), e1002477.

Rohovie, M.J., Nagasawa, M., Swartz, J.R., 2017. Virus-like particles: Next-generation nanoparticles for targeted therapeutic delivery. Bioeng. Transl. Med. 2 (1), 43–57.

Rols, M.P., Delteil, C., Golzio, M., Dumond, P., Cros, S., Teissie, J., 1998. In vivo electrically mediated protein and gene transfer in murine melanoma. Nat. Biotechnol. 16 (2), 168–171.

Rybicki, E.P., 2010. Plant-made vaccines for humans and animals. Plant Biotechnol. J. 8 (5), 620–637.

Saeboe-Larssen, S., Fossberg, E., Gaudernack, G., 2002. mRNA-based electrotransfection of human dendritic cells and induction of cytotoxic T lymphocyte responses against the telomerase catalytic subunit (hTERT). J. Immunol. Methods 259 (1–2), 91–203.

Sahoo, J.P., Mishra, P., Sahoo, S., Samal, K.C., 2021. Historic Moment: WHO Approves the world's first malaria vaccine "Mosquirix or RTS, S/AS01". Biotica Res. Today 3 (10), 892–896.

Salford, L.G., Persson, B.R.R., Brun, A., Ceberg, C.P., Kongstad, P.C., Mir, L.M., 1993. A new brain tumor therapy combining bleomycin with in vivo electropermeabilization. Biochem Biophys. Res. Commun. 194 (2), 938–943.

T. L. Schlick, Z. Ding, E.W. Kovacs and M. B. Francis, *J. Am. Chem. Soc.*, 2005, 127, 3718–3723.

Scotti, P.D., Dearing, S., Mossop, D.W., 1983. *Flock House virus*: A nodavirus isolated from*costelytra zealandica* (white) (Coleoptera: Scarabaeida). Arch. Virol. 75, 181–189.

Segel, M., Lash, B., Song, J., Ladha, A., Liu, C.C., Jin, X., Mekhedov, S.L., Macrae, R.K., Koonin, E.V., Zhang, F., 2021. Mammalian retrovirus-like protein PEG10 packages its own MRNA and can be pseudotyped for MRNA delivery. Science 373, 882–889.

Serša, G., Čemažar, M., Miklavčič, D., 1995. Antitumor effectiveness of electrochemotherapy with cis-diamminedichloroplatinum (II) in mice. Cancer Res. 55 (15), 3450–3455.

Shan, W., Zhang, D., Wu, Y., Lv, X., Hu, B., Zhou, X., et al., 2018. Modularized peptides modified HBc virus-like particles for encapsulation and tumor-targeted delivery of doxorubicin. Nanomed.: Nanotech., Biol. and Med. 14 (3), 725–734.

Shao, W., Paul, A., Abbasi, S., Chahal, P.S., Mena, J.A., Montes, J., Kamen, A., Prakash, S., 2012. Int. J. Nanomed. 7, 1575–1586.

Shenton, W., Douglas, T., Young, M., Stubbs, G., Mann, S., 1999. Adv. Mater. 11, 253–256.

Shirbaghaee, Z., Bolhassani, A., 2016. Different applications of virus-like particles in biology and medicine: vaccination and delivery systems: Different applications of virus-like particles. Biopolymers 105, 113–132.

Simpson, R.J., Jensen, S.S., Lim, J.W., 2008. Proteomic profiling of exosomes: Current perspectives. Proteomics 8 (19), 4083–4099.

Singh, P., Gonzalez, M.J., Manchester, M., 2006a. Viruses and their uses in nanotechnology. Drug Dev. Res. 67, 23e41.

Singh, P., Destito, G., Schneemann, A., Manchester, M., 2006b. Canine parvovirus-like particles, a novel nanomaterial for tumor targeting. J. of nanobiotech. 4, 1–11.

Singsuksawat, E., Onnome, S., Posiri, P., Suphatrakul, A., Srisuk, N., Nantachokchawapan, R., Siridechadilok, B., 2021. Potent programmable antiviral against dengue virus in primary human cells by Cas13b RNP with short spacer and delivery by VLP. Mol. Ther. Methods Clinical Dev. 21, 729–740.

Skachkov, I., Luan, Y., Van Der Steen, A.F., De Jong, N., Kooiman, K., 2014. Targeted microbubble mediated sonoporation of endothelial cells in vivo. IEEE Trans. Ultrason. Ferroelectr. Freq. Control 61 (10), 1661–1667.

Song, C., Phuengkham, H., Kim, Y.S., Dinh, V.V., Lee, I., Shin, I.W., Shin, H.S., Jin, S.M., Um, S.H., Lee, H., Hong, K. S., Jin, S.-M., Lee, E., Kang, T.H., Park, Y.-M., Lim, Y.T., 2019. Syringeable immunotherapeutic nanogel reshapes tumor microenvironment and prevents tumor metastasis and recurrence. Nat. Commun. 10, 1–15.

Speir, A., Munshi, S., Wang, G., Baker, T.S., Johnson, J.E., 1995. Structure 3, 63.

Spiller, D.G., Giles, R.V., Grzybowski, J., Tidd, D.M., Clark, R.E., 1998. Improving the intracellular delivery and molecular efficacy of antisense oligonucleotides in chronic myeloid leukemia cells: a comparison of streptolysin-O permeabilization, electroporation, and lipophilic conjugation. Blood J. Am. Soc. Hematol. 91 (12), 4738–4746.

Steele, J.F.C., et al., 2017. Synthetic plant virology for nanobiotechnology and nanomedicine. Wiley Interdiscip. Rev. Nanomed. Nanobiotechnol. 9 (4).

Steinmetz, N.F., 2010. Viral nanoparticles as platforms for next-generation therapeutics and imaging devices. Nanomed.: Nanotechnol. Biol. Med. 6, 634–641.

Steinmetz, N.F., Evans, D.J., 2007. Utilisation of plant viruses in bionanotechnology. Org. Biomol. Chem. 5 (18), 2891–2902.

Steinmetz, N.F., Lomonossoff, G.P., Evans, D.J., 2006a. Plant viral capsids as nanobuilding blocks: Construction of arrays on solid supports. Langmuir 22 (24), 10032–10037.

Steinmetz, N.F., Lomonossoff, G.P., Evans, D.J., 2006b. Decoration of cowpea mosaic virus with multiple, redoxactive, organometallic complexes. Small 2 (4), 530–533.

Steinmetz, N.F., et al., 2011. Intravital imaging of human prostate cancer using viral nanoparticles targeted to gastrin-releasing Peptide receptors. Small 7 (12), 1664–1672.

Stevenson, J., Hymas, W., Hillyard, D., 2008. The use of armored RNA as a multi-purpose internal control for RT-PCR. J. Virol. Methods 150, 73–76.

Stewart, M., Bhatia, Y., Athmaran, T.N., Noad, R., Gastaldi, C., Dubois, E., Russo, P., Thiéry, R., Sailleau, C., Breard, E., Zientara, S., 2010. Validation of a novel approach for the rapid production of immunogenic virus-like particles for bluetongue virus. Vaccine 28 (17), 3047–3054.

Stewart, M., Dovas, C.I., Chatzinasiou, E., Athmaram, T.N., Papadopoulos, M.P.O., Roy, P., 2012. Protective efficacy of Bluetongue virus-like and subvirus-like particles in sheep: Presence of the serotype-specific VP2, independent of its geographic lineage, is essential for protection. Vaccine 30 (12), 2131–2139.

Stewart, M., Dubois, E., Sailleau, C., Bréard, E., Viarouge, C., Desprat, A., Thiéry, R., Zientara, S., Roy, P., 2013. Bluetongue virus serotype 8 virus-like particles protect sheep against virulent virus infection as a single or multi-serotype cocktail immunogen. Vaccine 31 (3), 553–558. https://doi.org/10.1016/j.vaccine.2012.11.016.

Strable, E., Finn, M.G., 2009. Chemical modifications of viruses and virus-like particles, viruses and nanotechnology. Curr. Top. Microbiol. 327, 1–21.

Suffian, I.F., Al-Jamal, K.T., 2022. Bioengineering of virus-like particles as dynamic nanocarriers for in vivo delivery and targeting to solid tumours. Adv. Drug. Dev. Rev. 180, 114030.

Sukharev, S.I., Klenchin, V.A., Serov, S.M., Chernomordik, L.V., YuA, C., 1992. Electroporation and electrophoretic DNA transfer into cells. The effect of DNA interaction with electropores. Biophys. J. 63 (5), 1320–1327.

Sun, Y., Sun, Y., Zhao, R., 2017. Establishment of MicroRNA delivery system by PP7 bacteriophage-like particles carrying cell-penetrating peptide. J. Biosci. Bioeng. 124 (2), 242–249.

Tang, S., Xuan, B., Ye, X., Huang, Z., Qian, Z., 2016. A modular vaccine development platform based on sortase-mediated site-specific tagging of antigens onto virus-like particles. Sci. Rep. 6, 25741.

Tejeda-Rodríguez, J.A., Nunez, A., Soto, F., García-Gradilla, V., Cadena-Nava, R., Wang, J., Vazquez-Duhalt, R., 2019. Virus-based Nanomotors for cargo delivery. ChemNanoMat 5 (2), 194–200.

Tekle, E., Astumian, R.D., Chock, P.B., 1990. Electro-permeabilization of cell membranes: Effect of the resting membrane potential. Biochem. Biophy. Res. Commun. 172 (1), 282–287.

Terns, M.P., Goldfarb, D.S., 1997. Nuclear transport of RNAs in microinjected Xenopus oocytes. Methods Cell Biol. 53, 559–589.

Teruel, M.N., Blanpied, T.A., Shen, K., Augustine, G.J., Meyer, T., 1999. A versatile microporation technique for the transfection of cultured CNS neurons. J. Neurosci. Methods 93 (1), 37–48.

Teunissen, E.A., de Raad, M., Mastrobattista, E., 2013. Production and biomedical applications of virus-like particles derived from polyomaviruses. J Control Release 172 (1), 305–321.

Thong, Q.X., Biabanikhankahdani, R., Ho, K.L., Alitheen, N.B., Tan, W.S., 2019. Thermally-responsive virus-like particle for targeted delivery of cancer drug. Sci. Rep. 9, 3945.

Thuenemann, E.C., Le, D.H.T., Lomonossoff, G.P., Steinmetz, N.F., 2021. Bluetongue virus particles as Nanoreactors for enzyme delivery and cancer therapy. Mol. Pharm. 18, 1150–1156.

R.M. Du Toit, The transmission of blue-tongue and horse-sickness by Culicoides (1944).

Tomizawa, M., Shinozaki, F., Motoyoshi, Y., Sugiyama, T., Yamamoto, S., Sueishi, M., 2013. Sonoporation: Gene transfer using ultrasound. World J. Methodol. 3 (4), 39. https://doi.org/10.5662/wjm.v3.i4.39.

Tseng, R.J., Tsai, C., Ma, L., Ouyang, J., Ozkan, C.S., Yang, Y., 2006. Nat. Nanotechnol. 1, 72–77.

Tumban, E., Peabody, J., Tyler, M., Peabody, D.S., Chackerian, B., 2012. VLPs displaying a single L2 epitope induce broadly cross-neutralizing antibodies against human papilloma virus. PLoS One 7, e49751.

Uhde-Holzem, K., McBurney, M., Tiu, B.D., Advincula, R.C., Fischer, R., Commandeur, U., Steinmetz, N.F., 2016. Production of immunoabsorbent nanoparticles by displaying single-domain protein a on potato virus X. Macromol. Biosci. 16, 231e241.

Unger, E., Porter, T., Lindner, J., Grayburn, P., 2014. Cardiovascular drug delivery with ultrasound and microbubbles. Adv. Drug Deliv. Rev. 72, 110–126.

Vahdat, M.M., Hemmati, F., Ghorbani, A., Rutkowska, D., Afsharifar, A., Eskandari, M., et al., 2021. Hepatitis B core-based virus-like particles: A platform for vaccine development in plants. Biotechnol., Rep. 29, e00605.

Valegård, K., Liljas, L., Fridborg, K., Unge, T., 1991a. Structure determination of the bacteriophage MS2. Acta Crystallogr. B 47, 949–960.

Valegård, K., Liljas, L., Fridborg, K., Unge, T., 1991b. The three-dimensional structure of the bacterial virus MS2. Nature 345, 36–41.

Vega, R.A., Maspoch, D., Salaita, K., Mirkin, C.A., 2005. Angew. Chem., Int. Ed. 44, 6013–6015.

Verma, D., Gulati, N., Kaul, S., Mukherjee, S., Nagaich, U., 2018. Protein based nanostructures for drug delivery. J. Pharm. (Lahore) 2018, 9285854.

Verwoerd, D.W., Louw, H., Oellermann, R.A., 1970. Characterization of bluetongue virus ribonucleic acid. J. Virol. 5 (1), 1–7.

Verwoerd, D.W., Els, H.J., De Villiers, E.M., Huismans, H., 1972. Structure of the bluetongue virus capsid. J. Virol. 10 (4), 783–794.

Vuppu, S., Chavda, V.P., Mishra, T., Punetha, S., Sharma, N., Kamaraj, S., Raj, V., 2024. Nanovaccines for veterinary applications. Nanocarrier Vacc.: Biopharma.-Based Fast Track Dev. 423–464.

Wadsworth, P., 1998. Microinjection of mitotic cells. Methods Cell Biol. 61, 219–231.

Walper, S.A., Turner, K.B., Medintz, I.L., 2015. Enzymatic bioconjugation of nanoparticles: developing specificity and control. Curr. Opin. Biotechnol. 34, 232e241.

Wang, Y., Douglas, T., 2022. Bioinspired approaches to self-assembly of virus-like particles: From molecules to materials. Acc. Chem. Res. 55 (10), 1349–1359.

Wang, C., Fiering, S.N., Steinmetz, N.F., 2019. Cowpea mosaic virus promotes anti-tumor activity and immune memory in a mouse ovarian tumor model. Adv. Ther. 2, 1900003.

Wang, G., Li, R., Parseh, B., Du, G., 2021. Prospects and challenges of anticancer agents' delivery via chitosan-based drug carriers to combat breast cancer: A review. Carbohydr. Polym. 268, 118192. https://doi.org/10.1016/j.carbpol.2021.118192.

Warfeld, K.L., Bosio, C.M., Welcher, B.C., De, E.M., Mohamadzadeh, M., Schmaljohn, A., et al., 2003. Ebola virus-like particles protect from lethal Ebola virus infection. Proc. Natl. Acad. Sci. 100 (26), 15889–15894.

Warfeld, K.L., Posten, N.A., Swenson, D.L., Olinger, G.G., Esposito, D., Gillette, W.K., et al., 2007. Filovirus-like particles produced in insect cells: immunogenicity and protection in rodents. J. Infect. Dis. 196 (Suppl. ment_2), S421–S429, 155.

Watanabe, T., Watanabe, S., Neumann, G., Kida, H., Kawaoka, Y., 2002. Immunogenicity and protective efficacy of replication-incompetent influenza virus-like particles. J. Virol 76 (2), 767–773.

Watson, D.S., Endsley, A.N., Huang, L., 2012. Design considerations for liposomal vaccines: Influence of formulation parameters on antibody and cell-mediated immune responses to liposome associated antigens. Vaccine 30 (13), 2256–2272.

Wen, A.M., Rambhia, P.H., French, R.H., 2013. NF Steinmetz Design rules for nanomedical engineering: from physical virology to the applications of virus-based materials in medicine. J. Biol. Phys. 39, 1–25.

Woodward, B.J., Campbell, K.H., Ramsewak, S.S., 2008. A comparison of headfirst and tailfirst microinjection of sperm at intracytoplasmic sperm injection. Fertil. Steril. 89 (3), 711–714.

Wu, D.T., Roth, M.J., 2014. MLV based viral-like-particles for delivery of toxic proteins and nuclear transcription factors. Biomaterials 35, 8416–8426.

Wu, M., Sherwin, T., Brown, W.L., Stockley, P.G., 2005. Delivery of antisense oligonucleotides to leukemia cells by RNA bacteriophage capsids. Nanomed. Nanotechnol. Biol. Med. 1, 67–76.

Xu, R., Shi, M., Li, J., Song, P., Li, N., 2020. Construction of SARS-CoV-2 virus-like particles by mammalian expression system. Front. Bioeng. Biotechnol. 8, 862.

Yan, D., Wei, Y.Q., Guo, H.C., Sun, S.Q., 2015. The application of virus-like particles as vaccines and biological vehicles. Appl. Microbiol. Biotechnol. 99, 10415–10432.

Yang, S., Gao, H., 2017. Nanoparticles for modulating tumor microenvironment to improve drug delivery and tumor therapy. Pharma Res. 126, 97–108.

Yata, T., Lee, K.-Y., Dharakul, T., Songsivilai, S., Bismarck, A., Mintz, P.J., Hajitou, A., 2014. Hybrid nanomaterial complexes for advanced phage-guided gene delivery. Mol. Ther.-Nucleic Acids 3, e185.

Yildiz, I., Tsvetkova, I., Wen, A.M., Shukla S, S., Masarapu, M.H., Dragnea, B., et al., 2012. Engineering of brome mosaic virus for biomedical applications. RSC Adv. 2, 3670–3677.

Yoshida, N., Perry, A.C., 2007. Piezo-actuated mouse intracytoplasmic sperm injection (ICSI). Nat. Protoc. 2 (2), 296–304.

Yoshinaka, Y., Katoh, I., Copeland, T.D., Oroszlan, S., 1985. Murine leukemia virus protease is encoded by the gag-pol gene and is synthesized through suppression of an amber termination codon. Proc. Natl. Acad. Sci. 82 (6), 1618–1622.

Yuan, B., Liu, Y., Lv, M., Sui, Y., Hou, S., Yang, T., Sun, C., 2023. Virus-like particle-based nanocarriers as an emerging platform for drug delivery. J. Drug Target. 31 (5), 433–455.

Zeltins, A., 2013a. Construction and characterization of virus-like particles: Are view. Mol. Biotechnol. 53, 92–107.

Zeltins, A., 2013b. Construction and characterization of virus-like particles: A review. Mol. Biotechnol. 53, 92–107.

Zeng, Q., Saha, S., Lee, L.A., Barnhill, H., Oxsher, J., Dreher, T., Wang, Q., 2011. Chemoselective modification of turnip yellow mosaic virus by cu (I) catalyzed azide– alkyne 1, 3-dipolar cycloaddition reaction and its application in cell binding. Bioconjug. Chem. 22, 58–66.

Zepeda-Cervantes, J., Ramírez-Jarquín, J.O., Vaca, L., 2020. Interaction between virus-like particles (VLPs) and pattern recognition receptors (PRRs) from dendritic cells (DCs): Toward better engineering of VLPs. Front. Immunol. 11, 1100.

Zhai, L., Tumban, E., 2016. Gardasil-9: A global survey of projected efficacy. Antivir. Res. 130, 101–109.

Zhang, Z.G., Chopp, M., 2016. Exosomes in stroke pathogenesis and therapy. J. Clin. Investig. 126 (4), 1190–1197.

Zhang, Y., Yu, L.C., 2008. Microinjection as a tool of mechanical delivery. Curr. Opin. Biotechnol. 19 (5), 506–510.

Zhang, Y., Hong, Y., Bounhar, Y., Blacker, M., Roucou, X., Tounekti, O., Vereker, E., Bowers, W.J., Federoff, H.J., Goodyer, C.G., LeBlanc, A., 2003. p75 neurotrophin receptor protects primary cultures of human neurons against extracellular amyloid β peptide cytotoxicity. J. Neurosci. 23 (19), 7385–7394.

Zhang, Y., Champagne, N., Beitel, L.K., Goodyer, C.G., Trifiro, M., LeBlanc, A., 2004. Estrogen and androgen protection of human neurons against intracellular amyloid β1-42 toxicity through heat shock protein 70. J. Neurosci. 24 (23), 5315–5321.

Zhang, D., Das, D.B., Rielly, C.D., 2014. Potential of microneedle-assisted micro-particle delivery by gene guns: A review. Drug Deliv. 21 (8), 571–587.

Zhang, D., Sun, Y., Jia, T., Zhang, L., Wang, G., Zhang, R., Zhang, K., Lin, G., Xie, J., Wang, L., Li, J., 2015a. External quality assessment for the detection of measles virus by reverse transcription-PCR using armored RNA. PLoS One 10, e0134681.

Zhang, L., Sun, Y., Chang, L., Jia, T., Wang, G., Zhang, R., Zhang, K., Li, J., 2015b. A novel method to produce armored double-stranded DNA by encapsulation ofMS2 viral capsids. Appl. Microbiol. Biotechnol. 99, 7047–7057.

Zhang, M., Gao, S., Yang, D., Fang, Y., Lin, X., Jin, X., Liu, Y., Liu, X., Su, K., Shi, K., 2021a. Influencing factors and strategies of enhancing nanoparticles into tumors in vivo. Acta Pharm. Sin. B11 (8), 2265–2285.

Zhang, P., Narayanan, E., Liu, Q., Tsybovsky, Y., Boswell, K., Ding, S., Hu, Z., Follmann, D., Lin, Y., Miao, H., Schmeisser, H., 2021b. A multiclade env–gag VLP mRNA vaccine elicits tier-2 HIV-1-neutralizing antibodies and reduces the risk of heterologous SHIV infection in macaques. Nature Med. 27 (12), 2234–2245.

Zhang, M., Fu, M., Hu, Q., 2021c. Advances in human norovirus vaccine research. Vaccines 9 (7), 732.

Zhou, Q.L., Chen, Z.Y., Wang, Y.X., Yang, F., Lin, Y., Liao, Y.Y., 2014. Ultrasound-mediated local drug and gene delivery using nanocarriers. BioMed Res. Int. 2014 (1), 963891. https://doi.org/10.1155/2014/963891.

CHAPTER

# 20

# The role of sol-gel routes in the nanoparticle–protein interactions in drug delivery systems

*Cícero Coelho de Escobar*[1] *and João Henrique Z. dos Santos*[2]

**[1]Centro de Engenharias – Universidade Federal de Pelotas, Rua Benjamin Constant, Pelotas, RS, Brazil; [2]Instituto de Química – Universidade Federal do Rio Grande do Sul, Porto Alegre, RS, Brazil**

## 1. Introduction

The sol-gel process consists of any material synthesis route where, at a certain moment, the transition from a *sol* system (suspension of colloidal particles between 1 and 1000 nm) to a *gel* (rigid structure of colloidal particles) occurs. This is a two-step process of forming networks through polycondensation: Initially, oligomers, polymers, and cyclic structures are generated in the form of colloids (*sol*), which subsequently undergo condensation and cross-linking reactions (*gel*), leading to the formation of the end material. The sol-gel process has been well described and discussed in the literature in classic works such as those by Brinker and Scherer (1990), Schubert and Hüsing (2005), and Kickelbick (2007), as well as in reviews constantly published in the literature (Rex and dos Santos, 2023; Mahato et al., 2023; Goryunova et al., 2023; Subhayu, 2024; Sarmast et al., 2024).

Several factors influence the structural, textural, and morphological characteristics of the resulting materials, including the type of process (hydrolytic or nonhydrolytic), the nature of the catalyst (acidic or basic), temperature, and solvent, among others. In addition, such networking formation allows the resulting material preparation under several conditions, such as dip or spin coating, encapsulation, and precipitation, just to mention a few. Furthermore, the concept of molecular imprinting may also impinge some selectivity and specificity of the resulting surface (de Escobar et al., 2015). Besides aging and drying steps, other factors may also contribute to the broad potential of morphological or textural properties of the resulting materials. This makes sol-gel a versatile process that, combined with an appropriate

*Protein-Based Nanoparticles in Drug Delivery*
https://doi.org/10.1016/B978-0-443-33639-3.00009-X

deposition method, can be used to generate coatings deposited on particles, films, or surfaces to change their properties, increasing their catalyst, preconcentration, (bio)compatibility, (bio) corrosion protection, or antibacterial properties, just to mention a few.

From a synthesis point of view, in addition to the classic routes involving acid, basic, *two steps* (acid catalysis, followed by basic) and nonhydrolytic catalysis, it is worth highlighting the Stöber method for producing colloidal silica particles that has established itself as a reference method, due to the mild and well-controlled conditions during the synthesis steps. Briefly, the Stöber method is an optimization of the sol-gel process in a basic medium, which uses ideal dilution conditions in order to guarantee the formation of spherical particles with high colloidal stability and, in this way, minimization of aggregation processes (Stöber et al., 1968). The Stöber process is based on the hydrolysis of the silica precursor, commonly tetraethyl orthosilicate (TEOS), in the presence of water and ammonium hydroxide, both at critically controlled concentrations. In general, the synthesis occurs in a closed system, under controlled temperature and stirring, using anhydrous ethanol as the solvent. At the end of the synthesis process, the particles can be separated by ultracentrifugation and purified by dehydration. Although this approach seems simple, it is not trivial, and some important aspects should be considered when employing this method (Silva and Santos, 2023, 2024).

Sol-gel synthesis has attracted considerable attention due to its straightforwardness, scalability, precise control, and efficiency in terms of time and energy consumption. This method involves chemical reactions where colloidal particles form a sol or react with alkoxide precursors and water in a solution, yielding highly porous amorphous gel materials. These gels can exist in various physical forms, such as bulk (3D), films (2D), fibers (1D), powders, and nanoparticles (0D), retaining a liquid phase that includes solvent, catalyst, and excess reactants. The solution route, i.e., base- and acid-catalyzed, stands out as the most commonly used method in sol-gel synthesis of nanoparticles.

In the context of nanotechnology, the sol-gel process meets several prerequisites for its application in several basic research, applied research, and industrial process applications. A correlation map (Fig. 20.1) using the keywords "sol-gel," "nanotechnology," and "proteins" from abstracts was traced to promote the big picture of the most popular topics in the last 5 years of sol-gel nanoparticles and protein research and how they connect with each other.

The most prominent investigated topics dealing with the investigated themes show that silica remains the most investigated sol-gel-produced material, followed by titania (not shown). Furthermore, their clusters connect with their objectives, such as antibacterial or antioxidant activity, allied to the necessity of biocompatibility or biodegradability. One cannot neglect the historical milestone assigned to the works from Avnir et al. (1984, 1994) devoted to the encapsulation of organic dyes, and lately to proteins (and enzymes) by the sol-gel process in the 80s–90s of the last century.

## 2. Silica-based nanomaterials for drug delivery via the sol-gel process

The sol-gel process is a versatile technique for creating a diverse array of materials, including those used in drug delivery systems. A remarkable feature of the sol-gel method

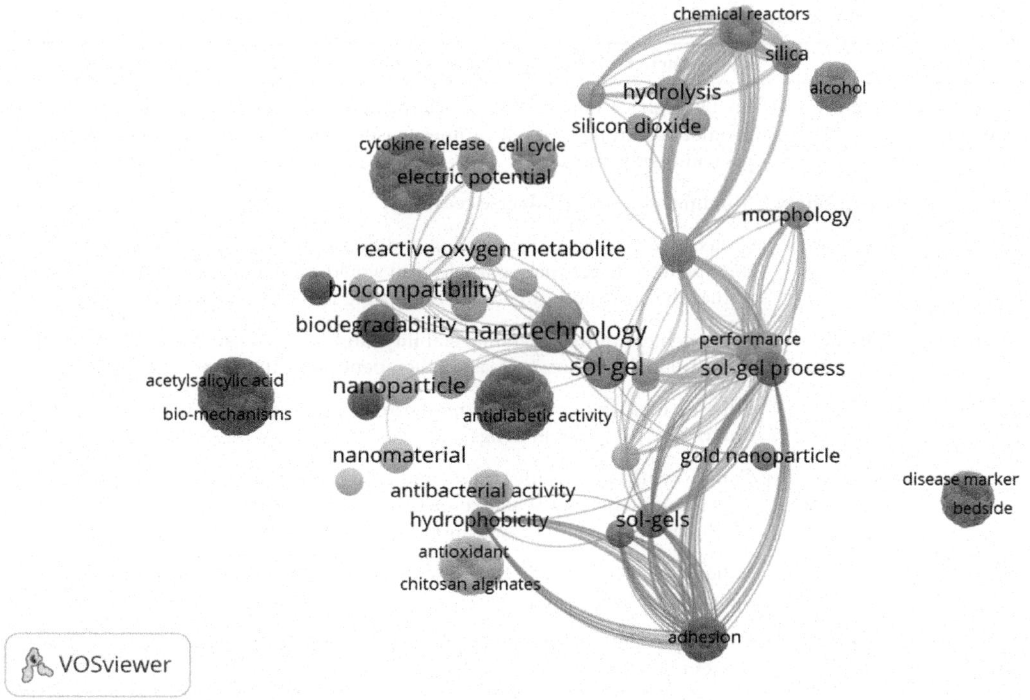


**FIGURE 20.1** Connection map using the words of article abstracts of the previous 5 years with the terms "sol-gel," "nano-," and "protein" in the Scopus database. The map was created using VOSviewer software.

is its ability to produce materials with specific micro- and nanostructures at lower temperatures compared to traditional ceramic and glass manufacturing techniques, resulting in highly uniform and chemically pure products (Owens et al., 2016). This low-temperature process, which uses chemical components to create uniform and pure glasses and ceramics, has garnered significant interest in the medical sector (Iqbal Janjua et al., 2023). Its multifunctionality and ability to produce materials with customizable properties make it a promising approach for innovative drug delivery systems and other advanced biomedical applications (Owens et al., 2016; Iqbal Janjua et al., 2023).

Sol-gel offers a multitude of advantages for drug and protein delivery applications (Table 20.1). These advantages include excellent biocompatibility, high specific surface areas ideal for drug adsorption, and the capability to facilitate precise biomolecular functionalization (Owens et al., 2016). By carefully controlling the thickness and pore-size distribution of silica coatings, the span and amount of drug release can be systematically managed (Barbé et al., 2011). Adjustments in sol composition allow for tailoring the porosity, which is a critical factor influencing drug diffusion and release rates. This method ensures consistent material homogeneity and uniform surface characteristics (Barbé et al., 2011).

In biomedical applications, the sol-gel approach is particularly valuable for producing bioactive glasses. These nanoporous materials enhance bioactivity and cellular response

**TABLE 20.1** Main advantages of sol-gel silica-based nanomaterials in protein delivery.

| Advantages | Consequences for protein drug delivery |
|---|---|
| **High surface area and porosity** | Enable high loading capacities for protein drugs, making them excellent carriers, and promote controlled release profiles, ensuring sustained and consistent delivery of protein therapeutics. |
| **Biocompatibility and safety** | Minimize the risk of adverse reactions. |
| **Stability and protection** | Protect proteins from degradation and denaturation, thus preserving their therapeutic efficacy; nanoparticles can shield proteins from enzymatic degradation within the gastrointestinal tract, enhancing their bioavailability. |
| **Surface functionalization** | Improvement of the targeting, stability, and release characteristics of the encapsulated proteins; increasing therapeutic effectiveness and reducing side effects. |
| **Controlled particle size** | Enhance their absorption and uptake in the gastrointestinal tract, facilitating efficient oral delivery of protein drugs. |
| **Easy synthesis and scalability** | Can be synthesized under mild conditions, which is beneficial for preserving the structural integrity of sensitive protein drugs; there is potential for large-scale production and commercialization of protein drug formulations. |
| **Improved bioavailability** | Enhance the solubility of the proteins and promote their transport across biological membranes. |
| **Thermal and chemical stability** | Can help maintain the stability and potency of protein drugs throughout the delivery process. |

Source: *Abeer, M.M., Rewatkar, P., Qu, Z., Talekar, M., Kleitz, F., Schmid, R., Linden, M., Kumeria, T., Popat, A., 2020. Silica nanoparticles: A promising platform for enhanced oral delivery of macromolecules. J. Contr. Release. 326 (2020), 544–555, https://doi.org/10.1016/j.jconrel.2020.07.021; Liu, H.J., Xu, P., 2019. Smart mesoporous silica nanoparticles for protein delivery. Nanomaterials 9 (4). https://doi.org/10.3390/nano9040511. https://www.mdpi.com/2079-4991/9/4/511/pdf; Xu, C., Lei, C., Yu, C., 2019. Mesoporous silica nanoparticles for protein protection and delivery. Front. Chem. 7. https://doi.org/10.3389/fchem.2019.00290. https://www.frontiersin.org/articles/10.3389/fchem.2019.00290/full; Yu, M., Gu, Z., Ottewell, T., Yu, C., 2017. Silica-based nanoparticles for therapeutic protein delivery. J. Mater. Chem. B 5 (18), 3241–3252. https://doi.org/10.1039/c7tb00244k; Xu, B., Li, S., Shi, R., Liu, H., 2023. Multifunctional mesoporous silica nanoparticles for biomedical applications. Springer Nature, China Signal Transduction and Targeted Therapy 8 (1). Available from: https://doi.org/10.1038/s41392-023-01654-7. https://www.nature.com/sigtrans; Tilkin, R.G., Mahy, J.G., Grandfils, C., Lambert, S.D., 2022b. Tissue engineering using scaffolds for bone reconstruction: a review of sol-gel silica materials for bone morphogenetic proteins (BMP) encapsulation and release. J. Sol. Gel Sci. Technol. 103 (2), 616–636. https://doi.org/10.1007/s10971-022-05868-z; Kirla, H., Henry, D.J., Jansen, S., Thompson, P.L., Hamzah, J., 2023. Use of silica nanoparticles for drug delivery in cardiovascular disease. Clin. Ther. 45 (11), 1060–1068. https://doi.org/10.1016/j.clinthera.2023.08.017; Castillo, R.R., Lozano, D., Gonzalez, B., Manzano, M., Izquierdo-Barba, I., Vallet-Regí, M., 2019. Advances in mesoporous silica nanoparticles for targeted stimuli-responsive drug delivery: An update. Expert Opin. Drug Deliv. 16 (4), 415–439. https://doi.org/10.1080/17425247.2019.1598375.*

due to their large specific surface area, which is greater than that of materials produced using conventional methods. Additionally, sol-gel technology allows for the creation of hybrid materials at the nanoscale, combining inorganic and organic components to overcome the limitations of traditional multiphasic composites (Owens et al., 2016; Barbé et al., 2011).

Recent studies have highlighted the potential of sol-gel-derived materials in several biomedical applications. For instance, hybrid sol-gel matrices incorporating organic polymers have shown improved mechanical properties and drug compatibility (Castillo et al., 2019). Moreover, sol-gel-derived silica nanoparticles (SNPs) have been employed for the targeted delivery of anticancer drugs, demonstrating enhanced therapeutic efficacy and reduced side effects (Abu-Dief et al., 2022; Yang and Yu, 2016; Gnoatto et al., 2022; Druzian et al., 2024).

Nanoparticles comprise a large range of materials, including metals, polymers, ceramics, and biomolecules. Their diminutive size conveys distinct physical, chemical, and biological properties that are markedly different from those of larger-scale materials (Khan et al., 2019; Chaudhary et al., 2023). Among its unique characteristics, one can highlight a high surface area-to-volume ratio, quantum mechanical effects, and the capability to interact at the molecular or atomic level.

Nanoparticles offer several advantages in drug delivery systems, enhancing both drug performance and patient outcomes. By improving the solubility of drugs with poor water solubility, nanoparticles significantly increase their bioavailability and therapeutic effect (Chaudhary et al., 2023; Chaudhari, 2012). Engineered for controlled and sustained release, they minimize the need for frequent dosing, thereby boosting patient adherence (Kamaly et al., 2016). Functionalization of nanoparticles enables precise targeting to specific tissues or cells, which reduces side effects and enhances therapeutic efficiency (Shi et al., 2017). Additionally, encapsulation protects drugs from environmental degradation, thereby improving their stability and shelf life (Chaudhary et al., 2023). The small size of nanoparticles allows them to traverse biological barriers, such as the blood–brain barrier (Saraiva et al., 2016), rendering easier drug delivery to previously inaccessible areas. In cancer treatment, they exploit the enhanced permeability and retention (EPR) effect to concentrate drugs within tumor tissues (Jasim et al., 2017). Moreover, nanoparticles can be multifunctional (Liong et al., 2008; Gao et al., 2023), serving roles in both imaging and therapy, and they reduce toxicity (Chaudhary et al., 2023) by specifically targeting diseased cells, minimizing adverse effects. Their adaptability permits them to carry a wide range of therapeutic agents, including small molecules, peptides, proteins, nucleic acids, and genes, thereby broadening the spectrum of treatable conditions (Khan et al., 2019). Furthermore, with their small size and unique surface characteristics, nanoparticles greatly enhance cellular uptake. They can penetrate cell membranes effectively and are often engineered to utilize endocytosis pathways, leading to increased drug concentrations at intracellular targets (Idrees et al., 2020).

Inorganic drug carriers, such as quantum dots, iron oxide, carbon, metal-organic frameworks (MOFs), silicon, and silica, have emerged as promising alternatives to organic systems. Among these, SNPs are particularly notable for their highly adjustable surface chemistry, proven biocompatibility, cost-effective synthesis, and resistance to chemical and enzymatic degradation (Abeer et al., 2020). Specifically, mesoporous silica nanoparticles (MSNs) offer significant advantages due to their unique structural and functional properties, including customizable porosity, pore sizes, pore structures, and particle dimensions and shapes (Abu-Dief et al., 2022). MSNs feature a highly ordered porous structure, providing an exceptionally high surface area and large pore volume, which is ideal for loading substantial amounts of therapeutic agents (Xu et al., 2023). The uniform pore size distribution allows for precise control over drug release kinetics, enhancing the efficiency and effectiveness of drug delivery systems. The presence of silanol (Si-OH) groups on the surface of MSNs facilitates diverse surface modifications, further enhancing their tunable particle size and morphology. Additionally, MSNs can be synthesized under mild conditions, allowing precise control over their structural parameters (Abeer et al., 2020; Abu-Dief et al., 2022). This capability enables the efficient loading or adsorption of drug payloads, with the drug loading capacity accurately measurable using established methods such as thermogravimetric analysis (TGA) to determine the mass ratio of organic payload to inorganic silica.

Another important aspect is the nanosilica market size, which is estimated to grow by USD 1.90 billion at a CAGR (compound annual growth rate) of 6.78% between 2023 and 2028. The scope of its application is wide. The demand for nanosilica is increasing, particularly in developing countries, due to its role in enhancing the properties of cement, glass, and other construction materials. In addition, the healthcare sector is investing heavily in nanotechnology, including the use of nanosilica in drug delivery systems and diagnostics, further fueling the demand. These trends are leading to increased investments in the production of nanosilica, making it a promising area for business growth (Technavio, 2024).

## 3. Nanoparticles for protein delivery systems via sol-gel routes

Table 20.2 shows recent works applying nanoparticles prepared via sol-gel routes for protein delivery systems. Several proteins have been studied for their potential therapeutic applications in protein delivery systems. For example, cytochrome *c* has been explored for cancer therapy due to its ability to induce apoptosis in tumor cells. Soybean trypsin inhibitor is under investigation for its potential in bone reconstruction, assisting in the regeneration and strengthening of bones. Insulin is widely recognized for its critical role in diabetes management, as it regulates blood glucose levels and enhances disease control. Serum albumin is essential for maintaining plasma oncotic pressure, which helps regulate fluid balance and prevent edema. Additionally, lysozyme is crucial to the body defense systems, functioning as an antimicrobial enzyme that combats bacterial infections and contributes to overall pathogen protection.

Therapeutic proteins are widely used in therapies due to their specificity and low side effects, but they face challenges such as low stability and difficulty in cellular penetration. Hollow nanocarriers can overcome these issues by providing a large space for biomolecules and protection against degradation. In this sense, hollow bioactive glass nanospheres were synthesized using a soft-template-assisted ultrasound-coupled sol-gel method (El-Fiqi, 2022). For the synthesis, polyethylene glycol (PEG) was dissolved in methanol (MeOH) and ammonium hydroxide, then a solution of calcium nitrate tetrahydrate (CaNT) and TEOS in MeOH was added dropwise while applying ultrasound. After 24 h of stirring, the precipitate was separated, washed, dried overnight at 70°C, and heat-treated at 700°C for 5 h. The final material showed favorable properties (CYC) for the intracellular delivery of therapeutic proteins.

Mesoporous bioactive glass microspheres (MBGMs) have gained attention for their spherical morphology, good dispersion, fluidity, and biocompatibility, making them useful as bioactive additives in composite scaffolds and drug/protein delivery carriers. They can efficiently load and release biomacromolecules, such as growth factors, such as bone morphogenetic protein (BMP), for bone tissue regeneration. In the study conducted by Miao et al. (2019), MBGMs were synthesized using a combination of base-catalyzed sol-gel and water-in-oil microemulsion, aiming for applications as drug/protein (serum albumin) carriers for bone tissue regeneration. This method enables the production of SNPs without the use of template agents. Sol-gel synthesis was carried out in "two steps." The first step involved the preparation of the bioactive glass sol through the hydrolysis of TEOS, triethyl

TABLE 20.2 Recent works (2019–2024) using nanoparticles for protein delivery systems via sol-gel routes.

| System | Silica precursor/ catalyst/template | Protein loading and release assays | Main finding | Ref. |
|---|---|---|---|---|
| Hollow bioactive glass nanospheres | TEOS/ammonium hydroxide/polyethylene glycol | CYT | Protein capacity ~570 mg of CYC per 1 g of follow bioactive nanosphere, in addition to controlled protein release over 5 days. | El-Fiqi (2022) |
| Mesoporous bioactive glass microspheres with different compositions | TEOS/HCl and ammonium hydroxide/ polyacrylic acid | BSA | Loading capacity of 202.17 mg/g and sustained release property for BSA up to 15 days. | Miao et al. (2019) |
| Mesoporous silica with isobutyramide as a "glue" molecule of biomacromolecule | TEOS/ammonium hydroxide/ cetyltrimethylammonium p-toluene sulfonate | HA, PS, IG, and PL | High loading capacity for SA and PS (≥ca. 350 μg.mg−1) but a moderate one for IG and PL. Efficient and promising materials for sustained protein release (HA and PS) upon incubation for 4 days at three different temperatures (25, 37, and 45 °C). | Bizeau et al. (2022) |
| Silica gel (xerogel) | TEOS/ammonium hydroxide or HCl | STI | Impregnation method (base-catalyzed) showed higher values of encapsulated protein amounts (up to 23.7 mg/g), while the in situ method (acid-catalyzed) allowed for better control of the release rate over the first 24 h. | Tilkin et al. (2020) |
| Mesocellular silica nanoparticle foams (MCFs) | TEOS/ammonium hydroxide | INS, LYS, and BSA | Protein release was tunable depending on the pore size. LYS-loaded MCFs could release 87% intact protein after incubation with pancreatin for 0.5 hours. | He et al. (2020) |
| Degraded mesoporous silica nanoparticles | TEOS/sodium hydroxide/cetyl trimethyl ammonium bromide (CTAB) | CYT | The initial release was rapid, releasing 62% at pH 5.0% and 34% at pH 5.0 within 24 h. | (Choi et al., 2020) |
| Structured mesoporous silica | TEOS/HCl/P123 | STI | Unstructured silica (disorganized mesopores) samples had higher protein loading than structured ones due to differences in pore interconnectivity. For TEOS-based samples, STI was released rapidly within the first 24 h, with the release rate slowing and reaching a plateau thereafter. In contrast, structured samples released STI more steadily over 28 days. | Tilkin et al. (2022) |

(Continued)

**TABLE 20.2** Recent works (2019–2024) using nanoparticles for protein delivery systems via sol-gel routes.—cont'd

| System | Silica precursor/ catalyst/template | Protein loading and release assays | Main finding | Ref. |
|---|---|---|---|---|
| Zinc-doped hollow mesoporous bioactive nanospheres | TEOS/HCl | BSA | BSA loading ranged from 62.3 mg/g to 110.3 mg/g. All samples had mesopores larger than 14 nm, facilitating protein entry. Best result showed a slower (up to 2 days) sustained release compared to other systems. | Hu et al. (2024) |
| Large-pore mesoporous silica particles | TEOS/HCl/Pluronic F127 | HP | PEG-coated carriers released the enzyme more quickly in an acidic environment due to the protonation of PEG at low pH that catalyzes the polymer hydrolysis reaction. | Banche-Niclot et al. (2021) |
| Ensilicated lysozyme | TEOS/HCl | LYS | Clear differences were found between native-heated lysozyme and ensilicated-then-released protein, indicating that long-term storage of ensilicated lysozyme at room temperature does not harm protein stability. | Doekhie et al. (2020) |
| Hollow silica nanoparticles | TEOS/HCl/Tween 80 | BSA | It was possible to directly encapsulate the protein without loss of its native structure, which releases according to the zero-order law for about 3 days. | Dolinina et al. (2019) |
| Functionalized sol-gel silica: | TEOS/HCl | STI | In situ method allowed the release rate of protein over the first 24 hours, followed by a sustained release up to 85 days. | Tilkin et al. (2021) |

*BSA*: Serum albumin; *CYT*: Cytochrome C; *HP*: Horseradish peroxidase; *INS*: Insulin; *IG*: Immunoglobulin; *LYS*: Lysozyme; *PL*: Polylysine; *PS*: Peroxidase; *STI*: Soybean trypsin inhibitor.

phosphate, and calcium nitrate in an acidic solution (HCl). The second step occurred after this solution was added dropwise to liquid paraffin, followed by the addition of a mixture of ammonia and 1,4-dioxane, which promotes the sol-gel transition and the formation of gel particles.

In the study conducted by Bizeu et al. (2022), large-pore mesoporous SNPs modified with isobutyramide (IBAM) were produced to enhance protein delivery. Effective protein delivery systems must interact with therapeutics in a manner that ensures efficient loading while being sufficiently labile to enable controlled release (Bizeau et al., 2022). Thus, the functionalization of SNP surfaces is a crucial aspect of the protein delivery method. Developing an intelligent anchoring strategy that functions as a glue molecule, facilitating both the efficient retention and sustained release of proteins, is an ongoing challenge. The IBAM "glue" molecule was tested for its ability to immobilize and sustainably release proteins, including human bovine serum albumin (BSA), horseradish peroxidase (HP), immunoglobulin G (IG), and polylysine (PL). Using three detection techniques (proteins with fluorescein isothiocyanate labeling, intrinsic tryptophan fluorescence, and bicinchoninic acid assay), the study demonstrated high loading capacities for BSA and HP and moderate capacities for IG and PL. The study evaluated the physicochemical properties and stability of the loaded nanoparticles, confirming their colloidal stability and reproducibility over washings. Protein release was tested under static and dynamic conditions at various temperatures, showing sustained release capabilities and retention of biological activity for RP. The findings suggest that IBAM nanoparticles are promising for sustained protein release, with potential applications in therapeutic systems, including those involving magnetic nanoparticles for enhanced functionalities like magnetic resonance imaging (MRI) and hyperthermia without affecting protein release.

In recent years, bone repair has gained significant importance, with a focus on using therapeutic biomolecules for tissue regeneration (Armiento et al., 2020). More specifically, bone has the ability to self-regenerate, enabling repair without scarring. However, large fracture defects demand external assistance for complete recovery. Several materials have been developed to enhance bone healing, with recent attention on therapeutic biomolecules such as BMPs, which are effective in promoting bone reconstruction (Bauso et al., 2024). BMPs regulate cell adhesion, proliferation, differentiation, and apoptosis in bone tissue. Controlled release of BMPs is crucial to prevent undesirable effects, and silica gels have gained interest for their capacity to provide sustained release of biomolecules in tissue engineering. BMPs cannot be administered directly to the fracture site because they are rapidly cleared from the body (El Bialy et al., 2017). Additionally, administering excessively high doses could result in undesirable tumor growth or neovascularization of unintended tissues (Jung et al., 2014). Consequently, developing delivery systems with tailored textural and chemical characteristics could help achieve longer BMP delivery.

The study led by Tilkin et al. (2020) investigated the influence of different encapsulation methods on the release kinetics and inhibitory activity of a model protein, Soybean Trypsin Inhibitor (STI), which was chosen due to its similarities with BMP in size, molecular weight, point of zero charge, hydrophobic properties, and release kinetics. The authors explored two methods: impregnation of presynthesized silica gels with the protein solution and direct incorporation of the protein during gel synthesis (in situ method). In the impregnation method, the synthesis occurred in a basic medium using aqueous $NH_3$ as the catalyst (Fig. 20.2A). Conversely, the in situ method was conducted in an acidic medium, using a dilute HCl solution. The impregnation method afforded the creation of different types of silica gels (Imp-Dry, Imp-450, and Imp-550) by adjusting drying and calcination conditions, offering flexibility in the design of the silica matrix, although it is more time-consuming. Contrarily, the in situ method involves a one-pot synthesis, reducing processing time but limiting optimization due to the need to protect the protein from denaturation.

The synthesis method strongly influences the silica surface chemistry, charge density, and textural properties, affecting STI's immobilization efficiency, release kinetics, and activity. It

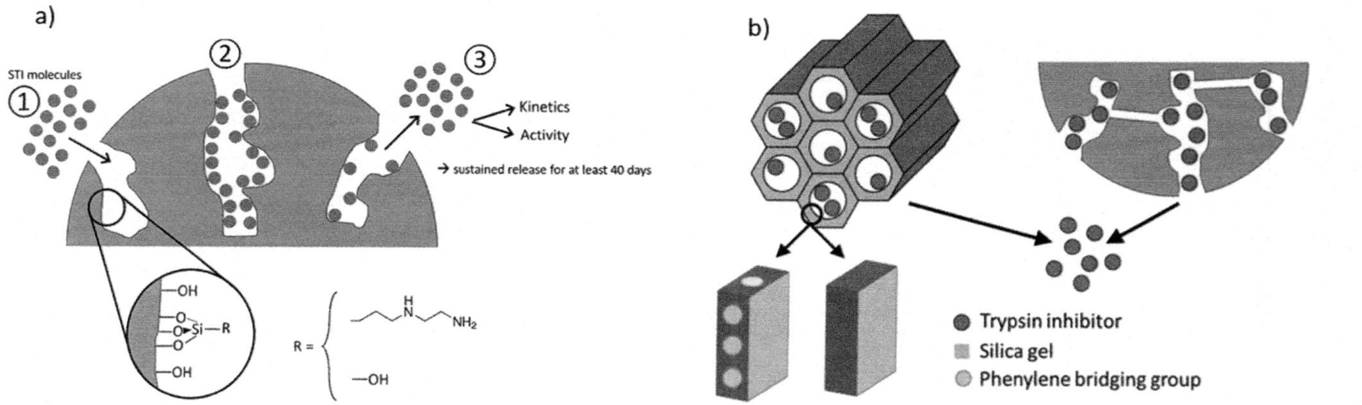


**FIGURE 20.2** Different mechanisms for protein release: (a) basic route, reproduced with permission from *R.G. Tilkin, X. Colle, A. Argento Finol, N. Régibeau, J.G. Mahy, C. Grandfils, S.D. Lambert, Protein encapsulation in functionalized sol-gel silica: Effect of the encapsulation method on the release kinetics and the activity. Microporous Mesoporous Mater. 308 (2020), https://doi.org/10.1016/j.micromeso.2020.110502* and (b) acid route, reproduced with permission from *R.G. Tilkin, J.G. Mahy, A.P.F. Monteiro, A. Belet, J. Feijóo, M. Laird, C. Carcel, N. Régibeau, B. Goderis, C. Grandfils, M. Wong Chi Man, S.D. Lambert, Protein encapsulation in mesoporous silica: influence of the mesostructured and pore wall properties. Colloids Surf. A Physicochem. Eng. Asp.. 642 (2022a), https://doi.org/10.1016/j.colsurfa.2022.128629; R.G. Tilkin, J.G. Mahy, C. Grandfils, S.D. Lambert, Tissue engineering using scaffolds for bone reconstruction: a review of sol-gel silica materials for bone morphogenetic proteins (BMP) encapsulation and release. J. Sol. Gel Sci. Technol.. 103 (2) (2022b), 616–636, https://doi.org/10.1007/s10971-022-05868-z.*

was observed that impregnation resulted in a rapid release of STI under physiological conditions, while the in situ method allowed for better control of the protein's release rate over the first 24 h. Additionally, no significant change in protein activity was observed with the in situ method, whereas the impregnated silica showed partial or total loss of activity after 4 weeks. More importantly, the study demonstrates the potential for sustained STI release over 40 days (Fig. 20.3), with both encapsulation techniques applicable to other proteins, although results may vary based on protein characteristics.

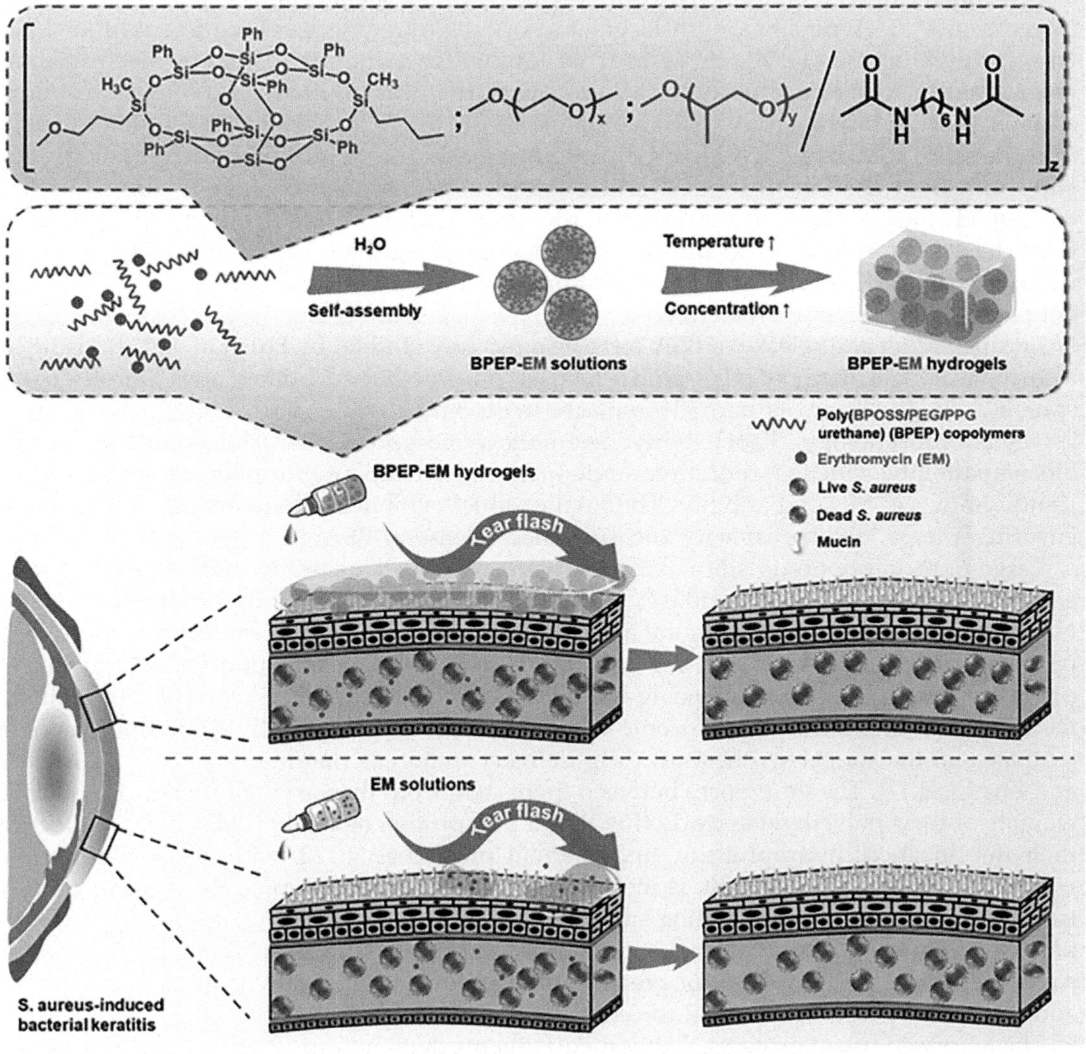


**FIGURE 20.3** Release kinetics profile of STI from silica gels. Reproduced with permission from *R.G. Tilkin, X. Colle, A. Argento Finol, N. Régibeau, J.G. Mahy, C. Grandfils, S.D. Lambert, Protein encapsulation in functionalized sol-gel silica: Effect of the encapsulation method on the release kinetics and the activity. Microporous Mesoporous Mater. 308 (2020), https://doi.org/10.1016/j.micromeso.2020.110502.*

Following the early study, the same research group continued with a focus on understanding how structured mesoporous silica scaffolds influence the encapsulation and release of STI, now using an acid sol-gel route (Tilkin et al., 2022a,b). SBA-15 silica samples were synthesized using TEOS with P123 as the surfactant in an acidic environment (HCl). The study examined the effect of adding a swelling agent to increase pore size, discovering that incorporating the agent with TEOS produced ordered mesoporous silica, whereas adding it during surfactant dissolution resulted in an unstructured material (Fig. 20.2B). Additionally, mesoporous silica was synthesized with phenylene-bridged silica precursors (1,4-bis(triethoxysilyl)benzene, BTEB) to investigate their impact on STI encapsulation, given their hydrophobic nature. The second phase of the study aimed to create SBA-15-type silica with larger mesopores by using swelling agents like 1,3,5-triisopropylbenzene (TIPB), chosen for its low water solubility. This approach enabled the formation of SMS (siliceous mesoporous structures) with well-defined structures and larger pores. The study also evaluated BTEB for incorporating phenylene groups into the silica matrix, which affected protein release due to altered hydrophobicity. Results indicated that unstructured silica samples had higher protein loading but less controlled release, while structured samples provided a more sustained release profile. BTEB-based samples showed limited STI release due to the high affinity of STI for phenylene groups. The findings suggest that optimizing silica surface hydrophobicity could enhance protein release efficiency.

Encapsulation and release of BSA were also recently studied by Hu et al. (2024), using an acid-route sol-gel method. This study focuses on zinc-doped hollow mesoporous nanospheres, where calcium is partially replaced with 5 mol% zinc. This doping strategy preserves the morphology, dispersibility, and hollow mesoporous structure while enhancing biocompatibility. Zinc incorporation moderately impacts apatite-forming ability but significantly improves biocompatibility. The final product exhibited a high specific surface area, ensuring a large loading capacity and sustained release of BSA.

Large-pore mesoporous silica particles were produced using an acid sol-gel route to encapsulate horseradish peroxidase, employing Pluronic F127 as the template (Banche-Niclot et al., 2021). In this paper, the authors highlight the development of large-pore mesoporous silica particles tailored for efficient protein delivery and underscore the role of pH-responsive coatings in enhancing biomolecule release kinetics, essential for biomimetic tissue engineering strategies. Pluronic F127 and P123 are commonly used copolymers as templates in the sol-gel synthesis of drug delivery materials (Jaquilin P J et al., 2022; Zhao and Zhang, 2017). The differences between them stem from the varying ratios and molecular weights of their polyethylene oxide (PEO) and polypropylene oxide (PPO) blocks, affecting their micellization, hydrophilicity, and thermal properties. P123, with a lower molecular weight and higher PPO content, is more hydrophobic and forms micelles at lower concentrations, making it ideal for creating smaller pore sizes. In contrast, F127 has a higher molecular weight and PEO content, making it more hydrophilic and suitable for forming larger pore sizes. Both are beneficial for creating mesoporous structures with high surface areas and controlled porosity, essential for effective and controlled drug release.

The increased use of proteins as therapeutic agents demands an efficient oral delivery system due to the drawbacks of injections, such as pain, infection risk, and high costs (Chen et al., 2022). Oral delivery faces challenges like enzymatic hydrolysis in the gastrointestinal tract and poor permeability of the intestinal epithelium. In this context, MSNs offer a promising solution due to their large surface areas, tunable pore sizes, and excellent stability (Carvalho et al., 2020). Their porous structures can enhance protein loading and protect proteins from enzymatic degradation, preventing aggregation and preserving biological activity. Despite advancements in controlling MSN morphology, challenges remain in encapsulating a wide range of proteins effectively, especially with MSNs having pores smaller than 3 nm or larger than 1–2 μm, which can impact protein protection and release behaviors. Unlike MSNs, which may be less effective for protein delivery due to their small pore sizes and limited protective capabilities, mesocellular silica foams (MCFs) present a promising alternative (He et al., 2020).

The research led by He et al. (2020) evaluated the loading and release behaviors of three model proteins with different molecular weights and sizes: INS, LYS, and BSA. Synthesized MCFs showed large and tunable pores (8–23 nm), but these are relatively small. MCFs demonstrated rapid and high drug loading, with capacities reaching up to 43%. The release profiles were dependent on pore size, with MCFs featuring larger pores allowing for more controlled and extended release. For example, MCFs could release 87% of the lysozyme intact after 0.5 h of incubation with pancreatin, and insulin release was significantly slower in MCFs with larger pores. The protective properties of MCFs were assessed through various assays to evaluate their effectiveness in preventing enzymatic hydrolysis and conformational changes of the proteins (Fig. 20.4). Sodium dodecyl sulfate polyacrylamide gel electrophoresis (SDS-PAGE) and high-performance liquid chromatography (HPLC) revealed that MCFs could protect proteins from enzymatic degradation. Specifically, MCFs with smaller pores showed better protection against protease activity, with MCF-8 allowing 87% of lysozyme to remain intact after pancreatin exposure, compared to lower protection in MCFs with larger pores. Insulin degradation was also reduced, with MCFs slowing its breakdown in acidic conditions and minimizing conformational changes. In vivo studies on diabetic mice demonstrated the efficacy of insulin-loaded MCFs in reducing blood glucose levels by up to 69%. The results highlighted that MCFs could effectively protect loaded proteins from aggregation and enzymatic hydrolysis, making them viable carriers for oral protein delivery. This research underscores the potential of MCFs in enhancing the stability and bioavailability of therapeutic proteins, addressing critical challenges in protein delivery systems and paving the way for improved oral medication options.

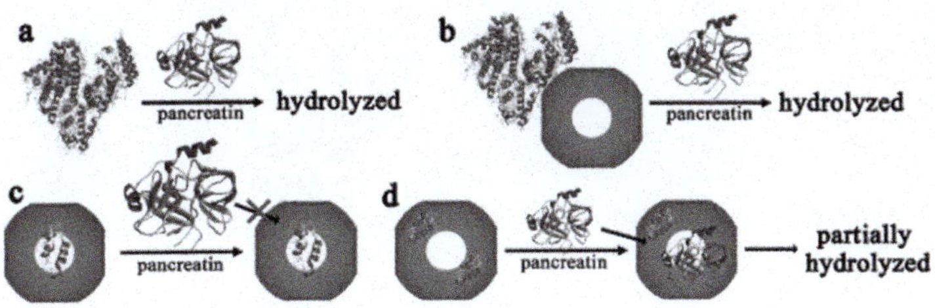


FIGURE 20.4 Schematic of the protective properties of MCF against enzymatic hydrolysis of (a) naked proteins, (b) proteins adsorbed outside the pores, (c) proteins loaded in small pores, and (d) proteins loaded in large pores. Reproduced with permission from [45].

Another approach for dealing with the drawbacks associated with MSNs, mainly due to their pores being insufficient for large biomolecules, is to degrade them physically to expand the pores. In the study conducted by Choi et al. (2020), a novel method using hydrolytic degradation under phosphate-buffered saline solution at 37 °C at a concentration of 1 mg/mL for 24 h (Fig. 20.5) was explored to expand the pores of MSNs (D-MSNs) to approximately 10 nm and roughen their surface. The study investigated the release of CYT from silica carriers, comparing degraded MSNs (CYT@D-MSNs) and conventional MSNs (CYT@MSNs). The release was tested at different pH levels (7.4 and 5.0) to explore pH-dependent behavior. Results indicated that CYT@D-MSNs released much more CYT (151 μg/mL at pH 5.0 and 82 μg/mL at pH 7.4) compared to CYT@MSNs (51 μg/mL at pH 5.0 and 28 μg/mL at pH 7.4), with greater release observed under acidic conditions due to the pH sensitivity of the silicate surface. The initial release was rapid, with CYT@D-MSNs releasing 62% at pH 5.0% and 34% at pH 7.4 within 24 h. Surface charge measurements revealed minimal impact of CYT loading and release on D-MSNs' surface charge, indicating that CYT is loaded on the inner surface of D-MSNs. The authors also investigated the cytotoxicity of particles against SKOV3 cancer cells. After 24 h of incubation with particles (20 μg/mL), cell viability was assessed. The results showed that free CYT and conventional MSNs had minimal cytotoxic effects, with over 95% of cancer cells surviving, whereas CYT@D-MSNs significantly reduced cell viability to approximately 56%, indicating effective intracellular delivery of CYT and induction of apoptosis. This characteristic is advantageous for intracellular delivery and rapid release in acidic environments, such as those found within cancer cells.

Proteins maintain their correct function through intramolecular interactions between amino acid side chains, forming a specific three-dimensional structure. These proteins can degrade due to environmental factors like pH and temperature changes, leading to unfolding, aggregation, and precipitation (Díaz-Villanueva et al., 2015). Strategies to increase protein stability in solution include excipients, buffer compositions, ionic liquids, and encapsulation, with lyophilization being the gold standard for biomolecule preservation (Akbarian and Chen, 2022). Most protein-based biopharmaceuticals need to be stored and distributed at 2–8 °C to remain biologically active (Cappelletto et al., 2024), with temperature changes outside this range often causing inactivation, especially in low-income countries

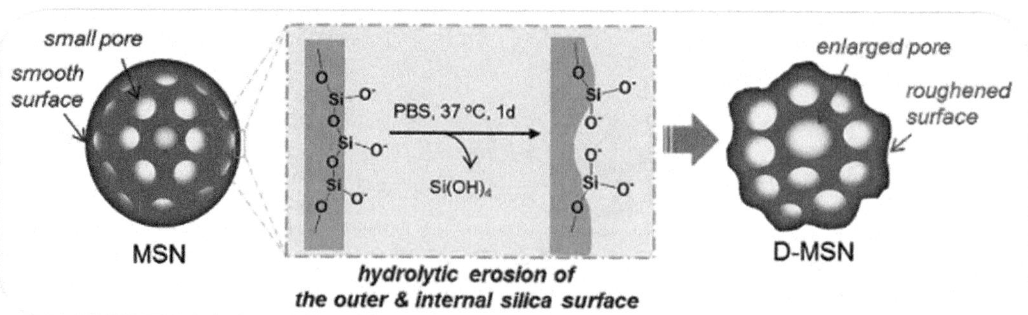


FIGURE 20.5 Schematic illustration of hydrolytic surface erosion of MSNs. Reproduced with permission from [46].

due to cold chain failures. Doekhie et al. (2020) aimed to support the future application of ensilication as a novel approach to biopharmaceutical stabilization. Ensilication offers an alternative that does not involve freeze/vacuum drying but rather uses electrostatic attachment and room temperature drying. The method applied in this study used TEOS as a precursor in acid-catalyzed sol-gel, creating a protein-loaded dry silica powder. The authors utilized calorimetric methods, such as differential scanning calorimetry (DSC), to investigate the thermal resilience of ensilicated LYS. The thermal midpoint (Tm) of transition for native lysozyme was found at 72.9°C, and released ensilicated lysozyme showed similar Tm values, confirming their observations with Tm for native at $73.47 \pm 0.12$°C and released at $72.10 \pm 0.99$°C. TGA demonstrated that the mass loss of ensilicated LYS during heating was associated with water liberation, averaging 4.6%, compared to 6.5% for lyophilized material.

LYS can trigger an immune response when injected into mice. In their study, the authors used LYS samples that had been ensilicated and stored for 1 month and 3 years. Powerful immune responses were detected 1 week after a booster shot, with the most representative data collected on day 42. They found clear differences between native-heated LYS and ensilicated-then-released protein, showing that long-term storage of ensilicated LYS at room temperature does not harm protein stability. Enzyme activity tests also showed that ensilicated lysozyme retained similar activity to the native form, with activity levels of 34,533 U $mg^{-1}$ after 1 month and 29,826 U $mg^{-1}$ after 3 years, compared to 31,747 U $mg^{-1}$ for the native form (Fig. 20.6). In contrast, native-heated lysozyme lost almost all

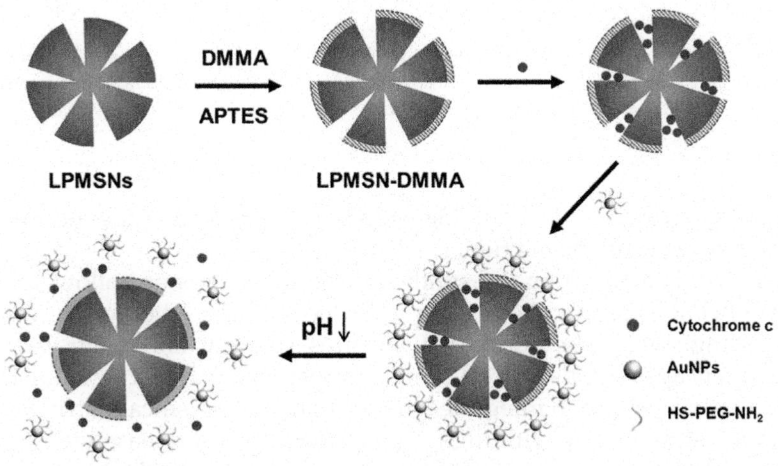


**FIGURE 20.6** LISA serum responses at day 42 of the in vivo mice trial. Responses ($n = 5$ per group) displayed in relative units (RUs) to the HyHel-10 monoclonal antibody against HEWL. ANOVA with post hoc Tukey shows statistically significant difference between ensilicated samples and native heated ($P < .01$). No significant difference was calculated for the comparison between ensilicated materials ($P > .05$). Reproduced with permission from *A. Doekhie, M.N. Slade, L. Cliff, L. Weaver, R. Castaing, J. Paulin, Y.-C. Chen, K.J. Edler, F. Koumanov, K.J. Marchbank, J.M.H. van den Elsen, A. Sartbaeva, Thermal resilience of ensilicated lysozyme via calorimetric and in vivo analysis. RSC Adv.. 10 (50) (2020), 29789–29796, https://doi.org/10.1039/d0ra06412b.*

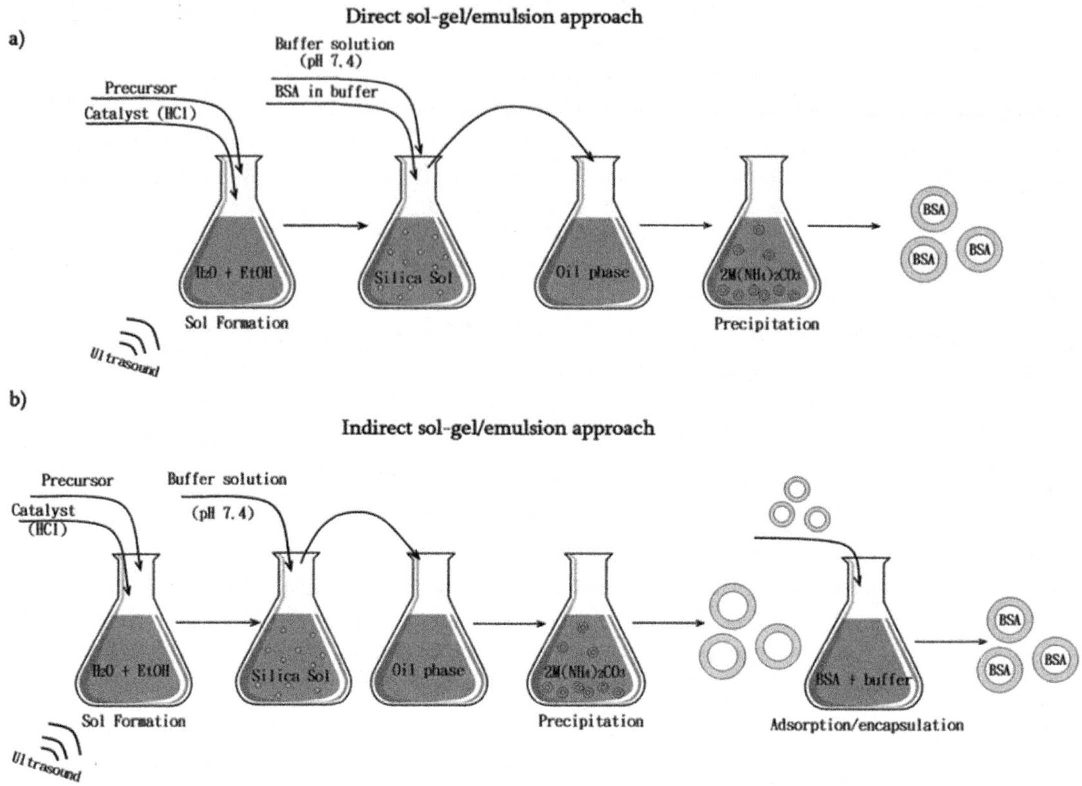


FIGURE 20.7 Schemes of direct (a) and indirect (b) BSA encapsulation using sol-gel/emulsion approaches. Reproduced with permission from *E.S. Dolinina, E.Y. Akimsheva, E.V. Parfenyuk, Silica microcapsules as containers for protein drugs: Direct and indirect encapsulation. J. Mol. Liq.. 287 (2019), 110938, https://doi.org/10.1016/j.molliq.2019.110938.*

functionality, with an activity level of just 66 U $mg^{-1}$, supporting the authors' findings that ensilication preserves protein function.

Dolina et al. (2019) focused on the synthesis and properties of hollow silica particles for biomedical applications, particularly drug delivery systems. The hollow core enables efficient drug loading, while the silica shell ensures stability and controlled release. They compared two encapsulations: direct and indirect, using sol-gel/emulsion technology (Fig. 20.7). Direct encapsulation integrates the protein into the silica matrix during synthesis, resulting in a one-step process with high protein loading and release via silica degradation, which enhances safety. Indirect encapsulation first synthesizes hollow silica particles, which are then loaded with protein, preserving the protein's native structure and providing prolonged, controlled release, but it involves a more complex two-step process. The results demonstrated that encapsulation methods significantly influence the functional properties of silica capsules loaded with proteins. Although indirect encapsulation allows for the preparation of particles without loss of the native structure of the encapsulated protein and exhibits a more prolonged controlled release of BSA (about 13%–22% of indirectly encapsulated BSA is released compared to 60%–65% of directly encapsulated protein over 150 h), direct encapsulation showed notable advantages such as a one-step encapsulation process, time efficiency, high protein loading, and release accompanied by silica particle degradation, making the systems safer for the body.

Tilkin et al. (2021) also examined the impact of different encapsulation methods and surface modifications on the release kinetics of STI, a model protein that has similarities with one morphogenetic protein (Tilkin et al., 2021). They employed two techniques: (i) impregnating silica gels with a protein solution after drying or calcination and (ii) directly incorporating the protein during silica gel synthesis (in situ). They utilized various organosilanes (i.e., functionalized silanes containing amine, ethylene diamine, or phenyl groups) and silica precursors (methoxy or ethoxy groups) to alter surface chemistry and textural properties. For the impregnation method, TEOS or TMOS (Trimethoxy(octyl)silane) was used as the main silica precursor in a basic route ($NH_3$), whereas in the in situ method, only TMOS was used in an acidic route (HCl), since TEOS could not be used in this case due to its insolubility in water. Their findings revealed that silica gels from impregnation displayed a diverse range of pore sizes, whereas in situ samples were primarily micro- and mesoporous. The results showed that phenyl-modified samples achieved a high level of STI encapsulation with minimal release over 85 days. In contrast, other functional groups led to lower encapsulation yields. For the impregnation method, STI release was initially rapid with a burst effect, followed by sustained release up to 30 days. Conversely, the in situ method offered better control over the release rate in the first 24 h and provided a more prolonged, sustained release extending to 85 days. It is noteworthy that the in situ method is similar to the direct one used in the work of Dolinina et al. (2019), as in both cases the protein is incorporated during the synthesis of the silica gel. In this sense, both studies agree in suggesting that adding the protein during synthesis results in better performance regarding protein release.

The analysis of the textural properties of materials synthesized via basic and acid sol-gel routes revealed variations in surface area, pore size, pore volume, protein loading, and cumulative protein release, as shown in Fig. 20.8. It can be observed that the textural parameters showed considerable variability across studies, regardless of the synthesis route. For example, both low values ranging from 20 to 120 $m^2/g$ and high values ranging from 550 to 600 $m^2/g$ were found for both routes. However, when considering the average values across the routes, little variation is observed. For instance, for pore size, the average values between the two routes are also quite similar, with 12 nm for the basic route and 15 nm for the acid route.

Materials synthesized via the acid route exhibited slightly higher average values for both surface area and pore size (Fig. 20.8A, B) compared to those obtained via the basic route. However, the difference in particle size was more pronounced, with the average particle size for the samples synthesized via the acid route being 1745 nm—nearly 8 times larger than that of the basic route (Fig. 20.8C). These results suggest that the acid route may facilitate the formation of a more extensive porous network. Nonetheless, materials synthesized via the basic route exhibited, on average, a higher pore volume (Fig. 20.8D), which could enhance the matrix capacity for biomolecule loading. In fact, the average protein loading (Fig. 20.8E) was slightly higher (1.86-fold) in the basic route samples, likely due to the

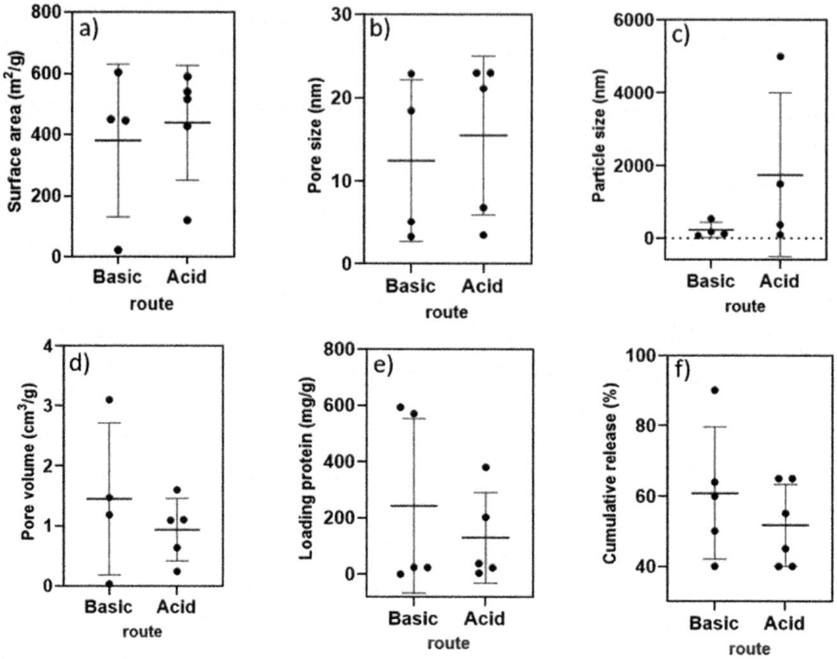


**FIGURE 20.8** Comparative analysis of surface area (BET method) (a), pore size (BJH method) (b), particle size (TEM, SEM, or DLS) (c), pore volume (BJH method) (d), protein loading (e), and release profiles (f) in materials synthesized via basic and acid sol-gel routes, based on references (El-Fiqi, 2022; Bizeau et al., 2022; Tilkin et al., 2020; He et al., 2020; Choi et al., 2020; Tilkin et al., 2022; Hu et al., 2024; Banche-Niclot et al., 2021; Doekhie et al., 2020; Dolinina et al., 2019; Tilkin et al., 2021). The thick horizontal lines in each graph represent the mean values of the respective measurements, while the black dots represent the individual data points obtained from the studies.

increased pore volume or other factors, such as surface chemistry, rather than surface area alone.

Interestingly, the basic route also showed a higher cumulative protein release trend (Fig. 20.8F), almost 20% higher, which could be attributed to a matrix structure that facilitates faster or more complete protein release. This enhanced release might be due to the larger pore volume observed in the basic route, allowing for easier diffusion of proteins from the matrix. Additionally, differences in surface chemistry between the two routes may also play a role in influencing the protein release kinetics.

Despite the above observed trends, statistical analysis (*t*-test for parametric data or Mann–Whitney *U* test for nonparametric data) indicated that the differences between the two synthesis routes were not significant. This suggests that both approaches are able to produce materials with similar functional performance in terms of protein loading capacity and release profile. In other words, this indicates that, within the tested experimental conditions of the analyzed studies, the choice between the basic or acid route can be made based on other considerations, such as process simplicity, cost, or specific application needs, without significantly affecting material performance. This reinforces the idea that both basic and acid sol-gel routes, despite their procedural differences, can be equally effective in preparing materials for controlled protein release, providing greater flexibility in the development of drug delivery systems.

## 4. Challenges in toxicity, biocompatibility, and potential side effects in nanoparticle protein delivery via sol-gel routes

Designing nanoparticles presents significant challenges, particularly regarding their potential toxicity (Tran et al., 2024). Due to their small size, nanoparticles can traverse biological barriers and interact with cellular structures in unpredictable ways, potentially causing harmful effects (Tran et al., 2024; Xuan et al., 2020). The surface chemistry of these particles, including aspects like charge and functional groups, is critical in shaping their interactions with cells and proteins, which can either reduce or increase their toxic potential (Tran et al., 2024). Additionally, the accumulation of nanoparticles in essential organs such as the liver, spleen, and kidneys raises concerns, as this buildup can result in toxicity (Huang et al., 2024). The body's ability to clear nanoparticles is influenced by their size, shape, and surface characteristics; ineffective clearance may lead to long-term adverse consequences. Furthermore, many nanoparticles, especially those made from metals, can produce reactive oxygen species (ROS), leading to oxidative stress, inflammation, and cellular damage (Min et al., 2023).

SNPs are generally regarded as less toxic compared to other nanoparticle types, particularly metal-based ones (Iqbal Janjua et al., 2023; Zhang et al., 2022). Silica is known for its biocompatibility and inert nature, meaning it typically does not trigger reactions within biological systems or provoke an immune response (Rascol et al., 2018; Hagman et al., 2020). The lethal dose 50 ($LD_{50}$) for SNPs is reported to be over 1000 mg/kg, suggesting a relatively high safety margin (Liu et al., 2011). For instance, research has shown that human corneal tissue culture exposed to up to 100 μg/mL concentrations of SNP for 72 hours revealed no significant endothelial toxicity (Kim et al., 2017). Similarly, in vivo studies in animal models have indicated that SNPs under 150 nm were biocompatible and safe for in vivo use in mice at concentrations below 300 mg/kg (Chan et al., 2017).

The toxicity of silica-based nanoparticles for protein delivery can be influenced by several structural factors, including the aspect ratio, porosity, and surface features (Yu et al., 2017). For example, a study assessed the in vivo toxicity of mesoporous hollow SNPs with a size of 110 nm administered via intravenous injection (Huang et al., 2011). The results indicated that nanoparticles had low toxicity in mice, whether given as a single dose or multiple doses. No fatalities were observed in mice that received intravenous doses of 20, 40, or 80 mg/kg over a period of 14 days. However, particles were primarily found in the liver and spleen 24 h after injection, with resident macrophages potentially facilitating their removal through phagocytosis. Moreover, about 50% of the mesoporous hollow silica nanoparticles (MHSNs) were cleared from the body within 4 weeks. Another investigation (Yu et al., 2012) focused on how porosity, aspect ratio, and surface properties affect the acute toxicity of SiNPs in immune-competent mice after a single intravenous dose. This research revealed that the maximum tolerated dose (MTD) of porous, bare MCM-41-type SiNPs ranged between 30 and 65 mg/kg. In contrast, the MTD for amine-modified SiNPs was higher, ranging from 100 to 150 mg/kg, indicating reduced toxicity. On the other hand, nonporous Stöber spheres with a diameter of 120 nm exhibited the lowest systemic toxicity, with the highest MTD of 450 mg/kg, regardless of any amine modification.

SNPs, while relatively inert, are not entirely free from toxicity, with several factors influencing their safety profile. The size and shape of these nanoparticles can affect their toxicity, with smaller particles being more reactive and able to penetrate biological barriers more easily, potentially posing a higher toxic risk (Tran et al., 2024; Abbasi et al., 2023). Nevertheless, very small and very large particles can increase cellular stress or inflammation. Additionally, the surface chemistry and functionalization of SNPs play a significant role in their potential toxicity (Xuan et al., 2020; Lérida-Viso et al., 2023). While some surface modifications can enhance biocompatibility, others may lead to adverse effects due to altered interactions with cells and tissues. Dose and exposure duration are also critical in determining the safety of SNPs (Morais et al., 2022). Even nontoxic materials can become harmful if used in excessive doses or over extended periods. Accumulation in organs, particularly when the body's clearance mechanisms are overwhelmed, may result in toxic effects. In this sense, some reports claim that the tolerable concentration range for repeated systemic injections of SNPs is typically between 20 and 80 mg/kg (Liu et al., 2011; Yu et al., 2019).

Although SNPs are less prone to generating ROS compared to metal-based ones, they can still induce oxidative and cytotoxic stress under certain conditions, particularly if they disrupt normal cellular functions (Yang et al., 2019). Furthermore, in biological environments, these nanoparticles tend to aggregate, forming larger particles that may cause blockages or localized toxicity, potentially impairing the body's ability to clear them effectively (Lérida-Viso et al., 2023; Napierska et al., 2010).

Considering the context above, some recent studies have explored the biocompatibility of various nanoparticle compositions aimed at protein delivery using the sol-gel route synthesis, with promising results in terms of cell viability. For example, in the study conducted by Miao et al. (2019), MBGMs were investigated for BSA release. The researchers used the CCK-8 assay (a colorimetric assay used to assess cell viability and proliferation) to assess the biocompatibility and impact of different MBGM compositions on cell proliferation. Over 1, 3, and 5 days of culture with 50 and 100 μg/mL MBGMs, there were no significant differences in cell proliferation between the control and experimental groups, except for MBGMs-60S at 100 μg/mL, which significantly inhibited cell growth on day 3 (Fig. 20.9). Overall, the findings suggest that MBGMs possess good cytocompatibility.

BSA load and release was also investigated by Hu et al. (2024). To assess biocompatibility, the authors conducted assays using MC3T3-E1 pro-osteoblasts. Both hollow mesoporous bioactive glass nanospheres (HMBGS) and zinc-doped hollow mesoporous bioactive glass nanospheres (Zn-HMBGS) significantly increased cell viability compared to the control at concentrations of 0.1 mg/mL and 0.05 mg/mL. Notably, the Optical Density (OD) values for Zn-HMBGS were higher than those for HMBGS at both concentrations, with Zn-HMBGS at 0.05 mg/mL showing even higher OD values than at 0.1 mg/mL. These results suggest that both samples exhibit good biocompatibility, and moderate zinc doping enhances cell viability.

In summary, although SNPs tend to be less toxic than other types, particularly those made of metals, their safety is heavily dependent on factors like particle size, shape, surface

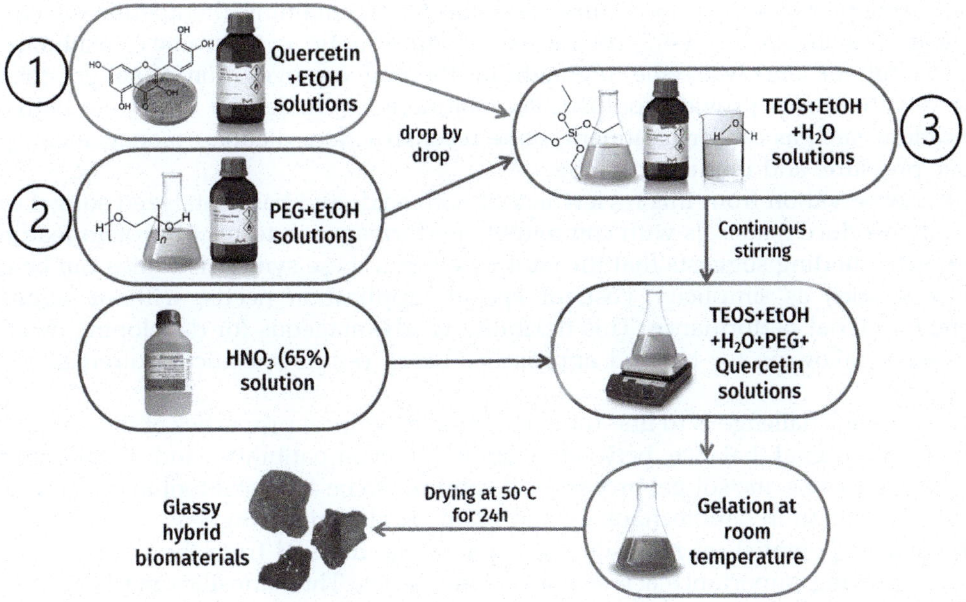


**FIGURE 20.9** Cell viability of MG63 after culturing with different concentrations of MBGMs. (a) 50 μg/mL, (b) 100 μg/mL. Reproduced with permission from *G. Miao, Z. Li, Y. Meng, J. Wu, Y. Li, Q. Hu, X. Chen, X. Yang, X. Chen, Preparation, characterization, in vitro bioactivity and protein loading/release property of mesoporous bioactive glass microspheres with different compositions. Adv. Powder Technol. 30 (9) (2019), 1848–1857, https://doi.org/10.1016/j.apt.2019.06.002.*

properties, and dosage. These factors can either reduce or heighten their toxic potential, especially in terms of generating ROS and accumulating in critical organs. Recent research on sol-gel synthesized nanoparticles for protein delivery applications has shown encouraging biocompatibility, indicating that with thoughtful design and surface modifications, nanoparticles can be optimized to achieve a balance between efficacy and safety in these applications.

## 5. Concluding remarks

This review explores the role of sol-gel routes in the development of nanoparticles for protein delivery systems. It specifically examines how proteins interact with SNPs, which are crucial for the efficiency of drug delivery by influencing the structural and textural properties of these materials. Advances such as the Stöber method have refined the sol-gel process, enabling more controlled and efficient production of colloidal silica particles. This process has proven versatile and effective across a broad range of applications, from synthesizing SNPs to encapsulating proteins for therapeutic use.

Extensive research on sol-gel-derived materials, particularly mesoporous silica, underscores their potential in drug delivery systems. These materials offer controlled release and protection of bioactive molecules, essential for maintaining therapeutic effectiveness. Recent studies have focused on proteins like serum albumin, cytochrome *c*, insulin, soybean trypsin inhibitor, and lysozyme, highlighting the ongoing evolution of sol-gel chemistry. These advancements provide sophisticated solutions to challenges in protein delivery for applications such as cancer treatment, bone reconstruction, diabetes management, plasma oncotic pressure, and immune defense.

A key observation from this review is that both acid- and base-catalyzed sol-gel systems generally produce materials with comparable performance in terms of protein loading and release. This finding suggests that the choice between these synthesis routes can be guided by factors such as simplicity, cost, or specific application needs, without significantly affecting material performance. This flexibility is advantageous for developing drug delivery systems, allowing for tailored approaches based on the specific requirements of each application.

The ongoing challenge is to fine-tune the physicochemical properties of these materials to achieve an optimal balance between stability, biocompatibility, and functionality. As research progresses, the sol-gel process will continue to be a pivotal tool in material science, driving innovation in nanotechnology and biomedical engineering.

The market potential for nanosilica, a key material derived from the sol-gel process, reflects its growing importance across various industries. The nanosilica market is projected to expand significantly, driven by its diverse applications in sectors such as construction and healthcare. This trend underscores the broader impact of sol-gel chemistry, not only in scientific research but also in industrial applications, marking it as a promising area for future business opportunities.

In conclusion, the sol-gel process remains a cornerstone in the development of advanced materials, with extensive applications ranging from construction to healthcare. As research continues to explore the complexities of sol-gel chemistry, the field is likely to witness the emergence of even more sophisticated materials designed to meet the evolving demands of both science and industry.

## Acknowledgments

C.C. de Escobar thanks CNPq (405411/2023-5) for financial support. J. H. Z. dos Santos thanks CNPq (421181/2023-0) for financial support.

## References

Abbasi, R., Shineh, G., Mobaraki, M., Doughty, S., Tayebi, L., 2023. Structural parameters of nanoparticles affecting their toxicity for biomedical applications: A review. J. Nanoparticle Res. 25 (3). https://doi.org/10.1007/s11051-023-05690-w. https://www.springer.com/journal/11051.

Abeer, M.M., Rewatkar, P., Qu, Z., Talekar, M., Kleitz, F., Schmid, R., Lindén, M., Kumeria, T., Popat, A., 2020. Silica nanoparticles: A promising platform for enhanced oral delivery of macromolecules. J. Contr. Release 326, 544–555. www.elsevier.com/locate/jconrel. doi: 10.1016/j.jconrel.2020.07.021.

Abu-Dief, A.M., Alsehli, M., Al-Enizi, A., Nafady, A., 2022. Recent advances in mesoporous silica nanoparticles for targeted drug delivery applications. Curr. Drug Deliv. 19 (4), 436–450. https://doi.org/10.2174/1567201818666210708123007.

Akbarian, M., Chen, S.H., 2022. Instability challenges and stabilization strategies of pharmaceutical proteins. Pharmaceutics 14 (11). https://doi.org/10.3390/pharmaceutics14112533. http://www.mdpi.com/journal/pharmaceutics.

Armiento, A.R., Hatt, L.P., Sanchez Rosenberg, G., Thompson, K., Stoddart, M.J., 2020. Functional biomaterials for bone regeneration: A lesson in complex biology. Adv. Funct. Mater. 30 (44). https://doi.org/10.1002/adfm.201909874. http://onlinelibrary.wiley.com/journal/10.1002/(ISSN)1616-3028.

Avnir, D., Levy, D., Reisfeld, R., 1984. The nature of the silica cage as reflected by spectral changes and enhanced photostability of trapped Rhodamine 6G. J. Phys. Chem. 88 (24), 5956–5959. https://doi.org/10.1021/j150668a042.

Avnir, D., Braun, S., Lev, O., Ottolenghi, M., 1994. Enzymes and other proteins entrapped in sol-gel materials. Chem. Mater. 6 (10), 1605–1614. https://doi.org/10.1021/cm00046a008.

Banche-Niclot, F., Montalbano, G., Fiorilli, S., Vitale-Brovarone, C., 2021. PEG-coated large mesoporous silicas as smart platform for protein delivery and their use in a collagen-based formulation for 3D printing. Int. J. Mol. Sci. 22 (4), 1–18. https://doi.org/10.3390/ijms22041718.

Barbé, C., Calleja, S., Kong, L., Drabarek, E., Bush, A., Sizgek, E., Finnie, K., 2011. Sol-gel silica particles for controlled release applications. MRS Online Proceedings Library 1314, mrsf10-1314-ll03-01. https://doi.org/10.1557/opl.2011.664.

Bauso, L.V., La Fauci, V., Longo, C., Calabrese, G., 2024. Bone tissue engineering and nanotechnology: a promising combination for bone regeneration. Biology 13 (4). https://doi.org/10.3390/biology13040237. www.mdpi.com/journal/biology.

Bizeau, J., Adam, A., Nadal, C., Francius, G., Siniscalco, D., Pauly, M., Bégin-Colin, S., Mertz, D., 2022. Protein sustained release from isobutyramide-grafted stellate mesoporous silica nanoparticles. Int. J. Pharm. X (4), 100130. https://doi.org/10.1016/j.ijpx.2022.100130.

Brinker, C., Scherer, G.W., 1990. Sol-gel Science: The Physics andChemistry of Sol-Gel Processing. Academic Press.

Cappelletto, E., Kwok, S.C., Sorret, L., Fuentes, N., Medina, A.M., Burleigh, S., Fast, J., Mackenzie, I.S., Fureby, A.M., Paulsson, M., Wahlgren, M., Elofsson, U., Flynn, A., Miolo, G., Nyström, L., De Laureto, P.P., De Paoli, G., 2024. Impact of post manufacturing handling of protein-based biologic drugs on product quality and user centricity. J. Pharmaceut. Sci. 113 (8), 2055–2064. https://doi.org/10.1016/j.xphs.2024.05.027.

Carvalho, G.C., Sábio, R.M., de Cássia Ribeiro, T., Monteiro, A.S., Pereira, D.V., Ribeiro, S.J.L., Chorilli, M., 2020. Highlights in mesoporous silica nanoparticles as a multifunctional controlled drug delivery nanoplatform for infectious diseases treatment. Pharm. Res. 37 (10). https://doi.org/10.1007/s11095-020-02917-6. www.wkap.nl/journalhome.htm/0724-8741.

Castillo, R.R., Lozano, D., González, B., Manzano, M., Izquierdo-Barba, I., Vallet-Regí, M., 2019. Advances in mesoporous silica nanoparticles for targeted stimuli-responsive drug delivery: An update. Expert Opin. Drug Deliv. 16 (4), 415–439. https://doi.org/10.1080/17425247.2019.1598375.

Chan, W.T., Liu, C.C., Chiau, J.S.C., Tsai, S.T., Liang, C.K., Cheng, M.L., Lee, H.C., Yeung, C.Y., Hou, S.Y., 2017. In vivo toxicologic study of larger silica nanoparticles in mice. Int. J. Nanomed. 12, 3421–3432. https://doi.org/10.2147/IJN.S126823.

Chaudhari, Y.S., 2012. Nanoparticles - A paradigm for topical drug delivery. Chronicles Young Sci. 3 (1), 82. https://doi.org/10.4103/2229-5186.94311.

Chaudhary, V., Verma, N., Panda, P., Rai, A., Khan, W., 2023. Nanoparticles based drug delivery system. A Review) 5, 952–958.

Chen, G., Kang, W., Li, W., Chen, S., Gao, Y., 2022. Oral delivery of protein and peptide drugs: From non-specific formulation approaches to intestinal cell targeting strategies. Theranostics 12 (3), 1419–1439. https://doi.org/10.7150/thno.61747.

Choi, E., Lim, D.K., Kim, S., 2020. Hydrolytic surface erosion of mesoporous silica nanoparticles for efficient intracellular delivery of cytochrome c. J. Colloid Interface Sci. 560, 416–425. https://doi.org/10.1016/j.jcis.2019.10.100.

de Escobar, C.C., Dallegrave, A., Lasarin, M.A., Zimnoch dos Santos, J.H., 2015. The sol-gel route effect on the preparation of molecularly imprinted silica-based materials for selective and competitive photocatalysis. Colloids Surf. A Physicochem. Eng. Asp. 486, 96–105. https://doi.org/10.1016/j.colsurfa.2015.09.027.

Díaz-Villanueva, J.F., Díaz-Molina, R., García-González, V., 2015. Protein folding and mechanisms of proteostasis. Int. J. Mol. Sci. 16 (8), 17193–17230. https://doi.org/10.3390/ijms160817193.

Doekhie, A., Slade, M.N., Cliff, L., Weaver, L., Castaing, R., Paulin, J., Chen, Y.-C., Edler, K.J., Koumanov, F., Marchbank, K.J., van den Elsen, J.M.H., Sartbaeva, A., 2020. Thermal resilience of ensilicated lysozyme via calorimetric and in vivo analysis. RSC Adv. 10 (50), 29789–29796. https://doi.org/10.1039/d0ra06412b.

Dolinina, E.S., Akimsheva, E.Y., Parfenyuk, E.V., 2019. Silica microcapsules as containers for protein drugs: Direct and indirect encapsulation. J. Mol. Liq. 287, 110938. https://doi.org/10.1016/j.molliq.2019.110938.

Druzian, D., Silva, M., da Silva, W., Zimnoch Dos Santos, J.H., 2024. Sol-Gel Technologies for Drug Delivery in Potential Cancer Treatments.

El Bialy, I., Jiskoot, W., Reza Nejadnik, M., 2017. Formulation, delivery and stability of bone morphogenetic proteins for effective bone regeneration. Pharm. Res. 34 (6), 1152–1170. https://doi.org/10.1007/s11095-017-2147-x.

El-Fiqi, A., 2022. Sol-gel synthesis, properties and protein loading/delivery capacity of hollow bioactive glass nanospheres with large hollow cavity and mesoporous shell. Front. Mater. Sci. 16.

Gao, Y., Wang, K., Zhang, J., Duan, X., Sun, Q., Men, K., 2023. Multifunctional nanoparticle for cancer therapy. https://doi.org/10.1002/mco2.187.

Gnoatto, J.A., Morás, A.M., Vitor de Oliveira, J., Arndt, E., Dallegrave, A., Borba da Cunha, A.C., Moura, D.J., dos Santos, J. H, Zimnoch, 2022. PEGylated and zwitterated silica nanoparticles as doxorubicin carriers applied in a breast cancer cell line: Effects on protein corona formation. J. Drug Deliv. Sci. Technol. 71.

Goryunova, K., Gahramanli, Y., Gurbanova, R., 2023. Adsorption properties of silica aerogel-based materials. RSC Adv. 13 (27), 18207–18216. https://doi.org/10.1039/d3ra02462h.

Hagman, E., Elimam, A., Kupferschmidt, N., Ekbom, K., Rössner, S., Iqbal, M.N., Johnston, E., Lindgren, M., Bengtsson, T., Danielsson, P., Nägeli, H., 2020. Oral intake of mesoporous silica is safe and well tolerated in male humans. PLoS One 15 (10), e0240030. https://doi.org/10.1371/journal.pone.0240030.

He, Y., Wang, M., Zhang, H., Zhang, Y., Gao, Y., Wang, S., 2020. Protective properties of mesocellular silica foams against aggregation and enzymatic hydrolysis of loaded proteins for oral protein delivery. J. Colloid Interface Sci. 560, 690–700. https://doi.org/10.1016/j.jcis.2019.10.118.

Hu, Q., Tang, H., Wu, H., Xu, Y., Li, W., Wang, X.J., Feng, G., Jiang, F., Liang, J., Liu, J., 2024. Facile synthesis, characterization, biocompatibility and protein loading/release property of zinc-doped hollow mesoporous bioactive glass nanospheres. J. Sol–Gel Sci. Technol. 110 (2), 518–531. https://doi.org/10.1007/s10971-024-06374-0.

Huang X. Li L. Liu T. H.N. L.H. Chen D. Tang F. 2011 *7 26 2011/07/26 ACS Nano 10.1021/nn200365a 1936086X 7 5390 5399 China the Shape Effect of Mesoporous Silica Nanoparticles on Biodistribution, Clearance, and Biocompatibility in Vivo 5.*

Huang, Y., Guo, X., Wu, Y., Chen, X., Feng, L., Xie, N., Shen, G., 2024. Nanotechnology's frontier in combatting infectious and inflammatory diseases: prevention and treatment. Signal Transduct. Target. Ther. 9 (1). https://doi.org/10.1038/s41392-024-01745-z. https://www.nature.com/sigtrans.

Idrees, H., Zaidi, S.Z.J., Sabir, A., Khan, R.U., Zhang, X., Hassan, S.U., 2020. A review of biodegradable natural polymer-based nanoparticles for drug delivery applications. Nanomaterials 10 (10), 1–22. https://doi.org/10.3390/nano10101970.

Iqbal Janjua, T., Cao, Y., Kleitz, F., Linden, M., Yu, C., Popat, A., 2023. Silica nanoparticles: A review of their safety and current strategies to overcome biological barriers. Adv. Drug Deliv. Rev. 203, 115115. https://doi.org/10.1016/j.addr.2023.115115.

Jaquilin P J, R., Oluwafemi, O.S., Thomas, S., Oyedeji, A.O., 2022. Recent advances in drug delivery nanocarriers incorporated in temperature-sensitive Pluronic F-127–A critical review. J. Drug Deliv. Sci. Technol. 72. https://doi.org/10.1016/j.jddst.2022.103390. http://www.editionsdesante.fr/category.php?id_category=48.

Jasim, A., Abdelghany, S., Greish, K., 2017. Current update on the role of enhanced permeability and retention effect in cancer nanomedicine nanotechnology-based approaches for targeting and delivery of drugs and genes. Elsevier Inc., Bahrain, pp. 62–109. https://doi.org/10.1016/B978-0-12-809717-5.00002-6. http://www.sciencedirect.com/science/book/9780128097175.

Jung, H.D., Yook, S.W., Han, C.M., Jang, T.S., Kim, H.E., Koh, Y.H., Estrin, Y., 2014. Highly aligned porous Ti scaffold coated with bone morphogenetic protein-loaded silica/chitosan hybrid for enhanced bone regeneration. J. Biomed. Mater. Res. - Part B Appl. Biomater. 102 (5), 913–921. https://doi.org/10.1002/jbm.b.33072. http://onlinelibrary.wiley.com/journal/10.1002/(ISSN)1552-4981.

Kamaly, N., Yameen, B., Wu, J., Farokhzad, O.C., 2016. Degradable controlled-release polymers and polymeric nanoparticles: Mechanisms of controlling drug release. Chem. Rev. 116 (4), 2602–2663. http://pubs.acs.org/journal/chreay. doi: 10.1021/acs.chemrev.5b00346.

Khan, I., Saeed, K., Khan, I., 2019. Nanoparticles: Properties, applications and toxicities. J. Chem. 12 (7), 908–931. https://doi.org/10.1016/j.arabjc.2017.05.011.

Kickelbick, G., 2007. Introduction to hybrid materials. In: Hybrid Materials: Synthesis, Characterization, and Applications, pp. 1–48. https://doi.org/10.1002/9783527610495.ch1. http://onlinelibrary.wiley.com/book/10.1002/9783527610495.

Kim, J.Y., Park, J.H., Kim, M., Jeong, H., Hong, J., Chuck, R.S., Park, C.Y., 2017. Safety of nonporous silica nanoparticles in human corneal endothelial cells. Sci. Rep. 7 (1). https://doi.org/10.1038/s41598-017-15247-2. www.nature.com/srep/index.html.

Kirla, H., Henry, D.J., Jansen, S., Thompson, P.L., Hamzah, J., 2023. Use of silica nanoparticles for drug delivery in cardiovascular disease. Clin. Ther. 45 (11), 1060–1068. https://doi.org/10.1016/j.clinthera.2023.08.017.

Lérida-Viso, A., Estepa-Fernández, A., García-Fernández, A., Martí-Centelles, V., Martínez-Máñez, R., 2023. Biosafety of mesoporous silica nanoparticles; towards clinical translation. Adv. Drug Deliv. Rev. 201, 115049. https://doi.org/10.1016/j.addr.2023.115049.

Liong, M., Lu, J., Kovochich, M., Xia, T., Ruehm, S.G., Nel, A.E., Tamanoi, F., Zink, J.I., 2008. Multifunctional inorganic nanoparticles for imaging, targeting, and drug delivery. ACS Nano 2 (5), 889–896. https://doi.org/10.1021/nn800072t.

Liu, H.J., Xu, P., 2019. Smart mesoporous silica nanoparticles for protein delivery. Nanomaterials 9 (4). https://doi.org/10.3390/nano9040511. https://www.mdpi.com/2079-4991/9/4/511/pdf.

Liu, T., Li, L., Teng, X., Huang, X., Liu, H., Chen, D., Ren, J., He, J., Tang, F., 2011. Single and repeated dose toxicity of mesoporous hollow silica nanoparticles in intravenously exposed mice. Biomaterials 32 (6), 1657–1668. https://doi.org/10.1016/j.biomaterials.2010.10.035.

Mahato, S., Mahata, D., Panda, S., Mahata, S., 2023. Perspective chapter, sol-gel science and technology in context of nanomaterials – recent advances.

Miao, G., Li, Z., Meng, Y., Wu, J., Li, Y., Hu, Q., Chen, X., Yang, X., Chen, X., 2019. Preparation, characterization, in vitro bioactivity and protein loading/release property of mesoporous bioactive glass microspheres with different compositions. Adv. Powder Technol. 30 (9), 1848–1857. https://doi.org/10.1016/j.apt.2019.06.002.

Min, Y., Suminda, G.G.D., Heo, Y., Kim, M., Ghosh, M., Son, Y.O., 2023. Metal-based nanoparticles and their relevant consequences on cytotoxicity cascade and induced oxidative stress. Antioxidants 12 (3). https://doi.org/10.3390/antiox12030703. www.mdpi.com/journal/antioxidants.

Morais, R.P., Hochheim, S., de Oliveira, C.C., Riegel-Vidotti, I.C., Marino, C.E.B., 2022. Skin interaction, permeation, and toxicity of silica nanoparticles: Challenges and recent therapeutic and cosmetic advances. Int. J. Pharm. 614. https://doi.org/10.1016/j.ijpharm.2021.121439.

Napierska, D., Thomassen, L.C.J., Lison, D., Martens, J.A., Hoet, P.H., 2010. The nanosilica hazard: another variable entity. Part. Fibre Toxicol. 7. https://doi.org/10.1186/1743-8977-7-39Belgium. http://www.particleandfibretoxicology.com/content/7/1/39.

Owens, G.J., Singh, R.K., Foroutan, F., Alqaysi, M., Han, C.M., Mahapatra, C., Kim, H.W., Knowles, J.C., 2016. Sol-gel based materials for biomedical applications. Prog. Mater. Sci. 77, 1–79. https://doi.org/10.1016/j.pmatsci.2015.12.001.

Rascol, E., Pisani, C., Dorandeu, C., Nyalosaso, J.L., Charnay, C., Daurat, M., Da Silva, A., Devoisselle, J.M., Gaillard, J.C., Armengaud, J., Prat, O., Maynadier, M., Gary-Bobo, M., Garcia, M., Chopineau, J., Guari, Y., 2018. Biosafety of mesoporous silica nanoparticles. MDPI Multidisciplinary Digital Publishing Institute, France Biomimetics. https://doi.org/10.3390/biomimetics3030022. https://res.mdpi.com/d_attachment/biomimetics/biomimetics-03-00022/article_deploy/biomimetics-03-00022-v2.pdf.

Rex, A., dos Santos, J.H.Z., 2023. The use of sol–gel processes in the development of supported catalysts. J. Sol. Gel Sci. Technol. 105 (1), 30–49. https://doi.org/10.1007/s10971-022-05975-x.

Saraiva, C., Praça, C., Ferreira, R., Santos, T., Ferreira, L., Bernardino, L., 2016. Nanoparticle-mediated brain drug delivery: Overcoming blood-brain barrier to treat neurodegenerative diseases. J. Contr. Release 235, 34–47. https://doi.org/10.1016/j.jconrel.2016.05.044.

M. Sarmast, D. Hoey, D. Biak, N. Abdullah, S. Kamarudin, H. Zainuddin, Sol–gel-templated bioactive glass scaffold: A review . (2024),

Schubert, U., Hüsing, N., 2005. Synthesis of inorganic materials, 2nd, revised and, Updated Edition.

Shi, J., Kantoff, P.W., Wooster, R., Farokhzad, O.C., 2017. Cancer nanomedicine: Progress, challenges and opportunities. Nat. Rev. Cancer 17 (1), 20–37. https://doi.org/10.1038/nrc.2016.108.

Silva, D.S.da, Santos, J.H.Z., 2023. Stöber method and its nuances over the years, p. 314.
Silva, A.d.S.d., Santos, J.H.Z.d., 2024. Silica particle size and polydispersity control from fundamental practical aspects of the Stöber method. Colloids Surf. A Physicochem. Eng. Asp. 702. https://doi.org/10.1016/j.colsurfa.2024.135190. https://www.sciencedirect.com/science/journal/09277757.
Stöber, W., Fink, A., Bohn, E., 1968. Controlled growth of monodisperse silica spheres in the micron size range. J. Colloid Interface Sci. 26 (1), 62–69. https://doi.org/10.1016/0021-9797(68)90272-5.
Subhayu, C., 2024. A review of the sol-gel process and its application. Int. Educ. Res. J. (IERJ) 10 (1), 15–19.
Technavio, UK - Size and forecast. (2024),
Tilkin, R.G., Colle, X., Argento Finol, A., Régibeau, N., Mahy, J.G., Grandfils, C., Lambert, S.D., 2020. Protein encapsulation in functionalized sol-gel silica: Effect of the encapsulation method on the release kinetics and the activity. Microporous Mesoporous Mater. 308. https://doi.org/10.1016/j.micromeso.2020.110502.
Tilkin, R.G., Mahy, J.G., Régibeau, N., Vandeberg, R., Monteiro, A.P.F., Grandfils, C., Lambert, S.D., 2021. Protein encapsulation in functionalized sol–gel silica: influence of organosilanes and main silica precursors. J. Mater. Sci. 56 (25), 14234–14256. https://doi.org/10.1007/s10853-021-06182-9.
Tilkin, R.G., Mahy, J.G., Monteiro, A.P.F., Belet, A., Feijóo, J., Laird, M., Carcel, C., Régibeau, N., Goderis, B., Grandfils, C., Wong Chi Man, M., Lambert, S.D., 2022a. Protein encapsulation in mesoporous silica: influence of the mesostructured and pore wall properties. Colloids Surf. A Physicochem. Eng. Asp. 642. https://doi.org/10.1016/j.colsurfa.2022.128629.
Tilkin, R.G., Mahy, J.G., Grandfils, C., Lambert, S.D., 2022b. Tissue engineering using scaffolds for bone reconstruction: a review of sol-gel silica materials for bone morphogenetic proteins (BMP) encapsulation and release. J. Sol. Gel Sci. Technol. 103 (2), 616–636. https://doi.org/10.1007/s10971-022-05868-z.
Tran, T.K., Nguyen, M.K., Lin, C., Hoang, T.D., Nguyen, T.C., Lone, A.M., Khedulkar, A.P., Gaballah, M.S., Singh, J., Chung, W.J., Nguyen, D.D., 2024. Review on fate, transport, toxicity and health risk of nanoparticles in natural ecosystems: Emerging challenges in the modern age and solutions toward a sustainable environment. Sci. Total Environ. 912. https://doi.org/10.1016/j.scitotenv.2023.169331. https://www.sciencedirect.com/science/journal/00489697.
Xu, C., Lei, C., Yu, C., 2019. Mesoporous silica nanoparticles for protein protection and delivery. Front. Chem. 7. https://doi.org/10.3389/fchem.2019.00290. https://www.frontiersin.org/articles/10.3389/fchem.2019.00290/full.
Xu, B., Li, S., Shi, R., Liu, H., 2023. Multifunctional mesoporous silica nanoparticles for biomedical applications. Springer Nature, China Signal Transduction and Targeted Therapy 8 (1). https://doi.org/10.1038/s41392-023-01654-7. https://www.nature.com/sigtrans.
Xuan, L., Ju, Z., Skonieczna, M., Zhou, P.K., Huang, R., 2020. Nanoparticles-induced potential toxicity on human health: Applications, toxicity mechanisms, and evaluation models, 4.
Yang, Y., Yu, C., 2016. Advances in silica based nanoparticles for targeted cancer therapy. Nanomed. Nanotechnol. Biol. Med. 12 (2), 317–332. https://doi.org/10.1016/j.nano.2015.10.018.
Yang, Y., Du, X., Wang, Q., Liu, J., Zhang, E., Sai, L., Peng, C., Lavin, M.F., Yeo, A.J., Yang, X., Shao, H., Du, Z., 2019. Mechanism of cell death induced by silica nanoparticles in hepatocyte cells is by apoptosis. Int. J. Mol. Med. 44 (3), 903–912. https://doi.org/10.3892/ijmm.2019.4265.
Yu, T., Greish, K., McGill, L.D., Ray, A., Ghandehari, H., 2012. Influence of geometry, porosity, and surface characteristics of silica nanoparticles on acute toxicity: Their vasculature effect and tolerance threshold. ACS Nano 6 (3), 2289–2301. https://doi.org/10.1021/nn2043803.
Yu, M., Gu, Z., Ottewell, T., Yu, C., 2017. Silica-based nanoparticles for therapeutic protein delivery. J. Mater. Chem. B 5 (18), 3241–3252. https://doi.org/10.1039/c7tb00244k.
Yu, Y., Zhu, T., Li, Y., Jing, L., Yang, M., Li, Y., Duan, J., Sun, Z., 2019. Repeated intravenous administration of silica nanoparticles induces pulmonary inflammation and collagen accumulation via JAK2/STAT3 and TGF-β/Smad3 pathways in vivo. Int. J. Nanomed. 14, 7237–7247. https://doi.org/10.2147/IJN.S209458.
Zhang, N., Xiong, G., Liu, Z., 2022. Toxicity of metal-based nanoparticles: Challenges in the nano era . Frontiers Media S.A. Front. Bioeng. Biotechnol. 10. https://doi.org/10.3389/fbioe.2022.1001572.
Zhao, L.Y., Zhang, W.M., 2017. Recent progress in drug delivery of pluronic P123: pharmaceutical perspectives. J.7nbsp;Drug Target. 25 (6), 471–484. https://doi.org/10.1080/1061186X.2017.1289538.

# PART III

# Recent advances and regulatory aspects of protein-based nanoparticles in drug delivery

CHAPTER

# 21

# Recent advancement in the codelivery of proteins and small-molecule drugs for targeted therapy

*Sahar Salehi*[1] *and Seyed Morteza Naghib*[2]

[1]Department of Biomedical Engineering, Shahab Danesh University, Qom, Iran;
[2]Nanotechnology Department, School of Advanced Technologies, Iran University of Science and Technology (IUST), Tehran, Iran

## 1. Introduction

Among the various approaches pursued to combat life-threatening or debilitating diseases in humans and animals, the advancement of drug delivery systems (DDS) emerges as a particularly impactful approach (Jain, 2008). A DDS is outlined as a technological formulation or device to deliver therapeutic substances into the body that enhances its efficacy and safety by precisely controlling the rate, timing, extent, and location of drug release (Urbán-Morlán et al., 2020). The aims and approaches of DDS are often classified into three main categories: (1) selection of the administration route and enhancement of absorption, (2) controlled release of the drug from formulations, and (3) targeting the drug to the site of action (Hashida, 2020). In recent years, DDS have shown remarkable therapeutic potential across a wide spectrum of diseases, including diabetes, cancerous tumors, cardiovascular and cerebrovascular diseases, as well as bacterial or viral infections and wounds (Tang et al., 2023; Zhu et al., 2024). In general, there are different routes for DDS, such as the transdermal, transmucosal, rectal, pulmonary, parenteral, intra-articular, and intravesical routes (Srikrishna and Cardozo, 2013). The DDS exhibits varied morphologies, with sizes ranging from the nanoscale to centimeter-scale dimensions. The aim of DDS is to enhance the bioavailability of a molecular drug while minimizing its side effects. In general, the DDS offers a broad design space and can be tailored according to varied diseases to achieve optimal therapeutic effects (Ezike et al., 2023).

*Protein-Based Nanoparticles in Drug Delivery*
https://doi.org/10.1016/B978-0-443-33639-3.00012-X

# 2. Different drug delivery formulations

## 2.1 Localized drug delivery

Localized drug delivery refers to a targeted approach in drug administration, where the therapeutic agent is delivered directly to a specific site within the body. This method allows for reduced systemic exposure, thereby limiting side effects and providing greater control over the treatment (Rolfes et al., 2012). This method enables the controlled release of a drug at a specific site over an extended duration, achieved through the application of a polymer coating or the incorporation of the drug into a polymer-based matrix (Rolfes et al., 2012; Hariharan and Tran, 2023). This kind of regional therapy is typically administered to naturally confined areas, such as the bladder or the vitreous fluid within the eye. However, there are techniques for localized drug delivery, such as hydrogels (Norouzi et al., 2016), micelles (Kumar, 2021), liposomes (Kannavou et al., 2024), and nano/microparticles (Ji and Kohane, 2019), that can limit the release of therapeutic agents at a specific site.

## 2.2 Targeted drug delivery

Targeted drug delivery represents the most precise mechanism of controlled drug delivery that refers to various methods used to enhance the concentration of a drug at a specific site within the body compared to other tissues. In general, its primary purpose is to amplify therapeutic benefits while reducing unwanted side effects (Tewabe et al., 2021). Targeted drug delivery is used in many diseases. But among them, cancer continues to be one of the most common causes of death. Therefore, advancements in targeted drug delivery have often been spearheaded by the development of anticancer therapies. In fact, such treatments are frequently associated with high toxicity and severe side effects, which can greatly diminish the patient's quality of life. Therefore, by increasing the concentration of these drugs specifically at the tumor site while minimizing exposure to the rest of the body, it is possible to achieve significantly enhanced therapeutic effects at the cancerous tumor, even at the same or reduced dosage levels (Rolfes et al., 2012; Lammers et al., 2012). One widely discussed approach to achieve this is to create or incorporate components in cancer drugs that specifically bind to tumor tissues. More specifically, the identification of distinct characteristics on the endothelial surfaces of growing cancerous tumors has facilitated the development of cancer drugs that selectively bind to these surfaces within the tumor's vasculature, thereby enhancing the desired therapeutic effects. This leads to reduced exposure of nontarget tissues to the drug compared to what was previously achievable (Zhao et al., 2020; Li et al., 2023).

An innovative approach to cancer drug delivery involves the use of nanoparticles (sized in the nanometer range) as carriers. These nanocarriers, as carriers, can pass through openings in tumor vasculature, providing direct access to the cancer cells (Yao et al., 2020). In general, these particles allow for acceptable customization for binding to the membranes of cancer cells, the microenvironment, and cytoplasmic or nuclear receptor sites. Consequently, the targeted cancer cells receive high concentrations of the drug, while minimizing harm to healthy tissue (Boisseau and Loubaton, 2011). There are mainly two ways for targeting of nanocarriers for cancer treatment: (1) passive targeting and (2) active targeting (Alavi and Hamidi, 2019). The schematic of passive targeting and active targeting is shown in Fig. 21.1.

### 2.2.1 *Passive targeting*

Passive targeting enables the accumulation of nanocarriers within the tumor microenvironment due to unique characteristics inherent to the tumor milieu that are not typically found in healthy tissues (Alavi and Hamidi, 2019; Bazak et al., 2014). In fact, passive targeting is the primary mechanism through which nanocarriers deliver their payload selectively to cancerous tumors. In this method, the delivery of nanocarriers is influenced by factors related to the tumor microvasculature, as well as properties inherent to the nanocarriers themselves, such as size, shape, and surface charge (Bazak et al., 2014; Kreuter, 2007). In passive targeting, nanocarriers accumulate in tumor tissues due to the enhanced permeability and retention (EPR) effect. The EPR effect was initially described by Maeda and Matsumura in 1986 (Maeda, 2021). This effect relies on the nanometer scale of nanocarriers and two key features of cancerous tumors: restricted lymphatic drainage and leaky vasculature. These characteristics allow nanocarriers to be excellent candidates for passive targeting, enhancing drug accumulation at tumor sites (Maeda, 2021; Subhan et al., 2021). After intravenous injection, nanocarriers with molecular weights of approximately between 40 and 70 kDa

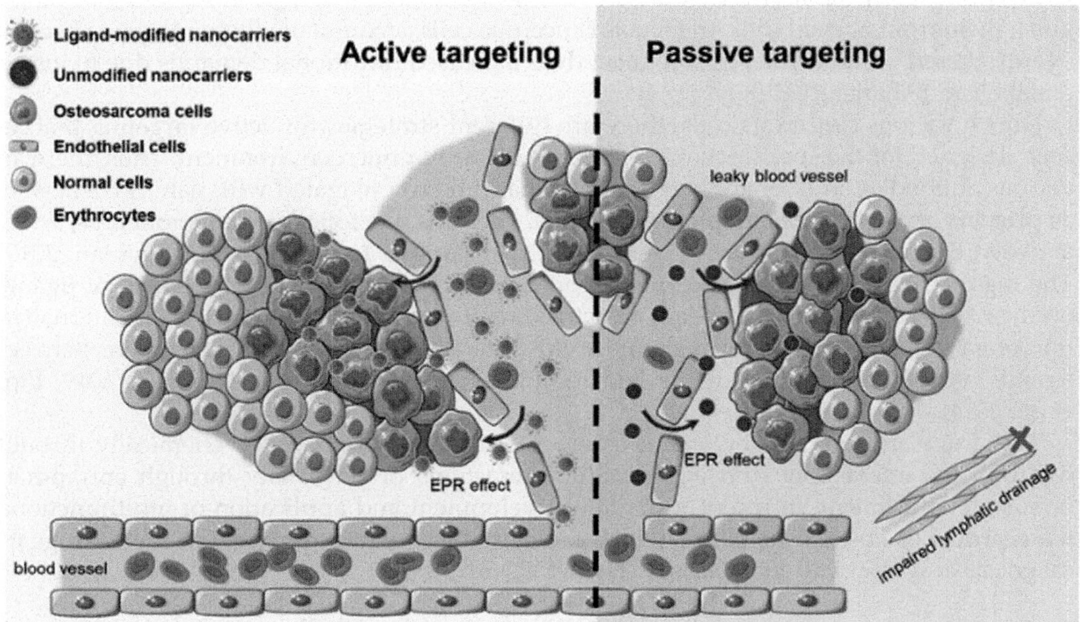


FIGURE 21.1 Schematic illustration of the active and passive targeting mechanisms of nano-delivery systems for antitumor therapy. *Adapted from P. Shi, Z. Cheng, K. Zhao, Y. Chen, A. Zhang, W. Gan, Y. Zhang, Active targeting schemes for nano-drug delivery systems in osteosarcoma therapeutics. Journal of Nanobiotechnology. 21 (1) (2023), https://doi.org/10.1186/s12951-023-01826-1.*

tend to accumulate in cancerous tumors. In fact, this unique phenomenon results from the abnormal vasculature and impaired lymphatic drainage within cancerous tumors (Durymanov et al., 2015). In passive targeting, although nanocarriers deliver their drug in cancerous tumors via the EPR effect, limitations like the lack of precise targeting and inefficient drug diffusion to cancer cells render passive targeting an inadequate strategy (Marques et al., 2020).

### 2.2.2 *Active targeting*

Active targeting addresses many of the systemic side effects caused by nonspecific distribution by modifying ligands, which enables more precise and efficient accumulation of the drug in cancerous tumors (Shi et al., 2023). Nanocarriers can interact with their target cells only when a ligand capable of binding to specific antigens is attached to their surface (Yu et al., 2010). The use of active targeting is essential for delivering genes and therapeutic agents, such as proteins and small-molecule drugs, directly to the target area. This approach significantly reduces damage to normal tissues, thereby enhancing therapeutic efficacy and minimizing unwanted side effects (Shi et al., 2023). In fact, active targeting has the potential to substantially enhance the amount of drug delivered to target cells, surpassing the effectiveness of both free drugs and passively targeted nanocarriers. In active targeting, ligands that specifically bind to receptors or biomarkers on the surface of cancerous cells are coated on the surfaces of nanocarriers. Cancerous cells often exhibit unique receptors that distinguish them from normal cells. In fact, as cancerous cells accumulate, these receptors become overexpressed on cancerous cells to meet their increased nutritional demands due to hypermetabolism (Anarjan, 2019).

Due to various cancerous cells, there are different strategies for active targeting that are each designed for the specific characteristics of the tumor microenvironment. Thus, there are various antibodies and nonantibody ligands that can be conjugated with nanocarriers, such as proteins like transferrin, peptides like RGD, vitamins like folic acid, and aptamers, which are used to enhance the selective delivery of nanocarriers to specific cells (Anarjan, 2019). The high surface-area-to-volume ratio of nanocarriers allows for a high density of ligands on their surface. Thus, the efficiency of active targeting increases. Typically, the internalization of nanocarriers occurs through endocytosis, facilitated by specific interactions between ligands on the nanocarrier surface and receptors on the target cells (Anarjan, 2019; Ling et al., 2014).

The drugs and therapeutic agents interact with nanocarriers either chemically through hydrophobic interactions and electrostatic interactions or physically through entrapment or surface attachment. In recent years, the development and application of multifunctional nanocarriers has been considered, which can simultaneously exploit two or more drugs for diagnosis and treat various diseases (Hsu et al., 2023).

## 2.3 Combination therapy

Combination therapy is a treatment approach that combines two or multiple drugs, each with a distinct mechanism of action, used in a single dosage form to achieve higher therapeutic efficacy than one drug alone (Dai et al., 2017). Combination drug therapy allows for the targeting of multiple pathways, leading to enhanced drug synergy. This approach results in therapeutic benefits that far exceed the mere additive effects of individual drugs. In fact, synergistic drug combinations allow for the reduction of individual drug dosages, minimizing drug toxicities and reducing the development of drug resistance (Dai et al., 2017; Duarte and Vale, 2022). Numerous studies show that drug combinations have been utilized to treat complex and multifaceted diseases such as severe bacterial or fungal infections (Spitzer et al., 2017), cancer (Dai et al., 2017), and other diseases that are difficult to treat with single-drug treatments.

### 2.3.1 *Combination therapy in the treatment of bacterial or fungal infections*

The discovery of antimicrobial drugs to combat infections caused by bacterial and fungal pathogens is a significant challenge. In fact, invasive fungal and bacterial infections are a significant health threat, causing high rates of disease and death, particularly among immunocompromised individuals. Despite the critical need, there remains a paucity of antifungal and antibacterial drug treatments available to combat these fungal and bacterial pathogens. Therefore, a promising therapeutic approach to enhance drug efficacy and reduce the emergence of drug resistance is the use of combination therapy. In fact, combining drugs can enhance efficacy and specificity compared to single-drug therapies. Further, the combination of drugs can delay or even prevent the development of resistance in many infectious diseases by promptly reducing the pathogen population (Spitzer et al., 2017).

### 2.3.2 *Combination therapy in the treatment of cancer*

Drug resistance in cancer is a well-known phenomenon that occurs when cancer cells develop tolerance to pharmaceutical treatments. Resistance to anticancer drugs stems from a range of factors, including genetic mutations, epigenetic changes, enhanced drug efflux, and other cellular and molecular mechanisms activated through specific signaling pathways. Thus, cancer treatment resistance is a major contributor to mortality, highlighting the urgent need for the development of new combination therapies (Wang et al., 2019). Combination treatments for cancer have the potential to enhance cancer cell death and lead to deeper and more durable responses in patients. In fact, these therapies combine two or more anticancer drugs with distinct mechanisms of action to enhance their anticancer effects, minimize potential side effects, and help prevent the emergence of drug resistance. Generally, combination therapy with anticancer drugs has been demonstrated to enhance the synergistic anticancer response by effectively combining different drugs and preventing the onset of drug resistance. In this method, due to the synergistic effects, side effects associated with high doses of single drugs are reduced (Dai et al., 2017; Mokhtari et al., 2017).

Despite the benefits of combination therapy, challenges remain, such as low bioavailability and the absence of tumor-specific strategies, which can lead to reduced therapeutic efficacy in patients (Zhang et al., 2024). The use of nanocarrier-based systems with combination therapy is essential to provide an effective strategy for the codelivery of anticancer drugs to the cancerous tumors. Additionally, this strategy aids in reducing blood and renal clearance, thereby enhancing the bioavailability of drugs in tumor tissues and minimizing toxicity to healthy surrounding tissues. In fact, to enhance the therapeutic benefits of codelivery systems, it is essential to achieve high drug-loading efficiency in nanocarriers. Furthermore, the therapeutic effectiveness of drug combinations depends heavily on the release kinetics of each drug, so the controlled release of drugs is essential in codelivery systems (Al Bostami, Abuwatfa and Husseini, 2022; Chen et al., 2023). Additionally, the use of nanoparticles as nanocarrier systems can effectively address the problem of low water solubility that is common among many anticancer drugs and improve their biodistribution around cancerous tumors (Chen et al., 2023).

In recent decades, various nanocarriers made from materials like lipids, polymers, and inorganic substances have been developed to enable the codelivery of anticancer drugs to cancerous tumors (Chen et al., 2023; Zeinali et al., 2020).

## 3. Molecular targeted drugs in the treatment of cancer

Molecular targeted therapy demonstrates exceptional specificity, enabling it to selectively interact with molecules directly involved in tumor progression. These target molecules may be unique to tumor cells, overexpressed, or mutated within the cancerous cells. In fact, targeted molecular therapy is a treatment strategy that inhibits the growth of cancer cells by interfering with specific molecules essential for the proliferation and survival of cancer or tumor cells. Using this approach, the drug is introduced into the body and precisely targets carcinogenic sites, effectively suppressing the growth and spread of malignant cells or inducing apoptosis in tumor tissues. As a result, due to their precision in targeting cancerous cells while sparing healthy tissues, molecularly targeted anticancer drugs are often referred to as "biological missiles." Targeted therapies are broadly categorized into two main types: small-molecule targeted drugs and macromolecular therapies (Li, Li and Ji, 2020a).

### 3.1 Small-molecule drugs

Small-molecule drugs are low-molecular-weight chemical compounds, typically ranging between 0.1 and 1 kDa. In fact, they are smaller than biologics or bio-therapeutic modalities, which generally have molecular sizes exceeding 1 kDa, as illustrated in Fig. 21.2. This size difference highlights their distinct mechanisms of action and applications in medical treatments (Chhabra, 2021). Due to their small size, small-molecule drugs have an advantage over biologics in both extracellular components, such as cell surface receptors or membrane-bound proteins like glycoproteins, as well as intracellular proteins like various kinases. In fact, their ability to traverse the outer plasma membrane allows them to target intracellular molecules, effectively regulating cellular functions. Additionally, small-molecule drugs are relatively easy to synthesize by chemical reactions and are inexpensive, more stable, and offer improved reproducibility compared to biological drugs (Li, Li and Ji, 2020a; Chhabra, 2021).

Due to their ability to travel through the body easily, transferring from the gastrointestinal tract into the bloodstream and reaching their site of action by permeating cell membranes to access intracellular targets, small-molecule drugs can treat a broad spectrum of diseases, including hypertension, cardiovascular diseases, neurological disorders, diabetes, infectious diseases, cancer, and more (Ma et al., 2021).

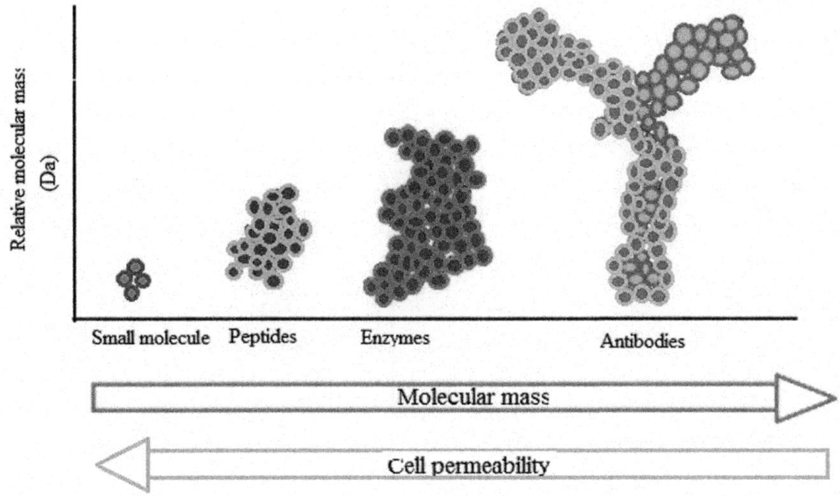


**FIGURE 21.2** Biological therapeutic modalities: From small-molecules to biological macromolecules.

### 3.1.1 *Small-molecule drugs in targeted cancer therapy*

In recent years, notable advancements have been achieved in the development of small-molecule targeted therapies for cancer treatment. In contrast to conventional drugs, small-molecule drugs primarily function as signal transduction inhibitors, selectively targeting and blocking pathways essential for tumor growth and proliferation. In fact, these drugs are targeted specifically at membrane receptors, cell cycle regulators, signaling pathway components, other critical proteins, and production-related factors. Due to their great selectivity, these drugs inflict minimal damage to normal cells, making them a key spot for anticancer drug development. Consequently, they are effective at relatively low doses. As of June 2021, there are a total of 98 small molecules with anticancer properties approved in the United States and China. Fig. 21.3 presents an overview of small-molecule anticancer drugs that have been approved by the US Food and Drug Administration (FDA) and the National Medical Products Administration (NMPA) of China since 2001 (Zhong et al., 2021; Yang et al., 2024).

Compared with macromolecule drugs, small-molecule targeted drugs offer several advantages in certain areas, including patient acceptability, pharmacokinetic characteristics, prices, and drug storage and transportation. In fact, small-molecule targeted drugs have demonstrated significant advancements, particularly when compared to macromolecular treatments represented by monoclonal antibodies (Zhong et al., 2021). Small-molecule targeted drugs encompass a diverse array of inhibitors, such as kinase inhibitors, proteasome inhibitors, and matrix metalloproteinase inhibitors, and offer the potential to treat various types of cancer effectively. Despite the development and widespread use of numerous small-molecule anticancer drugs in clinical practice, significant challenges remain, such as low response rates and the development of drug resistance, which hinder the overall effectiveness of these therapies (Liu et al., 2022).

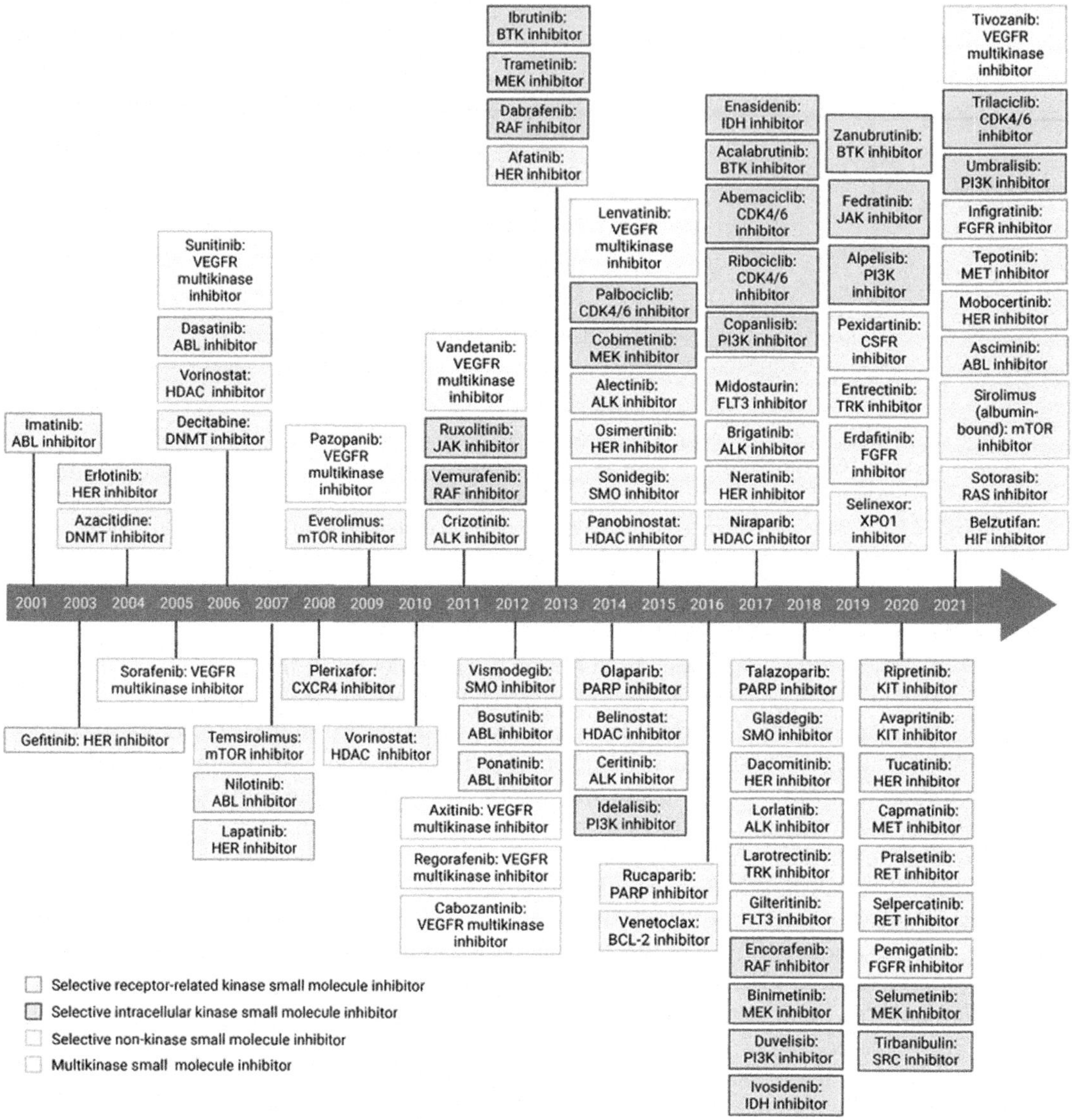


**FIGURE 21.3** Timeline for the US FDA-approved small-molecule inhibitors targeting cancers. *Adapted from G.H. Liu, T. Chen, X. Zhang, X.L. Ma, H.S. Shi, Small molecule inhibitors targeting the cancers. MedComm. 3 (4) (2022), https://doi.org/10.1002/mco2.181.*

To advance the development of small-molecule targeted anticancer drugs, the strategy of dual/multiple targeted small-molecule drugs refers to designing a single agent that is capable of simultaneously acting on two or more targets, thereby effectively blocking multiple oncogenic pathways. This approach can increase their antitumor efficiency and overcome resistance mechanisms. Therefore, the use of combination therapy shows significant promise in improving therapeutic efficacy, reducing drug-induced toxicity, and overcoming drug resistance in the treatment of cancer (Yang et al., 2024).

## 4. Protein drug delivery

Proteins are complex biological macromolecules composed of one or more polypeptide chains. They play crucial roles in living organisms by facilitating a wide range of functions, including catalyzing metabolic reactions, aiding in DNA replication, responding to cellular signals, and transporting molecules throughout the body. Due to their highly specific mechanisms of action, proteins hold great promise as therapeutic agents, often enabling effective treatment with relatively low doses (Panta et al., 2014).

Protein-based drugs can be categorized into various types, including antibody-based drugs, Fc fusion proteins, interferons, blood factors, hormones, anticoagulants, interleukins, and thrombolytics (Carter, 2011; Ebrahimi and Samanta, 2023). The use of protein-based drugs has revolutionized the treatment of numerous critical human diseases, including diabetes, hypertension, and cancer. In fact, protein therapies offer several advantages over traditional small-molecule drugs, which have long been dominant in the pharmaceutical industry. These advantages include greater specificity, enhanced therapeutic activity, and reduced toxicity. However, the exceptional specificity of proteins often relies on their intricate three-dimensional structure, which can be challenging to preserve during modification (Ebrahimi and Samanta, 2023; Gurevich and Gurevich, 2014). Unlike low molecular weight drugs, proteins possess a complex three-dimensional structure that plays a critical role in determining their biological activity. In fact, any disturbance in the primary (amino acid sequence), secondary (2D structure), tertiary (folding), and quaternary structure (assembly of peptide subunits) can lead to the loss of a protein's biological activity. These disruptions can be caused by even the smallest alterations in the protein's environment or microenvironment. The primary factors that can influence protein structure and stability include temperature, pH, solvent conditions, the presence of other solutes, and the protein's crystallinity state (Branden and Tooze, 2012).

Moreover, delivering therapeutic proteins, such as enzymes and cytokines, to specific disease sites faces significant challenges due to their susceptibility to enzymatic breakdown, short circulation half-lives, and poor membrane permeability. Protein drug delivery involves the use of specialized carriers designed to protect protein drugs, control their release, and improve their retention and biological activity, ultimately improving their therapeutic efficacy in the body (Yu et al., 2016).

Nanotechnology has demonstrated extensive potential in the field of protein delivery, offering advanced strategies to enhance stability, regulate release, and improve the therapeutic efficacy of protein-based therapies. Moreover, it has broadened the therapeutic window of protein drugs, enabling the administration of higher doses without increasing toxicity. So far, numerous nanomedicines have been granted approval for clinical application, such as lipidic nanoparticles, polymer nanoparticles, and inorganic nanomaterials. These nanoscale carriers, typically ranging from 10 to 150 nm in size, offer distinct advantages as DDS, especially for protein therapeutics (Yu et al., 2016; Yau et al., 2021).

## 4.1 The role of protein in the treatment of cancer

The role of proteins in cell biology and cancer mechanisms has become a critical area of research in oncology, particularly regarding their application in diagnosis, prognosis, and targeted therapies. In oncology, proteins are vital both as diagnostic biomarkers and therapeutic agents (Kędzierska and Bańkosz, 2024). In fact, cancer cells are characterized by specific cell surface receptors that can be effectively targeted in cancer therapies. An effective strategy for cancer therapy is surface receptor-dependent endocytosis, where macromolecular drug ligands bind to specific receptors on cancer cells. This binding facilitates the release of therapeutic proteins directly at the tumor site, enabling targeted destruction of cancer cells while preventing tumor metastasis (Bajracharya et al., 2022). To date, numerous proteins have demonstrated significant therapeutic potential and are being actively employed in cancer treatment strategies. These proteins play crucial roles in targeting cancer-specific mechanisms and enhancing treatment efficacy. Protein therapies offer a significantly larger binding surface area compared to small-molecule drugs, enabling them to interact with a wider range of protein targets. This characteristic expands their therapeutic potential, allowing for precise targeting of complex biological pathways and mechanisms. In fact, protein biologics enhance the active targeting of cancer cells by selectively binding to cell surface receptors and other markers that are either uniquely present or overexpressed in tumors, as opposed to healthy tissues. This selective interaction enhances therapeutic precision while minimizing off-target effects (Kintzing et al., 2016).

Although protein-based drugs have shown immense promise as candidates for treating various diseases, particularly cancer, several challenges persist (Kintzing et al., 2016; Wu et al., 2022):

1. **Limited Cellular Permeability**: Proteins with intracellular targets often exhibit low permeability through the cell membrane due to their high molecular weight and the presence of charged amino acid residues.
2. **Susceptibility to Degradation**: Proteins are prone to degradation and denaturation in harsh environments, such as exposure to proteolytic enzymes or low pH conditions, which significantly reduces their bioavailability and effectiveness.
3. **Rapid Metabolism**: Fast metabolism and the dissociation of protein subunits further contribute to a decrease in their effective bioavailability, posing hurdles for sustained therapeutic efficacy.

Protein-based therapies are vital in biomedicine due to their pharmacological effects and highly selective biological activity. Their ability to precisely target specific biological pathways makes them effective in treating a wide range of diseases (Su et al., 2018). However, proteins often exhibit unfavorable physical and chemical properties, including delicate tertiary structures, large molecular sizes, and poor membrane permeability. These characteristics pose significant challenges to the efficient delivery of proteins into cells (Qin et al., 2019). So far, protein delivery systems have mainly concentrated on targeting extracellular sites. However, many potential applications require the efficient delivery of proteins into the cytoplasm to achieve therapeutic effects (Scaletti et al., 2018). Currently, protein-based therapies for clinical use are primarily restricted to those that operate outside the cell, such as cytokines and monoclonal antibodies. In fact, these therapies target extracellular proteins or cell surface receptors to exert their effects. Currently, protein biologics with intracellular anticancer activity face limited clinical application due to their poor permeability across cell membranes, which hinders their ability to effectively reach intracellular targets (Cheng et al., 2022).

# 5. Combination therapy of small-molecule drugs and protein

Administering drugs in combination is a promising strategy to enhance efficacy through therapeutic synergy. Among the most widely used drug categories in medicine are small-molecule drugs and protein-based therapeutics, each offering distinct advantages. In fact, the codelivery approach of small-molecule drugs and protein-based therapeutics has demonstrated significant potential in cancer therapy and immunotherapy (Huang et al., 2022).

## 5.1 Codelivery of proteins and small-molecule drugs for cancer therapy

Given the complexity of cancer mechanisms, relying on a single anticancer drug for treatment may not be sufficient to achieve optimal therapeutic outcomes. Consequently, research efforts have increasingly focused on combining multiple therapeutic agents to amplify anticancer efficacy. Notably, combination therapy employing various anticancer drugs demonstrates superior effectiveness compared to single-drug treatments due to their synergistic mechanisms of action (Mokhtari et al., 2017). The potential synergistic effects arising from the simultaneous targeting of multiple pathways in tumor cells and tissues can significantly enhance tumor inhibition efficiency, increase sensitivity of tumors to therapeutic agents, reduce dosages of toxic drugs, minimize adverse side effects, and extend patient survival (He et al., 2016). Up to now, numerous codelivery platforms have been designed and implemented to treat tumors, incorporating combinations of antineoplastic drugs. These systems can include two chemotherapeutics, a combination of chemotherapeutic and gene therapies, or chemotherapeutic and protein-based therapies. In recent years, combination therapies utilizing chemotherapeutic agents and proteins have been explored extensively for treating various types of tumors (Qin et al., 2018). Compared with chemotherapeutic agents, proteins exhibit unique characteristics such as exceptional specificity, the capability to perform complex biological functions, and reduced toxicity to normal tissues. Unlike the nonspecific cytotoxicity associated with chemotherapeutic agents, proteins exert their anticancer effects primarily by directly inducing apoptosis in tumor cells via specific signaling pathways. Additionally, proteins can indirectly inhibit tumors by activating immune responses or targeting tumor vasculature and stromal components, further enhancing their therapeutic potential. Due to the potential for synergistic anticancer effects from the combined actions on multiple molecular targets of both chemotherapeutics and therapeutic proteins, the integration of these two strategies has garnered considerable attention in recent experimental studies and clinical trials (He et al., 2016; Jiang et al., 2014). However, despite promising experimental and clinical outcomes from codelivering chemotherapeutic drugs and proteins, the anticancer efficacy often falls due to the limitations of traditional delivery methods. These include short blood circulation time, severe systemic toxicity, inadequate tumor accumulation, and differences in distribution patterns between small-molecule drugs and macromolecular proteins (He et al., 2016). To optimize synergistic anticancer effects, significant efforts have been made to develop novel strategies for codelivering chemotherapeutic drugs and proteins to tumor tissues, ensuring consistent in vivo pharmacokinetics and precise targeting of tumor sites. Overall, the coencapsulation of small-molecule drugs and macromolecular proteins presents a substantial challenge due to their differing physicochemical properties, including molecular size, hydrophilic/hydrophobic balance, charge, stability, and permeability across cell membranes (He et al., 2016; Kim et al., 2015).

In recent years, numerous codelivery systems have been designed to efficiently encapsulate small chemotherapeutic agents alongside proteins, ensuring their controlled release precisely at targeted sites. Furthermore, remarkable advancements have been achieved in developing and applying these systems for both systemic and localized combination therapies, enabling effective tumor treatment in both in vitro and in vivo models (He et al., 2016).

### 5.1.1 *Nanocarriers for systemic codelivery*

Over recent decades, nanoscale carriers have become crucial tools in advancing cancer therapy. Their advantages include significantly extending the circulation time of drug-loaded nanocarriers in the bloodstream, enhancing drug accumulation at tumor sites, improving the efficiency of intracellular drug delivery, and reducing systemic side effects (He et al., 2016; Elsabahy and Wooley, 2012). Furthermore, controlled drug delivery can be accomplished through the design of advanced nanocarriers that are tailored to respond to the distinctive microenvironments of tumor tissues. In fact, these carriers can be tailored to react to specific conditions such as pH levels, enzymatic activity, and intracellular reducing environments, thereby enabling precise and efficient drug release at the tumor site (He et al., 2016; Du et al., 2011).

In general, there are various nanocarriers for codelivery of chemotherapeutic drugs and proteins with anticancer efficacy and potential synergistic effects, such as lipid-based nanocarriers, polymer-based nanocarriers, and antibody-conjugated nanocarriers (He et al., 2016).

#### 5.1.1.1 Lipid-based nanocarriers

Lipid-based nanocarriers are among the most effective nano-delivery vehicles that are widely utilized in medical research and pharmacology. These nanocarriers can encapsulate a wide range of therapeutic agents, including both small-molecule and macromolecular drugs for numerous medical applications. Lipid-based nanocarriers provide multiple advantages, including protecting drugs from degradation in the body, enhancing their solubility, controlling drug release, allowing targeted delivery to specific disease sites, and modifying drug biodistribution for optimized therapeutic outcomes (Mehta et al., 2023). There are several types of lipid-based nanocarriers, including liposomes, lipid nanoemulsions, solid lipid nanoparticles, and nanostructured lipid carriers. Among them, liposomes are spherical or multilayered vesicles formed through the self-assembly of phospholipid chains or lipid bilayers in aqueous solutions. In this structure, the bilayer phospholipid membrane is made up of hydrophobic tails and hydrophilic heads, which creates an amphiphilic structure (He et al., 2016; Mehta et al., 2023). Due to their ability to encapsulate hydrophilic drugs in the aqueous core and incorporate hydrophobic drugs within the lipid bilayers, along with their ease of synthesis, high bioavailability and biocompatibility, stability, passive and active targeting capabilities, and high drug loading efficiency, liposomes are considered promising nanocarriers for codelivery of various small-molecule drugs and biomacromolecules, including proteins, for treatment of cancer (He et al., 2016; Ashrafizadeh et al., 2022). For example, PEGylated liposomal tumor necrosis factor-α (Peg-LP TNF-α) was administered intravenously alongside Doxil in BN rats with subcutaneous BN175 sarcomas. Results revealed that the coadministration of Doxil and Peg-LP TNF-α significantly enhanced tumor suppression while reducing adverse effects compared with the combination of Doxil and free TNF-α. This outcome highlights the advantages of using PEGylated liposomal carriers to improve drug synergy and minimize toxicity (ten Hagen et al., 2002).

#### 5.1.1.2 Polymer-based nanocarriers

Polymer-based nanocarriers are a unique and innovative class of nanocarriers that could revolutionize the field of medicine. The initial and most crucial step in the fabrication and design of polymeric-based nanocarriers is choosing the best polymer. In fact, the selection of the polymer depends on the properties desired for the nanocarrier. These properties can include biocompatibility, biodegradability, stability, high drug-loading capacity, controlled release kinetics, and characteristics that facilitate targeted delivery of the nanocarrier to the specific sites in the body (Idris et al., 2023). Polymer-based nanocarriers are constructed from natural or synthetic polymers in the nanoscale range. Natural polymers such as polysaccharides and polypeptides are highly valued for their low toxicity, high biocompatibility, and biodegradability in comparison to synthetic polymers. However, controlling the physical and chemical properties of natural polymers can be challenging, which might limit their applications in specific fields (Idris et al., 2023; Haider et al., 2022). Generally, polymer-based nanocarriers are incredibly small systems that can deliver small-molecule drugs, peptides, proteins, nucleic acids, and other molecules to targeted cells or specific sites in the body. They are engineered to be biocompatible and biodegradable, allowing for safe use in the body. They can also specifically target areas without damaging healthy tissues or cells (Idris et al., 2023).

***5.1.1.2.1 Amphiphilic block copolymer-based nanocarriers*** Generally, there are different polymeric-based nanocarriers for DDS. Among them, amphiphilic block copolymer-based nanocarriers are extensively utilized in pharmaceutical applications, spanning from sustained drug release systems to gene delivery platforms (Letchford and Burt, 2007). Amphiphilic block copolymers are highly effective for delivering therapeutic agents due to their unique chemical composition. Each amphiphilic block copolymer typically consists of a hydrophilic block covalently bonded to a hydrophobic block. In fact, amphiphilic block copolymers are composed of at least two chemically distinct polymer chains that undergo phase separation due to chain association in solvents that selectively dissolve only one of the blocks. This characteristic allows them to self-assemble into nanoscale core–shell structures (Letchford and Burt, 2007; Adams et al., 2003). There are varieties of polymeric core–shell nanocarriers, including micelles, nanospheres, nanocapsules, and polymersomes, designed for the codelivery of hydrophilic and hydrophobic drugs to tumor cells for the treatment of cancer (Letchford and Burt, 2007).

***5.1.1.2.1.1 Polymeric micelles*** Polymeric micelles are promising drug delivery carriers that effectively overcome the bioavailability challenges of hydrophobic drugs while also facilitating the codelivery of hydrophilic drugs (Croy and Kwon, 2006). These nanocarriers are core–shell structures at the nanoscale, made from amphiphilic block copolymers. In aqueous solutions, amphiphilic block copolymers self-assemble to reduce free energy, forming a hydrophilic shell that prolongs circulation time and enhances solubility. Generally, the hydrophobic core of micelles provides an optimal environment for the solubilization and encapsulation of hydrophobic small-molecule drugs. Meanwhile, hydrophilic molecules, particularly large-sized proteins, are typically incorporated into micelles through covalent conjugation or physical interactions, enabling efficient codelivery within a single nanocarrier (Kuperkar et al., 2022). Due to their remarkable characteristics, including biocompatibility, low toxicity, nanoscale size, and considerable stability, polymeric micelles are extensively utilized in the treatment of a range of diseases, including cancer, in estrogen therapy, and even as carriers for antiinfluenza antiviral therapies (Kuperkar et al., 2022; Yadav et al., 2018).

In a recent study conducted by Chen and coworkers, a multistage cooperative nanoplatform was synthesized using a specifically engineered triblock copolymer, mPEG-*b*-PGCA-*b*-PGTA, for the intracellular codelivery of hydrophilic ribonuclease A (RNase A) and hydrophobic doxorubicin (DOX) (Fig. 21.4). In this system, DOX was loaded into the micelle cores through hydrophobic interactions, while RNase A was modified into RNBC (RNase A conjugated with nitrophenyl tetramethyl-dioxaborolanyl benzyl carbamate groups). This modification allowed RNase A to be attached to the micelle via reversible covalent bonding. Upon cellular uptake, codelivery of DOX and RNase A from the triblock copolymer nanoparticles is designed to occur through a multistage process. First, the acidic environment within the endosomes facilitates the initial release. Following this, the intracellular ROS (reactive oxygen species) environment, enhanced by DOX, further promotes the release of both drugs, enabling synergistic anticancer effects in both in vitro and in vivo (Zhang et al., 2020a).

***5.1.1.2.1.2 Polymeric nanospheres*** Polymeric nanospheres are usually defined as matrix-type structures that can encapsulate the therapeutic agents within their core or absorb them onto their surface. Most nanospheres are fabricated using biodegradable, biocompatible, and synthetic amphiphilic block copolymers. Due to their amorphous or crystalline structure, polymeric nanospheres can safeguard encapsulated drugs from enzymatic and chemical degradation. In fact, this structure is specifically tailored to enable efficient drug encapsulation and controlled release, thereby making them valuable in a wide range of therapeutic applications (Verma et al., 2010).

***5.1.1.2.1.3 Polymeric nanocapsules*** In recent years, nanocapsules have attracted more interest in medical, biological, and pharmaceutical applications, benefiting from their core–shell microstructure. In fact, nanocapsules consist of a core region, which may be either

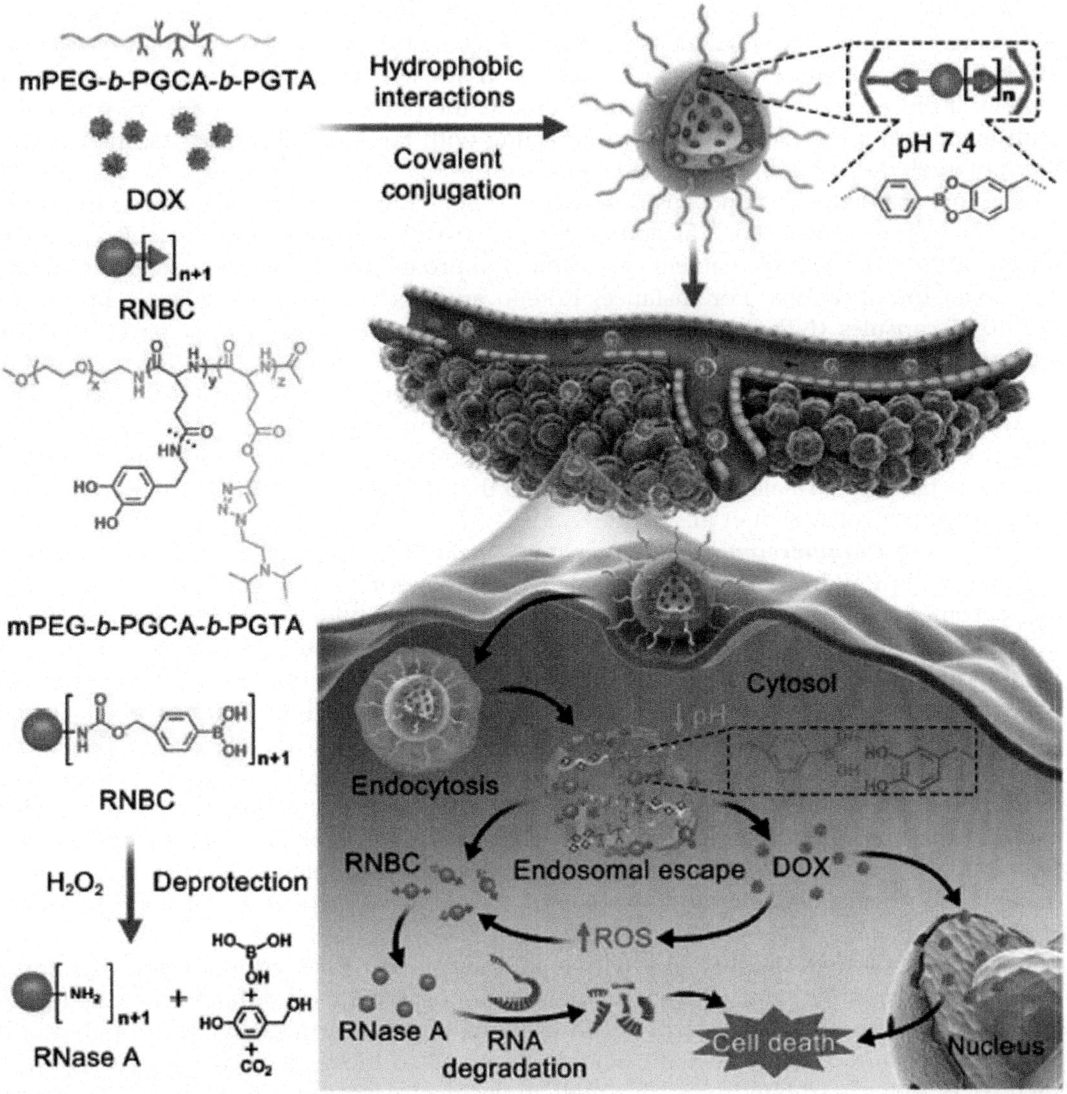


FIGURE 21.4 Schematic illustration of the intracellular codelivery of RNase A and DOX using a multistage cooperative drug delivery nanoplatform formed by mPEG-*b*-PGCA-*b*-PGTA for combination cancer therapy. *Adapted from P. Zhang, Y. Zhang, X. Ding, W. Shen, M. Li, E. Wagner, C. Xiao, X. Chen, A multistage cooperative nanoplatform enables intracellular co-delivery of proteins and chemotherapeutics for cancer therapy. Advanced Materials. 32 (46) (2020), https://doi.org/10.1002/adma.202000013.*

hollow or filled, surrounded by a shell-forming material that covers the encapsulated substance (Deng et al., 2020). The shells of nanocapsules can be constructed from various materials, including lipids, phospholipids, and polymers. Among them, polymeric nanocapsules are the most promising nanocapsules due to their exceptional capacity for achieving high drug loading, robust protection against degradation, and high biocompatibility. This is particularly attributed to the low tissue irritation and strong interaction with biological fluids of some polymers. Additionally, the polymeric shell can be functionalized with intelligent molecules capable of interacting with targeted biomolecules, thereby facilitating targeted drug delivery (Lima et al., 2022).

The core of polymeric nanocapsules can be designed to enable the delivery of hydrophobic or hydrophilic drugs such as gemcitabine hydrochloride and DOX, as well as proteins like albumin. However, to enable the codelivery of proteins and drugs, nanocapsules require additional modifications. For instance, Rotello and his coworker designed nanoparticle-stabilized capsules (NPSCs) to codeliver small-molecule drugs, such as paclitaxel (PTX) and protein caspase-3 (CASP3), into the cytoplasm. Apoptosis studies and in vitro cell viability measurements demonstrated that the codelivery of PTX and CASP3 via NPSCs resulted in a higher apoptosis rate in HeLa cells compared to NPSCs loaded with either PTX or CASP3 alone, indicating a higher killing rate in tumor cells. In addition, the final results from the Chou-Talalay analysis confirmed that PTX and CASP3 exhibited a synergistic effect on tumor cells (Kim et al., 2015).

***5.1.1.2.1.4 Polymersomes*** Polymersomes are hollow spherical structures similar to liposomes with a hydrophilic core enclosed by a polymeric bilayer membrane. These structures, complemented by a hydrophilic corona, can enable the encapsulation of both hydrophilic and hydrophobic drugs. In fact, polymersomes are nanocarriers composed of amphiphilic block copolymers with high molecular weights that can self-assemble into nanoscale vesicular structures (Lee and Feijen, 2012). In fact, these high molecular weight polymers exhibit amphiphilic properties similar to lipids but are comprised of polymer chains covalently bonded in sequences of two or more blocks. As a result, these structures form a denser membrane, providing rigidity and improved stability to the vesicles compared to liposomes. In addition, these vesicular structures exhibit remarkable resistance to oxidation and hydrolysis reactions, as well as exceptional stability against deformation during bodily transport, cellular division, and fusion processes (Lee and Feijen, 2012; Aibani et al., 2020).

Owing to their high stability, ability to load multiple drugs, exceptional biocompatibility, and robust membrane structure, polymersomes are promising candidates for drug delivery applications. Also, these nanocarriers can facilitate targeted drug delivery through modification of the surface function with ligands designed to bind specifically to cell receptors such as proteins, carbohydrates, or small molecules. Also, the development of stimuli-responsive polymersomes has garnered significant attention due to their ability to regulate drug release by modulating membrane stability and permeability in response to a specific target (Lee and Feijen, 2012). Up to now, numerous block copolymers responsive to various stimuli, including pH, temperature, magnetic fields, ionic strength, and glucose concentration, have been developed and used for the synthesis of stimuli-responsive polymersomes. As a result, these polymersomes can release drugs when exposed to external stimuli at the target site, thereby improving therapeutic effectiveness and minimizing potential side effects (García, 2019).

Therefore, polymersomes as nanocarriers for DDS possess the ability to encapsulate a wide variety of therapeutic agents, such as small-molecule and macromolecule drugs for codelivery to tumor cells (Cheng et al., 2022).

Cheng and colleagues designed a biodegradable chimeric polymersome using asymmetric poly(ethyleneglycol)-*b*-poly(ε-caprolactone)-*b*-poly(2-(diethylamino)ethyl methacrylate) (PEG-PCL-PDEA) triblock copolymers. This nanocarrier is capable of simultaneously encapsulating and transporting both proteins and DOX to the cytoplasm and/or nucleus of target cells. In this design, the PEG block was positioned on the surface of the polymersomes, ensuring superior biocompatibility and enhanced stability during circulation. The cationic PDEA blocks were placed inside the polymer structure, facilitating the effective encapsulation and stabilization of proteins. Meanwhile, the hydrophobic PCL block served as the compartment for loading DOX. In vitro studies demonstrated that the polymersomes delivered both the protein and DOX simultaneously into the cytosol and cell nuclei. This capability underscores their potential as effective codelivery systems for enhancing cancer therapy outcomes (Cheng et al., 2011).

#### 5.1.1.3 Antibody-conjugated nanoparticles

Therapeutic antibodies have demonstrated their ability to promote tumor necrosis and regression via multiple mechanisms, such as directly triggering apoptosis by blocking specific receptors, mediating immune-driven tumor cell destruction, and exerting targeted effects on tumor vasculature and stromal components. In fact, antibodies, owing to their tumor-targeting capabilities, can be conjugated with nanocarriers to facilitate the targeted delivery of therapeutic agents directly to tumor sites. This approach enhances anticancer efficacy by increasing tumor selectivity and achieving synergistic therapeutic effects (LoRusso et al., 2011).

In recent years, monoclonal antibody-based therapies have demonstrated significant success in cancer treatment. At the moment, several monoclonal antibodies have been approved by the US FDA or are currently undergoing various phases of clinical trials for the treatment of different types of cancer (He et al., 2016). For example, rituximab, a chimeric monoclonal antibody, has been approved by the US FDA for the treatment of non-Hodgkin lymphomas. It functions by inhibiting the expression of the immunosuppressive cytokine IL-10 and the antiapoptotic protein Bcl-2. Additionally, rituximab has demonstrated the ability to reverse drug resistance in various tumor cell lines (Qin et al., 2018; Alas et al., 2001).

## 5.2 Codelivery of proteins and small-molecule drugs for immunotherapy

Cytokines are a group of immune system proteins that play a crucial role in cancer immunotherapy by stimulating the immune system to detect and eliminate tumor cells effectively. In fact, due to their ability to induce apoptosis directly in tumor cells and exert indirect antitumor effects by modulating immune responses, various cytokines, particularly tumor necrosis factors (TNFs), interleukins (ILs), and interferons (IFNs), have been extensively utilized in clinical cancer therapies. Additionally, to enhance anticancer effectiveness and reduce adverse effects, studies have focused on the synergistic effects of combining cytokines with small-molecule chemotherapeutic drugs (Sousa, 2024). For example, TNF-α demonstrated synergistic anticancer activity with DOX in treating BN175 fibrosarcoma and ROS-1 osteosarcoma. This was achieved through codelivery of isolated limb perfusion (ILP), likely due to TNF-α enhancing the local concentration of DOX at tumor sites (Van Der Veen et al., 2000).

Systemic administration of cytokines offers potent immunotherapeutic benefits but is frequently hindered by severe dose-limiting toxicities. To overcome this limitation, cytokines have been encapsulated within polymeric nanocarriers, enabling improved intratumoral retention and localized therapeutic action following targeted delivery (Fu et al., 2023; Aznar et al., 2017).

### 5.2.1 Nano carriers for localized codelivery

The main obstacles in systemic chemotherapy are the inadequate concentration of drugs at tumor sites and the insufficient uptake of drugs by the target cells. In contrast, locoregional treatment for solid tumors, which involves the localized delivery of anticancer agents, offers advantages such as significantly increased drug concentration in tumor tissues and reduced systemic toxicity due to limited distribution in healthy tissues. At present, localized delivery of anticancer drugs has emerged as a key strategy for treating several types of cancer, including liver cancer, soft tissue tumors, peritoneal cancer, glioblastoma, and serosal malignancies. A variety of polymeric materials, such as injectable hydrogels, have been studied as potential carriers for the localized delivery of anticancer drugs. Furthermore, regional combination cancer therapy, which involves the localized and sustained codelivery of multiple anticancer agents, can promote prolonged synergistic antitumor effects while reducing systemic side effects (He et al., 2016; Budker et al., 2014).

#### 5.2.1.1 Injectable hydrogels

Biodegradable and injectable hydrogels have garnered considerable interest in biomedical research due to their potential as reservoirs for the localized and sustained delivery of small-molecule drugs and proteins. In fact, injectable hydrogels offer several key advantages for localized drug delivery, including minimally invasive administration, targeted and sustained drug release, reduced systemic toxicity, and the capacity to encapsulate and deliver both hydrophilic and hydrophobic therapeutic drugs. In recent studies, injectable hydrogels have been investigated as a platform for the localized codelivery of small-molecule chemotherapeutic drugs and proteins, aiming to achieve sustained synergistic anticancer effects (He et al., 2016; Ko et al., 2013).

Localized and sustained codelivery of small-molecule chemotherapeutic drugs and immunostimulating agents, such as cytokines, directly to tumor tissues has the potential to enhance chemo-immunotherapy. This approach can increase local drug concentrations while minimizing the systemic toxicity of small-molecule chemotherapeutic drugs to the host immune system. For example, a thermosensitive chitosan-based hydrogel was developed to enable localized combination chemo-immunotherapy. This system combined small-molecule drugs such as DOX, cisplatin (CDDP), or cyclophosphamide (CTX), along with granulocyte-macrophage colony-stimulating factor (GMCSF), to enhance therapeutic efficacy in tumor tissues. In vivo anticancer studies demonstrated that a chitosan-based hydrogel coloaded with a chemotherapeutic drug and GMCSF significantly improved and sustained tumor suppression compared with hydrogels loaded with either the drug or the protein alone (He et al., 2016; Seo et al., 2009).

# 6. Other advances in codelivery of proteins and small-molecule drugs

According to the said content, the codelivery of proteins and small-molecule drugs has emerged as a promising strategy for targeted therapy, offering synergistic effects by combining the unique mechanisms of action of these agents. Recent advancements in nanotechnology have enabled the development of novel platforms that overcome the inherent challenges of codelivery, such as differences in solubility, stability, and pharmacokinetics (Huang et al., 2022).

In recent years, cancer therapies combining protein therapy with photodynamic therapy (PDT) have garnered significant attention, showing promising results in both preclinical and clinical studies. A multifunctional nanocarrier incorporating a photosensitizer (PS) drug was designed, facilitating the targeted intracellular codelivery of both the PS and the protein. This system leveraged reversible protein engineering responsive to ROS to enhance therapeutic precision and efficacy. For the preparation of nanoparticles, RNase A, a protein drug, was conjugated at its lysine residues using a phenylboronic acid linker that is cleavable by $H_2O_2$. This process resulted in the formation of an inactivated prodrug known as RNBC (Fig. 21.5). Ketal-crosslinked, acid-degradable polyethyleneimine (KPEI), a cationic polymer, was employed to form nanocomposites (NCS) with RNBC via electrostatic interactions. This strategy enhances protein stability and significantly promotes cellular internalization. Hyaluronic acid (HA) was coupled with hematoporphyrin (HP), forming a photosensitizer (HA-HP), which was then coated onto the surface of the NCS. This coating improves serum stability by neutralizing positive charges, allowing for prolonged circulation in the bloodstream. Additionally, it enhances tumor accumulation via the EPR effect. Both in vitro and in vivo studies demonstrated that the synergistic combination of PDT mediated by PS and protein-mediated therapy significantly improves anticancer effects (He et al., 2018).

Mitochondria, often referred to as the powerhouses of the cell, are essential organelles responsible for supporting cellular function and metabolism. Mitochondrial dysfunction leads to a range of diseases, including cancer, cardiovascular conditions, and neurodegenerative disorders. As a result, targeting mitochondria represents a promising approach for therapeutic development. Up to now, numerous techniques have been developed to design nanocarriers specifically for mitochondria-targeted drug delivery (Rossmann et al., 2021). In recent years, Liew and colleagues introduced an innovative approach using glutathione (GSH)-responsive nanogel-based carriers for mitochondria-targeted delivery of native proteins and antibodies.

Additionally, they successfully demonstrated the coencapsulation of a protein (RNase A) and a small-molecule drug (DOX) in dual-cargo nanocapsules, enabling mitochondria-targeted combination therapy.

Although significant progress has been made, the codelivery of proteins and drugs remains a considerable challenge due to the contrasting environments required for encapsulating hydrophobic small-molecule drugs and hydrophilic proteins. In fact, hydrophobic small molecules like DOX, containing electron-donating groups (e.g., $-NH_2$ and $-OH$), can conjugate with phenyl boronic acid (BB)-modified polymers through "reversible click" chemistry. Previously, BB-modified RNase A was employed as an ROS-responsive protein

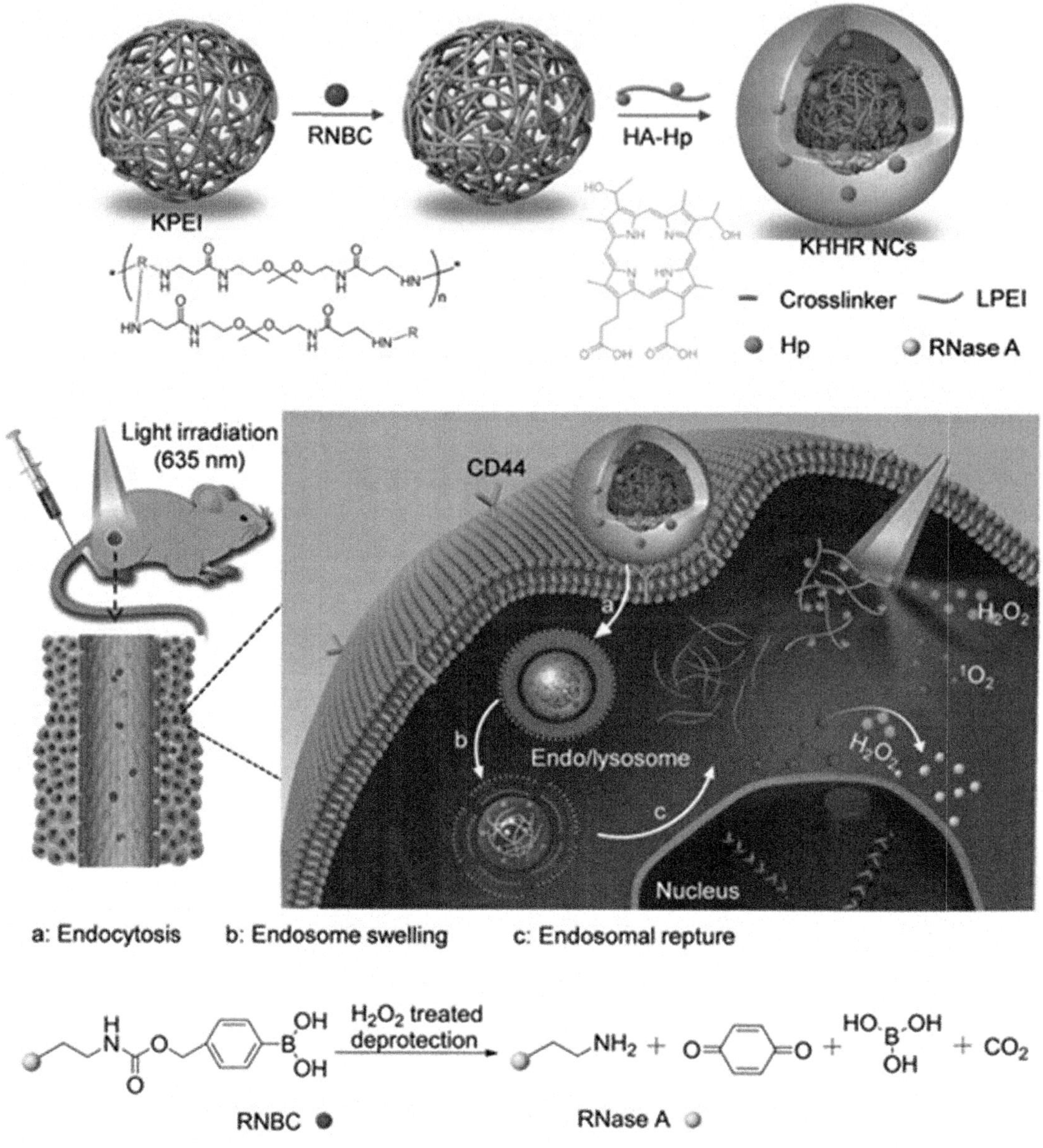


FIGURE 21.5 Schematic presentation of multifunctional nanocarrier incorporating a photosensitizer drug, facilitating the targeted intracellular codelivery of both the photosensitizer and the protein. *Adapted from H. He, Y. Chen, Y. Li, Z. Song, Y. Zhong, R. Zhu, J. Cheng, L. Yin, Effective and selective anti-cancer protein delivery via all-functions-in-one nanocarriers coupled with visible light-responsive, reversible protein engineering. Advanced Functional Materials. 28 (14) (2018), https://doi.org/10.1002/adfm.201706710.*

prodrug. Building on this concept, BB-modified RNase A was utilized to enable the coencapsulation of DOX, resulting in the creation of a dual-cargo, mitochondria-targeted nanotherapeutic with promising potential for combination therapy applications (Liew et al., 2021).

The cornea serves as the primary refractive element of the eye, with its transparency and avascular nature being essential for allowing light to enter. Corneal neovascularization (CNV), characterized by the growth of new blood vessels from the pericorneal vasculature, often arises as a consequence of various corneal disorders. This pathological condition has emerged as one of the major causes of blindness worldwide. Currently, CNV and associated conditions impact the daily lives of millions, posing a significant challenge to ocular health and vision quality globally. A primary therapeutic event in this process is the recruitment of inflammatory cells, which serves as the cornerstone of CNV development (Chen et al., 2020). In a study, Huang and coworkers developed nanosized hexahistidine-metal assemblies (HmA) to encapsulate a broad spectrum of drugs with high loading efficiency. Using a one-pot coassembly approach, they successfully coencapsulated the small-molecule drug dexamethasone phosphate (Dexp) and the protein drug bevacizumab (BVZ) into a single carrier, named Dexp&BVZ@HmA. The results demonstrated that Dexp and BVZ were efficiently loaded into the HmA system. Additionally, the nanocarrier substantially enhanced the bioavailability of both BVZ and Dexp. Most importantly, combination therapy using Dexp&BVZ@HmA outperformed monotherapy in both in vitro and in vivo studies, demonstrating remarkable therapeutic outcomes. This innovative codelivery strategy has great promise for the treatment of anterior segment diseases and other related disorders (Huang et al., 2022).

Recent developments in DDS have enhanced the effectiveness of existing chemotherapy drugs by improving their availability at tumor sites. However, small-molecule drugs typically target only a limited number of tumor-associated factors, overlooking the crucial tumor transcription factors. Cancer, being a genetic disease, has shown promising responsiveness to therapies utilizing short-interfering RNA (siRNA) (Pallathadka et al., 2024). In fact, siRNA has demonstrated its potential as an effective tool for selectively inhibiting specific targets within tumor cells. However, the intrinsic characteristics of siRNA have introduced considerable challenges to its effective therapeutic application. Unmodified naked siRNA, when delivered systemically, is susceptible to rapid degradation by enzymatic digestion. Additionally, siRNA has a molecular weight of approximately 13 kDa, which makes it small enough to be rapidly cleared by the kidneys (Dong et al., 2019). However, due to its larger molecular weight compared to small-molecule drugs, this difference presents challenges for codelivery systems, particularly in terms of biodistribution and pharmacokinetics. Recent advancements in nanomaterials have significantly improved the codelivery of siRNA and small-molecule drugs for cancer treatment. These innovative nanocarriers aim to address the challenges of delivering both therapeutic agents simultaneously, ensuring enhanced efficacy while minimizing side effects (Chung et al., 2021).

Overall, the study by Chung and coworkers provides valuable innovative strategies being explored for the codelivery of siRNA and small-molecule drugs, with the potential to improve the efficacy of cancer therapies and overcome the challenges of drug resistance and side effects. Table 21.1 shows recent nanocarrier systems for codelivery of small-molecule drugs and siRNA in the treatment of cancer (Li et al., 2020b).

**TABLE 21.1** Recent nanocarrier systems for codelivery of small-molecule drugs and siRNA for cancer therapy.

| Ref. | Cell line | Type of cancer | siRNA target | Small-molecule drug | Type of nanocarrier material |
|---|---|---|---|---|---|
| Li et al. (2020a, b) | SKOV3 | Ovarian cancer | siRNA | Doxorubicin | Polymeric micelles |
| Yan et al. (2020) | HUVEC, HepG2 | Liver cancer | BCL2 | Doxorubicin | Polymeric micelles |
| Nasab et al. (2021) | MCF-7, BT-474 | Breast cancer | FAM group | Paclitaxel | Polymeric micelles |
| Xu et al. (2020) | HeLa | Cervical cancer | SPDYE7P | Paclitaxel | Polymeric micelles |
| Zhang et al. (2020b) | NCI-H460 | Lung cancer | BIRC5 | Paclitaxel | Liposome |
| Zhang et al. (2020c) | A2780 ADR, HCT 116, MDA-MB-231 | Ovarian cancer, colorectal carcinoma, and breast cancer | ABCB1 | Doxorubicin | Dendrimer |
| Ghaffari et al. (2020) | HeLa | Cervical cancer | BCL2 | Curcumin | Dendrimer |

## 7. Conclusion

This review presents a comprehensive overview of recent advancements in codelivery systems designed and evaluated for the simultaneous delivery of proteins and small-molecule drugs, aiming to enhance the effectiveness of cancer therapy through synergistic mechanisms. In fact, the synergistic anticancer effects observed in combination therapy result from the interplay between the broad cytotoxic effects of small-molecule drugs and the precise, targeted actions of proteins. However, achieving optimal synergistic effects remains a significant challenge when using conventional methods that involve the simultaneous administration of free proteins and small-molecule drugs. Despite their potential, these approaches are often hindered by limitations such as mismatched pharmacokinetics and biodistribution between the proteins and small-molecule drugs, limited tumor accumulation, inefficient intracellular drug delivery to tumor cells, suboptimal drug-to-protein ratios, short in vivo half-lives, and substantial systemic toxicity. To enhance synergistic effects, numerous nanocarriers have been designed to enable the codelivery of proteins and small-molecule drugs. These nanocarriers are expected to improve the stability of proteins and small-molecule drugs both in vitro and in vivo, optimize the loading amounts and ratios of the therapeutic agents, enhance drug accumulation and precise distribution at tumor sites, and enable the controlled release of multiple therapeutic payloads at specific target locations. In nanocarrier systems, incorporating suitable physical interactions such as electrostatic forces and hydrogen bonding, as well as crosslinking networks or covalent conjugation, has been shown to enhance nanoparticle stability. These approaches facilitate the effective incorporation of proteins, which have significantly distinct physicochemical characteristics compared to small-molecule drugs. Overall, emerging codelivery strategies, including tumor-targeting multifunctional nanocarriers, hold great promise for the precise and efficient delivery of proteins and small-molecule drugs to tumor cells by effectively overcoming multiple biological barriers.

## References


Adams, M.L., Lavasanifar, A., Kwon, G.S., 2003. Amphiphilic block copolymers for drug delivery. J. Pharmaceut. Sci. 92 (7), 1343–1355. https://doi.org/10.1002/jps.10397.

Aibani, N., Khan, T.N., Callan, B., 2020. Liposome mimicking polymersomes; A comparative study of the merits of polymersomes in terms of formulation and stability. Int. J. Pharm. X 2, 100040. https://doi.org/10.1016/j.ijpx.2019.100040.

Al Bostami, R.D., Abuwatfa, W.H., Husseini, G.A., 2022. Recent advances in nanoparticle-based co-delivery systems for cancer therapy. Nanomaterials 12 (15). https://doi.org/10.3390/nano12152672.

Alas, S., Emmanouilides, C., Bonavida, B., 2001. Inhibition of interleukin 10 by rituximab results in down-regulation of Bcl-2 and sensitization of B-cell non-Hodgkin's lymphoma to apoptosis. Clin. Cancer Res. 7 (3), 709–723.

Alavi, M., Hamidi, M., 2019. Passive and active targeting in cancer therapy by liposomes and lipid nanoparticles. Drug Metabolism and Personalized Therapy 34 (1). https://doi.org/10.1515/dmpt-2018-0032.

Anarjan, F.S., 2019. Active targeting drug delivery nanocarriers: Ligands. Nano-Struct. Nano-Objects 19.

Ashrafizadeh, M., Delfi, M., Zarrabi, A., Bigham, A., Sharifi, E., Rabiee, N., Paiva-Santos, A.C., Kumar, A.P., Tan, S. C., Hushmandi, K., Ren, J., Zare, E.N., Makvandi, P., 2022. Stimuli-responsive liposomal nanoformulations in cancer therapy: Pre-clinical & clinical approaches. J. Contr. Release 351, 50–80. https://doi.org/10.1016/j.jconrel.2022.08.001.

Aznar, M.A., Tinari, N., Rullán, A.J., Sánchez-Paulete, A.R., Rodriguez-Ruiz, M.E., Melero, I., 2017. Intratumoral delivery of immunotherapy - act locally, think globally. J. Immunol. 198 (1), 31–39. https://doi.org/10.4049/jimmunol.1601145.

Bajracharya, R., Song, J.G., Patil, B.R., Lee, S.H., Noh, H.M., Kim, D.H., Kim, G.L., Seo, S.H., Park, J.W., Jeong, S.H., Lee, C.H., Han, H.K., 2022. Functional ligands for improving anticancer drug therapy: Current status and applications to drug delivery systems. Drug Deliv. 29 (1), 1959–1970. https://doi.org/10.1080/10717544.2022.2089296.

Bazak, R., Houri, M., El Achy, S., Hussein, W., Refaat, T., 2014. Passive targeting of nanoparticles to cancer: a comprehensive review of the literature. Molecular and Clinical Oncology 2 (6), 904–908. https://doi.org/10.3892/mco.2014.356.

Boisseau, P., Loubaton, B., 2011. Nanomedicine, nanotechnology in medicine. C. R. Phys. 12 (7), 620–636. https://doi.org/10.1016/j.crhy.2011.06.001.

Branden, C.I., Tooze, J., 2012. Introduction to Protein Structure. Garland Science.

Budker, V.G., Monahan, S.D., Subbotin, V.M., 2014. Loco-regional cancer drug therapy: Present approaches and rapidly reversible hydrophobization (RRH) of therapeutic agents as the future direction. Drug Discov. Today 19 (12), 1855–1870. https://doi.org/10.1016/j.drudis.2014.08.009.

Carter, P.J., 2011. Introduction to current and future protein therapeutics: A protein engineering perspective. Exp. Cell Res. 317 (9), 1261–1269. https://doi.org/10.1016/j.yexcr.2011.02.013.

Chen, M., Bao, L., Zhao, M., Cao, J., Zheng, H., 2020. Progress in research on the role of FGF in the formation and treatment of corneal neovascularization. Front. Pharmacol. 11. https://doi.org/10.3389/fphar.2020.00111.

Chen, D., Liu, X., Lu, X., Tian, J., 2023. Nanoparticle drug delivery systems for synergistic delivery of tumor therapy. Front. Pharmacol. 14. https://doi.org/10.3389/fphar.2023.1111991.

Cheng, R., Liu, G., Ma, S., Li, S., Meng, F., Liu, H., Zhong, Z., 2011. Biodegradable chimaeric polymersomes mediate highly efficient delivery of exogenous proteins into cells. J. Contr. Release 152, e136. https://doi.org/10.1016/j.jconrel.2011.08.046.

Cheng, Z., Li, Y., Zhao, D., Zhao, W., Wu, M., Zhang, W., Cui, Y., Zhang, P., Zhang, Z., 2022. Nanocarriers for intracellular co-delivery of proteins and small-molecule drugs for cancer therapy. Front. Bioeng. Biotechnol. 10. https://doi.org/10.3389/fbioe.2022.994655.

Chhabra, M., 2021. Biological Therapeutic Modalities Translational Biotechnology: A Journey from Laboratory to Clinics. Elsevier, United States, pp. 137–164. https://doi.org/10.1016/B978-0-12-821972-0.00015-0.

Chung, S.L., Yee, M.S.L., Hii, L.W., Lim, W.M., Ho, M.Y., Khiew, P.S., Leong, C.O., 2021. Advances in nanomaterials used in co-delivery of sirna and small molecule drugs for cancer treatment. Nanomaterials 11 (10). https://doi.org/10.3390/nano11102467.

Croy, S., Kwon, G., 2006. Polymeric micelles for drug delivery. Curr. Pharm. Des. 12 (36), 4669–4684. https://doi.org/10.2174/138161206779026245.

Dai, W., Wang, X., Song, G., Liu, T., He, B., Zhang, H., Wang, X., Zhang, Q., 2017. Combination antitumor therapy with targeted dual-nanomedicines. Adv. Drug Deliv. Rev. 115, 23–45. https://doi.org/10.1016/j.addr.2017.03.001.

Deng, S., Gigliobianco, M.R., Censi, R., Di Martino, P., 2020. Polymeric nanocapsules as nanotechnological alternative for drug delivery system: Current status, challenges and opportunities. Nanomaterials 10 (5). https://doi.org/10.3390/nano10050847.

Dong, Y., Siegwart, D.J., Anderson, D.G., 2019. Strategies, design, and chemistry in siRNA delivery systems. Adv. Drug Deliv. Rev. 144, 133–147. https://doi.org/10.1016/j.addr.2019.05.004.

Du, J.Z., Du, X.J., Mao, C.Q., Wang, J., 2011. Tailor-Made dual pH-sensitive polymer-doxorubicin nanoparticles for efficient anticancer drug delivery. J. Am. Chem. Soc. 133 (44), 17560–17563. https://doi.org/10.1021/ja207150n.

Duarte, D., Vale, N., 2022. Evaluation of synergism in drug combinations and reference models for future orientations in oncology. Curr. Res. Pharmacol. Drug Discov. 3, 100110. https://doi.org/10.1016/j.crphar.2022.100110.

Durymanov, M.O., Rosenkranz, A.A., Sobolev, A.S., 2015. Current approaches for improving intratumoral accumulation and distribution of nanomedicines. Federation Theranostics 5 (9), 1007–1020. https://doi.org/10.7150/thno.11742.

Ebrahimi, S.B., Samanta, D., 2023. Engineering protein-based therapeutics through structural and chemical design. Nat. Commun. 14 (1). https://doi.org/10.1038/s41467-023-38039-x.

Elsabahy, M., Wooley, K.L., 2012. Design of polymeric nanoparticles for biomedical delivery applications. Chem. Soc. Rev. 41 (7), 2545–2561. https://doi.org/10.1039/c2cs15327k.

Ezike, T.C., Okpala, U.S., Onoja, U.L., Nwike, C.P., Ezeako, E.C., Okpara, O.J., Okoroafor, C.C., Eze, S.C., Kalu, O.L., Odoh, E.C., Nwadike, U.G., Ogbodo, J.O., Umeh, B.U., Ossai, E.C., Nwanguma, B.C., 2023. Advances in drug delivery systems, challenges and future directions. Heliyon 9 (6). https://doi.org/10.1016/j.heliyon.2023.e17488.

Fu, Y., Tang, R., Zhao, X., 2023. Engineering cytokines for cancer immunotherapy: a systematic review. Front. Immunol. 14. https://doi.org/10.3389/fimmu.2023.1218082.

García, M.C., 2019. Stimuli-Responsive Polymersomes for Drug Delivery Applications. Elsevier BV, pp. 345–392. https://doi.org/10.1016/b978-0-08-101995-5.00019-2.

Ghaffari, M., Dehghan, G., Baradaran, B., Zarebkohan, A., Mansoori, B., Soleymani, J., Ezzati Nazhad Dolatabadi, J., Hamblin, M.R., 2020. Co-delivery of curcumin and Bcl-2 siRNA by PAMAM dendrimers for enhancement of the therapeutic efficacy in HeLa cancer cells. Colloids Surf. B Biointerfaces 188. https://doi.org/10.1016/j.colsurfb.2019.110762.

Gurevich, E.V., Gurevich, V.V., 2014. Therapeutic potential of small molecules and engineered proteins. Handb. Exp. Pharmacol. 219, 1–12. https://doi.org/10.1007/978-3-642-41199-1_1.

Haider, M., Zaki, K.Z., El Hamshary, M.R., Hussain, Z., Orive, G., Ibrahim, H.O., 2022. Polymeric nanocarriers: a promising tool for early diagnosis and efficient treatment of colorectal cancer. J. Adv. Res. 39, 237–255. https://doi.org/10.1016/j.jare.2021.11.008.

Hariharan, A., Tran, S.D., 2023. Localized drug delivery systems: an update on treatment options for head and neck squamous cell carcinomas. Pharmaceutics 15 (7). https://doi.org/10.3390/pharmaceutics15071844.

Hashida, M., 2020. Role of pharmacokinetic consideration for the development of drug delivery systems: a historical overview. Adv. Drug Deliv. Rev. 157, 71–82. https://doi.org/10.1016/j.addr.2020.06.015.

He, C., Tang, Z., Tian, H., Chen, X., 2016. Co-delivery of chemotherapeutics and proteins for synergistic therapy. Adv. Drug Deliv. Rev. 98, 64–76. https://doi.org/10.1016/j.addr.2015.10.021.

He, H., Chen, Y., Li, Y., Song, Z., Zhong, Y., Zhu, R., Cheng, J., Yin, L., 2018. Effective and selective anti-cancer protein delivery via all-functions-in-one nanocarriers coupled with visible light-responsive, reversible protein engineering. Adv. Funct. Mater. 28 (14). https://doi.org/10.1002/adfm.201706710.

Hsu, C.Y., Rheima, A.M., Kadhim, M.M., Ahmed, N.N., Mohammed, S.H., Abbas, F.H., Abed, Z.T., Mahdi, Z.M., Abbas, Z.S., Hachim, S.K., Ali, F.K., Mahmoud, Z.H., Kianfar, E., 2023. An overview of nanoparticles in drug delivery: Properties and applications. S. Afr. J. Chem. Eng. 46, 233–270. https://doi.org/10.1016/j.sajce.2023.08.009.

Huang, W., Wang, L., Yang, R., Hu, R., Zheng, Q., Zan, X., 2022. Combined delivery of small molecule and protein drugs as synergistic therapeutics for treating corneal neovascularization by a one-pot coassembly strategy. Mater. Today Bio 17, 100456. https://doi.org/10.1016/j.mtbio.2022.100456.

Idris, D.S., Roy, A., Pandit, S., Alghamdi, S., Almehmadi, M., Alsaiari, A.A., Abdulaziz, O., Alsharif, A., Khandaker, M.U., Faruque, M.R.I., 2023. Polymer-based nanocarriers for biomedical and environmental applications. E-polymers 23 (1). https://doi.org/10.1515/epoly-2023-0049.

Jain, K.K., 2008. Drug delivery systems - an overview. Methods Mol. Biol. 437, 1–50. https://doi.org/10.1007/978-1-59745-210-6_1.

Ji, T., Kohane, D.S., 2019. Nanoscale systems for local drug delivery. Nano Today 28, 100765. https://doi.org/10.1016/j.nantod.2019.100765.

Jiang, T., Mo, R., Bellotti, A., Zhou, J., Gu, Z., 2014. Gel-liposome-mediated co-delivery of anticancer membrane-associated proteins and small-molecule drugs for enhanced therapeutic efficacy. Adv. Funct. Mater. 24 (16), 2295–2304. https://doi.org/10.1002/adfm.201303222.

Kannavou, M., Natsaridis, E., Missirlis, A., 2024. Liposomes for drug delivery by localized routes of administration liposomes. In: Drug Delivery: what, where, How and when to Deliver. Elsevier, Greece, pp. 329–362. https://doi.org/10.1016/B978-0-443-15491-1.00025-0.

Kędzierska, M., Bańkosz, M., 2024. Role of proteins in oncology: Advances in cancer diagnosis, prognosis, and targeted therapy—a narrative review. J. Clin. Med. 13 (23), 7131. https://doi.org/10.3390/jcm13237131.

Kim, C.S., Mout, R., Zhao, Y., Yeh, Y.C., Tang, R., Jeong, Y., Duncan, B., Hardy, J.A., Rotello, V.M., 2015. Co-delivery of protein and small molecule therapeutics using nanoparticle-stabilized nanocapsules. Bioconjug. Chem. 26 (5), 950–954. https://doi.org/10.1021/acs.bioconjchem.5b00146.

Kintzing, J.R., Filsinger Interrante, M.V., Cochran, J.R., 2016. Emerging strategies for developing next-generation protein therapeutics for cancer treatment. Trends Pharmacol. Sci. 37 (12), 993–1008. https://doi.org/10.1016/j.tips.2016.10.005.

Ko, D.Y., Shinde, U.P., Yeon, B., Jeong, B., 2013. Recent progress of in situ formed gels for biomedical applications. Prog. Polym. Sci. 38 (3–4), 672–701. https://doi.org/10.1016/j.progpolymsci.2012.08.002.

Kreuter, J., 2007. Nanoparticles—a historical perspective. Int. J. Pharm. 331 (1), 1–10. https://doi.org/10.1016/j.ijpharm.2006.10.021.

Kumar, A., 2021. A comprehensive review on polymeric micelles: a promising drug delivery carrier. Journal of Analytical & Pharmaceutical Research 10 (3), 102–107. https://doi.org/10.15406/japlr.2021.10.00372.

Kuperkar, K., Patel, D., Atanase, L.I., Bahadur, P., 2022. Amphiphilic block copolymers: their structures, and self-assembly to polymeric micelles and polymersomes as drug delivery vehicles. Polymers 14 (21). https://doi.org/10.3390/polym14214702.

Lammers, T., Kiessling, F., Hennink, W.E., Storm, G., 2012. Drug targeting to tumors: Principles, pitfalls and (pre-) clinical progress. J. Contr. Release 161 (2), 175–187. https://doi.org/10.1016/j.jconrel.2011.09.063.

Lee, J.S., Feijen, J., 2012. Polymersomes for drug delivery: Design, formation and characterization. J. Contr. Release 161 (2), 473–483. https://doi.org/10.1016/j.jconrel.2011.10.005.

Letchford, K., Burt, H., 2007. A review of the formation and classification of amphiphilic block copolymer nanoparticulate structures: micelles, nanospheres, nanocapsules and polymersomes. Eur. J. Pharm. Biopharm. 65 (3), 259–269. https://doi.org/10.1016/j.ejpb.2006.11.009.

Li, R., Li, Q., Ji, Q., 2020a. Molecular targeted study in tumors: from western medicine to active ingredients of traditional Chinese medicine. Biomed. Pharmacother. 121. https://doi.org/10.1016/j.biopha.2019.109624.

Li, Z., Feng, H., Jin, L., Zhang, Y., Tian, X., Li, J., 2020b. Polymeric micelle with pH-induced variable size and doxorubicin and siRNA co-delivery for synergistic cancer therapy. Appl. Nanosci. 10 (6), 1903–1913. https://doi.org/10.1007/s13204-020-01263-8.

Li, J., Wang, Q., Xia, G., Adilijiang, N., Li, Y., Hou, Z., Fan, Z., Li, J., 2023. Recent advances in targeted drug delivery strategy for enhancing oncotherapy. Pharmaceutics 15 (9). https://doi.org/10.3390/pharmaceutics15092233.

Liew, S.S., Zhou, J., Li, L., Yao, S.Q., 2021. Co-delivery of proteins and small molecule drugs for mitochondria-targeted combination therapy. Chem. Commun. 57 (26), 3215–3218. https://doi.org/10.1039/d0cc08020a.

Lima, A.L., Gratieri, T., Cunha-Filho, M., Gelfuso, G.M., 2022. Polymeric nanocapsules: a review on design and production methods for pharmaceutical purpose. Methods 199, 54–66. https://doi.org/10.1016/j.ymeth.2021.07.009.

Ling, D., Hackett, M.J., Hyeon, T., 2014. Surface ligands in synthesis, modification, assembly and biomedical applications of nanoparticles. Nano Today 9 (4), 457–477. https://doi.org/10.1016/j.nantod.2014.06.005.

Liu, G.H., Chen, T., Zhang, X., Ma, X.L., Shi, H.S., 2022. Small molecule inhibitors targeting the cancers. MedComm 3 (4). https://doi.org/10.1002/mco2.181.

LoRusso, P.M., Weiss, D., Guardino, E., Girish, S., Sliwkowski, M.X., 2011. Trastuzumab emtansine: a unique antibody-drug conjugate in development for human epidermal growth factor receptor 2-positive cancer. Clin. Cancer Res. 17 (20), 6437–6447. https://doi.org/10.1158/1078-0432.CCR-11-0762.

Ma, Y.S., Xin, R., Yang, X.L., Shi, Y., Zhang, D.D., Wang, H.M., Wang, P.Y., Liu, J.B., Chu, K.J., Fu, D., 2021. Paving the way for small-molecule drug discovery. Am. J. Tourism Res. 13 (3), 853–870.

Maeda, H., 2021. The 35th anniversary of the discovery of EPR effect: a new wave of nanomedicines for tumor-targeted drug delivery—personal remarks and future prospects. J. Personalized Med. 11 (3), 229. https://doi.org/10.3390/jpm11030229.

Marques, A.C., Costa, P.J., Velho, S., Amaral, M.H., 2020. Functionalizing nanoparticles with cancer-targeting antibodies: a comparison of strategies. J. Contr. Release 320, 180–200. https://doi.org/10.1016/j.jconrel.2020.01.035.

Mehta, M., Bui, T.A., Yang, X., Aksoy, Y., Goldys, E.M., Deng, W., 2023. Lipid-based nanoparticles for drug/gene delivery: an overview of the production techniques and difficulties encountered in their industrial development. ACS Mater. Au 3 (6), 600–619. https://doi.org/10.1021/acsmaterialsau.3c00032.

Mokhtari, R.B., Homayouni, T.S., Baluch, N., Morgatskaya, E., Kumar, S., Das, B., Yeger, H., 2017. Combination therapy in combating cancer. Oncotarget 8 (23), 38022–38043. https://doi.org/10.18632/oncotarget.16723.

Nasab, S.H., Amani, A., Ebrahimi, H.A., Hamidi, A.A., 2021. Design and preparation of a new multi-targeted drug delivery system using multifunctional nanoparticles for co-delivery of siRNA and paclitaxel. J. Pharm. Anal. 11 (2), 163–173. https://doi.org/10.1016/j.jpha.2020.04.005.

Norouzi, M., Nazari, B., Miller, D.W., 2016. Injectable hydrogel-based drug delivery systems for local cancer therapy. Drug Discov. Today 21 (11), 1835–1849. https://doi.org/10.1016/j.drudis.2016.07.006.

Pallathadka, H., Hsu, C.Y., Obaid Saleh, R., Renuka Jyothi, S., Kumar, A., Yumashev, A., Sinha, A., Hussein Zwamel, A., Abed Jawad, M., Alsaadi, S.B., 2024. Specific small interfering RNAs (siRNAs) for targeting the metastasis, immune responses, and drug resistance of colorectal cancer cells (CRC). Int. Immunopharmacol. 140. https://doi.org/10.1016/j.intimp.2024.112730.

Panta, P., Kim, D.Y., Kwon, J.S., Son, A.R., Lee, K.W., Kim, M.S., 2014. Protein drug-loaded polymeric nanoparticles. J. Biomed. Sci. Eng. 07 (10), 825–832. https://doi.org/10.4236/jbise.2014.710082.

Qin, S.Y., Cheng, Y.J., Lei, Q., Zhang, A.Q., Zhang, X.Z., 2018. Combinational strategy for high-performance cancer chemotherapy. Biomaterials 171, 178–197. https://doi.org/10.1016/j.biomaterials.2018.04.027.

Qin, X., Yu, C., Wei, J., Li, L., Zhang, C., Wu, Q., Liu, J., Yao, S.Q., Huang, W., 2019. Rational Design of nanocarriers for intracellular protein delivery. Adv. Mater. 31 (46). https://doi.org/10.1002/adma.201902791.

Rolfes, C., Howard, S., Ryan, G., Paul, A., 2012. Localized Drug Delivery for Cardiothoracic Surgery. InTech. https://doi.org/10.5772/48577.

Rossmann, M.P., Dubois, S.M., Agarwal, S., Zon, L.I., 2021. Mitochondrial function in development and disease. DMM Disease Models and Mechanisms 14 (6). https://doi.org/10.1242/dmm.048912.

Scaletti, F., Hardie, J., Lee, Y.W., Luther, D.C., Ray, M., Rotello, V.M., 2018. Protein delivery into cells using inorganic nanoparticle-protein supramolecular assemblies. Chem. Soc. Rev. 47 (10), 3421–3432. https://doi.org/10.1039/c8cs00008e.

Seo, S.H., Han, H.D., Noh, K.H., Kim, T.W., Son, S.W., 2009. Chitosan hydrogel containing GMCSF and a cancer drug exerts synergistic anti-tumor effects via the induction of CD8+ T cell-mediated anti-tumor immunity. Clin. Exp. Metastasis 26 (3), 179–187. https://doi.org/10.1007/s10585-008-9228-5.

Shi, P., Cheng, Z., Zhao, K., Chen, Y., Zhang, A., Gan, W., Zhang, Y., 2023. Active targeting schemes for nano-drug delivery systems in osteosarcoma therapeutics. J. Nanobiotechnol. 21 (1). https://doi.org/10.1186/s12951-023-01826-1.

Sousa, F., 2024. Emerging cytokine delivery with nanomedicine for brain cancer treatment. Expet Opin. Drug Deliv. 21 (4), 513–516. https://doi.org/10.1080/17425247.2024.2347320.

Spitzer, M., Robbins, N., Wright, G.D., 2017. Combinatorial strategies for combating invasive fungal infections. Virulence 8 (2), 169–185. https://doi.org/10.1080/21505594.2016.1196300.

Srikrishna, S., Cardozo, L., 2013. The vagina as a route for drug delivery: a review. International Urogynecology Journal 24 (4), 537–543. https://doi.org/10.1007/s00192-012-2009-3.

Su, S., Wang, Y.Y., Du, F.S., Lu, H., Li, Z.C., 2018. Dynamic covalent bond-assisted programmed and traceless protein release: high loading nanogel for systemic and cytosolic delivery. Adv. Funct. Mater. 28 (48). https://doi.org/10.1002/adfm.201805287.

Subhan, M.A., Yalamarty, S.S.K., Filipczak, N., Parveen, F., Torchilin, V.P., 2021. Recent advances in tumor targeting via epr effect for cancer treatment. J. Personalized Med. 11 (6). https://doi.org/10.3390/jpm11060571.

Tang, P., Shen, T., Wang, H., Zhang, R., Zhang, X., Li, X., Xiao, W., 2023. Challenges and opportunities for improving the druggability of natural product: why need drug delivery system? Biomed. Pharmacother. 164. https://doi.org/10.1016/j.biopha.2023.114955.

ten Hagen, T.L.M., Seynhaeve, A.L.B., van Tiel, S.T., Ruiter, D.J., Eggermont, A.M.M., 2002. Pegylated liposomal tumor necrosis factor-α results in reduced toxicity and synergistic antitumor activity after systemic administration in combination with liposomal doxorubicin (Doxil®) in soft tissue sarcoma-bearing rats. Int. J. Cancer 97 (1), 115–120. https://doi.org/10.1002/ijc.1578.

Tewabe, A., Abate, A., Tamrie, M., Seyfu, A., Siraj, E.A., 2021. Targeted drug delivery — from magic bullet to nanomedicine: Principles, challenges, and future perspectives. J. Multidiscip. Healthc. 14, 1711–1724. https://doi.org/10.2147/JMDH.S313968.

Urbán-Morlán, Z., Serrano-Mora, L.E., Martínez-Acevedo, L., Leyva-Gómez, G., Mendoza-Muñoz, N., Quintanar-Guerrero, D., 2020. New Developments in Intrauterine Drug Delivery Systems and Devices Drug Delivery Devices and Therapeutic Systems. Elsevier, Mexico, pp. 601–622. https://doi.org/10.1016/B978-0-12-819838-4.00018-3.

Van Der Veen, A.H., De Wilt, J.H.W., Eggermont, A.M.M., Van Tiel, S.T., Seynhaeve, A.L.B., Ten Hagen, T.L.M., 2000. TNF-α augments intratumoural concentrations of doxorubicin in TNF-α-based isolated limb perfusion in rat sarcoma models and enhances anti-tumour effects. Br. J. Cancer 82 (4), 973–980. https://doi.org/10.1054/bjoc.1999.1027.

Verma, A.K., Chanchal, A., Maitra, A., 2010. Co-polymeric hydrophilic nanospheres for drug delivery: Release kinetics, and cellular uptake. Indian J. Exp. Biol. 48 (10), 1043–1052.

Wang, X., Zhang, H., Chen, X., 2019. Drug resistance and combating drug resistance in cancer. Cancer Drug Resistance 2 (2), 141–160. https://doi.org/10.20517/cdr.2019.10.

Wu, J., Sahoo, J.K., Li, Y., Xu, Q., Kaplan, D.L., 2022. Challenges in delivering therapeutic peptides and proteins: a silk-based solution. J. Contr. Release 345, 176–189. https://doi.org/10.1016/j.jconrel.2022.02.011.

Xu, C., Liu, W., Hu, Y., Li, W., Di, W., 2020. Bioinspired tumor-homing nanoplatform for co-delivery of paclitaxel and siRNA-E7 to HPV-related cervical malignancies for synergistic therapy. Theranostics 10 (7), 3325–3339. https://doi.org/10.7150/thno.41228.

Yadav, H.K.S., Almokdad, A.A., Shaluf, S.I.M., Debe, M.S., 2018. Polymer-Based Nanomaterials for Drug-Delivery Carriers Nanocarriers for Drug Delivery: Nanoscience and Nanotechnology in Drug Delivery. Elsevier Science Ltd., United Arab Emirates, pp. 531–556. https://doi.org/10.1016/B978-0-12-814033-8.00017-5.

Yan, T., Zhu, S., Hui, W., He, J., Liu, Z., Cheng, J., 2020. Chitosan based pH-responsive polymeric prodrug vector for enhanced tumor targeted co-delivery of doxorubicin and siRNA. Carbohydr. Polym. 250, 116781. https://doi.org/10.1016/j.carbpol.2020.116781.

Yang, Y., Liu, P., Zhou, M., Yin, L., Wang, M., Liu, T., Jiang, X., Gao, H., 2024. Small-molecule drugs of colorectal cancer: Current status and future directions. Biochim. Biophys. Acta Mol. Basis Dis. 1870 (1), 166880. https://doi.org/10.1016/j.bbadis.2023.166880.

Yao, Y., Zhou, Y., Liu, L., Xu, Y., Chen, Q., Wang, Y., Wu, S., Deng, Y., Zhang, J., Shao, A., 2020. Nanoparticle-based drug delivery in cancer therapy and its role in overcoming drug resistance. Front. Mol. Biosci. 7. https://doi.org/10.3389/fmolb.2020.00193.

Yau, A., Lee, J., Chen, Y., 2021. Nanomaterials for protein delivery in anticancer applications. Pharmaceutics 13 (2), 155. https://doi.org/10.3390/pharmaceutics13020155.

Yu, B., Tai, H.C., Xue, W., Lee, L.J., Lee, R.J., 2010. Receptor-targeted nanocarriers for therapeutic delivery to cancer. Mol. Membr. Biol. 27 (7), 286–298. https://doi.org/10.3109/09687688.2010.521200.

Yu, M., Wu, J., Shi, J., Farokhzad, O.C., 2016. Nanotechnology for protein delivery: Overview and perspectives. J. Contr. Release 240, 24–37. https://doi.org/10.1016/j.jconrel.2015.10.012.

Zeinali, M., Abbaspour-Ravasjani, S., Ghorbani, M., Babazadeh, A., Soltanfam, T., Santos, A.C., Hamishehkar, H., Hamblin, M.R., 2020. Nanovehicles for co-delivery of anticancer agents. Drug Discov. Today 25 (8), 1416–1430. https://doi.org/10.1016/j.drudis.2020.06.027.

Zhang, C., Zhang, S., Zhi, D., Zhao, Y., Cui, S., Cui, J., 2020a. Co-delivery of paclitaxel and survivin siRNA with cationic liposome for lung cancer therapy. Colloids Surf. A Physicochem. Eng. Asp. 585, 124054. https://doi.org/10.1016/j.colsurfa.2019.124054.

Zhang, P., Zhang, Y., Ding, X., Shen, W., Li, M., Wagner, E., Xiao, C., Chen, X., 2020b. A multistage cooperative nanoplatform enables intracellular co-delivery of proteins and chemotherapeutics for cancer therapy. Adv. Mater. 32 (46). https://doi.org/10.1002/adma.202000013.

Zhang, X., Pan, J., Yao, M., Palmerston Mendes, L., Sarisozen, C., Mao, S., Torchilin, V.P., 2020c. Charge reversible hyaluronic acid-modified dendrimer-based nanoparticles for siMDR-1 and doxorubicin co-delivery. Eur. J. Pharm. Biopharm. 154, 43–49. https://doi.org/10.1016/j.ejpb.2020.06.019.

Zhang, Y., Zhang, Y., Zhang, G., Wu, J., Wang, L., Dong, Z., Yi, Z., Huang, Q., Zou, M., Liao, R., Wang, F., Liang, P., 2024. Recent advances and clinical challenges of phototherapeutic nanoparticles in cancer monotherapy or combination therapy. Coord. Chem. Rev. 518, 216069. https://doi.org/10.1016/j.ccr.2024.216069.

Zhao, Z., Ukidve, A., Kim, J., Mitragotri, S., 2020. Targeting strategies for tissue-specific drug delivery. Cell 181 (1), 151–167. https://doi.org/10.1016/j.cell.2020.02.001.

Zhong, L., Li, Y., Xiong, L., Wang, W., Wu, M., Yuan, T., Yang, W., Tian, C., Miao, Z., Wang, T., Yang, S., 2021. Small molecules in targeted cancer therapy: advances, challenges, and future perspectives. Signal Transduct. Targeted Ther. 6 (1). https://doi.org/10.1038/s41392-021-00572-w.

Zhu, Y., Xu, L., Kang, Y., Cheng, Q., He, Y., Ji, X., 2024. Platelet-derived drug delivery systems: Pioneering treatment for cancer, cardiovascular diseases, infectious diseases, and beyond. Biomaterials 306, 122478. https://doi.org/10.1016/j.biomaterials.2024.122478.

CHAPTER

# 22

# Antibody–drug conjugated (ADC) nanoparticles for target-specific drug delivery nanocarriers in drug delivery

*Mahsa Nikbakht*[1], *Morteza Hosseini*[1], *Hodjattallah Rabbani*[2] *and Masoud Montazer*[1]

[1]Nanobiosensors Lab, Department of Life Science Engineering, Faculty of New Sciences & Technologies, University of Tehran, Tehran, Iran; [2]Monoclonal Antibody Research Center, Avicenna Research Institute, ACECR, Tehran, Iran

## 1. An overview of drug delivery

Developing an effective drug delivery system involves four critical steps: retention, evasion, targeting, and release. For such a system to function optimally, the therapeutic payload must remain stable throughout the processes of formulation and administration. Furthermore, the delivery system must successfully evade immune system detection, allowing it to circulate through the bloodstream long enough to reach its intended site of action. Targeting, whether passive or active, is crucial to ensure the drug selectively accumulates in the target tissue, organ, or cell, thereby minimizing off-target effects and maximizing therapeutic efficacy. Lastly, the system must be designed to release the drug at a controlled rate, ensuring that the therapeutic agent remains at the site of action long enough to achieve the desired effect while avoiding premature release or dose dumping (Mills and Needham, 1999).

Historically, the targeting step posed a significant challenge in the design of optimal drug delivery systems. While retention, evasion, and release had been addressed to some degree,

*Protein-Based Nanoparticles in Drug Delivery*
https://doi.org/10.1016/B978-0-443-33639-3.00013-1

the precise targeting of drugs remained elusive. The idea of targeted therapy, however, is not a recent concept and dates back to 1906, when Paul Ehrlich introduced the pioneering notion of a "magic bullet," a therapeutic agent capable of specifically homing in on diseased cells while sparing healthy ones (Mills and Needham, 1999; Fahmy et al., 2005).

Since then, significant advances have been made in the field of targeted drug delivery. However, the development of an ideal system remains challenging due to numerous biological and physiological barriers encountered en route to the target site. A successful targeted delivery system must effectively evade the immune system, particularly by avoiding recognition and clearance by the reticuloendothelial system (RES). Additionally, it should be biodegradable, ensuring that it is safely metabolized and eliminated from the body after fulfilling its therapeutic purpose. Moreover, the system must exhibit high specificity, selectively accumulating at the intended site of action while minimizing off-target effects. These challenges—immune evasion, biodegradability, and specificity—represent some of the most significant obstacles that continue to hinder the optimization of an ideal targeted drug delivery system. To overcome these challenges, various strategies have been developed to equip drug delivery platforms with precise targeting capabilities.

To explore the novel advancements in targeted drug delivery systems, particularly the focus of this chapter on antibody–drug conjugated nanoparticles, it is essential first to define the three primary strategies used to achieve targeted delivery of therapeutic agents.

1. Physical targeting
2. Chemical targeting
3. Biological targeting

A thorough understanding of these strategies provides the necessary foundation for discussing the mechanisms by which drugs are directed to specific sites within the body. This also leads to the core focus of this chapter: the use of antibody-drug conjugated nanoparticles as a promising platform for targeted drug delivery (Mills and Needham, 1999).

## 1.1 Physical targeting

This strategy refers to drug delivery systems that exploit the physical properties of the therapeutic agent, such as its size, composition, or structural characteristics, to facilitate preferential accumulation at target sites, rather than relying on specific ligand–receptor interactions. In some cases, these systems can be further enhanced by applying external stimuli, such as magnetic fields or thermal energy, to increase drug concentration at the desired location. This method results in spatial targeting and spatiotemporal control compared to nontargeted therapies, through minimal invasiveness. Physical targeting can be categorized into two subgroups (Mills and Needham, 1999; Sun et al., 2020).

## 1.2 Nonspecific mechanisms

This subtype relies on the inherent physical characteristics of the drug carrier—such as particle size, shape, surface charge, or a combination of these factors—to influence its distribution and retention within specific areas of the body. These factors enable passive targeting through phenomena like the enhanced permeability and retention (EPR) effect, which promotes accumulation in tumor tissues due to leaky vasculature (Mills and Needham, 1999).

The EPR effect, first proposed by Matsumura and Maeda in 1986, describes how defective tumor vasculature, along with the overproduction of vascular mediators, allows drug carriers of suitable size to accumulate within the tumor microenvironment. This phenomenon enables drug delivery systems to selectively penetrate and retain tumor tissue. Furthermore, it is now well established that conditions beyond solid tumors, such as inflammation and hypoxia, can also increase vascular permeability and lead to leakage, facilitating similar accumulation of therapeutic agents in these affected regions (Torchilin, 2011; Zi et al., 2022).

## 1.3 External control

External stimuli, such as magnetic fields, ultrasound, or electric fields, can be applied to guide and enhance the accumulation of therapeutic agents at the target site. These externally controlled methods provide a level of precision in drug delivery, allowing for greater control over where and when the drug is concentrated in the body, thus potentially reducing off-target effects (Mills and Needham, 1999).

Ultrasound waves, which propagate through a medium by inducing compression and pressure fluctuations, have long been employed in clinical practice as noninvasive imaging modalities, typically at frequencies around 2 MHz. More recently, therapeutic applications of ultrasound at lower frequencies, ranging from 20 kHz to 2 MHz, have garnered significant attention. These applications encompass tumor and neurological ablation, sonodynamic therapy, wound healing, bone fracture repair, and more. In addition to its direct therapeutic effects, ultrasound can also act as a physical trigger to enhance the targeted delivery of drugs, improving their localization and efficacy at the intended site of action (Sun et al., 2020).

In a recent study, Du and colleagues developed an innovative ultrasound- and pH-responsive polymersome based on the self-assembly of poly(ethylene oxide)-block-poly(2-(diethylamino)ethyl methacrylate)-stat-poly(methoxyethyl methacrylate) [PEO-b-P (DEA-stat-MEMA)]. In this design, the MEMA component confers ultrasound responsiveness, while the poly(2-(diethylamino) ethyl methacrylate) (PDEA) segment imparts pH sensitivity. This dual-responsive strategy leverages the benefits of noninvasive ultrasound waves, which can penetrate tissues at any depth and be applied externally to a targeted organ, as well as the acidic tumor microenvironment to enhance drug release (Wei et al., 2020).

Experiments showed that ultrasound sonication facilitated the rearrangement of hydrophobic segments within the block copolymers, resulting in alterations to the size of the polymersome. Additionally, in vivo experiments revealed that sonication significantly accelerated the release of the encapsulated drug from the polymersomes, leading to a 95% reduction in tumor growth without observed side effects. This approach underscores the potential of ultrasound-responsive drug delivery systems for effective and safe tumor treatment (Wei et al., 2020).

Light is another commonly employed physical trigger in therapeutic interventions due to its ability to elicit diverse effects, such as heat generation, degradation of photosensitive molecules, chemical structure modification, dye bleaching, and luminescence. These unique properties have made light a valuable tool in both diagnostic and therapeutic applications, particularly in dermatology, where its limited tissue penetration is advantageous for treating superficial skin conditions. Moreover, light can function as a precise trigger for targeted drug delivery, enabling site-specific activation of therapeutic agents, thereby enhancing treatment efficacy and minimizing off-target effects (Sun et al., 2020).

Sodano and colleagues developed a hybrid, mixed-micelle-like nanoparticle platform capable of delivering doxorubicin (DOX) alongside a light-regulated release of nitric oxide (NO). This system combines an NO photodonor with an amphiphilic block copolymer, enabling the synergistic release of both DOX and NO under light exposure. This dual-release mechanism enhances the therapeutic efficacy of the platform for treating cancers of the lung, intestine, and skin by providing controlled, on-demand release that increases localized drug and NO concentrations, potentially improving therapeutic outcomes (Sun et al., 2020; Sodano et al., 2020).

Magnetic fields represent another class of physical triggers, distinguished by their unique properties. Unlike other triggers, magnetic fields interact minimally with biological tissues, rendering them biologically inert. Additionally, their ability to penetrate deep into tissues offers significant advantages for therapeutic applications. The efficacy of magnetic fields in enhancing drug targeting primarily depends on the design of the drug carrier system, which typically consists of conventional carrier materials integrated with magnetically responsive components, such as paramagnetic, ferromagnetic, or superparamagnetic materials. These magnetic components enable precise control over the localization and release of therapeutic agents, improving the specificity and effectiveness of drug delivery (Sun et al., 2020; Torchilin, 2011).

Lu and colleagues developed a dual-responsive thermosensitive magnetic liposome (TML) system designed to coencapsulate Camptosar (CPT-11) and citric acid-coated magnetic $Fe_3O_4$ nanoparticles within its aqueous core. The surface of the liposomes was conjugated with Cetuximab (CET) to target the overexpressed epidermal growth factor receptor (EGFR) on human primary glioblastoma cells (U87). Upon exposure to a high-frequency alternating magnetic field (AMF), the temperature of the TMLs increases, triggering controlled drug release. This release occurs following CET-mediated endocytosis, allowing the targeted delivery of CPT-11 to glioblastoma cells. This approach demonstrates the potential of dual-responsive nanocarriers for targeted, on-demand drug delivery in cancer therapy (Lu et al., 2019).

Electrically based drug delivery represents an innovative class of physical targeting approaches, encompassing technologies such as iontophoresis and electroporation. Additionally, materials with intrinsic responsiveness to electrical stimuli are being investigated to enhance targeted delivery and controlled release of payloads. These approaches have shown promising results in transdermal and ocular drug delivery systems, where controlled electrical stimulation can facilitate precise and targeted drug administration across biological barriers (Sun et al., 2020).

In a recent study, Qu and colleagues developed a dual-responsive injectable hydrogel as a smart drug delivery platform for model drugs amoxicillin and ibuprofen. This hydrogel was synthesized by cross-linking a chitosan-graft-polyaniline (CP) copolymer with oxidized dextran (OD), resulting in a system with both electro- and pH-responsive properties, as well as intrinsic antibacterial activity. As an electrically responsive platform, the hydrogel exhibited an “on–off” pulsatile drug release when exposed to high voltage, highlighting its potential as a controlled, stimulus-responsive drug carrier (Qu et al., 2018) (Fig. 22.1).

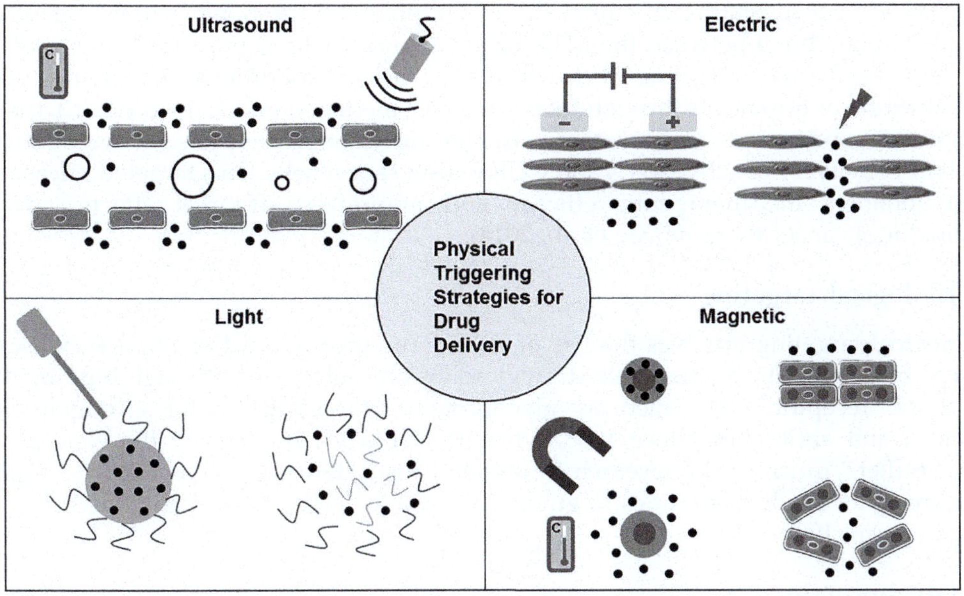


FIGURE 22.1 External stimuli for physical targeting: ultrasound, electric field, light, and magnetic field can be applied to guide and enhance the accumulation of therapeutic agent state target site. *Reprinted from Sun, T., Dasgupta, A., Zhao, Z., Nurunnabi, M., Mitragotri, S., 2020. Physical triggering strategies for drug delivery. Adv. Drug Deliv. Rev. 158, 36–62 with permission from Elsevier, © 2020.*

## 1.4 Chemical targeting

Chemical targeting can be achieved through the use of prodrugs, which are pharmacologically inactive compounds that require chemical or enzymatic transformation to become therapeutically active. Prodrugs can be designed for site-specific delivery, where they are transported to the target site and subsequently activated by enzymes that are present in the target tissue, organ, or cells. Alternatively, prodrugs may be administered systemically, with the conversion to the active form occurring only at the target site due to a specific chemical reaction or enzymatic process. In both approaches, the prodrug must remain at the target site long enough to undergo the necessary transformation into its active form. One of the key advantages of using prodrugs is their ability to reduce systemic toxicity and minimize side effects, as the inactive form of the drug poses less of a burden on nontarget tissues. By confining drug activation to the target site, prodrugs offer a more controlled and precise therapeutic effect, improving the safety and efficacy of treatment.

In addition to the role of enzymatic and chemical reactions in activating prodrugs, these strategies can also be employed to target a delivery vehicle or regulate the controlled release of a therapeutic agent (Mills and Needham, 1999).

Xie and colleagues developed an innovative pH-sensitive drug delivery system for combinatorial cancer therapy. This system employs a methotrexate (MTX) prodrug linked to 1,2-distearoyl-sn-glycero-3-phosphoethanolamine-N-[aldehyde(polyethylene glycol)-2000] via a Schiff base reaction. The resulting complex can self-assemble into micellar nanoparticles, encapsulating curcumin (CUR) within its hydrophobic core in aqueous solutions. The imine bond between the MTX prodrug and the lipid-polyethylene glycol conjugate is pH-sensitive, allowing it to cleave in acidic conditions. Following selective internalization of the carrier through folate receptor-mediated endocytosis (RME), the acidic conditions in endosomes and lysosomes trigger cleavage of the pH-sensitive bond, facilitating the codelivery of active MTX and CUR within cancer cells. This targeted release mechanism enhances the therapeutic efficacy and minimizes off-target effects, advancing combinatorial cancer therapy (Xie et al., 2018).

## 1.5 Biological targeting

Biological targeting involves the use of ligand–receptor interactions to achieve selective delivery of therapeutic agents. This strategy relies on molecules with high binding affinity to specific receptor sites, such as glycoproteins, targeting peptides, oligonucleotide aptamers, and antibodies. Since 1906, when Paul Ehrlich introduced the concept of the "magic bullet," much of the research in targeted drug delivery has focused on exploiting ligand–receptor binding affinities to guide therapeutic agents to their intended sites (Mills and Needham, 1999).

## 1.6 Glycoproteins

Transferrin (Tf) is an iron-binding glycoprotein that facilitates the transport into cells. The overexpression of Tf receptors on cancerous cells—up to 100-fold higher than in normal cells—along with its extracellular availability and capacity for cellular internalization, makes Tf a promising target for drug delivery applications. In 2016, Nag and colleagues reported the development of PEGylated chitosan nanoparticles functionalized with transferrin and loaded with paclitaxel (PTX), a chemotherapeutic agent, to evaluate their efficacy in targeting the lung cancer cell line HOP-62. Through a combination of MTT assays, cellular uptake studies, and biodistribution analysis, the results demonstrated that PTX-loaded chitosan-PEG-transferrin nanoparticles (PTX-Cs-PEG-Tf) effectively targeted lung cancer cells, delivering higher concentrations of PTX compared to normal lung cells. This selective targeting enhanced therapeutic outcomes, highlighting the potential of Tf-functionalized nanoparticles for cancer treatment (Yoo et al., 2019; Nag et al., 2016).

## 1.7 Targeting peptides

Peptides are short chains of amino acids, typically composed of fewer than 50 residues, that serve a variety of roles in biological systems. They have gained significant attention as therapeutic agents, with insulin being a well-known example. Roger Brent was one of the first to propose the concept of "targeting peptides," advocating their potential as targeting molecules in drug delivery. Due to their small size, ease of chemical modification, and relatively low production costs, peptides are ideal candidates for targeted drug delivery. They also exhibit favorable stability and low immunogenicity, enhancing their suitability for clinical applications. Advances in artificial intelligence have further streamlined peptide design, enabling the development of more precise and effective delivery systems (Todaro et al., 2023).

TH1902 and TH1904 are peptide-based drug delivery systems specifically designed to target sortilin1 (SORT1) receptors, which are overexpressed in various cancer types. TH1902 delivers a docetaxel payload for the treatment of ovarian cancer and triple-negative breast cancer, while TH1904 carries DOX for targeted ovarian cancer therapy. In vivo studies for both platforms demonstrate selective accumulation at the target site, significantly reducing off-target effects and enhancing therapeutic precision (Cooper et al., 2021).

## 1.8 Oligonucleotide aptamers

Aptamers are single-stranded oligonucleotides (DNA or RNA) that can adopt specific three-dimensional conformations, enabling them to bind their targets—such as nucleic acids, phospholipids, whole cells, and proteins—with high specificity and affinity. Due to their ease of production, low cost, thermal stability, and low immunogenicity, aptamers are attractive candidates for targeted drug delivery (Zununi Vahed et al., 2019; Zavareh et al., 2020). In a recent study, Ommen and colleagues developed aptamer-functionalized liposomes designed to deliver a combination of vancomycin and rifampicin to eradicate *Staphylococcus aureus* biofilm. They screened six DNA aptamers with binding affinity for *S. aureus*, assessing their antibacterial efficacy. Results indicated that one aptamer significantly enhanced the accumulation of drug-loaded liposomes at the biofilm site, effectively eradicating the biofilm within 24 h of treatment. This targeted delivery platform shows promise in addressing antibiotic resistance by ensuring localized, high-concentration antibiotic exposure while limiting off-target effects (Ommen et al., 2022).

## 1.9 Antibodies

Antibodies, or immunoglobulins, are proteins produced by the vertebrate immune system to recognize and neutralize foreign molecules (antigens) as part of the defense response. A defining characteristic of the immune response is the ability of antibodies to discriminate among antigens, even those with high molecular similarity. The immune system is remarkably sensitive to a broad range of molecules, capable of recognizing them as antigens, which reflects its capacity to generate a vast repertoire of immunoglobulins to combat these diverse threats. Despite this extensive diversity, antibodies are classified into five primary classes: IgA, IgD, IgE, IgM, and IgG, all of which share a similar basic structure (Cohen and Milstein, 1967; Wang et al., 2007).

Structurally, antibodies consist of distinct domains, each serving specific functions in immune recognition and response. One key domain is responsible for antigen recognition and exhibits high specificity for binding to antigens. This region is known as the Fab fragment (fragment antigen-binding) or the variable region. It contains the complementarity-determining regions (CDRs), which are the most variable and hyperdivergent segments directly involved in antigen binding. The CDRs are interspersed with more conserved sequences known as framework regions (FRs), which provide structural support to maintain the antibody's overall configuration (M Cardoso et al., 2012; Arruebo et al., 2009).

The other major domain of the antibody is the Fc region (fragment crystallizable), or the constant region, which is involved in mediating effector functions such as interaction with immune cells and the complement system. The Fab and Fc regions are connected by a

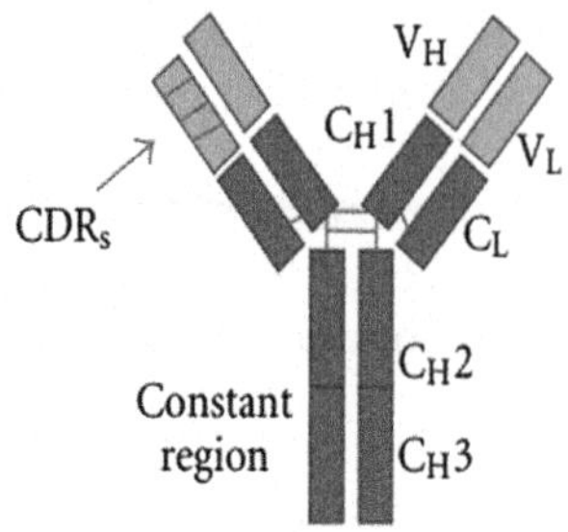


**FIGURE 22.2** molecule, consisting of two heavy chains (H) and two light chains (L). Each heavy chain contains a variable domain (V H) and three or four constant domains (CH1, CH2, CH3). Each light chain contains a variable domain (VL) and a constant domain (CL). The variable domains of both heavy and light chains include three complementarity- determining regions (CDRs), which are essential for antigen binding. *Reprinted from Arruebo, M., Valladares, M., González-Fernández, Á., 2009. Antibody-conjugated nanoparticles for biomedical applications. J. Nanomater. 2009 (1), 439389 with permission from Wiley, © 2009.*

flexible hinge region, allowing the antibody to adapt its conformation during antigen binding and enhance its interaction with other components of the immune system (M Cardoso et al., 2012; Arruebo et al., 2009) (Fig. 22.2).

Among the diverse molecules used in ligand–receptor interactions, antibodies have garnered significant attention due to their remarkable specificity and dual functionality as both targeting and therapeutic agents. Inspired by Paul Ehrlich's "magic bullet" concept, target-specific antibodies have been developed to deliver potent cytotoxic agents selectively to diseased cells, thereby enhancing therapeutic efficacy while minimizing off-target effects. This approach laid the foundation for ADCs. In this chapter, we will explore the role of antibodies in targeted drug delivery and their essential function in achieving precise therapeutic targeting. This discussion will set the stage for an in-depth examination of ADCs, their derivative antibody-conjugated nanoparticles (ACNPs), and their transformative potential in the targeted delivery of therapeutics in the following sections (Mills and Needham, 1999; Lambert and van Delft, 2021; Wang et al., 2015).

## 2. Antibody–drug conjugates

### 2.1 History of antibody–drug conjugates

As previously discussed, over a century ago, Paul Ehrlich proposed the concept of the "magic bullet," hypothesizing that specific molecules or antigens, unique to tumors and bacterial cells, could be targeted with precision by therapeutic agents. This foundational idea laid the groundwork for the development of ADCs, where targeted drug delivery would enhance therapeutic efficacy while minimizing off-target effects. However, despite the potential of Ehrlich's concept, ADC development progressed slowly for nearly 50 years, hindered by technical limitations. The isolation, purification, and large-scale production of antibodies suitable for therapeutic use presented significant challenges that stalled early ADC research efforts (Wang et al., 2015; van Delft and Lambert, 2021; Olivier and Hurvitz, 2016).

A significant breakthrough occurred in 1975, when Georges Köhler and César Milstein introduced hybridoma technology, a method that revolutionized antibody production. This technique involved the fusion of antibody-producing spleen cells with myeloma cells, allowing the combination of the antibody-generating capability of spleen cells with the rapid growth properties of myeloma cells. This innovation enabled the large-scale production of monoclonal antibodies with high specificity, overcoming a major obstacle in ADC development and providing the essential tools needed for clinical applications (Wang et al., 2015; van Delft and Lambert, 2021; Olivier and Hurvitz, 2016).

In the early development of ADCs, murine antibodies were utilized; however, they often elicited strong immune responses in humans, leading to reduced therapeutic efficacy. The advent of genetic engineering technologies partially addressed these limitations by enabling the development of second-generation ADCs using chimeric antibodies, which have mouse variable regions fused to human constant regions. This "humanized chimeric antibody" approach, which retains murine light and heavy variable domains connected to human constant regions, improved the efficacy and decreased immunogenicity. However, the presence of murine components sometimes still triggered a human antichimeric antibody response, limiting their effectiveness in some patients (Ponziani et al., 2020). To overcome these challenges, research efforts focused on creating fully humanized monoclonal antibodies. These next-generation antibodies either retained only murine CDRs grafted onto human variable regions or were entirely human in origin. This progression toward fully humanized or human monoclonal antibodies significantly enhanced the therapeutic potential of ADCs by reducing immunogenicity while maintaining target specificity (Ponziani et al., 2020).

The introduction of hybridoma technology and subsequent innovations significantly advanced the field, transforming ADCs into a viable and promising therapeutic strategy. These key developments, summarized in the timeline below, captured the interest of the pharmaceutical industry and spurred stepwise advancements in ADC research and development (Wang et al., 2015; van Delft and Lambert, 2021; Olivier and Hurvitz, 2016) (Table 22.1).

## 2.2 The ADC construction

ADCs are a class of targeted therapeutic agents designed to selectively deliver cytotoxic drugs to cancer cells, thereby enhancing the efficacy of treatment while minimizing off-target toxicity. ADCs are structurally composed of three components: a cytotoxic payload, a monoclonal antibody, and a linker that connects the two. Each element is critical for ensuring ADCs' targeted action and therapeutic potency (Perez et al., 2014).

## 2.3 Cytotoxic payload

An effective cytotoxic payload for ADCs must meet several key criteria.

1. Aqueous Solubility: The payload should be sufficiently soluble in aqueous solutions to facilitate conjugation with the antibody and to maintain solubility under physiological conditions.

**TABLE 22.1** Timeline of key developments in ADCs.

| Date | Key development | Research group | Ref. |
|---|---|---|---|
| 1907 | Introduction of "magic bullet" idea | Paul Ehrlich | Wang et al. (2015) |
| 1957 | Evaluating Ehrlich's idea for the first time by conjugation of methotrexate (MTX) to antibodies that target L1210 leukemia cells | Mathé | Wang et al. (2015) |
| 1970 | Demonstrated the necessity of a covalent bond between the drug and the immunoglobulin to achieve the targeted therapy | Ghose et al.<br>Rowland et al. | van Delft and Lambert (2021)<br>van Delft and Lambert (2021) |
| 1975 | Demonstrated for the first time that the activity of ADC is dependent on the conjugation method | Hurwitz et al. | Olivier and Hurvitz (2016) |
| 1975 | Production of mouse monoclonal antibodies with the hybridoma technology | Köhler and Milstein | Ponziani et al. (2020) |
| 1986 | First antibody–drug conjugate (Muromonab-CD3 (OKT3®)) approved by the FDA | Ortho Multicenter Transplant Study Group | Ponziani et al. (2020) |
| 1988 | Humanized monoclonal antibody reported | Riechmann et al. | Olivier and Hurvitz (2016) |

2. Apoptosis Induction: It should induce apoptotic cell death specifically in cancer cells, thereby promoting targeted cytotoxicity.
3. Conjugation Capability: The payload should possess functional groups that allow stable and efficient conjugation to the antibody.
4. High Cytotoxic Potency: A potent payload is essential, with an optimal half-maximal inhibitory concentration ($IC_{50}$) in the range of 0.01–0.1 nM, significantly more potent than traditional chemotherapeutics, to ensure strong anticancer activity (Ponziani et al., 2020).

Two primary categories of cytotoxic payloads are commonly employed in ADC development.

### 2.3.1 *Microtubule-disrupting agents*

These agents target and disrupt the microtubule structures in rapidly dividing cells, making them particularly effective against proliferative cancer cells. Key payloads in this category include auristatins and maytansines, which act as tubulin inhibitors to halt cell division selectively in cancer cells. Within this category, microtubule-disrupting agents can be further classified by their mechanism of action.

- Tubulin Polymerization Promoters (Microtubule Stabilizers): These agents bind to the β-subunit of α–β tubulin dimers, promoting microtubule formation in an uncontrolled manner, which interferes with cellular division.

- Tubulin Polymerization Inhibitors (Microtubule Destabilizers): These agents inhibit the polymerization of tubulin, preventing the formation of mature microtubules and thus blocking cell division at a critical structural level (Ponziani et al., 2020; Chen et al., 2017) (Fig. 22.3).

### 2.3.2 *DNA-damaging agents*

These highly potent agents target DNA within the cell, inducing apoptosis by directly damaging the DNA structure. Payloads in this group, such as calicheamicins and pyrrolobenzodiazepines (PBDs), possess a potency in the picomolar range, which enables them to be effective, especially when the target antigen expression on cancer cells is low. Their cytotoxic effects are exerted through the following mechanisms (Ponziani et al., 2020) (Fig. 22.4).

- DNA Double-Strand Breakage (DNA Cleavage)
- Mono-Adduct

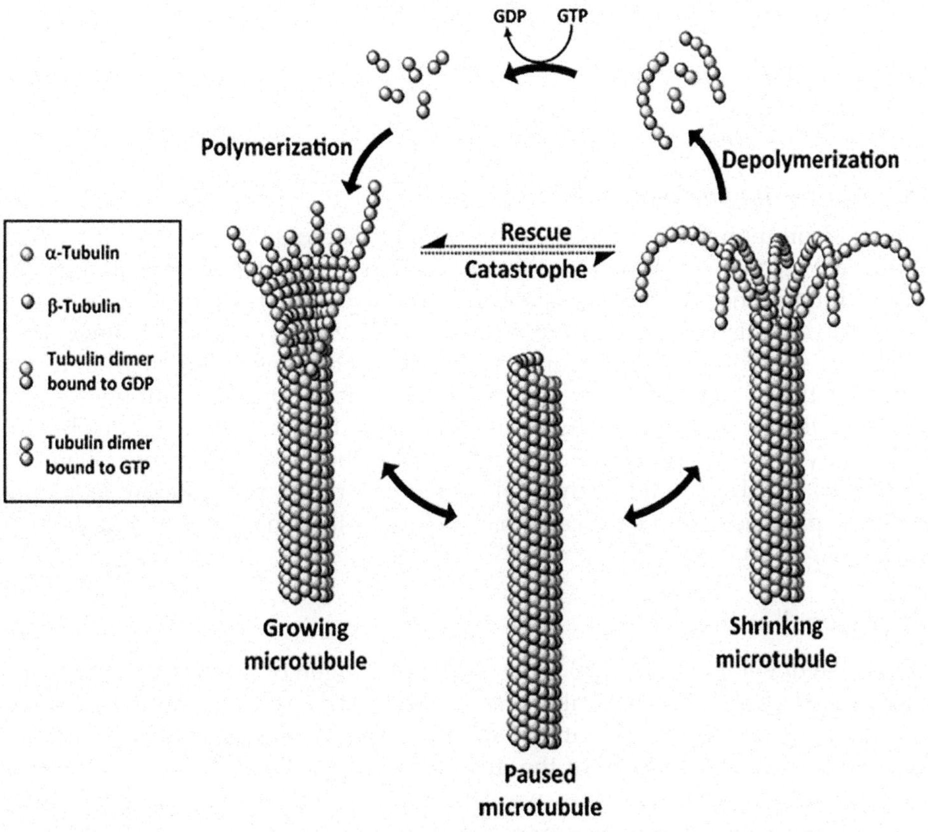


**FIGURE 22.3** Structure, polymerization, and depolymerization of microtubules. These processes can be affected by DNA-targeting payloads in antibody-drug conjugates (ADCs). *Reprinted from Chen, H., Lin, Z., Arnst, K. E., Miller, D.D., Li, W., 2017. Tubulin inhibitor-based antibody-drug conjugates for cancer therapy. Molecules 22 (8), 1281 with permission from MDPI, ©2017.*

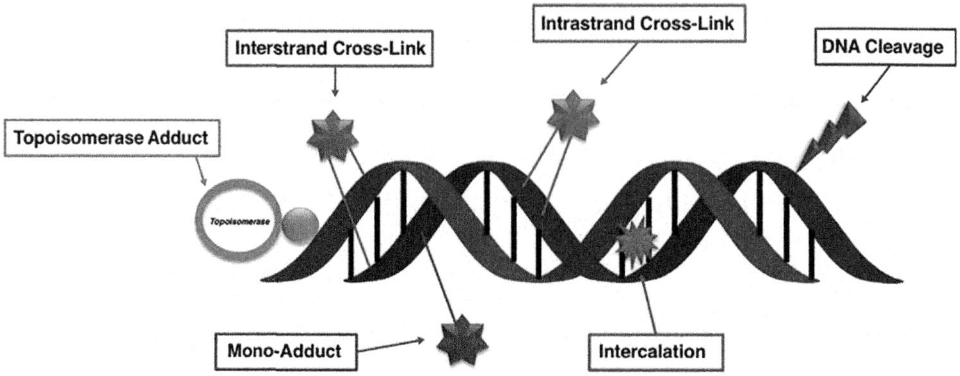


FIGURE 22.4 Different types of DNA damage that can result from the interaction of DNA-targeting payloads with tumor cells. *Reprinted from Jackson, P.J., Kay, S., Pysz, I., Thurston, D.E., 2018. Use of pyrrolobenzodiazepines and related covalent-binding DNA-interactive molecules as ADC payloads: is mechanism related to systemic toxicity? Drug Discov. Today Technol. 30, 71–83 with permission from Elsevier, © 2018.*

- DNA Intercalation
- DNA Cross-Linking
- Topoisomerase Adduct

### 2.3.3 *Alternative payloads*

Besides the commonly used classes, other potent cytotoxic molecules target tumor cells through unique mechanisms, such as direct induction of apoptosis, inhibition of RNA polymerase, and interference with the spliceosome. These payloads disrupt cancer cell proliferation via pathways distinct from microtubule destabilization or DNA damage, broadening the therapeutic strategies available for targeted cancer treatment (Ponziani et al., 2020).

Among the three main categories of payloads, microtubule-disrupting agents are the most widely utilized in commercially available ADCs. This preference is attributed to their selective toxicity toward rapidly dividing cancer cells, thereby minimizing collateral damage to normal cells, which generally exhibit slower proliferation rates. Below is a summary of representative payloads from each category, including their names and molecular formulas (Ponziani et al., 2020) (Table 22.2).

## 2.4 Monoclonal antibody

A key step in developing an ADC is the choice of antigen of interest and consequently, its corresponding antibody. Theoretically, the antibody should have the ability to recognize and bind to the overexpressed antigen on the surface of tumor cells (antigen density $>10^5$/cell) and avoid the delivery of the drug to normal cells, but as the field grows, these parameters are refining. For example, we don't need to find an antigen that has no expression on normal tissues while is overexpressed on tumor cells. It has become clear that the expression of antigen on normal tissues can be tolerated if it has no expression or minimal expression on vital organs. The FDA-approved ADC Kadcyla, which is for the treatment of HER2-negative breast cancer, highlights this point, since the targeted antigen, HER2-neu, is

**TABLE 22.2** Commonly used payloads in ADCs and their mechanism of action.

| Drug (payload) | Mechanism of action | Chemical structure | Ref. |
|---|---|---|---|
| Monomethyl auristatin E (MMAE) | Microtubule-targeting agent | | Köhler and Milstein (1975) |
| Monomethyl auristatin F (MMAF) | Microtubule-targeting agent | | Ortho Multicenter Transplant Study Group (1985) |
| Colchicine | Microtubule-targeting agent | | Hamann et al. (2002) |
| Maytansine | Microtubule-targeting agent | | (Riechmann et al., 1988; Dorywalska et al., 2016) |
| Camptothecin | DNA-targeting agent | | Thomas et al. (2004) |
| Calicheamicin | DNA-targeting agent | | (Ghose et al., 1972; Rowland et al., 1975) |
| Duocarmycin A | DNA-targeting agent | | Hurwitz et al. (1975) |
| Pyrrolobenzodiazepines | DNA-targeting agent | | Ortho Multicenter Transplant Study Group (1985) |
| Thailanstatin A | Spliceosome-targeting agent | | Donaldson (2020) |
| β-amanitin | Transcription inhibitor | | Tyagi et al. (2019) |

expressed in breast tissue as well as skin, heart, and epithelial cells in the gastrointestinal, respiratory, and urinary tracts (Chau et al., 2019).

After the specific binding of an ADC to its targeted tumor site, various factors can affect the amount of internalization: the chosen epitope of the target antigen, the affinity of the interaction between ADC and target antigen, and the intracellular trafficking pattern induced by the ADC complex (Beck et al., 2017).

The formulated ADC can have two destinies and can be divided into two groups based on its pathway.

### *2.4.1 Internalizing ADCs*

ADCs can be categorized based on the fate of the ADC following antibody binding to its target antigen. In internalizing ADCs, the interaction between the antibody and its target antigen triggers internalization via RME. Most ADCs utilize this pathway, wherein the antibody plays a pivotal role in facilitating internalization. In some cases, the binding of antibody and its receptor and subsequently the internalization of this complex can alone induce apoptosis, as in the case of the anti-HER3 antibody EV20. The internalization process typically involves distinct pathways such as clathrin-mediated endocytosis (CME), caveolae-mediated endocytosis, or alternative clathrin- and caveolae-independent mechanisms. In CME, the receptor plays a central role in mediating the endocytic process, while other pathways may operate independently of the receptor's mediation (Ponziani et al., 2020; Beck et al., 2017).

The majority of internalizing ADCs follow the CME pathway to access the cytoplasm. Once internalized, ADC-containing early endosomes mature into late endosomes. The acidic environment within late endosomes induces the dissociation of the ADC–antigen complex, allowing the antigen to be recycled back to the cell membrane. The late endosomes then fuse with lysosomes, where the ADC is degraded, leading to the release of the cytotoxic payload. The lysosomal enzymes degrade the ADC, liberating the drug, which then passively diffuses into the cytosol. Once in the cytoplasm, the payload exerts its pharmacological effect, ultimately leading to the targeted destruction of the cancer cell. It is worth noting that in some cases, the binding of antibody and its receptor and subsequently the internalization of this complex can alone induce apoptosis, as in the case of the anti-HER3 antibody EV20 (Ponziani et al., 2020).

#### 2.4.2 *Noninternalizing ADCs*

The efficacy of noninternalizing ADCs largely relies on the bystander effect. In this approach, proteolytic enzymes or reducing conditions within the tumor's extracellular matrix trigger the release of the cytotoxic payload from the antibody. Following this extracellular release, mechanisms such as pinocytosis or simple diffusion allow the free drug to enter neighboring tumor cells. Once inside the tumor cell, the payload exerts its cytotoxic action, leading to cell death. The subsequent exposure of the cell contents to extracellular reducing agents or proteases can cause further release of the drug, enabling it to affect adjacent cells—a mechanism advantageous in targeting heterogeneous tumor populations. However, the bystander effect has potential drawbacks. If the payload has a prolonged half-life, the bystander effect can be amplified, leading to off-target cytotoxicity and increased systemic side effects. Balancing the benefits of enhanced tumor penetration with the risks of nonspecific toxicity is critical in the design of effective noninternalizing ADCs (Beck et al., 2017) (Fig. 22.5).

### 2.5 Linker

The linker is a critical component of an ADC, serving as the bridge between the cytotoxic payload and the targeting antibody. The design of an effective linker is pivotal, as it must remain stable in the bloodstream to prevent premature drug release, yet facilitate efficient payload release upon reaching the targeted tumor cells. This dual requirement, though seemingly straightforward, presents one of the primary challenges in ADC development (Tsuchikama and An, 2018). Linkers are generally classified into two main categories: cleavable and noncleavable.

#### 2.5.1 *Cleavable linkers*

These are the most commonly utilized in FDA-approved ADCs due to their ability to trigger payload release through specific chemical reactions within the tumor microenvironment or inside target cells. These chemical triggers are carefully designed to respond to the unique conditions of tumor cells, ensuring selective drug release. The cleavable linkers are divided into two major groups: chemically labile linkers and enzyme-cleavable linkers. Below is a table summarizing the various chemical structures in cleavable linkers and the specific reactions they employ to achieve targeted drug release (Ponziani et al., 2020; Perez et al., 2014; Beck et al., 2017; Tsuchikama and An, 2018).

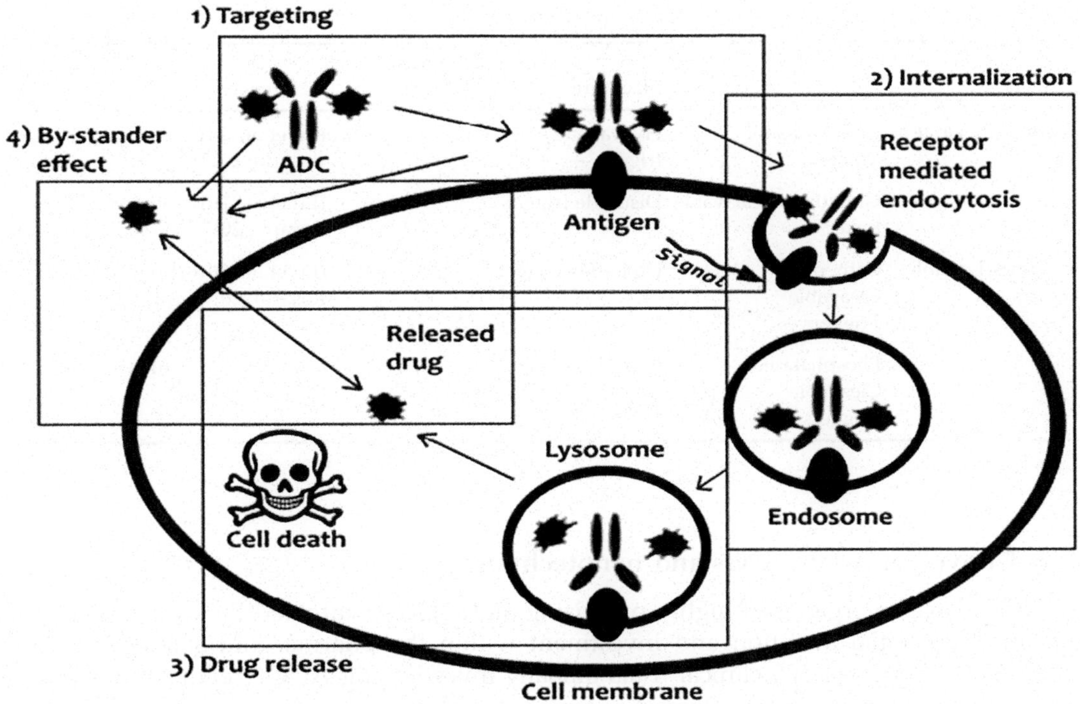


FIGURE 22.5 The mechanism of action for internalizing and non-internalizing ADC. *Reprinted from Ponziani, S., Di Vittorio, G., Pitari, G., Cimini, A.M., Ardini, M., Gentile, R., Giansanti, F., 2020. Antibody-drug conjugates: the new frontier of chemotherapy. Int. J. Mol. Sci. 21 (15), 5510 with Permission from MDPI, © 2020.*

### 2.5.2 Noncleavable linkers

In contrast to cleavable linkers, this group has no chemical trigger, and the linker is part of the payload. Typical noncleavable linkers incorporate structures like thioether or maleimidocaproyl groups, which are known for their stability. A prominent example of an FDA-approved ADC using a noncleavable linker is monomethyl auristatin F (MMAF), previously discussed in earlier sections. Noncleavable linkers are notable for their enhanced stability in plasma, which significantly reduces the risk of off-target toxicity. This stability ensures that the cytotoxic payload remains securely attached to the antibody while circulating in the bloodstream. For the payload to be released, the antibody must undergo internalization into the target tumor cell, followed by degradation within cellular compartments, such as lysosomes. This intracellular degradation can provide a greater therapeutic potency, as the payload derivatives can affect the targeted cell.

However, due to the requirement for internalization and intracellular processing, noncleavable ADCs generally lack the ability to produce a bystander effect, where the drug can diffuse to and kill neighboring tumor cells. This limitation arises because the degradation of the antibody releases fragments that are incapable of binding to antigens on adjacent cells, thereby restricting the cytotoxic impact on the initially targeted cell (Ponziani et al., 2020; Perez et al., 2014; Chau et al., 2019; Tsuchikama and An, 2018) (Table 22.3).

TABLE 22.3 Examples of cleavable linkers and their trigger.

| Category | Chemical trigger | Structure | Schematic structure | Reference |
|---|---|---|---|---|
| Chemically labile linkers | Acid cleavable Triggers | Hydrazone trigger | | (Lu et al., 2016; Su et al., 2021; Rosario, 2017) |
| | Glutathione-cleavable linker | Disulfide trigger | | (Lu et al., 2016; Su et al., 2021; Rosario, 2017) |
| Enzyme-cleavable linkers | Cathepsin Cleavable Triggers | Dipeptide trigger | | (Lu et al., 2016; Su et al., 2021; Rosario, 2017) |
| | Phosphatase Cleavable Triggers | Pyrophosphate trigger | | (Lu et al., 2016; Su et al., 2021; Rosario, 2017) |

## 2.6 Convergence of ADCs and nanotechnology

ADCs have emerged as a highly promising and effective targeted therapeutic platform, gaining substantial attention and investment within the pharmaceutical industry. As of 2018, there were over 600 clinical trials globally investigating ADCs, reflecting the intense focus on optimizing this technology (Liu et al., 2024; M Cardoso et al., 2012). Currently, there are 15 FDA-approved ADCs available on the market, some of which are summarized in the table below (Liu et al., 2024) (Table 22.4).

Despite their potential, several factors continue to challenge the development of ADCs. For example, one major challenge lies in selecting an appropriate payload. The cytotoxic agent must exhibit high potency along with reduced susceptibility to efflux mechanisms like multidrug resistance protein 1 (MDR1), a key pathway that can mediate resistance in ADCs. In addition, linker optimization remains a critical hurdle. The linker must be stable during systemic circulation to avoid premature drug release while ensuring efficient cleavage and drug delivery upon reaching the target cells (Liu et al., 2024). Nanotechnology is a rapidly evolving field with significant potential in drug delivery. Several nanocarriers for chemotherapeutic agents are already available on the market, including liposomes, polymeric nanoparticles, and micelles. A prime example is Doxil, a liposomal formulation of the chemotherapeutic drug DOX, which has been FDA-approved since 1995 for the treatment of Kaposi's sarcoma and later for ovarian cancer (Sakhalkar et al., 2003; Hu et al., 2010).

The integration of ADC technology with nanotechnology offers a promising strategy for enhancing therapeutic efficacy. This combination could give rise to a novel class of therapeutics known as ACNPs, designed for the targeted delivery of encapsulated drug cargo (Juan et al., 2020).

Compared to traditional ADCs, ACNPs offer several significant advantages. One major benefit is the controlled release of the therapeutic agent, allowing for a more precise and sustained delivery. Unlike ADCs, where the chemical stability of the payload can be compromised during formulation, ACNPs maintain the integrity of the drug's chemical structure,

**TABLE 22.4** Overview of FDA-approved ADCs with permission of Liu et al. (2024).

| Brand name | Target | Antibody | Payload | Tumor type | Approval date |
|---|---|---|---|---|---|
| Mylotarg | CD33 | Hydrazone | Calicheamicin | AML | 2000 |
| Adcetris | CD33 | Mc-VC-PABC | MMAE | HL, ALCL | 2011 |
| Kadcyla | HER2 | SMCC | DM1 | Breast cancer | 2013 |
| Besponsa | CD22 | Hydrazone | Calicheamicin | ALL | 2017 |
| Lumoxiti | CD22 | Mc-VC-PABC | PE38 | HCL | 2018 |
| Polyvi | CD79b | Mc-VC-PABC | MMAE | DLBCL | 2019 |
| Padcev | Nectin-4 | Mc-VC-PABC | MMAE | UC | 2019 |
| Enhertu | HER2 | Tetrapeptide | DXD | Breast cancer | 2019 |
| Trodelvy | TROP2 | CL2A | SN-38 | Breast cancer<br>UC | 2020 |
| Aidixi | HER2 | Mc-VC-PABC | MMAE | GC<br>UC | 2021 |
| Zynlonta | CD19 | Mc-VC-PABC | PBD SG3199 | DLBCL | 2021 |
| Tivdak | TF | Mc-VC-PABC | MMAE | Cervical cancer | 2021 |
| Elahere | FR a | Sulfo-SPDB | DM4 | Ovarian cancer | 2022 |

thereby minimizing the risk of generating harmful metabolites. Additionally, because the antibody is directly conjugated to the nanocarrier rather than being dependent on a specific linker, the release of the drug is not reliant on linker chemistry. This independence from linker optimization can expedite the development of ACNPs, bypassing one of the major bottlenecks faced by traditional ADCs (Johnston and Scott, 2018).

Another advantage of ACNPs is their ability to deliver multiple therapeutic agents simultaneously, thanks to the versatility of nanostructured carriers. Furthermore, ACNPs allow for a significantly higher drug-to-antibody ratio—often exceeding 100:1, compared to the 4:1 ratio typical of optimized ADCs. This increased drug payload capacity is particularly beneficial when the expression of the target antigen on the cell surface is low, as ACNPs can enhance the internalization of a sufficient quantity of the therapeutic agent into target cells (Johnston and Scott, 2018).

## 3. Nanoparticle functionalization with antibody

Functionalization of nanoparticles with antibodies can be achieved through three main strategies: adsorption, covalent binding, and the use of adaptor molecules. Regardless of the chosen approach, the functionalized nanoparticles must ensure an optimal density of antibodies per nanoparticle as well as the correct orientation of the antibodies. Achieving the correct antibody density is critical, as excessively high antibody densities can result in steric hindrance, limiting the spatial accessibility of the antigen and potentially reducing binding efficiency. Furthermore, the conjugation between the antibody and the nanoparticle must maintain stability throughout the therapeutic process while preserving the biological activity of the antibody. Proper orientation and functionality of the antibodies are crucial for effective targeting and to maximize the therapeutic potential of the nanoparticle–antibody conjugates (Polo et al., 2013).

## 3.1 Adsorption

Adsorption, a noncovalent technique, is the most simple and time-efficient method for nanoparticle functionalization, as it does not require chemical modification of the antibody or activation of nanoparticle functional groups. This approach relies on two main methods: physical adsorption and ionic binding. Physical adsorption involves the attachment of antibodies to the nanoparticle surface through weak, noncovalent interactions, such as electrostatic forces, hydrophobic interactions, hydrogen bonding, and van der Waals forces. These interactions do not involve any chemical alterations of the antibody or nanoparticle, making the process straightforward. Ionic binding relies on the formation of ionic linkages between oppositely charged antibodies and nanoparticles, where electrostatic attraction plays a dominant role in securing the antibody to the nanoparticle surface. While adsorption is advantageous due to its simplicity, it has several limitations compared to other functionalization methods. Noncovalent interactions are inherently less stable, making the conjugation more susceptible to disruption under physiological conditions. Additionally, achieving sufficient antibody coverage often requires high concentrations of antibodies. The random orientation of antibodies, a common outcome in adsorption-based methods, can hinder effective antigen binding, while poor reproducibility remains a challenge, particularly in applications that demand precise and consistent antibody presentation (Polo et al., 2013; Mathé et al., 1958, January).

## 3.2 Covalent binding

Covalent binding is another effective method for antibody immobilization, requiring the prior activation of nanoparticles. The most common covalent conjugation strategies involve carbodiimide chemistry, maleimide chemistry, and "click" chemistry. This approach provides more stable and reproducible antibody–nanoparticle conjugations compared to noncovalent methods (Marques et al., 2020).

Carbodiimide chemistry is one of the most widely used methods for the covalent conjugation of antibodies to nanoparticles. This strategy relies on the formation of amide bonds between the primary amine groups of antibodies and the carboxyl groups on the surface of the nanoparticles, eliminating the need for chemical modifications of the antibody. The process begins with the activation of the carboxyl groups on the nanoparticles using a cross-linking agent, most commonly one-ethyl-3-(3-dimethylaminopropyl) carbodiimide (EDC). EDC reacts with the carboxyl groups, forming reactive intermediates that subsequently react with the primary amine groups of the antibody, leading to stable amide bond formation, which is the basis of carbodiimide chemistry.

To improve the efficiency of this coupling, N-hydroxysuccinimide (NHS) or its water-soluble variant, N-hydroxysulfosuccinimide (sulfo-NHS), can be added. While not strictly necessary, NHS or sulfo-NHS help stabilize the reactive intermediates formed between EDC and the carboxyl groups, increasing the overall coupling efficiency and yield. However, despite its advantages, this method has some limitations. One major drawback is the non-selectivity of the coupling reaction, as it targets any available primary amine groups, leading to potential off-target conjugations. Additionally, the random orientation of antibodies on the nanoparticle surface can result in suboptimal antigen-binding efficiency and unpredictable biological activity (Polo et al., 2013; Marques et al., 2020).

Maleimide chemistry leverages the reactivity of sulfhydryl (thiol) groups (-SH), which are found on the side chains of cysteine residues in proteins. Cysteines are less abundant than primary amines, making them valuable targets for selective conjugation. Within proteins, cysteine residues often form disulfide bonds (-S-S-) through oxidative processes, stabilizing the tertiary and quaternary structures. However, disulfide-linked sulfhydryl groups are not directly accessible for conjugation. Only free or reduced sulfhydryls are suitable for binding with thiol-reactive compounds. To access these reactive sulfhydryl groups, disulfide bonds in antibodies can be selectively cleaved using reducing agents such as β-mercaptoethanol (β-ME) or dithiothreitol (DTT). This reduction process cleaves the antibody into two halves, each consisting of one heavy chain paired with a light chain, while preserving the antigen-binding site. The cleavage exposes reactive sulfhydryl groups that are available for selective conjugation (Polo et al., 2013; Marques et al., 2020).

Maleimide-based cross-linkers are highly effective for targeting these reactive sulfhydryl groups. Maleimide groups exhibit high selectivity for thiol groups, reacting up to 1000 times faster with free sulfhydryls than with primary amines at physiological pH. This rapid and selective reaction forms a stable thioether linkage, which is resistant to hydrolysis and enhances the stability of the conjugate. Among the various sulfhydryl-reactive reagents, maleimide-activated cross-linkers, particularly heterobifunctional linkers containing both NHS and maleimide groups, are commonly used. Examples include.

- NHS-PEG-Maleimide: A PEGylated analogue that improves solubility and biocompatibility.
- SMCC (succinimidyl 4-(N-maleimidomethyl)cyclohexane-1-carboxylate): A classic cross-linker providing a stable and selective conjugation.
- Sulfo-SMCC: A water-soluble version of SMCC for use in aqueous environments.

These linkers enable precise and efficient attachment of antibodies to nanoparticle surfaces, facilitating targeted drug delivery applications (Polo et al., 2013; Marques et al., 2020).

Click chemistry comprises a set of highly selective and efficient chemical reactions that result in the formation of stable bonds. The primary mechanisms include.

1. **Copper(I)-Catalyzed Azide-Alkyne Cycloaddition (CuAAC):** This is a $[3 + 2]$ cycloaddition reaction between an azide and a terminal alkyne, facilitated by a copper (I) catalyst. This reaction occurs under mild conditions, typically at room temperature, and is known for its high efficiency and selectivity.

2. **Strain-Promoted Azide-Alkyne Cycloaddition (SPAAC):** A variant of CuAAC, SPAAC eliminates the need for a copper catalyst by utilizing a strained alkyne, such as a cyclooctyne. The absence of copper ions reduces toxicity concerns, making SPAAC particularly advantageous for biological applications, as it allows the reaction to proceed under physiological conditions.
3. **Diels–Alder (DA) Reactions:** These are [4 + 2] cycloaddition reactions involving a diene and a dienophile, leading to the formation of cyclic compounds. The DA reaction proceeds efficiently at room temperature and mild conditions, offering a reliable method for creating irreversible covalent bonds.
4. **Inverse Electron Demand Diels–Alder (iEDDA) Reactions:** A subset of the DA reaction, where an electron-poor dienophile reacts with an electron-rich diene. This reaction is rapid and selective, making it highly suitable for bioconjugation applications under ambient conditions.

These reactions are characterized by their efficiency, selectivity, and mild reaction conditions, generally proceeding at room temperature and resulting in irreversible chemical bonds (Marques et al., 2020).

To functionalize nanoparticles for click chemistry, **EDC/NHS coupling reactions** are frequently employed. This method facilitates the attachment of azide or alkyne groups to the nanoparticle surface. These functional groups are particularly advantageous in biological environments because they are rare and inert toward most biomolecules. This reduces off-target interactions and enhances the specificity of click reactions. Consequently, click chemistry has become an ideal tool for bioconjugation, drug delivery, and the synthesis of multifunctional nanomaterials (Marques et al., 2020).

## 3.3 Binding with adaptor molecules

This strategy utilizes adaptor biomolecules to bind the Fc region of antibodies, enabling their immobilization on the surface of nanoparticles in an oriented manner, with the Fab regions remaining accessible for antigen recognition. One of the most common methods for functionalizing antibodies with adaptor molecules involves the streptavidin–biotin interaction, a rapid and robust noncovalent binding mechanism. This interaction occurs naturally with exceptionally high affinity and is highly resistant to various physiological conditions (Polo et al., 2013; Marques et al., 2020).

Biotin, an essential molecule for cell growth and signaling, is overexpressed in many cancer cells, making it particularly relevant for targeted therapies. In this approach, the nanoparticle surface is functionalized with streptavidin, while the antibodies are labeled with biotin, ensuring their oriented attachment on the nanoparticle surface for optimal antigen binding. Beyond the streptavidin–biotin system, other Fc-binding proteins, such as Protein A and Protein G, can also facilitate the oriented immobilization of antibodies on nanoparticle surfaces. These proteins bind specifically to the Fc region, preserving the antigen-binding capability of the Fab regions, and offering an alternative strategy for antibody functionalization in targeted drug delivery systems (Polo et al., 2013; Marques et al., 2020).

## 3.4 Therapeutic applications of antibody–drug conjugated nanoparticles

ACNPs have demonstrated significant potential in targeted therapies for various diseases. Below are some examples of specific applications of ACNPs in the treatment of different diseases.

### 3.4.1 *Cancer therapy*

ACNPs can play a crucial role in the targeted delivery of chemotherapeutic agents to tumor cells for enhanced efficacy and reduced systemic toxicity. In 2010, Hu and colleagues synthesized lipid-polymer hybrid NPs conjugated with anticarcinoembryonic antigen half-antibodies (HAb-NPs). These NPs targeted pancreatic cancer cells (BxPC-3), achieving an $IC_{50}$ of 251 nM compared to 526 nM for nontargeted NPs. This resulted in a two-fold improvement in therapeutic efficacy by exploiting the overexpression of carcinoembryonic antigen (CEA) in tumor cells (Yurko et al., 2009; Tyagi et al., 2019).

### 3.4.2 *Inflammatory diseases*

Targeting cell adhesion molecules using ACNPs to deliver antiinflammatory drugs directly to inflamed tissues can have great potential in the treatment of inflammatory diseases. In a rheumatoid arthritis model, antibody-conjugated NPs were functionalized with anti-E-selectin antibodies. These NPs targeted inflamed joints, reducing leukocyte adhesion and directly delivering drugs to the site of inflammation. Preclinical models showed a significant decrease in joint damage and inflammation compared to nontargeted treatments (Yurko et al., 2009; Tyagi et al., 2019).

### 3.4.3 *Infectious diseases*

Targeting infected cells or pathogens through ACNPs for improved drug delivery and treatment outcomes can be an efficient method. In tuberculosis (TB) research, NPs conjugated with antibodies recognizing activated macrophages were used to enhance the delivery of anti-TB drugs. These NPs improved drug efficacy and reduced side effects by focusing delivery on infected macrophages. In preclinical trials, this approach demonstrated higher bacterial clearance rates with lower drug doses (Kern et al., 2016; Mills and Gago, 2021).

### 3.4.4 *Thrombosis*

ACNPs can be used for localized delivery of anticoagulant or thrombolytic drugs to reduce systemic exposure and risks. Antibody-conjugated NPs were engineered to target fibrin, a key protein at thrombus sites. In preclinical studies, these NPs efficiently delivered thrombolytic agents directly to clots, achieving faster clot resolution and minimizing systemic bleeding risks compared to traditional therapies (Yurko et al., 2009; Tyagi et al., 2019).

### 3.4.5 *Neurological disorders*

Crossing the blood–brain barrier (BBB) for targeted drug delivery using ACNPs to treat central nervous system diseases can be a promising approach to pass through the BBB. Antibody-coated NPs targeting transferrin receptors on brain endothelial cells facilitated the transport of large-molecule drugs into the brain. For example, in multiple sclerosis models, these NPs effectively delivered therapeutic agents to inflamed brain tissues, reducing neuroinflammation and improving motor functions in animal studies (Yurko et al., 2009; Tyagi et al., 2019).

## 4. Conclusion and future perspectives

The field of ACNPs is rapidly advancing, offering a transformative approach to targeted drug delivery by combining nanotechnology and immunology. Despite significant progress, challenges such as scalable production, regulatory compliance, and long-term safety remain. To achieve clinical translation, continuous interdisciplinary research is essential, encompassing molecular and cellular immunology, material science, proteomics, and intracellular trafficking. Future work should focus on refining conjugation techniques, improving nanoparticle stability, conducting long-term in vivo studies, and developing cost-effective manufacturing processes to ensure the successful integration of ACNPs into clinical practice.

## References

Arruebo, M., Valladares, M., González-Fernández, Á., 2009. Antibody-conjugated nanoparticles for biomedical applications. J. Nanomater. 2009 (1), 439389.

Beck, A., Goetsch, L., Dumontet, C., Corvaïa, N., 2017. Strategies and challenges for the next generation of antibody–drug conjugates. Nat. Rev. Drug Discov. 16 (5), 315.

Chau, C.H., Steeg, P.S., Figg, W.D., 2019. Antibody–drug conjugates for cancer. Lancet 394 (10200), 793–804.

Chen, H., Lin, Z., Arnst, K.E., Miller, D.D., Li, W., 2017. Tubulin inhibitor-based antibody-drug conjugates for cancer therapy. Molecules 22 (8), 1281.

Cohen, S., Milstein, C., 1967. Structure of antibody molecules. Nature 214 (5087), 449–452.

Cooper, B.M., Iegre, J., O'Donovan, D.H., Halvarsson, M.Ö., Spring, D.R., 2021. Peptides as a platform for targeted therapeutics for cancer: peptide–drug conjugates (PDCs). Chem. Soc. Rev. 50 (3), 1480–1494.

Donaldson, W.A., 2020. Syntheses of spliceostatins and thailanstatins: a review. Beilstein J. Org. Chem. 16 (1), 1991–2006.

Dorywalska, M., Dushin, R., Moine, L., Farias, S.E., Zhou, D., Navaratnam, T., Strop, P., 2016. Molecular basis of valine-citrulline-PABC linker instability in site-specific ADCs and its mitigation by linker design. Mol. Cancer Therapeut. 15 (5), 958–970.

Fahmy, T.M., Fong, P.M., Goyal, A., Saltzman, W.M., 2005. Targeted for drug delivery. Mater. Today 8 (8), 18–26.

Ghose, T., Path, M.R.C., Nigam, S.P., 1972. Antibody as carrier of chlorambucil. Cancer 29 (5), 1398–1400.

Hamann, P.R., Hinman, L.M., Hollander, I., Beyer, C.F., Lindh, D., Holcomb, R., Bernstein, I., 2002. Gemtuzumab ozogamicin, a potent and selective anti-CD33 antibody– calicheamicin conjugate for treatment of acute myeloid leukemia. Bioconjug. Chem. 13 (1), 47–58.

Hu, C.M.J., Kaushal, S., Cao, H.S.T., Aryal, S., Sartor, M., Esener, S., Zhang, L., 2010. Half-antibody functionalized lipid– polymer hybrid nanoparticles for targeted drug delivery to carcinoembryonic antigen presenting pancreatic cancer cells. Mol. Pharm. 7 (3), 914–920.

Hurwitz, E., Levy, R., Maron, R., Wilchek, M., Arnon, R., Sela, M., 1975. The covalent binding of daunomycin and adriamycin to antibodies, with retention of both drug and antibody activities. Cancer Res. 35 (5), 1175–1181.

Johnston, M.C., Scott, C.J., 2018. Antibody conjugated nanoparticles as a novel form of antibody drug conjugate chemotherapy. Drug Discov. Today Technol. 30, 63–69.

Juan, A., Cimas, F.J., Bravo, I., Pandiella, A., Ocaña, A., Alonso-Moreno, C., 2020. An overview of antibody conjugated polymeric nanoparticles for breast cancer therapy. Pharmaceutics 12 (9), 802.

Kern, J.C., Cancilla, M., Dooney, D., Kwasnjuk, K., Zhang, R., Beaumont, M., Garbaccio, R.M., 2016. Discovery of pyrophosphate diesters as tunable, soluble, and bioorthogonal linkers for site-specific antibody–drug conjugates. J. Am. Chem. Soc. 138 (4), 1430–1445.

Köhler, G., Milstein, C., 1975. Continuous cultures of fused cells secreting antibody of predefined specificity. Nature 256 (5517), 495–497.

Lambert, J.M., van Delft, F.L., 2021. Introduction to antibody–drug conjugates.

Liu, K., Li, M., Li, Y., Li, Y., Chen, Z., Tang, Y., Liu, H., 2024. A review of the clinical efficacy of FDA-approved antibody–drug conjugates in human cancers. Mol. Cancer 23 (1), 62.

Lu, J., Jiang, F., Lu, A., Zhang, G., 2016. Linkers having a crucial role in antibody–drug conjugates. Int. J. Mol. Sci. 17 (4), 561.

Lu, Y.J., Chuang, E.Y., Cheng, Y.H., Anilkumar, T.S., Chen, H.A., Chen, J.P., 2019. Thermosensitive magnetic liposomes for alternating magnetic field-inducible drug delivery in dual targeted brain tumor chemotherapy. Chem. Eng. J. 373, 720–733.

M Cardoso, M., N Peca, I., Ca Roque, A., 2012. Antibody-conjugated nanoparticles for therapeutic applications. Curr. Med. Chem. 19 (19), 3103–3127.

M Cardoso, M., N Peca, I., Ca Roque, A., 2012. Antibody-conjugated nanoparticles for therapeutic applications. Curr. Med. Chem. 19 (19), 3103–3127.

Marques, A.C., Costa, P.J., Velho, S., Amaral, M.H., 2020. Functionalizing nanoparticles with cancer-targeting antibodies: a comparison of strategies. J. Contr. Release 320, 180–200.

Mathé, G., Lou, T.B., Bernard, J., January 1958. Effet sur la leucemie 1210 de la souris dune combinaison par diazotation da-methopterine et de gamma-globulines de hamsters porteurs de cette leucemie par heterogreffe. Presse Med. 66 (25), 571, 120 BLVD SAINT-GERMAIN, 75280 PARIS 06, FRANCE: MASSON EDITEUR.

Mills, A., Gago, F., 2021. Structural and mechanistic insight into DNA bending by antitumour calicheamicins. Org. Biomol. Chem. 19 (30), 6707–6717.

Mills, J.K., Needham, D., 1999. Targeted drug delivery. Expert Opin. Ther. Pat. 9 (11), 1499–1513.

Nag, M., Gajbhiye, V., Kesharwani, P., Jain, N.K., 2016. Transferrin functionalized chitosan-PEG nanoparticles for targeted delivery of paclitaxel to cancer cells. Colloids Surf. B Biointerfaces 148, 363–370.

Olivier, K.J., Hurvitz, S.A., 2016. Antibody-Drug Conjugates: Fundamentals, Drug Development, and Clinical Outcomes to Target Cancer. John Wiley & Sons.

Ommen, P., Hansen, L., Hansen, B.K., Vu-Quang, H., Kjems, J., Meyer, R.L., 2022. Aptamer-targeted drug delivery for Staphylococcus aureus biofilm. Front. Cell. Infect. Microbiol. 12, 814340.

Ortho Multicenter Transplant Study Group, 1985. A randomized clinical trial of OKT3 monoclonal antibody for acute rejection of cadaveric renal transplants. N. Engl. J. Med. 313 (6), 337–342.

Perez, H.L., Cardarelli, P.M., Deshpande, S., Gangwar, S., Schroeder, G.M., Vite, G.D., Borzilleri, R.M., 2014. Antibody–drug conjugates: current status and future directions. Drug Discov. Today 19 (7), 869–881.

Polo, E., Puertas, S., Moros, M., Batalla, P., Guisán, J.M., de la Fuente, J.M., Grazú, V., 2013. Tips for the functionalization of nanoparticles with antibodies. IEC: Third Edition 1051, 149–163.

Ponziani, S., Di Vittorio, G., Pitari, G., Cimini, A.M., Ardini, M., Gentile, R., Giansanti, F., 2020. Antibody-drug conjugates: the new frontier of chemotherapy. Int. J. Mol. Sci. 21 (15), 5510.

Qu, J., Zhao, X., Ma, P.X., Guo, B., 2018. Injectable antibacterial conductive hydrogels with dual response to an electric field and pH for localized "smart" drug release. Acta Biomater. 72, 55–69.

Riechmann, L., Clark, M., Waldmann, H., Winter, G., 1988. Reshaping human antibodies for therapy. Nature 332 (6162), 323–327.

Rosario, G., 2017. Decoupling stability and release in disulfide bonds with antibody-small molecule conjugates. Chem. Sci. 8 (1), 366–370.

Rowland, G.F., O'neill, G.J., Davies, D.A.L., 1975. Suppression of tumour growth in mice by a drug–antibody conjugate using a novel approach to linkage. Nature 255 (5508), 487–488.

Sakhalkar, H.S., Dalal, M.K., Salem, A.K., Ansari, R., Fu, J., Kiani, M.F., Goetz, D.J., 2003. Leukocyte-inspired biodegradable particles that selectively and avidly adhere to inflamed endothelium in vitro and in vivo. Proc. Natl. Acad. Sci. 100 (26), 15895–15900.

Sodano, F., Cavanagh, R.J., Pearce, A.K., Lazzarato, L., Rolando, B., Fraix, A., Sortino, S., 2020. Enhancing doxorubicin anticancer activity with a novel polymeric platform photoreleasing nitric oxide. Biomater. Sci. 8 (5), 1329–1344.

Su, Z., Xiao, D., Xie, F., Liu, L., Wang, Y., Fan, S., Li, S., 2021. Antibody–drug conjugates: recent advances in linker chemistry. Acta Pharm. Sin. B 11 (12), 3889–3907.

Sun, T., Dasgupta, A., Zhao, Z., Nurunnabi, M., Mitragotri, S., 2020. Physical triggering strategies for drug delivery. Adv. Drug Deliv. Rev. 158, 36–62.

Thomas, C.J., Rahier, N.J., Hecht, S.M., 2004. Camptothecin: current perspectives. Bioorg. Med. Chem. 12 (7), 1585–1604.

Todaro, B., Ottalagana, E., Luin, S., Santi, M., 2023. Targeting peptides: the new generation of targeted drug delivery systems. Pharmaceutics 15 (6), 1648.

Torchilin, V., 2011. Tumor delivery of macromolecular drugs based on the EPR effect. Adv. Drug Deliv. Rev. 63 (3), 131–135.

Tsuchikama, K., An, Z., 2018. Antibody-drug conjugates: recent advances in conjugation and linker chemistries. Protein Cell 9 (1), 33–46.

Tyagi, P., Pechenov, S., RiosDoria, J., Masterson, L., Dickinson, N.J., Howard, P., Subramony, J.A., 2019. Evaluation of pyrrolobenzodiazepine-loaded nanoparticles: a targeted drug delivery approach. J. Pharmaceut. Sci. 108 (4), 1590–1597.

van Delft, F., Lambert, J.M., 2021. Chemical Linkers in Antibody-Drug Conjugates (ADCs). Royal Society of Chemistry, USA.

Wang, W., Singh, S., Zeng, D.L., King, K., Nema, S., 2007. Antibody structure, instability, and formulation. J. Pharmaceut. Sci. 96 (1), 1–26.

Wang, J., Shen, W.C., Zaro, J.L., 2015. Antibody-Drug Conjugates: The 21st Century Magic Bullets for Cancer. Springer, New York, NY, USA.

Wei, P., Sun, M., Yang, B., Xiao, J., Du, J., 2020. Ultrasound-responsive polymersomes capable of endosomal escape for efficient cancer therapy. J. Contr. Release 322, 81–94.

Xie, J., Fan, Z., Li, Y., Zhang, Y., Yu, F., Su, G., Hou, Z., 2018. Design of pH-sensitive methotrexate prodrug-targeted curcumin nanoparticles for efficient dual-drug delivery and combination cancer therapy. Int. J. Nanomed. 13, 1381–1398.

Yoo, J., Park, C., Yi, G., Lee, D., Koo, H., 2019. Active targeting strategies using biological ligands for nanoparticle drug delivery systems. Cancers (Basel) 11.

Yurko, Y., Maximov, V., Andreozzi, E., Thompson, G.L., Vertegel, A.A., 2009. Design of biomedical nanodevices for dissolution of blood clots. Mater. Sci. Eng. C 29 (3), 737–741.

Zavareh, H.S., Pourmadadi, M., Moradi, A., Yazdian, F., Omidi, M., 2020. Chitosan/carbon quantum dot/aptamer complex as a potential anticancer drug delivery system towards the release of 5-fluorouracil. Int. J. Biol. Macromol. 165, 1422–1430.

Zi, Y., Yang, K., He, J., Wu, Z., Liu, J., Zhang, W., 2022. Strategies to enhance drug delivery to solid tumors by harnessing the EPR effects and alternative targeting mechanisms. Adv. Drug Deliv. Rev. 188, 114449.

Zununi Vahed, S., Fathi, N., Samiei, M., Maleki Dizaj, S., Sharifi, S., 2019. Targeted cancer drug delivery with aptamer-functionalized polymeric nanoparticles. J. Drug Target. 27 (3), 292–299.

## Further reading

Jackson, P.J., Kay, S., Pysz, I., Thurston, D.E., 2018. Use of pyrrolobenzodiazepines and related covalent-binding DNA-interactive molecules as ADC payloads: is mechanism related to systemic toxicity? Drug Discov. Today Technol. 30, 71–83.

Tan, L., Li, Y., Deng, F., Pan, X., Yu, H., Marina, M.L., Jiang, Z., 2020. Highly sensitive determination of amanita toxins in biological samples using β-cyclodextrin collaborated molecularly imprinted polymers coupled with ultra-high performance liquid chromatography tandem mass spectrometry. J. Chromatogr. A 1630, 461514.

CHAPTER

# 23

# Recent updates in protein nanoparticle vaccine platforms

*Samira Sabzi*[1], *Shahla Shahbazi*[2], *Roghayeh Mohammadzadeh*[3], *Fatemeh Mottaghitalab*[4] and *Mehdi Farokhi*[5]

[1]Medical Microbiology Research Center, Qazvin University of Medical Sciences, Qazvin, Iran; [2]Department of Molecular Biology, Pasteur Institute of Iran, Tehran, Iran; [3]Department of Microbiology and Virology, School of Medicine, Mashhad University of Medical Sciences, Mashhad, Iran; [4]Nanotechnology Research Centre, Faculty of Pharmacy, Tehran University of Medical Sciences, Tehran, Iran; [5]National Cell Bank of Iran, Pasteur Institute of Iran, Tehran, Iran

## 1. Introduction

Vaccines are fundamental to global health, successfully preventing and eradicating numerous infectious diseases. Additionally, in recent years, they have played a vital role in cancer immunotherapy (Hajj Hussein et al., 2015). Traditional vaccine methodologies predominantly utilize live attenuated organisms, inactivated pathogens, or specific microbial components to evoke protective immune responses. Despite their success, these strategies present several limitations, including risks of adverse effects, suboptimal immune responses, and other safety challenges (Jorge and Dellagostin, 2017). Recent advancements in technology, particularly protein nanoparticle vaccines (PNPs), are transforming the vaccine industry by enhancing effectiveness, safety, and the capacity to address both new and recurring pathogens, as well as cancer (Butkovich et al., 2021).

Originating from the theoretical exploration of matter manipulation at the atomic scale, concepts first presented by physicist Richard Feynman in his landmark lecture, *"There's Plenty of Room at the Bottom,"* laid the groundwork for the field of nanotechnology (Feynman, 2018). Subsequently, K. Eric Drexler's propositions from 1981 regarding protein engineering led to important progress in the design and application of nanoparticles (NPs) for vaccine

*Protein-Based Nanoparticles in Drug Delivery*
https://doi.org/10.1016/B978-0-443-33639-3.00015-5

development (Drexler, 1981). These PNPs, which function at sizes ranging from 10 to 1000 nm, can effectively engage with biological systems, boosting the immune response while ensuring a good safety profile (Nguyen and Tolia, 2021).

PNP vaccines operate by utilizing protein assemblies derived from various biological sources, including heat shock proteins (HSPs), ferritin, virus-like particles (VLPs), silk fibroin, gelatin, and albumin, to present antigens in a well-structured format. This arrangement increases immune recognition and response. PNPs are capable of serving multiple roles: serving as adjuvants, antigen carriers, and platforms for antigen presentation that stimulate robust humoral and cellular immunity (Pandey et al., 2024). By employing different anchoring strategies such as physical adsorption, encapsulation, or chemical conjugation researchers can optimize the presentation of antigens, enhance stability, and control the timing of immune responses (Li et al., 2020). Moreover, innovative design strategies facilitate the tailoring of PNPs to improve immunogenicity. Advanced techniques like genetic modification and bioconjugation enable the integration of specific targeting motifs or therapeutic agents within PNPs, allowing for precise delivery of antigens to antigen-presenting cells (APCs). This targeted delivery significantly enhances vaccine efficacy while minimizing off-target effects, ultimately contributing to improved patient outcomes (Diaz et al., 2018).

In recent times, many different types of PNPs have been developed. For instance, HSPs are recognized for their dual role as both chaperone proteins and immunogenic carriers (Zininga et al., 2018). Ferritin NPs have gained attention for their exceptional stability and ability to present multiple antigens simultaneously (Reutovich et al., 2023). Additionally, VLPs and engineered bacteriophages are utilized to elicit significant immune responses across various pathogens, including HIV, hepatitis B, and different strains of influenza (Plummer and Manchester, 2011).

PNPs have clinical applications in cancer vaccines, where engineered NPs targeting tumor-associated antigens (TAAs) show potential in eliciting robust antitumor immune responses (Neek et al., 2019). By harnessing the natural ability of these NP systems to enhance antigen exposure, researchers can create multivalent vaccines tailored to target multiple strains of pathogens or different tumor antigens, enabling innovative cancer therapies.

In contrast to conventional vaccines, which may raise significant safety concerns and frequently require multiple doses for adequate protection, PNPs provide numerous advantages. They enhance antigen presentation and cell-mediated immunity, and their structural modifications allow them to act as intrinsic adjuvants, eliminating the need for conventional adjuvant formulations that can cause adverse effects (Neek et al., 2019; Zhao et al., 2014). PNP systems also offer various routes of administration, including intranasal or oral delivery providing less invasive immunization methods and leading to improve patient compliance (Du et al., 2023).

Although PNP vaccines show great promise, they have some drawbacks. Challenges such as maintaining the stability and integrity of PNPs during production and transportation, along with ensuring consistent immune responses across diverse populations, require ongoing research efforts. Additionally, addressing manufacturing scalability while controlling costs remains vital for making PNP vaccines accessible worldwide (Xu et al., 2018; Velev and Gupta, 2009).

This chapter explores the advancements in PNP vaccine platforms, highlighting specific examples and comparing them to conventional vaccine approaches. The discussion encompasses the underlying design principles, delivery systems, and the clinical potential of these platforms in revolutionizing immunization strategies for infectious diseases and cancer treatment. By focusing on these key areas, we aim to underscore the significance of PNP technologies in advancing the future of vaccines.

## 2. The advantages of PNP vaccines

While traditional vaccines, which often utilize live weakened organisms, inactivated pathogens, or specific microbial components, have proven effective in disease prevention, they also present various safety concerns. For instance, live-attenuated vaccines can revert to virulence, as evidenced by cases of vaccine-derived poliovirus (Duintjer Tebbens et al., 2013). A historical example involves live attenuated oral poliovirus vaccines, which have been associated with cases of paralytic poliomyelitis (Peng et al., 2018). Similarly, Dengvaxia, a live attenuated vaccine for dengue fever, revealed potential challenges only after a large-scale vaccination for children in the Philippines, despite extensive preclinical and clinical testing (Thomas and Yoon, 2019). In contrast, inactivated or killed vaccine pathogens cannot replicate or revert to virulent forms, but this leads to a generally weaker immune response that often requires multiple doses, presenting a significant practical challenge (Zepp, 2010). Subunit vaccines frequently face challenges in eliciting strong immune responses during immunization (Foged, 2011; Sabzi et al., 2023). Currently, aluminum-based adjuvants, the most widely employed options for subunit vaccines, have been associated with localized reactions and may not effectively stimulate robust cell-mediated immunity (HogenEsch, 2013). Therefore, there is a need for innovative adjuvants and delivery mechanisms to support the evolution of the next generation of vaccines.

PNPs, typically measuring between 10 and 1000 nm, offer versatile platforms that enhance both the efficacy and safety of vaccine formulations. This specific size range is crucial because NPs exhibit effective interactions with biological systems, thereby driving increased research into their applications in biology and medicine. In vaccinology, PNPs play three primary roles: acting as adjuvants, carriers, or presentation platforms, depending on how vaccine antigens are incorporated (Fig. 23.1) (Nguyen and Tolia, 2021). The structural design of PNPs can be tailored to optimize their interactions with the immune system, thereby boosting immune responses to a wide array of pathogens and tumors.

Recent advancements have also focused on the integration of targeting moieties into PNPs, enabling the selective delivery of antigens to specific immune cells. This targeted approach not only enhances immune response but also minimizes off-target effects and potential adverse reactions (Conniot et al., 2014; Sabzi et al., 2024).

## 3. Immune response activation

To ensure the effectiveness of a prophylactic vaccine, it is crucial to generate a durable T-cell-dependent IgG antibody response (Zinkernagel, 2003). This process begins with the activation of T-cells by APCs. In turn, activated T-cells facilitate the activation of B-cells through

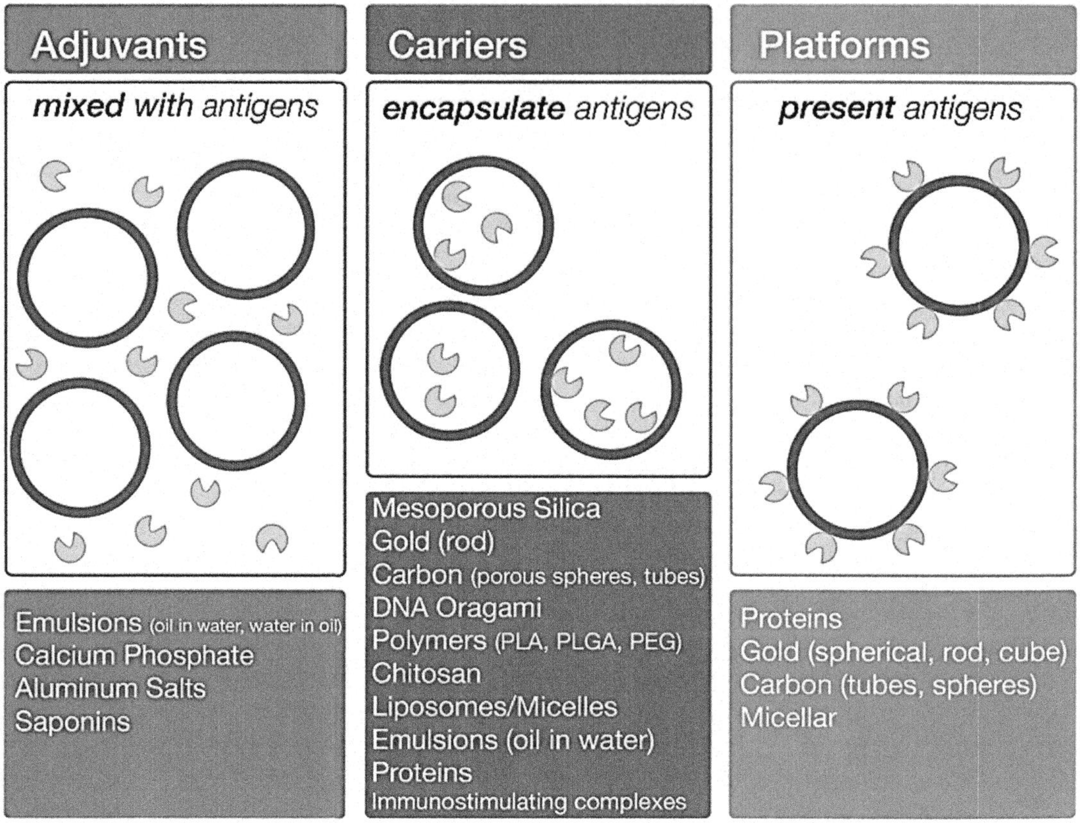


**FIGURE 23.1 Classifications of PNPs' roles in vaccines.** Three classifications of PNPs' roles in vaccines are based on their function as adjuvants, carriers, and platforms (Nguyen and Tolia, 2021). *From Nguyen, B. & Tolia, N. H. (2021). Protein-based antigen presentation platforms for nanoparticle vaccines. Npj Vaccines, 6(1). https://doi.org/10.1038/s41541-021-00330-7.*

the engagement of antigens and T follicular helper (TFH) cells, which are specialized T helper cells (Parker, 1993).

APCs play a vital role in the immune response by performing phagocytosis, processing, and presenting antigens to T-cells. When specific T-cells identify their target antigens, they get activated and differentiate into T helper cells. Naive B-cells need two essential signals to mature into high-affinity IgG-secreting plasma cells. First, an antigen presented by an APC enters directly into the lymph node and crosslinks multiple B-cell receptors (BCRs), leading to endocytosis and subsequent presentation of the processed antigen on the B-cell surface (signal 1). Second, the B-cell then interacts with a TFH cell, which helps promote its maturation into an IgG-producing plasma cell (signal 2) (Fig. 23.2) (Parker, 1993). This coordinated interaction among APCs, T-cells, and B-cells is essential for generating a strong and lasting immune response.

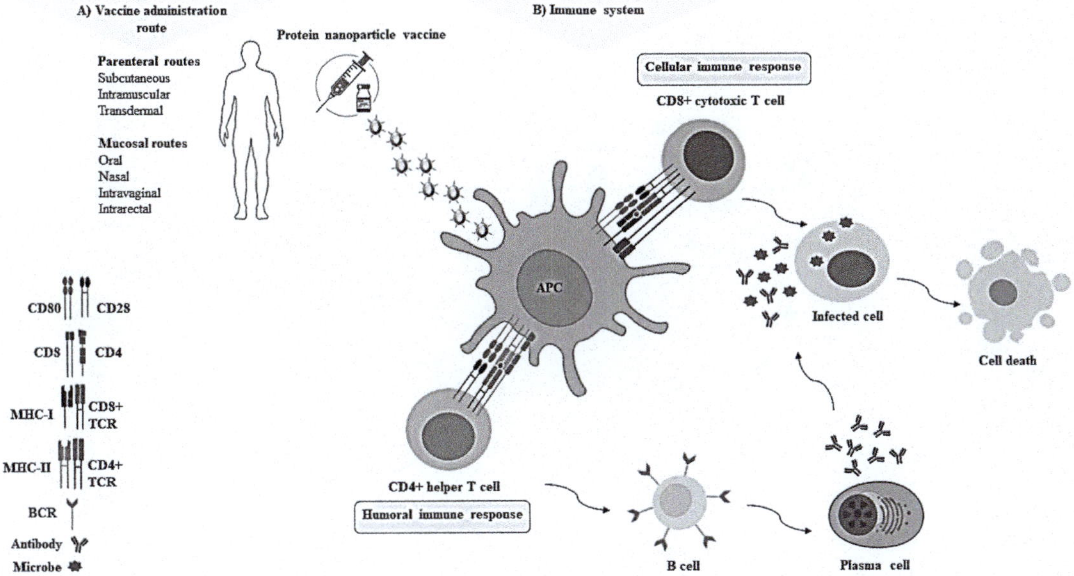


FIGURE 23.2 **PNP vaccine administration route and induction of the immune system.** (A) PNP vaccine administration routes, (B) upon vaccination, recognition of PAMPs by PRRs facilitates the uptake of the pathogen antigen(s) incorporated in the vaccine formulation by APCs, which process and load epitope peptides onto MHC. The epitope-MHC complex then travels to the cell membrane and is presented to naive T cells for their activation. Once T cells are activated, downstream signaling events lead to effector T-cell generation and B-cell activation. $CD8^+$ T cells directly kill the infected cells, while the interaction between $CD4^+$ T cells and B cells leads to the maturation of the B cells into antibody-producing plasma cells. These neutralizing antibodies are specific to the pathogens and block their pathogenicity. The interaction between the PNP vaccines with the immune system establishes immunological memory and protects the host against subsequent infections (*Created with* BioRender.com). PAMPs, pathogen-associated molecular patterns; APC, antigen-presenting cell; MHC, major histocompatibility complex; TCR, T-cell receptor; BCR, B-cell receptor.

## 4. The immunological impact of adjuvants

Adjuvants are components added to vaccines to boost the immunogenicity of antigens. Various types have been studied, including mineral salts, microbial substances, emulsions, saponins, synthetic small molecule agonists, polymers, NPs, and liposomes (O'Hagan and Valiante, 2003). Notable classical human vaccine adjuvants include aluminum salts, AS01 (Quillaja saponaria + MPL), AS03 (squalene-based emulsion), AS04 (aluminum hydroxide + MPL), MF59 (squalene-based emulsion), and CpG ODN 1018 (synthetic immunostimulatory oligonucleotide). These adjuvants enhance vaccine antibody responses and cellular immunity, improving the strength, breadth, and durability of immune responses (Del Giudice, Rappuoli and Didierlaurent, 2018; Pulendran, S. Arunachalam and O'Hagan, 2021). They activate innate immune cells and promote the generation of antigen presentation signals (signal 1) along with co-stimulatory signals (signal 2), which are essential for initiating the activation of naive T cells and enhancing the adaptive immune response (Fig. 23.3) (Janeway, 1989; Pollard

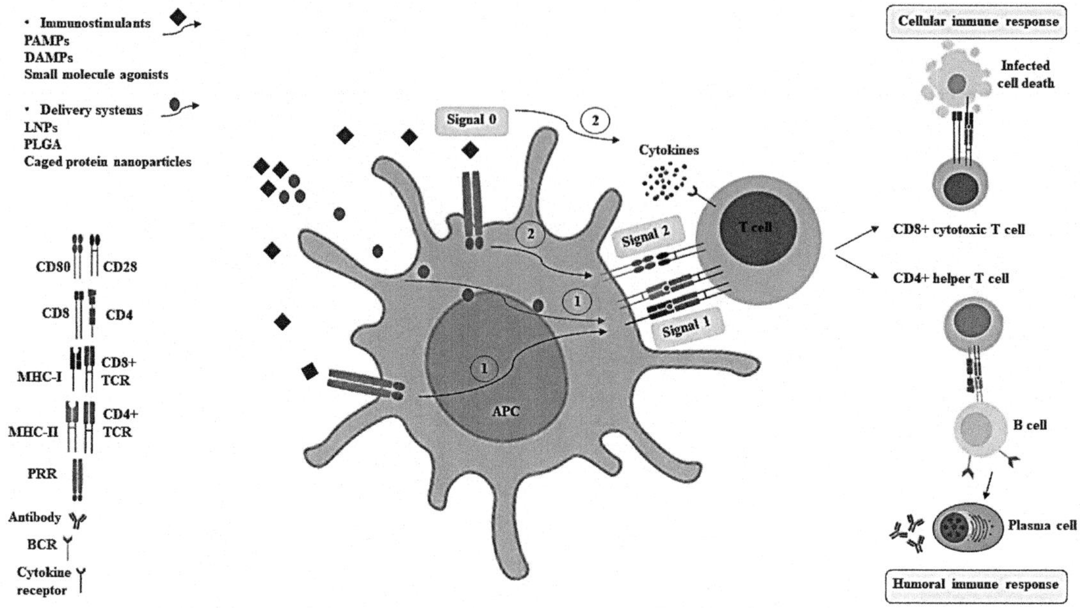


FIGURE 23.3 **The mechanisms of adjuvants function.** Adjuvants are categorized into two main groups: Immunostimulants and delivery systems. Immunostimulants, such as PAMPs, DAMPs, and various small molecule agonists, generate danger signals (signal 0) that activate pattern recognition receptors (PRRs) on antigen-presenting cells (APCs). This activation enhances the presentation of antigens on MHC molecules (signal 1). PRR activation also leads to an increase in the expression of cytokines and co-stimulatory molecules, thereby enhancing co-stimulatory signaling (signal 2). Meanwhile, delivery systems, which include lipid nanoparticles (LNPs), poly (lactic-co-glycolic acid) (PLGA), and self-loaded polymeric nanoparticles (PNPs), primarily work by improving the presentation of antigens on MHC molecules (signal 1) (*Created with* BioRender.com). PAMPs, pathogen-associated molecular patterns; DAMPs, damage-associated molecular patterns; PRR, pattern recognition receptor; APC, antigen-presenting cell; MHC, major histocompatibility complex; TCR, T-cell receptor; BCR, B-cell receptor.

and Bijker, 2021). PNPs, as nano adjuvants, provide controlled and sustained release of antigens, facilitating prolonged exposure of the immune system to these antigens. This extended exposure can boost the adaptive immune response, ultimately leading to better memory formation. Another advantage is the potential for targeted delivery. These NPs can be engineered to direct antigens specifically to immune cells or tissues, thereby increasing the likelihood of effective immune recognition and response (Molino et al., 2013).

## 5. Application of PNPs-based vaccines in infectious diseases and cancer

To date, a variety of protein structures have been used in the development of PNP vaccines. Previous studies have examined various types of PNPs, including self-assembling NPs, bacteriophage-VLP NPs, plant-derived NPs, and human virus-based vectors for their potential for vaccine development against various pathogens, including viral, bacterial, fungal, and parasitic infections (Fig. 23.4) (Butkovich et al., 2021; Diaz et al., 2018).

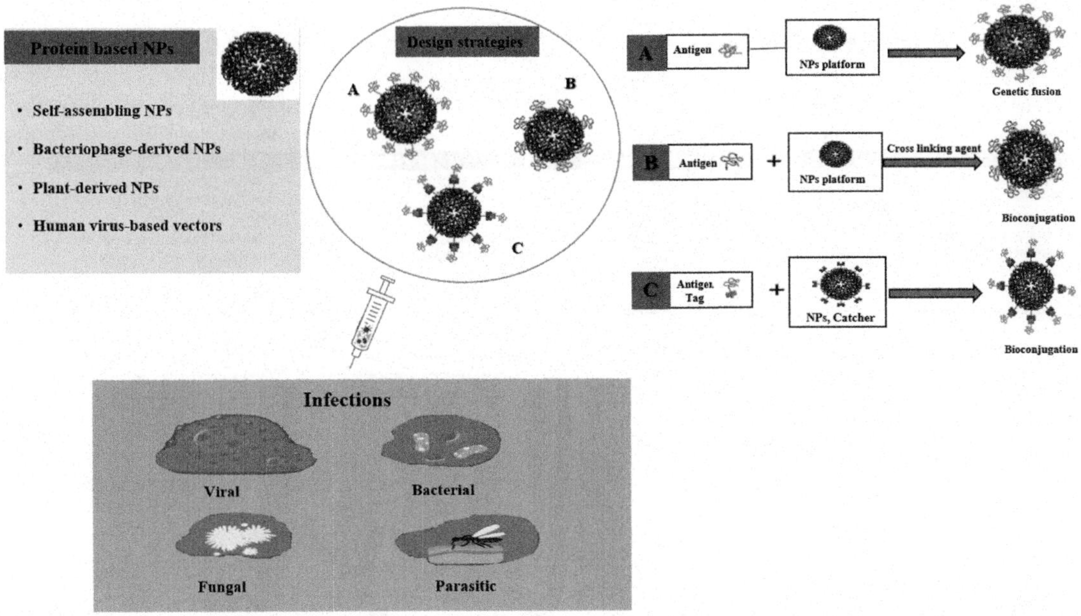


FIGURE 23.4 **Overview of PNP vaccine platforms and their applications in the prevention of infectious disease.** The figure illustrates various types of protein-based NPs, including self-assembling NPs, bacteriophage-derived NPs, plant-derived NPs, and human virus-based vectors. The NP platforms are engineered to present antigens using different approaches: (A) Genetic fusion and (B and C) bioconjugation. The NPs can be applied to target a range of infections, including viral, bacterial, fungal, and parasitic pathogens (*Created with* BioRender.com).

The continued exploration of PNP platforms is crucial for developing vaccines for diseases with limited prophylactic options and for preparing rapid responses to emerging infectious diseases. By harnessing the distinctive structural and functional attributes of NPs, PNP-based anticancer vaccines significantly boost the immune system's capacity to recognize and destroy cancer cells, representing a major advancement in immunotherapy (Rosenberg et al., 2004). These vaccines are designed to deliver TAAs efficiently, addressing the challenge of low immunogenicity often seen in the tumor microenvironment. The NPs, particularly VLPs and caged protein (CP) structures, mimic the organization and size of natural viruses, which makes them ideal for antigen delivery and uptake by APCs (Molino et al., 2017) (Fig. 23.5).

## 6. Important PNP-based vaccines

### 6.1 Heat shock proteins (HSPs)

HSPs are a group of highly conserved proteins that are produced by cells in response to stressful conditions, such as elevated temperatures, oxidative stress, and infections. These proteins play critical roles in protein folding, protection against cellular stress, and immune

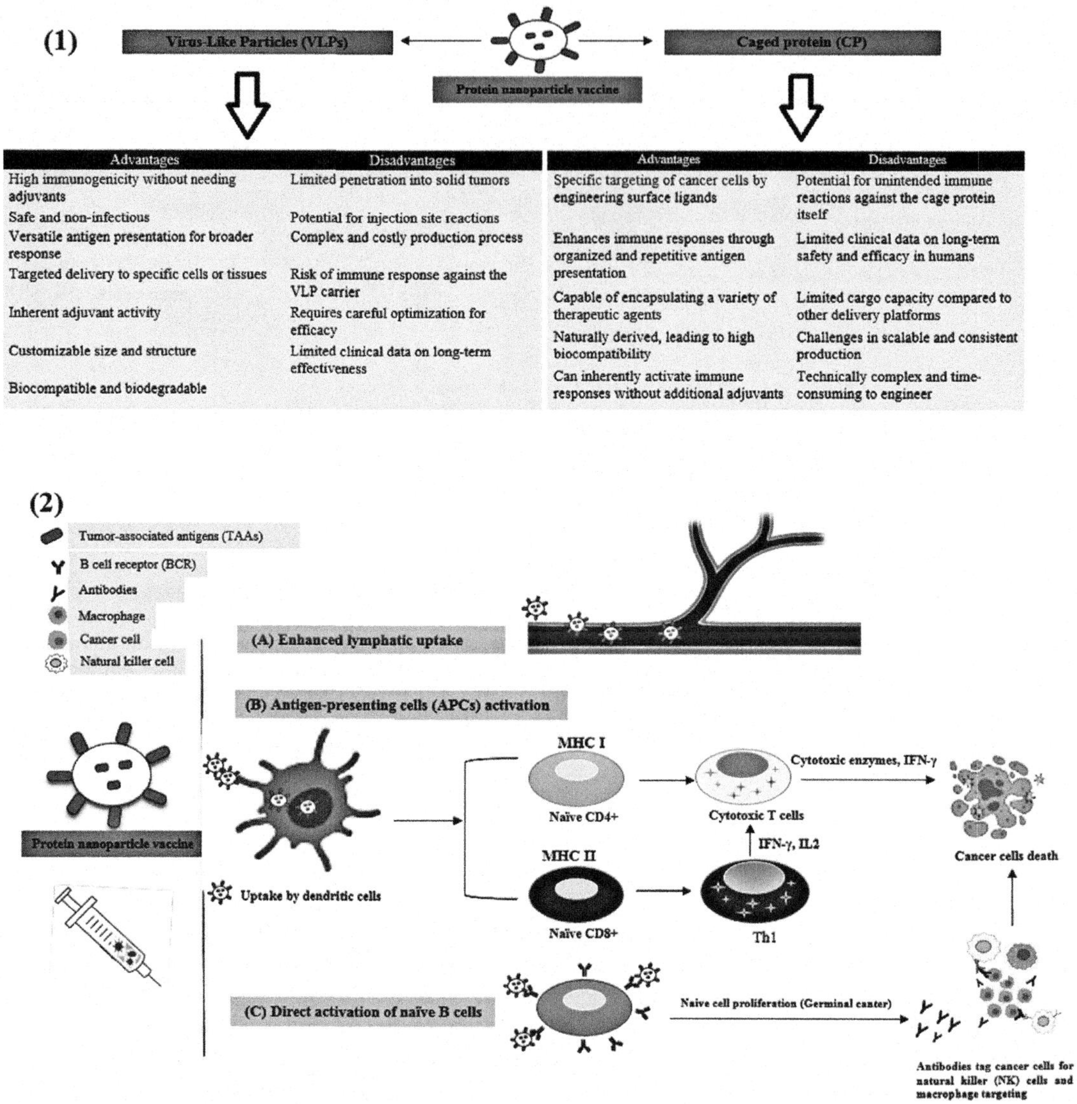


**FIGURE 23.5** **Overview of anti-cancer vaccines utilizing PNPs.** (1): VLPs and caged proteins (CP)-based PNP, highlighting their advantages and disadvantages. (2): Mechanisms of action for PNP vaccines, including enhanced lymphatic uptake, activation of antigen-presenting cells (APCs), and direct activation of naive B cells, leading to a coordinated immune response that targets and destroys cancer cells (*Created with* BioRender.com).

responses (Pockley and Henderson, 2018). In recent years, advancements in HSP-based vaccine development have garnered interest due to their potential to enhance immunogenicity and improve the effectiveness of vaccines against various pathogens, including viruses, bacteria, and tumors. These proteins are categorized based on their molecular weight; for instance, the 70-kilodalton heat shock proteins (HSP70s) are present in nearly all living organisms and play a crucial role in cellular behaviors (Kampinga and Craig, 2010). HSPs serve multiple functions in immunology. They possess chaperone activity, assisting in the proper folding of proteins and preventing misfolding and aggregation. Among the different types of HSPs, HSP70 and HSP90 are critical in stress responses, binding a wide array of client proteins, including tumor antigens (Das et al., 2019). HSPs are effective in stimulating both innate and specific immune responses. Their function as 'danger signals' that activate various host defense mechanisms is being utilized in the development of vaccines for infectious diseases and cancer (Dubaniewicz, 2013). Another characteristic unique to HSP-based vaccines in cancer prophylaxis is their ability to reduce the expression of molecular chaperones in tumor cells, thereby diminishing their tumorigenic characteristics and malignant potential (Didenko et al., 2018). Ito et al. found that hyperthermia using magnetic NPs induced necrotic cell death in rats and led to the release of protein HSP70, which elicited strong antitumor immunity. This suggests that magnetic NPs, as nanocarriers, can enhance HSP70 expression and facilitate in situ vaccination, contributing to novel antitumor prophylaxis (Ito et al., 2003). Additionally, when the conjugation of magnetic NPs with HSP70 is administered systemically into animals with C6 glioma, they preferentially concentrate in the tumor tissue, significantly enhancing the contrast in magnetoresonance imaging of the tumor. These conjugates are expected to improve the outcomes of glioma surgeries and serve as a targeted therapeutic vaccine (Shevtsov et al., 2014).

In the context of infectious diseases, HSPs can function as adjuvants. The co-administration of HSPs with vaccine antigens has demonstrated enhanced immune responses in viral infections, with HSP70 evaluated as an adjuvant in protein-based nanovaccines against HIV (Milani et al., 2024; Akbari et al., 2022). Recently, small heat shock protein 16.5 (sHsp16.5) from the thermophilic archeon *Methanocaldoccus jannaschii* assembles into a 24-subunit caged NP, which acts as a scaffold for enhancing immune responses (Richert et al., 2013). Research has demonstrated that conjugating sHsp16.5 with antigens, such as ovalbumin (OVA), significantly boosts immune responses, including a marked increase in OVA-specific IgG levels during influenza challenges. This nonspecific adjuvant activity enhances both local and systemic immune responses, as evidenced by increased trafficking of immune cells to the lungs and lymph nodes.

While HSP-based vaccines hold great promise, research shows that HSP-chaperoned peptides primarily induce protective immunity against autologous tumors rather than allogeneic tumors. Consequently, their effectiveness may vary depending on the specific disease context and individual patient characteristics (Srivastava, 1994). Ongoing studies are exploring whether HSP-based vaccines could be more effective as therapeutic agents administered after disease onset or as prophylactic measures given before disease development.

## 6.2 Ferritin NPs

Ferritin is a widely distributed self-assembling protein that can be genetically modified to present particular antigens. Ferritin is found in almost all living organisms, such as bacteria, fungi, plants, and animals. Its primary role is to store iron in a nontoxic, insoluble form while maintaining its bioavailability within cells by converting it into a soluble form

(Bhaskar and Lim, 2017). This function is crucial for regulating iron levels in the body. Additionally, ferritin helps protect cells from the harmful effects of free iron, which can cause oxidative stress and potentially damage cellular components, leading to cell death (Pantopoulos et al., 2012). The primary type of ferritin measures 12 nm in diameter and comprises 24 subunits. Antigens can be genetically linked to the N-terminal of an individual ferritin subunit (Wang et al., 2019c). In addition to its ability to self-assemble, the ferritin protein complex demonstrates impressive stability under varying thermal conditions and pH levels, enduring temperatures between 80 and 100 °C and pH values ranging from 3 to 10. It exhibits features such as monodispersity, small and uniform size, biocompatibility, biodegradability, cost-effective large-scale production, and compatibility with surface conjugation through different methods (Khoshnejad et al., 2018). The extraction of iron from the internal cavity of ferritin creates a hollow cage structure that can be filled with various bioactive compounds. This characteristic makes it a promising carrier, offering numerous benefits (Palombarini et al., 2020).

Ferritin NPs have three unique interfaces that can be utilized: the inner surface, the outer surface, and the areas between subunits. These interfaces can be altered using chemical and genetic engineering techniques, which enhances their potential as nanocages for vaccine applications in biotechnology (Fig. 23.6).

The H- and L-chains of ferritin can be combined with various antigens to create recombinant vaccine particles that incorporate multiple antigens, facilitating the development of multivalent nanovaccines. For example, *Staphylococcus aureus* (SA) alpha-hemolysin is often responsible for harmful cytotoxic effects associated with SA infections. To address this, a synthetic DNA segment coding for Hla121-138 was linked to the N-terminus of the ferritin coding sequence. This construct was then cloned into the pET-28A plasmid and introduced into *E. coli* BL21 (DE3) cells, enabling the production of an epitope-based NP (EpNP). The NPs effectively triggered the generation of potent neutralizing antibodies against hemolysin and provided significant protection in a mouse model subjected to SA as a bacterial skin infection (Von Hoven et al., 2016).

Various studies also have shown that ferritin-based nanovaccines can induce robust humoral immune responses against viral infections such as H2 influenza (Houser et al., 2022), and SARS-CoV-2 (Powell et al., 2021), which are presently undergoing clinical trials. The design of an influenza nanovaccine can be found in the research conducted by Kanekiyo et al. where trimeric hemagglutinin (HA) was incorporated into the three-fold axis of ferritin NPs, leading to the creation of particles that displayed eight trimeric viral spikes on their surfaces (Kanekiyo et al., 2013). This was achieved by fusing the HA gene to the N-terminal region of ferritin, strategically placed around the three-fold axis, which allowed HA monomers to be positioned closely enough to facilitate interactions. This proximity enabled the reciprocal stabilization necessary for the oligomerization of the conformation-dependent trimeric antigens. The resulting ferritin-HA NPs not only exhibited favorable physical characteristics such as uniformity, preservation of native conformation, and symmetric presentation but also demonstrated a significantly enhanced immunogenic response. In fact, the NP-based vaccine elicited HA antibody levels that were over 10 times greater in immunized mice compared with those generated by the currently licensed inactivated vaccine. The encouraging outcomes from this approach include the development of three influenza vaccines that are set to undergo phase 1 clinical trials (Kanekiyo et al., 2013). Several

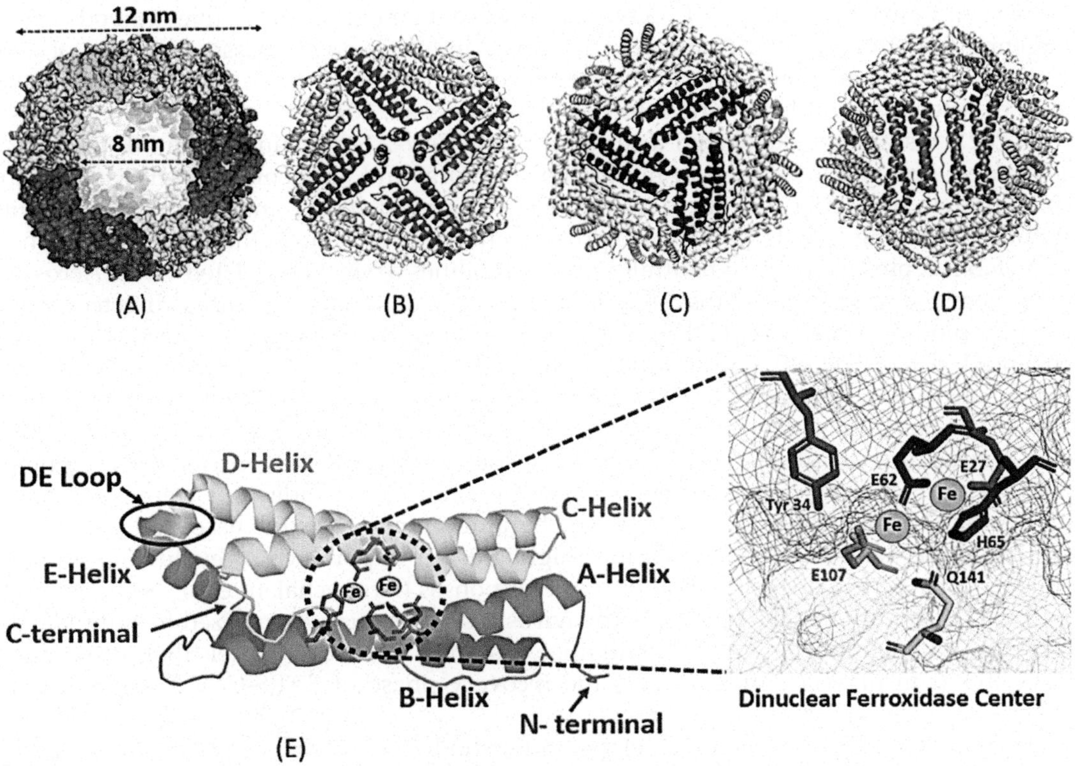


**FIGURE 23.6 A computer-generated representation of a human heteropolymer ferritin.** (A) A computer-generated representation of a human heteropolymer ferritin, comprised of 70% H subunits (shown in cyan) and 30% L subunits (shown in red). Views of the ferritin are presented through the 4-fold (B), 3-fold (C), and 2-fold (D) channels. (E) a schematic illustration of a single ferritin subunit, highlighting its five helices (labeled A, B, C, D, and E) as well as the residues located at the di-iron ferroxidase center (Reutovich et al., 2023). *From Reutovich, A.A., Srivastava, A.K., Arosio, P. & Bou-Abdallah, F. (2023). Ferritin nanocages as efficient nanocarriers and promising platforms for COVID-19 and other vaccines development. Biochimica et Biophysica Acta - General Subjects, 1867(3). https://doi.org/10.1016/j.bbagen.2022.130288.* For Interpretation of the references to color in this figure legend, please refer online version of this title.

ferritin-based influenza vaccine candidates have undergone evaluation in phase 1 clinical trials, demonstrating a wide range of responses similar to those seen in preclinical animal studies (Houser et al., 2022; Andrews et al., 2022).

Recently, Nie et al. developed a multiepitope nanovaccine for influenza, called MHF, which integrates linear epitopes derived from HA and matrix protein 2 with bacterial ferritin. The MHF formulation self-assembles into consistent NPs and has been shown to elicit cross-reactive neutralizing antibodies, promote cellular immunity, and generate long-term memory B-cell responses in mice. This intranasal multiepitope nanovaccine provides complete protection against the H3N2 strain and partial protection against H1N1 (Nie et al., 2024). Furthermore, Yassine et al. fabricated a fusion protein combining the H1 HA stem with ferritin, which was then organized into an NP known as H1-SS-NP. Immunization of mice and rabbits with this H1-SS-NP led to the generation of protective antibody levels targeting the HA stem. Either the H1-SS-NP vaccine itself or the passive transfer of antibodies produced in response to the vaccine provided protection for mice against a lethal dose of heterozygous H5N1 viral infection (Yassine et al., 2015).

In 2021, researchers developed a series of SARS-CoV-2 S-domain-ferritin NP utilizing a structure-based vaccine design to mimic the structural and antigenic characteristics of the spike protein of SARS-CoV. These immunogens triggered strong antibody responses with significant binding activity to the spike protein, effective blockade of the human angiotensin 2 (ACE2) receptor, and robust neutralization capabilities against the related virus. Across all immunogen design groups, they found noteworthy antibody responses directed at the receptor-binding domain (RBD), which demonstrated ACE2-blocking effects that likely enhanced neutralization. Furthermore, experiments aimed at dose reduction indicated that a substantial decrease in antigen could still produce strong antibody responses, while also maintaining high levels of neutralizing antibodies against the heterologous SARS-CoV-1 virus (Joyce et al., 2021). The immune responses generated by ferritin NPs combined with the ALFQ (army liposome formulation containing QS21) adjuvant were consistently more effective than those produced with the aluminum-hydroxide-based adjuvant. This finding aligns with various studies that highlight the importance of evaluating antigen-adjuvant pairing to achieve optimal immune responses (Arunachalam et al., 2021; Wørzner et al., 2021). Additionally, the novel coronavirus fusion ferritin was utilized to stimulate the production of neutralizing antibodies in mice, resulting in antibody levels that were double those found in plasma donors during the recovery phase of SARS-CoV-2 (Powell et al., 2021).

Another study by Chen et al. developed a ferritin-based vaccine candidate for foot-and-mouth disease virus utilizing Sf-9 cells. However, the vaccine provided only limited protection in mice compared to the commercially available inactivated vaccine. It was noted that enhancements to the expression system are necessary to improve the solubility of the resultant NPs (Chen et al., 2020). When developing a ferritin-based vaccine, incorporating antigens at the terminal ends of ferritin can lead to solubility issues. This problem often arises because the added antigen sequences may form hydrophobic regions or disrupt the overall charge distribution of the ferritin, resulting in unwanted interactions and aggregation. To address these solubility challenges, several strategies can be employed. One effective approach is to incorporate flexible linker sequences that connect the ferritin subunit to the antigen. Another strategy involves engineering the antigen itself by modifying its sequence to enhance solubility while maintaining its immunogenic properties. This could include introducing more polar amino acids or reducing hydrophobic areas. Furthermore, expressing and purifying the engineered ferritin-antigen fusion proteins in the presence of solubility-enhancing agents, such as specific buffer systems or co-expressed chaperones, can help maintain solubility and promote proper folding (Chakraborti and Chakrabarti, 2019; Uchida et al., 2010).

In the context of a ferritin-based nanovaccine for cancer prophylaxis, the ferritin NPs carrying HPV16 oncogene E7 peptide or MC38 tumor-derived neoantigens elicited a significantly stronger antigen-specific cytotoxic T lymphocyte response, around two to three times greater, compared to soluble peptide antigens. These ferritin NPs are quickly transported to the lymph nodes and specifically target DCs, with a particular emphasis on the $CD8\alpha^{+}$

subset, following subcutaneous immunization (Wang et al., 2019b). Furthermore, ferritin NPs are specifically designed for the targeted delivery of chemotherapeutic agents, effectively reducing associated risks. The benefits of ferritin include straightforward surface modification, a high capacity for drug loading, and excellent biocompatibility. These characteristics make ferritin a versatile nanocarrier suitable for advancing research and development in PNP vaccines and targeted drug delivery systems (Bhushan et al., 2014). It is essential to establish standardized protocols to ensure the reproducibility of the biological production process, making ferritin-based nanovaccines more accessible. However, a challenge arises as many self-assembled sequences originate from nonhuman species, potentially resulting in unintended immune reactions when used as vaccines (Attarilar et al., 2020). Table 23.1 reviews other ferritin NP-based vaccines targeting infectious diseases.

**TABLE 23.1** Other examples of Ferritin NP-based vaccines for infectious diseases.

| NP | Type of infectious disease | Disease | Specific immune responses | Reference |
|---|---|---|---|---|
| Ferritin | Viral | ZIKV infections | Robust humoral and cellular immune responses and protect mice from lethal virus challenge. | Pattnaik et al. (2023) |
| Ferritin | Viral | CSF | Induced robust and sustained antibody responses; increased IFN-γ and IL-4 levels; protected rabbits from viremia and fever after challenge. | Song et al. (2024) |
| Ferritin | Viral | Zika virus infection | Induced high antigen-specific IgG antibody levels; enhanced T/B lymphocyte activation and memory cell generation; safe and effective with adjuvants. | Liu et al. (2024) |
| Ferritin | Viral | Influenza | Neutralizing abs. | Georgiev et al. (2018) |
| Ferritin | Viral | Chronic hepatitis B | IgG abs, antigen-specific abs, protection against challenge. | Wang et al. (2020) |
| Ferritin | Viral | Hepatitis C | Antigen-specific abs, neutralizing abs. | Yan et al. (2020) |
| Ferritin | Bacterial | *P. aeruginosa* pneumonia | Induced quick and efficient immunity; provided protection against *Pseudomonas aeruginosa* pneumonia; enhanced mucosal immunity with intranasal administration. | Li et al. (2023) |
| Ferritin | Bacterial | *P. aeruginosa* lung infection | Induced a Th1-predominant immune response; enhanced protection against A-type and B-type flagellin strains; demonstrated good biocompatibility and safety. | Wei et al. (2023) |
| Ferritin | Bacterial | Lyme disease | Strong bacterial-specific antibody responses. | Kamp et al. (2020) |

## 6.3 VLPS: Bacteriophage platforms

Bacteriophages or phages, are viruses that specifically target bacteria and do not affect human cells. They consist of nucleic acid (either DNA or RNA) surrounded by a protein shell. Bacteriophage VLPS are highly diverse and can be used in a variety of applications, including vaccine development, drug delivery, and gene editing. There are various kinds of bacteriophages, each differing in shape and size. Notably, platforms such as P22, Qβ, λ, and T4 phages have been engineered for use in vaccines to combat a wide range of infectious diseases caused by pathogens as well as tumor cells. Bacteriophages demonstrate exceptional stability in challenging environments, can be produced in large quantities, pose no harm to humans or animals, and have a proven safety record for mammalian use (Razazan et al., 2019; Esmaeilzadeh et al., 2022).

The *Salmonella enterica* bacteriophage P22 is considered one of the most promising candidates for creating VLP nanocages. This phage is characterized by an icosahedral capsid that houses double-stranded DNA and features a tail region (Wang et al., 2019a). The phage's morphogenesis involves self-assembly using the scaffolding protein (SP, gp8) and coat protein (CP, gp5), along with minor proteins (gp7, gp16, and gp20) and a portal complex made of 12 gp1 copies. The SP interacts with the CP through coulomb interactions to facilitate assembly (Cortines et al., 2014). A key aspect of P22 VLP's application as an NP is its role as a nanocarrier for targeted delivery. While this use has been previously demonstrated with other VLPs, Kang et al. were pioneers in suggesting the bacteriophage P22 capsid as a framework for developing such nanoplatforms (Kang et al., 2008). The P22 VLP's ability to incorporate various components through genetic modifications of the SP protein has been demonstrated with the inclusion of the nucleoprotein from the influenza A virus (Patterson et al., 2013) as well as a poly antigen made up of matrix proteins from the respiratory syncytial virus (RSV) (Schwarz et al., 2016). Additionally, researchers have explored the possibility of presenting antigens on the exterior surface of the P22 VLP. This approach presents an advantage over traditional methods, especially since the intricate structure of some viruses can complicate and increase production costs. In contrast, external antigens can be easily attached to the P22 VLP's surface, making it a more versatile and cost-effective vaccine platform for various viral targets (Essus et al., 2023). A study found that pretreatment with the P22 phage before a single dose of OVA-sHsp significantly increased OVA-specific serum IgG just 4 days after exposure to influenza A (Richert et al., 2012). This suggests that P22, being potentially immunogenic even without modifications, shows promise as a vaccine platform for eliciting targeted immune responses. Another study found that P22 VLP is a promising platform for delivering peptide antigens in cancer vaccines. VLP-$OVA_T$, displaying a T-cell epitope, effectively induced CTL responses and inhibited tumor growth in mice, demonstrating its potential for personalized cancer immunotherapy (Li et al., 2021).

The dimensions of bacteriophage-based VLPs, around 30 nm, play a crucial role in their ability to efficiently drain to lymph nodes and effectively activate B cells. Additionally, these VLPs offer significant benefits as both their external surfaces and internal components can be tailored. This versatility allows for the presentation of various epitopes on the surface, while the interior can be engineered to contain TLR ligands, including RNA or DNA sequences that can stimulate TLR7/8 and TLR9, respectively (Klimek et al., 2018). Qβ VLPs are obtained from the Qβ phage of *Escherichia coli (E. coli)*, and both their structure and immunogenic properties have been thoroughly studied. This versatile platform supports the incorporation of a wide range of antigens, such as peptides, proteins, and carbohydrates. Additionally, it facilitates the rational design and enhancement of the antigenic structure integrated into the carrier. Qβ has been utilized as a framework for vaccine development in both infectious diseases and cancer, such as HPV (Josi et al., 2024) and COVID-19 (Guo et al., 2021).

Tailed bacteriophages, like T4, are the most numerous and broadly distributed organisms on the planet. T4, a bacteriophage belonging to the Myoviridae family, specifically targets *E. coli*. It has been an invaluable model organism in molecular biology and biotechnology for several reasons.

T4 phage is known for its relatively simple structure, consisting of a DNA genome and a protein coat, which makes it an excellent subject for studying viral replication and gene expression. Moreover, T4 has served as a powerful tool for genetic engineering, particularly in the development of cloning vectors and the study of gene function. Researchers have utilized its robust genomic tools, leading to advances in fields such as synthetic biology and vaccine design (Miller et al., 2003). Table 23.2 presents some examples of various phage VLPs in protein-based nanovaccine developments.

**TABLE 23.2** Examples of application of various phage VLPs in protein-based nanovaccine.

| VLP phage | Vaccine name | Infection/cancer | Administration | Specific immune response | Reference |
|---|---|---|---|---|---|
| P22 | EscC-P22 | Enterohemorrhagic *E. coli* (EHEC) | Intranasal | Bactericidal activity of serum from mice vaccinated | Huerta-Saquero et al. (2023) |
| | Hcp1-P22 VLP | *Burkholderia pseudomallei* infection | Intranasal | Specific IgG, IgG1, IgG2c, and IgA antibody responses | Khakhum et al. (2024) |
| | BTZ-loaded SP94-catechol-P22 WB | Human hepatocellular carcinoma (HCC) | - | Cytotoxic effects in a dose-dependent manner | Min et al. (2014) |
| Qβ | Qβ-HPVag | Human papillomavirus (HPV) carcinoma | Subcutaneous | Systemic increase in both $CD8^+$ and $CD4^+$ T cells | Josi et al. (2024) |
| | Qβ-muc-1 | Cancer | Subcutaneous | High IgG levels/cytotoxic T-cell production | Yin et al. (2018) |
| λ | λ-HPV-16 E7 | Cancer | Subcutaneous | Anti-tumor effects of vaccinated mice against challenge with E7-expressing tumor cell line, TC-1 | Ghaemi et al. (2010) |
| | λF7-gpD: E75 | Cancer | Subcutaneous | High level of IL-4 and IFN-γ, enhanced $CD8^+$ T cells, increased Foxp3 in $CD25+/CD4^+$ | Arab et al. (2018) |
| T4 | T4–SARS-CoV-2 | SARS-CoV-2 | Intramuscular | Balanced TH1- and TH2-derived IgG responses | Zhu et al. (2021) |
| | 3M2e-T4 | Influenza | Intranasal | IgA/$CD4^+$ T cells production | Mengling Li et al. (2023) |

## 6.4 Silk fibroin

Silk fibroin (SF) is an FDA-approved biopolymer derived from silkworms, most commonly the species *Bombyx mori*. Silk protein mainly consists of SF, making up about 70%–80%, and sericin, which accounts for 20%–30%. The structure of silk includes two parallel monofilaments, with sericin surrounding the outer surface of the SF fibers, effectively creating a monofilament. Sericin contributes to the stability of the cocoon by linking the two SF fibers together, serving both protective and adhesive functions for SF. The distinctive amino acid makeup and spatial configuration of SF enable it to possess flexible molecular chains, outstanding biocompatibility, low allergenicity, and environmentally friendly properties, positioning it as a promising option for applications in drug delivery and tissue engineering (Daneshvar et al., 2024; Mottaghitalab et al., 2015a, 2015b; Shirangi et al., 2023). Silk fibroin nanoparticles (SFNPs) possess numerous modifiable sites, allowing for their utilization either individually or in conjunction with a variety of antigen or drug delivery methods (Hassani Besheli et al., 2018; Rezaei et al., 2020). Our research team has conducted some studies on the application of SFNPs as a nano-adjuvant in vaccine development targeting both bacterial and viral infections. For example, in our previous study, we investigated a PNP vaccine based on SFNPs targeting urinary tract infections (UTIs) caused by uropathogenic *Escherichia coli* (UPEC), a major contributor to UTI prevalence. The resulting particles, termed Fusion-e-SFNPs, had a diameter of approximately 180 nm and achieved an impressive encapsulation efficiency of antigen of about 88%. The SFNP vaccine formulations successfully elicited robust humoral and cellular immune responses, evidenced by the production of key cytokines such as IFN-$\gamma$, IL-4, and IL-17 compared with control groups. Mice immunized with these antigen-encapsulated SFNPs showed a significant increase in total IgG levels and an elevated IgG2a/IgG1 ratio. Importantly, the antigen's incorporation within the SFNPs acted as an effective nano-adjuvant, protecting the bladder and kidneys against experimental UTIs over 6 months (Hasanzadeh et al., 2020). In 2021, we also used SFNPs as a nano-adjuvant to deliver recombinant hepatitis B surface antigen (HBsAg). HBsAg was successfully loaded onto SFNPs using both physical and chemical methods. Specifically, approximately 45.6% of HBsAg was released from physical-SFNPs, while about 34.1% was released from chemical-SFNPs, suggesting that the physical loading method allows for a more favorable release profile. After 28 and 56 days postinjection, mice immunized with physical SFNPs exhibited significantly higher levels of specific total IgG, IgG1, and IgG2a antibodies against HBsAg compared to those immunized with the chemically loaded SFNPs and the commercial hepatitis B vaccine (Rezaei et al., 2021). In 2023, we also evaluated the efficacy of a multi-epitope vaccine encapsulated in SFNPs against UTIs caused by *Pseudomonas aeruginosa,* the second most common UTI pathogen. This vaccine formulation achieved an encapsulation efficiency of 85%, enhancing the stability and targeted delivery of the antigen. The mean particle size of these SFNPs was determined to be 130 nm, which promotes better recognition and uptake by the immune system. After 35 days, 24% of the encapsulated multi-epitope antigen was released, indicating a sustained release profile conducive to prolonging the immune response. Notably, the IgG response following vaccination was sustained for at least 110 days, demonstrating long-lasting immunity. Mice receiving this multi-epitope vaccine exhibited significant protection against *P. aeruginosa* during bladder challenge assays, highlighting the vaccine's efficacy

(Rezvanirad et al., 2023). In another study, we also assessed a novel intranasal vaccine candidate based on recombinant protein encapsulated in SF-sodium alginate NPs (SF-SANPs), against respiratory infection (Pneumonia) caused by *Klebsiella pneumoniae*. Taking advantage of the unique properties of SF polymer and the mucoadhesive characteristics of alginate polymer, this study demonstrated enhanced systemic and mucosal antibody production. Antigen encapsulated in SF-SANPs induced a similar response to alum but with higher IFN-$\gamma$ production. Additionally, in vivo studies showed that the SF-SANPs vaccine candidate effectively protected the lungs of mice from experimental Pneumonia caused by *K. pneumoniae*, significantly mitigating lung inflammation (Shahbazi et al., 2023). Our findings from different studies indicate that SFNPs could serve as effective adjuvants or carriers for vaccines, highlighting the way for the development of novel and more efficient PNP nano-vaccine formulations against various infections.

In the cancer vaccine, the study by Bari et al. investigated an innovative immunotherapy approach using SFNPs to redirect preexisting immune responses against a nontumor-associated antigen, OVA, toward tumor cells. By loading SFNPs with OVA and the adjuvant CpG, the researchers demonstrated that these NPs effectively promoted the internalization of the antigen by both tumor cells and dentritic cells (DCs), eliciting robust OVA-specific cytotoxic T-cell responses, and significantly modifying the tumor microenvironment. The administration of SFNPs-OVA and SFNPs-CpG not only delayed tumor growth in murine melanoma and bladder cancer models but also resulted in complementary effects, enhancing the immune response and downregulating proteins associated with tumor progression. The findings indicate the potential for translating this "Trojan horse" strategy into clinical settings as a universal cancer treatment, leveraging recall antigens from standard vaccinations to engage the immune system against various solid tumors (Bari et al., 2023). Additionally, the potential of the targeted SFNP system as an effective approach for the specific delivery of anticancer therapies was suggested in our previous study for future treatment of malignant lung cancers (Mottaghitalab et al., 2017).

## 6.5 Gelatin

Gelatin is FDA-approved for use in pharmaceuticals, cosmetics, and food due to its long history of safety (Kommareddy et al., 2007). It is classified as a polyampholyte due to its balance of cationic and anionic groups. Gelatin is a denatured protein derived from collagen through hydrolysis, resulting in two types: type A, produced via acidic hydrolysis, and type B, obtained through basic hydrolysis. These types differ in their isoelectric points (IEPs); type A has an IEP of 7–9, while type B has an IEP of 4–5. Research indicates that type B gelatin NPs (GNPs) demonstrate superior drug delivery capabilities compared with type A. Researchers are particularly interested in gelatin polymer because of its high concentration of amino acids, specifically glycine, proline, and alanine. These amino acids occur in repeating sequences and contribute to the characteristic triple-helical structure of gelatin (Sahoo et al., 2015; Rajabnejadkeleshteri et al., 2021). Some properties of GNPs, including thermal stability and swelling behavior, are influenced by the amphoteric interactions within the gelatin. Furthermore, recent reports indicate that murine bone marrow DCs exhibit a substantial uptake of GNPs, making them effective for delivering antigens specifically to DCs (Coester et al., 2006). These promising findings, along with the biocompatibility, nontoxic nature, and cost-effectiveness of gelatin, position it as a viable option for assessment as an immunoadjuvant.

Intranasal and oral vaccination, in contrast to systemic methods, eliminates the pain and risk of infections that can occur with injections. It is also more cost-effective and facilitates the immunization of large populations, particularly for respiratory infections (Mangla et al., 2022). A similar study focuses on the development of oral vaccine formulations using urease-loaded and Omp31-loaded gelatin micro/nanoparticles (MNPs) to combat brucellosis, a disease with significant medical and economic implications. The researchers created distinct formulations, which included individual urease/gelatin and Omp31/gelatin MNPs, as well as a combination of both (referred to as the MNP cocktail), and administered these orally to mice. The immunological assessments demonstrated that all vaccine formulations prompted the production of specific IgG and IgA antibodies while promoting a Th1–Th17 immune response, evidenced by cytokine measurements and lymphocyte proliferation assays. Notably, splenocytes isolated from the immunized mice showed a strong recall proliferative response upon challenge with the virulent *B. melitensis* strain. The results suggest that the MNPs cocktail holds promise as a candidate for subunit vaccine development against brucellosis, while the gelatin MNPs serve as an effective delivery system for the oral administration of Brucella antigens (Abkar et al., 2023). In another study, the administration of tetanus toxoid (TT) encapsulated in GNPs in BALB/c mice successfully stimulated a systemic IgG response and resulted in a notably greater cytokine response (IL-2 and IFNγ) compared to the alum-TT vaccine. Following their uptake by APCs, GNPs are broken down by the lysosomal enzyme collagenase, which releases TT inside the cells. Additionally, GNPs are capable of delivering a substantial quantity of antigen to APCs, promoting a specific immune response against the antigen (Sudheesh et al., 2011).

By successfully conjugating the NS2 gene (nonstructural protein 2) of Hepatitis C Virus (HCV) with GNPs, a research study demonstrates this conjugation not only protects the gene from degradation but also facilitates transformation efficacy as an initial step to serve as a delivery system for an HCV vaccine. The findings advocate for the potential of GNPs as a safe, efficient, and cost-effective system for gene and vaccine delivery, particularly for addressing the public health challenge posed by HCV (Sabet et al., 2017).

The protein structure of gelatin is rich in functional groups, making it suitable for attaching antigens. This enables the creation of comprehensive vaccine formulations that combine antigens with immunostimulatory oligonucleotides as adjuvants, which could be used to target cancer or infections. For example, Zwiorek et al. focus on the development and evaluation of cationized GNPs as effective carriers for immunostimulatory CpG oligodeoxynucleotides (CpG-ODNs). The study demonstrates that these NPs enhance the uptake and immunostimulatory effects of CpG-ODNs in both murine and human immune cells, particularly in DCs and B cells. The positive charge on the NPs promotes phagocytosis and subsequent activation of immune responses (Zwiorek et al., 2008). A similar research study explored the development of nanovaccine using polyethyleneimine (PEI)-modified GNPs as carriers for the mucosal delivery of the antigen OVA and the immunostimulant polyinosinic: polycytidylic acid (poly (I: C) against cancer. The positive charge introduced by PEI on the GNPs enhances cellular uptake by APCs, such as macrophages and DCs, and enables effective adsorption of negatively charged antigens like OVA and poly (I: C). The results indicate that when mice are intranasally immunized with these OVA/poly (I: C)-loaded GNPs, there is a significant increase in the production of specific IgG in serum, as well as secretory IgA in nasal and lung lavages. This immunization strategy also demonstrates efficacy in inhibiting tumor growth in a cancer model, indicating that the combination of GNPs with poly(I: C) serves not only as an effective vaccine delivery system but also as a potential therapeutic approach against tumors and infections (Lin et al., 2019).

## 6.6 Albumin

Albumin is a protein that constitutes approximately 50%–60% of the total protein found in plasma and lymph (Elsadek and Kratz, 2012). Albumin is a natural nanocarrier that can create noncovalent complexes with various natural and synthetic substances. This protein is characterized by its biocompatibility, biodegradability, and nontoxic nature. Because of these properties, albumin-based nanocarriers have garnered significant interest for applications in drug or antigen delivery. Furthermore, albumin NPs can be produced easily under mild conditions through methods such as coacervation, controlled desolvation, or emulsion processes. They typically have a smaller diameter, ranging from 50 to 300 nm, and generally offer enhanced controlled-release characteristics over liposomes, potentially leading to improved patient acceptance and adherence. On a commercial scale, albumins are primarily sourced in significant amounts from egg whites (ovalbumin), bovine serum (bovine serum albumin, BSA), and human serum (human serum albumin, HSA), but they can also be extracted from soybeans, milk, and various grains (Elzoghby et al., 2012).

Due to the specific primary structure, albumin NPs can be easily modified on their surface, thanks to the presence of various functional groups such as carboxylic and amino groups. Typically, the attachment of ligands for surface modification of albumin NPs is performed through the formation of covalent bonds between the ligands and the functional groups found on the albumin surface. Alternatively, techniques such as surface coating or electrostatic adsorption can also be employed to modify the NP surfaces (Loureiro et al., 2016). For example, in the study, two types of nanocarriers, including adenovirus (Ad) and HSA-NP were developed. The surface of these negatively charged nanocarriers was modified by coating them with a positively charged HPV16 E7 MHC I–specific epitope, aiming to facilitate effective delivery to APCs. The authors conclude that these modified heterologous nano complexes are a promising strategy for vaccination against HPV-induced cervical cancer, showing potential for stimulating strong immune responses and effectively inhibiting tumor growth (Ghanaat et al., 2023). Another recent study investigated the potential of a vaccine formulation combining domain III of the Zika virus envelope protein (zEDIII) with BSA-NPs containing polyinosinic–polycytidylic acid (NPPI) to elicit an effective immune response against the Zika virus (ZIKV). The research demonstrates that NPPI can be effectively taken up by immature bone marrow DCs in vitro, leading to an increased cellular immune response as determined by histological analysis of treated mouse skin. Mice that were immunized with the zEDIII antigen alongside NPPI generated neutralizing antibodies, which were shown to confer protective effects when transferred to neonatal mice infected with ZIKV (Piva-Amaral et al., 2024). These antibodies mitigated weight loss and clinical symptoms related to the infection, significantly improved survival rates, and were associated with reductions in viable infectious ZIKV, inflammatory cytokines, and tissue damage in the brains of the infected mice.

The dual role of BSA-NPs in provoking an inflammatory response and enhancing the efficacy of antigen delivery suggests their potential as innovative platforms for vaccine development targeting infectious diseases or cancer. For instance, the study assessed the immunostimulant potential of BSA-NPs in conjunction with a recombinant nonstructural protein from Dengue virus (rNS1). Mice immunized with rNS1 in combination with BSA-NPs exhibited a significantly higher seroconversion rate, indicating improved immune response against the antigen compared to those receiving rNS1 alone (da Silva et al., 2018). In a similar study on nanovaccine design against *P. aeruginosa*, researchers investigated the efficacy of BSA-NPs loaded with antigens from *P. aeruginosa* as a potential vaccine to mitigate lung pathology in mice following nasal infection with this opportunistic pathogen. The researchers immunized mice with either empty BSA-NPs, BSA-NPs containing *P. aeruginosa* antigens, or other control formulations. Their findings demonstrated that mice vaccinated with BSA-NPs containing antigens exhibited a significant increase in *anti-Pseudomonas* IgG antibodies, particularly IgG1, and a notable production of IgG2a, which are indicative of a strong humoral response. Histopathological analysis of lung tissues from the immunized mice revealed substantial reductions in inflammation, edema, and other pathological signs when compared to control groups (Rodrigues et al., 2013; Maria de Souza Morais et al., 2018). These findings suggest the potential of BSA-NPs as a novel vaccine platform to induce protective immunity and mitigate lung inflammation, offering promise for treating infections in immunocompromised patients and those with cystic fibrosis.

## 7. Safety and efficacy of PNP vaccines

PNP vaccines are recognized for their strong safety profile, which is largely attributed to their biocompatibility and biodegradability. The materials used in PNPs are generally well-tolerated by the body, reducing the risk of severe adverse reactions. This makes them suitable for use in populations that are often more vulnerable to side effects, such as the elderly or those with compromised immune systems (Tapia et al., 2023). One of the primary safety benefits of PNPs is the reduced likelihood of inducing harmful immune responses. Unlike some traditional vaccine platforms, PNPs can be engineered to minimize the risk of triggering excessive or inappropriate immune activation. For instance, nonviral PNPs can be designed to avoid the risk of pathogenicity, a common concern with live-attenuated or inactivated virus vaccines. Furthermore, PNPs can also be designed to degrade into nontoxic byproducts after they have fulfilled their function, which adds a layer of safety. Clinical studies have generally reported low rates of severe side effects, with most adverse reactions being mild, such as temporary soreness at the injection site or mild flu-like symptoms. Despite their favorable safety profile, some challenges remain.

The efficacy of PNP vaccines has been shown in multiple studies, particularly in their ability to generate strong and long-lasting immune responses (Hasanzadeh et al., 2020; Rezvanirad et al., 2023). Nanovaccines are effective at lower antigen doses compared to traditional vaccines, which is a significant advantage in resource-limited settings and for rapid production (Yun and Cho, 2020). One of the key features of PNPs is their ability to mimic the structural characteristics of pathogens, which enhances their recognition by the immune system. This mimicry facilitates efficient uptake by APCs, leading to robust activation of both B cells and T cells. This results in a comprehensive immune response that includes the production of high-affinity antibodies and the development of memory cells, which are essential for long-term protection (Yun and Cho, 2020). Moreover, PNPs allow for the incorporation of multiple antigens within a single vaccine, enabling the creation of multivalent vaccines that can target various strains of a pathogen or different antigens associated with cancer (Butkovich et al., 2021; Neek et al., 2019; Tapia et al., 2023). This capability enhances the versatility and efficacy of PNP-based vaccines (Tapia et al., 2023). The overview of the safety and efficacy of PNP vaccines is shown in Fig. 23.7.

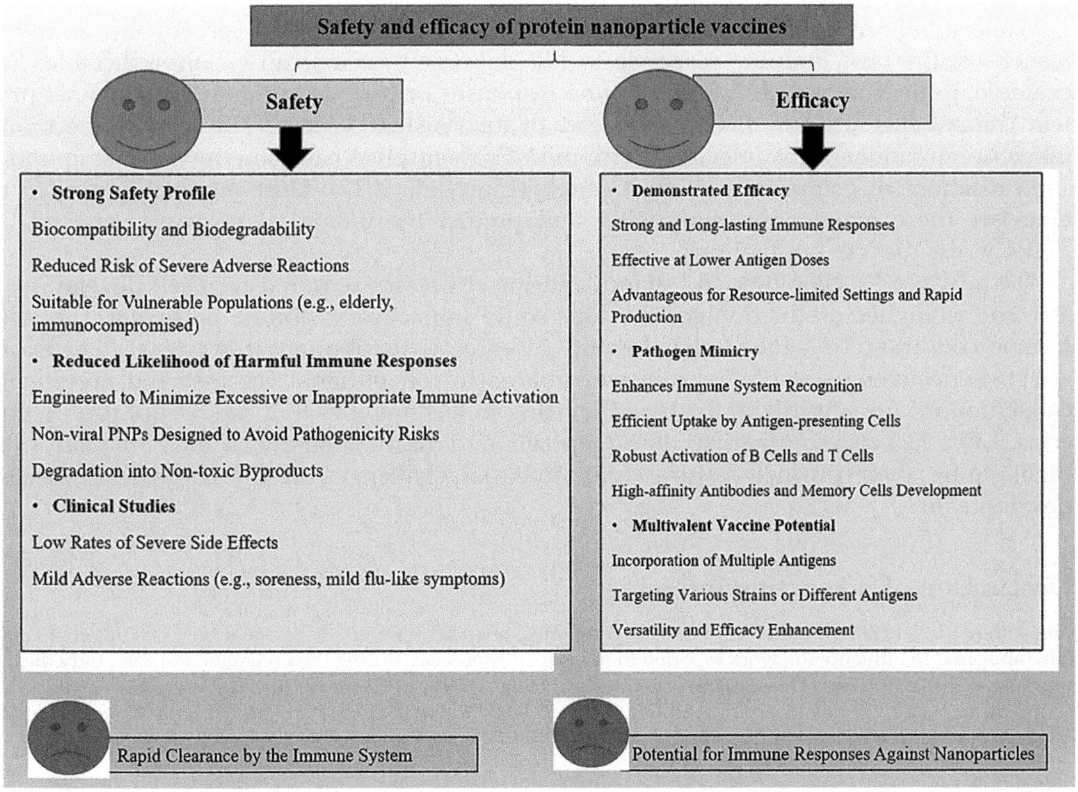


**FIGURE 23.7** Overview of the safety and efficacy of PNP vaccines.

## 8. Conclusion, challenges, and future directions

The successful application of PNPs in various fields, such as infectious diseases and cancer immunotherapy, suggests their versatility and potential. Numerous studies in this field illustrate the efficacy of PNP-based vaccines in eliciting robust immune responses and offering enhanced protection against diverse pathogens and cancer cells. It is crucial to maintain a focus on safety, efficacy, and equitable access to ensure that these advancements can be transformed into meaningful solutions for the prevention and treatment of infectious diseases and cancer. However, there are some challenges in the development of PNPs. For example, the structural integrity of PNPs can be compromised by environmental factors such as temperature, pH, and ionic strength, leading to aggregation or denaturation. Research must focus on optimizing formulations to enhance the stability and shelf life of PNPs under various storage conditions while minimizing the need for complex temperature control (Pulido-Reyes et al., 2017). Furthermore, many PNPs are produced using protein recombinant technology, which can be time-consuming and costly. The development of robust, scalable production methods is crucial to ensure that PNP vaccines can be manufactured efficiently and affordably to meet global needs (Pulido-Reyes et al., 2017; de Pinho Favaro et al., 2022).

While significant efforts have been made to understand how NPs can enhance immune responses, the host immune response to NP delivery systems can be unpredictable. For example, individual variability in immune responses or preexisting immunity against protein components used in PNPs may lead to inconsistent vaccine efficacy. Furthermore, inherent immunogenicity associated with the NPs themselves can sometimes result in undesired reactions or compromised effectiveness (Liu et al., 2017). More research is needed to elucidate these interactions thoroughly and predict the biological responses elicited by PNPs across diverse populations.

The advanced technology and manufacturing processes required for PNP development can lead to higher production costs, which could impact accessibility, particularly in low-income countries. To achieve global equity in vaccine distribution, it is crucial to evaluate the cost-effectiveness of PNP vaccines compared to conventional vaccines and investigate collaborations for subsidizing costs or investing in technologies that can reduce production costs. Table 23.3 also summarizes the advantages and disadvantages of some PNP platforms, highlighting their distinct features and potential challenges in the context of vaccine development.

## Declaration of competing interest

The authors declare that they have no known competing financial interests or personal relationships that could have appeared to influence the work reported in this paper. Moreover, during the preparation of this study the authors used ChatGPT 3.5 and DeepSeek in order to paraphrase, revise, and improve the English quality of the manuscript. After using this tool/service, the authors reviewed and edited the content as needed and take full responsibility for the content of the publication.

**TABLE 23.3** Advantages and disadvantages of PNP platforms.

| Platform | Advantages | Disadvantages | Reference |
|---|---|---|---|
| Self-assembling NPs | Uniform shape, monodispersity, thermal/pH stability, reversible assembly, ease of functionalization, biocompatibility, low toxicity, enhanced lymph node trafficking, scalable. | Steric hindrance, improper antigen orientation/misfolding, incomplete decoration, conformational changes, process optimization challenges. | (Pandey et al., 2024; Liu et al., 2021) |
| Bacteriophage-VLP NPs | Customizable, ordered antigen presentation, natural adjuvant properties, biocompatibility, low toxicity, and ability to carry multiple antigens. | Potential immunogenicity of bacteriophage, antigen misfolding/presentation issues, limited large-scale production potential depending on bacteriophage type. | (Pandey et al., 2024; Tapia et al., 2023; Huang et al., 2024; Sun et al., 2024) |
| Plant-derived NPs | Scalable, cost-effective, natural adjuvant properties, biodegradable, biocompatible, multivalent antigen presentation. | Variability in NP quality, differing glycosylation patterns, regulatory challenges. | (Tapia et al., 2023; Filipić et al., 2023) |
| Virus-based vectors | Efficient antigen presentation, strong humoral and cellular responses, established safety profiles for some vectors; high structural stability, resistance to degradation, immunocompatibility, and biomimetic properties. | Preexisting immunity to the vector, risk of recombination/integration into the host genome, potential for strong immune responses against the vector, limiting booster doses. | (Pandey et al., 2024; Filipić et al., 2023) |

## Acknowledgments

The authors would like to express their gratitude to the National Cell Bank of the Pasteur Institute of Iran for their invaluable support in this study.

## References

Abkar, M., Alamian, S., Sattarahmady, N., 2023. Gelatin micro/nanoparticles-based delivery of urease and omp31 in mice has a protective role against brucella melitensis 16 M infection. BioNanoScience 13 (2), 686–694. https://doi.org/10.1007/s12668-023-01073-6.

Akbari, E., Ajdary, S., Mirabzadeh Ardakani, E., Agi, E., Milani, A., Seyedinkhorasani, M., Khalaj, V., Bolhassani, A., 2022. Immunopotentiation by linking Hsp70 T-cell epitopes to Gag-Pol-Env-Nef-Rev multiepitope construct and increased IFN-gamma secretion in infected lymphocytes. Pathogens and Disease 80 (1). https://doi.org/10.1093/femspd/ftac021.

Andrews, S.F., Raab, J.E., Gorman, J., Gillespie, R.A., Cheung, C.S.F., Rawi, R., Cominsky, L.Y., Boyington, J.C., Creanga, A., Shen, C.H., Harris, D.R., Olia, A.S., Nazzari, A.F., Zhou, T., Houser, K.V., Chen, G.L., Mascola, J.R., Graham, B.S., Kanekiyo, M., Ledgerwood, J.E., Kwong, P.D., McDermott, A.B., 2022. A single residue in influenza virus H2 hemagglutinin enhances the breadth of the B cell response elicited by H2 vaccination. Nat. Med. 28 (2), 373–382. https://doi.org/10.1038/s41591-021-01636-8.

Arab, A., Nicastro, J., Slavcev, R., Razazan, A., Barati, N., Nikpoor, A.R., Momtazi Borojeni, A.A., Mosaffa, F., Badiee, A., Jaafari, M.R., Behravan, J., 2018. Lambda phage nanoparticles displaying HER2-derived E75 peptide induce effective E75-CD8+ T response. Immunol. Res. 66 (1), 200–206. https://doi.org/10.1007/s12026-017-8969-0.

Arunachalam, P.S., Walls, A.C., Golden, N., Atyeo, C., Fischinger, S., Li, C., Aye, P., Navarro, M.J., Lai, L., Edara, V. V., Röltgen, K., Rogers, K., Shirreff, L., Ferrell, D.E., Wrenn, S., Pettie, D., Kraft, J.C., Miranda, M.C., Kepl, E., Sydeman, C., Brunette, N., Murphy, M., Fiala, B., Carter, L., White, A.G., Trisal, M., Hsieh, C.L., Russell-Lodrigue, K., Monjure, C., Dufour, J., Spencer, S., Doyle-Meyers, L., Bohm, R.P., Maness, N.J., Roy, C., Plante, J.A., Plante, K.S., Zhu, A., Gorman, M.J., Shin, S., Shen, X., Fontenot, J., Gupta, S., O'Hagan, D.T., Van Der Most, R., Rappuoli, R., Coffman, R.L., Novack, D., McLellan, J.S., Subramaniam, S., Montefiori, D., Boyd, S.D., Flynn, J.A.L., Alter, G., Villinger, F., Kleanthous, H., Rappaport, J., Suthar, M.S., King, N.P., Veesler, D., Pulendran, B., 2021. Adjuvanting a subunit COVID-19 vaccine to induce protective immunity. Nature 594 (7862), 253–258. https://doi.org/10.1038/s41586-021-03530-2.

Attarilar, S., Yang, J., Ebrahimi, M., Wang, Q., Liu, J., Tang, Y., Yang, J., 2020. The toxicity phenomenon and the related occurrence in metal and metal oxide nanoparticles: a brief review from the biomedical perspective. Front. Bioeng. Biotechnol. 8. https://doi.org/10.3389/fbioe.2020.00822.

Bari, E., Ferrera, F., Altosole, T., Perteghella, S., Mauri, P., Rossi, R., Passignani, G., Mastracci, L., Galati, M., Astone, G.I., Mastrogiacomo, M., Castagnola, P., Fenoglio, D., Di Silvestre, D., Torre, M.L., Filaci, G., 2023. Trojan-horse silk fibroin nanocarriers loaded with a re-call antigen to redirect immunity against cancer. J. Immunother. Cancer 11 (1). https://doi.org/10.1136/jitc-2022-005916.

Bhaskar, S., Lim, S., 2017. Engineering protein nanocages as carriers for biomedical applications. NPG Asia Mater. 9 (4), e371. https://doi.org/10.1038/am.2016.128, 1884-4049.

Bhushan, B., Kumar, S.U., Matai, I., Sachdev, A., Dubey, P., Gopinath, P., 2014. Ferritin nanocages: a novel platform for biomedical applications. J. Biomed. Nanotechnol. 10 (10), 2950–2976. https://doi.org/10.1166/jbn.2014.1980.

Butkovich, N., Li, E., Ramirez, A., Burkhardt, A.M., Wang, S.W., 2021. Advancements in protein nanoparticle vaccine platforms to combat infectious disease. Wiley Interdiscip. Rev. Nanomed. Nanobiotechnol. 13 (3). https://doi.org/10.1002/wnan.1681.

Chakraborti, S., Chakrabarti, P., 2019. Self-assembly of ferritin: structure, biological function and potential applications in nanotechnology. Adv. Exp. Med. Biol. 1174, 313–329. https://doi.org/10.1007/978-981-13-9791-2_10.

Chen, Y., Hu, Y., Chen, H., Li, X., Qian, P., 2020. A ferritin nanoparticle vaccine for foot-and-mouth disease virus elicited partial protection in mice. Vaccine 38 (35), 5647–5652. https://doi.org/10.1016/j.vaccine.2020.06.063.

Coester, C., Nayyar, P., Samuel, J., 2006. In vitro uptake of gelatin nanoparticles by murine dendritic cells and their intracellular localisation. Eur. J. Pharm. Biopharm. 62 (3), 306–314. https://doi.org/10.1016/j.ejpb.2005.09.009.

Conniot, J., Silva, J.M., Fernandes, J.G., Silva, L.C., Gaspar, R., Brocchini, S., Florindo, H.F., Barata, T.S., 2014. Cancer immunotherapy: nanodelivery approaches for immune cell targeting and tracking. Front. Chem. 2. https://doi.org/10.3389/fchem.2014.00105.

Cortines, J.R., Motwani, T., Vyas, A.A., Teschke, C.M., 2014. Highly specific salt bridges govern bacteriophage p22 icosahedral capsid assembly: identification of the site in coat protein responsible for interaction with scaffolding protein. J. Virol. 88 (10), 5287–5297. https://doi.org/10.1128/JVI.00036-14.

da Silva, N.I.O., Salvador, E.A., Rodrigues Franco, I., de Souza, G.A.P., de Souza Morais, S.M., Prado Rocha, R., Dias Novaes, R., Paiva Corsetti, P., Malaquias, L.C.C., Leomil Coelho, L.F., 2018. Bovine serum albumin nanoparticles induce histopathological changes and inflammatory cell recruitment in the skin of treated mice. Biomed. Pharmacother. 107, 1311–1317. https://doi.org/10.1016/j.biopha.2018.08.106.

Daneshvar, A., Farokhi, M., Bonakdar, S., Vossoughi, M., 2024. Synthesis and characterization of injectable thermosensitive hydrogel based on Pluronic-grafted silk fibroin copolymer containing hydroxyapatite nanoparticles as potential for bone tissue engineering. Int. J. Biol. Macromol. 277, 134412. https://doi.org/10.1016/j.ijbiomac.2024.134412.

Das, J.K., Xiong, X., Ren, X., Yang, J.M., Song, J., 2019. Heat shock proteins in cancer immunotherapy. J. Oncol. 2019. https://doi.org/10.1155/2019/3267207.

de Pinho Favaro, M.T., Atienza-Garriga, J., Martínez-Torró, C., Parladé, E., Vázquez, E., Corchero, J.L., Ferrer-Miralles, N., Villaverde, A., 2022. Recombinant vaccines in 2022: a perspective from the cell factory. Microb. Cell Fact. 21 (1). https://doi.org/10.1186/s12934-022-01929-8.

Del Giudice, G., Rappuoli, R., Didierlaurent, A.M., 2018. Correlates of adjuvanticity: a review on adjuvants in licensed vaccines. Semin. Immunol. 39, 14–21. https://doi.org/10.1016/j.smim.2018.05.001.

Diaz, D., Care, A., Sunna, A., 2018. Bioengineering strategies for protein-based nanoparticles. Genes 9 (7). https://doi.org/10.3390/genes9070370.

Didenko, G., Kruts, O., Skivka, L., Prylutskyy, Y., 2018. The Effectiveness of Antitumor Vaccine Enriched with a Heat Shock Protein 70. Springer Science and Business Media LLC, pp. 325–345. https://doi.org/10.1007/978-3-319-89551-2_17.

Drexler, K.E., 1981. Molecular engineering: an approach to the development of general capabilities for molecular manipulation. Proc. Natl. Acad. Sci. 78 (9), 5275–5278. https://doi.org/10.1073/pnas.78.9.5275.

Du, G., Qin, M., Sun, X., 2023. Recent progress in application of nanovaccines for enhancing mucosal immune responses. Acta Pharm. Sin. B 13 (6), 2334–2345. https://doi.org/10.1016/j.apsb.2022.08.010.

Dubaniewicz, A., 2013. Microbial and human heat shock proteins as 'danger signals' in sarcoidosis. Hum. Immunol. 74 (12), 1550–1558. https://doi.org/10.1016/j.humimm.2013.08.275.

Duintjer Tebbens, R.J., Pallansch, M.A., Kim, J.H., Burns, C.C., Kew, O.M., Oberste, M.S., Diop, O.M., Wassilak, S.G. F., Cochi, S.L., Thompson, K.M., 2013. Oral poliovirus vaccine evolution and insights relevant to modeling the risks of circulating vaccine-derived polioviruses (cVDPVs). Risk Anal. 33 (4), 680–702. https://doi.org/10.1111/risa.12022.

Elsadek, B., Kratz, F., 2012. Impact of albumin on drug delivery - new applications on the horizon. J. Contr. Release 157 (1), 4–28. https://doi.org/10.1016/j.jconrel.2011.09.069.

Elzoghby, A.O., Samy, W.M., Elgindy, N.A., 2012. Albumin-based nanoparticles as potential controlled release drug delivery systems. J. Contr. Release 157 (2), 168–182. https://doi.org/10.1016/j.jconrel.2011.07.031.

Esmaeilzadeh, M.R., Sabzi, S., Hajihossein Tabrizi, A., 2022. Isolation and in vitro characterization of specific bacteriophages against methicillin-resistant staphylococcus aureus. Infection Epidemiology and Microbiology 8 (2), 121–128. https://doi.org/10.52547/iem.8.2.121.

Essus, V.A., Souza Júnior, G.S.e., Nunes, G.H.P., Oliveira, J.d.S., de Faria, B.M., Romão, L.F., Cortines, J.R., 2023. Bacteriophage P22 capsid as a pluripotent nanotechnology tool. Viruses 15 (2). https://doi.org/10.3390/v15020516.

Feynman, R., 2018. There's Plenty of Room at the Bottom Feynman and Computation. CRC Press, pp. 63–76. https://doi.org/10.1201/9780429500459.

Filipić, B., Pantelić, I., Nikolić, I., Majhen, D., Stojić-Vukanić, Z., Savić, S., Krajišnik, D., 2023. Nanoparticle-based adjuvants and delivery systems for modern vaccines. Vaccines 11 (7), 1172. https://doi.org/10.3390/vaccines11071172.

Foged, C., 2011. Subunit vaccines of the future: the need for safe, customized and optimized particulate delivery systems. Ther. Deliv. 2 (8), 1057–1077. https://doi.org/10.4155/tde.11.68.

Georgiev, I.S., Joyce, M.G., Chen, R.E., Leung, K., McKee, K., Druz, A., Van Galen, J.G., Kanekiyo, M., Tsybovsky, Y., Yang, E.S., Yang, Y., Acharya, P., Pancera, M., Thomas, P.V., Wanninger, T., Yassine, H.M., Baxa, U., Doria-Rose, N.A., Cheng, C., Graham, B.S., Mascola, J.R., Kwong, P.D., 2018. Two-component ferritin nanoparticles for multimerization of diverse trimeric antigens. ACS Infect. Dis. 4 (5), 788–796. https://doi.org/10.1021/acsinfecdis.7b00192.

Ghaemi, A., Soleimanjahi, H., Gill, P., Hassan, Z., Jahromi, S.R.M., Roohvand, F., 2010. Recombinant λ-phage nanobioparticles for tumor therapy in mice models. Genet. Vaccine Ther. 8. https://doi.org/10.1186/1479-0556-8-3Iran.

Ghanaat, M., Kaboosi, H., Negahdari, B., Fattahi, E., Malekshahi, Z.V., 2023. Heterologous prime-boost vaccination using adenovirus and albumin nanoparticles as carriers for human papillomavirus 16 E7 epitope. Curr. Pharm. Biotechnol. 24 (9), 1195–1203. https://doi.org/10.2174/1389201023666220922122531.

Guo, Y., Guo, R., Ma, Y., Chang, W., Ming, S., Yang, G., Guo, Y., 2021. Chimeric virus-like particles of universal antigen epitopes of coronavirus and phage qβ coat protein trigger the production of neutralizing antibodies. Curr. Top. Med. Chem. 21 (14), 1235–1250. https://doi.org/10.2174/1568026621666210618145411.

Hajj Hussein, I., Chams, N., Chams, S., El Sayegh, S., Badran, R., Raad, M., Gerges-Geagea, A., Leone, A., Jurjus, A., 2015. Vaccines through centuries: major cornerstones of global health. Front. Public Health 3. https://doi.org/10.3389/fpubh.2015.00269.

Hasanzadeh, S., Farokhi, M., Habibi, M., Shokrgozar, M.A., Ahangari Cohan, R., Rezaei, F., Asadi Karam, M.R., Bouzari, S., 2020. Silk fibroin nanoadjuvant as a promising vaccine carrier to deliver the fimh-iuta antigen for urinary tract infection. ACS Biomater. Sci. Eng. 6 (8), 4573–4582. https://doi.org/10.1021/acsbiomaterials.0c00736.

Hassani Besheli, N., Damoogh, S., Zafar, B., Mottaghitalab, F., Motasadizadeh, H., Rezaei, F., Shokrgozar, M.A., Farokhi, M., 2018. Preparation of a Codelivery system based on vancomycin/silk scaffold containing silk nanoparticle loaded VEGF. ACS Biomater. Sci. Eng. 4 (8), 2836–2846. https://doi.org/10.1021/acsbiomaterials.8b00149.

HogenEsch, H., 2013. Mechanism of immunopotentiation and safety of aluminum adjuvants. Front. Immunol. 3. https://doi.org/10.3389/fimmu.2012.00406.

Houser, K.V., Chen, G.L., Carter, C., Crank, M.C., Nguyen, T.A., Burgos Florez, M.C., Berkowitz, N.M., Mendoza, F., Hendel, C.S., Gordon, I.J., Coates, E.E., Vazquez, S., Stein, J., Case, C.L., Lawlor, H., Carlton, K., Gaudinski, M.R., Strom, L., Hofstetter, A.R., Liang, C.J., Narpala, S., Hatcher, C., Gillespie, R.A., Creanga, A., Kanekiyo, M., Raab, J.E., Andrews, S.F., Zhang, Y., Yang, E.S., Wang, L., Leung, K., Kong, W.P., Freyn, A.W., Nachbagauer, R., Palese, P., Bailer, R.T., McDermott, A.B., Koup, R.A., Gall, J.G., Arnold, F., Mascola, J.R., Graham, B.S., Ledgerwood, J.E., Casazza, J., Holman, L., Ola, A.O., Costner, P., Cunningham, J., Larkin, B., Novik, L., Saunders, J., Whalen, W., Wang, X., Eshun, A.M., Taylor, A., Cheng, K.C., Laurencot, C., Cox, J.H., Sitar, S., Le, L., Pittman, I., Vasilenko, O., Rothwell, R.S., Yamshchikov, G., Burch, E., Hickman, S., Trofymenko, O., Boyd, C., Apte, P., Cartagena, C.T., Hicks, R., Williams, P., Blaku, Z., Tran, C., 2022. Safety and immunogenicity of a ferritin nanoparticle H2 influenza vaccine in healthy adults: a phase 1 trial. Nat. Med. 28 (2), 383–391. https://doi.org/10.1038/s41591-021-01660-8.

Huang, Y., Guo, X., Wu, Y., Chen, X., Feng, L., Xie, N., Shen, G., 2024. Nanotechnology's frontier in combatting infectious and inflammatory diseases: prevention and treatment. Signal Transduct. Targeted Ther. 9 (1). https://doi.org/10.1038/s41392-024-01745-z.

Huerta-Saquero, A., Chapartegui-González, I., Bowser, S., Khakhum, N., Stockton, J.L., Torres, A.G., 2023. P22-Based nanovaccines against enterohemorrhagic Escherichia coli. Microbiol. Spectr. 11 (2). https://doi.org/10.1128/spectrum.04734-22.

Ito, A., Shinkai, M., Honda, H., Yoshikawa, K., Saga, S., Wakabayashi, T., Yoshida, J., Kobayashi, T., 2003. Heat shock protein 70 expression induces antitumor immunity during intracellular hyperthermia using magnetite nanoparticles. Cancer Immunol. Immunother. 52 (2), 80–88. https://doi.org/10.1007/s00262-002-0335-x.

Janeway, C., 1989. Immunogenecity signals 1,2,3. and 0. Immunol. Today 10 (9), 283–286. https://doi.org/10.1016/0167-5699(89)90081-9.

Jorge, S., Dellagostin, O.A., 2017. The development of veterinary vaccines: a review of traditional methods and modern biotechnology approaches. Biotechnology Research and Innovation 1 (1), 6–13. https://doi.org/10.1016/j.biori.2017.10.001.

Josi, R., Speiser, D.E., de Brot, S., Vogt, A.C., Sevick-Muraca, E.M., Tolstonog, G.V., Bachmann, M.F., Mohsen, M.O., 2024. A tetravalent nanovaccine that inhibits growth of HPV-associated head and neck carcinoma via dendritic and T cell activation. iScience 27 (4). https://doi.org/10.1016/j.isci.2024.109439.

Joyce, M.G., Chen, W.H., Sankhala, R.S., Hajduczki, A., Thomas, P.V., Choe, M., Martinez, E.J., Chang, W.C., Peterson, C.E., Morrison, E.B., Smith, C., Chen, R.E., Ahmed, A., Wieczorek, L., Anderson, A., Case, J.B., Li, Y., Oertel, T., Rosado, L., Ganesh, A., Whalen, C., Carmen, J.M., Mendez-Rivera, L., Karch, C.P., Gohain, N., Villar, Z., McCurdy, D., Beck, Z., Kim, J., Shrivastava, S., Jobe, O., Dussupt, V., Molnar, S., Tran, U., Kannadka, C.B., Soman, S., Kuklis, C., Zemil, M., Khanh, H., Wu, W., Cole, M.A., Duso, D.K., Kummer, L.W., Lang, T.J., Muncil, S.E., Currier, J.R., Krebs, S.J., Polonis, V.R., Rajan, S., McTamney, P.M., Esser, M.T., Reiley, W.W., Rolland, M., de Val, N., Diamond, M.S., Gromowski, G.D., Matyas, G.R., Rao, M., Michael, N.L., Modjarrad, K., 2021. SARS-CoV-2 ferritin nanoparticle vaccines elicit broad SARS coronavirus immunogenicity. Cell Rep. 37 (12). https://doi.org/10.1016/j.celrep.2021.110143.

Kamp, H.D., Swanson, K.A., Wei, R.R., Dhal, P.K., Dharanipragada, R., Kern, A., Sharma, B., Sima, R., Hajdusek, O., Hu, L.T., Wei, C.J., Nabel, G.J., 2020. Design of a broadly reactive lyme disease vaccine. Npj Vaccines 5 (1). https://doi.org/10.1038/s41541-020-0183-8.

Kampinga, H.H., Craig, E.A., 2010. The HSP70 chaperone machinery: J proteins as drivers of functional specificity. Nat. Rev. Mol. Cell Biol. 11 (8), 579–592. https://doi.org/10.1038/nrm2941.

Kanekiyo, M., Wei, C.J., Yassine, H.M., McTamney, P.M., Boyington, J.C., Whittle, J.R.R., Rao, S.S., Kong, W.P., Wang, L., Nabel, G.J., 2013. Self-assembling influenza nanoparticle vaccines elicit broadly neutralizing H1N1 antibodies. Nature 499 (7456), 102–106. https://doi.org/10.1038/nature12202.

Kang, S., Lander, G.C., Johnson, J.E., Prevelige, P.E., 2008. Development of bacteriophage P22 a platform for molecular display: genetic and chemical modifications of the procapsid exterior surface. Chembiochem 9 (4), 514–518. https://doi.org/10.1002/cbic.200700555.

Khakhum, N., Baruch-Torres, N., Stockton, J.L., Chapartegui-González, I., Badten, A.J., Adam, A., Wang, T., Huerta-Saquero, A., Yin, Y.W., Torres, A.G., Bäumler, A.J., 2024. Decoration of burkholderia hcp1 protein to virus-like particles as a vaccine delivery platform. Infect. Immun. 92 (3). https://doi.org/10.1128/iai.00019-24.

Khoshnejad, M., Parhiz, H., Shuvaev, V.V., Dmochowski, I.J., Muzykantov, V.R., 2018. Ferritin-based drug delivery systems: hybrid nanocarriers for vascular immunotargeting. J. Contr. Release 282, 13–24. https://doi.org/10.1016/j.jconrel.2018.02.042.

Klimek, L., Kündig, T., Kramer, M.F., Guethoff, S., Jensen-Jarolim, E., Schmidt-Weber, C.B., Palomares, O., Mohsen, M.O., Jakob, T., Bachmann, M., 2018. Virus-like particles (VLP) in prophylaxis and immunotherapy of allergic diseases. Allergo Journal International 27 (8), 245–255. https://doi.org/10.1007/s40629-018-0074-y.

Kommareddy, S., Shenoy, D.B., Amiji, M.M., Gelatin nanoparticles and their biofunctionalization, nanotechnologies for the life sciences: Online. (2007).

Li, Q., Li, X., Zhao, C., 2020. Strategies to obtain encapsulation and controlled release of small hydrophilic molecules. Front. Bioeng. Biotechnol. 8. https://doi.org/10.3389/fbioe.2020.00437.

Li, W., Jing, Z., Wang, S., Li, Q., Xing, Y., Shi, H., Li, S., Hong, Z., 2021. P22 virus-like particles as an effective antigen delivery nanoplatform for cancer immunotherapy. Biomaterials 271, 120726. https://doi.org/10.1016/j.biomaterials.2021.120726.

Li, M., Chen, C., Wang, X., Guo, P., Feng, H., Zhang, X., Zhang, W., Gu, C., Zhu, J., Wen, G., Feng, Y., Xiao, L., Peng, G., Rao, V.B., Tao, P., 2023. T4 bacteriophage nanoparticles engineered through CRISPR provide a versatile platform for rapid development of flu mucosal vaccines. Antivir. Res. 217, 105688. https://doi.org/10.1016/j.antiviral.2023.105688.

Li, Y., Pu, R., Zhang, Y., Zhang, Y., Wei, Y., Zeng, S., Gao, C., Wang, Y., Yin, D., Zhang, Y., Wan, J., Zou, Q., Gu, J., 2023. Self-assembled ferritin nanoparticles displaying PcrV and OprI as an adjuvant-free pseudomonas aeruginosa vaccine. Front. Immunol. 14. https://doi.org/10.3389/fimmu.2023.1184863.

Lin, S.F., Jiang, P.L., Tsai, J.S., Huang, Y.Y., Lin, S.Y., Lin, J.H., Liu, D.Z., 2019. Surface assembly of poly(I:C) on polyethyleneimine-modified gelatin nanoparticles as immunostimulatory carriers for mucosal antigen delivery. J. Biomed. Mater. Res. B Appl. Biomater. 107 (4), 1228–1237. https://doi.org/10.1002/jbm.b.34215.

Liu, Y., Hardie, J., Zhang, X., Rotello, V.M., 2017. Effects of engineered nanoparticles on the innate immune system. Semin. Immunol. 34, 25–32. https://doi.org/10.1016/j.smim.2017.09.011.

Liu, Z.H., Xu, H.L., Han, G.W., Tao, L.N., Lu, Y., Zheng, S.Y., Fang, W.H., He, F., 2021. A self-assembling nanoparticle: Implications for the development of thermostable vaccine candidates. Int. J. Biol. Macromol. 183, 2162–2173. https://doi.org/10.1016/j.ijbiomac.2021.06.024.

Liu, T., Li, M., Yang, T., Dong, Y., Liu, N., Wang, Z., Zhang, H., Zheng, A., Cui, C., 2024. Immunogenicity and safety of a self-assembling ZIKV nanoparticle vaccine in mice. Int. J. Pharm. 660, 124320. https://doi.org/10.1016/j.ijpharm.2024.124320.

Loureiro, A., Azoia, N.G., Gomes, A.C., Cavaco-Paulo, A., 2016. Albumin-based nanodevices as drug carriers. Curr. Pharm. Des. 22 (10), 1371–1390. https://doi.org/10.2174/1381612822666160125114900.

Mangla, B., Javed, S., Sultan, M.H., Ahsan, W., Aggarwal, G., Kohli, K., 2022. Nanocarriers-assisted needle-free vaccine delivery through oral and intranasal transmucosal routes: a novel therapeutic conduit. Front. Pharmacol. 12. https://doi.org/10.3389/fphar.2021.757761.

Maria de Souza Morais, S., Ferreira Rodigues, N., da Silva, N.I.O., Aparecido Salvador, E., Franco, I.R., Pires de Souza, G.A., da Silva, P.H.C., de Almeida, L.G.N., Rocha, R.P., da C Pereira, A.C.T., Ferreira, G.P., Veras Quelemes, P., Pereira de Araújo, M., Fornias Sperandio, F., Júnia de Souza Santos, L., Filho, O.A.M., Malaquias, L.C.C., Coelho, L.F.L., 2018. Serum albumin nanoparticles vaccine provides protection against a lethal Pseudomonas aeruginosa challenge. Vaccine 36 (43), 6408–6415. https://doi.org/10.1016/j.vaccine.2018.08.070.

Milani, A., Akbari, E., Pordanjani, P.M., Jamshidi, F., Ghayoumi, S., Sadeghi, S.A., Bolhassani, A., 2024. Immunostimulatory effects of Hsp70 fragments and Hsp27 in design of novel HIV-1 vaccine formulations. HIV Med. 25 (2), 276–290. https://doi.org/10.1111/hiv.13576.

Miller, E.S., Kutter, E., Mosig, G., Arisaka, F., Kunisawa, T., Rüger, W., 2003. Bacteriophage T4 genome. Microbiol. Mol. Biol. Rev. 67 (1), 86–156. https://doi.org/10.1128/MMBR.67.1.86-156.2003.

Min, J., Moon, H., Yang, H.J., Shin, H.H., Hong, S.Y., Kang, S., 2014. Development of P22 viral capsid nanocomposites as anti-cancer drug, bortezomib (BTZ), delivery nanoplatforms. Macromol. Biosci. 14 (4), 557–564. https://doi.org/10.1002/mabi.201300401.

Molino, N.M., Anderson, A.K.L., Nelson, E.L., Wang, S.W., 2013. Biomimetic protein nanoparticles facilitate enhanced dendritic cell activation and cross-presentation. ACS Nano 7 (11), 9743–9752. https://doi.org/10.1021/nn403085w.

Molino, N.M., Neek, M., Tucker, J.A., Nelson, E.L., Wang, S.W., 2017. Display of DNA on nanoparticles for targeting antigen presenting cells. ACS Biomater. Sci. Eng. 3 (4), 496–501. https://doi.org/10.1021/acsbiomaterials.7b00148.

Mottaghitalab, F., Farokhi, M., Shokrgozar, M.A., Atyabi, F., Hosseinkhani, H., 2015a. Silk fibroin nanoparticle as a novel drug delivery system. J. Control. Release 206, 161–176. https://doi.org/10.1016/j.jconrel.2015.03.020.

Mottaghitalab, F., Hosseinkhani, H., Shokrgozar, M.A., Mao, C., Yang, M., Farokhi, M., 2015b. Silk as a potential candidate for bone tissue engineering. J. Control. Release 215, 112–128. https://doi.org/10.1016/j.jconrel.2015.07.031.

Mottaghitalab, F., Kiani, M., Farokhi, M., Kundu, S.C., Reis, R.L., Gholami, M., Bardania, H., Dinarvand, R., Geramifar, P., Beiki, D., Atyabi, F., 2017. Targeted delivery system based on gemcitabine-loaded silk fibroin nanoparticles for lung cancer therapy. ACS Appl. Mater. Interfaces 9 (37), 31600–31611. https://doi.org/10.1021/acsami.7b10408.

Neek, M., Kim, T.I., Wang, S.W., 2019. Protein-based nanoparticles in cancer vaccine development. Nanomed. Nanotechnol. Biol. Med. 15 (1), 164–174. https://doi.org/10.1016/j.nano.2018.09.004.

Nguyen, B., Tolia, N.H., 2021. Protein-based antigen presentation platforms for nanoparticle vaccines. Npj Vaccines 6 (1). https://doi.org/10.1038/s41541-021-00330-7.

Nie, J., Wang, Q., Li, C., Zhou, Y., Yao, X., Xu, L., Chang, Y., Ding, F., Sun, L., Zhan, L., Zhu, L., Xie, K., Wang, X., Shi, Y., Zhao, Q., Shan, Y., 2024. Self-assembled multiepitope nanovaccine provides long-lasting cross-protection against influenza virus. Adv. Healthcare Mater. 13 (10). https://doi.org/10.1002/adhm.202303531.

O'Hagan, D.T., Valiante, N.M., 2003. Recent advances in the discovery and delivery of vaccine adjuvants. Nat. Rev. Drug Discov. 2 (9), 727–735. https://doi.org/10.1038/nrd1176.

Palombarini, F., Di Fabio, E., Boffi, A., Macone, A., Bonamore, A., 2020. Ferritin nanocages for protein delivery to tumor cells. Molecules 25 (4), 825. https://doi.org/10.3390/molecules25040825.

Pandey, K.K., Sahoo, B.R., Pattnaik, A.K., 2024. Protein nanoparticles as vaccine platforms for human and zoonotic viruses. Viruses 16 (6). https://doi.org/10.3390/v16060936.

Pantopoulos, K., Porwal, S.K., Tartakoff, A., Devireddy, L., 2012. Mechanisms of mammalian iron homeostasis. Biochemistry 51 (29), 5705–5724. https://doi.org/10.1021/bi300752r.

Parker, D.C., 1993. T cell-dependent B cell activation. Annu. Rev. Immunol. 11 (1), 331–360. https://doi.org/10.1146/annurev.iy.11.040193.001555.

Patterson, D.P., Rynda-Apple, A., Harmsen, A.L., Harmsen, A.G., Douglas, T., 2013. Biomimetic antigenic nanoparticles elicit controlled protective immune response to influenza. ACS Nano 7 (4), 3036–3044. https://doi.org/10.1021/nn4006544.

Pattnaik, A., Sahoo, B.R., Struble, L.R., Borgstahl, G.E.O., Zhou, Y., Franco, R., Barletta, R.G., Osorio, F.A., Petro, T. M., Pattnaik, A.K., 2023. A ferritin nanoparticle-based zika virus vaccine candidate induces robust humoral and cellular immune responses and protects mice from lethal virus challenge. Vaccines 11 (4). https://doi.org/10.3390/vaccines11040821.

Peng, X., Hu, X., Salazar, M.A., 2018. On reducing the risk of vaccine-associated paralytic poliomyelitis in the global transition from oral to inactivated poliovirus vaccine. Lancet 392 (10147), 610–612. https://doi.org/10.1016/S0140-6736(18)30483-5.

Piva-Amaral, R., Augusto Pires de Souza, G., Vilela Vieira Júnior, J.C., Goulart de Castro, R.F., Gozzi, W.P., Neto, S. P.L., Cauvilla dos Santos, A.L., Cassiano, H.P., Silva, L.C.F.da, Dias Novaes, R., Abrahão, J.S., Oliveira, C.E.de, Silva, B.de M., Costa, G.de P., Malaquias, L.C.C., Coelho, L.F.L., 2024. Bovine serum albumin nanoparticles containing poly (I:C) can enhance the neutralizing antibody response induced by envelope protein of Orthoflavivirus zikaense. Int. Immunopharmacol. 128, 111523. https://doi.org/10.1016/j.intimp.2024.111523.

Plummer, E.M., Manchester, M., 2011. Viral nanoparticles and virus-like particles: platforms for contemporary vaccine design. Wiley Interdiscip. Rev. Nanomed. Nanobiotechnol. 3 (2), 174–196. https://doi.org/10.1002/wnan.119.

Pockley, A.G., Henderson, B., 2018. Extracellular cell stress (heat shock) proteins—immune responses and disease: an overview. Phil. Trans. Biol. Sci. 373 (1738).

Pollard, A.J., Bijker, E.M., 2021. A guide to vaccinology: from basic principles to new developments. Nat. Rev. Immunol. 21 (2), 83–100. https://doi.org/10.1038/s41577-020-00479-7.

Powell, A.E., Zhang, K., Sanyal, M., Tang, S., Weidenbacher, P.A., Li, S., Pham, T.D., Pak, J.E., Chiu, W., Kim, P.S., 2021. A single immunization with spike-functionalized ferritin vaccines elicits neutralizing antibody responses against SARS-CoV-2 in mice. ACS Cent. Sci. 7 (1), 183–199. https://doi.org/10.1021/acscentsci.0c01405.

Pulendran, B., Arunachalam, P.S., O'Hagan, D.T., 2021. Emerging concepts in the science of vaccine adjuvants. Nat. Rev. Drug Discov. 20 (6), 454–475. https://doi.org/10.1038/s41573-021-00163-y.

Pulido-Reyes, G., Leganes, F., Fernández-Piñas, F., Rosal, R., 2017. Bio-nano interface and environment: a critical review. Environ. Toxicol. Chem. 36 (12), 3181–3193. https://doi.org/10.1002/etc.3924.

Rajabnejadkeleshteri, A., Basiri, H., Mohseni, S.S., Farokhi, M., Mehrizi, A.A., Moztarzadeh, F., 2021. Preparation of microfluidic-based pectin microparticles loaded carbon dots conjugated with BMP-2 embedded in gelatin-elastin-hyaluronic acid hydrogel scaffold for bone tissue engineering application. Int. J. Biol. Macromol. 184, 29–41. https://doi.org/10.1016/j.ijbiomac.2021.05.148.

Razazan, A., Nicastro, J., Slavcev, R., Barati, N., Arab, A., Mosaffa, F., Jaafari, M.R., Behravan, J., 2019. Lambda bacteriophage nanoparticles displaying GP2, a HER2/neu derived peptide, induce prophylactic and therapeutic activities against TUBO tumor model in mice. Sci. Rep. 9 (1). https://doi.org/10.1038/s41598-018-38371-z.

Reutovich, A.A., Srivastava, A.K., Arosio, P., Bou-Abdallah, F., 2023. Ferritin nanocages as efficient nanocarriers and promising platforms for COVID-19 and other vaccines development. Biochim. Biophys. Acta Gen. Subj. 1867 (3). https://doi.org/10.1016/j.bbagen.2022.130288.

Rezaei, F., Damoogh, S., Reis, R.L., Kundu, S.C., Mottaghitalab, F., Farokhi, M., 2020. Dual drug delivery system based on pH-sensitive silk fibroin/alginate nanoparticles entrapped in PNIPAM hydrogel for treating severe infected burn wound. Biofabrication 13 (1). https://doi.org/10.1088/1758-5090/abbb82.

Rezaei, F., Keshvari, H., Shokrgozar, M.A., Doroud, D., Gholami, E., Khabiri, A., Farokhi, M., 2021. Nano-adjuvant based on silk fibroin for the delivery of recombinant hepatitis B surface antigen. Biomater. Sci. 9 (7), 2679–2695. https://doi.org/10.1039/d0bm01518k.

Rezvanirad, A., Habibi, M., Farokhi, M., Asadi Karam, M.R., 2023. Immunogenic potential and therapeutic efficacy of multi-epitope encapsulated silk fibroin nanoparticles against pseudomonas aeruginosa-mediated urinary tract infections. Macromol. Biosci. 23 (9). https://doi.org/10.1002/mabi.202300074.

Richert, L.E., Servid, A.E., Harmsen, A.L., Rynda-Apple, A., Han, S., Wiley, J.A., Douglas, T., Harmsen, A.G., 2012. A virus-like particle vaccine platform elicits heightened and hastened local lung mucosal antibody production after a single dose. Vaccine 30 (24), 3653–3665. https://doi.org/10.1016/j.vaccine.2012.03.035.

Richert, L.E., Harmsen, A.L., Rynda-Apple, A., Wiley, J.A., Servid, A.E., Douglas, T., Harmsen, A.G., 2013. Inducible bronchus-associated lymphoid tissue (ibalt) synergizes with local lymph nodes during antiviral CD4+ T Cell Responses. Lymphatic Res. Biol. 11 (4), 196–202. https://doi.org/10.1089/lrb.2013.0015.

Rodrigues, N.F., Van Tilburg Bernardes, E., Rocha, R.P., Da Costa, L.C.F., Coutinho, A.C.A., Dos Santos Muniz, M., Pereira, A.A.O.C., Da Silva, P.H.B., Malaquias, L.C.C., Coelho, L.F.L., 2013. Bovine serum albumin nanoparticle vaccine reduces lung pathology induced by live Pseudomonas aeruginosa infection in mice. Vaccine 31 (44), 5062–5066. https://doi.org/10.1016/j.vaccine.2013.08.078.

Rosenberg, S.A., Yang, J.C., Restifo, N.P., 2004. Cancer immunotherapy: moving beyond current vaccines. Nat. Med. 10 (9), 909–915. https://doi.org/10.1038/nm1100.

Sabet, S., George, M.A., El-Shorbagy, H.M., Bassiony, H., Farroh, K.Y., Youssef, T., Salaheldin, T.A., 2017. Gelatin nanoparticles enhance delivery of hepatitis C virus recombinant NS2 gene. PLoS One 12 (7). https://doi.org/10.1371/journal.pone.0181723.

Sabzi, S., Badmasti, F., Noori Goodarzi, N., Habibi, M., Shahbazi, S., Asadi Karam, M.R., Farokhi, M., 2023. In silico evaluation, cloning, and expression of omp22 as a promising vaccine candidate against acinetobacter baumannii. Vaccine Res. 10 (1), 11–17. https://doi.org/10.61186/vacres.10.1.11.

Sabzi, S., Habibi, M., Badmasti, F., Shahbazi, S., Karam, M.R.A., Farokhi, M., 2024. Polydopamine-based nano adjuvant as a promising vaccine carrier induces significant immune responses against acinetobacter baumannii-associated pneumonia. Int. J. Pharm. 654, 123961. https://doi.org/10.1016/j.ijpharm.2024.123961.

Sahoo, N., Sahoo, R.K., Biswas, N., Guha, A., Kuotsu, K., 2015. Recent advancement of gelatin nanoparticles in drug and vaccine delivery. Int. J. Biol. Macromol. 81, 317–331. https://doi.org/10.1016/j.ijbiomac.2015.08.006.

Schwarz, B., Morabito, K.M., Ruckwardt, T.J., Patterson, D.P., Avera, J., Miettinen, H.M., Graham, B.S., Douglas, T., 2016. Viruslike particles encapsidating respiratory syncytial virus M and M2 proteins induce robust T cell responses. ACS Biomater. Sci. Eng. 2 (12), 2324–2332. https://doi.org/10.1021/acsbiomaterials.6b00532.

Shahbazi, S., Habibi, M., Badmasti, F., Sabzi, S., Farokhi, M., Asadi Karam, M.R., 2023. Design and fabrication of a vaccine candidate based on rOmpA from Klebsiella pneumoniae encapsulated in silk fibroin-sodium alginate nanoparticles against pneumonia infection. Int. Immunopharmacol. 125, 111171. https://doi.org/10.1016/j.intimp.2023.111171.

Shevtsov, M.A., Yakovleva, L.Y., Nikolaev, B.P., Marchenko, Y.Y., Dobrodumov, A.V., Onokhin, K.V., Onokhina, Y. S., Selkov, S.A., Mikhrina, A.L., Guzhova, I.V., Martynova, M.G., Bystrova, O.A., Ischenko, A.M., Margulis, B.A., 2014. Tumor targeting using magnetic nanoparticle Hsp70 conjugate in a model of C6 glioma. Neuro Oncol. 16 (1), 38–49. https://doi.org/10.1093/neuonc/not141.

Shirangi, A., Sepehr, A., Kundu, S.C., Moradi, A., Farokhi, M., Mottaghitalab, F., 2023. Recent Trends in Controlled Drug Delivery Based on Silk Platforms Silk-Based Biomaterials for Tissue Engineering, Regenerative, and Precision Medicine, second ed. Elsevier, Iran, pp. 417–444. https://doi.org/10.1016/B978-0-323-96017-5.00029-7.

Song, Y., Yuan, Z., Ji, J., Ruan, Y., Li, X., Wang, L., Zeng, W., Wu, K., Hu, W., Yi, L., Ding, H., Zhao, M., Fan, S., Li, Z., Chen, J., 2024. Development of a ferritin-based nanoparticle vaccine against classical swine fever. Vaccines 12 (8), 948. https://doi.org/10.3390/vaccines12080948.

Srivastava, P.K., 1994. Heat shock proteins in immune response to cancer: the fourth paradigm. Experientia 50 (11–12), 1054–1060. https://doi.org/10.1007/bf01923461.

Sudheesh, M.S., Vyas, S.P., Kohli, D.V., 2011. Nanoparticle-based immunopotentiation via tetanus toxoid-loaded gelatin and aminated gelatin nanoparticles. Drug Deliv. 18 (5), 320–330. https://doi.org/10.3109/10717544.2010.549525.

Sun, M., Pratama, A.C., Qiu, H., Liu, Z., He, F., 2024. Toward innovative veterinary nanoparticle vaccines. Animal Diseases 4 (1). https://doi.org/10.1186/s44149-024-00119-w.

Tapia, D., Reyes-Sandoval, A., Sanchez-Villamil, J.I., 2023. Protein-based nanoparticle vaccine approaches against infectious diseases. Arch. Med. Res. 54 (3), 168–175. https://doi.org/10.1016/j.arcmed.2023.02.003.

Thomas, S.J., Yoon, I.K., 2019. A review of Dengvaxia®: development to deployment. Hum. Vaccines Immunother. 15 (10), 2295–2314. https://doi.org/10.1080/21645515.2019.1658503.

Uchida, M., Kang, S., Reichhardt, C., Harlen, K., Douglas, T., 2010. The ferritin superfamily: Supramolecular templates for materials synthesis. Biochim. Biophys. Acta Gen. Subj. 1800 (8), 834–845. https://doi.org/10.1016/j.bbagen.2009.12.005.

Velev, O.D., Gupta, S., 2009. Materials fabricated by micro- and nanoparticle assembly - the challenging path from science to engineering. Adv. Mater. 21 (19), 1897–1905. https://doi.org/10.1002/adma.200801837.

Von Hoven, G., Rivas, A.J., Neukirch, C., Klein, S., Hamm, C., Qin, Q., Meyenburg, M., Fuser, S., Saftig, P., Hellmann, N., Postina, R., Husmann, M., 2016. Dissecting the role of ADAM10 as a mediator of Staphylococcus aureus α-toxin action. Biochem. J. 473 (13), 1929–1940. https://doi.org/10.1042/BCJ20160062.

Wang, C., Tu, J., Liu, J., Molineux, I.J., 2019a. Structural dynamics of bacteriophage P22 infection initiation revealed by cryo-electron tomography. Nat. Microbiol. 4 (6), 1049–1056. https://doi.org/10.1038/s41564-019-0403-z.

Wang, W., Liu, Z., Zhou, X., Guo, Z., Zhang, J., Zhu, P., Yao, S., Zhu, M., 2019b. Ferritin nanoparticle-based SpyTag/SpyCatcher-enabled click vaccine for tumor immunotherapy. Nanomed. Nanotechnol. Biol. Med. 16, 69–78. https://doi.org/10.1016/j.nano.2018.11.009.

Wang, Z., Xu, L., Yu, H., Lv, P., Lei, Z., Zeng, Y., Liu, G., Cheng, T., 2019c. Ferritin nanocage-based antigen delivery nanoplatforms: epitope engineering for peptide vaccine design. Biomater. Sci. 7 (5), 1794–1800. https://doi.org/10.1039/c9bm00098d.

Wang, W., Zhou, X., Bian, Y., Wang, S., Chai, Q., Guo, Z., Wang, Z., Zhu, P., Peng, H., Yan, X., Li, W., Fu, Y.X., Zhu, M., 2020. Dual-targeting nanoparticle vaccine elicits a therapeutic antibody response against chronic hepatitis B. Nat. Nanotechnol. 15 (5), 406–416. https://doi.org/10.1038/s41565-020-0648-y.

Wei, Y., Cheng, X., Liao, Y., Zeng, S., Li, Y., Zhang, Y., Gao, C., Zhang, Y., Wan, J., Gu, J., Zou, Q., 2023. Recombinant Pseudomonas aeruginosa flagellin delivered using ferritin nanoparticles provides enhanced cross-protection against lung infection in mice. Mol. Immunol. 163, 235–242. https://doi.org/10.1016/j.molimm.2023.10.005.

Wørzner, K., Sheward, D.J., Schmidt, S.T., Hanke, L., Zimmermann, J., McInerney, G., Hedestam, G.B.K., Murrell, B., Christensen, D., Pedersen, G.K., 2021. Adjuvanted SARS-CoV-2 spike protein elicits neutralizing antibodies and CD4 T cell responses after a single immunization in mice. EBioMedicine 63. https://doi.org/10.1016/j.ebiom.2020.103197.

Xu, L., Liang, H.W., Yang, Y., Yu, S.H., 2018. Stability and reactivity: positive and negative aspects for nanoparticle processing. Chem. Rev. 118 (7), 3209–3250. https://doi.org/10.1021/acs.chemrev.7b00208.

Yan, Y., Wang, X., Lou, P., Hu, Z., Qu, P., Li, D., Li, Q., Xu, Y., Niu, J., He, Y., Zhong, J., Huang, Z., 2020. A nanoparticle-based hepatitis c virus vaccine with enhanced potency. JID (J. Infect. Dis.) 221 (8), 1304–1314. https://doi.org/10.1093/infdis/jiz228.

Yassine, H.M., Boyington, J.C., McTamney, P.M., Wei, C.J., Kanekiyo, M., Kong, W.P., Gallagher, J.R., Wang, L., Zhang, Y., Joyce, M.G., Lingwood, D., Moin, S.M., Andersen, H., Okuno, Y., Rao, S.S., Harris, A.K., Kwong, P.D., Mascola, J.R., Nabel, G.J., Graham, B.S., 2015. Hemagglutinin-stem nanoparticles generate heterosubtypic influenza protection. Nat. Med. 21 (9), 1065–1070. https://doi.org/10.1038/nm.3927.

Yin, Z., Wu, X., Kaczanowska, K., Sungsuwan, S., Comellas Aragones, M., Pett, C., Yu, J., Baniel, C., Westerlind, U., Finn, M.G., Huang, X., 2018. Antitumor humoral and T cell responses by mucin-1 conjugates of bacteriophage Qβ in wild-type mice. ACS Chem. Biol. 13 (6), 1668–1676. https://doi.org/10.1021/acschembio.8b00313.

Yun, C.H., Cho, C.S., 2020. Nanoparticles to improve the efficacy of vaccines. Pharmaceutics 12 (5). https://doi.org/10.3390/pharmaceutics12050418.

Zepp, F., 2010. Principles of vaccine design-Lessons from nature. Vaccine 28 (3), C14. https://doi.org/10.1016/j.vaccine.2010.07.020.

Zhao, L., Seth, A., Wibowo, N., Zhao, C.X., Mitter, N., Yu, C., Middelberg, A.P.J., 2014. Nanoparticle vaccines. Vaccine 32 (3), 327–337. https://doi.org/10.1016/j.vaccine.2013.11.069.

Zhu, J., Ananthaswamy, N., Jain, S., Batra, H., Tang, W.C., Lewry, D.A., Richards, M.L., David, S.A., Kilgore, P.B., Sha, J., Drelich, A., Tseng, C.T.K., Chopra, A.K., Rao, V.B., 2021. A universal bacteriophage T4 nanoparticle platform to design multiplex SARS-CoV-2 vaccine candidates by CRISPR engineering. Sci. Adv. 7 (37). https://doi.org/10.1126/sciadv.abh1547.

Zininga, T., Ramatsui, L., Shonhai, A., 2018. Heat shock proteins as immunomodulants. Molecules 23 (11), 2846. https://doi.org/10.3390/molecules23112846.

Zinkernagel, R.M., 2003. On natural and artificial vaccinations. Annu. Rev. Immunol. 21, 515–546. https://doi.org/10.1146/annurev.immunol.21.120601.141045.

Zwiorek, K., Bourquin, C., Battiany, J., Winter, G., Endres, S., Hartmann, G., Coester, C., 2008. Delivery by cationic gelatin nanoparticles strongly increases the immunostimulatory effects of CpG oligonucleotides. Pharm. Res. 25 (3), 551–562. https://doi.org/10.1007/s11095-007-9410-5.

CHAPTER

# 24

# Recent advances in protein based nano delivery systems in overcoming the challenges associated with metastatic cancers

*Mohammad Doroudian[1], Sana Rahimian[1], Elham Abbasgholinejad[1] and Hossein Najafi[2]*

[1]**Department of Cell and Molecular Sciences, Faculty of Biological Sciences, Kharazmi University, Tehran, Iran; [2]Department of Industrial and Environmental Biotechnology, National Institute of Genetic Engineering and Biotechnology (NIGEB), Tehran, Iran**

## 1. Introduction

### 1.1 Historical perspective

Richard Feynman, an American physicist and Nobel Prize winner, first introduced the concept of nanotechnology in his 1959 lecture titled "There's Plenty of Room at the Bottom" during the annual meeting of the American Physical Society. This presentation is recognized as the inaugural academic discussion on nanotechnology, sparking significant advancements in the field (Baig et al., 2021). Nanoparticles, due to their submicroscopic dimensions, exhibit unique material properties (Doroudian et al., 2021) and have practical applications across various domains, including engineering, drug delivery, nanomedicine, environmental protection, and catalysis. They also target diseases such as melanoma, cardiovascular conditions, skin disorders, liver diseases (Jung et al., 1999), and more. The link between nanoparticles and biomedicine was established in the late 1970s (Afzal, no date).

In recent decades, effective drug delivery has remained a major challenge within medical science and targeted therapies (Ezike et al., 2023b; Rahimian, Najafi, Afzali, et al., 2024a; Rahimian, Najafi, Webber, et al., 2024b). The development of a drug is just the initial step in treating a disease; once an effective treatment is identified, the critical questions arise:

*Protein-Based Nanoparticles in Drug Delivery*
https://doi.org/10.1016/B978-0-443-33639-3.00003-9

How can we minimize side effects while maximizing accuracy and effectiveness? This is where drug delivery systems (DDSs) become essential (Odiba et al., 2016). In 1906, Paul Ehrlich introduced the concept of the "magic bullet," which effectively established the foundation for targeted drug delivery. Ehrlich's vision has evolved into what we now recognize as nanomedicine, where nanoparticles are designed to deliver therapeutic agents directly to specific cells or tissues (A.A. Tewabe et al., 2021). The modern era of drug delivery technology began in 1952 with the introduction of Spansule technology by SmithKline Beckman (Saif et al., 2023). The first generation (1950–1980) was notably productive, resulting in the creation of various oral and transdermal controlled-release formulations for clinical applications (Yun et al., 2015).

Speiser is recognized as the pioneer of pharmaceutical nanotechnology, having discussed nanoparticles in drug delivery as early as 1976 (Peppas, 2013). The launch of the first PEGylated protein, Adagen, in 1990 ushered in a new phase of PEGylation (Gao, 2024). In 2000, the U.S. government initiated the National Nanotechnology Initiative, which was soon adopted globally (Park et al., 2022). DDSs focus on administering pharmaceutical substances, including therapeutic medications, to targeted regions within the body to improve both efficacy and safety (Malamatari, 2023). This process enhances therapeutic outcomes by optimizing pharmacokinetics, enabling controlled release, and facilitating localized delivery (Adepu and Ramakrishna, no date).

Recently, nanomaterials have shown great potential for enhancing disease diagnosis and treatment specificity (Malik et al., 2023). Their application in drug delivery has proven advantageous in various aspects, including improving drug solubility, targeting drugs effectively, controlling drug release, and facilitating transport across cellular barriers (Jung et al., 1999). Various nanomaterials can serve as drug delivery vehicles, including metal nanoparticles, dendrimers, polymeric nanoparticles, magnetic nanoparticles (Jung et al., 1999), carbon nanotubes, quantum dots, and inorganic vectors (Jung et al., 1999).

Among these nanomaterials, protein nanoparticles stand out as highly effective DDSs (Hong et al., 2020a). Proteins and peptides are among the most versatile programmable polymers available. Composed of linear peptide chains that fold into complex three-dimensional structures, proteins play crucial roles in nearly all biological processes—from transporting small molecules that contribute to cellular signaling and provide structural support within cells (Movileanu et al., 2002; Ulijn and Jerala, 2018). Protein nanoparticles offer several advantages over other nanomaterials, including easy accessibility to resources, renewability, biocompatibility, biodegradability, reduced immunogenicity, and lower cytotoxicity—making them favorable candidates for drug delivery applications (Jung et al., 1999).

## 1.2 Current trends

Proteins are vital natural molecules recognized for their diverse functionalities and promising applications in biological and material sciences. Their role in enhancing the biocompatibility of inorganic nanoparticles has been well-established (Sahoo and Labhasetwar, 2003; Ravindran et al., 2013; Ezpeleta et al., 1996). Additionally, proteins have shown greater efficacy as drug carriers compared to inorganic nanoparticles, particularly in drug delivery contexts (Hawkins et al., 2008). This is largely attributed to their nanoscale size, well-defined structural configurations, abundance of modifiable functional groups, and biodegradability (Elzoghby et al., 2012; Panyam and Labhasetwar, 2003; Sripriyalakshmi et al., 2014).

PNPs, encompassing both natural and synthetic types, show promise in biomedicine for applications such as vaccines and DDSs. Although altering the outer surface of polymeric nanoparticles (PNPs) has proven effective for vaccine development, encapsulating target molecules within PNPs presents greater difficulties. For example, virus-like particles (VLPs) have been effectively created and utilized as vaccines, where the outer surface is altered through chemical or genetic modifications to enhance the immunogenicity of the attached antigens (Heddle et al., 2017).

Traditional drug therapies frequently lack precise targeting and optimal biodistribution, leading to unwanted side effects and diminished clinical effectiveness (Bae and Park, 2011). To ensure effective and localized treatment for patients, it is essential for drugs to be accurately targeted and distributed and released in a controlled manner at their main site of action, such as tumors. DDSs aim to address these limitations by altering the drug's solubility, pharmacokinetics, and biodistribution (Sahandi Zangabad et al., 2017).

Innovative nanotechnologies, especially nanoparticles, hold significant potential as DDSs for cancer therapy (Singh and Lillard, 2009). However, only a limited number of synthetic nanoparticles have progressed to approved clinical therapies due to various challenges, including physicochemical heterogeneity, difficulties in functionalization, instability, inadequate tumor penetration, and toxicity (Bertrand et al., 2014). The utilization of polymeric nanoparticles (PNPs) as nanocarriers presents a promising alternative, as they can be engineered to release their cargo in response to multiple stimuli, including pH, chemical changes, redox potential, and temperature (Kan-Davelaar, 2014). The majority of PNP delivery system development has concentrated on cancer therapy, particularly involving the incorporation of cancer drugs along with targeting peptides (Diaz, Care and Sunna, 2018b).

Biopolymer-based nanoparticles, especially those composed of proteins, have gained considerable recognition for their diverse applications as pharmaceutical agents and functional tools. Their appeal is largely due to their low toxicity and capacity for biodegradation, making them advantageous for a wide range of biomedical applications (Jacob et al., 2018; Lohcharoenkal et al., 2014). These nanoparticles offer several advantages as DDSs, including enhanced stability, biodegradability, ease of particle size manipulation, and a reduction in toxicity-related concerns, such as immunogenicity (Langer et al., 2003). PNPs improve the stability, activity, and half-life of drugs by shielding them from enzymatic degradation and renal clearance. Their nonantigenic properties allow for their application in various targeted therapies, including lung delivery (Mottaghitalab et al., 2017), cancer treatment (Saleh et al., 2019), tumor therapy (Sabra et al., 2018), and vaccines (Sahoo et al., 2015), due to their nonantigenic properties (Verma and Garg, 2001). Protein nanoparticles (PNPs) can also be integrated into biodegradable polymer microspheres, enabling a controlled and prolonged release of their cargo (Table 24.1).

The primary objective in designing nanoparticles is to regulate their particle size, surface area, and surface properties to ensure effective delivery of the necessary drug amounts while exhibiting the desired pharmacological effects through targeted release of active agents. Various approaches have been developed to achieve this goal (Davidov-Pardo et al., 2015; Hong et al., 2020b).

**TABLE 24.1** Comprehensive overview of protein nanoparticles: varieties, cargoes, therapeutic applications, and challenges.

| Protein nanoparticle type | Cargo | Therapeutic application | Advantages | Limitations | Ref. |
|---|---|---|---|---|---|
| Albumin-based nanoparticles | Chemotherapeutic drugs (e.g., paclitaxel), siRNA | Cancer treatment, gene therapy | Biodegradable, nontoxic, FDA-approved (e.g., Abraxane) | Stability issues in storage | (Tincu, no date) |
| Ferritin nanoparticles | Anticancer agents, contrast agents | Cancer therapy, imaging | High stability, tunable surface | Complex production process | Mohanty et al. (2022) |
| Silk fibroin nanoparticles | Small molecules, peptides | Wound healing, drug delivery | Biocompatible, slow-release | Limited solubility in some environments | Farokhi et al. (2020) |
| Elastin-like polypeptides | Nucleic acids, peptides | Gene delivery, regenerative medicine | Thermo-responsive, versatile | Production scalability issues | Rana and De la Hoz Siegler (2024) |
| Casein nanoparticles | Hydrophobic drugs | Cancer, cardiovascular diseases | Low-cost, easily adaptable | Potential immunogenicity | Mittal (2023) |
| Zein nanoparticles | Hydrophobic drugs | Cancer, diabetes | Natural origin, strong drug retention | Limited bioavailability | (Reboredo, no date) |
| Collagen nanoparticles | Growth factors, peptides | Tissue engineering, wound healing | Biocompatible, promotes cell adhesion | Susceptible to enzymatic degradation | Klimek and Ginalska (2020) |
| Gelatin nanoparticles | Proteins, nucleic acids | Vaccine delivery, cancer therapy | Biodegradable, safe for systemic use | Limited mechanical strength | Madkhali (2023) |
| Keratin nanoparticles | Antioxidants, chemotherapeutic drugs | Antioxidant delivery, cancer treatment | Biocompatible, high drug loading | Limited clinical data | Sezgin-Bayindir et al. (2023) |
| Histone-derived nanoparticles | DNA, RNA | Gene therapy, immunotherapy | High nucleic acid binding capacity | Toxicity concerns at high doses | Somase et al. (2024) |

Serum proteins have garnered particular interest as naturally derived drug nanocarriers with biocompatible and biodegradable characteristics, especially for applications in cancer nanomedicine (Jain et al., 2018). Owing to their low toxicity and immunogenicity, serum proteins—especially those found endogenously—are frequently employed as carriers for imaging agents and small-molecule therapeutics. They also serve as excellent candidates for pharmaceutical formulations and vaccine excipients (Yewale et al., 2013).

A variety of protein-based nanoparticles are currently utilized in cancer immunotherapy, each with distinct significance. Notable examples include albumin-based nanocarrier systems such as Abraxane, cationic bovine serum albumin (CBSA), gliadin, zein, milk protein nanoparticles, casein nanoparticles, and doxorubicin (DOX)-loaded lactoferrin nanoparticles (Verma et al., 2020; Wang et al., 2021; Kariduraganavar et al., 2019).

Proteins are regarded as ideal materials for nanoparticle preparation due to their unique functionalities and amphiphilicity, which enhance their interaction with both drugs and solvents (Jahanshahi, 2004; Marty et al., 1978). Nanoparticles derived from natural proteins are biodegradable and metabolizable, allowing for straightforward surface modifications that facilitate the attachment of drugs and targeting ligands (Weber et al., 2000). They have been successfully synthesized from a variety of proteins, including water-soluble proteins such as bovine and human serum albumin (HSA), as well as insoluble proteins like zein and gliadin (Ezpeleta et al., 1996; Weber et al., 2000). Despite this, there have been relatively few review articles on protein nanoparticles, with most focusing on the preparation and characterization of nanoparticles derived from gelatin, albumin, and gliadin (Lohcharoenkal et al., 2014).

## 2. Challenges in metastatic cancer treatment

Cancer metastasis is the leading cause of cancer-related morbidity and mortality, accounting for approximately 90% of cancer deaths (Seyfried and Huysentruyt, 2013; Guan, 2015). Although advancements in early detection and treatment have improved overall survival rates, significant challenges remain in effectively managing metastatic disease. Current treatment options primarily include chemotherapy and radiotherapy, with newer anticancer drugs—such as neutralizing antibodies and small molecule kinase inhibitors—showing potential effects on both tumor growth and metastasis (Guan, 2015).

The metastatic process begins with the detachment of cancer cells from the primary tumor, followed by their migration through blood or lymphatic vessels to distant sites where they can settle and grow. This complex journey involves four critical steps: detachment, migration, invasion, and adhesion, all of which are interrelated and influenced by various biochemical factors. Despite advancements in our understanding of tumor biology, metastasis continues to be a significant hurdle, and the mechanisms that govern this process remain largely elusive (Parker et al., 2022).

Patients with solid tumors often face the inevitability of metastasis, which can occur at varying times after diagnosis, ranging from immediate detection of metastatic lesions to decades later. While some patients may remain free from macrometastasis during their clinical course, micrometastasis can often be detected at different stages of the disease (Jiang and Ablin, 2011).

Metastatic tumors are particularly challenging to treat due to their diffuse localization in multiple organs, rendering conventional surgical and radiotherapeutic approaches less effective. Furthermore, these tumors often exhibit resistance to standard cytotoxic therapies. Despite significant technological advances in imaging and cancer cell identification, the molecular mechanisms underlying metastasis and chemoresistance remain poorly understood. Alarmingly, none of the over 200 approved anticancer drugs specifically target and inhibit metastatic progression (Steeg, 2016).

Several obstacles hinder the development of effective antimetastatic drugs. First, there is a lack of high-throughput screening technologies to identify potential antimetastatic compounds (Qian et al., 2017). Recent studies, such as those conducted by Polireddy et al. (2016), have sought to address this gap by utilizing specific markers to identify inhibitors of cancer cell invasion. Second, pharmaceutical companies often lack standardized techniques for employing appropriate animal models in preclinical assessments, despite these models being well established in academic settings (Wang et al., 2016; Li et al., 2011, 2012; Zheng et al., 2017). Additionally, clinical trial designs may need to shift to prioritize metastasis-free survival as a primary endpoint to facilitate the development of antimetastatic therapies (Qian et al., 2017).

Given these challenges, a promising strategy is to focus on preventing metastasis rather than treating it after it has occurred. Adjuvant or neoadjuvant therapy aims not only to shrink the primary tumor but also to prevent the dissemination of tumor cells that could lead to metastatic growth (Zong et al., 2017).

Recent studies have highlighted the potential of protein-based nanoparticles (PNPs) as vehicles for encapsulating various anticancer agents, including paclitaxel and daunorubicin, as well as other therapies like hormones and immunotherapies.

However, the application of PNPs in metastatic cancer treatment is not without its challenges. Issues such as biological barriers and the need for targeted delivery must be carefully considered to enhance the efficacy of these nanoparticles.

## 2.1 Overcoming barriers in treating metastatic cancer

Despite significant advancements in cancer diagnostics and therapeutics, metastasis remains a formidable challenge, casting a shadow over patient prognoses. The metastatic cascade is a complex, multistage process that involves the journey of cancer cells from primary tumors to remote sites (Shen et al., 2023). This process begins with the detachment of tumor cells, followed by invasion into the surrounding stroma, entry into the bloodstream, extravasation into distant tissues, and eventual colonization of new niches. Each of these steps presents unique obstacles for therapeutic interventions (Mohammadi-Motlagh et al., 2023).

### 2.1.1 *Blood–brain barrier (BBB)*

One critical barrier to effective treatment is the BBB, especially concerning brain metastases, which are among the most lethal forms of cancer (Zoghbi et al., 2024). The BBB comprises a unique microvascular system that protects the brain from toxins, including systemic chemotherapy (Wu, 2023). In many cases, tumor cells utilize the brain as a sanctuary from systemic treatments, resulting in relapses (Steeg et al., 2011). Thus, the successful treatment or prevention of brain metastasis, particularly in breast cancer, necessitates innovative strategies to facilitate the transport of chemotherapeutic agents across the BBB.

### 2.1.2 *Heterogeneity of tumor cells*

In addition to the BBB, the heterogeneity of tumor cells complicates treatment efforts. Cancers are characterized by a heterogeneous composition of cell populations that manifest varying characteristics at phenotypic, epigenetic, and genetic levels (Dagogo-Jack and Shaw, 2018). This intratumor heterogeneity (ITH) has been recognized for decades and is now understood to be a significant contributor to treatment resistance (Marusyk et al., 2020). As tumors evolve, it becomes almost mathematically certain that a subset of cells will develop a therapy-resistant phenotype, leading to treatment failures (Gay et al., 2026). This variability in tumor cell populations highlights the necessity for personalized treatment approaches.

### 2.1.3 Tumor microenvironment

The tumor microenvironment (TME) is another critical factor that significantly influences cancer progression, invasion, and treatment resistance. is an interactive cellular milieu made up of immune and inflammatory cells, stromal fibroblasts, and endothelial cells that constitute blood vessels (Anderson and Simon, 2020; Mun et al., 2022). These components release a range of extracellular signaling molecules that influence TME, creating a pathological environment that adapts to promote cancer progression (Patel et al., 2018). The TME plays a crucial role in influencing tumor growth and the potential for metastasis, affecting both primary and acquired resistance to treatments, including cytotoxic chemotherapies and targeted treatments (Neophytou, no date).

Resistance mechanisms mediated by the TME include preventing immune clearance of tumor cells, hindering drug absorption, and stimulating paracrine growth factors that promote cancer cell survival and proliferation (Wu et al., 2021a; Vasan et al., 2019). The critical role of immune evasion is emphasized by the success achieved through checkpoint blockade immunotherapy, which highlights the need to devise strategies that disrupt these protective mechanisms within the TME (Yao, Wang and Ma, no date; Berland et al., 2024).

### 2.1.4 Systemic distribution of drugs

Moreover, the systemic distribution of therapeutic agents poses significant challenges. The pharmacokinetics of drugs can greatly affect their distribution and accumulation in metastatic sites, often leading to suboptimal therapeutic levels at the tumor site (Rizk et al., 2017). While an optimal DDS would reduce sequestration in healthy organs and enhance accumulation in tumors, achieving this balance is challenging (Cheng et al., 2023). Combination therapies often necessitate separate infusions, which can hinder the simultaneous delivery of multiple drugs to target cells (Mokhtari et al., 2017). Consequently, there is an increasing interest in creating combination nanoparticles that can deliver several active drugs through a single pharmaceutical carrier (Yu et al., 2022).

### 2.1.5 Limited drug penetration

Limited drug penetration is another major obstacle in effective cancer treatment. Many therapies do not penetrate tumor tissues effectively due to poor vascularization and high interstitial pressure within tumors (Munir, no date). The vascular system of solid tumors is often chaotically arranged, characterized by tortuous and heterogeneous vessels with uneven diameters (Siemann, 2011). This disorganized structure can vary significantly depending on the type of tumor, its growth rate, and its location (Awad et al., 2023). For example, as tumors grow, their vascular density often decreases, leading to areas of ischemia (Nagy et al., 2009). Reports indicate that blood vessels are more numerous at the tumor–host interface than in central regions, complicating drug delivery (Paresishvili and Kakabadze, 2023).

Additionally, blood flow within tumors is not constant; it can change direction or flow patterns within minutes, leading to perfusion heterogeneity (Rajput et al., 2023). This variability can create avascular necrotic regions, seminecrotic regions, and stabilized microcirculation areas, all of which pose challenges for optimal delivery of anticancer agents to all tumor cells (Paresishvili and Kakabadze, 2023; Tindall et al., 2008; Yamamoto, no date). The vascular permeability and hydraulic conductivity of tumors further complicate drug distribution within tumor parenchyma (Yang and Zhan, 2022). Variability in permeability can occur within the same tumor and is influenced by tumor growth rates, regression, recurrence, and the host's production of cytokines such as vascular permeability factor (VPF) and vascular endothelial growth factor (VEGF). These factors can alter the tumor's microenvironment and impact how effectively drugs can be delivered (Dvorak, no date). An additional challenge lies in the development and formulation of protein-based nanoparticles themselves. These nanoparticles must be engineered to ensure stability, biocompatibility, and efficient cellular uptake (Diaz, Care and Sunna, 2018a). Factors such as particle size, surface charge, and hydrophobicity can influence how well the nanoparticles interact with both the tumor cells and the surrounding TME (Sabourian et al., 2020). Furthermore, the potential for immunogenic responses to the nanoparticles must be considered, as unwanted immune reactions can lead to rapid clearance from circulation and reduce treatment efficacy (Aljabali et al., 2023; Zolnik et al., 2010). Addressing these formulation challenges is crucial for enhancing the therapeutic potential of protein-based nanoparticles and ensuring their successful application in metastatic cancer treatment. In summary, the treatment of metastatic cancer using protein-based nanoparticles faces numerous interconnected challenges. Overcoming the barriers posed by the TME, ITH, systemic drug distribution, vascular architecture, and nanoparticle formulation is crucial for enhancing therapeutic efficacy. As research continues to explore innovative nanoparticle designs and delivery strategies, addressing these obstacles will be vital for improving treatment outcomes in metastatic cancer.

## 3. Structural properties and mechanisms of drug delivery in protein-based nanoparticles

Protein-based nanoparticles signify a notable progression in nanomedicine, providing a diverse platform for the administration of therapeutic drugs (Aljabali et al., 2022). Several proteins, including albumin, gelatin, silk fibroin, and casein, which ensure biocompatibility and biodegradability while offering significant functional diversity, make up these nanoparticles (Ferraro et al., 2024). These proteins' intrinsic structural properties facilitate the meticulous construction of nanoparticles with customized attributes that can be adjusted for specific drug delivery applications (Mitchell et al., 2021).

### 3.1 Structural properties

The structural characteristics of protein-based nanoparticles are crucial to their efficacy as medication delivery platforms (Hong et al., 2020b). Particle size is a vital consideration, generally ranging from 10 to 200 nm. This size range is very beneficial for drug administration because it promotes extended blood circulation time and allows nanoparticles to utilize the enhanced permeability and retention (EPR) effect for passive tumor targeting (Zi et al., 2022). Furthermore, you can alter the dimensions during the manufacturing process to enhance cellular absorption or avoid phagocytic elimination using the mononuclear phagocyte system (Lu et al., 2023).

Surface charge, or zeta potential, is a crucial structural feature affecting the stability and interaction of nanoparticles with biological membranes (Kamble et al., 2022). A slightly negative surface charge usually helps blood flow for a longer time, while a positive charge can increase cellular absorption by interacting electrostatically with negatively charged cell membranes (Alfei and Schito, 2020). Polyethylene glycol (PEG) can alter the surfaces of protein-based nanoparticles to enhance stability and minimize nonspecific interactions, a process known as PEGylation (Li et al., 2021). PEGylation promotes the biocompatibility of nanoparticles and imparts a stealth property, enabling evasion of immune detection (Zalba et al., 2022).

The protein's structural complexity, encompassing its secondary, tertiary, and quaternary structures, is crucial for drug encapsulation and release (Falsafi et al., 2022). These structures alter the protein's binding affinity for drug molecules, thereby influencing encapsulation efficiency (Moraru, no date). Proteins with hydrophobic pockets are particularly adept at encapsulating hydrophobic medicines, ensuring their stability and protection within the nanoparticle until they reach their target location (Sun et al., 2021). Furthermore, we can design protein folding patterns to respond to environmental cues such as pH variations or the presence of specific enzymes, thereby facilitating the regulated release of the encapsulated medicine (Devnarain et al., 2021).

## 4. Mechanisms of drug delivery

Protein-based nanoparticles transport medications to their target locations through intricate techniques, generally classified into passive and active targeting strategies (Yetisgin, 2020).

The EPR effect is used for passive targeting. This effect makes nanoparticles preferentially stick to tumor tissues because tumors usually have damaged blood vessels and poor lymphatic drainage (Guo et al., 2021). Because of this feature, protein-based nanoparticles can gather in tumors, increasing the concentration of the medicine there while lowering its exposure to the body as a whole and reducing its adverse effects (Iqbal et al., 2021). The design of these nanoparticles, encompassing their dimensions and surface characteristics, is essential for optimizing the EPR effect (Kang, no date).

Active targeting involves adding certain ligands to the surfaces of protein-based nanoparticles so they can attach to overexpressed receptors on the surfaces of target cells (Nguyen et al., 2021). These ligands may comprise antibodies, peptides, or tiny compounds that identify and attach to receptors such as folate, transferrin, or integrins (Anthony et al., 2021). These receptors engage to absorb nanoparticles into target cells through receptor-mediated endocytosis, increasing drug administration's selectivity and efficiency

(Kunjiappan et al., 2021). This technique is especially effective for targeting cancer cells, which frequently overexpress certain receptors relative to normal cells (Ali et al., 2021).

Multiple processes can activate the liberation of the medication from the protein-based nanoparticle once it enters the cell (Kaltbeitzel and Wich, 2023). To make sure the drug is released in the right way at the right time, different methods are used, such as using enzymes to break down the protein matrix, disassembly that is sensitive to pH, and redox-sensitive release (Sun and Davis, 2021). The acidic milieu of lysosomes can initiate the liberation of pharmaceuticals from pH-sensitive nanoparticles, while enzymes such as proteases can dismantle the protein shell, facilitating the regulated release of the medication (Zou et al., 2021).

The formation of a protein corona, which happens when nanoparticles enter the bloodstream and interact with plasma proteins, can also have a big impact on how the drug is distributed, how well it is absorbed by cells, and how well the system works overall (Chen et al., 2020). Making a protein corona might cover up the targeting ligands on the nanoparticle surface. Careful planning and surface modification can fix this problem, though, and make sure the nanoparticles get to where they're supposed to go (Pinals et al., 2020).

For the most part, the way drugs are delivered and how they are structured in protein-based nanoparticles make them a strong and flexible way to develop new therapies (Liang et al., 2022). Researchers can make these nanoparticles more useful for targeted therapeutic purposes by carefully changing their sizes, surface charges, and protein composition (Wang et al., 2021). Protein-based nanoparticles are much more effective and specific at delivering drugs because they can use both passive and active targeting strategies and drug release mechanisms that are sensitive to their surroundings. Research in this domain is progressing, positioning these nanoparticles to play a pivotal role in treating various diseases such as cancer, cardiovascular disorders, and infectious diseases (Cao et al., 2020).

## 4.1 Drug-loading strategies for protein-based nanoparticles

The effective delivery of therapeutic agents using protein-based nanoparticles (PNPs) hinges on their ability to encapsulate drugs efficiently. Various strategies have been developed to enhance drug loading, which is critical for maximizing therapeutic efficacy while minimizing the required dosage. These strategies can be categorized into three main groups: chemical, physical, and self-assembly strategies. Each category encompasses distinct methods and mechanisms that influence the drug-loading capacity of nanoparticles, tailored to meet the specific requirements of targeted therapies, particularly in the treatment of metastatic cancers (Fig. 24.1).

### *4.1.1 Chemical strategies*

#### 4.1.1.1 Emulsion/solvent extraction

Emulsion/solvent extraction methods are widely utilized to produce both polymer and protein nanoparticles. An emulsion refers to a combination of two or more liquids that do not mix, in which one liquid is distributed in the form of small droplets throughout the other (Scheffel et al., 1972; Yang et al., 2007). In basic applications, a polymer solution or a protein

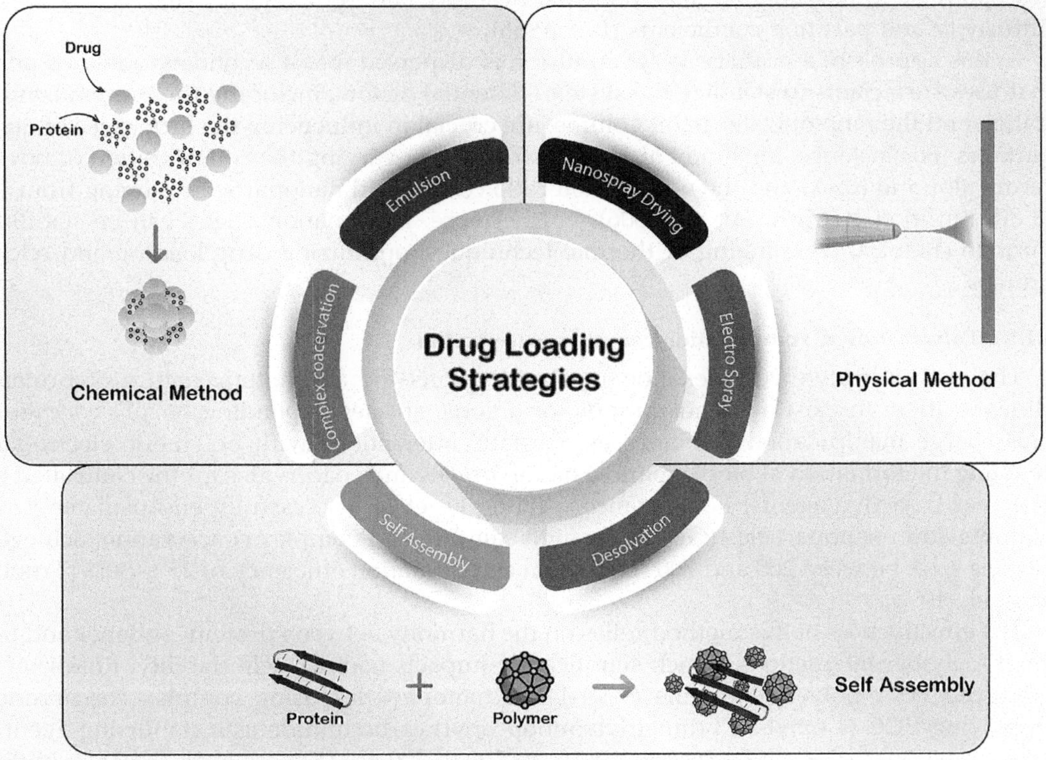


**FIGURE 24.1 Classification of techniques for drug loading into protein-based nanoparticles.** (a) The chemical method involves the formation of protein nanoparticles through chemical reactions, encompassing techniques such as emulsion and complex coacervation. (b) The physical method entails the aggregation of proteins into nanosized particles, utilizing approaches like electrospray and nano spray drying. (c) The self-assembly method relies on the spontaneous agglomeration of proteins to create nanoparticles, with the desolvation method being a notable example. The figure was created by the author using Adobe Photoshop (version 21.1.3) and Adobe Illustrator (version 28.3).

solution is dispersed through sonication or mechanical agitation, creating an emulsion system, either oil-in-water (O/W) or water-in-oil (W/O). Subsequent removal of the solvent or nonsolvent leads to the formation of nanoparticles. However, specific organic solvents, including chloroform and ethyl acetate, along with surfactants like Tween 80 and polyvinyl alcohol (PVA), can adversely impact the biological activity of protein therapeutics, potentially causing adverse reactions (Sturesson and Carlfors, 2000; Raghuvanshi et al., 1998).

Recent developments include the water-in-oil-in-water double emulsion method, which significantly enhances encapsulation efficiency for therapeutic payloads (Wang and Uludag, 2008). This is particularly important given the advancements in biotechnology and genetic engineering (Hutchinson and Furr, 1990), which have highlighted the therapeutic potential of peptides and proteins. However, these agents often face hurdles such as short half-lives, susceptibility to degradation, and poor permeability across biological barriers due to low diffusivity and partition coefficients (Lee, 1988).

In this approach, a primary W/O emulsion is dispersed into a secondary aqueous phase that uses surfactants to stabilize the system. Essential factors, including the protein concentration and the ratio of water to oil volume, are crucial in influencing the properties of nanoparticles. For instance, Mishra et al. demonstrated that varying the concentration of bovine serum albumin (BSA) and the water-to-oil ratio could yield nanoparticles ranging from 100 to 800 nm in size (Mishra et al., 2006). Furthermore, these nanoparticles can be stabilized through chemical crosslinking or thermal techniques, optimizing drug loading and release profiles.

#### 4.1.1.2 Polyelectrolyte complexation/complex coacervation

The polyelectrolyte complexation method exploits the amphoteric nature of proteins, allowing them to exist as either cationic or anionic species depending on pH conditions. This charge manipulation facilitates electrostatic interactions with polymeric electrolytes, enabling the formation of biocompatible nanoparticles and coacervates for the controlled delivery of bioactive agents. For instance, Truong-Le et al. successfully encapsulated DNA within gelatin nanoparticles (GNPs) through salt-induced complex coacervation, achieving particle sizes between 200 and 700 nm and an encapsulation efficiency of 25%–30% (Truong-Le et al., 1998).

The effectiveness of this method relies on the harmony between protein–polymer and polymer–polymer interactions, which significantly impacts nanoparticle stability. Rhaese et al. produced HSA–polyethylenimine (PEI)–DNA nanoparticles using complex coacervation, employing EDC (1-ethyl-3-(3-dimethylaminopropyl) carbodiimide as a stabilizing agent to achieve nanoparticles with sizes ranging from 300 to 700 nm (Rhaese et al., 2003). Additionally, Ren et al. explored the impacts of ultrasonic treatment on zein-chitosan complexes, demonstrating improvements in encapsulation efficiency, reaching up to 65.2%, while also reducing particle size and enhancing thermal stability (Ren et al., 2019). This approach provides a versatile strategy for tailoring nanoparticle properties, making it a promising method for drug delivery uses, particularly in relation to metastatic cancers (Hong et al., 2020b).

### *4.1.2 Physical strategies*

#### 4.1.2.1 Nano spray drying

Nano spray drying is an effective technique for processing nanoparticles from liquid samples for drug delivery applications. This method combines the principles of spray drying with the ability to produce nanoscale particles, making it particularly suitable for pharmaceuticals that require precise control over particle size and morphology (Arpagaus et al., 2018).

The nano spray drying process consists of several basic steps: (1) heating the drying gas, (2) generating droplets, (3) drying the droplets, and (4) collecting the particles (Arpagaus et al., 2017). At the beginning of the process, liquid samples are converted into an aerosol within a chamber, where streams of heated nitrogen and carbon dioxide gases are directed toward the spray generated by the nozzle (Oliveira et al., 2013). An electrode positioned at the base of the chamber collects the nanoparticles, and as the droplets travel downward, they become electrostatically charged. This technique is both rapid and cost-effective, making it suitable for small-scale production of protein particles. One significant application is in DDSs, in which hydrophilic pharmaceuticals can be packaged into these spray-dried nanoparticles. The process is advantageous for heat-sensitive compounds since solvent evaporation maintains the temperature of the nanoparticle droplets (Haggag and Faheem, 2015). Particle size can be regulated by modifying parameters such as nozzle diameter and spraying rate. For protein nanoparticles, the addition of surfactants is often necessary for stabilization. For instance, Lee et al. created BSA nanoparticles using a Nano Spray Dryer B-90, incorporating Tween 80 as a surfactant. This inclusion transformed the particles into a stable spherical shape, with size primarily influenced by spray mesh size and BSA concentration (Lee et al., 2011).

#### 4.1.2.2 Electrospray technique

Electrospray (ES), also referred to as electrohydrodynamic atomization, has become a cutting-edge method for creating particles intended for drug delivery. While similar to electrospinning, ES typically utilizes more dilute polymer solutions and employs the same basic equipment, including a high-voltage power supply, a glass syringe, a syringe pump, and a grounded conductive surface (Nikolaou and Krasia-Christoforou, 2018). Electrospraying is a liquid atomization method that enables the manipulation of materials at the submicron scale. This technique involves applying high voltage to a protein solution, allowing the formation of aerosolized droplets as the liquid jet is extruded through a nozzle (Gulfam et al., 2012; Wu et al., 2008). The resulting droplets consist of colloidal-sized protein nanoparticles, facilitating the integration of drugs and nucleic acids with high efficacy. Solid nanoparticles are created through solvent evaporation (Champion et al., 2007). Key parameters, including flow rate, operating distance, needle gauge diameter, and applied voltage, can be adjusted to tailor the DDS. The electrospraying technique is based on the use of high voltage to facilitate the ejection of polymers from syringes as nanoparticles (Bock et al., 2011; Dorozhkin, 2010). The benefits of this technique include high encapsulation efficiency, reproducibility, and cost-effectiveness, along with the ability to synthesize carbohydrate polymer nanoparticles or stable proteins that maintain biocompatibility (Yang et al., 2018).

### *4.1.3 Self-assembly strategies*

#### 4.1.3.1 Self-assembly

Self-assembly of protein micelles occurs when separate protein chains are solubilized in a solution that surpasses the critical solution temperature (CMT) and at the critical micelle concentration (CMC), resulting in the formation of nanosized aggregates (Hong et al., 2020b). The stability of these micelles can be enhanced through a solidification process that bridges the protein chains. By modifying albumin—a hydrophilic protein—to introduce amphiphilic properties, it can self-assemble into micelle nanoparticles upon introduction to aqueous environments. The hydrophobic cores of these micelles have the ability to effectively encapsulate active molecules.

For instance, Gong et al. successfully created protein micelle nanoparticles by reacting the primary amino groups of albumin with acetaldehyde, leading to a core–shell nanomicelle structure (Gong et al., 2009). This system was then dissolved in water and filtered through a fine porous membrane with a pore size of 0.45 μm. Paclitaxel was incorporated into the protein micelles using a dialysis technique, achieving a drug loading of 33.1% and an encapsulation efficiency of 90.5%. Additionally, in a study by Mukherjee et al., the protein-loading capacity of nanoparticles was determined by adding a known number of protein-loaded nanoparticles to a 5% SLS-NaOH (sodium lauryl sulfate-sodium hydroxide) solution, separating the dispersed phase from the continuous phase by centrifugation, and then spectrophotometrically assaying the released protein in the supernatant (Mukherjee et al., 2008). The results showed that increasing the speed of homogenization and the amount of polymer enhanced the protein-loading capacity of the formulation (Mittal et al., 2007; Basarkar et al., 2007). Furthermore, Sabra et al. created zein-lactoferrin (zein-Lf) micelles that successfully encapsulated hydrophobic drugs like wogonin (WOG) and rapamycin (RAP) using hydrophobic coupling reactions (Sabra et al., 2018). The inclusion of hydrophilic lactoferrin expanded the range of tumor-targeting potential, enhancing stability and hemocompatibility while maximizing the cytotoxic effects of RAP and WOG on MCF-7 breast cancer cells (Hong et al., 2020b).

#### 4.1.3.2 Desolvation

Desolvation is a widely used method for producing protein-based nanoparticles, leveraging the addition of desolvating agents like ethanol and acetone to protein solutions containing pharmaceutics (Weber et al., 2000; Zhao et al., 2015). These agents modify the protein structure and decrease solubility, leading to the formation of nanoparticles through precipitation. The process leads to an increase in particle size by gradually augmenting the number of similarly sized particles (Zhao et al., 2015). Once formed, nanoparticles can be stabilized using bridging agents, such as glutaraldehyde (Hong et al., 2020b).

The desolvation technique offers several advantages over other nanoparticle production methods, including emulsification, thermal gelation, nano spray drying, nanoparticle albumin-bound (NAB) technology, and self-assembly. Notably, it is an easy and reproducible process that results in nanoparticles with more controllable drug release characteristics (Elzoghby et al., 2012). This method is particularly advantageous for encapsulating therapeutic agents that are sensitive to heat or other harsh conditions, as it operates under mild conditions (Kouchakzadeh et al., 2014).

Key factors influencing particle size include protein concentration, the rate of desolvating agent addition, pH, and temperature. Generally, higher pH levels and lower protein concentrations result in smaller nanoparticles. Although desolvation does not directly synthesize nanoparticles, it is considered a self-assembly method because it concentrates proteins by reducing their solubility. This technique is often applied in generating albumin nanoparticles. Langer et al. utilized desolvating agents for HSA at pH levels between 7 and 9, employing acetone to create particles, which were then stabilized with GA (glutaraldehyde) (Langer et al., 2003). Furthermore, water-soluble drugs like DOX and 5-fluorouracil have been effectively incorporated into albumin nanoparticles using the desolvation method (Dreis et al., 2007; Maghsoudi et al., 2008; Dreis et al., 2007; Maghsoudi et al., 2008). Further optimization of parameters such as ethanol addition speed and protein concentration allowed to produce HSA nanoparticles ranging from 100 to 300 nm. Lee et al. demonstrated the encapsulation of α-galactosidase into HSA and recombinant 30Kc19 protein nanoparticles, achieving a loading efficiency of 80%–95% and nanoparticle diameters between 230 and 310 nm (Lee et al., 2016).

## 4.2 Targeted delivery approaches

### 4.2.1 *Active targeting through ligands and antibodies*

Active targeting techniques often include adding a variety of ligands, peptides, or antibodies to the surface of protein-based nanoparticles that can selectively interact with receptors that are overexpressed on metastatic cancer cells (Li, no date). A common example is the active targeting of HER2-positive breast cancer cells using nanoparticles coated with trastuzumab, a monoclonal antibody that targets the HER2 receptor. This improves absorption at metastatic areas and ultimately boosts therapeutic efficacy (Sitia, 2022).

Folic acid is another example of a targeted ligand whose use depends on the overexpression of folate receptors in many metastatic cancers (Farran et al., 2020). The attachment of folic acid to albumin or casein nanoparticles exhibits increased drug uptake in metastatic breast and ovarian cancers (Hussain et al., 2023). Such ligand-functionalized PNPs may reduce harmful effects on healthy tissues while increasing drug accumulation in malignant cells. The accuracy of this scale could reduce systemic toxicity and improve the therapeutic index of the encapsulated medications, such as DOX or paclitaxel (Yang et al., 2021; Mustafa et al., 2023).

### 4.2.2 *Passive targeting via enhanced permeability and retention effect*

The passive accumulation of these protein-based nanoparticles in tumor tissues would depend upon the EPR effect. Both leaking vasculature and compromised lymphatic drainage characterize metastatic tumors, allowing nanoparticles that are appropriately sized to extravasate and thereby result in accumulation at the tumor site (Iqbal et al., 2021; Sun et al., 2020). Albumin-bound nanoparticles of paclitaxel (nab-paclitaxel) have successfully exploited the EPR effect in treating metastatic breast cancer. However, EPR per se may not be sufficient in cases of metastases with poor vascularization or cancers that do not present obvious EPR (Cho, 2022; Sharifi et al., 2022). In that case, higher precision is achieved by a combination of passive targeting through EPR with active targeting using receptor–ligand interaction (Fig. 24.2) (Rasel et al., 2022).

### 4.2.3 *Stimuli-responsive protein nanoparticles*

The responsiveness of the PNPs is actually engineered against specific TME triggers, such as pH, temperature, or enzymatic activity of the TME (Roma-Rodrigues, 2021). These nanoparticles undergo certain changes in structure or degradation upon encountering stimuli, leading to site-specific drug release. This approach has proved very effective in the context of metastatic cancers, whose microenvironments differ quite significantly from those of healthy tissues (Fig. 24.3) (Nazir et al., 2022).

### 4.2.4 *Dual-functional nanoparticles for imaging and therapy (theranostic approach)*

Theranostic nanoparticles combine therapeutic agents with diagnostic ones in one delivery system and hence allow for simultaneous treatment and monitoring. Protein-based theranostic nanoparticles are usually conjugated with imaging agents such as fluorescent dyes or magnetic nanoparticles, which may facilitate real-time tracking of the nanoparticles regarding their distribution and accumulation at metastatic sites (Borlan et al., 2021). This is especially useful in treating metastatic cancer, where the monitoring of drug delivery and

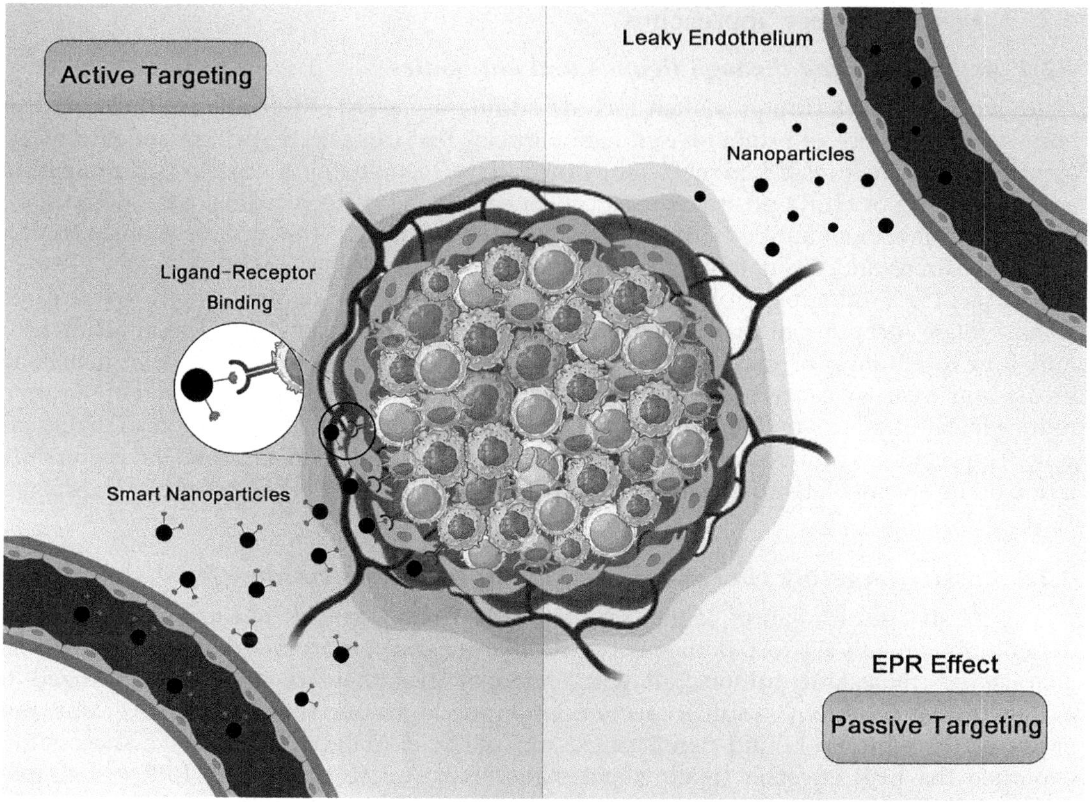


FIGURE 24.2 **Targeting cancer cells: Passive versus active approaches.** Passive targeting of cancer cells relies on the enhanced permeability and retention (EPR) effect, while active targeting involves facilitating the uptake of nanotherapeutics through receptor-mediated endocytosis. For example, nanoparticles can be functionalized with ligands that specifically bind to receptors or other molecules that are overexpressed on the surface of cancer cells. The figure was created by the author using Adobe Photoshop (version 21.1.3) and Adobe Illustrator (version 28.3).

tumoral response may guide the treatment strategy more precisely. The designs are so varied, for example, that theranostic nanoparticles containing both cisplatin and a near-infrared dye were able to effectively detect and treat metastatic lung cancer lesions in preclinical models (Manzari et al., 2021).

### *4.2.5 Targeted delivery of gene therapies and immune modulators*

Beyond the delivery of small-molecule drugs, protein-based nanoparticles have been used to deliver gene therapies and immune-modulating agents. Most gene therapy approaches involve the delivery of siRNA or mRNA to metastatic cancer cells that subsequently suppress oncogenes via silencing or upregulation of tumor-suppressor genes (Ebrahimi et al., 2023). Albumin-based nanoparticles have been studied for the delivery of siRNA that targets KRAS mutations in metastatic pancreatic cancer. Positive results

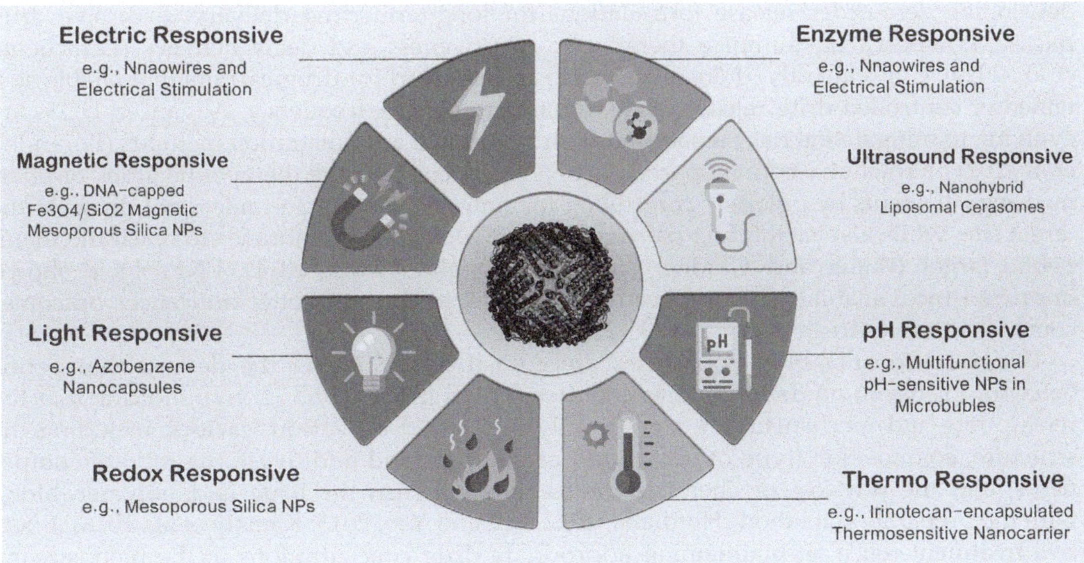


FIGURE 24.3 **Types of stimuli-responsive protein-based nanoparticles.** Types of stimuli-responsive protein-based nanoparticles. The figure was created by the author using Adobe Photoshop (version 21.1.3) and Adobe Illustrator (version 28.3).

achieved from localized gene therapy include a reduction in tumor growth with improved survival (Tarannum and Vivero-Escoto, 2022).

Moreover, nanoparticles carrying immune checkpoint inhibitors, such as antibodies against PD-1/PD-L1, can be fabricated (Ratajczak et al., 2023). Such nanoparticles may be engineered to codeliver immune checkpoint inhibitors together with chemotherapeutic agents by creating a synergistic effect in modulating the immune response against metastatic cancer cells. Ferritin-based nanoparticles, for instance, have been functionalized with anti-PD-L1 antibodies, demonstrating improved efficacy in preclinical models of metastatic melanoma (Wang et al., 2024).

## 4.3 Controlled release mechanism

Throughout treatment, the primary objective of drug therapy is to maximize efficacy and reduce adverse effects. The effectiveness of a drug primarily depends on its availability at the target site, ensuring a concentration and frequency that optimize therapeutic effects while minimizing side effects for the patient (Stielow, 2023a). The therapeutic window is defined as the range between the minimum toxic concentration (MTC) and the minimum effective concentration (MEC) (Colombo and Rich, 2022; Goldstein et al., 2021). Administering a large single dose of a medication can lead to dangerous side effects and a rapid decline in drug levels below the MEC. To achieve greater stability in plasma drug levels, multiple doses of a formulation can be beneficial; however, patient noncompliance may arise with intermittent dosing regimens (Otimenyin, no date). There is an ongoing interest in developing zero-order release formulations for long-term drug delivery. Excessive drug release, however, can diminish therapeutic effectiveness and delay delivery (Laracuente et al., 2020). Consequently, there is an increasing demand for drug carriers that enable sustained or controlled drug release while minimizing dosing frequency. Advanced DDSs are evolving to mitigate the risks associated with traditional administration methods (Borandeh et al., 2021). Protein-based nanoparticles (PNPs) can enhance the therapeutic index of pharmacological agents by precisely controlling the amount, timing, and release of drugs at the target site, while also facilitating passage through biological membranes to reach the therapeutic target (Wang and Uludag, 2008; Molino and Wang, 2014). PNPs have shown improved bioavailability and reduced side effects, leading to better anticancer outcomes compared to free drugs (Verma et al., 2018).

The characteristics of nanoparticles are crucial for achieving the desired therapeutic behavior (Yetisgin, no date). Studies conducted both in vitro and in vivo indicate that the release rate and mechanism are significantly influenced by various factors, including the structure, composition (type of drug, kind of polymer, and additives), the ratio of components, and the physical or chemical interactions between the drug and polymer, along with the preparation method (Herdiana, 2022; Lee and Yeo, 2015; Kamaly et al., 2016). Effective treatment relies on maintaining appropriate drug concentrations in the bloodstream, along with the release of active substances at a controlled rate (Stielow, 2023b). The transport of poorly soluble drugs using PNPs is facilitated by their reduced particle size, which improves dissolution in the bloodstream and enables targeted delivery to specific cells or tissues (Hong et al., 2020a).

For PNPs, drug release can be categorized into five mechanisms based on how the drug escapes from the carrier: diffusion, solvent interaction, chemical reaction, stimuli-responsive release, and intracellular delivery, as briefly summarized below.

### 4.3.1 *Diffusion-controlled release*

The diffusion-controlled mechanism is a prominent method for drug release. This type of release typically occurs in a capsule-type reservoir system, where the drug is enclosed within a core that is surrounded by a polymeric membrane (Sanopoulou and Papadokostaki, 2017; Lee and Good, 1987). In this mechanism, the drug or active substance passes through the polymer nanoparticle matrix, which acts as a controlled release system. Initially, the drug dissolves in the core and then diffuses through the membrane, driven by concentration gradients (Price, 2023).

### 4.3.2 *The swelling-controlled release*

In swelling-controlled release systems, the polymer matrix expands as it interacts with the surrounding medium, facilitating drug release. Prior to degradation, the polymer swells, which influences the diffusion of the drug based on factors like hydrophilicity and polymer chain density (Siepmann and Siepmann, 2012). In the swelling process, drug delivery occurs through both erosion and diffusion (Ko et al., 2019). The relaxation constant of the polymer matrix is crucial in influencing the rate of drug release, with larger values leading to slower release rates (Viswanadha et al., 2024).

### 4.3.3 *Erosion and degradation-controlled release*

Erosion mechanisms involve a combination of swelling, diffusion, and dissolution processes. Erosion can be categorized as homogeneous, where the polymer erodes evenly, or heterogeneous, where degradation occurs from the surface inward (Kamaly et al., 2016). Factors such as the chemical properties of the surrounding medium, enzymatic activity, and polymer composition influence the rate of erosion (Lamoudi et al., 2016). Biodegradable polymers are preferred in DDSs, as their breakdown products can be safely eliminated from the body without causing long-term adverse effects (Tsung et al., 2023). The drug release kinetics are primarily influenced by the polymer's degradation rate, which depends on factors like molecular weight, end groups, and crystallinity (Lamoudi et al., 2016).

### 4.3.4 *Stimuli-controlled release*

Stimuli-controlled release mechanisms utilize either internal or external triggers to release drugs. Internal stimuli can target diseased tissue, enhancing drug selectivity and action (Wang et al., 2014). This approach requires the incorporation of specific substances into PNPs that respond to endogenous stimuli, such as the acidic environment or elevated enzyme levels found in tumor tissues (Wang et al., 2014; Rosenkranz and Slastnikova, 2023). Conversely, external stimuli like light or ultrasound can prompt drug release in designated areas. Smart-responsive PNPs typically remain inactive in normal tissues but become activated in TMEs, facilitating controlled drug release as needed (Wells et al., 2019).

### 4.3.5 *Intracellular delivery with virus-like particles*

Viruses, particularly VLPs, have emerged as innovative drug carriers due to their robustness and ability to release their genetic material in response to cellular signals (Martins et al., 2022). VLPs are self-assembled from the coat proteins of native viruses and can encapsulate a variety of therapeutic agents, including chemotherapy drugs and genes (Ikwuagwu and Tullman-Ercek, 2022). Through genetic engineering, specific targeting motifs can be displayed on VLP surfaces to enhance delivery to cancer cells (Kim et al., 2023).

The internalization of VLPs into target cells typically occurs via receptor-mediated endocytosis, followed by either direct fusion with the plasma membrane or fusion with endosomal membranes (Kalia and Jameel, 2011). Some VLPs exhibit natural tissue tropism based on their viral origin—for instance, hepatitis B virus (HBV)-derived VLPs target liver cells due to the virus's natural infection patterns, while rotavirus-derived VLPs preferentially deliver drugs to intestinal tissue (Nooraei et al., 2021). Enhanced targeting can be achieved by chemically or genetically attaching receptor-binding domains to VLP surfaces, allowing for selective binding to cancer cells that express specific receptors (Laomeephol et al., 2024; Shahgolzari, no date).

The use of VLPs for drug delivery presents significant advantages, including increased drug accumulation at targeted sites and improved bioavailability. This targeted approach can minimize toxicity to healthy cells and enhance treatment efficacy (Kim, no date). For example, MS2 VLPs modified with a targeting peptide (SP94) have been shown to selectively deliver chemotherapeutic drugs such as DOX to human hepatocellular carcinoma cells, demonstrating high specificity and significantly improved cytotoxicity compared to free DOX (Chung et al., 2020a).

# 5. Functional groups and their roles

## 5.1 Chemical modifications

Protein-based nanoparticles (PNPs) are becoming more popular as platforms for drug delivery, diagnostics, and other biomedical uses because they are biocompatible, biodegradable, and can do a lot of different things (Ferraro et al., 2024). Chemical modifications in these nanoparticles aim to improve their stability, functionalization, and targeting ability. Researchers have developed a variety of chemical techniques to enhance the effectiveness of protein-based nanoparticles in medical applications (Kaltbeitzel and Wich, 2023).

A common chemical modification involves the covalent attachment of PEG to the protein's surface, referred to as PEGylation (Sun et al., 2021). PEGylation improves the stability and solubility of PNPs by inhibiting protein aggregation and proteolytic degradation while diminishing immunogenicity and prolonging circulation duration in the bloodstream (Jana et al., 2021). The modification includes the integration of targeting ligands, such as peptides or antibodies, which can be chemically conjugated to nanoparticles to improve their selectivity for particular tissues or cell types (Yetisgin, no date). These targeting ligands enhance the nanoparticles' capacity to deliver medications directly to the illness site, hence augmenting therapeutic efficacy (Raj et al., 2021).

Additional chemical alterations include protein crosslinking to create more stable nanoparticle formations (Zhang et al., 2021). For instance, glutaraldehyde or carbodiimide-mediated cross-linking fortifies the protein matrix and ensures structural integrity of the nanoparticles, particularly under diverse physiological settings (Steiert, 2020). Furthermore, researchers have used chemical modifications like phosphorylation and acetylation to modify the surface charge and hydrophilicity of protein-based nanoparticles, thereby influencing their interaction with biological membranes and cellular absorption (Bashiri et al., 2023).

The developments in chemical modification technologies have improved the functionality of protein-based nanoparticles for targeted drug delivery, cancer therapy, and vaccine production (Fig. 24.4) (Alam et al., 2022).

## 5.2 Impact of hydrophilicity and hydrophobicity on drug efficacy

### *5.2.1 Applications in medicine*

Protein-based nanoparticles (PNPs) are a good choice for DDSs because they are biocompatible, biodegradable, and can be modified to work in specific therapeutic ways (Ferraro et al., 2024). Hydrophilicity and hydrophobicity are two critical factors that significantly affect the effectiveness of PNPs (Ngouangna et al., 2022). These characteristics influence the interaction of nanoparticles with biological systems, their capacity for drug encapsulation, and the release kinetics of therapeutic substances (Yusuf et al., 2023). Comprehending the influence of hydrophilicity and hydrophobicity on PNPs facilitates the systematic creation of nanoparticles customized to the pharmacokinetics and pharmacodynamics of their associated pharmaceuticals (Haripriyaa and Suthindhiran, 2023).

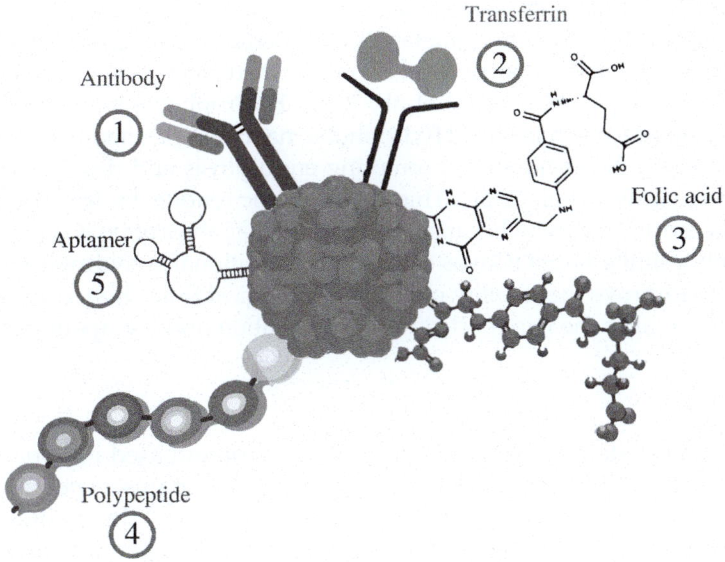


**FIGURE 24.4 Chemical modifications of PNPs to enhance targeting and therapeutic efficacy.** This figure illustrates the functionalization of PNPs with: (1) antibodies for specific antigen recognition, (2) transferrin for targeting transferrin receptors on cancer cells and neurons, (3) folic acid to target folate receptors commonly found on cancer cells, (4) polypeptides for enhancing cellular uptake, and (5) aptamers for precise targeting of biomolecules. These modifications, therefore, improve nanoparticle specificity, stability, and efficiency for different therapeutic applications. The figure was created by the author using Adobe Illustrator (version 28.3).

### *5.2.2 Hydrophilicity in protein-based nanoparticles*

Hydrophilicity is essential for enhancing the solubility, circulation duration, and stability of PNPs, especially for pharmaceuticals with limited aqueous solubility (Bhalani, 2022). A prevalent strategy for augmenting the hydrophilicity of PNPs involves surface modification, namely PEGylation, wherein PEG chains are covalently bonded to the nanoparticle surface (Sun et al., 2021). PEGylation improves the nanoparticle's hydrophilicity and provides a steric shield, reducing opsonization and immune recognition, thereby prolonging the nanoparticle's circulation half-life (Guo et al., 2023). This is particularly important for drugs that require prolonged systemic exposure to achieve therapeutic effects. Hydrophilic PNPs have demonstrated the capacity to diminish fast clearance by the reticuloendothelial system (RES), facilitating prolonged release and bioavailability of pharmaceuticals (Elsewedy et al., 2021).

Hydrophilic PNPs are particularly effective in the delivery of proteins, peptides, and nucleic acids, which are intrinsically hydrophilic substances (Luther et al., 2020). These therapeutic agents benefit from increased solubility and stability when encapsulated in hydrophilic nanoparticles. Moreover, hydrophilic surface changes can improve nanoparticles' capacity to traverse biological barriers, including the BBB, facilitating targeted distribution to specific organs (Teixeira et al., 2023). This is essential in the management of conditions such as cancer and neurological illnesses, where precise administration can reduce off-target effects and improve therapeutic effectiveness (Mukherjee, no date).

### *5.2.3 Hydrophobicity in protein-based nanoparticles*

Conversely, hydrophobic protein-based nanoparticles are more effective for administering hydrophobic medicines, which constitute a significant fraction of small-molecule therapies (Ledesma, 2022). Hydrophobic modifications can be introduced to the protein backbone through chemical conjugation or by using hydrophobic proteins as the nanoparticle's core material. Hydrophobic nanoparticles effectively encapsulate poorly water-soluble medicines, safeguarding them against premature breakdown or metabolism (Rocha et al., 2023). Hydrophobic nanoparticles efficiently encapsulate poorly water-soluble medicines, safeguarding them against premature breakdown or metabolism (Li et al., 2020). Hydrophobic interactions also play a critical role in cellular uptake mechanisms. Hydrophobic nanoparticles demonstrate improved interactions with lipid-rich cell membranes, promoting endocytosis and drug transport to intracellular compartments (Amini et al., 2021). This characteristic renders hydrophobic PNPs especially advantageous in cancer treatment because effective cellular absorption is crucial for the medication to attain its intracellular target (Gavas et al., 2021). Additionally, hydrophobic modifications have been shown to improve the stability of PNPs in biological fluids by reducing protein corona formation, which can alter the nanoparticle's biodistribution and therapeutic efficacy (Rampado et al., 2020).

#### 5.2.4 *Applications in medicine*

The dual characteristics of hydrophilicity and hydrophobicity in protein-based nanoparticles have resulted in their extensive utilization across multiple medical domains, especially in medication delivery and oncological treatment (Kaltbeitzel and Wich, 2023). In oncological therapy, hydrophobic polymeric nanoparticles (PNPs) have been employed to transport chemotherapy drugs like paclitaxel and DOX, which have low solubility in aqueous environments. These nanoparticles improve drug solubility, protect the drug from degradation, and facilitate controlled release, leading to enhanced therapeutic outcomes with reduced systemic toxicity (Doxorubicin nanoformulations on therapy against cancer: An overview from the last 10 years, 2022). Hydrophilic PNPs are extensively utilized in the administration of biologics, including monoclonal antibodies, enzymes, and nucleic acids, where solubility and stability are very important (Silvestre et al., 2021).

Additionally, hydrophilic and hydrophobic PNPs are being explored for targeted drug delivery applications. By altering the surface of PNPs with targeting ligands, such as peptides or antibodies, nanoparticles can preferentially adhere to certain cells or tissues, hence enhancing the accuracy of drug delivery (Mitchell et al., 2021). This method is very beneficial in treating complicated diseases, including cancer and neurological disorders, as focused administration can greatly enhance therapeutic efficiency while reducing side effects (Akhtar et al., 2021).

The equilibrium between hydrophilicity and hydrophobicity in protein-based nanoparticles is essential for ascertaining their functionality in biological systems and their viability as drug delivery mechanisms (Zhang et al., 2022). Advancements in nanoparticle design and surface modification techniques have facilitated the creation of PNPs with customized hydrophilic and hydrophobic characteristics, enhancing medication efficacy and broadening their medical applications (Ahmad, 2022).

## 6. Hydrophilicity and hydrophobicity applications in medicine

### 6.1 Lung delivery systems

Inhalation therapy provides an effective, noninvasive approach for delivering therapeutics directly to the lungs, particularly beneficial for treating pulmonary diseases (Kuzmov and Minko, 2015; Rasul et al., 2020). This method allows for cell- and organelle-specific drug delivery by attaching targeting ligands to drug carriers, which minimizes exposure to healthy lung tissue and other systemic organs. Such specificity can reduce required drug dosages and mitigate adverse side effects (Senapati et al., 2018; Majumder et al., 2019). The lung is especially suited for protein and gene-based therapeutics due to its lower levels of intracellular and extracellular drug-metabolizing enzymes compared to the gastrointestinal tract and liver (Lee et al., 2015a, 2015b). Currently, various inhalation devices—including pressurized metered-dose inhalers, dry powder inhalers, nebulizers, and soft mist inhalers—are employed to facilitate pulmonary drug delivery (Ruigrok et al., 2016).

The deposition of inhaled particles within the lungs is influenced by factors such as inertial impaction, gravitational sedimentation, and diffusion, which are primarily determined by the aerodynamic particle size distribution of the aerosolized drugs (Alhajj et al., 2020; Youngren-Ortiz et al., 2016). One significant challenge in this delivery method is the complex branching of the airways, which varies in length and diameter. As inhaled particles navigate these branched pathways, they are prone to collide with airway walls rather than reaching deeper lung regions, primarily due to increased particle velocity (Fröhlich, 2019; Lam et al., 2012).

A promising strategy involves the use of GNPs as drug carriers, which can enhance delivery efficiency while minimizing mucociliary clearance effects. Tseng et al. (2009) demonstrated that inhalable GNPs do not induce lung inflammation, as evidenced by myeloperoxidase activity assays, confirming their safety for pulmonary use. This capability makes inhaled GNPs a suitable vehicle for delivering cisplatin in lung cancer treatment, with the potential for improved therapeutic outcomes and reduced side effects. Notably, GNPs can achieve high concentrations of cisplatin in cancerous lung tissues (Tseng et al., 2009).

Despite their advantages, the application of nano-sized delivery systems poses challenges owing to their mass median aerodynamic diameter (MMAD), which might not be ideal for effective inhalation. Consequently, a significant portion of the inhaled dose can be exhaled, leading to minimal lung deposition. To address this issue, Sham et al. (2004) investigated the application of spray-dried micrometer-sized carrier particles to deliver GNPs to the lower respiratory tract using dry powder inhalers. In this method, GNPs were combined with lactose as the carrier matrix, which dissolves rapidly upon contact with the lung's aqueous environment, facilitating immediate release of the nanoparticles. The average particle size of the spray-dried GNPs expanded from 242.2 to 319.9 nm, resulting in a fine particle fraction (FPF) of 40% and a suitable MMAD of 3.0 μm for effective lung delivery (Sham et al., 2004).

Additionally, an aerosol formulation of cationized GNPs loaded with immunostimulating agents, specifically cytosine–phosphate–guanine–oligodeoxynucleotides (CpG–ODN), was developed to enhance immunotherapy efficacy against hypersensitivity, particularly in treating equine recurrent airway obstruction (Fuchs et al., 2012; Klier et al., 2012). Following nebulization, the GNPs showed sizes between 222.3 and 248.2 nm, with an FPF reaching 65.7%. The nebulized CpG–ODN-loaded GNPs effectively triggered IL-10 release in vitro from equine alveolar lymphocytes, significantly enhancing the expression of the regulatory antiinflammatory cytokine IL-10 after five consecutive inhalations (Zhao et al., 2012).

Moreover, GNPs were investigated as a system for pulmonary insulin administration. Research indicates that intratracheal instillation of insulin-loaded GNPs enhances insulin absorption in the lungs and prolongs the duration of the hypoglycemic effect while minimizing insulin deposition in lung tissues (Elzoghby, 2013).

Beyond GNPs, the lung's unique anatomy and physiology present various challenges for drug delivery. The complex branching of airways, characterized by varying lengths and diameters, affects particle deposition due to inertial impact and the dynamics of airflow (Fröhlich, 2019). Mucociliary clearance mechanisms, along with alveolar macrophage activity, further reduce the likelihood of particles interacting with target lung cells (Roy and Vij, 2010; Sanders et al., 2009). Consequently, inhaled particles often struggle to reach deeper lung regions, particularly when considering the rapid clearance mechanisms at play (Youngren-Ortiz et al., 2016).

To enhance the effectiveness of protein-based therapies, various strategies have been employed, including chemical modifications and encapsulation in nanoparticles. The physicochemical properties of these carriers significantly influence delivery efficacy, and ongoing research aims to refine these systems for better therapeutic outcomes in pulmonary applications (Zhao, Liu and Lu, no date).

## 6.2 Cancer and tumor therapies

Traditional fabrication techniques for protein-based nanoparticles (PNPs) commonly utilize toxic solvents and crosslinking agents, which can lead to considerable toxicity and diminished drug stability. To address these challenges, innovative strategies for the noncovalent self-assembly of proteins have been introduced, employing hydrophobic interactions and manipulation of disulfide bonds to produce nontoxic, crosslinker-free drug-loaded protein nanoparticles. Approaches such as thermal-mediated unfolding, the use of reducing agents, pH modulation, and photochemical techniques effectively facilitate this self-assembly process (Hassanin and Elzoghby, 2020).

A well-known FDA-approved example of protein nanoparticles is Abraxane (nab-paclitaxel), a 130 nm albumin-based formulation developed to stabilize the hydrophobic paclitaxel, an anticancer agent (Ibrahim et al., 2002; Fu et al., 2009). Due to paclitaxel's poor solubility, traditional formulations often require toxic solvents like Cremophor EL (Weiss et al., 1990). In contrast, Abraxane is created by dissolving paclitaxel in chloroform and mixing it with a water-based solution of unprocessed HSA. This technique produces an emulsion using high-pressure homogenization, promoting nanoparticle formation and ensuring consistent protein-to-drug ratio. Provided as a freeze-dried powder, Abraxane shows excellent extended storage durability, lasting for as long as 36 months at room temperature. The drug forms a hydrophobic core within the albumin shell, which helps to reduce drug leakage. Although it was initially thought that the structural stability of the albumin proteins was maintained, recent studies indicate that partial degradation may occur during the preparation process (Hama et al., 2021). Following injection, Abraxane rapidly breaks down into separate albumin-bound drug complexes, altering the structural stability of the albumin proteins while improving delivery to tumors (Yang et al., 2013). Increased tumor accumulation and cellular uptake are linked to interactions with albumin-specific receptors such as Gp60 and SPARC (Yardley, 2013a, 2013b; Cortes and Saura, 2010), though alternative uptake pathways have also been proposed (Hama et al., 2021).

Isolated viral coat proteins can spontaneously assemble in vitro without including nucleic acid components, allowing for the encapsulation of various therapeutic agents within VLPs (Chung et al., 2020b). The integration of VLPs with CRISPR-Cas technology enables the development of effective systems for in vivo gene editing through the coencapsulation of guide RNA and mRNA that encodes Cas9 (Indikova and Indik, 2020; Lyu et al., 2020). Likewise, hydrophobic drugs such as Dox can be administered by genetically engineered VLPs containing hydrophobic amino acids in their interior. Additional enhancements to VLPs can be accomplished through surface modifications, which may involve the addition of targeting peptides and PEG chains to promote immune evasion (Ghosh and Banerjee, no date; Rohovie et al., 2017).

Li et al. demonstrated that artificial synthesis could reveal a peptide specific to the urokinase receptor presented on the surface of HSA nanoparticles. By denaturing the HSA fusion protein utilizing urea in a solution based on ethanol and then rapidly diluting it, they accomplished self-assembly into nanoparticles with a consistent size distribution of approximately 50 nm, which allowed for the encapsulation of the hydrophobic photosensitizer chlorpromazine (CPZ). This nanoparticle system effectively reduced tumor size in a mouse model that overexpresses uPAR, and in vitro studies showed that receptor-triggered disassembly and the introduction of the urokinase receptor prompted the activation of drug release (Bae et al., 2012).

Transferrin, an iron-binding transport protein, specifically interacts with the transferrin receptor, which is expressed at high levels in numerous cancer cell lines, making it a valuable component for nanoparticles (Wong et al., 2017; Li and Qian, 2002). Makwana et al. covalently linked an atom transfer radical polymerization (ATRP) initiator to transferrin, leading to the controlled polymerization of a PEG brush polymer and the creation of protein–polymer conjugates. These conjugates self-assemble into spherical nanoparticles that vary in size from 10 to 200 nm, depending on the number of polymer chains. Although an increased number of polymer chains on the protein reduced its affinity for the CD71 receptor, the nanoparticles effectively encapsulated paclitaxel, demonstrating greater cytotoxicity to cancer cells in comparison to the free drug, owing to improved transport mediated by the transferrin receptor (Makwana et al., 2017).

Villaverde et al. investigated the self-organization of protein nanoparticles in the absence of polymers through electrostatic interactions from short peptide tags that also function as targeting groups for CXCR4-overexpressing cancer cells (Céspedes et al., 2014). By attaching a cell-penetrating peptide to the N-terminus of green fluorescent protein (GFP) and a His-tag to the C-terminus, the constructs that have been genetically engineered readily form uniform nanostructures shaped like donuts (12–56 nm) through self-assembly that are efficiently internalized by target cells, accumulating in the perinuclear region following endosomal escape. Computational modeling of the interactions driving protein nano-assembly suggests two potential mechanisms: tail–tail interactions between the interactions of the peptide tags and the tail-barrel with the protein structure. The GFP nanoparticles facilitated in vivo tracking of nanoparticle distribution while also protecting GFP from photobleaching caused by UV light exposure (Kaltbeitzel and Wich, 2023; Unzueta et al., 2020).

Lie et al. also engineered nanoparticles of interferon alpha (IFN-α) featuring a radius of 65 nm. This was achieved by adjusting the C-terminus of IFN-α, which is linked to an amphiphilic block copolymer containing poly-PEG and poly-hydroxypropyl. through

ATRP, while preserving the protein's secondary structure. In vivo studies demonstrated significantly better outcomes than Pegasys, with a 100% survival rate among treated mice and 62.5% remaining cancer-free by the study's conclusion (Liu et al., 2018).

These advancements in protein-based nanoparticles underscore their potential as effective platforms for targeted cancer therapy, leveraging both hydrophobic and hydrophilic interactions to enhance drug delivery and therapeutic efficacy (Table 24.2). provides a comprehensive overview of recent clinical trials that explore the use of protein-based nanoparticles in the treatment of various types of metastatic cancers, sourced from https://clinicaltrials.gov/.

## 6.3 Vaccine delivery

With their unique properties of biocompatibility, encapsulation of a wide range of antigens, and efficiency in the enhancement of immune responses, PNPs have become one of the most studied vaccine carriers in the last decade (Kheirollahpour et al., 2020). Because of their nanoscale sizes, they enable advanced cellular uptake and precise distribution, hence assuring efficient antigen presentation. PNPs can also be engineered to mimic viruses with the addition of immunogenicity (Wang, Sun and Hou, 2021). For this reason, they also provide a solid backbone for the next generation in vaccine development and promise more effectiveness and safety in vaccination (Cid and Bolívar, 2021).

### *6.3.1 Antigen presentation and immune activation*

The primary role of protein nanoparticles in vaccine delivery is to improve antigen presentation to the immune system. Protein nanoparticles can be designed to transport antigens—complete proteins, peptides, or nucleic acids—that are capable of mimicking specific pathogens, including bacteria and viruses (Kim et al., 2021). After administration, the nanoparticles deliver these antigens to the antigen-presenting cells, such as macrophages and dendritic cells (DCs). The processing of these antigens by antigen presenting cell (APC) involves their delivery to the T cells, thus eliciting an adaptive immunological response (Est-Witte, 2021).

In the process of administration, these nanoparticles carry antigens into antigen-presenting cells, such as macrophages and DCs. The antigen-presenting cells then process antigens and present them to T cells, thus eliciting an adaptive immune response (Benne et al., 2022; Zhou et al., 2020).

### *6.3.2 Enhanced antigen stability and protection*

The protein nanoparticles protect the fragile antigens from degradation in biological environments (Shi and McHugh, 2023). If the route of administration involves circulation or the gastrointestinal tract, several antigens can be degraded by the enzymatic and pH fluctuations before they meet the immune cells (Peng and Fadeel, 2022). These antigens can be encapsulated into protein nanoparticles that will protect them from harmful conditions (Olshefsky et al., 2022).

Protection keeps them intact until the antigens arrive at their site of action—for example, lymph nodes—where they can be presented to the immune cells. Hence, protein

**TABLE 24.2** Clinical trials on metastatic cancer since January 1, 2015.

| Title | Type of cancer | Type of protein nanoparticle | Cargo | Number of patients | Date of start | Status | ClinicalTrials.gov ID |
|---|---|---|---|---|---|---|---|
| Trial of ascorbic acid (AA) + nanoparticle paclitaxel protein bound + cisplatin + gemcitabine (AA nabplagem) | Metastatic pancreatic cancer | Albumin | Paclitaxel | 27 | December 15, 2017 | Finished | NCT03410030 |
| Biologically optimized infusion schedule of gemcitabine and nab-paclitaxel for the treatment of metastatic pancreatic cancer | Metastatic pancreatic cancer | Albumin | Paclitaxel | 53 | June 24, 2020 | Ongoing | NCT04115163 |
| Nab-sirolimus and pazopanib hydrochloride in treating patients with advanced nonadipocytic soft tissue sarcomas | Metastatic nonadipocytic soft tissue sarcomas (STS) | Albumin | Sirolimus (Rapamycin) | 19 | April 1, 2019 | Ongoing | NCT03660930 |
| Nab-paclitaxel PIPAC in combination with paclitaxel and ramucirumab for the treatment of stomach cancer with peritoneal metastases | Metastatic stomach cancer | Albumin | Paclitaxel | 30 | October 17, 2025 | Start date is on October 17, 2025 | NCT06675136 |
| Hyperthermic intraperitoneal chemotherapy for the treatment of pancreatic cancer and peritoneal metastasis | Metastatic pancreatic cancer | Albumin | Paclitaxel | 40 | January 5, 2024 | Ongoing | NCT04858009 |
| Paricalcitol and hydroxychloroquine in combination with gemcitabine and nab-paclitaxel for advanced pancreatic cancer | Metastatic pancreatic cancer | Albumin | Paclitaxel | 12 | September 14, 2020 | Ongoing | NCT04524702 |
| Durvalumab in combination with chemotherapy in treating patients with advanced solid tumors (durva + study) | Metastatic malignant solid neoplasm | Albumin | Paclitaxel | 115 | July 16, 2019 | Ongoing | NCT03907475 |

(*Continued*)

TABLE 24.2 Clinical trials on metastatic cancer since January 1, 2015.—cont'd

| Title | Type of cancer | Type of protein nanoparticle | Cargo | Number of patients | Date of start | Status | ClinicalTrials.gov ID |
|---|---|---|---|---|---|---|---|
| Ceritinib and combination chemotherapy in treating patients with advanced solid tumors or locally advanced or metastatic pancreatic cancer | Metastatic pancreatic cancer | Albumin | Paclitaxel | 38 | January 8, 2015 | Finished On December 27, 2018 | NCT02227940 |
| Gemcitabine hydrochloride, cisplatin, and nab-paclitaxel in treating patients with advanced or metastatic biliary cancers | Metastatic biliary cancers | Albumin | Paclitaxel | 62 | April 2, 2015 | Finished On August 13, 2020 | NCT02392637 |
| Phase I study of tumor-treating fields (TTF) in combination with cabozantinib or with pembrolizumab and nab-paclitaxel in patients with advanced solid tumors involving the abdomen or thorax | Different types of metastatic cancers | Albumin | Paclitaxel | 43 | April 24, 2022 | Ongoing | NCT05092373 |
| Bats in combination with low dose IL-1 and GM-CSF for advanced pancreatic cancer | Metastatic pancreatic cancer | Albumin | Paclitaxel | 2 | December 2015 | Finished on June 21, 2021 | NCT02620865 |
| Pressurized intraperitoneal aerosolized nab-paclitaxel in combination with gemcitabine and cisplatin for the treatment of biliary tract cancer patients with peritoneal metastases | Metastatic biliary tract cancer | Albumin | Paclitaxel | 12 | September 19, 2022 | Ongoing | NCT05285358 |
| Comparing two treatment combinations, gemcitabine and nab-paclitaxel with 5-fluorouracil, leucovorin, and liposomal irinotecan for older patients with pancreatic cancer that has spread | Metastatic pancreatic cancer | Albumin | Paclitaxel | 176 | August 26, 2020 | Ongoing | NCT04233866 |

| | | | | | | | |
|---|---|---|---|---|---|---|---|
| High-dose radiation therapy with pembrolizumab and chemotherapy for the treatment of patients with PD-L1-positive metastatic triple-negative breast cancer | Metastatic TNBC (triple-negative breast carcinoma) | Albumin | Paclitaxel | 29 | October 1, 2024 | Ongoing | NCT06492759 |
| Testing the addition of the pill chemotherapy, cabozantinib, to the standard immunotherapy nivolumab compared to standard chemotherapy for nonsmall cell lung cancer | Metastatic nonsmall cell lung cancer | Albumin | Paclitaxel | 117 | July 13, 2020 | Ongoing | NCT04310007 |
| Testing the addition of an individualized vaccine to durvalumab and tremelimumab and chemotherapy in patients with metastatic triple-negative breast cancer | Metastatic TNBC (triple-negative breast carcinoma) | Albumin | Paclitaxel | 70 | April 13, 2021 | Ongoing | NCT03606967 |
| Evaluation of IPI-549 combined with front-line treatments in pts. with triple-negative breast cancer or renal cell carcinoma (Mario-3) | Metastatic TNBC (triple-negative breast carcinoma) and renal cell carcinoma | Albumin | Paclitaxel | | December 17, 2019 | Ongoing | NCT03961698 |
| Atezolizumab with chemotherapy in treating patients with anaplastic or poorly differentiated thyroid cancer | Metastatic thyroid gland carcinoma | Albumin | Paclitaxel | 50 | July 27, 2017 | Ongoing | NCT03181100 |
| Sonoporation and chemotherapy for the treatment of pancreatic cancer | Metastatic pancreatic cancer | Albumin | Paclitaxel | 120 | December 6, 2021 | Ongoing | NCT04821284 |

nanoparticles stabilize vaccines for an extended period, which in turn increases their efficacy, mainly for routes of administration that would otherwise be unpleasant, like oral or intranasal (Krishnamurty and Turley, 2020; Kumar et al., 2022).

### 6.3.3 *Targeted delivery to immune cells*

One of the major advantages of protein nanoparticles is the fact that they are able to target specific immune cells, such as DCs and macrophages, that have a very important role in developing a strong immunological response (Cifuentes-Rius et al., 2021). Targeting ligands attached to the surface of protein nanoparticles could bring about efficient targeting toward these cells. This increases specificity in vaccine delivery and ensures that the antigen targets the most suitable type of immune cells (Mitchell et al., 2021).

Mannose-modified protein nanoparticles are therefore capable of targeting the mannose receptors on DCs, which increases DC uptake and enhances immunological activation. Targeting in such a way is important for developing effective vaccination efficacy, especially for vaccines that would need Th1 cellular immunity—such as vaccines against HIV or cancer (Meng et al., 2023).

### 6.3.4 *Controlled antigen release*

Antigen released through protein nanoparticles in a regulated and sustained manner results in the enhancement of the immune response. Sustained antigen presentation in immunizations can achieve improved and prolonged immune responses, much closer to the natural response of the body to disease (Fan, 2022).

By design, protein nanoparticles—such as those with hydrophobic cores—can encapsulate antigens and provide a means for such release to be modulated by environmental stimuli, including pH or enzymatic activity (Ramos, 2022). In this sense, a regulated release can frequently maintain the body's antigen levels for an extended period of time, minimizing the need for repeated booster shots. As a result, the vaccine is more effective overall (Michaelides et al., 2023).

### 6.3.5 *Adjuvant properties*

As adjuvants, protein nanoparticles enhance the immune system's response to an antigen. The multivalent repeating structure in some proteins naturally recapitulates viral capsids, making them immunogenic by nature (Tariq et al., 2022). This is so because such symmetrical structures can directly activate the immune cells through pattern recognition receptors (PRRs) on APCs, thereby amplifying the immunological response without any supplementary adjuvants (Burn et al., 2020).

Surfaces of protein nanoparticles can be modified with conventional adjuvants, such as Toll-like receptor (TLR) agonists, to augment the immune response. The dual role played by protein nanoparticles, carrying and immune-stimulating, further enhances versatility in vaccine formulation (Huang, no date).

### 6.3.6 *Reduced toxicity and biocompatibility*

While most synthetic materials used liposomes or polymeric nanoparticles, protein-based nanoparticles are inherently biocompatible and biodegradable in nature (Wong et al., 2020). Naturally occurring proteins such as albumin, gelatin, and ferritin are already inside the body;

thus, they have a lower chance of producing any adverse immunological reaction or toxicity (Sharma et al., 2021). After serving their role of antigen transport, the protein nanoparticles get degraded into amino acids, which either get reused by the body or excreted (Varanko et al., 2020).

This biodegradability has made the protein nanoparticles an interesting vector in vaccine delivery, especially in populations described as at-risk, such as children, the elderly, and immunocompromised patients (Grego et al., 2020). Due to the low toxicity profiles, higher doses can be allowed without significant side effects and, therefore, enhance vaccine efficacy (Bitounis et al., 2024).

### 6.3.7 Applications in new vaccine technologies

Among the innovative vaccination technologies, protein nanoparticles play an active role in mRNA vaccines and subunit vaccinations. In mRNA vaccines, the protein nanoparticles serve as vectors by encapsulating and protecting mRNA molecules, enabling safe cellular entry where their translation gives the antigen of interest (Ramachandran et al., 2022). Subunit vaccines are effective only in those cases when protein nanoparticles expose multiple copies of a protein or peptide antigen on their surface in order to effectively mimic the structure of natural infection and thus favor immune recognition (Butkovich et al., 2021).

Ferritin-based nanoparticles represent one of the most promising tools in the development of next-generation vaccines against influenza, COVID-19, and other viral diseases due to their high efficiency in delivering viral antigens in a very immunogenic way (Zhu et al., 2023).

Protein nanoparticles are one of the imperatives in COVID-19 vaccine delivery for enhancing antigen presentation stability and tailored immune responses (Du et al., 2022). By encapsulating viral antigens, such as the spike protein of SARS-CoV-2, PNPs increase antigen recognition by APCs, thus inducing robust humoral and cellular immunity (Garcia-Soto et al., 2022). Typical examples include the NVX-CoV2373 protein subunit vaccine by Novavax, which utilizes PNPs to elicit vigorous immune responses and neutralizing antibodies (Vu, no date). By encapsulating fragile antigens, nanoparticles protect them from degradation, thereby allowing more specific targeting. Controlled release mechanisms further provide for prolonged exposure to the immune system—a very important factor in effective immunization (Lung et al., 2020).

Besides offering protection, PNPs can be designed for active targeting, increasing vaccine uptake by DCs and, consequently, immune stimulation (Liu et al., 2021). Their biocompatibility and biodegradability make them safer compared to synthetic nanoparticles. However, there are significant production and governmental approval obstacles to be faced (Geszke-Moritz and Moritz, 2024). In this regard, the present study has assessed the potential of protein nanoparticles for COVID-19 vaccine development by pointing out innovative formulations and combinations with other vaccine platforms with a view to enhancing efficacy and immune responses, adding to the vaccination strategy against the pandemic (Fig. 24.5) (Shin et al., 2020).

## 7. Future trends in drug delivery

The landscape of drug delivery is evolving, particularly in the context of treating metastatic cancers. Traditional systemic administration of therapeutic agents often results in

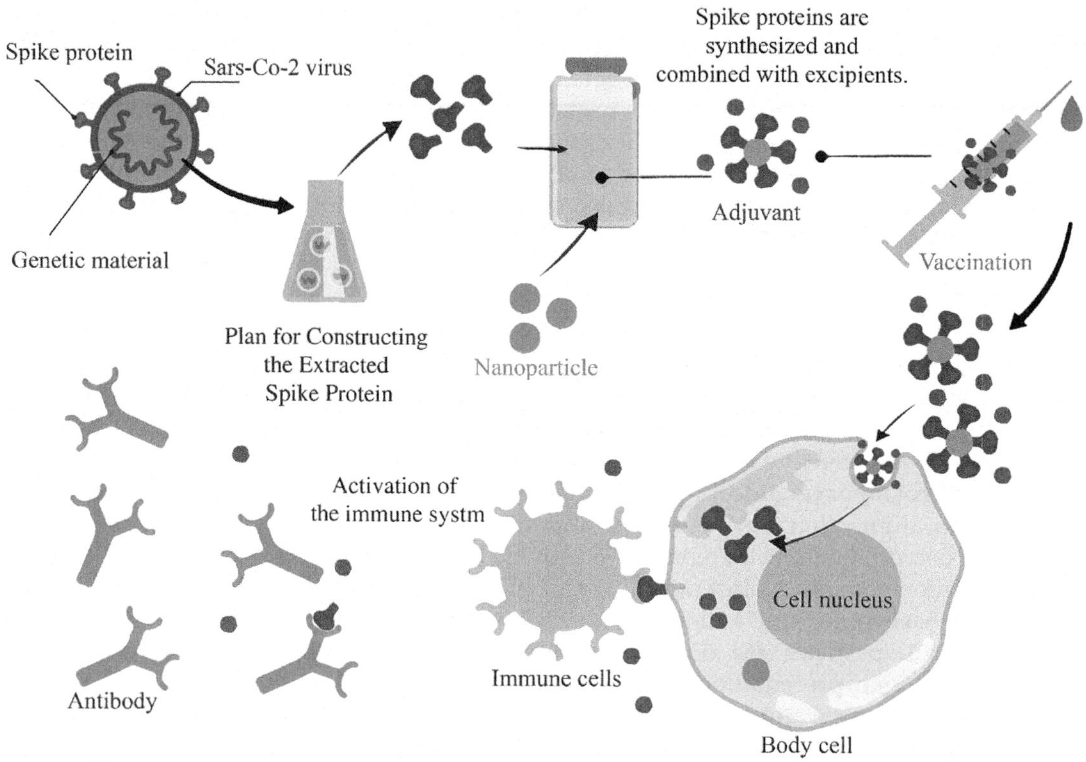


**FIGURE 24.5 Schematic representation of protein-based vaccines, outlining the mechanism behind the COVID-19 vaccine.** The spike protein, produced in cell cultures and purified in the lab, is combined with nanoparticles into nanostructures. An adjuvant enhances the immune response. Upon injection, the vaccine activates the immune system to produce antibodies and form long-lasting memory B cells for protection. The figure was created by the author using Adobe Illustrator (version 28.3).

widespread distribution, increasing the likelihood of side effects and diminishing the overall efficacy of treatment (Ezike et al., 2023a). In contrast, the advent of protein-based nanoparticles (PNPs) has opened new avenues for targeted delivery, enhancing the precision with which therapeutic agents can be directed to specific cells (Ashagrache Ashagrachew Tewabe et al., 2021; Veselov, no date).

Protein nanoparticles serve as effective carriers that improve cellular uptake and minimize off-target effects. By functionalizing these carriers with receptors that specifically bind to ligands on target cells, researchers can significantly increase the selectivity of drug delivery (Yoo et al., 2019; Nelemans and Gurevich, 2020). This advancement is particularly crucial for metastatic cancers, where the goal is to concentrate on treatment at tumor sites while sparing healthy tissues.

Recent studies have highlighted the potential of albumin-based carriers for encapsulating chemotherapeutic drugs, facilitating localized accumulation at affected sites (Jamroży et al., 2024). The versatility of protein nanoparticles allows for the delivery of various therapeutic agents—including genetic materials, anticancer drugs, and growth factors—while offering advantages such as stability and ease of manufacturing. The eco-friendly production processes associated with protein nanoparticles further enhance their appeal, as they typically require fewer chemicals than traditional nanoparticle formulations (Hong et al., 2020a).

Despite their advantages, the application of protein nanoparticles in the pharmaceutical sector is not without challenges (Lohcharoenkal et al., 2014; Huang et al., 2015; Elzoghby et al., 2011). One significant limitation is the inherent variability in natural proteins, which can lead to batch-to-batch inconsistencies during large-scale production. To address this issue, researchers are increasingly focusing on recombinant proteins produced through genetic engineering (Pang et al., 2019; Wu et al., 2021b). These engineered proteins can provide uniformity in size and molecular weight, improving the reproducibility of DDSs. Furthermore, the design of these proteins allows for the attachment of targeting moieties, which can fine-tune the release rates of the encapsulated drugs (Kianfar, 2021).

Immunogenicity remains another concern, as foreign proteins may elicit immune responses in the body. However, studies have shown that certain protein nanoparticles, particularly those derived from human sources like albumin and gelatin (Kianfar et al., 2018; Ehsa E. Kianfar, 2019), exhibit minimal immunogenicity (Wang et al., 2020), making them more suitable for clinical applications.

One of the critical challenges in drug delivery using protein nanoparticles is achieving a sustained release profile. Many natural proteins are hydrophilic and can swell upon absorbing water, leading to rapid drug release (Kianfar et al., 2015; Kianfar et al., 2017; Kianfar and Mahler, 2020; Kianfar et al., 2020; Ehsan Kianfar, 2019). To tackle this, researchers are exploring nontoxic chemical linkers to stabilize protein nanoparticles and extend their drug release capabilities. Additionally, the use of hydrophobic plant proteins has shown promise in developing nanoparticles that can effectively retain and release drugs over longer periods (Kianfar and Cao, 2021; Mousavian et al., 2020; Yang et al., 2020; Gao et al., 2021).

Another significant barrier to effective drug delivery is the rapid clearance of nanoparticles from circulation and poor penetration into target tissues (Barua and Mitragotri, 2014). A metaanalysis of various studies indicated that only a small fraction of administered nanoparticle doses successfully reaches solid tumors (Wilhelm et al., 2016). This underscores the urgent need for innovative designs that enhance the bioavailability and targeting efficiency of PNPs (Habibi, 2022).

Emerging trends in protein-based DDSs are focusing on leveraging the innate properties of proteins to create more effective carriers (Tripathi and Shrivastava, 2019). The use of engineered protein nanoparticles is particularly promising, as they can be tailored to address specific therapeutic needs while minimizing immunogenicity and production challenges (Habibi, no date). Additionally, the development of VLPs offers a safer alternative to traditional viral vectors, combining the advantages of viral delivery mechanisms (Chung et al., 2020b).

Recent advances in Nab technology, which allows for the encapsulation of hydrophobic drugs in albumin nanoparticles, demonstrate the commercial viability of protein nanoparticle systems. This method enhances drug solubility without the need for harmful solubilizers, marking a significant step forward in the field (Joshi et al., 2020).

As research progresses, the future of protein-based nanoparticles in drug delivery, especially for metastatic cancers, looks promising. The focus will likely shift toward refining these systems for better stability, targeted delivery, and controlled release, ultimately paving the way for more effective and safer therapeutic strategies.

## 8. Conclusion

The protein-based nanoparticles represent an important step forward in the nanomedicine area, offering a combination of biocompatibility, structural versatility, and functional adaptability. Their application in drug delivery, especially in complex conditions like metastatic cancer and respiratory diseases, underlines their transformative potential. Though significant challenges persist, such as overcoming biological barriers and attaining precise targeting, continuous innovation in design and functionalization holds promise for addressing these limitations. The integration of protein nanoparticles into clinical practice may revolutionize therapeutic strategies and drive progress toward more effective, personalized, and accessible healthcare solutions.

## References

Adepu, S., Ramakrishna, S. Controlled drug delivery systems: current status and future directions. Molecules. 26 (19).

Afzal, O. Nanoparticles in drug delivery: from history to therapeutic applications. Nanomaterials. 12.

Ahmad, F., 2022. Unique properties of surface-functionalized nanoparticles for bio-application: functionalization mechanisms and importance in application. Nanomaterials 12 (8).

Akhtar, A., Andleeb, A., Sher Waris, T., Bazzar, M., Moradi, A.-R., Awan, N.R., Yar, M., 2021. Neurodegenerative diseases and effective drug delivery: a review of challenges and novel therapeutics. J. Contr. Release 330, 1152–1167. https://doi.org/10.1016/j.jconrel.2020.11.021.

Alam, K., Rahman, M., Beg, S., Chauhan, D., Hafeez, A., Almalki, W.H., Ansari, M.J., Kumar, V., 2022. Advancement in Protein-Based Nanocarriers in Targeted Anticancer Therapy Nanotherapeutics in Cancer Vaccination and Challenges. Elsevier, India, pp. 95–102. https://doi.org/10.1016/B978-0-12-823686-4.00014-8.

Alfei, S., Schito, A.M., 2020. Positively charged polymers as promising devices against multidrug resistant gram-negative bacteria: a review. Polymers 12 (5), 1195. https://doi.org/10.3390/polym12051195.

Alhajj, N., Zakaria, Z., Naharudin, I., Ahsan, F., Li, W., Wong, T.W., 2020. Critical physicochemical attributes of chitosan nanoparticles admixed lactose-PEG 3000 microparticles in pulmonary inhalation. Asian J. Pharm. Sci. 15 (3), 374–384. https://doi.org/10.1016/j.ajps.2019.02.001.

Ali, E.S., Sharker, S.M., Islam, M.T., Khan, I.N., Shaw, S., Rahman, M.A., Uddin, S.J., Shill, M.C., Rehman, S., Das, N., Ahmad, S., Shilpi, J.A., Tripathi, S., Mishra, S.K., Mubarak, M.S., 2021. Targeting cancer cells with nanotherapeutics and nanodiagnostics: current status and future perspectives. Semin. Cancer Biol. 69, 52–68. https://doi.org/10.1016/j.semcancer.2020.01.011.

Aljabali, A.A.A., Rezigue, M., Alsharedeh, R.H., Obeid, M.A., Mishra, V., Serrano-Aroca, Á., Tambuwala, M.M., 2022. Protein-based drug delivery nanomedicine platforms: recent developments. Pharm. Nanotechnol. 10 (4), 257–267. https://doi.org/10.2174/2211738510666220817120307.

Aljabali, A.A., Obeid, M.A., Bashatwah, R.M., Serrano-Aroca, Á., Mishra, V., Mishra, Y., El-Tanani, M., Hromić-Jahjefendić, A., Kapoor, D.N., Goyal, R., Naikoo, G.A., Tambuwala, M.M., 2023. Nanomaterials and their impact on the immune system. Int. J. Mol. Sci. 24 (3). https://doi.org/10.3390/ijms24032008.

Amini, M.A., Ahmed, T., Liu, F.C.F., Abbasi, A.Z., Soeandy, C.D., Zhang, R.X., Prashad, P., Cummins, C.L., Rauth, A.M., Henderson, J.T., Wu, X.Y., 2021. Exploring the transformability of polymer-lipid hybrid nanoparticles and nanomaterial-biology interplay to facilitate tumor penetration, cellular uptake and intracellular targeting of anticancer drugs. Expet Opin. Drug Deliv. 18 (7), 991–1004. https://doi.org/10.1080/17425247.2021.1902984.

Anderson, N.M., Simon, M.C., 2020. The tumor microenvironment. Curr. Biol. 30 (16), R921. https://doi.org/10.1016/j.cub.2020.06.081.

Anthony, D.P., Hegde, M., Shetty, S.S., Rafic, T., Mutalik, S., Satish Rao, B.S., 2021. Targeting receptor-ligand chemistry for drug delivery across blood-brain barrier in brain diseases. Life Sci. 274, 119326. https://doi.org/10.1016/j.lfs.2021.119326.

Arpagaus, C., John, P., Collenberg, A., Rütti, D., 2017. Nanocapsules Formation by Nano Spray Drying Nanoencapsulation Technologies for the Food and Nutraceutical Industries. Elsevier, Switzerland, pp. 346–401. https://doi.org/10.1016/B978-0-12-809436-5.00010-0.

Arpagaus, C., Collenberg, A., Rütti, D., Assadpour, E., Jafari, S.M., 2018. Nano spray drying for encapsulation of pharmaceuticals. Int. J. Pharm. 546 (1–2), 194–214. https://doi.org/10.1016/j.ijpharm.2018.05.037.

Awad, N.S., Salkho, N.M., Abuwatfa, W.H., Paul, V., AlSawaftah, N.M., Husseini, G.A., 2023. Tumor vasculature vs tumor cell targeting: understanding the latest trends in using functional nanoparticles for cancer treatment. Open Nano 11, 100136. https://doi.org/10.1016/j.onano.2023.100136.

Bae, Y.H., Park, K., 2011. Targeted drug delivery to tumors: Myths, reality and possibility. J. Contr. Release 153 (3), 198–205. https://doi.org/10.1016/j.jconrel.2011.06.001.

Bae, S., Ma, K., Kim, T.H., Lee, E.S., Oh, K.T., Park, E.-S., Lee, K.C., Youn, Y.S., 2012. Doxorubicin-loaded human serum albumin nanoparticles surface-modified with TNF-related apoptosis-inducing ligand and transferrin for targeting multiple tumor types. Biomaterials 33 (5), 1536–1546. https://doi.org/10.1016/j.biomaterials.2011.10.050.

Baig, N., Kammakakam, I., Falath, W., Kammakakam, I., 2021. Nanomaterials: a review of synthesis methods, properties, recent progress, and challenges. Mater. Adv. 2 (6), 1821–1871. https://doi.org/10.1039/d0ma00807a.

Barua, S., Mitragotri, S., 2014. Challenges associated with penetration of nanoparticles across cell and tissue barriers: a review of current status and future prospects. Nano Today 9 (2), 223–243. https://doi.org/10.1016/j.nantod.2014.04.008.

Basarkar, A., Devineni, D., Palaniappan, R., Singh, J., 2007. Preparation, characterization, cytotoxicity and transfection efficiency of poly(dl-lactide-co-glycolide) and poly(dl-lactic acid) cationic nanoparticles for controlled delivery of plasmid DNA. Int. J. Pharm. 343 (1–2), 247–254. https://doi.org/10.1016/j.ijpharm.2007.05.023.

Bashiri, G., Padilla, M.S., Swingle, K.L., Shepherd, S.J., Mitchell, M.J., Wang, K., 2023. Nanoparticle protein corona: from structure and function to therapeutic targeting. Lab Chip 23 (6), 1432–1466. https://doi.org/10.1039/d2lc00799a.

Benne, N., Braake, D.ter, Jan Stoppelenburg, A., Broere, F., 2022. Nanoparticles for inducing antigen-specific T cell tolerance in autoimmune diseases. Front. Immunol. 13. https://doi.org/10.3389/fimmu.2022.864403.

Berland, L., Gabr, Z., Chang, M., Ilié, M., Hofman, V., Rignol, G., Ghiringhelli, F., Mograbi, B., Rashidian, M., Hofman, P., 2024. Further knowledge and developments in resistance mechanisms to immune checkpoint inhibitors. Front. Immunol. 15. https://doi.org/10.3389/fimmu.2024.1384121.

Bertrand, N., Wu, J., Xu, X., Kamaly, N., Farokhzad, O.C., 2014. Cancer nanotechnology: the impact of passive and active targeting in the era of modern cancer biology. Adv. Drug Deliv. Rev. 66, 2–25. https://doi.org/10.1016/j.addr.2013.11.009.

Bhalani, D.V., 2022. Bioavailability enhancement techniques for poorly aqueous soluble drugs and therapeutics. Biomedicines 10.

Bitounis, D., Jacquinet, E., Rogers, M.A., Amiji, M.M., 2024. Strategies to reduce the risks of mRNA drug and vaccine toxicity. Nat. Rev. Drug Discov. 23 (4), 281–300. https://doi.org/10.1038/s41573-023-00859-3.

Bock, N., Woodruff, M.A., Hutmacher, D.W., Dargaville, T.R., 2011. Electrospraying, a reproducible method for production of polymeric microspheres for biomedical applications. Polymers 3 (1), 131–149. https://doi.org/10.3390/polym3010131.

Borandeh, S., van Bochove, B., Teotia, A., Seppälä, J., 2021. Polymeric drug delivery systems by additive manufacturing. Adv. Drug Deliv. Rev. 173, 349–373. https://doi.org/10.1016/j.addr.2021.03.022.

Borlan, R., Focsan, M., Maniu, D., Astilean, S., 2021. Interventional NIR fluorescence imaging of cancer: review on next generation of dye-loaded protein-based nanoparticles for real-time feedback during cancer surgery. Int. J. Nanomed. 16, 2147–2171. https://doi.org/10.2147/ijn.s295234.

Burn, O.K., Prasit, K.K., Hermans, I.F., 2020. Modulating the tumour microenvironment by intratumoural injection of pattern recognition receptor agonists. Cancers 12 (12), 1–22. https://doi.org/10.3390/cancers12123824.

Butkovich, N., Li, E., Ramirez, A., Burkhardt, A.M., Wang, S.W., 2021. Advancements in protein nanoparticle vaccine platforms to combat infectious disease. Wiley Interdiscip. Rev. Nanomed. Nanobiotechnol. 13 (3). https://doi.org/10.1002/wnan.1681.

Cao, J., Huang, D., Peppas, N.A., 2020. Advanced engineered nanoparticulate platforms to address key biological barriers for delivering chemotherapeutic agents to target sites. Adv. Drug Deliv. Rev. 167, 170–188. https://doi.org/10.1016/j.addr.2020.06.030.

Céspedes, M.V., Unzueta, U., Tatkiewicz, W., Sánchez-Chardi, A., Conchillo-Solé, O., Álamo, P., Xu, Z., Casanova, I., Corchero, J.L., Pesarrodona, M., Cedano, J., Daura, X., Ratera, I., Veciana, J., Ferrer-Miralles, N., Vazquez, E., Villaverde, A., Mangues, R., 2014. In vivo architectonic stability of fully de novo designed protein-only nanoparticles. ACS Nano 8 (5), 4166–4176. https://doi.org/10.1021/nn4055732.

Champion, J.A., Katare, Y.K., Mitragotri, S., 2007. Particle shape: a new design parameter for micro- and nanoscale drug delivery carriers. J. Contr. Release 121 (1–2), 3–9. https://doi.org/10.1016/j.jconrel.2007.03.022.

Chen, A., Sack, M., Pokorski, J.K., Steinmetz, N.F., 2020. COVID-19 vaccine development and a potential nanomaterial path forward . Nature Research, United States Nature Nanotechnology. 17483395. 15 (8), 646–655. Available from: http://www.nature.com/nnano/index.html. https://doi.org/10.1038/s41565-020-0737-y.

Cheng, X., Xie, Q., Sun, Y., 2023. Advances in nanomaterial-based targeted drug delivery systems. Front. Bioeng. Biotechnol. 11. https://doi.org/10.3389/fbioe.2023.1177151.

Cho, H., 2022. Emerging albumin-binding anticancer drugs for tumor-targeted drug delivery: current understandings and clinical translation. Pharmaceutics 14 (4).

Chung, Y.H., Cai, H., Steinmetz, N.F., 2020. Viral nanoparticles for drug delivery, imaging, immunotherapy, and theranostic applications. Adv. Drug Deliv. Rev. 156, 214–235. https://doi.org/10.1016/j.addr.2020.06.024.

Cid, R., Bolívar, J., 2021. Platforms for production of protein-based vaccines: from classical to next-generation strategies. Biomolecules 11 (8), 1072. https://doi.org/10.3390/biom11081072.

Cifuentes-Rius, A., Desai, A., Yuen, D., Johnston, A.P.R., Voelcker, N.H., 2021. Inducing immune tolerance with dendritic cell-targeting nanomedicines. Nat. Nanotechnol. 16 (1), 37–46. https://doi.org/10.1038/s41565-020-00810-2.

Colombo, R., Rich, J.R., 2022. The therapeutic window of antibody drug conjugates: a dogma in need of revision. Cancer Cell 40 (11), 1255–1263. https://doi.org/10.1016/j.ccell.2022.09.016.

Cortes, J., Saura, C., 2010. 8, 1; d) DA Yardley. J. Controlled Release. 170.

Dagogo-Jack, I., Shaw, A.T., 2018. Tumour heterogeneity and resistance to cancer therapies. Nat. Rev. Clin. Oncol. 15 (2), 81–94. https://doi.org/10.1038/nrclinonc.2017.166.

Davidov-Pardo, G., Joye, I.J., Mcclements, D.J., 2015. Food-grade protein-based nanoparticles and microparticles for bioactive delivery: fabrication, characterization, and utilization. Adv. Protein Chem. Struct. Biol. 98, 293–325. https://doi.org/10.1016/bs.apcsb.2014.11.004.

Devnarain, N., Osman, N., Fasiku, V.O., Makhathini, S., Salih, M., Ibrahim, U.H., Govender, T., 2021. Intrinsic stimuli-responsive nanocarriers for smart drug delivery of antibacterial agents—an in-depth review of the last two decades. Wiley Interdiscip. Rev. Nanomed. Nanobiotechnol. 13 (1). https://doi.org/10.1002/wnan.1664.

Diaz, D., Care, A., Sunna, A., 2018a. Bioengineering strategies for protein-based nanoparticles. Genes 9 (7). https://doi.org/10.3390/genes9070370.

Diaz, D., Care, A., Sunna, A., 2018b. Bioengineering strategies for protein-based nanoparticles. Genes 9 (7), 370. https://doi.org/10.3390/genes9070370.

Doroudian, M., Azhdari, M.H., Goodarzi, N., O'Sullivan, D., Donnelly, S.C., 2021. Smart nanotherapeutics and lung cancer. Pharmaceutics 13 (11), 1972. https://doi.org/10.3390/pharmaceutics13111972.

Dorozhkin, S.V., 2010. Calcium orthophosphates as bioceramics: state of the art. J. Funct. Biomater. 1 (1), 22–107. https://doi.org/10.3390/jfb1010022.

Doxorubicin nanoformulations on therapy against cancer: an overview from the last 10 years. Biomater. Adv. 133, 2022.

Dreis, S., Rothweiler, F., Michaelis, M., Cinatl, J., Kreuter, J., Langer, K., 2007. Preparation, characterisation and maintenance of drug efficacy of doxorubicin-loaded human serum albumin (HSA) nanoparticles. Int. J. Pharm. 341 (1–2), 207–214. https://doi.org/10.1016/j.ijpharm.2007.03.036.

Du, L., Yang, Y., Zhang, X., Li, F., 2022. Recent advances in nanotechnology-based COVID-19 vaccines and therapeutic antibodies. Nanoscale 14 (4), 1054–1074. https://doi.org/10.1039/d1nr03831a.

Dvorak, H.F. Reconciling VEGF with VPF: the importance of increased vascular permeability for stroma formation in tumors, healing wounds, and chronic inflammation . Front. Cell Dev. Biol. 9.

Ebrahimi, N., Sadat Manavi, M., Nazari, A., Momayezi, A., Faghihkhorasani, F., Abdulwahid, A.-H.R.R., Rezaei-Tazangi, F., Kavei, M., Rezaei, R., Mobarak, H., Aref, A.R., Fang, W., 2023. Nano-scale delivery systems for siRNA delivery in cancer therapy: new era of gene therapy empowered by nanotechnology. Environ. Res. 239, 117263. https://doi.org/10.1016/j.envres.2023.117263.

Elsewedy, H.S., Al Dhubiab, B.E., Mahdy, M.A., Elnahas, H.M., 2021. A review article on the basic concepts of drug delivery systems as targeting agents. International Journal of Pharma Medicine and Biological Sciences 10 (1), 23–29. https://doi.org/10.18178/ijpmbs.10.1.23-29.

Elzoghby, A.O., 2013. Gelatin-based nanoparticles as drug and gene delivery systems: Reviewing three decades of research. J. Contr. Release 172 (3), 1075–1091. https://doi.org/10.1016/j.jconrel.2013.09.019.

Elzoghby, A.O., Abo El-Fotoh, W.S., Elgindy, N.A., 2011. Casein-based formulations as promising controlled release drug delivery systems. J. Contr. Release 153 (3), 206–216. https://doi.org/10.1016/j.jconrel.2011.02.010.

Elzoghby, A.O., Samy, W.M., Elgindy, N.A., 2012. Albumin-based nanoparticles as potential controlled release drug delivery systems. J. Contr. Release 157 (2), 168–182. https://doi.org/10.1016/j.jconrel.2011.07.031.

Est-Witte, S.E., 2021. Nanoparticles for Generating Antigen-specific T Cells for Immunotherapy Seminars in Immunology. Elsevier.

Ezike, T.C., Okpala, U.S., Onoja, U.L., Nwike, C.P., Ezeako, E.C., Okpara, O.J., Okoroafor, C.C., Eze, S.C., Kalu, O.L., Odoh, E.C., Nwadike, U.G., Ogbodo, J.O., Umeh, B.U., Ossai, E.C., Nwanguma, B.C., 2023a. Advances in drug delivery systems, challenges and future directions. Heliyon 9 (6). https://doi.org/10.1016/j.heliyon.2023.e17488.

Ezike, T.C., Solomon Okpala, U., Onoja, U.L., Nwike, C.P., Ezeako, E.C., Okpara, O.J., Okoroafor, C.C., Eze, S.C., Kalu, O.L., Odoh, E.C., Nwadike, U.G., Ogbodo, J.O., Umeh, B.U., Ossai, E.C., Nwanguma, B.C., 2023b. Advances in drug delivery systems, challenges and future directions. Heliyon 9 (6), e17488. https://doi.org/10.1016/j.heliyon.2023.e17488.

Ezpeleta, I., Irache, J.M., Stainmesse, S., Chabenat, C., Gueguen, J., Popineau, Y., Orecchioni, A.-M., 1996. Gliadin nanoparticles for the controlled release of all-trans-retinoic acid. Int. J. Pharm. 131 (2), 191–200. https://doi.org/10.1016/0378-5173(95)04338-1.

Falsafi, S.R., Rostamabadi, H., Samborska, K., Mirarab, S., Rashidinejhad, A., Mahdi Jafari, S., 2022. Protein-polysaccharide interactions for the fabrication of bioactive-loaded nanocarriers: chemical conjugates and physical complexes. Pharmacol. Res. 178, 106164. https://doi.org/10.1016/j.phrs.2022.106164.

Fan, J., 2022. Advances in infectious disease vaccine adjuvants. Vaccines 10.

Farokhi, M., Mottaghitalab, F., Reis, R.L., Ramakrishna, S., Kundu, S.C., 2020. Functionalized silk fibroin nanofibers as drug carriers: advantages and challenges. J. Contr. Release 321, 324–347. https://doi.org/10.1016/j.jconrel.2020.02.022.

Farran, B., Carvalho Montenegro, R., Kasa, P., Pavitra, E., Huh, Y.S., Han, Y.-K., Kamal, M.A., Nagaraju, G.P., Rama Raju, G.S., 2020. Folate-conjugated nanovehicles: strategies for cancer therapy. Mater. Sci. Eng. C 107, 110341. https://doi.org/10.1016/j.msec.2019.110341.

Ferraro, C., Dattilo, M., Patitucci, F., Prete, S., Scopelliti, G., Parisi, O., Puoci, F., 2024. Exploring protein-based carriers in drug delivery: a review. Pharmaceutics 16 (9), 1172. https://doi.org/10.3390/pharmaceutics16091172.

Fröhlich, E., 2019. Biological obstacles for identifying in vitro-in vivo correlations of orally inhaled formulations. Pharmaceutics 11 (7), 316. https://doi.org/10.3390/pharmaceutics11070316.

Fu, Q., Sun, J., Zhang, W., Sui, X., Yan, Z., He, Z., 2009. Nanoparticle albumin-bound (NAB) technology is a promising method for anti-cancer drug delivery. Recent Pat. Anticancer Drug Discov. 4 (3), 262–272. https://doi.org/10.2174/157489209789206869.

Fuchs, S., Klier, J., May, A., Winter, G., Coester, C., Gehlen, H., 2012. Towards an inhalative in vivo application of immunomodulating gelatin nanoparticles in horse-related preformulation studies. J. Microencapsul. 29 (7), 615–625. https://doi.org/10.3109/02652048.2012.668962.

Gao, Y., 2024. PEGylated therapeutics in the clinic. Bioeng. Transl. Med. 9 (1).

Gao, C., Liao, J., Lu, J., Ma, J., Kianfar, E., 2021. The effect of nanoparticles on gas permeability with polyimide membranes and network hybrid membranes: a review. Rev. Inorg. Chem. 41 (1), 1–20. https://doi.org/10.1515/revic-2020-0007.

Garcia-Soto, M.J., Farfan-Castro, S.I., Wong-Arce, A., Romero-Maldonado, A., Gonzalez-Ortega, O., Rosales-Mendoza, S., 2022. Particulate Vaccines Against SARS-CoV-2 Biomedical Innovations to Combat COVID-19. Elsevier, Mexico, pp. 153–171. https://doi.org/10.1016/B978-0-323-90248-9.00009-7.

Gavas, S., Quazi, S., Karpiński, T.M., 2021. Nanoparticles for cancer therapy: current progress and challenges. Nanoscale Res. Lett. 16 (1). https://doi.org/10.1186/s11671-021-03628-6.

Gay, L., Baker, A.M., Graham, T.A., 2026. Tumour cell heterogeneity.

Geszke-Moritz, M., Moritz, M., 2024. Biodegradable polymeric nanoparticle-based drug delivery systems: comprehensive overview, perspectives and challenges. Polymers 16 (17), 2536. https://doi.org/10.3390/polym16172536.

Ghosh, S., Banerjee, M. A smart viral vector for targeted delivery of hydrophobic drugs. Sci. Rep. 11.

Goldstein, M.J., Peters, M., Weber, B.L., Davis, C.B., 2021. Optimizing the therapeutic window of targeted drugs in oncology: Potency-guided first-in-human studies. Clin. Transl. Sci. 14 (2), 536–543. https://doi.org/10.1111/cts.12902.

Gong, J., Huo, M., Zhou, J., Zhang, Y., Peng, X., Yu, Di, Zhang, H., Li, J., 2009. Synthesis, characterization, drug-loading capacity and safety of novel octyl modified serum albumin micelles. Int. J. Pharm. 376 (1–2), 161–168. https://doi.org/10.1016/j.ijpharm.2009.04.033.

Grego, E.A., Siddoway, A.C., Uz, M., Liu, L., Christiansen, J.C., Ross, K.A., Kelly, S.M., Mallapragada, S.K., Wannemuehler, M.J., Narasimhan, B., 2020. Polymeric nanoparticle-based vaccine adjuvants and delivery vehicles. Springer Science and Business Media LLC 433, 29–76. https://doi.org/10.1007/82_2020_226.

Guan, X., 2015. Cancer metastases: challenges and opportunities. Acta Pharm. Sin. B 5 (5), 402–418. https://doi.org/10.1016/j.apsb.2015.07.005.

Gulfam, M., Kim, J.-eun, Lee, J.M., Ku, B., Chung, B.H., Chung, B.G., 2012. Anticancer drug-loaded gliadin nanoparticles induce apoptosis in breast cancer cells. Langmuir 28 (21), 8216–8223. https://doi.org/10.1021/la300691n.

Guo, D., Ji, X., Luo, J., 2021. Rational nanocarrier design towards clinical translation of cancer nanotherapy. Biomed. Mater. 16 (3).

Guo, C., Yuan, H., Wang, Y., Feng, Y., Zhang, Y., Yin, T., He, H., Gou, J., Xing, T., 2023. The interplay between PEGylated nanoparticles and blood immune system. Adv. Drug Deliv. Rev. 200, 115044. https://doi.org/10.1016/j.addr.2023.115044.

Habibi, N., 2022. Protein nanoparticles: uniting the power of proteins with engineering design approaches. Adv. Sci. 9 (8).

Haggag, Y.A., Faheem, A.M., 2015. Evaluation of nano spray drying as a method for drying and formulation of therapeutic peptides and proteins. Front. Pharmacol. 6. https://doi.org/10.3389/fphar.2015.00140.

Hama, M., Ishima, Y., Chuang, V.T.G., Ando, H., Shimizu, T., Ishida, T., 2021. Evidence for delivery of Abraxane via a denatured-albumin transport system. ACS Appl. Mater. Interfaces 13 (17), 19736–19744. https://doi.org/10.1021/acsami.1c03065.

Haripriyaa, M., Suthindhiran, K., 2023. Pharmacokinetics of nanoparticles: current knowledge, future directions and its implications in drug delivery. Future J. Pharmaceut. Sci. 9 (1). https://doi.org/10.1186/s43094-023-00569-y.

Hassanin, I.A., Elzoghby, A.O., 2020. Self-assembled non-covalent protein-drug nanoparticles: an emerging delivery platform for anti-cancer drugs. Expet Opin. Drug Deliv. 17 (10), 1437–1458. https://doi.org/10.1080/17425247.2020.1813713.

Hawkins, M.J., Soon-Shiong, P., Desai, N., 2008. Protein nanoparticles as drug carriers in clinical medicine. Adv. Drug Deliv. Rev. 60 (8), 876–885. https://doi.org/10.1016/j.addr.2007.08.044.

Heddle, J.G., Chakraborti, S., Iwasaki, K., 2017. Natural and artificial protein cages: design, structure and therapeutic applications. Curr. Opin. Struct. Biol. 43, 148–155. https://doi.org/10.1016/j.sbi.2017.03.007.

Herdiana, Y., 2022. Drug release study of the chitosan-based nanoparticles. Heliyon 8.

Hong, S., Choi, D.W., Kim, H.N., Park, C.G., Lee, W., Park, H.H., 2020. Protein-based nanoparticles as drug delivery systems. Pharmaceutics 12 (7), 604. https://doi.org/10.3390/pharmaceutics12070604.

Huang, W., Rollett, A., Kaplan, D.L., 2015. Silk-elastin-like protein biomaterials for the controlled delivery of therapeutics. Expet Opin. Drug Deliv. 12 (5), 779–791. https://doi.org/10.1517/17425247.2015.989830.

Hussain, A., Kumar, A., Uttam, V., Sharma, U., Sak, K., Saini, R.V., Saini, A.K., Haque, S., Singh Tuli, H., Jain, A., Sethi, G., 2023. Application of curcumin nanoformulations to target folic acid receptor in cancer: recent trends and advances. Environ. Res. 233, 116476. https://doi.org/10.1016/j.envres.2023.116476.

Hutchinson, F.G., Furr, B.J.A., 1990. Biodegradable polymer systems for the sustained release of polypeptides. J. Contr. Release 13 (2–3), 279–294. https://doi.org/10.1016/0168-3659(90)90018-o.

Ibrahim, N.K., Desai, N., Legha, S., Soon-Shiong, P., Theriault, R.L., Rivera, E., Esmaeli, B., Ring, S.E., Bedikian, A., Hortobagyi, G.N., Ellerhorst, J.A., 2002. Phase I and pharmacokinetic study of ABI-007, a Cremophor-free, protein-stabilized, nanoparticle formulation of paclitaxel. Clin. Cancer Res. 8 (5), 1038–1044.

Ikwuagwu, B., Tullman-Ercek, D., 2022. Virus-like particles for drug delivery: a review of methods and applications. Curr. Opin. Biotechnol. 78, 102785. https://doi.org/10.1016/j.copbio.2022.102785.

Indikova, I., Indik, S., 2020. Highly efficient 'hit-and-run' genome editing with unconcentrated lentivectors carrying Vpr.Prot.Cas9 protein produced from RRE-containing transcripts. Nucleic Acids Res. 48 (14), 8178–8187. https://doi.org/10.1093/nar/gkaa561.

Iqbal, H., Yang, T., Li, T., Zhang, M., Ke, H., Ding, D., Deng, Y., Chen, H., 2021. Serum protein-based nanoparticles for cancer diagnosis and treatment. J. Contr. Release 329, 997–1022. https://doi.org/10.1016/j.jconrel.2020.10.030.

Jacob, J., Haponiuk, J.T., Thomas, S., Gopi, S., 2018. Biopolymer based nanomaterials in drug delivery systems: a review. Mater. Today Chem. 9, 43–55. https://doi.org/10.1016/j.mtchem.2018.05.002.

Jahanshahi, M., 2004. Re-design of downstream processing techniques for nanoparticulate bioproducts. Iran. J. Biotechnol. 2 (1), 1–12.

Jain, A., Singh, S.K., Arya, S.K., Kundu, S.C., Kapoor, S., 2018. Protein nanoparticles: promising platforms for drug delivery applications. ACS Biomater. Sci. Eng. 4 (12), 3939–3961. https://doi.org/10.1021/acsbiomaterials.8b01098.

Jamroży, M., Kudłacik-Kramarczyk, S., Drabczyk, A., Krzan, M., 2024. Advanced drug carriers: a review of selected protein, polysaccharide, and lipid drug delivery platforms. Int. J. Mol. Sci. 25 (2), 786. https://doi.org/10.3390/ijms25020786.

Jana, S., Jana, S., Sanjeeb, K., 2021. Sahoo, PEGylated nanoparticles as a versatile drug delivery system. Nanoengineering of Biomaterials 1–2, 309–341. https://doi.org/10.1002/9783527832095.ch10.

Jiang, W.G., Ablin, R.J., 2011. Cancer metastasis, challenges, progress and the opportunities. Frontiers in Bioscience - Elite 3 (1), 391–394. https://doi.org/10.2741/e254.

Joshi, M., Nagarsenkar, M., Prabhakar, B., 2020. Albumin nanocarriers for pulmonary drug delivery: an attractive approach. J. Drug Deliv. Sci. Technol. 56, 101529. https://doi.org/10.1016/j.jddst.2020.101529.

Jung, T., Breitenbach, A., Kamm, W., Hungerer, K.D., Hundt, E., Kissel, T., 1999. Germany Oral and nasal administration of tetanus toxoid loaded nanoparticles consisting of novel charged biodegradable polyesters for mucosal vaccination. Proceedings of the Controlled Release Society 26, 347–348.

Kalia, M., Jameel, S., 2011. Virus entry paradigms. Amino Acids 41 (5), 1147–1157. https://doi.org/10.1007/s00726-009-0363-3.

Kaltbeitzel, J., Wich, P.R., 2023. Protein-based nanoparticles: from drug delivery to imaging, nanocatalysis and protein therapy. Angew. Chem., Int. Ed. 62 (44). https://doi.org/10.1002/anie.202216097.

Kamaly, N., Yameen, B., Wu, J., Farokhzad, O.C., 2016. Degradable controlled-release polymers and polymeric nanoparticles: mechanisms of controlling drug release. Chem. Rev. 116 (4), 2602–2663. https://doi.org/10.1021/acs.chemrev.5b00346.

Kamble, S., Agrawal, S., Cherumukkil, S., Sharma, V., Vir Jasra, R., Munshi, P., 2022. Revisiting zeta potential, the key feature of interfacial phenomena, with applications and recent advancements. ChemistrySelect 7 (1). https://doi.org/10.1002/slct.202103084.

Kan-Davelaar, A., 2014. Using viruses as nanomedicines. Br. J. Pharmacol. 171, 4001–4009.

Kang, H. Size-dependent EPR effect of polymeric nanoparticles on tumor targeting.

Kariduraganavar, M.Y., Heggannavar, G.B., Amado, S., Mitchell, G.R., 2019. Protein Nanocarriers for Targeted Drug Delivery for Cancer Therapy. Elsevier BV, pp. 173–204. https://doi.org/10.1016/b978-0-12-814033-8.00006-0.

kheirollahpour, M., Mehrabi, M., Mohammadpour Dounighi, N., Mohammadi, M., Masoudi, A., 2020. Nanoparticles and vaccine development. Pharm. Nanotechnol. 8 (1), 6–21. https://doi.org/10.2174/2211738507666191024162042.

Kianfar, E., 2019. Synthesizing of Vanadium Oxide Nanotubes: Using Hydrothermal and Ultrasonic Method. LAP LAMBERT Academic Publishing.

Kianfar, E., 2019. Comparison and assessment of zeolite catalysts performance dimethyl ether and light olefins production through methanol: a review. Rev. Inorg. Chem. 39 (3), 157–177. https://doi.org/10.1515/revic-2019-0001.

Kianfar, E., 2021. Protein nanoparticles in drug delivery: animal protein, plant proteins and protein cages, albumin nanoparticles. J. Nanobiotechnol. 19 (1). https://doi.org/10.1186/s12951-021-00896-3.

Kianfar, E., Cao, V., 2021. Polymeric membranes on base of PolyMethyl methacrylate for air separation: a review. J. Mater. Res. Technol. 10, 1437–1461. https://doi.org/10.1016/j.jmrt.2020.12.061.

Kianfar, E., Mahler, A., 2020. Zeolites: properties, applications, modification and selectivity. (Chapter).

Kianfar, E., Baghernejad, M., Rahimdashti, Y., 2015. Study synthesis of vanadium oxide nanotubes with two template hexadecylamin and hexylamine. in Biological Forum.

Kianfar, E., Pirouzfar, V., Sakhaeinia, H., 2017. An experimental study on absorption/stripping CO2 using mono-ethanol amine hollow fiber membrane contactor. J. Taiwan Inst. Chem. Eng. 80, 954–962. https://doi.org/10.1016/j.jtice.2017.08.017.

Kianfar, E., Salimi, M., Pirouzfar, V., Koohestani, B., 2018. Synthesis and modification of zeolite ZSM-5 catalyst with solutions of calcium carbonate (CaCO3) and sodium carbonate (Na2CO3) for methanol to gasoline conversion. Int. J. Chem. React. Eng. 16 (7). https://doi.org/10.1515/ijcre-2017-0229.

Kianfar, E., Hajimirzaee, S., Mousavian, S., Mehr, A.S., 2020. Zeolite-based catalysts for methanol to gasoline process: a review. Microchem. J. 156. https://doi.org/10.1016/j.microc.2020.104822.

Kim, K.R. Virus-like nanoparticles as a theranostic platform for cancer . Front. Bioeng. Biotechnol. 10.

Kim, D., Wu, Y., Kim, Y.B., Oh, Y.-K., 2021. Advances in vaccine delivery systems against viral infectious diseases. Drug Deliv. Transl. Res. 11 (4), 1401–1419. https://doi.org/10.1007/s13346-021-00945-2.

Kim, K.R., Lee, A.S., Kim, S.M., Heo, H.R., Kim, C.S., 2023. Virus-like nanoparticles as a theranostic platform for cancer. Front. Bioeng. Biotechnol. 10. https://doi.org/10.3389/fbioe.2022.1106767.

Klier, J., Fuchs, S., May, A., Schillinger, U., Plank, C., Winter, G., Gehlen, H., Coester, C., 2012. A nebulized gelatin nanoparticle-based cpg formulation is effective in immunotherapy of allergic horses. Pharm. Res. 29 (6), 1650–1657. https://doi.org/10.1007/s11095-012-0686-8.

Klimek, K., Ginalska, G., 2020. Proteins and peptides as important modifiers of the polymer scaffolds for tissue engineering applications—a review. Polymers 12 (4), 844. https://doi.org/10.3390/polym12040844.

Ko, S.W., Lee, J.Y., Lee, J., Son, B.C., Jang, S.R., Erik Aguilar, L., Oh, Y.M., Park, C.H., Kim, C.S., 2019. Analysis of drug release behavior utilizing the swelling characteristics of cellulosic nanofibers. Polymers 11 (9), 1376. https://doi.org/10.3390/polym11091376.

Kouchakzadeh, H., Shojaosadati, S.A., Shokri, F., 2014. Efficient loading and entrapment of tamoxifen in human serum albumin based nanoparticulate delivery system by a modified desolvation technique. Chem. Eng. Res. Des. 92 (9), 1681–1692. https://doi.org/10.1016/j.cherd.2013.11.024.

Krishnamurty, A.T., Turley, S.J., 2020. Lymph node stromal cells: cartographers of the immune system. Nat. Immunol. 21 (4), 369–380. https://doi.org/10.1038/s41590-020-0635-3.

Kumar, M., Dogra, R., Mandal, U.K., 2022. Nanomaterial-based delivery of vaccine through nasal route: opportunities, challenges, advantages, and limitations. J. Drug Deliv. Sci. Technol. 74. https://doi.org/10.1016/j.jddst.2022.103533.

Kunjiappan, S., Pavadai, P., Vellaichamy, S., Ram Kumar Pandian, S., Ravishankar, V., Palanisamy, P., Govindaraj, S., Srinivasan, G., Premanand, A., Sankaranarayanan, M., Theivendren, P., 2021. Surface receptor-mediated targeted drug delivery systems for enhanced cancer treatment: a state-of-the-art review. Drug Dev. Res. 82 (3), 309–340. https://doi.org/10.1002/ddr.21758.

Kuzmov, A., Minko, T., 2015. Nanotechnology approaches for inhalation treatment of lung diseases. J. Contr. Release 219, 500–518. https://doi.org/10.1016/j.jconrel.2015.07.024.

Lam, J.K.W., Liang, W., Chan, H.K., 2012. Pulmonary delivery of therapeutic siRNA. Adv. Drug Deliv. Rev. 64 (1), 1–15. https://doi.org/10.1016/j.addr.2011.02.006.

Lamoudi, L., Chaumeil, J.C., Daoud, K., 2016. Swelling, erosion and drug release characteristics of Sodium Diclofenac from heterogeneous matrix tablets. J. Drug Deliv. Sci. Technol. 31, 93–100. https://doi.org/10.1016/j.jddst.2015.12.005.

Langer, K., Balthasar, S., Vogel, V., Dinauer, N., von Briesen, H., Schubert, D., 2003. Optimization of the preparation process for human serum albumin (HSA) nanoparticles. Int. J. Pharm. 257 (1–2), 169–180. https://doi.org/10.1016/s0378-5173(03)00134-0.

Laomeephol, C., Tawinwung, S., Suppipat, K., Arunmanee, W., Wang, Q., Luckanagul, J.A., 2024. Surface functionalization of virus-like particles via bioorthogonal click reactions for enhanced cell-specific targeting. Int. J. Pharm. 660, 124332. https://doi.org/10.1016/j.ijpharm.2024.124332.

Laracuente, M.L., Yu, M.H., McHugh, K.J., 2020. Zero-order drug delivery: state of the art and future prospects. J. Contr. Release 327, 834–856. https://doi.org/10.1016/j.jconrel.2020.09.020.

Ledesma, F., 2022. Nanomaterial strategies for delivery of therapeutic cargoes. Adv. Funct. Mater. 32 (4).

Lee, V.H.L., 1988. Enzymatic barriers to peptide and protein absorption. Crit. Rev. Ther. Drug Carrier Syst. 5 (2), 69–97.

Lee, P.I., Good, W.R., 1987. Overview of Controlled-Release Drug Delivery Controlled-Release Technology. American Chemical Society, pp. 1–13.

Lee, J.H., Yeo, Y., 2015. Controlled drug release from pharmaceutical nanocarriers. Chem. Eng. Sci. 125, 75–84. https://doi.org/10.1016/j.ces.2014.08.046.

Lee, S.H., Heng, D., Ng, W.K., Chan, H.K., Tan, R.B.H., 2011. Nano spray drying: a novel method for preparing protein nanoparticles for protein therapy. Int. J. Pharm. 403 (1–2), 192–200. https://doi.org/10.1016/j.ijpharm.2010.10.012.

Lee, W.H., Loo, C.Y., Traini, D., Young, P.M., 2015a. Inhalation of nanoparticle-based drug for lung cancer treatment: advantages and challenges. Asian J. Pharm. Sci. 10 (6), 481–489. https://doi.org/10.1016/j.ajps.2015.08.009.

Lee, W.H., Loo, C.Y., Traini, D., Young, P.M., 2015b. Nano- and micro-based inhaled drug delivery systems for targeting alveolar macrophages. Expet Opin. Drug Deliv. 12 (6), 1009–1026. https://doi.org/10.1517/17425247.2015.1039509.

Lee, H.J., Park, H.H., Sohn, Y., Ryu, J., Park, J.H., Rhee, W.J., Park, T.H., 2016. α-Galactosidase delivery using 30Kc19-human serum albumin nanoparticles for effective treatment of Fabry disease. Appl. Microbiol. Biotechnol. 100 (24), 10395–10402. https://doi.org/10.1007/s00253-016-7689-z.

Li, Y. Intracellular antibody delivery mediated by lipids, polymers, and inorganic nanomaterials for therapeutic applications.

Li, H., Qian, Z.M., 2002. Transferrin/transferrin receptor-mediated drug delivery. Med. Res. Rev. 22 (3), 225–250. https://doi.org/10.1002/med.10008.

Li, X.J., Ong, C.K., Cao, Y., Xiang, Y.Q., Shao, J.Y., Ooi, A., Peng, L.X., Lu, W.H., Zhang, Z., Petillo, D., Qin, L., Bao, Y.N., Zheng, F.J., Chia, C.S., Iyer, N.G., Kang, T.B., Zeng, Y.X., Soo, K.C., Trent, J.M., Teh, B.T., Qian, C. N., 2011. Serglycin is a theranostic target in nasopharyngeal carcinoma that promotes metastasis. Cancer Res. 71 (8), 3162–3172. https://doi.org/10.1158/0008-5472.CAN-10-3557China.

Li, X.J., Peng, L.X., Shao, J.Y., Lu, W.H., Zhang, J.X., Chen, S., Chen, Z.Y., Xiang, Y.Q., Bao, Y.N., Zheng, F.J., Zeng, M.S., Kang, T.B., Zeng, Y.X., Teh, B.T., Qian, C.N., 2012. As an independent unfavorable prognostic factor, IL-8 promotes metastasis of nasopharyngeal carcinoma through induction of epithelial-mesenchymal transition and activation of AKT signaling. Carcinogenesis 33 (7), 1302–1309. https://doi.org/10.1093/carcin/bgs181.

Li, Q., Li, X., Zhao, C., 2020. Strategies to obtain encapsulation and controlled release of small hydrophilic molecules. Front. Bioeng. Biotechnol. 8. https://doi.org/10.3389/fbioe.2020.00437.

Li, H., Wang, Y., Qi, T., Yin, D., Tang, C., He, E., Zou, L., Peng, Q., 2021. The protein corona and its effects on nanoparticle-based drug delivery systems. Acta Biomater. 129, 57–72. https://doi.org/10.1016/j.actbio.2021.05.019.

Liang, Q., Zhou, L., Li, Y., Liu, J., Liu, Y., 2022. Nano drug delivery system reconstruct tumour vasculature for the tumour vascular normalisation. J. Drug Target. 30 (2), 119–130. https://doi.org/10.1080/1061186x.2021.1927056.

Liu, X., Sun, M., Sun, J., Hu, J., Wang, Z., Guo, J., Gao, W., 2018. Polymerization induced self-assembly of a site-specific interferon α-block copolymer conjugate into micelles with remarkably enhanced pharmacology. J. Am. Chem. Soc. 140 (33), 10435–10438. https://doi.org/10.1021/jacs.8b06013.

Liu, G., Zhu, M., Xiao, Z., Nie, G., 2021. Nanotechnology-empowered vaccine delivery for enhancing CD8+ T cells-mediated cellular immunity. Adv. Drug Deliv. Rev. 176, 113889. https://doi.org/10.1016/j.addr.2021.113889.

Lohcharoenkal, W., Wang, L., Chen, Y.C., Rojanasakul, Y., 2014. Protein nanoparticles as drug delivery carriers for cancer therapy. BioMed Res. Int. 2014, 1–12. https://doi.org/10.1155/2014/180549.

Lu, J., Gao, X., Wang, S., He, Y., Ma, X., Zhang, T., Liu, X., 2023. Advanced strategies to evade the mononuclear phagocyte system clearance of nanomaterials. Explorations 3 (1). https://doi.org/10.1002/exp.20220045.

Lung, P., Yang, J., Li, Q., 2020. Nanoparticle formulated vaccines: opportunities and challenges. Nanoscale 12 (10), 5746–5763. https://doi.org/10.1039/c9nr08958f.

Luther, D.C., Huang, R., Jeon, T., Zhang, X., Lee, Y.W., Nagaraj, H., Rotello, V.M., 2020. Delivery of drugs, proteins, and nucleic acids using inorganic nanoparticles. Adv. Drug Deliv. Rev. 156, 188–213. https://doi.org/10.1016/j.addr.2020.06.020.

Lyu, P., Wang, L., Lu, B., 2020. Virus-like particle mediated CRISPR/Cas9 delivery for efficient and safe genome editing. Life 10 (12), 366. https://doi.org/10.3390/life10120366.

Madkhali, O.A., 2023. Drug delivery of gelatin nanoparticles as a biodegradable polymer for the treatment of infectious diseases: perspectives and challenges. Polymers 15 (21), 4327. https://doi.org/10.3390/polym15214327.

Maghsoudi, A., Shojaosadati, S.A., Vasheghani Farahani, E., 2008. 5-Fluorouracil-loaded BSA nanoparticles: formulation optimization and in vitro release study. AAPS PharmSciTech 9 (4), 1092–1096. https://doi.org/10.1208/s12249-008-9146-5.

Majumder, J., Taratula, O., Minko, T., 2019. Nanocarrier-based systems for targeted and site specific therapeutic delivery. Adv. Drug Deliv. Rev. 144, 57–77. https://doi.org/10.1016/j.addr.2019.07.010.

Makwana, H., Mastrotto, F., Magnusson, J.P., Sleep, D., Hay, J., Nicholls, K.J., Allen, S., Alexander, C., 2017. Engineered polymer–transferrin conjugates as self-assembling targeted drug delivery systems. Biomacromolecules 18 (5), 1532–1543. https://doi.org/10.1021/acs.biomac.7b00101.

Malamatari, M., 2023. The importance of drug delivery in the clinical development and lifecycle of drug products with examples from authorised medicinal products. Processes 11 (10), 2919. https://doi.org/10.3390/pr11102919.

Malik, S., Muhammad, K., Waheed, Y., 2023. Emerging applications of nanotechnology in healthcare and medicine. Molecules 28 (18). https://doi.org/10.3390/molecules28186624.

Manzari, M.T., Shamay, Y., Kiguchi, H., Rosen, N., Scaltriti, M., Heller, D.A., 2021. Targeted drug delivery strategies for precision medicines. Nat. Rev. Mater. 6 (4), 351–370. https://doi.org/10.1038/s41578-020-00269-6.

Martins, S.A., Santos, J., Silva, R.D.M., Rosa, C., Cabo Verde, S., Correia, J.D.G., Melo, R., 2022. How promising are HIV-1-based virus-like particles for medical applications. Front. Cell. Infect. Microbiol. 12. https://doi.org/10.3389/fcimb.2022.997875.

Marty, J.J., Oppenheim, R.C., Speiser, P., 1978. Nanoparticles–a new colloidal drug delivery system. Pharm. Acta Helv. 53 (1), 17–23.

Marusyk, A., Janiszewska, M., Polyak, K., 2020. Intratumor heterogeneity: the rosetta stone of therapy resistance. Cancer Cell 37 (4), 471–484. https://doi.org/10.1016/j.ccell.2020.03.007.

Meng, L., Teng, Z., Yang, S., Wang, N., Guan, Y.H., Chen, X., Liu, Y., 2023. Biomimetic nanoparticles for DC vaccination: a versatile approach to boost cancer immunotherapy. Nanoscale 15 (14), 6432–6455. https://doi.org/10.1039/d2nr07071e.

Michaelides, K., Prasanna, M., Badhan, R., Mohammed, A.-U.-R., Walters, A., Keith Howard, M., Dulal, P., Al-Khattawi, A., 2023. Single administration vaccines: delivery challenges, in vivo performance, and translational considerations. Expet Rev. Vaccine 22 (1), 579–595. https://doi.org/10.1080/14760584.2023.2229431.

Mishra, V., Mahor, S., Rawat, A., Gupta, P.N., Dubey, P., Khatri, K., Vyas, S.P., 2006. Targeted brain delivery of AZT via transferrin anchored pegylated albumin nanoparticles. J. Drug Target. 14 (1), 45–53. https://doi.org/10.1080/10611860600612953.

Mitchell, M.J., Billingsley, M.M., Haley, R.M., Wechsler, M.E., Peppas, N.A., Langer, R., 2021. Engineering precision nanoparticles for drug delivery. Nat. Rev. Drug Discov. 20 (2), 101–124. https://doi.org/10.1038/s41573-020-0090-8.

Mittal, A., 2023. Development, characterization and evaluation of sorafenib loaded camel milk casein nanoparticles.

Mittal, G., Sahana, D.K., Bhardwaj, V., Ravi Kumar, M.N.V., 2007. Estradiol loaded PLGA nanoparticles for oral administration: effect of polymer molecular weight and copolymer composition on release behavior in vitro and in vivo. J. Contr. Release 119 (1), 77–85. https://doi.org/10.1016/j.jconrel.2007.01.016.

Mohammadi-Motlagh, H.-R., Sadeghalvad, M., Rezaei, N., 2023. Introduction on Cancerous Cells and Metastasis. Springer Science and Business Media LLC, pp. 1–24. https://doi.org/10.1007/978-3-030-80962-1_37-1.

Mohanty, A., Parida, A., Kumar Raut, R., Behera, R.K., 2022. Ferritin: a promising nanoreactor and nanocarrier for bionanotechnology. ACS Bio & Med Chem Au 2 (3), 258–281. https://doi.org/10.1021/acsbiomedchemau.2c00003.

Mokhtari, R.B., Homayouni, T.S., Baluch, N., Morgatskaya, E., Kumar, S., Das, B., Yeger, H., 2017. Combination therapy in combating cancer. Oncotarget 8 (23), 38022–38043. https://doi.org/10.18632/oncotarget.16723.

Molino, N.M., Wang, S.W., 2014. Caged protein nanoparticles for drug delivery. Curr. Opin. Biotechnol. 28, 75–82. https://doi.org/10.1016/j.copbio.2013.12.007.

Moraru, C. Understanding the factors influencing chitosan-based nanoparticles-protein corona interaction and drug delivery applications. Molecules. 25.

Mottaghitalab, F., Kiani, M., Farokhi, M., Kundu, S.C., Reis, R.L., Gholami, M., Bardania, H., Dinarvand, R., Geramifar, P., Beiki, D., Atyabi, F., 2017. Targeted delivery system based on gemcitabine-loaded silk fibroin nanoparticles for lung cancer therapy. ACS Appl. Mater. Interfaces 9 (37), 31600–31611. https://doi.org/10.1021/acsami.7b10408.

Mousavian, S., Faravar, P., Zarei, Z., azimikia, R., Ghasemi Monjezi, M., kianfar, E., 2020. Modeling and simulation absorption of CO2 using hollow fiber membranes (HFM) with mono-ethanol amine with computational fluid dynamics. J. Environ. Chem. Eng. 8 (4), 103946. https://doi.org/10.1016/j.jece.2020.103946.

Movileanu, L., Benevides, J.M., Thomas, G.J., 2002. Determination of base and backbone contributions to the thermodynamics of premelting and melting transitions in B DNA. Nucleic Acids Res. 30 (17), 3767–3777. https://doi.org/10.1093/nar/gkf471.

Mukherjee, S. Recent advancements of nanomedicine in neurodegenerative disorders theranostics.

Mukherjee, B., Santra, K., Pattnaik, G., Ghosh, S., 2008. Preparation, characterization and in-vitro evaluation of sustained release protein-loaded nanoparticles based on biodegradable polymers. Int. J. Nanomed. 3 (4), 487–496.

Mun, J.Y., Leem, S.H., Lee, J.H., Kim, H.S., 2022. Dual relationship between stromal cells and immune cells in the tumor microenvironment. Front. Immunol. 13. https://doi.org/10.3389/fimmu.2022.864739.

M.U. Munir, Nanomedicine penetration to tumor: challenges, and advanced strategies to tackle this issue. Cancers (Basel) 14.

Mustafa, G., Hassan, D., Ruiz-Pulido, G., Pourmadadi, M., Eshaghi, M.M., Behzadmehr, R., Tehrani, F.S., Rahdar, A., Medina, D.I., Pandey, S., 2023. Nanoscale drug delivery systems for cancer therapy using paclitaxel— a review of challenges and latest progressions. J. Drug Deliv. Sci. Technol. 84, 104494. https://doi.org/10.1016/j.jddst.2023.104494.

Nagy, J.A., Chang, S.H., Dvorak, A.M., Dvorak, H.F., 2009. Why are tumour blood vessels abnormal and why is it important to know? Br. J. Cancer 100 (6), 865–869. https://doi.org/10.1038/sj.bjc.6604929.

Nazir, F., Tabish, T.A., Tariq, F., Iftikhar, S., Wasim, R., Shahnaz, G., 2022. Stimuli-sensitive drug delivery systems for site-specific antibiotic release. Drug Discov. Today 27 (6), 1698–1705. https://doi.org/10.1016/j.drudis.2022.02.014.

Nelemans, L.C., Gurevich, L., 2020. Drug delivery with polymeric nanocarriers—cellular uptake mechanisms. Materials 13.

Neophytou, C.M. The role of tumor microenvironment in cancer metastasis: molecular mechanisms and therapeutic opportunities. Cancers. 13 (9).

Ngouangna, E.N., Zaidi Jaafar, M., Norddin, M.N.A.M., Agi, A., Oseh, J.O., Mamah, S., 2022. Surface modification of nanoparticles to improve oil recovery mechanisms: a critical review of the methods, influencing Parameters, advances and prospects. J. Mol. Liq. 360, 119502. https://doi.org/10.1016/j.molliq.2022.119502.

Nguyen, P.V., Allard-Vannier, E., Chourpa, I., Hervé-Aubert, K., 2021. Nanomedicines functionalized with anti-EGFR ligands for active targeting in cancer therapy: biological strategy, design and quality control. Int. J. Pharm. 605, 120795. https://doi.org/10.1016/j.ijpharm.2021.120795.

Nikolaou, M., Krasia-Christoforou, T., 2018. Electrohydrodynamic methods for the development of pulmonary drug delivery systems. Eur. J. Pharmaceut. Sci. 113, 29–40. https://doi.org/10.1016/j.ejps.2017.08.032.

Nooraei, S., Bahrulolum, H., Sadat Hoseini, Z., Katalani, C., Hajizade, A., Easton, A.J., 2021. Gholamreza Ahmadian, Virus-like particles: preparation, immunogenicity and their roles as nanovaccines and drug nanocarriers. J. Nanobiotechnol. 19 (1). https://doi.org/10.1186/s12951-021-00806-7.

Odiba, A., Ukegbu, C., Anunobi, O., Chukwunonyelum, I., Esemonu, J., 2016. Making drugs safer: improving drug delivery and reducing the side effect of drugs on the human biochemical system. Nanotechnol. Rev. 5 (2), 183–194. https://doi.org/10.1515/ntrev-2015-0055.

Oliveira, A.M., Guimaraes, K.L., Cerize, N.N.P., Tunussi, A.S., Poco, J.G.R., 2013. Nano spray drying as an innovative technology for encapsulating hydrophilic active pharmaceutical ingredients (API). J. Nanomed. Nanotechnol. 4 (6). https://doi.org/10.4172/2157-7439.1000186.

Olshefsky, A., Richardson, C., Pun, S.H., King, N.P., 2022. Engineering self-assembling protein nanoparticles for therapeutic delivery. Bioconjug. Chem. 33 (11), 2018–2034. https://doi.org/10.1021/acs.bioconjchem.2c00030.

Otimenyin, S.O. Chapter 15 - Dosage regimen, in Physico-Chemical Aspects of Dosage Forms. Academic Press, .251–274.

Pang, X., Gong, Kan, Zhang, X., Wu, S., Cui, Y., Qian, B.-Z., 2019. Osteopontin as a multifaceted driver of bone metastasis and drug resistance. Pharmacol. Res. 144, 235–244. https://doi.org/10.1016/j.phrs.2019.04.030.

Panyam, J., Labhasetwar, V., 2003. Biodegradable nanoparticles for drug and gene delivery to cells and tissue. Adv. Drug Deliv. Rev. 55 (3), 329–347. https://doi.org/10.1016/S0169-409X(02)00228-4.

Paresishvili, T., Kakabadze, Z., 2023. Challenges and opportunities associated with drug delivery for the treatment of solid tumors. Oncol. Rev. 17. https://doi.org/10.3389/or.2023.10577.

Park, H., Otte, A., Park, K., 2022. Evolution of drug delivery systems: from 1950 to 2020 and beyond. J. Contr. Release 342, 53–65. https://doi.org/10.1016/j.jconrel.2021.12.030.

Parker, A.L., Benguigui, M., Fornetti, J., Goddard, E., Lucotti, S., Insua-Rodríguez, J., Wiegmans, A.P., 2022. Current challenges in metastasis research and future innovation for clinical translation. Clin. Exp. Metastasis 39 (2), 263–277. https://doi.org/10.1007/s10585-021-10144-5.

Patel, H., Nilendu, P., Jahagirdar, D., Pal, J.K., Sharma, N.K., 2018. Modulating secreted components of tumor microenvironment: a masterstroke in tumor therapeutics. Cancer Biol. Ther. 19 (1), 3–12. https://doi.org/10.1080/15384047.2017.1394538.

Peng, G., Fadeel, B., 2022. Understanding the bidirectional interactions between two-dimensional materials, microorganisms, and the immune system. Adv. Drug Deliv. Rev. 188, 114422. https://doi.org/10.1016/j.addr.2022.114422.

Peppas, N.A., 2013. Historical perspective on advanced drug delivery: how engineering design and mathematical modeling helped the field mature. Adv. Drug Deliv. Rev. 65 (1), 5–9. https://doi.org/10.1016/j.addr.2012.09.040.

Pinals, R.L., Chio, L., Ledesma, F., Landry, M.P., 2020. Engineering at the nano-bio interface: harnessing the protein corona towards nanoparticle design and function. Analyst 145 (15), 5090–5112. https://doi.org/10.1039/d0an00633e.

Polireddy, K., Dong, R., McDonald, P.R., Wang, T., Luke, B., Chen, P., Broward, M., Roy, A., Qi, C., Ahmad, A., 2016. Targeting epithelial-mesenchymal transition for identification of inhibitors for pancreatic cancer cell invasion and tumor spheres formation. PLoS One 11 (10), e0164811. https://doi.org/10.1371/journal.pone.0164811.

Price, J.C., 2023. Diffusion Controlled Systems: Polymeric Microcapsules Polymers for Controlled Drug Delivery. CRC Press, Georgia, pp. 1–14. https://doi.org/10.1201/9781003418252-1.

Qian, C.N., Mei, Y., Zhang, J., 2017. Cancer metastasis: issues and challenges. Chin. J. Cancer 36 (1). https://doi.org/10.1186/s40880-017-0206-7.

Raghuvanshi, R.S., Goyal, S., Singh, O., Panda, A.K., 1998. Stabilization of dichloromethane-induced protein denaturation during microencapsulation. Pharmaceut. Dev. Technol. 3 (2), 269–276. https://doi.org/10.3109/10837459809028504.

Rahimian, S., Najafi, H., Webber, C.A., Jalali, H., 2024a. Advances in exosome-based therapies for the repair of peripheral nerve injuries. Neurochem. Res. 49 (8), 1905–1925. https://doi.org/10.1007/s11064-024-04157-1.

Rahimian, S., Najafi, H., Afzali, B., Doroudian, M., 2024b. Extracellular vesicles and exosomes: novel insights and perspectives on lung cancer from early detection to targeted treatment. Biomedicines 12 (1), 123. https://doi.org/10.3390/biomedicines12010123.

Raj, S., Khurana, S., Ramesh, C., Kumar Kesari, K., Kamal, M.A., Garg, N., Ruokolainen, J., Das, B.C., Kumar, D., 2021. Specific targeting cancer cells with nanoparticles and drug delivery in cancer therapy. Semin. Cancer Biol. 69, 166–177. https://doi.org/10.1016/j.semcancer.2019.11.002.

Rajput, S., Kumar Sharma, P., Malviya, R., 2023. Fluid mechanics in circulating tumour cells: role in metastasis and treatment strategies. Medicine in Drug Discovery 18, 100158. https://doi.org/10.1016/j.medidd.2023.100158.

Ramachandran, S., Satapathy, S.R., Dutta, T., 2022. Delivery strategies for mRNA vaccines. Pharm. Med. 36 (1), 11–20. https://doi.org/10.1007/s40290-021-00417-5.

Ramos, R., 2022. Protein-based encapsulation strategies: toward micro-and nanoscale carriers with increased functionality. Small Sci. 2 (3).

Rampado, R., Crotti, S., Caliceti, P., Pucciarelli, S., Agostini, M., 2020. Recent advances in understanding the protein corona of nanoparticles and in the formulation of "stealthy" nanomaterials. Front. Bioeng. Biotechnol. 8. https://doi.org/10.3389/fbioe.2020.00166.

Rana, Md M., De la Hoz Siegler, H., 2024. Evolution of hybrid hydrogels: next-generation biomaterials for drug delivery and tissue engineering. Gels 10 (4), 216. https://doi.org/10.3390/gels10040216.

Rasel, M.S.I., Mohona, F.A., Akter, W., Kabir, S., Chowdhury, A.A., Chowdhury, J.A., Hassan, M.A., Al Mamun, A., Ghose, D.K., Ahmad, Z., Khan, F.S., Bari, M.F., Rahman, M.S., Amran, M.S., 2022. Exploration of site-specific drug targeting - a review on EPR-, stimuli-, chemical-, and receptor-based approaches as potential drug targeting methods in cancer treatment. J. Oncol. 2022. https://doi.org/10.1155/2022/9396760.

Rasul, R.M., Tamilarasi Muniandy, M., Zakaria, Z., Shah, K., Chee, C.F., Ali, D., Rahman, N.A., Wong, T.W., 2020. A review on chitosan and its development as pulmonary particulate anti-infective and anti-cancer drug carriers. Carbohydr. Polym. 250, 116800. https://doi.org/10.1016/j.carbpol.2020.116800.

Ratajczak, K., Grel, H., Olejnik, P., Jakiela, S., Stobiecka, M., 2023. Current progress, strategy, and prospects of PD-1/PDL-1 immune checkpoint biosensing platforms for cancer diagnostics, therapy monitoring, and drug screening. Biosens. Bioelectron. 240, 115644. https://doi.org/10.1016/j.bios.2023.115644.

Ravindran, A., Chandran, P., Khan, S.S., 2013. Biofunctionalized silver nanoparticles: advances and prospects. Colloids Surf. B Biointerfaces 105, 342–352. https://doi.org/10.1016/j.colsurfb.2012.07.036.

Reboredo, C., 2021. Zein-based nanoparticles as oral carriers for insulin delivery. Pharmaceutics 14 (1).

Ren, X., Hou, T., Liang, Q., Zhang, X., Hu, Di, Xu, B., Chen, X., Chalamaiah, M., Ma, H., 2019. Effects of frequency ultrasound on the properties of zein-chitosan complex coacervation for resveratrol encapsulation. Food Chem. 279, 223–230. https://doi.org/10.1016/j.foodchem.2018.11.025.

Rhaese, S., von Briesen, H., Rübsamen-Waigmann, H., Kreuter, J., Langer, K., 2003. Human serum albumin–polyethylenimine nanoparticles for gene delivery. J. Contr. Release 92 (1–2), 199–208. https://doi.org/10.1016/s0168-3659(03)00302-x.

Rizk, M.L., Zou, L., Savic, R.M., Dooley, K.E., 2017. Importance of drug pharmacokinetics at the site of action. Clin. Transl. Sci. 10 (3), 133–142. https://doi.org/10.1111/cts.12448.

Rocha, B., Aparecida de Morais, L., Costa Viana, M., Carneiro, G., 2023. Promising strategies for improving oral bioavailability of poor water-soluble drugs. Expet Opin. Drug Discov. 18 (6), 615–627. https://doi.org/10.1080/17460441.2023.2211801.

Rohovie, M.J., Nagasawa, M., Swartz, J.R., 2017. Virus-like particles: next-generation nanoparticles for targeted therapeutic delivery. Bioeng. Transl. Med. 2 (1), 43–57. https://doi.org/10.1002/btm2.10049.

Roma-Rodrigues, C., 2021. Combined cancer therapeutics—Tackling the complexity of the tumor microenvironment. Wiley Interdisciplinary Reviews: Nanomedicine and Nanobiotechnology. 13 (5).

Rosenkranz, A.A., Slastnikova, T.A., 2023. Prospects of using protein engineering for selective drug delivery into a specific compartment of target cells. Russian Federation Pharmaceutics 15 (3). https://doi.org/10.3390/pharmaceutics15030987.

Roy, I., Vij, N., 2010. Nanodelivery in airway diseases: challenges and therapeutic applications. Nanomed. Nanotechnol. Biol. Med. 6 (2), 237–244. https://doi.org/10.1016/j.nano.2009.07.001.

Ruigrok, M.J.R., Frijlink, H.W., Hinrichs, W.L.J., 2016. Pulmonary administration of small interfering RNA: the route to go? J. Contr. Release 235, 14–23. https://doi.org/10.1016/j.jconrel.2016.05.054.

Sabourian, P., Yazdani, G., Sajad Ashraf, S., Frounchi, M., Mashayekhan, S., Kiani, S., Kakkar, A., 2020. Effect of physico-chemical properties of nanoparticles on their intracellular uptake. Int. J. Mol. Sci. 21 (21), 8019. https://doi.org/10.3390/ijms21218019.

Sabra, S.A., Elzoghby, A.O., Sheweita, S.A., Haroun, M., Helmy, M.W., Eldemellawy, M.A., Xia, Y., Goodale, D., Allan, A.L., Rohani, S., 2018. Self-assembled amphiphilic zein-lactoferrin micelles for tumor targeted co-delivery of rapamycin and wogonin to breast cancer. Journal of Pharmaceutics and Biopharmaceutics 128, 156–169. https://doi.org/10.1016/j.ejpb.2018.04.023.

Sahandi Zangabad, P., Karimi, M., Mehdizadeh, F., Malekzad, H., Ghasemi, A., Bahrami, S., Zare, H., Moghoofei, M., Amin, H., Hamblin, M.R., 2017. Nanocaged platforms: modification, drug delivery and nanotoxicity. Opening synthetic cages to release the tiger. Nanoscale 9 (4), 1356–1392. https://doi.org/10.1039/c6nr07315h.

Sahoo, S.K., Labhasetwar, V., 2003. Nanotech approaches to drug delivery and imaging. Drug Discov. Today 8 (24), 1112–1120. https://doi.org/10.1016/S1359-6446(03)02903-9.

Sahoo, N., Sahoo, R.K., Biswas, N., Guha, A., Kuotsu, K., 2015. Recent advancement of gelatin nanoparticles in drug and vaccine delivery. Int. J. Biol. Macromol. 81, 317–331. https://doi.org/10.1016/j.ijbiomac.2015.08.006.

Saif, A., Anjum, L., Faisal, Z., Akram, N., Abbas Shah, Y., Irfan, R., Saeed, F., Afzaal, M., Shah, M.A., 2023. Recent advances in protein-based nanoparticles and their applications in the delivery of bioactive compounds. Int. J. Food Prop. 26 (2), 2866–2880. https://doi.org/10.1080/10942912.2023.2261662.

Saleh, T., Soudi, T., Shojaosadati, S.A., 2019. Aptamer functionalized curcumin-loaded human serum albumin (HSA) nanoparticles for targeted delivery to HER-2 positive breast cancer cells. Int. J. Biol. Macromol. 130, 109–116. https://doi.org/10.1016/j.ijbiomac.2019.02.129.

Sanders, N., Rudolph, C., Braeckmans, K., De Smedt, S.C., Demeester, J., 2009. Extracellular barriers in respiratory gene therapy. Adv. Drug Deliv. Rev. 61 (2), 115–127. https://doi.org/10.1016/j.addr.2008.09.011.

Sanopoulou, M., Papadokostaki, K.G., 2017. Controlled Drug Release Systems: Mechanisms and Kinetics Biomedical Membranes and (Bio)artificial Organs. World Scientific Publishing Co. Pte. Ltd., Greece, pp. 1–33.

Scheffel, U., Rhodes, B.A., Natarajan, T.K., Wagner, H.N., 1972. Albumin microspheres for study of the reticuloendothelial system. J. Nucl. Med. 13 (7), 498–503.

Senapati, S., Kumar Mahanta, A., Kumar, S., Maiti, P., 2018. Controlled drug delivery vehicles for cancer treatment and their performance. Signal Transduct. Targeted Ther. 3 (1). https://doi.org/10.1038/s41392-017-0004-3.

Seyfried, T.N., Huysentruyt, L.C., 2013. On the origin of cancer metastasis. Crit. Rev. Oncog. 18 (1–2), 43–73. https://doi.org/10.1615/CritRevOncog.v18.i1-2.40.

Sezgin-Bayindir, Z., Losada-Barreiro, S., Fernández-Bravo, S., Bravo-Díaz, C., 2023. Innovative delivery and release systems for antioxidants and other active substances in the treatment of cancer. Pharmaceuticals 16 (7), 1038. https://doi.org/10.3390/ph16071038.

Shahgolzari, M. Multifunctional plant virus nanoparticles for targeting breast cancer tumors. Vaccines (Basel) 10.

Sham, J.O.-H., Zhang, Y., Finlay, W.H., Roa, W.H., Löbenberg, R., 2004. Formulation and characterization of spray-dried powders containing nanoparticles for aerosol delivery to the lung. Int. J. Pharm. 269 (2), 457–467. https://doi.org/10.1016/j.ijpharm.2003.09.041.

Sharifi, M., Cho, W.C., Ansariesfahani, A., Tarharoudi, R., Malekisarvar, H., Sari, S., Bloukh, S.H., Edis, Z., Amin, M., Gleghorn, J.P., ten Hagen, T.L.M., Falahati, M., 2022. An updated review on EPR-based solid tumor targeting nanocarriers for cancer treatment. Cancers 14 (12), 2868. https://doi.org/10.3390/cancers14122868.

Sharma, S., Parveen, R., Chatterji, B.P., 2021. Toxicology of nanoparticles in drug delivery. Current Pathobiology Reports 9 (4), 133–144. https://doi.org/10.1007/s40139-021-00227-z.

Shen, K., Song, W., Wang, H., Wang, L., Yang, Y., Hu, Q., Ren, M., Gao, Z., Wang, Q., Zheng, S., Zhu, M., Yang, Y., Zhang, Y., Wei, C., Gu, J., 2023. Decoding the metastatic potential and optimal postoperative adjuvant therapy of melanoma based on metastasis score. Cell Death Discov. 9 (1). https://doi.org/10.1038/s41420-023-01678-6.

Shi, M., McHugh, K.J., 2023. Strategies for overcoming protein and peptide instability in biodegradable drug delivery systems. Adv. Drug Deliv. Rev. 199, 114904. https://doi.org/10.1016/j.addr.2023.114904.

Shin, M.D., Shukla, S., Chung, Y.H., Beiss, V., Chan, S.K., Ortega-Rivera, O.A., Wirth, D.M., Chen, A., Sack, M., Pokorski, J.K., Steinmetz, N.F., 2020. COVID-19 vaccine development and a potential nanomaterial path forward. Nat. Nanotechnol. 15 (8), 646–655. https://doi.org/10.1038/s41565-020-0737-y.

Siemann, D.W., 2011. The unique characteristics of tumor vasculature and preclinical evidence for its selective disruption by Tumor-Vascular Disrupting Agents. Cancer Treat Rev. 37 (1), 63–74. https://doi.org/10.1016/j.ctrv.2010.05.001.

Siepmann, J., Siepmann, F., 2012. Swelling Controlled Drug Delivery Systems Fundamentals and Applications of Controlled Release Drug Delivery. Springer US, France, pp. 153–170. https://doi.org/10.1007/978-1-4614-0881-9_7.

Silvestre, A.L.P., Oshiro-Júnior, J.A., Garcia, C., Turco, B.O., Leite, J.M.D.S., Damasceno, B.P.G.D.L., Soares, J.C.M., Chorilli, M., 2021. Monoclonal antibodies carried in drug delivery nanosystems as a strategy for cancer treatment. Curr. Med. Chem. 28 (2), 401–418. https://doi.org/10.2174/0929867327666200121121409.

Singh, R., Lillard, J.W., 2009. Nanoparticle-based targeted drug delivery. Exp. Mol. Pathol. 86 (3), 215–223. https://doi.org/10.1016/j.yexmp.2008.12.004.

Sitia, l., 2022. HER-2-targeted nanoparticles for breast cancer diagnosis and treatment. Cancers 14 (10).

Somase, V., Desai, S.A., Patel, V.P., Patil, V., Bhosale, K., 2024. Antimicrobial peptides: potential alternative to antibiotics and overcoming limitations for future therapeutic applications. Int. J. Pept. Res. Therapeut. 30 (4). https://doi.org/10.1007/s10989-024-10623-9.

Sripriyalakshmi, S., Jose, P., Ravindran, A., Anjali, C.H., 2014. Recent trends in drug delivery system using protein nanoparticles. Cell Biochem. Biophys. 70 (1), 17–26. https://doi.org/10.1007/s12013-014-9896-5.

Steeg, P.S., 2016. Targeting metastasis. Nat. Rev. Cancer 16 (4), 201–218. https://doi.org/10.1038/nrc.2016.25.

Steeg, P.S., Camphausen, K.A., Smith, Q.R., 2011. Brain metastases as preventive and therapeutic targets. Nat. Rev. Cancer 11 (5), 352–363. https://doi.org/10.1038/nrc3053.

Steiert, E., 2020. Dynamic protein-based nanoparticles for drug delivery applications.

Stielow, M., 2023a. The bioavailability of drugs—the current state of knowledge. Molecules 28 (24).

Stielow, M., 2023b. The bioavailability of drugs—the current state of knowledge. Molecules 24.

Sturesson, C., Carlfors, J., 2000. Incorporation of protein in PLG-microspheres with retention of bioactivity. J. Contr. Release 67 (2–3), 171–178. https://doi.org/10.1016/S0168-3659(00)00205-4.

Sun, Y., Davis, E., 2021. Nanoplatforms for targeted stimuli-responsive drug delivery: a review of platform materials and stimuli-responsive release and targeting mechanisms. Nanomaterials 11 (3), 746. https://doi.org/10.3390/nano11030746.

Sun, X., Ni, N., Ma, Y., Wang, Y., Tai Leong, D., 2020. Retooling cancer nanotherapeutics' entry into tumors to alleviate tumoral hypoxia. Small 16 (41). https://doi.org/10.1002/smll.202003000.

Sun, T., Zhang, Y.S., Pang, B., Hyun, D.C., Yang, M., Xia, Y., 2021. Engineered Nanoparticles for Drug Delivery in Cancer Therapy. Informa UK Limited, pp. 31–142. https://doi.org/10.1201/9780429027819-2.

Tarannum, M., Vivero-Escoto, J.L., 2022. Nanoparticle-based therapeutic strategies targeting major clinical challenges in pancreatic cancer treatment. Adv. Drug Deliv. Rev. 187, 114357. https://doi.org/10.1016/j.addr.2022.114357.

Tariq, H., Batool, S., Asif, S., Ali, M., Haider Abbasi, B., 2022. Virus-like particles: revolutionary platforms for developing vaccines against emerging infectious diseases. Front. Microbiol. 12. https://doi.org/10.3389/fmicb.2021.790121.

Teixeira, M.I., Lopes, C.M., Amaral, M.H., Costa, P.C., 2023. Surface-modified lipid nanocarriers for crossing the blood-brain barrier (BBB): a current overview of active targeting in brain diseases. Colloids Surf. B Biointerfaces 221, 112999. https://doi.org/10.1016/j.colsurfb.2022.112999.

Tewabe, A., Abate, A., Tamrie, M., Seyfu, A., Siraj, E.A., 2021. Targeted drug delivery — from magic bullet to nanomedicine: principles, challenges, and future perspectives. J. Multidiscip. Healthc. 14, 1711–1724. https://doi.org/10.2147/JMDH.S313968.

Tewabe, A., Abate, A., Tamrie, M., Seyfu, A., Abdela Siraj, E., 2021. Targeted drug delivery — from magic bullet to nanomedicine: principles, challenges, and future perspectives. J. Multidiscip. Healthc. 14, 1711–1724. https://doi.org/10.2147/jmdh.s313968.

Tincu, C.-E. Recent advancements and strategies for overcoming the blood–brain barrier using albumin-based drug delivery systems to treat brain cancer, with a focus on glioblastoma. Polymers. 15.

Tindall, M.J., Please, C.P., Peddie, M.J., 2008. Modelling the formation of necrotic regions in avascular tumours. Math. Biosci. 211 (1), 34–55. https://doi.org/10.1016/j.mbs.2007.09.002.

Tripathi, N.K., Shrivastava, A., 2019. Recent developments in bioprocessing of recombinant proteins: expression hosts and process development. Frontiers Media S.A., India Frontiers in Bioengineering and Biotechnology 7. https://doi.org/10.3389/fbioe.2019.00420.

Truong-Le, V.L., Thomas August, J., Leong, K.W., 1998. Controlled gene delivery by DNA-gelatin nanospheres. Hum. Gene Ther. 9 (12), 1709–1717. https://doi.org/10.1089/hum.1998.9.12-1709.

Tseng, C.L., Su, W.Y., Yen, K.C., Yang, K.C., Lin, F.H., 2009. The use of biotinylated-EGF-modified gelatin nanoparticle carrier to enhance cisplatin accumulation in cancerous lungs via inhalation. Biomaterials 30 (20), 3476–3485. https://doi.org/10.1016/j.biomaterials.2009.03.010.

Tsung, T.H., Tsai, Y.C., Lee, H.P., Chen, Y.H., Lu, D.W., 2023. Biodegradable polymer-based drug-delivery systems for ocular diseases. Int. J. Mol. Sci. 24 (16). https://doi.org/10.3390/ijms241612976.

Ulijn, R.V., Jerala, R., 2018. Peptide and protein nanotechnology into the 2020s: beyond biology. Chem. Soc. Rev. 47 (10), 3391–3394. https://doi.org/10.1039/c8cs90055h.

Unzueta, U., Roldán, M., Pesarrodona, M., Benitez, R., Sánchez-Chardi, A., Conchillo-Solé, O., Mangues, R., Villaverde, A., Vázquez, E., 2020. Self-assembling as regular nanoparticles dramatically minimizes photobleaching of tumour-targeted GFP. Acta Biomater. 103, 272–280. https://doi.org/10.1016/j.actbio.2019.12.003.

Varanko, A., Saha, S., Chilkoti, A., 2020. Recent trends in protein and peptide-based biomaterials for advanced drug delivery. Adv. Drug Deliv. Rev. 156, 133–187. https://doi.org/10.1016/j.addr.2020.08.008.

Vasan, N., Baselga, J., Hyman, D.M., 2019. A view on drug resistance in cancer. Nature 575 (7782), 299–309. https://doi.org/10.1038/s41586-019-1730-1.

Verma, R.K., Garg, S., 2001. Drug delivery technologies and future directions. Pharm. Technol. 25 (2), 1–14.

Verma, D., Gulati, N., Kaul, S., Mukherjee, S., Nagaich, U., 2018. Protein based nanostructures for drug delivery. J. Pharm. 2018, 1–18. https://doi.org/10.1155/2018/9285854.

Verma, M.L., Dhanya, B.S., Rani, V., Thakur, M., Jeslin, J., Kushwaha, R., 2020. Carbohydrate and protein based biopolymeric nanoparticles: current status and biotechnological applications. Int. J. Biol. Macromol. 154, 390–412. https://doi.org/10.1016/j.ijbiomac.2020.03.105.

Veselov, V.V., 2022. Targeted delivery methods for anticancer drugs. Cancers 14 (3).

Viswanadha, L.S., Arcot, Y., Lin, Y.-T., Akbulut, M.E.S., 2024. A comparative investigation of release kinetics of paclitaxel from natural protein and macromolecular nanocarriers in nanoscale drug delivery systems. JCIS Open 15, 100120. https://doi.org/10.1016/j.jciso.2024.100120.

Vu, M.N. Current and future nanoparticle vaccines for COVID-19. EBioMedicine 74.

Wang, G., Uludag, H., 2008. Recent developments in nanoparticle-based drug delivery and targeting systems with emphasis on protein-based nanoparticles. Expet Opin. Drug Deliv. 5 (5), 499–515. https://doi.org/10.1517/17425247.5.5.499.

Wang, Y., Shim, M.S., Levinson, N.S., Sung, H.-W., Xia, Y., 2014. Stimuli-responsive materials for controlled release of theranostic agents. Adv. Funct. Mater. 24 (27), 4206–4220. https://doi.org/10.1002/adfm.201400279.

Wang, M.Y., Lin, Z.R., Cao, Y., Zheng, L.S., Peng, L.X., Sun, R., Meng, D.F., Xie, P., Yang, J.P., Cao, L., Xu, L., Huang, B.J., Qian, C.N., 2016. PDZ binding kinase (PBK) is a theranostic target for nasopharyngeal carcinoma: driving tumor growth via ROS signaling and correlating with patient survival. Impact Journals LLC, China Oncotarget 7 (18), 26604–26616. https://doi.org/10.18632/oncotarget.8445.

Wang, B., Kong, B., Li, F., Liu, Q., Zhang, H., Xia, X., 2020. Changes in the thermal stability and structure of protein from porcine longissimus dorsi induced by different thawing methods. Food Chem. 316, 126375. https://doi.org/10.1016/j.foodchem.2020.126375.

Wang, J., Li, Y., Nie, G., 2021. Multifunctional biomolecule nanostructures for cancer therapy. Nat. Rev. Mater. 6 (9), 766–783. https://doi.org/10.1038/s41578-021-00315-x.

Wang, S., Sun, Z., Hou, Y., 2021. Engineering nanoparticles toward the modulation of emerging cancer immunotherapy. Adv. Healthcare Mater. 10 (5).

Wang, Z., Zhi, K., Ding, Z., Sun, Y., Li, S., Li, M., Pu, K., Zou, J., 2021. Emergence in protein derived nanomedicine as anticancer therapeutics: More than a tour de force. Semin. Cancer Biol. 69, 77–90. https://doi.org/10.1016/j.semcancer.2019.11.012.

Wang, Y., Liu, Y., Zhang, J., Peng, Q., Wang, X., Xiao, X., Shi, K., 2024. Nanomaterial-mediated modulation of the cGAS-STING signaling pathway for enhanced cancer immunotherapy. Acta Biomater. 176, 51–76. https://doi.org/10.1016/j.actbio.2024.01.008.

Weber, C., Coester, C., Kreuter, J., Langer, K., 2000. Desolvation process and surface characterisation of protein nanoparticles. Int. J. Pharm. 194 (1), 91–102. https://doi.org/10.1016/s0378-5173(99)00370-1.

Weiss, R.B., Donehower, R.C., Wiernik, P.H., Ohnuma, T., Gralla, R.J., Trump, D.L., Baker, J.R., Van Echo, D.A., Von Hoff, D.D., Leyland-Jones, B., 1990. Hypersensitivity reactions from taxol. J. Clin. Oncol. 8 (7), 1263–1268. https://doi.org/10.1200/jco.1990.8.7.1263.

Wells, C.M., Harris, M., Choi, L., Murali, V.P., Guerra, F.D., Jennings, J.A., 2019. Stimuli-responsive drug release from smart polymers. J. Funct. Biomater. 10 (3). https://doi.org/10.3390/jfb10030034.

Wilhelm, A. Tavares, Q.D. Ohta, S. Audet, J. Dvorak, Chan, WC W., 2016. Nat. Rev. Mater. 1.

Wong, A.S.M., Czuba, E., Chen, M.Z., Yuen, D., Cupic, K.I., Yang, S., Hodgetts, R.Y., Selby, L.I., Johnston, A.P.R., Such, G.K., 2017. pH-responsive transferrin-phlexi particles capable of targeting cells in vitro. ACS Macro Lett. 6 (3), 315–320. https://doi.org/10.1021/acsmacrolett.7b00044.

Wong, K.H., Lu, A., Chen, X., Yang, Z., 2020. Natural ingredient-based polymeric nanoparticles for cancer treatment. Molecules 25 (16), 3620. https://doi.org/10.3390/molecules25163620.

Wu, et al., Molecular Genetics and Genomics. (1) (2008), 19–24.
Wu, D., 2023. The blood–brain barrier: structure, regulation and drug delivery. Signal Transduct. Targeted Ther. 8 (1).
Wu, P., Gao, W., Su, M., Nice, E.C., Zhang, W., Lin, J., Xie, N., 2021. Adaptive mechanisms of tumor therapy resistance driven by tumor microenvironment. Front. Cell Dev. Biol. 9. https://doi.org/10.3389/fcell.2021.641469.
Yamamoto, A. Metastasis from the tumor interior and necrotic core formation are regulated by breast cancer-derived angiopoietin-like 7. Proc. Natl. Acad. Sci. 120 (10).
Yang, Y., Zhan, W., 2022. Role of tissue hydraulic permeability in convection-enhanced delivery of nanoparticle-encapsulated chemotherapy drugs to brain tumour. Pharm. Res. 39 (5), 877–892. https://doi.org/10.1007/s11095-022-03261-7.
Yang, L., Cui, F., Cun, D., Tao, A., Shi, K., Lin, W., 2007. Preparation, characterization and biodistribution of the lactone form of 10-hydroxycamptothecin (HCPT)-loaded bovine serum albumin (BSA) nanoparticles. Int. J. Pharm. 340 (1–2), 163–172. https://doi.org/10.1016/j.ijpharm.2007.03.028.
Yang, X., Ye, Z., Yuan, Y., Zheng, Z., Shi, J., Ying, Y., Huang, P., 2013. Insights into the binding of paclitaxel to human serum albumin: multispectroscopic studies. Luminescence 28 (3), 427–434. https://doi.org/10.1002/bio.2522.
Yang, Y.Y., Zhang, M., Liu, Z.P., Wang, K., Yu, D.G., 2018. Meletin sustained-release gliadin nanoparticles prepared via solvent surface modification on blending electrospraying. Appl. Surf. Sci. 434, 1040–1047. https://doi.org/10.1016/j.apsusc.2017.11.024.
Yang, Z., Zhang, L., Zhou, Y., Wang, H., Wen, L., Kianfar, E., 2020. Investigation of effective parameters on SAPO-34 nanocatalyst in the methanol-to-olefin conversion process: a review. Rev. Inorg. Chem. 40 (3), 91–105. https://doi.org/10.1515/revic-2020-0003.
Yang, H.Y., Li, Y., Lee, D.S., 2021. Functionalization of magnetic nanoparticles with organic ligands toward biomedical applications. Advanced NanoBiomed Research 1 (5). https://doi.org/10.1002/anbr.202000043.
Yao, L. Wang, Q. Ma, W. Navigating the immune maze: pioneering strategies for unshackling cancer immunotherapy resistance. Cancers (Basel) 15.
Yardley, D.A., 2013. Nab-Paclitaxel mechanisms of action and delivery. J. Contr. Release 170 (3), 365–372. https://doi.org/10.1016/j.jconrel.2013.05.041.
Yetisgin, A.A., 2020. Therapeutic nanoparticles and their targeted delivery applications. Molecules 25.
Yewale, C., Baradia, D., Vhora, I., Misra, A., 2013. Proteins: emerging carrier for delivery of cancer therapeutics. Expet Opin. Drug Deliv. 10 (10), 1429–1448. https://doi.org/10.1517/17425247.2013.805200.
Yoo, J., Park, C., Yi, G., Lee, D., Koo, H., 2019. Active targeting strategies using biological ligands for nanoparticle drug delivery systems. Cancers 11 (5), 640. https://doi.org/10.3390/cancers11050640.
Youngren-Ortiz, S.R., Gandhi, N.S., España-Serrano, L., Chougule, M.B., 2016. Aerosol delivery of siRNA to the lungs. Part 1: Rationale for gene delivery systems. KONA Powder and Particle Journal 2016 (33), 63–85. https://doi.org/10.14356/kona.2016014.
Yu, J., Mu, Q., Fung, M., Xu, X., Zhu, L., Ho, R.J.Y., 2022. Challenges and opportunities in metastatic breast cancer treatments: nano-drug combinations delivered preferentially to metastatic cells may enhance therapeutic response. Pharmacol. Therapeut. 236, 108108. https://doi.org/10.1016/j.pharmthera.2022.108108.
Yun, Y.H., Lee, B.K., Park, K., 2015. Controlled drug delivery: Historical perspective for the next generation. J. Contr. Release 219, 2–7. https://doi.org/10.1016/j.jconrel.2015.10.005.
Yusuf, A., Almotairy, A.R.Z., Henidi, H., Alshehri, O.Y., Aldughaim, M.S., 2023. Nanoparticles as drug delivery systems: a review of the implication of nanoparticles' physicochemical properties on responses in biological systems. Polymers 15 (7), 1596. https://doi.org/10.3390/polym15071596.
Zalba, S., ten Hagen, T.L.M., Burgui, C., Garrido, M.J., 2022. Stealth nanoparticles in oncology: Facing the PEG dilemma. J. Contr. Release 351, 22–36. https://doi.org/10.1016/j.jconrel.2022.09.002.
Zhang, R., Han, Y., Xie, W., Liu, F., Chen, S., 2022. Advances in protein-based nanocarriers of bioactive compounds: from microscopic molecular principles to macroscopical structural and functional attributes. J. Agric. Food Chem. 70 (21), 6354–6367. https://doi.org/10.1021/acs.jafc.2c01936.
Zhang, T., Xu, J., Chen, J., Wang, Z., Wang, X., Zhong, J., 2021. Protein nanoparticles for pickering emulsions: a comprehensive review on their shapes, preparation methods, and modification methods. Trends Food Sci. Technol. 113, 26–41. https://doi.org/10.1016/j.tifs.2021.04.054.
Zhao, Y. Liu, S. Lu, X. Advances in pulmonary protein delivery systems. Advanced NanoBiomed Research 4.

Zhao, Y.Z., Li, X., Lu, C.T., Xu, Y.Y., Lv, H.F., Dai, D.D., Zhang, L., Sun, C.Z., Yang, W., Li, X.K., Zhao, Y.P., Fu, H.X., Cai, L., Lin, M., Chen, L.J., Zhang, M., 2012. Experiment on the feasibility of using modified gelatin nanoparticles as insulin pulmonary administration system for diabetes therapy. Acta Diabetol. 49 (4), 315–325. https://doi.org/10.1007/s00592-011-0356-z.

Zhao, Z., Li, Y., Xie, M.B., 2015. Silk fibroin-based nanoparticles for drug delivery. Int. J. Mol. Sci. 16 (3), 4880–4903. https://doi.org/10.3390/ijms16034880.

Zheng, L.S., Yang, J.P., Cao, Y., Peng, L.X., Sun, R., Xie, P., Wang, M.Y., Meng, D.F., Luo, D.H., Zou, X., Chen, M.Y., Mai, H.Q., Guo, L., Guo, X., Shao, J.Y., Huang, B.J., Zhang, W., Qian, C.N., 2017. SPINK6 promotes metastasis of nasopharyngeal carcinoma via binding and activation of epithelial growth factor receptor. Cancer Res. 77 (2), 579–589. https://doi.org/10.1158/0008-5472.CAN-16-1281.

Zhou, J., Kroll, A.V., Holay, M., Fang, R.H., Zhang, L., 2020. Biomimetic nanotechnology toward personalized vaccines. Adv. Mater. 32 (13). https://doi.org/10.1002/adma.201901255.

Zhu, Y., Zhu, Y., Cao, T., Liu, X., Liu, X., Yan, Y., Shi, Y., Wang, J.-C., 2023. Ferritin-based nanomedicine for disease treatment. Medical Review 3 (1), 49–74. https://doi.org/10.1515/mr-2023-0001.

Zi, Y., Yang, K., He, J., Wu, Z., Liu, J., Zhang, W., 2022. Strategies to enhance drug delivery to solid tumors by harnessing the EPR effects and alternative targeting mechanisms. Adv. Drug Deliv. Rev. 188, 114449. https://doi.org/10.1016/j.addr.2022.114449.

Zoghbi, M., Jad Moussa, M., Dagher, J., Haroun, E., Qdaisat, A., Singer, E.D., Karam, Y.E., Yeung, S.-C.J., Chaftari, P., 2024. Brain metastasis in the emergency department: epidemiology, presentation, investigations, and management. Cancers 16 (14), 2583. https://doi.org/10.3390/cancers16142583.

Zolnik, B.S., González-Fernández, A., Sadrieh, N., Dobrovolskaia, M.A., 2010. Minireview: nanoparticles and the immune system. Endocrinology 151 (2), 458–465. https://doi.org/10.1210/en.2009-1082.

Zong, Y., Wu, J., Shen, K., 2017. Nanoparticle albumin-bound paclitaxel as neoadjuvant chemotherapy of breast cancer: a systematic review and meta-analysis. Oncotarget 8 (10), 17360–17372. https://doi.org/10.18632/oncotarget.14477.

Zou, T., Lu, W., Mezhuev, Y., Lan, M., Li, L., Liu, F., Cai, T., Wu, X., Cai, Y., 2021. A review of nanoparticle drug delivery systems responsive to endogenous breast cancer microenvironment. Eur. J. Pharm. Biopharm. 166, 30–43. https://doi.org/10.1016/j.ejpb.2021.05.029.

CHAPTER

# 25

# Conclusion and future prospective of protein-based nanoparticles

*Alookika Agarwal[1], Payel Shil[1], K.G. Abishek[1], Garima Gupta[2], Prakash Kumar Sarangi[3], Muskan Leharwani[4], Prashant Kesharwani[4,5], Ulduza Gurbanova[6], Aziz Eftekhari[7,8] and Rambabu Dandela[1]*

[1]Department of Industrial and Engineering Chemistry, Institute of Chemical Technology, Indian Oil Campus, Bhubaneswar, Odisha, India; [2]School of Allied Medical Sciences, Lovely Professional University, Phagwara, Punjab, India; [3]College of Agriculture, Central Agricultural University, Imphal, Manipur, India; [4]Next-Generation Translational Nanomedicine Laboratory, Department of Pharmaceutical Sciences, Dr. Harisingh Gour Vishwavidyalaya (A Central University), Sagar, Madhya Pradesh, India; [5]University Institute of Pharma Sciences, Chandigarh University, Mohali, Punjab, India; [6]Institute of Molecular Biology, Ministry of Science and Education of the Republic of Azerbaijan, Baku, Azerbaijan; [7]Department of Biochemistry, Faculty of Science, Ege University, Izmir, Turkiye; [8]Nanobiomedicine Research Center, Azerbaijan Medical University, Baku, Azerbaijan

## 1. Introduction

### 1.1 Overview of protein-based nanoparticles

Proteins are a highly defined linear peptide chain packed in a complicated three-dimensional structure (1, 2). Protein-based nanoparticles (PBNPs) are now a feasible carrier for drug delivery and nanomedicine. The phrase "nanotechnology" refers to the approaches and procedures used to research, create, and manufacture objects at the nanoscale, including particles, electronics, etc. Nanoplatforms vary in size from 1 to 1000 nm (nm) (Jain et al., 2018). These nanostructures, typically ranging from 10 to 1000 nm, are composed of natural

*Protein-Based Nanoparticles in Drug Delivery*
https://doi.org/10.1016/B978-0-443-33639-3.00016-7

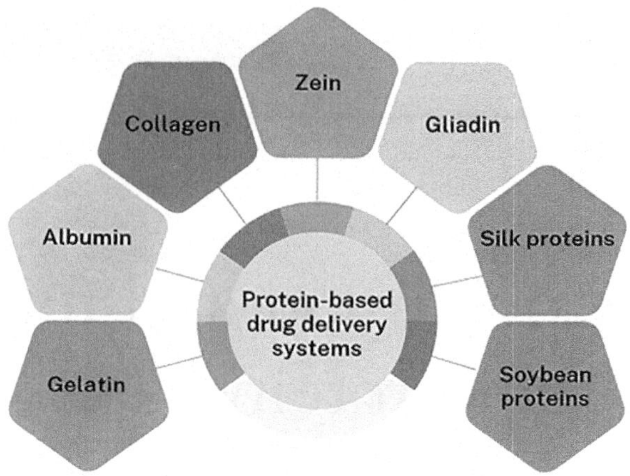


FIGURE 25.1 Examples of proteins used in drug delivery systems. Reused from Ferraro, C., Dattilo, M., Patitucci, F., Prete, S., Scopelliti, G., Parisi, O.I., Puoci, F., 2024. Exploring protein-based carriers in drug delivery: a review. Pharmaceutics 16 (9). Under CC BY license.

or engineered proteins that can be precisely designed and manipulated at the molecular level.

The inherent biocompatibility, biodegradability, and structural tunability of PBNPs have made them a very flexible and attractive platform in drug distribution and nanomedicine. Usually made from naturally occurring proteins as represented in (Fig. 25.1), like albumin, gelatin, casein, or zein, these nanoparticles have outstanding safety records and may encapsulate various medicinal substances.

History of PBNPs.

## 1.2 1990s: early developments

Researchers started the path in the 1990s by highlighting the inherent qualities of proteins in fundamental studies. Albumin and gelatin are two examples of proteins chosen for their biocompatibility, which means they are safe for the body to utilize, and biodegradability, which means they may naturally decompose after serving their purpose. This time was significant because it established the possibility that proteins may function as efficient transporters of medicinal drugs, laying the foundation for further study as depicted in Fig. 25.2. This decade saw the crucial discovery of protein nanoparticles in the pharmaceutical industry, which sparked interest in their possible use in drug delivery methods (Hong et al., 2020; Afzal et al., 2022).

## 1.3 2000–05: Formulation and characterization

Protein-based drug delivery saw tremendous formulation advances in the early 2000s, mainly thanks to techniques like coacervation (also called desolation or complex coacervation) and nanoprecipitation, which enabled exact control over the size of nanoparticles, the effectiveness of drug loading, and reproducibility. The coacervation technique has been widely employed to generate stable protein-based nanoparticles, particularly using carriers such as albumin and gelatin. In this approach, the addition of a desolvating agent (e.g., ethanol) induces phase separation, followed by cross-linking to stabilize the particles. The

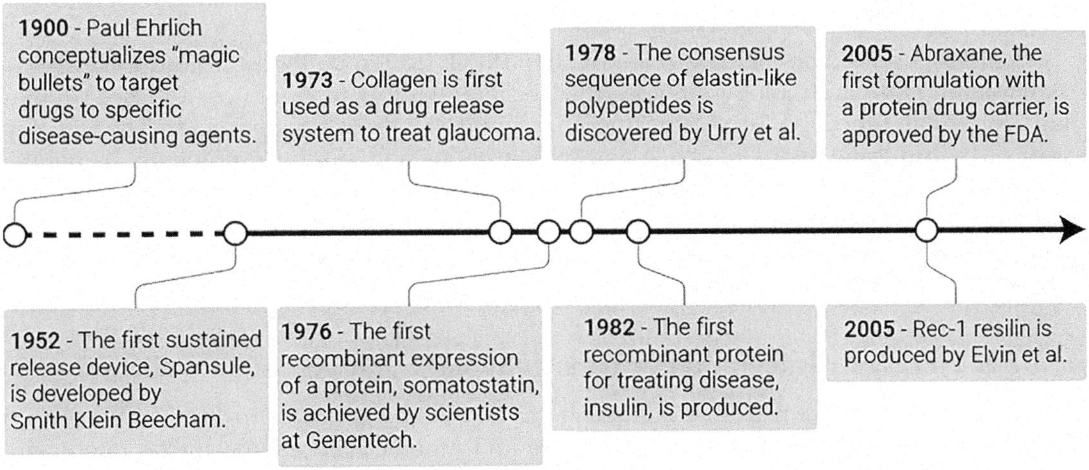


**FIGURE 25.2** Timeline of major advances in engineering protein-based biomaterials for controlled drug delivery. *Reused with permission from Varanko, A., Saha, S., Chilkoti, A., 2020. Recent trends in protein and peptide-based biomaterials for advanced drug delivery. Adv. Drug Deliv. Rev. 156, 133–187. Copyright @ Elsevier, 2020.*

nanoprecipitation technique also emerged as an effective alternative, offering the advantage of producing uniformly sized particles under relatively mild conditions. This method involves the controlled addition of a non-solvent into an aqueous protein solution, leading to supersaturation, nucleation, and subsequent nanoparticle formation. Alongside these developments, characterization methods such as Transmission Electron Microscopy (TEM) and Dynamic Light Scattering (DLS) became standard practice, enabling detailed assessment of particle morphology, structure, and size distribution. These tools ensured reproducibility and reliability in nanoparticle-based drug delivery systems (Verma et al., 2018; Tarhini et al., 2018).

## 1.4 2006–2010: Targeted delivery and functionalization

In the following phase, researchers worked to enhance the targeting capabilities of PBNPs. Nanoparticles were functionalized by attaching specific ligands, like peptides and antibodies, to their surfaces. This functionalization significantly enhanced the nanoparticles' selectivity for particular cell types, which is crucial in cancer treatments where targeted administration maximizes therapeutic efficacy while minimizing side effects. The planning and implementation of drug delivery systems were revolutionized by the advancements made during this period (Ruoslahti et al., 2010; Tang et al., 2025).

## 1.5 2011–15: Clinical trials and applications

The early 2010s marked a significant turning point with the start of clinical testing for several PBNP systems. These studies revealed their practical applications, particularly in delivering chemotherapeutic drugs and RNA-based therapies. By confirming both the effectiveness and safety of protein nanoparticles in controlled drug delivery, the results opened the door to their integration into conventional treatment plans. This period underscored the therapeutic advantages of protein nanoparticles (Jain et al., 2018; Hong et al., 2020).

## 1.6 2016–2020: Innovations in design and synthesis

Scientists observed an increase in innovative PBNP design methods around this time. As recombinant DNA technology advanced, it became possible to create customized proteins with particular functions, increasing the adaptability of these nanoparticles. The development of hybrid nanoparticles, which combine proteins and synthetic polymers, is another possible tactic to improve the stability and effectiveness of drug administration. These advancements not only improved the efficiency of drug delivery systems but also broadened the applications of PBNPs. This makes them suitable for a range of therapeutic areas (Defrates et al.; Varanko et al., 2020).

## 1.7 2021-Present: Integration of nanotechnology and precision medicine

PBNPs have seen tremendous advancement in recent years due to the combination of nanotechnology and precision medicine. More and more, advances in artificial intelligence and machine learning are being used to forecast the interactions of nanoparticles in biological systems, allowing for the creation of more individualized and effective drug delivery plans. The development of stimuli-responsive nanoparticles, which can release therapeutic payloads in response to particular biological triggers, is the focus of current research. These continuing developments demonstrate the field's dynamic character and its capacity to transform current methods of treatment (Mao et al., 2024; Li et al., 2023; Samathoti et al., 2025).

Overall, the timeline shows the remarkable advancement in PBNP engineering for controlled drug delivery, showing a sequential progression characterized by important discoveries and advancements. Therapeutic proteins, peptides, nucleic acids (like siRNA or mRNA), and small molecule medications can all be transported by PBNPs to improve their bioavailability and stability throughout systemic distribution (Zaher et al., 2023). As illustrated in Fig. 25.3, The combination of PBNPs' biological compatibility, morphological diversity, and targeting ability makes them an extremely powerful tool for achieving site-specific, controlled, and efficient therapeutic administration. These qualities make them particularly suitable for customized medications, which boost therapeutic efficacy while lowering side effects (Tarhini et al., 2017). Their methods of preparation can be enhanced to enhance drug loading and release patterns, thereby augmenting their therapeutic potential (Tarhini et al., 2017).

The ability of PBNPs to respond to environmental stimuli like pH, temperature, redox balance, or enzyme activity makes them an excellent platform for site-specific and controlled drug release. Because they are stimuli-responsive, PBNPs can remain stable in circulation while selectively releasing their therapeutic payload in challenging environments, such as the acidic tumor microenvironment or intracellular lysosomal compartments (Zaher et al., 2023; Konate et al., 2021). For example, gelatine and albumin nanoparticles that are sensitive to pH have been designed to swell or dissolve, releasing anticancer drugs only at the tumor site (Kobatake, 2022). Likewise, heat-labile polypeptide nanoparticles have also demonstrated encouraging outcomes for hyperthermia-assisted cancer therapy, where the release of drugs is stimulated by localized temperature rise (Shinn et al., 2022). The multifunctional nature of PBNPs has greatly expanded their applications in advanced biomedical fields,

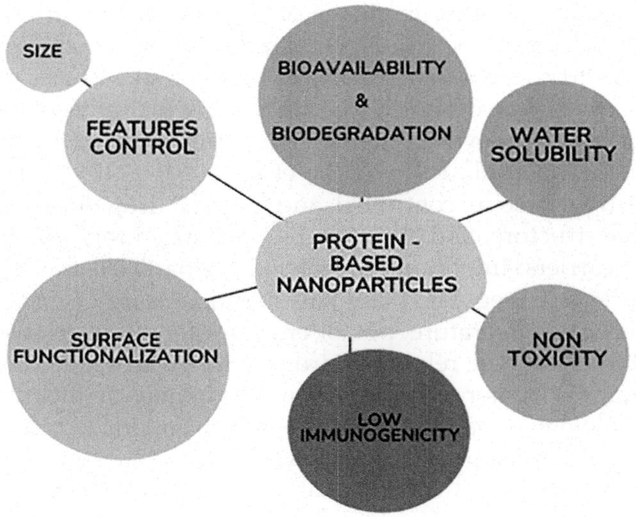


**FIGURE 25.3** Major advantages of protein-based nanoparticles for drug delivery. *Reused from Ferraro, C., Dattilo, M., Patitucci, F., Prete, S., Scopelliti, G., Parisi, O.I., Puoci, F., 2024. Exploring protein-based carriers in drug delivery: a review. Pharmaceutics 16 (9). Under CC BY license.*

including targeted cancer therapy, vaccine delivery, gene transfer, and immunomodulation (Ediriweera et al., 2025). In cancer therapy, PBNPs can be paired with tumor-targeting ligands to concentrate at the disease site and release drugs more effectively. In vaccine development, their biodegradable nature and ability to mimic pathogen-like structures boost antigen presentation and strengthen immune activation (Ferraro et al., 2024). As a result, the need for protein-based nanoparticles has increased dramatically in recent years, promoting studies on scalable production methods, safety evaluation, and clinical translation.

## 1.8 Importance in drug delivery system

PBNPs, are becoming a more creative and useful tool for modern drug delivery. They are very effective carriers because of their special capacity to combine biological compatibility with functional flexibility. These nanoparticles are a safer substitute for many synthetic polymer-based delivery systems because they are made from naturally occurring proteins like casein, albumin, gelatin, and silk fibroin and have outstanding biocompatibility, non-immunogenicity, and biodegradability (Zaher et al., 2023; Deivayanai et al., 2025). One of the biggest advantages of PBNPs is their capacity to transport a broad range of therapeutic agents, such as proteins, peptides, hydrophilic and hydrophobic small molecules, and nucleic acids. This adaptability enhances drug solubility, stability, and bioavailability, increasing the efficacy of treatments (Kianfar, 2021). Additionally, the presence of various reactive groups in proteins, such as amines, carboxyls, and thiols allow them to be chemically modified and linked with targeting ligands. This makes protein-based nanoparticles well-suited for delivering drugs directly to specific cells or tissues.

The accuracy of drug delivery can be increased by functionalising PBNPs with targeting ligands like antibodies, aptamers, peptides, or small molecules (like folic acid) in addition to their encapsulating capabilities. This enables receptor-mediated absorption in certain cell types (Eweje et al., 2024). Off-target toxicity and poor therapeutic index are two obstacles that this active targeting approach helps to address, particularly in illnesses like cancer or chronic inflammatory disorders. PBNP can also be designed to react to particular physiological signals, like pH, temperature, or enzyme levels, enabling the drug payload to be released in a precise and timely manner (Fan et al., 2017; Yadav et al., 2020). PNBPs offer a highly advanced and reliable approach for precise, controlled, and targeted drug delivery. Their excellent biocompatibility, flexible structure, and ability to be customized for specific targets make them especially effective carriers. Importantly, protein nanoparticles may be designed to respond to stimuli, which enables regulated and site-specific release of drugs in anticipation of physiological triggers like temperature, pH, or enzymes found in sick tissues (Li et al., 2023; Liu et al., 2022). To activate the release of drugs from protein nanocarriers solely at the target region, for example, tumor microenvironments frequently include an acidic pH or particular proteases. Protein nanoparticles can also exhibit prolonged blood circulation and avoid early filtration by the mononuclear phagocyte system (MPS), which enhances the therapeutic index and lowers off-target toxicity (Zaher et al., 2023). Clinically authorized examples of PBNP delivery systems, such Abraxane (albumin-bound paclitaxel), have confirmed their viability and potential for translation (Danhier et al., 2015). PBNPs are expected to play a key role in next-generation drug delivery systems as the need for customized and targeted therapies increases, particularly in the treatment of inflammation, cancer, and hereditary illnesses (Ediriweera et al., 2025; Yadav et al., 2020).

## 1.9 Advantages over traditional nanoparticles

PBNPs shine in the realm of drug delivery because they are naturally biodegradable and biocompatible, made from materials our bodies recognize and can safely break down (Defrates et al.). This means they are much less likely to trigger harmful immune reactions compared to synthetic carriers. Once they have done their job delivering medicine, our bodies can easily dismantle them, helping to minimize long-term accumulation and unwanted side effects (Outlook, 2023; Hua et al., 2024). Recent developments in self-assembling protein structures have made it possible to create modular, monodisperse nanoparticles that are structurally precise and reproducible in addition to effectively encasing therapeutic cargo. The next phase of personalized and bioinspired nanomedicines is being made possible by these advancements (Richards et al., 2024). Drug distribution to specific tissues or organs is made easier by the use of surface modification methods, which enhance targeting capabilities (Jain et al., 2018). Only under pathological conditions, such as the acidic tumor microenvironment or intracellular lysosomal compartments, can PBNPs release their therapeutic payload due to their stimuli-responsiveness, and they remain stable during circulation (Zaher et al., 2023; Konate et al., 2021). In addition to increasing treatment efficacy, this behavior reduces side effects and off-target toxicity, which are frequent problems in traditional drug delivery systems (Ganguly et al., 2024).

Protein-based nanoparticles are highly versatile: their structural and surface features can be tailored by genetic engineering or by chemical conjugation to introduce targeting ligands and functional groups, enabling controlled assembly and site-specific delivery (Richards et al., 2024; Habibi et al., 2022). Many protein scaffolds can be endowed with intrinsic cell-penetrating motifs or be fused to cell-penetrating peptides (CPPs), substantially improving intracellular uptake and transfection efficiency compared with many synthetic carriers. Finally, nanoparticles assembled from endogenous or well-characterized biomolecules (for example albumin, ferritin, or silk) generally show favorable biocompatibility and reduced immunogenicity in preclinical studies, lowering the risk of unfavorable immunological responses and long-term accumulation (Hong et al., 2020). Protein-based nanoparticles are exceptionally adaptable—a quality that lets researchers tailor their behavior to specific needs. For instance:

- They can be engineered to respond to environmental cues—such as pH or temperature changes—to trigger cargo release precisely at the target site (Li et al., 2023).
- Many proteins self-assemble into nanostructures under mild conditions, simplifying manufacturing and allowing tight control over particle size and geometry (Ediriweera et al., 2025; Fan et al., 2017).
- In some designs, the protein serves as both the structural matrix and the functional component, which reduces the need for extra modification steps and streamlines synthesis (Kaltbeitzel and Wich, 2023).

Protein nanoparticles greatly improve the stability of encapsulated drugs and biomolecules by shielding them from degradation and extending their circulating half-life. Additionally, these particles can be produced using renewable natural sources and eco-friendly manufacturing processes, aligning with principles of green chemistry and sustainability (Defrates et al.; Ferraro et al., 2024; Tivano and Chiono, 2023). These strengths—robust drug protection, green production, and versatility— PBNPs are emerging as up-and-coming platforms for applications in drug delivery, diagnostics, and tissue engineering.

## 2. Current state of protein-based nanoparticles

### 2.1 Critical application of protein based nanoparticles in drug delivery

Carrier proteins are important in drug delivery systems because they improve the solubility, stability, and targeting of medicinal drugs. Naturally derived proteins, such as ferritin, gelatin, fibroin, and, albumin are biocompatible and biodegradable, reducing toxicity and producing bio-friendly amino acids (Delivery, 2023). This makes protein PBNPs a safer and smarter alternative to many traditional drug delivery systems (3). They can be made without harsh chemicals using methods such as desolvation, emulsions, phase separation, electrospray, or even self-assembly (2). As depicted in below Fig. 25.4, one of the most commonly utilized is human serum albumin (HSA), which has many binding sites and a lengthy plasma half-life, allowing medications to circulate in the body for more extended periods (Ahire et al., 2025).

Protein chemistry allows proteins to form strong and stable connections through hydrophobic, electrostatic, and covalent bonds that help hold drugs securely in place. It facilitates the attachment of targeted molecules such as peptides or antibodies, enabling treatments to be directed toward the appropriate cells or tissues. This approach enhances precision and

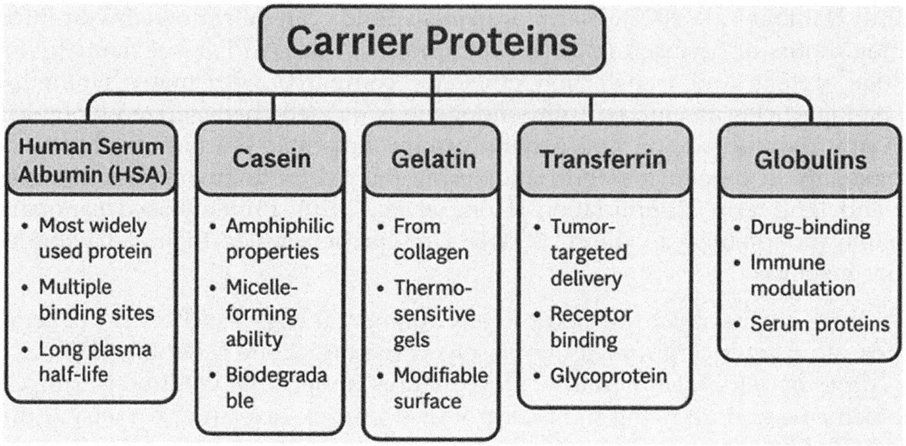


**FIGURE 25.4** Types of carrier proteins. *Reused from Ahire, E.D., Savaliya, N., Makwana, K.V., Salave, S., Banth, M. K., Bhavsar, B., Khunt, D., Prajapati, B.G., 2025. Protein-bound nano-injectable suspension: unveiling the promises and challenges. Appl. Nano 6 (2), 1–28. Under CC BY license.*

minimizes unwanted effects(Hong et al., 2020; Kianfar, 2021). In a study on tumor-targeting techniques, scientists discovered that some proteins, particularly albumin, have a natural ability to reach cancer cells. This is because albumin can bind to specific receptors, such as gp60 and SPARC, which are frequently overexpressed in malignancies. This natural affinity allows PBNPs to accumulate at tumor sites, infiltrate cancer cells more efficiently, and remain in circulation for extended periods as mentioned in Fig. 25.4. These characteristics make them highly well-suited to transporting cancer medicines directly to their targets (Miao et al., 2022). One well-known example is Abraxane, a cancer medication that contains paclitaxel in human albumin nanoparticles. This ingenious design eliminates the need for hazardous chemical solvents, allowing the medicine to concentrate more effectively in solid tumors (Can Karaca et al., 2023). Another innovation is zein-based nanoparticles that target LDL receptors, which are abundantly expressed in blood brain barrier (BBB) endothelial cells. These nanoparticles displayed strong receptor affinity and effective translocation across the barrier, supporting their potential for CNS drug delivery (Kesharwani and Gupta, 2023). Similarly, Silk fibroin nanoparticles have been designed to release therapeutic substances in acidic and enzyme-rich tumor environments. These systems have demonstrated in vivo sustained drug release for over 7 days, significantly extending therapeutic exposure (Bin et al., 2022). Gelatin nanoparticles are designed to detect and respond to matrix metalloproteinases (MMP-2 and MMP-9), which are often overexpressed in tumor tissues. This intelligent, enzyme-triggered breakdown ensures that the therapeutic payloads are released primarily at the tumor site, limiting interaction with healthy tissues and mitigating undesirable side effects (Ujnf et al., 2023). In a separate study, the effects of PBNPs on vaccines were investigated. The findings were unexpected. Administration of mRNA-based COVID-19 vaccines induced the endogenous production of nanoparticles, in which antigens were presented in a repetitive, multivalent arrangement. This layout attracts the attention of the immune system, resulting in a more robust and precise response (Hendricks et al., 2025). Their precise size and structure allow them to reach the lymph nodes more effectively, where antigen-presenting cells can readily take them up. This boosts B cell activation and sharpens the immune system's ability to target the threat (Wang et al., 2017).

PBNPs provide clear benefits for infectious disease vaccines, including oral delivery. In practice, this means that a vaccine might be administered as a capsule or drink rather than through a needle, making the process significantly more comfortable for patients, more straightforward to distribute, and easier to scale up for mass immunization programs (Paiva and Vicentini, 2023). Studies have shown that loading insulin into zein nanoparticles can significantly enhance its absorption when administered orally (Reboredo et al., 2022). Casein nanoparticles have shown great potential in increasing the efficacy of orally consumed drugs like resveratrol. In one study, resveratrol encapsulated in casein nanoparticles stayed in circulation for up to 8 h, with an oral bioavailability of around 26.5%, which is almost 10 times higher than unformulated resveratrol. This improvement permits the body to absorb and use the molecule more effectively (Peñalva et al., 2018). Another study on vaccination performance discovered an additional benefit of PBNPs as they might boost immunity in the body on their own, essentially serving as built-in adjuvants and avoiding the need for extra immuno-stimulants (Pati et al., 2018).

## 2.2 Major challenges and limitations of protein based nanoparticles

Proteins may denature or aggregate during nanoparticle formulation or storage, leading to loss of structural integrity, reduced therapeutic efficacy, and potential activation of immune responses. This compromises the overall stability and functionality of the nanoparticle system (Ahire et al., 2025). Protein aggregation increases the complexity of the formulation because clumped proteins may not function properly and may produce undesirable immunological responses. Stability of proteins during formulation and storage is crucial for therapeutic value of nanoparticles. In addition, nanoparticles can become immunogenic if they include foreign proteins or have altered protein structures, leading the immune system to mistake them. This threatens the safety of the formulation by potentially causing allergic symptoms or other hypersensitive reactions. To maximize the efficacy and safety of protein-based drug delivery systems, immunogenicity must be reduced (Wang et al., 2017). Adopting various techniques to increase the stability and solubility of the specific proteins is a beneficial way to stop agglomerates forming. One example is encouraging the use of protective biopolymers or surfactants by concentrating on the analysis of their particular interactions that can stabilize them (Soane et al., 2018).

When PBNPs enter biological settings, they quickly form a "protein corona" consisting of adsorbed biomolecules. This dynamic layer can cause conformational changes, obscure targeting ligands, alter biodistribution, and expose novel epitopes, lowering targeting efficiency while raising the likelihood of immune detection and systemic clearance (Mayordomo et al., 2025). Natural proteins exhibit inherent heterogeneity in terms of size, structure, and molecular weight, resulting in significant batch-to-batch differences during nanoparticle manufacturing. This heterogeneity impairs reproducibility, complicates quality control, and leads to uneven therapeutic performance, posing a significant obstacle for clinical translation and large-scale PBNP production (Kianfar, 2021). Scaling up PBNP synthesis from laboratory to industrial levels poses considerable challenges. These include maintaining a uniform size distribution, consistent drug-loading efficiency, and sterility during large-scale synthesis. Furthermore, the complexity of the processes and the associated high production costs hinder their commercialization and widespread clinical application (Ahire et al., 2025). Because proteins are naturally hydrophilic, protein-based nanoparticles frequently have a limited capacity for long-term drug release. These nanocarriers can reduce the effectiveness of treatment because they easily absorb water, inflate quickly, and explode when their payload is released. Table 25.1 lists the main difficulties and restrictions related to PBNPs. Advanced techniques for regulated protein-based medication delivery are needed to overcome these limitations. Methods like ligand attachment or antibody conjugation surface modification can improve the stability of the nanocarrier and allow for longer, more effective drug releasee (Ferraro et al., 2024).

## 2.3 Recent innovations in protein nanoparticles

As research into PBNP progresses, researchers are becoming increasingly interested in their potential applications beyond traditional ones. Recent research has demonstrated that PBNPs have considerable promise for applications such as targeted protein degradation (TPD) and precision medication delivery. Researchers revealed that these nanoparticles may specifically transport drugs and break down disease-causing proteins, allowing for more efficient and accurate therapies (Hill et al., 2024). This innovative approach makes use of the special qualities of protein nanoparticles, particularly their capacity to self-assemble into stable structures and their biocompatibility, which qualifies them for application in delicate biological settings (Lee, 2018).

A recent study demonstrated that engineered PBNPs can deliver proteolysis-targeting chimeras (PROTACs) to effectively degrade challenging cancer-related proteins such as Ras and c-Myc, which were previously belived as "undruggable" (Hill et al., 2024). Using targeted light exposure, light-activated PROTAC nanoparticles cause protein degradation and photodynamic therapy, which helps eliminate tumors while directing the immune

**TABLE 25.1** Major challenges and limitations of protein-based nanoparticles.

| Limitations of PBNP | Description | Reference |
|---|---|---|
| **Protein denaturation & aggregation** | Loss of structure and clumping during formulation/storage, reducing efficacy and stability. | Ahire et al. (20225) |
| **Immunogenicity & Hypersensitivity** | Foreign or altered proteins may trigger immune or allergic reactions. | Wang et al. (2017) |
| **Protein corona formation** | Adsorbed biomolecules can mask targeting ligands and alter biodistribution. | Mayordomo et al. (2025) |
| **Drug–Protein binding variability** | Natural protein heterogeneity affects drug release and consistency. | Kianfar (2021), Ahire et al. (2025) |
| **Scale-up & reproducibility issues** | Difficult to maintain uniform quality and efficiency in large-scale production. | Ferraro et al. (2024) |

system's reaction and preventing harm to healthy tissue. The ClickRNA-PROTAC systems acted as precision tools that were switched on only upon detecting unique genetic signals within cancer cells, dismantling tumor-promoting proteins while leaving healthy cells largely unaffected. Similarly, ultrasound-activated PROTAC prodrugs remain dormant as they circulate through the body and are activated only when ultrasound is applied to the tumor. This allows protein breakdown to occur precisely at the disease site, treating deep-seated cancers while keeping healthy tissues safe. In addition, self-assembling nano-molecular glues (nano-mGlu) are designed to detect unique chemical clues inside tumors, such as unusually high levels of glutathione or hydrogen peroxide. When they pick up these signals, they switch on and stick to harmful proteins, breaking them apart to slow or stop tumor growth (Wang et al., 2023a). Carrier-free chemoimmunotherapy nanoparticles (DPA NPs) are made by directly combining the cancer drug doxorubicin, a tumor-targeting peptide (iRGD), a linker that responds to tumor enzymes, and an immune-activating molecule (MPLA). Once they reach the tumor, they destroy cancer cells in a way that alerts the immune system (Deng et al., 2025).

It has been discovered that ferritin nanocages (FNs) spontaneously seek for transferrin receptor-1, which is commonly observed in tumor cells. Researchers can use genetic or chemical modifications to change these cages into targeted carriers that carry medications or imaging agents directly to malignancies, as illustrated in Fig. 25.5. Active-targeted PBNPs have surface molecules, such as antibodies, peptides (e.g., RGD, EGFR, and SP94), or nanobodies, that direct them to specific receptors on tumor cells. This focused method boosts the extent to which the particles are taken up and the depth of their penetration into tumors, and in certain situations, they can even traverse the BBB to reach cancers in the central nervous system (Sun et al., 2021).

A new technique called photoreactive electrohydrodynamic (EHD) jetting has been developed for the fabrication of PBNPs. Referer to Table 25.2, in this process, a protein solution mixed with light-sensitive crosslinkers is jetted while being continuously exposed to ultraviolet (UV) light. This triggers the proteins to link together mid-air, forming soft, nanogel-like particles in just minutes, rather than the hours or days required by traditional methods

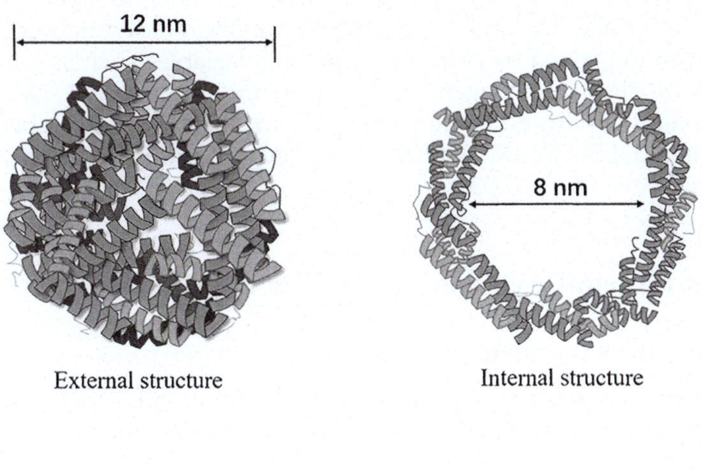


**FIGURE 25.5** External and internal structure of ferritin. *Reused from Sun, X., Hong, Y., Gong, Y., Zheng, S., Xie, D., 2021. Bioengineered ferritin nanocarriers for cancer therapy. Int. J. Mol. Sci. 22 (13). Under CC BY license.*

TABLE 25.2 Recent innovations in protein nanoparticles.

| Innovation | Description & advantages | Reference |
|---|---|---|
| Targeted Protein degradation (TPD) with PROTAC-loaded PNBPs | Delivers PROTACs to break down "undruggable" proteins like c-Myc and Ras; highly precise therapy. | Hill et al. (2024) |
| Light-activated PROTAC nanoparticles | Uses targeted light for combined photodynamic therapy and protein degradation; minimizes damage to healthy tissue. | Lee (2018), Wang et al. (2023a) |
| ClickRNA-PROTAC systems | Activates only in cancer cells with specific genetic signals; spares healthy cells. | Wang et al. (2023a) |
| Ultrasound-activated PROTAC prodrugs | Switches on only with ultrasound at tumor site; enables deep-tissue targeting with minimal side effects. | Wang et al. (2023a) |
| Self-assembling nano-molecular glues (nano-mGlu) | Detect tumor-specific chemical signals to bind and degrade harmful proteins; tumor-specific action. | Wang et al. (2023a) |
| Carrier-free chemoimmunotherapy nanoparticles (DPA NPs) | Combines drug, targeting peptide, enzyme-responsive linker, and immune stimulant; kills cancer and activates immunity. | Deng et al. (2025) |
| Ferritin nanocages for active targeting | Naturally target tumor receptors; can be modified for drug or imaging delivery; potential to cross blood-brain barrier. | Sun et al. (2021) |
| Photoreactive EHD jetting | Rapid UV crosslinking during jetting to create nanogels in minutes; fast and scalable. | Wang et al. |
| Self-driving MTBO synthesis platform | AI-driven optimization speeds PNBP design and testing. | Wang et al. |

A self-driving synthesis platform as in Table 25.2, has been created that builds on knowledge from earlier experiments and applies multitask Bayesian optimization (MTBO) to accelerate protein nanoparticle design (Wang et al.). The process of making albumin-based nanoparticles through desolvation has been improved by carefully adjusting variables such as temperature, pH, and the selection of desolvating agent (such as ethanol or acetone). Once produced, the particles are thoroughly analyzed using techniques such as UV–visible spectroscopy, dynamic light scattering (DLS), FT-IR, FESEM, and TEM to confirm their size, structure, and overall quality (Galiyeva et al., 2023).

# 3. Future prospects of protein-based nanoparticles in drug delivery

## 3.1 Emerging technologies for targeted drug delivery

In recent years, targeted drug delivery systems have drawn major attention for their ability to boost treatment effectiveness while minimizing side effects. Among the different approaches, nanoparticle-based delivery systems are especially promising. They can improve the solubility of poorly water-soluble drugs, enable controlled and sustained release, and allow drugs to be directed more selectively to specific tissues or cells (Yao et al., 2020). A major advantage of nanoparticle-based carriers is that they can be engineered to respond to specific stimuli. This means they can be designed to release a drug only when triggered by certain physiological signals, such as changes in temperature, pH, or enzyme activity. This ensures the medicine is delivered mainly at the intended site of action (Mi, 2020). This strategy cuts down on unwanted side effects by reducing exposure in healthy tissues and makes the drug more effective at the site of disease. New technologies are reshaping modern treatment strategies, especially in the field of targeted drug delivery. Stimuli-responsive nanoparticle systems, which encapsulate medicinal medications in nanoscale carriers that release their contents in response to particular triggers like pH or temperature, are among the most promising. This smart design reduces toxicity, ensures controlled release at the intended site, and improves both solubility and bioavailability (Wang et al., 2023b).

Many applications, including cancer therapy, are now being investigated for these smart nanocarriers. Tumor microenvironments frequently produce distinct chemical and biological reactions that may be utilized to precisely release drugs. Multi-stimuli-responsive designs are becoming more and more common as research progresses because they provide even more safety and control over drug delivery (Das et al., 2020).

Another approach that shows promise for targeted medication delivery is the use of cell-based carriers. By using their natural ability to target specific locations, engineered cells—such as immune cells or modified stem cells—can transport therapeutic substances directly to sick regions. This approach has shown a lot of promise in both regenerative medicine and cancer therapy (Wang et al., 2021). Meanwhile, novel approaches to drug delivery are being made possible by developments in gene-editing technologies, especially CRISPR-Cas9. By changing genes related to medication metabolism or cellular absorption, researchers can create new therapeutic approaches and increase the efficacy of current therapies. Additionally, integrating CRISPR-Cas9 with systems based on nanoparticles improves distribution accuracy and has a lot of potential for the advancement of personalized medicine (Kim et al., 2020; Fengqian et al., 2019). Artificial intelligence (AI) and machine learning (ML) are revolutionizing the design and use of PBNP. These tools let scientists quickly identify the optimal arrangements for producing nanoparticles by analyzing large databases of protein interactions and structures (Singh et al., 2023).

If ML algorithms could also identify critical characteristics like drugloading capacity, release kinetics, and nanoparticle stability, then long-term laboratory testing would be superfluous (Kopac, 2025). AI makes it possible to tailor protein nanoparticle designs according to the unique characteristics of each patient, increasing therapeutic efficacy while reducing side effects. Another tried-and-true method for targeted medication delivery is liposomes. Because of their amphiphilic qualities, these spherical vesicles made of lipid bilayers may encapsulate both hydrophilic and hydrophobic medications, expanding their therapeutic uses. Their innate capacity to engage with cellular membranes promotes better intracellular medication absorption, which raises the efficacy of therapy. Additionally, it has been demonstrated that liposomal formulations maximize pharmacokinetic characteristics, such as extended circulation duration, increased bioavailability, and decreased systemic toxicity, which eventually improves therapeutic results, especially in cancer (Rudnicka et al., 2024; Beltrán-Gracia et al., 2019). ADCs, or antibody-drug conjugates, represent a major advancement in the administration of targeted medications. These bioconjugates enable precise therapeutic delivery to cancerous cells while preserving healthy organs by combining potent cytotoxic medications with monoclonal antibodies that specifically target tumor-associated proteins. By lowering systemic toxicity and increasing therapeutic effectiveness, this approach solidifies ADCs as a fundamental component of precision oncology. Trastuzumab and deruxtecan in HER2-positive tumors are two recent clinical successes that show their increasing importance and therapeutic effect in the treatment of cancer (Zhang, 2019). Personalized medicine is changing as a result of gene-editing strategies like CRISPR-Cas9 and gene-silencing strategies like RNA interference (RNAi). By precisely manipulating DNA sequences, these technologies open the door to customized medications based on each patient's unique genetic profile. By targeting the fundamental causes of hereditary disorders and cancers instead of merely their symptoms, they are laying the foundation for highly individualized therapies (Wang et al., 2016).

In conclusion, the quick development of targeted medication delivery is being driven by developments in molecular medicine, biomaterials, and nanotechnology. These advancements are creating new opportunities for the development of personalized medicine and the treatment of chronic diseases by increasing the therapeutic impact, safety, and accuracy of therapies. Because of ongoing research integrating techniques like gene-editing technologies, liposomal carriers, antibody–drug conjugates, and nanoparticle systems, targeted delivery is anticipated to become a distinctive feature of next-generation therapeutics (Wang et al., 2021, 2023b; Zhang, 2019).

## 3.2 Protein nanoparticles in personalized medicine

Because PBNPs are naturally biocompatible, biodegradable, and structurally versatile, they have drawn a lot of interest as prospective platforms for personalized medicine. Treatment accuracy may be increased by designing these nanocarriers to precisely distribute therapeutic payloads, target certain cells or tissues, and react to physiological cues. PBNPs have the potential to be customized to each patient's unique profile within the context of personalized medicine, optimizing therapeutic benefit and reducing side effects (Hua et al., 2024; Olshefsky et al., 2022). The capacity of PBNPs to encapsulate and transport a variety of therapeutic substances, including as proteins, nucleic acids, and tiny molecules, is one of its main advantages. This adaptability makes it possible to create multipurpose nanocarriers that can combine therapeutic and diagnostic purposes in addition to co-delivering many medications (Kaltbeitzel and Wich, 2023; Zhang et al., 2021). Because they enable simultaneous therapy and real-time monitoring of illness development and therapeutic response, these theranostic applications are particularly beneficial in personalized medicine (Qu et al., 2024; Spada et al., 2021; Obozina et al., 2023).

PBNPs' capacity to identify and attach to particular cell types or tissues is improved by surface targeting ligands. Targeted delivery is a crucial part of individualized therapy because it reduces off-target interactions and makes it easier to distribute medications precisely to sick locations. Protein nanoparticles coupled with aptamers, peptides, or antibodies can preferentially identify cancer cell signals, increasing the therapeutic efficacy of chemotherapy and significantly reducing systemic toxicity (Qu et al., 2024; Obozina et al., 2023). Beyond ligand targeting, the development of stimuli-responsive protein nanoparticles enhances the accuracy of drug delivery. Many times, these nanocarriers are designed to release their payload in reaction to physiological or pathological cues, such pH, temperature, or enzyme activity. By enabling medication release to be adjusted to the microenvironment of sick tissues or the particular physiological factors of each patient, this responsive behavior optimizes therapeutic advantages and reduces adverse effects (Hua et al., 2024; Wu et al., 2020). PBNPs are becoming more widely recognized as adaptable platforms for the creation of vaccines and immunotherapy in the field of personalized medicine. By exhibiting antigens on their surface or encasing immunomodulatory substances, they can elicit specific immune responses. This makes it possible to create vaccinations or immunotherapies that are specifically tailored to a patient's genetic background or traits linked to the disease (Neek et al., 2020; Feng et al., 2024; Xu et al., 2024). In addition to its therapeutic use, PBNPs have significant promise for diagnostic applications. They may be made to recognize biomarkers and molecular signatures connected to illness, enabling real-time monitoring of the course of the condition and the efficacy of therapy (Mao et al., 2024). Such theranostic applications, which integrate therapy and diagnostics, are especially valuable for advancing precision healthcare.

Widespread clinical application is still severely hampered despite these advancements. The conversion of laboratory research into clinical practice is still hampered by regulatory approval, batch-to-batch repeatability, and large-scale manufacture (Xu et al., 2024). To fully utilize protein PBNPs' potential in individualized therapy, these restrictions must be addressed. Nonetheless, they are among the most promising opportunities in the development of nanomedicine because to their capacity to offer individualized therapies, improve patient outcomes, and create quality healthcare. Since PBNPs may mimic normal biological processes and have great biocompatibility and structural tunability, they are becoming an important feature of personalized medicine. The biomimetic surfaces of these nanocarriers, which are derived from proteins like ferritin and albumin, facilitate efficient cellular uptake and extended circulation in vivo. They can be specifically engineered to transport a variety of therapeutic substances, such as small molecules, nucleic acids, and peptides (Eweje et al., 2024; Xu et al., 2023). Furthermore, a lot of protein nanoparticles behave in a stimuli-responsive manner, releasing their therapeutic payload in response to specific triggers at the illness site, such as enzyme activity or an acidic pH. Localized and regulated medication distribution is made possible by this method, which is particularly advantageous for treating difficult illnesses including cancer and genetic disorders (Xu et al., 2023). By tailoring treatments to each patient's own molecular profile, these nanoparticles can dramatically increase therapy efficacy while reducing off-target interactions and negative effects.

Microfluidic technology has gained recognition for increasing medication delivery precision in addition to creating protein nanoparticles. Because microfluidic systems allow for accurate control over mixing, flow, and reaction conditions, they can produce highly uniform, reproducible nanoparticles (Zhang et al., 2023; Ma et al., 2022). This level of control not only simplifies the fabrication of complex delivery systems such as carriers combining multiple therapeutic agents or diagnostics, but also allows real-time monitoring and adjustment, fundamentally enhancing treatment personalization.

### 3.3 Advances in protein engineering for better drug loading and releasing

Protein engineering is now recognized as a promising approach for the development of medication delivery systems. Researchers can develop extremely effective carriers that improve drug loading and offer regulated release by modifying the structural and functional features of proteins (Soheil et al., 2022). The application of self-assembling protein nanoparticles, which spontaneously form stable nanostructures capable of covering therapeutic molecules and preventing them from deterioration during circulation, is one noteworthy advancement in this field (Soheil et al., 2022; Frokjaer and Otzen, 2005).

One of the most important areas of improved medication delivery is the development of stimuli-responsive protein carriers. These carriers undergo conformational changes or controlled disassembly in response to physiological signals such pH variations, temperature changes, or enzymatic activity. Because of its responsiveness, medicinal medicines may be precisely released at targeted bodily locations, increasing efficacy and reducing systemic adverse effects (Torchilin, 2014). All of these developments show how protein engineering may be used to develop next-generation drug delivery systems that combine target selectivity, stability, and accuracy. The construction of fusion proteins, which combine drug-binding domains with targeting modules, is another recent development in protein engineering. These modified structures serve as dual-purpose systems that not only enable effective drug encapsulation but also identify certain receptors on target cells. This dual feature reduces off-target toxicity and offers considerable therapeutic benefits by improving the precision of medication delivery to sick tissues or organs. In cancer and other illnesses where tailored delivery is crucial to optimizing therapy results, such techniques hold special promise (Mahmood et al., 2023).

Additionally, the creation of protein-based drug carriers has changed as a result of advancements in computational protein design. Conventional approaches mostly used naturally occurring proteins with little variation, but the combination of molecular modeling and artificial intelligence now enables the de novo design of proteins that are suited to particular therapeutic needs (Langan et al., 2019). Researchers can design carriers with specific binding sites for accurate drug encapsulation or programmed conformational transitions for stimuli-responsive release by using algorithms that forecast protein folding, stability, and intermolecular interactions. This rational design strategy offers significant advantages over conventional approaches, optimizing drug-loading efficiency, release kinetics, and stability under physiological conditions (Son et al., 2024). Recent research additionally highlighted the feasibility of building protein switches and self-assembled scaffolds from scratch, thus increasing the availability of protein carriers over naturally occurring templates (Langan et al., 2019). Furthermore, with the increasing expansion of AI-powered platforms like as AlphaFold and RoseTTAFold, the reliability of protein structure prediction has drastically improved, expediting the discovery of innovative drug delivery systems (Lu et al., 2024). All of the above developments in computational protein design are opening the door to highly adaptable, practical, and clinically accessible next-generation delivery systems.

In conclusion, remarkable novel opportunities for drug delivery have been made possible by the combination of protein engineering with supportive platforms like hydrogels and nanomaterials. These hybrid systems bring together the structural strength and versatility of synthetic materials with the biocompatibility, specificity, and responsiveness of engineered proteins. Such composites can accomplish multipurpose capabilities that neither system could yield alone by utilizing the advantages of both constituents (Koseva et al., 2015). For example, protein–nanoparticle hybrids have been used to enhance drug encapsulation efficiency and prolong circulation time, while hydrogel–protein composites enable localized, sustained release at the target site (Koseva et al., 2015; Raza et al., 2018; Weiwei et al., 2017). Typically, these systems exhibit greater stability in physiological environments, higher drug loading capacity, and precisely controllable release profiles, making them highly attractive for applications in cancer therapy, regenerative medicine, and chronic disease management (Sun et al., 2023).

## 3.4 Integration with gene therapy and MRNA-based vaccines

The integration of protein-based nanoparticles with gene therapy and mRNA-based vaccines represents a promising frontier in biomedical research and therapeutic development. While lipid nanoparticles (LNPs) have dominated the clinical landscape, particularly following the success of COVID-19 mRNA vaccines (Lin et al., 2024), protein-based systems offer unique advantages that warrant comprehensive investigation. These systems take advantage of natural biocompatibility and biodegradability of protein, while simultaneously serving as platforms for targeted distribution and increased therapeutic efficacy (Pati et al., 2018). A variety of platforms, such as synthetic protein assemblies, non-viral protein nanocages (PNCs), and viral capsids, can be used to create protein-based nanoparticles (PBNPs) (Wang et al., 2024). These systems have several special qualities that make them attractive for therapeutic applications. Protein nanoparticles have controlled assembly processes, a uniform size distribution, and modifiable inner and outer surfaces (Wang et al., 2024). The ability to modify both genetic and post-translational changes allows for the incredibly flexible design of multifunctional drug delivery vehicles. Compared to synthetic polymers, protein-based systems are more biocompatible and biodegradable, which reduces concerns about adverse effects and prolonged accumulation (Li et al., 2020). Another feature is the types of Protein based systems. The field is divided into three main groups: artificial protein assemblies that are computationally constructed, non-viral protein nanocages made from biological proteins, and viral capsids that use natural assembly techniques (Wang et al., 2024). With viral capsids delivering well-characterized structures, non-viral PNCs lowering immunogenicity concerns, and artificial assemblies allowing for precise engineering for particular uses, each group has unique benefits (Hendricks et al., 2025).

PBNPs are designed to encapsulate and shield nucleic acids, such therapeutic genes or plasmid DNA, from deterioration in the circulation in the context of gene therapy (Wang et al., 2024). By targeting certain cell types or tissues, these nanocarriers can maximize gene transport efficiency while reducing off-target consequences. Surface alterations improve treatment specificity and decrease off-target effects by enabling tailored administration to particular cell types (Xiao et al., 2022). Recent developments show how several treatment modalities may be integrated with protein nanoparticles. Cholesteryl-based biodegradable cationic lipidoid nanoparticles, for example, have been successfully used to distribute proteins and mRNA through genome engineering in the tissues of the brain, spleen, lung, and skeletal muscle (Li et al., 2020). Despite achieving transfection efficacies that are on par with established techniques, these systems show noticeably lower cytotoxicity (Li et al., 2020). To facilitate distribution to certain cell types, protein nanoparticles can be functionalized with peptides, antibodies, or other targeting ligands (Wittena et al., 2023). In gene therapy, where accurate cellular localization is crucial for both therapeutic effectiveness and safety, PBNPs are very useful. Two essential steps for effective gene delivery are cellular uptake and endosomal escape, which can be improved by surface functionalizing PBNPs with cell-penetrating peptides or ligands (Wittena et al., 2023). The therapeutic potential of mRNA-based vaccines has been emphasized by their effectiveness during the COVID-19 pandemic. However, issues including instability, enzymatic degradation susceptibility, and strict cold-chain requirements continue to restrict broad use. By stabilizing and delivering mRNA vaccines, protein nanoparticles provide a viable platform to overcome these constraints. Encapsulation in protein-based nanostructures improves intracellular trafficking, promotes effective cellular absorption, and shields mRNA from nucleases. In addition to boosting vaccine potency, this strategy may also enhance immunogenicity, lower dose requirements, and streamline production and delivery procedures (Lin et al., 2024; Pardi et al., 2018).

The protein shell of PBNPs functions as a barrier to ribonuclease activity, effectively preventing extracellular mRNA degradation and maintaining mRNA integrity throughout storage and transportation (Lin et al., 2024). The integrity of mRNA is maintained throughout storage and transit by the protein shell, which serves as a barrier to stop ribonuclease destruction (Wang et al., 2024). In situations with limited resources, this protection is crucial for preserving the effectiveness of immunizations and for room-temperature storage. Protein nanoparticles may enhance immune responses in a number of ways. They can function as adjuvants, promoting immune cell activation and antigen presentation (Lin et al., 2024). In environments with limited resources, this protective effect is especially crucial for preserving vaccination efficacy and for storage in ambient conditions. Furthermore, by acting as adjuvants, enhancing antigen presentation, and stimulating immune cells, protein nanoparticles can improve immune responses. Because of their nanoscale size, antigen-presenting cells may more easily absorb them, enhancing T and B cell-mediated immunity (Hendricks et al., 2025). A particularly innovative approach is the use of computationally generated mRNA-launched PBNP vaccines. These approaches combine the advantages of mRNA vaccines' rapid synthesis with the enhanced immunogenicity of PBNP display (Hendricks et al., 2025). The method offered protection against both vaccine-matched and mismatched viral challenges and showed neutralizing antibody levels that were 5–28 times greater than those of membrane-anchored spike protein vaccines (Hendricks et al., 2025). The integration of several fields, such as immunology, materials science, and computational biology, will determine the direction of PBNP delivery systems in the future (Wang et al., 2024). In order to overcome present constraints and fully utilize these systems, an interdisciplinary approach is necessary. The goal of emerging technologies is to create hybrid systems that integrate the benefits of many distribution methods. The next step in therapeutic delivery is the combination of immune modulation capabilities, controlled release characteristics, and targeting mechanisms (Carvalho et al., 2024). Cost-effectiveness, regulatory concerns, and manufacturing scalability must all be addressed for clinical translation to be successful. To get these technologies closer to clinical use, standardized production processes and quality assurance procedures must be established (Wang et al., 2024). Nanoparticles based on proteins have special prospects for personalized medical strategies. They may be tailored to meet the demands of each patient because to their modular architecture, especially in cancer immunotherapy where patient-specific antigens can be added (Pati et al., 2018; Wittena et al., 2023).

A potential yet complex area is the combination of PBNP with mRNA vaccinations and gene therapy. Even while present methods show much promise, further study and improvement are required to get over current obstacles and succeed clinically. Computational design, advanced engineering methods, and interdisciplinary collaboration are required to fully achieve the therapeutic potential of these innovative delivery systems.

## 4. Potential areas of expansion

PBNPs are versatile enough to allow for substantial surface modification and the conjugation of medicinal compounds. They may also be formulated into gels, emulsions, or dried particles, which improve stability in biological settings and during storage. In targeted drug delivery applications, including as cancer therapy, vaccine administration, and pulmonary therapies, PBNPs have demonstrated exceptional potential. They may also be combined with biodegradable polymers to create microspheres, which allow for the controlled and prolonged release of medicinal substances. PBNPs are especially well-suited for clinical applications because of their many benefits, which include biodegradability, low toxicity, and minimum antigenicity. Particle size, surface properties, and surface area are carefully optimized in the design of nanoparticle-based drug delivery systems in order to increase drug-loading efficiency and guarantee accurate pharmacological results. Predictable performance across a range of biological contexts depends on achieving targeted release of active compounds at the desired site of action, as well as maintaining high levels of purity and consistency in particle size and shape. This constancy reduces immunological reactions and reaffirms PBNPs' appropriateness for therapeutic use (Tarhini et al., 2018).

The potential uses of PBNPs have been extended into fields like as cancer, neurological disorders, infectious illnesses, and regenerative medicine by recent developments in nanotechnology and molecular biology. The increasing focus on precision medicine, which customizes treatments to meet the unique requirements of each patient, is also consistent with these advancements. The subsequent sections will highlight the transformational potential of protein-based nanoparticles in tackling intricate healthcare issues by examining important areas where they may be further developed.

### 4.1 Protein nanoparticles in oncology

PBNPs have a lot of potential to improve the effectiveness of cancer vaccinations. These nanoparticles efficiently trigger antigen-specific immune responses against tumor cells by enabling the co-delivery of significant amounts of adjuvants and antigens. Even though this field has seen tremendous advancements, further optimization and a better comprehension of the underlying mechanics are still needed. Combining PBNP-based vaccines with other FDA-approved immunotherapies, including checkpoint inhibitors or immune-modulating drugs, is one way to increase their therapeutic potential (Neek et al., 2019). The enhanced permeability and retention (EPR) effect, which is impacted by tumor-specific pathophysiology and microenvironmental features like leaky vasculature, aberrant angiogenesis, and impaired lymphatic drainage, is primarily responsible for the improved accumulation and deep tissue penetration of PBNPs in solid tumors. To optimize tumor localization by the EPR effect, nanoparticles must be continuously circulated in the bloodstream (Vogel et al., 2001; Maeda et al., 2000). It is crucial to remember that while the EPR effect's effectiveness in passive tumor targeting varies significantly depending on the kind of tumor and patient-specific heterogeneity, it is more noticeable in xenograft mice models (Shi et al., 2020). Receptor-mediated active targeting is a viable strategy for accurate PBNP delivery in addition to passive targeting. This tactic makes use of interactions between protein ligands and receptors that are overexpressed on tumor or endothelial cells, including osteonectin, scavenger receptor class B type 1 (SR-B1), albondin (gp60), low-density lipoprotein receptors (LDLRs), and transferrin receptors (TfRs) (Ho et al., 1978; Elzoghby et al., 2012; Dufès et al., 2013). Nanoparticles are actively taken up by receptor-mediated endocytosis or transcytosis. For example, gp60 (albondin) on endothelial surfaces is the particular binding site for albumin, which causes internalization and active transport into tumor tissues. Albondin and intracellular caveolin-1 interact in this process, causing the cell membrane to invaginate and transcytosis vesicles known as caveolae to develop. The components of albumin and plasma are transported into the extravascular region more easily by these vesicles. As a result, anticancer medications conjugated with or integrated into albumin nanoparticles are effectively transported to the area around tumor cells (Zhao et al., 2018; Motevalli et al., 2019; Kimura et al., 2018).

Hydrophobic anticancer drugs delivered intravenously via solvent-based systems are widely used for treating solid tumors. Although these formulations have contributed to notable clinical advancements, their effectiveness is frequently limited by the toxicities associated with the solvent-based carriers (Horwitz, 2004). Additionally, these delivery methods often restrict tumor penetration due to the formation of large polar micelles, which can result in nonlinear pharmacokinetics and a reduced proportion of unbound drug available for therapeutic action. To overcome these challenges, advanced drug delivery systems have been developed, paving the way for innovative and promising formulations in cancer treatment (Liu et al., 2021).

## 4.2 Applications in neurological disorders

Protein-based nanoparticles (PBNPs) are drawing much attention in neurology because they are naturally compatible with the body, can be engineered for specific purposes, and most importantly, can cross the blood–brain barrier (BBB). This makes them well-suited for carrying medicines straight to the brain (Jain et al., 2018). Fig. 25.6 below illustrates how nanoparticles cross the BBB through different transport pathways.

In Alzheimer's disease (AD), as depicted in Fig. 25.7 below, researchers discovered that gold nanoparticles coated with β-casein can help stop amyloid-beta (Aβ) proteins from clumping together (Sim et al., 2020). β-casein (βCas) is a whey protein with a chaperone-

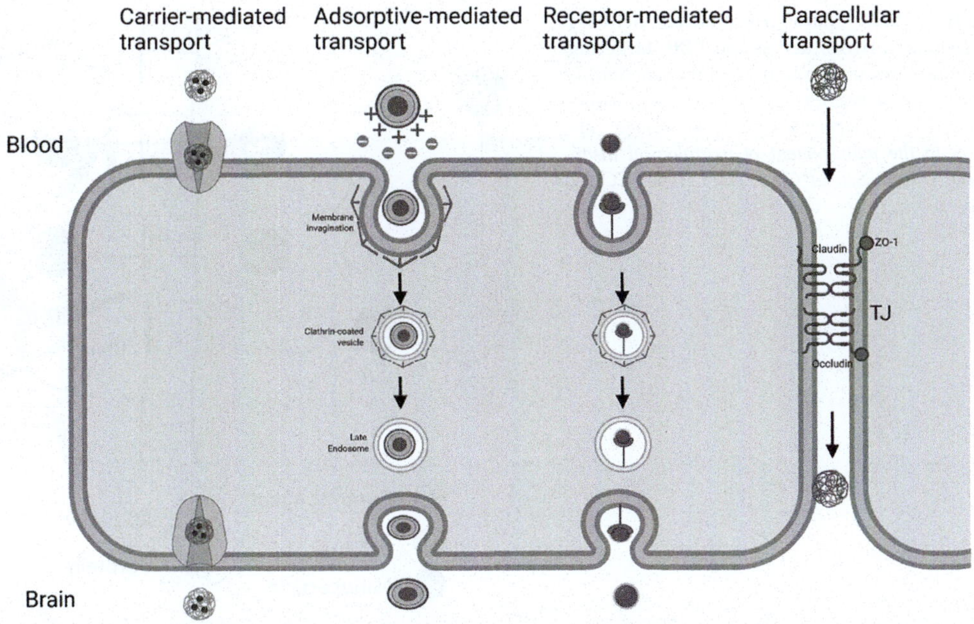


**FIGURE 25.6** Nanoparticles (NPs) cross the blood–brain barrier via paracellular, carrier-mediated, adsorptive-mediated, and receptor-mediated transport, involving tight junctions, membrane interactions, and receptor recognition leading to transcytosis. *Reused from Hersh, A.M., Alomari, S., Tyler, B.M., 2022. Crossing the blood-brain barrier: advances in nanoparticle technology for drug delivery in neuro-oncology. Int. J. Mol. Sci. 23 (8). Under CC BY license.*

like function. The flexible and partially disordered conformation of βCas exposes hydrophobic areas that can interact with a variety of partially folded or misfolded polypeptides, including amyloid beta. βCas attaches to aggregation-prone regions of Aβ, preventing the peptide from forming oligomers and fibrils (Javed et al., 2019). The accumulation of tau proteins is also linked to the advancement of AD and other neurological disorders (Nam et al., 2020). Researchers have found that protein-capped calcium sulfide and iron oxide nanoparticles can prevent tau polymerization and reduce neurofibrillary tangle development (Ngowi et al., 2021).

Parkinson's disease (PD) is another neurological condition characterized by the gradual and selective destruction of nigrostriatal dopaminergic neurons, which results in a lack of the neurotransmitter dopamine (Siracusa et al., 2018). Lactoferrin-coated nanoparticles were developed to take advantage of lactoferrin receptors identified on both the BBB and neurons producing substantia nigra. As seen in Fig. 25.7 above, nanoparticles can penetrate the BBB more efficiently by utilizing this natural transport pathway. In one study, rotigotine was bundled into these lactoferrin-modified nanoparticles and delivered through the nose, resulting in higher and longer-lasting amounts in the brain, particularly in the striatum, than with conventional nanoparticles. This targeted delivery protected neurons and alleviated Parkinson's disease symptoms in a rat model (Wu and Sun, 2018; Bi, 2016). In addition to lactoferrin-modified nanoparticles, numerous other protein-based nanosystems have shown potential for PD treatment. In a study, it was found that albumin/PLGA nanoparticles

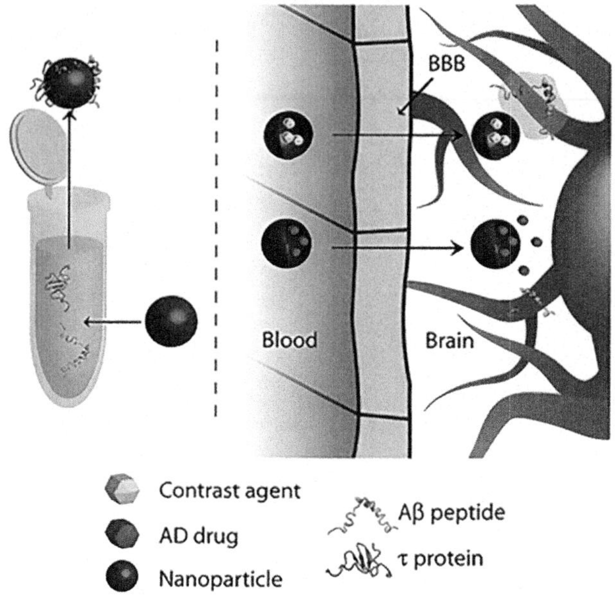


**FIGURE 25.7** Nanoparticle-based delivery of Alzheimer's drugs across the BBB, targeting Aβ peptides and tau proteins. *Reused from Sim, T. M., Tarini, D., Dheen, S.T., Bay, B.H., Srinivasan, D.K., 2020. Nanoparticle-based technology approaches to the management of neurological disorders. Int. J. Mol. Sci. 21 (17), 1–32. Under CC BY license.*

loaded with dopamine (ALNP-DA) can cross the BBB via receptor-mediated transcytosis. In preclinical PD models, ALNP-DA refilled dopamine levels in the nigrostriatal pathway and dramatically improved motor coordination, balance, and sensorimotor performance (Fuentes et al., 2021). Additionally, engineered selenium-human serum albumin nanoparticles have been produced to provide antioxidant and neuroprotective benefits when taken orally, specifically targeting PD (Xu et al., 2023).

The expansion of the CAG trinucleotide repeat in exon one of the huntingtin (HTT) gene located on chromosome four leads to Huntington's disease (HD), which is an autosomal dominant, progressive, and fatal neurological illness (Mignani et al., 2017; Mariane et al., 2022). The production of a mutant huntingtin protein (mHTT) with an unusually long N-terminal polyglutamine (polyQ) tract occurs when the number of CAG repeats in exon one of the HTT gene reaches 40 or more. Primarily through β-sheet structures and polar zipper interactions, this expansion encourages protein misfolding and aggregation, which, in turn, causes the specific neuronal dysfunction and degeneration that characterize Huntington's disease (Priya and Gromiha, 2019). To reduce the production of toxic huntingtin protein aggregates, silk fibroin nanoparticles (SFNs) have been engineered to encapsulate small interfering RNAs (siRNAs) and antisense oligonucleotides (ASOs) to silence the mHTT gene (Mendonça et al., 2023). The β-sheet-rich structure of silk fibroin offers stability and controlled degradation, extending therapeutic exposure and improving neuronal uptake in preclinical HD models (Huang et al., 2023). Similarly, albumin nanoparticles have been used to deliver antioxidant molecules and neuroprotective peptides by effectively penetrating the BBB through albumin's natural receptor-mediated transcytosis (Spada et al., 2021). It has also been demonstrated that peptide-loaded nanoparticle carriers can prevent mHTT aggregation by directly interfering with the misfolding process (Joshi et al., 2019). All of these studies highlight that PBNPs not only improve the bioavailability and brain-targeting of therapeutic agents, but they also offer a platform for combinatorial approaches in HD, where neuroprotection, aggregation inhibition, and gene silencing can be combined in a synergistic way (Riccardi et al., 2021).

In multiple sclerosis (MS), an autoimmune neurodegenerative illness, PBNP have been developed to function as both drug carriers and immune modulators. Albumin nanoparticles coupled with myelin antigens, such as myelin basic protein (MBP), have been shown to develop immunological tolerance by increasing the identification of myelin as self. This method lowered autoimmune reactions and helped restore immunological homeostasis in experimental autoimmune encephalomyelitis (EAE), the standard preclinical MS model (Al-ghobashy et al., 2017).

Amyotrophic lateral sclerosis (ALS), commonly known as motor neuron disease (MND) or Lou Gehrig's disease, is a fast progressive neurodegenerative illness caused by malfunction of neurons that control muscle movement (Wang et al., 2020; Hardiman et al.). In ALS, upper and lower motor neurons gradually degenerate, with TDP-43 and SOD1 aggregation being the two main pathogenic characteristics. Antisense oligonucleotides (ASOs) that target mutant SOD1 are among the therapeutic compounds that have been studied for delivery using albumin nanoparticles. PBNPs improve CNS delivery and extend therapeutic action because albumin naturally bridges the BBB through receptor-mediated transcytosis (Wang et al., 2020). These findings highlight PBNP as an potentially valuable therapy option for neurological diseases, as it improves bioavailability and targeted administration while also reducing the gap between preclinical research and clinical application (Jain et al., 2018; Sim et al., 2020). The following Table 25.3 is an overview of protein-based nanoparticles (PNBPs) in neurological diseases.

**TABLE 25.3** Protein-based nanoparticles (PNBPs) in neurological disorders.

| Neurological disorder | PBNP type | Mechanism of action | References |
|---|---|---|---|
| **Alzheimer's disease (AD)** | β-casein/gold NPs, protein-capped CaS/FeO NPs | Inhibit Aβ aggregation; reduce tau polymerization | Sim et al. (2020), Javed et al. (2019), Nam et al. (2020), Ngowi et al. (2021) |
| **Parkinson's disease (PD)** | Lactoferrin-modified rotigotine NPs; Albumin/PLGA-Dopamine NPs; Selenium-HSA NPs | Nose-to-brain delivery, DA replenishment, antioxidant effects | Siracusa et al. (2018), Wu and Sun (2018), Fuentes et al. (2021), Xu et al. (2023) |
| **Huntington's disease (HD)** | Silk fibroin NPs (siRNA/ASO); Albumin NPs; Peptide-loaded NPs | Gene silencing (mHTT), antioxidant delivery, aggregation inhibition | Spada et al. (2021), Huang et al. (2023) |
| **Multiple sclerosis (MS)** | Albumin NPs conjugated with myelin antigens | Immune tolerance induction, reduced autoimmunity | Al-ghobashy et al. (2017) |
| **Amyotrophic lateral sclerosis (ALS)** | Albumin NPs carrying ASOs | Cross BBB via receptor-mediated transcytosis, prolonged ASO activity | Wang et al. (2020) |

## 4.3 Use in infectious diseases and vaccine delivery

Vaccination is a highly successful public health intervention that prevents millions of deaths and reduces the worldwide burden of infectious diseases. Better vaccination platforms and delivery strategies are essential, as infectious diseases continue to cause substantial mortality and morbidity worldwide (Pathogen and Group, 2024). PBNPs improve vaccine efficacy by imitating the structural characteristics of pathogens and stimulating immune responses via multivalent antigen presentation. Antigens organized repetitively on nanoparticle scaffolds enable efficient crosslinking of B-cell receptors. This recurrent antigen presentation promotes robust germinal center development and affinity maturation compared to soluble antigen forms (Kelly et al., 2020). In addition to the advantages of immunology, PBNP platforms provide valuable benefits, such as scalability and structural stability (Nguyen, 2021). Additionally, PBNPs are being investigated for mucosal vaccine delivery. They are promising candidates for needle-free immunization strategies because of their stability, biocompatibility, and structural flexibility, which could increase access and boost vaccination campaign compliance worldwide (J et al., 2025). From preclinical testing to clinical success, PBNP vaccines have made significant strides in the treatment of various infectious diseases. A computationally created I53-50 nanoparticle containing the SARS-CoV-2 spike protein on an icosahedral scaffold produced strong protective immunity in non-human primates in the case of COVID-19 (Brouwer et al., 2021). Preclinical efficacy was demonstrated in a non-human primate model using ferritin-based constructs exhibiting the receptor-binding domain (RBD), which produced robust immune responses in rhesus macaques (Li et al., 2021). Clinically, the recombinant spike protein nanoparticle vaccine NVX-CoV2373 (Novavax) achieved approximately 90% efficacy in a Phase 3 trial conducted in the United Kingdom and provided significant protection in concurrent Phase 3 investigations in the United States and Mexico (Chadwick et al., 2021). Additional efficacy was confirmed in a randomized trial in South Africa against the Beta (B.1.351) variant (Shinde et al., 2021). The R21/Matrix-M vaccine for malaria, a ferritin-based circumsporozoite nanoparticle mixed with the saponin adjuvant Matrix-M, showed good safety and strong immunogenicity in phase 1 clinical trials in the UK and Burkina Faso (Venkatraman et al., 2025).

In addition to COVID-19 and malaria, several infectious diseases are being treated with PBNP platforms, the most clinically developed of which are virus-like particles (VLPs). Hepatitis B, hepatitis E, and HPV vaccines that are licensed already contain VLPs, and new VLP-based vaccine candidates for HIV, influenza, and norovirus have shown promising results (Mohsen et al., 2017). As stated in Table 25.4, PBNP based on ferritin scaffolds has shown excellent results in improving influenza vaccine effectiveness (Houser et al., 2022). Protein nanoparticles generated from bacteriophages, such as AP205 VLPs, have been investigated using antigens from HIV, SARS-CoV-2, West Nile virus, and influenza (M2e). These particles can also carry long peptide. Since these particles are incapable of replicating, they elicit potent B cell responses while remaining totally harmless (Zhang et al., 2020; Neilsen et al.). Scientists are using encapsulin nanoparticles as vaccine platforms, which are protein cages made by bacteria. This makes it easier for immune cells to obtain antigens and greatly increases T cell responses to specific antigens in preclinical models (Michel-souzy et al., 2021; Lagoutte et al., 2018). Overall, the versatility of protein-based nanoparticles lies in their capacity to display antigens and their potential to address issues of cost-effective

**TABLE 25.4** Protein-based nanoparticles (PNBPs) for infectious disease vaccines.

| PNP system | Target disease | Reference |
|---|---|---|
| **Ferritin nanoparticles** | Influenza, COVID-19, Malaria | Li et al. (2021), Houser et al. (2022) |
| **Virus-like particles (VLPs)** | Hepatitis B, Hepatitis E, HPV, HIV, Influenza, Norovirus | Mohsen et al. (2017) |
| **Encapsulin nanocages** | HIV, Influenza, SARS-CoV-2 | Michel-souzy et al. (2021), Lagoutte et al. (2018) |
| **Protein nanocages (I53-50, AP205, etc.)** | COVID-19, HIV, West Nile virus | Brouwer et al. (2021), Zhang et al. (2020), Neilsen et al. |
| **NVX-CoV2373 (Novavax)** | COVID-19 (incl. Beta variant) | Chadwick et al. (2021), Shinde et al. (2021) |
| **R21/Matrix-M** | Malaria | Venkatraman et al. (2025) |

manufacturing, equitable access, and innovative delivery systems, making them key components of future vaccine strategies in veterinary and human medicine (Shetty et al., 2024). Below mentioned Table 25.4 summarizes the role of protein-based nanoparticles (PNBPs) for infectious disease vaccines.

## 4.4 Opportunities in tissue engineering and regenerative medicine

Tissue engineering and regenerative medicine offer transformative potential in healthcare by overcoming the inherent limitations of conventional therapeutic approaches. Advancements in biomaterials, stem cell technology, and 3D bioprinting have enabled the production of functional tissue and organ structures, giving new possibilities for treating severe injuries and degenerative diseases (Loukelis et al., 2024). Recent studies underscore significant progress in 3D bioprinting while also pointing to the rise of 4D and 5D approaches that allow the creation of dynamic, adaptable constructs designed to replicate better the complexity of native tissue structures (Stanislav and Hammer, 2025; Agarwal et al., 2025). PBNPs, which are made from naturally occurring biomolecules such as collagen, elastin, albumin, and silk fibroin, have shown significant promise as powerful tools to promote therapeutic outcomes in recent developments in tissue engineering and regenerative medicine (Hogan et al., 2023). Among the most commonly researched systems, silk fibroin nanoparticles have proven to be extraordinarily useful in the regulated administration of growth factors, thus boosting cellular proliferation and lineage-specific differentiation to accelerate tissue regeneration (Luo et al., 2023). Similarly, as referred in Table 25.5, albumin-based nanoparticles are being investigated for their dual utility as therapeutic carriers and cellular scaffolds, affording the benefit of simultaneously encapsulating bioactive chemicals while producing a matrix conducive to cell adhesion and migration (Murphy et al., 2025). As stated in Table 25.5, Collagen nanoparticles provide scaffolding and adjustable drug release. They have been used as vehicles for systemic therapeutic delivery, in the healing of skin

TABLE 25.5 Protein-based nanoparticles (PNBPs) in tissue engineering and regenerative medicine.

| Material/PNBP | Application area | References |
|---|---|---|
| **Silk fibroin nanoparticles** | Wound healing, tissue regeneration | Luo et al. (2023) |
| **Albumin nanoparticles** | Scaffold & drug delivery | Murphy et al. (2025) |
| **Collagen nanoparticles** | Skin, vascular, bone, cartilage repair | Arun et al. (2021) |
| **Casein-derived nanoparticles** | Bone tissue engineering | Zhang et al. (2024), Khatun et al. (2022) |
| **Elastin-incorporated nanostructures** | Vascular scaffolds | Selvaras et al. (2023), Wang et al. (2023c) |

wounds, in the construction of vascular and bone tissue, and in the repair of cartilage and nerves (Arun et al., 2021).

In bone tissue applications, casein-derived nanoparticles have also shown increased osteogenic differentiation by mesenchymal stem cells and are being integrated into composite designs that facilitate bone regeneration (Zhang et al., 2024; Khatun et al., 2022). In vascular tissue engineering, elastin-incorporated nanostructures offer significant mechanical and functional advantages. Electrospun polyurethane membranes containing a chitosan/elastin blend have better integration potential, controlled biodegradation, and antithrombogenic properties (Selvaras et al., 2023; Wang et al., 2023c). On a larger scale, extracellular matrix (ECM) components, such as collagen, gelatin, fibrin, and glycosaminoglycans, are used to create nanoparticles that enhance medication delivery, alter immune responses, and promote tissue-specific reconstruction (Hogan et al., 2023).

## 5. Conclusion

PBNPs have emerged as a transformative class of biomaterials that combine natural compatibility with advanced engineering possibilities. Their inherent biocompatibility, biodegradability, and structural tunability give them a distinct edge over synthetic carriers, enabling safe, stable, and efficient drug delivery systems. Over the years, research has demonstrated their ability to encapsulate small molecules, proteins, nucleic acids and, peptides, thereby addressing critical challenges in solubility, stability, and controlled release of therapeutics. These advantages have made PBNPs increasingly relevant not only in oncology, where they are already clinically established, but also across a spectrum of biomedical applications. Current advances highlight how specific proteins such as gelatin, casein, albumin, silk fibroin, ferritin, and zein—are being exploited for their multifunctional roles Albumin-based systems have already proved their therapeutic effectiveness, with formulations such as Abraxane demonstrating both safety and efficacy in cancer therapy via receptor-mediated cellular absorption. Additionally, ferritin nanocages, elastin-based constructions, and silk fibroin nanoparticles each bring unique physicochemical properties that increase the possibilities for targeted drug delivery and controlled release. Collectively, these examples demonstrate how PBNPs can be used as both drug delivery platforms and flexible functional biomaterials. One prominent feature of these nanoparticles is their capacity to cross biological barriers, particularly BBB making them extremely promising for treating neurological illnesses. Preclinical studies have demonstrated that casein- and albumin-based systems can reduce harmful protein aggregation, deliver neuroprotective substances, and aid in the restoration of neurotransmitter balance in conditions such as Parkinson's, Alzheimer's, Huntington's disease, multiple sclerosis, and amyotrophic lateral sclerosis.

PBNPs have demonstrated great potential in both vaccine delivery and the treatment of infectious illnesses. Their ability to display several antigens at once and act as natural immune boosters makes them perfect for generating long-lasting immune protection. This potential is already shown by clinical successes: the R21/Matrix-M malaria vaccine and the Novavax COVID-19 vaccine (NVX-CoV2373) both rely on PBNP platforms and have shown effectiveness. The development of ferritin scaffolds, virus-like particles, and encapsulin nanocages as viable vaccination candidates against influenza, HIV, and other viral threats highlights the long-term relevance of PBNPs in preventive medicine. Proteins including collagen, albumin, elastin, and silk fibroin are used as scaffolding and delivery systems in the rapidly developing disciplines of tissue engineering and regenerative medicine. In the form of nanoparticles, they can stimulate cell adhesion, development, and specialization while also releasing growth factors and other bioactive compounds in a regulated way. These characteristics make them useful for a number of procedures, such as wound healing, vascular grafting, bone and cartilage regeneration, and nerve restoration. It is anticipated that characteristics including ligand-based targeting, stimuli responsiveness, and AI-guided design would improve the therapeutic accuracy of PBNPs in the future. While microfluidic methods offer solutions for repeatability and scale-up manufacturing, hybrid technologies that mix proteins with polymers or inorganic materials may enhance stability and make large-scale production more feasible. Long-term safety, possible immunological responses, regulatory approval, and the need for economical production procedures are some of the major obstacles that still need to be overcome.

In conclusion, the paradigm change from traditional, one-size-fits-all therapy to precision and personalized care is best shown by protein-based nanoparticles. They are vital tools for treating complicated disorders ranging from cancer and neurodegeneration to infectious diseases and tissue damage because of their inherent compatibility with biological systems and sophisticated engineering techniques. Clinical translation still faces obstacles, but as biotechnology, nanotechnology, and computational sciences continue to combine, their full promise should be realized. As a result, PBNPs have the potential to become essential components of next-generation therapeutic and preventative healthcare solutions, rather than merely supporting agents.

## Acknowledgment

The author (Prashant Kesharwani) acknowledges the financial support from the Indian Council of Medical Research (ICMR), New Delhi, India, through Extramural Research Grants.

## References


Afzal, O., Altamimi, A.S.A., Nadeem, M.S., Alzarea, S.I., Almalki, W.H., Tariq, A., Mubeen, B., Murtaza, B.N., Iftikhar, S., Riaz, N., and Kazmi, I. (2022) Nanoparticles in Drug Delivery: From History to Therapeutic Applications. 1–27.

Agarwal, T., Onesto, V., Banerjee, D., Guo, S., Polini, A., Vogt, C., Viswanath, A., Esworthy, T., Cui, H., O'Donnell, A., Vajanthri, K.Y., Moroni, L., Ozbolat, I.T., Panoskaltsis-Mortari, A., Zhang, L.G., Costantini, M., Maiti, T.K., 2025. 3D bioprinting in tissue engineering: current state-of-the-art and challenges towards system standardization and clinical translation. Biofabrication 17 (4), 042003.

Ahire, E.D., Savaliya, N., Makwana, K.V., Salave, S., Banth, M.K., Bhavsar, B., Khunt, D., Prajapati, B.G., 2025. Protein-bound nano-injectable suspension: Unveiling the promises and challenges. Applied Nano 6 (2), 1–28.

Al-ghobashy, M.A., Elmeshad, A.N., Abdelsalam, R.M., Nooh, M.M., 2017. Development and pre-clinical evaluation of recombinant human myelin basic protein nano therapeutic vaccine in experimental autoimmune encephalomyelitis mice animal model. Sci. Rep. 1–16 (October 2016).

Arun, A., Malrautu, P., Laha, A., and Luo, H. (2021) applied sciences Collagen Nanoparticles in Drug Delivery Systems and Tissue Engineering.

Beltrán-Gracia, E., López-Camacho, A., Higuera-Ciapara, I., Velázquez-Fernández, J.B., Vallejo-Cardona, A.A., 2019. Nanomedicine Review: Clinical Developments in Liposomal Applications. Springer, Vienna.

Bi, C., 2016. Intranasal delivery of rotigotine to the brain with lactoferrin-modified PEG-PLGA nanoparticles for Parkinson ' s disease treatment. Int. J. Nanomed. 6547–6559.

Bin, L., Yang, Y., Wang, F., Wang, R., Fei, H., Duan, S., Huang, L., Liao, N., Zhao, S., Ma, X., 2022. Biodegradable silk fibroin nanocarriers to modulate hypoxia tumor microenvironment favoring enhanced chemotherapy. Front. Bioeng. Biotechnol. 10 (July), 1–12.

Brouwer, P.J.M., Brinkkemper, M., Maisonnasse, P., Gils, M.J. Van, Grand, R. Le, and Sanders, R.W. (2021) Article Two-component spike nanoparticle vaccine protects macaques from SARS-CoV-2 infection ll Two-component spike nanoparticle vaccine protects macaques from SARS-CoV-2 infection. 1188–1200.

Can Karaca, A., Assadpour, E., Jafari, S.M., 2023. Plant protein-based emulsions for the delivery of bioactive compounds. Adv. Colloid Interface Sci. 316 (June), 1–2.

Carvalho, H.M.B., Fidalgo, T.A.S., Acúrcio, R.C., Matos, A.I., Satchi-Fainaro, R., Florindo, H.F., 2024. Better, faster, stronger: Accelerating mRNA-based immunotherapies with nanocarriers. Wiley Interdiscip. Rev. Nanomed. Nanobiotechnol. 16 (6).

Chadwick, D.R., Clark, R., Cosgrove, C., Galloway, J., Goodman, A.L., Heer, A., Higham, A., Iyengar, S., Jamal, A., Jeanes, C., Kalra, P.A., Kyriakidou, C., Mcauley, D.F., Meyrick, A., Minassian, A.M., Minton, J., Moore, P., Munsoor, I., Nicholls, H., Osanlou, O., Packham, J., Pretswell, C.H., Ramos, A.S.F., Saralaya, D., Sheridan, R. P., Smith, R., Soiza, R.L., Swift, P.A., Thomson, E.C., Turner, J., Viljoen, M.E., Albert, G., Cho, I., Dubovsky, F., Glenn, G., Rivers, J., 2021. Safety and efficacy of NVX-CoV2373 Covid-19 vaccine. N. Engl. J. Med. 1172–1183.

Danhier, F., Feron, O., Préat, V., 2015. To exploit the tumor microenvironment: passive and active tumor targeting of nanocarriers for anti-cancer drug delivery. J. Contr. Release 148 (2010), 135–146.

Das, S.S., Bharadwaj, P., Bilal, M., Barani, M., Rahdar, A., Taboada, P., Bungau, S., Kyzas, G.Z., 2020. Stimuli-responsive polymeric nanocarriers for drug. Polymers 12, 1–45.

Defrates, K., Markiewicz, T., Gallo, P., Rack, A., Weyhmiller, A., Jarmusik, B., and Hu, X. Protein polymer-based nanoparticles: fabrication and medical applications. Int. J. Mol. Sci. 1–20.

Deivayanai, V.C., Thamarai, P., Karishma, S., Saravanan, A., Yaashikaa, P.R., Vickram, A.S., 2025. Advances in nanoparticle-mediated cancer therapeutics: Current research and future perspectives. Cancer Pathog. Ther. 3 (September 2024), 293–308.

Delivery, C. (2023) Organic and Biogenic Nanocarriers as Bio-Friendly Systems.

Deng, B., Kong, Y., Ma, Y., Zhan, Y., Sun, Y., Wang, R., Huang, P., Liu, L., 2025. A novel carrier-free nanoparticle with stable distinctive three-dimensional structure for tumor-targeted precision chemoimmunotherapy. J. Nanobiotechnol. 23 (1).

Dufès, C., Al Robaian, M., Somani, S., 2013. Transferrin and the transferrin receptor for the targeted delivery of therapeutic agents to the brain and cancer cells. Ther. Deliv. 4 (5), 629–640.

Ediriweera, G.R., Chang, Y., Yang, W., Whittaker, A.K., Fu, C., 2025. Self-assembled protein – polymer nanoparticles via photoinitiated polymerization-induced self-assembly for targeted and enhanced drug delivery in cancer therapy. Molecules 30 (4), 856.

Elzoghby, A.O., Samy, W.M., Elgindy, N.A., 2012. Protein-based nanocarriers as promising drug and gene delivery systems. J. Contr. Release 161 (1), 38–49.

Eweje, F., Walsh, M.L., Ahmad, K., Ibrahim, V., Alrefai, A., Chen, J., Chaikof, E.L., 2024. Protein-based nanoparticles for therapeutic nucleic acid delivery. Biomaterials 305 (December 2023).

Fan, T., Yu, X., Shen, B., Sun, L., 2017. Peptide self-assembled nanostructures for drug delivery applications. J. Nanomater. 2017, 16.

Feng, T., Hu, J., Wen, J., Qian, Z., Che, G., Zhou, Q., Zhu, L., 2024. Personalized nanovaccines for treating solid cancer metastases. J. Hematol. Oncol. 4.

Fengqian, C., Martin, A., and Qi, L. (2019) Strategies for nonviral nanoparticle-based delivery of CRISPR Cas9.

Ferraro, C., Dattilo, M., Patitucci, F., Prete, S., Scopelliti, G., Parisi, O.I., Puoci, F., 2024. Exploring protein-based carriers in drug delivery: A review. Pharmaceutics 16 (9).

Frokjaer, S., Otzen, D.E., 2005. Protein drug stability: A formulation challenge. Nat. Rev. Drug Discov. 4 (4), 298–306.

Fuentes, V.M., Mayer, A.B., Lima, M.R., Geraldes, L.R., Zanotto, L.N., Moreira, K.G., Martins, O.P., Piva, H.L., Sueli, M., Felipe, S., Amaral, A.C., Bocca, A.L., Tedesco, A.C., Mortari, M.R., 2021. Dopamine - loaded nanoparticle systems circumvent the blood – brain barrier restoring motor function in mouse model for Parkinson ' s disease. Sci. Rep. 1–16.

Galiyeva, A., Daribay, A., Zhumagaliyeva, T., Zhaparova, L., Sadyrbekov, D., Tazhbayev, Y., 2023. Human serum albumin nanoparticles: Synthesis, optimization and immobilization with antituberculosis drugs. Polymers 15 (13).

Ganguly, S.C., Mahanti, B., Ganguly, S., Majumdar, S., 2024. Potential paradigm of proteins and polypeptides-based nanostructures in drug delivery and management of maladies: a review. J. Nanoparticle Res. 26 (4), 1–21.

Habibi, N., Mauser, A., Ko, Y., Lahann, J., 2022. Protein nanoparticles: Uniting the power of proteins with engineering design approaches. Adv. Sci. (Weinh.) 2104012, 1–34.

Hardiman, O., Al-chalabi, A., Chio, A., Corr, E.M., Robberecht, W., Shaw, P.J., and Simmons, Z. Amyotrophic lateral sclerosis.

Hendricks, G.G., Grigoryan, L., Navarro, M.J., Catanzaro, N.J., Hubbard, M.L., Powers, J.M., Mattocks, M., Treichel, C., Walls, A.C., Lee, J., Ellis, D., Wang, J.Y.J., Cheng, S., Miranda, M.C., Valdez, A., Chao, C.W., Chan, S., Men, C., Johnson, M.R., Zepeda, S.K., Ols, S., Hui, H., Wu, S.-Y., Lujan, V., Muramatsu, H., Lin, P. J.C., Sung, M.M.H., Tam, Y.K., Leaf, E.M., Pardi, N., Baric, R.S., Pulendran, B., Veesler, D., Schäfer, A., King, N.P., 2025. Computationally designed mRNA-launched protein nanoparticle immunogens elicit protective antibody and T cell responses in mice. Sci. Transl. Med. 17 (820), eadu2085.

Hill, S.K., England, R.M., Perrier, S., 2024. Modular design of cyclic peptide – polymer conjugate nanotubes for delivery and tunable release of anti-cancer drug compounds. J. Contr. Release 367 (January), 687–696.

Ho, Y.K., Smith, R.G., Brown, M.S., Goldstein, J.L., 1978. Low-density lipoprotein (LDL) receptor activity in human acute myelogenous leukemia cells. Blood 52 (6), 1099–1114.

Hogan, K.J., Perez, M.R., Mikos, A.G., 2023. Extracellular matrix component-derived nanoparticles for drug delivery and tissue engineering. J. Contr. Release 360 (March), 888–912.

Hong, S., Choi, D.W., Kim, H.N., and Park, C.G. (2020) Protein-Based Nanoparticles as Drug Delivery Systems. 1–29.

Horwitz, S.B., 2004. Personal recollections on the early development of Taxol. J. Nat. Prod. 67 (2), 136–138.

Houser, K. V, Chen, G.L., Carter, C., Crank, M.C., Nguyen, T.A., Claudia, M., Florez, B., Berkowitz, N.M., Mendoza, F., Hendel, C.S., Gordon, I.J., Coates, E.E., Vazquez, S., Stein, J., Case, C.L., Lawlor, H., Carlton, K., Gaudinski, M.R., Strom, L., Hofstetter, A.R., Liang, C.J., Narpala, S., Hatcher, C., Gillespie, R.A., Creanga, A., Kanekiyo, M., Raab, J.E., Andrews, S.F., Zhang, Y., Yang, E.S., Wang, L., Leung, K., Kong, W., Freyn, A.W., Nachbagauer, R., Palese, P., Bailer, R.T., Mcdermott, A.B., Koup, R.A., Gall, J.G., Arnold, F., Mascola, J.R., Graham, B.S., Ledgerwood, J.E., and Team, S. (2022) adults: a phase 1 trial. 28 (February).

Hua, Y., Qin, Z., Gao, L., Zhou, M., Xue, Y., Li, Y., Xie, J., 2024. Protein nanoparticles as drug delivery systems for cancer theranostics. J. Contr. Release 371 (June), 429–444.

Huang, X., An, Y., Yuan, S., Chen, C., Shan, H., Zhang, M., 2023. Silk fibroin carriers with sustained release capacity for treating neurological diseases. Front. Pharmacol. 1–17. May.

J, L.A.A., Pa, P., Seng, C.Y., Haeng, J., Lee, S.E., 2025. Protein nanocages: A new frontier in mucosal vaccine delivery and immune activation. Hum. Vaccines Immunother. 21 (1).

Jain, A., Singh, S.K., Arya, S.K., Kundu, S.C., Kapoor, S., 2018. Protein nanoparticles: promising platforms for drug delivery applications. ACS Biomater. Sci. Eng. 4 (12), 3939–3961.

Javed, I., Peng, G., Xing, Y., Yu, T., Zhao, M., Kakinen, A., Faridi, A., Parish, C.L., Ding, F., Davis, T.P., Ke, P.C., Lin, S., 2019. Inhibition of amyloid beta toxicity in zebrafish with a chaperone-gold nanoparticle dual strategy. Nat. Commun. 10 (1).

Joshi, A.S., Singh, V., Gahane, A., Thakur, A.K., 2019. Biodegradable nanoparticles containing mechanism based peptide inhibitors reduce polyglutamine aggregation in cell models and alleviate motor symptoms in a drosophila model of huntington' s disease. ACS Chem. Neurosci. 10 (3), 1603–1614.

Kaltbeitzel, J., Wich, P.R., 2023. Protein-based nanoparticles: From drug delivery to imaging, nanocatalysis and protein therapy. Angew. Chem., Int. Ed. 62 (44).

Kelly, H.G., Kent, S.J., Wheatley, A.K., Kelly, H.G., Tan, H., Juno, J.A., Esterbauer, R., Ju, Y., Jiang, W., Wimmer, V. C., Duckworth, B.C., Groom, J.R., Caruso, F., Kanekiyo, M., Kent, S.J., Wheatley, A.K., 2020. Self-assembling influenza nanoparticle vaccines drive extended germinal center activity and memory B cell maturation. germinal center activity and memory B cell maturation JCI Insight 5 (10).

Kesharwani, P., Gupta, N., 2023. Recent advances in nanocarriers for pancreatic cancer therapy. Recent Advances in Nanocarriers for Pancreatic Cancer Therapy 1–461.

Khatun, S., Appidi, T., Rengan, A.K., 2022. Food bioscience casein nanoformulations - potential biomaterials in theranostics. Food Biosci. 50 (PB), 102200.

Kianfar, E., 2021. Protein nanoparticles in drug delivery: animal protein, plant proteins and protein cages, albumin nanoparticles. J. Nanobiotechnol. 19 (1), 1–32.

Kim, D., Le, Q.V., Wu, Y., Park, J., Oh, Y.K., 2020. Nanovesicle-mediated delivery systems for crispr/cas genome editing. Pharmaceutics 12 (12), 1–42.

Kimura, K., Yamasaki, K., Nakamura, H., Haratake, M., Taguchi, K., Otagiri, M., 2018. Preparation and in vitro analysis of human serum albumin nanoparticles loaded with anthracycline derivatives. Chem. Pharm. Bull. 66 (4), 382–390.

Kobatake, E., 2022. Construction of protein nanoparticles for targeted delivery of drugs to cancer cells. Mater. Adv. 6262–6269.

Konate, K., Josse, E., Viv, E., and Deshayes, S. (2021) Peptide-Based Nanoparticles for Therapeutic Nucleic.

Kopac, T., 2025. Leveraging artificial intelligence and machine learning for characterizing protein corona, nanobiological interactions, and advancing drug discovery. Bioengineering 12 (3).

Koseva, N.S., Rydz, J., Stoyanova, E.V., Mitova, V.A., 2015. Hybrid Protein–Synthetic Polymer Nanoparticles for Drug Delivery. Elsevier Inc.

Lagoutte, P., Mignon, C., Stadthagen, G., Potisopon, S., Donnat, S., Mast, J., Lugari, A., Werle, B., 2018. Simultaneous surface display and cargo loading of encapsulin nanocompartments and their use for rational vaccine design. Vaccine 36 (25), 3622–3628.

Langan, R.A., Boyken, S.E., Ng, A.H., Samson, J.A., Dods, G., Westbrook, A.M., Nguyen, T.H., Lajoie, M.J., Chen, Z., Berger, S., Mulligan, V.K., Dueber, J.E., Novak, W.R.P., El-Samad, H., Baker, D., 2019. De novo design of bioactive protein switches. Nature 572 (7768), 205–210.

Lee, E.J., 2018. Recent advances in protein-based nanoparticles. Kor. J. Chem. Eng. 35 (9), 1765–1778.

Li, H., Guo, L., Zheng, H., Li, J., Zhao, X., Li, J., Liang, Y., Yang, F., Zhao, Y., Yang, J., Xue, M., Zuo, Y., Zhou, J., Chen, Y., Yang, Z., Li, Y., Jin, W., Shi, H., He, Z., Li, Q., Liu, L., 2021. Self-assembling nanoparticle vaccines displaying the receptor binding domain of SARS-CoV - 2 Elicit robust protective immune responses in rhesus monkeys. Bioconjug. Chem. 32 (10), 2268.

Li, Y., Yang, G., Gerstweiler, L., Thang, S.H., and C.-X.Z. (2023) Design of Stimuli-Responsive Peptides and Proteins.pdf.

Li, Y., Jarvis, R., Zhu, K., Glass, Z., Ogurlu, R., Gao, P., Li, P., Chen, J., Yu, Y., Yang, Y., Xu, Q., 2020. Protein and mRNA delivery enabled by cholesteryl-based biodegradable lipidoid nanoparticles. Angew. Chem. Int. Ed. 59 (35), 14957–14964.

Lin, Y., Chen, X., Wang, K., Liang, L., Zhang, H., 2024. An overview of nanoparticle-based delivery platforms for mRNA vaccines for treating cancer. Vaccines 12 (7), 1–22.

Liu, G., Yang, L., Chen, G., Xu, F., Yang, F., Yu, H., Li, L., Dong, X., Han, J., Cao, C., Qi, J., Su, J., Xu, X., Li, X., Li, B., 2021. A review on drug delivery system for tumor therapy. Front. Pharmacol. 12.

Liu, T., Li, L., Cheng, C., He, B., Jiang, T., Bokjoh, P.G., Ijob, B., 2022. Emerging prospects of protein/peptide-based nanoassemblies for drug delivery and vaccine development. Nano Res. 15 (8), 7267–7285.

Loukelis, K., Koutsomarkos, N., Mikos, A.G., Chatzinikolaidou, M., 2024. Advances in 3D bioprinting for regenerative medicine applications. Regen. Biomater. 11 (March).

Lu, L., Gou, X., Tan, S.K., Mann, S.I., Yang, H., Zhong, X., Gazgalis, D., Valdiviezo, J., Jo, H., Wu, Y., Diolaiti, M.E., Ashworth, A., Polizzi, N.F., DeGrado, W.F., 2024. De novo design of drug-binding proteins with predictable binding energy and specificity. Science 384 (6691), 106–112.

Luo, L., Zhang, H., Zhang, S., Luo, C., Kan, X., Lv, J., Zhao, P., 2023. Extracellular vesicle - derived silk fibroin nanoparticles loaded with MFGE8 accelerate skin ulcer healing by targeting the vascular endothelial cells. J. Nanobiotechnol. 1–27.

Ma, Z., Li, B., Peng, J., Gao, D., 2022. Recent development of drug delivery systems through microfluidics: From synthesis to evaluation. Pharmaceutics 14 (2), 434.

Maeda, H., Wu, J., Sawa, T., Matsumura, Y., Hori, K., 2000. Tumor vascular permeability and the EPR effect in macromolecular therapeutics: a review. J. Contr. Release 65 (1), 271–284.

Mahmood, T., Shahbaz, A., Hussain, N., Ali, R., Bashir, H., Rizwan, K., 2023. Recent advancements in fusion protein technologies in oncotherapy: A review. Int. J. Biol. Macromol. 230 (November 2022).

Mao, Y., Xie, J., Yang, F., Luo, Y., Du, J., 2024. Advances and prospects of precision nanomedicine in personalized tumor theranostics. Front. Cell Dev. Biol. (December), 1–15.

Mariane, K., Valadão, G., Okabaiasse, B., Mirian, L., Yamaguchi, U., Carolina, A., Bernuci, M.P., 2022. Nanotechnology in improving the treatment of huntington ' s disease: A systematic review. Neurotox. Res. 636–645.

Mayordomo, N.M., Zatarain-Beraza, A., Valerio, F., Álvarez-Méndez, V., Turegano, P., Herranz-García, L., López de Aguileta, A., Cattani, N., Álvarez-Alonso, A., Fanarraga, M.L., 2025. The protein corona paradox: Challenges in achieving true biomimetics in nanomedicines. Biomimetics 10 (5), 1–21.

Mendonça, M.C.P., Sun, Y., Cronin, M.F., Lindsay, A.J., Cryan, J.F., Driscoll, C.M.O., 2023. Cyclodextrin-based nanoparticles for delivery of antisense oligonucleotides targeting huntingtin. Pharmaceutics 15 (2), 520.

Mi, P., 2020. Stimuli-responsive nanocarriers for drug delivery, tumor imaging, therapy and theranostics. Theranostics 10 (10), 4557–4588.

Miao, Y., Yang, T., Yang, S., Yang, M., Mao, C., 2022. Protein nanoparticles directed cancer imaging and therapy. Nano Converg. 9 (1).

Michel-Souzy, S., Hamelmann, N.M., Zarzuela-Pura, S., Paulusse, J.M.J., Cornelissen, J.J.L.M., 2021. Introduction of surface loops as a tool for encapsulin functionalization. Biomacromolecules 22 (12), 5234–5242.

Mignani, S., Bryszewska, M., Zablocka, M., Klajnert-maculewicz, B., Cladera, J., Shcharbin, D., Majoral, J., 2017. Progress in polymer science can dendrimer based nanoparticles fight neurodegenerative diseases ? Current situation versus other established approaches. Prog. Polym. Sci. 64, 23–51.

Mohsen, M.O., Zha, L., Cabral-miranda, G., Bachmann, M.F., 2017. Seminars in immunology major fi ndings and recent advances in virus – like particle ( VLP ) -based vaccines. Semin. Immunol. 34 (August), 123–132.

Motevalli, S.M., Eltahan, A.S., Liu, L., Magrini, A., Rosato, N., Guo, W., Bottini, M., Liang, X.-J., 2019. Co-encapsulation of curcumin and doxorubicin in albumin nanoparticles blocks the adaptive treatment tolerance of cancer cells. Biophys. Rep. 5 (1), 19–30.

Murphy, G., Brayden, D.J., Cheung, D.L., Liew, A., Fitzgerald, M., 2025. Albumin-based delivery systems: Recent advances , challenges , and opportunities. J. Contr. Release 380 (August 2024), 375–395.

Nam, E., Lee, Y.B., Moon, C., Chang, K.A., 2020. Serum tau proteins as potential biomarkers for the assessment of alzheimer's disease progression. Int. J. Mol. Sci. 21 (14), 1–20.

Neek, M., Kim, T.I., Wang, S.-W., 2019. Protein-based nanoparticles in cancer vaccine development. Nanomed. Nanotechnol. Biol. Med. 15 (1), 164–174.

Neek, M., Wang, S., and Comprehensive, F. (2020) HHS Public Access. 15 (1), 164–174.

Neilsen, G., Mathew, A.M., Castro, J.M., Mcfadden, W.M., Wen, X., Ong, Y.T., and Tedbury, P.R. biocontainment level using replicons and virus-like particles. (15).

Ngowi, E.E., Wang, Y.Z., Qian, L., Helmy, Y.A.S.H., Anyomi, B., Li, T., Zheng, M., Jiang, E.S., Duan, S.F., Wei, J.S., Wu, D.D., Ji, X.Y., 2021. The application of nanotechnology for the diagnosis and treatment of brain diseases and disorders. Front. Bioeng. Biotechnol. 9 (March), 1–19.

Nguyen, B. (2021) Protein-based antigen presentation platforms for nanoparticle vaccines.

Obozina, A.S., Komedchikova, E.N., Kolesnikova, O.A., Iureva, A.M., Kovalenko, V.L., Zavalko, F.A., Rozhnikova, T.V., Tereshina, E.D., Mochalova, E.N., Shipunova, V.O., 2023. Genetically encoded self-assembling protein nanoparticles for the targeted delivery in vitro and in vivo. Pharmaceutics 15 (1), 231.

Olshefsky, A., Richardson, C., Pun, S.H., King, N.P., 2022. Engineering self-assembling protein nanoparticles for therapeutic delivery. Bioconjug. Chem. 33 (11), 2018–2034.

Outlook, F. (2023) Biodegradable Biopolymeric Nanoparticles for Biomedical Applications-Challenges and Future Outlook.

Paiva, N.F., Vicentini, F.T.M., 2023. Oral and nasal vaccination: Current prospects, challenges, and impact of nanotechnology-based delivery systems. Braz. J. Pharm. Sci. 59.

Pardi, N., Hogan, M.J., Porter, F.W., Weissman, D., 2018. mRNA vaccines-a new era in vaccinology. Nat. Rev. Drug Discov. 17 (4), 261–279.

Pathogen, I., Group, C., 2024. Global burden associated with 85 pathogens in 2019: A systematic analysis for the Global Burden of Disease Study 2019. Lancet Infect. Dis. 24 (August).

Pati, R., Shevtsov, M., Sonawane, A., 2018. Nanoparticle vaccines against infectious diseases. Front. Immunol. 9 (OCT).

Peñalva, R., Morales, J., González-Navarro, C.J., Larrañeta, E., Quincoces, G., Peñuelas, I., Irache, J.M., 2018. Increased oral bioavailability of resveratrol by its encapsulation in casein nanoparticles. Int. J. Mol. Sci. 19 (9).

Priya, S.B., Gromiha, M.M., 2019. Structural insights into the aggregation mechanism of huntingtin exon 1 protein fragment with different polyQ-lengths. J. Cell. Biochem. 120 (6), 10519–10529.

Qu, N., Song, K., Liu, M., Chen, L., Lee, R.J., Teng, L., 2024. Albumin nanoparticle-based drug delivery systems. Int. J. Nanomed. (May).

Raza, F., Zafar, H., Zhu, Y., Ren, Y., Ullah, A., Khan, A.U., He, X., Han, H., Aquib, M., Boakye-Yiadom, K.O., Ge, L., 2018. A review on recent advances in stabilizing peptides/proteins upon fabrication in hydrogels from biodegradable polymers. Pharmaceutics 10 (1).

Reboredo, C., González-Navarro, C.J., Martínez-López, A.L., Martínez-Ohárriz, C., Sarmento, B., Irache, J.M., 2022. Zein-based nanoparticles as oral carriers for insulin delivery. Pharmaceutics 14 (1).

Riccardi, C., Napolitano, F., Montesarchio, D., Sampaolo, S., Melone, M.A.B., 2021. Nanoparticle-guided brain drug delivery: Expanding the therapeutic approach to neurodegenerative diseases. Pharmaceutics 13 (11), 1897.

Richards, B.A., Goncalves, A.G., Sullivan, M.O., Chen, W., 2024. Engineering protein nanoparticles for drug delivery. Curr. Opin. Biotechnol. 86.

Rudnicka, K., Lemieszek, P., Krukar, K., Pustelniak, M., Miga-Orczykowska, N., Sajkiewicz, I., Wójtowicz, J., Jasiuk, I., Łukaszewska, E., Kister, K., 2024. Targeted cancer therapy: The role of liposomes in oncology: A literature review. Katarzyna. (February) 4–6.

Ruoslahti, E., Bhatia, S.N., Sailor, M.J., 2010. Targeting of drugs and nanoparticles to tumors. J. Cell Biol. 188 (6), 759–768.

Samathoti, P., Komarla, R., Sarad, K., Naik, P., 2025. The Role of Nanomedicine and Artificial Intelligence in Cancer Health Care: Individual Applications and Emerging Integrations — a Narrative Review. Springer US.

Selvaras, T., Ali, S., Rathosivan, A., Kumar, S., Sivakumar, J., Suhaini, S., Saidin, S., 2023. Biodegradable and antithrombogenic chitosan/elastin blended polyurethane electrospun membrane for vascular tissue integration. J. Biomed. Mater. Res. B Appl. Biomater. 1171–1181. December 2022.

Shetty, S., Alvarado, P.C., Pettie, D., Collier, J.H., 2024. Next-generation vaccine development with nanomaterials: Recent advances, possibilities, and challenges. Annu. Rev. Biomed. Eng. 273–306.

Shi, Y., van der Meel, R., Chen, X., Lammers, T., 2020. The EPR effect and beyond: strategies to improve tumor targeting and cancer nanomedicine treatment efficacy. Theranostics 10 (17), 7921–7924.

Shinde, V., Bhikha, S., Hoosain, Z., Archary, M., Bhorat, Q., Fairlie, L., Lalloo, U., Masilela, M.S.L., Moodley, D., Hanley, S., Fouche, L., Louw, C., Tameris, M., Singh, N., Goga, A., Dheda, K., Grobbelaar, C., Kruger, G., Ganey, N.C., Baillie, V., Oliveira, T. De, Koen, A.L., Lombaard, J.J., Mngqibisa, R., Bhorat, A.E., Benadé, G., Lalloo, N., Pitsi, A., Vollgraaff, P., Luabeya, A., Esmail, A., Petrick, F.G., Jose, A.O., Foulkes, S., Ahmed, K., Thombrayil, A., Fries, L., Clark, S.C., Zhu, M., Bennett, C., Albert, G., Faust, E., Plested, J.S., Robertson, A., Neal, S., Cho, I., Glenn, G.M., Dubovsky, F., Madhi, S.A., Group, S., 2021. Efficacy of NVX-CoV2373 Covid-19 vaccine against the B.1.351 variant. N. Engl. J. Med. 1899–1909.

Shinn, J., Kwon, N., Ah, S., Yonghyun, L., 2022. Smart pH - responsive nanomedicines for disease therapy. J. Pharm. Investig. 52 (4), 427–441.

Sim, T.M., Tarini, D., Dheen, S.T., Bay, B.H., Srinivasan, D.K., 2020. Nanoparticle-based technology approaches to the management of neurological disorders. Int. J. Mol. Sci. 21 (17), 1–32.

Singh, A.V., Varma, M., Laux, P., Choudhary, S., Datusalia, A.K., Gupta, N., Luch, A., Gandhi, A., Kulkarni, P., Nath, B., 2023. Artificial intelligence and machine learning disciplines with the potential to improve the nanotoxicology and nanomedicine fields: a comprehensive review. Arch. Toxicol. 97 (4), 963–979.

Soane, D.S., Mahoney, R.P., Wuthrich, P., and Greene, D.G. (2018) Stabilizing Excipients for Therapeutic Protein Formulations. 2.

Siracusa, R., Paterniti, I., Cordaro, M., Crupi, R., Bruschetta, G., Campolo, M., Cuzzocrea, S., Esposito, E., 2018. Neuroprotective effects of temsirolimus in animal models of Parkinson 's disease. Mol. Neurobiol. 55 (3), 2403–2419.

Soheil, H., Farid, D., Andreas, B.-S., 2022. Oral delivery of therapeutic peptides and proteins. Oral Delivery of Therapeutic Peptides and Proteins 182, 1–296.

Son, A., Park, J., Kim, W., Yoon, Y., Lee, S., Park, Y., Kim, H., 2024. Revolutionizing molecular design for innovative therapeutic applications through artificial intelligence. Molecules 29 (19), 1–40.

Spada, A., Emami, J., Tuszynski, J.A., Lavasanifar, A., 2021. The uniqueness of albumin as a carrier in nanodrug delivery. Mol. Pharm. 18 (5), 1862–1894.

Stanislav, Ž., Hammer, N., 2025. Editorial: Tissue engineering and regenerative medicine: Advances , controversies , and future directions. Front. Bioeng. Biotechnol. 1–3. March.

Sun, X., Hong, Y., Gong, Y., Zheng, S., Xie, D., 2021. Bioengineered ferritin nanocarriers for cancer therapy. Int. J. Mol. Sci. 22 (13).

Sun, Q., Yang, Z., Qi, X., 2023. Design and application of hybrid polymer-protein systems in cancer therapy. Polymers 15 (9).

Tang, S., Han, E.L., Mitchell, M.J., 2025. Peptide - functionalized nanoparticles for brain - targeted therapeutics. Drug Deliv. Transl. Res. (0123456789).

Tarhini, M., Greige-Gerges, H., Elaissari, A., 2017. Protein-based nanoparticles: from preparation to encapsulation of active molecules. Int. J. Pharm. 522 (1–2), 172–197.

Tarhini, M., Benlyamani, I., Hamdani, S., Agusti, G., and Fessi, H. (2018) Protein-Based Nanoparticle Preparation via. 1–18.

Tivano, F., Chiono, V., 2023. Zein as a renewable material for the preparation of green nanoparticles for drug delivery. Front. Biomater. Sci 1–21. May.

Torchilin, V.P., 2014. Multifunctional, stimuli-sensitive nanoparticulate systems for drug delivery. Nat. Rev. Drug Discov. 13 (11), 813–827.

Ujnf, D., Vodpouspmmfe, B.O.E., and Esvh, J. (2023) SFMFBTF BOE FOIBODFE QFOFUSBUJPO GPS BOUJDBODFS UIFSBQZ. 16 (8), 11186–11196.

Varanko, A., Saha, S., Chilkoti, A., 2020. Recent trends in protein and peptide-based biomaterials for advanced drug delivery. Adv. Drug Deliv. Rev. 156, 133–187.

Venkatraman, N., Tiono, A.B., Bowyer, G., Bellamy, D.G., Stockdale, L.K., Powlson, J., Collins, K.A., Coulibaly, S., Datoo, M.S., Silman, D., Ouedraogo, A., Nébié, I., Imoukhuede, E.B., Brod, F., Folegatti, P., Dickinson-craig, E., Jamieson, S., Bougouma, E.C., Wright, D., Diarra, A., Bliss, C.M., Morter, R., Glenn, G., Fries, L.F., Reimer, J.M., Lövgren-bengtsson, K., Baker, M., Poulton, I., Moyle, S., Berrie, E., Green, N., Mukhopadhyay, E., Viebig, N.K., Angus, B., Lawrie, A., Roberts, R., Gilbert, S.C., Lewis, D.J.M., Sirima, S.B., Ewer, K.J., Hill, A.V.S., 2025. Evaluation of a novel malaria anti-sporozoite vaccine candidate , R21 in Matrix-M adjuvant, in the UK and Burkina Faso: two phase 1 , first-in-human trials. Articles Lancet Microbe 6 (March), 1–11.

Verma, D., Gulati, N., Kaul, S., Mukherjee, S., Nagaich, U., 2018. Protein based nanostructures for drug delivery. J. Pharm. 2018 (1), 9285854.

Vogel, S.M., Minshall, R.D., Pilipović, M., Tiruppathi, C., Malik, A.B., 2001. Albumin uptake and transcytosis in endothelial cells in vivo induced by albumin-binding protein. Am. J. Physiol. Lung Cell. Mol. Physiol. 281 (6 25–6), L1512–L1522.

Wang, F., Parhizkar, M., Harker, A., and Edirisinghe, M. Constrained composite Bayesian optimization for rational synthesis of polymeric particles.

Wang, H., La Russa, M., Qi, L.S., 2016. CRISPR/Cas9 in genome editing and beyond. Annu. Rev. Biochem. 85, 227–264.

Wang, Y., Cheetham, A.G., Angacian, G., Su, H., Xie, L., Cui, H., 2017. Peptide–drug conjugates as effective prodrug strategies for targeted delivery. Adv. Drug Deliv. Rev. 110–111, 112–126.

Wang, G.Y., Rayner, S.L., Chung, R., Shi, B.Y., Liang, X.J., 2020. Materials today bio advances in nanotechnology-based strategies for the treatments of amyotrophic lateral sclerosis. Mater. Today Bio 6 (May), 100055.

Wang, J., Chen, P., Dong, Y., Xie, H., Wang, Y., Soto, F., Ma, P., Feng, X., Du, W., Liu, B.F., 2021. Designer exosomes enabling tumor targeted efficient chemo/gene/photothermal therapy. Biomaterials 276 (July), 121056.

Wang, W., Zhu, C., Zhang, B., Feng, Y., Zhang, Y., Li, J., 2023a. Self-assembled nano-PROTAC enables near-infrared photodynamic proteolysis for cancer therapy. J. Am. Chem. Soc. 145 (30), 16642–16649.

Wang, T., Wu, C., Hu, Y., Zhang, Y., Ma, J., 2023b. Stimuli-responsive nanocarrier delivery systems for Pt-based antitumor complexes: a review. RSC Adv. 13 (24), 16488–16511.

Wang, X., Bai, Z., Li, K., Dong, J., Zhang, H., Liu, X., Han, W., Li, Q., 2023c. Bioinspired PLCL/elastin nanofibrous vascular tissue engineering scaffold enhances endothelial cells and inhibits smooth muscle cells. Biomacromolecules 24 (6), 2741–2754.

Wang, X., Gao, R., Wang, X., Zhou, J., Zhang, X.E., Li, F., 2024. mRNA delivery systems based on protein nanocages: How far can we go? BioDesign Research 6, 32.

Weiwei, G., Yue, Z., Qiangzhe, Z., Liangfang, Z., 2017. Nanoparticle-hydrogel: A hybrid biomaterial system for localized drug delivery. Physiology & behavior 176 (3), 139–148.

Wittena, J., Hub, Y., Langera, R., Anderson, D.G., 2023. Recent Advances in Nanoparticulate RNA Delivery Systems. Proceedings of the National Academy of Sciences, 2017.

Wu, Z., Sun, K., 2018. Lactoferrin-modified rotigotine nanoparticles for enhanced nose-to-brain delivery: LESA-MS/MS- based drug biodistribution. Pharmacodynamics , and Neuroprotective Effects 273–281.

Wu, L., Wang, D., Li, Z., 2020. Grand challenges in nanomedicine. Mater. Sci. Eng. C 106 (August 2018).

Xiao, Y., Tang, Z., Huang, X., Chen, W., Zhou, J., Liu, H., Liu, C., Kong, N., Tao, W., 2022. Emerging mRNA technologies: delivery strategies and biomedical applications. Chem. Soc. Rev. 51 (10), 3828–3845.

Xu, Z., Zhang, X., Dong, W., Zuo, L., Zhu, L., Wang, R., and Ma, X. (2023) pH-responsive protein nanoparticle as potential platform for targeted tumor therapy. (May), 1–9.

Xu, K., Huang, P., Wu, Y., Liu, T., Shao, N., Zhao, L., Hu, X., Chang, J., Peng, Y., Qu, S., 2023. Engineered selenium/human serum albumin nanoparticles for efficient targeted treatment of Parkinson's disease via oral gavage. ACS Nano 17 (20), 19961–19980.

Xu, M., Wei, S., Duan, L., Ji, Y., Han, X., 2024. The recent advancements in protein nanoparticles for immunotherapy. Nanoscale 11825–11848.

Yadav, S., Sharma, A.K., Kumar, P., 2020. Nanoscale self-assembly for therapeutic delivery. Front. Bioeng. Biotechnol. 8 (February), 1–24.

Yao, Y., Zhou, Y., Liu, L., Xu, Y., Chen, Q., Wang, Y., Wu, S., Deng, Y., Zhang, J., Shao, A., 2020. Nanoparticle-based drug delivery in cancer therapy and its role in overcoming drug resistance. Front. Mol. Biosci. 7 (August), 1–14.

Zaher, S., Soliman, M.E., Elsabahy, M., Hathout, R.M., 2023. Protein nanoparticles as natural drugs carriers for cancer therapy. Advances in Traditional Medicine 23 (4), 1035–1064.

Zhang, F., 2019. Development of CRISPR-Cas systems for genome editing and beyond. Q. Rev. Biophys. 52.

Zhang, N., Li, C., Jiang, S., 2020. Recent advances in the development of virus-like particle-based flavivirus vaccines. Vaccines (Basel) 1–21.

Zhang, Q., Zhang, J., Song, J., Liu, Y., Ren, X., and Zhao, Y. (2021) Protein-Based Nanomedicine for Therapeutic Bene fi ts of Cancer.

Zhang, H., Yang, J., Sun, R., Han, S., Yang, Z., Teng, L., 2023. Microfluidics for nano-drug delivery systems: From fundamentals to industrialization. Acta Pharm. Sin. B 13 (8).

Zhang, M., Li, X., and Lin, H. (2024) Magnetic casein/CaCO3/Fe3O4 microspheres stimulate osteogenic differentiation. (November 2011).

Zhao, Y., Lv, F., Chen, S., Wang, Z., Zhang, J., Zhang, S., Cao, J., Wang, L., Cao, E., Wang, B., Hu, X., 2018. Caveolin-1 expression predicts efficacy of weekly nab-paclitaxel plus gemcitabine for metastatic breast cancer in the phase II clinical trial. BMC Cancer 18 (1), 1019.

# Further reading

Ahire, E.D., Savaliya, N., Makwana, K.V., Salave, S., Banth, M.K., Bhavsar, B., 2025. Protein-Bound Nano-Injectable Suspension: Unveiling the Promises and Challenges. Appl Nano. 6 (2), 1–28.

Ferraro, C., Dattilo, M., Patitucci, F., Prete, S., Scopelliti, G., Parisi, O.I., 2024. Exploring Protein-Based Carriers in Drug Delivery: A Review. Pharmaceutics 16 (9).

Hersh, A.M., Alomari, S., Tyler, B.M., 2022. Crossing the Blood-Brain Barrier: Advances in Nanoparticle Technology for Drug Delivery in Neuro-Oncology. Int J Mol Sci. 23 (8).

Sim, T.M., Tarini, D., Dheen, S.T., Bay, B.H., Srinivasan, D.K., 2020. Nanoparticle-based technology approaches to the management of neurological disorders. Int J Mol Sci. 21 (17), 1–32.

Sun, X., Hong, Y., Gong, Y., Zheng, S., Xie, D., 2021. Bioengineered ferritin nanocarriers for cancer therapy. Int J Mol Sci 22 (13).

Varanko, A., Saha, S., Chilkoti, A., 2020. Recent trends in protein and peptide-based biomaterials for advanced drug delivery. Adv Drug Deliv Rev 156, 133–187. https://doi.org/10.1016/j.addr.2020.08.008.

# Index

*Note:* Page numbers followed by *f* indicate figures and *t* indicate tables.


**A**

Abraxane (ABI-007), 4, 8–9, 25, 29–30, 38–39, 96–97, 98f, 125–126, 180, 196–198, 229t, 254–256, 298–299, 312–313, 315–316, 354, 365–366
  approved status, 229t, 254–256
  indication, 229t, 254–256
Acidity-responsive protein nanoparticles, 220
  extracellular pH in tumors, 220
  pH-responsive nanomaterials, 220
  Warburg effect, 220
*Acinetobacter baumannii*, 421, 537
ACLU. *See* American Civil Liberties Union
Active targeting, 27–28, 415, 421–422, 424
  against cancer cells, 415
  in combinational therapy, 421–422
  ligand-conjugated targeting, 27
  in nanomedicine, 414
  receptor-mediated endocytosis, 27
  stimuli-responsive systems, 27
  of tumor, 415
Adjuvants, 692–693, 694f, 695–696, 699, 706–709
  immunostimulants, 695–696, 696f
  nano adjuvants, 695–696
  types, 695–696
Adsorption, 684
Advanced glycation end products (AGEs), 564–566
Aggregation, 62–63, 66–67, 71, 73
  prevention, 73
Albumin, 4, 5t–7t, 8, 10–14, 16–30, 32t–33t, 36–39, 84–85, 85f, 96–97, 139–140, 143–145, 144t, 150–151, 153–156, 159t, 161t, 168–169, 180–181, 186, 194t–195t, 196–199, 211–212, 224–227, 257, 298–300, 303, 307–309, 312–316, 319, 409–410, 709–710
  active targeting, 224–225
  albumin-bound paclitaxel, 298–299, 312–313, 315–316
  bovine serum albumin (BSA), 4, 14, 17t–23t, 34t–35t, 36, 88f, 89, 709–710
  drug delivery, 224
  human serum albumin (HSA), 4, 16–24, 17t–23t, 29–30, 34t–35t, 37–38, 85–86, 91, 180, 196–198, 709–710
  human serum albumin (HSA) nanoparticles, 303
  lactalbumin, 5t–7t, 8, 17t–23t, 24
  nanoparticle albumin-bound paclitaxel, 96–97, 98f
  nanoparticles, 303, 309, 312–314
  ovalbumin, 709
  properties, 224
  serum albumin-coated TMV particles, 186
Albumin-based nanoparticles, 125–128, 276–277, 279f, 284, 287f, 337–338
  bovine serum albumin (BSA), 276–277
  gene vaccination, 338
  human serum albumin (HSA), 276–277
  ovalbumin (OVA), 276–277
  surface modification, 337–338
Alexandria University, 333–334
Alginate nanoparticles, 336–337
  functionalization, 337
  gene delivery process, 337
  vaccine carriers, 337
Alzheimer's disease. *See* Diseases; Alzheimer's
American Civil Liberties Union (ACLU)
  member nations, 347
  provisions of treaty, 428
Amination, 414
Amphiphilic diblock ELP, 554–557, 555f
Amphiphilic nature, 409–410
Anatomical barriers, 112
Angiogenesis, 413–414, 449, 451–452
Animal protein-based nanoparticles, 299–300
  casein, 299–300
  gelatin, 299–300
  silk fibroin, 299–300
Antibodies, 673–675, 678–680
  Fab fragment, 673
  Fc region, 673–674, 686
  monoclonal, 675, 676t, 678–680
Antibody-conjugated nanoparticles (ACNPs), 276, 279, 279f, 287f, 655, 674, 682–683, 687
  EGFR receptors, 279
  HER2 receptors, 279
  therapeutic applications, 687
  VCAM-1, 279

Antibody-drug conjugates (ADCs), 197, 667, 674–683, 676t, 679t, 682t–683t
construction of, 675
FDA-approved, 682, 683t
history of, 674–675, 676t
Antigen-presenting cells (APCs), 692–697, 695f–696f, 698f, 702–703, 707–711
activation, 698f
pattern recognition receptors (PRRs) on, 695f–696f
uptake by, 711
Antimicrobial activity, 444–446
Antimicrobial drugs, 421
applications, 421
AP/Cas-NPs, 422
APCs. *See* Antigen-presenting cells (APCs)
Apigenin (AP), 422
Apolipoprotein-related nanoparticles, 276–277, 279f, 287f
apolipoprotein A1 (ApoA1), 277
apolipoprotein E, 277
Zr-mA1, 277
Application in cosmeceuticals, 512–513
Aptamers, 673
oligonucleotide, 673
Area under the curve, 416
Arthritis, 423
Artificial intelligence (AI), 371
Atomizing/antisolvent precipitation process (AAP), 467t, 470
ATP production, 414
AuNCs. *See* Gold nanoclusters
AuNPs. *See* Gold nanoparticles

## B

Bacteriophages, 704–705, 705t, 713t
P22, 704, 705t
Q, 704–705, 705t
T4, 704–705, 705t
BBB. *See* Blood-brain barrier (BBB)
B-cell receptor (BCR), 695f–696f
B-cells, 693–694, 695f–696f, 698f, 703t, 704–705, 708–709, 711
activation, 695f, 698f
memory cell generation, 703t
BCR. *See* B-cell receptor (BCR)
Bevacizumab (BVZ), 659
Bioavailability, 16, 25, 28–29, 37–38, 55–56, 60, 62–63, 68–70, 78, 378–379, 387–388, 392–393, 397–400, 413, 421–422, 428, 614t, 615, 623
absorption barriers, 68–70
poor, 68–69
technological advances to enhance, 111
Biocompatibility, 275–276, 278, 281, 283, 286–288, 290, 378–379, 384, 393, 398–400, 409–410, 413, 435–436, 438, 442–445, 449–451, 611–618, 614t, 622, 629–632
cell viability, 624, 630, 631f
cytotoxicity, 624, 630
toxicity, 629–631
Biodegradability, 275–276, 282, 286, 288, 290, 409–410, 436, 438, 442–443, 450
Biodegradable polymers, 409–410
Bioimaging, 588f, 596–597
computed tomography (CT), 596–597
magnetic resonance imaging (MRI), 596–597
optical imaging, 597
Biological barriers, 181, 182f, 183–184
circulatory system, 181, 183
endothelial barriers, 183
extracellular matrix (ECM), 183–184, 186–188
Biological roles
of curcumin, 423
of phenolic compounds, 423–424
Biological targeting, 672
Bioluminescence imaging (BLI), 283
Biomarker detection, 309
Bioorthogonal chemistry, 311
click chemistry, 311
Blood-brain barrier (BBB), 95–96, 119–121, 350, 377–378, 397–398, 534–535, 687
Blood coagulation, 424, 427–428
*Bluetongue virus (BTV)*, 194t–195t, 587–588
BODIPY, 413, 415
BODIPY-loaded casein NPs, 415
*Bombyx mori*, 89, 125–126, 299–300
Bone morphogenetic protein (BMP), 614t, 616–619
Bovine serum albumin (BSA), 378–379, 384–400, 385f, 389t, 394t, 395f
conformational changes, 384–386, 391, 393–397, 395f
drug-binding properties, 386–387, 398–399
synthesis methods, 388–390, 396–397, 399–400
BSA. *See* Albumin
BT-549 cells, 415
Bystander effect, 680–681

## C

$CaCl_2$, 414–416
Calcium chloride. *See* $CaCl_2$
Calcium ferrite NPs, 416
Calcium phosphate, 410–411
Camel milk casein NPs, 414–415
Camptothecin, 424–425
Cancer, 297–299, 415, 421–422, 424
breast, 413, 415, 424–425

cells, 413–414, 421–422
colorectal, 414
diagnosis, 273–275, 281–282, 284, 290–291
drug resistance, 297, 319
gene therapy, 304–308, 305t, 334, 336, 339–341
glioblastoma, 416
hepatocellular carcinoma, 414–415
oral, 416
theranostics, 298–308, 310–312, 315, 322
Cancer imaging, 273–286
preoperative, 273–274
real-time, 279, 281–283
tumor specificity, 281
Cancer immunotherapy, 691–692, 697–699, 698f, 702–705, 705t, 707–712
anticancer vaccines, 697, 702–703, 707–710
tumor-associated antigens (TAAs), 692, 697
Cancer therapeutic modalities, 212–217
chemotherapy, 211–213
immunotherapy, 213–214
radiotherapy, 211, 216–217
Cancer therapy, 96–98, 139–140, 143–145, 150–151, 153, 155–157, 161–162, 161t, 165–168, 365–366, 509–511, 520–536, 528t–529t, 594–596, 687
anticancer drugs, 88, 90, 96–97
combination therapy, 596
cyclophosphamide, 509
doxorubicin, 510
lung cancer treatment, 97–98
metastatic breast cancer, 96–97
monotherapy, 595–596
paclitaxel, 510
tumor microenvironment (TME), 596
Cancer treatment, 57–59, 67, 74–77, 379–384, 386–388, 390–393, 395–399, 448–454
anticancer drugs, 384, 386–390, 392–393, 397–398
doxorubicin, 386–390, 392–393, 397–398
immunooncology agents, 45
paclitaxel, 386, 395–396
protein-based nanoparticles for, 76–77
Capsules, 413
Carbodiimide conjugation, 416
Carbohydrate recognition domains (CRDs), 519–520
Cargoes, 409–411
hydrophilic, 409–410
hydrophobic, 409–410
Casein, 5t–7t, 9–11, 17t–23t, 24–25, 32t–33t, 88, 88f, 211–212, 243–244, 247t–250t, 409–411, 414, 416
hydrolysate (Cas), 423
micellar structure, 243
micelles, 9, 11–12, 24–25, 32t–33t
nano-micelles, 409–411
NPs, 414–416, 421, 423–424
properties, 243
protein, 409–413, 421
as template for AuNCs preparation, 424
types, 243
K-Casein, 410–412
Casein-based nanoparticles, 125–126
Casein/chitosan (Cas/CHI), 427–428
Casein micelles, 144t, 145, 151, 168–169
Casein nanoparticles, 339
codelivery techniques, 339
DNA delivery, 339
CD44, 415
receptors, 415
Celecoxib, 413–414
Celiac disease, 502, 513
Cell-penetrating peptides (CPPs), 548, 553, 556–557
Cell surface, 520–521, 523–525, 525f, 527–533, 536–537
Cellular immunity, 692, 695–696, 695f–696f, 698f, 700–702, 703t, 705t, 706–710, 713t
T-cell activation, 693–694
Cellular uptake, 180–181, 184–193, 200, 415–416
mechanisms, 189–191, 190f
size-dependent, 187
Characterization, 321
Characterization of nanocarriers, 12–16
drug loading capacity, 12–15
encapsulation efficiency, 12–15
particle size, 12–13
Characterization of zein-based nanoparticles, 471–472
intermolecular interactions, 472
particle morphology, 471–472
particle size and surface charge, 472
Characterization parameters, 119–125, 128
biocompatibility and toxicity, 124–125, 128–129
encapsulation efficiency and drug loading, 122–123, 128
particle size and distribution, 119–120, 128
Chemical conjugation, 553–554
Chemical modifications, 387–388, 398–400
folic acid conjugation, 387–388, 391–392, 395–400
PEGylation, 387
Chemical targeting, 671–672
Chemotherapy, 211–217, 221, 223–224, 230–231, 234–235, 237, 257
adverse effects, 212–213
multidrug resistance (MDR), 212–213
nonspecific distribution, 212–213
Chitosan (CHI), 423, 427–428, 473, 486
Chitosan coatings, 350, 363, 368, 370

Chitosan nanoparticles, 334–336
encapsulation effectiveness, 335
functionalization, 335
plasma stability, 335
Chrysin, 421
Chrysin-loaded casein, 421
Circular dichroism (CD), 356, 362, 368
Cisplatin, 415
CL4 aptamer, 415
CL4-conjugated dye-loaded caseinate NPs, 415
Click chemistry, 684–686
Copper (I)-Catalyzed Azide-Alkyne Cycloaddition (CuAAC), 413
Diels–Alder (DA) reactions, 373
Inverse electron demand Diels–Alder (iEDDA) reactions, 61
Clinical trials, 25–26, 28, 31, 32t–33t, 37–39
Coacervation method, 411–412, 414, 416, 467t, 468
Collagen, 87–88, 88f
Colloidal calcium phosphate, 410–411
Combination therapy, 642–644, 646–647, 649–650, 654, 656–661
in cancer treatment, 643–644
synergistic effects, 642–644, 646–647, 649–651, 654–657, 659–661
Commercial and regulatory considerations, 78–80
cold chain logistics and storage, 84
cost of delivery technologies, 85
pricing and reimbursement, 80
Concanavalin-A (Con-A), 520, 522–523, 527, 528t–529t, 530–532, 536–538
Controlled drug delivery, 85–86
Controlled drug release, 377–379, 384–388, 390–393, 396–400
Controlled particle size, 614t
Controlled release, 52, 67, 72–73, 76–78, 409–411, 428, 440–446, 448–451, 453–454
challenges with, 72–73
crosslinking, 411–412, 416
mechanisms, 409–410
property, 428
protein-based systems, 52
Copper sulfide-ferritin nanocages (CuS-Fn NCs), 283–284
photothermal conversion efficiency, 284
photothermal treatment (PTT), 284
radionuclides, 284
Core/shell nanostructure, 428
Corneal neovascularization (CNV), 659
Covalent binding, 684–686
carbodiimide chemistry, 684–685
maleimide chemistry, 684–685
Covalent conjugation, 192, 197
antibody–drug conjugate, 197
chemical reactions, 197
Covalent interactions, 140, 147–150, 148t, 153–156, 158, 161–162, 164f
Cowpea chlorotic mottle virus (CCMV), 573f, 574
Cowpea mosaic virus (CPMV), 194t–195t, 317, 573f, 574–575
CP. *See* Virus-like particles (VLPs)
CPMV. *See* Cowpea mosaic virus (CPMV)
Critical micellization temperature (CMT), 555
Cross-linking, 10–12, 14–16, 24, 28–29, 31, 39, 351, 353, 355, 360, 363, 370
*Curcuma longa*, 564
Curcumin, 423–424, 534–535
CUR/SC nano-micelles, 423
CYT. *See* Cytochrome c (CYT)
Cytochrome c (CYT), 616, 617t–618t, 624, 631–632
Cytokines, 421, 423, 647–649, 655–656
interferons (IFNs), 655–656
interleukins (ILs), 655–656
tumor necrosis factors (TNFs), 655–656
Cytotoxic effect, 414–415, 421–422
Cytotoxic payloads, 675–678, 679t
DNA-damaging agents, 677–678
microtubule-disrupting agents, 676–677

## D

Damage-associated molecular patterns (DAMPs), 213–214, 215f, 696f
danger signals, 696f
DAMPs. *See* Damage-associated molecular patterns (DAMPs)
Dasatinib, 413–414
Daunorubicin, 414
DCs. *See* Dendritic cells (DCs)
DDS. *See* Drug delivery systems (DDS)
Degradation-mediated release, 199
enzymatic activity, 199
hydrolysis, 199
Delivery, 410–413, 424
agents, 409–410
of anticancer drugs, 413
of antidiabetic drugs, 422
of antiinflammatory drugs, 423
of antimicrobial drugs, 421
of antioxidant drugs, 423–424
smart nutraceutical and drug, 409–410
vehicles, 409–410
Dendritic cells (DCs), 213–214, 215f, 250–251
Deoxyribonucleic acid (DNA), 437–438, 449–453, 452f
Desolvation method, 350–352, 411, 416, 438–439, 439f

Device dependency, 74
Dexamethasone phosphate (Dexp), 659
Diabetes, 522, 538
Diabetes management, 75
glucagon-like peptide 1 (GLP-1) agonists, 83
long-acting insulin analogs, 81
Diabetes mellitus type II, 564–566
Diagnostic applications, 308–310
molecular beacons, 309
real-time monitoring, 310, 314
Dialysis method, 416, 467t, 468, 469f
Diffusion-controlled release, 199, 362, 362t
Diseases
Alzheimer's, 421–422, 522, 538–539
chronic inflammatory, 423
respiratory tract infection, 421
DNA damage, 414, 424–425
DNA vaccines, 126–127
Doxorubicin (Dox), 125–126, 553–556, 652, 653f, 654–659, 670, 673, 682
Drug delivery, 139–141, 144t, 148t, 149–169, 159t, 161t, 180–181, 185–186, 193–198, 200, 365, 377–380, 381f–383f, 384, 386–393, 389t, 394t, 396–400, 435–436, 439–455, 521–539, 612–616, 618–619, 622–624, 626–632, 667–675, 682–683, 685–688
nasal administration, 378–379, 387
oral, 528t–529t, 530–532, 536–538
protein encapsulation, 612, 619–622, 620f, 626–627, 626f, 631–632
protein release, 613, 615–624, 620f–621f, 626–632, 628f
sol-gel process, 611–629, 617t–618t, 631–632
systems, 180, 185–186, 193–198, 200
targeted, 180, 192–193, 196–200, 377–379, 384–388, 390–393, 395–400, 521–539, 667–675, 682, 685–688
Drug delivery systems (DDSs), 83–84, 86–87, 428, 465–466, 473, 475, 477–481, 483, 485–487, 548, 554, 556, 559, 566, 639. *See also* Protein-based nanocarriers
aims and approaches, 639
controlled release, 302–306, 312, 319
curcumin, 302–303, 302f
morphologies, 639
nanocarrier-based delivery, 83–84
nanocarriers, 549–554, 559–566, 560f
oral administration, 83
pH-responsive, 474, 478
redox-responsive, 479
reduction of toxicity, 303
routes, 639
sustained drug release, 85–86
targeted, 470, 471f, 473–475, 476f, 477–478, 480, 483–485
Drug loading, 151–160, 159t, 165–169, 181, 193–198, 200
covalent drug conjugation, 155–156, 159t
covalent interactions, 197
encapsulation and entrapment, 197–198
noncovalent interactions, 196–197
physical encapsulation, 155–156, 159t
Drug loading mechanisms, 357–361
Drug release, 140–141, 143, 147–149, 152–162, 159t, 165–169
enzyme-mediated, 157–158, 159t, 165–167
pH-responsive, 156–157, 159t, 161–163
triggered, 140–141, 147–149, 148t, 155–156, 160–163, 164f, 169
Drug release kinetics, 508–509
diffusion-controlled release, 509
stimuli-responsive release, 509
Dynamic light scattering (DLS), 119, 128

E

Easy synthesis and scalability, 612, 614t
*E. coli. See Escherichia coli (E. coli)*
EDC/NHS conjugation, 414–416
EDC/NHS coupling reactions, 686
Efficacy, 692–693, 697, 706–712, 711f
long-lasting immune responses, 711
lower antigen doses, 711
EGFR. *See* Epidermal growth factor receptor
Egypt, 691
Egypt-Japan University of Science and Technology, 693
Ehrlich ascites tumor, 413–414, 421–422
Elastin-like polypeptide nanoparticles (ELPs), 276, 278, 279f, 287f
heat sensitivity, 278
pentapeptide sequences, 278
thermal responsiveness, 278
Elastin-like polypeptides (ELPs), 211–212, 252–254, 255t–256t, 257, 547–566, 550f, 552f, 555f, 558f, 560f
architectures, 554–559, 560f
biomedical applications, 253
functionalization, 553
properties, 253
purification, 551–553, 552f
self-assembly, 253
Elastin nanoparticles, 339
functionalization, 339
gene therapy applications, 339
Electrical field, 413, 426
Electroporation, 578–580, 579f

Electroporation (*Continued*)
DNA electrotransfer, 580
in vitro, 579
in vivo, 579–580
Electroporation technique, 328f, 329
Electrospinning, 413, 426–428, 444–446, 449, 453–454
Electrospraying, 467t, 470, 486–487, 502t–503t, 504–506, 505f
nanoparticle morphology, 504
Electrospun, 426
Electrostatic attractions, 409–410
ELP-based micelles, 553–557, 555f, 560f, 561–562
ELP coacervates, 548, 554, 558f, 559–561, 560f, 564–566
ELP polyplexes, 548, 554, 557–558, 558f, 560f
ELPs. *See* Elastin-like polypeptides (ELPs)
Emulsification, 409–410, 412–413, 421–422
solvent evaporation technique, 412
Emulsification method, 354–355
Encapsulation efficiency (EE), 467–470, 484t, 486t, 506–508
Endocytosis, 183, 186–187, 189–193, 190f
caveola-mediated, 187, 189–190
clathrin-mediated, 187, 189–190
macropinocytosis, 183, 189–190
Endosomal escape, 183, 189–191
fusogenic peptides, 189–190
histidine-rich peptides, 189–191
Energy-independent manner, 409–410
Engineered protein nanoparticles, 126–127
Enhanced permeability and retention (EPR) effect, 4, 13, 24, 26, 119–120, 125–126, 217, 223, 227, 548, 641–642, 641f, 657, 668–669
passive targeting, 217, 227
PEGylation, 217
tumor accumulation, 217
Enhanced permeation and retention (EPR) effect, 86–87, 92, 95–96, 281, 298, 303
Enhancement of oral, 421–422
Enzymatic degradation, 55–56, 64–65, 67–68, 366
proteolytic degradation, 55–56, 64–65, 67–68
Enzymatic hydrolysis, 502t–503t, 504–506
Enzyme activity and stability, 396
Enzyme replacement therapy (ERT), 98–99
Enzyme-responsive protein nanoparticles, 223–224
hyaluronidase (HAdase), 223–224
matrix metalloproteinases (MMPs), 219f, 223–224, 230–231
targeted drug release, 223–224
Epidermal growth factor receptor (EGFR), 415
EPR. *See* Enhanced permeation and retention (EPR) effect
ERT. *See* Enzyme replacement therapy (ERT)
*Escherichia coli (E. coli)*, 51–52, 55, 549–551, 700, 704–707, 705t
enterohemorrhagic *E. coli (EHEC)*, 705t
uropathogenic *E. coli* (UPEC), 706–707
Etoposide, 421–422
Eugenol, 414
Exosomes, 584–585, 585f
Expanding into nutraceutical delivery, 512–513
Extracellular matrix (ECM), 183–184, 186–188

## F

Factors influencing drug-loading capacity, 506–508
Fc fusion proteins, 60, 69
Ferritin, 139–140, 144t, 145, 152–153, 156–157, 159t, 161t, 180–181, 186, 189, 194t–195t, 300, 308–311, 313, 316–318
Ferritin nanoparticles (Ferritin NPs), 276, 279f, 284, 287f, 692, 699–703, 701f, 703t
antigen incorporation, 702
apoferritin, 276
hollow cavity, 276
iron oxide core, 276
multivalent nanovaccines, 700
stability, 699–700
Ferritin NPs. *See* Ferritin nanoparticles (Ferritin NPs)
Ferulic acid, 423–424
Fibers, 413, 426
Fibroblast cells, 414, 423–425
Fibroin, 5t–7t, 8–9, 11–12, 15–16, 17t–23t, 29–30, 38, 143, 144t, 145, 155–156, 159t, 161t
silk fibroin, 8–9, 11–12, 15–16, 17t–23t, 29–30, 38
Flash nanoprecipitation, 467t, 471, 511–513
Flock house virus (FHV), 577–578
Fluorescence imaging, 273–274, 275f
fluorophores, 273
live cell imaging, 273–274
multiplex imaging, 273–274
Folate, 473–474, 477, 483
Food and Drug Administration (FDA), 213–214, 222–223, 254–256, 436, 450
Food-borne pathogenic bacteria, 421
Food packaging, 426–427
active antimicrobial, 427
Freeze-drying, 350, 370–371
Functional flexibility, 74
Functional groups, 180, 188–189, 409–410
Functionalization of nanoparticles, 683–687
adaptor molecules, 686
adsorption, 684
covalent binding, 684–686
Functionalized drug-loaded casein NPs, 415
FYARRO, 25–26, 38–39, 229t, 254–256, 354
approved status, 229t, 254–256
indication, 229t, 254–256

## G

Γ-Glutamyl transpeptidase (GGT) receptors, 424–425
Gastrointestinal delivery, 509–511
  *Helicobacter pylori infection*, 510
Gelatin, 5t–7t, 10–11, 14–16, 17t–23t, 29–31, 32t–35t, 37–39, 139–140, 144t, 145, 151–152, 157–158, 159t, 161t, 167–169, 211–212, 229–231, 231t, 257, 409–410, 707–709
  drug and gene carriers, 230
  properties, 229
  types, 229, 707–708
Gelatin nanoparticles (GNPs), 125–128, 333–334, 707–709
  cancer gene therapy, 334
  cellular uptake, 333–334
  siRNA delivery, 334
Gelation, 409–410
Gene delivery, 145–146, 151–153, 161t, 167, 169
Gene guns/biolistic delivery, 582–583, 583f
Gene gun technique, 328f, 330
Gene therapy, 304–308, 305t, 436, 449–455
  apoptosis induction, 305t, 306–307
  immunotherapy, 305t, 307–308
  oncogene silencing, 305–306, 305t
Genetic disorders, 76
  enzyme replacement therapy (ERT), 469
  hemophilia treatment, 467
Genetic material delivery systems, 327–330, 328f
  electroporation, 328f, 329
  gene gun, 328f, 330
  microinjection, 328f, 329–330
Genetic synthesis, 548–551, 550f, 558
  PRe-RDL method, 550f, 551
  recursive directional ligation (RDL), 549–551, 550f
GGT, 424–425
  glutamate, 416
  vitamin D3, 421–422
Gliadin, 5t–7t, 11, 17t–23t, 85f, 88f, 90, 211–212, 232, 233t
  properties, 232
  subtypes, 232
  tumor therapy, 232, 233t
Gliadin nanocarriers, 499–500, 502, 504–513
  characterization, 508–509
  manufacture, 502, 504–506
  stabilization, 506–508
Gliadin nanocarrier stabilization with gum arabic, 506–508
Gliadin nanocarrier stabilization with surfactants, 506–508
Gliadins, 499–503, 499t, 500f–501f, 502t, 513
  chemical structure and composition, 500–501
  extraction methods, 503
  role in celiac disease, 502
Glucagon-like peptide 1 (GLP-1), 564–566
Glutamic acid, 416
Glutaraldehyde, 351, 351f, 360, 361f, 363
Glutathione, 424–425
Glutathione (GSH)-responsive protein nanoparticles, 223
  redox homeostasis, 223
  TME concentration, 223
Glycan structures, 519–533, 525f, 535–537
  cancer-associated, 521–523, 535–536
  disease-associated, 522
  fucosylated, 522–523, 535–536
Glycoengineering, 67, 69
Glycoproteins, 672
GNPs. *See* Gelatin
Goat milk casein NPs, 424
Gold nanoclusters (AuNCs), 424
Gold nanoparticles (AuNPs), 424
GRAS, 409–410
Green tea essential oil, 426–427
Growth factors, 449–450, 453–454
GSH. *See* Glutathione (GSH)-responsive protein nanoparticles
Gum arabic (GA), 422

## H

Heat shock proteins (HSPs), 692, 697–699
  HSP70, 697–699
  sHsp16.5, 699
HeLa, 416
*Helicobacter pylori*, 90
  infections, 500, 502t–503t, 509–511, 528t–529t, 536–537
Hemolytic potential, 413, 421–422
Hemostasis, 427–428
Hepatocellular carcinoma, 414–415
HepG2 cells, 414–415
Heterogeneous nuclear ribonucleoprotein A1 (hnRNPA1), 413
Hexahistidine-metal assemblies (HmA), 659
Hibiscus chlorotic ringspot virus, 192–193
High-performance liquid chromatography (HPLC), 185
High-pressure homogenization, 332
High surface area and porosity, 613–615, 614t, 622–623, 627–628
Histones, 5t–7t, 8, 17t–23t
Homogenization, 412
Horseradish peroxidase (HP), 617t–618t, 618–619, 622
HP. *See* Horseradish peroxidase (HP)

HPV. *See* Human papillomavirus (HPV)
HSA. *See* Albumin
HSPs. *See* Heat shock proteins (HSPs)
Human immunodeficiency virus (HIV-1), 586–587
Humanization of therapeutic proteins, 493
Human papillomavirus (HPV), 702–705, 705t, 709–710
  cervical cancer, 709–710
  HPV-16 E7, 705t
Human serum albumin (HSA), 349–350
Humoral immunity, 692, 695f–696f, 698f, 700–701, 703t, 705t, 706–708, 710, 713t
  antibody production, 695f, 698f
  IgG antibody response, 693–694, 699–702, 703t, 705t, 706–708, 710
  immunological memory, 695f, 701–702, 711
Hyaluronic acid (HA), 360, 361f, 363–365, 367f, 415, 474, 477, 482
Hybridoma technology, 675, 676t
Hybrid zein-based drug delivery systems, 480–481
  zein-inorganic hybrid nanoparticles, 481
  zein-protein hybrid nanoparticles, 480
  zein-surfactant hybrid nanoparticles, 480
Hydrodynamic diameter, 187
Hydrodynamic particle size, 413–414
Hydrogel-based systems, 127–128
Hydrogel systems, 45
Hydrogen bonding, 140, 147, 148t, 149–152, 154, 409–410, 423–424
Hydrolytic degradation, 624, 624f
Hydrophilic, 409–411
  portion, 418
  section, 409–410
Hydrophobic, 409–411
  interactions, 140, 144t, 147, 148t, 149–154, 156–158, 161–162, 409–410, 416, 423–425
  portion, 417
  section, 409–410
Hydrophobicity/hydrophilicity, 186–187, 189
Hydroxyl camptothecin, 414
Hypoglycemic activity, 422
Hypoxia-inducible factor (HIF), 212–213, 220–221
Hypoxia-responsive protein nanoparticles, 221
  HIF-1, 221
  reoxygenation strategies, 221
  tumor angiogenesis, 221

## I

IC50, 413
ICD. *See* Immunogenic cell death (ICD)
IG. *See* Immunoglobulin G (IG)
Immune checkpoint inhibitors (ICIs), 213–214
Immune responses, 520, 523–524, 531–532, 536, 538
Immunogenic cell death (ICD), 213–214
Immunogenicity, 51–56, 59–60, 62–63, 66–71, 73–74, 692–693, 695–705, 698f, 712, 713t
  adverse immune reactions, 70
  antigen misfolding, 713t
  minimizing, 70–71
  preexisting immunity, 713t
  of therapeutic proteins, 70
Immunoglobulin G (IG), 617t–618t, 618–619
Immunostimulants, 696f
  damage-associated molecular patterns (DAMPs), 696f
  pathogen-associated molecular patterns (PAMPs), 695f–696f
Immunosuppressive effects, 416
Immunotherapy, 649, 655–656
Impact of pH on nanocarrier morphology, 506–508
Improved bioavailability, 614t
Infectious diseases, 687, 691–693, 696–699, 697f, 702–712, 703t, 705t
  bacterial infections, 697f, 703t, 705t
  fungal infections, 697f
  *Staphylococcus aureus*, 673
  viral infections, 697f, 703t, 705t
Inflammation, 413, 415
Inflammatory diseases, 687
Injectable hydrogels, 656
Inorganic nanoparticles, 328f, 329
INS. *See* Insulin (INS)
Institute of Graduate Studies and Research, 331
Insulin (INS), 51–52, 55, 61–62, 68, 75, 617t–618t, 623, 631–632
Intermolecular interactions, 386–388, 391, 394–397, 399–400
  electrostatic interactions, 386–387, 391, 394–397, 399–400
  hydrogen bonding, 386–387, 391, 399–400
  hydrophobic interactions, 386–387, 391, 395–396, 399–400
Intracellularly, 409–410
Intracellular traffic, 191
  nuclear localization signal (NLS), 191
  proteasome-inhibitory peptides, 191
Intratumoral localization, 425–426
Inverse transition cycling (ITC), 551–553, 552f
Inverse transition temperature (Tt), 547–548, 551–555, 559–561, 563–566
In vitro accumulation, 416
In vitro cellular uptake, 415
In vitro cytotoxic effect, 414
In vitro drug release, 414, 416
In vitro studies, 413–415
In vivo pharmacokinetics, 416

In vivo properties of protein-based nanocarriers, 12–13, 16–39
In vivo studies, 413–415, 421–422
IR 797 dye, 424–425
Isoelectric point (pI), 410–411

## K

*K. pneumoniae*. *See* Infectious diseases

## L

Lactoferrin, 5t–7t, 12, 17t–23t, 37, 211–212, 245–246, 247t–250t, 409–410, 473, 477–478
  properties, 245–246
  receptors, 245–246
  targeted delivery, 245–246
Lauric acid, 421
Lectin-based nanocarrier systems, 524–527, 525f
  advantages, 527–533
  challenges, 533–534
  materials, 524
Lectins, 519–539
  animal lectins, 520
  microbial lectins, 520
  nanoparticles, 340
  plant lectins, 520
Legumin, 139–140, 144t, 145, 161t
Leukemia, 414
L929 fibroblast cells, 414, 424–426
Linalool, 422
Linkers, 675, 680–683, 682t
  cleavable, 680, 682t
  noncleavable, 681
Lipid film hydration, 502t–503t, 504–506, 505f
Lipid nanoparticles, 328f, 329
Lipid oxidation, 421
Lipophilic, 409–410
Lipophilic dye, 415
Liposomes, 85–86, 95, 97f, 443, 454–455, 524–525, 525f, 528t–529t, 535–536, 538, 583–584, 584f
Liquid-liquid dispersion, 467t, 469
Listeria monocytogenes, 421, 427
Localized drug delivery, 640
  hydrogels, 640
  liposomes, 640
  micelles, 640
LPS, 423
Luc-linker@HFn, 282–283
  bioluminescent signal, 282–283
  human ferritin (HFn), 282
  luciferin-linker system, 282
Lung infection, 421
Lyophilization, 332
LYS. *See* Lysozyme (LYS)
Lysozyme (LYS), 211–212, 232–235, 235t, 617t–618t, 623–626, 625f, 631–632
  nanocomposites, 234
  properties, 232–234
  sources, 232–234

## M

*Macrobrachium rosenbergii nodavirus*, 251t–252t
Macrophages, 423
Magic bullet, 667–668, 672, 674, 676t
Magnetic field, 416
Magnetic hyperthermia, 425–426
Magnetic imaging, 425–426
Magnetic nanoparticles (MNPs), 231t, 244, 244f, 425–426, 474, 480
Major histocompatibility complex (MHC), 694–696, 695f–696f, 698f, 709–710
  epitope peptides, 695f
  MHC class I, 698f
  MHC class II, 698f
M13 bacteriophage, 573f, 577
MBGMs. *See* Mesoporous bioactive glass microspheres (MBGMs)
M cells (microfold cells), 523–524, 528t–529t, 531–532
MCF-7, 413–414
MCFs. *See* Mesocellular silica foams (MCFs)
MDA-MB-231 breast cancer cells, 413, 415
MDR. *See* Multidrug resistance (MDR)
Meat preservation, 421, 427
Membrane potential, 414
Menthol essential oil (MEO), 427
Mesocellular silica foams (MCFs), 617t–618t, 622–623, 623f
Mesoporous bioactive glass microspheres (MBGMs), 616–618, 617t–618t, 630, 631f
Mesoporous silica nanoparticles (MSNs), 615, 622–624, 624f
Mesoporous silica NPs (MSNs), 414
Metal organic framework (MOF), 428
Metastasis, 414–415
Methods for drug incorporation, 506–508
Methods of preparation, 115–119, 115f, 122–123, 128
  coacervation method, 116–117, 122–123
  desolvation method, 115–116
  self-assembly, 118–119
Methotrexate (MTX), 229t, 231t, 232, 233f
MHC. *See* Major histocompatibility complex (MHC)
Micellar architectures, 412
Micelles, 9, 24–25, 32t–33t, 412
  casein micelles, 9, 11–12, 24–25, 32t–33t
Microfluidic technique, 332, 333f, 352, 467t, 471
Microinjection method, 328f, 329–330, 581–582, 582f

Microneedles, 442, 454–455
Migration, 413–414
Milk, 409–410, 414–415
Milk proteins, 243–246, 409–410
casein, 243
lactoferrin, 245–246
whey proteins, 244–245
Mitochondria, 414, 657–659
MNPs. *See* Magnetic nanoparticles (MNPs)
Molecular weight, 410–411
of the hydrolyzed hyaluronic acid, 415
Monoclonal antibodies (mAbs), 55–59, 645, 648–649, 655
rituximab, 655
Mononuclear phagocyte system (MPS), 92, 95, 120–121, 125
Morphology and surface properties, 121–122, 128
MPS. *See* Mononuclear phagocyte system (MPS)
MRNA, 413
MS2 bacteriophage, 194t–195t, 573f, 576
MSNs. *See* Mesoporous silica nanoparticles (MSNs)
MTX. *See* Methotrexate (MTX)
Mucociliary clearance, 576
Multidrug resistance (MDR), 212–213, 225
Multifunctional platforms, 310–315
Multimodal imaging platforms, 376
Multivalent vaccines, 692, 700, 711, 711f
Murine leukemia virus (MLV), 585–586
Mycobacterium tuberculosis, 556

## N

Nab technology. *See* Nanoparticle albumin bound (nab) technology
Nano-capsules, 413
Nanocarrier drug delivery systems, 499–500
Nanocarriers (NCs), 377–400, 381f–383f, 389t, 394t, 409–411, 435–436, 438–455, 465–466, 475, 477–478, 480, 482, 521, 523–539, 525f, 572–578, 573f, 640–644, 641f, 647–648, 650–652, 654–657, 659–661, 682–683
active targeting, 640–642, 641f
BSA-based nanocarriers, 378–400, 381f–383f, 389t, 394t
gliadin nanoparticles, 528t–529t, 536–537
gold nanoparticles, 528t–529t, 535–536
hybrid, 572–573
hydrogel nanoparticles, 526, 528t–529t
inorganic, 572–573
multicompartment nanocarriers, 399
organic, 572–573
passive targeting, 640–642, 641f
stimuli-sensitive nanocarriers, 388, 398
for systemic codelivery, 650–655
zein-based, 466, 475, 476f, 477, 480
Nano-delivery, 409–410
Nanodiamonds, 524, 525f, 526–527, 528t–529t
Nanoemulsions, 354
Nanofibers, 413, 426–428
Nanomaterials (NMs), 83–84
Nanomedicine, 425–426
Nano-micelles, 409–411
Nanoparticle albumin bound (nab) technology, 12, 25–26, 31, 38–39, 353–354
Nanoparticle charge analysis, 504, 508–510
Nanoparticle production methods, 330–333
chemical cross-linking, 331
electrospray, 332–333
electrostatic assembly, 331–332
Nanoparticles (NPs), 8–39, 17t–23t, 32t–35t, 54, 55f, 60, 64–68, 65f, 76–78, 83–87, 87f, 92–96, 97f, 99–100, 99t, 274, 276–284, 286–291, 350, 411–416, 421–427, 612, 615–632, 617t–618t
carbon nanoparticles, 276, 286
ceramic nanoparticles, 276, 286
chemistry, 95–96
elasticity, 96
encapsulation, 93
lipid-based, 276, 286
protein-based, 76–77
shapes, 93–94, 183–185, 187–188
size, 180, 183–185, 187–188
stability, 78
Nanoprecipitation, 332, 502t–503t, 504–506, 505f
Nano-reservoir, 412
Nano-sized aggregates, 412
Nano spray drying, 412
Nanotechnology, 83–87, 298, 571–572, 612, 613f, 615–616, 632, 682–683, 688
nanosilica market, 616, 632
Nasomucosal toxicity, 632
National Medical Products Administration (NMPA) of China, 645
National Research Centre, 646
Natural antimicrobials, 421
Natural proteins, 409–410
Near-infrared (NIR) imaging, 274, 275f, 277, 280–281, 283
NIR probes, 274
wavelength range, 274, 280–281
Nerve growth factors, 127–128
Neurodegenerative diseases, 76
antiamyloid and antitau therapies, 73
neurotrophic factors, 57
Neuroinflammation, 554, 560f, 564

Neurological disorders, 526–527, 528t–529t, 534–535, 687
NIH-3T3, 414, 424–427
Nile red, 414, 425–426
NMs. *See* Nanomaterials (NMs)
Nonantigenicity, 409–410
Non-aqueous phase, 409–410
Noncovalent interactions, 196–197
Nontoxicity, 409–410
Nose-to-brain drug delivery, 368
NPs. *See* Nanoparticles
Nucleic acid delivery, 593–594
  microRNA (miRNA), 594
  mRNA, 593–594
  small interfering RNAs (siRNAs), 594
Nutraceuticals, 576

## O

Ocular drug delivery, 554, 560f, 562–564
OJP-loaded NPs, 423
Ontak, 97–98
Ophiopogon japonicus polysaccharides (OJPs), 423
Optical imaging, 273–275, 275f, 280–286
  contrast mechanisms, 273–274
  light interaction with biological tissues, 273–274, 280
  types, 273, 275f
Oral bioavailability, 421
Oral drug suspension, 416
Oral glucose tolerance, 422
Orange oil, 422
O/w emulsion, 412
Oxidative stress, 421, 424

## P

Paclitaxel (PTX), 85f, 88, 96–97, 98f, 99, 298–299, 315–316, 415–416, 562
*P. aeruginosa. See Pseudomonas aeruginosa (P. aeruginosa)*
PAMPs. *See* Pathogen-associated molecular patterns (PAMPs)
PARP protein, 414
Passive targeting, 4, 26, 416
Pathogen-associated molecular patterns (PAMPs), 695f–696f
  danger signals, 696f
Pattern recognition receptors (PRRs), 695f–696f
PC3 cancer cells, 416
PCL. *See* Polycaprolactone
PDI. *See* Polydispersity index (PDI)
PDT. *See* Photodynamic therapy; Photodynamic therapy (PDT)
PEG. *See* Polyethylene glycol (PEG)
PEGylation, 14, 29, 52–53, 53f, 55–56, 60, 62–63, 67–69, 73–74, 120–122, 185–186, 197, 318–319
  extended half-life and improved pharmacokinetics, 376
  shielding from immune system, 581
  site-specific, 478
PEO. *See* Polyethylene oxide
Peptides, 140–143, 147, 149–153, 161–167, 442, 451–454
Pharmaceutical applications, 125–129
  drug delivery systems, 125–126, 128–129
  gene therapy, 115, 126–129
  tissue engineering, 115, 127–129
Pharmaceutical sciences, 106
Pharmacodynamics, 64–66, 74
  dose–response relationship, 16
  target specificity and mechanism of action, 31
  therapeutic window, 45
Pharmacokinetics, 55–56, 64–65, 65f, 73–74, 416, 422, 523–524, 530–531, 534, 537
  absorption, 457
  distribution, 456
  metabolism and excretion, 516
Pharmacological actions, 421
Pharm D Program, 416
PH-dependent manner, 409–410
PH-driven method, 467t, 468, 486–487
Phenolic compounds, 414, 423–424
Pheophorbide a (Pba), 425
Photoacoustic imaging (PAI), 273–274, 275f, 280, 283–284
  acoustic waves, 274, 280
  endogenous contrast agents, 274
  exogenous contrast agents, 274
Photodynamic therapy (PDT), 213–216, 215f, 221, 222f, 227, 227t–228t, 230–231, 239t–240t, 298–299, 308, 424–425, 657
  combination therapy, 213–216
  hypoxia impediment, 214–216
  photosensitizers, 214–216
Photo-responsive nanoparticles, 475
Photosensitizer (PS), 657
Phototherapy, 424
Photothermal effect, 424–425
Photothermal therapy (PTT), 214–218, 227, 230–231, 237, 298–299, 308
  photothermal agents, 216
  tumor ablation, 227
PH-shifting mechanism, 424
PH values, 384–385, 387–400, 395f
Physical targeting, 668
  external control, 669–670
  nonspecific mechanisms, 668–669

PI. *See* Isoelectric point
*Pichia pastoris*, 232–234
PL. *See* Polylysine (PL)
Plant protein-based nanoparticles, 300
gliadin, 300
soy proteins, 300
zein, 300
Plasmid DNA (pDNA), 126–127
*Plasmodium berghei*, 163–165
Platelet coalescence, 427–428
PNPs. *See* Protein nanoparticles
PNPs vaccines, 691–693, 694f–698f, 696–712, 711f, 713t
advantages, 692–693
design principles, 692–693
disadvantages, 692, 713t
Polycaprolactone (PCL), 426–427
Polydispersity index (PDI), 414. *See also* Size and morphology analysis
Polyethylene glycol (PEG), 95
Polyethylene oxide (PEO), 427
Polylysine (PL), 617t–618t, 618–619
Polymeric micelles, 650–652, 660t
Polymeric nanocapsules, 652–654
Polymeric nanoparticles, 328f, 329, 524–526, 525f
Polymers, 409–410, 435–436, 439–443, 450–451, 454–455
Polymersomes, 654–655
Polyphenol, 423–424
Polyvinyl alcohol (PVA), 426–428
Positron emission tomography (PET), 274–279, 284, 286–291, 287f, 289f
annihilation mechanism, 289, 289f
image acquisition, 287f
radiotracers, 274–278, 286–291
Preparation methods of nanocarriers, 10–12
desolvation (precipitation), 10
electrospinning deposition, 11
self-assembly, 11–12
Preparation of zein-based nanoparticles, 466–471
Prodigiosin, 413
Prodrugs, 671–672
Proliferation levels, 413–414, 426
Proline, 410–411
Protamine-based nanoparticles, 126–127
Protamine-DNA complexes, 126–127
Protease Operated Depot (POD), 564–566
Proteases, 416
Protein A, 686
Protein-based drug delivery, 85–87, 96–99
history, 85–87
materials, 87–92
therapeutic applications, 96–99
Protein-based nanocarriers, 3–39
Protein-based nanoparticles (PBNPs), 113–129, 179–200, 298–305, 298f, 308–315, 319–322, 333–341
advantages, 114, 301t, 319
animal proteins, 180–181
challenges, 341
disadvantages, 301t, 319
factors affecting the size, 301t
future prospects, 115, 341
gene therapy potential, 333–341
historical development, 114
interactions, 179, 181–191, 198–200
plant proteins, 180–181
virus like nanoparticles (VLN), 180–181, 192
Protein-based vaccines, 77
adjuvant enhancements, 76
subunit and recombinant, 63
Protein cages, 299–300, 340–341
viral protein cages, 340–341
Protein corona, 29–31, 78, 120–121, 124–125, 181, 184–189, 200, 533
hard corona, 184–185
modifications for, 185–186
soft corona, 184–185
Protein delivery, 436, 449–455
Protein drug conjugates, 300
Protein engineering, 56, 60–61, 66, 68–69, 140–149, 151–154, 160, 168–169, 398–399
advanced engineering, 68
de novo design, 141–143, 153
directed evolution, 141–142
rational design, 141–142
Protein folding, 143, 146–147, 148t
Protein G, 686
Protein nanoparticles (PNPs), 84–86, 85f, 87f–88f, 89, 96–97, 97f–98f, 99–100, 99t, 211–212, 214–257, 275–291, 411
advantages, 284, 290
biocompatibility, 211–212, 257
disadvantages, 285, 290–291
drug delivery systems (DDSs), 211–212, 257
future prospects, 285–286, 291
properties, 211–212
Protein/peptide delivery, 593
Protein polymer conjugates, 300–301
Protein-polymer hybrid nanocarriers, 153, 160–163, 164f
Proteins, 3–39, 5t–7t, 647–652, 654–661
classification, 4–8
heteroproteins, 4, 5t–7t

holoproteins, 4
Limited cellular permeability, 648
rapid metabolism, 648
susceptibility to degradation, 648
Protein stability, 62–63, 66–68, 71–73, 76–78
denaturation, 62–63, 66, 71
increased solubility and, 77
strategies for enhancing, 67
Protein structure, 62–64, 63f, 71
primary, 63–64, 63f
quaternary, 63–64, 63f
tertiary, 63–64, 63f
Protein therapeutics, 59–80
drug delivery, 51–62, 68, 70–71, 73–74, 76–78
fundamental concepts, 59–61
recombinant, 54–59, 61–62
Protein unfolding, 368
Proteolysis, 409–410
PRRs. *See* Pattern recognition receptors (PRRs)
*Pseudomonas aeruginosa (P. aeruginosa)*, 482–483, 526, 528t–529t, 703t, 706–708, 710
lung infection, 703t
pneumonia, 703t
PTT. *See* Photothermal therapy (PTT)
PTT values, 428
Pulmonary infections, 421
PVA. *See* Polyvinyl alcohol

## Q

Quantum dots (QDs), 273–274, 276, 278, 286

## R

Radiotherapy, 211, 216–217, 221, 237, 257
glioblastoma therapy, 216–217
ionizing radiation, 216–217
STAT3 downregulation, 216–217
Rapamycin (Rapa), 561, 563–564
Reactive oxygen species (ROS), 213–216, 219f, 221–223, 222f, 230, 238, 244, 247t–250t, 629–630, 652, 653f, 657, 658f
Re-bleeding, 427–428
Receptor-mediated endocytosis, 523–524, 527–530, 534
Receptors, 409–410, 415
Recombinant biopolymers, 547–548
Recombinant DNA technology, 51–55, 54f
*Escherichia coli (E. coli)*, 51–52, 55
Red clover necrotic mosaic virus (RCNMV), 575
Redox response, 479
Red pigment, 413
Regulatory aspects and clinical translation, 511–512
Reh lymphoblastic cells, 414
Release kinetics, 123–124, 128
Release pattern, 421–422
Responsive zein-based drug delivery systems, 474–475, 480
magnetic response, 474, 480
photo response, 475, 479
pH response, 474, 478
Resveratrol, 423–424
Reticuloendothelial system (RES), 183, 189, 668
Reversed-phase high-performance liquid chromatography, 677
Reversible addition-fragmentation chain transfer (RAFT), 413
polymerization, 162–163, 164f, 413
Reversible deactivation radical polymerization (RDRP), 413
Reversible inhibition fragmentation transfer (RIFT), 413
polymerization, 413
Reversible termination, 413
Reversible transfer, 413
Rhein, 423–424
Rhodamine B, 416, 421–422
*Ribonuclease A (RNase A)*, 652, 653f, 657–659, 658f
RNS generation, 421
ROS. *See* Reactive oxygen species; Reactive oxygen species (ROS)
ROS-responsive protein nanoparticles, 222–223
multibioresponsive behavior, 222–223
oxidative stress, 223

## S

Sabra and Agwa, 409–410
Safety, 421
Safety and efficacy, 321–322
Safety profile, 691–693, 699–700, 704, 707–708, 710–711, 711f, 713t
biocompatibility, 710, 711f
biodegradability, 710, 711f
reduced adverse reactions, 710, 711f
*Salmonella*, 421
Salting-out method, 438–439, 439f
SARS-CoV-2. *See* Severe acute respiratory syndrome coronavirus 2 (SARS-CoV-2)
Scaffolds, 127–128
Scalability, 319–320
Scalable process, 412
Scanning electron microscopy (SEM), 122, 128
SCC7 tumor cells, 425
SC/GA. *See* Sodium caseinate/gum arabic
SCL-1 cells, 425–426
Scratch wound closure, 426
Self-assembling nanocarriers, 139–141, 144t, 148t, 149–169, 159t, 161t, 164f

Self-assembling nanocarriers (*Continued*)
hydrogels, 151–152, 165–167
micelles, 139–140, 144t, 147, 150–151, 156–157, 165–168
nanocages, 152–153, 156–157, 159t, 161t
Self-assembly, 139–141, 143, 144t, 145, 147–169, 148t, 159t, 161t, 164f, 409–410, 412, 416, 425–428
covalent interactions. *See* Covalent interactions
noncovalent interactions, 140, 144t, 147–156, 148t, 158, 164f
techniques, 330–331
Self-stabilized silk sericin-based nanoparticles (SSC@NPs), 281–283
cryoprotective properties, 282
pH sensitivity, 281–282
silk sericin, 281
Serum albumin (BSA), 617t–618t, 618–619, 622–623, 626–627, 626f, 630
Severe acute respiratory syndrome coronavirus 2 (SARS-CoV-2), 700–702, 705t
S-domain-ferritin NP, 702
spike protein, 702
SF. *See* Silk fibroin (SF)
SFNPs. *See* Silk fibroin (SF)
SFNs. *See* Silk fibroin nanoparticles (SFNs)
Shelf life, 421, 426–427
Short-interfering RNA (siRNA), 659, 660t
Side effects, 413, 425
Silica, 612–613, 614t, 615–624, 617t–618t, 626–627, 631–632
silica gel, 617t–618t, 619–621, 620f–621f, 627
silica nanoparticles (SNPs), 614–619, 629–631
Silk, 88f, 89, 211–212, 235–238, 239t–240t, 435–455
biomedical applications, 236
properties, 236
sources, 235
Silk elastin-like polymers (SELPs), 449–451
Silk fibroin (SF), 211–213, 216, 235–237, 239t–240t, 436–446, 437f, 439f–440f, 446f–447f, 448–455, 452f, 706–707
drug delivery, 236
properties, 236
silk fibroin nanoparticles (SFNPs), 706–707
structure, 706–707
tumor treatment, 237, 239t–240t
Silk fibroin nanoparticles (SFNs), 125–126, 212–213, 239t–240t, 338–339
cellular entrance, 338
gene delivery vehicle, 338
genetic vaccines, 338–339
Silk polylysine copolymers, 449–451
Silk sericin (SSs), 237–238, 239t–240t, 436–438
chemical reactivity, 237
nanocarriers, 237
properties, 237
Silver nanoparticles (Ag NPs), 426
Singlet oxygen, 425
SiRNA, 126–127
Size and morphology analysis, 508–512
Size control, 396–397, 399–400
Skin delivery, 509–511
*all-trans retinoic acid*, 510–511
alpha-tocopherol, 510–511
Small-molecule drugs, 644–647, 645f–646f, 649–652, 654–661
advantages, 644–645
challenges, 645
in targeted cancer therapy, 645–647
Smart Bibliometrics systematic review methodology, 379–383, 380f–383f
SmURFP nanoparticles, 280–281
biocompatible, 281
cyanobacterial origin, 280–281
nontoxic, 281
Sodium azide, 416
Sodium caseinate, 413–415, 422, 426–427, 472–473, 483–485, 484f
Sodium caseinate/gum arabic (SC/GA), 422
Sol-gel method, 416
Sol-gel process, 611–629, 617t–618t, 631–632
acid route, 611–613, 619–622, 624–625, 627–629, 628f, 632
base route, 611–613, 616–619, 627–629, 628f, 632
Stöber method, 612, 629–631
Solubility, 378–379, 384–388, 392–393, 398–400, 412, 421–424, 428
Solubilization, 428
Solution reservoir, 409–410
Solvent evaporation, 332, 412–415, 421–422
Solvent/nonsolvent method, 467–468, 467t, 486–487
Solvents, 412–413
Sonic hedgehog (Shh), 413
Sonoporation. *See* Ultrasound-assisted (sonoporation) methods
Sorafenib, 414–415
Soybean trypsin inhibitor (STI), 617t–618t, 619–622, 620f–621f, 627, 631–632
Spectroscopy, 273
Spray drying, 412, 414, 467t, 469
SSs. *See* Silk sericin (SSs)
Stability, 377–379, 384–388, 390–400, 421, 423–424
and protection, 614t, 615, 622–627, 631–632
*Staphylococcus aureus*, 233t, 426–428
STI. *See* Soybean trypsin inhibitor (STI)
Stimuli-responsive protein delivery systems, 78
Stimuli-responsive release, 198–199

pH-sensitive, 198–199
temperature-sensitive, 198–199
Stimuli-responsive systems, 370
Storage, 421, 424, 426
Strain-Promoted Azide-Alkyne Cycloaddition (SPAAC), 437
Streptavidin–biotin interaction, 686
*Streptococcus mutans*, 482–483
Streptozotocin, 422
Supercritical antisolvent process (SAS), 467t, 470
Superior hypoglycemic activity, 422
Suppression of *L. monocytogenes*. *See Listeria monocytogenes*
Surface charge (zeta potential), 120–121, 128, 183–185, 187–188
Surface functionalization, 613, 614t, 615, 618–619, 627, 629–631
Surface modification, 139–140, 147–149, 152–157, 169
ligand attachment, 152–154
PEGylation, 147–149, 154, 161–162, 165–167
surface charge modulation, 154–155, 158, 167
Surface-to-volume proportion, 426
Swiss CD1 female mice, 413–414, 421–422
Synthetic polymers, 409–410

## T

Targeted delivery, 54, 60, 64–65, 68–69, 73–78
Targeted drug delivery, 640–642
for cancer, 640
nanoparticles as carriers, 640–641
Targeting, 416, 421–422
Targeting peptides, 672–673
Targeting strategies, 180–181, 192–200
cell surface receptors, 192–193
ligand–receptor interactions, 188–189
Targeting strategies for protein-based nanocarriers, 26–27. *See also* Active targeting; Passive targeting
*Taxus brevifolia*, 315–316
T-cell receptor (TCR), 695f–696f
T-cells, 693–696, 695f–696f, 698f, 702–705, 705t, 707, 711
CD4+ T cells, 695f, 698f, 705t
CD8+ T cells, 695f, 698f, 705t
T follicular helper (TFH) cells, 693–694
TCR. *See* T-cell receptor (TCR)
Techniques
antisolvent, 413
coacervation, 414, 416
desolvation, 411, 416
dialysis, 416
EDC/sulfo-NHS reaction, 414
electrospinning, 413, 426–428
emulsification, 412, 421–422
freeze-drying, 416
nano spray drying, 412
solvent evaporation, 412–415, 421–422
ultrasonication/freeze-drying, 416
Technological applications, 421
Temperature-dependent variability, 368
TEOS. *See* Tetraethyl orthosilicate (TEOS)
Tetraethyl orthosilicate (TEOS), 612, 616–619, 617t–618t, 622, 624–625, 627
Theranostics, 281, 284, 291, 379, 388, 397–399, 526–527, 532
Therapeutics, 409–411
genes, 126–127
materials, 409–410
potential, 409–410, 421–422, 424–425
Thermal and chemical stability, 614t, 624–625
Thermal responsive, 548, 551–553, 559–566
Thermo-responsive polymers, 413
Thrombosis, 687
Thymol, 421, 427
Thymoquinone, 416
Tissue engineering, 141–142, 144t, 161t
Tissue regeneration, 435–436, 443–444, 449–454
TME. *See* Tumor microenvironment; Tumor microenvironment (TME)
Tobacco mosaic virus (TMV), 573f, 575
Toll-like receptors (TLRs), 531–532
Toxicity, 409–410, 413–414, 416, 422
Transfection reagents, 330
Transferrin (Tf), 672
Transferrin nanoparticles, 276–277, 279f, 287f
iron requirements, 277
transferrin receptor, 277
tumor marker, 277
Transferrin receptor 1 (TfR1), 282–283
Treating various diseases, 409–410
Treatment of infections, 37–38
Treatment of neurodegenerative diseases, 37
Treatment of tumors, 31–37
Triptolide, 416
Trout fillets, 427
Trypsin, 416
Tuberculosis, 528t–529t, 535, 537
Tumor cells, 413–414, 424–425
Tumor growth inhibition, 415
Tumor microenvironment (TME), 183–184, 198–199, 212–214, 218–224, 219f, 227t–228t, 234–235, 239t–240t, 243–246, 250–257, 298–300, 306–307, 313–314, 416, 424–425
acidosis, 218–220
hallmarks, 218–220, 219f
hypoxia, 218–221
Tumor necrosis factor alpha (TNF-?), 564
Tumor-targeting strategies, 217–218
active targeting, 217–218
passive targeting, 217
protein corona, 217–218

Tumor therapy, 548, 553, 555–557, 559–562, 560f
Turnip yellow mosaic virus (TYMV), 577
Tyrosine kinase inhibitor, 413–414

## U

Ultrasonication, 412, 416, 423
Ultrasound-assisted (sonoporation) methods, 330, 331f
Uptake, 414–416
US Food and Drug Administration (FDA), 645, 646f, 655
Utilization in food technology, 512–513

## V

Vaccination, 28–31, 38
Vaccine delivery, 449, 454–455, 692–693, 695–696, 702–703, 706–710
  intranasal, 692, 701–702, 706–709
  oral, 692, 708
  targeted, 692–693, 695–696, 702–703, 706–707, 709–710
Vaccines, 99, 99t, 142, 161t, 163–165, 523–524, 528t–529t, 531–532, 571–572, 573f, 589–591, 589f–590f, 691–693, 708, 712
  commercial, 589–591
  conventional, 692–693, 712
  COVID-19 vaccine, 99t
  development, 334, 336–340
  *Helicobacter pylori*, 590–591
  influenza vaccine, 99t
  live attenuated, 691, 693, 710
  subunit, 693, 708
  VLP-based, 589–591, 590f
Viral capsid nanocages, 316–318
  cowpea mosaic virus (CPMV), 317
Viral vectors, 328, 328f
Virus-like particles (VLPs), 9–12, 84, 91, 98–99, 126–127, 153, 161t, 165, 571–572, 572f, 588–598, 588f–590f, 592f, 595f, 692, 697, 698f, 704–705, 705t, 713t
  applications, 588–597, 588f
  bacteriophage-derived, 696, 697f, 713t
  caged proteins (CP), 697, 698f
  human virus-based vectors, 696, 697f, 713t
  immunogenicity, 588–589
  loading/unloading, 592–593, 592f
Virus-like polypeptides (VLPs), 211–212, 250–251, 251t–252t, 253, 257
  drug delivery, 250–251
  noninfective, 250
  structure, 250
Virus-like protein nanoparticles (VLPs), 276, 278, 279f, 284, 287f
  cancer-targeting molecules, 278
  noninfectious, 278
  Physalis mottle virus (PhMV) VLPs, 278
Vitamin D3, 421–422
  receptors, 421–422
VLPs. *See* Virus-like particles (VLPs)
Volatility, 421

## W

Water-binding capacity, 409–410
Water-in-oil-in-water emulsion, 412
Water solubility, 421–424
WGA. *See* Wheat germ agglutinin (WGA)
Wheat germ agglutinin (WGA), 17t–23t, 25, 525–527, 528t–529t, 530–531, 533–538
Whey protein nanoparticles, 409–410
Wound dressing, 426, 428
Wound healing, 426, 436, 443, 445–446
W/o/w emulsion. *See* Water-in-oil-in-water emulsion

## Z

Zein, 5t–7t, 8, 11, 13–14, 17t–23t, 32t–35t, 37–38, 88f, 89–90, 211–212, 238–241, 242t, 413, 465–475, 467t, 469f, 471f, 476f, 477–487, 479f, 481f, 484f, 484t, 485f, 486t
  amphiphilic and hydrophobic characteristics, 465–466
  drug carriers, 238–241
  Generally Recognized as Safe (GRAS), 465–466
  properties, 238–241
  storage protein of corn, 465–466
  types, 238–241
Zein nanoparticles (ZNPs), 238–241, 242t, 339–340, 466–475, 471f, 477–487, 481f, 484f, 484t, 485f, 486t
  applications, 481–483
  cancer gene therapy, 339–340
  modification, 472–475, 477–478, 483–486
  vaccine development, 339–340
Zeta potential, 414–415, 421–422, 424–425. *See also* Nanoparticle charge analysis
Zika virus (ZIKV), 703t, 709–710
  envelope protein (zEDIII), 709–710
  infections, 703t
ZIKV. *See* Zika virus (ZIKV)
ZnO NPs, 426
ZNPs. *See* Zein nanoparticles (ZNPs)
Zwitterionic polypeptides (ZIPPs), 562